EDWARD AND LANE
ON
EUROPEAN UNION LAW

EDWARD AND LANE ON EUROPEAN UNION LAW

DAVID EDWARD
Professor Emeritus, School of Law, University of Edinburgh, UK and Judge of the European Court of Justice 1989–2004

ROBERT LANE
School of Law, University of Edinburgh, UK

Edward Elgar
Cheltenham, UK • Northampton, MA, USA

Published by
Edward Elgar Publishing Limited
The Lypiatts
15 Lansdown Road
Cheltenham
Glos GL50 2JA
UK

Edward Elgar Publishing, Inc.
William Pratt House
9 Dewey Court
Northampton
Massachusetts 01060
USA

A catalogue record for this book
is available from the British Library

Library of Congress Control Number: 2012942063

This book is available electronically in the ElgarOnline.com Law Subject Collection,
E-ISBN 978 0 85793 105 4

ISBN 978 0 85793 104 7 (cased)

Typeset by Columns Design XML Ltd, Reading
Printed and bound in Great Britain by T.J. International Ltd, Padstow

CONTENTS

v

EXTENDED TABLE OF CONTENTS

PART A
THE ORIGINS AND DEVELOPMENT OF THE EUROPEAN UNION

11. THE FREE MOVEMENT OF PERSONS AND SERVICES

FOREWORD

Legal bookshops are full of texts in which the practitioner, wishing to supplement his understanding of a difficult subject that he never really got to grips with during his university course, can invest. Some are strikingly slim volumes that promise, nevertheless, to tell you all you really need to know to deal with that unexpected application tomorrow morning ('why, oh why, do the papers always come in so late?'). Some more closely resemble doorstops, but have the advantage (obvious to any lawyer who wants a life as well as a practice) that they may save you hours of flailing about on the internet using random search terms before you hit the vein of case law that addresses the problem at hand. Why another tome – this one definitely at the heavyweight end of the scale – which offers to cover all EU law ('but that goes well beyond what I need for my practice: I only ever deal with [fill in the blank]!')?

A difficulty that practitioners often bemoan, having proudly described themselves as 'just an ordinary' advocate/barrister/solicitor/legal adviser (etc.), is that they do not – cannot – understand how to interpret EU law, advise their clients about it and base arguments upon it in court because EU law has a weird logic that is not the same as national law and therefore defies both explanation and comprehension. The short answer is that EU law cannot be grasped and understood on the basis of a lucky dip into the specific sub-, sub-, sub-topic that is the problem of the moment. It is an organic whole. To illustrate the point: EU employment law does not live in a separate, watertight compartment labelled 'employment law'. It is put together with building blocks that are drawn from diverse parts of the treaty: from social rights for workers to the importance of ensuring, within a single common market, that enterprises in different Member States compete on a level playing field with each other. It is permeated with fundamental principles (such as proportionality). The actual texts cannot be construed literally like a UK statute, because the different linguistic versions are sure, sooner or later, to differ; and compromises during the negotiating process may have wreaked havoc with the original drafting and left ambiguities (or downright omissions) just where one would have hoped to find a neat, tightly-draw definition. EU employment law is therefore to be approached, analytically, like any other area of EU law. And if one is going to do that, it is really almost essential to try to get a 'feel' for how EU law works as a whole.

This book sets about the problem at its root. It starts with a short, but beautifully crafted, description of the history: from the beginnings in the aftermath of the 1939–45 war and the visionary foresight of Monnet, Adenauer and Schuman to the seventh accession (Croatia will join the EU on 1 July 2013). By the end of those first 27 pages – which should be compulsory reading for anyone wanting to sound off publicly about

'Europe' – the reader is given a real understanding of the contradictions that make up the EU: idealism and pragmatism, federal vision and the ferocious defence of national interests, apparent movement towards a particular goal endorsed politically by all Member States followed by stalemate as the details get thrashed out in the too-early hours of the morning at a 'three shirt' summit. The description is neither Euro-starry-eyed nor British Euro-sceptic: it is refreshingly balanced: 'the Union institutions and national governments have struggled to contain and redress the [sovereign debt] crisis in a number of ways, not wholly successfully. It has emerged as a significant test of the political will of both the Union and the member states, and particularly of the wisdom, and perhaps the survival, of economic and monetary union and the euro'. The quality of writing is also a delight: thus, 'the Reform, or Lisbon, Treaty … stumbled eventually to universal ratification and entered into force in 2009. Since then the Union has been beset by decidedly choppy economic waters'.

The substantive chapters live up to the promise of the Introduction. They manage to convey an encyclopaedic knowledge of the case law with pithy accuracy, leading the reader through the labyrinth and not hesitating to point out that the Court is bold and timid by turns – sometimes, it pushes the boat out; sometimes, it keeps below the parapet. Looking at areas that I know well (such as citizenship of the Union), I cannot fault the coverage. I would therefore feel very comfortable about using it as a way into an area that I knew less well (and, despite a professional and academic life spent in EU law, I find that every week in my current job I am reading some legislative text that I haven't encountered before and that I need to construe).

One of the many good things about the present offering is that is does not wear the usual blinkers. It is not 'EU law as seen through the eyes of an English common lawyer'. Of course the case law of the Bundesverfassungsgericht gets suitable mention. That one would expect: all serious EU law texts pause to mention 'Solange I' and 'Solange II' (even though some of the authors may be a little hesitant about what the nickname 'Solange' actually means auf Deutsch). But there are also significant references to decisions of (for example) the Polish and Czech constitutional courts. There are – as there should be – Scottish cases as well as cases from south of the border.

Along the way, there are little gems to delight the heart of the reader with a roving eye and an inquisitive mind. Thus, one single footnote addresses (albeit tersely) why the original Reinheitsgebot contains no mention of yeast, Louis Pasteur and the fact that the first King of the Hellenes was a Bavarian prince. It is very rare to find a book on EU law that manages to combine such deep scholarship, accurate insider knowledge and truly comprehensive coverage with readability. This is a learned text that wears its learning lightly.

My own favourite, I must admit, is the footnote informing us that the correct tempo for the European anthem (the 'Ode to Joy' from Beethoven's Ninth Symphony) is 'allegretto' ($♩$ = 112 – 124). Perhaps my amateur orchestra here in Luxembourg plays it a tad too slowly: we're more andante moderato ($♩$ = 104 – 112). But the best way may be with a variable tempo, reflecting the changes in mood as it progresses. At the risk of distracting you from what you really intended to check out when you acquired this book, why not have a look at Som Sabadell (Plaça de Sant Roc, 19 May 2012):

http://www.youtube.com/watch_popup?v=GBaHPND2QJg&feature=youtube.be

and judge for yourselves?

Eleanor Sharpston
Advocate-General
Court of Justice of the European Union
Luxembourg

PREFACE

The first edition of our book *European Community Law: An Introduction*, published in 1991, was essentially a reprint of the article on 'European Community Law and Institutions' that we contributed to the Stair Memorial Encyclopaedia of the Laws of Scotland. It was addressed primarily to a Scottish audience, although we believed that it would have wider appeal.

As we said in the Preface to the second edition in 1995, our exposition of Community law was founded on two beliefs. The first was that Community law must be seen as a whole in its historical context; that the institutional and substantive law were inseparable; and that a grasp of the structure of the EC Treaty was essential to a proper understanding of what it contained. The second was that the basic principles of Community law could be mastered in a relatively short time by any reasonably intelligent person who was not blinded by preconceived ideas: Community law was a new type of law, designed to deal with the problems of the late twentieth century and *ought* to be accessible.

Although the second edition was published after the Treaty of Maastricht came into force, that Treaty did not seriously affect our approach because the Community pillar of the Union remained the only part of the structure that had any form of direct legal effect. Many people, students, academics and practitioners told us that they found our book very useful and we were urged to produce a third edition. But we found ourselves in a constantly changing legal landscape that was no longer susceptible to straightforward description.

Throughout the whole period from 1995 to 2009 when the Treaty of Lisbon entered into force, there was hardly a moment when a new Treaty was not under negotiation or awaiting ratification. The numbering of Treaty articles was changed by the Treaty of Amsterdam, would have been changed again by the Constitutional Treaty had it come into force and was changed yet again by the Lisbon Treaty. The underlying logical structure of the original EEC Treaty was overlaid by an incoherent patchwork of political wish lists, *culs de sac* and compromises.

For the first time since 1995, it is now possible to state the essential features of the institutional and substantive law of the EU without having to explain that they may soon be changed or the articles of the treaties renumbered. But the scope of EU law has in the meantime widened and deepened to such an extent that a work that began as a book of 100 pages has grown to 1000 pages. Essentially this is a new book.

The new book is entirely the work of Robert Lane adhering as far as possible to the aim of the original – to state the law as simply as possible and provide the reader with quick access to the primary materials: provisions of the Treaties, secondary legislation including new forms of instrument of differential legal character and effects and the decisions of the courts.

Our thanks to Ms Juliette Brelsford for her help in collating the tables and to all at Edward Elgar for bringing it to fruition.

The law is stated as at 1 September 2012.

David Edward and Robert Lane
Edinburgh

TABLE OF CASES

I

The Civil Service Tribunal

Alphabetical List of Cases before the European Courts

OTHER COURTS

Permanent Court of International Justice

International Court of Justice

European Court of Human Rights

EFTA Court

NATIONAL COURTS

Belgium

Canada

Czech Republic

Denmark

Germany

Estonia

Greece

Spain

Italy

Cyprus

Latvia

Hungary

Isle of Man

Austria

Poland

United States

China

TABLE OF TREATIES

Treaty of 25 March 1957 establishing the European Atomic Energy Community (the Euratom Treaty)

Treaty of 25 March 1957 on the Functioning of the European Union (the TFEU) (2009–)

TABLE OF LEGISLATION

Directives

Decisions

Representatives of the governments of the member states

European Council

Conventions

B. NATIONAL LEGISLATION

Belgium

Bulgaria

Czech Republic

Part A

THE ORIGINS AND DEVELOPMENT OF THE EUROPEAN UNION

1

THE HISTORY

A. THE BEGINNINGS

In the aftermath of the 1939–45 war a number of bodies and institutions were **1.01**
set up to promote European reconciliation and economic recovery and to
avoid the risks of further conflicts between the nations of Europe. The latter
half of the 1940s saw, in the economic sphere, the creation of the Organisation for European Economic Cooperation (OEEC, 1948) (subsequently
the Organisation for Economic Cooperation and Development (OECD))
and the Benelux customs union (1948), and in the military sphere, the
creation of the Western European Union (the Brussels Pact, 1948) and the
North Atlantic Treaty Organisation (NATO, 1949) – which came subsequently to be mirrored in the East with the creation of the Warsaw Pact
(1955). The primary forum for political cooperation was envisaged to be the

Council of Europe, created in 1949:[1] from an original ten signatory states its membership now numbers 47 and it has become truly pan-European, excluding now only Belarus (which has applied for membership), Kazakhstan, the Vatican (although the Holy See has observer status) and Kosovo (if it is an independent state), and reaching even deep into the Caucasus – indeed, with accession of the Russian Federation in 1996, to Kamchatka. But it has not otherwise fulfilled expectations, save for its great achievement, the promulgation in 1950 of the European Convention on Human Rights (ECHR)[2] and the creation, in the European Commission and European Court of Human Rights, of machinery for its enforcement. There were also a number of initiatives, some ambitious, which failed to progress beyond the drawing-board.

1.02 All of the organisations which saw first light in that decade were based upon traditional methods of intergovernmental negotiation and cooperation. But there were many – primary amongst them the French civil servant Jean Monnet, the head of the new *Commissariat du Plan*, who had the ear of the French Foreign Minister Robert Schuman – who believed that these traditional methods were inadequate to solve the structural problems of the European economies and provide lasting political cohesion. In particular, the division of Germany and the Berlin blockade of 1949 underlined the need to bind the new Federal Republic of Germany more firmly into the political structure of Western Europe.

1.03 The fundamental change was engineered by Mr Monnet and put into play by Mr Schuman, with the foreknowledge and support of Dr Adenauer. On 9 May 1950, in a statement which has come to be known as the 'Schuman Declaration',[3] he announced that:

> the French government proposes that action be taken immediately on one limited but decisive point.

> The French government proposes that the entirety of Franco-German production of coal and steel be placed under a common High Authority within an organisation open to the participation of the other countries of Europe.

---

1 Statute of the Council of Europe (Treaty of London), 87 UNTS 103, CETS No. 1; signed 5 May 1949, in force 3 August 1949.

2 Convention of 4 November 1950 for the Protection of Human Rights and Fundamental Freedoms, 213 UNTS 221.

3 The Schuman Declaration – 'the alpha of European integration' – repays careful study. It is terse yet remarkably prescient, containing the seeds of nearly all the ideas which have gone into the making of the European Communities which were to follow. The text can prove elusive; it is therefore reproduced in Annex I. It is from the date of the Schuman Declaration that 9 May is recognised in some quarters as 'Europe Day' – coincidentally also Victory Day in the Soviet Union.

Coal and steel were then the 'basic elements of industrial production' both in peace and in war, and the principal coal and steel producing areas lay along fault lines between various states, not least between France and Germany. Implementation of the Schuman Plan would force them to cooperate economically and make it impossible to develop armaments unilaterally, at the expense of others. According to the declaration,

> The solidarity in production thus established will make it plain that any war between France and Germany becomes not merely unthinkable, but materially impossible.

Yet it is fundamental to an understanding of what followed that the proposal was intended to be, and was seen to be, only the first step in a much more ambitious project:

> Europe will be made neither at a stroke, nor according to a uniform model: it will be built through concrete achievements which first create a de facto solidarity ...

> The pooling of coal and steel production should provide immediately for the setting up of common foundations for economic development, a first step in the federation of Europe ...

> In this way there will be brought about simply and speedily that fusion of interest which is indispensable to the establishment of a common economic system; it may be the leaven from which may grow a wider and deeper community between countries long riven by bloody division ...

> [T]his proposal will lead to the realisation of the first concrete foundation of a European federation indispensable to the preservation of peace.

The Schuman Plan led to a treaty signed in Paris on 18 April 1951 establishing **1.04** the European Coal and Steel Community (the ECSC Treaty, or Treaty of Paris),[4] of which the signatory states were 'the original Six' – Belgium, (the Federal Republic of) Germany, France, Italy, Luxembourg and the Netherlands. Other European states were invited to take part but for a variety of reasons declined. Upon deposit of all instruments of ratification, the Treaty entered into force, and the Community into being, on 24 July 1952.

B. EUROPEAN COAL AND STEEL COMMUNITY

The essential feature of the European Coal and Steel Community (ECSC) was **1.05** the creation of a new entity (a 'Community') with legal personality and

---

4   261 UNTS 140.

autonomous institutions, in which the member states pooled portions of the authority normally exercised by states in the enjoyment of their sovereignty for limited but defined purposes. The production and distribution of coal and steel were brought under the control of a High Authority with supranational powers, including the power to make legally binding 'decisions' and 'recommendations'. The other institutions of the Community were a Common Assembly with supervisory powers, representing the peoples of the states brought together in the Community; a Special Council of Ministers, whose powers were partly legislative and partly consultative, representing the governments of the member states; and a Court of Justice whose function was to 'ensure that in the interpretation and application of this Treaty ... the law is observed'.[5] The Treaty was concluded for a period of 50 years[6] – in 1951, in its context and ambition, an incalculably long period of time; the ECSC therefore dissolved on 24 July 2002.

C. THE ROME TREATIES AND THE THREE COMMUNITIES

1.06 The setting up of the ECSC was followed by attempts to establish along similar lines a European Defence Community[7] ('the Pleven Plan') and ancillary to it a European Political Community,[8] support for which receded with the détente of the mid-1950s, and both failed ultimately for want of French agreement. In 1955, in order to overcome a mood of early euroscepticism, an inter-governmental conference of the original Six met at Messina (the 'Messina Conference') under the chairmanship of the Belgian Foreign Minister Mr Paul-Henri Spaak. Some other European governments sent observers but, again, none elected to take part.

1.07 The outcome of the Messina Conference was the Spaak Report,[9] which, like the Schuman Declaration, repays careful reading. It led to two treaties signed in Rome on 25 March 1957 (the Rome Treaties) establishing amongst the Six the European Economic Community (the EEC Treaty)[10] and the European Atomic Energy Community (the EAEC or Euratom Treaty).[11] Both entered into force on 1 January 1958. There were therefore then constituted three legally distinct Communities. As the EEC and Euratom Treaties were, unlike

---

5   ECSC Treaty, art. 31.
6   *Ibid.* art. 97.
7   Traité du 27 mai 1952 instituant la Communauté Européenne de Défense.
8   Traité du 10 mars 1953 instituant la Communauté Politique Européenne.
9   Comité intergouvernemental créé par la conférence de Messine, *Rapport des chefs de délégations aux ministres des Affaires étrangères* (Brussels, 21 April 1956).
10   298 UNTS 11.
11   298 UNTS 167.

the ECSC Treaty, concluded for 'an unlimited period',[12] those two Communities survived the 2002 dissolution of the ECSC and continued in being until restructured by the Lisbon Treaty in 2009, the Atomic Energy Community emerging from that intact and surviving still. The depositary of the Rome Treaties, and all subsequent amending treaties, is the government of Italy.

The immediate purpose of Euratom was to create 'the conditions necessary for **1.08** the speedy establishment and growth of nuclear industries',[13] whilst that of the EEC – championed particularly by the three Benelux states – was to establish over a 12-year transition period a 'common market' for all forms of economic activity[14] (excepting those in the coal, steel and nuclear energy sectors). But it is again of the first importance to understand their longer-term political aims. Drawing inspiration from the Schuman Declaration, the Preamble to the ECSC Treaty had referred to 'a broader and deeper Community among peoples long divided by bloody conflicts' and that of the EEC Treaty to a determination of its signatories 'to lay the foundations of an ever closer union among the peoples of Europe'. The aim of the treaties was to achieve political ends through economic means. Coal and steel were then the basic elements of industrial production, and atomic energy, then in its infancy, was seen as the principal source of energy – indeed, the panacea – of the future. It was believed that the bringing of coal and steel and atomic energy, as well as economic activity generally, under common rules and common institutions would lead to economic interdependence and, eventually, to the political integration of the member states. Subsequent events were to prove that economic, not to speak of political, integration would be more difficult to achieve than the immediate and short-term aims of the Treaties.

D. INSTITUTIONS OF THE COMMUNITIES

The EEC and Euratom Treaties followed the same general scheme as the **1.09** ECSC Treaty in (each) establishing a Community with legal personality and four autonomous institutions to exercise the powers conferred upon the Communities. As before, the institutions included an Assembly representing the peoples, a Council and a Court of Justice. The institution equivalent to the High Authority of the ECSC was, however, called the Commission. From the beginning a single Assembly and a single Court of Justice served all three Communities, and in 1967 the three Councils were merged into one and the

---

12 EEC Treaty, art. 240; Euratom Treaty, art. 208.
13 Euratom Treaty, art. 1.
14 EEC Treaty, art. 2.

ECSC High Authority and the EEC and Euratom Commissions into a single body, the Commission of the European Communities. In other respects the three Communities remained legally distinct. The EEC soon became the predominant of the three, and was, for most purposes, if inaccurately, referred to as 'the European Community' or simply 'the Community'.

E. SUBSEQUENT DEVELOPMENTS

1.10 Since founded in 1958 the three Communities have undergone significant development as a result both of formal amendment to the founding Treaties and of a natural historical, institutional and political evolution and growth. These developments are perhaps best described by means of a simple chronology of the most important of these events, as a means of introducing, or clarifying, institutions and concepts which are discussed in greater detail in the following chapters. The chronology is not, and does not pretend to be, comprehensive.

1. Common Agricultural Policy

1.11 According to the Spaak Report, a common market which excluded agriculture was 'inconceivable'.[15] The adoption of an agricultural policy was therefore designated one of the main activities of the EEC;[16] it was to be developed 'by degrees' during the transition period and in force at its close at the latest.[17] The broad lines it was to follow were agreed at an intergovernmental conference in Stresa in 1958, and the first detailed regulations giving effect to it were agreed by agricultural ministers during December 1961–January 1962, the product of a 'marathon session' of the Council which was working under French and Dutch threats to block progress in other areas. The result was rules for the 'common organisation' of six markets (cereals, pigmeat, eggs, poultry, fruit and vegetables, and wine) as well as agreement on the basic financial regulations. Other common organisations were to follow, but the pattern set by the 1961/62 agreement was to shape the Common Agricultural Policy (CAP), and so much of Community expenditure and internecine wrangling, over the next 30 years.

---

15 'On ne peut concevoir l'établissement d'un marché commun général en Europe que l'agriculture s'y trouve incluse'; Spaak Report, n. 9 above, p. 44.

16 EEC Treaty, art. 3(d).

17 *Ibid.* art. 40(1).

2. The Luxembourg Compromise

There developed an early crisis in Community affairs when in 1965 France **1.12** adopted 'the policy of the empty chair', absenting herself from meetings of the Council and effectively bringing the legislative machinery of the Community to a standstill. This was a product of President de Gaulle's dissatisfaction with the workings and development of the Communities generally, concern at the impending move, at the beginning of the third stage of the transition period, from unanimity to majority voting in the Council,[18] and alarm in particular at the ambition, and successes, of the EEC Commission under the presidency of Mr Walter Hallstein – in de Gaulle's view, 'a technocratic Areopagus, stateless and unaccountable'.[19] The crisis was papered over in 1966 with the so-called 'Luxembourg Compromise',[20] which, although it had no legal status and was little more than an agreement to disagree, allowed Council business to resume but allowing any member state thereafter to veto any legislative proposal which it conceived to affect its 'very important interests'. It thus altered the balance between the institutions which had been intended by the Treaty and crippled the Community machinery for the next 20 years.[21]

3. Completion of the transition period

The EEC Treaty provided for the progressive creation of the common market **1.13** over a three-stage transition period of 12 years.[22] In the event the timetable was 'accelerated',[23] so that many of the relevant rules were put in place 18 months early. And even though the common market was not (and in fine detail is still not) fully achieved by the end of the third stage, the passing of the transition period, on 1 January 1970, had significant relevance for the manner in which the Court of Justice was to interpret thereafter the Treaty obligations borne by the member states.

---

18 EEC Treaty, art. 8(1); on the transitional period see immediately below. Of particular concern here was the move to majority voting, and so the end of a French veto, in the agricultural sector; EEC Treaty, art. 43(2).

19 For its full flavour: 'Or on sait, Dieu sait si on le sait! qu'il y a une conception différente au sujet d'une fédération européenne dans laquelle, suivant les rêves de ceux qui l'ont conçue, les pays perdraient leur personnalité nationale, et où, faute d'un fédérateur, tel qu'à l'Ouest tentèrent de l'être – chacun d'ailleurs à sa façon – César et ses successeurs, Charlemagne, Othon, Charles Quint, Napoléon, Hitler, et tel qu'à l'Est s'y essaya Staline, ils seraient régis par quelque aréopage technocratique, apatride et irresponsable'; from a press conference at the Elysée Palace, 9 September 1965.

20 For the (brief) text of the Luxembourg Compromise (or Luxembourg Accords) see *Bulletin EC* 3–1996, 9 ff.

21 See 3.41 below.

22 EEC Treaty, art. 8.

23 Council Decision 66/532 [1966] JO 2971 (the 'acceleration decision').

4. The first accessions

1.14   Mindful of the advantages of economic cooperation but unwilling to undertake the profound degree of integration of the sort into which the Community member states had entered, in 1960 seven other European states (Denmark, Norway, Austria, Portugal, Switzerland, Sweden and the United Kingdom) had formed the European Free Trade Association (EFTA).[24] Shortly thereafter three of the seven (the United Kingdom, Denmark (both in 1961) and Norway (1962)) plus Ireland (1961) applied to join the Communities.[25] Because of the close economic ties amongst them, particularly within the EFTA, the success of the applications of the latter three was seen by all parties to be inextricably linked to that of the United Kingdom.[26] Parallel accession negotiations began in 1961 but, owing to the antipathy of President de Gaulle to British accession, in 1963 the French delegation demanded cessation of the UK negotiations,[27] and for practical purposes negotiations with all four were 'suspended' *sine die*. Renewed applications from each in 1967 were stonewalled for a time owing to a French veto in the Council. Negotiations resumed only in 1970 (Mr Pompidou now in the Elysée Palace), and led to a Treaty of Accession signed in Brussels in January 1972 between the six member states and each of the four applicant states. Following a 'no' vote in a national referendum, Norway declined to deposit instruments of ratification. On 1 January 1973, Denmark, Ireland and the United Kingdom became member states of the three Communities subject to transitional arrangements which expired at the end of 1977. In 1975 a referendum was held in the United Kingdom on continued membership – a device a primary purpose of which was to contain internal political fissures in the governing Labour party. A thumping majority (67:33 per cent) voted 'yes'.

5. Budgetary reform

1.15   In 1970 the financial provisions of the Treaties were amended so as to confer upon the Assembly (by this time known as the Parliament)[28] greater powers in

---

24   Convention of 4 January 1960 establishing the European Free Trade Association (Stockholm Convention), 370 UNTS 4; in force 3 May 1960. The EFTA was joined subsequently by Iceland (1970), Finland (1986) and Liechtenstein (1991), and the founding treaty was significantly overhauled in 2001 (Vaduz Convention of 21 June 2001, LGBl. 2003 Nr. 189, in force 1 June 2002).

25   On accession see 2.68–2.74 below.

26   See Opinion (of the Commission) concerning the Applications for Membership from the United Kingdom, Denmark, Ireland and Norway, *Bulletin EC* 9/10–1969, para. 5.

27   For the Commission view of the event, and in particular excoriating comment from Mr Hallstein on the conduct of the French government, see *Bulletin EC* 2–1963, 8–18.

28   See 3.45 below.

relation to the Community budget.[29] This marked the first stage in a long process of gradual accretion of power to, and assertion of that power by, the Parliament. At the same time the Community as a whole gained financial independence from the member states, the system under which its revenue was raised by financial contributions from the member states being replaced by a system known as 'own resources'.[30] Under own resources, the Union budget is now financed almost entirely[31] from customs duties (including, from 2007, substantial agricultural duties, previously a distinct customs classification), levies derived from the sugar market, a percentage of the value added tax levied by the member states and, from 2002,[32] payments derived from rates of gross national income (GNI).[33] There exist draft proposals for a new system with effect, the Commission hopes, from January 2014.[34]

6. Political cooperation and the European Council

The early 1970s saw the beginnings of a process of extra-Community political **1.16** cooperation amongst the member states in the field of foreign policy, and of regular meetings of the heads of state and government of the member states known as 'summits' or, since 1974, as meetings of the 'European Council'. The European Council increasingly assumed overall policy-making authority, although it had neither legal status in the framework of the Community nor any power to take binding decisions. Its existence was first recognised, then re-affirmed, in subsequent amending treaties.

7. European Monetary System

In 1978 a Resolution of the European Council[35] established the European **1.17** Monetary System (EMS) for the promotion of monetary stability, including a mechanism for stabilising (but not fixing) exchange rates (the Exchange Rate Mechanism, or ERM) and a new unit of monetary value (the European

---

29 See the (first) Treaty of Luxembourg of 22 April 1970, in force 1 January 1971; provisions replaced by the (second) Treaty of Luxembourg of 22 July 1975, in force 1 June 1977; see now TFEU, arts 310–324.

30 See Council Decision 70/243 on the replacement of financial contributions from the Member States by the Communities' own resources [1970] JO L94/19; replaced as of January 2007 by Council Decision 2007/436 [2007] OJ L163/17.

31 There are minor sources of Union revenue (e.g., a (modest) tax upon the income of its employees, financial penalties imposed by the Commission, sale and rental of property) but they are insignificant in relation to the budget as a whole.

32 Decision 2000/597 [2000] OJ L253/42.

33 Decision 2007/436, n. 30 above, art. 2.

34 See COM(2011) 510 final. The budgetary procedure is complex (and of course important) but will not be considered in this book in detail.

35 *Bulletin EC* 12–1978, 10 ff.

Currency Unit, or ECU) based on a 'basket' of values of national currencies.[36] The EMS was to unravel during the currency crisis of 1992, restabilised subsequently, was largely overtaken by the economic and monetary union (EMU) entered into by most (but not all) member states, yet came to be replaced in 1997 with a new system ('ERM-II') which remains instrumental for those member states not yet part of, but wishing to join, EMU.

8. Direct elections to the Parliament

1.18 1979 saw the first direct elections to the European Parliament, which had thitherto consisted of nominees of the parliaments of the member states. Although the Parliament had for some years begun to call the Commission more effectively to account by parliamentary questions, it remained a consultative assembly unwilling to use the two draconian powers conferred upon it by the treaties: the power to reject the budget prepared by the Commission and approved by the Council[37] and the power to force the resignation of the Commission as a body.[38] It first made use of its power in relation to the budget in 1980, thereby complicating a financial situation already fraught by demands of the United Kingdom for a reduction in her financial contribution and by impending Greek accession. It has also since toyed frequently, and sometimes quite seriously, with using its power of censure in relation to the Commission.[39] Since direct elections and the legitimacy that comes with them the Parliament has waged an unceasing struggle, with some success, to increase its powers within the Community/Union machinery.

9. The second accession

1.19 On 1 January 1981, Greece became the tenth member state, subject to transitional arrangements which expired at the end of 1985.

10. Greenland secession

1.20 Unlike the Færoe Islands, which had enjoyed sufficient autonomy under the Danish Crown to resist, Greenland became an integral part of the Community upon Danish accession in 1973. In 1979 it was granted 'home rule' within the

---

36 The value of the ECU was fixed by Regulation 3180/78 [1978] OJ L379/1 and varied relative to a national currency with currency fluctuations.

37 See 3.57 below.

38 See 3.34 below.

39 See 3.34 below.

national community (*Rigsfælleskabet*),[40] a status similar to that enjoyed by the Færoes, and bringing with it the power to opt out of Danish treaty obligations. Never enthusiastic 'Europeans', and with the Common Fisheries Policy about fully to bite,[41] in a 1982 referendum Greenlanders voted (by 12,615 votes to 11,180) to withdraw from the Community, and did so with formal treaty amendment in 1985.[42] At a stroke the Community lost 57 per cent of its territory, if only 0.02 per cent of its population. It remains, to date, the sole instance of formal secession of a territory from the Community.

11. Reinvigoration

Emerging from the recession of the 1970s, the first half of the 1980s was, for the Communities, a period of political and institutional ferment and resurgence. At the Copenhagen Summit in December 1982 the European Council instructed the Council to move promptly on a vast backlog of Commission proposals for legislation, and the logjam began to break up. In the meanwhile the (now directly elected) Parliament had begun to press for radical reform of the institutional machinery with a view, inter alia, to its being given an equal if not predominant part in the process of legislation. To this end it adopted a 'draft Treaty establishing the European Union' (the Spinelli Treaty) in 1984.[43] At the Fontainebleau Summit in the same year the European Council settled the long-running dispute about the United Kingdom's financial contribution and set up an '*Ad hoc* Committee on Institutional Affairs' (the Dooge, or Spaak II, Committee) comprising representatives of the heads of state and government (most of them foreign ministers) and of the president of the Commission 'to make suggestions for the improvement of the operation of European cooperation in both the Community field and that of political, or any other, cooperation'.[44]   **1.21**

The Dooge Committee reported in Spring 1985 and proposed that an inter-   **1.22**
governmental conference be convened (the first step in the process of treaty

---

40 Lov nr. 577 af 29. november 1978 om Grønlands hjemmestyre. In a subsequent referendum in 2008 Greenlanders voted decisively (76:24 per cent) for a further (very extensive) degree of autonomy, but not full independence, from Denmark, as a result graduating in 2009 from 'home' to 'self' rule; see Lov nr. 473 af 12. juni 2009 om Grønlands selvstyre.

41 See 10, 107 below, n. 598.

42 Treaty of 13 March 1984 amending, with regard to Greenland, the Treaties establishing the European Communities [1985] OJ L29/1; in force 1 February 1985.

43 The draft Treaty was drawn up by a panel of experts and had no official status, but exerted significant influence upon the treaty revision which was to follow. It is often referred to as the Spinelli Treaty because it was based upon a proposal from the veteran Italian politician Altiero Spinelli. For the text see [1984] OJ C77/33.

44 *Bulletin EC* 6–1984, 11.

amendment)[45] 'to negotiate a draft European Union Treaty … guided by the spirit and method of' the Spinelli Treaty.[46] In the meanwhile, a new Commission under the presidency of Mr Jacques Delors had taken office in January 1985. Shortly thereafter Lord Cockfield, the Commissioner with responsibility for the internal Community market, produced his White Paper 'on completing the internal market'[47] – probably the most influential Community document since the Spaak Report – which identified the remaining barriers to trade within the Community and some 300 measures necessary to remove them, and proposed a timetable for doing so over the lifetime of two Commissions, that is, by the end of 1992 (hence, the '1992 Programme'). Despite some (British, Danish and Greek) opposition, in June the European Council resolved to convene an intergovernmental conference for the purpose of implementing both the Dooge recommendations and the Cockfield White Paper.[48] The conference met in Luxembourg and Brussels during the autumn of 1985.

12. The third accession

1.23 The conference included the participation of Spain and Portugal, which formally acceded to membership of the Communities on 1 January 1986, so bringing the number of member states to 12, subject to transitional arrangements which expired at the end of 1993.

13. Single European Act

1.24 The outcome of the conference was a new Treaty known as the Single European Act,[49] so called because it dealt with a number of separate matters in a single treaty. The Single European Act (SEA) was signed on 17 and 28 February 1986 and came into force on 1 July 1987.

1.25 The Single European Act formally recognised the existence of the European Council, although it assigned no powers or functions to it. It provided for a number of amendments to the founding treaties, and gave institutional form to the machinery of political cooperation in the field of foreign policy. The machinery of European Political Cooperation (EPC, or PoCo) was established parallel to, but not as part of, the institutional machinery of the Community.

---

45   See 2.62 below.
46   Report from the ad hoc Committee on Institutional Affairs, *Bulletin EC* 3–1985, 102, at 110.
47   COM(85) 310.
48   See *Bulletin EC* 6–1985, 13–17.
49   For the text, see [1987] OJ L169/1.

Institutionally, the SEA amended the EEC Treaty so as to create greater **1.26** opportunity for legislative decisions to be taken by qualified majority vote in the Council and involve the Parliament more closely in certain aspects of the legislative process. It contained no reference to the Luxembourg Compromise – which apparently was not mentioned throughout the negotiations – and neither recognised, nor provided any machinery for, the exercise of any right of veto. The risk of any such right being exercised was in any event reduced by allowing a measure of 'variable geometry',[50] which eased the political process of agreement, but created its own difficulties.

The Single European Act also created a new concept of 'the internal market' **1.27** and injected into the EEC Treaty the legislative mechanisms considered necessary to achieve it by the implementation of the recommendations of the Cockfield White Paper. The legislative programme envisaged by the White Paper for the completion of the internal market was largely (but not entirely) achieved by the end of 1992.

14. Social Charter

The Commission became concerned that implementation of the internal **1.28** market as proposed by the Cockfield White Paper would have serious social repercussions which were inadequately addressed by the EEC Treaty. Accordingly, it put forward a Community Charter of Fundamental Social Rights of Workers, or the Social Charter, which was adopted by 11 of the then 12 member states – the United Kingdom opposing – in December 1989. The Social Charter has no legal force; it was intended rather as a blueprint for the subsequent adoption of Community legislation in the social sphere.

15. German reunification

In October 1990, Germany was (re)unified. Whilst requiring (and gaining) the **1.29** consent of the four occupying powers,[51] as a matter of (Federal) German constitutional law unification was achieved within the mechanisms of the Basic Law by the dissolution of the Democratic Republic, the recreation of its five historic *Länder* and their absorption into the Federal Republic,[52] and

---

50   As to variable geometry see 2.34 below.
51   Treaty of 12 September 1990 on the final settlement with respect to Germany (the 'two plus four treaty'), BGBl. 1990 II S. 1317.
52   See the 'unification treaty' (Vertrag vom 31. August 1990 zwischen der Bundesrepublik Deutschland und der Deutschen Demokratischen Republik über die Herstellung der Einheit Deutschlands, BGBl. 1990 II S. 889) and the 'unification treaty law' (Gesetz zu den Vertrag vom 31. August 1990 – Einigungsvertragsgesetz vom 23. September 1990, BGBl. 1990 II S. 885). For the recreation of the five eastern *Länder* see Verfassungsgesetz vom

Community law tacitly accepted this construct. The territory and the people of the erstwhile Democratic Republic therefore became part of the Community without Treaty amendment and with no formal accession procedure. As a practical matter, it meant that Germany became by far the most populous member state – which came to be recognised with the subsequent allocation to Germany of a greater number of members of the European Parliament, but otherwise afforded no further institutional advantage.

16. The 1990 intergovernmental conferences

1.30 The Community ambition, both tacit and sometimes express, of realisation of economic and monetary union (EMU) was reconfirmed at the Hanover Summit in 1988, at which the European Council charged a committee chaired by the President of the Commission, Mr Delors, to study the matter. The Delors Committee reported in 1989,[53] identifying three stages necessary for the achievement of EMU. An intergovernmental conference was convened in December 1990 to consider incorporation of the 'Delors Plan' into the treaties. At the same time a number of member states were unwilling to proceed to EMU without an extension of Community competences and enhancement of the democratic accountability of its institutions. Accordingly, a parallel inter-governmental conference was convened to consider these issues and those of foreign affairs, defence and collective security.

17. European Union

1.31 Whilst there was little interaction between the two conferences, their deliberations resulted in a single treaty, the Treaty on European Union (TEU), signed at Maastricht (hence known also as the Maastricht Treaty) on 7 February 1992.[54] Following legal challenges to ratification in four member states,[55]

---

14. August 1990 zur Bildung von Ländern in der Deutschen Demokratischen Republik – Ländereinführungsgesetz, GBl der DDR I, Nr. 51, which transformed the DDR into a federation ('Die Deutsche Demokratische Republik ist ein Bundesstaat, in dem die Gewaltenteilung garantiert ist', § 3 I) which never saw the light of day.

53 For the text see *Report of the Committee for the Study of Economic and Monetary Union* (1989); summarised in *Bulletin EC* 4–1989, 8.

54 For the text see [1992] OJ C191/1. In another (see n. 3 above) transeurasian chronological quirk, although signed on 7 February 1992 the TEU (and so the creation of the European Union) was actually agreed by the heads of state and government in Maastricht on 9 December 1991 – the day after the dissolution of the Soviet Union was formally declared by the Belavezha Accords.

55 In the United Kingdom there were unsuccessful petitions for injunction/interdict in both the English (*R v Secretary of State for the Foreign and Commonwealth Office, ex parte Rees-Mogg* [1994] 1 All ER 457 (QBD)) and the Scottish (*Monckton v Lord Advocate* 1995 SLT 1201 (OH)) courts. Rather more sophisticated constitutional challenges were mounted in France (Conseil Constitutionnel, décisions no. 92–308 du 9 avril 1992, JO du 11 avril 1992, p 5354 et no. 92–312 du 2 septembre 1992, JO du 3 septembre 1992, p 12095), in Spain (TC,

referendums in three (two consecutive referendums in Denmark)[56] and constitutional amendments in three, the Treaty came into force on 1 November 1993. It too is concluded for an unlimited period.[57]

The TEU – marking yet another 'new stage in the process of European **1.32** integration'[58] – created the 'European Union' and the so-called 'pillar structure' which, until 2010, comprised it. The central pillar is the existing Communities and their law (as amended significantly by the TEU).[59] The two other, flanking pillars comprised provisions on common foreign and security policy (the second pillar) and on various aspects of justice and home affairs (the third pillar). The latter two pillars, like European Political Cooperation under the Single European Act, embrace areas in which the member states agreed to cooperate and undertook to pursue common action, but outwith the Community framework and its democratic and judicial machinery, and upon a traditional, intergovernmental basis. The non-Community pillars of the Union were, and remain, nonetheless treaty obligations amongst the member states, if subject (primarily but not wholly) to the enforcement machinery of public international law and not Community law. The constitutional structure of the Union (as it was) is therefore very complex, and such clarity as there was is diminishing with the gradual emergence of a Union legal personality and a blurring of the distinction amongst the pillars. It will be considered in greater detail in Chapter 2.

Within the 'first pillar' the TEU also amended the treaties founding the **1.33** Communities, and in particular the EEC Treaty, in a number of significant respects. Chief amongst these amendments were:

Declaración 1/1992 de 1 de julio de 1992 (BOE núm. 177, de 24 de julio de 1992)) and in Germany (BVerfG, 12. Oktober 1993 (*Maastricht*), BVerfGE 89, 155). The irony is that both the French and the Spanish Constitutions were found to require amendment before proceeding to ratification (which were duly secured) whilst the German Constitution did not, yet it was the German judgment which, by laying down limits beyond which further integration would be constitutionally impermissible in Germany, generated the greatest furore.

56 In a June 1992 referendum the Danes voted narrowly (50.7:49.3 per cent) against ratification of the Treaty, primarily, it is thought, owing to fears of its defence implications. But following a number of undertakings given to Denmark at a meeting of the European Council in December 1992 (the Edinburgh Summit) which involved no alterations to the treaty (Conclusions of the Presidency, *Bulletin EC* 12–1992, 9, Part B), a second referendum in May 1993 produced a vote in favour (57:43 per cent) of ratification. A constitutional challenge was raised subsequent to ratification, but was unsuccessful; see *Højesteret*, dom af 6. april 1998 (*Carlsen m.fl. mod Statsminister*), U1998.800H. There were referendums also in Ireland (a constitutional necessity) and in France (not legally required but thought politically expedient, in the event carried by only a narrow (51:49 per cent) majority).

57 TEU, art. 51.

58 *Ibid.* Preamble, 1st indent.

59 *Ibid.* Titles II–IV.

- recognising its pre-eminence amongst the three Communities and the conferral upon it of new competences in areas which are not primarily economic, the EEC was restyled the 'European Community' (EC);
- citizenship of the Union was created;
- provision was made, institutionally and substantively, for the achievement of economic and monetary union (EMU) and the single currency over a transitional period;
- provision was made for the development of a significant social policy within the framework of the 1989 Social Charter; and
- a number of changes were made to the institutional and judicial mechanisms of the Community.

1.34 It was anticipated that the peculiar constitutional structure of the Union, a product of the inability of all member states to agree on the way forward, was a leap into the unknown and might well require adjustment in the light of experience. There were also a number of contentious issues upon which the conferences failed to reach agreement. The TEU itself therefore provided that another intergovernmental conference was to be convened in 1996 in order to consider further revisions.[60]

18. European Economic Area

1.35 Unconnected to but contemporaneous with the process leading up to the TEU, the (then) seven member states of the European Free Trade Association (EFTA)[61] had sought closer economic relations with the Community. As a result, an agreement was signed in May 1992 between the EEC, the ECSC (but not Euratom) and the Community member states on the one part and each of the EFTA states on the other with the purpose of creating a European Economic Area (EEA).[62] In a December 1992 referendum the Swiss voted against ratification. Following ratification by the two Communities, all Community member states and all the EFTA states except Switzerland, the EEA Agreement entered into force, and the EEA came into being, on 1 January 1994.

19. The fourth accession

1.36 In June 1994, a fourth accession treaty (the Corfu Accession Treaty) was signed between the European Union and its member states and four EFTA (and

---

60 *Ibid.* art. N(2) (now repealed).
61 I.e., at the time, Austria, Finland, Iceland, Liechtenstein, Norway, Sweden and Switzerland.
62 For the text see [1994]OJ L1/3.

EEA) member states: Norway, Austria, Finland and Sweden. Referendums were held in each of the applicant states. The Austrians, Finns and Swedes voted in favour of accession, but in late 1994 Norwegians voted, once again, not to join. Following ratification by Austria, Finland and Sweden and by all existing member states, the treaty entered into force on 1 January 1995, so bringing the number of member states to 15 (and at the same time reducing the EFTA component of the EEA to a rump of Iceland, Liechtenstein and Norway). Transitional arrangements for the three new member states expired for the most part in 1998.

The 1990s also saw a flurry of accession applications from a number of states of central and eastern Europe, many of them newly independent, in which the system of centrally planned economies had collapsed. **1.37**

20. Schengen

In 1985 the governments of five of the then ten member states (Belgium, Germany, France, Luxembourg and the Netherlands) had signed the Schengen Agreement on the gradual abolition of checks on the movement of persons across their common borders. It could come fully into force only after significant legal and technical groundwork was laid, and duly did so in Spring 1995. Within the Schengen area (or 'Schengenland'), persons now cross internal borders free of checks or other controls; checks at external borders are to a common Schengen standard. Since the Agreement was signed most (but not all) member states – and four non-member states – have acceded to it. Originally existing alongside but independent of the Community, Schengen was absorbed ('incorporated') into Community/Union competences by the Treaty of Amsterdam. **1.38**

21. Treaty of Amsterdam

The intergovernmental conference called for by the Treaty on European Union convened in March 1996 in Turin. It led eventually to a treaty signed in Amsterdam (Treaty of Amsterdam) on 2 October 1997, which entered into force on 1 May 1999.[63] The Treaty made a number of changes to the constitutional and institutional structures of the European Union and of the Communities, principally: **1.39**

- increasing significantly the powers of the Parliament in the adoption of Community legislation;

---

63   For the text see [1997] OJ C340/1.

- creating new (EC) Treaty provisions on the progressive establishment of 'an area of freedom, security and justice', incorporating the Schengen *acquis* into the Community and Union spheres and amending substantially the TEU provisions regulating third pillar (justice and home affairs) matters, renaming it Police and Judicial Cooperation in Criminal Matters, and at the same time bringing about a significant diminution of their direct importance, by providing for much of it to be drawn into the first (Community) pillar;

- creating a new institutional variable geometry with the provision that, where some (but not all) member states wished to pursue 'closer cooperation' (now 'enhanced cooperation') amongst them, they could in certain circumstances use the Community institutions and machinery to that end; and

- sowing significant confusion by causing all Treaty articles of the EC Treaty (but not of the ECSC or Euratom Treaties) and the Treaty on European Union to be renumbered.

However, the Treaty failed to address the pressing issue of the constitutional/ institutional reform made necessary by the steady growth of the Community/ Union and made urgent by the looming expansion of Union membership; instead it merely called for yet another intergovernmental conference to carry out a 'comprehensive review' of 'the composition and functioning of the institutions' prior to enlargement beyond 20 member states.[64]

22. Resignation of the Santer Commission

1.40 The Commission which took up office in 1995 under the presidency of Mr Jacques Santer became dogged by accusations of corruption and incompetence. Immediately following the release of a damning report by an *ad hoc* committee of 'independent experts', in March 1999, with only nine months remaining in its mandate, the Commission resigned *en bloc*. It was replaced six months later by a new Commission under the presidency of Mr Romano Prodi. The repercussions of the event for the institutions are resounding still.

---

64 Protocol [attached to the Community Treaties and to the TEU] on the Institutions with the Prospect of Enlargement of the European Union. The figure of 21 or more member states ('before … membership … exceeds twenty') anticipated a first tranche of five accession states (which events proved to have been a conservative projection) and was intended to allow some breathing space.

23. The Lisbon Strategy

At the Lisbon summit in March 2000, the European Council adopted the **1.41** 'Lisbon Strategy' (alternatively, the Lisbon Agenda, the Lisbon Process), an action and development plan for the Community/Union with the purpose of creating, by 2010, 'the most competitive and dynamic knowledge-based economy in the world, capable of sustainable economic growth with more and better jobs and social cohesion'.[65] As a counter to decreasing productivity and stagnation of economic growth, key to the strategy is innovation, education and training ('the learning economy'), social and environmental renewal and sustainability. It was intended to inform much of Community and Union policy-making over the decade. However, a 2004 report of a 'high level group' indicated that progress had been sluggish,[66] and there were complaints that the social and environmental aspects of the Lisbon Agenda were allowed to fall away, the priority focusing on purely economic concerns. It has, to an extent, been discredited, and partially abandoned. In 2010 it was rebranded by the Commission as 'Europe 2020', a self-proclaimed ten-year strategy for 'smart, sustainable and inclusive growth'.[67] It is yet to be seen whether Europe 2020 will fare better than the Lisbon Strategy.

24. Treaty of Nice

In order to sort out the 'Amsterdam leftovers', the institutional reform baton **1.42** was taken up by another intergovernmental conference which first met in February 2000, and in fairly quick time produced a text which was adopted at the Nice Summit in December and signed, at Nice, on 26 February 2001.[68] The Treaty of Nice marked agreement on significant issues of the institutional machinery of the Union in anticipation of the impending accession of up to 12 new member states, such as the size of the Commission and the Parliament, the abolition of the power of veto for almost all matters and, of particular political sensitivity, the weighting of member states' votes in the Council and the national allocation of members of the Parliament.[69] Nice also provided for the adoption of significant reforms of the structure and jurisdiction of the Court of

---

65 Lisbon European Council, Conclusions of the Presidency, *Bulletin EU* 3–2000, 8. For the full text see 7–15.
66 *Facing the Challenge: The Lisbon Strategy for Growth and Employment* (Kok Report) (Luxembourg, 2004).
67 COM(2010) 2020. For further detail see *Towards a Single Market Act*, COM(2010) 608 final; *EU Citizenship Report 2010*, COM(2010) 603 final.
68 For the text see [2001] OJ C80/1.
69 It should be noted that the agreement was reached amongst the 15, with no representation of or consultation with the candidate countries; such is their difference in bargaining power that the latter had little choice but to accept the agreed formulae in subsequent accession negotiations.

Justice. Following a wait upon Irish ratification,[70] it entered into force on 1 February 2003.

25. Charter of Fundamental Rights

1.43 Following years of pressure from a number of quarters, a European Union Charter of Fundamental Rights was adopted ('declared' or 'solemnly proclaimed') in December 2000 at the Nice Summit.[71] The Charter is essentially a codification of a number of provisions of the European Convention on Human Rights and, to a lesser extent, the 1989 Social Charter. It represents a compromise amongst the disparate views of the various governments as to what such an instrument ought to be, and, as a result, its exact status was, and in some measure remains still, unclear. It is discussed below.[72]

26. Economic and monetary union: the Euro

1.44 Using powers conferred by the Treaty on European Union, the Council caused the third and final stage of economic and monetary union to begin on 1 January 1999. Accordingly on 1 January 2002, the euro entered formally into circulation and became the sole currency of 12 of the then 15 member states.

27. End of the Coal and Steel Community

1.45 In accordance with article 97 of the ECSC Treaty, the Coal and Steel Community died a natural death on 24 July 2002. All matters governed (for 50 years) by the *lex specialis* of the ECSC Treaty were therefore then absorbed into the more general economic regime of the European Community. The assets of the ECSC in liquidation reverted to the member states, but fell under Commission management with a view to their transfer to the European Community for the creation of a 'Research Fund for Coal and Steel',[73] eventually established in 2008.[74] The European Community succeeded to the rights and obligations of treaties entered into by the ECSC with third countries.[75]

---

70 Irish constitutional law requires a popular referendum to be held prior to Irish ratification (*Crotty* v *An Taoiseach* [1987] IR 713 (SC)). A referendum was held in June 2001, and the Irish (by 54:46 per cent) rejected Nice; but in a second referendum in October 2002 they comfortably (63:37 per cent) approved it.

71 For the text see [2000] OJ C364/1.

72 See 6.114–6.118 below.

73 Decision [of the representatives of the governments of the member states] 2002/234 [2002] OJ L79/42; Protocol (No. 37) on the Financial Consequences of the Expiry of the ECSC Treaty; Decision 2003/76 [2003] OJ L29/22; Decision 2003/77 [2003] OJ L29/25; Decision 2003/78 [2003] OJ L29/28.

74 Decision 2008/376 [2008] OJ L130/7.

75 Decision 2002/595 [2002] OJ L194/35; Decision 2002/596 [2002] OJ L194/36.

28. Constitutional Convention

At the Laeken Summit in December 2001, the European Council called for the **1.46** convening of a 'constitutional convention' in order 'to consider the key issues arising for the Union's future development' and make appropriate recommendations therefor. Issues identified for the agenda included:[76] the division of Union/member state competences; the status of the Charter of Fundamental Rights; simplification, or rationalisation, of the treaties; the role of national parliaments; simplification of legislative instruments; and democracy, transparency and efficiency in the Union. The Convention, properly 'the Convention on the Future of Europe', was convened in February 2002 under the presidency of former French president Mr Giscard d'Estaing, and comprised 105 members drawn from the governments and parliaments of the member states and the candidate countries, the European Parliament and the Commission, plus observers from other Community organs. In June/July 2003 it agreed a draft 'Treaty establishing a Constitution for Europe' which proposed the fusion of the basic Community and Union treaties, other than the Euratom Treaty, into a single 'constitution' of the European Union. The draft was submitted to the European Council for consideration in summer 2003.

29. The fifth accession

By the end of 2002 there were 13 states which had applied and were in the **1.47** queue for accession to the Union: Bulgaria, the Czech Republic, Estonia, Cyprus, Latvia, Lithuania, Hungary, Malta, Poland, Romania, Slovakia, Slovenia and Turkey. At the Copenhagen Summit in December 2002 political agreement was reached that ten of the 13 – all of them save Bulgaria, Romania and Turkey – ought to be admitted to the Union in 2004. In April 2003, a Treaty of Accession was signed in Athens (hence, a second Athens Accession Treaty) between the Union and its member states on the one hand and each of the ten applicant states (sometimes 'the EU-10') on the other, and, following referendums in each of the latter, on 1 May 2004 the ten acceded to the Union, bringing the number of member states to 25. The fifth accession, and subsequent and future accessions, follow a different pattern than previously; this is discussed below.[77]

---

76   Declaration on the Future of the Union included in the Final Act of the [Nice] Conference; The Future of the European Union – Laeken Declaration, *Bulletin EU* 12–2001, 19.
77   See 2.74 below.

30. The sixth accession

1.48 In April 2005, a Treaty of Accession was signed with Bulgaria and Romania, which provided for accession to the Union of those two states on 1 January 2007. It required that a number of conditions be met, absent which accession could be delayed for one year. The conditions were duly deemed to be met and the two were admitted to the Union as scheduled, bringing the number of member states to 27.

31. Constitution for Europe

1.49 In autumn 2003 an intergovernmental conference was called in order to consider the draft Treaty proposed by the constitutional convention. At a first attempt, in late 2003, the conference failed to reach agreement, owing essentially to a stalemate on the weighting of member states' voting rights in the institutions. But following minor alterations (and a change of government in Spain) a final text was agreed by the conference in June 2004. The 'Treaty Establishing a Constitution for Europe'[78] was signed on 29 October 2004 in Rome (in the Sala degli Orazi e Curiazi in the Campidoglio, where the original Rome Treaties were signed), and its fate then turned upon ratification by the member states, anticipated to be completed by, and so allowing the 'constitution' to come into force on, 1 November 2006.[79]

1.50 Immediately there were judicial challenges to ratification in a number of member states.[80] By mid-May 2005 the Constitutional Treaty had been ratified

---

78 For the text see [2004] OJ C310/1.

79 Treaty establishing a Constitution for Europe, art. IV-447(2).

80 There had been an opening judicial salvo in the United Kingdom prior to agreement on the text, with a (profoundly unsuccessful) attempt to restrain the government from introducing a future Bill in Parliament to give the Constitutional Treaty effect (*R (Southall and anor) v Secretary of State for the Foreign and Commonwealth Office* [2003] EWCA Civ 1002, [2003] EuLR 832). Following signature of the Treaty, petitions against ratification were raised before the constitutional courts in Germany, Spain, France, the Czech Republic and Slovakia. Two were lodged before the *Bundesverfassungsgericht*, the first in the form of both a 'constitutional complaint' (*Verfassungsbeschwerde*) and an 'institutional complaint' (*Organstreitverfahren*) seeking to interdict the placing of the matter on the *Bundestag*'s order paper, and both were dismissed as inadmissible (BVerfG, 28. April 2005 (*Verfassungsvertrag*), BVerfGE 112, 363). The second, also a constitutional complaint and institutional complaint, sought the setting aside of the ratification law (approved by both *Bundestag* and *Bundesrat*) prior to its signature by the President; it was suspended *sine die*, the *Bundesverfassungsgericht* indicating it would not proceed until the status of the Treaty became clearer. Essentially the same situation obtained in Slovakia, the treaty being approved by the Parliament in May 2005 but ratification waiting upon the judgment of the *Ústavný Súd*. The *Tribunal Constitucional* (TC, Declaración 1/2004 de 13 de diciembre de 2004 (BOE núm. 3, de 4 de enero de 2005)) found no Spanish constitutional impediment, but the *Conseil Constitutionnel* determined (décision no. 2004-505 de 19 novembre 2004, JO du 24 novembre 2004, p. 19885) that French ratification could not proceed without constitutional amendment (which was quickly secured: loi constitutionnelle no. 2005-204 du 1er mars 2005, JO du 2 mars 2005, p. 3696). The petition before the Czech *Ústavní Soud* withered away.

by nine member states.[81] But in referendums held in France and the Netherlands in May and June respectively, a significant majority in each (55:45 per cent in France, 62:38 per cent in the Netherlands) voted against.

As its entry into force required ratification by all member states,[82] this left the **1.51** Constitutional Treaty, if not dead, on critical life support. It rallied with ratification by Latvia the day after the Dutch referendum and within weeks by Malta and Luxembourg (on the back of a referendum, in which 57 per cent voted in favour), followed in 2006 by Estonia. The ratification procedure was also completed by the parliaments in Germany, Slovakia and Finland and waited upon formal signature by the respective presidents.[83] As the 2005 accession Treaty presumed the constitution would be in force by the time of Bulgarian and Romanian accession their primary ratification was in fact of the Constitutional Treaty, providing for accession to the Union and Communities only in the event that the Constitutional Treaty was not in force on the date of accession.[84] This brought the total of assenting member states to 15, with three more on the brink awaiting only judicial/regional parliament approval. But planned referendums in six others[85] were postponed indefinitely, the European Council accepted that the anticipated date for the entry into force of the Treaty was no longer 'tenable' and it called for a period of reflection, explanation and discussion in all member states.[86]

32. Reform Treaty

In June 2007 the European Council agreed that 'the time had come to resolve **1.52** the issue and for the Union to move on'.[87] Another intergovernmental conference was convened and charged with negotiating a new treaty, drawing in significant measure upon the Constitutional Treaty and moderated in

---

81 That is, Belgium, Greece, Spain (following a non-binding referendum, in which 77 per cent voted 'yes'), Italy, Cyprus, Lithuania, Hungary, Austria and Slovenia.

82 See 2.62 below.

83 For Germany and Slovakia see n. 80, above; the Finns were waiting upon the consent of *Ålands Lagtinget* in the Åland Islands, unnecessary for ratification but necessary in order to make the treaty effective there; Ahvenanmaan Itsehallintolaki 1991/1144, 59 §.

84 2005 Treaty of Accession, arts 1 and 2.

85 That is, the Czech Republic, Denmark, Ireland, Poland, Portugal and the United Kingdom. The member states ratify amending treaties each in accordance with its own constitutional procedures; see 2.62 below. Of the member states only Ireland, possibly Slovakia, and since 2011 (in some spheres) the United Kingdom (see 2.62 below, n. 254), are obliged to hold a referendum. But a number elected to hold referendums – for the Dutch, the first in their history – in most cases of an advisory, non-binding character, and in many cases in order to evade the political responsibility of and for ratification.

86 European Council, Brussels, 16–17 June 2005, Declaration by the Heads of State or Government, *Bulletin EU* 6–2005, 25. See Communication from the Commission to the European Council, *The Period of Reflection and Plan D*, COM(2006)212.

87 European Council, Brussels, 21–22 June 2007, Presidency Conclusions, *Bulletin EU* 6–2007, 8, para. 8.

accordance with a mandate the European Council itself agreed and set.[88] The IGC assembled in summer 2007, a text was agreed at the Lisbon Council in October and the Treaty signed in Lisbon, at the Jerónimos Monastery, on 13 December 2007.[89] Throughout its negotiation it was called (in short style) the Reform Treaty, but has since become known more commonly as the Treaty of Lisbon. The process of ratification by the member states then began anew, hoped initially (by its supporters) to be completed before parliamentary elections and appointment of a new Commission in summer/autumn 2009. Judicial challenges (of varying degrees of merit) to ratification in France,[90] the United Kingdom,[91] Austria,[92] the Czech Republic,[93] Belgium,[94] Latvia,[95] Germany (perhaps most seriously),[96]

---

88   *Ibid.* Annex I.

89   For the text see [2007] OJ C306/1.

90   Conseil constitutionnel, décision no. 2007–560 du 20 décembre 2007, JO du 29 décembre 2007, p. 21813. The extension of Community competences into new areas would, for much the same reasons as the Conseil identified in its decision on ratification of the Treaty establishing a Constitution for Europe (see n. 80 above), require constitutional amendment; secured by loi constitutionnelle no. 2008–724 du 23 juillet 2008, JO du 24 juillet 2008, p. 11890.

91   *R (Wheeler)* v *Office of the Prime Minister and anor* [2008] EWHC 1409 (Admin), [2008] All ER (D) 333. The action sought to compel a referendum on ratification of the treaty on the ground that one had been promised by the government prior to ratification of the Treaty establishing a Constitution for Europe, to which, it was claimed, the Lisbon Treaty was materially identical.

92   VfGH, 30. September 2008 – SV 2/08, 3/08. Individual petitions seeking to have the approval of the treaty by the *Nationalrat* set aside and a declaration that a referendum was constitutionally required for such approval were dismissed as premature and so inadmissible, the treaty not yet having been published in the *Bundesgesetz-blatt* (and so of no force) as required by Art. 49 Abs 1 B-VG.

93   Pl. ÚS 19/08 ze dne 26. listopadu 2008 (*Lisabonská smlouva*). The petition, raised by the Senate, concerned essentially whether Czech ratification of Lisbon imperilled the attributes of a democratic state governed by the rule of law (the inviolable 'material core' (*materiální ohnisko*) of the Constitution (arts 1, 9(2)) such that it would exceed the power of conferral the state enjoys (and was created in 2001 expressly to allow for accession to the Union) under art. 10a. It did not. See further n. 98 below.

94   Grondwettelijk Hof, Arrest Nr. 58/2009, van 19 maart 2009 (*Sleeckx e.a. t/ Vlaamse Gewest*). Belgium had already ratified the treaty, a petition seeking the annulment of the decree by which the Flemish region consented to it raised subsequently, claiming (ambitiously, and unsuccessfully) that it breached various provisions of the Constitution, of the EU Charter of Fundamental Rights and of Belgian organic law.

95   Satversmes tiesa, 2009 gada 7 aprīļa spriedums lietā Nr. 2008–35–1 (*Lisabonas līgum*); no injury to the principles of 'constitutional integrity' (*Satversmes vienotības*) or of popular sovereignty (art. 2 of the Constitution), nor a substantial change (*būtiskas izmaiņas*) to Union membership requiring a referendum (art. 68(4)), no consequent violation of the principle of democratic participation (art. 101).

96   BVerfG, 30. Juni 2009 (*Lissabon-Vertrag*), BVerfGE 123, 267. The *Bundesverfassungsgericht* found the German law approving the treaty to be compatible with the Basic Law but that the law which regulated the privileges of the *Bundestag* and the *Bundesrat* in European matters (Gesetz vom 17. November 2005 über die Ausweitung und Stärkung der Rechte des Bundestages und des Bundesrates in Angelegenheiten der Europäischen Union, Bundestagsdrucksache 16/8489) would require amendment prior to ratification in order to shore up and better to elaborate those privileges so that both houses could properly discharge the responsibilities to be borne under the Treaty in a manner compliant with the Basic Law. The necessary changes were effected by means of three laws adopted in September (Gesetze vom 22. September 2009 über die Ausweitung und Stärkung der Rechte des Bundestages und des Bundesrates in Angelegenheiten der Europäischen Union; zur Änderung des Gesetzes über die Zusammenarbeit von Bundesregierung und Deutschem Bundestag in Angelegenheiten der Europäischen Union; zur Änderung des Gesetzes über die Zusammenarbeit von Bund und Ländern in Angelegenheiten der Europäischen Union; BGBl. 2009 I Se. 3022, 3026, 3031) and German ratification

Denmark[97] and the Czech Republic (again)[98] were all seen off over 2008/09. But en route, with only eight member states 'in the bag' (chronologically Hungary, Malta, France, Romania, Slovenia, Bulgaria, Austria and Denmark), in June 2008 the Irish in their (compulsory) referendum voted (by 53.4 per cent to 46.6 per cent) against ratification. There followed frantic recrimination and apportioning of blame, both within Ireland and beyond. Meanwhile other ratifications were slowly totting up. Following a number of 'legal guarantees and assurances' (of questionable reliability) made by the 27 heads of state and government in order to entice the Irish electorate[99] a second referendum was held in October 2009, this time the Irish voting decisively (67 to 33 per cent) 'yes'. There followed Polish (Mr Kaczyński having pledged to wait upon the Irish result, so signing the instrument of ratification 557 days after parliamentary approval), Irish, and finally, after much eleventh hour grandstanding by Mr Klaus, more promises from the heads of state and government[100] and the second blessing of the *Ústavní Soud*, Czech ratification in November. The Lisbon Treaty accordingly entered into force on 1 December 2009. There were *post natum* throws of the dice in

---

entered at the end of that month. Like the *Maastricht* judgment before it, the *Lisbon* judgment contains extensive discussion as to limits beyond which further Union integration will be constitutionally impermissible in Germany.

97 A number of petitioners challenged the compatibility of the Danish law of incorporation of Lisbon with § 20 of the Constitution, claiming change so fundamental as to require an election/referendum in accordance with § 88. The *Østre Landsret* dismissed the action as inadmissible for lack of petitioners' interest in the outcome (dom af 28. oktober 2009 (*Hausgaard m.fl. mod Statsminister & Udenrigsminister*), j.no. B-1889–08, 14. afdeling). That finding was reversed by the *Højesteret* (Sag 336/2009, dom af 11. januar 2011, 1. afdeling) and the case referred back to the *Østre Landsret*, which found Lisbon not to have altered the Union's identity so fundamentally as to exceed the limits of § 20 (dom af 15. juni 2012, j.no. B-222–11, 7. afdeling). The judgment is likely to be appealed. In any event, Denmark having already deposited instruments of ratification, it is likely that any judicial disapprobation will, at most, indicate constitutional limits to future Union development, as the *Højesteret* did previously, dom af 6. april 1998 (*Carlsen m.fl. mod Statsminister*), U1998.800H.

98 Pl. ÚS 29/09 ze dne 3. listopadu 2009 (*Lisabonská smlouva II*). This was a second constitutional complaint, raised by a number of disgruntled *Občanská demokratická* senators, dismissed as partly *res judicata*, partly inadmissible and partly unfounded. The court declined the request to identify a catalogue of 'non-transferable' (*nepřenositelných*) competences or define the substantive limits to the transfer of competence which would take a ratification law beyond the limits permitted by the constitution. Perhaps the most interesting plea in the complaint, that the decision of the European Council by which it afforded undertakings to Ireland (n. 99 below) constituted a material change to the treaty so that the ratification process would require to start anew, was inadmissible.

99 Decision of the Heads of State or Government of the 27 Member States of the EU, meeting within the European Council, on the concerns of the Irish people on the Treaty of Lisbon, *Bulletin EU* 6–2009, 14, Annex I; see 2.66 below.

100 Brussels European Council, 29–30 October 2009, Presidency Conclusions, para. I.2 and Annex I; see 2.66 below.

the constitutional courts of Austria (again),[101] Hungary[102] and Poland,[103] but in none was a constitutional incompatibility found.

33. Sovereign debt crisis

1.53 The post-Lisbon period has been marked by economic difficulties and a worsening sovereign debt crisis, first in Iceland, then notably in Ireland, Portugal and, first and foremost, in Greece. It had immediate impact for the 17 member states which had adopted the euro, but with the interlocking exposure to debt it spilled over across the whole Union, and beyond. The Union institutions and national governments have struggled to contain and redress the crisis in a number of ways, not wholly successfully. It has emerged as a significant test of the political will of both the Union and the member states, and particularly of the wisdom, and perhaps survival, of economic and monetary union and the euro.

34. The seventh accession

1.54 In December 2011 a Treaty of Accession was signed with Croatia. Provided that all instruments of ratification are deposited as anticipated, Croatia will join the Union on 1 July 2013, bringing the number of member states to 28.

F. RECAPITULATION

1.55 The European Union, which came into being in 1993, now comprises 27 member states. It started life in the 1950s as one, then three, Communities which constituted a 'new legal order' and developed a significant and sophisticated quasi-constitutional legal system of their own. In 1993 the Communities

---

101 VfGH, 12. Juni 2010 – SV 1/10, EuGRZ 2010, 493, a petition from a number of right-wing (FPÖ and BZÖ) *Nationalrat* deputies claiming the breadth of the Lisbon changes was tantamount to a total revision (*Gesamtänderung*) of the Constitution, so requiring a referendum (art. 44 Abs 3 B-VG). It was dismissed as inadmissible for failing to show with sufficient specificity an injury to personal (constitutional) rights.

102 143/2010 (VII. 14) AB *határozat*, an individual constitutional complaint claiming that Lisbon entailed a surrender of authority in a manner which would imperil Hungarian independence, sovereignty and adherence to the rule of law as guaranteed by 2 § of the (then) constitution. It was dismissed, the court emphasising that all constitutional propriety had been adhered to in the ratification of Lisbon and adoption of enabling legislation.

103 K 32/09, Wyrok z dnia 24 listopada 2010 r. (*Traktat z Lizbony*), 2010 Nr. 229, poz. 1506, a petition raised by a number of *Sejm* deputies and Senators claiming that Lisbon extended Union competences, principally through art. 48 TEU and art. 352 TFEU (as to which see 2.62 and 6.52–6.54 below), so as to injure national constitutional procedures in a manner which exceeded the 'normative anchors' (*kotwice normatywne*) of art. 90(1) (delegation or transfer (*przekazać*) of state authority to an international organisation) of the Constitution. It did not.

were absorbed into the new Union, comprising the central of the three 'pillars' which constituted the Union. With the end of the European Coal and Steel Community in 2002, and the Atomic Energy Community being of such specialised application and in some measure moribund, the EC (before 1993, the EEC) was pre-eminent; for virtually all purposes it was the first pillar, the central core of the Union. The Community Treaties had created institutions with broad legislative powers; they were competent to act also under the Treaty on European Union, but their powers under the Community Treaties were of an entirely different character from those under the non-Community pillars of the Union – although this is a distinction which was beginning to blur. The Union underwent massive expansion in 2004, further minor expansion in 2007, incorporating 12 southern, central and eastern European states, with a thirteenth agreed to join in 2013 and others still waiting in the wings. Following an *ad hoc* constitutional convention to map the way forward, a 'Constitution for Europe' was signed late in 2004; it provided for further change, and fundamentally the fusion of the three pillars into one (except for the Atomic Energy Community, which would survive independently, remaining outside but alongside the reformed Union). Following rejection by the French and the Dutch in referendums, the constitution went cold. It was resuscitated in 2007 in the form of the Reform, or Lisbon, Treaty, which stumbled eventually to universal ratification and entered into force on 1 December 2009. Since then the Union has been beset by decidedly choppy economic waters.

2

THE EUROPEAN UNION: STRUCTURE AND BASIC RULES

2.01 The three Communities, at the forefront of which was the European Economic Community, developed a sophisticated constitutional structure over the years to which the European Union succeeded in 2009. The development and nature of that constitutional structure will be considered in detail in Chapter 6. A new dimension was added in 1993 with the creation by the Maastricht Treaty of the European Union (in its first incarnation), built originally around the Communities. Although the European Community and the European Union were (re-)married by Lisbon – alternatively, Lisbon was the Union's genephagia of the Community whence it sprang – the consequences of Maastricht (and the failure of the Constitutional Treaty) still inform the Union's framework and the structure of the Treaties which now govern it. They can be understood only with an appreciation of those developments which led us hither. It is proposed in this chapter to consider the nature and structure of the Treaties and a number of the fundamental, or constitutional, rules set out (primarily) in the first of them.

A. CONSTITUTIONAL STRUCTURE OF THE EUROPEAN UNION

1. European Union 1993–2009

At the 1990/91 intergovernmental conferences which laid the groundwork for **2.02**
the Treaty on European Union there were some member states enthusiastic to
broaden significantly the spheres of Community activity into new fields:
primarily, economic and monetary union, the social arena, and the conduct of
foreign policy and coordination of police and judicial matters. But there were
other member states adamantly opposed. Since Treaty amendment requires the
approval of all member states,[1] the choice was therefore to abandon the
initiative or to reach some sort of accommodation. A twofold solution was
adopted. First, certain fields and activities were drawn into the Community
sphere, but the member states opposed were authorised to 'opt out' of the Treaty
rules adopted or to be adopted. This was a new variation on variable geometry –
a permanent, or at least indefinite, exclusion for defined member state(s) from
the operation of Community rules. It applied, and applies still, to economic and
monetary union (Denmark and the United Kingdom opting out)[2] and applied –
but no longer – to various social provisions (the United Kingdom opting out,
but 'opting in' subsequently).[3] It also applied to certain member states in certain
defined narrow areas, providing derogation from Treaty rules for the Danish law
on ownership of second homes[4] and the Irish law regulating abortion.[5] The
same technique was adopted subsequently to similar purpose, for example: the
insulation from Community rules by the 1994 Corfu Accession Treaty of
certain Sami rights[6] and its special dispensation for Sweden (alone) permitting
the sale of *snus* (oral tobacco) there;[7] certain provisions of the Treaty of
Amsterdam on the free movement of persons (Denmark, Ireland and the
United Kingdom opting out, the former partly, the latter two reserving the right
to opt in on an *à la carte* basis);[8] the special rules in the 2003 Athens Accession
Treaty on acquisition of property[9] and on abortion[10] in Malta; and the partial
(non-)application of the Charter of Fundamental Rights in Poland and the

---

1 See 2.62 below.
2 See 14.16 below.
3 See 14.34 below.
4 Protocol [annexed to the EC Treaty] on the Acquisition of Property in Denmark; now Protocol (No. 32) on the Acquisition of Property in Denmark.
5 Protocol (No. 17) annexed to the Treaty on European Union and the Treaties establishing the European Communities; now Protocol (No. 35) on article 40.3.3 of the Constitution of Ireland.
6 1994 Accession Treaty, Protocol No. 3 on the Sami people.
7 1994 Accession Treaty, art. 151, Annex XV, ch. X.
8 See 11.178–11.181, 11.188–11.190 below.
9 Protocol No. 6 on the Acquisition of Secondary Residences in Malta.
10 Protocol No. 7 on Abortion in Malta.

United Kingdom (and the Czech Republic).[11] And it informs the rules on 'enhanced cooperation' amongst various member states, first made possible by Amsterdam,[12] and those on common security and defence policy introduced by Lisbon.[13]

2.03 The second solution was more radical. In order to accommodate the disparate interests of the (governments of the) member states, the response was the creation of the 'European Union' and the so-called 'pillar structure' which comprised it. The central pillar was the existing Communities and their law (as amended significantly by Maastricht). The two other, flanking pillars address areas which (some) member states were unwilling to entrust to, and submit to the democratic and judicial discipline of, the Community system. They were, first, a common foreign and security policy, which was a continuation of the extra-Community system of European Political Cooperation formally recognised by, and given rudimentary institutional machinery in, the Single European Act; and, second, cooperation in the fields of justice and home affairs, thought necessary fully and effectively to ensure the achievement of the internal market (a primary goal of the Community), principally the free movement of persons.

2.04 Under the Maastricht scheme, the three pillars 'supported' the over-arching pediment, or constitutional order, of the Union. The second and third pillars extended the areas in which the member states undertook to pursue common action, but in areas which lie at the heart of the sovereignty of the state – the crown jewels, its foreign and defence policies and its power of coercion – and so not to be ceded to an autonomous Community legal order. Therefore, although the Union was 'founded on' the Communities,[14] was served by the existing Community institutions,[15] and was bound to respect and build upon the *acquis communautaire*,[16] its non-Community competences escaped in most respects the autonomous democratic and judicial machinery inherent in the first pillar – sometimes called in the pan-Union context, for sake of comparison, 'the Community method' or the Community way.[17] The other two pillars

---

11 See 6.118 below.
12 See 2.41–2.46 below.
13 See 2.52–2.58 below.
14 *TEU* (pre-Lisbon), art. 1.
15 *Ibid.* art. 3; see Part B, Introduction, below.
16 *Ibid.* art. 3, 1st para.; as to the *acquis communautaire* see Part B, Introduction, below.
17 Article I-1(1) of the draft Treaty establishing a Constitution for Europe as presented by the constitutional convention provided that '[t]he Union … shall exercise in the Community way the competences … confer[red] on it', but in the final text signed in October 2004 'in the Community way' had been altered (prosaically, and unhelpfully) to 'on a Community basis'; other languages remained unchanged (*sur le mode communautaire; in gemeinschaftlicher Weise*). The term did not survive into the Lisbon Treaty.

comprised, in effect, traditional intergovernmental treaty obligations amongst the member states, so were sometimes called the 'intergovernmental pillars' of the Union, and relied upon the rules of public international law to make them effective. They were not, for example, incorporated into UK law[18] and were not recognised by or enforceable in British courts – although the courts of other, monist, member states may have taken a more generous view. In any event they were unlike the provisions of the Community pillar in that they laid down few burdens; they were rather a blueprint for, and a promise of, future (inter-governmental) cooperation, implementation of which would be a matter for the competent institutions of the member states. Insofar as there was a constitu-tional hierarchy between Community law and (non-Community) Union law, the operation of the former took priority.[19]

This once (relatively) clear distinction slowly became blurred. There was, for example, no provision in the Treaties conferring legal personality upon the Union as there was, from the beginning, for the Community.[20] Yet in the 15 years following its creation the Union developed a distinct, if embryonic, legal personality and method of its own – what the president of the German *Bundesverfassungsgericht* called 'a partial legal order characterised by inter-national law';[21] there was the (intended) haemorrhaging of third pillar activities into the Community sphere and under the Community method – in sometime jargon, '*communautairisation*'; and Community techniques (and the Court of Justice) edged into Union activities. **2.05**

With Lisbon the process of dismantling the intergovernmental pillars was completed. But in order properly to understand the result it is useful, briefly, to address what was during a 15-year interregnum Union law but *not* Community law. **2.06**

Intergovernmental pillars

The two intergovernmental pillars created by Maastricht, upon which the member states could not agree a common (Community) approach, were Union **2.07**

---

18 See the European Communities Act 1972 (as amended), s. 1(2), which recognised as a 'Community Treaty', and so to be given legal effect, only Titles II, III and IV of the TEU, other provisions insofar as they relate to those Titles, and protocols attached by the TEU to the Community Treaties.

19 TEU (pre-Lisbon), art. 47: '[N]othing in this Treaty shall affect the Treaties establishing the European Communities or the subsequent Treaties and Acts modifying or supplementing them', and art. 29: the Union's objectives in third pillar matters shall be achieved '[w]ithout prejudice to the powers of the European Community'.

20 EEC Treaty, art. 210 (art. 281 EC (post-Amsterdam)).

21 'Eine völkerrechtlich geprägte Teilrechtsordnung': H.-J. Papier, 'Europas Neue Nüchterheit: Der Vertrag von Lissabon', a speech delivered to the Forum Constitutionis Europae, Humboldt University, Berlin, 21 February 2008.

collaboration in the fields of foreign and security policy ('second pillar' or 'Title V', after the relevant title in the text of the Treaty) matters; and justice and home affairs ('third pillar' or 'Title VI').

(i) Common Foreign and Security Policy (CFSP)

2.08 Title V of the Treaty on European Union provided the 'Provisions on Common Foreign and Security Policy' (CFSP; thought by some to be better rendered by GASP, for *Gemeinsame Außen- und Sicherheitspolitik*). CFSP grew out of the less formal European Political Cooperation under the Single European Act (and the rudimentary arrangements which preceded it),[22] covered 'all areas of foreign and security policy'[23] and was part of a Union ambition, commensurate with its economic stature, 'to assert … its identity on the international scene'.[24] To this end the member states undertook to work together, to support the Union's external and security policy 'actively and unreservedly in the spirit of loyalty and mutual solidarity' and to refrain from any action contrary to the interests of the Union or likely to impair its effectiveness as a cohesive force in international relations.[25] The 'objectives' were the safeguarding of the common values, fundamental interests, independence and integrity of the Union, the strengthening of the Union's security, the preservation of peace and international security, the promotion of international cooperation, and development and consolidation of democracy, the rule of law, and respect for human rights and fundamental freedoms.[26]

2.09 As action under CFSP effectively required the unanimous agreement of the governments of the member states, it is perhaps no surprise that experience showed unreserved cooperation, let alone unreserved enthusiasm, in foreign policy sometimes to be lacking. To give only one example, a Treaty duty of 'loyalty and mutual solidarity' does not best describe the events leading to the 2003 invasion of Iraq. Even more remote was, and is, the 'progressive framing' of a common defence policy. There is, of course, an irony in nine member states (five of them in previous guises) and part of another (Germany) having been party to the Warsaw Pact. But there were real difficulties for some member states in which neutrality is, or was, a constitutional imperative, a matter of state policy, or an ingrained habit.[27] Nevertheless significant progress was made,

---

22 See 1.16 above. The TEU (pre-Amsterdam), art. P(2) repealed the provisions of the Single European Act dealing with EPC, which were subsumed into the more sophisticated provisions of Title V.
23 TEU (pre-Lisbon), art. 11.
24 *Ibid.* art. 2, 2nd indent.
25 *Ibid.* art. 11(2).
26 *Ibid.* art. 11.
27 See e.g., the Staatsvertrag vom 15. Mai 1955 (Staatsvertrag von Wien), BGBl. 152/1955 and the Bundesverfassungsgesetz vom 26. Oktober 1955 über die Neutralität Österreichs (Neutralitätsgesetz–NeutrG), BGBl. 211/1955 which, being the price of the end of the four power occupation, guaranteed Austrian 'permanent

sometimes quietly, on creating coherent policies and projecting and protecting them abroad.

(ii) Justice and Home Affairs (JHA)

The third pillar, or Title VI matters, was originally 'Provisions on Cooperation **2.10** in the Fields of Justice and Home Affairs' (JHA). It constituted recognition that the (Community) goal of the free movement of persons could not be wholly achieved without addressing matters ancillary to free movement but which trench upon sensitive areas still within the sphere of national sovereignty. JHA drew into the Union sphere and declared to be matters of common interest issues ancillary to the free movement of persons (which was a Community goal) asylum, external border controls, immigration and the status and rights of third country nationals, customs cooperation, police cooperation and judicial cooperation.[28] It was materially altered in 1999 by the Treaty of Amsterdam which created the concept of the area of freedom, security and justice which spanned Community and Union activities, so providing for the severing of some JHA matters (asylum, immigration, rights of third country nationals and judicial cooperation in civil matters) and their transfer from the third pillar to the first – put otherwise, their *communautairisation*.

The remaining third pillar was thus narrowed and thereafter renamed 'Pro- **2.11** visions on Police and Judicial Cooperation in Criminal Matters', but the shorthand 'JHA' survived. It addressed thereafter common action amongst the member states in the fields of police and judicial cooperation in criminal matters,[29] specifically closer cooperation between police forces, customs authorities and other competent authorities, both directly and through Europol,[30] and closer cooperation between judicial and other competent national authorities, including cooperation within a 'European Judicial Cooperation Unit' (Eurojust).[31] Europol was established in 1995,[32] Eurojust in 2002.[33] Union activity was not to trench upon the responsibilities of member states with regard to maintenance of law and order and safeguarding internal

---

[*immerwährende*] neutrality' and a ban on accession to any military alliance, and was long thought to constitute an ineluctable constitutional bar to Austrian accession to the Communities; *cf.* the present art. 23f. B-VG. The problem is one shared, in varying ways and degrees, also by Sweden, Finland, Ireland (in which the issue is thought to have contributed significantly to the failure of the 'yes' vote in the first Lisbon referendum) and Malta, which ensures that the CFSP is marked, effectively, by permanent variable geometry.

28   TEU (pre-Amsterdam), art. K.1.
29   TEU (pre-Lisbon), art. 29, 1st para.; see also art. 2, 4th indent.
30   *Ibid.* art. 29, 2nd para., 1st indent; art. 30.
31   *Ibid.* art. 29, 2nd para., 2nd indent; art. 31.
32   For the text see [1995] OJ C316/2.
33   Decision 2002/187 [2002] OJ L63/1.

security.[34] As with CFSP, action under Title VI generally required the unanimous consent of the governments of the member states, although this principle was subject to a slow erosion. JHA activity was in the event significantly more successful and significantly more robust than CFSP. Much was achieved over the 16 years of its operation, and this contributed to the palatability of its (almost) complete *communautairisation* by Lisbon.

2. The Lisbon Treaty

2.12 The Treaty establishing a Constitution for Europe which grew out of the 2002/03 constitutional conference and was signed in 2004 proposed that the Community and the non-Community pillars of the Union be (re-)fused into one. Following its failure, the Treaty of Lisbon cannibalised it and reproduced much of its substance, but there are two major differences: first, Lisbon removed or downgraded much of the 'sting' of the Constitutional Treaty, its trappings which smacked too much, in some quarters, of ambition to statehood: a flag,[35] an anthem[36] (although both of these existed and continue to exist unofficially, and for a resolute 16 member states 'continue as symbols to express the sense of community of the people in the European Union and their allegiance to it'),[37] an office of Minister for Foreign Affairs,[38] an express provision on the primacy of Union law,[39] a Treaty-entrenched Charter of Fundamental Rights[40] and, perhaps most incendiary, the very name 'constitution'. Lisbon downplays these and is intentionally modest in ambition. If compared to the ringing preambular aspirations of its predecessors:

- 'RESOLVED ... to create ... the basis for a deeper and broader community among peoples long divided by bloody conflicts; and to lay the

---

34 TEU (pre-Lisbon), art. 33.

35 Treaty establishing a Constitution for Europe, art. I-8. The flag – comprising a circle of 12 gold stars on a blue field – originated in the Council of Europe in 1955 and is used by it and the Union both.

36 *Ibid.*, being the 'Ode to Joy' from the fourth movement of Beethoven's Ninth Symphony (arr. von Karajan, *allegretto* (originally *allegro assai*), without lyrics). The anthem too was adopted by the Council of Europe in 1972.

37 So recognised in a declaration annexed to the Final Act of the Lisbon Treaty, and extending to the flag, the anthem, the Union's 'motto' ('united in diversity') and the euro as its currency; Declaration (No. 52) by the Kingdom of Belgium, the Republic of Bulgaria, the Federal Republic of Germany, the Hellenic Republic, the Kingdom of Spain, the Italian Republic, the Republic of Cyprus, the Republic of Lithuania, the Grand-Duchy of Luxembourg, the Republic of Hungary, the Republic of Malta, the Republic of Austria, the Portuguese Republic, Romania, the Republic of Slovenia and the Slovak Republic on the symbols of the European Union. The symbols of the Union are also 'recognised and espoused' by the European Parliament (Rules of Procedure, rule 213.1) which 'celebrates' Europe day (rule 213.2).

38 Treaty establishing a Constitution for Europe, art. I-28.

39 *Ibid.* art. I-6.

40 *Ibid.* Part II (arts II-61–114).

foundations for institutions which will give direction to a destiny henceforward shared' (1951);[41]

- 'DETERMINED to lay the foundations of an ever closer union among the peoples of Europe' (1957);[42]

- 'RESOLVED to mark a new stage in the process of European integration', 'DESIRING to deepen the solidarity between their peoples' and 'RESOLVED to continue the process of creating an ever closer union' (1992);[43]

- 'CONVINCED that … the peoples of Europe are determined to transcend their former divisions and, united ever more closely, to forge a common destiny' (2004),[44]

the sole indent of the Lisbon Preamble is prosaic, almost tired:

- 'DESIRING to complete the process started by the Treaty of Amsterdam and by the Treaty of Nice with a view to enhancing the efficiency and democratic legitimacy of the Union and to improving the coherence of its action'.

Secondly, and more importantly, the two are structured very differently. The Constitutional Treaty was one of global amendment: it would dismantle the existing (Union and European Community) Treaties and embody them, and the future Union, in a single instrument ('the constitution') which formed a wholly new, and comprehensive, text. Lisbon follows instead the traditional technique of a series of amendments to the existing Treaties: it does not abandon them, rather it simply (if extensively) amends them. Formally styled the 'Treaty of Lisbon amending the Treaty on European Union and the Treaty establishing the European Community', it consists of seven articles only: the vast bulk of it (124 pages in the *Official Journal*) comprises articles 1 and 2, which list the amendments to the then existing Union and Community Treaties, respectively. They present thus an impenetrable maze of cross-referenced numbered articles, possible to read intelligently only with copious cross-referencing to the texts they amend or replace. Thereafter, articles 3 through 7 are simple, brief provisions, addressing the normal paraphernalia of treaties and providing for: **2.13**

---

41 ECSC Treaty, Preamble, 5th para.
42 EEC Treaty, Preamble, 1st para.
43 TEU (pre-Lisbon), Preamble, 1st, 4th and 11th paras.
44 Treaty establishing a Constitution for Europe, Preamble, 3rd para.

- duration of the Treaty itself – like the Treaties it amended, unlimited (article 3);
- a protocol on amendments to the existing protocols attached to the various Treaties (article 4(1));
- a protocol providing for amendment to the Euratom Treaty (article 4(2));
- renumeration of Treaty articles upon entry into force, in order (like Amsterdam before it) once again to streamline the jumble of Treaty articles resulting from the amendment process (article 5);
- ratification and entry into force: on 1 January 2009, or, failing ratification by all member states by that date, on the first day of the month following deposit of instrument of ratification by the last member state to do so (article 6); and
- authentic languages and depositary (article 7).

2.14 Articles 1 and 2 provided for a new 'Treaty establishing the European Union' which is a significantly amended version of the previous TEU, and a companion 'Treaty on the Functioning of the European Union', which is in large measure a chopped and changed EC Treaty; the continuity of the predecessor Treaties is apparent in that the latter is represented still as having six contracting parties and to have been signed ('done') at Rome on 25 March 1957, similarly the new TEU as having 12 contracting parties and to have been signed at Maastricht on 7 February 1992. A Treaty on the 'functioning' of the Union does no favours to the English ear, but a Treaty on the *Arbeitsweise* or the *werking* of the Union sounds less ill, and conveys more clearly what it is about. The two taken together establish and define the European Union, or 'the Union':

> The Union shall be founded on the present Treaty [establishing the European Union] and on the Treaty on the Functioning of the European Union ... The Union shall replace and succeed the European Community.[45]

Thus the European Community disappeared, absorbed by the European Union with a single legal personality[46] which assumed the complex, quasi-constitutional system which had characterised the Community way. The pillar structure is disassembled, police and judicial cooperation in criminal matters made (almost) wholly subject to the Community method (or wholly *communautairised*, which term is useful but will presumably now fall out of use and favour); and common foreign and security policy (buttressed by additional new provisions on the Union's external action generally and on a subset of CFSP

---

45   Amended TEU, art. 1, 3rd para.
46   *Ibid.* art. 47.

addressing common security and defence policy) brought within the Union umbrella but subject still to special rules and procedures which cannot be characterised as *communautaire*. The amended Treaty on European Union provides the basic constitutional rules of the Union across six Titles and 55 articles; the (much more extensive, 358 article) Treaty on the Functioning of the Union organises the way in which it operates, determining the areas of, delimitation of and arrangements for exercising its competences.[47] This construction suggests a subordination of the latter to the former, but the two Treaties 'have the same legal value'[48] so must be read as one. Together they are referred to as 'the Treaties'.[49] In order to distinguish between them (and from pre-existing treaties), where they are cited henceforward in this book, the Treaty establishing the European Union as amended will be referred to as the 'TEU', its predecessor as the 'TEU (pre-Lisbon)', and the Treaty on the Functioning of the European Union as the 'TFEU'. Where reference is made to the latter's predecessor it will be to the 'EEC Treaty' (as it was 1958–1993) or the 'EC Treaty' (1993–2009), as appropriate.

The Atomic Energy Community survives Lisbon and continues to exist **2.15** alongside but legally distinct from the Union, the member states 'recalling the necessity that the provisions of the Treaty establishing the European Atomic Energy Community should continue to have full legal effect'.[50] As previously, Euratom is *lex specialis*, the provisions on the Union Treaties not to derogate from the Euratom Treaty.[51] A declaration of five member states attached to the Lisbon Treaty notes that the Euratom Treaty has not been substantially amended since its entry into force in 1958, that it should therefore be 'brought up to date' and supports the convening of an intergovernmental conference to that purpose 'as soon as possible'.[52]

B. TREATY ON EUROPEAN UNION

Notwithstanding the same legal value adhering to both there is still a logic of **2.16** hierarchy between the Treaties, for the Treaty on European Union consists primarily of 'constitutional' provisions, those classically a function of and

---

47 Treaty on the Functioning of the European Union, art. 1(1).
48 Amended TEU, art. 1, 3rd para.; Treaty on the Functioning of the European Union, art. 1(2).
49 *Ibid.*
50 Treaty of Lisbon, Protocol (No. 12) amending the Treaty establishing the European Atomic Energy Community, Preamble, 1st para.
51 Euratom Treaty, art. 106a(3).
52 Declaration (No. 54) by the Federal Republic of Germany, Ireland, Republic of Hungary, Republic of Austria and the Kingdom of Sweden. Amendment of the Euratom Treaty is to be secured by what the TEU calls the ordinary revision procedure; Euratom Treaty, art. 106a (carrying over TEU, art. 48(2)–(5)).

typically set out in a basic law, and fundamental principles of general application to which the operation of the Union, the detail of it set out in the Treaty
on the Functioning of the Union, is made subject. Put otherwise, there is a
precedent in the scheme of the original EEC Treaty which was to progress from
the general to the specific: Part One, called the 'Principles' (*Grundsätze*), set out
the basic aims of the Community, the institutions and the principles in the light
of which what followed was to be interpreted and applied. The Court of Justice
would often refer to Part One, and put great store by it, in interpreting the later
provisions. Much of it was drawn by Lisbon into the Treaty on European
Union, which now performs that function.

2.17 The Treaty itself is fairly succinct. It consists of six Titles, as follows:

- Title I: Common provisions
- Title II: Provisions on democratic principles
- Title III: Provisions on the institutions
- Title IV: Provisions on enhanced cooperation
- Title V: Provisions on the Union's external action and the Common
  Foreign and Security Policy
- Title VI: Final provisions.

Annexed to the Treaty are 37 protocols; they are also annexed to the TFEU and
some of them to the Euratom Treaty; and still more may be found annexed to
the various accession Treaties. The protocols form an integral part of,[53] and
have the same legal status as,[54] the treaty to which they are annexed. Some have
disappeared, some are spent, but some remain of great legal and practical
importance. Also noted alongside the Treaties are 65 declarations which were
annexed to the Final Act of the Lisbon Intergovernmental Conference; many
more declarations annexed to previous amending/accession treaties survive still.
Declarations indicate a policy intent or gloss on the part of one or more of the
governments of the member states, of the intergovernmental conference which
precedes treaty amendment, or of the Union institutions. The Vienna Convention on the Law of Treaties recognises declarations as part of the 'context' in
which the express terms of a treaty find themselves for purposes of interpreting
the treaty,[55] the Court of Justice sometimes takes notice of them 'as being

---

53   TEU, art. 51 (ex art. 311 EC).
54   This is implicit in cases in which the Court of Justice interprets and applies various protocols; e.g., Cases T-7
     etc./98 *de Nicola* v *Banca europea per gli investimenti* [2001] ECR-SC II-185; Case C-469/03 *Criminal
     proceedings against Miraglia* [2005] ECR I-2009.
55   Vienna Convention of 23 May 1969 on the Law of Treaties, 1155 UNTS 331, in force 27 January 1980, art.
     31(2)(b).

instruments for the interpretation of the … Treaty',[56] but they are not binding as part, and in the manner, of the Treaty texts.

It is proposed to consider the six Titles of the TEU in turn. **2.18**

1. Title I: Common provisions

(a) The Union's values and objectives

Articles 2 and 3 of the TEU represent significant restructuring of the introduc- **2.19** tory provisions of the previous Treaties. But they are not new to Lisbon, rather they were lifted *verbatim* from the Treaty establishing a Constitution for Europe. Article 2 provides:

> The Union is founded on the values of respect for human dignity, freedom, democracy, equality, the rule of law and respect for human rights, including the rights of persons belonging to minorities.

> These values are common to the Member States in a society in which pluralism, non-discrimination, tolerance, justice, solidarity and equality between women and men prevail.

The Treaty articles in Part I of the Constitutional Treaty each having a heading (those of the TEU do not), article 2 was called 'the Union's values'.[57]

Article 3 provides what the Constitutional Treaty called 'the Union's object- **2.20** ives'.[58] It begins:

> 1. The Union's aim [*but*; *Ziel*] is to promote peace, its values and the well-being of its peoples.

Previously neither the Union nor the Community had (in English) an aim, and certainly not this one. Rather the Union had a number of objectives (*objectifs*; *Ziele*)[59] and the Community a 'task' (*mission*; *Aufgabe*),[60] the latter corresponding roughly to what follows in article 3:

> 2. The Union shall offer its citizens an area of freedom, security and justice without internal frontiers, in which the free movement of persons is ensured in conjunction

---

56 Case C-135/08 *Rottmann* v *Freistaat Bayern* [2010] ECR I-1449, at para. 40.
57 Treaty establishing a Constitution for Europe, art. I-2; which was in fact drawn partly from the then existing TEU, art. 6(1).
58 Treaty establishing a Constitution for Europe, art. I-3.
59 TEU (pre-Lisbon), art. 2.
60 EC Treaty, art. 2.

with appropriate measures with respect to external border controls, asylum, immigration and the prevention and combating of crime.

3. The Union shall establish an internal market. It shall work for the sustainable development of Europe based on balanced economic growth and price stability, a highly competitive social market economy, aiming at full employment and social progress, and a high level of protection and improvement of the quality of the environment. It shall promote scientific and technological advance.

It shall combat social exclusion and discrimination, and shall promote social justice and protection, equality between women and men, solidarity between generations and protection of the rights of the child.

It shall promote economic, social and territorial cohesion, and solidarity among Member States.

It shall respect its rich cultural and linguistic diversity, and shall ensure that Europe's cultural heritage is safeguarded and enhanced.

4. The Union shall establish an economic and monetary union whose currency is the euro.

5. In its relations with the wider world, the Union shall uphold and promote its values and interests and contribute to the protection of its citizens.

There followed in the EC Treaty a list of Community 'activities',[61] essentially the fields in which the Community was competent to act in order to achieve its task. They are now restructured, rechristened ('competences') and remain in the TFEU.

(b) Relations between the Union and the member states

2.21 Article 4, also lifted in the main from the Constitutional Treaty, begins:

1. In accordance with Article 5, competences not conferred upon the Union in the Treaties remain with the Member States.

Article 5 repeats the primary clause *verbatim*.[62] It is a device for greater certainty (a 'residual power' clause) common to most (but not all) federal constitutions but previously implicit only in the Treaties. For some reason it is now worth saying twice, and repeated, quite unnecessarily, in a declaration annexed to the Final Act of the Lisbon IGC.[63]

---

61 *Ibid.* art. 3.
62 TEU, art. 5(2), final sentence.
63 Declaration (No. 18) in relation to the delimitation of competences.

Mutual respect and sincere cooperation

Whilst the institutions created by the Treaties act autonomously of the author- **2.22** ities of the member states – this being a facet of the 'autonomy' of Union law, an important constitutional principle in its conduct[64] – and the authorities of the member states certainly act independently of the Union, they share a duty to respect the other and cooperate fully in order that Union law be made effective. The duty owed by the member states and their authorities was derived from article 5 of the EEC Treaty, and creates significant burdens for them; this is discussed below.[65] There was equivalent express provision in neither the Euratom Treaty nor the pre-Lisbon TEU, but the principle 'is also applicable in respect of [the Euratom Treaty]'[66] and 'applie[d] in [pre-Lisbon] Union law, without needing to be expressly mentioned'.[67] Indeed

> [t]hat principle is of general application and is especially binding in the area of police and judicial cooperation in criminal matters (commonly known as 'Justice and Home Affairs') (JHA) governed by Title VI of the [pre-Lisbon] EU Treaty, which is moreover entirely based on cooperation between Member States and the institutions.[68]

On the flipside of the coin the only Treaty reference appeared in the TEU, which provided that '[t]he Union shall respect the national identities of its Member States',[69] a provision included in the Treaties only with Maastricht. Nonetheless 'the … duty of loyal cooperation flow[s] in both directions: [it] appl[ies] to the Community as well as to the Member States'.[70] On both sides it is normally called the duty of 'sincere cooperation',[71] occasionally 'genuine cooperation'[72] (in both cases *cooperation loyale*; *loyale Zusammenarbeit*), and is analogous to the fundamental German constitutional principle of *Bundestreue* (*Grundsatz des bundesfreundlichen Verhaltens*), or 'federal fidelity'; hence, sometimes use of the terms (by German speakers) *Gemeinschaftstreue* and, even

---

64 See 6.12 below.
65 See 6.31–6.33 below.
66 Case C-115/08 *Land Oberösterreich* v *ČEZ* [2009] ECR I-10265, at para. 138.
67 Case C-105/03 *Criminal proceedings against Pupino* [2005] ECR I-5285, *per* A-G Kokott, at para. 27 of her opinion; accepted by the Court, at paras 39–42 of the judgment.
68 Case T-284/08 *People's Mojehadin Organization of Iran* v *Council* [2008] ECR II-3487, at para. 53.
69 TEU (pre-Lisbon), art. 6(3).
70 Cases C-402 and 415/05P *Kadi and Al Bakaraat* v *Council and Commission* (Kadi II) [2008] ECR I-6351, *per* A-G Poiares Maduro, at para. 32 of his opinion.
71 Case 230/81 *Luxembourg* v *Parliament* [1983] ECR 255; Case 2/88 Imm *Zwartveld and ors* [1990] ECR I-3365; [1990] ECR I-4405; Case C-234/89 *Delimitis* v *Henninger Bräu* [1991] ECR I-935; Case C-344/98 *Masterfoods* v *HB Ice Cream* [2000] ECR I-11363; Case C-94/00 *Roquette Frères* v *Directeur Général de la Concurrence* [2002] ECR I-9011; Case T-339/04 *France Télécom* v *Commission* [2007] ECR II-521.
72 Case C-45/07 *Commission* v *Greece* [2009] ECR I-701, at para. 25; Case C-246/07 *Commission* v *Sweden* [2010] ECR I-3317, at para 71. It has also been called by the British Supreme Court 'wholehearted cooperation': *Inntrepreneur Pub Co. and ors* v *Crehan* [2006] UKHL 38, [2007] 1 AC 333, *per* Lord Bingham at 339.

before Lisbon, *Unionstreue*.[73] The relationship was written into the Treaties by Lisbon as part of article 4 thus:

> 2. The Union shall respect the equality of Member States before the Treaties as well as their national identities, inherent in [inhérente à zum Ausdruck kommt] their fundamental structures, political and constitutional, inclusive of regional and local self-government. It shall respect their essential State functions, including ensuring the territorial integrity of the State, maintaining law and order and safeguarding national security. In particular, national security remains the sole responsibility of each Member State.
> 3. Pursuant to the principle of sincere cooperation, the Union and the Member States shall, in full mutual respect, assist each other in carrying out tasks which flow from the Treaties.

On the Union side the duty applies principally to the Commission, mirroring that of the member states and largely to assist national authorities in the effective application of Union law. Even where no duty can be said to exist, the Commission 'should in principle warmly welcome any invitation by a national court to cooperate, on a voluntary basis' in its proceedings.[74] It was in service of this logic that the Court improbably ordered the Commission to collaborate with a Dutch criminal court investigation in *Zwartveld*,[75] for the duty of sincere cooperation borne by the institutions is 'of particular importance' where that cooperation involves national courts responsible for ensuring the application of Union law.[76] The Commission has in a number of spheres adopted notices in order to codify and give greater definition to it. It was also declared by the intergovernmental conference which led to the Treaty of Nice to apply to relations between the institutions themselves[77] and Lisbon cemented this in the Treaties, requiring that they 'practice [*sic*] mutual sincere cooperation'.[78]

2.23   The obligation of article 4(2) that the Union respect the national identities of the member states (hence sometimes the 'identity clause') is now, according to the Polish *Trybunał Konstytucyjny*, 'the principal axiological basis of the European Union': a bold formulation, too early to measure its accuracy; but maybe augmented – certainly not diminished – by appearing alongside the duty of sincere cooperation 'in full mutual respect'.[79] It has been expressly recognised

---

73   Case C-105/03 *Pupino*, n. 67 above, *per* A-G Kokott, at para. 25 ff. of her opinion (in its original (and authentic) German; rendered 'loyalty to the Union' in English and '*le devoir de loyauté à l'égard de l'Union*' in French).
74   Case C-275/00 *European Community* v *First and Franex* [2002] ECR I-10943, at para. 34.
75   Case 2/88 Imm *Zwartveld*, n. 71 above; see 5.30 below, n. 158.
76   Case 2/88 Imm *Zwartveld*, n. 71 above ([1990] ECR I-3365), at para. 18; Case C-429/07 *Inspecteur van de Belastingdienst* v *X* [2009] ECR I-4833, at para. 21.
77   Declaration No. 3 on Article 10 of the Treaty establishing the European Community.
78   TEU, art. 13(2).
79   K 32/09, Wyrok z dnia 24 listopada 2010 r. (*Traktat z Lizbony*), 2010 Nr 229, poz. 1506, at para. 2.1 ('zasadniczą podstawę aksjologiczną Unii Europejskiej').

and applied directly by the Court of Justice in determining whether an Austrian ban on noble titles and privileges is a legitimate means of safeguarding national identity and republican status[80] and recognising the legitimacy of measures to protect a member state's official national language.[81] The (express) principle of the equality of the member states before the Treaties is new with Lisbon, and it is not clear what, if any, ramifications it may have.

Finally, and certainly not least, article 4(3) continues, imposing upon the **2.24** member states two general obligations, one positive, the other negative:

> The Member States shall take any appropriate measure, general or particular, to ensure fulfilment of the obligations arising out of the Treaties or resulting from the acts of the institutions of the Union.

> The Member States shall facilitate the achievement of the Union's tasks and refrain from any measure which could jeopardise the attainment of the Union's objectives.

From the beginning this had been a self-standing Treaty article.[82] It could be read simply as a statement of *pacta sunt servanda*. But the terms, and particularly the second limb, said sometimes to embody a duty of good faith (*Loyalitätspflicht*),[83] were co-opted by the Court as a means of identifying substantial duties for the member states – and *all* public authorities of the member states, including, in circumstances, the courts – across a wide range of activities; in fact, '[i]n all the areas corresponding to the objectives of the Treaty'.[84] The breadth of these duties will be discussed below.[85] The Lisbon reorientation, bundling it into a larger paragraph which is itself only part of a wider article dealing with the relationship between the Union and the member states, may have dealt it a disservice should it cause the central importance it has long been accorded – it has been called the most important general principle of Community law[86] – to diminish.

---

80 Case C-208/09 *Sayn-Wittgenstein* v *Landeshauptmann von Wien* [2010] ECR I-13693, at para. 92.
81 Case C-391/09 *Runevič-Vardyn and anor* v *Vilniaus miesto savivaldybės administracija*, judgment of 12 May 2011, not yet reported, at para. 86; Case C-51/08 *Commission* v *Luxembourg*, judgment of 24 May 2011, not yet reported, at para. 124. The issue of safeguarding the national language had been recognised previously as a matter of legitimate public policy, long before Lisbon and long before the Charter, in Case 379/87 *Groener* v *Minister for Education and anor* [1989] ECR 3967. Article 4(2) has been cited in one other case, Case C-3/10 *Affatato* v *Azienda Sanitaria Provinciale di Cosenza* [2010] ECR I-121* but peripherally only.
82 EEC Treaty, art. 5 (subsequently art. 10 EC).
83 C-531/07 *Fachverband der Buch- und Medienwirtschaft* v *LIBRO Handelsgesellschaft* [2009] ECR I-3717, *per* A-G Trstenjak, at para. 125 of her opinion.
84 Case C-246/07 *Commission* v *Sweden* [2010] ECR I-3317, at para. 69.
85 See 6.31–6.33 below.
86 J. Temple-Lang, 'Article 10 EC: The Most Important "General Principle" of Community Law', in U Bernitz et al., *General Principles of EC Law in a Process of Development* (Kluwer, 2008), p. 75.

(c) Fundamental principles

2.25 Article 5 of the TEU is also lifted *verbatim* (except replacing 'Constitution' with 'Treaties') from the Constitutional Treaty, setting out what the latter called 'fundamental principles' of Union competences.[87] They are three: the principle of conferral, which articulates the limits of Union competences, and the principles of subsidiarity and proportionality, which govern their use.[88]

(i) Conferral

2.26 The Union enjoys no inherent sovereignty. It is seen for the most part as a species of confederation, deriving its personality and authority from the Treaties, the creators of which continue to exist (and continue to be, and to be recognised to be, states in international law); and although it is a very wide personality and authority, it must act always in accordance with and within the limits set by the Treaties. In other words, Union authority is a *compétence d'attribution*. This was inherent in the original Community system although made express only in 1993, the EC Treaty thereafter providing that '[t]he Community shall act within the limits of the powers conferred upon it by this Treaty and of the objectives assigned to it therein'.[89] It was emphasised as such by the Court of Justice, recognising in an advisory opinion of high constitutional significance that '[i]t follows from Article 3b of the Treaty … that the Community … has only those powers which have been conferred upon it'.[90] It is a principle which of course applied even more strictly to the pre-Lisbon Union, although the then TEU, oddly, did not say it expressly. In its present formulation:

1. The limits of Union competences are governed by the principle of conferral …
2. Under the principle of conferral, the Union shall act only within the limits of the competences conferred upon it by the Member States in the Treaties to attain the objectives set out therein.[91]

A conference declaration notes that the legal personality conferred upon the Union does not 'in any way' extend its authority beyond these limits.[92] There is no clue as to why it is rendered (awkwardly) as 'conferral' in English, which appears to have started life in the constitutional convention's 2003 draft Constitutional Treaty; it remains in French *le principe d'attribution* – or perhaps clearest, *der Grundsatz der begrenzten Einzelmächtigung*. The Treaties now, with

---

87 Treaty establishing a Constitution for Europe, art. I-11.
88 TEU, art. 5(1).
89 EC Treaty (pre-Amsterdam), art. 3b, 1st para. (subsequently art. 5, 1st para.).
90 Opinion 2/94 *Re Accession to the ECHR* [1996] ECR I-1759, at para. 23.
91 TEU, art. 5; see also TFEU, art. 7.
92 Declaration (No. 24) concerning the legal personality of the European Union.

Lisbon, go on to define three categories of competences conferred upon the Union;[93] in one of them harmonisation of national law by the Union is expressly excluded,[94] this being a constitutional device first introduced by Maastricht[95] and one (of several) designed to prevent 'competence creep'.

The principle is all at the same time simple, fundamental – and yet a Pandora's **2.27** box. It gives rise to a number of theoretical and practical difficulties which vex a number of constitutional courts, such as the fluidity of the *Grundnorm*, the determination of the limits it sets, the power, if any, of the Union to (re-)set the limits of its powers (*Kompetenz-Kompetenz*), the identification of the correct (and by what tests?) basis in the treaties for action, theories of implied powers, and a serious risk of chafing against various principles of constitutional law, some fundamental, in a number of member states. That some constitutional/ supreme courts cannot resist articulating their own views is unsurprising, for if the Treaty formula is that the Union may act 'only within the limits of the competences conferred upon it by the Member States' it is almost inviting them to explore, and set down markers, on what, in accordance with their own constitutional law, it is permissible to confer. It may therefore appear to have the effect, or may indeed have it, of making Union law *de facto* a prisoner of national constitutional law. It also reinforces the status and responsibilities of the Court of Justice as a constitutional court, for

> [o]ne of the most difficult but, at the same time, fundamental tasks of this Court is that of controlling the boundaries of the Union's actions. This is fundamental to the preservation of the balance of power between the States and the Union.[96]

These are matters of highest constitutional importance, adhering to the development of the Community legal order now inherited by the Union. They will be discussed in some detail in Chapter 6.

(ii) Subsidiarity

If conferral defines whether the Union has authority to act, subsidiarity and **2.28** proportionality define, respectively, whether it *should* act and the restraint, or finesse, it should show when it does so. Unlike proportionality, subsidiarity was not inherent in the Treaties, although it is a common enough device of constitutional law, not least that of federations, as a means of entrenching

---

93 TFEU, arts 2–4, 6; see 7.06–7.10 below.
94 *Ibid.* art. 2(5).
95 EC Treaty (pre-Amsterdam), arts 126(4), 127(4), 128(5), 129(4).
96 Case C-58/08 *R (Vodaphone and ors)* v *Secretary of State for Business, Enterprise and Regulatory Reform* [2010] ECR I-4999, *per* A-G Poiares Maduro, at para. 1 of his opinion.

regional autonomy against incursion from the centre.[97] It came latterly to Community law, first recognised in the European Parliament's 1984 Draft (Spinelli) Treaty on European Union,[98] and seducing in particular the framers of the Maastricht Treaty.

2.29 Subsidiarity is a principle of social ordering which posits that matters ought to be regulated by the lowest or least centralised of competent authorities or organisations suitable to the task at hand. In other words, each (successively) higher authority should have a subsidiary function, performing only those tasks which cannot be performed effectively at a more immediate or local (or, in Catholic social philosophy, personal)[99] level. It was first bent to Union purpose by Maastricht which formally incorporated it as a principle in both the Union and the EC Treaties[100] and emphasised it at the outset of the former by its noting a Union 'in which decisions are taken ... as closely as possible to the citizen'.[101] That admonition survived Lisbon.[102] The principle itself is now formulated thus:

> Under the principle of subsidiarity, in areas which do not fall within its exclusive competence, the Union shall act only if and in so far as the objectives of the proposed action cannot be sufficiently achieved by the Member States, either at central level or at regional and local level, but can rather, by reason of the scale or effects of the proposed action, be better achieved at Union level.[103]

In its Treaty version there is therefore a twofold test: Union action is justified only if it serves an end which both (a) cannot be achieved satisfactorily at the national/regional/local level *and* (b) can be achieved better at Union level. It applies only in fields in which the Union and the member states share concurrent jurisdiction; expressly, and then logically, it can apply neither where the Union enjoys exclusive competence nor in areas remaining within member state sovereignty and untouched by the Treaties. Whether the new Lisbon formulation, which for the first time expressly enjoins regional and local authorities to the Union task (for which it won approbation from the Bundes-verfassungsgericht),[104] requires the member states to import the principle into national law or practice in concurrent fields (hitherto it has been an (ironic)

---

97 See especially § 72 II GG; similarly, Ahvenanmaan Itsehallintolaki 1991/1144, 18.27 §.
98 Draft Treaty establishing the European Union, Preamble, 9th para. and art. 12(2).
99 It forms a core principle of Catholic social philosophy on the nature of the relationship of the individual to the wider community and the state; see Pius XI, *Quadragesimo Anno* (1931), p. 79.
100 TEU (pre-Amsterdam), art. B, 2nd para.; EC Treaty, art. 3b, 2nd para.
101 TEU (pre-Amsterdam), art. A, 2nd para.
102 TEU, art. 1, 2nd para.
103 *Ibid.* art. 5(3). See also Preamble, 13th para. and art. 10(3), which provide further reference to subsidiarity.
104 BVerfG, 30. Juni 2009 (*Lissabon-Vertrag*), BVerfGE 123, 267.

exercise of subsidiarity that member states are not obliged to do so) has not yet been addressed.

Since its introduction into the Treaties subsidiarity has generated much heat **2.30** but little light. The European Council and the Commission indicated their views on its meaning,[105] the three political institutions had, even prior to Maastricht's entry into force, agreed a procedure amongst them in order to take account of its requirements,[106] and it was addressed for that purpose in an Amsterdam protocol.[107] Yet a previous president of the Court of Justice pronounced the original Maastricht formula to be 'gobbledygook'.[108] Whilst the Germans are able happily to apply their no less woolly formula,[109] how far the Treaty principle is, as such, justiciable remains fully to be tested. It has been seriously argued before the Court on only a few occasions,[110] and in each the Court pronounced itself, fairly peremptorily, satisfied that the institutions had taken due and proper account of its requirements.[111] This suggests a fairly cautious, or gentle, view of intensity of review, if not of justiciability of the principle itself. Certainly it would be difficult to identify a perceptible self-restraint on the part of the Union institutions flowing from it.

However, Lisbon provided it with fresh blood. The Treaties now require the **2.31** Union institutions to apply it (they 'shall apply the principle of subsidiarity') in accordance with the amended protocol,[112] the protocol requiring that all draft

---

105 European Council in Edinburgh, Conclusions of the Presidency, *Bulletin EC* 12–1992, 12–18; Commission Communiqué on Subsidiarity, *Bulletin EC* 10–1992, 116–26.

106 Interinstitutional agreement of 25 October 1993, *Bulletin EC* 10–1993, 119.

107 Protocol on the Application of the Principles of Subsidiarity and Proportionality. Even prior to 1999, the Parliament scrutinised every legislative proposal in order to determine whether it complied with the principle; see now its Rules of Procedure, rule 58.

108 A. Mackenzie Stuart, 'A Formula for Failure', *The Times* (London), 11 December 1992.

109 § 72 II GG was brought expressly within the jurisdiction of the *Bundesverfassungsgericht* in 1994 (§ 93 I Abs. 2a GG) which has since set aside federal legislation for breach of the principle: BVerfG, 9. Juni 2004 (*Ladenschlussgesetz III*), BVerfGE 111, 10; BVerfG, 26. Januar 2005 (*Studiengebühren*), BVerfGE 112, 226.

110 Why this is so was considered by the European Convention working group on the principle of subsidiarity: Working Document 11 (12 August 2002), pp. 7–8.

111 Case C-84/94 *United Kingdom* v *Council (Working Time Directive)* [1996] ECR I-5755; Case C-233/94 *Germany* v *Parliament and Council (Deposit Guarantee Schemes)* [1997] ECR I-2405; Cases C-154 and 155/04 *R (Alliance for Natural Health and ors)* v *Secretary of State for Health and anor* [2005] ECR I-6451; Case C-58/08 *R (Vodaphone and ors)* v *Secretary of State for Business, Enterprise and Regulatory Reform*, [2010] ECR I-4999; Case T-18/10 *Inuit Tapiriit Kanatami and ors* v *Parliament and Council*, order of 6 September 2011 (dismissed for inadmissibility); Case T-526/10 *Inuit Tapriiit Kanatami and ors* v *Commission*, pending. There are other judgments in which it could be said the Court has considered and applied the principle implicitly: Case C-376/98 *Germany* v *Parliament and Council* (Tobacco Advertising) [2000] ECR I-8419, especially *per* A-G Fennelly, at paras 131–45 of his opinion (if the judgment may be characterised as an (implicit) application of subsidiarity it is the only instance of a Union measure to be annulled on that ground); Case C-377/98 *Netherlands* v *Parliament and Council* (Biotechnological Inventions) [2001] ECR I-7079; Case C-491/01 *R* v *Secretary of State for Health, ex parte British American Tobacco and ors* [2002] ECR I-11453.

112 TEU, art. 5(3).

legislation contain ('should contain'; *devrait comporter*) a detailed statement making it possible to appraise compliance with the principle[113] and that drafts be forwarded in good time to all national parliaments. Any parliament or chamber of a parliament may adopt a reasoned opinion as to why the proposed legislation fails to comply with the principle,[114] and the Union institutions 'shall take account' of that opinion;[115] a muster of one-third of them may require it to be reviewed (*ré-examiné*).[116] Although the time limits are short this introduced pre-legislative monitoring for the first time. The Court of Justice is expressly recognised to have jurisdiction to review a Union legislative act 'on grounds of infringement of the principle of subsidiarity' and special rules apply as to who may raise the issue before the Court.[117]

(iii) Proportionality

2.32 The principle of proportionality derives from the administrative law of a number of member states, particularly that of Germany. At its simplest it requires that a person subject to the law should be subjected to no greater burdens than are reasonably necessary to achieve its (legitimate) aim; that, for a public authority, measures adopted should be appropriate for attaining the objectives pursued and must not go beyond what is necessary to achieve them. It was recognised (very) early on as a general principle of Community law,[118] was expressly written into the EC Treaty by Maastricht,[119] and in its present formulation,

> [u]nder the principle of proportionality, the content and form of Union action shall not exceed what is necessary to achieve the objectives of the Treaties.[120]

It is foreshadowed by another construction which directs that the Union 'shall pursue its objectives by appropriate means commensurate with the competences … conferred upon it'[121] but put with greater precision by the Court of Justice:

> By virtue of that principle, the lawfulness of the prohibition of an economic activity is subject to the condition that the prohibition measures are appropriate and necessary in

---

113   Protocol (No. 2) on the Application of the Principles of Subsidiarity and Proportionality, art. 5.
114   *Ibid.* art. 6.
115   *Ibid.* art. 7(1).
116   *Ibid.* art. 7(2).
117   *Ibid.* art. 8, 1st and 2nd paras; see 5.74 below, n. 465.
118   Case 8/55 *Fédération Charbonnière de Belgique* v *High Authority* [1954–56] ECR 245; see further Case 11/70 *Internationale Handelsgesellschaft mbH* v *Einfuhr- und Vorratsstelle für Getreide und Futtermittel* [1970] ECR 1125, including the opinion of A-G Dutheillet de Lamothe.
119   EC Treaty (pre-Amsterdam), art. 3b, 3rd para. (subsequently art. 5, 3rd para).
120   TEU, art. 5(4).
121   *Ibid.* art. 3(6).

order to achieve the objectives legitimately pursued by the legislation in question; when there is a choice between several appropriate measures, recourse must be had to the least onerous, and the disadvantage caused must not be disproportionate to the aims pursued.[122]

Proportionality is pervasive: 'there are few areas of Community law, if any at all, where [it] is not relevant'.[123] It applies both to Union institutions when exercising legislative or administrative functions – even where unstated it 'is none the less a criterion for the lawfulness of any act of the institutions of the Union'[124] – and to any and all national authorities when implementing them. It applies also to member states when seeking to exercise a permitted derogation from general Union rules, the extent of which must be limited to that which is necessary to achieve the legitimate and intended purpose of the derogation.[125] Penalties (or other sanctions) imposed by a Union institution[126] or by a member state in a Union sphere[127] must be proportionate to the gravity of the offence. In the legislative arena, where complex assessment of political, economic and social criteria is required, the Union institutions enjoy a broad margin of appreciation, and will act disproportionately only if a measure is manifestly inappropriate having regard to the objective being pursued.[128] A protocol was added by the Treaty of Amsterdam[129] which seeks to ensure that the institutions are mindful of it, and comply with it, in the discharge of their activities.

122   Case 331/88 *R* v *Minister of Agriculture, Fisheries and Food, ex parte FEDESA* [1990] ECR I-4023, at para. 13.
123   Case C-120/94 *Commission* v *Greece* (Macedonia) [1996] ECR I-1513, *per* A-G Jacobs, at para. 70 of his opinion.
124   Case C-441/07P *Commission* v *Alrosa* [2010] ECR I-5949, at para. 36.
125   E.g., Case 104/75 *de Peijper* [1976] ECR 613; Case 124/81 *Commission* v *United Kingdom* (UHT Milk) [1983] ECR 203; Case C-55/94 *Gebhard* v *Consiglio dell'Ordine degli Avvocati e Procuratori di Milano* [1995] ECR I-4165; Case C-100/01 *Ministre de l'Intérieur* v *Oteiza Olazabal* [2002] ECR I-10981; Case C-320/03 *Commission* v *Austria* [2005] ECR I-7929; in UK courts, *Her Majesty's Advocate* v *Riganti* 1992 SCCR 891; *Gough and anor* v *Chief Constable of the Derbyshire Constabulary* [2002] EWCA Civ 351, [2002] QB 1213.
126   EU Charter of Fundamental Rights ('EU Charter'), art. 49(3); Case 8/55 *Fédération Charbonnière de Belgique* v *High Authority* [1954–56] ECR 292; discussed extensively in Case T-31/99 *ABB Asea Brown Boveri* v *Commission* [2002] ECR II-1881; Case T-306/00 *Conserve Italia* v *Commission* [2003] ECR II-5705.
127   EU Charter, art. 49(3); Case 430/77 *R* v *Boucbereau* [1977] ECR 1999; Case C-193/94 *Criminal proceedings against Skanavi and Chryssanthakopoulos* [1996] ECR I-929; Case C-348/96 *Criminal proceedings against Calfa* [1998] ECR I-11.
128   Case 331/88 *R* v *Minister of Agriculture, Fisheries and Food, ex parte FEDESA* [1990] ECR I-4023, at paras 12–18; Case C-84/94 *United Kingdom* v *Council* (Working Time Directive) [1996] ECR I-5755; Case C-157/96 *R* v *Ministry of Agriculture, Fisheries and Food, ex parte National Farmers' Union and ors* [1998] ECR I-2211; Case C-189/01 *Jippes and ors* v *Minister van Landbouw, Natuurbeheer en Visserij* [2001] ECR I-5689; Case C-491/01 *R* v *Secretary of State for Health, ex parte British American Tobacco and ors* [2002] ECR I-11453; Cases C-453 etc./03 *R (ABNA and ors)* v *Secretary of State for Health and ors* [2005] ECR I-10423; Case C-310/04 *Spain* v *Council* [2006] ECR I-7285.
129   Protocol [annexed to the EC Treaty] on the Application of the Principles of Subsidiarity and Proportionality; now Protocol (No. 2) on the Application of the Principles of Subsidiarity and Proportionality.

2.33 There are two further constructs abroad, not expressly recognised as principles (indeed, not expressly recognised) in the Treaties but no less fundamental to a proper understanding of Union law. They are as follows.

(iv)   Variable geometry

2.34 The uniform application of law is a general principle, sometimes of constitutional standing, that persons and jurisdictions subject to the law be treated equally, absent objective justification. This was originally so for Community law, so that Community legislation could be struck down if it purported to apply differently in different member states.[130] But the uniformity began to break up with the Single European Act (1987): for the first time the EEC Treaty expressly permitted the application of Community law differently, and at different times, in different member states[131] – a scheme usually called variable geometry or 'multi-speed' or 'differentiated' integration. There was a presumption in variable geometry that whilst integration and the rules giving effect to it may proceed more rapidly as amongst some member states, the laggards will eventually catch up and Community rules would apply uniformly thereafter:[132] '[t]he ... derogations introduced by the contested directive constitute measures whose sole object and purpose ... is to postpone temporarily the effective application of the Community act concerned'.[133] But subsequently the term has been applied to situations whereby some member states enjoy in one sphere or another a right of permanent derogation from Union rules, usually the price of their consent to Treaty amendment or to legislation, as the case may be. The Treaties are now riddled with it, and in its various permutations it sits ill with the general admonition, introduced expressly by Lisbon, of the equality of the member states before the Treaties.[134] Variable geometry by direct authority of Treaty provisions is sometimes characterised as 'primary flexibility', to be distinguished from variable geometry effected by the institutions where they have that option ('secondary flexibility'). Post-Lisbon, its incidence is only likely to increase.

(v)   The 'acquis communautaire'

2.35 From the start Community law has been an evolving legal order. Its substantive rules, rights, obligations and remedies develop over time, and the Court of Justice has frequently used the formula 'in the present state of Community law' when determining the outcome of a dispute. However, there is a presumption

---

130   E.g., Case 41/84 *Pinna* v *Caisse d'allocations familiales de la Savoie* [1986] ECR 1.
131   See in particular, EEC Treaty, arts 7c and 100a(4) (now TFEU, arts 27 and 114(4)–(8)).
132   See EEC Treaty, art. 7c, 2nd para. (TFEU, art. 27, 2nd para.): permitted derogation from internal market legislation 'must be of a temporary nature'.
133   Case C-413/04 *Parliament* v *Council* (Estonian Energy) [2006] ECR I-11221, at para. 60.
134   TEU, art. 4(2).

that evolution is in one direction, and that at any point in time there could be identified a state of the development of the law which embodies the principles and objectives, essential rights, obligations, remedies and substantive rules of Community law and which, absent Treaty amendment, cannot – certainly should not – be reversed.[135] This accumulated bank of Community patrimony, or heritage, was referred to as the *acquis communautaire*,[136] and its entrenchment and continuous development was fundamental to the nature of the Community legal order. The Union created by Maastricht was committed expressly, as one of its primary objectives, 'to maintain[ing] in full the *acquis communautaire* and build[ing] on it';[137] even the Constitution for Europe, which would kill off the Community, set out 'to continue the work accomplished ... by ensuring the continuity of the Community *acquis*'.[138] Yet it has never had a Treaty definition[139] and, more curiously given the importance previously attached to it, the term is virtually abandoned with the Lisbon Treaty: it is gone from the Preamble and introductory articles of both Treaties and appears in the texts proper only twice, once alluding to the *acquis* (without modifier) only indirectly, to indicate that enhanced cooperation measures are excluded from it,[140] the second time to the Schengen *acquis*, which is something different and specific;[141] otherwise it surfaces only in protocols.[142] It has hitherto coloured much of the thinking of the Court of Justice. Whether the intention, or effect, of Lisbon is to diminish its relevance – elsewhere the Treaties now speak for the first time of proposals for Treaty amendment which 'serve ... to reduce the competences conferred on the Union by the Treaties'[143] – and whether the Court will shake off the habit, remains to be seen.

---

135 Arguably the Court of Justice has identified a core of Union law which is beyond even the constituent power to reverse: Opinion 1/91 *Re the EEA Agreement* [1991] ECR I-6079; Case C-459/03 *Commission v Ireland* (MOX) [2006] ECR I-4635; see 2.63 below.

136 Of the 23 Treaty languages, almost half (Czech, Estonian, English, Irish, Italian, Latvian, Lithuanian, Maltese, Dutch, Romanian and Slovak) could muster no autochthonous version of *acquis communautaire*; others which essayed an attempt tended to speak of Community (indivisible) assets (e.g., *acervo communitario*; *gemeinschaftlicher Besitzstand*) or simply Community rule of law (*gemenskapens regelverk*). It should be noted that the term is sometimes used in a narrower sense, to signify merely the positive Treaty rules and the (voluminous) substantive legislation adopted by the Union institutions.

137 TEU (pre-Lisbon), art. 2.

138 Treaty establishing a Constitution for Europe, Preamble, 5th para.

139 The closest there is to an 'official' definition is a joint declaration (No. 1) on Common Foreign and Security Policy annexed to the Final Act of the 1994 Accession Treaty whereby the *acquis communautaire* was defined, limply and prosaically, as 'the rights and obligations attaching to the Union and its institutional framework'.

140 TEU, art. 20(4); as to enhanced cooperation see 2.41–2.46 below.

141 TFEU, art. 87(3). As to the Schengen *acquis* see 11.185 below.

142 Protocol (No. 19) on the Schengen *Acquis* integrated into the Framework of the European Union. Also Protocol (No. 21) on the Position of the United Kingdom and Ireland in respect of the Area of Freedom, Security and Justice and Protocol (No. 22) on the Position of Denmark, which simply note (art. 2 of each) the partial exclusion of those member states from the area of freedom, security and justice and thus that the creation of applicable rules cannot 'in any way affect the Community or Union *acquis*' as it applies there.

143 TEU, art. 48(2); as to amendment see 2.62–2.67 below.

(d) Fundamental rights

2.36 Maastricht introduced with the original TEU a commitment to 'respect fundamental rights, as guaranteed by the European Convention for the Protection of Human Rights and Fundamental Freedoms ... and as they result from the constitutional traditions common to the member states'.[144] It was, in part, a codification of the work of the Court of Justice in developing an implied bill of rights as part of Community law. Originally it was exhortatory only, the teeth (such as they are) came later. Its present formulation is as follows:

> 1. The Union recognises the rights, freedoms and principles set out in the Charter of Fundamental Rights of the European Union ... which shall have the same legal value as the Treaties.
>
> ...
>
> 3. Fundamental rights, as guaranteed by the European Convention for the Protection of Human Rights and Fundamental Freedoms and as they result from the constitutional traditions common to the Member States, shall constitute general principles of the Union's law.[145]

Previously it had said also that '[t]he Union is founded on the principles of liberty, democracy, respect for human rights and fundamental freedoms, and the rule of law, principles which are common to the Member States',[146] but this was severed by Lisbon and incorporated into the new article 2. Article 7, introduced by the Treaty of Amsterdam and altered significantly by Nice (only minimally by Lisbon), then provides mechanisms for the adoption of sanctions against a member state responsible for a 'serious and persistent' breach of the 'values' (previously 'principles') of article 2. The new (trump?) card introduced by Lisbon is the elevation to 'the same legal value as the Treaties' of the EU Charter of Fundamental Rights. Articles 6 and 7, and the Convention, and the Charter, will be considered in detail below.

2. Title II: Democratic principles

2.37 The Treaties have always provided a number of checks and balances in the legislative process. Many of them, and in particular the compulsory participation of the Parliament in that process, serve to entrench and defend the 'principle of democracy', which is 'one of the cornerstones of the Community edifice' and common to the constitutional principles of all member states,[147]

---

144 TEU (pre-Amsterdam), art. F.
145 TEU, art. 6.
146 TEU (pre-Lisbon), art. 6(1).
147 Case C-59/94 *Netherlands* v *Council* [1996] ECR I-2169, *per* A-G Tesauro, at para. 19 of his opinion.

and a 'founding principle of the European Union'.[148] Breach of the principle could constitute a procedural irregularity in the legislative process meriting annulment of a measure which failed to take adequate account of it.[149] The General Court went further, recognising it to be a self-standing principle, so that even where the Treaties do not require participation with the Parliament in the course of legislation, a failure to consult it might nevertheless breach the principle and so lead to its annulment.[150] It also leads to further refinements such as transparency and openness of the institutions which is recognised by the Treaties,[151] 'strengthen[s]' the principle of democracy,[152] 'contributes to strengthening the principles of democracy and respect for fundamental rights as laid down in Article 6 of the EU Treaty and in the Charter of Fundamental Rights'[153] and 'guarantees that the administration enjoys greater legitimacy and is more effective and more accountable to the citizen in a democratic system'.[154]

But the Treaties themselves were, surprisingly, long lukewarm on this: **2.38** Maastricht first recognised the member states' governments to be 'founded on the principles of democracy'[155] but neither attributed it to nor required it of the Union; the Union garnered that status only with Amsterdam.[156] Lisbon promotes it to one of the values upon which the Union is founded (article 2) and introduces the new Title II on 'Provisions on Democratic Principles', addressing directly for the first time in Treaty texts the issues, and enhancement, of democratic control and accountability. To this end the TEU provides that

- the functioning of the Union is founded upon representative democracy;[157]
- every citizen has the right to participate in the democratic life of the Union;[158] and
- the Union's institutions must:

---

148 Cases T-222 etc./99 *Martinez and ors* v *Parliament* [2001] ECR II-2823, at para. 200.
149 Case 138/79 *Roquette Frères* v *Council* [1980] ECR 3333; see 5.68 below.
150 Case T-135/96 *Union Européenne de l'Artisanat et des Petites et Moyennes Entreprises* v *Council* [1998] ECR II-2335.
151 TEU (pre-Lisbon), art. 1, 2nd para. (now TEU, art. 1, 2nd para.); see Part B, Introduction, below.
152 Case T-211/00 *Kuijer* v *Council* [2002] ECR II-485, at para. 52; see also Cases T-3/00 and 337/04 *Pitsiorlas* v *Council* [2007] ECR II-4779, at paras 218–23.
153 Regulation 1049/2001 [2001] OJ L145/43, Preamble, 2nd para.; also Case C-506/08P *Sweden* v *MyTravel and Commission*, judgment of 21 July 2011, not yet reported, at para. 72 and cases cited.
154 Case T-18/10R *Inuit Tapiriit Kanatami and ors* v *Parliament and Council* [2010] ECR II-75* at para. 20.
155 TEU (pre-Amsterdam), art. F.
156 TEU (pre-Lisbon), art. 6(1).
157 TEU, art. 10(1).
158 *Ibid.* art. 10(3).

> – give citizens and representative associations the opportunity to make known and exchange their views in all areas of Union action,[159] and
> – maintain an open, transparent and regular dialogue with representative associations and civil society.[160]

In addition, national parliaments 'contribute actively to the good functioning of the Union'[161] by exercising an enhanced role in the adoption and supervision of the institutions,[162] and there is a first brush with direct democracy via a 'European citizens initiative' whereby a number of citizens may invite the institutions to adopt legislation which they consider 'required' for Union purposes.[163]

2.39   The introduction of Title II is in part an implementation of the Laeken call for greater democracy in Union machinery. But it is also a response to the concern which began increasingly to be voiced by a number of constitutional courts that the democratic accountability of the Community system fell materially short of that which applied in, and is fundamental to, their own constitutions – and, implied, a possibility of rebellion. Certainly the constitutional courts in the Czech Republic,[164] Latvia,[165] Germany[166] and Poland[167] noted the Lisbon changes with approbation, and they at the least suggest that the institutions will be held more firmly to account democratically. How far it will extend, what, if any, changes it will bring about, and how justiciable these provisions will prove to be, is yet to be seen. It is worth recalling that the Council long resisted the simplest of steps towards democratic accountability, now achieved (partially) by Lisbon,[168] that it deliberate and vote in public.

---

159   *Ibid.* art. 11(1).
160   *Ibid.* art. 11(2).
161   *Ibid.* art. 12.
162   *Ibid.*; see 3.67–3.73 below.
163   *Ibid.* art. 11(4); see 3.74 below.
164   Pl. ÚS 19/08 ze dne 26. listopadu 2008 (*Lisabonská smlouva*), at paras 206–17.
165   Satversmes tiesa, 2009 gada 7 aprīļa spriedums lietā Nr 2008–35–1 (*Lisabonas līgum*), at paras 18.3–18.4.
166   BVerfG, 30. Juni 2009 (*Lissabon-Vertrag*), BVerfGE 123, 267 (363–9). A perennial concern of the *Bundesverfassungsgericht* is its constitutional duty to protect the autonomy and integrity of the *Länder* (and so the federation) which on one view are under threat of erosion once removed, by a Union machinery insufficiently supple to accommodate the interests, and legitimacy, of states/regions within the member states. It saw Lisbon provisions on democracy and subsidiarity as (small) mitigation of that threat.
167   K 32/09, Wyrok z dnia 24 listopada 2010 r. (*Traktat z Lizbony*), 2010 Nr 229, poz. 1506, at paras 2.3, 4.1.
168   TEU, art. 16(8); TFEU, art. 15(2).

3. Title III: The institutions

Title III of the TEU establishes the 'institutional framework' by which the **2.40**
Union is to be governed.[169] It does little more than identify the institutions and
provide the bare bones of their constitution. The detail is set out in the TFEU.
Consideration of the institutions will therefore be reserved for Chapters 3–5.

4. Title IV: Enhanced cooperation

Title IV of the TEU provides for the possibility of 'enhanced cooperation' **2.41**
amongst the member states.[170] Introduced by the Treaty of Amsterdam as
'closer cooperation', the Title was amended significantly by Nice. A debate
generated upon the semantics of upgrading by Nice from 'closer' to 'enhanced'
cooperation is one reserved to English speakers: most other languages have
used the same term (e.g., *coopération renforcée; verstärkte Zusammenarbeit*) from
the start.

Enhanced cooperation is frequently described by the rubrics differentiated or **2.42**
flexible integration, and is a type of constitutional variable geometry. Where
some member states wish to pursue initiatives whither others are unwilling to
go, resulting otherwise in political stalemate, enhanced cooperation permits the
enthusiastic member states to have recourse to the institutions, mechanisms
and procedures set out in the Treaties in order to proceed as they will – but on
their own: rules adopted are binding upon participating member states only. It
is 'a legal expression of the balancing exercise between making the Union wider
and making it deeper'.[171] There are a number of strict conditions: generally,
action undertaken must

- be competent under the Treaties and concern areas not within exclusive
  Union competences;
- comply with the Treaties and Union law and be consistent with Union
  policies;
- further the objectives of the Union, protect its interests and reinforce its
  integration process; and
- neither undermine the internal market or economic, social and territorial
  cohesion, constitute a barrier to or discrimination in trade between
  member states nor distort competition amongst them.[172]

---

169   TEU, arts 13–19.
170   TEU, art. 20; TFEU, arts 326–34.
171   Case C-137/05 *United Kingdom* v *Council* [2007] ECR I-11593, *per* A-G Trstenjak, at para. 77 of her opinion.
172   TEU, art. 20; TFEU, arts 326, 329(1), 334.

It may be undertaken only as a last resort, where normal Union action has proved unattainable within a reasonable period;[173] it requires the participation of at least nine member states;[174] and it must be open to all, both at its formation ('establishment')[175] and 'at any other time' subsequently,[176] subject to compliance with any conditions laid down in the authorising decision and in measures (if any) already adopted with that framework.[177] The widest possible participation is to be 'promoted'.[178] All members of the Council participate in deliberations but voting is reserved to those member states taking part (following a special formula for Council voting),[179] although MEPs from non-participating member states continue to take part in debates and in voting in the European Parliament in the relevant area. Participating member states bear the cost of any resulting expenditure (other than administrative costs of the institutions) unless the Council by unanimity decides otherwise.[180] Measures adopted bind only the participating member states and do not form part of the *acquis* to be borne by candidate countries.[181] Enhanced cooperation must respect the competences, rights and obligations of non-participating member states, which in turn must do nothing to impede it.[182]

2.43 Member states wishing to establish enhanced cooperation must submit a request to the Commission, which may (but need not) submit a proposal to that effect to the Council; if the Commission elects not to submit a proposal it must inform the member states why.[183] Authorisation to proceed may then be granted by the Council with the consent of the Parliament.[184] A member state wishing subsequently to opt into ('participate in') enhanced cooperation in progress must notify the Council and the Commission to that effect, and it is the Commission which authorises ('confirms') it, subject to being satisfied as to fulfilment of requisite conditions and of any transitional measures it may see fit to impose,[185] this perhaps in order to dissuade the faint-hearted. A Commission rejection may be overridden by the Council.[186]

---

173 TEU, art. 20(2).
174 *Ibid*. Prior to Lisbon it required eight member states, prior to Nice a majority of member states.
175 TEU, art. 20(1); TFEU, art. 328(1).
176 *Ibid*.
177 TFEU, art. 328(1), 1st para.
178 *Ibid*. art. 328(1), 2nd para.
179 TEU, art. 20(3); TFEU, arts 330 and 238(3).
180 TFEU, art. 332.
181 TEU, art. 20(4). This is one of very few references in the Treaties to an *acquis*.
182 TFEU, art. 327.
183 *Ibid*. art. 329(1).
184 *Ibid*.
185 *Ibid*. art. 331(1).
186 *Ibid*.

Specific rules apply to enhanced cooperation within the framework of the **2.44** Common Foreign and Security Policy, which became at all possible only with the Treaty of Nice. The request is submitted not to the Commission but the Council, which forwards it to the High Representative for foreign affairs and security policy and to the Commission for opinions on consistency with, respectively, the CFSP and other Union policies.[187] Authorisation to proceed is for the Council, acting unanimously.[188] A member state wishing to opt in subsequently must notify the Council, the High Representative and the Commission, and it is the Council which approves, by moderated unanimity, after consulting the High Representative (who may propose transitional measures).[189] There are special rules for a variation of enhanced cooperation in the European Defence Agency and permanent structure cooperation in security and defence policy.[190]

The purpose of enhanced cooperation is to ensure that the integration process is **2.45** not held back by the slowest ship(s) in the convoy, unwilling, or unable, to proceed at a pace promoted by the majority. Its critics fear fissures in Union solidarity, the emergence of core 'pioneer groups' of member states and the culture of a 'Europe *à la carte*' – and that the rudimentary beginnings of variable geometry in the Single European Act may grow to resemble a complex of n-dimensional space. But its supporters will claim that it recognises and accommodates diversity, and that solidarity is safeguarded by the stringent criteria provided and the right of non-participating member states to opt in. It is not clear if, how and when a member state may withdraw from enhanced cooperation.

For whatever reason, except for measures adopted under the analogous but **2.46** more specific rules on economic and monetary union, JHA and the Schengen agreement which are marked by 'automatic enhanced cooperation',[191] enhanced cooperation had its maiden outing only in 2010: in 2008 eight member states (Greece, Spain, Italy, Luxembourg, Hungary, Austria, Romania and Slovenia), others thought to be sympathetic, initiated an enhanced cooperation measure in the matter of common rules for divorce between couples of different Union nationalities ('Rome III')[192] and requested the Commission to adopt a proposal

---

187 *Ibid.* art. 329(2).
188 *Ibid.*
189 *Ibid.* art. 331(2).
190 See 2.57 below.
191 See 11.178–11.181 and 11.188–11.190 below.
192 See Council press release 11653/08, p. 23. Originally proposed by the Commission in 2006 as an amendment to a Regulation on mutual recognition and enforcement of judgments in matrimonial matters (the 'Brussels II *bis* Regulation'; see 11.169 below), the necessary Council unanimity (EC Treaty, art. 65(3) (now TFEU, art.

to that end. The Commission complied in spring 2010,[193] and, the consent of the Parliament secured,[194] the Council authorised it in the summer,[195] with 14 member states participating (the original eight plus Belgium, Bulgaria, Germany, France, Latvia, Malta and Portugal having in the meanwhile come on board, but Greece having withdrawn) and adopted the substantive measure at the end of the year.[196] A second venture is in train, the adoption of regulation creating the EU patent, which was deadlocked in the Council owing primarily to its language arrangements (which require Council unanimity).[197] A Commission proposal authorising enhanced cooperation was adopted at the end of 2010[198] and secured parliamentary consent[199] and Council approval,[200] with 25 member states (all but Spain and Italy) participating, in spring 2011; the Council approval has been challenged by both as an abuse of process.[201] Next in the queue is thought likely to be a harmonised corporate tax base and/or a harmonised financial transaction tax. It is anticipated that enhanced cooperation will see greater play as the Lisbon provisions on judicial cooperation in criminal matters and police matters bed down.[202]

5. Title V: External action and the Common Foreign and Security Policy

2.47 The acorn from which Title V of the TEU grew was the informal cooperation within the European Council (that body itself at chrysalis stage at the time) on matters of foreign policy which developed in the 1970s. The machinery of European Political Cooperation (EPC, or PoCo), as it had become known, was established by the Single European Act but parallel to, not as part of, the institutional machinery of the Community. It was given greater substance by Maastricht, comprising the second pillar, or Title V, of the Treaty on European Union on 'Provisions on Common Foreign and Security Policy' (CFSP). With Lisbon the field has been (nominally) *communautairised*, yet it resembles far more accurately the scheme of CFSP which preceded it.

81(3))) proved impossible to achieve owing to opposition from the Nordic member states generally and the Swedes in particular.

193   COM(2010) 105 final.
194   Legislative resolution of 16 June 2010, 2010/066 (NLE).
195   Decision 2010/405 [2010] OJ L189/12.
196   Regulation 1259/2010 [2010] OJ L343/10; applies from June 2012.
197   TFEU, art. 118, 2nd para. On the EU Patent see 10.79 below.
198   COM(2010) 790 final.
199   Legislative resolution of 15 February 2011, A7–0021/2011.
200   Decision 2011/167 [2011] OJ L76/53.
201   Cases C-274 and 295/11 *Spain and Italy* v *Council*, pending.
202   See 11.171–11.176 below.

It should be said at the outset that external economic aspects of the common/ **2.48**
internal market – primarily the common customs tariff, the common commercial policy and related activities – were addressed by the EEC/EC Treaties and
fell within Community competence (and the Community method) from the
start. Following Maastricht they became instruments for the implementation of
the CFSP (where it could be agreed) and, with Lisbon, consolidated into a
distinct Part (Part V) of the TFEU, rationalised within the umbrella of, and
more expressly subordinated to, the Union's 'external action'.

Title V TEU is divided into two chapters, on general provisions on external **2.49**
action and specific provisions on the CFSP. Thus the first chapter applies to
both CFSP and external action under the TFEU. Chapter 2 is in turn divided
into two sections, on provisions on the CFSP and provisions on the Common
Security and Defence Policy.

(a) General provisions

The Union's 'action on the international scene' (it sounds less fatuous in other **2.50**
languages) is guided by the principles of democracy, the rule of law, the
universality and indivisibility of human rights and fundamental freedoms,
respect for human dignity, the principles of equality and solidarity, and respect
for the principles of the United Nations Charter and international law,[203] being
those, we discover, which inspired the Union's creation, development and
enlargement and which it seeks to advance in the wider world.[204] It is
underpinned as a Union objective in article 3, these being values and interests
the Union is to uphold and promote internationally. It seeks to develop relations
and build partnerships with third countries and international organisations
which share those principles and define and pursue common policies and action
to cooperate internationally to safeguard and promote them, preserve peace,
strengthen international security, foster the development of developing countries, encourage integration, preserve and improve the quality of the environment and assist populations, countries and regions confronting natural or
man-made disasters.[205] Upon this basis the strategic interests and objectives of
the Union are identified by the European Council by decisions, which may
relate to the CFSP and/or to other areas of external action; are adopted by
unanimity upon a recommendation from the Council or jointly from the High
Representative for foreign affairs and security policy and the Commission;[206]
and are implemented by the various means provided in the Treaties.[207]

---

203 TEU, arts 21(1), 23.
204 *Ibid.*
205 *Ibid.*
206 *Ibid.* art. 22.
207 *Ibid.*

2.51 Lisbon introduced a new provision at the top of the Treaties (in Title I of the TEU) directing the Union to develop a 'special relationship' (*relations priv-ilégiées*) with neighbouring countries, marked by close and peaceful relations with a view to establishing an area of prosperity and good neighbourliness.[208] What it will produce, what it means, and even to whom it applies,[209] is too early to project.

(b) Common Foreign and Security Policy

2.52 The Union's competence in matters of common foreign and security policy covers all areas of foreign policy and all questions relating to Union security, including the progressive framing of a common defence policy which might lead to a common defence (*sic*).[210] The Union conducts the CFSP by defining general guidelines;[211] adopting decisions defining actions to be undertaken and positions to be taken by the Union and arrangements for their implementation;[212] decisions defining the Union approach to a particular matter of a geographic or thematic nature to which 'positions' member states must 'ensure that their national policies conform';[213] and strengthening systematic cooperation between member states in the conduct of policy.[214] The operation of the CFSP falls to the European Council, the Council and the High Representative for foreign affairs and security policy, its implementation to the High Representative, assisted by the European External Action Service (EEAS), and the member states; the other institutions get barely a look in.[215] The administrative and operating costs of the CFSP are charged to the Union budget,[216] other costs are charged to the member states in accordance with a GNP scale unless the Council decides otherwise.[217] Enhanced cooperation is possible within CFSP but subject to specific rules.[218]

2.53 The question is now whether it will be a success. Much will turn on the degree of agreement reached and detail of the decisions adopted by the European Council and the Council; the general requirement of unanimity across the

---

208 *Ibid.* art. 8.
209 There has been in place since 2004 a 'European Neighbourhood Policy' (ENP) which defines the Union's 'immediate neighbours' as most of the Mediterranean littoral (excluding Turkey (subject to more different rules) and the Turkish Republic of Northern Cyprus (unrecognised)) and several former Soviet republics, including Russia; see 14.95–14.96 below. Article 8 may, or may not, adopt the same approach.
210 TEU, art. 24(1).
211 *Ibid.* art. 25(a).
212 *Ibid.* art. 25(b).
213 *Ibid.* art. 29.
214 *Ibid.* art. 25(c).
215 See 3.75–3.78 below.
216 TEU, art. 41(1), (2), 2nd para.
217 *Ibid.* art. 41(2), 2nd para.
218 See 2.44 above.

field[219] might suggest frequent stalemate. Yet action under the pre-Lisbon CFSP, certainly no easier, managed a record probably best described as one which disappointed its supporters but confounded the cynics. There is now new machinery in place, a new supporting and autonomous body (the EEAS), a higher profile adhering to it, and perhaps a general predisposition that some, and increasing, areas of concern justify, even require, a coherent Union response. Collateral encouragement may be had by a more vigorous application of article 4(3) TEU to foreign policy.[220] At the same time there is being created a triangular tension amongst the European Council/Council, the member states (both directly and by means of the temporary agents seconded from national ministries) and the new, previously untried post of High Representative. A great deal of the success of CFSP will turn upon her skill.

It should be noted that, as was the case with all previous incarnations, the CFSP **2.54** is not recognised by and in the United Kingdom. The European Union (Amendment) Act 2008 incorporated the Treaty of Lisbon, including its annex and protocols, amongst the instruments which comprise 'the Treaties' for purposes of the European Communities Act 1972, but 'excluding any provision that relates to, or in so far as it relates to could be applied in relation to, the Common Foreign and Security Policy'.[221] As a result the provisions on CFSP bind the United Kingdom as a matter of public international law and of Union law, but they are accorded no force of law within the United Kingdom so are unenforceable (indeed, unrecognised) by UK courts. Other member states are less hostile.

(c)   Common Security and Defence Policy

An 'integral part of the common foreign and security policy'[222] is the Common **2.55** Security and Defence Policy (CSDP), which 'include[s] the progressive framing of a common Union defence policy. This will lead to a common defence'.[223] But that will occur, if ever, only when the European Council decides it is so and the member states agree in accordance with their constitutional requirements.[224] Generally the Treaty provisions on CSDP provide no compulsion and no timetable. This was emphasised by the heads of state and government in their 'decision' to placate Irish concerns as to the defence implications of

---

219   See TEU, arts 22(1), 24(1) below.
220   See 14.75 below.
221   European Union (Amendment) Act 2008, s. 1(2)(s).
222   TEU, art. 42(1).
223   *Ibid.* art. 42(2).
224   *Ibid.*

Lisbon:[225] the CSDP neither prejudices the security and defence policies of the member state nor creates obligations for them; it does not provide for the creation of a European army; it does not affect the rights of member states to determine the nature and volume of defence and security expenditure and the nature of their defence capabilities; and it does not affect or prejudice Ireland's traditional policy of military neutrality. Ireland is not alone in its wariness to the invitation of the CSDP to depart from long habit in matters of military and defence policies.[226]

2.56 In the shorter term, the provisions on CSDP are to provide the Union with the operational capacity to undertake missions outside the Union for purposes of peace keeping, conflict prevention and strengthening international security in accordance with the principles of the UN Charter.[227] This includes joint disarmament operations, humanitarian and rescue tasks, military advice and assistance, conflict prevention and peace keeping, combat forces in crisis management, and through all of them a contribution to combating terrorism.[228] The military assets necessary to these tasks are to be made available by the member states.[229]

2.57 Member states wishing to do so may establish 'permanent structured cooperation'.[230] In order to do so they must have advanced military capabilities ('fulfil higher criteria'),[231] meet further criteria and make commitments as set out in a Treaty protocol[232] and meet the approval of the Council, acting by qualified majority.[233] Other member states may join later with the qualified majority approval of the Council comprising participating member states.[234] A participating member state which no longer fulfils the criteria or meets the commitments may be suspended by that Council,[235] and a participating member state may withdraw unilaterally.[236]

---

225 Decision of the Heads of State or Government of the 27 Member States of the EU, meeting within the European Council, on the concerns of the Irish People on the Treaty of Lisbon, *Bulletin EU* 6–2009, 14, Annex I, Section C. See now the 'Irish Protocol' (2.66 below), art. 3.
226 See 2.09 above, n. 27.
227 TEU, art. 42(1).
228 *Ibid.* art. 43(1).
229 *Ibid.* art. 42(1), (3).
230 *Ibid.* arts 42(6), 46.
231 *Ibid.* art. 42(6).
232 Protocol (No. 10) on Permanent Structured Cooperation established by Article 42 of the Treaty on European Union.
233 TEU, *ibid.* art. 46(2).
234 *Ibid.* art. 46(3).
235 *Ibid.* art. 46(4).
236 *Ibid.* art. 46(5).

The member states undertake progressively to improve their military capabil- **2.58** ities working in close cooperation with the European Defence Agency[237] but participation in its work and in projects initiated by it is wholly voluntary.[238]

If a member state is a victim of armed aggression on its territory other member **2.59** states bear an obligation of aid and assistance 'by all means in their power' in accordance with article 51 of the UN Charter.[239] If the object of a terrorist attack or victim of a natural or man-made disaster, the Union and the member states are obliged to act jointly in a spirit of solidarity, mobilise all instruments at its disposal and assist it at the request of its political authorities.[240] Both reflect the collective security provision of article 5 of the North Atlantic Treaty, and response to armed aggression in fact made subject to NATO commitments, that organisation remaining, for the member states its members, 'the foundation of their collective defence and the forum for its implementation'.[241] It is for each member state to determine the nature of aid and assistance to be furnished.[242] For terrorist attacks and natural or man-made disasters the response, including military resources made available by member states, is coordinated by the Council and arrangements for its implementation defined by Council decision upon a joint proposal from the Commission and the High Representative.[243]

6. Title VI: Final provisions

Title VI of the Treaty on European Union lays down final provisions, some **2.60** standard treaty paraphernalia (duration (unlimited), ratification, authentic languages and depositary) but others on key constitutional issues of Treaty amendment, accession to and secession from the Union. They are matters which have been addressed in one way or another from the beginning. Lisbon made two significant changes.

(a) Legal personality

Article 47 of the TEU provides simply that '[t]he Union shall have legal **2.61** personality'. This was a quality which had adhered previously only to the Communities[244] and was quite deliberately withheld from the Union, although

---

237   *Ibid.* art 42(3), 2nd para.
238   Implicit in TEU, art. 46(2); emphasised in the national declaration by Ireland 'associated with' its ratification of Lisbon, *Bulletin EU* 6–2009, 16.
239   TEU, art. 42(7).
240   TFEU, art. 222(1), (2).
241   TEU, art. 42(7), 2nd para.
242   Decision of the Heads of State or Government, n. 225 above, Section C, 5th para.
243   TFEU, art. 222(3).
244   EEC Treaty, art. 210 (subsequently art. 281 EC); Euratom Treaty, art. 184.

paradoxically it did enjoy express treaty making authority with one or more third states or international organisations '[w]hen it is necessary' for 'implementation' of Title V (CFSP)[245] or of Title VI (JHA)[246] matters. The treaty making power in CFSP matters is expressly retained elsewhere by Lisbon,[247] whilst article 47 makes it clear that the single Union has succeeded to the (single) personality long enjoyed by the European Community. That of Euratom continues to survive independently.[248]

(b) Amendment

2.62 Prior to Maastricht each of the Community Treaties provided its own (essentially identical) mechanism for its amendment.[249] Maastricht gathered these into a single provision which applied to 'the amendment of the Treaties on which the Union is founded'.[250] That single provision was sundered again by Lisbon, article 48 of the Treaty on European Union providing the mechanisms for amendment ('revision') of 'the Treaties', the Euratom Treaty regaining its own authority for amendment.[251] Eight years in gestation, Lisbon itself followed the procedures as laid down in the (previous) TEU scrupulously, and entered into force with the requisite ratification by all member states.[252] But it altered significantly the process of future Treaty amendment, introducing:

- an 'ordinary revision procedure',[253] a close variation of the procedure which existed previously, as follows: a proposal for amendment of the Treaties may be initiated by a member state, the Commission or the Parliament, submitted then by the Council to the European Council, the national parliaments being notified; the European Council decides by simple majority whether to proceed, and if so decides calls for an (unquantified) 'convention' comprising representatives of the national parliaments, the heads of state or government, the Parliament and the Commission; if involving institutional change in the monetary sphere the European Central Bank is to be consulted. The convention examines the proposal and adopts, by consensus, a 'recommendation' to an intergovernmental conference (IGC), an *ad hoc* conference of representatives of the governments of the member states convened by the president of the Council for the purpose of determining the amendments, if any, to be made to the

---

245   TEU (pre-Lisbon), art. 24.
246   *Ibid.* art. 38.
247   *Ibid.* art. 37.
248   Euratom Treaty, art. 184.
249   ECSC Treaty, art. 96; EEC Treaty, art. 236; Euratom Treaty, art. 204.
250   TEU (pre-Lisbon), art. 48.
251   Euratom Treaty, art. 106a(1).
252   TEU (pre-Lisbon), art. 48; Lisbon Treaty, art. 6.
253   TEU, art. 48(1)–(5).

Treaties. Post-Lisbon the European Council may by simple majority, with the consent of the Parliament, decide not to convene the convention if the 'extent' (*ampleur*) of the changes does not justify it, in which case the 'terms of reference' for the IGC are set by the European Council itself. If the IGC agrees ('by common accord') a text, which is then agreed and signed by the member states, the amendments enter into force following ratification by all of them each in accordance with its constitutional requirements.[254] If after two years of its signature four-fifths of the member states have ratified it and one or more member states encounter(s) 'difficulties in proceeding with ratification', the matter is referred to the European Council (without indication or hint as to what the European Council should or can do);

- a 'simplified revision procedure':[255] applying to only Part Three of the TFEU (and not all of it),[256] amendment may be secured by a decision of the European Council, acting by unanimity after consulting the Parliament and the Commission (and the Central Bank in the monetary area), duly ratified by all member states.

The Euratom Treaty may be amended through the ordinary revision procedure only.[257]

There are other provisions in the Treaties for the amendment of a small number **2.63** of minor housekeeping matters by the European Council, the Council or the

---

254 Ratification in the United Kingdom is (as it must be) accompanied by legislation in order to give effect to the changes. This could in the past be done by Order in Council (approved by resolutions of both Houses of Parliament) made by authority of s. 1(3) of the European Communities Act 1972 which adds the new instrument to the list therein of 'EU Treaties' and which is therefore to be given legal effect, and this method has been used for minor Treaty amendment. Major change was by statute: the European Communities (Amendment) Acts 1986 (giving effect to the SEA), 1993 (Maastricht), 1998 (Amsterdam), 2002 (Nice) and the European Union (Amendment) Act 2008 (Lisbon). There were statutory bars prohibiting UK assent to ratification of a treaty which increases the powers of the European Parliament (European Parliamentary Elections Act 2002, s. 12) and (post-Lisbon) amendment by the ordinary revision procedure (European Union (Amendment) Act 2008, s. 5) without express approval by Act of Parliament. Now, by virtue of the European Union Act 2011, ratification of any amendment treaty requires in all cases to be preceded by an Act of Parliament, and in many cases, depending upon its subject matter and scope (see s. 4 of the Act), by a referendum (the 'referendum lock'). The Act is shot through with further statutory bars limiting the freedom of UK ministers to consent to a number of (European) Council acts without parliamentary approval, a number of them also requiring a referendum. The Act was a means of containing the (substantial) anti-Europe wing of the Conservative party, and marks a significant sea-change in British constitutional practice.
255 TEU, art. 48(1), (6)–(7).
256 TFEU, art. 353. Reserved to the ordinary revision procedure are amendments to arts 311, 3rd and 4th paras (adoption of rules regulating the Union's own resources), 312(2), 1st subpara (adoption of rules regulating the multiannual financial framework), 352 (the 'flexibility clause') and 354 (adoption of sanctions for breach of fundamental rights).
257 Euratom Treaty, art. 106a(1).

Parliament and Council,[258] otherwise amendment is secured by means of the procedures of article 48. It will therefore be observed that Treaty amendment, as with constitutional amendment generally, is entrenched against casual whim. The Commission and the Parliament have a veto in the intergovernmental convention, or the Parliament must consent to bypassing it; each national government has a veto at the convention and at the IGC, each national parliament a veto (assuming it has that authority in constitutional law) at the stage of ratification; and in those member states which must have, or elect to have, a referendum, there is a popular veto. On occasion the entry into force of an agreed Treaty amendment has been delayed considerably waiting upon ratification by a single member state – the Single European Act and the Treaty of Nice waiting upon Ireland,[259] the Maastricht Treaty upon Germany.[260] And a 1970 amendment drawn up and agreed in accordance with (then) proced-ures[261] never entered into force because it was never ratified by Italy. Because the power of amendment, and so the constituent, normative power (*pouvoir constituant*) remains, and lies essentially, with the member states (acting in concert), they are in this context often called the '*Herren der Verträge*' (masters, or lords, of the Treaties); the *Bundesverfassungsgericht* put particular store by this in consenting to ratification of the Lisbon Treaty: that so long as the member states remain *Herren der Verträge* they have yielded no *Kompetenz-Kompetenz* to the Union, the Union remains a *Staatenverbund* (≅ confederation) and German participation remains within the limits permitted by the Basic Law.[262] The Court of Justice once hinted that there is a core of fundamental provisions of Community law which, like the 'inviolable core content' of the Basic Law[263] or

---

258 For example: alteration of the composition of the Commission (TEU, art. 17(5)); of the powers of the European Public Prosecutor's Office (TFEU, art. 86(4)); of the number of Advocates-General in the Court of Justice (TFEU, art. 252) and of judges in the General Court (Statute of the Court of Justice, art. 48 and TFEU, art. 281) and the Civil Service Tribunal (Statute of the Court of Justice, Annex I, art. 2); of the territories listed in Annex II (TFEU, art. 355(6)); and amendment of certain provisions of various Protocols (e.g., the Protocol on the Statute of the Court (TFEU, art. 281), on the Statute of the ESCB and ECB (art. 10.6) and on the Statute of the EIB (by the Board of Governors; arts 4.3, 5.2).

259 Irish ratification of the SEA was delayed pending a constitutional challenge which went up to the Supreme Court (*Crotty* v *An Taoiseach* [1987] IR 713) and a subsequent referendum, which, the Court determined, was required by Irish constitutional law. Nice (and Lisbon) each required two referendums; see 1.42, n. 70 and 1.52 above.

260 German ratification turned upon the outcome of a constitutional challenge in the *Bundesverfassungsgericht*; see BVerfG, 12. Oktober 1993 (*Maastricht*), BVerfGE 89, 155.

261 Treaty of 15 October 1970 amending the Protocol on the European Investment Bank.

262 BVerfG, 30. Juni 2009 (*Lissabon-Vertrag*), BVerfGE 123, 267, especially 324. It had characterised the Community as a *Staatenverbund* previously in the *Maastricht* judgment (n. 260 above), *passim*, the term coined by Judge Kirchhof and its exact meaning still a matter of debate.

263 That is, the *unantastbare Kerngehalt* preserved by § 79 III GG (the 'eternity clause' (*Ewigkeitsklausel*)); see also 6.54, n. 323 below.

the 'material core' of the Czech Constitution,[264] are beyond the authority even of the constituent power to alter.[265] But article 48 now (post-Lisbon) provides that 'proposals [for amendment] may, *inter alia*, serve ... to reduce the competences conferred on the Union in the Treaties',[266] and the more commonly held view is that the *Herren der Verträge* may, in accordance with the prescribed procedure, amend or alter the treaties in any way they see fit: they may reverse the *acquis communautaire*,[267] or even, should they choose to do so, dismantle and extinguish the Union. *But* because they may act, and change may be brought about, only by unanimity, any such outcome could be held at bay by, say, the government or the parliament of Malta – representing 0.083 per cent of the population of the Union. Starker still, since the Belgian Constitution requires the consent of the governments of the communities and/or regions which make up the Kingdom if the subject matter falls within their constitutional competences,[268] an amending treaty meeting that criterion could be vetoed by refusal or failure of the 'German speaking community', population about 73,000, to adopt the requisite decree. Or, in real historical terms: the outcome of the 2008 referendum by which the Irish voted against ratification of the Lisbon Treaty was 752,451 for, 862,415 against. This means that the Treaty fell (more accurately, was delayed) as a result of 109,964 Irish votes, or the wishes of 0.02 per cent of the population of the Union.

From 1958 to 1986 the Community treaties suffered no serious alteration, **2.64** amended on six occasions but each time effecting only minor change.[269] Since 1986 there have been six amendments, five substantial. The five were made by:

---

264 '*Doktríny materiálního ohnisko ústavy*'; see arts 1 and 9(2) Úst and Pl. ÚS 19/08 ze dne 26 listopadu 2008 (*Lisabonská smlouva*), at para. 89; also Pl. ÚS 27/09 ze dne 10 září 2009 (*Věc Melčák*), not an EU case but the first time a constitutional law was struck down for breach of art. 9(2).

265 Opinion 1/91 *Re the European Economic Area Agreement* [1991] ECR I-6079. It is thought that the principle of non-discrimination is so central to Union endeavour, even prior to its elevation by Lisbon to Part Two of the TFEU, that it cannot be abandoned.

266 TEU, art. 48(2). See also Declaration (No. 18) in relation to the Delimitation of Competences, 3rd para.

267 An amendment introduced by the Maastricht Treaty (the 'Barber Protocol') was a response to a judgment of the Court of Justice which recognised (generous) widowers' pension rights and could be said to reverse an element of the *acquis*. On the Barber Protocol see 14.53 below, on the *acquis communautaire* see 2.35 above.

268 Constitution of Belgium, art. 167 § 4; loi spéciale de réformes institutionnelles, loi du 8 août 1980, Moniteur Belge du 15 août 1980, art. 92*bis*, § 4*ter*.

269 The Netherlands Antilles Convention of 13 November 1962 ([1964] JO 2414), adding the Netherlands Antilles to an EEC Treaty Annex; the Merger Treaty of 8 April 1965 ([1967] JO L152/2), fusing the three Councils and the two Commissions and the High Authority into a single Council and a single Commission; the First Budgetary Treaty of 22 April 1970 ([1971] JO L2/1), amending budgetary procedures; the European Investment Bank Treaty of 10 July 1975 ([1975] OJ L91/1), amending the EEC Treaty Protocol on the Bank; the Second Budgetary Treaty of 22 July 1975 ([1977] OJ L359/1), amending again budgetary procedures and creating the Court of Auditors; and the Greenland Treaty of 13 March 1984 ([1985] OJ L29/1), recognising and implementing the withdrawal of Greenland from the Communities (as to which see 1.20 above).

- the Single European Act (1986);[270]
- the Treaty on European Union (Treaty of Maastricht) (1992);[271]
- the Treaty of Amsterdam (1997);[272]
- the Treaty of Nice (2001);[273] and
- the Treaty of Lisbon (2007).[274]

? all this way –

Each was secured by strict adherence to the article 48 (or its predecessors in the Community treaties) procedure. There therefore remains the question of whether article 48 constitutes a 'closed system' such that Treaty amendment may be secured by its procedure and it alone, to the exclusion of any other means. There are early precedents of the latter: the ECSC Treaty was amended twice in 1958 but not by the procedures equivalent to article 48,[275] rather by treaty, duly ratified, amongst the six member states[276] – in other words by the traditional treaty making power theirs by virtue of statehood in accordance with applicable rules of public international law;[277] misspellings and minor linguistic infelicities in the modern Treaties have been corrected ('rectified') by *procès-verbal* agreed by the governments of all member states;[278] and there is one modern (1993/94) – aberrant? – example of Treaty amendment, very minor, secured by agreement amongst the member states without recourse to article 48.[279] These aside, the Court of Justice appears to support the closed system of article 48: it said in 1976 on amendment of the EEC Treaty, albeit *obiter*:

---

270 Treaty of 17 and 28 February 1986 [1987] OJ L169/1; in force 1 July 1987.
271 Treaty of 7 February 1992 [1992] OJ C191/1; in force 1 November 1993.
272 Treaty of 2 October 1997 [1997] OJ C340/1; in force 1 May 1999.
273 Treaty of 26 February 2001 [2001] OJ C80/1; in force 1 February 2003.
274 Treaty of 19 December 2007 [2007] OJ C306/1; in force 1 December 2009.
275 ECSC Treaty, arts 95 (the *petite révision* procedure) and 96.
276 Traité de 27 octobre 1956 portant modification au Traité instituant la CECA conséquente du retour de la Sarre à l'Allemagne, in force 9 October 1958; Convention of 27 March 1957 on Certain Institutions Common to the European Communities, attached to the Rome Treaties, in force 1 January 1958. As for the former, France returned the Saar to German authority with effect from 1 January 1957 (Traité de 27 octobre 1956 entre la France et l'Allemagne réglant la question de la Sarre, 1053 UNTS 4; Gesetz vom 23. Dezember 1956 über die Eingliederung des Saarlandes, BGBl. 19I S. 1956 101), but the time lag for the entry into force of the amending Treaty (owing to delay in Italian and Dutch ratification) means that the ECSC either (a) permitted member states unilaterally to (re)define themselves (or recognised the 'moving frontier rule' part of customary international law), or (b) recognised the two countries as differently constituted for the first nine months of 1958 than did the other two Communities.
277 See the Vienna Convention on the Law of Treaties, art. 39.
278 See e.g., [2004] OJ L126/1 and 2; [2007] OJ L60/1; [2007] OJ L149/18; the extensive rectification of the Lisbon Treaty, [2009] OJ C290/1, [2010] OJ C81/1.
279 The Protocol on the Statute of the European Investment Bank was amended, by the addition of a single article, in 1994 by an 'Act' of representatives of the heads of state of the member states followed by ratification by each member state; see [1994] OJ L173/14. No authority for the adoption of the 'Act' was cited.

> In fact, apart from any specific provisions, the Treaty can only be modified by means of the amendment procedure carried out in accordance with Article 236.[280]

It is a matter which is unlikely now seriously to be tested.

The most recent chapter in the 25-year saga of regular fundamental change, a **2.65** state of affairs which might be called protracted, semi-permanent Treaty revision, is of course the Lisbon Treaty, born of Laeken and the Treaty establishing a Constitution for Europe. Unlike previous amendments, the IGC which agreed the text of the Constitutional Treaty was able to work swiftly because the preparatory work had been completed in the form of the draft treaty proposed by the constitutional convention.[281] Equally, the IGC convened in 2007 to agree a Reform Treaty was able to work from the carcass of the Constitutional Treaty and the mandate given it by the European Council (the 'Draft IGC Mandate'),[282] and so was able to negotiate and agree a text in under four months. Lisbon now in place, three further, mercifully simple, Treaty amendments have been initiated, and one completed: first, a proposal to amend a Treaty protocol by ordinary revision procedure (necessarily; but bypassing a convention) so as to permit an agreed increase in the number of members of the Parliament, which came into force in December 2011.[283] Second, in early 2011 the European Council adopted a decision for amendment (by simplified procedure) of article 136 TFEU, adding a new paragraph to allow for the creation of a stability mechanism to be available 'if indispensable to safeguard the stability of the euro area as a whole';[284] ratification and so entry into force is

---

280　Case 43/75 *Defrenne* v *SABENA* [1976] ECR 455, at para. 58 (art. 236 being the EEC Treaty precursor of TEU, art. 48). This is consistent with the amendment to the EIB Statute (*ibid.*) only if that could be characterised as a trifle, so admitting some form of *de minimis* exception to art. 48. (This could perhaps apply equally to the Saar case (n. 276 above), the changes effected by the 1956 amending Treaty being only deletion of a subparagraph attributing parliamentary delegates from the Saar to the French total and altering a weighting of Council voting from 20 per cent to one-sixth.) Alternatively, that amendment was improperly secured, and the European Investment Fund purported to be created by its authority (see [1994] OJ L173/1) does not exist. As the 'Act' in issue is one of the member states outwith any machinery foreseen by the Treaties it cannot be annulled (or interpreted) by the Court of Justice (on annulment see 5.66–5.87 below), but the Court could treat it as non-existent, and not part of the Treaties. The EIB Statute has been untouched from 1994 until Lisbon, which reproduces the amended Statute in a protocol (Protocol (No. 5) on the Statute of the European Investment Bank), so causing the issue (probably) to disappear.

281　The process by which the Constitutional Treaty was produced is also to be lauded for its relative transparency and openness, to be compared with the secrecy, stealth and spin which frequently attend an IGC.

282　European Council, Brussels, 21/22 June 2007, Presidency Conclusions, *Bulletin EU* 6–2007, 8, Annex I.

283　The European Council Decision calling an IGC was adopted in June 2010 (Decision 2010/350 [2010] OJ L160/5), agreement of the IGC reached six days later (Protocol amending the Protocol on Transitional Provisions annexed to the TEU, the TFEU and the Euratom Treaty [2010] OJ C263/1), the Protocol hoped to be ratified by the member states by December 2010 but, owing to delay in Greek, British and, finally, Belgian ratification, the process was completed only in November 2011. For the detail on numbers of MEPs see 3.50 below.

284　Decision 2011/199 [2011] OJ L91/1, art. 1.

anticipated to be secured by January 2013.[285] Both amendments, it will be observed, adhere correctly to the procedures of article 48. Since they do no more than add a single article to a Treaty protocol and a single paragraph to a Treaty article, respectively, they lend weight to the view that article 48 is in fact a closed system for Treaty amendment.

2.66 Ratification of Lisbon witnessed a new phenomenon, that of bribing (not too strong a word) the Irish voters and the Czech President into ratification by means of promises from the 27 heads of state and government as to future Treaty amendment. For the Irish, in order 'to provide reassurance and to respond to the concerns of the Irish people' identified by the Taoiseach as having resulted in a 'no' vote in the first referendum, a 'decision' was agreed by the European Council[286] and adopted by the heads of state and government meeting within the European Council[287] purporting to define the application of the Treaty in certain spheres[288] and a promise was made (by the European Council) that a decision would be taken 'in accordance with the necessary legal procedures' that the old system of one Commissioner appointed from each member state, abandoned by both Nice and Lisbon (from 2014), would be re-instituted.[289] For the Czechs it was a promise (from the heads of state and government) of moderation of the effects of the Charter of Fundamental Rights, to be made 'at the time of the conclusion of the next Accession Treaty'.[290] This is a constitutional morass: undertakings given, promises made

---

285 *Ibid.* art. 2. However the Supreme Court in Ireland has now asked the Court of Justice whether Decision 2011/199 is invalid for its material provisions going beyond that permitted by the simplified revision procedure; Case C-370/12 *Pringle v Government of Ireland*, pending; which, even if the proceedings are accelerated (as the Supreme Court has requested), will delay ratification for months.

286 European Council, Brussels, 18/19 June 2009, Presidency Conclusions, *Bulletin EU* 6–2009, 8, para. 1.3.4.

287 *Ibid.* para. 1.3–4 and Annex I.

288 The areas of concern addressed by the heads of state and government were the right to life, family and education; taxation; security and defence policy and neutrality. A solemn declaration on workers' rights was added by the European Council (Annex II).

289 European Council, Brussels, 11/12 December 2008, Presidency Conclusions, *Bulletin EU* 12–2008, 8, para. I.4.2. At the time it was made there was no Treaty authority for the European Council to deliver on its promise; post-Lisbon it (probably) has the power on its own initiative to alter the number of Commissioners as promised without Treaty amendment; TEU, art. 17(5); see n … below.

290 European Council, Brussels, 29–30 October 2009, Presidency Conclusions, para. I.2 and Annex I. The concern appeared to be the possibility of judicial challenges to the 'Beneš decrees' on expropriation of German and Hungarian property, made by the Czechoslovak government in exile, subsequently 'ratified' by the national assembly and homologated by a 'constitutional law' of the parliament of Czechoslovakia in 1946 (Ustavní zákon č. 57/1946 Sb. ze dne 28. března 1946), to which both the Czech Republic and Slovakia succeeded. It is not clear that these fears were well founded, even the Court of Human Rights dismissing (as inadmissible) a claim for reparation as the property expropriation preceded the entry into force of the relevant provisions of the ECHR and Czechoslovak ratification of it: *Bergauer and ors v Czech Republic* (Application No. 17120/04), judgment of 13 December 2005, unreported. The solution was to (promise to) extend the agreed Polish and UK 'opt-outs' from part of the Charter to the Czech Republic (see 6.118 below) but it is equally unclear how this will cure the (perceived) problem. The remedy, if remedy it be, does not apply to Slovakia.

and measures adopted by the European Council and the heads of state and government meeting within the European Council (*not* the same body)[291] which neither has the authority to make or, ultimately, the power to keep.[292] The next accession Treaty now having been concluded (with Croatia),[293] the text now published in the *Official Journal*[294] betrays no mention of the Czech undertaking – which means that text is incomplete, the heads of state and government reneged on their promise, or everyone forgot about it. Even had it come to pass, it is possible that the inclusion in an accession treaty of terms giving effect to the promise made to the Czechs would be an abuse of process as a matter which ought properly to have been adopted by the mechanisms of article 48, and so go unrecognised by the Court of Justice.[295] It is also richly ironic, and should be a serious embarrassment to them, that Lisbon should enter into force, the signatories still 'confirming [the Union's] attachment to … respect for human rights and fundamental freedoms',[296] by grace of an undertaking from their heads of government selectively to scrap some of those rights for some of its citizens. As of Autumn 2012 a new Treaty protocol noting the Irish concerns ('Protocol on the concerns of the Irish people on the Treaty of Lisbon' or 'the Irish Protocol') has been agreed by a (perfunctory) IGC, signed by all member states and is undergoing ratification. An equivalent 'Czech Protocol' stumbled shortly out of the blocks owing to opposition from the Czech Senate, and is now delayed indefinitely.

The close of 2011 witnessed a second phenomenon. Discussion within the **2.67** European Council to amend the Treaties (by simplified procedure) with a view to strengthening economic convergence in the euro area, improving financial discipline and deepening economic union as a prudent response to the eurozone debt crisis was met with a British veto. The other 26 member states promptly decided to venture outside the Union,[297] proposing a new treaty creating a 'Fiscal Compact' which was signed by 25 of them (the Czechs joining the British in staying out) in early 2012[298] and anticipated (optimistically) to enter into force in January 2013.[299] Other than some supervisory jurisdiction

---

291 For the difference see 3.37 below.
292 Unless the decisions taken could be construed as treaties in public international law; which, given the constitutional safeguards over the power of the executive in most member states, it is submitted they cannot; and in no circumstance can they circumvent the obligatory procedures of TEU, art. 48.
293 See immediately below.
294 [2012] OJ L112/10.
295 See immediately below.
296 TEU, Preamble, 4th para.
297 A '17+' group of the 17 eurozone countries plus Bulgaria, Denmark, Latvia, Lithuania, Poland and Romania opted straightaway for this course, the Czech Republic, Hungary and Sweden indicating support but electing to withhold a decision pending parliamentary approval.
298 Treaty of 2 March 2012 on Stability, Coordination and Governance in the Economic and Monetary Union.
299 *Ibid.* art. 14(2). For the detail see 14.25 below.

conferred upon the European Commission and the Court of Justice,[300] the Treaty is wholly unconnected with the Union, its jurisdiction and methods – but at the same time will cut across its material competences significantly. The objective remains that it be incorporated into the Union Treaties 'as soon as possible'[301] – in other words, that it gain Czech and United Kingdom assent and participation – and it is anticipated this will happen within five years 'at most'.[302] It is not unprecedented in principle: the member states have entered into other treaties in matters (still) within their competence, some of which came to be absorbed subsequently by the Community/Union; and the creation of the Union in 1993 and enhanced cooperation (most apposite the Social Protocol introduced by Maastricht, by which the United Kingdom was excluded from certain social legislation for a time but signed up to it five years later)[303] may be said to be variations on the theme. But the alacrity with which the 17+ turned to the *hors-traité* option, the close intermingling of Union and fiscal compact competences and the attendant risks to Union continuity and cohesion make this, however carefully matters (and Union priority) are delineated in the new Treaty, a more complex and delicate operation than any previously.[304]

(c) Accession

2.68 As with Treaty amendment, the Community Treaties each provided its own mechanism for accession of new member states to the respective Community.[305] They were replaced by and in the Treaty on European Union at Maastricht with a single provision which applies to membership of the Union,[306] so barring accession *à la carte*, which was for practical purposes possible only to the Union in its entirety and not to either or both of the remaining Communities. With the entry into force of Lisbon, Euratom was severed from the Union and this uniformity once again sundered so that accession to the Union and accession to the (extant) Atomic Energy Community are now governed by separate (if

---

300 *Ibid.* art. 8. The (limited) supervisory authority of the Commission came in later drafts and met with some surprise.

301 European Council, 9 December 2011, Statement by the Euro Area heads of state or government, p. 7.

302 Fiscal Compact Treaty, n. 298 above, art. 16.

303 See 14.34–14.35 below.

304 Art. 2 of the Treaty provides that it is to be applied and interpreted, and applies insofar as it is compatible with, the Treaties on which the European Union is founded and with European Union law; nevertheless the Supreme Court in Ireland (sitting as seven judges) has asked the Court of Justice whether Irish ratification is compatible with its obligations under the Union Treaties: *Pringle v Government of Ireland* [2012] IESC 47, decision of 31 July 2012; lodged as Case C-370/12 *Pringle v Government of Ireland*, pending; it is a question the Court of Justice may be unable to answer.

305 ECSC Treaty, art. 98; EEC Treaty, art. 237; Euratom Treaty, art. 205; all now repealed.

306 TEU (pre-Lisbon), art. 49.

materially identical) provisions,[307] so (re-)opening the legal possibility of accession to the Union but not Euratom, or to Euratom but not the Union. It is by no means certain that a third country would never find accession to Euratom alone (and not the Union) an attractive proposition, but given the constitutional/institutional Laocoön it would create it is an option unlikely ever to be on the table.

Application for accession is addressed by the 'applicant state' (or 'candidate country') to the Council; in order to proceed it requires at this initial stage the unanimous support of the Council (after consulting the Commission) and the assent of the European Parliament acting by absolute majority of its members. It will be observed that the constitutional hurdles of accession of a new member state are higher than those of Treaty amendment, requiring from the start a unanimous Council (which is why French opposition was enough to blackball the Danish, Irish, Norwegian and UK applications through the 1960s);[308] and (since 1987) the consent of the Parliament. Negotiations are conducted on the Union side by the Council, latterly on the basis of (some three dozen) 'chapters' of an 'accession package' which are 'opened' (negotiations commence) and 'closed' (agreement reached). In the event of final agreement, the mechanism of accession is signature of a terse 'treaty of accession' by all member states and the applicant state(s), setting out the basic agreement and key principles of admission to the Union, to which is appended an extensive 'act of accession' (which is an 'integral part' of the Treaty of Accession)[309] detailing terms, conditions and transitional arrangements. The package is then subject to ratification by all member states and by the applicant state(s) in accordance with respective constitutional requirements. There is no case of a treaty of accession, once agreed, failing to find ratification by all member states; but Norwegian accession fell at this final hurdle, twice, for want of Norwegian ratification. **2.69**

Being an act of the member states and not of the EU institutions, the terms of an accession treaty cannot be called into question before the Court of Justice.[310] Upon its entry into force the rule is that the provisions of Union law, and the full *acquis*, apply *ab initio* and *in toto* to a new member state, 'derogations being **2.70**

---

307 That is, TEU, art. 49 and Euratom Treaty, art. 106a. Article 49 governs admission to the Union but its provisions are carried over (they 'shall apply to') the Euratom Treaty *mutatis mutandis* (art. 106a).

308 See 1.14 above.

309 E.g., the second Brussels Accession Treaty (n. 323 below), art. 1(3); Case C-161/06 *Skoma-Lux* v *Celní ředitelství Olomouc* [2007] ECR I-10841, at para. 3.

310 Case 313/89 *Commission* v *Spain* [1991] ECR I-5231.

allowed only in so far as they are expressly laid down by transitional pro-visions';[311] the public international law character of the accession instruments thus gives way to the Union constitutional order.

2.71 Notwithstanding express rules on amendment in article 48, an accession treaty may also effect Treaty amendment insofar as it comprises 'adjustments to the Treaties … which such admission entails'.[312]

2.72 Accession to the Union is open to any European state which respects the principles set out in article 2 of the Treaty on European Union and is committed to promoting them.[313] The quality of 'European' appears to be elastic, as Turkey (with 3 per cent of its territory in the European continent) is a serious candidate for accession and Cyprus, physiographically Asian if cultur-ally (for the most part) European, has already joined; but a 1987 application from Morocco was politely declined. Respect for the principles of article 2 is more difficult: in 1978 the Court of Justice was asked to determine whether Greece, Spain and Portugal, all fresh from military/authoritarian government, were eligible for accession in the light of the (rudimentary) Treaty conditions then in force, but found the question premature and non-justiciable.[314] At the 1993 Copenhagen Summit the European Council adopted a resolution setting out the criteria (the 'accession criteria' or 'Copenhagen criteria') by which fitness for accession is to be judged, being: stability of institutions guaranteeing democracy, the rule of law and human rights including respect for minorities; a functioning market economy; the capacity to cope with Community/Union market forces; and adherence to the aims of political, economic and monetary

---

311 Case C-233/97 *KaapAhl* [1998] ECR I-8069, at para. 15; Case C-420/07 *Apostolides* v *Orams and Orams* [2009] ECR I-3571, at para. 33; Cases C-424 and 425/10 *Ziolkowski & Szeja* v *Land Berlin*, judgment of 21 December 2011, not yet reported, at para. 56. Derogations must be interpreted restrictively and must be limited to what is 'absolutely necessary' in order to attain their objectives; *Apostolides*, at para. 35. Assurances (claimed to be) given in the course of accession negotiations will cut no ice with the Court; Case C-76/08 *Commission* v *Malta* [2009] ECR I-8213, at para. 67.

312 TEU, art. 49(2). Thus it is that the promises made by the 27 heads of state and government to the Irish and the Czechs in order to secure their consent to the Lisbon Treaty which require Treaty amendment, envisaged by and half promised to the Irish, and expressly promised to the Czechs 'at the time of the conclusion of the next Accession Treaty', to be secured by affixing a putative 'Irish Protocol' (if necessary) and a 'Czech Protocol' (clearly necessary) to the next (in the event Croatian) accession treaty may have proven constitutionally impermissible, for if they are not 'adjustments … which [Croatian] admission entails' they may, if slipped in the back door via art. 49 (rather than by art. 48 and in accordance with the procedures it requires), have been an abuse of process. The issue will not arise as the Irish and Czech protocols follow another route; see 2.66 above.

313 TEU, art. 49.

314 Case 93/78 *Mattheus* v *Doego Fruchtimport und Tiefkühlkost* [1978] ECR 2203. But terms of accession, once agreed, cannot be challenged before the Court of Justice; Cases 31 and 35/86 *Levantina Agricola Industria and anor* v *Council* [1978] ECR 2285.

union.[315] The constitutional requirement for adherence to the principles of article 6(1) EC (respect for fundamental rights) was then introduced by the Treaty of Amsterdam in 1999, and an obligation to consider the Copenhagen criteria was written into the Treaties by Lisbon.[316] Whilst the justiciability of these provisions remains an open question, doubtless they would inform the political judgments of the Union institutions and the member states in deciding whether to consent.

Since creation of the European Communities there have been, to date, seven **2.73** accession treaties, those accommodating the accessions of:

- Denmark, Ireland and the United Kingdom (1973);[317]
- Greece (1981);[318]
- Spain and Portugal (1986);[319]
- Austria, Finland and Sweden (1995);[320]
- the Czech Republic, Estonia, Cyprus, Latvia, Lithuania, Hungary, Malta, Poland, Slovakia and Slovenia (2004);[321]
- Bulgaria and Romania (2007);[322] and
- Croatia (2013).[323]

The citizens and territory of the German Democratic Republic were absorbed into those of the Federal Republic in 1990 by unilateral German act and so joined the Community without formal accession.[324] The political agreement on the 2004 and 2007 enlargements reached at the Copenhagen Summit in 2002 included a decision that if Turkey (which has enjoyed an 'association' with the Community since 1964[325] and applied for full membership in 1987) came to

---

315 *Bulletin EC* 6–1993, 13. The Madrid Summit in 1995 added an administrative infrastructure capable of bearing the burdens of giving proper effect to Community law. From 1997 the Commission read active resistance to corruption, particularly in the public sector, into these conditions.

316 TEU, art. 49(1): 'The conditions of eligibility agreed upon by the European Council shall be taken into account'.

317 Treaty of 22 January 1972 (Brussels Accession Treaty) [1972] JO L73/1.

318 Treaty of 28 May 1979 (Athens Accession Treaty) [1979] OJ L291/9.

319 Treaty of 12 June 1985 [1985] OJ L302/9 (signed coterminously in Madrid and Lisbon, so lacking an informal shorthand title).

320 Treaty of 24 June 1994 (Corfu Accession Treaty) [1994] OJ C241/9.

321 Treaty of 16 April 2003 ([Second] Athens Accession Treaty) [2003] OJ L236/17.

322 Treaty of 25 April 2005 (Luxembourg Accession Treaty) [2005] OJ L157/11.

323 Treaty of 9 December 2011 ([Second] Brussels Accession Treaty) [2012] OJ L112/10.

324 See 1.29 above. The same issue, if on a smaller scale, arises with the (re-)absorption of Bonaire, Saba and Sint Eustatius into *land Nederland* in 2010 (see 10.05 below, n. 39) and Mayotte becoming a French overseas *département* in 2011 (14.83 below, n. 457), so bringing all these territories into the Union by, ostensibly, unilateral Dutch and French action. But there is now express provision in the Treaties (TFEU, art. 355(6)) for dealing with it; see 10.05 below, n. 37. Nor does it extend citizenship of the Union, a status already enjoyed by the peoples of those islands.

325 See 11.151 below.

fulfil the Copenhagen criteria by the end of 2004, negotiations ought to follow, and following agreement in the European Council in December 2004 which recognised Turkey's 'candidate status', negotiations commenced, after a shaky start,[326] in autumn 2005; they are open-ended, without formal commitment, and not expected to be speedy. Croatia submitted its application for accession in 2003, was granted candidate status in 2004, negotiations began in 2005, saw off hurdles on the surrender of suspected war criminals to the jurisdiction of the International Criminal Court and a maritime (and riparian) boundary dispute with Slovenia, were completed in June 2011, approved by the European Parliament in early December and a Treaty of Accession signed a week later; it anticipates completion of ratification (requiring a referendum in Croatia[327] and possibly elsewhere) by, and so Croatian accession on, 1 July 2013.[328] In 2004 (the Former Yugoslav Republic of) Macedonia applied for accession and was granted candidate status in late 2005, but no date has been set for the start of negotiations; the very name of the country will be a formidable sticking point in winning Greek consent at least.[329] At the end of 2008 Montenegro formally applied, was granted candidate status at the end of 2010 and negotiations opened in 2012;[330] Albania applied in spring 2009, Serbia at the end of 2009. Following the economic turmoil of 2008 (and ongoing) and a change of government (to a majority left-leaning government for the first time since gaining home rule in 1874), Iceland submitted an application for accession in

---

326 Just prior to commencement of negotiations the Austrian government withdrew its support for accession, pushing instead for an (undefined) 'special association' between Turkey and the Union, and relented only on the day negotiations were scheduled to begin. Both the Austrian and French governments of the day promised referendums on Turkish accession, and in 2005 the French constitution was amended so as to require any future accession to be approved by referendum (art. 88–5), although this requirement may (since 2008) be circumvented by a three-fifths vote of approval of the Parliament meeting in congress (*le Parlement convoqué [ou réuni] en Congrès*) (arts 88–5 and 89, 3ᵉ alinéa). (Bulgarian and Romanian accessions were not subject to referendums as art. 88–5 applies only to accessions, a product of an accession IGC convened by the Council after 1 July 2004; loi constitutionnelle no. 2005–204 du 1er mars 2005 modifiant le titre XV de la Constitution, JO du 2 mars 2005, p. 3696, art. 4.) There are proposals to alter the referendum provision limiting its application to candidate countries with a population of more than 5 per cent of that of the Union; (partly) European countries outwith the Union which would be caught by this threshold are Russia, Ukraine and Turkey.

327 Constitution of Croatia, art. 142. The referendum took place in January 2012, accession supported by 66 per cent (against 33 per cent) of votes on a 43.5 per cent turnout.

328 (Brussels) Accession Treaty of 9 December 2011, art. 3.

329 However, in 2011 the International Court of Justice found Greece to have violated the 'interim accord' with Macedonia (Interim Accord of 13 October 1995, 1891 UNTS I-32193) in objecting to Macedonian admission to NATO by other than the name accorded it by the Security Council ('the former Yugoslav Republic of Macedonia'): *Former Yugoslav Republic of Macedonia* v *Greece*, judgment of 5 December 2011, not yet reported. As the accord applies to 'international, multilateral and regional organizations and institutions of which [Greece] is a member' albeit permitting it to object to membership other than by the name accorded it by the Security Council (art. 11(1)), whilst other EU member states are divided on the issue (between 'former Yugoslav Republic of Macedonia' and 'Republic of Macedonia'), it is not clear how the Court of Justice (or indeed the ICJ, which has jurisdiction to interpret the interim accord, but the Court of Justice has not) would, if asked, respond to the equivalent question of admission to the Union.

330 European Council, Brussels, 28/29 January 2012, Presidency Conclusions, para. IV.(b).

the summer of 2009, candidate status was granted in spring 2010 and negotiations begun that summer; should Iceland join it would replace Malta as the least populous member state and Icelandic would become the least spoken official language (depending upon how Irish speakers are counted). Switzerland applied to join in 1992 but following referendum rejection of the EEA no further action has been taken and the application is largely forgotten, if never officially withdrawn.

It should be noted that the 2004 and subsequent accessions follow a different **2.74** pattern than previously. The general approach of the first four accession treaties was to provide for accession effective upon an agreed date, following which the new member state(s) would adjust to the requirements of membership in accordance with the terms set out in the act of accession, which provided a substantial transition period therefor. By comparison, the 2003, 2005 and 2011 accession treaties followed a lengthy period during which the accession states were required, by political agreement with the Union, to adhere to a 'pre-accession strategy' of adjustment to (then) Community discipline prior to accession – indeed, prior to formal agreement upon accession – so that they could hit the ground running and require relatively little by way of a post-accession transition period.[331] This caused some disquiet, for it required significant sacrifice on the part of the accession states without binding promise of membership. But it may be assumed that future accessions will follow this model. There may also have set in a sense of 'enlargement fatigue', or 'absorption saturation', that digestion of the 13 new member states will be burden enough, and enthusiasm for prompt inclusion of yet more which follow in the queue is muted.[332]

---

331 For the transition provisions applying to the 2004, 2007 and 2013 accessions (involving the movement of persons, agriculture, transport, tax and environmental provisions of the Treaty) see Annexes V, VI, VII–X, and XII–XIV of the 2003 Act of Accession [2003] OJ L236/803–924, Annexes VI and VII of the 2005 Act of Accession, [2005] OJ L157/278–368, and arts 36–42 and Annex V of the 2011 Act of Accession. For three years following the 2007 accessions the Commission had authority to adopt safeguard measures in the face of 'serious economic difficulties' (2005 Act of Accession, art. 36), 'a serious breach of the functioning of the internal market' (art. 37) or 'serious shortcomings' in areas falling within Title VI of the EC Treaty (art. 38) occasioned by failures of the new member states to comply with Community discipline. It did so as regards problems of air transport with Bulgaria (Regulation 1962/2006 [2006] OJ L408/8; repealed two years later, Regulation 875/2008 [2008] OJ L240/3) and indicated it might do so (but in the event didn't) owing to concerns about judicial reform and control of corruption and organised crime there (COM(2006) 549; COM(2008) 495 final).

332 See *Enlargement Strategy and Main Challenges 2006–2007* COM(2006) 649, in which the Commission emphasises the difficulties of further enlargement. Also European Parliament, *Report [of the Foreign Affairs Committee] on the Commission's 2007 Enlargement Strategy Paper*, A6–0226/2008.

(d) Secession

2.75 Prior to Lisbon there was no provision in the Treaties addressing secession of a member state. Treaties establishing international organisations commonly do provide for withdrawal or denunciation, usually requiring only a period of notice. The Community and Union Treaties did not; rather, they were concluded for 'an unlimited period'[333] and silent on the matter of withdrawal of a member state. The principal precedents for secession are:

- the departure of Greenland from the Communities in 1985. But that was a function of the internal constitutional re-ordering of a member state and the cessation of the application of the Treaties to part (and a non-European part) of its territory. Even so, it was effected by formal Treaty amendment in accordance with the then existing procedures; it was universally accepted that this was necessary in order to give effect to the wishes of Greenlanders to secede, and that it was beyond the powers of Greenland and/or Danish authorities to do so unilaterally. This was reflected in reverse in 2011, Mayotte acquiring the status of a French *département d'outre-mer* by unilateral French law and so becoming an integral part of French territory but *not* by that act becoming part of the territory of the Union, that being a matter reserved to the European Council by authority of and in conformity with the Treaties;[334]

- the departure of Saint-Barthélemy from the Union in 2012. But this too was cessation of the application of the Treaties to a non-European part (a *collectivité d'outre-mer*) of a member state and secured by decision of the European Council under Treaty authority.[335] More interesting is its status (alongside Saint-Martin) from 2007 to 2009: in 2007 a constitutional reorganisation of overseas territories[336] saw both withdraw from the administrative authority of Guadeloupe (a *département d'outre-mer*), becoming *collectivités d'outre-mer*. As Guadeloupe formed part of the territory of the Community but the overseas collectivities did (and do) not,[337] this either (a) marked their secession from the Community or (b) did not, notwithstanding the French law which severed them from Guadeloupe, in the absence of formal Community recognition of that fact. The situation was reversed (on supposition (a)) or formally re-affirmed (on supposition (b)) in 2009 by the Lisbon Treaty which

---

333 EEC Treaty, art. 240; Euratom Treaty, art. 208; TEU (pre-Lisbon), art. 51; Lisbon Treaty, art. 3; TEU, art. 53; TFEU, art. 356. The exception was the ECSC Treaty; see 1.05 above.

334 See 10.05 below.

335 Decision 2010/718 [2010] OJ L325/4; see 10.05 below, n. 37.

336 Loi organique no. 2007–223 du 21 février 2007 portant dispositions statutaires et institutionnelles relatives à l'outre-mer 2007, JO du 22 février 2007, p. 3220.

337 EC Treaty, art. 299(2): 'The provisions of this Treaty shall apply to the French overseas departments'. The formula is now different; see 10.05 below, n. 37.

expressly recognised both, still *collectivités d'outre-mer*, to be part of Union territory[338] – a status Saint-Barthélemy (but not Saint-Martin) lost again in 2012. None of this had an effect upon rights of citizenship (the Saint-Martinois and Saint-Barthinois are fully French, and so Union, citizens) and no legal repercussion of the interregnum is recorded. If (a) is the correct interpretation of the events, it remains the sole instance of (temporary) departure of a territory from the Community by unilateral (French) act.

Three other precedents may be identified but their peculiarity makes them uninstructive.[339] All are fundamentally different from the issue of secession of a member state. It is submitted that in the state of Community law (the arguments for the Union were less strong) as it was prior to Lisbon, secession of a member state would require Treaty amendment in order to remove the provisions throughout the treaties expressly recognising it to be a member state; and that owing to the nature of the treaties and the rights and duties created by them as interpreted and applied, any purported unilateral secession from the Community of a member state or part of a member state would be unlawful absent Treaty amendment – which required, and requires, the unanimous consent of the governments and parliaments of the member states and so, again, conferring a veto upon Malta. This would be consistent with applicable rules of **2.76**

---

338   TFEU, art. 355(1).

339   First, the Saar case (n. 276 above) indicates that the ECSC *may* have recognised a moving frontier rule, but even if so it occurred long before a Community legal order began to take shape. The second is Algeria, at the time of the entry into force of the EEC Treaty an integral part of France (in French constitutional law) and subject to some, but not all, Treaty rules (EEC Treaty, art. 227(2)). Following the Algerian War (of Independence) it seceded from France in 1962 acquiring independent statehood, following which its relationship with the Community was in limbo until the entry into force of a cooperation agreement in 1978 (Cooperation Agreement of 26 April 1976 between the EEC and the People's Democratic Republic of Algeria [1978] OJ L263/2). No Community action was taken to alter its status, and in fact the various Treaty provisions purported to apply to Algeria still (when they clearly did not) until art. 227(2) was amended in 1993 by the Maastricht Treaty. However Algeria was never wholly and integrally part of the Community, and its relationship with France was one of dependency, so entitling it upon independence to a 'clean slate' denunciation of French treaty obligations; see the Vienna Convention of 23 August 1978 on Succession in Respect of Treaties, 1946 UNTS 3, in force 1 November 1996, art. 16. (Only five EU member states (Czech Republic, Estonia, Cyprus, Slovakia, Slovenia) have ratified the Convention; Poland and the German Democratic Republic signed but never ratified it.) The third case is Saint-Pierre-et-Miquelon which became a *département d'outre-mer* in 1976 (Loi no. 76–664 du 19 juillet 1976, JO du 20 juillet 1976, p. 4323) but in 1985 reassumed the status of a *territoire d'outre mer* (Loi no. 85–595 du 11 juin 1985, JO du 14 juin 1985, p. 6551). Its status in Community law was thus altered by unilateral French action. But it was not until the Amsterdam Treaty that the *départements d'outre-mer* were made fully part of Community territory (text to n. 334 above), prior to which the provisions of Community law applied there only partially (EEC Treaty, art. 227(2)); nor, as with Saint-Martin and Saint-Barthélemy, were there any repercussions for the rights of Community nationality, the Saint-Pierrais and Miquelonnais being French citizens throughout. The event should therefore perhaps be seen as altering, at the time, not Community territory but the (partial) application of Community law to a third territory, and may be compared with the more correct treatment of Mayotte and Saint-Barthélemy today.

public international law,[340] but of course contrary to the conventional UK view of the supremacy of Parliament,[341] and of similar constitutional constructions in other member states. Whether or not UK courts would have given effect to an Act of Parliament purporting, in express terms, to amend or repeal the statutory underpinning making Community law effective in the United Kingdom in order unilaterally to take it out of the Union – and more specifically the Community – is a question of both theological nicety and, now, historical interest.

2.77 Lisbon wrought significant change, providing for 'voluntary withdrawal' of a member state from the Union.[342] It is the first time the Treaties formally countenance Union membership prefaced not upon a marriage for life, and it puts the Union in odd company: of modern federal constitutions only that of the Soviet Union expressly recognised the right of the several republics freely to secede from the USSR.[343] Yet it was noted with approval, notwithstanding the open-ended commitment of articles 53 TEU and 356 TFEU, by the *Bundesverfassungsgericht*, calling it a principle of 'reversible autolimitation' (*umkehrbare Selbstbindung*) inherent in the *Staatenverbund* it recognises the Union to be, which ought to be hindered by neither Union authority nor other member states.[344] Optimally, withdrawal would gain the consent of the European Parliament and a (double) qualified majority of the Council, following which it would be made effective by an agreement between the seceding member state and the Council which establishes the conditions for withdrawal and a framework for its future relationship with the Union.[345] But absent agreement a member state may nevertheless secede unilaterally two years after notifying its intention to do so,[346] no provision being made to address the legal vacuum which would ensue, although elsewhere Lisbon has, probably unintentionally,

---

340 The Vienna Convention on the Law of Treaties provides (art. 56(1)) that denunciation of or withdrawal from a treaty is possible only where the founding treaty makes express provision for it, the parties can be shown to have intended it, or it is implied by the nature of the treaty – or, of course, if it is agreed subsequently by the contracting parties. An exception may have applied to the withdrawal of Greenland, for even though still a Danish 'dependent territory for international relations', it too might upon elevation to home rule have been entitled to a clean slate and so a right of unilateral denunciation of Danish treaties. The fact that the Greenland and Saint-Barthélemy secession were engineered not unilaterally but in accordance with art. 236 EEC and art. 255(6) TFEU is an indication of the displacement of public international law by a more sophisticated Community/Union regime, and one resembling a constitutional order.

341 For discussion see 6.18 below.

342 TEU, art. 50.

343 Конституция (Основно́й Зако́н) СССР (от 7 октября 1977 г.), ст. 72. And so a double irony: of all federal constitutions the only one in which the right was expressly provided, but widely thought to be the one in which it was least likely ever to be exercised; yet over the events of 1990–91, it *was* exercised.

344 BVerfG, 30. Juni 2009 (*Lissabon-Vertrag*), BVerfGE 123, 267 (349).

345 TEU, art. 50(2),(3).

346 *Ibid.* art. 50(3).

made the task less fraught.[347] This clarifies and eases – remarkably generously, some would say dangerously – the question of a right of secession from the Union. A state having withdrawn from the Union, but wishing to rejoin, would enjoy no special privileges, and be required to apply anew for accession through normal procedures.[348]

It is not clear whether this logic assists in the question of the outcome of the **2.78** dissolution, or dismemberment, of a member state. Should a member state unilaterally be dismembered in accordance with its own constitutional rules, and one, some, or all of the resulting parts then claim automatic succession to full Union membership in its/their own right, it is submitted that the Union legal order could not cope. This is *not* consistent with public international law, which generally prescribes continuity of membership.[349] But to allow one part of a dissolving member state, to the exclusion of another, to succeed to its membership would be to deprive the other part(s) of acquired rights and their populations of citizenship rights; in the face of multiple succession, a Union which recognises the member states (as presently constituted) and allocates to them seats and voting rights in the institutions, cannot accept a unilateral *fait accompli* by conjuring from the ether, for example, additional seats in the Parliament and the advisory committees and weightings different from those painstakingly agreed and now provided; rather it would require agreement, in accordance with article 48, to do so. But it might be argued that the Lisbon provisions permitting voluntary withdrawal, unilaterally if need be, permit also the withdrawal of part of a member state (if agreed internally); and that the institutional changes which make unilateral withdrawal easier also make easier adaptation to dismemberment of a member state and (multiple?) secession of what results. The Treaty commitment to respect for the equality of the member states and their national identities,[350] combined with the international legal right to self-determination, may well produce a legal obligation to achieve that result.

---

347 The Treaties post-Lisbon are more amenable to change of this sort than previously in terms of institutional balance. For example, whilst in the past voting in the Council was in many areas by weighted majority, each member state accorded a Treaty-determined weighting the result of sometimes laborious negotiation, a new system (to be fully operative by 2017) operates rather by minimum number and percentages of member states and of population sizes (see 3.42 below); similarly, the number of Commissioners and of judges in the Court of Justice comprises not a set number (as previously) but 'one national of each Member State' (TEU, art. 17(4)) and 'one judge from each Member State' (TEU, art. 19(2)), and the allocation of seats in the Parliament is not Treaty-determined but agreed within the European Council subject to a Treaty cap (TEU, art. 14(2); see 3.47 below). Thus, unnegotiated secession of a member state may be less of a Treaty rupture than in the past.

348 TEU, art. 50(5).

349 See the 1978 Vienna Convention, n. 339 above, art. 34.

350 TEU, art. 4(2).

2.79 This is, of course, a projection only, and one which may (although may not) remain untested.

Part B

THE INSTITUTIONAL FRAMEWORK

INTRODUCTION

The Treaties establish an 'institutional framework' consisting of seven institutions (properly so-called) charged with 'promot[ing the Union's] values, advanc[ing] its objectives, serv[ing] its interests, those of its citizens and those of the Member States, and ensur[ing] the consistency, effectiveness and continuity of its politics'.[1] They are:

- the European Parliament;
- the European Council;
- the Council;
- the European Commission;
- the Court of Justice of the European Union;
- the European Central Bank;
- the Court of Auditors.

Each of the three original Community Treaties established four institutions: an Assembly (which became the Parliament), a Council, a Commission (the High Authority under the European Coal and Steel Treaty) and a Court of Justice. A convention signed alongside the Rome Treaties[2] fused the three Assemblies and the three Courts of Justice so that all three Communities were served by a single Assembly and a single Court of Justice from the outset. There remained a distinct High Authority/Commission and a distinct Council for each Community until 1967 when they were merged into a single Commission and a single Council (each 'of the European Communities').[3] The Court of Auditors was created in 1975 and elevated to the status of an institution, by Maastricht, in 1993. Otherwise Maastricht created no new institutions to govern the new European Union, rather it adopted, or 'borrowed', the existing Community institutions and charged them with carrying out the new tasks of the second and third pillars of the Union (the 'single institutional framework').[4] But the working of the institutions, the nature of the law they create, and the rules which apply to its enforcement, were fundamentally different under the Community Treaties and under the Union Treaty. With the European Union and European Community fused into one by Lisbon this distinction largely disappears, although second pillar matters under the pre-Lisbon TEU (Common Foreign and Security Policy) continue to be subject to specific rules and

---

1   TEU, art. 13(1).
2   Convention of 25 March 1957 on Certain Institutions common to the European Communities.
3   (Brussels) Treaty of 8 April 1965 establishing a single Council and a Single Commission of the European Communities (the Merger, sometimes 'Fusion', Treaty), [1967] JO L152/2, in force 1 July 1967, arts 1 and 9.
4   See TEU (pre-Amsterdam), art. C.

procedures closer to those of the TEU as it was than to the Community method. With Lisbon, the five existing institutions survive and two others, the European Council and the European Central Bank, both already in existence but in different guise, were added to their number. The Union's institutional framework is carried over and 'applies' to the Atomic Energy Community.[5]

Four of the institutions are 'political institutions', involved primarily in the initiation, formulation, adoption and execution of Union policy and legislation. A fifth, the European Central Bank, is a peculiar hybrid, discharging advisory, legislative and enforcement functions within its spheres of competence. The remaining two (the 'supervisory institutions') exercise judicial and financial control of and over the means by which the political institutions operate. There are, however, supervisory aspects to the work of the Commission.

The Treaties establish a number of other organs with significant powers and which are autonomous for budgetary purposes[6] but are not 'institutions'. These are, principally, the Economic and Social Committee and the Committee of the Regions (the 'advisory bodies') but also a perplexing number of offices, agencies and other bodies (without formal or uniform classification)[7] created by legislation to develop and supervise aspects of the work of the Union. Taken together they form what is sometimes called the 'multi-level architecture' of the Union.

As is the case with the Union itself,[8] each of the institutions is required to act within the limits of the powers conferred upon it by the Treaties.[9] This includes adherence to general principles of Union law developed from a number of sources to define the way in which powers should be exercised.[10] Within these parameters, each institution operates in accordance with its own Rules of Procedure; failure to comply with them may render its conduct unlawful.[11] The institutions have a duty to cooperate amongst themselves and fully with national authorities, administrative and judicial, to assist in the implementation of Union rules (the duty of 'sincere cooperation').[12]

---

5 Euratom Treaty, art. 106a(1).

6 Regulation of 21 December 1977 ('the Financial Regulation') [1977] OJ L356/1, as amended.

7 There is no reliable store to be put by nomenclature. For example, for 'institutions' the German text of the Treaties uses *Organe*; in discussing judicial control of Union authorities TFEU, arts 263 and 265 provide for review of acts and omissions of the institutions and of 'bodies, offices or [and; art. 265] agencies of the Union', but 'organes et organismes de l'Union' and 'Einrichtungen oder [und] sonstigen Stellen der Union'; Eurojust (see 4.31 below) is a body/*organe/bezeichnete Stelle* of the Union.

8 See 2.26 above.

9 TEU, art. 13(2) (ex art. 7 EC).

10 See 6.101–6.138 below.

11 See e.g., Case C-137/92P *Commission* v *BASF and ors (PVC)* [1994] ECR I-2555; Cases T-3/00 and 337/04 *Pitsiorlas* v *Council* [2007] ECR II-4779, at paras 178–257.

12 See 2.22 above.

The seats of the institutions, a matter for concensus amongst the governments of the member states,[13] were for many years provisional. They were finally fixed at a meeting of the European Council (the Edinburgh Summit) in 1992[14] and codified in the Treaties by Amsterdam.[15]

1. Transparency and openness of the institutions

Since Maastricht the TEU has recognised the objective of transparency in the decision-making process, the Union being one 'in which decisions are taken as openly as possible'.[16] In 1993 the Council and Commission approved a Code of Conduct[17] concerning public access to the documents of the two institutions which stated the 'general principle' that 'the public will have the widest possible access to documents held by the Commission and the Council'.[18] Significant litigation followed. In order to regularise matters the EC Treaty was amended by Amsterdam, and the TFEU now provides amongst its provisions of general application:

1. In order to promote good governance and ensure the participation of civil society, the Union institutions, bodies, offices and agencies shall conduct their work as openly as possible.
2. The European Parliament shall meet in public, as shall the Council when considering and voting on a draft legislative act.
3. Any citizen of the Union, and any natural or legal person residing or having its registered office in a Member State, shall have a right of access to documents of the Union institutions, bodies, offices and agencies, whatever their medium, subject to the principles and the conditions to be defined in accordance with this paragraph.

   General principles and limits on grounds of public or private interest governing this right of access to documents shall be determined by the European Parliament and the Council, by means of regulations, acting in accordance with the ordinary legislative procedure.

   Each institution, body, office or agency shall ensure that its proceedings are transparent and shall elaborate in its own Rules of Procedure specific provisions regarding access to its documents, in accordance with the regulations referred to in the second subparagraph.

   The Court of Justice of the European Union, the European Central Bank and the

---

13 TFEU, art. 341 (ex art. 289 EC).
14 Decision of the Representatives of the Governments of the Member States on the Location of the Seats of the Institutions [1992] OJ C341/1.
15 Protocol (No. 6) on the Location of the Seats of the Institutions and of Certain Bodies, Offices, Agencies and Departments of the European Union.
16 TEU, art. 1, 2nd para.
17 [1993] OJ L340/41; implemented for and by the Council by Decision 93/731 [1993] OJ L340/43, and for and by the Commission by Decision 94/90 [1994] OJ L46/58, now repealed.
18 Code of Conduct, 1st para.

European Investment Bank shall be subject to this paragraph only when exercising their administrative tasks.[19]

The first paragraph of subsection (3) is reproduced in the Charter of Fundamental Rights with no reference to limitations.[20] In 2001 a Regulation was adopted giving effect to (the predecessor of) these provisions;[21] it applies to documents held by the Commission, the Council and the Parliament, and the Rules of Procedure of each have been amended to accommodate it,[22] but as a general rule not to the Court of Justice and the financial institutions owing to the different nature of the responsibilities they discharge.[23] The general rule is that there is a right of access to documents,[24] except where disclosure would undermine the protection of the public interest (as defined), the privacy and integrity of the individual, commercial interests, judicial proceedings and legal advice, the purpose of inspections, investigations and audits and, in the event of 'internal' documents, the decision-making process.[25] The exceptions are to be interpreted and applied strictly.[26] Generally the activities of the Union acting in an administrative capacity (so in most case the Commission) give rise to less extensive access to documents than when acting in a legislative capacity.[27] The Court of Justice is only now addressing the extent to which Commission documents are protected by a privilege adhering to the confidentiality of private commercial interests.[28] A person requesting access to a document is not required to justify it[29] and so need not demonstrate an interest in having access to it.[30] A presumption of legality attaches to any statement made by an institution relating to the non-existence of documents requested, but it is a

---

19   TFEU, art. 15 (ex art. 255 EC).

20   EU Charter of Fundamental Rights, art. 42; as to the Charter, see 6.114–6.118 below.

21   Regulation 1049/2001 [2001] OJ L145/43.

22   See, for the Council, Decision 2001/840 [2001] OJ L313/40 and RP, Annex II; for the Commission, Decision 2001/937 [2001] OJ L345/94; for the Parliament, Bureau Decision of 28 November 2001 [2001] OJ C374/1 and RP, rules 96 and 97. Provision has also been made for (limited) access to European Central Bank documents: Decision 2004/258 [2004] OJ L80/42.

23   So, contrary to the recommendation of A-G Poiares Maduro, the Commission cannot be compelled to make available to third parties pleadings it has lodged before the Court; Cases C-514 etc./07P *Sweden and Association de la presse internationale* v *Commission* [2010] ECR I-8533.

24   Regulation 1049/2001, art. 2(1).

25   *Ibid.* art. 4(1–3).

26   Case T-471/09 *Toland* v *Parliament*, judgment of 7 June 2011, not yet reported, at para. 28 and case law cited.

27   Case C-139/07P *Commission* v *Technische Glaswerk Ilmenau* [2010] ECR I-5885, at para. 60; Cases C-514 etc./07P *Sweden and Association de la presse internationale*, n. 23 above, at para. 77.

28   Case T-237/05 *Éditions Odile Jacob* v *Commission* [2010] ECR II-2245; Case C-360/09 *Pfleiderer* v *Bundeskartellamt*, judgment of 14 June 2011, not yet reported; Case T-437/08 *CDC Hydrogene Peroxide Cartel Damage Claims* v *Commission*, judgment of 15 December 2011, not yet reported; Case T-344/08 *EnBW Energie Baden-Württemberg* v *Commission*, judgment of 22 May 2012, not yet reported; Case T-380/08 *Netherlands* v *Commission*, pending.

29   Regulation 1049/2001, art. 6(1).

30   Cases T-391/03 and 70/04 *Francher and Byk* v *Commission* [2006] ECR II-2023, at para. 82 and case law cited.

'simple' presumption which the applicant may rebut in any way on the basis of relevant and consistent evidence.[31] The presumption applies by analogy where an institution declares that it is not in possession of documents requested.[32] A 30-year limitation rule applies.[33] Disclosure remains a problem and a source of spirited litigation before the Court of Justice,[34] and the Commission has been criticised by the Ombudsman for its resistance and obstruction in releasing documents: in one case alone on access to documents regarding carbon emissions he found the Commission had failed in its duty of sincere cooperation,[35] its 'uncooperative attitude ... runs counter to the very principle of the rule of law, on which the Union is, *inter alia*, founded'[36] and declared it, twice, to be guilty of maladministration.[37]

A great leap forward was agreement at Lisbon, against significant resistance, that the Council deliberate and vote in public on the adoption of legislative acts.[38] Even then the Council has fought a rearguard action to keep its deliberations under wraps.[39] An exercise in review and amendment of Regulation 1049/2001 is underway but is proving acrimonious.

---

31 Cases T-110, 150 and 405/03 *Sison and ors* v *Council* [2005] ECR II-1429, para. 29 and case law cited; Case T-380/04 *Terezakis* v *Commission* [2008] ECR II-11*.

32 Cases T-355 and 446/04 *Co-Frutta* v *Commission* [2010] ECR II-1.

33 Regulation 1049/2001, art. 4(7).

34 The cases are too numerous to list. For the most important and/or recent see Case T-194/94 *Carvel and Guardian Newspapers* v *Council* [1995] ECR II-2765; Case T-105/95 *WWF UK* v *Commission* [1997] ECR II-313; Case T-174/95 *Svenska Journalistförbundet* v *Council* [1998] ECR II-2289; Cases C-174 and 189/98P *Netherlands and van der Wal* v *Commission* [2000] ECR I-1; Case C-41/00P *Interporc Im- und Export* v *Commission* [2003] ECR I-2125; Case C-64/05P *Sweden* v *Commission* [2007] ECR I-11389; Cases C-39 and 52/05P *Sweden and Turco* v *Council* [2008] ECR I-4723; Case C-345/06 *Heinrich* [2009] ECR I-1659; Case C-362/08P *Internationaler Hilfsfonds* v *Commission* [2010] ECR I-669; Case C-139/07P *Technische Glaswerk Ilmenau*, n. 27 above; Case C-28/08 *Commission* v *The Bavarian Lager Co.* [2010] ECR I-6055; Cases C-514 etc./07P *Sweden and Association de la presse internationale*, n. 23 above; Case T-233/09 *Access Info Europe* v *Council*, judgment of 22 March 2011, not yet reported; Case T-471/08 *Toland*, n. 26 above; Case C-506/08P *Sweden* v *MyTravel and Commission*, judgment of 21 July 2011, not yet reported; Case C-135/11P *IFAW Internationaler Tierschutz-Fonds* v *Commission*, judgment of 21 June 2012, not yet reported. See also Report from the Commission on the implementation of the principles in EC Regulation No. 1049/2001, COM(2004) 45 final.

35 Special Report of 24 February 2010 from the European Ombudsman to the European Parliament concerning lack of cooperation by the Commission in Complaint 676/2008/RT, para. 1.

36 *Ibid.* para. 39.

37 Decision of 7 July 2010 the European Ombudsman closing his inquiry into complaint 676/2008/RT; follow-up Decision of 24 September 2010.

38 TEU, art. 16(8); TFEU, art. 15(2).

39 See Case T-233/09 *Access Info Europe*, n. 34 above, in which the General Court ordered disclosure of national positions taken in Council working groups in deliberations upon a proposal for amendment of Regulation 1049/2001. The Council has appealed (Case C-280/11P *Council* v *Access Info Europe*, pending), and at the time of writing fully 20 member states are reported to be preparing to intervene in its support.

2. European governance

In 2001 the Commission produced a White Paper on 'European Governance',[40] envisaging fundamental reform of the manner in which the Community, and the Union, were governed. More precisely, the White Paper identified five principles – openness, participation, accountability, effectiveness and coherence – which 'underpin democracy and the rule of law' and suggests improvements, requiring significant change to the institutions and the manner in which they operate, to each. The principles were taken up in the Laeken Declaration[41] and so commended to the Constitutional Convention, surviving the Lisbon Treaty in the form, primarily, of the provisions on democratic principles in Title II of the TEU.[42] The general debate on European governance is ongoing.

3. Languages

Something must be said of the language regime which applies to the institutions. The Treaties exist in 23 authentic versions,[43] the 23 Treaty languages being also the 'official languages and working languages' of the institutions.[44] This produces 253 different language combinations; the addition of Croatian in 2013[45] will take it to 276, and one more (Icelandic, say) to 300. This presents frightening difficulties for the (smooth) operation of the institutions, yet it is a matter of Union policy that the institutions[46] can function, and are seen to function, in all languages; hence the Treaty right of any citizen of the Union to write to any institution or to the Ombudsman in any official language and have a reply in that language.[47]

---

40   White Paper on European Governance, COM(2001) 428 final.
41   Declaration on the Future of the Union included in the Final Act of the [Nice] Conference; the Future of the European Union – Laeken Declaration, *Bulletin EU* 12–2001, 19.
42   See 2.37–2.39 above.
43   See 6.09 below.
44   Regulation 1, [1958] JO 385, art. 1, as amended. From accession in 1973 to 2007 Irish was an official language of the Court of Justice only (see 5.25 below); in 2004 the Irish government formally sought full official status for Irish, and Regulation 1 was amended accordingly in 2005 (Regulation 920/2005 [2005] OJ L156/3), so that from January 2007 Irish is an official and working language of the institutions and (some) Union legislation is drafted and published in Irish (see 6.10 below, n. 67). Shortly after the Irish initiative the Spanish government proposed that Catalan/Valencian, Basque and Galician also be elevated to similar status. This has not yet happened, but since 2006 the Parliament and the Ombudsman allow speakers of those languages to use them, and receive answers in them, in correspondence with either.
45   2011 Act of Accession, art. 14.
46   The language regime of the Union 'organs', of a status inferior to that of the institutions, may be less comprehensive; see Case C-361/01P *Kik* v *OHIM* [2003] ECR I-8283; Case C-160/03 *Spain* v *Eurojust* [2005] ECR I-2077.
47   TFEU, art. 24, 4th para. (ex art. 21, 3rd para. EC).

Having said this, the institutions remain free to determine narrower internal linguistic rules as they see fit,[48] and the institutional machinery actually functions in a smaller number of languages. The Parliament and to a lesser extent the Council require to work in all or most languages, for linguistic ability of their members (and the political readiness to use it) cannot be presumed, but the Court of Justice works essentially in French, the college of Commissioners has decided (informally) to work in German, English and French, and these are recognised to be the *de facto* 'internal working languages' of the Commission and its services. However discrimination on grounds of language in (access to) employment in an institution is expressly prohibited[49] save where justified on objective and reasonable grounds and aimed at legitimate objectives in the general interest in the framework of staff policy[50] or connected with the proper functioning of the service.[51] Notices of vacancies may therefore (with objective justification) be published in full in some languages only, but adequate notice of a notice, affording all potential candidates effective knowledge of its existence and content, must be published in all languages.[52] In all cases in contentious dealings with an official in its service (for example, in disciplinary matters), an institution is bound to use a language which the official understands 'thoroughly'.[53]

4. Plan of this part

Chapter 3 deals with the political institutions, so, in turn:

- the European Council;
- the Commission;
- the Council;
- the Parliament;

and considers the legislative process in which they are, in their various ways, involved. Chapter 4 considers the Court of Auditors, the European Central

---

48 Regulation 1, arts 6 and 7.
49 Staff Regulations of Officials of the European Communities, art. 1d(1).
50 *Ibid.* art. 1d(6).
51 Case 15/63 *Lassalle* v *Parliament* [1964] ECR 31; Case T-117/08 *Italy* v *European Economic and Social Committee*, judgment of 31 March 2011, not yet reported.
52 Case T-185/05 *Italy* v *Commission* [2008] ECR II-3207; Case T-117/08 *Italy* v *EESC, ibid.* cf. Cases T-156 and 232/07 *Spain* v *Commission* [2010] ECR II-191* and Cases T-166 and 285/07 *Italy* v *Commission* [2010] ECR II-193*.
53 Case T-197/98 *Rudolph* v *Commission* [2000] ECR-SC II-241, at para. 46 ('une langue que celui-ci maîtrise d'une façon approfondie') ; alternatively, 'une maîtrise de la langue ... lui ayant permis de prendre effectivement et facilement connaissance du contenu des lettres qui lui ont été transmises par l'administration au cours de la procédure disciplinaire': Case T-203/03 *Rasmussen* v *Commission* [2005] ECR-SC II-1287, at para. 64.

Bank and the myriad other committees, organs and agencies. Chapter 5 describes the Court of Justice, its jurisdiction and its procedures.

3

THE POLITICAL INSTITUTIONS AND PROCEDURES

A. EUROPEAN COUNCIL

The European Council has existed for some time but was formally recognised **3.01** as an institution of the Union only in 2009 with Lisbon. It developed in the early 1970s through a series of 'summits' of heads of state and government held outside the machinery laid down in the Community Treaties.[1] This evolved in part because of a policy vacuum created by the gradual completion of 'first generation' Treaty objectives, and in part to a desire to reassert the predominance of national governments in defining future Community development.

---

1 The original, rudimentary 'constitution' of the European Council can be said to have been set out at the Paris Summit of 1974; see *Bulletin EC* 12–1974, 7 ff.

The European Council was formally recognised by the Single European Act, which assigned to it no specific powers or functions. In 2002 it was agreed that it would meet in principle four times a year, but may be convened for an extraordinary meeting in exceptional circumstances.[2] Since 2003 all 'ordinary' summits are held in Brussels.[3]

3.02 The Treaty on European Union now provides:

1. The European Council shall provide the Union with the necessary impetus for its development and shall define the general political directions and priorities thereof. It shall not exercise legislative functions.
2. The European Council shall consist of the Heads of State or Government of the Member States, together with its President and the President of the Commission. The High Representative of the Union for Foreign Affairs and Security Policy shall take part in its work.
3. The European Council shall meet twice every six months, convened by its President. When the agenda so requires, the members of the European Council may decide each to be assisted by a minister and, in the case of the President of the Commission, by a member of the Commission. When the situation so requires, the President shall convene a special meeting of the European Council.[4]

Prior to Lisbon the Treaties made (virtually) no provision for the European Council taking a formal vote,[5] and it acted always by consensus. The present, now codified, rule is decisions to be taken by concensus except where the Treaties provide otherwise.[6] Where a vote is taken the president and the Commission president do not vote.[7] One member may act on behalf of another (but only one other) and abstentions by members present or represented do not prevent the adoption of a unanimous vote.[8] Where it acts by qualified majority

---

2 European Council, Seville, Conclusions of the Presidency, *Bulletin EU* 6–2002, 8, Annex I. Examples of circumstances meriting an extraordinary European Council meeting are the issues relating to the 2001 terrorist attacks in the United States (September 2001), the impending invasion of Iraq (February 2003), the Russian/Georgian dispute in South Ossetia and Abkhazia (September 2008), the 2008 (and ongoing) financial crisis (March 2009) and the insurrection in Libya (March 2011).

3 See Declaration [annexed to the Final Act of the Treaty of Nice] on the venue for European Councils. Previously the first of the two six-monthly meetings was held in Brussels, the second in the member state holding the presidency of the Council; hence, reference is made to, for example, deliberations of and decisions adopted at 'the Edinburgh Summit' (or 'Edinburgh Council'), the Copenhagen Summit, the Tampere Summit, and so on. In 2010 Mr Rompuy (see immediately below) suggested re-establishing the convention.

4 TEU, art. 15.

5 The sole exception was TEU (pre-Lisbon), art. 23(2), which provided that in the adoption of legislation giving effect to CFSP measures, the Council may take no vote but 'request that the matter be referred to the European Council for decision by unanimity'.

6 TEU, art. 15(4).

7 TFEU, art. 235(1).

8 *Ibid.*

the rules which regulate Council voting apply.[9] It plays an active role in the initiation and formulation of the Common Foreign and Security Policy[10] but otherwise takes no part in the formal legislative machinery of the Union, and as it has no competence to adopt legally binding acts ('[i]t shall not exercise legislative functions')[11] it is, in principle, immune from the jurisdiction of the Court of Justice. Its role and importance, though of primary significance to the Union, are therefore restricted largely to the political arena.

From its inception the presidency of the European Council was assumed by the presidency of the Council.[12] With Lisbon, the European Council 'elects' a president by qualified majority for a term of two and a half years, renewable once.[13] He or she can be dismissed by the same procedure in the event of an impediment or serious misconduct.[14] The president chairs and drives forward (*anime; gibt ihnen Impulse*) the work of the European Council; ensures its preparation and continuity in cooperation with the president of the Commission; endeavours to facilitate cohesion and consensus within it; and, without prejudice to the powers of the High Representative for foreign affairs and security policy,[15] ensures (*assure; nimmt wahr*) the external representation of the Union on issues concerning its Common Foreign and Security Policy. Immediately Lisbon entered into force, Mr van Rompuy was elected president.[16] **3.03**

B. EUROPEAN COMMISSION

The single Commission 'of the European Communities' came into being in 1967 with the merger of the ECSC High Authority and the two EEC and Euratom Commissions.[17] In subsequent Treaty texts it remained simply 'the Commission' but retained in formal usage the 'Commission of the European Communities' until Lisbon, which rechristened it 'the European Commission', albeit 'hereinafter referred to as "the Commission"'.[18] **3.04**

---

9 *Ibid*. For further detail see the Rules of Procedure of the European Council, Decision 2009/882 [2009] OJ L315/51.
10 TEU, arts 24, 26, 31.
11 *Ibid*. art. 15(1).
12 See 3.39 below.
13 TEU, art. 15(5).
14 *Ibid*.
15 *Ibid*. art. 15(6). On the High Representative see 3.11 below.
16 Decision 2009/879 [2009] OJ L315/48; re-elected in 2012, Decision 2012/151 [2012] OJ L77/17.
17 Merger Treaty (see Part B, Introduction, no. 3 above), art. 9.
18 TEU, art. 13.

3.05   The Commission is not, as sometimes suggested, the civil service or bureau-cracy of the Union. It is an autonomous political institution consisting of, at present, 27 Commissioners 'chosen on the ground of their general competence and European commitment from persons whose independence is beyond doubt'.[19] Prior to Lisbon the Commissioners were required to be 'completely independent in the performance of their duties' and 'neither seek nor take instructions from any government or from any other body';[20] now it is the Commission itself which '[i]n carrying out its responsibilities ... shall be completely independent'.[21] A Commissioner still 'neither seek[s] nor take[s] instructions from any Government or other institution, body, office or entity' (except for the High Representative for foreign affairs and security policy in its midst, who discharges in part a Council mandate) and 'shall refrain from any action incompatible with [his] duties or the performance of [his] tasks'.[22] Previously, each member state 'undertakes to respect this principle and not to seek to influence the Members of the Commission in the performance of their tasks'[23] but this was abandoned by Lisbon; it was in any event an undertaking thought commonly to be honoured in the breach.

3.06   It is important therefore to distinguish between the Commissioners who collectively constitute the Commission properly so-called and exercise a politi-cal and legislative role in discharging the tasks assigned to that institution, and the Commission 'services' which constitute the civil service. It is also important to note that each of the institutions, and particularly the Council and the Parliament, have the support of their own extensive staff of civil servants (their 'secretariats'). That of the Council has grown considerably since 1993 with its responsibilities of administering and executing non-Community Union activ-ities.

1.   The Commissioners

3.07   From 2004 the Commission comprised (and was required to comprise)[24] a national of each member state. So, the first Barroso Commission which held office from 2004 to 2010 consisted first of 25, then with Bulgarian and

---

19   TEU, art. 17(3) (ex art. 213(1) EC) (or, grammatically, *sont choisis … parmi des personnalités; unter Persönli-chkeiten ausgewählt*).

20   EC Treaty, art. 213(2).

21   TEU, art. 17(3).

22   *Ibid.*

23   EC Treaty, art. 213(2).

24   *Ibid.* art. 213(1). See also 2003 Act of Accession, art. 45(1): 'Any State which accedes to the Union shall be entitled to have one of its nationals as a member of the Commission'.

Romanian accession 27, Commissioners.[25] By virtue of a protocol adopted at Nice, upon membership of the Union reaching 27 (as happened in 2007), the next appointed Commission (so scheduled for appointment in autumn 2009) was to have fewer Commissioners than member states, the number to be set by a unanimous Council subject to a composition which 'reflect[s] satisfactorily the demographic and geographic range of all the Member States of the Union'.[26] With the term of the outgoing Commission due (by virtue of primary Treaty law) to end on 31 October 2009,[27] but political events in flux owing to the last minute flurry of Lisbon ratifications, no new Commission was appointed in accordance with that procedure; instead the existing Barroso Commission simply stayed in office, by grace, it was claimed, of a principle of continuity of public service, competent in such circumstances to 'deal with current business' (*expédier des affaires courantes*),[28] and allowing the Lisbon Treaty to enter into force and its different rules on appointment to apply. Lisbon reneged on the Nice agreement and reverts to the one Commissioner–one member state rule for '[t]he Commission appointed between the date of the entry into force of the Treaty of Lisbon and 31 October 2014';[29] thereafter the Commission is to consist of a membership corresponding to two-thirds of the number of member states, upon a basis of 'strictly equal rotation' amongst them, reflecting their demographic and geographical range, the detail to be determined by the European Council by unanimity,[30] *unless* the European Council, again by unanimity, decides to alter this number.[31] As the looming loss of a Commissioner from each member state, in accordance with the Nice protocol and the Lisbon provisions on the post-2014 Commission, was perceived to be a significant contributing factor to the Irish 'no' in the 2008 Lisbon referendum, to counter this dissatisfaction the European Council undertook to ensure, 'in accordance with the necessary legal procedures', that the Commission will

---

25 Until 2004 each of the larger member states (Germany, Spain, France, Italy and the United Kingdom) was afforded the privilege of nominating two Commissioners, with one from each of the others. Thus, from 1995 to 2004 the Commission comprised 20 members (from 15 member states), and, for a short period following enlargement in May 2004 until the appointment of the (first) Barroso Commission in November of that year, it was 30-strong.

26 Protocol [annexed to the TEU (pre-Lisbon), the EC and Euratom Treaties] on the Enlargement of the European Union, art. 4(2)–(3).

27 2003 Act of Accession, art. 45(2)(b).

28 The expression comes from art. 201 EC (now TFEU, art. 234) which addresses the functioning of the Commission following its dismissal but prior to its replacement. As to what is legitimate 'current business' which the Commission may discharge in these circumstances see Case T-219/99 *British Airways* v *Commission* [2003] ECR II-5917; Cases T-228 and 233/99 *Westdeutsche Landesbank Girozentrale and anor* v *Commission* [2003] ECR II-435.

29 TEU, art. 17(4).

30 TEU, art. 17(5); TFEU, art. 244.

31 TEU, art. 17(5).

continue to consist of one member from each member state.[32] So, the second Barroso Commission which took up office in February 2010 consists of 27 members in accordance with Lisbon. A Croatian will be added upon accession,[33] and it may be assumed that the European Council will, before 2014, take the necessary steps to ensure that future Commissions will be of like size, or grow with new member states.[34]

3.08 A Commission's term of office is five years.[35]

3.09 Whilst it acts as a college, the Commission works under the 'political guidance' of its president, who lays down the guidelines within which it is to work and determines its internal organisation with a view to ensuring its consistency, efficency and collegiality.[36] He, or she, therefore exercises significant authority over the college, not unlike that of a prime minister in cabinet government. Like a prime minister, he or she also plays a significant role in its appointment.

2. Appointment of the Commission

3.10 The method of appointment of the Commission has changed regularly with each treaty amendment since 1993, such that each Commission since has been appointed by a different procedure. Under the present system, introduced by Lisbon and applied for the first time to the appointment of the (second) Barroso Commission in 2010, the first step is nomination ('proposal') of a president by the European Council by qualified majority vote, the president-nominate then 'elected' by the European Parliament by a majority of its component members.[37] Should he or she fail to win parliamantary approval a new candidate must be nominated.[38] The rest, drawn from names put forward ('suggestions') by each of the remaining member states (other than that of the president-nominate), are then adopted by the Council and 'by common accord

---

32 Brussels European Council, 11–12 December 2008, Presidency Conclusions, *Bulletin EU* 12–2008, 8, para. 1.4.2.

33 2011 Act of Accession, art. 21.

34 The Treaties nevertheless continue to provide that the Commission is to consist of a number corresponding to two-thirds of the number of member states from 2014 'unless the European Council … decides to alter this number' (TEU, art. 17(5)) and to speak of rotation of membership, demographic and geographic range and sequence of Commissioners (art. 17(5), 2nd para; TFEU, art. 244). It is thus not wholly certain that the European Council has the power to alter the number to 28+ without amendment of these provisions, although the Court of Justice could be expected to view a decision doing so benignly.

35 TEU, art. 17(3) (ex art. 214(1) EC). Prior to 1994 it was four years.

36 *Ibid.* art. 17(6).

37 *Ibid.* art. 17(7). Prior to 2004 it required the unanimous agreement of the governments of the member states, which was why Mr Dehaene could be blackballed in 1994 by a single member state (the United Kingdom).

38 *Ibid.*

with the President-elect'[39] (so conferring upon the latter a veto), the entire Commission-nominate is subject as a body to a vote of consent by the Parliament,[40] and it is then formally appointed by the European Council acting by qualified majority vote.[41] It is worth recalling that the first Barroso Commission (subject to similar procedural rules) was appointed several weeks late, so extending of the term of the outgoing (Prodi) Commission, because Mr Barroso at first declined to put the Commission-nominate to parliamentary approval in the face of likely rejection, and did so only after three of its proposed number were replaced.

High Representative of the Union for Foreign Affairs and Security Policy

The Constitutional Treaty had proposed the appointment of a 'Union Minister **3.11** for Foreign Affairs'[42] but the post was widely perceived as unnecessarily provocative and contributing significantly to the Treaty's rejection. The more modest Lisbon equivalent is the 'High Representative of the Union for Foreign Affairs and Security Policy', appointed by the European Council by qualified majority with the agreement of the president of the Commission.[43] The term of office is not prescribed, the Treaties providing simply that it may be ended (*mettre fin*) by the same procedure.[44] The High Representative is *ex officio* a member of the Commission and one of its vice-presidents[45] (so sometimes referred to in short form jargon as the 'VP/HR') but is also responsible for conducting the Union's external action, Common Foreign and Security Policy and Common Security and Defence Policy within a mandate set by the Council;[46] in this task she is assisted by a (newly created) European External Action Service (EEAS), which acts independently of the other institutions. The two hats she is required to wear, with the collegiate loyalty she bears to the Commission, may prove problematic. Immediately Lisbon entered into force Baroness Ashton was appointed to the post.[47]

---

39 *Ibid.*
40 *Ibid.* To this end the Parliament now (since the appointment of the Prodi Commission in 1999) holds a series of hearings in which each Commissioner-nominate appears before and is questioned by the parliamentary committee responsible for the subject matter for which he or she is to be given the Commission portfolio. If portfolios are reshuffled during the life of a Commission the president must inform the Parliament in due time for 'relevant parliamentary consultation', although the decision may take effect immediately; Framework Agreement on Relations between the European Parliament and the European Commission [2010] OJ L304/47, para. 7.
41 *Ibid.*
42 Treaty establishing a Constitution for Europe, art. I-28.
43 TEU, art. 18(1).
44 *Ibid.*
45 *Ibid.* art. 18(4).
46 *Ibid.* art. 18(2).
47 Decision 2009/880 [2009] OJ L315/49. In an inauspicious start the decision was badly drafted and had to be re-adopted three days later; Decision 2009/950 [2009] OJ L328/69.

3.12   Prior to Nice an individual Commissioner could be dismissed ('compulsorily retired') only by the Court of Justice, upon application by the Council or the Commission, and only if he or she failed to fulfil the conditions for the performance of his or her duties or was guilty of serious misconduct.[48] In light of the antics of (some) members of the Santer Commission (1994–99)[49] this was altered by Nice, so that an individual Commissioner could also be dismissed by the president, with the approval of the college of Commissioners;[50] with Lisbon the requirement of that approval disappeared, and the power exercised for the first time in 2012 when Mr Dalli was sacked by Mr Barroso amidst allegations of selling influence.[51] In 2010 an agreement was made with the Parliament which requires the president 'seriously [to] consider' asking an individual Commissioner to step down if he or she has lost the confidence of the Parliament, and to explain their reasons for not doing so.[52] A Commissioner guilty of impropriety in office may also be deprived of his or her pension rights or other benefits, again by the Court upon application by the Council or Commission.[53]

---

48   EC Treaty, art. 216. The procedure was put in train for the first time in 1999, in order to sack Mr Bangemann for (perceived) impropriety in accepting the offer of a private sector post in an area related to his Commission responsibilities whilst still a member of the (lame duck) Commission – the duty to behave with integrity 'in particular' as regards the acceptance of appointments or benefits being written into the Treaties (TFEU, art. 245, 2nd para; ex art. 213(2) EC); see the Council petition in Decision 1999/493 [1999] OJ L192/53 and Mr Bangemann's challenge of it (Case T-208/99 *Bangemann v Council*). The affair was resolved politically, if not amicably, and the litigation abandoned; the events are discussed in Cases T-227/99 and 134/00 *Kvaerner Warnow Werft v Commission* [2002] ECR II-1205. Latterly, a number of ex-Commissioners, not least those stepping down in 2009/10 (and in Mr Verheugen's case, accompanied by his mistress *devenue chef de cabinet*), have been seen to emulate Mr Bangemann in acquiring 'revolving door' new posts, if in a manner marginally less blatant, with little censure from the Commission.

49   See 3.34 below.

50   EC Treaty, art. 217(4).

51   TEU, art. 17(6), 2nd para. The High Representative can be sacked only by the European Council (art. 18(1)) but must be if the president requests it; art. 17(6), 2nd para.

52   Framework Agreement on Relations between the European Parliament and the European Commission [2010] OJ L304/47, para. 5.

53   TFEU, arts 245, 2nd para and 247 (ex arts 213(2) and 216 EC). This too happened with Mr Bangemann (Case C-290/99 *Council v Bangemann*), but was settled. In 2004 the Commission raised proceedings seeking to deprive Mrs Cresson of pension rights for favouritism and/or gross negligence during her term of office (1995–99), Case C-432/04 *Commission v Cresson* [2006] ECR I-6387. The Court found that a breach of the propriety incumbent upon a Commissioner 'of a certain degree of gravity is required' (para. 72), that Mrs Cresson's misconduct had met that standard, but did not deprive her of pension rights as 'the finding of the breach constitutes, of itself, an appropriate penalty' (para. 150), without explanation as to why this was so. (She, her dentist and eight cabinet officials and Commission agents were also charged (*inculpé*) with forgery (*faux et usage de faux*), fraud and corruption (*prise illégale d'intérêt*) by a Belgian *juge d'instruction* in connection with the events but the charges were in the end discontinued (*non-lieu*)). There is one (but only one) instance of a Commission official being deprived of pension rights (being reduced by one-third), for corruption; see Case T-197/00 *Onidi v Commission* [2002] ECR-SC II-325.

In the event of the resignation, compulsory retirement or death of a Commis- **3.13** sioner, he or she is replaced for the remainder of his or her term by Council decision.[54]

3. Collegiality

In taking decisions the Commission acts by simple majority[55] and always as a **3.14** 'college'.[56] Collegiality is a fundamental principle of Commission activities: it presumes the equal participation and the collective deliberation of all Commissioners in the adoption of decisions, and the collective responsibility at the political level therefor.[57] An act of the Commission may be challenged on the ground that the principle was not properly respected.[58] No legislative power may be delegated by the Commission but authority to adopt management or administrative measures may be conferred upon an individual Commissioner (the 'empowerment procedure') or upon a Director-General or Head of Service within Commission services (the 'delegation procedure'), 'provided the principle of collective responsibility is fully respected'[59] and always within a framework of very tightly defined checks and balances.[60]

In practice the president assigns to each Commissioner one or more 'responsi- **3.15** bilities'[61] – that is, portfolios for one or more areas of Union activity. The responsible Commissioner may, and frequently does, issue statements or make speeches on aspects of Commission policy falling within his or her portfolio, and such statements and speeches are a guide to the way in which the Commission will seek to develop and apply Union law. *Ad hoc* working groups of Commissioners may be appointed by the president.[62]

---

54 TFEU, art. 246, 2nd para (ex art 215, 2nd para. EC). The replacement is appointed by qualified majority vote by
    common accord with the Commission president. The Council may by unanimity determine that the vacancy
    need not be filled ('in particular where the remainder of the Member's term of office is short'), but this is not a
    common course of action: in 2009 Mr Figel' resigned with only one month to run in the first Barroso
    Commission yet was replaced by Mr Šefčovič to serve from 1 to 31 October – hardly worth the trip from
    Bratislava.
55 TFEU, art. 250 (ex art 219, 2nd para. EC).
56 Rules of Procedure (RP) of the Commission, art. 1. Opposition or dissent is not formally recorded, although it
    is frequently made public by informal means.
57 Case C-191/95 *Commission* v *Germany* [1998] ECR I-5449; Case C-1/00 *Commission* v *France* (BSE) [2001]
    ECR I-9989; Case T-57/01 *Solvay* v *Commission* [2009] ECR II-4621, at paras 151–8; Case T-58/01 *Solvay* v
    Commission [2009] ECR II-4781, at paras 126–39.
58 E.g., Case C-137/92P *Commission* v *BASF and ors* (PVC) [1994] ECR I-2555; Case C-191/95 *Commission* v
    Germany, *ibid*.; Cases C-287 and 288/95P *Commission* v *Solvay* (Soda Ash) [2000] ECR I-2391; Case C-1/00
    BSE, *ibid*.
59 RP Commission, arts 13 and 14.
60 Case 9/56 *Meroni* v *High Authority* [1957–58] ECR 133; Cases 32, 33/58 *SNUPAT* v *High Authority* [1959]
    ECR 127; Case 5/85 *AKZO* v *Commission* [1986] ECR 2585.
61 TFEU, art. 248 (ex art. 217(2) EC).
62 RP Commission, art. 3, 2nd para.

3.16 Each Commissioner is assisted by a *cabinet*, or a private office, working under a *chef de cabinet*. The Commissioner is free to choose the members of his or her *cabinet*, but it has become a convention that at least some be of different nationalities.

4. Organisation

3.17 The internal organisation of the Commission is the responsibility of the president, 'ensuring that it acts consistently, efficiently and as a collegiate body'.[63] It adopts its own Rules of Procedure;[64] they are binding and contrary practice does not cause them to fall into desuetude.[65] The seat of the Commission is Brussels, although some of its services are situated in Luxembourg. It meets weekly, or more often 'whenever necessary'.[66]

5. Services of the Commission

3.18 Much of the work of the Commission is carried out by the Commission's 'services' – that is, by the officials (sometimes 'servants', frequently *fonctionnaires*), employed by the Commission. The Commission employs about 33,000 staff of all grades across its services, of whom about one-tenth are involved in the work of translation and interpretation.[67] The bulk of the Commission's services are organised under Directorates-General (under Directors-General), which are divided into Directorates (under Directors) and Directorates into Units (under Heads of Unit). There are at present 33 Directorates-General, each of which is responsible for a general area of policy, for example, internal market, competition, agriculture and rural development, and so on. A list of the Directorates-General is provided in Annex II. Long designated by Roman numerals (these three just mentioned being, for example, D-G III, D-G IV and D-G VI) the style was abandoned in 1999, and the normal shorthand now is simply, for example, 'D-G Agriculture', or, internally, 'DG AGRI'. Five of the 33 (the 'external relations D-Gs') are concerned with foreign policy matters and are in a state of flux as the EEAS evolves. The responsibilities of the Directorates-General do not necessarily correspond to the portfolios of the Commissioners, two or more of whom may be responsible for aspects of the work of a single Directorate-General. Conversely, one Commissioner may have

---

63   TEU, art. 17(6)(b) (ex art. 217(1) EC).
64   TFEU, art. 249(1) (ex art. 218(2) EC); for the present Rules of Procedure see [2010] OJ L55/61.
65   Case C-137/92P *Commission v BASF and ors* (PVC) [1994] ECR I-2555.
66   RP Commission, art. 5.
67   As at January 2012 the Commission employed a staff of 33,033, 2,424 (7.3 per cent) in D-G Translation (the second largest D-G, after D-G Development and Cooperation) and 829 (2.5 per cent) in D-G Interpretation (or D-G SCIC); European Commission, *Human Resources Key Figure Card* (2012).

responsibility for more than one Directorate-General. Subject to that, the Directorates-General of the Commission may be compared with UK ministries, the Commissioner being analogous to the Minister and the Directorate-General to the Permanent Secretary.

Outwith the D-G structure the Commission has: **3.19**

(a) a Secretariat-General, under the direction of a Secretary-General, corresponding roughly to the Cabinet Office in the United Kingdom. The Secretary-General 'assists' the president in preparing the proceedings and meetings of the Commission and has overall responsibility for coordination within the Commission and for relations between the Commission on the one hand and the other institutions and the member states on the other.[68] He is present or represented as of right at all Commission meetings;[69]

(b) a Legal Service, which provides independent legal advice to the Commission and its services. The Commission relies heavily upon this advice, especially in matters of enforcement of Treaty obligations, and the Legal Service must be consulted upon all drafts or proposals for legal instruments, the initiation of (virtually) all decision-making procedures and upon all documents which may have legal implications.[70] It is organised, under a Director-General, in 'teams' (*équipes*), each of which is responsible for giving advice on a particular area or areas of the law. The Commission is normally represented before the European Court of Justice by a member of the relevant team (its 'agent').

There are a number of other administrative services, most of them internal to the Commission. The administrative structure of the Commission services is described in Annex II.

6. Powers and functions of the Commission

The Commission promotes the general interests of the Union and adopts **3.20** appropriate measures to that end, exercising the coordinating, executive and management functions conferred upon it by the Treaties.[71]

(a) Legislation

The Commission plays a pivotal role in the Union legislative process. It has, in **3.21** particular, a virtual monopoly upon the initiation of primary legislation, a

---

68 RP, art. 17.
69 RP, arts 20.3, 26. So too is the president's *chef de cabinet*; art. 10.
70 RP, art. 23.4.
71 TEU, art. 17(1).

legislative act being adopted 'only ... on the basis of a Commission proposal, except where the Treaties provide otherwise';[72] exceptions are few. A proposal is developed by the Directorate-General in charge of the file (*dossier*) on the basis of a mandate set by the college of Commissioners under the authority of the relevant Commissioner and in consultation with other services of the Commission as necessary. The Directorate-General will also, whenever desirable, obtain help and advice from experts from the member states (whether from the national administration or from the private sector), from professional or trade union organisations (for example BUSINESSEUROPE (a pan-European employers' federation, previously the *Union des Industries de la Communauté européenne*, UNICE) and the European Trade Union Confederation (ETUC)), and from a variety of other sources. When the file is ready, the draft proposal is submitted by the responsible Commissioner or Commissioners to the Commission itself and there approved, with or without amendment. In practice, amendments at this level can be very extensive, reflecting the political composition of the Commission.

3.22 Once adopted by the college of Commissioners, a proposal is submitted to the Council and (ordinarily) the Parliament. The Commission may, and frequently does, amend its proposal in the course of its subsequent legislative progress. It may in any event alter its proposal at any time until the Council has acted,[73] and in most cases the Council may amend the proposal only by unanimity.[74] In consequence the Council must in practice negotiate with the Commission (and the Parliament) on amendments it wishes to have incorporated. Because it may withdraw a proposal at any time, the Commission remains 'master of the text' to a significant extent throughout the legislative process.

3.23 Whilst the Commission has, at present, almost sole power to initiate legislation, the legislative programme is sometimes inspired from elsewhere. It has frequently drawn from a political agenda set by the European Council, and this *de facto* power of policy-making can only increase with the latter's recognition in the Treaties (and so its legitimacy) and its own institutional autonomy, president and budget. Legislation may be introduced in order to give effect to international obligations into which the Union has entered (another matter largely for the European Council/Council and/or the High Representative for Foreign Affairs and Security Policy), or to update existing legisation in light of changing circumstances. Member states wishing to pursue enhanced cooperation (outside the sphere of Common Foreign and Security Policy) must

---

72   *Ibid.* art. 17(2).
73   TFEU, art. 293(2) (ex art. 250(2) EC).
74   *Ibid.* art. 293(1) (ex art. 250(1) EC).

submit a request to that effect to the Commission, which 'may' submit the necessary proposal to the Council;[75] the Parliament may request that the Commission introduce legislation,[76] indeed the Council may request the Commission to undertake any studies it (the Council) considers desirable and to submit to it any appropriate proposals for legislation or repeal of legislation;[77] the European Central Bank may 'recommend' and the Court of Justice and the European Investment Bank may 'request' the adoption of legislation;[78] and a popular petition may 'invite' the Commission to submit a proposal for legislation on matters on which the signatories consider that action is required for purposes of implementing the Treaties.[79] But the Commission need not comply with any such request, recommendation or invitation. Uniquely to the area of judicial cooperation in criminal matters and police cooperation, the Commission may be bypassed completely, legislation proposed by ('on the initiative of') a muster of one-quarter of the member states.[80]

(b) Subordinate legislation; 'comitology'

Whilst it enjoys virtually no autonomous legislative authority under the Treaties,[81] the Commission exercises 'executive functions'[82] when properly authorised to do so. This occurs in two contexts. **3.24**

First, and new with Lisbon, it may be authorised by a legislative act adopted by **3.25** the Parliament and Council to adopt 'non-legislative acts of general application' to supplement or amend non-essential elements of the legislative act,[83] the enabling act defining the objectives, content, scope, duration and conditions of the delegation of power and reserving its own essential elements.[84] It may set conditions to which the delegated authority is subject, being (a) the possibility of revocation by the Parliament (by a majority of its component members) or the Council (by qualified majority) and/or (b) the delegated act may enter into

---

75 *Ibid.* art. 329(1) (ex art. 11 EC); as to enhanced cooperation see 2.41–2.46 above.

76 *Ibid.* art. 225 (ex art. 192, 2nd para EC; introduced by the TEU (pre-Lisbon) in 1993). If it elects not to submit a proposal the Commission must inform the Parliament of the reasons.

77 *Ibid.* art. 241 (ex art. 208 EC). Likewise it must inform the Council of its reasons for not doing so. The Commission has undertaken to devote 'particular attention' to Council suggestions for the repeal of legislation so as better to ensure respect for subsidiarity and proportionality; Declaration (No. 18) in relation to the Delimitation of Competences, 2nd para.

78 TFEU, art. 289(4).

79 TEU, art. 11(4); see 3.74 below.

80 TFEU, art. 76; see 11.163 below.

81 The exceptions are TFEU, art. 45(3)(d) (ex art. 39(3)(d) EC) (dealing with workers' post-retirement rights of residence in another member state) and TFEU, art. 106(3) (ex art. 86(3) EC) (adjustment of national legislation regulating monopoly service providers).

82 TEU, art. 17(1).

83 TFEU, art. 290(1).

84 *Ibid.* art. 290(2), (3).

force only absent objection by the Parliament or Council (by the same majorities) within a set period.[85]

3.26 Secondly, where uniform conditions for the implementation of a legally binding Union act are needed (*nécessaires*) it is, except in the field of the Common Foreign and Security Policy, a task for the Commission.[86] This conferral of subordinate authority upon the Commission by enabling legislation predates Lisbon and is now 'an established legislative technique' and 'established practice of the Community legislature'.[87] However, in order that some control over the exercise of Commission delegated authority be retained by the member states,[88] the former's powers for the implementation of acts of the Council (or Council and Parliament) are exercised normally in accordance with a procedure known as 'comitology', involving a host of committees ('comitology committees') composed of representatives of the member states and chaired by an official of the Commission, which 'assist' the Commission in its deliberations. This enhances the dialogue between the Commission and national administrations and inculcates a transnational habit in national decision-making, but also limits the Commission's autonomy.

3.27 With comitology the enabling measure ('the basic act') will normally specify the committee procedure to be followed, as codified in a 2003 regulation.[89] Prior to 2011 there were five types of procedure,[90] in 2011 they were narrowed ('simplified')[91] to two, as follows:[92]

- 'advisory procedure': when acting in accordance with the advisory procedure the committee is consulted, adopts an 'opinion', if necessary by a vote (by simple majority), but the opinion, of which the Commission must take 'utmost account', is not binding upon it.[93] The advisory procedure survives unchanged from previously and applies to all but implementing acts of a general scope, other implementing acts relating to programmes

---

85   *Ibid.* art. 290(2).

86   *Ibid.* art. 291(2); under the CFSP the task is delegated to the Council and/or the member states; TEU, arts 24, 26.

87   Case C-133/06 *Parliament* v *Council* (Safe Country Lists) [2008] ECR I-3189, at paras 32, 41.

88   TFEU, art. 291(3); Regulation 182/2011 [2011] OJ L55/13, art. 1.

89   Regulation 1882/2003 [2003] OJ L284/1.

90   Decision 1999/468 [1999] OJ L184/23 ('the second comitology decision', replacing the original 1987 comitology decision, Decision 87/373 [1987] OJ L197/33). The procedures were, in ascending order of procedural complexity, the advisory procedure (Directive 1999/468, art. 3), management procedure (art. 4), regulatory procedure (art. 5), regulatory procedure with scrutiny (art. 5a) and safeguard procedure (art. 6).

91   Regulation 182/2011, n. 88 above, replacing the second comitology decision, n. 90 above, Preamble, 8th para.

92   Regulation 182/2011, n. 88 above.

93   *Ibid.* art. 4. As to voting in the institutions see 3.41 below. Where a vote is taken the (Commission) chair does not vote; art 3(2).

with 'substantial implications', agriculture and fisheries, environment, security and safety or protection of health and safety of humans, animals or plants, common commercial policy, taxation,[94] and even these in duly justified cases;[95]

- 'examination procedure': these matters are subject to the examination procedure which replaces the previous management and regulatory procedures and by which the committee may, by qualified majority vote:
  - adopt an opinion which approves the draft measure, in which case the Commission must adopt it[96] unless, in very exceptional circumstances and in the face of new circumstances, it declines to do so, having duly informed the committee and the legislator;[97]
  - do nothing, in which case the Commission may adopt the measure except in certain excluded areas which go to an appeal committee;[98] or
  - reject the draft measure, in which case the Commission cannot adopt it but may resubmit it to the committee within two months or take it to the appeal committee within one month.[99] If it goes to the appeal committee the Commission must adopt the measure if approved, may adopt the measure if the committee fails or declines to act, and cannot adopt the measure if it votes against.[100]

However, a measure may be adopted in the face of initial rejection if necessary to avoid significant disruption of agricultural markets or a risk to the Union's financial interests but it must be taken to the appeal committee immediately and be repealed forthwith if the committee votes against.[101] A variation of the previous safeguard procedure, where the basic act so authorises, the Commission may upon 'duly justified imperative grounds of urgency' adopt an implementing act with immediate effect, but if subject to examination procedure must be submitted to the committee and, if rejected by the latter, repealed immediately.[102] A variation of the previous regulatory procedure with scrutiny, where the basic act is adopted under the ordinary legislative procedure the Parliament or the Council may at any time object on the ground that a draft implementing measure exceeds the implementing powers provided in the former, in which case the Commission must review the latter taking account of **3.28**

---

94   *Ibid.* art. 2(2).
95   *Ibid.* art. 2(3).
96   *Ibid.* art. 5(2).
97   Statement by the European Parliament, the Council and the Commission [2011] OJ L55/19.
98   Regulation 182/2011, art. 5(4). As to the appeal committee see art. 3(7).
99   *Ibid.* art. 5(3).
100   *Ibid.* art. 6(3).
101   *Ibid.* art. 7.
102   *Ibid.* art. 8.

the views expressed and informing the Parliament and the Council whether it intends to maintain, amend or withdraw the implementing measure.[103]

3.29 The new procedures applied from March 2011 to all new committee deliberations under pre-existing basic acts[104] save where they call for the regulatory procedure with scrutiny, which will survive for that purpose.[105] Prior to Lisbon, the Parliament and Council could depart from the criteria laid down but were required to justify doing so,[106] and the Council could reserve the right itself to exercise implementing powers but was required to explain, properly and in detail, why it was justified in derogating from the normal rule.[107] It is not clear if either discretion survives.[108]

(c) Enforcement

3.30 It is the duty of the Commission to 'ensure the application of the Treaties' and 'oversee [*surveiller, überwachen*] the application of Union law under the control of the Court of Justice of the European Union'.[109] To this end it monitors the activities of the member states and is empowered to raise against them enforcement proceedings before the Court for failure to meet an obligation imposed by Union law.[110] In this context the Commission is sometimes called the custodian or the guardian of the Treaties and of Union law.

(d) European Economic Area

3.31 The Commission is charged by the Agreement creating the European Economic Area (EEA) with its enforcement within the territory of the Union. Commission powers under the EEA Agreement are discussed below.[111]

---

103   *Ibid.* art. 11.
104   *Ibid.* art. 13.
105   *Ibid.* art. 12. The regulatory procedure with scrutiny was introduced in 2006 to draw the Parliament, thitherto with limited influence, more fully into comitology procedures. A measure proposed by the Commission is subject to the adoption by the committee of a preliminary opinion which is referred for scrutiny to the Council and the Parliament, the purpose being to allow for opposition where it appears to exceed the implementing powers provided for in the basic instrument, is incompatible with its aim, or is disproportionate or inconsistent with the principle of subsidiarity. Either institution may 'oppose', and ultimately veto, the measure.
106   Case C-378/00 *Commission* v *Parliament and Council* (LIFE) [2003] ECR I-937; Case C-122/04 *Commission* v *Parliament and Council* (Forest Focus) [2006] ECR I-2001.
107   Case C-257/01 *Commission* v *Council* (Visa Border Checks) [2005] ECR I-345, at para. 50; Case C-133/06 *Parliament* v *Council* (Safe Country Lists) [2008] ECR I-3189, at para. 46. Notwithstanding the stated requirement of 'detailed', the justification on offer could be thin ('general and laconic'; *Visa Border Checks*, para. 53) yet still satisfy the Court.
108   See, as to the latter, TFEU, art. 291(2): 'Where uniform conditions for implementing legally binding Union acts are needed, those acts *shall* confer implementing powers on the Commission' (emphasis added).
109   TEU, art. 17(1). Previously the Commission 'ensure[d] that the provisions of this Treaty and the measures taken by the institutions pursuant thereto are applied'; EC Treaty, art. 211.
110   TFEU, art. 258 (ex art. 226 EC); see 5.48–5.65 below.
111   See 14.86 below.

(e) International representation

Except where relating exclusively or principally to Common Foreign and **3.32**
Security Policy the Commission initiates treaty negotiations with third countries[112] and negotiates commercial agreements with them, within a framework
established, and in consultation with a committee appointed, by the Council.[113]
This applies equally to an international agreement in any field falling within
internal Union competence *ratione materiae*,[114] as well as the Union component
of any 'mixed agreement'.[115] In other than Common Foreign and Security
Policy the Commission 'ensure[s] the Union's external representation',[116] so
represents the Union in various international fora. Prior to Lisbon it also
represented the Community in many third states through 'delegations' there,
where the Commission 'representative' was normally treated as an accredited
member of the diplomatic corps. However, in 2010 the Commission delegations were renamed 'EU delegations' and authority over them transferred to
the High Representative for Foreign Affairs and Security Policy, marking the
opening salvo in the scrap between the Commission and the EEAS as the
post-Lisbon CFSP beds in.

(f) Legal representation

The Commission acts for the Union in legal proceedings in which Union **3.33**
interests are in issue[117] except in matters relating to the operation of an
institution, in which case, owing to a principle of administrative and operational
autonomy, the institution acts for itself.[118] The Commission may raise civil
actions in the courts of third states in order to protect Union interests.[119]

7. Accountability to the Parliament

The Commission is, as a body, responsible to the Parliament.[120] This manifests **3.34**
itself in three ways:

---

112   TFEU, art. 218(3).
113   *Ibid.* art. 207(3) (ex art. 300(2) EC).
114   Case 22/70 *Commission* v *Council* (ERTA) [1971] ECR 263; Case C-466/98 *Commission* v *United Kingdom* [2002] ECR I-9427.
115   See 14.74 below.
116   TEU, art. 17(1).
117   TFEU, art. 335 (ex art. 282 EC); see Case C-199/11 *European Union* v *Otis and ors*, pending.
118   *Ibid.*; this proviso was added by Lisbon, prior to which authority was required to be delegated by the Commission, as to which see Case C-137/10 *European Communities* v *Région de Bruxelles-Capitale*, judgment of 5 May 2011, not yet reported.
119   Cases T-377 etc./00 *Philip Morris International* v *Commission* [2003] ECR II-1.
120   TEU, art. 17(8).

(1) *Appointment*: The president of the Commission is elected by the Parliament and its membership subject to parliamentary consent, as discussed above.[121]

(2) *Censure*: The Parliament has the power, by a two-thirds majority of votes cast and an absolute majority of its members, to pass a motion of censure upon the Commission, in which event the Commission must resign as a body.[122] This is the Parliament's 'nuclear option'. Motions of censure have been raised on a number of occasions but never carried. In 1999, a motion was tabled against the Santer Commission, but, following loss of the support of the Socialist Group, was defeated.[123] Two months later an *ad hoc* 'committee of independent experts' established by the Parliament delivered a damning report on Commission practices,[124] which led (although did not compel) the Commission to resign *en bloc*.[125] It was these events which led to the introduction by the Treaty of Nice of provisions enabling the dismissal of an individual Commissioner by the president with the support of the college of Commissioners,[126] the support no longer necessary.[127] Where an individual Commissioner loses the confidence of the Parliament it may now require the Commission president 'seriously [to] consider' sacking him him or her, and to explain his reasons if he chooses not to do so.[128]

(3) *Parliamentary questions*: The Commission is required to reply orally or in writing to questions put to it by the Parliament or by its members.[129] The replies to such questions are a guide to the legislative policy of the Commission and to its thinking on points of Union law. The members of the Commission and the Council are entitled to be given the opportunity to be heard by the Parliament, and the speeches made on these occasions may again be a guide to the policy aspects of law-making. Parliamentary answers and speeches may also be helpful in assessing the prospects of Union legislation being enacted and, if so, on what timescale.

---

121 See 3.10 above.

122 TEU, art. 17(8) and TFEU, art. 234 (ex art. 201 EC).

123 OJ, Debates of the European Parliament, 1999 Session, No. 4-531/256 ff.

124 *First Report by the Committee of Independent Experts on Allegations regarding Fraud, Mismanagement and Nepotism in the European Commission* (15 March 1999). The report is available only at www.europarl.eu.int/ experts; extracts in *Bulletin EU* 3–1999, 139.

125 Yet in accordance with art. 215 of the EC Treaty it remained in office (under the acting presidency of Mr Marín González) in order to deal with 'current business' (as to which see n. 28 above) until replaced by a new Commission six months later.

126 EC Treaty, art. 217(4).

127 TEU, art. 17(6).

128 Framework Agreement on Relations between the European Parliament and the European Commission [2010] OJ L304/47, para. 5.

129 TFEU, art. 230. Oddly for a body with a claim to democratic credentials, oral questions are in the control of the Conference of Presidents (Rules of Procedure of the Parliament (RP EP), rule 115.1) and oral and written questions may be rejected by the president for 'inadmissibility' (RP EP, rules 116.3, 117.2).

C. THE COUNCIL

1. Name and function

'The Council' is formally so styled in the Treaties, but is commonly known as **3.35** the Council of Ministers. In 1993 it renamed itself 'the Council of the European Union' in recognition of its (significant and sole) responsibilities in non-Community Union spheres of activity[130] and continues to do so, although without Treaty authority. At the beginning it was the sole, latterly the predominant, Community legislative authority. Hence the venerable description 'the Commission proposes, the Council disposes', which expresses the symbiotic nature of the relationship between the two institutions in the promulgation of law: the Commission proposes but cannot enact; the Council, absent express Treaty authority which bypasses normal procedures, cannot enact without a Commission proposal. With Treaty amendment the Council primacy has gradually been pared away, so that it now shares a rough equality with the Parliament in spheres of general legislation and cedes autonomous power of legislation to the European Central Bank in the monetary sphere.

2. Composition

In terms of the Treaties: **3.36**

> The Council shall consist of a representative of each Member State at ministerial level, who may commit the government of that Member State in question and cast its vote.[131]

The composition depends upon the subject matter under discussion. In 2002 the Council established nine 'configurations' (previously 'formations') in which it was to sit.[132] Two configurations (general affairs and foreign affairs) were formally established by the Lisbon Treaty,[133] the rest made subject to the authority of the European Council.[134] Immediately Lisbon entered into force the existing list of configurations was 'adapted' provisionally[135] and fixed subsequently as follows:

---

130 Council Decision 93/591 [1993] OJ L281/18.
131 TEU, art. 16(2) (ex art. 203, 1st para. EC).
132 RP Council, Annex 1 (pre-2009), added following agreement at the 2002 Seville Summit.
133 TEU, art. 16(6).
134 TFEU, art. 236.
135 Decision 2009/878 [2009] OJ L315/46; RP Council, Annex I. The decision was adopted by the Council by provisional authority pending the adoption by the European Council of an authoritative list; Protocol (No. 36) on Transitional Provisions, art. 4.

- general affairs;
- foreign affairs;
- economic and financial affairs (including budget);
- justice and home affairs (including civil protection);
- employment, social policy, health and consumer affairs;
- competitiveness (internal market, industry, research and space);
- transport, telecommunications and energy (including nuclear energy, so most Euratom business);
- agriculture and fisheries;
- environment; and
- education, youth, culture and sport.[136]

Reference is sometimes made to, for example, the activities of the general affairs Council, the 'Relex' (foreign affairs, from *relations extérieures*) Council, the 'Ecofin' (economic and financial affairs) Council or the JHA (justice and home affairs) Council as a shorthand for identifying the configuration in which it sits (although this has no bearing upon its power and procedures). The general affairs Council, the Relex Council (prior to 2009 bound together as a single configuration) and the Ecofin Council are the 'senior' bodies, meeting monthly (as does the agricultural Council normally), the remainder meeting from time to time. The general affairs Council ensures consistency in the work of the different configurations, deals with matters crossing configuration boundaries and prepares and ensures the follow-up to meetings of the European Council, in liaison with the president of the European Council and the Commission; the Relex Council 'elaborates' the Union's external action on the basis of strategic guidelines laid down by the European Council and ensures that the Union's action is consistent.[137] Both normally comprise the foreign ministers of the member states, the Ecofin Council the finance ministers. Other configurations normally comprise the ministers holding the relevant portfolio in national government. One configuration may bring together several ministers from each member state, each participating in turn as a full member, the agenda and organisation of proceedings adjusted accordingly.[138] Since 1993 a member state may be represented by ministers from regional government so long as they were 'authorised' to bind the member state[139] – a (small) step, owing primarily to pressure from the German *Länder* and the Belgian autonomous communities, towards greater regional influence in Community decision-making. There may

---

136 Decision 2010/594 [2010] OJ L263/12, amending RP Council, Annex I. For want of a better home 'Competitiveness (internal market, industry, research and space)' includes tourism and 'Education, youth, culture and sport' includes audiovisual affairs.
137 TEU, art. 16(6).
138 RP Council, Annex I, 2nd para., statement (m).
139 EC Treaty, art. 203, 1st para.

be national laws or conventions regulating central/regional representation in the Council in light of it.[140] It is preserved but unnecessarily muddled by Lisbon, the present formula being so long as he or she 'may commit the government of the Member State in question and cast its vote'.[141] Whatever its configuration and composition, all decisions are taken in the name of the Council as such.

3. Member States meeting in the (European) Council

Some provisions of the Treaties provide for decisions to be taken by the **3.37** 'common accord of the governments of the Member States'. Where this applies, and sometimes where the member states wish to cooperate from time to time on a matter outwith Union competences, representatives of the 27 governments will meet using the facilities of the Council but adopt such measures as decisions of the representatives of the member states 'meeting in the Council' (*au sein du Conseil*) or, latterly, if the heads of states and government, 'meeting in the European Council'. But it is important to note that they are acting not in their capacity as members of the Council (or European Council) but as representatives of their governments, and thus collectively exercising the powers of the member states, therefore measures they produce may have legal effects, but are not subject to judicial review by the Court of Justice.[142]

4. Organisation

The Council is 'assisted' by its own General Secretariat under the responsibility **3.38** of a Secretary-General and a Deputy Secretary-General who are responsible for its operation; each is appointed by the Council.[143] The Council Secretariat also assists the European Council.[144] Following the Treaty of Amsterdam, the Secretary-General also held the office of High Representative for the Common Foreign and Security Policy,[145] and as the importance and burdens of that office (held from its inception in 1993 to 2009 by Mr Solana de Madariaga) increased,

---

140 E.g., Accord de 8 mars 1994 de coopération entre l'Etat fédéral, les Communautés et les Régions, relatif à la représentation du Royaume de Belgique au sein du Conseil de Ministres de l'Union européenne, MB du 17 novembre 1994, p. 28209.

141 TEU, art. 16(2). The (potential) difficulties may arise in that, whilst it is for each member state to determine who represents it in Council proceedings (RP Council, Annex I), the TFEU provides (art. 10(2)) that member states are represented in the Council 'by their governments'. There may also be national constitutional difficulties in, for example, a Scottish or a Bavarian minister 'commit[ting] the government' of the United Kingdom or of Germany.

142 Cases C-181 and 248/91 *Parliament* v *Council and Commission* (Bangladesh) [1993] ECR I-3685.

143 TFEU, art. 240(2) (ex art. 207(2) EC).

144 *Ibid.* art. 235(4).

145 TEU (pre-Lisbon), art. 18(3).

de facto responsibility for Council administration passed to the Deputy Secretary-General. The appointment of a permanent High Representative for Foreign Affairs and Security Policy in 2009 enables the Secretary-General (initially Mr de Boissieu, then Mr Corsepius from 2011 to 2015) to reassume his original responsibilities. The seat of the Council is in Brussels, but it meets in Luxembourg in April, June and October.[146] Meetings are closed to the public except for those deliberating legislative acts[147] and first deliberation on (many, not all) matters relating to rules which are legally binding in and for the member states.[148] The Council adopts its own Rules of Procedure.[149]

5. Presidency

3.39 The Council meets when convened by its president, on his or her own initiative or at the request of one of its members or of the Commission.[150] Prior to Lisbon, the presidency of the Council was held for six months at a time by each member state in strict rotation, the order determined by the Council.[151] The powers of the presidency are significant, since the president controls the agenda of Council meetings and the vote.[152] Member states have sometimes been criticised for arranging the legislative programme of the Council in a manner which best suits their (or their governments') interests. Certainly, the political skills of presidency ministers, and not least those of the prime minister, were and are instrumental to the discharge of a 'successful' presidency. The presidency also chairs (with the assistance of the Council secretariat) an intergovernmental conference on treaty amendment which happens to fall within its term of office, so with skill may be able to bend (future) treaty texts to its will. The presidency also represented the European Union prior to Lisbon in matters coming within the CFSP,[153] that task now assumed by the High Representative for Foreign Affairs and Security Policy.[154]

---

146 Protocol (No. 6) on the Location of the Seats of the Institutions and of Certain Bodies, Offices, Agencies and Departments of the European Union; RP Council, art. 1(3). This was part of a trade-off with Luxembourg for abandoning its claim to host occasional plenary sessions of the Parliament.

147 TEU, art. 16(8); RP Council, art. 5(1).

148 RP Council, art. 8.

149 TFEU, art. 240(3) (ex art. 207(3) EC); for the present Rules of Procedure see Decision 2009/937 [2009] OJ L325/35.

150 TFEU, art. 237; RP Council, art. 1(1).

151 EC Treaty, art. 203, 2nd para. The order, fixed barring alteration until July 2020, was set out in Decision 2007/5 [2007] OJ L1/11.

152 The Council votes 'on the initiative of the president' (RP Council, art. 11(1)); but a vote may be forced by a majority of its members (*ibid.*).

153 TEU (pre-Lisbon), art. 18(1).

154 TEU, art. 27(2).

With the increasing Council workload, including general or specific European **3.40** Council business, and not least that of the CFSP, there were concerns that the burdens of the presidency had become too great for even the larger member states. Lisbon therefore introduced significant change. The High Representative now presides over (although exercises no vote in) the Relex Council permanently.[155] Council presidencies are otherwise held by pre-established groups of three member states for a period of 18 months.[156] This reflects, and regularises, a *de facto* practice (informally the 'trio presidency') which began in January 2007 as a means of enhancing continuity, the then incoming German presidency agreeing with the following two (Portuguese and Slovenian) presidencies a joint working programme for a number of matters over the following 18 months. The groups are made up 'on a basis of equal rotation' among the member states, taking into account their diversity and geographical balance within the Union.[157] Each member of the group in turn 'chairs' for a six-month period all Council configurations (excepting Relex), the other members assisting the chair in all its responsibilities on the basis of an 18-month common programme.[158] The three may decide alternative arrangements among themselves,[159] practical arrangements to that end determined by each group by common accord.[160]

6. Voting in the Council

In some areas the Council acts by simple majority; in a few important (or **3.41** sensitive) areas the Treaties require unanimity. Where unanimity applies neither abstentions by members present in person or represented[161] nor absences[162] are counted; and of course each member state has, and may exercise, a veto.[163] But the normal rule, except where the Treaties specify otherwise, is

---

155   *Ibid.* art. 18(3).
156   Decision 2009/881 [2009] OJ L315/50 ('European Council Decision'), art. 1.
157   TEU, art. 16(9); Decision 2009/881, art. 1. The groups are established by Decision 2009/908 [2009] OJ L322/28 (implementing the European Council Decision), art. 1 and Annex I, which reproduces the order determined in 2007 by Decision 2007/5 (n. 151 above).
158   Decision 2009/881, art. 1(2); Decision 2009/908, art. 2(1).
159   Decision 2009/908, art. 2(2).
160   *Ibid.* art. 2(3).
161   TFEU, art. 238(4) (ex art. 205(3) EC).
162   By no means are all Council meetings fully attended by representatives from all member states; diplomats from the permanent representatives' offices may attend, but they may not vote. A proxy vote may be cast by a Council member on behalf of not more than one other member state; TFEU, art. 239 (ex art. 206 EC); RP Council, art. 11(3).
163   For some time there was a *de facto* veto, a product of the 1965/66 Luxembourg Compromise which was said, even in areas in which the Treaty allowed for majority voting, to allow any member state to veto a proposal which it considered to affect its 'very important interests'. The Council adhered to this *modus vivendi* for some time. But from a legal point of view no such right of veto ever existed, and around the time of agreement on the

that the Council acts by qualified majority vote (QMV).[164] When acting by QMV, the votes of the member states represented in the Council are, from the beginning and presently, weighted by reference to their population sizes, the weighting a matter of perennial scrapping amongst the member states at intergovernmental/accession conferences when they come up for alteration. Since 1 January 2007 (with Bulgarian and Romanian accession) the total of all weighted votes is 345, ranging from three for Malta to 29 each for Germany, France, Italy and the United Kingdom.[165] Where the Council acts upon a Commission proposal (which is normally the case), the adoption of a measure by QMV requires 255 of the 345 votes (260 of 352 votes post-Croatian accession) and, in order to prevent the smaller member states being over-whelmed by the larger, a simple majority of member states (the so-called 'double majority');[166] otherwise it requires 255 (260) votes and the support of at least two-thirds of the member states.[167] Put another way, a muster of 91 (93) Council votes constitutes a blocking minority. A member state may, by requesting 'verification', further require that the member states voting for the measure represent amongst them at least 62 per cent of the population of the Union.[168] It should be noted that, QMV notwithstanding, the political culture of the Council is one in which there is a marked tendency towards seeking a widest possible consensus: in the Council's own words, 'devot[ing] every effort to strengthening the democratic legitimacy of decisions taken by qualified majority'.[169]

3.42 Lisbon recasts significantly, and complicates even further, the arithmetic of QMV. A qualified majority is now to be attained:

(a)   until 31 October 2014, as under the present weighting and verification system,[170] except where under the Treaties not all the members of the

---

Single European Act in the mid-1980s, QMV again became the normal practice; the Luxembourg Compromise has not been formally invoked in Council proceedings since 1984. Yet it would be safer to describe it as dormant rather than dead and buried: in response to a parliamentary question, in 2001 the Council responded cryptically: 'As for what is commonly called the "Luxembourg Compromise" ..., its status will remain the same after the entry into force of the Nice Treaty'; [2001] OJ C364E/48. Put otherwise, it is gone, but a wraith remains.

164   TEU, art. 16(3). Prior to Lisbon simple majority was the default procedure; EC Treaty, art. 205(1).

165   Protocol (No. 36) on Transitional Provisions, art. 3(3) (ex art. 205(2) EC). Croatia is to be afforded seven votes upon accession, bringing the total to 352. A table of present voting weight in the Council is provided in Annex III.

166   *Ibid.* (as amended by the 2011 Act of Accession, art. 20). The second limb of the double majority was introduced only in 2004.

167   *Ibid.*

168   *Ibid.* For the tabulation of population sizes, upon which the computation is based, see RP Council, Annex III (which is amended annually).

169   Decision 2009/859 [2009] OJ L314/73, Preamble, 2nd para.

170   TEU, art. 16(5) and Protocol (No. 36) on Transitional Provisions, art. 3(3).

Council participate in voting (that is, in areas in which one or more member states enjoy the privilege of an opt-out, or under enhanced cooperation or its variations), in which case it is attained with the support of at least 55 per cent of the representatives participating accounting amongst them for at least 65 per cent of the population of the Union, a blocking minority comprising more than 35 per cent of the population of participating member states plus one member;[171]

(b) from 1 November 2014 to 31 March 2017, with the votes of at least 15 members, comprising at least 55 per cent of their total number and representing at least 65 per cent of the population of the Union, a blocking minority comprising at least four members, except in cases where not all members participate, in which the rule in (a) applies; *unless*, in either case, a member of the Council requests that it revert to the present weighting and system, in which case that is done; and *unless* the Council is acting not upon a proposal from the Commission or the High Representative, in which case 72 per cent of Council members representing at least 65 per cent of the population is required;[172]

(c) from 1 April 2017, as in (b) without possibility of recourse to the present system;[173]

(d) however, should members of the Council representing at least three-quarters of the population or three-quarters of the member states (from 1 November 2014 to 31 March 2017, thereafter both thresholds dropping to 55 per cent) necessary to constitute a blocking minority indicate opposition to the Council adopting a measure by qualified majority, the Council is required to 'discuss the issue' and 'do all in its power to reach … a satisfactory solution to address concerns raised by the [minority] members of the Council'.[174] This marks a resurrection of the Ioannina Compromise, thought buried.[175] The Council decision implementing these procedures is entrenched to a degree, any future modification

---

171 Protocol (No. 36) on Transitional Provisions, art. 3(4).

172 TEU, art. 16(4); Protocol (No. 36) on Transitional Provisions, art. 3(2); TFEU, art. 238(3).

173 Protocol (No. 36) on Transitional Provisions, art. 3(2) thereafter being inoperative.

174 Decision 2009/859, n. 169 above; pre-ordained by Declaration (No. 7) on Article 16(4) of the TEU and Article 238(2) of the TFEU.

175 The Ioannina Compromise was an 'emergency brake' agreed during the Corfu accession negotiations (1994) whereby in the event of a proposed measure which just met the (then) QMV arithmetic for adoption but no more, the Council would do 'all in its power' to reach a satisfactory solution which could be adopted by a majority including at least one more member state. Unlike the Luxembourg Compromise, the Ioannina Compromise was recognised by a Council 'decision' ([1994] OJ C105/1) and by a Declaration in the Final Act of the Amsterdam Treaty (Declaration relating to the Protocol on the Institutions with the Prospect of Enlargement of the European Union). But, according to the latter, it was to apply '[u]ntil the entry into force of the first enlargement … and, by that date, a solution to [the issue of QMV weighting] will be found'. Therefore it presumably lapsed with the accessions on 1 May 2004 or, at the latest, on 1 November 2004 when the new (and present) QMV weightings came into force. But it is difficult to say, as it was never formally used.

requiring the 'preliminary deliberation' of the European Council acting by consensus.[176]

None of this labyrinth could be said remotely to serve the simplification and efficiency in decision-making which was a primary clarion call of the Laeken Declaration. But it does bring the huge benefit of avoiding the (often fraught) recalibration of weighted votes previously necessary upon accession of a new member state; and, although doubtless not the purpose, secession of a member state.

7. Bridging clauses

3.43 Prior to Lisbon, the EC Treaty contained three 'bridging clauses' (*clauses passerelles*),[177] authority enabling the Council, acting by unanimity, to alter a Treaty requirement of unanimity to less burdensome procedures for the adoption of future measures in the fields. They applied in some areas of social policy,[178] environmental policy[179] and visas, asylum and immigration.[180] A further bridging clause in the EU Treaty provided for the transfer of third pillar matters to the first pillar by a unanimous Council decision subsequently approved ('adopted') by each member state.[181] In the event, a bridging measure was adopted only once, in the sphere of visas, asylum and immigration.[182] There is now, however, a general bridging clause, whereby a requirement of a unanimous vote for the Council to act may be altered by the European Council (acting by unanimity and with the consent of the Parliament acting by a majority of its component members) so that in a particular case, or generally henceforward, measures may be adopted by simple majority vote or by ordinary legislative procedure, provided there is no opposition from any national parliament.[183] The constitutional importance is reflected in the fact it is contained in a Treaty article dealing otherwise with Treaty revision.[184] There remain in the Treaties a number of bridging clauses *de lege speciali*, most requiring merely a

---

176 Protocol (No. 9) on the Decision of the Council relating to the Implementation of Article 16(4) of the TEU and Article 238(2) of the TFEU.
177 '*Passerelle*' is normally translated (if at all) as 'bridge'; in some bilingual jurisdictions it is commonly rendered 'springboard'. Those wary of it may call it a 'ratchet' clause, and in 2006 the Select Committee on European Scrutiny of the UK House of Commons attracted some attention, and opprobrium, for translating it matter-of-factly as 'gangplank'.
178 EC Treaty, art. 137(2).
179 *Ibid.* art. 175(2).
180 *Ibid.* art. 67(2).
181 TEU (pre-Lisbon), art. 42.
182 Decision 2004/927 [2004] OJ L396/45; see 11.160 below.
183 TEU, art. 48(7).
184 See 2.62 above.

unanimous Council vote to be put into effect.[185] In the United Kingdom there is in place a statutory bar to a minister voting in favour or otherwise supporting any of them without parliamentary approval,[186] and in 2011 the bar was raised so as to require in many cases prior approval by both Act of Parliament and referendum.[187] Similar rules/conventions apply elsewhere.

8. COREPER

The Treaties recognise the existence of a committee consisting of the 'perma- **3.44** nent representatives' (effectively ambassadors) of the member states (commonly called COREPER, from *COmité des REprésentants PERmanents*),[188] permanently based in Brussels. COREPER is 'responsible for preparing the work of the Council and for carrying out the tasks assigned to it by the latter'.[189] Much of the preparatory work of the Council is done by committees of national civil servants, the 'preparatory bodies' (or working groups) subordinate to COREPER and set up by it or with its approval.[190] Their work is then deliberated in COREPER, which meets extensively, as either the permanent representatives themselves (COREPER II) or, more commonly, their deputies (COREPER I). It is chaired by the member state representative holding the chair of the general affairs Council[191] except when discussing Relex matters, when it is normally (but not always) chaired by a representative of the High Representative for Foreign Affairs and Security Policy. A number of decisions of the Council are, for practical purposes, taken by COREPER and rubber-stamped by the Council. The efficiency of COREPER, the eye of the needle through which most business passes, is therefore fundamental to the work of the Council.

---

185   TEU, art. 31(3) (CFSP); TFEU, art. 81(3), 2nd para (family law); art. 153(2), 4th para. (social policy); art. 192(2), 2nd para. (environment); art. 312(2), 2nd para (finance); arts 333(1) and 331(2) (enhanced cooperation).
186   European Union (Amendment) Act 2008, s. 6. Approval is secured by a motion moved in each House and agreed without amendment.
187   European Union Act 2011, s. 6(1), (5)(b).
188   TEU, art. 16(7); TFEU, art. 240(1) (ex art. 207 EC).
189   TFEU, art. 240(1).
190   RP Council, art. 19(3). There are at present some 160 such groups, assigned to specific Council configurations – for example, about 40 to the foreign affairs Council and 30 to the agricultural Council. Special note should be taken of the Special Committee on Agriculture (SCA), established in 1960 not by COREPER but by the member states, which in practice prepares more than half of the work of the agricultural Council. For a complete list of preparatory bodies see Council Doc. 11602/09, Annex I.
191   Decision 2009/881, art. 2.

D. EUROPEAN PARLIAMENT

3.45   Each of the original Community Treaties established an 'Assembly', a single Assembly serving all three Communities from the start. The Assembly came to be called the Parliament in normal, and sometimes official, usage as early as 1962,[192] and the Single European Act (1986) formally, if obliquely, restyled it the 'European Parliament'.[193] It has been called that in Treaty texts since.

1. Membership

3.46   The Treaties provide that the functioning of the Union is founded upon representative democracy,[194] citizens are directly represented at Union level in the Parliament[195] and the Parliament is composed of 'representatives of the Union's citizens',[196] called 'members' (*membres*; *Mitgliedern*) elsewhere in the Treaties[197] and 'members [but *députés*] of the European Parliament' in other instruments[198] and in its own Rules of Procedure,[199] and, universally (in English), MEPs. Since 1979, they are elected by direct universal adult suffrage by a free and secret ballot for a fixed five-year term.[200] With the extension of the Commission's term of office to five years in 1994 appointment/election to the two institutions is now roughly synchronised, parliamentary elections in June and Commission appointment in the autumn of the same year. Whilst the Treaties recognise elsewhere that the franchise is a right accruing to citizens of the Union,[201] the Court of Justice found, perhaps surprisingly, that it is for the member states to determine eligibility to vote, so that they may grant that right to third country nationals 'who have close links to them'.[202] The Treaties require the adoption of a uniform voting procedure;[203] this has not yet been achieved, but in 2002 procedures were partially harmonised with the adoption of some 'common principles' on proportional representation by list or single transferable

---

192   See e.g., Assembly resolution of 30 March 1962 [1962] JO 1045.
193   The change of name was engineered by reference throughout the SEA to 'Parliament' rather than 'Assembly', with a rider (art. 3) regarding the institutions 'henceforth designated as referred to hereafter'.
194   TEU, art. 10(1).
195   *Ibid.* art. 10(2).
196   *Ibid.* art. 14(1).
197   TEU, art. 14(2); TFEU, arts 223–4.
198   Act concerning the Election of the Representatives of the Assembly by Direct Universal Suffrage [1976] OJ L278/10, as amended by Decision 2002/772 [2002] OJ L283/1.
199   For the present version see European Parliament, Rules of Procedure, 7th parliamentary term (March 2011) [2011] OJ L116/1, rule 1.2.
200   TEU, art. 14(3) (ex art. 190(3) EC). Prior to 1979 they were appointed from amongst deputies sitting in national parliaments.
201   TFEU, art. 22 (ex art. 19 EC); see 8.14 below.
202   Case C-145/04 *Spain* v *United Kingdom* [2006] ECR I-7917, at para. 78; see 8.14 below.
203   TFEU, art. 223(1) (ex art. 190(4) EC).

vote, the period for holding elections and the timing of the counting of votes,[204] otherwise leaving the member states 'free to apply their national provisions'.[205]

The number of MEPs has grown, from an original 410 in 1979, with progressive enlargement (and German unification), peaking at 785 MEPs from 2007 to 2009,[206] then pared back to, and capped at, 736 as of the June 2009 election[207] but increased to 754 in 2011. There is a fixed allocation amongst the member states in a manner degressively proportionate to population size with a weighting in favour of the smaller states, ranging from (at present) six from Malta, Luxembourg, Estonia and Cyprus (and so, for Malta, one MEP per 69,000 population) to 99 from Germany (one per 830,000).[208] Lisbon amends the cap upwards to 751 MEPs ('[t]hey shall not exceed seven hundred and fifty in number, plus the President'),[209] with a minimum of six and a maximum of 96 from any one member state.[210] The actual number (its 'composition') is to be determined by the European Council acting by unanimity upon the initiative and with the consent of the Parliament.[211] However, a political decision was reached in December 2008 that their number should be increased by 18,[212] the allocation of the additional seats agreed in June 2009[213] (a fortnight after the election) and the 18 'designated' by the affected member states. The new total is thus 754, three beyond the Lisbon cap unless three (German) MEPs are jettisoned, as was agreed by the European Council but for which no mechanism is in place to achieve. Thus from 2009, there existed 18 'reserve' or 'phantom' MEPs who could not take up their seats (although they drew salary and allowances) until the Treaties were amended to allow them to do so. A

3.47

---

204 Decision 2002/772 [2002] OJ L283/1; the rules therefore applied in and from the 2004 elections.

205 *Ibid.*, Preamble, first recital.

206 The 2004 elections produced 732 MEPs. Their number was increased to 785 in 2007 in order to accommodate incoming Bulgarian and Romanian MEPs (2005 Act of Accession, art. 24(1)), initially appointed but replaced by directly elected MEPs following elections in Bulgaria and in Romania in August and November 2007, respectively.

207 EC Treaty, art. 190, as amended by the 2005 Act of Accession, art. 9(2). The total 'shall not exceed 736'; art. 189, 2nd para.

208 EC Treaty, art. 190(2). Under the European Parliamentary Elections Act 2002 (as amended) the 73 (from 2011) United Kingdom MEPs are further subdivided, at present into 60 from England (including, since 2004, Gibraltar), six from Scotland, four from Wales and three from Northern Ireland, elected (since the 1999 election) from 12 multi-member constituencies ('electoral regions') on the basis of proportional representation by list and tabulated by the d'Hondt system (in the 11 British regions) and by single transferable vote (Northern Ireland).

209 TEU, art. 14(2). This peculiar formula is a product of an unseemly row at the Lisbon IGC by which Italy secured a promise of an MEP in addition to that previously agreed; see Declaration (No. 4) on the Composition of the European Parliament.

210 TEU, art. 14(2).

211 *Ibid.*

212 European Council, Brussels, 11–12 December 2008, *Bulletin EU* 12–2008, 8, Presidency Conclusions, Declaration of the European Council: Treaty of Lisbon – Transitional measures concerning the composition of the European Parliament.

213 European Council, Brussels, 18–19 June 2009, *Bulletin EU* 6–2009, 8, Presidency Conclusions, Annex 4.

conference of representatives of the governments of the member states agreed the change in June 2010,[214] subject to ratification by the member states which was hoped to be completed by December 2010[215] but, waiting upon Greek, UK and, finally, Belgian ratification, it was only in December 2011 that the 18 took their seats. As it was effected by amendment not of the Treaties proper but of the Protocol on Transitional Provisions the arrangement will apply to the 2009–14 term only, and the allocation of seats will require to be reduced thereafter in order to be Treaty compliant. On top of the 754, Croatia is to be accorded 12 MEPs from accession until the end of the 2009–14 session,[216] which will make it necessary to recrunch the numbers anew. The European Council is to adopt a decision determining the composition of the Parliament 'in good time before the 2014 European Parliament elections'.[217]

3.48 Since direct elections, an MEP's salary was equivalent to that of a member of (the lower house of) his or her home parliament, and was met by that member state. This meant very significant disparities – an Italian MEP, for example, on a salary of four times that of his or her Spanish colleagues. A Statute for Members of the European Parliament,[218] adopted by the Parliament in 2005 and applying from the start of the present (2009–14) term,[219] provides that MEPs are entitled to 'an appropriate salary to safeguard their independence'[220] which is uniform, fixed at 38.5 per cent of the salary of a judge at the Court of Justice,[221] or (in 2011) €7,956.87 per month (€6,200.72 after tax and accident insurance contribution), and drawn from the general Union budget.[222] This is intended to blunt widespread public unease with perceived excessive salaries, but fails to address the issue of the (extreme in some cases) generosity MEPs are thought to show themselves (honestly or otherwise)[223] in matters of the perquisites of office. A new Code of Conduct requiring greater transparency

---

214 Protocol amending the Protocol on Transitional Provisions annexed to the TEU, the TFEU and the Euratom Treaty [2010] OJ C263/1.

215 *Ibid.* art. 2.

216 2011 Act of Accession, art. 19.

217 Protocol (No. 36) on Transitional Provisions, art. 2(3) as amended by the amending Protocol.

218 Decision 2005/684 [2005] OJ L262/1.

219 *Ibid.* art. 30.

220 *Ibid.* art. 9(1).

221 *Ibid.* art. 10.

222 *Ibid.* art. 23.

223 See e.g., Case T-149/09 *Dover* v *Parliament*, judgment of 24 March 2011, not yet reported, in which the General Court required a UK Conservative MEP to repay £345,289 in improper allowance claims made over the course of two parliamentary terms. For years the Parliament resisted granting access to the bulk of the 2006 annual report of its internal audit service, until (effectively) ordered by the General Court to do so (Case T-471/09 *Toland* v *Parliament*, judgment of 7 June 2011, not yet reported) for fear, it is widely anticipated, of exposing avarice on a grand scale.

and disclosure was agreed provisionally in 2011 (following corruption allegations and consequent resignation of two MEPs)[224] and is expected to enter into
force some time in 2013.[225]

MEPs enjoy a large measure of diplomatic immunity,[226] which may be lifted by **3.49**
the Parliament.[227]

2. Political parties

MEPs normally stand for election by reference to national political parties (and **3.50**
at present are drawn from some 160 different parties); it was only in the 2009
election that a (somewhat) pan-Union political party (Libertas) was organised
and ran for the Parliament on that basis, fielding 520 candidates across 14
member states, and was rewarded with one seat (in France) for its troubles.
However, MEPs sit in the Parliament not as national deputies but in transnational 'political parties at European level' (prior to Lisbon 'political groups',
still called that in the Rules of Procedure) which 'contribute to forming
European political awareness and to expressing the will of the citizens of the
Union'.[228] The incentive to form political parties (which must include a
minimum number and transnational spread of MEPs)[229] is that various initiatives, appointment to parliamentary committees, speaking time and disbursement of funding is on a party basis. There must be a genuine political affiliation
(which is presumed)[230] amongst the members of a party, it cannot be formed as
a mere technical expedient.[231] In the 2004 elections the right-leaning parties

---

224 Mr Strasser (PPE-DE) and Mr Thaler (S&D). A third implicated MEP (S&D) remains in post.
225 For the draft see Code of Conduct for Members of the European Parliament, PE 463.760/BUR/GT.
226 Protocol (No. 7) on the Privileges and Immunities of the European Union, arts 7–9; RP EP, rule 5.1.
227 RP EP, rules 6, 7. See e.g., Case T-345/05R *V v Parliament* [2007] ECR II-25*; Case T-345/05 *Mote v
Parliament* [2008] ECR II-2849; Cases C-200 and 201/07 *Marra v De Gregorio and Clemente* [2008] ECR
I-7929; *R v Mote* [2007] EWCA Crim 3131, [2008] Crim LR 797. For all the (personal) corruption widely
attributed to MEPs, only one (Mr Tom Wise, UKIP) has ever been sentenced to a term of imprisonment for
criminal conduct in post, in 2009 of two years, imposed by an English court, for false accounting and money
laundering. (Mr Mote (also UKIP) was convicted of fraud and deception in 2007 and sentenced to a
nine-month term of imprisonment, but for conduct prior to his taking up his seat.) In 2012 Mr Ernst Strasser
(ÖVP) was charged by a special prosecutor (*Korruptionsstaatsanwaltschaft*) with corruption; a conviction
carries a penalty of up to ten years' imprisonment.
228 TEU, art. 10(4).
229 From 2009 a political group must comprise at least 25 MEPs drawn from at least one-quarter of the member
states; RP EP, rule 30.2. Previously it was 20 MEPs drawn from at least one-fifth of the member states.
230 RP EP, rule 30.1.
231 Cases T-222 etc./99 *Martinez and ors v Parliament* [2001] ECR II-2823; partially set aside on appeal in Case
C-486/01P *Front National v Parliament* [2004] ECR I-6289 on admissibility grounds.

dominated, and this may have indirectly secured the presidency of the Commission for Mr Barroso.[232] In 2009 they did so again, contributing, again, to Mr Barroso's fortunes and renomination. As at 1 January 2012, there are seven political parties, with MEPs as follows:

Group of the European Peoples' Party (Christian Democrats) and European Democrats (PPE-DE):	272
Progressive Alliance of Socialists and Democrats (S&D):	190
Group of the Alliance of Liberals and Democrats for Europe (ADLE):	85
Group of the Greens/European Free Alliance (Verts/ALE):	58
European Conservative and Reformist Group (ECR):	57
Confederal Group of the European United Left/Nordic Green Left (GUE/NGL):	34
Europe of Freedom and Democracy Group (F&D):[233]	28

3.51 It will be observed that the right dominates, the PPE-DE with by far the largest number of seats and from the ranks of which emerged the president in 2009 (Mr Buzek); he was replaced in 2012 by Mr Schultz from the S&D. The PPE-DE and the (broadly) like-minded groups (the essentially Eurosceptic F&D and 'anti-federalist' ECR) enjoy a majority of 357 seats to 282 over the left (the S&D, the Verts/ALE and the GUE/NGL), although party loyalties are fissile and more fluid than is generally the case in national parliaments. There remain 30-odd 'non-attached' (*non-inscrit*) MEPs, a few political outcasts but mostly extreme nationalist/racists unpalatable to any party and, perhaps, to themselves.[234] With Nice, regulatory control of the political parties was subsumed by the Parliament and Council together,[235] but they are in some measure self-governing.

3. Procedures and organisation

3.52 The Parliament itself, with Council approval, lays down the regulations and general conditions governing the performance of the duties of MEPs,[236] now

232 Mr Barroso was nominated in July 2004 (one month after parliamentary elections), and it is likely the Council (which then discharged that task) settled upon a centre-right candidate as one reflecting the political make-up of, and so politically acceptable to, the new Parliament.

233 Formed in 2009 from the remnants of the Union for the Europe of Nations Group (UEN) and the Independence/Democracy Group (IND/DEM), both of which fared poorly at the election that year.

234 A grouping of far-right MEPs mustered the 20 of their number (then) necessary to form a political group, the Identity, Tradition and Sovereignty Group (ITS), in early 2007 but it collapsed within the year, ironically a result of internecine racial squabbling.

235 TFEU, art. 224 (ex art. 191, 2nd para. EC); see Regulation 2004/2003 [2003] OJ L297/1.

236 TFEU, art. 223(2) (ex art. 190(5) EC).

embodied in the 2005 Statute (although it is long on privileges and short on duties), and adopts its own Rules of Procedure.[237] Except where otherwise provided in the Treaties the Parliament acts by an absolute majority of votes cast;[238] the quorum is one-third of its membership[239] or, at present, 252 MEPs. However, in many important areas a positive vote by a majority of its members (i.e., at present at least 377 votes) is required, so that the Parliament sometimes finds itself unable to act because it fails to muster the necessary number of votes.[240]

Preliminary work is done by the standing parliamentary committees, of which **3.53** there are currently 21; they have become increasingly influential in the process of legislation and now work very closely with the services of the Council and of the Commission. The committees report to the plenary session of the Parliament, which is in annual session,[241] in practice sitting 12 times a year (twice in September, as there is no August sitting). The Parliament may establish *ad hoc* temporary committees and committees of inquiry.

The president and officers of the Parliament are elected from amongst its **3.54** members,[242] and in practice hold office for two and a half years. Much of the work of organisation is undertaken by the Parliament's 'governing bodies': the Bureau, consisting of the officers of the Parliament (the president and the 14 vice-presidents, assisted by the five quaestors, responsible for administrative and financial matters directly affecting its members) and by the Conference of Presidents, consisting of the president and the chairmen (*sic*)of the political groups.[243] It is widely perceived that parliamentary machinery, through appointment of office bearers and membership of committees (and the presidency), is stitched up by agreement between the EPP-DE and the S&D.[244]

---

237 TFEU, art. 232 (ex art. 199 EC).
238 TFEU, art. 231 (ex art. 198 EC).
239 RP EP, rule 155.2. The Parliament is presumed to be quorate whatever the number of MEPs present and voting unless the president, on a request from at least 40 MEPs, determines that it is not; RP EP, rule 155.3.
240 For example, a January 2007 plenary vote on the 'third railway package' (opening up international passenger rail services to competition, a certification system for train drivers and minimum rights for passengers) supported by the Council, the transport committee of the Parliament and agreed by the PPE-DE and the PSE (as the S&D then was) was carried by 358 to 195 votes but the proposed measures died because the vote was short of the 393 (then) required as more than 200 MEPs had failed to attend – because the threat of inclement weather jeopardised their weekend travel plans. The package was eventually adopted in the autumn of that year; see 11.209 below.
241 TFEU, art. 229 (ex art. 196 EC).
242 TEU, art. 14(4) (ex art. 197, 1st para. EC).
243 See generally RP EP, rules 20–9.
244 Since direct elections in 1979, for example, only two presidents (Mrs Veil (1979–81) and Mr Cox (2002–04)) have been drawn from parties other than the EPP-DE or the S&D (or their predecessors).

3.55 The seat of the Parliament is in Strasbourg, where the 12 monthly plenary sessions are held; additional plenary sessions are held in Brussels.[245] The General Secretariat and its departments are in Luxembourg and the committees of the Parliament meet in Brussels. This 'two-seat arrangement' or, to its (many) critics, travelling circus, does little to reduce the administrative (and environmental) costs of the institution, is stoutly detested by the MEPs themselves, but would require an amendment to the protocol, or at the least the unanimous agreement of the governments of the member states, to be altered, and the French government has long been firmly resolved that the Parliament not be allowed to quit Strasbourg. In 1995 the Parliament voted to hold only 11 of its 1996 plenary sessions in Strasbourg but the decision was annulled by the Court of Justice at French initiative.[246] It has now tried again, voting to shorten two of its 12 Strasbourg sessions from four to two days in 2012 and 2013 and holding them both in October;[247] unsurprisingly France promptly challenged these too.[248]

4.   Powers of the Parliament

3.56 The Parliament exercises legislative and budgetary functions (jointly with the Council) and 'functions of political control and consultation as laid down in the Treaties'.[249] It does so across four broad categories. First, it enjoys a degree of political control over the Commission, discussed above.[250] Secondly, it has significant powers in relation to the Union budget. Thirdly, it exercises general supervisory powers. And fourthly, it plays an important role in the adoption of Union legislation.

(a)   Powers with respect to the budget

3.57 The budgetary procedure under the treaties involves an intricate process of power sharing amongst the Parliament, the Council and the Commission.[251] Ultimately it is the president of the Parliament who declares the budget to be finally 'adopted'.[252] The Parliament may reject the budget outright by a majority of its component members so requiring the Commission to submit a new draft budget;[253] it has done so on a number of occasions (in all cases but

---

245   Protocol (No. 6) on the Location of the Seats of the Institutions and of Certain Bodies, Offices, Agencies and Departments of the European Union.

246   Case C-345/95 *France* v *Parliament* [1997] ECR I-5215.

247   [2011] OJ C165E/151.

248   Cases C-237 and 238/11 *France* v *Parliament*, pending.

249   TEU, art. 14(1).

250   See 3.34 above.

251   TFEU, art. 314 (ex art. 272 EC).

252   TFEU, art. 314(9).

253   TFEU, art. 314(7) (ex art. 272(8) EC). Prior to Lisbon it required the votes of three-fifths of MEPs.

two involving supplementary budgets), leading to temporary financial paralysis. It may also override the Council, post-concilation, by a majority of its component members and three-fifths of the votes cast.[254] Prior to Lisbon it had limited control over 'compulsory expenditure' (those areas of the Community budget in which there was a legal obligation to disburse Community funds, the great bulk of it in the agricultural sector), with greater influence over lesser 'non-compulsory' (optional) spending. With Lisbon the distinction is abandoned, so increasing significantly the Parliament's control of Union finances. Further, the multiannual financial framework is given Treaty status (previously it existed only as a function of interinstitutional agreement) and its adoption requires the Parliament's consent.[255] Within the constraints of the Treaties, the budgetary procedure is governed by an agreement amongst the three institutions.[256]

(b) General supervisory powers

Since Maastricht the Parliament has power to establish temporary Committees **3.58** of Inquiry to investigate alleged contraventions of or maladministration in the implementation of Community, now Union, law;[257] it was the report of one such committee which led to the resignation of the Commission in 1999.[258] Any citizen of the Union or any natural or legal person residing or having its registered office in a member state may address a petition to the Parliament on any matter within the fields of Union activity which affects him, her or it directly.[259]

The Parliament appoints an Ombudsman with powers to investigate alle- **3.59** gations of maladministration in the activities of the Union institutions other than the judicial activities of the Court of Justice.[260] The Ombudsman is responsible to the Parliament, and is appointed after each election for the duration of its term of office.[261] A complaint may be lodged with him by any citizen of the Union or by any natural or legal person residing or having its registered office in the Union.[262] If he finds maladministration he is required to

---

254 TFEU, art. 314(7)(d).

255 *Ibid.* art. 312(2).

256 See the Interinstitutional Agreement of 17 May 2006 on budgetary discipline and sound financial management [2006] OJ C139/1, which is a revision of a series of previous agreements. See also Council Regulation 2040/2000 [2000] OJ L244/27 on budgetary discipline.

257 TFEU, art. 226 (ex art. 193 EC); RP EP, rule 185 and Annex IX.

258 See 3.34 above.

259 TFEU, arts 24 and 227 (ex arts 21, 1st para., 194 EC); RP EP, rules 201–3.

260 TFEU, art. 228 (ex art. 195 EC); RP EP, rules 204–6.

261 TFEU, art. 288(2). In 1994 Mr Söderman was appointed, and in 1999 reappointed, the Ombudsman; he was replaced (upon retirement) by Mr Diamandouros in 2003, who was reappointed following the 2004 and 2009 elections.

262 TEU, art. 24, 3rd para.; TFEU, art. 288(1).

report to the Parliament, and may, if he considers it appropriate, make recommendations therein. Such a report produces of itself no legal effects for third parties, who therefore cannot compel the Ombudsman to produce it.[263] But he may be held accountable for injury caused by his own misconduct.[264]

(c) Powers with respect to legislation

3.60 From the outset a number of articles of the Treaties required that, before acting, the Council must 'consult' the Parliament. The opinion thus obtained was not binding upon the Council, it was advisory only. Notwithstanding, the Court of Justice held that the requirement to consult the Parliament, far from being a mere formality, 'reflects at Community level the fundamental democratic principle that the peoples should take part in the exercise of power through the intermediary of a representative assembly',[265] so that a failure to consult was a mandatory procedural flaw justifying the annulment of the resulting (purported) measure.[266] The Court has also found that the Council is required to reconsult the Parliament if the Commission has amended a draft proposal, or the Council itself intends to amend it, and the resulting text departs substantially from the text upon which the Parliament has already been consulted, unless the amendments correspond essentially to the wishes of the Parliament itself.[267] Even where the Treaties do not require consultation the Commission will urge the Council to consult the Parliament in important matters.[268] In this context the Court of First Instance has referred to procedural requirements as a function of 'the principle of democracy', breach of which could lead to the annulment of a Union act.[269]

3.61 The right of the Parliament to be consulted only afforded it a minor role in the legislative process and resulted in prolonged criticism of a 'democratic deficit' in the Community system. This led eventually to an increase, by progressive Treaty

---

263 Case T-103/99 *Associazione delle Cantine Sociali Venete* v *Ombudsman and Parliament* [2002] ECR II-4165.

264 Case C-234/02P *European Ombudsman* v *Lamberts* [2004] ECR I-2803; Case T-412/05 *M* v *European Ombudsman* [2008] ECR II-197*.

265 Case 138/79 *Roquette Frères* v *Council* [1980] ECR 3333 at 3360. See also Case 70/88 *Parliament* v *Council* ('Chernobyl') [1990] ECR I-2041.

266 *Ibid.*

267 Case C-65/90 *Parliament* v *Council* [1992] ECR I-4593; Cases C-13–16/92 *Driessen en Zonen* v *Minister van Verkeer en Waterstaat* [1993] ECR I-4751; Case C-388/92 *Parliament* v *Council* [1994] ECR I-2067; Case C-21/94 *Parliament* v *Council* [1995] ECR I-1827; Case C-408/95 *Eurotunnel and ors* v *SeaFrance* [1997] ECR I-6315.

268 See e.g., Cases C-181 and 248/91 *Parliament* v *Council and Commission* (Bangladesh) [1993] ECR I-3685.

269 Case T-135/96 *Union Européenne de l'Artisanat et des Petites et Moyennes Entreprises* v *Council* [1998] ECR II-2335.

amendment, in the Parliament's legislative functions.[270] Prior to Lisbon there were four distinct procedures by which the Parliament took part in the adoption of Community legislation:[271]

- *consultation* (or 'advisory opinions'), as just described;
- the *cooperation* procedure, introduced by the Single European Act;[272]
- the *co-decision* procedure, introduced by Maastricht;[273] and
- *assent*, introduced by the Single European Act, whereby, in a small number of areas, the positive approval of the Parliament is required before action can be taken.

The cooperation procedure all but died out with Amsterdam, with few excep- **3.62** tions[274] replaced by the co-decision procedure; Lisbon delivered it the *coup de grâce*. Consultation still exists, as does assent (now 'consent'); and what was co-decision became the 'ordinary legislative procedure',[275] defined as 'the joint adoption by the European Parliament and the Council of a [measure] on a proposal from the Commission'.[276] By comparison, a (new) 'special legislative procedure' consists in the adoption of a measure by the Parliament 'with the participation of the Council' or by the Council 'with the participation of the Parliament'.[277] There is nothing 'special' about the special legislative procedure, it denotes merely the adoption of legislation by the two institutions in a manner different from the (ordinary) norm, prescribed upon a case-by-case basis by a given legal base.

---

270 It was fear in (some quarters of) the United Kingdom of the growth of the powers of the Parliament which led to the adoption of that rare constitutional device, a statutory bar to ratification of any future treaty increasing those powers without express approval by Act of Parliament; see now the European Parliamentary Elections Act 2002, s. 12.

271 EC Treaty, art. 192, 1st para.

272 *Ibid.* art. 252. The term 'cooperation' was used in the EEC Treaty (when amended by the SEA) from 1987 to 1993 when it was abandoned with the entry into force of Maastricht.

273 *Ibid.* art. 251; nor did the term 'co-decision' appear in the Treaty, having been abandoned in the later Maastricht drafts.

274 The exceptions were arts 99(5), 102, 103(2) and 106(2) EC, all in the field of economic and monetary policy. These were provisions agreed at Maastricht, the detail delicate and the second/third stages of EMU ongoing, with which the Amsterdam IGC was therefore loathe to tinker.

275 TFEU, art. 289(1).

276 *Ibid.* art. 289(1).

277 *Ibid.* art. 289(2).

3.63 The ordinary legislative procedure operates as follows:[278]

Proposal: a Commission proposal is submitted to both the Council and the Parliament.

First reading: the Parliament adopts its 'position' (previously common position) and communicates it to the Council; the Council may approve the Parliament's position in which case the measure is adopted in that form; if it does not, it adopts its own position and communicates it to the Parliament, informing it fully of the reasons behind it.

Second reading: if within three months (extended to four at the initiative of either Council or Parliament) of these communications, the Parliament:

(a) approves the Council's first reading position or takes no decision, the measure is adopted in that form;

(b) rejects the Council's first reading position (by a majority of its component members), the measure dies;

(c) proposes amendments to the Council's first reading position (by a majority of its component members), the amended text is submitted to Council and Commission for their 'opinions'.

If within three (four) months of (c), the Council (by qualified majority or by unanimity on amendments of which the Commission disapproved):

(a) approves all the Parliament's amendments, the measure is thus adopted;

(b) does not approve all amendments, the president of the Council and the president of the Parliament must convene, within six weeks (extendable to eight), a meeting of a Conciliation Committee.

Conciliation: the Conciliation Committee, comprising members of the Council or their representatives and an equal number of MEPs,[279] seeks to agree a joint text by qualified majority (Council) and simple majority (Parliament) within six (eight) weeks upon a basis of the second reading opinions; the Commission takes part and 'take[s] all necessary initiatives' to reconcile the two; if no joint text is approved within six (eight) weeks the measure dies.

Third reading: if a joint text is approved by the Committee it is then subject to approval by the Parliament (simple majority) and the Council (qualified majority) within six (eight) weeks, at which point the measure is adopted; if either fails to approve, it falls.

---

278   *Ibid.* art. 294.

279   For appointment to the Parliament's 'delegation' to a Conciliation Committee see RP EP, rule 68. The exact number from each political party is determined by the conference of presidents.

It can be rendered diagrammatically as shown in Figure 3.1.

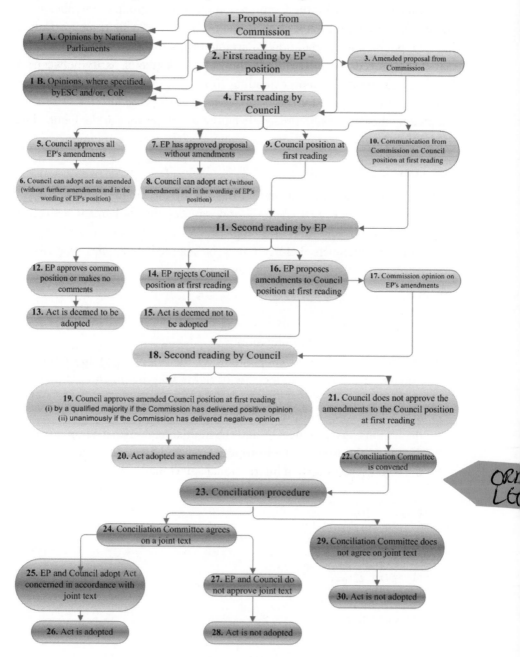

Note: Reproduced from http://ec.europa.eu/codecision/stepbystep/diagram_en.htm.

Figure 3.1   The ordinary legislative procedure

3.64 There are special provisions covering the (rare) cases in which the initial proposal comes not from the Commission but from a group of member states, the European Central Bank or the Court of Justice.[280] The three institutions have adopted a joint declaration on arrangements for good faith and efficient use of the procedure.[281] Because it allows for a degree of parity between the Council and the Parliament, extending to what is effectively a parliamentary veto, measures adopted by the ordinary legislative procedure (as were those adopted by the co-decision procedure before it) are acts not of the Council but of 'the European Parliament and the Council of the European Union'.

(d)   Consent

3.65 The assent procedure was introduced in 1987 by the Single European Act. It was restyled 'consent' by Lisbon,[282] and requires the Parliament actively to approve a decision, sometimes by simple majority, sometimes by a majority of its component members, before it may be adopted. It applies in a limited number of areas, all of which are of constitutional import and/or high political sensitivity:

- composition of [283] and method of election to[284] the Parliament itself;
- appointment of the Commission;[285]
- measures on enhanced cooperation,[286] the adoption of most (not all) bridging measures,[287] an increase of rights adhering to citizenship of the Union,[288] legislation to combat certain forms of discrimination[289] and use of the Treaty 'flexibility clause';[290]
- the Union's own resources[291] and the multiannual financial framework;[292]
- control of the assets of the European Coal and Steel Community;[293]
- the conclusion of certain international agreements;[294]

---

280   TFEU, art. 294(15).
281   Joint Declaration on practical arrangements for the codecision procedure [2007] OJ C145/5 (so predating Lisbon yet applicable still to the ordinary legislative procedure).
282   Most other languages suffered similar change, for example from *avis conforme* to *approbation*, but the German term (*Zustimmung*) remained unaltered.
283   TEU, art. 14(2), 2nd para.
284   TFEU, art. 223.
285   TEU, art. 17(4).
286   TFEU, art. 329(1).
287   TEU, art. 48(7).
288   TFEU, art. 25.
289   *Ibid.* art. 19(1).
290   *Ibid.* art. 352; see 6.52 below.
291   *Ibid.* art. 311.
292   *Ibid.* art. 312(2).
293   Protocol (No. 37) on the Financial Consequences of the Expiry of the ECSC Treaty and on the Research Fund for Coal and Steel, art. 2.
294   TFEU, art. 218(6). It is in this area that the Parliament frequently flexes its muscles.

- Union accession to the European Convention on Human Rights;[295]
- mutual recognition in criminal matters,[296] definition of criminal offences[297] and establishment and extension of powers of the European Public Prosecutor's Office;[298]
- determination of a risk or the existence of a breach of fundamental rights by a member state;[299]
- a decision to bypass an intergovernmental convention in Treaty amendment;[300]
- accession of new member states;[301] and
- secession of existing member states.[302]

(e)   Legal base

The Treaty article which empowers the institutions to legislate (the 'legal base', **3.66** or 'Treaty base', for the legislation) always specifies the procedure to be followed – normally, now, the ordinary legislative procedure. The choice of (correct) legal base is determined according to an objective, not a subjective, test. As it affects the Parliament's power to influence the outcome, the Parliament always examines draft legislation upon which it is consulted for 'the validity or the appropriateness' of the legal base,[303] and it is not uncommon to find the Parliament challenging legislation before the Court of Justice on the ground that it was adopted upon an incorrect legal base.[304]

E.   OTHER ASPECTS OF THE LEGISLATIVE PROCESS

1.   Role of national parliaments

There has long been concern in some quarters that the Community as was, and **3.67** *a fortiori* the Union as it was prior to Lisbon, failed to measure up to the principle of democracy which, according to the Treaties, is one which inspired

---

295   *Ibid.* art. 218(6)(a)(ii).
296   *Ibid.* art. 82(2)(d).
297   *Ibid.* art. 83(1).
298   *Ibid.* art. 86(1).
299   TEU, art. 7(1), (2).
300   *Ibid.* art. 48(3).
301   *Ibid.* art. 49.
302   *Ibid.* art. 50(2).
303   RP EP, rule 37.
304   E.g., Case C-295/90 *Parliament* v *Council* (Students) [1992] ECR I-4193; Cases C-164 and 165/97 *Parliament* v *Council* (Forest Pollution) [1999] ECR I-1139; Cases C-317 and 318/04 *Parliament* v *Council and Commission* (Passenger Name Records) [2006] ECR I-4721; Cases C-317 and 318/04 *Parliament* v *Council and Commission* [2006] ECR I-4721; Case C-166/07 *Parliament* v *Council* (International Fund for Ireland) [2009] ECR I-7135. On legal base see further 6.48–6.51 below.

the creation of the Union[305] and a value upon which it, and its functioning, is founded.[306] One response over the years is to increase the powers and influence of the Parliament, which has been incrementally in train since the 1980s. But another is an enhanced role in the Union machinery for national parliaments. This is what led to the creation in 1989 of the Conference of the Community and European Affairs Committees of the Parliaments of the EU, or COSAC (Conférence des organes spécialisés dans les affaires communautaires et européennes des Parlements de l'UE). COSAC comprises up to six members drawn from the European affairs committees of each of the various national parliaments plus six members from the European Parliament, meeting at least once every six months in the member state chairing the Council. Its purpose is to liaise amongst the (myriad committees of the) parliaments of the member states in the scrutiny of proposals for Union legislation. It operates now under Rules of Procedure agreed at the XXIX COSAC in Athens (to adopt its own style of designation) in May 2003.[307]

3.68 A protocol was added to the Treaties by Amsterdam which obliged the Commission to forward all consultation documents directly to the national parliaments (but not regional parliaments) of the member states and to make proposals for legislation available 'in good time' to national governments so that the latter 'may ensure that its own national parliament receives them as appropriate'.[308] It also expressly recognised COSAC, which was authorised to examine any legislative proposal in relation to the area of freedom, security and justice and make 'appropriate contributions' for the attention of the Parliament, the Council and the Commission, but they 'shall in no way bind national parliaments or prejudge their position'.[309]

3.69 An increased role for national parliaments was part of the Laeken agenda, and Lisbon provides them one general and three specific morsels. First, it incorporated a 'principle of representative democracy', and recognises the democratic legitimacy of the European Council, the Council and national parliaments thus:

    1. The functioning of the Union shall be founded on representative democracy.

    2. … Member States are represented in the European Council by their Heads of State

---

305 TEU, art. 21(1).

306 *Ibid.* arts 2, 10(1).

307 Published at [2008] OJ C27/6.

308 Protocol [annexed to the TEU (pre-Lisbon), the EC and Euratom Treaties] on the Role of National Parliaments in the European Union. The qualifications ('may ensure', 'as appropriate') suggested that this created no legal obligation for governments to comply.

309 Protocol (No. 13) on the Role of National Parliaments in the European Union, para. 7.

or Government and in the Council by their governments, themselves democratically accountable either to their national Parliaments, or to their citizens.[310]

It therefore increases incrementally the profile of national parliaments so that they may 'contribute actively to the good functioning of the Union'.[311] Commission consultation documents and draft legislative acts are required to be sent directly to the national parliaments (so bypassing national governments),[312] and except in urgent cases (for which due reasons must be given) the latter tabled before the Council only after a lapse of eight weeks.[313] A conference of Parliamentary Committees for Union Affairs (read COSAC, presumably with a new acronym) is to promote the exchange of information and best practice between national parliaments and the European Parliament, and may submit any contribution it deems appropriate for the attention of the Parliament, the Council and the Commission.[314]

Then, national parliaments enjoy substantial new powers in three particulars.[315] **3.70**

First, where a national parliament or a chamber of a national parliament (which **3.71** may, and perhaps must, consult regional parliaments)[316] takes the view that a legislative proposal is inconsistent with the principle of subsidiarity, it may transmit a 'reasoned opinion' to that effect to the presidents of the Parliament, the Council and the Commission, and they in turn are required to 'take account' of such opinion.[317] If, upon a basis of two votes per national parliament (where bicameral, one to each chamber), opinions transmitted represent at least one-third of all votes (or one-quarter in the area of freedom, security and justice), the Commission must 'review' (*réexaminer*) the proposal.[318] It is anticipated that COSAC will play an important liaison role here. Following review the Commission may maintain, amend or withdraw the proposal, but must give reasons for its decision.[319] This power has been christened the early warning mechanism or 'yellow card'. A slightly more robust version (the 'orange

---

310   TEU, art. 10.
311   *Ibid.* art. 12.
312   Protocol (No. 1) on the Role of National Parliaments in the European Union, arts 1, 2.
313   *Ibid.* art. 4.
314   *Ibid.* art. 10.
315   Protocol (No. 2) on the Application of the Principles of Subsidiarity and Proportionality.
316   *Ibid.* art. 6. It is unclear if there is an obligation to consult regional parliaments: cf. 'It will be for each national Parliament … to consult, where appropriate'; 'Il appartient à chaque parlement national … de consulter, le cas échéant'; but 'Dabei obliegt es dem jeweiligen nationalen Parlament … gegebenenfalls … zu konsultieren'. In any event there may be in place a national rule, convention and/or procedure which makes consultation obligatory.
317   *Ibid.* arts 6, 7(1).
318   *Ibid.* art. 7(2).
319   *Ibid.*

card') applies under the ordinary legislative procedure only, where objection is made by at least half the parliamantary votes; then, as with the yellow card, the Commission must review the proposal and may maintain, amend or withdraw it, but must add a reasoned opinion justifying why it believes it to comply with the principle of subsidiarity.[320] In all cases national parliaments must act quickly, within eight weeks from the date of transmission of the draft legislative act,[321] so it is not anticipated that bookings will occur frequently. First use of the yellow card occurred only in Spring 2012 in response to an (intrusive) draft regulation (the Monti II law) on a right to take collective industrial action.

3.72 Secondly, if an act is adopted in the face of the disapproval of a national parliament or of one of its chambers it appears that the parliament or chamber may instruct its government to raise a judicial challenge to the act, an option hitherto the exclusive preserve of (central) governments.[322]

3.73 Thirdly, national parliaments have a power of veto over the adoption of bridging measures: a proposal for any such measure in the context of the European Council's general bridging power[323] or the Council's bridging power in the sphere of family law[324] (but not others) must be notified to national parliaments at least six months prior to adoption, and should any one parliament make known its opposition within that period the measure cannot be adopted.

3.74 There is also the Union's first brush with direct democracy via the 'European citizens initiative', whereby a muster of not less (*sic*) than 1 million Union citizens, nationals of a 'significant number' of member states, may 'invite' the Commission to submit a proposal for legislation on matters on which they consider that action is required for purposes of implementing the Treaties.[325] The Commission need not do as invited but presumably has a duty properly to consider and give due weight to any such initiative. Detailed provisions, including the minimum number of member states from which the citizens must come, were to be set out in legislation.[326] A maiden outing was not auspicious: a petition organised by Greenpeace urging legislation banning the introduction in the Union of genetically engineered crops secured the requisite 1 million signatures and was submitted in late 2010 but ignored by the Commission (and

---

320   *Ibid.* art. 7(3).
321   *Ibid.* art. 6.
322   *Ibid.* art. 8, 1st para. The exact procedure is (intentionally?) unclear; see 5.74 below, n. 465.
323   TEU, art. 48(7); Protocol (No. 1), n. 312 above, art. 6.
324   TFEU, art. 81(3), 3rd para.
325   TEU, art. 11(4).
326   TFEU, art. 24, 1st para.

the Parliament) which viewed any such initiative a nullity pending the adoption of rules (they claimed) necessary to implement the procedure. It is by no mean clear that such legislation is necessary (put otherwise, whether article 11(4) TEU is directly effective) and that the Court of Justice, if asked, would agree. In any event implementing legislation is now adopted, and came into force on 1 April 2012.[327]

2. Common Foreign and Security Policy

The institutional framework which governs most of Union activity does not apply in the sphere of Common Foreign and Security Policy, which is subject to its own specific rules and procedures.[328] Within the framework of the CFSP the adoption of legislative acts is excluded.[329] Identification of the Union's strategic interests, determination of objectives and definition of general guidelines of the CFSP are for the European Council;[330] its framing (*élaboration*; *Gestaltung*) and the adoption of decisions necessary to define and implement it are for the Council.[331] The role in CFSP of the European Parliament and of the Commission is 'defined by the Treaties'[332] but they hardly bother: the Parliament is to be consulted regularly by the High Representative on the main aspects and the basic choices of the CFSP, its views are to be 'duly taken into consideration'[333] and it may put questions to the Council and the High Representative.[334] It has a foreign affairs (normally 'Afet', for *affaires étrangères*) committee; only five members of Afet (the 'special committee') are permitted (partial) access to (some) classified documents. The Commission is barely mentioned,[335] the jurisdiction of the Court of Justice almost wholly excluded.[336]

3.75

---

327 Regulation 211/2011 [2011] OJ L65/1; also Regulation 1179/2011 [2011] OJ L301/3, laying down technical specifications. The signatures must come from at least one-quarter of the member states and number in those member states at least the number of MEPs allocated to them multiplied by 750 (Regulation 211/2011, art. 7): so, at present (2012), 4,500 signatories from Malta, Luxembourg, Cyprus and Estonia, 6,000 from Slovenia, and so on up to 74,250 from Germany (Annex I). Annex I may be adjusted by the Commission in the light of changes in the composition of the Parliament.

328 TEU, art. 24(1).

329 *Ibid.* arts 24(1), 2nd para., 31(1).

330 *Ibid.* art. 26(1).

331 *Ibid.* art. 26(2).

332 *Ibid.* art. 24(1), 2nd para.

333 *Ibid.* art. 36.

334 *Ibid.* art. 36, 2nd para.

335 The Commission has a say in the staffing, organisation and functioning of the EEAS (art. 27(3)) and may support the High Representative in asking questions of the Council (art. 30(1)).

336 TEU, art. 24(1); TFEU, art. 275. See 5.29 below.

3.76 Under CFSP provisions both the European Council and the Council act by unanimity[337] except where the Council

- adopts a decision defining a Union action or position:
  - on the basis of a decision of the European Council relating to the Union's strategic interests and objectives; or
  - on a proposal presented by the High Representative at the specific request of the European Council;
- adopts a decision implementing any such decision;
- appoints a special representative in relation to a particular policy issue;
- adopts a procedural question;
- is directed to do so by the European Council (acting unanimously),

in which case it acts by qualified majority.[338] However even here a member of the Council may declare that, for vital and stated reasons of national policy, it intends to oppose the adoption of a decision, in which event no vote is taken; the High Representative then consults closely with that member state involved in order to reach an acceptable solution, failing which the Council may, by a qualified majority, request that the matter be referred to the European Council for a decision by unanimity.[339] No decision having military or defence implications may be taken by qualified majority.[340] In any circumstances a member state may abstain from a vote and qualify its abstention by making a formal declaration, in which case it is absolved from applying the decision, although it accepts the decision otherwise binds the Union and it must do nothing likely to conflict with or impede Union action based upon it.[341] If one-third of member states representing one-third of the population of the Union make such declaration a decision cannot be adopted.[342]

3.77 The High Representative for Foreign Affairs and Security Policy contributes to the development of the CFSP and ensures the implementation of decisions adopted in the field.[343] She chairs the Council when it sits in its Relex

---

337 TEU, art. 31(1).
338 *Ibid.* art. 31(2).
339 *Ibid.* art. 31(2), 2nd para.
340 *Ibid.* art. 31(4).
341 *Ibid.* art. 31(1), 2nd para.
342 *Ibid.*
343 *Ibid.* art. 27(1).

configuration[344] and represents the Union in CFSP matters.[345] In this she is assisted by the EEAS[346] and a Political and Security Committee.[347]

As for the Common Security and Defence Policy, decisions are taken by the **3.78** Council, acting (almost always) by unanimity on a proposal from the High Representative.[348] Where implementation of a task is entrusted to a group of member states they are to agree amongst themselves the management of the task in association with the High Representative.[349] Approval of the establishment of permanent structured cooperation is for the Council acting by qualified majority,[350] decisions thereafter for the Council comprising participating member states (by qualified majority thereof).[351] Participation in the work of the European Defence Agency and projects initiated by it is wholly voluntary.[352]

3. Euratom

The one surviving Community is the Atomic Energy Community, which has, **3.79** of course, always adhered to the Community method. The Euratom Treaty was amended by Lisbon and eviscerated of virtually all its existing provisions on the institutions, procedure and nature of legislation, the equivalent Union provisions being carried over and 'apply[ing] to' the Euratom Treaty.[353] The Atomic Energy Community is therefore governed by the institutions which (now) owe their existence to the Union Treaties, and the general institutional framework and the legislative procedures of the Union may be considered, for all practical purposes, to apply to it.

---

344   *Ibid.* See 3.40 above.
345   *Ibid.* art. 27(2).
346   *Ibid.* art. 27(3).
347   *Ibid.* art. 38.
348   *Ibid.* art. 42(4).
349   *Ibid.*
350   *Ibid.* art. 46(2).
351   *Ibid.* art. 46(3).
352   Implicit in TEU, art. 46(2); emphasised in the national declaration by Ireland 'associated with' its ratification of Lisbon, *Bulletin EU* 6–2009, 16.
353   Euratom Treaty, art. 106a(1).

4

OTHER BODIES

4.01 The Treaties, and some legislation adopted by Treaty authority, establish a host of other organs, agencies and bodies separate from the institutions which act with and/or alongside them in the political sphere. Some, particularly the 'financial institutions' (a widely used misnomer), wield formidable powers in their own right. They are as follows.

A. COURT OF AUDITORS

4.02 The first of these bodies is in fact an institution properly so-called. An independent Court of Auditors was first created in 1975 by a treaty amending various financial provisions of the EEC Treaty.[1] With Maastricht it was upgraded to the status of a full Community institution,[2] the fifth such and the first new 'institution' since the beginning. The Treaties require that it, like the Commission, consist of 'one national from each Member State',[3] who must be 'especially qualified' with experience of external audit bodies; it is appointed by

---

1 Treaty of 22 July 1975 amending certain financial provisions (the second budgetary treaty) [1977] OJ 1977 L359/1; see EEC Treaty, art. 206(1), now repealed.
2 EEC Treaty, art. 4.
3 TFEU, art. 285, 2nd para. (ex art. 247, 1st para. EC).

the Council from nominations ('proposals') from each member state, after consulting the Parliament, for a six-year term, renewable.[4]

The Court of Auditors is modelled upon the French *Cour des Comptes*. But it is **4.03** not a court, nor, as in the case with the equivalent bodies in some member states, are its members judges.[5] Its task is to carry out the audit.[6] To this end it is to 'examine the accounts of all revenue and expenditure of the Union'[7] and those of 'all bodies, offices or agencies set up by the Union',[8] and, in particular, 'examine whether all revenue has been received and all expenditure incurred in a lawful and regular manner and whether the financial management has been sound'.[9] It is thus sometimes characterised as the 'financial conscience' of the Union. The audit is carried out in liaison with national audit bodies or government departments.[10] The Court of Auditors is required to publish an annual report.[11] Its prominence has increased with allegations of financial mismanagement of Community and Union expenditure, and it has delivered a number of stinging rebukes to the responsible authorities. It adopts its Rules of Procedure (published for the first time in 2002)[12] and has its seat in Luxembourg.

B. 'FINANCIAL INSTITUTIONS'

1. European Central Bank

The European Central Bank (ECB) came into being in 1998 and assumed its **4.04** powers on 1 January 1999, the beginning of the third stage of economic and monetary union.[13] It replaced the European Monetary Institute (EMI), which was established in January 1994,[14] the beginning of the second stage, and assisted in progress towards the third stage, and which was liquidated at its commencement. It was elevated formally to the status of an institution by

---

4 TFEU, art. 286(2).
5 So, for example, the Greek Ελεγκτικό Συνέδριο is a court within the meaning of TFEU, art. 267 competent to seek preliminary rulings from the Court of Justice; Case C-443/93 *Vougioukas* v *Idryma Koinonikon Asfalisseon* [1995] ECR I-4033.
6 TFEU, art. 285.
7 *Ibid.* art. 287(1).
8 *Ibid.*
9 *Ibid.* art. 287(2).
10 *Ibid.* art. 287(3).
11 *Ibid.* art. 287(4).
12 See now [2010] OJ L103/1.
13 EC Treaty, arts 8 and 105–7 and Protocol (No. 4) on the European System of Central Banks and of the European Central Bank ('ESCB/ECB Statute'). As to EMU, see… below.
14 See EC Treaty, art. 117 and Protocol [annexed to the EC Treaty] on the Statute of the European Monetary Institute.

Lisbon.[15] The ECB has legal personality[16] and is completely independent in the performance of its tasks.[17] It is governed by an Executive Board, comprising six members (including president and vice-president) appointed by the common accord of the governments of the member states participating in EMU[18] for an eight-year non-renewable term,[19] and a Governing Council, comprising the Executive Board and the governors of each of the participating national central banks.[20] The president of the Council and a member of the Commission participate, but do not vote, in meetings of the Governing Council,[21] and the president of the ECB participates, but does not vote, in Council meetings at which Bank matters are discussed.[22] The ECB adopts its own Rules of Procedure.[23] Its seat is Frankfurt (Main).

4.05 The Treaties also established the European System of Central Banks (ESCB, or 'Eurosystem').[24] The ESCB is composed of the ECB and the national central banks and governed by the decision-making bodies of the ECB.[25] Its primary objective is the maintenance of price stability, to which end it defines and implements Union monetary policy, conducts foreign exchange operations, holds and manages foreign reserves and promotes the smooth operation of payments systems.[26]

4.06 The ECB has an advisory role in, and must be consulted by the Council before the adoption of, any Union legislation 'in its fields of competence';[27] it must also be consulted by national authorities over any relevant draft national legislation.[28] But, almost uniquely under the Treaties, it may also adopt legislation

---

15 TEU, art. 13.
16 TFEU, art. 282(3) (ex art. 107(2) EC); ESCB/ECB Statute, art. 9.
17 TFEU, art. 130 (ex art. 108 EC); ESCB/ECB Statute, art. 7.
18 See 14.10 below.
19 TFEU, art. 283 (ex art. 112 EC) and ESCB/ECB Statute, art. 11. The term of appointment is intended to promote the independence from political interference of the members of the Board.
20 TFEU, art. 283 and ESCB/ECB Statute, art. 10. The Governing Council therefore grows in size with each additional member state adopting the euro. At present each member of the Governing Council has one vote (ESCS/ECB Statute, art. 10.2). The Bank was to adopt an extraordinarily complex voting system involving a rotation of voting rights amongst the bank governors upon its membership exceeding 21 (also art. 10.2). This occurred in January 2009 with the adoption of the euro by Slovakia (see 14.18 below), but the new system has been put off until the number of governors in the Council exceeds 18, unlikely to happen before 2014; Decision 2009/5 [2009] OJ L3/4.
21 TFEU, art. 284(1) (ex art. 113(1) EC).
22 TFEU, art. 284(2).
23 Decision 2004/257 [2004] OJ L80/33. See also the Rules of Procedure of the Governing Council of the ECB [2004] OJ L230/61.
24 TFEU, arts 282 and 127–30 (ex arts 8 and 105–8 EC) and ESCB/ECB Statute.
25 TFEU, art. 129(1), (3); ESCB/ECB Statute, art. 8.
26 TFEU, art. 127; ESCB/ECB Statute, arts 2, 3.
27 TFEU, art. 127(4).
28 *Ibid.*

autonomously. In order to discharge the tasks assigned to it by the ESCB/ECB Statute, the ECB may adopt any appropriate legislative measure except a Directive.[29] It also enjoys powers of enforcement (over national central banks)[30] and financial sanction (over private persons)[31] which fail in their obligations under the Statute or under ECB legislation. All of these measures are subject to review before the Court of Justice.[32]

2. Economic and Financial Committee

At the beginning of the third stage of economic and monetary union (1 January **4.07** 1999) the Economic and Financial Committee came into being (replacing the Monetary Committee which had preceded it during the second stage).[33] It consists of 58 members, two each appointed by the member states (drawn from senior Ecofin civil servants or the national central banks), the Commission and the European Central Bank. It has advisory status, and delivers opinions to and at the request of the Commission and/or Council in the economic and financial sphere (especially on questions of budget deficits), reviews and reports upon the economic situation in the member states, assists the Council in the discharge of its economic and monetary duties, examines and reports upon the situation within the Union on payments and capital movements, and reviews and reports upon the economic and monetary policies of member states not participating in EMU.

3. European Investment Bank

The EEC Treaty established a European Investment Bank (EIB) with legal **4.08** personality.[34] Its task is 'to contribute by having recourse to the capital market and utilising its own resources, to the balanced and steady development of the internal market in the interest of the Union'. For this purpose the Bank 'shall, operating on a non-profit making basis, grant loans and give guarantees which facilitate the financing of …: (a) projects for developing less-developed regions; (b) projects for modernising or converting undertakings or for developing fresh activities; (c) projects of common interest to several Member States'.[35] Projects in the latter two categories must be 'of such size or nature that they cannot be entirely financed by the various means available in the individual Member

---

29 TFEU, art. 132(1) (ex art. 110(1) EC) and ESCB/ECB Statute, art. 34.
30 TFEU, art. 271(d) (ex art. 237(d) EC); ESCB/ECB Statute, art. 35.5 and 35.6.
31 TFEU, art. 132(3) (ex art. 110(3) EC); ESCB/ECB Statute, art. 34.3.
32 TFEU, art. 258 (ex art. 230 EC) and ESCB/ECB Statute, art. 35.1.
33 TFEU, art. 134 (ex art. 114(2) EC); established by Decision 98/743 [1998] OJ L358/109.
34 EEC Treaty, art. 129 (now TFEU, art. 308).
35 TFEU, art. 309 (ex art. 267 EC).

States'.[36] The Statute of the Bank establishes the system of direction and management and lays down more detailed rules as to the ways in which loan and guarantee operations may be carried out.[37] The Board of Directors of the Bank is competent to raise enforcement proceedings before the Court of Justice, analogous to article 258 proceedings, where member states fail in their obligations under the EIB Statute.[38] It has never happened. The seat of the EIB is Luxembourg.

4. European Investment Fund

4.09 In 1994 a European Investment Fund was created by the Board of Governors of the EIB.[39] The Fund has legal personality and financial autonomy. The founder members of the Fund are the European Community (represented by the Commission), the EIB and a number of financial institutions. Its task is to support financially the development of trans-European networks and small and medium-sized enterprises. The seat of the Fund is Luxembourg.

5. Supervisory authorities

4.10 In the wake of the 2008 (and ongoing) financial crisis the Union adopted a new 'European financial supervisory architecture', consisting in the creation out of existing advisory committees of three European Supervisory Authorities (ESAs): the European Supervisory Authority (European Banking Authority),[40] the European Supervisory Authority (European Insurance and Occupational Pensions Authority)[41] and the European Supervisory Authority (European Securities and Markets Authority).[42] Their seats are, respectively, London, Frankfurt (Main) and Paris.[43] Each is a Union body with legal personality.[44] Together with an ESA Joint Committee,[45] the European Systemic Risk Board (ESRB) (based in Frankfurt)[46] and the national financial supervisory authorities, they form a European System of Financial Supervisors (ESFS) and so contribute to a more efficient, integrated and sustainable

---

36 *Ibid.*
37 Protocol (No. 5) on the Statute of the European Investment Bank.
38 TFEU, art. 271 (ex art. 237 EC).
39 Statute of the European Investment Fund [1994] OJ L173/1. There may be some dispute as to the original legality of this body; see 2.64 above, n. 279 and accompanying text.
40 Regulation 1093/2010 [2010] OJ L331/12.
41 Regulation 1094/2010 [2010] OJ L331/48.
42 Regulation 1095/2010 [2010] OJ L331/84.
43 Regulation 1093/2010, art. 7; Regulation 1094/2010, art. 7; Regulation 1095/2010, art. 7.
44 Regulation 1093/2010, art. 5; Regulation 1094/2010, art. 5; Regulation 1095/2010, art. 5.
45 Regulation 1093/201, art. 54; Regulation 1094/2010, art. 54; Regulation 1095/2010, art. 54.
46 Regulation 1092/2010 [2010] OJ L331/1.

European system of supervision of the financial sectors. The Treaty base for the measures is article 114 TFEU which deals with harmonisation of national law,[47] and this may well lead to a constitutional challenge, of improper or inadequate legal authority, before the Court of Justice.

6. European Stability Mechanism

In 2011 the eurozone member states entered into a treaty for the creation of the **4.11** European Stability Mechanism (ESM),[48] to raise and mobilise funding and provide financial assistance to ESM members experiencing or threatened by severe financial problems. Membership consists of the contracting parties (the 17 eurozone member states) and is open to any other member state as and when it adopts the euro as its currency.[49] The ESM will have legal personality and legal capacity,[50] its own Board of Governors and Board of Directors[51] and its own staff.[52] Its seat will be Luxembourg.[53] Ratification and so entry into force of the treaty is anticipated (optimistically) by the end of 2012.[54]

C. ADVISORY BODIES

The EEC Treaty established at the start an Economic and Social Committee **4.12** with advisory status, the Maastricht Treaty created a Committee of the Regions, which came into being in 1994. Since Lisbon they are called the 'advisory bodies' of the Union.[55]

1. Economic and Social Committee

The Economic and Social Committee existed from the beginning with advisory **4.13** status, to 'assist' the Council and Commission[56] (and now also the Parliament).[57] Styling itself now the European Economic and Social Committee, it consists of 'representatives of organisations of employers, of the employed, and

---

47 See 10.68–10.77 below.
48 Treaty of 11 July 2011 establishing the European Stability Mechanism.
49 *Ibid.* arts 1, 2, 39; or technically when the Council acts to abrogate its derogation from adopting the euro; see 14.15 below.
50 *Ibid.* art. 27.
51 *Ibid.* art. 4.
52 *Ibid.* art. 28.
53 *Ibid.* art. 26.
54 *Ibid.* arts 42–3. See 14.25 below, n. 129.
55 TEU, art. 13(4); TFEU, art. 300.
56 EC Treaty, arts 7(2) and 257, 1st para.
57 TFEU, art. 300(1).

of other parties representative of civil society, notably in socio-economic, civic, professional and cultural areas'.[58] The Committee must be consulted by the Council before certain legislative acts are adopted. It has adopted its own Rules of Procedure[59] and has its own secretariat, chamber and offices in Brussels. The composition of the Committee is to be fixed by the Council by unanimity,[60] capped at 350,[61] for a five-year term of office.[62] Pending such decision, it consists of the previously sitting 344 members (to be increased 'temporarily' by nine upon Croatian accession),[63] drawn from the member states by fixed allocation[64] and, in practice, divided into three groups: Group I representing employers, Group II employees and Group III others.

2. Committee of the Regions

4.14 The Maastricht Treaty provided for the Committee of the Regions, which came into being in 1994.[65] Like the Economic and Social Committee, it has advisory status and assists the Pariament, the Council and the Commission.[66] Its composition, future and present, and term of office is as that of the Economic and Social Committee.[67] But the membership is drawn, by fixed allocation, from 'representatives of regional or local bodies who either hold a regional or local authority electoral mandate or are politically accountable to an elected assembly'.[68] It is required to be consulted by the Council before certain legislative acts are adopted, principally those which have an impact upon regional constitutional competences in various of the federal or devolved member states or upon local government.[69] It must also be informed each time an opinion is sought from the Economic and Social Committee and may issue an opinion if it considers that the proposal has regional implications.[70] It has

---

58 *Ibid.* art. 300(2). Prior to Lisbon it had a more common touch, consisting of 'representatives of the various economic and social components of organised civil society, and in particular representatives of producers, farmers, carriers, workers, dealers, craftsmen, professional occupations, consumers and the general interest'; EC Treaty, art. 257, 2nd para.
59 Consolidated in [2007] OJ L93/1.
60 TFEU, art. 301.
61 *Ibid.*
62 *Ibid.* art. 302.
63 2011 Act of Accession, art. 23.
64 Protocol (No. 36) on Transitional Provisions.
65 Decision 94/65 [1994] OJ L31/29.
66 TFEU, art. 300(1).
67 *Ibid.* art. 305.
68 *Ibid.* art. 300(3). Whether the national proposals for membership come from central authorities or directly from the regions is a matter for the member states.
69 For example, proposals in the fields of employment (TFEU, arts 148(2), 149), education (art. 165(4)), culture (art. 167(5)), public health (art. 168), trans-European networks (art. 172) and economic and social cohesion (arts 175, 177, 178). On all of these see Chap. 14 below.
70 TFEU, art. 307, 3rd para.

adopted its own Rules of Procedure[71] and its seat is in Brussels, sharing the same infrastructure as the Economic and Social Committee.[72] The creation of the Committee was a (modest) step towards bringing regional influence to bear upon the Community, now Union, legislative machinery.

D. EUROPEAN EXTERNAL ACTION SERVICE

The European External Action Service (EEAS) was created in 2010 following **4.15** the entry into force of the Lisbon Treaty which provided for it.[73] It is a 'functionally autonomous body' of the Union, distinct from the Commission and the general secretariat of the Council,[74] which 'assists'[75] and 'supports'[76] the High Representative for Foreign and Security Policy in her various tasks and operates under her authority.[77] It is made up of (*composé de*) a central administration, organised in Directorates-General and managed by an Executive Secretary-General, and the Union's external delegations (each under a head of delegation);[78] the 130+ external delegations 'represent the Union', are responsible to the High Representative, and cooperate closely with member states' diplomatic and consular missions.[79] A number of Directorates, and their functions, within the Commission (much of D-G External Relations, 'Relex') and the general-secretariat of the Council, previously responsible for the Union's foreign and security policy, were transferred to the EEAS upon its creation.[80] EEAS officials, reflecting adequate geographical and gender balance and comprising a meaningful presence of nationals from all member states,[81] include both its own officials, drawn in the first instance from existing Commission and Council *fonctionnaires*, and staff (about one-third of its strength) seconded from the national diplomatic services ('temporary agents').[82] As at January 2012 it has a staff of some 3,600, of which 40 per cent are in Brussels, 60 per cent in Union delegations abroad; when fully up and running (in 2012/13) it is expected to field a complement of some 6,000. Attached to the the EEAS is a

---

71 [2010] OJ L6/14.
72 See Protocol [annexed to the TEU (pre-Lisbon)] on the Economic and Social Committee and the Committee of the Regions.
73 TEU, art. 27(3); Decision 2010/427 [2010] OJ L201/30.
74 Decision 2010/427, art. 1(2).
75 TEU, art. 27(3).
76 Decision 2010/427, art. 2(1).
77 *Ibid.* art. 1(3).
78 *Ibid.* arts 1(4), 4, 5.
79 TFEU, art. 221.
80 Decision 2010/427, Annex I.
81 *Ibid.* art. 6(6).
82 TEU, art. 27(3); Decision 2010/427, art. 6.

Joint Situation Centre (SitCen), a department responsible to the High Representative, which provides the Council with 'high quality' information and analysis in matters of public security and liaises with the security services of the member states. The EEAS has the legal capacity necessary to perform its tasks and attain its objectives.[83]

E. OTHER BODIES

1. European Anti-Fraud Office (OLAF)

4.16 In 1999 the Commission created a European Anti-Fraud Office, or OLAF (*Office de lutte antifraude*).[84] Its purpose is to combat fraud, corruption and any other illegal activity which adversely affects the Union's financial interests. Based in Brussels, it operates under its own Director, has its own staff, and is assisted by a surveillance committee. It is kept very, very busy. And, it should be said, it has not shown itself to be wholly adept, having become embroiled in an embarrassing political scandal, *l'affaire Tillack*,[85] ill-befitting a body whose purpose is to root out impropriety.

2. Social Protection Committee

4.17 The Treaties, post-Nice, authorise the Council to create a Social Protection Committee with advisory status 'to promote cooperation on social protection

---

83 Decision 2010/427, art. 1(2).
84 Decision 1999/352 [1999] OJ L136/20.
85 In 2004 a German journalist (Mr Tillack) sought to challenge the Commission and OLAF following publication by the latter of allegations of his personal corruption (payment of a bribe to an OLAF official in exchange for confidential documents relating to his investigations into corruption in the statistical office) for which it could muster no proof, which led to his arrest and a raid and removal of documents from his private office by the Belgian police; Mr Tillack was not charged with any offence and eventually (in 2009) the *Procureur du Roi* abandoned all proceedings against him. His attempt to challenge the Commission before the Court of First Instance was inadmissible and his claim for damages unfounded: Case T-193/04 *Tillack* v *Commission* [2006] ECR II-3995. OLAF was censured by the Ombudsman for its conduct in the affair (Special Report following the draft recommendation to OLAF in complaint 2485/2004/GG, 12 May 2005), and the Court of Human Rights found searches carried out at Mr Tillack's home to be a violation of art. 10 of the European Convention (freedom of expression) and awarded him damages of €10,000 and costs; *Tillack* v *Belgium* (Application no. 20477/05), judgment of 27 November 2007, not yet reported. No apology has been forthcoming. In two other cases OLAF (a) leaked confidential information in the course of an inquiry into impropriety by a member of the Court of Auditors and (b) referred allegations of fraudulent invalidity claims from staff at the Joint Research Centre (in Ispra) to the Italian prosecuting authorities in a manner which so blatantly infringed, respectively, her right to confidentiality of personal data and their rights of defence as to justify the award of damages; Case T-259/03 *Nikolaou* v *Commmission* [2007] ECR II-99* and Cases F-5 and 7/05 *Violetti and Schmit* v *Commission*, judgment of 28 April 2009, not yet reported (but the latter set aside on admissibility grounds, Case T-261/09P *Commission* v *Violetti and Schmit*, judgment of 20 May 2010, not yet reported).

policies between Member States and with the Commission';[86] in fact the Committee was established by general Council powers in 2000[87] and re-established under specific Treaty authority, its task broadened in light of enlargement, in 2004.[88] The Committee monitors the social situation and social protection policies of the member states, promotes exchanges of information and good practice, and undertakes work generally within the field at the request of the Council or Commission or on its own initiative. It works closely with the Employment Committee established in 2000[89] and the Economic Policy Committee established in 1974.[90] It consists (as do the Employment Committee and the Economic Policy Committee) of two members appointed by each member state and two by the Commission; its secretariat is provided by the Commission.

3. European Personnel Selection Office (EPSO)

In order to promote, and to be seen to promote, fairness and transparency in recruitment to the services of the institutions, in 2002 a joint decision of the Parliament, the Council, the Commission, the Court of Justice, the Court of Auditors, the Economic and Social Committee, the Committee of the Regions and the Ombudsman created the European Personnel Selection Office (EPSO; 'the Office').[91] It is an 'interinstitutional body' charged with the selection, appointment and promotion of staff employed by each and all of them, exercising the 'powers of selection' under the Staff Regulations and acting in effect as their employment agent as well as that for 'any body, office or agency established by or in accordance with the Treaties which has delegated its powers to, or called on the services of, the Office'.[92] All appointments now run the gauntlet of competitions (*concours*) organised by EPSO, except that an institution may hold its own competition 'in exceptional cases … to meet specific needs for highly qualified staff' and with EPSO's consent.[93] Candidates satisfying the criteria set by EPSO are then entered on a 'reserve list', from which is drawn the successful candidate(s) appointed by the appropriate authorities of each institution.

4.18

---

86 TFEU, art. 160 (ex art. 144 EC).
87 Decision 2000/436 [2000] OJ L172/26.
88 Decision 2004/689 [2000] OJ L314/8 (replacing Decision 2000/436).
89 Decision 2000/98 [2000] OJ L29/21.
90 Decision 74/122 [1974] OJ L63/21; revised 'Statutes' in Decision 2000/604 [2000] OJ L257/28.
91 Decision 2002/620 [2002] OJ L197/53.
92 *Ibid.* art. 2(3).
93 *Ibid.* art. 2(1).

4.19 A 2010 judgment of the Civil Service Tribunal annulling a Commission decision not to appoint a candidate to a reserve list[94] suggests that EPSO's *concours* procedures are materially flawed. If not set aside on appeal[95] the judgment may have serious repercussions not only for candidates not admitted to the *concours* but for who did not gain employment with the institutions in accordance with those procedures, and those who did.

4.20 In 2005 a European Administrative School ('the School') was established, 'attached administratively' to EPSO.[96] Its task is the implementation of professional training 'activities' for all signatory institutions and bodies with a view to greater cooperation in training and staffing amongst them.

4. European Institute of Innovation and Technology

4.21 The European Institute of Innovation and Technology (EIT) was created in 2008 as a Community 'body'.[97] Its task is the promotion and integration of higher education, research and innovation 'of the highest standards' across the Union.[98] Its has its seat in Budapest.

5. Agencies

4.22 A number of 'agencies' have been created by the Council. They are distinct from the institutions and have their own legal personality, but are governed by and subject to the general principles which adhere to Union public law. Their purpose is the accomplishment of specific technical, scientific or managerial tasks as set out in their various founding regulations. They are thus part of a strategy of a wider delegatation of responsibility for Union activities, but there are concerns they may afford considerable opportunity for fraud and corruption.[99] At present the agencies (in chronological order of their creation, and with their seats) are:

- European Centre for the Development of Vocational Training (Thessaloniki);
- European Foundation for the Improvement of Living Conditions (Dublin);
- European Environment Agency (Copenhagen);

---

94   Case F-35/08 *Pachtitis* v *Commission*, judgment of 15 June 2010, not yet reported.
95   Case T-361/10P *Commission* v *Pachtitis*, pending.
96   Decision 2005/118 [2005] OJ L37/14.
97   Regulation 294/2008 [2008] OJ L97/1.
98   *Ibid.* art. 3.
99   See OLAF, *Annual Report 2010*, pp. 34–5.

- European Medicines Agency (London);[100]
- Office for Harmonisation in the Internal Market (Trade Marks and Designs) (Alicante);
- European Training Foundation (Turin);
- European Monitoring Centre for Drugs and Drug Addiction (Lisbon);
- Community Plant Variety Office (Angers);
- European Agency for Safety and Health at Work (Bilbao);
- Translation Centre for the Bodies of the European Union (Luxembourg);
- European Agency for Reconstruction (Thessaloniki);
- European Food Safety Authority (Parma);
- European Maritime Safety Agency (Lisbon);
- European Aviation Safety Agency (Cologne);
- European Railway Agency (Lille-Valenciennes);
- European Network and Information Security Agency (Heraklion);[101]
- European Centre for Disease Prevention and Control (Stockholm);
- European Chemicals Agency (Helsinki);
- European Agency for the Management of Operational Cooperation at the External Borders ('Frontex') (Warsaw);
- Community Fisheries Control Agency (Vigo);
- European GNSS Agency (Prague);[102]
- European Institute for Gender Equality (Vilnius);
- European Union Agency for Fundamental Rights (Vienna);[103]
- European Asylum Support Office (Valetta Harbour);
- Agency for the Cooperation of Energy Regulators (Ljubljana); and
- European Agency for the Management of Large-Scale IT Systems in the Area of Freedom, Security and Justice (Tallinn).

In 2002 the Council adopted a 'statute'[104] authorising the Commission to create **4.23** 'executive agencies', a particular species of agency to which the Commission delegates ('externalises') management of certain Union programmes. To date there are six executive agencies:

- Executive Agency for Competitiveness and Innovation (Brussels);[105]
- Education, Audiovisual and Culture Executive Agency (Brussels);

---

100 Prior to 2004 the European Agency for Evaluation of Medicinal Products; retained the acronym EMEA until 2009, now the EMA.
101 The Agency is (at present) scheduled to fold in September 2013, at which point it is expected to re-emerge in significantly different form, now the subject of debate.
102 Prior to 2010 the European GNSS [for Global Navigation Satellite System] Supervisory Authority.
103 The Fundamental Rights Agency succeeded a previous agency, the European Monitoring Centre on Racism and Xenophobia, created in 1997, which was wound down with the creation of the FRA in 2007.
104 Regulation 58/2003 [2003] OJ L11/1.
105 Replacing the Intelligent Energy Executive Agency in 2007.

- Executive Agency for Health and Consumers (Luxembourg);[106]
- European Research Council Executive Agency (Brussels);
- Trans-European Transport Network Executive Agency (Brussels); and
- Research Executive Agency (Brussels).

6. European Union bodies

4.24 A number of bodies were set up by or under Titles V and VI of the pre-Lisbon Treaty on European Union in order to assist in the coordination of second and third pillar matters. They are now undergoing a forced marriage into the Union, in its general capacity or under the Common Foreign and Security Policy (CFSP) provisions, as appropriate. Key amongst them are the following.

(a) CFSP bodies

(i) Political and Security Committee

4.25 The Political and Security Committee grew out of the Political Committee established by the Maastricht Treaty[107] (and which itself grew out of informal EPC practice predating Maastricht). It was envisaged by the Treaty of Nice,[108] but was established by general Council powers in 2001, two years before Nice entered into force[109] and is now written into the Treaties.[110] Composed of representatives of the member states at senior/ambassadorial level within the framework of their permanent representatives,[111] its task is to monitor the international situation in the areas falling within CFSP, deliver opinions to the Council in any such area at the request of the Council or upon its own initiative, and, under the authority and direction of the Council and of the High Representative, exercise political control and strategic direction of crisis management (i.e., military) operations. It therefore deals with and oversees CFSP matters on a day-to-day basis. It is, and is designed to be, the 'linchpin' of CFSP.[112]

(ii) Military Committee

4.26 At the same time the Council created the Military Committee (EUMC).[113] It is 'established within the Council', and comprises the Chiefs of Defence

---

106 Replacing the Executive Agency for the Public Health Programme in 2008.
107 TEU (pre-Amsterdam), art. J.8(5).
108 TEU (pre-Lisbon), art. 25 (as amended by Nice).
109 Decision 2001/78/CFSP [2001] OJ L27/1.
110 TEU, art. 38.
111 Decision 2000/143/CFSP [2000] OJ L49/1, art. 1.
112 Decision 2001/78/CFSP, Annex.
113 Decision 2001/79/CFSP [2001] OJ L27/4.

(CHODs) of each member state represented by their military representatives, but it meets at the level of CHODs as and when necessary. It is the forum for military consultation and cooperation amongst the member states in the fields of conflict prevention and crisis management, and provides, by consensus, the Political and Security Committee with military advice and recommendations upon all military matters of Union concern. It is assisted in terms of advice, planning and implementation by the Military Staff (EUMS).

(iii)   CFSP agencies

There were established by Council 'joint actions'[114] three agencies under CFSP: **4.27** the European Institute for Security Studies,[115] based in Paris; the European Union Satellite Centre,[116] based in Torrejón de Ardoz; and the European Defence Agency,[117] based (its 'headquarters') in Brussels; the profile of the Defence Agency was beefed up very considerably by Lisbon with a view to assisting in the improvement of military capabilities as part of the Common Security and Defence Policy.[118] There is also a European Security and Defence College (ESDC),[119] a network for the coordination and promotion of training of both civilian and military personnel in the field of security and defence policy (ESDP) as an essential component of CFSP.

(b)   Erstwhile JHA bodies

(i)   JHA Coordinating Committee

The TEU (pre-Lisbon) itself created a Coordinating Committee (or 'Article 36 **4.28** Committee', presumably now the 'Article 71 Committee') consisting of senior national officials to assist the Council in all deliberations in third pillar matters.[120] It is essentially a JHA equivalent of the Political and Security Committee, except that it has no responsibility for monitoring the implementation of agreed measures.

(ii)   European Police Office (Europol)

Europol was envisaged in Maastricht[121] as a means of ensuring the effectiveness **4.29** of cooperation amongst competent national authorities in matters of serious international organised crime. It was created by convention in 1995[122] and,

---

114   As to joint actions see 6.91 below.
115   Joint Action 2001/554/CFSP [2001] OJ L200/1.
116   Joint Action 2001/555/CFSP [2001] OJ L200/5.
117   Joint Action 2004/551/CFSP [2004] OJ L245/17; replaced by Decision 2011/411 [2011] OJ L183/16.
118   TEU, arts 42(3) and 45; Decision 411/2011.
119   Joint Action 2008/550/CFSP [2008] OJ L176/20.
120   TFEU, art. 71 (ex TEU (pre-Lisbon), art. 36).
121   TEU (pre-Lisbon), art. 29; see now TFEU, art. 88.
122   Convention on the Establishment of a European Police Office (Europol Convention) [1995] OJ C316/2.

following ratification by the member states, has been fully in operation since July 1999. In 2009 its constituent base was readopted in the form of a Council (JHA) decision[123] and with Lisbon it was *communautairised* and its control assumed by the Union institutions.[124] It has its seat in the Hague.

(iii)   European Police College (CEPOL)

4.30 In 2000 the Council established the European Police College, or CEPOL,[125] with the objective of training senior police officers and encouraging knowledge of and cooperation amongst their various national (and international) activities through establishment of a network of national training institutes. It is run by a governing board comprising the directors of the various national institutes, which is assisted by a permanent secretariat. It has its seat in Bramshill (England). It has been criticised roundly for its sloppy financial accounting.

(iv)   European Judicial Cooperation Unit (Eurojust)

4.31 The Treaty of Nice gave formal institutional recognition to the European Judicial Cooperation Unit, or 'Eurojust',[126] but Eurojust was established by the Council in 2002,[127] before Nice entered into force, 'with a view to reinforcing the fight against serious crime'. It is a 'body' (*organe*) of the European Union, with legal personality,[128] and comprises one member from each member state who is a prosecutor, a judge or a police officer 'of equivalent competence'.[129] Its objective is improved coordination and cooperation between the competent authorities of the member states in the investigation and prosecution of serious, and especially organised, crime.[130] Its seat is in the Hague.

4.32 In 1998 the Council set up the European Judicial Network,[131] comprising the central authorities of each member state responsible for international judicial cooperation and the judicial or other competent authorities with specific responsibilities for international cooperation.[132] The member states are to establish 'contact points' through which the Network operates, with a view to facilitating judicial cooperation between them, particularly in action to combat forms of serious crime.[133] They are to provide judicial authorities and other

---

123   Decision 2009/371/JHA [2009] OJ L121/37 ('Europol Decision').
124   TFEU, art. 88.
125   Decision 2000/820/JHA [2000] OJ L336/1; replaced by Decision 2005/681/JHA [2005] OJ L256/63.
126   TEU (pre-Lisbon), art. 29, 2nd para, 2nd indent; see now TFEU, art. 85.
127   Decision 2002/187/JHA [2002] OJ L63/1.
128   *Ibid.* art. 1.
129   *Ibid.* art. 2(1).
130   *Ibid.* art. 3.
131   Joint Action 98/428 [1998] OJ L191/4; now replaced by Decision 2008/976/JHA [2008] OJ L348/130.
132   Decision 2008/976, art. 2(1).
133   *Ibid.* art. 4(1).

competent authorities in their own member state the contact points in other member states, and the judicial authorities there with the legal and practical information necessary to enable them to prepare an effective request for judicial cooperation or to improve judicial cooperation in general.[134] The European Judicial Network and Eurojust are to maintain 'privileged relations' with each other, based on consultation and complementarity, with a view to ensuring efficient cooperation.[135]

7. Euratom organs

The Euratom Treaty establishes a number of specialist bodies. There are two agencies, a 'Supply Agency' with right of option on, and important administrative powers in, the supply of ores, source materials and special fissile materials[136] and the 'Fusion for Energy', or European Joint Undertaking for ITER and the Development of Fusion Energy, set up in 2007 to work with industry and research organisations on the development and manufacture of hi-tech components for the ITER (international thermonuclear experimental reactor) fusion project.[137] Then, there are an Arbitration Committee competent to award non-exclusive licences in respect of intellectual property rights in the nuclear sphere;[138] a Scientific and Technical Committee, of at present 39 members, attached to the Commission but appointed by the Council,[139] which advises the Commission upon all nuclear issues, across the range of Euratom activities and beyond, for example on radiation protection; and a High Level Group on Nuclear Safety and Waste Management, of 28 members (one from each member state, one from the Commission), which advises and assists the Commission on matters of the safety of nuclear installations and of spent fuel and radioactive waste.[140]

4.33

---

134   *Ibid.* art. 4(2).
135   *Ibid.* art. 10.
136   Euratom Treaty, arts 52–6; for the governing 'Statutes' see Decision 2008/114 [2008] OJ L41/15, Annex.
137   Decision 2007/198 [2007] OJ L90/58. The members are the member states plus Switzerland. Its seat is in Barcelona.
138   Euratom Treaty, arts 17–23.
139   *Ibid.* art. 134(2).
140   Decision 2007/530 [2007] OJ L195/44.

5

THE COURT OF JUSTICE

A. THE COURT

1. Treaty Provisions on the Court of Justice

Each of the Community Treaties established a 'Court of Justice', but, like the **5.01** Parliament, the three were fused into a single Court which served all three Communities from the outset.[1] It is now a creation of the Treaty on European Union,[2] the relevant provisions carried over to apply also to the Atomic Energy Community.[3] The jurisdiction of the Court is, as from the beginning, simply to 'ensure that in the interpretation and application of the Treaties the law is observed'.[4] It is not, however, a court of general jurisdiction. The nature and extent of its jurisdiction, and the conditions for its exercise, are laid down in the Treaties, more detailed provisions found in the Statute of the Court, various supplementary conventions, regulations and decisions, rules of procedure, supplementary rules and a number of practice directions adopted by the Court. The most relevant of these are gathered together in *Selected Instruments relating to the Organisation, Jurisdiction and Procedure of the Court*, published occasionally by the Court (most recently in an out-of-date 1999 edition), and all of them are available, updated, from its website. The Court has its seat in Luxembourg; it may choose (but never has) to hold one or more sittings elsewhere.[5] It is in permanent session.[6]

Originally the Statutes of the Court were contained in protocols appended to **5.02** the three Community Treaties, one for each. With Nice a single (significantly amended) Statute was annexed to the two (extant) Community Treaties and to the Treaty on European Union, and with Lisbon there is a single 'Statute of the Court of Justice of the European Union' likewise annexed to the TEU, the TFEU and the Euratom Treaty.[7] The Statute of the Court was alterable originally only by Treaty amendment, certain provisions (essentially those on

---

1 More accurately, from October 1958, when the judges took the oath of office and the (new) Court of Justice 'of the European Communities' assumed its duties, prior to which the Court of Justice of the ECSC carried on with business. In fact four (of the seven) judges and both Advocates-General in the ECSC Court were (re-)appointed to the new Court. The first judgments were delivered in February 1959 (Case 17/57 *Gezamenlijke Steenkolenmijnen in Limburg* v *High Authority* [1959] ECR 1 and Case 1/58 *Stork* v *High Authority* [1959] ECR 17), the first judgment under the EEC Treaty (a staff case) in July 1960 (Cases 43 etc./59 *von Lachmüller and ors* v *EEC Commission* [1960] ECR 463), and the first judgment on a substantive (non-staff case) EEC matter, almost four years after its creation, in December 1961 (Case 7/61 *EEC Commission* v *Italy* [1961] ECR 317).
2 TEU, arts 13, 19.
3 Euratom Treaty, art. 106a(1).
4 TEU, art. 19(1) (ex art. 220 EC). Other language versions refer, variously, to a duty to 'ensure respect of/for the law', 'safeguard the maintenance of the law', or 'preserve law and justice' in the interpretation and application of the Treaties.
5 Rules of Procedure of the Court of Justice, art. 23.
6 Statute of the Court of Justice, art. 15.
7 Protocol (No. 3) on the Statute of the Court of Justice of the European Union.

procedure) subsequently by unanimous Council vote,[8] then most provisions by unanimous Council vote,[9] and now by the ordinary legislative procedure.[10] In a like manner the Rules of Procedure were originally adopted by the Court subject to approval of a unanimous Council[11] but altered by Nice to a qualified majority[12] and by Lisbon to a simply majority.[13] The Court long pressed for these changes, which significantly speed up any streamlining of rules which the Court thinks appropriate. The Rules of Procedure have been altered from time to time but their structure remained fundamentally unchanged since adopted by the ECSC Court in 1953,[14] and a cold reading offered a skewed perception of what the Court actually did. An exercise at root and branch reorganisation was undertaken, and in 2011 amendments to both the Statute of the Court and to the Rules of Procedure of the Court of Justice were formally proposed by the Court[15] and were adopted in 2012.[16]

2. Court of Justice/General Court/Civil Service Tribunal

5.03 By the mid-1980s the Court was coming under an increasingly heavy workload. In order to ease the pressure the Single European Act amended the founding treaties so as to provide authority (to the Council) to create and 'attach' to the Court of Justice a court with first instance jurisdiction in certain forms of action.[17] This Court, styled the 'Court of First Instance', was established in 1989.[18] In the same manner a single subject matter (disputes between a

---

8   EC Treaty, art. 188, 2nd para. (1993–99), art. 245, 2nd para. (1999–2003); Euratom Treaty, art. 160 (1993–2003).

9   EC Treaty, art. 245, 2nd para. (2003–09). Only the core provisions of Title I (arts 1–8) were entrenched.

10 TFEU, art. 281. Only the core provisions of Title I (arts 1–8) and art. 64 (language arrangements) are entrenched, reserved to formal Treaty amendment and a unanimous Council, respectively.

11 EEC Treaty, art. 188, 2nd para. The unanimity requirement could lead to serious delay, even in uncontentious areas. For example, Austria, Finland and Sweden joined the Union with effect from January 1995, but owing to a backlog of Council business the Rules of Procedure were not amended to recognise the use of Finnish and Swedish until June 1997 ([1997] OJ L103/1). Until then they could be used only by special dispensation of the Court, which, technically, it probably did not have the authority to grant. The 11 new languages resulting from the 2004 and 2007 accessions were, by contrast, recognised by the Court from the date of enlargement (Decision 2004/405 [2004] OJ L132/2; Decision 2006/955 [2006] OJ L386/44).

12 EC Treaty (post Nice), art. 223, 6th para.

13 TFEU, art. 253, 6th para.

14 JO de la CECA, le 7 mars 1953, p. 37.

15 Draft Amendments to the Statute of the Court of Justice of the European Union and to Annex I Thereto; Draft Rules of Procedure of the Court of Justice; both unpublished; proposed to the Council and Parliament on 28 March 2011 (for adoption) and to the Council on 25 May 2011 (for approval), respectively; latest version of the latter now published in Council Doc. 8020/12. Some measures adopted by Regulation 741/2012 [2012] OJ L228/1.

16 Regulation 741/2012 [2012] OJ L228/1; Rules of the Procedure of the Court of Justice [2012] OJ L265/11, in force 1 November 2012.

17 EC Treaty, art. 225 (pre-Nice).

18 Decision 88/591 [1989] OJ C215/1.

Community institution and its officials, or 'staff cases') was later carved from the jurisdiction of the Court of First Instance and conferred upon a third court (technically then a judicial panel) 'attached' to it, the 'Civil Service Tribunal', in 2005. The term 'Court of Justice' was therefore used to refer either to the Court of Justice as a Community institution, in which case it included the Court of First Instance and the Civil Service Tribunal, or to the Court of Justice as a judicial body separate, and with distinct jurisdiction, from the subsidiary courts. The three taken together were sometimes referred to as 'the Community judicature' or 'the Community courts'; the former at least appears to have survived Lisbon, the Court having since referred to the jurisdiction of 'the judicature of the European Union' (*la Cour*),[19] 'the European Union judicature' (*le juge de l'Union; der Unionsrichter*)[20] and 'the Union judicature' (*les juridictions de l'Union; le juge de l'Union*).[21] With the creation of the Court of First Instance, cases brought before the Court of Justice were numbered 'C- …' (for *Cour de Justice*) and those brought before the Court of First Instance 'T- …' (*Tribunal de première instance*) to distinguish between them; for the same reason the Court of First Instance was sometimes called, informally, 'the Tribunal'. Cases before the Civil Service Tribunal are distinguished by the prefix 'F- …' (for *fonction publique*). The three courts share a common site and common services (such as translation and interpretation), but each has its own Registrar, Registry and Rules of Procedure.[22] The Statute of the Court of Justice provides for the situations where an action is raised before the wrong court or the same material issue is raised (competently) before two courts.[23]

---

19 Case C-550/09 *Criminal proceedings against E and F* [2010] ECR I-6213, at para. 44.
20 Cases C-201 and 216/09P *ArcelorMittal Luxembourg and ors v Commission*, judgment of 29 March 2011, not yet reported, at paras 60 and 142 (*Unionsrichter*). In Cases C-463 and 475/10P *Deutsche Post and Germany v Commission*, judgment of 13 October 2011, not yet reported, A-G Bot referred (at para. 54 of his opinion) to *le juge de l'Union* but it came out *das Unionsgericht* in German and 'the Courts of the Union' in English. Subsequently *le juge de l'Union* and *les juridictions de l'Union* have been rendered 'the Courts of the European Union': Case C-272/09P *KME Germany and ors v Commission*, judgment of 8 December 2011, not yet reported, at paras 94, 104 and 106; Case C-386/10P *Chalkor Epexergasias Metallon v Commission*, judgment of 8 December 2011, not yet reported, at paras 63, 64 and 67; Case C-389/10P *KME Germany and ors v Commission*, judgment of 8 December 2011, not yet reported, at paras 121, 130, 131 and 133.
21 Case C-506/08P *Sweden v MyTravel and Commission*, judgment of 21 July 2011, not yet reported, at paras 116, 117 (*les juridictions de l'Union*); Case T-341/07 *Sison v Council* (Sison III), judgment of 23 November 2011, not yet reported, at para. 40 (*le juge de l'Union*).
22 TFEU, art. 254 (ex art. 224 EC) for the General Court, art. 257 (ex art. 225a EC) for a specialised court. The present Rules of Procedure of the General Court were adopted in 1991 and last consolidated in [2010] OJ C177/37. These may now (post Lisbon), like those of the Court of Justice, be amended by the Council by simple majority vote (TFEU, art. 254, 5th para). For the Rules of Procedure of the Civil Service Tribunal see [2010] OJ C177/71.
23 Statute of the Court of Justice, art. 54 and Annex I, art. 8.

5.04   The rules governing the Court of First Instance were originally contained essentially in the 1989 Decision which created it. The Court, and those rules, were written by Nice more fully into the EC Treaty,[24] so 'detaching' it from the Court of Justice and granting it institutional autonomy (if maintaining its judicial subservience). The Civil Service Tribunal was likewise attached to the Court of First Instance, and is still so,[25] but is now recognised, as a specialised court, to be part of the trinity which taken together form 'the Court of Justice of the European Union'.[26] The Court of Justice and the Civil Service Tribunal continue to be known as just that, the Court of First Instance rechristened by Lisbon 'the General Court' (*le Tribunal*; *das Gericht*).[27]

3.   Court of Justice

(a)   Composition

5.05   The Court of Justice consists now of 27 judges ('one judge from each Member State')[28] and eight Advocates-General who 'assist' the Court.[29] The Treaties provide that:

> The Judges and Advocates-General of the Court of Justice shall be chosen from persons whose independence is beyond doubt and who possess the qualifications required for appointment to the highest judicial offices in their respective countries or who are jurisconsults of recognised competence; they shall be appointed by common accord of the governments of the Member States for a term of six years.[30]

In practice, each member state nominates one judge.[31] By convention five of the Advocates-General are nominated by (and from) the larger member states, the remaining three by (and from) the smaller member states in rotation.[32] In order

---

24   EC Treaty, arts 220–5.

25   TFEU, art. 257, 1st para.

26   TEU, art. 19(1).

27   *Ibid.*

28   *Ibid.* art. 19(2) (ex art. 221, 1st para. EC).

29   *Ibid.*

30   TFEU, art. 253, 1st para. (ex art. 223, 1st para. EC); see also TEU, art. 19(2).

31   Prior to the first accession beyond six member states in 1973 the Court consisted of seven judges (and two Advocates-General), the convention being that the extra judge was Italian and the Advocates-General German and French (in the ECSC Court of Justice the extra judge had been Dutch). Between 1981 and 1995, when there was again an even number of member states, an additional judge, nominated from one of the five larger member states (Germany, France, Spain, Italy and the United Kingdom) in rotation, was appointed in order to ensure an uneven number of judges in the full Court. The practice is probably unnecessary for future accessions given the unlikelihood of even the whole Court ever sitting as all judges, and no provision is made for an extra (29th) judge upon Croatian accession in 2013.

32   It was anticipated that the larger member states would lose this privilege following the 2004 accessions, the Advocates-General drawn thereafter from all member states in some form of equal rotation, but this did not happen. Poland made no claim to the privilege of a permanent Advocate-General, possibly simply an oversight; a declaration attached to the Lisbon Treaty (Declaration No. 38 on Article 252 of the TFEU on the Number of

to assist continuity appointment is staggered, half of the judges and half of the Advocates-General coming up for renewal every three years.[33] Appointment is renewable,[34] except (in practice) for Advocates-General from smaller member states. A judge or Advocate-General may be dismissed only if 'he no longer fulfils the requisite conditions or meets the obligations arising from his office' and upon the unanimous decision of all other members of the Court.[35]

Whilst the number of judges will grow automatically with any future accession ('one judge from each Member State') – and so, for example, Croatia gains a judge upon accession without need for Treaty or legislative change – the number of Advocates-General is to remain fixed at eight, unless that number is increased by a unanimous Council.[36] **5.06**

Lisbon introduced a vetting system, making appointment of judges and Advocates-General subject to the (non-binding) 'opinion' of a panel (*comité*) (appointment 'after consultation of [*sic*] the panel')[37] as to suitability to the discharge of the duties of judge or Advocate-General.[38] The panel (now informally 'the article 255 committee') comprises seven members drawn from former members of the Court or of the General Court, judges of national supreme courts and lawyers of 'recognised competence', one member to be proposed by the Parliament.[39] First appointed in February 2010 for a four-year term,[40] it is an eclectic group of two former judges at the Court (one from the Court of Justice, one from the General Court), four judges from national supreme/constitutional/administrative courts and a former MEP/national minister of foreign affairs. In fact a similar body (a 'committee' in permanent session) predates Lisbon,[41] having been appointed in January 2005[42] in order to consider appointment (and 2008, 2009 and 2011 re-appointment) to the Civil **5.07**

Advocates-General in the Court of Justice) anticipates an increase in their number from eight to 11 (and, if requested, 'the Council will ... agree on such an increase'), in which case it is understood Poland will acquire a permanent Advocate-General. The smaller member states from which the rotating Advocates-General are appointed seem now to have settled into an alphabetical order, the present three from Slovenia (Ms Trstenjak), Slovakia (Mr Mazák) and Finland (Mr Jääskinen) replacing, respectively, outgoing Dutch and Austrian Advocates-General in 2006 and a Portuguese Advocate-General in 2009. If the convention holds, Ms Trstenjak and Mr Mazák will be replaced with a Swede and a Belgian in autumn 2012.

33 TFEU, art. 253, 2nd para. (ex art. 223, 2nd para. EC); Statute of the Court of Justice, art. 9.
34 TEU, art. 19(2).
35 Statute of the Court of Justice, art. 6.
36 TFEU, art. 252, 1st para. (ex art. 222, 1st para. EC). But see Declaration No. 38, n. 32 above.
37 TFEU, art. 253, 1st para.
38 *Ibid.* art. 255, 1st para.
39 *Ibid.* art. 255, 2nd para.
40 Decision 2010/125 [2010] OJ L50/20; Decision 2010/124 [2010] OJ L50/18, Annex, para. 3; the panel's 'operating rules' are provided in the latter Annex.
41 See Statute of the Court of Justice, Annex I, art. 3(3).
42 Decision 2005/151 [2005] OJ L50/9.

Service Tribunal.[43] It was anticipated by some that this committee would mutate into the article 255 committee for vetting appointments to the two senior courts, but this did not happen; nor does it now appear, as was also anticipated, that the latter will come to absorb the the duties of the former.

(b) President and vice-president

5.08 The president of the Court of Justice is elected by the judges themselves from amongst their number.[44] The term of office is three years, and is renewable.[45] The president fixes the dates and times of sittings of the Court, presides over deliberations in which he takes part, is responsible for the business and administration of the Court and represents the Court before other institutions, the member states and the outside world. He is also competent, sitting alone, to determine applications to the Court for interim or interlocutory measures and certain appeals from the General Court.[46] From 2012 there is a vice-president of the Court, also elected for a (renewable) three-year period, to 'assist' the president and stand in for the latter when he is indisposed or otherwise prevented from discharging his duties, or when the office of president is vacant.[47]

(c) Collegiality; Chambers

5.09 Except where the president can act alone, the Court acts always as a college, sitting either:

- in plenary session (the 'whole' or 'full' Court; *l'assemblée plénière*) consisting of all the judges, for which the quorum is 17 ('*petit plenum*');[48]
- in the 'Grand Chamber' (a Nice innovation) of 15 judges[49] (with a quorum of 11);[50] or
- in chambers of five (currently the first, second, third and fourth chambers) or three (the fifth, sixth, seventh and eighth chambers) judges.[51]

---

43 Decision 2005/49 [2005] OJ L21/13. Appointment is for four years, renewable; Annex, para. 2. Its present composition (see Decision 2009/69 [2009] OJ L24/11), for November 2008–November 2012, is two former judges of the Court of Justice, one of the General Court, one of both (Mr Schintgen, who served consecutively on both courts) and three (primarily) academic lawyers.

44 TFEU, art. 253, 3rd para. (ex art. 223, 3rd para. EC). Election is by secret ballot; Rules of Procedure (RP) of the Court of Justice, art. 8(3).

45 *Ibid.* Normally a president enjoys two terms as such, latterly (Judges Rodriguez Iglésias (1994–2003) and Skouris (2003–12)) three.

46 See 5.39 and 5.111 below.

47 Statute of the Court of Justice, art. 9a; RP Court of Justice, art. 10(1). The 'judicial functions' of the vice-president are set out in Decision 2012/671 [2012] OJ L300/47.

48 Statute of the Court of Justice, art. 17, 4th para. Prior to 2012 the quorum was 15.

49 *Ibid.* art. 16, 2nd para. (previously 13).

50 *Ibid.* art. 17, 3rd para. (previously 9).

51 *Ibid.* art. 16, 1st para.

In the Rules of Procedure these are called the various 'formations' of the Court.[52] The president of the Court sits as president of the Grand Chamber;[53] the presidents of the chambers, who discharge within the chamber the powers of the president of the Court,[54] are elected for a three-year period (chambers of five)[55] or annually (chambers of three)[56] by the judges. The judges which sit in the Grand Chamber or in the smaller chambers are determined by lists of their number drawn up annually by the Court.[57] There is neither provision for, nor habit of, selection of a judge in a given case by nationality as there is in the Court of Human Rights.[58]

Each case, as it arrives, is assigned by the president of the Court to a **5.10** 'judge-rapporteur', one of the judges of the Court who assumes significant responsibility for it thereafter. The judge-rapporteur (sometimes called, if the context is clear, simply rapporteur or, rarely, the judge responsible for the case) presents a preliminary report (*rapport préalable*) to a 'general meeting' of the Court, which then decides whether the case should be assigned to a chamber or kept before the Court, sitting as the full Court or in the Grand Chamber.[59] In all cases the formation chosen includes the judge-rapporteur,[60] who is subsequently responsible for producing a second, more substantial report, the 'Report for the Hearing' (*rapport d'audience*), which outlines the facts of the case and the arguments of the parties preparatory to the oral hearing,[61] and ultimately drafts the final judgment.[62] The Court is required to sit in the formation of the full

---

52 RP Court of Justice, arts 11(3), 27–31, 60.

53 Statute of the Court of Justice, art. 16, 2nd para.

54 RP Court of Justice, art. 11(4).

55 Statute of the Court of Justice, art. 16, 1st para.; RP Court of Justice, art. 12(1).

56 RP Court of Justice, art. 12(2).

57 *Ibid.* arts 27, 28. Thus the chambers consist not of named judges but of pools of judges. The Grand Chamber consists of the president and vice-president of the Court, the presidents of three chambers of five judges, the judge-rapporteur and the remainder drawn in rotation from the 'list' drawn up by the Court (art. 11b); for the smaller chambers the president of each is named but seven (second and third chambers), six (first and fourth, sixth and seventh chambers) or five (fifth and eighth chambers) judges are assigned to the chamber, which is composed in a given case by the president, the judge-rapporteur and an additional three or one judge(s) designated in accordance with their own lists (art. 28). This scheme limits the possibility of the development of 'specialist' chambers as were thought to evolve in the past. It also means that the Grand Chamber consists of five 'permanent' members (over the three year period of the president of the Court and presidents of chambers of five judges holding office), the remainder rotating; there are concerns that this may be injurious to the continuity and consistency the Court is thought previously to have enjoyed.

58 ECtHR, Rules of Court, rule 24(2)(b).

59 RP Court of Justice, art. 59. For criteria see art. 60.

60 *Ibid.* arts 27(1), 28(1).

61 Until 1994 the Report for the Hearing was published with the judgment of the Court; it is no longer published, and is now available only in the language of proceedings (p… below) and directly from the Court. As a result a judgment of the Court, and particularly a judgment of the General Court which is normally not assisted by an Advocate-General, contains a more extensive recitation of facts and argument than previously.

62 An interesting but so far unstudied question is the influence a particular judge-rapporteur, by drafting it, may bring to bear upon a judgment. The rapporteur in each case is identified in the published judgments of the

Court for only a very small number of (disciplinary) matters,[63] otherwise it is reserved to cases 'of exceptional importance';[64] it has done so only once since the 2004 accessions in a contentious case,[65] although previously (with a Court of 15 judges, quorate with 11) it was not uncommon. By comparison opinions sought from it under article 218(11) TFEU[66] are, owing to their constitutional character, normally heard and delivered by the full Court. A member state or institution party to proceedings may require that a case be heard by the Grand Chamber;[67] individuals have no such standing.[68] Whatever its formation, all judgments are published as judgments of the Court, and no dissenting opinions are expressed or published. As with acts of all Union institutions, a judgment of the Court must be reasoned: it 'shall state the reasons on which [it is] based',[69] or, more succinctly, '*Les arrêts sont motivés*'.

(d) Advocate-General

5.11 To each case that comes before the Court is assigned an Advocate-General. His (or, now, her)[70] function is 'acting with complete impartiality and independence, to make, in open court, reasoned submissions on cases [raised before the Court]';[71] in so doing he or she 'assists' the Court,[72] originally 'assist[ed] the Court in the performance of the task assigned to it',[73] and whilst this latter formula was abandoned by Nice it still holds true. Modelled upon the office of the *commissaire du gouvernement* in the French *Conseil d'Etat*, the Advocate-General is not an advocate, still less comparable to the British law officer called the Advocate General. He or she is, in the fullest sense, a member of the court and (since 1973) ranks with the judges in order of appointment:

Court of Justice. For long the General Court declined to follow suit, probably a function of no more than habit and inertia; but with identification of the rapporteur by the Civil Service Tribunal (for whom it is obligatory; RP Civil Service Tribunal, art. 79) the General Court fell into line (for the most part, but not wholly consistently) in 2008.

63 Statute of the Court of Justice, art. 16, 4th para.
64 *Ibid.* art. 16, 5th para.
65 Case C-432/04 *Commission* v *Cresson* [2006] ECR I-6387.
66 See 5.153 below.
67 Statute of the Court of Justice, art. 16, 3rd para. But the Court will not comply with a demand for assignment of a case to the Grand Chamber if it comes at a 'very advanced' stage of proceedings; Case C-310/04 *Spain* v *Council* [2006] ECR I-7285.
68 Case C-292/05 *Lechouritou and ors* v *Dimosio tis Omospondiakis Dimokratias tis Germanias* [2007] ECR I-1519.
69 Statute of the Court of Justice, art. 36.
70 The Court was a uniquely male institution until the appointment of A-G Rozès in 1981, who completed only part of her term before being recalled to high judicial office (premier président de la Cour de Cassation) in France; thereafter it reassumed its resolute masculinity until the appointments of Judges Macken (1999) and Colneric (2000) and A-G Stix-Hackl (2000); as at January 2012 it comprises four female judges and three female Advocates-General. The General Court fared slightly better, in the appointments of Judges Tiili and Lindh with Finnish and Swedish accession in 1995; it now boasts seven female judges.
71 TFEU, art. 252, 2nd para. (ex art. 222, 2nd para. EC).
72 TEU, art. 19(2).
73 EEC Treaty, art. 166, 2nd para. (art. 222, 2nd para. EC (pre-Nice)).

[T]he Opinion of the Advocate General ... is not ... an opinion addressed to the judges or to the parties which stems from an authority outside the Court or which derives its authority from that of the Procureur Général's department ... Rather, it constitutes the individual reasoned opinion, expressed in open court, of a Member of the Court of Justice itself.[74]

The Advocate-General in a particular case is selected by the 'first Advocate-General', a titular post which rotates annually amongst the Advocates-General and is appointed by the Court.[75]   **5.12**

The Advocate-General's 'opinion' in a case is delivered, usually, several weeks after the oral pleadings (the 'hearing'; *audience*, or *plaidoirie*). It is part, and marks the end, of the submissions phase of proceedings[76] (hence the opinion is *conclusions* in French and, clearer still, *Schlußanträge* in German) and the opening of the deliberation phase, in which the Advocate-General takes no further part. Although the analogy is not exact and must be treated with some caution, an Advocate-General's opinion can be likened to the judgment of a single judge at first instance, to be followed by a compulsory and definitive appeal – the judgment of the Court. The opinion in a case is published in the European Court Reports (see below) together with the judgment. In comparison with the relative terseness of a judgment of the Court, the opinions of the Advocates-General are more discursive, and similar in style to the opinions or judgments of common law judges; this is in part due to the privilege of logical narrative, a quality sometimes lacking in a judgment which is the product of the necessary deliberations and agreement (and absorption of dissent) amongst the judges. Opinions therefore 'make it easier to understand the judgments delivered and influence the establishment and development of Community case-law'.[77] They also allow for exploration of issues not necessarily considered in the judgment. Although barely (if at all) acknowledged, certainly not analysed, in the ensuing judgment, and in no way binding upon the judges, opinions are a source of Union law and may be a valuable guide to the reasoning of the Court.   **5.13**

There is no provision or mechanism for parties to submit observations in response to an Advocate-General's opinion.[78] The Court may re-open the oral   **5.14**

---

74   Case C-17/98 *Emesa Sugar* v *Aruba* [2000] ECR I-665, at para. 14.
75   RP Court of Justice, art. 14.
76   *Ibid.* art. 82(2).
77   Case C-466/00 *Kaba* v *Secretary of State for the Home Department* [2003] ECR I-2219, *per* A-G Ruiz-Jarabo Colomer at para. 115 of his opinion.
78   Case C-266/09 *Stichting Natuur en Milieu and ors* v *College voor de toelating van gewasbeschermingsmiddelen en biociden*, [2010] ECR I-13119, at para. 28.

procedure,[79] and parties have sought this in order to 'correct errors' in the opinion, but the Court need not do so, and such efforts are usually without success.[80]

5.15 Prior to Nice each judgment (but not reasoned order)[81] of the Court required to be preceded by an Advocate-General's opinion. The EC Treaty was then amended to call for an opinion in cases 'which, in accordance with the Statute of the Court of Justice ..., require his involvement',[82] and the Court may now waive that requirement, after hearing the Advocate-General, '[w]here it considers that the case raises no new point of law'.[83] Since 2004 roughly one-third of judgments are delivered without formal opinion, speeding up significantly the time it requires for the Court to come to judgment.

(e) The Registrar

5.16 The Court appoints a registrar, who holds office for a term of six years, renewable.[84] He is responsible, under the authority of the president, for the

---

79 RP Court of Justice, art. 83.
80 E.g., Case C-17/98 *Emesa Sugar* v *Aruba* [2000] ECR I-665; Case C-309/99 *Wouters* v *Algemene Raad van de Nederlandse Orde van Advokaten* [2002] ECR I-1577; C-466/00 *Kaba*, n. 77 above; Case C-210/03 *R (Swedish Match AB and anor)* v *Secretary of State for Health* [2004] ECR I-11893; Case C-292/05 *Lechouritou and ors* v *Dimosio tis Omospondiakis Dimokratias tis Germanias* [2007] ECR I-1519; Case C-491/06 *Danske Svineprodu-center* v *Justitsministeriet* [2008] ECR I-3339; Case C-210/06 *CARTESIO Oktató és Szolgáltató* [2008] ECR I-9641; Case C-42/07 *Liga Portuguesa de Futebol Profissional and anor* v *Departamento de Jogos da Santa Casa da Misericórdia de Lisboa* [2009] ECR I-7633; Cases C-201 and 216/09P *ArcelorMittal Luxembourg and ors* v *Commission*, judgment of 29 March 2011, not yet reported. For rare examples of a successful request (in the first case made by nine intervening governments) see Case C-475/03 *Banca Popolare di Cremona* v *Agenzia Entrate Ufficio Cremona*, order of 21 October 2005, unreported; Case C-292/04 *Meilicke and ors* v *Finanzamt Bonn-Innenstadt*, order of 7 April 2006, unreported. Of course, a request to re-open the procedure is discussed by at least the Advocate-General (who is 'heard' on the matter; RP Court of Justice, art. 83) and the judge-rapporteur, and even where it fails it is unlikely the judges are unaware of the arguments put forward. The Court may also re-open the oral procedure upon a proposal from the Advocate-General or of its own motion (RP Court of Justice, art. 83; see e.g., Case C-280/00 *Altmark Trans and anor* v *Nahverkehrsgesellschaft Altmark and anor* [2003] ECR I-7747; Case C-227/04P *Lindorfer* v *Council*, order of 26 April 2006, unreported; Case C-110/05 *Commission* v *Italy*, order of 7 March 2007, unreported; Case C-382/08 *Neukirchinger* v *Bezirkshaut-pmannschaft Grieskirchen*, order of 21 April 2010, unreported) and will do so where it lacks sufficient information, a new fact is submitted of a 'decisive' nature, an important but unforeseen question arises in the course of proceedings, or the case must be dealt with upon the basis of arguments not debated by the parties; sometimes it expressly invites submissions from the parties, the institutions and the member states on a particular question. However, there is no obligation to re-open the oral procedure even where an Advocate-General raises a point of law which was not the subject of debate between the parties '[s]ince the Court is not bound either by the Advocate General's Opinion or by the reasoning on which it is based' (Case C-249/06 *Commission* v *Sweden* [2009] ECR I-1335, at para. 13), which seems to discount the persuasive powers of the Advocate-General.
81 See 5.32 below.
82 TFEU, art. 252, 2nd para (ex art. 222, 2nd para. EC).
83 Statute of the Court of Justice, art. 20, 5th para. The judge-rapporteur makes a preliminary recommendation in the *rapport préalable* as to whether to dispense with an opinion; RP Court of Justice, art. 59(2).
84 RP Court of Justice, art. 18(1), (4).

acceptance, transmission and custody of documents,[85] for keeping the register,[86] and for effecting service;[87] he assists the Court, the chambers, the president and the judges in all their official functions.[88] He himself may be supported by a deputy registrar.[89]

4. General Court

(a) Composition

The General Court consists now of 27 judges[90] 'whose independence is beyond doubt and who possess the ability required for appointment to high judicial office'.[91] However, the Treaties provide that it shall 'include *at least* one judge per Member State',[92] so permitting an increase in the number of judges beyond that of the number of member states, by Council decision. Like the Court of Justice, judges are appointed by the common accord of the governments of the member states and following consultation with the article 255 panel;[93] equally, the method and term of appointment and the election and powers of the president and vice-president,[94] of those of the presidents of chambers,[95] and the office and function of the registrar[96] are as those of the Court of Justice. There is no separate office of Advocate-General, but one of the judges may be called upon to perform the task of Advocate-General in a given case.[97] This happens hardly at all – at the time of writing only four times, and none since 1992; but Advocates-General may be appointed to the General Court should its jurisdiction be altered.[98] The Court may sit in plenary session[99] (and did so in its early

5.17

---

85 *Ibid.* art. 20.
86 *Ibid.* art. 21(1).
87 *Ibid.* arts 20(1), 48; RP Court of Justice, art. 79. Service of documents may now be by electronic means subject to criteria yet to be determined by the Court; art. 48(4).
88 *Ibid.* art. 20(2). See generally, Instructions to the Registrar [1974] OJ L350/33.
89 *Ibid.* art. 19.
90 Statute of the Court of Justice, art. 48. This will be altered to 28 as at Croatian accession; 2011 Act of Accession, art. 9(2).
91 TFEU, art. 254, 2nd para. (ex art. 224, 2nd para. EC).
92 TEU, art. 19(2), 2nd para. (ex art. 224, 1st para. EC); emphasis added.
93 TFEU, art. 254, 2nd para.
94 *Ibid.* art. 254, 3rd para.
95 RP General Court, arts 15, 16. The presidents of chambers of five judges are elected for a term of three years, renewable once (art. 15(2)), the president of a chamber of three for a 'defined term' (art. 15(3)).
96 Statute of the Court of Justice, art. 52; Instructions to the Registrar [2007] OJ L232/1.
97 TFEU, art. 254, 6th para.; Statute of the Court of Justice, art. 49. Because there is no Advocate-General both the preliminary report and the report for the hearing tend to be more extensive than in the Court of Justice, the judge-rapporteur assuming (tacitly) some of the responsibilities borne by an Advocate-General.
98 The Treaty now (post-Nice) envisages full-time Advocates-General to 'assist' the General Court; TFEU, art. 254, 1st para. (ex art. 224, 1st para. EC). None has yet been appointed, but it is anticipated that this will come about if and when the Court is granted jurisdiction to hear preliminary references under art. 267.
99 Statute of the Court of Justice, art. 50, 2nd para.

days) and in a Grand Chamber[100] (of 13 judges,[101] quorum of which is nine),[102] but normally sits in chambers of three (four in five judgments of the General Court being decided by a chamber of three) or, in difficult or important cases, five judges ('extended composition').[103] There is an appeal chamber (of three or five judges) to hear appeals from an (inferior) specialised court.[104]

5.18 Since 1999 certain categories of cases[105] may be 'delegated' by a chamber to a single judge (always the judge-rapporteur) where the questions of law or fact raised present little difficulty, the case is of limited importance, and there are no other special circumstances;[106] a single judge may not hear a case which addresses the legality of an act of general application,[107] and a member state or institution party to proceedings may veto delegation to a single judge.[108] The Court sits as a single judge very rarely: since 1999 only in staff cases under article 270, jurisdiction in which passed to the Civil Service Tribunal in 2005, and a very few other cases of exceptional simplicity and tedium.[109]

---

100   *Ibid.* art. 50, 3rd para. The Grand Chamber has sat only three times, in a group of complicated cases heard together involving international trade law and the non-contractual liability of the Union (Case T-69/00 *Fabbrica italia accumulatori motocarri Montecchio and anor* v *Council and Commission* [2005] ECR II-5393; Case T-151/00 *Laboratoire du Bain* v *Council and Commission* [2005] ECR II-23*; Case T-301/00 *Groupe Fremaux and anor* v *Council and Commission* [2005] ECR II-25*; Case T-320/00 *Cartondruck* v *Council and Commission* [2005] ECR II-27*; Case T-383/00 *Beamglow* v *Parliament, Council and Commission* [2005] ECR II-5459; Case T-135/01 *Fedon & Figli and anor* v *Council and Commission* [2005] ECR II-29*), in a politically sensitive case involving access to Union documents (Case T-36/04 *Association de la presse internationale* v *Commission* [2007] ECR II-3201) and in a competition case involving the (then) highest ever fine imposed by the Commission (Case T-201/04 *Microsoft* v *Commission* [2007] ECR II-3601).

101   RP General Court, art. 10(1). The Grand Chamber now comprises the president of the Court, the seven presidents of those chambers not entrusted with the case and the judges of the chamber, extended composition (see n. 103 below) which would have sat had it been assigned to a chamber of five judges.

102   *Ibid.* art. 32(3), 2nd para.

103   Statute of the Court of Justice, art. 50, 1st para. At present the Court comprises eight chambers of three judges and eight chambers of five judges, styled the first through eighth chambers (the chambers of three) and the first through eighth chambers, extended composition (the chambers of five). The method varies from that of the Court of Justice: the presidents of the eight chambers are elected for a three-year period (RP General Court, art. 15) and act as such whether the chamber is sitting as three judges or in extended composition; the *puisne* judges of each formation are now assigned to it following three separate rotas, (a) competition, state aids and trade protection cases, (b) intellectual property cases and (c) all other cases; [2011] OJ C232/2.

104   As to specialised courts see immediately below. The appeal chamber is excluded from the procedures *ibid.*, rather it is composed of the president of the Court and, in rotation, two presidents of chambers; if sitting in extended composition, the three judges in the formation to which the case was first assigned and, in rotation, two presidents of chambers; [2011] OJ C232/2.

105   Staff cases, annulment or compulsion proceedings against a Union institution raised by private persons, claims in non-contractual liability and disputes on arbitration clauses in contracts with the Union.

106   Statute of the Court of Justice, art. 50, 2nd para.; RP General Court, arts 11(1) and 14(2)(1). The first judgment of the Court sitting in the composition of a single judge was rendered in 1999: Case T-180/98 *Cotrim* v *Centre Européen pour le Développement de la Formation Professionnelle* [1999] ECR-SC II-1077.

107   RP General Court, art. 14(2)(2)(a). Where a case has been delegated to a single judge where the rules do not allow it, his judgment may be set aside on appeal; Case C-171/00P *Libéros* v *Commission* [2002] ECR I-451.

108   *Ibid.* art. 51(2), 2nd para.

109   Case T-429/93 *Le Goff and ors* v *Council* [2000] ECR II-2439 and Case T-537/93 *Tromeur* v *Council and Commission* [2000] ECR II-2457 (non-contractual liability); Case T-68/99 *Toditec* v *Commission* [2001] ECR

Faced with an increasing workload and a growing backlog of cases, the **5.19** proposals put forward in 2011 included one for an increase in the number of judges in the General Court from 27 to 39. Should it be adopted it would likely result in significant change to the organisation and working of the Court.

(b) Jurisdiction

The jurisdiction originally conferred upon the Court of First Instance was **5.20** limited to staff cases, certain matters involving coal and steel production governed by the ECSC Treaty, and actions for annulment of Community acts raised by a natural or legal person in the field of competition[110] – areas in which a substantial amount of fact finding and/or complex economic analysis is normally required. By 1994 it was extended to include all actions raised directly before the Court by a natural or legal person.[111] That is still the case, but the Treaty of Nice provided for significant further extension. Article 256 of the TFEU now reads:

> The General Court shall have jurisdiction to hear and determine at first instance actions or proceedings referred to in Articles 263, 265, 268, 270 and 272, with the exception of those assigned to a specialised court ... or those reserved in the Statute for the Court of Justice. The Statute may provide for the General Court to have jurisdiction for other classes of action or proceeding ...

> The General Court shall have jurisdiction to hear and determine questions referred for a preliminary ruling under Article 267, in specific areas laid down by the Statute.[112]

At present there is one specialised court;[113] and the Statute of the Court does **5.21** not, yet, countenance and accord the General Court jurisdiction under article 267. But it has now been granted jurisdiction in all actions otherwise adumbrated in article 256(1) excepting those falling under articles 263 or 265 (essentially judicial review proceedings) and raised (in accordance with an unnecessarily complex and confusing formula):

II-1443, Case T-138/05 *Commission v Impetus* [2007] ECR II-136* and Case T-259/09 *Commission v Arci Nuova associazione comitato di Cagliari and Gessa* [2010] ECR II-284 (disputes over arbitration clauses); Case T-190/07 *KEK Diavlos v Commission* [2010] ECR II-33* (reimbursement of a sum owed under contract) and Case T-162/04 *Branco v Commission* [2006] ECR II-102* and Case T-388/07 *Comune di Napoli v Commission* [2010] ECR II-79* (annulment of Commission decisions).

110 Decision 88/591, art. 3(1). On annulment of Union acts see 5.66–5.87 below.
111 Decision 88/591, as amended by Decision 93/350 [1993] OJ L144/21, itself amended in turn by Decision 94/149 [1994] OJ L66/29.
112 TFEU, art. 256 (ex art. 225 EC).
113 See immediately below.

(a)   by a member state:

    (i)   against an act or failure to act of the Parliament and/or the Council, unless it is

       – a Council decision approving a state aid under article 108(2) TFEU;

       – a Council measure imposing safeguard measures under article 207 TFEU; or

       – a Council measure exercising implementing powers it has conferred upon itself under article 291(2) TFEU (that is, in the field of the Common Foreign and Security Policy(CFSP));

    (ii)   against an act or failure to act by the Commission under article 331 TFEU on enhanced cooperation; and

(b)   by a Union institution against an act or failure to act of the Parliament and/or the Council, the Commission or the European Central Bank.[114]

At a risk of oversimplification the General Court may therefore be characterised as the administrative court of the Union. Judgments are open to appeal to the Court of Justice, on points of law only.[115]

5.   Specialised courts

5.22   The EC Treaty post-Nice also provided for the creation, by a unanimous Council, of 'judicial panels' (*chambres juridictionelles*) to be 'attached' to the Court of First Instance, to hear and determine at first instance certain classes of action or proceeding brought in specific (but undefined) areas within its jurisdiction.[116] With Lisbon they were restyled 'specialised courts' (*tribunaux spécialisés*)[117] and the power to create them shared between Council and Parliament.[118] They are now recognised as formally part of the Court of Justice of the European Union.

5.23   The first, and so far only, specialised court to be created is the European Union Civil Service Tribunal (*Tribunal de la fonction publique*),[119] with first instance jurisdiction in matters of employment disputes between a Union institution, or any Union organ or body, and its servants ('staff cases').[120] The Tribunal

---

114   Statute of the Court of Justice, art. 51.
115   TFEU, art. 256(1) (ex art. 225(1) EC) and Statute of the Court of Justice, art. 58; on appeals see 5.110–5.118 below.
116   TFEU, art. 257 (ex art. 225a EC).
117   TEU, art. 19.
118   TFEU, art. 257, 1st para.
119   Decision 2004/752 [2004] OJ L333/7.
120   See 5.91–5.92 below.

assumed its duties in 2005 and delivered its first judgment in early 2006.[121] It consists of seven judges (which number may be increased by the Council upon a request from the Court of Justice),[122] appointed not by the governments of the member states but by the Council (by unamity)[123] upon the recommendation of the vetting committee of previous judges. Uniquely amongst the Union courts appointment is by relatively open recruitment, the Council calling for qualified persons to apply.[124] Given the small number of judges and the significant inconvenience of the temporary indisposal of one or more of them, temporary judges (*juges par intérim*) may be appointed to the Tribunal (and to any specialised court) to cover any such absence.[125] The Tribunal sits normally in chambers of three, but may sit as the full court (quorate with five judges), in a chamber of five (three judges), or as a single judge;[126] a case is referred to the full court or a chamber of five where the difficulty of the questions of law raised or the importance of the case or special circumstances so justify,[127] to a single judge (the judge-rapporteur) where it raises no factual or legal difficulty, is of limited importance and presents no other special circumstances.[128] A judgment is open to appeal to the General Court (heard by its appeals chamber) on points of law only,[129] although a decision creating a specialised court may provide for appeal also on points of fact.[130] An appeal judgment of the General Court is subject in turn to 'review' by the Court of Justice, itself sitting in an appeal chamber, but only exceptionally.[131]

---

121 Decision 2004/752, art. 4; Decision of the President of the Court of Justice, OJ 2005 L325/1. The first judgment was in Case F-16/05 *Falcione* v *Commission* [2006] ECR-SC II-A-1–7.

122 Statute of the Court of Justice, Annex (added by Decision 2004/752), art. 2(1).

123 TFEU, art. 257, 4th para. (ex art. 225a, 4th para. EC).

124 Decision 2005/150 OJ 2005 L50/7, Annex. For the outcome of the procedure see Decision 2005/577 OJ 2005 L197/28.

125 Statute of the Court of Justice, art. 62c and Annex I, art. 2(2). The Council is to draw up a list of three temporary judges drawn from previous members of the Court who are able to place themselves at the disposal of the Tribunal, from which term previous judges will be called upon to 'assist' it as necessary. Appointment is for four years, renewable. For the detail see Regulation 979/2012 [2012] OJ L303/83.

126 Statute of the Court of Justice, Annex, art. 4(2); Rules of Procedure of the Civil Service Tribunal ([2010] OJ L177/71), arts 9, 24. The Rules of Procedure were adopted in 2007, prior to which the Tribunal adhered to those of the General Court *mutatis mutandis*; Decision 2004/752, art. 3(4). As with the senior courts, there are now published instructions to the Registrar of the Tribunal[2007] OJ L249/3.

127 RP Civil Service Tribunal, art. 13. In Case F-16/05 *Falcione*, n. 121 above, the Tribunal sat as the full court (of seven judges), but this was more for ceremonial purposes. It sits as the full court occasionally, when the issues are difficult or of significant practical or political consequence (e.g., Case F-105/05 *Wils* v *Parliament* [2007] ECR-SC II-A-I-1187 (seven judges); Cases F-124/05 and 96/06 *A and G* v *Commission*, judgment of 13 January 2010, not yet reported (five judges)), but infrequently.

128 RP Civil Service Tribunal, art. 14. It has done so only once: Case F-1/10 *Marcuccio* v *Commission*, judgment of 14 December 2010, not yet reported.

129 Statute of the Court of Justice, Annex, art. 11(1).

130 TFEU, art. 257, 3rd para. (ex art. 225a, 2nd para. EC).

131 See 5.117 below.

Given the small number of judges and so the significant inconvenience of the temporary indisposal of one or more of them, the 2011 amendments envisage the drawing up of a short list of previous judges at the Court from which could be drawn temporary judges to sit in the Tribunal should the need arise.

5.24 The second specialised court envisaged is a specialised patent tribunal with first instance jurisdiction over disputes on validity and infringements under the (not yet established) Union patent system, long styled provisionally the Community Patent Court (*Tribunal de brevet communautaire*).[132] But the field is one in significant disarray and it is likely to be some time before the dust settles and the court created, if ever.[133]

6. Languages

5.25 Pleadings before any of the courts may be in any of the 23 official Union languages.[134] Unless the Court authorises otherwise, they must be conducted in the 'language of the case', which is, depending upon the form of action, (a) chosen by the applicant, (b) the language (or one of the languages) of a defendant member state, (c) the language of the referring national court, or (d) the language of a judgment under appeal.[135] However, so long as the application is drafted entirely in the language of the case, supporting documents, if lengthy, may be in another language providing extracts in the former

---

132 Proposal for a Council Decision establishing the Community Patent Court, COM(2003) 828 final. The proposed Treaty base was art. 225a EC but would now be art. 262 TFEU, for the conferring of jurisdiction upon the Court of Justice over disputes arising in the area of European intellectual property rights.

133 The EU patent itself has been long deadlocked in the Council, and is now the subject of an enhanced cooperation measure; see 2.46 above, and, on the Union patent system generally, 10.79 below. A Draft Agreement on the European and EU Patent Court and Draft Statute, Council Doc. 14970/08, which is proposed to have both Union and European Patent Convention jurisdiction, to which the Union would accede and which would create a 'European and EU Patents Court'. But owing to that court and the proposed judicial structure the Court of Justice found the draft agreement to be inconsistent with both the TEU and the TFEU (Opinion 1/09 *Re the European Patent Convention*, opinion of 8 March 2011, not yet reported) so derailing the project. Presumably the failure of the wider Patents Court breathes new life into the Community (or EU) Patent Court. In Summer 2012 the European Council agreed upon the creation of a 'Unified Patent Court' (UPC) (*Juridiction unifée en matière des brevets*), consisting of a 'Central Division of the Court of First Instance of the UPC' with its seat (and that of the president) in Paris, with 'thematic clusters' (*chambres spécialisées*) sitting in London (for litigation involving chemistry, including pharmaceuticals, and human necessities) and Munich (mechanical engineering); see Brussels European Council, 28–29 June 2012, Presidency Conclusions, para. 3. It is not yet clear if the UPC is a specialised court or a distinct court outside the Court of Justice of the EU. The (outline) proposal is chaotic from the start, and has already met serious opposition from the Parliament.

134 RP Court of Justice, art. 36; RP General Court, art. 35; RP Civil Service Tribunal, art. 29; on official languages see Part B, Introduction above. Uniquely amongst the institutions, Irish has been an official language of the Court of Justice since accession in 1973. However, to date it has been used for ceremonial (e.g., swearing in) purposes only, it has never served as the language of a case and has never been used by an Advocate-General or in pleadings by the Irish (or any other) government.

135 RP Court of Justice, art. 37; RP General Court, art. 35; RP Civil Service Tribunal, art. 29.

are supplied.[136] An intervening member state[137] may use its own language irrespective of the language of the case;[138] the Union institutions enjoy no such privilege as they are irrebuttably presumed to be able, and so required, to plead in all 23 languages.[139] Whilst reported officially in 22 languages,[140] judgments are formally delivered in the language of the case (which is identified at the outset in each reported judgment), and that text constitutes the only authentic version of the judgment (unless the Court directs otherwise).[141] But in practice the 'working language of the Court' is French, and most judgments are drafted and agreed in French. The French text of a judgment ought therefore to be consulted if, as sometimes happens, the meaning of the English (or any other) text is not clear.

The Advocate-General may, irrespective of the language of the case, use any **5.26** official language,[142] and opinions are normally written and delivered in his or her own language. However, in order to speed up proceedings there is now a convention developing by which Advocates-General from the (linguistically) smaller member states are encouraged to write opinions in one of the 'big five' languages.[143]

7. Reporting

Judgments of the Court of Justice (together with the opinions of the **5.27** Advocates-General), of the General Court and of the Civil Service Tribunal are reported officially in *Reports of Cases before the Court of Justice of the European Union* – normally referred to as the European Court Reports (ECR). The ECR

---

136 RP Court of Justice, art. 38; RP General Court, art. 35(3); RP Civil Service Tribunal, art. 29; Case C-526/08 *Commission* v *Luxembourg* [2010] ECR I-6151.

137 As to intervention see 5.35 below.

138 RP Court of Justice, art. 38(4); RP General Court, art. 35(3); RP Civil Service Tribunal, art. 29. Where a non-member state has a right of intervention in the preliminary ruling procedure (see Statute of the Court of Justice, art. 23, 3rd and 4th paras; art. 40, 3rd para.) it must use one of the official languages of the Court; RP Court of Justice, art. 38(5), (6); RP General Court, art. 35(3).

139 RP Court of Justice, art. 37(1); RP General Court, art. 35(2)(c); RP Civil Service Tribunal, art. 29.

140 By derogation from the general rule (which must be reviewed every five years and may be ended by a unanimous Council), judgments of the Court are not translated into or reported in Irish; Regulation 920/2005 [2005] OJ L156/3; the derogation extended now to 2017, Regulation 1257/2010 [2010] OJ L343/5.

141 RP Court of Justice, art. 41; RP General Court, art. 37; RP Civil Service Tribunal, art. 29. See e.g., Case T-184/01R *IMS Health* v *Commission* [2001] ECR II-3193, at para. 92. But see Case C-167/04P *JCB Service* v *Commission* [2006] ECR I-8925, at para. 221, in which the Court of Justice interprets the authentic (English) version of a judgment of the General Court by reference to other (non-authentic) language versions.

142 RP Court of Justice, art. 38(3).

143 Thus, in recent practice, Mr Poiares Maduro frequently delivered his opinions in English or French, Mr Mazák delivers his frequently in English (or occasionally French), Ms Trstenjak hers in German (occasionally French) and Mr Jääskinen his in French (occasionally English). The courtesy is infectious, Ms Sharpston having turned her hand to Spanish and German and Mr Mengozzi to Spanish and French.

exists now in 22 official languages. Since 2004 reporting of judgments has been selective, and some are now reported in summary form. The *dispositif* of each judgment and order is published in the *Official Journal*, normally within a month or two of judgment. Judgments in staff cases are since 1994 reported in a specialist series of the ECR (ECR-SC). All judgments, opinions and orders since 1997 are available in full (but not immediately in all languages) in electronic form on the Court's website. A guide to reports of the Court may be found in Annex IV.

8. Court of Justice and the Atomic Energy Community

5.28 In what follows, reference will be made to the jurisdiction conferred upon the Court by the TEU and the TFEU. Jurisdiction is also conferred by the Euratom Treaty which is, in most respects, materially the same. The Euratom provisions are to be interpreted by analogy to the Union provisions.[144]

9. Court of Justice and excluded fields

5.29 It should be noted that the Court of Justice had very little jurisdiction over the pre-Lisbon TEU. That Treaty set out (exhaustively)[145] the scope of its powers (*compétences*; *Zuständigkeit*), which generally did *not* extend to matters falling within the non-Community fields of Union activities save for the exceptions provided expressly therein.[146] Post-Lisbon the general rule is inclusive jurisdiction across both Union Treaties, but it is ousted:

- as regards the substance (but not procedure) of measures adopted by the European Council or the Council acting under article 7 of the TEU (determination of and sanctions for breaches of fundamental rights by member states);[147]
- with respect to the provisions on foreign and security policy and measures adopted under it, save (a) monitoring the frontier between the Union's competences and the CFSP, for the implementation of the latter must not affect the exercise of Union competences or the powers of the institutions in respect to them, and (b) reviewing the legality of decisions adopted by the Council providing for restrictive measures (for example, freezing of assets) against third country natural or juristic persons;[148]

---

144 Case T-219/95R *Danielsson and ors* v *Commission* [1995] ECR II-3051.
145 Case T-231/04 *Greece* v *Commission* [2007] ECR II-63, at para. 73.
146 TEU (pre-Lisbon), art. 46.
147 TFEU, art. 269; see 6.105 below.
148 TEU, art. 24(1); TFEU, art. 275.

- as regards review of the validity or proportionality of operations carried out by the police or other national law enforcement services or the exercise of the responsibilities of a member state regarding maintenance of law and order and safeguarding internal security;[149] and
- as regards pre-Lisbon acts of the Union in the field of police cooperation and judicial cooperation in criminal matters, if ousted immediately prior to the entry into force of Lisbon, for a transitional period of five years.[150] Presumably this also means that the immunity enjoyed by the institutions in non-contractual liability for injury caused when acting under the pre-Lisbon TEU[151] survives during this period.

B. FORMS OF ACTION BEFORE THE COURT

1. General

The authority of the Court of Justice is set out in the TEU as follows: **5.30**

> The Court of Justice of the European Union shall, in accordance with the Treaties:
>
> (a) rule on [*statue sur*] actions brought by a Member State, an institution or a natural or legal person;
> (b) give preliminary rulings, at the request of courts or tribunals of the Member States, on the interpretation of Union law or the validity of acts adopted by the institutions;
> (c) rule [*statue*] in other cases provided for in the Treaties.[152]

This betrays little of the depth and breadth of the jurisdiction of the Court. In 'ensur[ing] that … the law is observed'[153] the Court exercises judicial control over, first, the Union and its institutions, in order to ensure their compliance with the law:

> [T]he European Union is based on the rule of law and the acts of its institutions are subject to review by the Court of their compatibility with EU law and, in particular, with the Treaty on the Functioning of the European Union and the general principles of law. The Treaty on the Functioning of the European Union has established a complete system of legal remedies and procedures designed to confer on the judicature of the

---

149 TFEU, art. 276.
150 Protocol (No. 36) on Transitional Measures, art. 10.
151 Case C-354/04P *Gestoras Pro Amnistía and ors* v *Council* [2007] ECR I-1579; Case C-355/04P *Segi and ors* v *Council* [2007] ECR I-1657; see 5.100 below.
152 TEU, art. 19(3).
153 *Ibid.* art. 19(1).

European Union jurisdiction to review the legality of acts of the institutions of the European Union.[154]

Secondly, available procedures also make it possible to test the compatibility with the requirements of Union law of the conduct of the member states, in order to ensure that they too comply with the obligations they bear under the Treaties. In rare circumstances the Court has jurisdiction over the conduct of individuals, insofar as they are subjects of Union law. However, each of the forms of process before the Court of Justice (and before the General Court and Civil Service Tribunal where they have jurisdiction) is distinct, and is subject to rules which are set out in some detail in the TFEU, the Statute of the Court and the Rules of Procedure. It is for the applicant raising the action to select the correct form of process and adequately (sufficiently clearly and precisely) define the subject matter of the claim, and not for the Court to do it for him;[155] failure properly to do so renders the action inadmissible.[156] The Court has smoothed over some shortcomings or unfairness in its procedures, but it is not a court of general jurisdiction and its authority is limited to that expressly conferred upon it;[157] it cannot create new forms of process, for that would be to usurp the authority of the framers of the Treaties.[158] However, where the Court has jurisdiction, it is compulsory and privative: the member states 'undertake not to submit a dispute concerning the interpretation or application of the Treaties to

---

154 Case C-550/09 *Criminal proceedings against E and F* [2010] ECR I-6213, at para. 44. The *dictum* on the 'complete system of legal remedies and procedures' first appeared in Case 294/83 *Parti Ecologiste 'Les Verts' v European Parliament* [1986] ECR 1339, at para. 23, and has been repeated many times since; most recently, Opinion 1/09 *Re the European Patent Convention*, opinion of 8 March 2011, not yet reported, at para. 70.

155 Statute of the Court of Justice, art. 21; RP Court of Justice, art. 120(c), (d); RP General Court, art. 44(1)(c), (d); RP Civil Service Tribunal, arts 35, 36.

156 Case 175/73 *Union Syndicale and ors v Council* [1974] ECR 917; Case T-348/94 *Enso Española v Commission* (Cartonboard) [1998] ECR II-1875; Case T-319/03 *French and ors v Council and Commission* [2004] ECR II-769; Case C-160/03 *Spain v Eurojust* [2005] ECR I-2077; Case T-28/03 *Holcim (Deutschland) v Commission* [2005] ECR II-1357.

157 TEU, art. 13(2) (ex art. 7(1) EC); Case C-376/98 *Germany v Parliament and Council* [2000] ECR I-8419, at para. 83; Case T-338/02 *Segi and ors v Council* [2004] ECR II-1647, at para. 38.

158 Case C-50/00P *Unión de Pequeños Agricultores v Council* [2002] ECR I-6677; Cases T-377 etc./00 *Philip Morris International and ors v Commission* [2003] ECR II-1; Case T-28/03 *Holcim (Deutschland)*, n. 156 above. There is one aberrant exception to this rule in Case 2/88 Imm *Zwartveld and ors* [1990] ECR I-3365; [1990] ECR I-4405, in which the Court, at the request (for 'judicial cooperation') of a *Rechter-commissaris* (examining judge) in Dutch criminal proceedings involving fisheries fraud, ordered the Commission to make documents available to the judge and authorise its officials to appear as witnesses. The Court had no apparent power to make the order, justified it by reference to a duty of sincere cooperation borne by the Commission, and has not repeated the exercise. (It also affixed to the case number the suffix '-Imm', for immunity, which is unknown.) Other, if less marked, exceptions may be identified in Case 70/88 *Parliament v Council* (Chernobyl) [1990] ECR I-2041 (extension to the Parliament of (partial) standing to seek annulment of a Union measure) and Case C-47/07P *Masdar (UK) v Commission* [2008] ECR I-9811 (recognition of a remedy in restitution for unjust enrichment even though (at para. 50) 'the EC Treaty does not make express provision for a means of pursuing that type of action').

any method of settlement other than those provided for therein',[159] and an attempt to do so is a breach of that provision combined with article 4(3) TEU.[160] This marks

> the autonomy of the Community legal system, observance of which is ensured by the Court by virtue of the exclusive jurisdiction conferred on it by Article [19(1) TEU], jurisdiction [which] form[s] part of the very foundations of the Community.[161]

The available forms of process fall into, principally, four categories: **5.31**

- direct actions;
- appeals;
- references for preliminary rulings; and
- opinions.

In direct actions the 'application' (*requête*) must contain the subject matter of the proceedings, the form of order sought and a summary of the pleas in law in a manner sufficiently clear and precise so as to enable the defendant to prepare a defence and the Court to rule on it, if necessary, without further information, otherwise the action is inadmissible.[162] The same applies *mutatis mutandis* to appeals.[163] Matters come before the Court via references for preliminary rulings and requests for opinions by means other than application, and different rules apply.

The Court cannot decline jurisdiction when seised competently of a case. **5.32** However it may, after hearing the Advocate-General, dispose of a case by 'reasoned order' without proceeding to judgment (or waiting upon an Advocate-General's opinion) where:

- it is clear that there is an absolute bar to proceedings, where the Court has no jurisdiction or the action is manifestly inadmissible;[164]
- an action raised before the General Court or the Civil Service Tribunal lacks any foundation in law;[165]

---

159 TFEU, art. 344 (ex art. 292 EC).
160 Case C-459/03 *Commission* v *Ireland* (MOX Plant) [2006] ECR I-4635.
161 Cases C-402 and 415/05P *Kadi and Al Bakaraat* v *Council and Commission* (Kadi II) [2008] ECR I-6351, at para. 282.
162 E.g., Case 175/73 *Union Syndicale and ors* v *Council* [1974] ECR 917; Case T-348/94 *Enso Española* v *Commission* (Cartonboard) [1998] ECR II-1875; Case T-319/03 *French and ors* v *Council and Commission* [2004] ECR II-769; Case C-160/03 *Spain* v *Eurojust* [2005] ECR I-2077; Case T-28/03 *Holcim (Deutschland)* v *Commission* [2005] ECR II-1357.
163 RP Court of Justice, art. 168(1)(d); see 5.112 below.
164 RP Court of Justice, arts 150, 53(2); RP General Court, art. 111; RP Civil Service Tribunal, art. 76.
165 RP General Court, art. 111; RP Civil Service Tribunal, art. 76.

- an appeal to the Court of Justice or the General Court is manifestly clearly inadmissible or manifestly clearly unfounded;[166] or
- in a reference to the Court of Justice from a national court under article 267 it is clear the Court has no jurisdiction or the action is manifestly inadmissible,[167] or the question is identical to one upon which the Court has already ruled or the answer may be clearly deduced from existing case law or admits of no reasonable doubt.[168]

Orders can be rendered much more speedily than judgments.

5.33 Pleadings before the Court are by written and oral procedure.[169] Written procedure predominates; in the Court of Justice a hearing is held only at the 'reasoned' request of a party,[170] with which the Court need not comply if it considers it already has sufficient information to decide the case.[171] That said, most cases do have a hearing. But counsel are afforded as a general rule no more than 20 minutes ('20 minutes maximum') to plead before the full Court, the Grand Chamber or a chamber of five judges of the Court of Justice, and no more than 15 minutes before a chamber of three.[172] The general rule is 15 minutes for pleading before the General Court, which may be extended, by leave, where the complexity of a case requires it,[173] and 'normally' 15 or 30 minutes before the Civil Service Tribunal before chambers of three and five judges respectively. [174]

---

166 RP Court of Justice, art. 181 ('manifestly'); RP General Court, art. 145 ('clearly'). In a series of appeals in 2002 (the *Cement* cases) the Court for the first time dismissed a number of pleas raised by the appellants as clearly inadmissible or clearly unfounded by order, reserving the 'runnable' pleas for subsequent argument and judgment; see Case C-204/00P *Aalborg Portland* v *Commission*, order of 5 June 2002, unreported. But the efficiency gained was not thought to be significant, and the exercise has not been repeated.

167 RP Court of Justice, art. 53(2).

168 RP Court of Justice, art. 99. Article 99 was introduced as art. 104(3) in 1991; it originally applied only to references which were identical to one already ruled upon; in 2000 the criteria 'clearly deducible from existing case law' and 'admits of no reasonable doubt' were added, the latter criterion dropped in 2005 but restored in 2012. From 2002 to September 2012, 181 references (about one in 15) were dealt with by art. 104(3) reasoned order.

169 RP Court of Justice, arts 57–85; RP General Court, arts 43–63; RP Civil Service Tribunal, arts 33–53.

170 RP Court of Justice, art. 76(1).

171 *Ibid.*, art. 76(2).

172 Practice Directions relating to direct actions and appeals [2004] OJ L361/15 (as amended), para. 51; Notes for the Guidance of Counsel in Written and Oral Proceedings before the Court of Justice of the European Communities, January 2007, unpublished, para. C.5. The latter still provides for 30 minutes before the full Court, the Grand Chamber or chambers of five judges, as did the former until amended in 2009; presumably the former is definitive.

173 Notes for the Guidance of Counsel at the Hearings of Oral Argument [before the General Court], undated, unpublished, para. II.4. An example of the flexibility of this rule is Case T-201/04 *Microsoft* v *Commission* [2007] ECR II-3601, in which five full days were set aside for the hearing, in the event extending on some of them into the evening.

174 Notes for the guidance of parties and their representatives for the hearing of oral argument before the EU Civil Service Tribunal, June 2006, unpublished, para. 3.5.

The three Courts have issued practice directions which 'reflect, explain and **5.34** complement' their rules of procedure[175] and notes for the guidance of counsel in cases before them.[176]

(a) Parties and interveners

Strictly speaking there are 'parties' only in direct actions before the three courts **5.35** and in appeals taken to the upper two: the person(s) bringing the action (or the appeal) and those against whom it is brought. In such actions member states and Union institutions have the right to be heard as interveners;[177] the right is extended to other EEA member states and the EFTA Surveillance Authority if a case concerns 'one of the fields of application of [the EEA] Agreement',[178] a courtesy reciprocated with a right of intervention by EU member states and the Commission before the EFTA Court of Justice.[179] Other persons may apply to be heard but must show sufficient interest;[180] permission is normally granted (or refused) by the president by way of interim order.[181] In all cases the scope of an intervener's pleadings is limited to supporting the submissions of one or another of the parties.[182] In references to the Court of Justice for preliminary

---

175 Practice Directions, n. 172 above (for the Court of Justice); Practice Directions to parties before the General Court [2012] OJ L68/23; Practice directions to parties on judicial proceedings before the European Union Civil Service Tribunal [2008] OJ L69/13.

176 See for the Court of Justice, n. 172 above; the General Court, n. 173 above and Notes of Guidance for Counsel for the Written Procedure [before the General Court] [1994] OJ C120/16; the Civil Service Tribunal, n. 174 above.

177 Statute of the Court of Justice, art. 40, 1st para. Member states are not shy in using this privilege; the 'record' to date is Case C-440/05 *Commission* v *Council* [2007] ECR I-9097, a sensitive case on criminal jurisdiction (see 6.57 below), in which 19 member states intervened (in vain) in support of the Council.

178 Statute of the Court of Justice, arts 23, 3rd para. and 40, 3rd para. The right is extended further to other non-member states which have concluded an agreement with the Council, the subject matter of the agreement is in issue in a case before the Court, and the agreement expressly so provides; Decision 2002/653 [2002] OJ L218/1; Statute of the Court of Justice, art. 23, 4th para.

179 Statute of the EFTA Court of Justice, art. 36; on the EEA and its institutions, see 14.85–14.86 below.

180 Statute of the Court of Justice, art. 40, 2nd para; for extensive discussion see Case T-201/04R *Microsoft* v *Commission* [2004] ECR II-4463. A person whose application to intervene before the General Court is refused may appeal that decision to the Court of Justice by way of summary procedure; Statute of the Court of Justice, art. 57, 1st and 3rd paras.

181 RP Court of Justice, art. 131(3); RP General Court, art. 116(1); RP Civil Service Tribunal, art. 109(6).

182 An intervener may use arguments new or different from those of the party litigant, so long as in support of the form of order sought by the latter; Case C-150/94 *United Kingdom* v *Council* [1998] ECR I-7235; Case C-248/99P *France* v *Monsanto and Commission* [2002] ECR I-1; Case C-28/09 *Commission* v *Austria*, judgment of 21 December 2011, not yet reported, at para. 50. But it may not raise arguments or pleas completely unconnected with the issues underlying the dispute, as established by the applicant and defendant (Case C-155/91 *Commission* v *Council* [1993] ECR I-939) and may not raise an objection that the action before the Court is inadmissible (Case T-174/95 *Svenska Journalistförbundet* v *Council* [1998] ECR II-2289; Case C-13/00 *Commission* v *Ireland* [2002] ECR I-2943). At the hearing before the Court of Justice an intervener's submissions are restricted to 15 minutes maximum whatever its formation; Practice Directions relating to direct actions and appeals [2004] OJ L361/15 (as amended), para. 51.

rulings, the parties to the main action before the national court,[183] member states, other EEA member states, and the Union and EFTA institutions are entitled to be heard ('to submit statements of case [*mémoires*] or written observations');[184] the Commission always makes use of this right, certainly by lodging written observations and usually also by representation at a hearing by an 'agent', a member of its legal service. Persons other than a member state or a Union institution must be represented by a lawyer authorised to practise before a court of a member state (or an EEA member state),[185] except that, in references, those entitled to appear before the referring national court (a party litigant, for example) may appear before the Court of Justice.

(b) Expedited and urgent procedures

5.36 Since 2001 the president of the General Court may exceptionally, upon the application of a party, order that a case be heard by 'expedited' (or 'fast-track') procedure where the particular urgency of a case requires judgment with a minimum of delay;[186] in the case of a reference to the Court of Justice under article 267 the president may do likewise where the referring court requests it

---

183   It is for the referring court to identify the parties to the main action in accordance with national law; Case 9/74 *Casagrande* v *Hauptzollamt München* [1974] ECR 773. In principle it cannot be fettered in the parties it sees fit to join in the action, who will thereby acquire a right to be heard before the Court of Justice. But a problem is developing of abuse of process in the joining of parties to litigation who have no real interest in the main action but seek (and gain, where it is generously afforded, e.g., the English Civil Procedure Rules (CPR), r. 54.17) that status in order to be heard by the Court. For example in *Football Association Premier League* v *QC Leisure and ors* [2008] EWHC 2897 (Ch), [2009] 1 WLR 1603, the English High Court (Kitchen J) joined several parties to the action but the Court of Justice refused so to recognise them: Cases C-403 and 429/08 *Football Association Premier League* v *QC Leisure and ors*, order of 16 December 2009, unreported. Kitchen J parried with an additional reference from a case initiated by one of the rebuffed parties: *Union of European Football Associations (UEFA)* v *Euroview Sport* [2010] EWHC 1066 (Ch), [2010] EuLR 583, registered as Case C-228/10 *Union of European Football Associations (UEFA) and anor* v *Euroview Sport* but withdrawn by him following the judgment in *QC Leisure* (removed from the register by order of 11 January 2012). The issues were discussed by Ouseley J in *R (Air Transport Association of America and ors)* v *Secretary of State for Energy and Climate Change* [2010] EWHC 1554 (Admin), judgment of 27 May 2010, at paras 4–21.

184   Statute of the Court of Justice, art. 23, 2nd and 3rd paras. Upon arrival of a reference at the Court Registry, each member state (and EFTA state) is notified in order that it may take proper advantage of this privilege; Statute of the Court of Justice, art. 23; RP Court of Justice, art. 98(2). In order to speed up proceedings, since 2005 the notification may be in summary form.

185   Statute of the Court of Justice, art. 19. This includes university teachers if nationals of a member state the law of which accords them rights of audience. An action raised by a party purportedly represented by someone unqualified (Case T-445/04 *Energy Technologies* v *OHIM* [2005] ECR II-677), and any documents submitted by a party in an otherwise competent action not drafted and signed by a lawyer (Case T-320/07 *Jones and ors* v *Commission*, judgment of 23 November 2011, not yet reported), are inadmissible, and a defect which cannot be rectified at a later time (Case C-163/07P *Diy-Mar Insaat Sanayi ve Ticaret Ltd Sirketi and anor* v *Commission* [2007] ECR I-10125). Counsel wear their home court dress before the Courts; British and Irish counsel sometimes find that the earphones supplied (for listening to simultaneous interpretation) wear ill with a wig.

186   Statute of the Court of Justice, art. 23a; RP General Court, art. 76a. A similar procedure applied in the Court of Justice from 2000 but was abandoned in 2012; (previous) RP Court of Justice, art. 62a.

and circumstances require judgment 'within a short time'.[187] A request for either procedure will be refused (by reasoned order of the president) if the case merits no special attention (or no case has been made that it does so)[188] or if it gives rise to complicated and delicate legal issues.[189] In both there is greater emphasis upon oral pleadings than is normally the case. A judgment can be furnished under the expedited procedure in four to 12 months, and the General Court is significantly more generous than was the Court of Justice in granting it.[190] This is to be compared with the 25 months which is the average life span of a case before the General Court.[191] As for the accelerated (now expedited) procedure before the Court of Justice under article 267, to the end of 2007 the

---

187   Statute of the Court of Justice, art. 23a; RP Court of Justice, art. 105. From 2000 to 2012 this was the accelerated procedure which applied where a judgment was required as 'a matter of exceptional urgency'; (previous) RP, art. 104a.

188   E.g., Case C-344/04 *R (International Air Transport Association and ors)* v *Department of Transport*, order of 24 September 2004, unreported; Case C-341/05 *Laval un Partneri* v *Svenska Byggnadsarbetareförbundet and ors* (Vaxholm), order of 15 November 2005, unreported.

189   E.g., Case T-306/01 *Yusuf* v *Council and Commission* [2005] ECR II-3533; Case T-464/04 *Independent Music Publishers and Labels Association (Impala)* v *Commission* [2006] ECR II-2289.

190   The Court of Justice applied the (now abandoned) expedited procedure of art. 62a only three times, twice in a direct action (Case C-39/03P *Commission* v *Artegodan and ors* [2003] ECR I-7885 and Case C-27/04 *Commission* v *Council* [2004] ECR I-6649, both of which took five and a half months from lodging of application to judgment); once in an appeal case (Case C-503/07P *Saint-Gobain Glass Deutschland* v *Commission* [2008] ECR I-2217; five months). The General Court has been much more accommodating: see Cases T-195 and 207/01 *Government of Gibraltar* v *Commission* [2002] ECR II-2309 (the first case heard by expedited procedure, eight months); Cases T-346 and 347/02 *Cableuropa and ors* v *Commission* [2003] ECR II-4251 (ten months); Case T-87/05 *Energias de Portugal* v *Commission* [2005] ECR II-3745 (ten months); Case T-178/05 *United Kingdom* v *Commission* [2005] ECR II-4807 (six and a half months); Case T-417/05 *Endesa* v *Commission* [2007] ECR II-2533 (seven and a half months); Cases T-376 and 383/05 *TEA-SEGOS and anor* v *Commission* [2007] ECR II-205 (four months); Case T-170/06 *Alrosa Company* v *Commission* [2007] ECR II-2601 (12 and a half months); Case T-182/06 *Netherlands* v *Commission* [2007] ECR II-1983 (11 and a half months); Case T-282/06 *Sun Chemical Group* v *Commission* [2007] ECR II-2149 (nine months); Case T-28/07 *Fels-Werke and ors* v *Commission* [2007] ECR II-98* (seven months); Case T-206/07 *Foshan Shunde Yongjian Housewares & Hardware Co.* v *Council* [2008] ECR II-1 (seven and a half months); Case T-284/08 *People's Mojahedin Organization of Iran* v *Council* [2008] ECR II-3487 (four and a half months; including the exceptional achievement of delivering judgment the day after the oral hearing); Cases T-246 and 332/08 *Melli Bank* v *Council* [2009] ECR II-2629 (11 and a half months); Case T-390/08 *Bank Melli Iran* v *Council* [2009] ECR II-3967 (13 months) Case T-86/11 *Bamba* v *Council*, judgment of 8 June 2011, not yet reported (4 months); Case T-12/12 *Laboratoires CTRS* v *Commission*, judgment of 4 July 2012, not yet reported (6 months). It must be said that some expedited judgments are, owing to procedural or other quirks, not very: Case T-341/07 *Sison* v *Council* (Sison II) [2009] ECR II-3625 (23 months); Case T-85/09 *Kadi* v *Commission* (Kadi III) [2010] ECR II-5177 (18 months).

191   But there is, of course, a wide variation here: a staff case (in which the General Court had first instance jurisdiction until 2005) can be dealt with quite expeditiously, whilst a complicated (or sensitive) competition case (or one to which no urgency adheres and is always at the back of the queue) can take several years; e.g., Case T-41/96 *Bayer* v *Commission* [2000] ECR II-3383 (four and a half years); Cases T-122/02 *Bolloré and ors* v *Commission* [2007] ECR II-947 (five years); Case T-145/89 *Baustahlgewebe* v *Commission* [1995] ECR II-987 (five and a half years); Case T-13/03 *Nintendo and anor* v *Commission* [2009] ECR II-947 (six and a quarter years); Case T-419/03 *Altstoff Recycling Austria* v *Commisson*, judgment of 22 March 2011, not yet reported (seven and a quarter years); Cases T-57/01 and T-58/01 *Solvay* v *Commission (Soda Ash)* [2009] ECR II-4621 and II-4781 (eight and three-quarters years); Case T-66/01 *Imperial Chemical Industries* v *Commission (Soda Ash)* [2010] ECR II-2631 (nine and a half years).

only judgment adopting it (out of 31 requests) was delivered in 2001,[192] the exceptional urgency being a function of measures to combat the spread of foot and mouth disease, and the case took a very impressive 11 weeks from arrival at the Registry to judgment. Two further accelerated judgments were delivered in 2008, four in 2010 and two in 2011, involving

- the execution by a German court of a Polish arrest warrant;[193]
- residence permits of non-Union nationals married to Union citizens in Ireland;[194]
- an ongoing criminal trial on terrorist-related offences;[195]
- a claim for doubling the period of maternity leave from employment following the birth of twins;[196]
- a hybrid case involving extension of the term of detention of third country nationals 'irregularly' present in France but also the compatibility with Union law of French procedural rules;[197]
- enforcement of a custody order;[198]
- removal of third country nationals, family members of home nationals, for unauthorised residence;[199] and
- imprisonment of a third country national for illegal entry and residence.[200]

The judgments were delivered, respectively, within 20, 14, 17, 17, 6(!), $16^{1}/_{2}$, $9^{1}/_{2}$ and $9^{1}/_{2}$ weeks of the decision to apply the procedure; a preliminary ruling requires, on average, 17 months from lodging of reference to judgment.

5.37 In 2008 there came into being an 'urgent preliminary ruling procedure', informally the ppu (*procédure préjudicielle d'urgence*), in order to deal with preliminary references in cases concerning specifically the area of freedom, security and justice (*justice, liberté, securité*, JLS)[201] in which a ruling is required

---

192 Case C-189/01 *Jippes* v *Minister van Landbouw, Natuurbeheer en Visserij* [2001] ECR I-5689.

193 Case C-66/08 *Kozłowski* [2008] ECR I-6041.

194 Case C-127/08 *Metock and ors* v *Minister for Justice, Equality and Law Reform* [2008] ECR I-6241.

195 Case C-550/09 *Criminal proceedings against E and F* [2010] ECR I-6213.

196 Case C-149/10 *Chatzi* v *Ipourgos Ikonomikon* [2010] ECR I-8489.

197 Cases C-188 and 189/10 *Melki and Abdeli* [2010] ECR I-5667. Owing to those procedural rules it was 'essential' (Cases C-188 and 189/10 *Melki and Abdeli*, order of 12 May 2010, unreported, at para. 16) that the preliminary ruling be supplied within three months.

198 Case 296/10 *Purrucker* v *Vallés Pérez* (Purrucker II) [2010] ECR I-11163.

199 Case C-256/11 *Dereci and ors* v *Bundesministerium für Inneres*, judgment of 15 November 2011, not yet reported.

200 Case C-329/11 *Achughbabian* v *Préfet du Val-de-Marne*, judgment of 6 December 2011, not yet reported.

201 See 11.164–11.176 below.

as a matter of urgency[202] (so the 'urgent procedure', not to be confused with the confusing 'exceptional urgency' under the accelerated procedure). The referring national court may request that the matter be dealt with by the ppu or the Court itself may, exceptionally, elect it.[203] The reference goes to a chamber of five judges designated (on an annual basis) for that purpose[204] which considers the urgency of the matter, decides whether the procedure is merited, and may hear the case as three or five judges or refer it to the Court of Justice for re-assignment to a larger bench.[205] In cases of 'extreme urgency' the written procedure may be dispensed with,[206] and in all cases the hearing is crucial, affording other member states the first effective opportunity to make representation to the Court and being generally longer and more interactive than the norm. The Advocate-General is 'heard'[207] but produces no formal opinion, only a 'view' or *prise de position* (which is expected to be made available within 48 hours of the hearing). The Court has supplemented its general guidance on preliminary references in light of adoption of the ppu.[208] The Treaties provide that if a reference is made from a court or tribunal of a member state 'with regard to a person in custody, the Court of Justice ... shall act with the minimum of delay',[209] in which case the (extreme) urgent procedure is presumably to be put into play.[210]

5.38 The first case in which the ppu was requested arrived at the Court in February 2008 but the request was premature as the procedure had not yet come into force (on 1 March 2008), so the Court elected instead the accelerated procedure.[211] As of September 2012 there have been 14 ppu judgments, six on fathers seeking to enforce custody/residence/guardianship/return orders of German, Italian, German, Irish, Spanish and English courts in Lithuania, Slovenia, Austria, England, Germany and England, respectively, whither the mothers

---

202 Statute of the Court of Justice, art. 23a; RP Court of Justice, arts 107–114. For discussion of the circumstances which will justify it see Case C-491/10 PPU *Aguirre Zarraga* v *Pelz*, [2010] ECR I-14247, at paras 38–41.

203 RP Court of Justice, art. 107(1). This compares with the accelerated procedure under art. 104a which required to be requested by the referring court.

204 *Ibid.* art. 11(2).

205 *Ibid.* art. 113.

206 *Ibid.* art. 111.

207 *Ibid.* art. 112.

208 [2008] OJ C64/1; see now Information Note on References by National Courts for a Preliminary Ruling [2011] OJ C160/1, Part II.

209 TFEU, art. 267, 4th para.

210 But see Case C-329/11 *Achughbabian*, n. 200 above, in which the ppu was requested by the referring court but refused without reasons given. Mr Achughbabian had, however, been released from detention at the time the reference was made, and the case was already subject to an accelerated procedure.

211 Case C-66/08 *Kozłowski*, order of 22 February 2008, unreported.

had absconded with their infant/young daughters/sons;[212] three requests for interpretation of the framework decision on the European arrest warrant,[213] on extradition of individuals arrested (and held) for terrorist offences, serious drugs offences and other multiple offences in France, Spain and Finland;[214] three on imprisonment of illegally staying third country nationals in Bulgaria, Italy and the Netherlands either pending deportation or following failure to obey an order to quit the country;[215] one on parental responsibility and an order to place an Irish child habitually in care in Ireland in a secure institution in England;[216] and on imprisonment in Germany of a human smuggler for supplying forged visas.[217] Judgments were delivered in 49, 49, 51, 55, 55, 55, 36, 77, 65, 38, 70, 38 57 and 42 days respectively from the decision to apply the procedure.[218] Two other cases were accorded ppu status but were not carried to judgment, one withdrawn by the referring court,[219] the other deprived (by a national ministry changing its mind) of purpose.[220] The accelerated procedure remains, applicable for matters 'of exceptional urgency' not related (wholly)[221] to JLS, but is thought unikely to be deployed often; with ever-increasing Union activity in JLS fields, the frequency of recourse to the ppu can only increase.

---

212 Case C-195/08 PPU *Rinau* [2008] ECR I-5271; Case C-403/09 PPU *Detiček* v *Sgueglia* [2009] ECR I-12193; Case C-211/10 PPU *Povse* v *Alpago* [2010] ECR I-6669; Case C-400/10 PPU *JMcB* v *LE* [2010] ECR I-8965; Case C-491/10 PPU *Aguirre Zarraga* v *Pelz* [2010] ECR I-14247; Case C497/10 PPU *Mercredi* v *Chaffe* [2010] ECR I-14309 (which turned upon not enforcement but the competence of an English court to order the return of the daughter from Réunion, France). The cases concerned Regulation 2201/2003 [2003] OJ L338/1 on jurisdiction and recognition and enforcement of judgments in matrimonial matters and matters of parental responsibility.

213 Framework Decision 2002/584 OJ 2002 L190/1.

214 Case C-296/08 PPU *Santesteban Goicoechea* [2008] ECR I-6307; Case 388/08 PPU *Criminal proceedings against Leymann & Pustovarov* [2008] ECR I-8993; Case C-192/12 PPU *West*, judgment of 28 June 2012, not yet reported.

215 Case C-357/09 PPU *Kadzoev* v *Direktsia 'Migratsia' pri Ministerstvo na vatreshnite raboti* [2009] ECR I-11189 (unlike other ppu cases referred to and heard and determined by the Grand Chamber); Case C-61/11 PPU *Criminal proceedings against El Dridi*, judgment of 28 April 2011, not yet reported; Case C-278/12 PPU *Adil* v *Minister voor Immigratie, Integraite en Asiel*, judgment of 28 April 2011, not yet reported; Case C-278/12 PPU *Adil* v *Minister voor Immigratie, Integratie en Asiel*, judgment of 19 July 2012, not yet reported.

216 Case C-92/12 PPU *Health Service Executive* v *SC & AC*, judgment of 26 April 2012, not yet reported.

217 Case C-83/12 PPU *Criminal proceedings against Vo*, judgment of 10 April 2012, not yet reported.

218 The (exceptional) speed of the judgement in Case C-296/08 PPU *Santesteban Goicoechea* (36 days) may be attributable in part to the language of the referring court (French), so obviating the need for translation. The same advantage accrued to Cases C-188 & 189/10 *Melki & Abdeli* (n. 197 above), accorded the accelerated procedure and judgement rendered in 39 days. Yet the court managed to dispose of Case C-278/12 PPU *Asil*, in Dutch, in 38 days.

219 Case C-105/10 PPU *Virallinen syyttäjä* v *Gataev and Gataeva*, involving refugee status; removed from the register by order of 3 April 2010.

220 Case C-155/11 PPU *Mohammed Imran* v *Minister van Buitenlandse Zaken*, involving family integration; order of 7 June 2011, not yet reported.

221 Cases C-188 and 189/10 *Melki and Abdeli*, n. 197 above, suggests that the accelerated, and not urgent, procedure is the correct procedure to be applied to hybrid cases.

(c)   Interim measures

5.39 An action raised before the Court of Justice has no suspensory effect.[222] However, the Court may, upon an application from a party to a case before it, order that the application of a contested Union act be suspended 'if it considers that the circumstances so require'[223] or in any action order any 'necessary' interim or interlocutory measures:[224]

> Such broad wording is obviously intended to grant sufficient powers to the judge hearing an application for interim measures to prescribe any measure which he deems necessary to guarantee the full effectiveness of the definitive future decision, in order to ensure that there is no lacuna in the legal protection provided by the Community Courts. [225]

Interim measures cannot be sought without raising a 'main action' (or main proceedings) to which the application for interim measures is ancillary.[226] An application for interim order is by way of summary procedure,[227] and the ensuing decision (*sic*) is made by reasoned order.[228] It may be, and normally is, heard and determined by the president sitting alone.[229] As an interim order cannot prejudge the outcome in the main action[230] the Court may not, as a rule, examine issues of admissibility, although that may be necessary where the action is argued to be manifestly inadmissible in order to rebut it.[231] Where circumstances justify/require it, the Court may, as a precautionary measure, adopt provisional interim measures.[232]

5.40 The Court is competent to suspend the application of any Union act (including a judgment of the General Court or the Civil Service Tribunal) or of any national measure which is in issue in the main action, and it will do so where

---

222 TFEU, art. 278 (ex art. 242 EC).

223 *Ibid.*

224 *Ibid.* art. 279 (ex art. 243 EC).

225 Case T-411/07R *Aer Lingus Group* v *Commission* [2008] ECR II-411, at para. 56.

226 RP Court of Justice, art. 160(1), (2); RP General Court, art. 104(1); RP Civil Service Tribunal, art. 102(1). An application for interim measures is given the same number as the main action but is distinguished by an additional letter 'R', for *référé*.

227 Statute of the Court of Justice, art. 39.

228 RP Court of Justice, art. 102(1); RP General Court, art. 107(1); RP Civil Service Tribunal, art. 105(1).

229 Statute of the Court of Justice, art. 39. For an exception see Case C-180/96R *United Kingdom* v *Commission* (BSE) [1996] ECR I-3903, which, owing to commercial importance and high political sensitivity, was heard and determined by the full court.

230 RP Court of Justice, art. 162(4); RP General Court, art. 107(4); RP Civil Service Tribunal, art. 105(4).

231 Case T-18/10R *Inuit Tapiriit Kanatami and ors* v *Parliament and Council* [2010] ECR II-75*, at para. 38 and case law cited.

232 Case C-320/03R *Commission* v *Austria* [2003] ECR I-7929, made permanent (until date of judgment in the main action) in Case C-320/03R *Commission* v *Austria* [2004] ECR I-3593; Case T-18/10R II *Inuit Tapiriit Kanatami and ors* v *Parliament and Council*, order of 19 August 2010, unreported, at para. 2 and case law cited, cancelled (*rapporté*) in Case T-18/10R II, [2010] ECR II-235.

there is a *prima facie* case (or *fumus boni juris*), urgency and a likelihood of serious and irreparable injury by the continuing application of that measure.[233] Urgency is to be assessed in relation to the necessity for interim relief in order to prevent serious and irreparable damage to the party requesting it;[234] it is for him to adduce sound evidence that he cannot wait for the outcome of the main proceedings without suffering, or very likely suffering, damage of that kind.[235] Damage of a pecuniary nature is irreparable only exceptionally, where the applicant's existence would otherwise be imperilled.[236] The conditions are cumulative, so that an application for interim relief must be dismissed if any one of them is absent;[237] there is no pre-established scheme of analysis for their consideration and the Court may consider them in any manner and order it sees fit.[238] It must also, where appropriate, balance the interests concerned.[239] Generally there can be no suspension of a negative administrative measure since an order to that effect may not change an applicant's legal position.[240] The Court may require the lodging of a cross-undertaking in damages or caution (a 'security'), the 'amount and nature to be fixed in the light of the circumstances'.[241] Orders of the General Court or of the Civil Service Tribunal granting or refusing interim measures may be appealed directly to the Court of Justice or to the General Court, as the case may be, by way of summary procedure.[242]

5.41 The exception to the general rule is in the context of proceedings before the Court of Justice by virtue of the preliminary ruling procedure of article 267: here the Court will order no interim suspension, that being a matter for the referring national court.[243]

---

233 RP Court of Justice, art. 160(3); RP General Court, art. 104(2); RP Civil Service Tribunal, art. 102(2). For good discussion of the issues see Case C-149/95P(R) *Commission* v *Atlantic Container Line* [1995] ECR I-2165; Case T-41/96R *Bayer* v *Commission* [1996] ECR II-381; Case C-393/96P(R) *Antonissen* v *Council and Commission* [1997] ECR I-441; Case T-65/98R *van den Bergh Foods* v *Commission* [1998] ECR II-2641; Case T-184/01R *IMS Health* v *Commission* [2001] ECR II-3193; Case C-481/01P(R) *NDC Health and anor* v *IMS Health and anor* [2002] ECR I-3401; Case C-7/04P(R) *Commission* v *Akzo Nobel Chemicals and anor* [2004] ECR I-8739; Case T-201/04R *Microsoft* v *Commission* [2004] ECR II-4463.

234 Cases T-195 and 207/01R *Government of Gibraltar* v *Commission* [2001] ECR II-3915, at para. 95.

235 Case T-34/02R *B* v *Commission* [2002] ECR II-2803, at para. 85; Case C-355/99P(R) *HFB Holding für Fernwärmetechnik Beteiligungsgesellschaft and ors* v *Commission* [1999] ECR I-8705, at para. 67.

236 Case T-181/02R *Neue Erba Lautex* v *Commission* [2002] ECR II-5081, at para. 84.

237 Case C-268/96P(R) *Stichting Certificatie Kraanverhuurbedrijf and anor* v *Commission* [1996] ECR I-4971; Case C-7/04P(R) *Akzo Nobel Chemicals*, n. 233 above; Case T-411/07R *Aer Lingus Group* v *Commission* [2008] ECR II-411, at para. 33.

238 Case C-149/95P(R) *Commission* v *Atlantic Container Line and ors* [1995] ECR I-2165, at para. 23.

239 Case C-445/00R *Austria* v *Council* [2001] ECR I-1461, at para. 73.

240 Case C-206/89R *S* v *Commission* [1989] ECR 2841, at para. 14; Case C-488/01P(R) *Front national and anor* v *Parliament* [2002] ECR I-1843, at para. 73.

241 RP Court of Justice, art. 162(2); RP General Court, art. 107(2); RP Civil Service Tribunal, art. 105(2).

242 Statute of the Court of Justice, art. 57, 2nd and 3rd paras; Annex I, art. 10(2) and (3).

243 See 5.140 below.

(d) Costs/expenses

5.42 A final judgment or order which closes proceedings always includes a direction as to costs or expenses (*dépens*).[244] The losing party is ordered to pay the costs provided that the winning party has applied for them in its pleadings.[245] A party which loses in the General Court but succeeds on appeal may recover costs of proceedings in both courts.[246] Recoverable costs are those 'necessarily incurred', or 'objectively necessary', for the purpose of the proceedings at issue;[247] in the event of dispute between the parties, costs may be taxed by the appropriate Court, and by the chamber which decided the case.[248] Costs may be split at the Court's discretion where each party succeeds in part and fails in part.[249] Interveners generally pay their own costs.[250] A successful party may be ordered to bear its own costs where circumstances are exceptional or where it caused the other side to incur costs unreasonably or vexatiously,[251] and in 2003, for the first time, the General Court ordered (essentially) successful parties to do so because it found the length of their written submissions to be so extensive as to amount to an abuse.[252] Where a case does not proceed to judgment (or order) costs are at the discretion of the Court.[253] There are special rules for staff cases raised under article 270.[254] No costs are awarded in preliminary ruling proceedings under article 267, they being a matter for the referring national court.

---

244 In proceedings seeking interim remedies costs are reserved.

245 RP Court of Justice, art. 138(1); RP General Court, art. 87(2); RP Civil Service Tribunal, art. 87(1). Applying for costs only at the hearing stage appears not to debar their award; Cases T-225 etc./06 *Budějovický Budvar* v *OHIM* [2008] ECR II-3555, at para. 206 and case law cited.

246 RP Court of Justice, art. 138(1) with art. 184(1). If a case is remitted back to the General Court by the Court of Justice costs are reserved.

247 See Case T-290/94-DEP *Kaysersberg* v *Commission* [1998] ECR II-4105.

248 RP Court of Justice, art. 148; RP General Court, art. 92(1); RP Civil Service Tribunal, art. 92(1). An application for taxation of costs may be identified by the suffix 'DEP', for *dépens*. For examples see Case T-290/94-DEP *Kaysersberg*, ibid.; Case C-286/95P-DEP *Imperial Chemical Industries* v *Commission* [2004] ECR I-6469; Case T-342/99-DEP *Airtours* v *Commission* [2004] ECR II-1785.

249 RP Court of Justice, art. 138(2); RP General Court, art. 87(3); RP Civil Service Tribunal, art. 89(2).

250 RP Court of Justice, art. 140; RP General Court, art. 87(4); RP Civil Service Tribunal, art. 89(4).

251 RP Court of Justice, art. 139; RP General Court, art. 87(3); RP Civil Service Tribunal, art. 88.

252 Cases T-191 etc./98 *Atlantic Container Line and ors* v *Commission* [2003] ECR II-3275.

253 RP Court of Justice, art. 142; RP General Court, art. 87(6); RP Civil Service Tribunal, art. 89(6).

254 Before the General Court an institution met its own costs in a staff case irrespective of the outcome (RP General Court, art. 88). First instance jurisdiction in staff cases now assumed by the Civil Service Tribunal, in cases raised before it since its own Rules of Procedure entered into force (1 November 2007) the losing party is liable for costs (RP Civil Service Tribunal, arts 87(1) and 122) unless equity (*equité, Billigkeit*) requires otherwise (art. 87(2)). If a judgment of the Civil Service Tribunal is appealed by an institution to the General Court the institution bears its own costs irrespective of the outcome (RP General Court, arts 88 and 148, 2nd para.; if raised (unsuccessfully) by an official costs are borne by him or her unless apportioned where equity requires it (RP General Court, art. 148, 2nd para.

(e) Legal aid

5.43 Legal aid is available directly from each Court[255] to a party who is 'wholly or in part unable to meet the costs of proceedings'.[256] A party may apply for legal aid prior to or in the course of proceedings, evidence of need is required, and the application need not be made through a lawyer; application forms are available from the Courts, the Civil Service Tribunal form accessible to be downloaded from the Court's website. The Court of Justice has stated a view on the circumstances in which legal aid must be provided for the effective protection of a Union law right in a national court,[257] which presumably apply *mutatis mutandis* to the Union Courts. The decision on the application is made in the Court of Justice by a chamber (the chamber of three to which the judge-rapporteur belongs), in the General Court and the Civil Service Tribunal by the president.[258] Reasons are given for a refusal.[259] There is no appeal.[260]

(f) Discontinuance

5.44 The president will order a case to be removed (*radiée*) from the register if, in direct actions, the applicant informs the Court in writing that he wishes to discontinue,[261] the agreement of the defendant not being required;[262] or, except in the case of (judicial review) proceedings raised under articles 263 or 265,[263] if the parties settle before a judgment is delivered and abandon their claims.[264] In cases of preliminary references under article 267 settlement and/or discontinuance is a matter for the referring national court.[265]

(g) Interpretation; revision; rectification; third party proceedings

5.45 If the meaning or scope of a judgment (or order)[266] is unclear or in doubt, the Court 'shall construe it' (*dieses ... auszulegen; il appartient à la Cour de l'interpréter*) upon application of a party or a Union institution with sufficient

---

255 RP Court of Justice, art. 115; RP General Court, arts 94–7; RP Civil Service Tribunal, art. 95.
256 RP Court of Justice, arts 115(1), 185(1); RP General Court, art. 94(2); RP Civil Service Tribunal, art. 95(2). An application for legal aid may be identified by a case number with the suffix AJ (*aide judiciaire*) attached.
257 Case C-279/09 *DEB Deutsche Enrgiehandels- und Beratungsgesellschaft* v *Bundesrepublik Deutschland*, [2010] ECR I-13849.
258 RP Court of Justice, arts 116(1), 187(1); RP General Court, art. 96(2); RP Civil Service Tribunal, art. 97(2).
259 RP Court of Justice, arts 116(4), 187(3); RP General Court, art. 96(2), 2nd para.; RP Civil Service Tribunal, art. 97(2), 2nd para. Neither the Court of Justice nor the General Court gave reasons until a change to their Rules of Procedure in 2005.
260 RP General Court, art. 96(6); RP Civil Service Tribunal, art. 97(6).
261 RP Court of Justice, art. 148; RP General Court, art. 99.
262 See e.g., Case C-120/94 *Commission* v *Greece* (Macedonia) [1996] ECR I-1513.
263 RP Court of Justice, art. 147(2); RP General Court, art. 98.
264 RP Court of Justice, art. 147(1); RP General Court, art. 98; RP Civil Service Tribunal, art. 69.
265 See 5.137 below.
266 Case C-114/08P(R)-INT *Pellegrini* v *Commission* [2010] ECR I-48*.

interest.[267] The application goes to the same Court and same chamber which produced the original judgment[268] and is, if successful, decided in the form of a second judgment.[269] In order to be admissible it must concern the operative part of the judgment in question and the essential grounds thereof, and seek to resolve an obscurity or ambiguity that may affect the meaning or scope of that judgment insofar as the Court was required to decide the particular case before it; it is inadmissible where it relates to matters not decided by the judgment or seeks to obtain from the Court an opinion on the application, implementation or consequences of the judgment.[270] An application for interpretation is very rare, its admissibility rarer still.[271]

A judgment (or order)[272] of the Court may also be 'revised' (*révisé; wieder-* **5.46** *aufnahmen*), by the Court which issued it, upon 'discovery of a fact which is of such a nature as to be a decisive factor, and which, when the judgment was given, was unknown to the Court and to the party claiming it'.[273] Revision is *not* an appeal procedure; rather it is

> an exceptional review procedure that allows the authority of *res judicata* attaching to a final judgment or to an order ... to be called into question on the basis of the findings of fact relied upon by the Court. Revision presupposes the discovery of elements of a factual nature which existed prior to the judgment or the order and which were unknown at that time to the Court which delivered the judgment or the order as well as to the party applying for revision and which, had the Court been able to take them into consideration, could have led it to a different determination of the proceedings.[274]

---

267 Statute of the Court of Justice, art. 158; RP Court of Justice, art. 102; RP General Court, art. 129; RP Civil Service Tribunal, art. 118.

268 RP General Court, art. 129(2); RP Civil Service Tribunal, art. 118(2); the Rules of Procedure of the Court of Justice are silent on the matter. The application is given the original case number and, sometimes (there is no consistent style), a suffix 'A' (for '*application*'), a number (to reflect the relevant provision of the Rules of Procedure), or 'INT' or 'INTP', for *interprétation*.

269 RP Court of Justice, art. 159(6); RP General Court, art. 129(3); RP Civil Service Tribunal, art. 118(3). An application is normally found and declared inadmissible by reasoned order.

270 Case T-22/91 INT *Raiola-Denti and ors v Council* [1993] ECR II-817; Case T-573/93(129) *Caballero Montoya v Commission* [1997] ECR-SC II-761, at para. 27 and case law cited; Case F-1/05 INT *Landgren v Fondation européenne pour la formation*, order of 13 July 2007, unreported; Case T-284/08 INTP *People's Mojahedin Organization of Iran v Council* [2008] ECR II-334*; Case T-348/05 INTP *JSC Kirovo-Chapetsky Khimichesky Kombinat v Council* [2009] ECR II-116*.

271 The only reported successes are Cases 41 etc./73 INT *Société anonyme Générale sucrière and ors v Commission* [1977] ECR 445; Case C-245/95P INT *NSK and ors v Commission* [1999] ECR I-1; Case T-348/05 INTP *JSC Kirovo-Chapetsky Khimichesky Kombinat*, ibid.

272 Cases C-199 and 200/94REV *Compañia Internacional de Pesca y Derivados v Commission* [1998] ECR I-831.

273 Statute of the Court of Justice, art. 44.

274 Case C-255/06P-REV *Yedaş Tarim ve Otomotiv Sanayi ve Ticaret v Council and Commission* [2009] ECR I-53*, at para. 16.

An application for revision must be made within three months of the date on which the relevant fact(s) became known to the applicant[275] and is time-barred after ten years.[276] Admissibility is considered (in the General Court and the Civil Service Tribunal) upon the basis of written pleadings alone;[277] this is 'a first phase ..., which opens with a judgment expressly recording the existence of a new fact, recognising that it is of such a character as to lay the case open to revision, and declaring the application admissible on that ground'.[278] If admissible, the Court then proceeds to judgment on the merits as normally.[279] In no case, following only a handful of attempts, has the Court found a petition for revision admissible. However, the Court may also, of its own motion or upon application by a party made within two weeks of delivery of a judgment, 'rectify' (*rectifier*, *berichtigen*) 'clerical mistakes, errors in calculation and obvious inaccuracies slips in it',[280] and this does happen from time to time.[281]

5.47 Exceptionally, a judgment of the Court may be challenged by third parties ('third party proceedings'; *tierce opposition*) who were not heard and whose rights were prejudiced by the judgment.[282] A successful challenge causes the judgment to be varied (*modifié*, *ändern*) on the points on which the submissions are upheld.[283] This 'extraordinary, even exceptional' remedy is justified by considerations of legal certainty and efficient administration of justice, to safeguard the rights of any person who may have a legitimate interest in proceedings before the Court.[284] In order to be admissible a third party must therefore show 'valid reasons'[285] for which he was unable to take part (by, for example, intervention) in the original proceedings before the Court and demonstrate not only that there is a legitimate interest to protect but that the judgment is prejudicial to his rights.[286] There has never been a successful challenge.

---

275 RP Court of Justice, art. 159(2); RP General Court, art. 125; RP Civil Service Tribunal, art. 119(1).
276 Statute of the Court of Justice, art. 44, 3rd para.
277 RP Court of Justice, art. 100(1); RP General Court, art. 127(2); RP Civil Service Tribunal, art. 119(3). Prior to 2012 also in the Court of Justice, and in closed session; (previous) RP, art. 100(1).
278 Case 116/78REV *Bellintani and ors* v *Commission* [1980] ECR 23, at para. 3.
279 RP Court of Justice, art. 159(6); RP General Court, art. 127(3); RP Civil Service Tribunal, art. 119(3).
280 RP Court of Justice, arts 108(1), 154(1) 'inaccuracies'; RP General Court, art. 84(1) ('slips'); RP Civil Service Tribunal, art. 84(1) ('slips').
281 E.g., recently, Case T-289/03REC *BUPA* v *Commission*, order of 29 April 2008, unreported; Case T-321/07REC *Lufthansa AirPlus Servicekarten* v *Office for Harmonisation in the Internal Market (Trade Marks and Designs) (OHIM)*, order of 19 May 2010, unreported.
282 Statute of the Court of Justice, art. 157; RP Court of Justice, art. 97; RP General Court, art. 123; RP Civil Service Tribunal, art. 117.
283 RP Court of Justice, art. 157(5); RP General Court, art. 123(3); RP Civil Service Tribunal, art. 117(3).
284 Case T-35/98TO *Ascasibar Zubizarreta and ors* v *Albani and ors* [1992] ECR II-1599, at para. 31; Case T-284/08TO *Avaki and ors* v *People's Mojahedin Organization of Iran and Council* [2009] ECR II-161*, at para. 14.
285 Case T-35/98TO *Ascasibar Zubizarreta*, n. 284 above, at para. 33; Case T-284/08TO *Avaki*, n. 284 above, at para. 16.
286 RP Court of Justice, art. 157(1); RP General Court, art. 123(1); RP Civil Service Tribunal, art. 117(2).

2.   Direct actions

(a)   Action for failure to fulfil an obligation (articles 258–60 TFEU)

The action for failure to fulfil an obligation is an action brought against a **5.48** member state by the Commission under article 258 or by another member state under article 259 of the TFEU. However, enforcement proceedings raised by one member state against another have not proved a popular form of action, article 259 seeing action only six times.[287] The purpose of the action is to obtain an authoritative declaration that the defendant member state has failed to fulfil an obligation incumbent upon it under Union law. It thus created a mechanism of autonomous enforcement of Treaty obligations, for its time a radical solution to the traditional weakness of public international law in drawing compliance from intransigent contracting parties; it 'plays an essential role in guaranteeing the correct application of the law'[288] and is 'the *ultima ratio* enabling the Community interests enshrined in the Treaty to prevail over the inertia and resistance of Member States'.[289]

An action may be raised under article 258 for virtually any failure to comply **5.49** with a Treaty obligation, save where the Treaties provide, *lege speciali*, other means of enforcement in specific areas.[290] The failure may be one of omission – frequently a failure to implement a Directive within the prescribed time limit or failure to implement it properly – or of commission – the adoption or enforcement of national legislation or the implementation of national policy in a manner incompatible with Union law. In keeping with general principles, article 258 does not distinguish amongst the various regions or authorities within the state: even if the failure is attributable, as a matter of constitutional law, to a province, a region or a municipality, the action is *not* raised against, and defended by, them, it is raised against the member state as an indivisible

---

287   Two of these cases (Case 58/77 *Ireland* v *France* and Case C-349/92 *Spain* v *United Kingdom*) were settled before judgment and withdrawn; the rest led to a judgment (Case 141/78 *France* v *United Kingdom* [1979] ECR 2923; Case C-388/95 *Belgium* v *Spain (Rioja)* [2000] ECR I-3123; Case C-145/04 *Spain* v *United Kingdom* [2006] ECR I-7917). The latter was an action which, owing to 'the sensitivity of the underlying bilateral issue' (at para. 32; the issue being voting rights in Gibraltar for European elections), the Commission would not raise. The sixth, Case C-364/10 *Hungary* v *Slovakia*, judgment of 16 October 2012, not yet reported, was even more sensitive, involving the latter's ban upon an unofficial visit of the Hungarian president to the (Slovak but ethnically Hungarian) border town of Komárno; see 8.10 below, n. 23. It should be noted that member states may, and frequently do, intervene (see 5.35 above) from time to time in support of (or against) the Commission in an action raised under TFEU, art. 258 against another member state; see e.g., Case C-304/02 *Commission* v *France* [2005] ECR I-6263, in which 16 of the then 25 member states intervened.
288   *26th Annual Report on Monitoring the Application of Community Law*, COM(2009) 675 final, at para. 2.2.
289   Case 20/59 *Italy* v *High Authority* [1960] ECR 325 at 339; Case 25/59 *Netherlands* v *High Authority* [1960] ECR 355 at 374 (referring to art. 88 ECSC = art. 258 TFEU).
290   See 5.64 below.

person;[291] in this, Union law cleaves to the public international law view of the state.[292] So, Belgium must answer for a failure attributable (as a matter of Belgian law) to a community or region,[293] Italy for its municipalities (*comuni*),[294] regions[295] and autonomous provinces,[296] Spain for its autonomous communities,[297] Germany for the various *Länder*,[298] the United Kingdom for Gibraltar,[299] and Finland for the Åland islands,[300] notwithstanding these regions may have their own parliaments with sole constitutional responsibility for the substantive area in question and immune from the authority of the centre:

> [T]he fact that a Member State has conferred on its regions the responsibility for giving effect to directives cannot have any bearing on the application of Article [258]. The Court has consistently held that a Member State cannot plead conditions existing within its own legal system in order to justify its failure to comply with obligations and time-limits resulting from Community directives. While each Member State may freely allocate internal legislative powers as it sees fit, the fact remains that it alone is responsible towards the Community under Article [258] for compliance with obligations arising under Community law.[301]

Perhaps it should be otherwise:

> [A] Member State cannot use its decentralised structure as a cloak in order to justify a failure to comply with its obligations under Community law. It might be said that, if so, decentralised authorities of Member States need some mechanism by which to participate in the elaboration of EU law, especially when the Member State itself is not competent ... That is a fair point.[302]

---

291 For a definition of 'member state' for purposes of proceedings before the Court see Case C-95/97 *Région Wallonne* v *Commission* [1997] ECR I-1787, at paras 6 and 7.

292 See *Polish Nationals in Danzig* [1932] PCIJ Ser. A/B, No. 44, at 24.

293 Cases 227 etc./85 *Commission* v *Belgium* [1988] ECR 1; Case C-435/09 *Commission* v *Belgium*, judgment of 24 March 2011, not yet reported.

294 Case 199/85 *Commission* v *Italy* [1987] ECR 1039.

295 Case C-87/02 *Commission* v *Italy* [2004] ECR I-5975; Case C-173/05 *Commission* v *Italy* [2007] ECR I-4917; Case C-508/09 *Commission* v *Italy*, judgment of 3 March 2011, not yet reported.

296 Case C-439/99 *Commission* v *Italy* [2002] ECR I-305.

297 Case C-419/01 *Commission* v *Spain* [2003] ECR I-4947; Case C-516/07 *Commission* v *Spain* [2009] ECR I-76*; Case C-400/08 *Commission* v *Spain*, judgment of 24 March 2011, not yet reported.

298 Case C-58/89 *Commission* v *Germany* [1991] ECR I-4983.

299 Case C-349/03 *Commission* v *United Kingdom* [2005] ECR I-7321; Case C-457/08 *Commission* v *United Kingdom* [2009] ECR I-137*.

300 Case C-343/05 *Commission* v *Finland* [2006] ECR I-66*; Case C-159/06 *Commission* v *Finland* [2006] ECR I-114*. But the Åland government must be consulted by the Finnish government and liaise in preparation of the defence to any enforcement proceedings involving Åland matters; Ahvenanmaan Itsehallintolaki 1991/1144, 59 c §.

301 Case C-87/02 *Commission* v *Italy* [2004] ECR I-5975, at para. 38.

302 Case C-212/06 *Government of the French Community and Walloon Government* v *Flemish Government* [2008] ECR I-1683, *per* A-G Sharpston at paras 105–7 of her opinion.

It is especially fair in the context of enforcement proceedings, in circumstances where the (alleged) failure falls to a decentralised authority yet for political or other reasons the member state (the central authorities) elects not to contest the Commission complaint, in which case the responsible regional authority may (at best) intervene, but with no submission of a party to support it cannot advance, and so the Court will not hear, arguments defending the contested conduct. In its turn a member state may encounter internal difficulties, of very significant practical importance, in identifying the competent authority at fault (and maybe liability in reparation for injury caused). But these are issues not addressed adequately by present Union machinery, and they are not a concern of Union law.[303]

Exceptionally, a member state may be censured under article 258 for a persistent **5.50** failure of the police to ensure the effective enjoyment by private persons of a Union right.[304] Even conduct of the courts, if it amounts to (wilful) consistent interpretation and application of law in a manner at variance with the requirements of Union law, may properly fall within the purview of article 258 proceedings.[305]

Although many (about half of)[306] proceedings under article 258 follow a **5.51** complaint to the Commission (and there is now in place a registration system, the CHAP ('Complaints Handling – Accueil des Plaignants') for complaints and enquiries), it cannot be forced to act. It is true that the language of article 258 appears to impose upon the Commission an obligation to initiate at least the administrative (pre-litigation) phase[307] of proceedings should it apprehend a breach of the Treaties by a national authority ('If [it] considers that a Member State has failed to fulfil an obligation under the Treaties, it *shall* deliver a

---

303 The problem may be addressed in national constitutional law: in Belgium, for example, the federal authorities ('the State') may assume the powers of ('*peut se substituer à*') a community or region in order to give effect to a judgment of the Court finding Belgium to have failed in a Treaty obligation; Constitution of Belgium, art. 169 and loi spéciale de réformes institutionnelles, loi du 8 août 1980, MB du 15 août 1980, p. 9434, art. 16 § 3.

304 Case C-265/95 *Commission v France* (Spanish Strawberries) [1997] ECR I-6959; see 10.63 below.

305 Case C-129/00 *Commission v Italy* [2003] ECR I-14637; Case C-154/08 *Commission v Spain* [2009] ECR I-187*; Opinion 1/09 *Re the European Patent Convention*, opinion of 8 March 2011, not yet reported, at para. 87. In 2004 the Commission initiated enforcement proceedings against Sweden on the ground that the paucity of references from the supreme courts (*Högsta domstolen* and *Regeringsrätten* (now *Högstaförvaltnings-domstolen*)) and the absence of procedural rules for the identification and determination of cases which must be referred to the Court of Justice under 267 (as to which see 5.139–5.140 below) left Sweden in breach of Community law; Commission docket No. 2003/2161, C(2004)3988. This is the only such case ever raised under art. 258, it is by no means clear the Commission would have prevailed, and it was abandoned after changes to Swedish procedural law.

306 At the end of 2009, 53 per cent of active cases originated from complaints, dropping by the end of 2011 to around 43 per cent; *29th Annual Report on Monitoring the Application of EU Law (2011)*, COM(2012) 714 final para. 2.1.3.

307 See immediately below.

reasoned opinion on the matter'), although this does not extend to a duty to proceed to the judicial phase ('[it] *may* bring the matter before the Court of Justice'). But a wide degree of discretion even over the pre-litigation phase is secured by the requirement that it (subjectively) 'considers' that there has been a failure, so that it appears that a complainant cannot force the Commission to launch, and certainly not to continue, enforcement proceedings.[308] Whether this would be different in a case in which a Commission decision not to proceed is wholly unreasonable – where it declined to take action in the face of an egregious and intentional Treaty infringement – is not known: there is no precedent to the contrary. Nor, on the other side of the coin, may a decision to initiate proceedings, again one wholly within Commission discretion, be challenged.[309] So, an argument that a Union right could be more expediently protected by proceedings in a national court is quite irrelevant,[310] and the Commission need show no particular interest in the outcome:

> It is settled case-law that in exercising its powers under Article [258] the Commission does not have to show that there is a specific interest in bringing an action. The provision is not intended to protect the Commission's own rights. The Commission's function, in the general interest of the Community, is to ensure that the Member States give effect to the Treaty and the provisions adopted by the institutions thereunder and to obtain a declaration of any failure to fulfil the obligations deriving therefrom with a view to bringing it to an end.[311]

Nor may a member state object that it is being unfairly singled out for Commission attention:

> If the Commission considers that a Member State has infringed provisions of the Treaty, it is for it to determine whether it is expedient to take action against that State and what provisions the State has infringed, and to choose the time at which it will initiate infringement proceedings; the considerations which determine its choice of time cannot affect the admissibility of its action.

> Given this discretion, the Commission is free to initiate infringement proceedings against only some of the Member States which are in a comparable position from the point of view of compliance with Community law. It may thus, in particular, decide to initiate infringement proceedings against other Member States subsequently, after becoming aware of the outcome of the earlier proceedings.[312]

---

308 Case 48/65 *Lütticke* v *EEC Commission* [1966] ECR 19; Case 247/87 *Star Fruit* v *Commission* [1989] ECR 291; Case C-29/92 *Asia Motor France* v *Commission* [1992] ECR I-3935; Case T-194/04 *Bavarian Lager Co.* v *Commission* [2007] ECR II-4523.

309 Case C-191/95 *Commission* v *Germany* [1998] ECR I-5449.

310 Case C-456/05 *Commission* v *Germany* [2007] ECR I-10517.

311 Cases C-20 and 28/01 *Commission* v *Germany* [2003] ECR I-3609, at para. 29; to similar effect, Case C-445/06 *Danske Slagterier* v *Bundesrepublik Deutschland* [2009] ECR I-2119, at para. 43.

312 Case C-531/06 *Commission* v *Italy* [2009] ECR I-4103, at paras 23–4.

Given this wide discretion there are concerns, not necessarily unfounded, that the Commission is not immune to political pressures from various quarters. Because the Commission is under no legal obligation to initiate enforcement proceedings, a decision not to do so cannot engage the non-contractual liability of the Union;[313] but it cannot be ruled out that a decision to launch proceedings could, in exceptional circumstances, do so.[314] In keeping with the principle of Commission collegiality, the decision to raise article 258 proceedings must be taken by the college of Commissioners, and the information upon which the decision is based must be available to each Commissioner.[315]

Whilst contentious proceedings, the procedure under article 258 falls into two distinct stages: **5.52**

- the administrative phase:
  - investigation by the Commission;
  - the formal letter of complaint or notice (*lettre de mise en demeure*, sometimes rendered 'letter before action') identifying an alleged breach and inviting the member state to submit observations;
  - the 'reasoned opinion' (*avis motivé*), a reasoned statement identifying the alleged breach and allowing the member state a reasonable time to reply to it, to remedy the breach, or, where appropriate, to prepare a rebuttal to it;[316]
- the judicial phase:
  - written procedure;
  - oral procedure, up to and including the opinion of the Advocate-General;
  - judgment of the Court, which either:
    - dismisses the action as inadmissible for procedural impropriety;
    - dismisses the action as unfounded, that is, there has been no breach by the member state of a Union law obligation as libelled and made out by the Commission; or
    - declares the existence of the breach.

---

313 Case C-72/90 *Asia Motor France* v *Commission* [1990] ECR I-2181; Case T-202/02 *Makedoniko Metro and Michaniki* v *Commission* [2004] ECR II-181.

314 Cases T-440 etc./03 *Arizmendi and ors* v *Council and Commission* [2009] ECR II-4883.

315 Case C-191/95 *Commission* v *Germany*, n. 309 above; Case C-1/00 *Commission* v *France* (BSE) [2001] ECR I-9989.

316 Case C-289/94 *Commission* v *Italy* [1996] ECR I-4405. As to what is reasonable time, which may be brief if circumstances justify it, see Case 74/82 *Commission* v *Ireland* [1984] ECR 317; Case 293/85 *Commission* v *Belgium* [1988] ECR 305; Case C-56/90 *Commission* v *United Kingdom* (Bathing Water) [1993] ECR I-4109; Case C-473/93 *Commission* v *Luxembourg* [1996] ECR I-3207; Case C-1/00 *Commission* v *France* (BSE), ibid.; Case C-320/03 *Commission* v *Austria* [2005] ECR I-9871.

The purpose of the administrative phase (latterly sometimes called the 'pre-litigation procedure'; *procédure précontentieuse*) is to identify the alleged breach and to enable the defendant member state to explain why there is no breach or, if the breach is admitted, to remedy it. The proper conduct of the administrative phase 'constitutes an essential guarantee required by the EC Treaty'[317] both to protect the rights of the member state and to ensure that a contentious procedure has a clearly defined dispute as its subject matter.[318] It follows that the failure, if failure there be, is to be determined by reference to the situation prevailing at the end of the period laid down in the reasoned opinion,[319] and the Commission cannot raise during the judicial phase any complaint not set out in the reasoned opinion or any point upon which the defendant member state has not had the opportunity to comment during the administrative phase. Thus

> [t]he reasoned opinion ... must contain a coherent and detailed exposition of the reasons which led the Commission to the conclusion that the Member State concerned had failed to fulfil one of its obligations under the Treaty.

> The reasoned opinion and therefore the action, which, according to settled case-law, ... may not be based on pleas and grounds other than those put forward in that opinion, must therefore set out the complaints coherently and precisely in order that the Member State and the Court may appreciate exactly the scope of the infringement of Community law complained of, a condition which is necessary in order to enable the Member State to avail itself of its right to defend itself and the Court to determine whether there is a breach of obligations as alleged.[320]

But the requirement cannot be stretched so far as to mean that in every case the statement of the complaints set out in the letter of formal notice, the operative part of the reasoned opinion and the form of order sought in the application must be exactly the same, provided that the subject matter of the proceedings has not been extended or altered.[321] Nor need the Commission, in either application or reasoned opinion, indicate the steps which ought to be taken in order to eliminate the impugned conduct.[322] A measure taken

---

317 Case C-145/01 *Commission v Italy* [2003] ECR I-5581, at para. 17.
318 Case C266/94 *Commission v Spain* [1995] ECR I-1975; Case C-1/00 *Commission v France* (BSE), n. 315 above; Case C-362/01 *Commission v Ireland* [2002] ECR I-11433; Case C-145/01 *Commission v Italy*, n. 317 above; Case C-350/02 *Commission v Netherlands* [2004] ECR I-6213.
319 Case C-200/88 *Commission v Greece* [1990] ECR I-4299; Case C29/01 *Commission v Spain* [2002] ECR I-2503; Case C-145/01 *Commission v Italy*, n. 317 above.
320 Case C-98/04 *Commission v United Kingdom* [2006] ECR I-4003, at paras 17, 18.
321 Case C-147/03 *Commission v Austria* [2005] ECR I-5969, at paras 23–4; Case C-33/04 *Commission v Luxembourg* [2005] ECR I-10629, at para. 37.
322 Case C-247/89 *Commission v Portugal* [1991] ECR I-3659, at para. 22; Case C-559/07 *Commission v Greece* [2009] ECR I-47, at para. 23.

by the Commission during the pre-litigation procedure creates no binding force or legal obligation,[323] so enjoys immunity from judicial review by the Court.

Once the judicial phase is opened, the function of the Court is to ensure that the **5.53** Commission has complied with procedural propriety throughout the administrative phase,[324] and then to decide whether, in the circumstances disclosed, it has adduced sufficient evidence to establish that an obligation has not been fulfilled. The essential points of law and of fact upon which it bases its case must be indicated coherently and intelligibly in the application and the heads of claim (*conclusions de la requête*) put forward unambiguously so that the Court does not rule *ultra petita* or fail to rule on a complaint.[325] It is for the Commission to make out the breach:

> It is established case-law that, in proceedings for failure to fulfil obligations, it is for the Commission to prove the existence of the alleged infringement and to provide the Court with the information necessary for it to determine whether the infringement is made out, and the Commission may not rely on any presumption for that purpose.[326]

---

323 Case 48/65 *Alfons Lütticke and ors* v *EEC Commission* [1966] ECR 27; Case T-258/06 *Germany* v *Commission* [2010] ECR II-2027, at para. 152.

324 See e.g., Case C-341/97 *Commission* v *Netherlands* [2000] ECR I-6611; Case C-145/01 *Commission* v *Italy*, n. 317 above; Case C-98/04 *Commission* v *United Kingdom*, n. 320 above. Because it is an essential formal requirement of the art. 258 procedure the Court may raise this question of its own motion; Case C-362/90 *Commission* v *Italy* (Public Supply Contracts) [1992] ECR I-2353; Case C-98/04 *Commission* v *United Kingdom*, n. 320 above; Case C-160/08 *Commission* v *Germany* [2010] ECR I-3713; Case C-271/09 *Commission* v *Poland*, judgment of 21 December 2011, not yet reported, at para. 25 and case law cited. Exceptionally, excessive duration of the pre-litigation procedure may be a defect rendering the action inadmissible; Case C-287/03 *Commission* v *Belgium* [2005] ECR I-3761. Cf. Case C-523/04 *Commission* v *Netherlands* [2007] ECR I-3267 (more than six years between offending act and *lettre de mise en demeure* and more than four years between reasoned opinion and initiation of judicial phase not, in the circumstances, excessive). It appears that inadmissibility will turn upon the defendant member state's rights of defence being compromised by the accretion of time, which it is for the member state to show; Case C-33/04 *Commission* v *Luxembourg* [2005] ECR I-10629, at para. 76; Case C-490/04 *Commission* v *Germany* [2007] ECR I-6095, at para. 26. That the Commission does not take action upon a reasoned opinion immediately or shortly after its issue does not create a legitimate expection for the member state that the procedure has been closed; Case C-317/92 *Commission* v *Germany* [1994] ECR I-2039, at para. 4; Case C-546/07 *Commission* v *Germany* [2010] ECR I-439, at para. 26.

325 Case C-255/04 *Commission* v *France* [2006] ECR I-5251, at para. 24; Case C-195/04 *Commission* v *Finland* [2007] ECR I-3351, at para. 22; Case C-127/05 *Commission* v *United Kingdom* [2007] ECR I-4619, at para. 56; Case C-211/08 *Commission* v *Spain* [2010] ECR I-5267, at para. 32; Case C-400/08 *Commission* v *Spain*, judgment of 24 March 2011, not yet reported, at para. 36; see also the opinion of A-G Sharpston in Case C-195/04 (*Finland*), *supra*, at paras 41–9.

326 Case C-287/03 *Commission* v *Belgium*, n. 324 above, at para. 27; see also Case C-475/01 *Commission* v *Greece* (Ouzo) [2004] ECR I-8923, *per* A-G Tizzano, at para. 107 of his opinion; Case C-507/03 *Commission* v *Ireland* [2007] ECR I-9777, at para. 33.

On (rare) occasion in the past involving complex issues of law and fact the Court declined to find one way or the other, instead adopting an interim judgment (*sic*) determining points of law and inviting the Commission and the member state(s) to re-examine the matter in light of them and make submissions afresh, following which a second, final judgment was issued;[327] now it is more likely to dismiss the action as not proven.

5.54 If the breach alleged is one of failure to comply with Union legislation it is not open to the member state to raise a defence that the measure is unlawful, for that would be an abuse of process, illegality of a Union act being a matter which falls properly within proceedings raised under article 263 to which member states enjoy unrestricted access;[328] the exception is compliance with a measure which is tainted with such particularly serious and manifest defects as to render it 'non-existent'.[329] This bar has been restricted thus far to measures addressed to the member state, so decisions[330] and Directives;[331] it is an open question whether the same rule applies in the case of a Regulation[332] or, post-Lisbon, a decision with no addressee.

5.55 Throughout the procedure settlement can be, and often is, reached between the Commission and the defendant member state, in which case the Commission may, even having seised the Court, withdraw the action ('discontinue proceedings').[333] But it need not: its interest remains alive even in the face of the infringement being (tardily) remedied[334] and it may legitimately elect to proceed, for example, in order to obtain a clarification of the law from the Court of Justice or to establish authoritatively the basis of any civil liability which the

---

327 E.g., Case 170/78 *Commission* v *United Kingdom* (Wine and Beer) (No. 1) [1980] ECR 417 and (No. 2) [1983] ECR 2265; Case 149/79 *Commission* v *Belgium* (Belgian Railways) (No. 1) [1980] ECR 3881 and (No. 2) [1982] ECR 1845.

328 Case C-74/91 *Commission* v *Germany* [1992] ECR I-5437; Case C-261/99 *Commission* v *France* [2001] ECR I-2537; Case C-1/00 *Commission* v *France* (BSE) [2001] ECR I-9989; Case C-404/00 *Commission* v *Spain* [2003] ECR I-6695; Case C-232/05 *Commission* v *France* [2006] ECR I-10071. As to art. 263 see 5.66–5.86 below. The judgment in Case C-475/01 *Ouzo* (n. 326 above) might be read as indicating that the Commission is also barred from pleading the illegality of a Union measure in art. 258 proceedings in the (rare) circumstances it might wish to do so.

329 Case C-404/00 *Commission* v *Spain* [2003] ECR I-6695, at para. 41 and case law cited. As to non-existence see n. 524 below.

330 E.g., Case 226/87 *Commission* v *Greece* [1988] ECR 3611; Case C-261/99 *Commission* v *France*, Case C-1/00 *BSE*, Case C-404/00 *Commission* v *Spain* and Case C-232/05 *Commission* v *France*, n. 328 above.

331 E.g., Case C-74/91 *Commission* v *Germany* [1992] ECR I-5437, n. 328 above; Case C-194/01 *Commission* v *Austria* [2004] ECR I-4579.

332 See the discussion of A-G Jacobs in Case C-11/00 *Commission* v *European Central Bank* [2003] ECR I-7147, at para. 191 of his opinion; also the discussion of art. 277, at 5.103–5.105 below.

333 RP Court of Justice, art. 148.

334 Case C-519/03 *Commission* v *Luxembourg* [2005] ECR I-3067, at para. 19; Case C-562/07 *Commission* v *Spain* [2009] ECR I-9553, at para. 23.

member state may incur.[335] By comparison, the Commission having elected to withdraw the action, a defendant member state cannot cause it to be sustained on the same grounds.[336] Following the close of written and oral procedure the Court may proceed to judgment even where the Commission seeks a discontinuance. And nowhere in the course of proceedings may the Commission afford guarantees or determine conclusively, by reasoned opinion or otherwise, the compatibility of the member state's conduct with Treaty obligations, that being a matter for the Court alone.[337]

It might be noted that, owing to the legal/political sensitivities which attend the censure of a member state, article 258 (and article 259) actions are amongst the narrowing category of cases reserved still by the Treaties to the (direct and sole) jurisdiction of the Court of Justice.   **5.56**

(i) Force of the judgment; sanctions (article 260 TFEU)

Judgment in a successful article 258 action follows, in the *dispositif*, a standard format: the Court declares that, by doing x, or failing to do y, the (named) member state has failed to fufil its obligations under, for example, article z of one of the Treaties, under provisions of a Regulation or a Directive, or sometimes (rarely) simply 'under Union law' as appropriate. The judgment is declaratory only; it cannot of itself set aside an offending national law, nor certainly conjure from the ether one which ought to, but doesn't, exist. The Commission has authority neither conclusively to identify the rights and duties of the defaulting member state nor provide guarantees that a given course of conduct will cure the breach.[338] Nor may the Court order specific action to achieve that end. However, the Treaties provide that: **5.57**

> If the Court of Justice of the European Union finds that a Member State has failed to fulfil an obligation under the Treaties, the State shall be required to take the necessary measures to comply with the judgment of the Court.[339]

There is no time limit specified but the Court has said consistently that 'the importance of immediate and uniform application of Community law means that the process of compliance must be initiated at once and completed as soon

---

335 E.g. Case 154/85 *Commission* v *Italy* [1987] ECR 2717; Case 240/86 *Commission* v *Greece* [1988] ECR 1835.

336 See e.g., Case C-120/94 *Commission* v *Greece* (Macedonia) [1996] ECR I-1513.

337 Case C-191/95 *Commission* v *Germany* [1998] ECR I-5449, at para. 45; Case T-139/06 *France* v *Commission*, judgment of 19 October 2011, not yet reported, at para. 32.

338 Cases 142/80 and 143/80 *Amministrazione delle Finanze dello Stato* v *Essevi and Salengo* [1981] ECR 1413, at para. 16; Case C-393/98 *Ministério Público and anor* v *Fazenda Pública* [2001] ECR I-1327, at para. 18.

339 TFEU, art. 260(1) (ex art. 228(1) EC).

as possible'.[340] The Court has no authority to derogate from this and set a time limit for compliance.[341] Furthermore, a declaration under article 260 that a member state has failed to fulfil an obligation under the Treaties has the force of *res judicata* and

> is a prohibition having the full force of law on the competent national authorities against applying a national rule recognized as incompatible with the Treaty and ... an obligation on them to take all appropriate measures to enable Community law to be fully applied.[342]

Even if the legislative or administrative authorities of the member state fail to take appropriate action, its courts are bound, if possible, to enforce the Court's judgment, and not the offending national rule.[343]

5.58 The Treaties provide no other sanction for a member state's failure to comply with Treaty obligations, and, until Maastricht, provided no sanction for failure to comply with a judgment of the Court finding and declaring the failure to exist. Open defiance of a judgment of the Court is very rare,[344] considerable delay in compliance less so. The Maastricht amendment introduced a 'special judicial procedure for the enforcement of judgments'[345] which authorises the Commission to raise a further action against a defaulting member state, identifying the failure in a letter of formal notice but (since Lisbon) requiring no reasoned opinion and recommending, in the event of failure to comply with the notice, a financial penalty (a 'lump sum or penalty payment', the one element dissuasive, the other persuasive[346] or

---

340   Case C-387/97 *Commission* v *Greece* [2000] ECR I-5047, at para. 82; Case C-278/01 *Commission* v *Spain* [2003] ECR II-14141, at para. 27; Case C-121/07 *Commission* v *France* [2008] ECR I-9159, at para. 21.

341   Case C-473/93 *Commission* v *Luxembourg* [1996] ECR I-3207.

342   Case 48/71 *Commission* v *Italy* (Second Art Treasures Case) [1972] ECR 527 at 532.

343   Cases 314–316/81 and 83/82 *Procureur de la République* v *Waterkeyn* [1982] ECR 4337.

344   Member states sometimes fail to comply with a judgment simply out of lethargy. For example, France was condemned by the Court of Justice in 1996 (Case C-334/94 *Commission* v *France* [1996] ECR I-1307) for failure to comply with a 1974 judgment (Case 167/73 *Commission* v *France* (Code du Travail Maritime) [1974] ECR 359), but that failure appears in the meanwhile to have attracted neither censure nor urgency from any quarter. As for outright defiance, there are only two examples: first, a flagrant refusal by France to comply with the judgment in Case 232/78 *Commission* v *France* [1979] ECR 2729, which condemned as a breach of art. 34 French barriers to the importation of British mutton and lamb; the 'crisis' was resolved politically, by the introduction of a common organisation of the market in sheepmeat in 1980 (Regulation 1837/80 [1980] OJ L183/1, as to which see 10.104 below); secondly (and again, art. 34), for about nine months France refused to admit imports of British beef in open defiance of the judgment in Case C-1/00 *Commission* v *France* (BSE) [2001] ECR I-9989.

345   Case C-304/02 *Commission* v *France* [2005] ECR I-6263, at para. 92; Case T-33/09 *Portugal* v *Commission*, judgment of 27 March 2011, not yet reported, at para. 60.

346   Case C-304/02 *Commission* v *France* [2005] ECR I-6263, *per* A-G Geelhoed at para. 41 of his (second) opinion; Case C-121/07 *Commission* v *France* [2008] ECR I-9159, at para. 33.

coercive)[347] which it considers appropriate; where the Court finds that the member state had not complied with its judgment, it may, at its (wide) discretion, impose such penalty.[348] Since Lisbon the Commission may bypass the requirement of a reasoned opinion, proceeding directly to the Court seeking a lump sum or penalty payment, required only first to allow the errant member state the opportunity to submit observations.[349] The reference date for assessing whether there has been a failure which attracts financial liability was the date of expiry of the period laid down in the Commission's reasoned opinion,[350] but it used sometimes to happen that a member state avoided a penalty if the breach was rectified by the time of the Court's examination of the facts.[351] Presumably now the reference date is the deadline indicated for submission of observations. In all cases to date in which a penalty payment has been imposed, it runs from the date of the judgment imposing it. The rule on the circumscription of the breadth of the judicial inquiry by the pre-litigation procedure developed by case law on article 258 applies equally to article 260(2) proceedings.[352] The Commission has published guidance as to calculation of both appropriate penalty payments and lump sum penalties.[353] In 2005 it warned that where a case raised under article 260(2) proceeded as far as the judicial phase, it intended thenceforth automatically to push for the imposition of a lump sum penalty and to persist in it, no longer withdrawing the application in the event of tardy compliance thereafter.[354] This is to obviate the risk, 'as tends to occur with increasing frequency in practice', that a member state would be encouraged not to comply with a judgment with all due diligence and

---

347 Case C-121/07 *Commission v France, ibid.*, at para. 56: 'an order for a penalty payment ... is essentially intended to be coercive as regards the ongoing breach ... in so far as the failure to comply with the judgment which originally established that failure continues'.

348 TFEU, art. 260(2) (ex art. 228(2) EC). It is important that the decision is taken by the Court of Justice, for the Treaty provides (TFEU, art. 299; ex art. 256 EC) that a decision of the Council, the Commission or the European Central Bank which imposes a financial penalty is enforceable by civil process, but only if imposed 'on persons other than States'. Commission proposals as to penalty do not bind the Court, 'and merely constitute a useful point of reference'; Case C-278/01 *Commission v Spain* [2003] ECR I-14141, at para. 41; Case C-119/04 *Commission v Italy* [2006] ECR I-6885, at para. 37.

349 TFEU, art. 260(2).

350 Case C-503/04 *Commission v Germany* [2007] ECR I-6153, at para. 19; Case C-121/07 *Commission v France*, n. 346 above, at para. 22.

351 Case C-503/04 *Commission v Germany, ibid.*

352 Case C-177/04 *Commission v France* [2006] ECR I-2461, at paras 37–9; Case C-457/07 *Commission v Portugal* [2009] ECR I-8091, at paras 56–7.

353 Communication on application of Article 260 of the TFEU, SEC(2010) 923. The communication is revised periodically to take account of inflation and changes in GDP; the present communication replaces predecessors adopted in 1996 ([1996] OJ C242/6) and 1997 ([1997] OJ C63/2), which met with approbation from the Court, Case C-387/97 (*Commission v Greece* [2000] ECR I-5047, at paras 84–92), and 'recast' in 2005 (SEC(2005) 1658).

354 Communication on application of Article 228 of the EC Treaty , SEC(2005) 1658.

systematically to adopt delaying tactics.[355] Presumably the period starts now with the lodging of the action before the Court. But imposition of a lump sum penalty does not follow automatically,[356] and is to be determined by the Court at its discretion. Where a periodic penalty payment is imposed it is normally 'from the date of delivery of the present judgment until the day on which the judgment in [the original article 258 action] is complied with', or similar formula. But the requirement to meet the penalty obligation is discharged once the defaulting member state complies with the operative part of the article 260 judgment, which may be narrower than full compliance with the article 258 judgment.[357]

5.59 From December 1996 to October 2005 the Commission issued, pursuant to article 260(2), 296 *lettres de mise en demeure*, leading to 125 reasoned opinions; it decided to initiate proceedings before the Court in 38 cases, and brought them in 23.[358] Detailed data thereafter are difficult to come by, but ten cases reached the Court in 2006,[359] seven in 2007,[360] and none in 2008, two in 2009,[361] one in 2010[362] and six in 2011.[363] At the beginning of 2012 there were 77 proceedings in train.[364] There have been, to date, 11 final judgments in which a penalty has been imposed, so discernable trends are beginning to emerge. They are:

- Greece, in 2000: failure to comply with a 1992 judgment on compliance with an environmental Directive on disposal of toxic and dangerous waste, a penalty payment of €20,000 per day pending full compliance;[365]
- Spain, in 2003: failure to comply with a 1998 judgment on compliance with a Directive on the quality of bathing water, a penalty payment of €624,160 per year and per 1 per cent of non-conforming bathing water sites;[366]

---

355 Case C-121/07 *Commission* v *France* [2008] ECR I-9159, at para. 30.

356 *Ibid.*, at para. 63.

357 Case T-33/09 *Portugal* v *Commission*, judgment of 29 March 2011, not yet reported.

358 Case C-121/07 *Commission* v *France*, n. 346 above, at para. 31. France was the leading offender, attracting one in six of the *lettres de mise en demeure*, one in five of the reasoned opinions, one in five of the Commission decisions to initiate judicial proceedings and one in four of those brought.

359 *25th Annual Report on Monitoring the Application of Community Law*, COM(2008) 777 final, para. 2.1.

360 *Ibid.*

361 Case C-401/09 *Commission* v *Greece*, n 374 below; Case C-489/09 *Commission* v *Italy*, n 375 below.

362 Case C-610/10 *Commission* v *Spain*, pending.

363 Case C-184/11 *Commission* v *Spain*, pending; Case C-241/11 *Commission* v *Czech Republic*, pending; Case C-270/11 *Commission* v *Sweden*, pending; Case C-279/11 *Commission* v *Ireland*, pending; Case C-374/11 *Commission* v *Ireland*, pending; Case C-576/11 *Commission* v *Luxembourg*, pending.

364 *29th Annual Report on Monitoring the Application of EU Law (2011)*, COM (2012) 714 final. Greece emerged as the head of the field, the subject of 13 proceedings, with Italy on 12 and Spain on 8.

365 Case C-387/97 *Commission* v *Greece* [2000] ECR I-5047.

366 Case C-278/01 *Commission* v *Spain* [2003] ECR I-14141.

- France, in 2005: failure to comply with a 1991 judgment on fisheries conservation measures, the failure being structural, 'particularly' serious and persistent, so the penalty being a lump sum (the first imposed) of €20 million plus a penalty payment of €57.8 million for each further six-month period of non-compliance;[367]
- France again, in 2006: (partial) failure to comply with a 2002 judgment on compliance with a Directive on liability for defective products, a penalty payment of €31,650 per day pending full compliance;[368]
- Portugal, in 2008: failure to comply with a 2004 judgment on compliance with a public procurement Directive, a penalty payment of €19,392 per day pending full compliance;[369]
- France yet again, in 2008: failure to comply (timeously) with a 2004 judgment on compliance with a Directive on deliberate release into the environment of genetically modified organisms, a lump sum penalty of €10 million;[370]
- Greece, thrice, in 2009: failure (timeously) to comply with a 2005 judgment on restrictions on the establishment and operation of opticians' shops, a lump sum penalty of €1 million;[371] failure to comply with a 2006 judgment on installation of computer games in venues other than casinos, a lump sum penalty of €3 million plus a penalty payment of €31,563 per day pending compliance;[372] and failure to comply with a 2005 judgment on recovery of state aid illegally disbursed to Olympic Airways, a lump

---

367 Case C-304/02 *Commission* v *France* [2005] ECR I-6263. The Commission had sought only the penalty payment (of €316,500 per day of non-compliance = €57.8 million per half year) from the date of delivery of the judgment; the Court therefore established that art. 260(2) permits it to exceed the Commission's recommended penalty and, notwithstanding the language – 'lump sum *or* penalty payment' – allows the imposition of both. A-G Geelhoed had recommended a lump sum fine of €1,15.5 million. In the view of the Commission, France continued to fail to remedy the situation, so it adopted a decision requiring payment of the first penalty payment, which decision was challenged (unsuccessfully) by France for lack of competence; Case T-139/06 *France* v *Commission*, judgment of 19 October 2011, not yet reported. The United Kingdom helpfully intervened in support of the Commission.

368 Case C-177/04 *Commission* v *France* [2006] ECR I-2461. France had complied partially with the judgment in the course of proceedings; the Court thus confirmed that reformulation of the Commission application is permissible in such circumstances. Yet the fine imposed was more than double that (€13,715 per day) proposed by the Commission and the Advocate-General.

369 Case C-70/06 *Commission* v *Portugal* [2008] ECR I-1. There arose subsequently a dispute as to when exactly Portugal complied fully, and so the amount of the penalty exigible; see Case T-33/09 *Portugal* v *Commission*, judgment of 29 March 2011, not yet reported.

370 Case C-121/07 *Commission* v *France* [2008] ECR I-9159. The Commission and Advocate-General had both sought a penalty payment but France complied (in stages, first partly and then completely) prior to judgment but well after the expiry of the reasoned opinion deadline, thus depriving a penalty payment of its purpose but justifying a lump sum fine.

371 Case C-568/07 *Commission* v *Greece* [2009] ECR I-4505. The Commission had proposed a penalty payment of €71,000 per day but (tardy) Greek compliance to the Commission's satisfaction rendered it otiose.

372 Case C-109/08 *Commission* v *Greece* [2009] ECR I-4657. The lump sum was half again as much as the €2 million proposed by the Advocate-General.

sum penalty of €2 million plus a penalty payment of €16,000 per day pending compliance;[373]

- Greece once more, in 2011: failure to comply with a 2007 judgment on implementation of a Directive on compensation for victims of crime, a lump sum penalty of €3 million;[374]
- Italy in 2011: failure to comply with a 2004 judgment on recovery of illegally disbursed state aid, a lump sum penalty of €30 million plus a penalty payment of €30 million multiplied by the perentage of still-unrecovered state aid every six months until full compliance.[375]

In other final judgments under article 260(2) Italy avoided a penalty because the Commission had failed to show that its failure to comply with the earlier judgment continued to persist;[376] and Germany by complying with the judgment following the Commission's reasoned opinion but prior to the date of examination of the facts by the Court.[377] Portugal did likewise by exposing sloppy Commission work in both failing adequately ('coherently and precisely') to specify in the reasoned opinion the points upon which there was (alleged to be) a failure to comply with the earlier judgment and exceeding the limits of the complaint as set out in it.[378]

5.60 Neither the Treaties nor legislation sets out detailed rules for the enforcement of a judgment imposing a penalty. It falls by default to the Commission, as the institution which implements the budget, to recover such sums.[379] Any measure doing so do is subject to challenge by normal review proceedings under article 263,[380] but the General Court can call into question neither the original infringement by the member state nor the lawfulness of the penalty imposed, they being *res judicatae* already determined by the Court of Justice.[381]

5.61 Failure to put right a breach of Union law following censure by the Court of Justice is also very likely to constitute a 'sufficiently serious' breach of its

---

373 Case C-369/07 *Commission v Greece* [2009] ECR I-5703.
374 Case C-407/09 *Commission v Greece*, judgment of 31 March 2011, not yet reported. The Commission had sought also a periodic penalty payment but abandoned that claim in the face of tardy compliance.
375 Case C-469/09 *Commission v Italy*, judgment of 17 November 2011, not yet reported.
376 Case C-119/04 *Commission v Italy* [2006] ECR I-6885.
377 Case C-503/04 *Commission v Germany* [2007] ECR I-6153; the Commission had abandoned its recommendation of a lump sum penalty (the case raised prior to its 2005 undertaking to do otherwise) and the Advocate-General had agreed.
378 Case C-457/07 *Commission v Portugal* [2009] ECR I-8091. The weakness of the Commission's case was thought sufficiently clear so as not to require an Advocate-General's opinion.
379 Case T-33/09 *Portugal v Commission*, judgment of 29 March 2011, not yet reported; Case T-139/06 *France v Commission*, n. 367 above.
380 See immediately below.
381 Case T-33/09 *Portugal v Commission*, n. 379 above.

obligations and so leave the member state open to claims in reparation from persons harmed by the failure.[382]

Since Lisbon enforcement proceedings raised under article 258 in 'non-communication cases', alleging a failure to notify measures adopted for the implementation of a Directive (this being a perennial failure across the member states by which they may conceal, for a time, a failure to implement and so a source of great frustration to the Commission) the Commission may, 'when it deems appropriate', propose that a penalty be imposed in that (initial) action, the penalty to be determined by the Court (but not exceeding the amount sought by the Commission), payable on a date set in its judgment.[383] The first nine such cases, against five member states, were to court in late 2011.   **5.62**

In keeping with the general approach, so far as Union law is concerned the liability lies with, and any penalty is imposed upon, the member state as an indivisible person. There may be legislation or conventions within a member state as to how and by whom it is borne.[384]   **5.63**

(ii)   Analogous enforcement provisions

The Treaties have other provisions whereby the Commission may raise enforcement proceedings against a member state in a manner similar to article 258 but bypassing the administrative phase. This applies where a member state fails to comply with a Commission decision in the area of state aids,[385] derogates from internal market legislation[386] or 'improperly' adopts national measures in the event of serious internal disturbance, serious international tension or war.[387] In the event of a member state failing in its duty to avoid excessive government deficits, the Treaties provide other, specific enforcement procedures and recourse to article 258 is in part expressly ousted.[388] The Governing Council of   **5.64**

---

382   See 6.37 below.

383   TFEU, art. 260(3). See Commission Communication, Implementation of Article 260(3) of the Treaty, TFEU (2010) 1371 final.

384   See e.g., in Belgium, loi spéciale de réformes institutionnelles, loi du 8 août 1980, MB du 15 août 1980, p. 9434, art. 16 § 3 3°, 2ᵉ alinéa, by which 'the State' may recover from a community or region the costs of a failure (*non-respect; niet-nakomen*) by the latter of a Treaty obligation. Presumably this applies both to penalties imposed by the Commission and to damages secured by individuals against the state, as to which see 6.34–6.40 below. A similar mechanism exists in Finland 'in so far as [the sanction] has arisen from an act or omission on the part of the province [of Åland]'; Ahvenanmaan Itsehallintolaki 1991/1144, 59 d §. In England and Wales a minister may require a local or public authority to pay (into the Consolidated Fund or the Welsh Consolidated Fund) all or part of an 'EU financial sanction' (that is, a penalty imposed under art. 260(2)) where the latter caused or contributed to the infraction for which the penalty was imposed; Localism Act 2011, ss. 48–67. Otherwise it is a matter addressed by 'concordats' amongst the four Parliaments/Assemblies.

385   TFEU, art. 108(2) (ex art. 88(2) EC); see 13.173 below.

386   TFEU, art. 114(9) (ex art. 95(9) EC); see 10.09 below.

387   TFEU, art. 348, 2nd para (ex art. 298, 2nd para. EC); see 10.32 below.

388   TFEU, art. 126(10) (ex art. 104(10) EC); see 14.21 below.

the European Central Bank has powers 'the same as those conferred upon the Commission in respect of Member States by Article 258' to raise enforcement proceedings before the Court of Justice where a national central bank has failed in its obligations under the ESCB/ECB Statute[389] and the Board of Directors of the European Investment Bank may do likewise where a member state has failed in its obligations under the EIB Statute.[390]

(iii)   Excluded areas

5.65   Barred from the enforcement procedure of article 258 are, owing to general ouster of the Court's jurisdiction, national compliance with any rules of the Common Foreign and Security Policy and police or other law enforcement operations and those carried out for the maintenance of law and order and internal security.[391] Barred provisionally is member state compliance with obligations arising from measures adopted prior to the entry into force of the Lisbon Treaty in the sphere of police and judicial cooperation in criminal matters;[392] the exclusion lapses after five years, that is in December 2014.[393]

(b)   Action of annulment (article 263 TFEU)

5.66   The action provided by article 263 is an action to annul a legislative or administrative act of a Union institution – to deprive it of legal effect. Whilst the EEC Treaty limited the institutions the acts of which could be challenged in this context,[394] the Court said that an act of *any* Community institution or body was susceptible to annulment proceedings,[395] for 'it cannot be acceptable, in a

---

389   TFEU, art. 271(d) (ex art. 237(d) EC); ESCB/ECB Statute, arts 35.5 and 35.6.

390   TFEU, art. 271(a) (ex art. 237(a) EC).

391   TEU, art. 24(1); TFEU, arts 275, 276; see 5.29 above.

392   Protocol (No. 36) on Transitional Provisions, art. 10(1). Amendment of any such measure will entail the immediate applicability of art. 258; art. 10(2).

393   *Ibid.* art. 10(3).

394   The EEC Treaty referred here to review only of acts of the Council and Commission (art. 173, 1st para), the EC Treaty latterly, in light of intervening case law, to review of (joint) acts of the European Parliament and the Council and acts of the Council, the Commission, the European Parliament and the European Central Bank (art. 230, 1st para.). Subsequent Treaty provisions provide expressly for review of acts of the Board of Governors and the Board of Directors of the European Investment Bank (art. 237 EC), and the Court has extended this to the Bank's Management Committee: Case C-15/00 *Commission* v *European Investment Bank* [2003] ECR I-7281, and of measures adopted by the organs of the European Investment Fund (Protocol on the Statute of the European Investment Bank, art. 30(6)), as does some legislation (e.g., review of decisions of the Board of Appeal of the Community Trade Mark Office (Regulation 207/2009 [2009] OJ L78/1, art. 65 and Regulation 6/2002 [2002] OJ L3/1, art. 61).

395   Case 294/83 *Parti Ecologiste 'Les Verts'* v *European Parliament* [1986] ECR 1339; Case C-314/91 *Weber* v *Parliament* [1993] ECR I-1093; Case C-319/91 *European Parliament* v *Council* [1994] ECR I-625; Case C-315/99P *Ismeri Europa* v *Court of Auditors* [2001] ECR I-5281, *per* A-G Ruiz-Jarabo Colomer; Case T-411/06 *Sogelma* v *European Agency for Reconstruction* [2008] ECR II-2771; Case T-117/08 *Italy* v *European Economic and Social Committee*, judgment of 31 March 2011, not yet reported; but cf. Case T-148/97 *Keeling* v *OHIM* [1998] ECR II-2217.

Community based on the rule of law, that such acts escape judicial review'.[396] The only requirements are (a) that the act in question is an act of the institutions: measures adopted by 'common accord of the governments of the Member States', for example, even where the Treaties provide for them and even where they produce legal effects, are acts not of the institutions but of the member states and beyond the review jurisdiction of the Court;[397] and (b) that the act be one which is capable of producing legal effects, and the Court takes a broad view of acts which meet the criterion.[398] Lisbon consolidated and extended the reach of article 263 expressly to review of the legality of legislative acts; of acts of the Council, the Commission or the Central Bank other than recommendations and opinions; and of acts of the Parliament and the Council, and of bodies, offices or agencies of the Union, intended to produce legal effect *vis-à-vis* third parties.[399] It is not necessary that the act in question continues to produce effects or is still in force, only that there is an interest in its annulment;[400] put another way, annulment is of itself capable of having legal consequences.[401]

(i) Prescription

The action of annulment is subject to a two-month time bar,[402] which is strictly enforced.[403] Time starts to run with the publication of the measure (calculated from the end of the 14th day after publication in the *Official Journal*)[404] or its   **5.67**

---

396 Case T-411/06 *Sogelma*, ibid., at para. 37.

397 Cases C-181 and 248/91 *Parliament* v *Council and Commission* (Bangladesh) [1993] ECR I-3685.

398 See e.g., Case 22/70 *Commission* v *Council* (ERTA) [1971] ECR 263; Case 60/81 *IBM* v *Commission* [1981] ECR 2639; Case C-25/94 *Commission* v *Council* [1996] ECR I-1469; Case C-123/03P *Commission* v *Greencore Group* [2004] ECR I-11647; Cases T-125 and 253/03 *Akzo Nobel Chemicals and anor* v *Commission* [2007] ECR II-3523; Case T-185/05 *Italy* v *Commission* [2008] ECR II-3207, at paras 51–3; Case C-370/07 *Commission* v *Council* (CITES) [2009] ECR I-8917; Case C-322/09P *NDSHT Nya Destination Stockholm Hotell & Teaterpaket* v *Commission*, [2010] ECR I-11911; Cases C-463 and 475/10P *Deutsche Post and Germany* v *Commission*, judgment of 13 October 2011, not yet reported; and especially Case C-131/03P *RJ Reynolds Tobacco Holdings and ors* v *Commission* [2006] ECR I-7797. The Court may clearly examine of its own motion whether an act under attack meets the necessary test; according to A-G Kokott it must do so: *CITES*, *supra*, at para. 21 of her opinion.

399 TFEU, art. 263, 1st para.

400 E.g., Case 53/85 *AKZO* v *Commission* [1986] ECR 1965; Case 207/86 *Asociación Profesional de Empresarios de Pesca Comunitarios* v *Commission* [1988] ECR 2151; Case C-370/07 *CITES*, n. 398 above.

401 Case 53/85 *AKZO*, ibid., at para. 21; Case T-102/96 *Gencor* v *Commission* [1999] ECR II-753, at para. 40.

402 TFEU, art. 263, 5th para.

403 E.g., Cases T-121 and 151/96 *Mutual Aid Administration Services* v *Commission* [1997] ECR II-1355; Case C-176/02P *Laboratoire Monique Rémy* v *Commission*, order of 30 January 2003, unreported. For the method of computation of time limits generally see Case 152/85 *Misset* v *Council* [1987] ECR 223; Case T-125/89 *Filtrona Española* v *Commission* [1990] ECR II-393; Case C-102/92 *Ferriere Acciaierie Sarde* v *Commission* [1993] ECR I- 801; Case T-233/09 *Access Info Europe* v *Council*, judgment of 22 March 2011, not yet reported; Case F-34/10 *Arango Jaramillo and ors* v *Banque européenne d'investissements*, order of 4 February 2011, not yet reported (annulment action inadmissible for arriving at the registry by email less than two minutes late).

404 RP Court of Justice, art. 50; RP General Court, art. 102.

notification to a party;[405] absent publication or notification it starts when it comes to his knowledge,[406] a more elusive 'subsidiary criterion'[407] which means the date on which he acquires precise knowledge of the content of the measure in question and of the reasons upon which it is based in such a way as to enable him effectively to exercise his right to challenge it.[408] There is an additional universal period of grace of ten days 'on account of distance';[409] owing to the increased speed of communications the 2011 amendments proposed that it be abolished, but it wasn't. It is for the party claiming an action is out of time to show when time began to run,[410] but the Court may raise the issue of time bar of its own motion even if no party has objected[411] and appears now to be under a duty to do so.[412] The Court recognises a concept of excusable error in time limits but it is strictly construed and applicable only exceptionally where an institution has given rise to pardonable confusion in the mind of a party acting on good faith and exercising all the diligence required of a normally experienced trader.[413] There is an argument that the time bar must be extended (presumably for a further two months) for a new member state upon its accession (prior to which it enjoys no standing) as regards a Union measure adopted following signature of the Treaty of Accession. The Court avoided settling it once by dismissing a case on the merits without addressing admissibility of the action;[414] but facing the question again without that possibility, it confirmed it.[415] The argument having succeeded, there is no reason why the principle ought to be, or can be, restricted to the member states, and it ought perhaps to be extended to any person who gains the necessary standing by virtue of accession of his or her member state who lacked it before.

(ii)   Grounds of review

5.68   The grounds of action, modelled upon and adhering closely to French adminis-trative law[416] but readily recognisable to any administrative lawyer, are:

---

405   TFEU, art. 263, 5th para.
406   *Ibid.*
407   Case T-354/05 *Télévision française 1* v *Commission* [2009] ECR II-471, at para. 33.
408   Case C-309/95 *Commission* v *Council* [1998] ECR I-655, at para. 18; Case C-403/05 *Parliament* v *Commission* [2007] ECR I-9045, at paras 28, 29; Case T-185/05 *Italy* v *Commission* [2008] ECR II-3207, at para. 68.
409   RP Court of Justice, art. 51; RP General Court, art. 102; RP Civil Service Tribunal, art. 100(3). Previously it varied with (postal) distance from Luxembourg, from two days for Belgium to a month from beyond Europe.
410   Case T-263/97 *GAL Penisola Sorrentina* v *Commission* [2000] ECR II-2041, at para. 47.
411   Case T-119/95 *Hauer* v *Council and Commission* [1998] ECR II-2713.
412   Cases T-121 and 151/ 96 *Mutual Aid Administration Services*, n. 403 above; Case T-185/05 *Italy* v *Commission*, n. 408 above.
413   Case T-392/05 *MMT Mecklenburg- Strelitzer Montag- und Tiefbau* v *Commission*, order of 11 December 2006, unreported, at para. 36 and case law cited.
414   Case C-273/04 *Poland* v *Council* [2007] ECR II-8925.
415   Case C-336/09P *Poland* v *Commission*, judgment of 26 June 2012, not yet reported.
416   The ECSC system of remedies from which those of the Communities were drawn was drafted by Mr Maurice Lagrange, a member of the Conseil d'Etat and subsequently an Advocate-General of the Court of Justice (of both the ECSC and of the Communities).

- lack of competence;
- infringement of an essential procedural requirement;
- infringement of the Treaties or of any rule of law relating to their application; and
- misuse of powers.[417]

The first two grounds relate to matters 'prior to the act' in the sense that the relevant question is whether the necessary enabling powers had been conferred upon the institution before it acted or whether the institution, in proceeding to act, complied with all (materially) relevant procedural rules. The first may be recognised as equivalent to substantive *ultra vires* in British administrative law, the second procedural *ultra vires*. The Court of Justice has annulled acts on a number of occasions on the ground that the institution purporting to act exceeded its powers as a matter of the allocation of institutional competences under the Treaties[418] or, where acting by authority of enabling legislation, the power conferred by and/or under the enabling act;[419] occasionally a measure may be annulled because the institution acted without authority *ratione temporis*.[420] But the Court has annulled an act because it went beyond *Community* competences very rarely.[421] Failure to comply with a mandatory procedural requirement is argued (and successfully) from time to time in the context of annulment of a general legislative act,[422] but it is more commonly raised where a Union institution discharges administrative functions which are made subject to strict procedures. Failure adequately to give reasons which justify the adoption of a measure, a Treaty requirement,[423] is infringement of an essential

---

417 TFEU, art. 263, 2nd para.

418 E.g., Cases 281 etc./85 *Germany and ors* v *Commission* [1987] ECR 3203; Case C-327/91 *France* v *Commission* [1994] ECR I-3641; Case C-106/96 *United Kingdom* v *Commission* [1998] ECR I-2729; Case C-110/02 *Commission* v *Council* [2004] ECR I-6333; Case C-133/06 *Parliament* v *Council* (Safe Country Lists) [2008] ECR I-3189.

419 E.g., Cases T-74 etc./00 *Artegodan and ors* v *Commission* [2002] ECR II-4945, upheld on appeal in Case C-39/03P *Commission* v *Artegodan and ors* [2003] ECR I-7885; Case C-11/00 *Commission* v *European Central Bank* [2003] ECR I-7147; Case C-46/03 *United Kingdom* v *Commission* [2005] ECR I-10167; Cases C-317 and 318/04 *Parliament* v *Council and Commission* (Passenger Name Records) [2006] ECR I-4721; Cases T-218 etc./03 *Boyle and ors* v *Commission* [2006] ECR II-1699; Cases C-14 and 295/06 *Parliament and Denmark* v *Commission* (DecaBDE) [2008] ECR I-1649; Case T-341/07 *Sison* v *Council* (Sison II) [2009] ECR II-3625.

420 E.g, Cases T-27 etc./03 *SP and ors* v *Commission* [2007] ECR II-4331.

421 Case C-376/98 *Germany* v *Parliament and Council* (Tobacco Advertising) [2000] ECR I-8419 (cf. Case C-380/03 *Germany* v *Parliament and Council* (Tobacco Advertising) [2006] ECR I-11573). The Court may be said to have done so implicitly in Case C-91/05 *Commission* v *Council* (Small Arms Weapons) [2008] ECR I-3651, by annulling a decision adopted by authority of the pre-Lisbon TEU on the ground that it should have had a dual treaty base (as to which see 6.48 below), one the EC Treaty, the other the TEU, the latter area falling outwith Community competences.

422 E.g., Case 138/79 *Roquette Frères* v *Council* [1980] ECR 3333; Case C-300/89 *Commission* v *Council* [1991] ECR I-2867.

423 See 6.45 below.

procedural requirement;[424] the Court has said (occasionally) that this involves a matter of public policy and so may, or must, be raised by the Court of its own motion.[425] However, in the case of administrative acts in particular, infringement of even an essential procedural requirement may result in annulment only if it can be shown that, but for the irregularity, the outcome of the procedure might have been different:[426] if it had 'any – even a small – chance of altering the outcome of the administrative procedure';[427] alternatively, 'the irregularity, however regrettable, vitiates the procedure only if it gives rise to harmful consequences for that person in the administrative procedure'.[428] Yet the Court is not consistent in this – saying sometimes that the Commission had infringed an essential procedural requirement in the adoption of a (purported) administrative act 'and it is not necessary also to establish that [the infringement] resulted in harm to the person relying on it'[429] – so prudence is called for.

5.69 The third ground relates to the applicable hierarchy of norms, and whether the act, as adopted, is consistent with the Treaties or any other higher rule of law to which it is subject. It is by application of this ground that Union legislation is measured against the fundamental principles set out in the TEU (the principle of subsidiarity meriting specific mention here)[430] and the provisions having general application set out in the TFEU; that the general principles of Union law are recognised and given effect;[431] and that the legal base of legislation may be reviewed – an incorrect legal base being an infringement of the Treaties.[432] The fourth ground, misuse of powers (*détournement de pouvoir*), 'has a very precise meaning':[433] it applies where, although the act appears to be the lawful act of a competent authority, on the basis of objective evidence the authority's

---

424 Case C-367/95P *Commission v Sytraval and Brink's France* [1998] ECR I-1719, at para. 67; Case T-168/01 *GlaxoSmithKline Services v Commission* [2006] ECR II-2969, at para. 54; Case T-112/05 *Akzo Nobel and ors v Commission* [2007] ECR II-5049, at para. 94.

425 Case C-166/95P *Commission v Daffix* [1997] ECR I-983, at para. 24; Case C-367/95P *Sytraval and Brink's France*, n. 424 above; Cases T-50 etc./06 *Ireland, France and Italy v Commission* [2007] ECR II-172* (set aide on appeal as Case C-89/08P *Commission v Ireland, France and Italy* [2009] ECR I-11245 but not on that point).

426 Case 142/87 *Belgium v Commission* [1990] ECR I-959. This is similar to the situation in both Scots and English administrative law; *Malloch v Aberdeen Corporation* 1971 SC (HL) 85.

427 Cases T-25 etc./95 *Cimenteries CBR and ors v Commission* (Cement) [2000] ECR II-491, at para. 247.

428 *Ibid.*, at para. 643.

429 Case C-286/95P *Commission v ICI* (Soda Ash) [2000] ECR I-2341, at para. 42; Cases C-287 and 288/95P *Commission v Solvay* (Soda Ash) [2000] ECR I-2391, at para. 46.

430 See Protocol (No. 2) on the Application of the Principles of Subsidiarity and Proportionality, art. 8, 1st para. ('The Court of Justice shall have jurisdiction in actions on grounds of infringement of the principle of subsidiarity by a legislative act in accordance with the rules laid down in Article 263').

431 See 6.101–6.103 below.

432 That is, TFEU, art. 296, 2nd para. (ex art. 253 EC); see 6.48 below. The Court of Justice appears sometimes to regard an incorrect legal base as an infringement of a procedural requirement, but the issue has not been fully clarified and could be argued both ways.

433 Case T-471/04 *Karatzoglou v European Agency for Reconstruction* [2008] ECR-SC I-A-2–35, at para. 49.

power has in truth been exercised for a purpose other than that for which it was conferred or with the sole, or at least decisive, aim of achieving purposes other than those stated.[434] It extends to an act purported to be adopted by authority of one legal base in order intentionally to evade the prescribed procedure of another,[435] to wilful failure to comply with a clearly prescribed procedure,[436] and would apply to a situation in which an institution acts corruptly or in bad faith. Its nearest British equivalent is misfeasance in public office.

There is no limit to the pleas in law (*moyens*) which may be advanced by a party **5.70** seeking annulment of a Union act, and it is not unknown for a party to fling everything it can into the fray. The practical disadvantage is that, should the applicant succeed in his main plea (or in an ancillary plea) but fail in others, he might not (at the Court's discretion) be awarded his full costs[437] – although this is an area marked by wild inconsistency from the Court. Nor is it unknown for a defendant institution to raise a plea of inadmissibility, fail, succeed on the merits, yet be ordered to bear part of the costs owing to the failure of its initial challenge.[438] Introduction of new pleas in the course of proceedings is prohibited unless based upon matters of law or fact which came to light only at that stage.[439] In some areas the Court may raise a plea of its own motion. This is perhaps surprising, not least because the Court has found Union law not to require a national court, in proceedings before it, to raise of its own motion a point of Union law not raised by the parties.[440] However, in annulment (or related) proceedings,

> the role of the Community judicature is not passive and cannot be limited to assessing the merits of the positions taken by each of the parties to the dispute in strict adherence to the pleas and arguments put forward by the parties. The Community judicature does not merely act as a referee between the parties. It must also, under Article [263], ensure compliance with Community law.
>
> The rules on procedure before each Community Court, and also the case-law, have thus identified several sets of circumstances in which the Community judicature, in

---

434   Case 8/57 *Groupement des hauts fourneaux et aciéries belges* v *High Authority* [1957–58] ECR 245 at 263; Case C-110/97 *Netherlands* v *Council* [2001] ECR I-8763, at para. 137; Case C-491/01 *R* v *Secretary of State for Health, ex parte British American Tobacco (Investments) and ors* [2002] ECR I-11453, at para. 189; Case C-342/03 *Spain* v *Council* [2005] ECR I-1975, at para. 64; Case T-471/04 *Karatzoglou*, n. 433 above, at paras 49–50.

435   Case 331/88 *R* v *Minister for Agriculture, Fisheries and Food, ex parte FEDESA* [1990] ECR I-4023; Case C-210/03 *R (Swedish Match AB and anor)* v *Secretary of State for Health* [2004] ECR I-11893.

436   Case T-284/08 *People's Mojahedin Organization of Iran* v *Council* [2008] ECR II-3487, at para. 44.

437   See 5.42 above.

438   E.g., Case T-138/03 *É.R. and ors* v *Council and Commission* [2006] ECR II-4923.

439   RP Court of Justice, art. 127(1); RP General Court, art. 48(2), RP Civil Service Tribunal, art. 43(1).

440   See 6.28 below.

order to fulfil its task as an arbiter of legality, has the power to raise an issue of law of its own motion.[441]

This is so where the issue is one of public policy which justifies active intervention from the Court, such as: proceedings which are manifestly inadmissible or lack any foundation in law;[442] where there exists an absolute bar to proceedings[443] by reason of, for example, time bar,[444] justiciability of the measure in dispute,[445] standing of the applicant[446] or *res judicata*;[447] or where the measure in issue is *ultra vires*[448] or is tainted by an infringement of an essential procedural requirement such as the obligation that it be (correctly) reasoned.[449] Consideration of the issues may take place at any stage in the proceedings.[450] Where the Court intervenes of its own motion it has a responsibility to ensure that the parties are heard on the matter, if necessary by re-opening proceedings.[451] Should the General Court fail in this duty its judgment may be set aside on appeal.[452]

5.71 It should be noted that the intensity of judicial review is generally of a light touch, certainly in general legislative acts involving questions of economic policy and evaluation, where the Union institutions enjoy a wide margin of appreciation and where the Court will usually test only for manifest error of appraisal:

> [W]here a Community authority is called upon, in the performance of its duties, to make complex assessments, it enjoys a wide measure of discretion, the exercise of which is subject to a limited judicial review in the course of which the Community judicature may not substitute its assessment of the facts for the assessment made by the authority concerned. Thus, in such cases, the Community judicature must restrict itself to examining the accuracy of the findings of fact and law made by the authority concerned and to verifying, in particular, that the action taken by that authority is not vitiated by

---

441 Case C-89/08P *Commission v Ireland, France and Italy* [2009] ECR I-11245, *per* A-G Bot at paras 60–1 of his opinion.
442 RP Court of Justice, art. 53(2); RP General Court, art. 111; RP Civil Service Tribunal, art. 76.
443 RP Court of Justice, art. 150; RP General Court, art. 113; RP Civil Service Tribunal, art. 77.
444 See nn. 411 and 412 above.
445 See n. 398 above.
446 See n. 495 below and accompanying text.
447 Cases C-442 and 471/03P *P & O European Ferries (Vizcaya) and anor v Commission* [2006] ECR I-4845, at paras 38–52.
448 Case C-210/98 *Salzgitter v Commission* [2000] ECR I-5843, at para. 56.
449 See n. 425 above and accompanying text.
450 Case C-290/07P *Commission v Scott* [2010] ECR I-7763, *per* A-G Mengozzi at para. 33 of his opinion.
451 Case C-89/08P *Commission v Ireland, France and Italy* [2009] ECR I-11245; Case C-197/09RX-II *M v European Medicines Agency* [2009] ECR I-12033, at para. 57.
452 *Ibid.*

manifest error or misuse of powers and that it did not clearly exceed the bounds of its discretion.[453]

But the Court may still bite: the Council has the broadest of discretion in matters of the Common Agricultural Policy so that review by the Court is limited to verifying that the Council has not manifestly exceeded the limits of its discretion and that measures are neither vitiated by manifest error or misuse of powers nor manifestly inappropriate in terms of the objective which the Council is seeking to pursue.[454] Having said that,

> even though such judicial review is of limited scope, it requires that the Community institutions which have adopted the act in question must be able to show before the Court that in adopting the act they actually exercised their discretion, which pre-supposes the taking into consideration of all the relevant factors and circumstances of the situation the act was intended to regulate.[455]

In one area the Court has adopted a new vigour in review of Union acts, that is where a measure may trench substantially upon fundamental rights guarantees. Here the Court will, and must, ensure the review, 'in principle the full review', of the lawfulness of the Union measure in the light of the fundamental rights forming an integral part of the general principles of Union law.[456] The General Court (in which the matter is first and most comprehensively contested) has interpreted this as requiring a standard and intensity of review which is 'full and rigorous'.[457]

Where an act under review is of an administrative rather than a legislative **5.72** character, review will be, as with administrative law generally, of a more intense quality.

(iii)   Title and interest

The action of annulment may be raised: **5.73**

- as of right, without need to demonstrate interest, by the Parliament, the Council, the Commission or a member state (the 'privileged applicants');[458]

---

453   Case C-120/97 *Upjohn* v *Medicines Licensing Authority and ors* [1999] ECR I-223, at para. 34.
454   Case C-310/04 *Spain* v *Council* [2006] ECR I-7285, at paras 96–9.
455   *Ibid.* at para. 122.
456   Cases C-402 and 415/05P *Kadi and Al Barakaat* v *Council and Commission* (Kadi II) [2008] ECR I-6351, at paras 326 and 327.
457   Case T-85/09 *Kadi* v *Commission* (Kadi III) [2010] ECR II-5177, at para. 151; and the extensive discussion at paras 112–51.
458   TFEU, art. 263, 2nd para.

- by the Court of Auditors, the European Central Bank or the Committee of the Regions where the act in question infringes their prerogatives ('semi-privileged applicants');[459] and
- by a natural or juristic person but subject to proof of title and interest or *locus standi* ('non-privileged applicants').[460]

5.74 *Privileged applicants*   Although there is some contrary authority,[461] the predominant view is that a privileged applicant need demonstrate no legal interest whatsoever in order to raise proceedings.[462] The Parliament was upgraded to a privileged applicant (previously it was 'semi-privileged') only in 2003 by Nice. As with article 258, 'member state' here means the central authorities of the state: *Land*, devolved, regional or local governments are not recognised to be privileged applicants.[463] There is disquiet as to the fairness of this, as it often falls (in federal member states in particular) to regional authorities to implement Union legislation, and to bear the financial cost of failing properly to do so,[464] yet they have no standing to challenge its legality (as well as sometimes limited, or no, influence in its adoption). A special rule applies to standing to challenge a legislative act on the ground that it infringes the principle of subsidiarity.[465]

---

459   *Ibid.* art. 263, 3rd para.

460   *Ibid.* art. 263, 4th para.

461   Case C-308/95 *Netherlands* v *Commission* [1999] ECR I-6513; Case C-164/02 *Netherlands* v *Commission* [2004] ECR I-1177.

462   Case 131/86 *United Kingdom* v *Council* [1988] ECR 905; Case 45/86 *Commission* v *Council* [1987] ECR 1493; Case C-208/99 *Portugal* v *Commission* [2001] ECR I-9183; Case C-301/03 *Italy* v *Commission* [2005] ECR I-10217, *per* A-G Jacobs at para. 52 of his opinion; Case C-77/05 *United Kingdom* v *Council* (Frontex) [2007] ECR I-11459 and Case C-137/05 *United Kingdom* v *Council* (Biometric Passports) [2007] ECR I-11593 (the United Kingdom challenging regulations which did not apply to it); Case T-185/05 *Italy* v *Commission* [2008] ECR II-3207; Case T-369/07 *Latvia* v *Commission*, judgment of 22 March 2011, not yet reported. The position taken by a member state or an institution at the time of the adoption of the measure has no relevance; Case 166/78 *Italy* v *Council* [1979] ECR 2575; Case C-378/00 *Commission* v *Parliament and Council* (LIFE) [2003] ECR I-937.

463   Case C-95/97 *Région Wallonne* v *Commission* [1997] ECR I-1787; Case T-214/95 *Vlaams Gewest* v *Commission* [1998] ECR II-717; Case T-238/97 *Comunidad Autónoma de Cantabria* v *Council* [1998] ECR II-2271; Cases T-132 and 143/96 *Freistaat Sachsen and ors* v *Commission* [1999] ECR II-3663; Cases T-32 and 41/98 *Nederlandse Antillen* v *Commission* [2000] ECR II-201 (overturned on appeal, Case C-142/00P *Commission* v *Nederlandse Antillen* [2003] ECR I-3483, but not on that point); Case T-37/04 *Região autónoma dos Açores* v *Council* [2008] ECR II-103*; for a rare exception to the rule see Case T-366/03 and 235/04 *Land Oberösterreich and Austria* v *Commission* [2005] ECR II-4005.

464   See 6.39 below.

465   Protocol (No. 2) on the Application of the Principles of Subsidiarity and Proportionality, art. 8, 1st para.: the action may be raised by a member state (in the normal sense, which is uncontentious) under art. 263 'or notified by them in accordance with their legal order on behalf of their national Parliament or a chamber thereof'. Whether this creates a duty of a member state to act, to adjust its 'legal order' accordingly, and whether an action once 'notified' is brought in the name of (and directed by) the member state or of its parliament, is not yet clear.

Semi-privileged applicants   The semi-privileged applicants enjoy standing to **5.75**
challenge legislation under article 263 TFEU insofar as it is claimed to infringe
their prerogatives. The 'prerogatives' of the institutions (*ses prérogatives; ihre
Rechte*) address essentially their proper role in the legislative process. The
principle was born in case law, the Court of Justice recognising an implicit right
of the Parliament to protect its prerogatives even before it was codified in article
263 (by Maastricht).[466] The Committee of the Regions was recognised as a
semi-privileged applicant only with Lisbon; it now appears to have an unhindered right to challenge a legislative act for breach of the principle of
subsidiarity provided the act was one which required that it be consulted.[467]

Non-privileged applicants   Article 263 underwent at casual glance minor but **5.76**
in fact significant amendment by Lisbon. Prior to Lisbon a non-privileged
applicant was entitled to raise an action for annulment of any act of which he
was personally the addressee (that is, necessarily, a decision), and this is still so.
Otherwise he could, according to the EC Treaty, challenge only 'a decision
which, although in the form of a regulation or a decision addressed to another
person, is of direct and individual concern to [him]'.[468] A private third party
seeking the annulment of a Community act therefore had three cumulative
hurdles to overcome.

The nature of a decision: The Court long held that the language (limited to 'a **5.77**
decision [even if] in the form of a regulation') meant that a Community act was,
irrespective of the merits of the claim, immune from review at the instance of a
non-privileged applicant if it was of general application, that is, it applies to
objectively determined situations and entails legal effects for persons regarded
generally and in the abstract.[469] Put more simply, it was of a legislative rather
than an administrative nature, or a true regulation, not in real terms a decision
whatever its designation.[470] There is significant overlap between the administrative character of a measure and its individual bearing upon a person (the third
test), but an act genuinely of general application may, in perhaps rare circumstances, affect only a narrow class of persons; an action of annulment was
nevertheless inadmissible failing the first test alone.[471] However, in 1994 the

---

466   Case 70/88 *Parliament* v *Council* (Chernobyl) [1990] ECR I-2041.

467   Protocol (No. 2), n. 465 above, art. 8, 2nd para.

468   EC Treaty, art. 230, 4th para.

469   Cases T-295 etc./04 *Centro Provincial de Jóvenes Agricultores de Jaén (ASAJA)* v *Council* [2005] ECR II-3151, at
       para. 31 and case law cited.

470   First considered in Cases 16 and 17/62 *Confédération Nationale des Producteurs des Fruits et Légumes* v *EEC
       Council* [1962] ECR 471.

471   E.g. Case C-298/89 *Government of Gibraltar* v *Council* [1993] ECR I-3605. The exception was review of
       anti-dumping measures, which are required to be in the form of a Regulation because of the legal framework
       by which they are adopted, but have been identified by the Court as a 'hybrid instrument', having some of the
       character of both a legislative and an administrative act, and so (sometimes) reviewable at the instance of an

Court of Justice found it possible to identify individual concern in a true legislative measure and allowed an action for its annulment to proceed (and succeed).[472] It followed suit a (small, but consistent) number of times thereafter.[473] The test therefore appeared to be abandoned and was formally dropped by Lisbon, article 263 now reading simply 'an act addressed to that person or which is of direct and individual concern to [him]'.

5.78 *Direct concern*: A person is 'directly' affected by a Union measure when it bears directly upon his legal rights or obligations without intervening authority, or, put another way, it leaves no real discretion to any authority – Union or national – charged with putting it into effect, it having a purely automatic character which derives solely from the measure in question without the application of any discretionary intervening or intermediate rule.[474] This means in theory that a Directive ought never to be subject of review at the instance of a non-privileged applicant, for a Directive always requires transformation into national law; but this is not necessarily so,[475] and in one case (so far) the Court has found the requisite direct concern in a Directive justifying the admissibility of an annulment action raised by a non-privileged applicant.[476] The measure must affect a person materially as well as legally: the adoption of an import ban will affect directly traders/importers of goods the subject of the ban, but not

---

affected non-privileged applicant; see Cases 239 and 275/82 *Allied Corporation and ors* v *Commission* [1984] ECR 1005; Case 264/82 *Timex* v *Council and Commission* [1985] ECR 849; Case C-358/89 *Extramet Industrie* v *Council* [1991] ECR I-2501; Case C-239/99 *Nachi Europe* v *Hauptzollamt Krefeld* [2001] ECR I-1197.

472   Case C-309/89 *Codorníu* v *Council* [1994] ECR I-1853.

473   Case T-484/93 *Exporteurs in Levende Varkens* v *Commission* [1995] ECR I-2941; Case C-451/98 *Antillean Rice Mills* v *Council* [2001] ECR I-8949; Case C-41/99P *Sadam Zuccherifici and ors* v *Council* [2001] ECR I-4239; Case T-43/98 *Emesa Sugar* v *Council* [2001] ECR II-3519; Cases T-94 etc./00 *Rica Foods* v *Commission* [2002] ECR II-4677; Case T-420/05 *Vischim* v *Commission* [2009] ECR II-3841; Case T-380/06 *Vischim* v *Commission* [2009] ECR II-3911. See also Case C-142/00P *Commission* v *Nederlandse Antillen* [2003] ECR I-3483, overturning Cases T-32 and 41/98 *Nederlandse Antillen* v *Commission* [2000] ECR II-201.

474   See e.g., Case 62/70 *Bock* v *Commission* [1971] ECR 897; Case 11/82 *Piraiki-Patraiki* v *Commission* [1985] ECR 207; Case C-386/96P *Dreyfus* v *Commission* [1998] ECR I-2309; Cases T-172 etc./98 *Salamander and ors* v *Parliament and Council* [2000] ECR II-2487; Cases T-198 etc./95 *Comafrica and ors* v *Commission* [2001] ECR II-1975; Case C-486/01P *Front National* v *Parliament* [2004] ECR I-6289; Case C-417/04P *Regione Siciliana* v *Commission* [2006] ECR I-3881; Case C-15/06P *Regione Siciliana* v *Commission* [2007] ECR I-2591; Case T-18/10 *Inuit Tapiriit Kanatami and ors* v *Parliament and Council*, order of 6 September 2011, not yet reported.

475   See e.g., Case T-135/96 *Union Européenne de l'Artisanat et des Petites et Moyennes Entreprises* v *Council* [1998] ECR II-2335 (a Directive *might* directly (and individually) affect a private person, but only exceptionally, and not here); Case T-223/01 *Japan Tobacco and anor* v *Parliament and Council* [2002] ECR II-3259, at para. 28 (the fact that a Directive is at issue 'in itself is not sufficient to render such actions inadmissible'). For an expression of the doctrinaire view see Cases T-172 etc./98 *Salamander*, n. 474 above.

476   Cases T-420/05 and T-380/06 *Vischim*, n. 473 above. The (closely related) actions were admissible but dismissed on their merits.

those who merely produce or process them;[477] the measure may well have consequences for the latters' economic activities but they do not result directly from it.[478]

Individual concern: A person is individually affected by a Union measure where **5.79** it affects him 'by reason of certain attributes which are peculiar to [him] or by reason of circumstances in which [he is] differentiated from all other persons and by virtue of these factors distinguishes [him] individually just as in the case of the person addressed'.[479] In contradistinction to the wide amplitude given to acts which were subject to review, this test for individual concern ('the *Plaumann* test') is read narrowly, and means that access to judicial review under article 263 is available, if at all, only rarely, and only to a (very) small and closed class of private persons. It has long been recognised by the Court itself to be 'clearly restrictive',[480] yet is applied rigorously and consistently;[481] the interests of persons deprived of access to the Court under article 263 are (claimed to be) protected by the availability of other remedies.[482] There is an argument that the *Plaumann* test so restricts access to judicial protection as to fall foul of the relevant provisions of both the European Convention on Human Rights and the EU Charter of Fundamental Rights.[483] With a nod to the logic of these arguments, in 2002 the General Court formally broke with the old rule, laying down a different, and much more generous, test of individual concern under article 263.[484] Advocate-General Jacobs was at the same time urging a similar (re)orientation[485] but the Court of Justice immediately restated the established construction of the rule,[486] so implicitly finding the existing avenues of judicial review of Community legislation satisfactory to the requirements of the Convention. Whether the Court of Human Rights would agree is a different

---

477 Case T-18/10 *Inuit Tapiriit Kanatami*, n. 474 above.

478 *Ibid.* at para. 75.

479 Case 25/62 *Plaumann* v *EEC Commission* [1963] ECR 95 at 107.

480 Case 40/64 *Sgarlata* v *EEC Commission* [1965] ECR 215 at 227.

481 E.g., Cases 106–7/63 *Toepfer* v *EEC Commission* [1965] ECR 405; Case 100/74 *CAM* v *Commission* [1975] ECR 1393; Case 11/82 *Piraiki-Patraiki* v *Commission* [1985] ECR 207; Case C-321/95P *Stichting Greenpeace Council and ors* v *Commission* [1998] ECR I-1651; Case T-135/96 *Union Européenne de l'Artisanat et des Petites et Moyennes Entreprises* v *Council* [1998] ECR II-2335; Case C-447/98P *Molkerei Großbraunshain and Bene Nahrungsmittel* v *Commission* [2000] ECR I-9097; Case T-47/00 *Rica Foods (Free Zone)* v *Commission* [2002] ECR II-113. But for a recent, more nuanced approach see Case C-260/05P *Sniace* v *Commission* [2007] ECR I-10005; Case C-125/06P *Commission* v *Infront WM* [2008] ECR I-1451.

482 See 5.95 below.

483 See 6.120 below, n. 629.

484 Case T-177/01 *Jégo-Quéré et Cie* v *Commission* [2002] ECR II-2365, reversed on appeal as Case C-263/02P *Commission* v *Jégo-Quéré et Cie* [2004] ECR I-3425.

485 See his opinion in Case C-50/00P *Unión de Pequeños Agricultores* v *Council* [2002] ECR I-6677.

486 Case C-50/00P *Unión de Pequeños Agricultores, ibid.*; re-affirmed in Case C-312/00P *Commission* v *Camar and Tico* [2002] ECR II-11355 and Case C-142/00P *Commission* v *Nederlandse Antillen* [2003] ECR I-3483; Case C-263/02P *Jégo-Quéré*, n. 484 above; Case C-167/02P *Rothley and ors* v *Parliament* [2004] ECR I-3149.

matter.[487] In *Unión de Pequeños Agricultores*, the Court of Justice said that a change to the rule was a matter for the member states, 'if necessary' by Treaty amendment.[488] They responded in Lisbon, extending the reach of the non-privileged applicant to 'a regulatory act [*acte règlementaire*; *Rechtsakte mit Verordungscharakter*] which is of direct concern to [him] and does not entail implementing measures'.[489] In the face of such an act it is no longer necessary to show individual concern, only legal effects and direct concern, and this is likely to increase significantly the admissibility (if not necessarily the success) of article 263 actions. First consideration of review of a regulatory act has now occurred but we are made little wiser by it.[490] The extension of standing may also turn out to be a poisoned chalice.[491] The Court of Justice is sometimes urged to relax the tests for admissibility where the measure at issue is particularly egregious ('measures that lack even the appearance of legality'),[492] but, so far, to no avail.

5.80   The repeal by an institution of a measure does not necessarily extinguish an applicant's interest in its annulment, for repeal does not constitute recognition of the unlawfulness of the measure and has only prospective effect, as compared to a judgment annulling it, by which it is eliminated retroactively from the legal order.[493] In addition, if a measure is annulled it will oblige the institution(s) to take the measures necessary to comply with the judgment, which may involve amendment to or repeal of subsequent measures,[494] and may have a bearing upon liability for injury caused by its adoption in the first place.

5.81   All actions of annulment raised by non-privileged applicants fall now within the jurisdiction of the General Court. As admissibility involves considerations

---

487 See *Bosphorus Hava Yollari Turizm v Ireland* (2006) 39 EHRR 1, and in particular the separate concurring judgment of Judge Ress.

488 Case C-50/00P *Unión de Pequeños Agricultores*, n. 485 above, at para. 45.

489 TFEU, art. 263, 4th para.

490 Case T-18/10 *Inuit Tapiriit Kanatami and ors v Parliament and Council*, order of 6 September 2011, not yet reported; the act at issue was found not to be a regulatory act. The Inuit have a second iron in the fire in Case T-526/10 *Inuit Tapiriit Kanatami and ors v Commission*, pending, challenging the first act's implementing Regulation. As to the (putative) meaning of 'regulatory act' see 6.99 below

491 This is because of the existing rule that a person who enjoyed clear standing under art. 230 EC (TFEU, art. 263) to seek annulment of a Community measure but failed to use it could not subsequently plead its illegality in a national court; see 5.142 below. The possibility is now that a person directly affected by a regulatory act which entails no implementing measures falls within this category, so has two months (from its publication in the *Official Journal*, not everyone's favourite reading) to raise an action under art. 263, and has no legal redress thereafter when, for example, the act is applied to him by a national authority.

492 Case C-131/03P *RJ Reynolds Tobacco Holdings and ors v Commission and anor* [2006] ECR I-7795, at paras 92–3.

493 Case T-256/07 *People's Mojahedin Organization of Iran v Council* [2008] ECR II-3019, at para. 48. As to the legal effects of annulment see immediately below.

494 Cases T-481 and 484/93 *Exporteurs in Levende Varkens and ors v Commission* [1995] ECR II 2941, at paras 46–8; Case T-228/02 *Organisation des Modjahedines du peuple d'Iran v Council* [2006] ECR I-4665, at para. 35.

of public policy and constitutes an absolute bar to proceedings, the Court may at any time and of its own motion consider whether an action is barred for want of the applicant's sufficient standing,[495] but it appears to apprehend no duty to do so,[496] and has said that it is free to decide that the proper administration of justice justifies the dismissal of an action on its merits without ruling on admissibility.[497] A party may apply to the Court to rule upon admissibility without hearing argument on the substance of the case.[498] A decision having been taken to consider the issue of admissibility separately, the remainder of the proceedings is oral unless the Court directs otherwise.[499]

It might be noted that there is no nationality or geographic limitation to standing under article 263, an applicant from anywhere in the world is competent to raise an action provided he or she meets the requisite (addressee or direct and (maybe) individual concern) tests. Thus it is that three Inuit from Qikiqtarjuaq off the east coast of Baffin Island may come to the Court seeking (so far unsuccessfully) annulment of an EU ban on the import of sealskin.[500] Anti-dumping measures in particular attract disgruntled third country companies to the Court, and not only the usual suspects but applicants from, for example, the Soviet Union[501] (a tricky one, as the Soviet Union did not

5.82

---

495 RP General Court, art. 113; Case T-174/95 *Svenska Journalistförbundet* v *Council* [1998] ECR II-2289; Case T-354/00 *Métropole Télévision* v *Commission* [2001] ECR II-3177; Case C-341/00P *Conseil national des professions de l'automobile and ors* v *Commission* [2001] ECR I-5263; Cases T-366/03 and 235/04 *Land Oberösterreich and Austria* v *Commission* [2005] ECR II-4005; Cases T-218 etc./03 *Boyle and ors* v *Commission* [2006] ECR II-1699; Case T-170/06 *Alrosa* v *Commission* [2007] ECR II-2601; Case T-289/03 *BUPA* v *Commission* [2008] ECR II-81, at paras 63–85.

496 See e.g., Cases T-195 and 207/01 *Government of Gibraltar* v *Commission* [2002] ECR II-2309. In one very peculiar case the Court of First Instance annulled a Council Regulation on the Community's common commercial policy in an action raised under art. 173 EC (pre-Amsterdam) (TFEU, art. 263) by a (pre-accession) Austrian company, it by any measure enjoying insufficient standing to do so, but it appearing never to have occurred to anyone, including the Court, to raise the issue of admissibility; Case T-115/94 *Opel Austria* v *Council* [1997] ECR II-39. A more recent *dictum* from the Court of First Instance indicates a duty of the Court to consider admissibility 'should such an issue arise'; Case T-209/01 *Honeywell International* v *Commission* [2005] ECR II-5527, at para. 53.

497 Case C-23/00P *Council* v *Boehringer Ingelheim Vetmedica and anor* [2002] ECR I-1873, at paras 51–2; Case C-273/04 *Poland* v *Council* [2007] ECR II-8925; Case T-319/05 *Switzerland* v *Commission* [2010] ECR II-4265.

498 RP Court of Justice, art. 151; RP General Court, art. 114. These provisions apply across the jurisdiction of the Courts, but arise most commonly in art. 263 proceedings.

499 RP Court of Justice, art. 151(4); RP General Court, art. 114(3).

500 Case T-18/10 *Inuit Tapiriit Kanatami and ors* v *Parliament and Council*, order of 6 September 2011, not yet reported; Case T-526/10 *Inuit Tapiriit Kanatami and ors* v *Commission*, pending.

501 Case 120/83R *Raznoimport* v *Commission* [1983] ECR 2573; Cases 294/86 and 77/87 *Technointorg* v *Commission and Council* [1988] ECR 6077.

recognise the Community (and so the Court of Justice) until 1988),[502] Russia,[503] Ukraine,[504] Korea,[505] China,[506] Thailand,[507] India[508] and Saudi Arabia.[509] In fact, because article 263 is likely to be the only avenue of judicial redress open to them, the Court takes a relatively lenient view as to individual concern in the field.[510] Nor is it uncommon to find third country firms before the Court seeking the annulment of Commission decisions adopted in the sphere of competition[511] and, increasingly, third country nationals the subject of repressive Union measures[512] – some seven dozen such actions were raised before the General Court in 2011, from, principally, Côte d'Ivoire, Iran and Syria.

(iv) Annulment

5.83 Should an action be competently and timeously raised, and, on substance, a Union act be found to be unlawful, it is annulled by declaration of the Court; in Treaty terms, it is declared 'void' (*nul et non avenu*).[513] The effect is, in principle, to deprive the act of all legal effect, past, present and future:

> Under the first paragraph of Article [264] when an action for annulment is well-founded, the Community court must declare the contested act void. It follows that the Community court's decision of annulment leads to the disappearance retroactively of the contested act with regard to all persons.[514]

---

502 Joint Declaration of 25 June 1988 on the Establishment of Official Relations between the European Economic Community and Council for Mutual Economic Assistance [1988] OJ L157/35.

503 Case T-87/98 *International Potash Co. v Council* [2000] ECR II-3179; Case T-170/06 *Alrosa Company v Commission* [2007] ECR II-2601.

504 Case T-249/06 *Interpipe Nikopolsky Seamless Tubes Plant Niko Tube and anor v Council* [2009] ECR II-383.

505 Case T-51/96 *Miwon Co. Ltd v Council* [2000] ECR II-184.

506 Case T-170/94 *Shanghai Bicycle v Council* [1997] ECR II-1383; Case 138/02 *Nanjing Metalink International v Council* [2006] ECR II-4347; Case T-498/04 *Zhejiang Xinan Chemical Industrial Group v Council* [2009] ECR II-1969.

507 Case T-118/96 *Thai Bicycle v Council* [1998] ECR II-2991.

508 Case T-88/98 *Kundan Industries and anor v Council* [2002] ECR II-4897.

509 Case 49/88 *Al-Jubail Fertilizer Co. v Council* [1991] ECR I-3187.

510 See 14.110 below.

511 See 13.103 below.

512 E.g., Case T-229/02 *Ocalan (on behalf of the Kurdistan Workers' Party (PKK)) v Council* [2008] ECR II-45*; Cases C-402 and 415/05P *Kadi and Al Barakaat v Council and Commission* [2008] ECR I-6351; Case T-284/08 *People's Mojahedin Organization of Iran v Council* [2008] ECR II-3487; Case T-390/08 *Bank Melli Iran v Council* [2009] ECR II-3967; Cases C-399 and 403/06P *Hassan and Ayadi v Council* [2009] ECR I-11393; Case T-85/09 *Kadi v Commission* (Kadi III) [2010] ECR II-5177.

513 TFEU, art. 264, 1st para (ex art. 231, 1st para. EC).

514 Case C-199/06 *Centre d'exportation du livre français and anor v Société internationale de diffusion et d'édition* [2008] ECR I-469, at para. 61.

The jurisdiction of the Court is limited to this declaration of nullity: it cannot order directions to the erring institution,[515] nor can it issue a (merely) declaratory judgment[516] or other directions[517] even if they concern the manner in and with which its judgment ought to be complied. The institution is, however, under a Treaty obligation to take all necessary measures to comply with the judgment of the Court,[518] the purpose being not 'the elimination of the act as such from the Community legal order, since that is the very essence of its annulment by the Court', but rather 'the removal of the effects of the illegalities found in the judgment annulling the act'.[519] Where a measure which has already been executed is annulled, the retroactive effect of the judgment normally requires the re-establishment of the legal position in which the applicant found himself prior to its adoption.[520] But prior to its annulment (or invalidation under article 267)[521] the act is presumed to be valid and must be given full force and effect,[522] unless the Court has suspended its operation by interim order[523] or, very exceptionally, the act is tainted with such serious and manifest defects as to render it 'non-existent'.[524] The quality of 'voidness' is further subject to two important exceptions:

---

515   Cases T-374 etc./94 *European Night Services and ors* v *Commission* [1998] ECR II-3141; Case C-390/95P *Antillean Rice Mills and ors* v *Commission* [1999] ECR I-769.

516   Case C-224/03 *Italy* v *Commission* [2003] ECR I-14751, at paras 20–2.

517   Cases C-199 and 200/94P *Pesquería Vasco-Montañesa and anor* v *Commission* [1995] ECR I-3709, at para. 24; Case T-145/06 *Omya* v *Commission* [2009] ECR II-145, at para. 23.

518   TFEU, art. 266, 1st para. (ex art. 233, 1st para. EC); see 5.90 below.

519   Case T-229/02 *Ocalan (on behalf of the Kurdistan Workers' Party (PKK))* v *Council* [2008] ECR II-45*, at para. 49.

520   Cases 97 etc./86 *Asteris and ors* v *Commission* [1988] ECR 2181; Case T-171/99 *Corus UK* v *Commission* [2001] ECR II-2967, at para. 50 and case law cited; Case F-1/05 *Landgren* v *Fondation européenne pour la formation* [2006] ECR-SC II-A-1–459, at para. 92.

521   See 5.141 below.

522   Case 101/78 *Granaria* v *Hoofdproduktschap voor Akkerbouwprodukten* [1979] ECR 623; Case C-137/92P *Commission* v *BASF and ors* (PVC) [1994] ECR I-2555; Case C-475/01 *Commission* v *Greece* (Ouzo) [2004] ECR I-8923; Case C-199/06 *Centre d'exportation du livre français and anor* v *Société internationale de diffusion et d'édition* [2008] ECR I-469, at para. 60; Case C-27/09P *France* v *People's Mojehadin Organization of Iran*, judgment of 21 December 2011, not yet reported, at para. 74.

523   See 5.40 above.

524   The construct of 'non-existence', derived from French and German administrative law, applies where a measure is tainted by an irregularity or defect the gravity of which is so obvious that it cannot be recognised or tolerated by the legal order. A (purported) act has been declared by the Court of Justice to be non-existent only once, in a pre-EEC coal and steel case, Cases 1 and 14/57 *Société des usines à tubes de la Sarre* v *High Authority* [1957–58] ECR 105. Ironically a non-existent measure cannot be annulled for it has produced no legal effects capable of annulment. In Union law the construct applies in exceptional circumstances only, and 'must be limited to the most extreme cases' (Case T-369/07 *Latvia* v *Commission*, judgment of 22 March 2011, not yet reported, at para. 61); see Cases T-79 etc./89 *BASF and ors* v *Commission* (PVC) [1992] ECR 315, in which the General Court declared a purported act non-existent but was reversed on appeal (although the act was annulled), Case C-137/92P *Commission* v *BASF and ors* (PVC) [1994] ECR I-2555; Case C-475/01 *Commission* v *Greece* (Ouzo) [2004] ECR I-8923; Case C-345/06 *Heinrich* [2009] ECR I-1659, *per* A-G Sharpston at paras 102–10 of her opinion.

- The Court may moderate the effect of annulment: having annulled a Union act, it may 'if it considers this necessary' declare some or all of its provisions to be operative (in Treaty terms, 'definitive'; *définitif, fortgeltend*).[525] It uses this power sparingly, in the interests of, for example, legal certainty or legitimate expectation, where rights and legal relationships have been established, in good faith, upon the basis of the law as thought to be good law,[526] or in other exceptional circumstances which justify it – up to and including, in (it is to be hoped) an exceptional case, sustaining the effects of an annulled measure 'for a brief period' even though its continued operation deprived individuals of their fundamental rights.[527] The effects of the measure are normally sustained until replaced by another competently adopted, sometimes with a requirement that the latter follow 'within a reasonable period'.[528]
- In the case of an administrative act addressed to several persons, if an addressee fails to raise a challenge under article 263, the act becomes definitive for him, even if it comes subsequently to be annulled in proceedings brought by another addressee.[529] In this case the interests of legal certainly override those of legality.

5.84   Generally it is only the *dispositif*, or operative part, of an act which is subject to annulment, as only it produces legal effects; the reasoning which led to the *dispositif* does not.[530] But exceptionally that reasoning may be challenged if it is

---

525   TFEU, art. 264, 2nd para.
526   See e.g., Case 45/86 *Commission* v *Council* (Generalised Tariff Preferences) [1987] ECR 1493; Case C-295/90 *European Parliament* v *Council* (Students) [1992] ECR I-4193; Case C-388/92 *European Parliament* v *Council* [1994] ECR I-2067; Case C-21/94 *European Parliament* v *Council* [1995] ECR I-1827; Case C-271/94 *European Parliament* v *Council* (Trans-European Networks) [1996] ECR I-1689; Case C-106/96 *United Kingdom* v *Commission* [1998] ECR I-2729 (Social Exclusion Projects); Case C-378/00 *Commission* v *Parliament and Council* (LIFE) [2003] ECR I-937; Case C-445/00 *Austria* v *Council* [2003] ECR I-8549; Cases C-317 and 318/04 *Parliament* v *Council and Commission* [2006] ECR I-4721; Case C-166/07 *Parliament* v *Council* (International Fund for Ireland) [2009] ECR I-7135; Case C-370/07 *Commission* v *Council* (CITES) [2009] ECR I-8917. Article 231 EC applied this declaratory power to Regulations only, but in the *Students* judgment the Court exercised it in relation to a Directive, and in *Trans-European Networks* (and subsequent judgments), to decisions. TFEU, art. 264 applies it to all Union acts. On legal certainty and legitimate expectation, see 6.134–6.135 below.
527   Cases C-402 and 415/05P *Kadi and Al Barakaat* v *Council and Commission* (Kadi II) [2008] ECR I-6351, at para. 375.
528   See e.g., Case C-166/07 *International Fund for Ireland*, n. 526 above, at para. 75 and in the *dispositif*, 2nd para.
529   Case C-310/97P *Commission* v *AssiDomän Kraft Products* [1999] ECR I-5363. This also applies in the (very rare) case in which a Regulation applies distinctly to identified individuals, a successful action resulting in its annulment 'insofar as it concerns the applicant'; see Case T-229/02 *Ocalan (on behalf of the Kurdistan Workers' Party (PKK))* v *Council* [2008] ECR II-45*; Cases C-402 and 415/05P *Kadi II*, n. 527 above; Case T-318/01 *Othman* v *Council and Commission* [2009] ECR II-1627; Case T-85/09 *Kadi* v *Commission* (Kadi III) [2010] ECR II-5177.
530   E.g., Cases T-125 and 127/97 *Coca-Cola* v *Commission* [2000] ECR II-1733; Case C-164/02 *Netherlands* v *Commission* [2004] ECR I-1177.

essential to an understanding of the *dispositif*,[531] and the General Court appears to be softening its general approach to this.[532] Of particular importance to administrative acts (but not restricted to them)[533] adopted following extensive economic analysis and reasoning, where some of the grounds provided are sufficient to justify the decision, errors which might invalidate other grounds do not result in its annulment.[534] Put another way, if the operative part of a decision is based upon several 'pillars' of reasoning each of which is sufficient to justify it, it should be annulled only if each pillar is vitiated by illegality.[535] If in the course of proceedings an institution repeals (usually 'withdraws'; *retire*) the measure in question such that no legal effect remains, the action is rendered without object and the Court may declare it unnecessary to give judgment;[536] but this will not be the case where the applicant retains an interest in the annulment of the measure.[537]

Portions of a Union measure may be annulled and the rest left intact and **5.85** operative, provided the former is severable from the whole,[538] and an action for partial annulment of a Union measure where the provisions sought to be annulled are not severable appears now to be inadmissible.[539] The Court has said that severability is not possible where the partial annulment of a measure would have the effect of altering its substance,[540] which is an objective, not subjective test.[541] Otherwise the only guidance comes from Advocate-General Fennelly:

> The Court has not laid down any general guidelines on the question of the severability of the valid and invalid parts of a legislative measure. None the less, it seems to me that it has chosen the route of partial annulment where two conditions are satisfied: first, where a particular provision is discrete and, thus, severable without altering the

---

531 Case T-251/00 *Lagardère & Canal+* v *Commission* [2002] ECR II-4825; Case T-474/04 *Pergan Hilfsstoffe für industrielle Prozesse* v *Commission* [2007] ECR II-4225; Cases T-265 etc./04 *Tirrenia di Navigazione and ors* v *Commission* [2009] ECR II-21*.

532 Case T-233/04 *Netherlands* v *Commission* (NOx Emissions) [2008] ECR II-591 (set aside on appeal as Case C-279/08P *Commission* v *Netherlands*, judgment of 8 September 2011, not yet reported, but not on admissibility grounds); Cases T-265 etc./04 *Tirrenia di Navigazione*, n. 531 above. However, both are state aids cases, in which the *dispositif* is bound ineluctably to the reasoning which led thither.

533 See e.g., Cases C-402 and 415/05P *Kadi II*, n. 527 above, at para. 233.

534 Cases C-302 and 308/99 *Commission and France* v *Télévision Française 1* [2001] ECR I-5603, at paras 26–9; Case T-209/01 *Honeywell International* v *Commission* [2005] ECR II-5527, at para. 48.

535 Case T-209/01 *Honeywell International*, ibid., at para. 49.

536 Case T-184/01 *IMS Health* v *Commission* [2005] ECR II-817.

537 See n. 493 above and accompanying text. It is for the applicant to show that his or her interest survives repeal of the measure; Case T-184/01 *IMS Health*, ibid.

538 Case C-540/03 *Parliament* v *Council* (Family Reunification) [2006] ECR I-5769, at para. 27 and case law cited.

539 Case C-36/04 *Spain* v *Council* [2006] ECR I-2981, at para. 9.

540 Case C-540/03 *Family Reunification*, n. 538 above, at para. 28 and case law cited.

541 Case C-239/01 *Germany* v *Commission* [2003] ECR I 10333, at para. 37.

remaining text; and, secondly, where the annulment of that provision does not affect the overall coherence of the legislative scheme of which it forms a part.[542]

In administrative matters, and especially competition cases, severance is quite common.[543]

5.86 Annulment (or repeal) of a measure does not deprive a person who has suffered consequential injury of the right to raise an action seeking damages.[544]

(v) Article 7 TEU measures

5.87 Where the European Council or the Council acts under article 7 of the Treaty on European Union ('determination' of a breach by a member state of fundamental rights and adoption of sanctions thereupon),[545] the Court of Justice may 'decide on' (*se prononcer sur*) its legality but only in respect of the procedural stipulations of article 7 and only at the request of the member state concerned.[546] The request must be made within one month of the determination and the Court must furnish its ruling (*sic*) within one month from the date of the request.[547] No measure having yet been adopted under article 7, no request has ever been made.

(c) Action for failure to act (article 265 TFEU)

5.88 In British terms the action under article 265 of the TFEU for failure to act is comparable to an application or petition for a mandatory order requiring the specific performance of a statutory duty. The purpose of the action is to compel a Union institution (here expressly the European Council, the Council, the Parliament, the Commission, the European Central Bank) and, since Lisbon, any body, office or agency of the Union,[548] to do something which, under Union law, it is legally obliged to do. The action is admissible only if the institution or body has first been called upon to act.[549] The rules as to title and interest are essentially the same as those applying to the action of annulment, except that the privileged applicants are 'the Member States and the other institutions of

---

542 Case C-376/98 *Germany v Parliament and Council* (Tobacco Advertising) [2000] ECR I-8419, *per* A-G Fennelly at para. 122 of his opinion.

543 See 13.106 below.

544 TFEU, art. 266, 2nd para. (ex art. 233, 2nd para. EC); see 5.94–5.102 below.

545 See 6.105 below.

546 TFEU, art. 269, 1st para. The member state 'concerned' presumably means the member state (or states) against which disciplinary measures have been adopted.

547 TFEU, art. 269, 2nd para. Because it is badly drafted it is not clear whether this applies equally to Council measures adopted (by authority of art. 7(3)) subsequently to a determination and in light of it.

548 TFEU, art. 265, 1st para. (ex art. 232, 1st para. EC). But the Court has confirmed that the Ombudsman is not subject to art. 265 proceedings; Case T-103/99 *Associazione delle Cantine Sociali Venete v European Ombudsman and European Parliament* [2000] ECR II-4165.

549 TFEU, art. 265, 2nd para.

the Union'.[550] A natural or juristic person must show that the institution had a duty to address an act to him – that is, take a decision which, if unfavourable, he could have challenged under article 263.[551] If the institution has acted after the lodging of the action but before judgment, the action is deprived of its purpose – it 'terminates the failure to act and renders the action devoid of purpose'[552] – and there is no longer any need to adjudicate.[553] It is immaterial if the position adopted by the institution is not one the substance of which satisfies the applicant.[554] Outwith the specific area of the duty of the Commission to respond to a complainant in competition and state aid matters,[555] it is a most difficult action successfully to pursue, and this has occurred very rarely.[556]

In a 2003 judgment the Court of Justice determined that where the Council was **5.89** required by regulation to act within a strict timetable but failed by the end of that time period to do so (owing to an inability to muster a majority within the Council to act), it was not a failure to act within the meaning of article 265 but a refusal to act, and so a positive act reviewable within the meaning of article 263.[557] The Court has not yet built upon this judgment.

(d) Compliance with annulment or a finding of failure to act (article 266 TFEU)

Article 266 TFEU requires that in the event of annulment of a measure or a **5.90** declaration that an institution has (unlawfully) failed to act, the offending institution is 'required to take the necessary measures to comply with the judgment of the Court of Justice of the European Union'.[558] It should therefore remove any effects of the illegal conduct identified in the judgment annulling the measure and restore the *status quo ante*,[559] or perform that which non-performance of which has been condemned, as the case requires; the obligation

---

550 *Ibid.* art. 265, 1st para. Yet more sloppy drafting, although there since the beginning (cf. art. 175 EEC) and not unique to English: grammatically it means that the privileged applicants are the Court of Justice and the Court of Auditors, which is not the case.

551 TFEU, art. 265, 3rd para; Case T-24/90 *Automec* v *Commission* [1992] ECR II-2223.

552 Case C-282/95P *Guérin Automomobiles* v *Commission* [1997] ECR I-1503, at para. 31; Cases T-344 and 345/00 *CEVA Santé Animale and Pharmacia* v *Commission* [2003] ECR II-229, at para. 85.

553 E.g., *Guérin Automomobiles* and *CEVA Santé Animale, ibid.*; also Case T-212/95 *Oficemen* v *Commission* [1997] ECR II-1161; Case T-17/96 *Télévision Française 1* v *Commission* [1999] ECR II-1757.

554 Case C-44/00P *Société de Distribution Mécanique et d'Automobiles* v *Commission* [2000] ECR I-11231, at para. 83 and case law cited.

555 See 13.89 below.

556 Case 13/83 *European Parliament* v *Council* [1985] ECR 1513; Case C-107/91 *ENU* v *Commission* [1993] ECR I-599 (a case under the corresponding provision of the Euratom Treaty); Case T-17/96 *Télévision Française 1* v *Commission* [1999] ECR II-1757; Case T-395/04 *Air One* v *Commission* [2006] ECR II-1343 (action admissible but dismissed on its merits). cf. Case 246/81 *Bethell* v *Commission* [1982] ECR 2277.

557 Case C-76/01P *Eurocoton and ors* v *Council* [2003] ECR I-10091.

558 TFEU, art. 266, 1st para. (ex art. 233, 1st para. EC).

559 Cases 97 etc./86 *Asteris and ors* v *Commission* [1988] ECR 2181; Case T-171/99 *Corus UK* v *Commission* [2001] ECR II-2967, at para. 50 and case law cited; Case F-1/05 *Landgren* v *Fondation européenne pour la formation* [2006] ECR-SC II-A-1–459, at para. 92.

applies under both articles 263 and 265 equally.[560] It is for the offending institution to determine the measures necessary to comply with the judgment,[561] and must do so by reference to the grounds of the judgment of annulment which identifies the exact provision regarded as unlawful and shows the exact reasons for the illegality found in the operative part.[562] It must also do so promptly, failing which it may become liable in damages (if it was not already) to any person suffering loss as a result.[563] If it adopts a measure to replace that which was annulled it must ensure that the former is not vitiated by the same defects or unlawfulness which led to the annulment.[564] The duty of compliance extends to an obligation to make restitution (*in integrum*) of any financial penalty (plus intervening interest) imposed by the measure.[565] However, article 266 cannot serve as an autonomous form of action:[566] should the institution fail to adopt measures complying, or complying adequately, with the judgment of the Court, the remedy is a subsequent action under article 265 (no compliance) or article 263 (inadequate compliance); alternatively (or concurrently), an action seeking damages.

(e)   Staff cases (article 270 TFEU)

5.91   The legal nexus between a Union institution and its officials is governed by the Staff Regulations (*Statut des fonctionnaires*) and/or the Conditions of Employment,[567] and not upon the contract of employment.[568] A dispute arising therefrom must be taken, first, to an internal complaints procedure[569] and thereafter to the Court under article 270 TFEU[570] which is, in effect, the jurisdiction of an employment tribunal. It applies to 'any dispute between the Union [including all bodies and agencies] and its servants',[571] or 'any dispute between the Communities and any person to whom these Staff Regulations

---

560   Case T-74/92 *Ladbroke Racing Deutschland* v *Commission* [1995] ECR II-115, at para. 75.

561   Cases 98 and 99/63R *Erba and Reynier* v *Commission* [1964] ECR 276.

562   Cases 97 etc./86 *Asteris*, n. 559 above, at para. 27; Cases T-305 etc./94 *Limburgse Vinyl Maatschappij and ors* v *Commission* (PVC II) [1999] ECR II-931, at para. 184.

563   See n. 614 below and accompanying text.

564   Cases 97 etc./86 *Asteris and ors* v *Commission* [1988] ECR 2181; Case T-256/07 *People's Mojahedin Organization of Iran* v *Council* [2008] ECR II-3019.

565   Case T-171/99 *Corus UK* v *Commission* [2001] ECR II-2967; Case T-86/03 *Holcim (France)* v *Commission* [2005] ECR II-1536.

566   Case T-28/03 *Holcim (Deutschland)* v *Commission* [2005] ECR II-1357.

567   Originally Regulation 31/62 [1962] JO 1385, now Staff Regulations for Officials of the European Union ('Staff Regulations') and Conditions of Employment of Other Servants of the Union (CEOS); published from time to time in booklet form (most recently 1 May 2004); available at ec.europa.eu/civil_service/docs/toc100_en.pdf.

568   Case 28/74 *Gillet* v *Commission* [1975] ECR 463. This means that the rights and obligations of officials may be altered at any time by the institutions, subject to protection of vested rights.

569   Staff Regulations, art. 90.

570   See *ibid.* art. 91 for the detail.

571   TFEU, art. 270; Statute of the Court of Justice, Annex I, art. 1.

apply regarding the legality of an act adversely affecting [him or her]'[572] which must be raised by means of this procedure, and not under article 263.[573] There is a three-month time bar, time starting at the termination of the complaints procedure.[574] In the interests of legal certainty the notion of a staff dispute is given a wide definition by the Court, extending to persons who have the status neither of official nor employee but claim or seek that status, so including challenges by disgruntled would-be recruits to the Union institutions.[575] Because failure to promote, or appoint, a *fonctionnaire* is subject to review, the conduct of the European Personnel Selection Office (EPSO)[576] now falls under scrutiny in this context, although the responsibility lies with the institution for which EPSO was acting. A 2010 judgment of the Civil Service Tribunal annulling a Commission decision not to appoint a candidate to a reserve list suggests that EPSO's procedures are materially flawed, and may open the way for multiple claims under article 270.[577]

Since 2005, staff cases go to the Civil Service Tribunal, so marking the first (as it **5.92** was envisaged to be)[578] jurisdiction transferred to a specialised court. Judgments in staff cases are, since 1994, reported separately from the main reports of the Court.[579] They are now reported in full only in the language of the case unless the Tribunal directs otherwise.

(f) Action of damages or indemnity (articles 268, 272 and 340 TFEU)

(i) Contractual liability

The contractual liability of the Union is governed by the proper law of the **5.93** contract in question.[580] The Court of Justice has jurisdiction to hear and determine a dispute involving an arbitration clause contained in a contract concluded by or upon behalf of the Union, irrespective of its being subject to public or private law,[581] otherwise it is a matter for national courts.[582]

---

572 Staff Regulations, art. 91(1).
573 Case T-208/00 *Barleycorn and Rivas* v *Parliament and Council* [2001] ECR-SC II-479.
574 Staff Regulations, art. 91(3).
575 Case 23/64 *Vandevyvere* v *Parliament* [1965] ECR 157; Case 116/78 *Bellintani and ors* v *Commission* [1979] ECR 1585; Case T-72/89 *Viciano* v *Commission* [1990] ECR II-57; Case T-144/02 *Eagle and ors* v *Commission* [2004] ECR II-3381; cf. Case F-53/06 *Gualtieri* v *Commission* [2006] ECR-SC II-A-1-399. So, the refusal of an institution to release documents relevant to a *fonctionnaire*'s complaint against it must be challenged under art. 270 and not through nomal procedures; Case F-121/07 *Strack* v *Commission*, judgment of 20 January 2011, not yet reported.
576 See 4.18 above.
577 Case F-35/08 *Pachtitis* v *Commission*, judgment of 15 June 2010, not yet reported; see 4.19 above.
578 See Declaration [No. 16, anned to the EC Treaty] on Article 225a of the Treaty establishing the European Community.
579 See Annex IV.
580 TFEU, art. 340, 1st para. (ex art. 288, 1st para. EC).
581 TFEU, art. 272 (ex art. 238 EC).

(ii) Non-contractual liability

5.94 The action for damages or indemnity (*demande en indemnité*) against the Union is provided by article 268 (conferral upon the Court of Justice of jurisdiction) and article 340, second paragraph (identification of the applicable law) of the TFEU. Here the jurisdiction of the Court of Justice is exclusive,[583] and no claim for damages may be raised in a national court.[584] As to the applicable law, rather than attempting a laborious task of creating and defining a system of pubic delictual liability, the Treaties draw entirely and expressly (and in this uniquely in the Treaties) upon 'the general principles common to the laws of the Member States'.[585] As it has developed so far, the action is one essentially in tort or of reparation, the ground of action being that the Union or its servants have in the performance of its/their duties[586] unlawfully caused loss or damage. Whilst article 340 refers to 'damage caused by [the Union's] institutions', the Court has made it clear that 'institutions' here does not mean institutions properly so-called, but also any body established by or under the Treaties, the (injurious) conduct of which is attributable to the Union;[587] and although the liability is the Union's, in the interests of the good administration of justice it is represented by the institution or institutions against which the matter giving rise to liability is alleged.[588] Liability may also arise in a failure to act.[589]

5.95 Whilst it goes in part to the legality of a Union act, the action in reparation is an independent form of action and unrelated to the action of annulment under article 263:

> [I]t is settled case-law that the action for damages provided for in the second paragraph of Article [340] is an independent form of action with a particular purpose to fulfil within the system of actions and subject to conditions as to its use dictated by its specific nature. It differs from an action for annulment in that its end is not the abolition of a particular measure but compensation for damage caused by an institution. The principle

---

582   TFEU, art. 274 (ex art. 240 EC); see e.g., the discussion in Case C-377/09 *Hanssens-Ensch* v *European Community* [2010] ECR I-7747.

583   Case C-275/00 *European Community* v *First and Franex* [2002] ECR I-10943, at para. 43 and case law cited.

584   See e.g., *Kearns and anor* v *European Commission* [2005] IEHC 324, [2006] EuLR 568.

585   TFEU, art. 340, 2nd para. (ex art. 288, 2nd para. EC); frequently but inaccurately cited as art. 340(2).

586   Damages for injury caused by the Union or its servants *not* in the performance of their duties are a matter for the law (and the courts) of the place where the injury occurred.

587   Case C-370/89 *Société Générale d'Entreprises Électromécaniques and Etroy* v *European Investment Bank* [1992] ECR I-6211. The liability of the European Central Bank is written expressly into the TFEU by Lisbon (art. 340, 3rd para.) in a peculiar manner which suggests that a different regime (extending beyond 'non-contractual liability') may apply to it.

588   Cases 63 etc./72 *Werhahn* v *Council* [1973] ECR 1229.

589   Cases T-344 and 345/00 *CEVA Santé Animale and Pharmacia Entreprises* v *Commission* [2003] ECR II-229 (overturned on appeal as Case C-198/03P *Commission* v *CEVA Santé Animale and Pfizer Enterprises* [2005] ECR I-6357, but not on the point of principle).

of the independent character of the action for damages is thus explained by the fact that the purpose of such an action differs from that of an action for annulment.[590]

In practice the two are sometimes raised together, or a claim in damages follows on from annulment of a measure;[591] an action for damages will fail when there is a close connection between it and an action for annulment which has been dismissed.[592] Alternatively, because not subject to the latter's strict rules on standing, the former is raised on its own. However, exceptionally an action for damages is inadmissible if in truth aimed at securing the withdrawal of a measure which has become definitive and would, if upheld, nullify the legal effects of that measure.[593] Even though an action raised under article 340 cannot bring about the annulment of a Union measure, and 'any finding as to the lawfulness of the act is entirely incidental',[594] it is nevertheless one of the avenues to the Union judicature which, taken together, ensure 'effective judicial protection' for the individual,[595] and, as with article 263, the erring institution must adopt the measures necessary to comply with a finding of illegality.[596] The action must be raised within five years of the occurrence of the injury or of the time when the injured party ought reasonably to have known of it.[597]

For an action in damages to succeed, four conditions: 5.96

- illegality;[598]

---

590 Case T-47/02 *Danzer and Danzer* v *Council* [2006] ECR II-1779, at para. 27. Also Case 5/71 *Zuckerfabrik Schöppenstedt* v *Council* [1971] ECR 975; Case 175/84 *Krohn* v *Commission* [1986] ECR 753.

591 See e.g., Case C-310/04 *Spain* v *Council* [2006] ECR I-7285 (annulment), followed up by Cases T-252 etc./07 *Sungro and ors* v *Council and Commission* [2010] ECR II-55 (damages). Alternatively a claim for damages may follow on from a finding of invalidity in art. 267 proceedings: Case 120/86 *Mulder* v *Minister van Landbouw en Visserij* [1988] ECR 2321 and Case C-104/89 *Mulder* v *Council and Commission* [1992] ECR I-3061.

592 Case T-340/99 *Arne Mathisen* v *Council* [2002] ECR II-2905, at para. 134 and case law cited.

593 Case 175/84 *Krohn*, n. 590 above; Case T-178/98 *Fresh Marine* v *Commission* [2000] ECR II-3331; Case T-47/02 *Danzer and Danzer*, n. 590 above.

594 Case C-63/89 *Les Assurances du Credit and anor* v *Council and Commission* [1991] ECR I-1799, *per* A-G Tesauro at para. 10 of his opinion.

595 Case C-50/00P *Unión de Pequeños Agricultores* v *Council* [2002] ECR I-6677; Case C-131/03P *RJ Reynolds Tobacco Holdings and ors* v *Commission and anor* [2006] ECR I-7795, at paras 82–4.

596 Case C-308/06 *R (International Association of Independent Tanker Owners (Intertanko) and ors)* v *Secretary of State for Transport* [2008] ECR I-4057, at paras 44–5; Cases C-120 and 121/06P *Fabbrica italiana accumulatori motocarri Montecchio (FIAMM) and anor* v *Council and Commission* [2008] ECR I-6513, at para. 124 ('There is nothing to suggest that the position should be any different in the case of a judgment delivered in an action for compensation').

597 Statute of the Court of Justice, art. 46; discussed in Case 145/83 *Adams* v *Commission* [1985] ECR 3539; Cases 256 etc./80 *Birra Wührer* v *Council and Commission* [1984] ECR 3693; Case T-20/94 *Hartmann* v *Council and Commission* [1997] ECR II-595; Cases T-8 and 9/95 *Pelle and Konrad* v *Council and Commission* [2007] ECR II-4117.

598 It should be noted that, as a function of constitutional principles of equality and solidarity, the law of some member states recognises non-contractual liability of a public authority even absent unlawful conduct (in particular, principles of *égalité devant les charges publiques* (in France), *responsabilidad patrimonial de la administración pública por los daños causados por el funcionamiento normal de los servicios públicos* (Spain) and *Sonderopfer* (Germany)); the Court of Justice counts 'barely half of the Member States' legal systems' to do so;

- fault (*culpa*);
- injury which is actual and certain;[599] and
- (direct) causation[600]

must be present and proven; they are cumulative, and the absence of any one of them causes the action to fail.[601] The Court (the General Court at any rate) will sometimes list these as three conditions, the second (fault) being absorbed into, although modifying, the first (illegality).[602] According to the tests developed early on by the Court, the claimant must show not just illegality ('it is not the purpose of [the] action … to make good damage caused by all unlawfulness'[603]) but, going to fault, a serious (or flagrant) breach on the part of the Union institution(s) of a superior rule of law (in effect, a breach of one of the general principles of EU law, read broadly) for the protection of the individual[604] in

---

Cases C-120 and 121/06P *FIAMM*, n. 596 above, at para. 141. After some prevarication (see e.g., Case 59/83 *Biovilac* v *European Economic Community* [1984] ECR 4057; Case C-237/98P *Dorsch Consult* v *Council and Commission* [2000] ECR I-4549, at para. 19; Cases T-64 and 65/01 *Afrikanische Frucht-Compagnie and anor* v *Council and Commission* [2004] ECR II-521, at paras 143–56; Case T-138/03 *ÉR and ors* v *Council and Commission* [2006] ECR II-4923) and 'systematically [leaving] the question to one side' (*FIAMM*, at para. 148) the Court of Justice seems finally to have bitten the bullet and determined that, contrary to the view of the General Court (Case T-69/00 *Fabbrica italiana accumulatori motocarri Montecchio and anor* v *Council and Commission* [2005] ECR II-5393; Case T-135/01 *Fedon & Figli and ors* v *Council and Commission* [2005] ECR II-29*) and the recommendation of A-G Poiares Maduro (at paras 54–83 of his opinion), 'as Community law currently stands' illegality is always necessary successfully to find liability for conduct falling within the sphere of its legislative competence: Cases C-120 and 121/06P *FIAMM*. This leaves the door ajar for a possibility of damages for injury caused by a lawful act in a non-legislative sphere (where it is unlikely to occur; see 5.97 below). The Court also laid down markers (at paras 181–4) describing where legislative action might infringe various general principles of Union law so leading (via illegality) to liability.

599 E.g, Case T-99/98 *Hameico Stuttgart and ors* v *Council and Commission* [2003] ECR II-2195, at para. 67. But 'certain' goes not to the exact extent of the damage claimed, rather the very existence of the injury; Cases C-243/05P *Agraz and ors* v *Commission* [2006] ECR I-10833. It must nevertheless be quantifiable; e.g., Case T-108/94 *Candiotte* v *Council* [1996] ECR II-87, at para. 54. Injury extends to loss of profits; Case C-104/89 *Mulder* v *Council and Commission* [1992] ECR I-3061. Loss of opportunity is not ruled out (Case T-47/93 *C* v *Commission* [1994] ECR–SC II-743, at para. 54) so long as the damage is actual and certain (Cases T-3/00 and 337/04 *Pitsiorlas* v *Council* [2007] ECR II-4779, at para. 319).

600 As to causation see Case T-138/03 *ÉR*, n. 598 above; *Pitsiorlas*, n. 599 above, at paras 296–326.

601 Case C-146/91 *Koinopraxia Enoseon Georgikon Synetairismon Diacheiriseos Enchorion Proïonton* v *Council and Commission* [1994] ECR I-4199; Case C-104/97P *Atlanta* v *European Community* [1999] ECR I-6983; Case T-341/07 *Sison* v *Council* (Sison III), judgment of 23 November 2011, not yet reported. The Court is not required to examine the conditions in any particular order (Case C-257/98P *Lucaccioni* v *Commission* [1999] ECR I-5251) and will frequently dismiss an action upon a finding that one is absent without considering the others.

602 E.g., Case T-138/03 *ÉR*, n. 598 above, at para. 99; Case T-333/03 *Masdar (UK)* v *Commission* [2006] ECR II-4377, at para. 61; Case T-162/07 *Pigasos Alieftiki Naftiki Etaireia* v *Council and Commission* [2009] ECR II-153*, at paras 45–7.

603 Case T-425/05 *Artegodan* v *Commission* [2010] ECR II-491, at para. 51.

604 The Court has used the formulae 'intended to confer rights on individuals', 'for the protection of the individual' and 'intended to protect individuals', but they are to be read synonymously, 'mere variations on a single legal concept'; Case T-341/07 *Sison* v *Council* (Sison III), judgment of 23 November 2011, not yet reported, at para. 33. The rule that liability requires breach of a provision intended to benefit the individual is derived from German principles of *Schutznormtheorie*; it is to be compared with rules of law intended for the

which the institution has manifestly and gravely disregarded the limits to its discretion.[605] In the legislative sphere, the institutions enjoy such a margin of appreciation that these were long difficult hurdles to overcome: the Court itself noted that they required conduct 'verging on the arbitrary',[606] their application 'has made for perplexity'[607] and they 'are so restrictive as to make it extremely difficult actually to obtain damages against a Community institution'.[608] In 1996 Advocate-General Tesauro could count only eight successful actions.[609] However, starting in 1996 with *Brasserie du Pêcheur*[610] and in the cases following, the Court has constructed and developed the tests for the non-contractual liability of the member states in the Union sphere,[611] tests which are probably less onerous in application than those which traditionally applied to Union liability, and, in line with *Brasserie du Pêcheur*, they have now been expressly recognised as carried over into, and so reformulating, article 340.[612] Thus is the Court now able to say:

> It is settled case-law that, in order for the Community to incur non-contractual liability within the meaning of the second paragraph of Article [340], a number of conditions must be met: the rule of law infringed must be intended to confer rights on individuals; the breach must be sufficiently serious; and there must be a direct causal link between the breach of the obligation resting on the author of the act and the damage sustained by the injured parties.[613]

The bar has thus been lowered somewhat. One principle transplanted from national liability successfully is that the obligation to ensure effective compliance with a judgment of the Court of Justice is 'so fundamental' to Union law

---

benefit of the general good. The closest British equivalent is the first limb of the twofold test set out by Lord Browne-Wilkinson in *X (Minors)* v *Bedfordshire County Council* [1995] 2 AC 633 at 731 for finding a private right of action in a breach of statutory duty, that is, whether a statutory obligation is imposed for the protection of a limited class of the public. 'Individual' must of course be read in its normal (if misleading) Union law meaning of both natural and juristic persons.

605 Case 5/71 *Schöppenstedt* v *Council* [1971] ECR 975; Cases 83 etc./76 *Bayerische HNL* v *Council and Commission* [1978] ECR 1209; Case 143/77 *Koninklijke Scholten-Honig* v *Council and Commission* [1979] ECR 3583; Case 238/78 *Ireks-Arkady* v *Council and Commission* [1979] ECR 2955. For an instance in which these tests have been satisfied see Case C-104/89 *Mulder* v *Council and Commission* [1992] ECR I-3061.

606 Cases 116 and 124/77 *Amylum* v *Council and Commission* [1979] ECR 3497, at para. 19.

607 Cases C-46 and 48/93 *Brasserie du Pêcheur* v *Germany* and *R* v *Secretary of State for Transport, ex parte Factortame* [1996] ECR I-1029, *per* A-G Tesauro at para. 64 of his opinion.

608 *Ibid.* para. 63.

609 *Ibid.* at n. 65.

610 *Ibid.*

611 See 6.34–6.40 below.

612 Case C-352/98P *Laboratoires Pharmaceutiques Bergaderm and anor* v *Commission* [2000] ECR I-5291; Case C-312/00P *Commission* v *Camar and Tico* [2002] ECR I-11355; Cases T-344 and 345/00 *CEVA Santé Animale and Pharmacia Entreprises* v *Commission* [2003] ECR II-229 (overturned on appeal as Case C-198/03P *Commission* v *CEVA Santé Animale and Pfizer Enterprises* [2005] ECR I-6357 but not on that point).

613 Case T-193/04R *Tillack* v *Commission* [2004] ECR II-3575, at para. 52.

that failure of an institution to comply promptly with a judgment of itself constitutes grounds for liability under article 340.[614] Another, drawn from the laws of the member states and recognised by the Court of Justice as absorbed into Union law, is the obligation of an injured party to show reasonable diligence in limiting the extent of his loss, otherwise he is at risk of having to bear the damage himself.[615]

5.97 As the determining factor in finding a sufficiently serious breach is not the general or individual nature of the Union measure[616] the test applies equally in the administrative sphere, but here such is the narrowness of the margin of discretion that it may be characterised as one of ordinary care and diligence;[617] mere illegality is not of itself enough, except where an institution 'has only considerably reduced, or even no, discretion, [so that] the mere infringement of Community law may be sufficient to establish the existence of a sufficiently serious breach'.[618] But in all cases in this (narrow) context liability, sometimes construed as a breach of the (higher) principle of sound administration, is relatively easy to find.[619] So

> [i]n particular, the finding of an irregularity which in comparable circumstances would not have been committed by a normally prudent and diligent administration permits the conclusion that the conduct of the institution constituted an illegality of such a kind as to involve the liability of the Community under Article [340].[620]

However, in 'delicate and controversial' areas (involving, for example, issues of public health) an institution may enjoy a broader discretion so as to avoid liability which would otherwise adhere.[621] The 'particular complexity' of a case

---

614 Case T-220/97 *H & R Ecroyd Holdings* v *Commission* [1999] ECR II-1677, at para. 43; Case T-11/00 *Hautem* v *European Investment Bank* [2000] ECR–SC II-1295; Cases F-44 and 94/06 *C and F* v *Commission* [2007] ECR-SC II-A-I-537; Case T-341/07 *Sison* v *Council* (Sison III), judgment of 23 November 2011, not yet reported, at para. 40.

615 Case C-104/89 *Mulder* v *Council and Commission* [1992] ECR I-3061; Case T-178/98 *Fresh Marine* v *Commission* [2000] ECR II-3331.

616 Case C-352/98P *Bergaderm*, n. 612 above; Case C-472/00P *Commission* v *Fresh Marine* [2003] ECR I-7541; Case C-282/05P *Holcim (Deutschland)* v *Commission* [2007] ECR I-2941.

617 Case T-178/98 *Fresh Marine*, n. 615 above, upheld on appeal in Case C-472/00P, *ibid.*

618 Case C-312/00P *Commission* v *Camar and Tico* [2002] ECR I-11355, at para. 54; Case C-282/05P *Holcim (Deutschland)*, n. 616 above, at para. 47; Case T-212/03 *MyTravel Group* v *Commission* [2008] ECR II-1967, at para. 39; Case T-19/07 *Systran and Systran Luxembourg* v *Commission*, [2010] ECR II-6083, at para. 127. The same applies where the defendant institution improperly applies the relevant substantive or procedural rules; *MyTravel*; Case C-440/07P *Commission* v *Schneider Electric* [2009] ECR I-6413.

619 Cases T-178/98 and C-472/00P *Fresh Marine*, nn. 615 and 616 above; Case C-312/00P *Camar and Tico*, *ibid.*; Case T-351/03 *Schneider Electric* v *Commission* [2007] ECR II-2237.

620 Cases T-198/95 *Comafrica and Dole Fresh Fruit Europa* v *Commission* [2001] ECR II-1975, at para. 134; Case T-285/03 *Agraz and ors* v *Commission* [2005] ECR II-1063, at para. 40.

621 Case C-198/03P *Commission* v *CEVA Santé Animale and Pfizer Enterprises* [2005] ECR I-6357.

may also serve to exculpate an erring institution in the administrative sphere.[622] So, in a case in which the Union was widely expected to be found liable in damages for the Commission having made a terrible hash (in a decision annulled as 'vitiated by a series of errors of assessment as to factors fundamental to any [proper] assessment')[623] of a proposed merger,

> it is necessary to bear in mind that the economic analyses necessary for the characterisation in competition law ... involve generally ... complex and difficult intellectual exercises, which may inadvertently contain some inadequacies, such as approximations, inconsistencies, or indeed certain omissions ...

> That does not mean ... that the Commission committed a manifest and grave infringement of its discretion ..., provided that – as in the present case – it is capable of explaining the reasons for which it could reasonably form the view that its assessments were well founded.[624]

As the Court has recognised that, in some circumstances, member state liability **5.98** may be engaged by the deprivation of a Union right by a judgment of a national court,[625] the same must in logic apply to deprivation of a Union right by the Court of Justice. This has now been formally recognised by the Court, in a case involving (unlawfully) excessive duration of proceedings before the General Court;[626] but it failed to address the serious problems (of *nemo iudex in causa sua*) this creates in identifying a court with (competent) jurisdiction to deal with it.[627]

The Court has now recognised (but has yet clearly to define) a remedy in **5.99** restitution for unjust enrichment (*de in rem verso*) which although it 'do[es] not fall under the rules governing non-contractual liability in the strict sense' is a logical and necessary extension of article 340,[628] otherwise there would be an unacceptable deprivation of effective judicial protection.[629] Unlike the normal

---

622 Case T-28/03 *Holcim (Deutschland)* v *Commission* [2005] ECR II-1357, at para. 114; upheld on appeal as Case C-282/05P, n. 616 above; Case T-341/07 *Sison* v *Council* (Sison III), judgment of 23 November 2011, not yet reported, at paras 37–40, 58–74.

623 Case T-342/99 *Airtours* v *Commission* [2002] ECR II-2585, at para. 294.

624 Case T-212/03 *MyTravel Group* v *Commission* [2008] ECR I-1967, at paras 81, 87. As to the rules on mergers, see 13.133–13.141 below.

625 See 6.38 below.

626 Case C-385/07P *Der Grüne Punkt – Duales System Deutschland* v *Commission* [2009] ECR I-6155, at para. 195; also Case C-583/08P *Gogos* v *Commission* [2010] ECR I-4469, at para. 56 and the opinion of A-G Kokott at paras 86–8.

627 But see the discussion of A-G Bot in *Der Grüne Punkt*, *ibid.*, who did address it, at paras 307–42 of his opinion.

628 Case C-47/07P *Masdar (UK)* v *Commission* [2008] ECR I-9811, at paras 47–9.

629 *Ibid.* at para. 50.

remedy in reparation a successful claim for unjust enrichment is 'not necessarily' conditional upon illegality or fault.[630]

5.100 The Union enjoyed immunity in non-contractual liability for injury caused when acting under the pre-Lisbon TEU.[631] This was because there was no equivalent in the TEU to article 288 EC (article 340 TFEU). Whilst such a remedy may have been desirable ('a system of legal remedies, in particular a body of rules governing non-contractual liability, other than that established by the treaties can indeed be envisaged'), its creation would require Treaty amendment.[632] Presumably this immunity lasts for any surviving Union measures until December 2014.[633]

5.101 A dispute between an official and an employer Union institution concerning compensation for injury is pursued, if it originates in the relationship of employment (construed broadly),[634] under article 270 TFEU and the Staff Regulations, not under article 340.[635] That having been said, the logic of article 340 applies equally, save that liability is strict(er), and arises if three conditions are satisfied: there is an illegal (presumably wrongful) act of the institution, actual harm is suffered, and there is a (direct and certain) causal link between the two.[636] The General Court has gone so far as to say that the first condition is fulfilled when an institution commits an unlawful act, without it being necessary to consider whether there has been sufficiently serious breach of the limits of its discretion.[637] Damages are available here for non-material harm (*préjudice moral*), for example injury to dignity and professional reputation, where that harm is severable from the illegality which merited annulment and not fully

---

630   *Ibid.* at para. 45.
631   Case C-354/04P *Gestoras Pro Amnistía and ors* v *Council* [2007] ECR I-1579; Case C-355/04P *Segi and ors* v *Council* [2007] ECR I-1657.
632   Case C-354/04P *Gestoras Pro Amnistía, ibid.,* at para. 50; Case C-355/04P *Segi, ibid.,* at para. 50.
633   TEU and TFEU, Protocol (No. 36) on Transitional Provisions, art. 10.
634   See 5.91 above.
635   Case 9/75 *Meyer-Burckhardt* v *Commission* [1975] ECR 1171; Case 48/76 *Reinartz* v *Council and Commission* [1977] ECR 291.
636   Case C-136/92P *Commission* v *Brazzelli Lualdi and ors* [1994] ECR I-1981; Case C-259/96P *Council* v *de Nil and Impens* [1998] ECR I-2915; Case T-45/01 *Sanders and ors* v *Commission* [2004] ECR II-3315; Cases F-5 and 7/05 *Violetti and Schmit* v *Commission,* judgment of 28 April 2009, not yet reported; Case F-30/08 *Nanopoulos* v *Commission,* judgment of 11 May 2010, not yet reported, at paras 128–33; Case F-46/09 *V* v *Parliament,* judgment of 5 July 2011, not yet reported.
637   Case T-143/09P *Commission* v *Petrilli,* judgment of 16 December 2010, not yet reported. This notwithstanding earlier case law (Case T-57/99 *Nardone* v *Commission,* judgment of 10 December 2008, not yet reported) which held these to be two different tests. The Court of Justice was invited to re-examine the judgment in *Petrilli* in light of this apparent inconsistency but declined to do so; Case C-17/11RX *Commission* v *Petrilli,* decision of 8 February 2011, unreported.

remedied by it.[638] The action must be raised in all events within the five-year time bar but also within a reasonable period of time.[639] Equally, an institution must prosecute a disciplinary case with due diligence, failure of which duty may result in damages.[640]

As no claim for damages may be raised against a Union institution in a national **5.102** court, the Court of Justice enjoying exclusive jurisdiction,[641] yet only a national court may order reparation from a national authority, very serious difficulties arise in attributing, and recovering from, (jointly) wrongful conduct where national authorities are responsible for administering an allegedly unlawful Union act.[642]

(g) Plea of illegality (article 277 TFEU)

Because it is very difficult for a non-privileged applicant to establish the **5.103** requisite title and interest to raise an action of annulment under article 263 of an act, and in particular of a legislative or general act, of a Union institution (unless one which entails no implementing measures), the Treaties provide for a collateral means of judicial protection in article 277 TFEU, called, normally, the plea of illegality (*exception d'illégalité*). It has as its purpose the protection of non-privileged applicants,[643] and is the expression of a general principle of law.[644] By it, the legality of a legislative act, beyond his direct reach under article 263, may be challenged incidentally by a private person if and when it is applied to him in an individual manner by a subsequent act of a Union institution: the subsequent, administrative act is challenged, and normally under article 263, not on the ground that it is unlawful *per se*, but that it relies for its authority upon the unlawful parent act which it implements. There is no time limit (as regards the parent act) to a plea of illegality, the only precondition being that it

---

638   See e.g., Case 343/97 *Culin* v *Commission* [1990] ECR I-225; Case T-259/03 *Nikolaou* v *Commission* [2007] ECR II-99*; Cases F-5 and 7/05 *Violetta and Schmit*, n. 636 above; Case T-12/08P *M* v *Agence européenne des médicaments*, judgment of 6 May 2009, not yet reported; Cases F-124/05 and 96/06 *A and G* v *Commission*, judgment of 13 January 2010, not yet reported; Case F-30/08 *Nanopoulos*, n. 636 above; Case F-46/09 *V*, n. 636 above.

639   Case T-144/02 *Eagle and ors* v *Commission* [2004] ECR II-3381; Case F-125/05 *Tsarnavas* v *Commission* [2007] ECR-SC II-A-I-231.

640   E.g., Cases F-124/05 and 96/06 *A and G*, n. 638 above.

641   See 5.94 above.

642   See e.g., Cases 5 etc./66 *Kampffmeyer and ors* v *EEC Commission* [1967] ECR 245; Case 281/82 *Unifrex* v *Commission and Council* [1984] ECR 1969; Case 175/84 *Krohn* v *Commission* [1986] ECR 753; Case C-282/90 *Industrie- en Handelsonderneming Vreugdenhil* v *Commission* [1992] ECR I-1937; Case C-104/89 *Mulder* v *Council and Commission* [1992] ECR I-3061; Cases C-106 etc./90 *Emerald Meats* v *Commission* [1993] ECR I-209; Cases T-481 and 484/93 *Exporteurs in Levende Varkens and ors* v *Commission* [1995] ECR II 2941; Case C-275/00 *European Community* v *First and Franex* [2002] ECR I-10943.

643   Case 92/78 *Simmenthal* v *Commission* [1979] ECR 777.

644   Case 92/78 *Simmenthal, ibid.*; Case 216/82 *Universität Hamburg* v *Hauptzollamt Hamburg-Kehrwieder* [1983] ECR 2771.

be raised within the context of other proceedings competently before the Court. Article 277 is therefore *not* an independent form of action,[645] rather an indirect, 'incidental'[646] or 'subordinate'[647] means of judicial review. But it does mean that any legislative (or similar) act is open perpetually to review, irrespective of age, so long as it is capable of forming the legal basis of a subsequent implementing (normally administrative) act.[648]

5.104 It is not open to a privileged applicant, who enjoyed unrestricted right to challenge the parent measure at the time of its adoption, to invoke a plea of illegality in order to challenge it *if* that applicant was a formal addressee of the measure.[649] This means, necessarily, a Directive or a decision. Having first opted for the contrary,[650] but after long prompting by several Advocates-General,[651] it appears now that it may invoke a plea of illegality where the parent measure is a Regulation.[652] If this is so it may be distinguished from the preliminary ruling procedure of article 267 wherein a privileged applicant is (or appears to be) barred from pleading in a national court the illegality of a measure which he could have, but didn't, challenge under article 263.[653] If the parent act is one which cannot be reviewed by the Court of Justice (*in casu* a joint action of the Council adopted under the CFSP provisions of the pre-Lisbon TEU which was given effect subsequently by a decision) the plea of illegality is inadmissible except insofar as it is a question of whether the Council trespassed into (then) Community authority.[654] As with the issue of admissibility generally,[655] the Court will sometimes dismiss an action in which a plea of

---

645 Cases 31 and 33/62 *Wöhrmann* v *EEC Commission* [1962] ECR 501.

646 Case C-442/04 *Spain* v *Council* [2008] ECR I-3517, *per* A-G Bot at paras 58 and 59 of his opinion.

647 *Ibid.* at paras 42 and 53.

648 Prior to Lisbon the text of art. 241 EC limited its application to (indirect) review of Regulations, but it applied to any act 'which … produce[d] similar effects', this wide interpretation justified by 'the need to provide those persons who are precluded by [art. 263] from instituting proceedings directly in respect of general acts with the benefit of judicial review'; Case 92/78 *Simmenthal*, n. 643 above, at paras 40, 41. Lisbon replaced 'regulation' with 'an act of general application'.

649 Case 2/59 *Germany* v *High Authority* [1960] ECR 53; Case 130/83 *Commission* v *Italy* [1984] ECR 2849; Case 93/84 *Commission* v *France* [1985] ECR 829; Case C-261/99 *Commission* v *France* [2001] ECR I-2537; Case C-404/00 *Commission* v *Spain* [2003] ECR I-6695.

650 E.g., Case 92/78 *Simmenthal*, n. 643 above.

651 Case 32/65 *Italy* v *Council and Commission* [1966] ECR 389 (A-G Roemer); Case 181/85 *France* v *Commission* [1987] ECR 689 (A-G Slynn); Case 204/86 *Greece* v *Council* [1988] ECR 5323 (A-G Mancini); Case C-11/00 *Commission* v *European Central Bank* [2003] ECR I-7147 (A-G Jacobs); Case C-91/05 *Commission* v *Council* (Small Arms Weapons) [2008] ECR I-3651 (A-G Mengozzi); Case C-442/04 *Spain* v *Council* [2008] ECR I-3517 (A-G Bot).

652 Case C-442/04 *Spain* v *Council*, *ibid.* The reasoning of the Court was peremptory but the subject of extensive discussion by A-G Bot (paras 24–67 of his opinion). Owing to peculiarities of the case (a previous action raised by Spain for partial annulment found to be inadmissible; Case C-36/04 *Spain* v *Council* [2006] ECR I-2981) it cannot be said with certainty that the issue is settled.

653 See 5.142 below.

654 Case C-91/05 *Commission* v *Council* (Small Arms Weapons), n. 651 above.

655 See 5.81 above.

illegality has been raised on its merits without ruling upon the the admissibility of the plea.[656] This it does where the proper administration of justice justifies it, without saying exactly what that means.

The grounds for review of the legality of the parent act are those of article 263. **5.105** If the plea is successful the act is not annulled, because a Union act cannot be annulled except by means of the article 263 procedure; rather it is declared 'inapplicable' in the instant case, and so the administrative act based upon it, deprived of its legal foundation, is annulled. Presumably the erring institution is nevertheless bound by article 266 to take the necessary measures to comply with the judgment of the Court as regards the parent act.[657]

(h) Review of financial penalties (article 261 TFEU)

The Treaties provide that Regulations adopted by the Council or the Parlia- **5.106** ment and Council which provide for (financial) penalties may confer upon the Court unlimited jurisdiction 'with regard to' those penalties.[658] This is not of itself an autonomous form of action,[659] the availability of review depending upon the terms of legislation adopted by the institutions. In practice, Regulations which provide for financial penalties *do* provide for unlimited review jurisdiction of the Court. This has especial importance in the area of competition law.[660]

(i) Censure of a Commissioner (articles 245, 247 TFEU)

An action may be raised before the Court of Justice in order compulsorily to **5.107** retire,[661] or to deprive of pension rights or other benefits,[662] a member of the Commission who no longer fulfils the conditions required for the performance of his or her duties or who has been guilty of serious misconduct. The application must come from the Council or the Commission. The first (and so far only) judgment of the Court under these provisions came in 2006.[663]

---

656 Case 181/85 *France* v *Commission* [1987] ECR 689; Case C-23/00P *Council* v *Boehringer Ingelheim Vetmedica and anor* [2002] ECR I 1873; Case T-36/06 *Bundesverband deutscher Banken* v *Commission* [2010] ECR II-537.

657 See the passage from Cases C-120 and 121/06P *Fabbrica italiana accumulatori motocarri Montecchio and anor* v *Council and Commission* [2008] ECR I-6513, cited at 5.141 below, applying to art. 267 preliminary rulings the obligations of art. 266 with logic that would apply equally to art. 277.

658 TFEU, art. 261 (ex art. 229 EC).

659 Case T-252/03 *Fédération nationale de l'industrie et des commerces en gros des viandes* v *Commission* [2004] ECR II-3795.

660 See 13.107 below.

661 TFEU, art. 247 (ex art. 216 EC). But this may now be done by the Commission president alone, without the intervention of the Court; see 3.12 above.

662 TFEU, art. 245(2) (ex art. 213(2) EC).

663 Case C-432/04 *Commission* v *Cresson* [2006] ECR I-6387; see 3.12 above, n. 53.

(j)   Garnishee orders

5.108   In accordance with a protocol attached to the Treaties, Union premises, buildings and archives are inviolable and the Union, its assets, revenues and other property exempt from direct taxation and largely exempt from indirect taxation.[664] There can therefore be no administrative or legal measure of constraint against Union property and assets unless this immunity is lifted by the Court of Justice.[665] This is obtained by way of application pursuant to that provision for authorisation to serve a garnishee order upon an institution in respect of certain sums alleged to be owed by it or by the Union. An action raised for this purpose may be identified by the suffix SA affixed to the case number, for *saisie-arrêt*.

(k)   Euratom jurisdiction

5.109   Virtually all of the jurisdiction of the Court of Justice as set out in the Treaties is carried over to (it 'shall apply to') the Euratom Treaty and the Atomic Energy Community.[666] There is additional jurisdiction for the Court over licensing and sub-licensing for disposal of nuclear materials over which the Commission holds intellectual property rights or contractual licences[667] and sanctions imposed by the Commission in the event of breach of the Treaty safeguard provisions.[668]

3.   Appeals

(a)   Appeal from the General Court

5.110   An appeal against any judgment of the General Court lies to the Court of Justice but on points of law only.[669] This includes (but is probably not restricted to) 'lack of competence of the General Court, a breach of procedure before it which adversely affects the interests of the appellant as well as the infringement of Union law by the General Court'.[670]

---

664   Protocol (No. 7) on the Privileges and Immunities of the European Union.
665   *Ibid.* art. 1.
666   Euratom Treaty, art. 106a; the only exceptions are TFEU, arts 271 (disputes involving the financial institutions), 275 and 276 (exclusion of the Court's jurisdiction over CFSP and (narrow) JLS matters), which have no equivalent provisions in the Euratom Treaty.
667   *Ibid.* art. 144(a).
668   *Ibid.* arts 144(b) and 145.
669   TFEU, art. 256(1) (ex art. 225(1) EC) and Statute of the Court of Justice, arts 49–54.
670   Statute of the Court of Justice, art. 58, 1st para.

Whilst a judgment of the General Court must be reasoned[671] and whether the grounds are inadequate or contradictory is a question of law,[672] it is not required 'to provide an account that follows exhaustively and one by one all the arguments articulated by the parties to the case',[673] so long as in all cases

> the statement of the reasons on which a judgment is based [*la motivation d'un arrêt*] must clearly and unequivocally disclose the Court of First Instance's thinking, so that the persons concerned can be apprised of the justification for the decision taken and the Court of Justice can exercise its power of review'.[674]

Further,

> [a]ccording to settled case-law, the Court of First Instance has exclusive jurisdiction to find the facts, save where a substantive inaccuracy in its findings is apparent from the documents submitted to it, and to appraise those facts. That appraisal thus does not, save where the clear sense of the evidence has been distorted, constitute a point of law which is subject, as such, to review by the Court of Justice on appeal.

> However, ... when the Court of First Instance has found or assessed the facts, the Court of Justice has jurisdiction under Article [256] to review the legal characterisation of those facts by the Court of First Instance and the legal conclusions it has drawn from them.[675]

So, whether the General Court was entitled to conclude, on the basis of the facts before it for assessment, that a Union institution had, or had not, failed in its duty to act diligently and itself to state reasons is a question of law open to appeal.[676]

An appeal must be lodged within two months of the notification of the General **5.111** Court judgment to the parties.[677] Where a judgment of the General Court has annulled a regulation the judgment takes effect only when an appeal becomes time-barred or, if raised, is dismissed.[678] An appeal may be raised by one of the

---

671   *Ibid.* arts 36 and 53, 1st para.
672   Case C-185/95P *Baustahlgewebe* v *Commission* [1998] ECR I-8417, at para. 25; Cases C-120 and 121/06P *Fabbrica italiana accumulatori motocarri Montecchio and anor* v *Council and Commission* [2008] ECR I-6513, at para. 90.
673   Case C-397/03P *Archer Daniels Midland and anor* v *Commission* [2006] ECR I-4429, at para. 60; Case C-3/06P *Groupe Danone* v *Commission* [2007] ECR I-1331, at para. 46.
674   Case C-202/07P *France Télécom* v *Commission* [2009] ECR I-2369, at para. 29.
675   Case C-76/06P *Britannia Alloys and Chemicals* v *Commission* [2007] ECR I-4405, *per* A-G Bot at paras 41–2 of his opinion.
676   Case C 535/06P *Moser Baer India* v *Council* [2009] ECR I-7051, at para. 34 and case law cited.
677   Statute of the Court of Justice, art. 56. A case taken on appeal to the Court of Justice is given a new 'C- ...' number and is distinguished by an additional letter 'P', for *pourvoi* (appeal).
678   *Ibid.* art. 60. Otherwise a judgment of the General Court can be suspended only by interim order of the Court of Justice; see below.

parties to proceedings before the General Court; by a member state or a Union institution, even where they were not parties to, and did not intervene in, proceedings at first instance; and by third parties if (apparently) they had intervened at first instance and if the judgment directly affects their interests.[679] An appeal against an interlocutory order of the General Court, for example a refusal to permit a third party to intervene or to grant interim measures, may be taken directly to the Court of Justice by way of summary procedure;[680] and an appeal against an interlocutory finding disposing of a procedural issue concerning a plea of lack of competence or inadmissibility may be raised before final judgment.[681] Because the Court of Justice may dispense with oral procedure even without the consent of the parties[682] and because they may be dismissed by reasoned order if 'manifestly' (prior to 2012 'clearly') inadmissible or unfounded,[683] appeals are often dealt with fairly speedily. Where no appeal is raised the judgment of the General Court, in both its operative part and *ratio decidendi*, become final[684] – or, put otherwise, *res judicata*.[685]

5.112 An appeal can raise no new pleas. Were it otherwise it would

> allow a party to put forward for the first time before the Court of Justice a plea in law which it has not raised before the Court of First Instance [and so] allow it to bring before the Court, whose jurisdiction in appeals is limited, a case of wider ambit than that which came before the Court of First Instance.[686]

So, for example, a party cannot aver breach of a procedural safeguard not raised before the General Court when it had the opportunity to do so, and is presumed to have waived its benefits.[687] The appeal must indicate the contested elements of the first instance judgment and the legal arguments advanced to that purpose,[688] otherwise it is inadmissible. If this merely reproduces pleas and arguments used at first instance it amounts to a request for re-examination, which the Court cannot undertake.[689] However

---

679 *Ibid.* art. 56.
680 *Ibid.* art. 57. On intervention and interim measures see 5.35 and 5.39 above.
681 *Ibid.* art. 56, 1st para; see e.g., Case C-263/02P *Commission v Jégo Quéré et Cie* [2004] ECR I-3425.
682 *Ibid.* art. 59.
683 RP Court of Justice, art. 181.
684 Cases C-442 and 471/03P *P & O European Ferries (Vizcaya) and anor v Commission* [2006] ECR I-4845, at paras 44 and 47.
685 Case C-308/07P *Gorostiage Atxalandabaso v Parliament* [2009] ECR I-1059, at para. 57.
686 Case C-202/07P *France Télécom v Commission* [2009] ECR I-2369, at para. 60.
687 Case C-64/98P *Petrides v Commission* [1999] ECR I-5187.
688 RP Court of Justice, art. 168(1)(d).
689 Case C-352/98P *Bergaderm and Goupil v Commission* [2000] ECR I-5291.

[b]y contrast, provided that the appellant challenges the interpretation or application of Community law by the Court of First Instance, the points of law examined at first instance may be discussed again in the course of an appeal. Indeed, if an appellant could not thus base his appeal on pleas in law and arguments already relied on before the Court of first Instance, an appeal would be deprived of part of its purpose.[690]

If based upon a challenge to the grounds of a judgment of the General Court which have no effect upon the operative part of the judgment ('vitiated by an error in law' but 'that error does not affect the Court of First Instance's conclusion'),[691] so even if legally correct cannot lead to its being set aside, the appeal is 'ineffective' (*inopérant*) and will fail.[692] Put another way, an appeal will fail if the General Court is shown to have erred in law, but the operative part of its judgment is shown to be well founded upon other (stated) grounds.[693] Thus the Court of Justice will reject outright complaints directed against grounds of judgment which the General Court included not to sustain its judgment but 'for the sake of completeness'.[694] Owing to the monopoly of the General Court on determination of fact, the Court of Justice may substitute its own reasoning only when it is able to base it upon facts found and established in its judgment by the former.[695] An appeal against costs alone, or the party ordered to pay them, is inadmissible.[696]

It appears that the Court of Justice must consider, of its own motion if **5.113** necessary, allegations of incorrect or improper composition of the formation of the General Court which delivered the judgment under appeal.[697] It may of its own motion consider any issue relating to admissibility of the appeal[698] or find

---

690   Case C-10/06P *De Bustamante Tello* v *Council* [2007] ECR I-10381, at para. 28.
691   Case C-113/07P *SELEX Sistemi Integrati* v *Commission* [2009] ECR I-2207, at para. 93.
692   Case C-35/92R *Parliament* v *Frederiksen* [1993] ECR I-991; Cases C-302 and 308/99P *Commission and France* v *Télévision Française 1* [2001] ECR I-5603; Cases C-120 aand 121/06P *Fabbrica italiana accumulatori motocarri Montecchio (FIAMM) and anor* v *Council and Commission* [2008] ECR I-6513. This applies equally where there was a breach of an appellant's procedural rights at first instance, an appeal succeeding only if the breach adversely affected his interests; Statute of the Court of Justice, art. 58, 1st para.; Case C-113/07P *SELEX, ibid.*.
693   Case C-320/92P *Finsider* v *Commission* [1994] ECR I-5697; Case C-265/97P *Coöperatieve Vereniging de Verenigde Bloemveilingen Aalsmeer* v *Florimex and ors* [2000] ECR I-2061; Case C-312/00P *Commission* v *Camar and Tico* [2002] ECR I-11355; Case C-93/02P *Biret International* v *Council* [2003] ECR I-10497; Case C-167/04P *JCB Service* v *Commission* [2006] ECR I-8935, at para. 186; Cases C-402 and 415/05P *Kadi and Al Bakaraat* v *Council and Commission* [2008] ECR I-6351, at paras 233–6; Cases C-120 and 121/06P *FIAMM, ibid.*, at para. 187; Case C-113/07P *SELEX*, n. 691 above, at para. 81; Case C-534/07P *William Prym* v *Commission* [2009] ECR I-7415, at para. 72; Case C-352/09P *ThyssenKrupp Nirosta* v *Commission*, judgment of 29 March 2011, not yet reported, at paras 114–57.
694   Case C-27/09P *France* v *People's Mojahedin Organization of Iran*, judgment of 21 December 2011, not yet reported, at paras 78–9.
695   Case C-294/95P *Ojha* v *Commission* [1998] ECR I-5863, *per* A-G Léger at paras 178–9 of his opinion.
696   Statute of the Court of Justice, art. 58, 2nd para; Case C-396/93P *Henrichs* v *Commission* [1995] ECR I-2611.
697   Cases C-341 and 342/06P *Chronopost and La Poste* v *UFEX and ors* [2008] ECR I-4777, at paras 46–9.
698   Case C-17/07P *Neirinck* v *Commission* [2008] ECR I-36*, at para. 38.

that a party having no interest in bringing or maintaining an appeal for an event occurring after the judgment of the General Court removes the prejudicial effect thereof as regards the appellant and so declare the appeal inadmissible or devoid of purpose.[699] Whether it may consider of its own motion issues of error of law in the General Court's reasoning which were not challenged on appeal is unclear.[700]

5.114 If an appeal is successful the Court of Justice sets aside the judgment of the General Court, and may either refer it back (*renvoyer*) for rehearing or, where the state of proceedings so permits (*le litige … est en état d'être jugé*), decide the case itself.[701] Where a case is referred back the General Court is bound by the judgment of the Court of Justice on points of law.[702] The Court of Justice is never overtly critical of the judgment of the General Court, but, just occasionally, an Advocate-General is.[703]

5.115 Should the General Court come to be granted jurisdiction to hear preliminary rulings under article 267, its judgment will be subject to 'review' (*réexamen*) by the Court of Justice but only 'exceptionally', where there is a serious risk to the unity or consistency of Union law.[704]

(b) Appeal to the General Court

5.116 Appeal lies from the Civil Service Tribunal, and any specialised court created in the future, to the General Court (which may, as with the Civil Service Tribunal, but need not be, limited to points of law).[705] Rules governing such appeals are similar to those applicable to appeals to the Court of Justice.[706] An appeal is heard by a chamber of the Court designated for the purpose.[707] If successful the

---

699 Case C-19/93P *Rendo and ors v Commission* [1995] ECR I-3319, at para. 13; Case C-535/06P *Moser Baer India v Council* [2009] ECR I-7051, at para. 24; Cases C-399 and 403/06P *Hassan and Ayaddi v Council* [2009] ECR I-11393, at para. 58.

700 See the opinion of A-G Mengozzi in Case C-290/07P *Commission v Scott* [2010] ECR I-7763.

701 Statute of the Court of Justice, art. 61. However, where the successful appeal has been raised by other than a party to proceedings before the General Court, the Court of Justice may, if it considers it necessary, declare some or all of the legal effects of the original judgment to be definitive for the parties; Statute of the Court of Justice, art. 61, 3rd para.

702 *Ibid.* art. 61, 2nd para. A case remitted back to the General Court reassumes its original 'T- …' number, explaining why some cases before the Court result in two judgments, several years apart. Latterly the two may be distinguished by the addition to the second judgment of the suffix 'RENV' (*renvoi*).

703 See the opinions of A-G van Gerven in Case C-137/92P *Commission v BASF and ors* (PVC) [1994] ECR I-2555 and of A-G Mengozzi in Case C-290/07P *Scott*, n. 700 above.

704 TFEU, art. 256(3). Such a review goes to the special chamber established to hear appeal judgments of the General Court (n. 710 below), and essentially the same procedures will apply. As to the 'urgent procedure' now governing review see Statute of the Court of Justice, arts 62a, 62b and RP Court of Justice, arts 191–195.

705 Statute of the Court of Justice, Annex, art. 11.

706 See RP General Court, arts 137–49. Thus an appeal from the Civil Service Tribunal (but not from boards of appeal of a Union agency) is given a new 'T- …' number before the General Court and the suffix 'P' (*pourvoi*).

707 See n. 104 above and accompanying text.

Court gives judgment in the case or, if the state of proceedings does not permit it, remits it back to the Tribunal;[708] where remitted back, the Tribunal is bound by the judgment of the General Court on points of law.[709]

An appeal judgment of the General Court is subject in turn to review by the **5.117** Court of Justice but only exceptionally, where there is, again, a serious risk to the unity or consistency of Union law.[710]

The creation, starting in 1994, of Community intellectual property rights (at **5.118** present Community trade marks,[711] Community designs[712] and Community plant varieties,[713] but their number is likely to increase post-Lisbon)[714] has brought with it bodies competent to regulate them. The Office for Harmonisation in the Internal Market (Trade Marks and Designs) (OHIM) and the Community Plant Variety Office each have a Board of Appeal for the settlement of disputes. Any determination of a Board of Appeal is subject to appeal before the General Court,[715] appeal lying thereafter to the Court of Justice by

---

708 Statute of the Court of Justice, Annex I, art. 13(1). A case remitted back reassumes its original 'F' number to which is added the suffix 'RENV'.

709 *Ibid.* art. 13(2).

710 TFEU, art. 256(2) (ex art. 225(2) EC). See Statute of the Court of Justice, arts 62a, 62b. The review goes to a special chamber of the president and four presidents of chambers of five judges (RP Court of Justice, art. 191) and special rules apply (arts 191–195). It is open to the first Advocate-General to suggest that such a risk exists so that a judgment be reviewed, but the decision remains with the appeal chamber; Statute of the Court of Justice, art. 62, RP Court of Justice, art. 193. A review decision (*sic*) may be identified by the suffix RX (for *réexamen*). For the eight existing examples to September 2012 see Case C-216/08RX *Combescot* v *Commission*, decision of 16 April 2008, unreported (the review heard by the full court because the review chamber had yet to be established); Case C-21/09RX *Belgium and Commission* v *Genette*, decision of 5 February 2009, unreported; Case C-180/09RX *Sanchez Ferriz and ors* v *Commission*, decision of 5 June 2009, unreported; Case C-197/09RX *Agence européenne des médicaments* v *M*, decision of 24 June 2009, unreported; Case C-183/10RX *Bianchi* v *Fondation européenne pour la formation*, decision of 5 May 2010, unreported; Case C-478/10RX *Marcuccio* v *Commission*, decision of 28 October 2010, unreported; Case C-17/11RX *Commission* v *Petrilli*, decision of 8 February 2011, unreported; Case C-334/12 ex *Arango Jaramillo* v *Banque euopéenne d'investissement*, decision of 12 July 2012, unreported. In only two cases (*M* and *Arango Jaramillo*) did the Court decide that a review should proceed; and, in *M*, succeed: Case C-197/09RX-II *M* v *European Medicines Agency* [2009] ECR I-12033. For procedure where a judgment of the General Court has been reviewed and referred back to it see RP General Court, arts 121a–121d, the discussion of the Court in *M* and Case T-12/08P-RENV-RX *M* v *Agence européenne des medicaments*, judgment of 8 July 2010, not yet reported (referring the case back to the Civil Service Tribunal (Case F-23/07 RENV-RX *M* v *Agence européenne des medicaments*, which was subsequently settled) as the state of proceedings did not permit the General Court to decide it itself).

711 Regulation 207/2009 [2009] OJ L78/1 (a consolidated version replacing Regulation 40/94 [1994] OJ L11/1); see 10.79 below.

712 Regulation 6/2002 [2002] OJ L3/1; see 10.79 below.

713 Regulation 2100/94 [1994] OJ L227/1; see 10.79 below.

714 See art. 118 TFEU, providing for the first time express authority (previously action was taken under the flexibility clause of art. 352) for the creation of European intellectual property rights and provision of uniform protection.

715 Regulation 207/2009, art. 65; Regulation 6/2002, art. 61; Regulation 2100/94, art. 73. The jurisdiction falls within that of the General Court even, since 2004, if raised by a Union institution or a member state; Statute of the Court of Justice, art. 51.

normal rules. Appeals against OHIM determinations on trade mark matters now make up an appreciable part of the General Court's list; this jurisdiction may come to be transferred to a specialised court.[716] Litigation is also generated (increasingly) from the activities of other Union agencies, particularly, under the REACH Regulation,[717] determinations of the Chemicals Agency Board of Appeal subject to appeal to the General Court.[718]

4. References for a preliminary ruling (article 267 TFEU)

5.119 The jurisdiction which accounts now for the largest number of cases before the Court of Justice (in 2011, for example, accounting for 423 of 688 cases brought) consists in requests for preliminary rulings under article 267 TFEU. Modelled upon German and Italian constitutional procedures[719] (it was the Italian delegation to the Messina conference which first proposed it), this form of process is known in French as the *renvoi préjudiciel* (roughly, reference before judgment) or, alternatively, *Vorabentscheidungsersuchen* (pre-decision entreaty), which more accurately describe what it involves. The procedure enables a national court, having encountered a question of Union law in the course of proceedings before it ('the main proceedings'; *l'affaire*, or *le litige, au principal*), to stay those proceedings and request and obtain from the Court of Justice an authoritative ruling on the (Union) law in issue. The ruling is then remitted to the national court, which applies it in disposing of the case.

5.120 Article 267 is therefore, contrary to a view held too widely, *not* an appellate jurisdiction, rather it is institution of a 'system of cooperation',[720] 'a dialogue between one court and another'[721] and an an interaction 'vital to the uniform interpretation and the effective application of Community law'.[722] It would be

---

716 See TFEU, art. 262 (ex art. 229a EC), by which the Council may, by unanimity, 'adopt provisions to confer jurisdiction … on the Court of Justice of the European Union in disputes relating to the application of acts adopted on the basis of the Treaties which create Community intellectual property rights'.

717 Regulation 1907/2006 [2006] OJ L396/1 concerning the registration, evaluation, authorisation and restriction of chemicals (REACH) and establishing the European Chemicals Agency.

718 *Ibid.* art. 94.

719 § 100 I GG and Gesetz vom 12. März 1951 über das Bundesverfassungsgericht (BVerfGG), Neugefaßt BGBl. 1993 I S. 1473, §§ 13 Nr. 11, 80–82a; Italian Constitution, art. 134; l. cost. 9 febbraio 1948, no. 1, GU no. 43 del 20 febbraio 1948, art. 1; l. cost. 11 marzo 1953, no. 87, GU no. 62 del 14 marzo 1953, art. 23; Norme integrative per i giudizi davanti alla Corte costituzionale, GU no. 261 del 7 novembre 2008, art. 1–23. A similar procedure exists in Spain: Spanish Constitution, art. 161; Ley Orgánica 2/1979, de 3 de octubre, del Tribunal Constitucional, BOE de 5 octubre 1979, arts 35–7.

720 Case C-210/06 *CARTESIO Oktató és Szolgáltató* [2008] ECR I-9641, at para. 70. See BVerfG, 12. Oktober 1993 (*Maastricht*), BVerfGE 89, 155 (175): 'Allerdings übt das Bundesverfassungsgericht seine Gerichtsbarkeit über die Anwendbarkeit von abgeleitetem Gemeinschaftsrecht in Deutschland in einem "Kooperationsverhältnis" zum Europäischen Gerichtshof aus'.

721 Case C-210/06 *CARTESIO*, *ibid.*, at para. 91.

722 *Ibid. per* A-G Poiares Maduro at para. 19 of his opinion.

difficult to overestimate its importance in the development of Community/ Union law. It is the national courts which normally first encounter issues of Union law – by virtue of the principle of direct effect they are all 'the courts of general jurisdiction in Community law' (*juge communautaire de droit commun*)[723] or the '"ordinary" courts within the European Union legal order' (*juges de 'droit commun' de l'ordre juridique de l'Union*);[724] by injecting the Court into national proceedings, it makes the meanest, as well as the highest, court in the land, in effect, a constitutional court, bypassing normal rules of judicial hierarchy and jurisdiction. Virtually all the key 'constitutional' judgments of the Court of Justice – first and foremost, *van Gend en Loos*[725] (direct effect) and *Costa*[726] (primacy) – and the case law which has given real substance to the internal market have arisen in the context of article 267 cases. It was, until Nice, the one head of jurisdiction of the Community judicature reserved to the Court of Justice by the EC Treaty,[727] and there seems no enthusiasm to take advantage of the possibility post-Nice of transferring jurisdiction in specific areas to the General Court.

It is important to note the twin, distinct, purposes of the procedure. Article 267 **5.121** provides:

> The Court of Justice of the European Union shall have jurisdiction to give preliminary rulings concerning:
>
> (a) the interpretation of the Treaties;
> (b) the validity and interpretation of acts of the institutions, bodies, offices or agencies of the Union.

A national court or tribunal may therefore seek the assistance of the Court of Justice, first, upon the correct interpretation of a provision of Union law (either the Treaties or legislation or principles springing therefrom) before it – the purpose being to (seek to) ensure the uniform interpretation of Union law,[728] so that 'in all circumstances [it] has the same effect in all Member States',[729] which is '[o]ne of the Court's essential tasks';[730] and secondly, a court or tribunal may request a preliminary ruling upon the 'validity' of an act of a Union institution

---

723 Case C-555/07 *Kücükdevici* v *Swedex* [2010] ECR I-365, *per* A-G Bot at para. 55 of his opinion.
724 Opinion 1/09 *Re the European Patent Convention*, opinion of 8 March 2011, not yet reported, at para. 80.
725 Case 26/62 *Algemene Transport- en Expeditie Onderneming van Gend en Loos* v *Nederlandse Administratie der Belastingen* [1963] ECR 1.
726 Case 6/64 *Costa* v *ENEL* [1964] ECR 585.
727 EC Treaty, art. 225(1) (pre-Nice).
728 Case 26/62 *van Gend en Loos*, n. 725 above.
729 Opinion 1/09 *Re the European Patent Convention*, opinion of 8 March 2011, not yet reported, at para. 83.
730 *Report of the Court of Justice on Certain Aspects of the Application of the Treaty on European Union* (1995), para. 11.

or body.[731] This constitutes an alternative avenue of judicial review of Union legislation – an important and, according to the Court of Justice, a sufficient one[732] given the difficulty of private persons meeting the strict tests for standing required under article 263. In this respect article 267 is an indirect route to the Court of Justice, a plea of illegality with a parallel to article 277: article 277 allows a 'non-privileged applicant' to challenge the legality of general legislation when it comes to be applied to him by a subsequent act of a Union institution; article 267 allows him to do so when it is applied to him by a subsequent act of a national authority. For,

> in proceedings before the national courts, every party has the right to plead before the court hearing the case the illegality of the provisions contained in legislative acts of the European Union which serve as the basis for a decision or act of national law relied upon against him and to prompt that court ... to put that question to the Court by means of a reference for a preliminary ruling.[733]

Since so much of Union law is applied or administered by national authorities, this is a not uncommon, if circuitous, avenue of judicial protection: of references under article 267, roughly one in six addresses a question of validity, rather than interpretation, of Union law. In the interests of the judicial protection article 267 affords, member states are under a duty to ensure that there is in place a system of remedies and procedures which ensures satisfactory access to the procedure,[734] and this was codified in the Treaties after a fashion by Lisbon.[735]

5.122 It will be observed that there are measures beyond the review jurisdiction of the Court of Justice which cannot be the subject of a preliminary ruling as to their validity, but which may nevertheless be referred to the Court on the matter of their interpretation. This applies of course to the Treaties themselves, but also to true opinions or recommendations, which lack the legal effects necessarily requisite to their annulment or invalidation,[736] and to treaties with third countries (including accession treaties and ancillary acts of accession) entered

---

731 Lisbon extended the reach of art. 267 to review (and interpretation) of acts of bodies, offices or agencies of the Union; previously it had been restricted to acts of the institutions or of the European Central Bank; art. 234(1) EC.

732 Case C-50/00P *Unión de Pequeños Agricultores* v *Council* [2002] ECR I-6677; Case C-167/02P *Rothley and ors* v *Parliament* [2004] ECR I-3149; Case C-263/02P *Commission* v *Jégo-Quéré et Cie* [2004] ECR I-3425.

733 Case C-550/09 *Criminal proceedings against E and F* [2010] ECR I-6213, at para. 45. The right is qualified in the next paragraph to exclude those who had standing to challenge the measure under art. 263; see 5.142 below.

734 Case C-50/00P *Unión de Pequeños Agricultores*, n. 732 above, at para. 41; Case C-263/02P *Jégo-Quéré*, n. 732 above, at para. 31; Case T-370/02 *Alpenhain-Camembert-Werk and ors* v *Commission* [2004] ECR II-2097, at para. 72.

735 TEU, art. 19(1), 2nd para.: 'Member States shall provide remedies sufficient to ensure effective legal protection in the fields covered by Union law'.

736 See 5.66 above.

into by the Union insofar as they form part of Union law[737] – although an interpretation of a Treaty provision rendered by the Court of Justice cannot be binding upon third states party to it. A national court may also refer a question seeking an interpretation of a previous judgment of the Court.[738]

The Court of Justice, however, has no jurisdiction under article 267 to rule upon **5.123** the interpretation purely of national law[739] and will refuse to respond to a reference which has that purpose. But there are three exceptions to the rule.

First, a question which on its face asks for an interpretation of national law but **5.124** which in reality is seeking guidance as to the correct interpretation of relevant Union law will (tacitly or otherwise) be reformulated by the Court (or the Court will 'extract' from it the relevant points) to that purpose and effect:

[I]n the event of questions' [*sic*] having been improperly formulated or going beyond the scope of the powers conferred on the Court of Justice by Article [267], the Court is free to extract from all the factors provided by the national court and in particular from the statement of grounds contained in the reference, the elements of Community law

737 This because the process by which a treaty is ratified by and for the Union is an 'act of the institutions', and once it enters into force it forms an integral part of the Union legal system, so amendable to an interpretative reference; Case 181/73 *Haegeman v Belgian State* [1974] ECR 449; Case C-27/96 *Danisco Sugar v Allmänna Ombudet* [1997] ECR I-6653; Cases C-23–25/04 *Sfakianakis v Elliniko Domisio* [2006] ECR I-1265; Case C-459/03 *Commission v Ireland* (MOX Plant) [2006] ECR I-4635; Case C-301/08 *Bogiatzi v Deutscher Luftpool and ors* [2009] ECR I-10185. This includes treaties signed and ratified not by the Union but by the member states and to which obligations the Union has succeeded: Cases 21–24/72 *International Fruit Company and ors v Produktschap voor Groenten en Fruit* [1972] ECR 1219; Case C-308/06 *R (International Association of Independent Tanker Owners(Intertanko) and ors) v Secretary of State for Transport* [2008] ECR I-4057; Case C-301/08 *Bogiatzi*, above. However, in the case of a 'mixed agreement' (as to which see 14.74 below) the Court has no jurisdiction to interpret those provisions of the agreement which pertain to the obligations of the member states (Case 12/86 *Demirel v Stadt Schwäbisch Gmünd* [1987] ECR 3719; Case C-53/96 *Hermès International v FHT Marketing Choice* [1998] ECR I-3603) except insofar as to address the exceptional question of whether the matter falls properly within Union, and not national, competence; Case C-431/05 *Merck Genéricos – Produtos Farmacêuticos v Merck and anor* [2007] ECR I-7001. See also the discussion of A-G Sharpston in Case C-240/09 *Lesoochranárske zoskupenie v Ministerstvo životného prostredia Slovenskej republiky*, judgment of 8 March 2011, not yet reported.

738 E.g., Case C-224/01 *Köbler v Austria* [2003] ECR I-10239; Case C-147/01 *Weber's Wine World and ors v Abgabenberufungskommission Wien* [2003] ECR I-11365; Case C-348/04 *Boehringer Ingelheim and ors v Swingward and anor* [2007] ECR I-3391; Case C-2/06 *Willy Kempter v Hauptzollamt Hamburg-Jonas* [2008] ECR I-411; Case C-478/07 *Budějovický Budvar v Rudolf Ammersin* [2009] ECR I-7221; Case C-205/09 *Criminal proceedings against Eredics and anor*, [2010] ECR I010231; Case C-400/09 *Orifarm and ors v Merck & Co. and ors*, judgment of 28 July 2011, not yet reported; Case C-398/09 *Lady & Kid and ors v Skatteministeriet*, judgment of 6 September 2011, not yet reported. A reference of this type is probably restricted to interpretation of the operative part of a judgment, or a part of the reasoning which leads ineluctably thereto.

739 E.g., Case C-346/94 *City of Glasgow District Council v Kleinwort Benson* [1995] ECR I-615; Case C-435/93 *Dietz v Stichting Thuiszorg Rotterdam* [1996] ECR I-5223, at para. 39; Case C-69/10 *Samba Diouf v Ministre de Travail, de l'Emploi et de l'Immigration*, judgment of 28 July 2011, not yet reported, at para. 59; Case C-457/09 *Chartry v État belge*, order of 1 March 2011, not yet reported; Case C-482/10 *Cicala v Regione Siciliana*, judgment of 21 December 2011, not yet reported.

requiring an interpretation – or, as the case may be, an assessment of validity – having regard to the subject-matter of the dispute.[740]

So, a question along the lines of 'Is national law x compatible with Union law?' – a question the Court has no jurisdiction to answer[741] – will be recast as 'the national court is asking, in effect, for the correct interpretation, and therefore requirements, of Union law in the light of the circumstances of a national law such as x' – which it does.[742] Put otherwise,

on a literal reading of the question referred for a preliminary ruling by the [national court], the Court is being asked to rule on the compatibility with Community law of a provision of national law. Nevertheless, although the Court cannot answer that question in the terms in which it is framed, there is nothing to prevent it from giving an answer of use to the national court by providing the latter with the guidance as to the interpretation of Community law necessary to enable that court to rule on the compatibility of those national rules with Community law.[743]

Or,

[i]t is true that it is not for the Court to rule on the compatibility of national rules with provisions of Community law in proceedings brought under Article [267]. Furthermore, under the system of judicial cooperation established by that provision the interpretation of national rules is a matter for the national courts and not the Court of Justice.

On the other hand, the Court does have jurisdiction to supply the national court with all the guidance as to the interpretation of Community law necessary to enable that court to rule on the compatibility of the national rules with the provisions of Community law.[744]

Nor has the Court jurisdiction under article 267 to invalidate a national law which is inconsistent with Union law: if a national court asks 'Is national law x invalid for incompatibility with Union law?', the Court will always respond (assuming it is the correct answer) that the Treaties, a Regulation, a Directive or simply Union law 'precludes [*s'oppose à*] national law such as that at issue in the main proceedings', and leave it to the national court, which alone has power to

---

740 Case 83/78 *Pigs Marketing Board* v *Redmond* [1978] ECR 2347, at para. 26; to the same effect, Case C-384/08 *Attanasio Group* v *Comune di Carbognano* [2010] ECR I-2055, at para. 18.

741 Case C-63/94 *Groupement National des Négociants en Pommes de Terre de Belgique (Belgapom)* v *ITM Belgium and anor* [1995] ECR I-2476, at para. 7; Case C-55/94 *Gebhard* v *Consiglio dell'Ordine degli Avvocati e Procuratori di Milano* [1995] ECR I-4165, at para. 19.

742 See e.g., Case 137/84 *Ministère public* v *Mutsch* [1985] ECR 2681; Case 14/86 *Pretore di Salò* v *Persons Unknown* [1987] ECR 2545; Cases C-10 etc./97 *Ministero delle Finanze* v *IN.CO.GE.'90 and ors* [1998] ECR I-6307.

743 Cases C-338 etc./04 *Criminal proceedings against Placanica and ors* [2007] ECR I-1891, at para. 37.

744 Case C-506/04 *Wilson* v *Ordre des avocats du barreau de Luxembourg* [2006] ECR I-8613, at paras 34–5.

do so, to set aside, or disapply, that law. The need for restructuring questions has diminished with the growing sophistication of national judges in the use of article 267, questions now sometimes betraying considerable understanding and forensic skill in Union law. And, it might be noted, the Court is sometimes criticised for reformulating a question which requires no reformulation in order to evade a difficult question.

Secondly, in a dispute involving solely national law, but national law which **5.125** expressly incorporates, or refers to, Union provisions, the Court may furnish a ruling, if requested, not on the national law but on the Union provisions relevant to its interpretation.[745]

Thirdly, in a dispute all aspects of which are confined to one member state, so, **5.126** owing to the 'wholly internal' rule, falling outwith the sphere of Union law,[746] the Court may furnish a ruling, if requested, on otherwise applicable Union law where national law provides that a home national enjoys the same rights which a national of another member state would derive from Union law in the same situation.[747]

Procedure and forms for use of article 267 have been adopted into British (and **5.127** other) rules of court.[748] The Court of Justice has itself issued a guidance note as an aid to its use.[749]

---

745 Cases 297/88 and 197/89 *Dzodzi v Belgium* [1990] ECR I-3763; Case C-28/95 *Leur-Bloem v Inspecteur der Belastingdienst/Ondernemingen Amsterdam 2* [1997] ECR I-4161; Case C-130/95 *Giloy v Hauptzollamt Frankfurt am Main-Ost* [1997] ECR I-4291; Case C-306/99 *Banque Internationale pour l'Afrique Occidentale v Finanzamt für Großunternehmen in Hamburg* [2003] ECR I-1; Case C-217/05 *Confederación Española de Empresarios de Estaciones de Servicio v Compañía Española de Petróleos* [2006] ECR I-11987; Case C-280/06 *Autorità Garante della Concorrenza e del Mercato v Ente tabacchi italiani and ors* [2007] ECR I-10893, including the extensive discussion of A-G Kokott at paras 19–64 of her opinion; cf. Case C-482/10 *Cicala v Regione Siciliana*, judgment of 21 December 2011, not yet reported. According to Ms Kokott (at para. 24 of her opinion in *Tabacchi italiani*), the interest in doing so is 'particularly strong' in the area of competition law owing to the frequent orientation of national law in the field to Union law.
746 See 10.66 and 11.90–11.95 below.
747 Case C-451/03 *Servizi Ausiliari Dottori Commercialisti v Califiori* [2006] ECR I-2941, at para. 29; Cases C-94 and 202/04 *Cipolla and ors v Fazari and ors* [2006] ECR I-11241, at para. 30; Joined Cases C-570 and 571/07 *Blanco Pérez and Chao Gómez v Consejería de Salud y Servicios Sanitarios and anor* [2010] ECR I-4629, at para. 39.
748 See e.g., in England and Wales, CPR, rr. 68.1–68.4 (supplemented by Practice Direction 68 – References to the European Court); Criminal Procedure Rules 2010, rr. 75.1–75.4; in Scotland, RC 65.1–65.5; Act of Adjournal (Consolidation) 1988, ss. 63–7 and 113–18; Sheriff Court Ordinary Cause Rules, rr. 38.1–38.5; in Northern Ireland, Rules of the Supreme Court (NI) 1979, Ord. 114; County Court Rules (NI) 1981, Ord. 23; Crown Court Rules (NI) 1979, rr. 39–42.
749 Information Note on References by National Courts for a Preliminary Ruling [2011] OJ C160/1; this is an updated version of a notice first issued in 1996, reissued in 2005 and 2009.

(a) Court or tribunal of a member state

5.128 The procedure may be put in train by any 'court or tribunal' of a member state (in other languages one word sufficing, e.g., *juridiction; Gericht*). The quality of court or tribunal is to be determined by reference to Union law alone, and turns upon, variously, whether: it is established by law, it is permanent, its jurisdiction is compulsory, its procedure is *inter partes*, it applies rules of law, and it is independent.[750] It is probably attributed a narrower meaning than the same terms under article 6(1) of the European Convention on Human Rights.[751] Arbitration tribunals or bodies generally do not satisfy the tests. A reference from a body which is not a court or tribunal is inadmissible.

5.129 As a reference may be made by a court or tribunal 'of a Member State', a reference from a court outwith the Union is inadmissible, even if that court is applying Union law (where, for example, the proper law of a contract is that of a member state, moderated by some provision of Union law) and may reasonably require advice upon its interpretation or validity.[752] However, the Court of Justice has extended article 267 to be available to courts or tribunals in other countries or territories in which the Treaties apply (in some cases only partially), and so has admitted references from French Polynesia,[753] Réunion,[754] the Isle of Man[755] and Jersey.[756] Although not strictly a court 'of a member state', the Court has also found a reference from the Benelux Court of Justice to be admissible,[757] but not one from the Complaints Board created by a convention

---

750   See Case 61/65 *Vaasen–Goebbels* v *Bestuur van het Beambtenfonds voor het Mijnbedrijf* [1966] ECR 261; Case 246/80 *Broekmeulen* v *Huisarts Registratie Commissie* [1981] ECR 2311; Case 14/86 *Pretore de Salò* v *Persons Unknown* [1987] ECR 2545; Case C-54/96 *Dorsch Consult Ingenieurgesellschaft* v *Bundesbaugesellschaft Berlin* [1997] ECR I-4961; Cases C-9 and 118/97 *Jokela and Pitkäranta* [1998] ECR I-6267; Cases C-110–147/98 *Gabalfrisa and ors* v *Agencia Estatal de Administración Tributaria* [2000] ECR I-1577; Case C-516/99 *Walter Schmid* [2002] ECR I-4573; Case C-53/03 *Synetairismos Farmakopoion Aitolias & Akarnanias and ors (Syfait)* v *Glaxosmithkline* [2005] ECR I-4609; Case C-256/05 *Telekom Austria*, order of 6 October 2005, unreported; Case C-96/04 *Standesamt Stadt Niebüll* [2006] ECR I-3561; Case C-109/07 *Pilato* v *Bourgault* [2008] ECR I-3503; Case C-14/08 *Roda Golf & Beach Resort* [2009] ECR I-5439. For an extensive discussion of the case law (and a plea for an urgent need for change in it, to which the Court did not respond) see the opinion of A-G Ruiz-Jarabo Colomer in Case C-17/00 *De Coster* v *Collège des Bourgmestres et Echevins de Watermael-Boitsfort* [2001] ECR I-9445; also the discussion of A-G Jacobs in Case C-53/03 *Syfait*, above.

751   See *Campbell and Fell* v *United Kingdom* (1985) 7 EHRR 16, at paras 76–85; *Findlay* v *United Kingdom* (1997) 24 EHRR 221.

752   See discussion in Cases T-377 etc./00 *Philip Morris International and ors* v *Commission* [2003] ECR II-1.

753   Cases C-100 and 101/89 *Kaefer and Procacci* v *French State* [1990] ECR I-4647; Case C-260/90 *Leplat* v *Territory of French Polynesia* [1992] ECR I-643.

754   Case C-163/90 *Administration des Douanes et Droits Indirects* v *Legros and ors* [1992] ECR I-4625; Cases C-407–411/93 *Dindar Confort and ors* v *Conseil Régional de la Réunion* [1994] ECR I-3957.

755   Case C-355/89 *Department of Health and Social Security* v *Barr & Montrose Holdings* [1991] ECR I-3479.

756   Case C-171/96 *Pereira Roque* v *Lieutenant Governor of Jersey* [1998] ECR I-4607; Case C-293/02 *Jersey Produce Marketing Organisation* v *States of Jersey* [2005] ECR I-9543. On the application of the Treaty to the Isle of Man and the Channel Islands see 10.05 below.

757   Case C-265/00 *Campina Melkunie* v *Benelux-Merkenbureau* [2004] ECR I-1699; the issue discussed at length previously in Case C-337/95 *Parfums Christian Dior* v *Evora* [1997] ECR I-6013. Not only is a reference

amongst the member states and the Communities for the resolution of disputes arising under the Statute of the European Schools,[758] which was in all other respects a court or tribunal, but not of a member state.[759]

(b) Decision to refer

Any national court or tribunal may request a preliminary ruling when it considers that a decision on a question of Union law 'is necessary to enable it to give judgment'.[760] It may do so at any stage in the course of proceedings it sees fit, and at its discretion alone, irrespective of the wishes of any or even all of the parties: **5.130**

> [T]he system established by Article [267] with a view to ensuring that Community law is interpreted uniformly in the Member States instituted direct cooperation between the Court of Justice and the national courts by means of a procedure which is completely independent of any initiative by the parties.[761]

Legitimate considerations of the national judge in deciding whether to refer may nevertheless include the wishes of the parties, as well as the difficulty of the question(s) to be answered, the need for uniform interpretation throughout the Union, the advantages enjoyed by the Court of Justice in construing Union instruments, the time required (delay sometimes being the primary purpose of a party urging that a reference be made), and the costs.[762] Equally, the framing of the question(s) is a matter wholly for the court, paying only such regard to the views of the parties as it thinks fit; normal practice in the United Kingdom is for counsel to be invited to play an active part in assisting the court in drafting the questions,[763] although the exercise is not always fruitful.[764]

---

admissible, it is compulsory, as there is no avenue of appeal from the Benelux Court of Justice; see 5.139 below. But this also means logically that the highest Belgian/Dutch/Luxembourg courts are absolved of a duty to refer if a matter might be appealed to the Benelux Court; discussed in *Christian Dior.*

758 Convention of 21 June 1994 defining the Statute of the European Schools [1994] OJ L212/3.

759 Case C-196/09 *Miles and ors* v *European Schools*, judgment of 14 June 2011, not yet reported. The subject matter of the dispute was taken up coterminously by the Commission in enforcement proceedings raised under art. 258; see Case C-545/09 *Commission* v *United Kingdom*, judgment of 2 February 2012, not yet reported.

760 TFEU, art. 267, 2nd para.

761 Case C-2/06 *Willy Kempter* v *Hauptzollamt Hamburg-Jonas* [2008] ECR I-411, at para. 41; Case C-210/06 *CARTESIO Oktató és Szolgáltató* [2008] ECR I-9641, at para. 90 (substituting 'throughout' for 'in').

762 See the 'guidelines' proposed by Denning MR in *Bulmer* v *Bollinger* [1974] Ch. 401, and the rather more helpful guidance given by Bingham MR in *R* v *International Stock Exchange of the United Kingdom and the Republic of Ireland, ex parte Else* [1993] 1 All ER 420; the latter cited with approval and adopted by the Inner House of the Court of Session in Scotland in *Booker Aquaculture* v *Secretary of State for Scotland* 2000 SC 9 (per the Lord President (Rodger)) and *Royal Bank of Scotland Group* v *Commissioners for Her Majesty's Revenue and Customs* [2007] CSIH 15, 2007 SC 401 (per the Lord Justice-Clerk (Gill)).

763 See e.g., *R (Air Transport Association of America and ors)* v *Secretary of State for Energy and Climate Change* [2010] EWHC 1554 (Admin).

764 See e.g., *Boehringer Ingelheim and anor* v *Swingward and ors* [2004] EWCA Civ 757, [2004] All ER (D) 151.

5.131 In setting the question(s) the national court delimits the scope of the reference, and thus, in principle, binds the Court of Justice. So, for example, when the question is one of interpretation the Court cannot examine a point of validity raised by one of the parties.[765] This means that the Court will interpret a provision of Union law which it might consider to be, and had the question been framed differently it might have found to be, unlawful. The Court has, rarely, extracted from an interpretative reference the authority to consider legality,[766] but this may be proper only where the order for reference makes it clear that the referring court had serious doubts as to the force of a Union measure and that those doubts led to the reference;[767] in such circumstances it may remain open to the national court not to apply the ruling. The Court has been known to invite the referring court to consider matters not raised in its reference ('the Court draws the national court's attention to the possible impact of [a particular measure] on the free movement of goods and persons'),[768] but this too is rare. It is also for the national court to define the legal context of the case: it is 'the factual and legislative context which the national court is responsible for defining and the accuracy of which is not a matter for this Court to determine'.[769] So the Court will proceed upon the basis of facts as presented by the referring court, even if they are contested by the parties,[770] and cannot question the correctness of the referring court's interpretation of national law.[771] But it will correct a 'false premiss' in the reference deriving from the national court's misapprehension of Union law.[772]

---

765   E.g. Case 44/65 *Hessische Knappschaft* v *Maison Singer et fils* [1965] ECR 965, especially the opinion of A-G Gand at 975–6; Case C-132/03 *Ministero della Salute* v *Codacons and anor* [2005] ECR I-4167. See also Case C-393/08 *Sbarigia* v *Azienda USL RM/A and ors* [2010] ECR I-6333, *per* A-G Jääskinen at paras 76–92 of his opinion.

766   Case 2/76 *Strehl* v *Nationaal Pensioenfonds voor Mijnwerkers* [1977] ECR 211; Case 145/79 *Roquette Frères* v *France* [1980] ECR 2917.

767   See the opinion of A-G Sharpston in Case C-345/06 *Heinrich* [2009] ECR I-1659, at paras 78–9.

768   Case C-12/02 *Criminal proceedings against Grilli* [2003] ECR I-11585, at para. 36.

769   Case C-300/01 *Salzmann* [2003] ECR I-4899, at para. 31; also Cases C-222 etc./05 *Van der Weerd and ors* v *Minister van Landbouw, Natuur en Voedselkwaliteit* [2007] ECR I-4233, at para. 22.

770   E.g., Case C-280/06 *Autorità Garante della Concorrenza e del Mercato* v *Ente tabacchi italiani and ors* [2007] ECR I-10893, at para. 27; Case C-291/05 *Minister voor Vreemdelingenzaken en Integratie* v *Eind* [2007] ECR I-10719; Cases C-378–80/07 *Angelidaki and ors* v *Organismos Nomarchiadi Aftodiikisi Rethimnis and anor* [2009] ECR I-3071, at para. 51; Case C-382/08 *Neukirchinger* v *Bezirkshautpmannschaft Grieskirchen* [2011] ECR I-139, at para. 41.

771   Case C-412/96 *Kainuun Liikenne* v *Pohjolan Liikenne* [1998] ECR I-5141, at paras 21–4; Case C-58/98 *Corsten* [2000] ECR I-7919, at para. 24; Cases C-482 and 493/01 *Orfanopoulos and ors* v *Land Baden-Württemberg* [2004] ECR I-5257, at para. 42; Cases C-378–80/07 *Angelidaki, ibid.*; Case C-115/08 *Land Oberösterreich* v *ČEZ* [2009] ECR I-10265.

772   Case C-420/06 *Jager* v *Amt für Landwirtschaft Bützow* [2008] ECR I-1315, at paras 48–58; Case C-515/07 *Vereniging Noordelijke Land- en Tuinbouw Organisatie* v *Staatssecretaris van Financiën* [2009] ECR I-839, at paras 29–40.

Assuming the reference to have come from a court or tribunal of a member **5.132** state, the Court of Justice may not question the competency of the action in the main proceedings or whether the national court is properly constituted or otherwise acting outwith its jurisdiction as a matter of national law,[773] nor may it question the decision to refer.[774] It must respond, save in the exceptional circumstances where:

- the matter falls clearly outwith its jurisdiction *ratione materiae*;[775]
- the question referred is too vague;[776]
- the reference amounts to an abuse of process as the questions are hypothetical or disclose no real legal dispute;[777]
- the questions asked bear no relation to the subject matter of the dispute;[778] and/or

---

773 Case 65/81 *Reina and Reina* v *Landeskreditbank Baden-Württemburg* [1982] ECR 33; Case C-116/00 *Criminal proceedings against Laguillaumie* [2000] ECR I-4979; Case C432/05 *Unibet (London) and anor* v *Justitiekanslern* [2007] ECR I-2271, at para. 33; Case C-550/09 *Criminal proceedings against E and F* [2010] ECR I-6213, at paras 34–6.

774 Case 26/62 *Algemene Transport- en Expeditie Onderneming van Gend en Loos* v *Nederlandse Administratie der Belastingen* [1963] ECR 1; Case C-415/93 *Union Royal Belge des Sociétés de Football Association and ors* v *Bosman* [1995] ECR I-4921; Case C-326/00 *Idryma Koinonikon Asfaliseon* v *Ioannidis* [2003] ECR I-1703.

775 Case C-253/94P *Roujansky* v *Council* [1995] ECR I-7; Case C-346/94 *City of Glasgow District Council* v *Kleinwort Benson* [1995] ECR I-615; Case C-291/96 *Criminal proceedings against Grado and Bashir* [1997] ECR I-5531; Case C-321/97 *Andersson and Wåkerås-Andersson* v *Svenska Staten* [1999] ECR I-3551; Case C-24/02 *Marseille Fret* v *Seatrano Shipping Co.* [2002] ECR I-3383; Case C-302/06 *Koval'ský* v *Mesto Prešov and ors* [2007] ECR I-11*; Case C-186/07 *Club Náutico de Gran Canaria* v *Comunidad Autónoma de Canarias* [2008] ECR I-60*; Case C-104/08 *Kurt* v *Bürgermeister der Stadt Wels* [2008] ECR I-97*; Case C-287/08 *Savia and ors* v *Ministero dell'Istruzione, dell'Università e della Ricerca and ors* [2008] ECR I-136*; Cases C-267 and 268/10 *Rossius and Collard* v *État belge – Service public fédéral Finances*, order of 23 May 2011, not yet reported (see 14.119 below, n. 671 and accompanying text). There may be a temporal element, the Court lacking jurisdiction because the Union law it is invited to interpret does not apply *ratione temporis*: Case C-324/04 *Criminal proceedings against Vajnai* [2005] ECR I-8577; Case C-302/04 *Ynos* v *Varga* [2006] ECR I-371; Case C-261/05 *Lakép and ors* v *Komárom-Esztergom Megyei Közigazgatási Hivatal* [2006] ECR I-20*.

776 Case C-157/92 *Pretore di Genova* v *Banchero* (Banchero I) [1993] ECR I-1085; Case C-387/93 *Criminal proceedings against Benchero* (Banchero II) [1995] ECR I-4663; Case C-116/00 *Criminal proceedings against Laguillaumie* [2000] ECR I-4979; Case C-75/04 *Ministerie van Financiën* v *Hanssens and ors*, order of 21 January 2005, unreported; Case C-237/04 *Enrisorse* v *Sotacarbo* [2006] ECR I-2843.

777 Case 104/79 *Foglia* v *Novello* (No. 1) [1980] ECR 745; Case 244/80 *Foglia* v *Novello* (No. 2) [1981] ECR 3045; Case C-83/91 *Meilicke* v *ORGA Meyer* [1992] ECR I-4871; Case C-111/94 *Job Centre Co-op* [1995] ECR I-3361; Case C-86/00 *HSB-Wohnbau* [2001] ECR I-5353; Case C-153/00 *Criminal proceedings against der Weduwe* [2002] ECR I-11319; Case C-318/00 *Bacardi-Martini* v *Newcastle United Football Co.* [2003] ECR I-905; cf. Case C-491/01 *R* v *Secretary of State for Health, ex parte British American Tobacco and anor* [2002] ECR I-11453; Case C-144/04 *Mangold* v *Helm* [2005] ECR I-9981. There are procedures in Scotland, Wales and Northern Ireland whereby a reference may be made by the Lord Advocate, Advocate General, Attorney-General or Counsel General (as appropriate) to the Supreme Court on the constitutional competence of the Parliament/Assembly to enact a bill (Scotland Act 1998, s. 33; Northern Ireland Act 1998, s. 11; Government of Wales Act 2006, s. 99), with provision for reference from the Supreme Court to the Court of Justice should it entail a point of Union law (ss. 34, 12 and 100, respectively). *Quaere* whether this is a 'legal dispute' susceptible to an art. 267 reference.

778 Case 286/88 *Falcolia Angelo* v *Comune di Pavia* [1990] ECR I-191; Case C-343/90 *Laurenço Dias* v *Director da Alfândega do Porto* [1992] ECR I-4673; Case C-83/91*Meilicke* v *ORGA Meyer, ibid.*; Case C-297/93 *Grau-Hupka* v *Stadtgemeinde Bremen* [1994] ECR I-5535; Case C-35/99 *Criminal proceedings against Arduino*

- the referring court has failed to provide sufficient information as to the factual and legal background to the case to enable the Court adequately to identify the issues.

5.133 This final condition in particular has seen the Court become increasingly strict over the years, so that it now says:

Concerning the information that must be provided to the Court in the context of a reference for a preliminary ruling, it should be noted that that information does not serve only to enable the Court to provide answers which will be of use to the national court; it must also enable the Governments of the Member States, and other interested parties, to submit observations in accordance with Article 23 of the Statute of the Court of Justice. For those purposes, according to settled case-law, it is firstly necessary that the national court should define the factual and legislative context of the questions it is asking or, at the very least, explain the factual circumstances on which those questions are based. Secondly, the referring court must set out the precise reasons why it was unsure as to the interpretation of Community law and why it considered it necessary to refer questions to the Court for a preliminary ruling. In consequence, it is essential that the referring court provide at the very least some explanation of the reasons for the choice of the Community provisions which it requires to be interpreted and of the link it establishes between those provisions and the national legislation applicable to the dispute in the main proceedings.[779]

[2002] ECR I-1529; Cases C-430 and 431/99 *Inspecteur van de Belastingdienst Douane, Rotterdam* v *Sea-Land Service and Nedlloyd Lijnen* [2002] ECR I-5235; Case C-318/00 *Bacardi-Martini, ibid.*; Case C-293/03 *My* v *Office National des Pensions* [2004] ECR I-12013; Case C-222/04 *Ministero dell'Economia e delle Finanze* v *Cassa di Risparmio di Firenze and ors* [2006] ECR I-289; Case C-500/06 *Corporación Dermoestética* v *To Me Group Advertising Media* [2008] ECR I-5785; Case C-3/10 *Affatato* v *Azienda Sanitaria Provinciale di Cosenza*, [2010] ECR I-121; Case C-310/10 *Ministerul Justiției și Libertăților Cetățenești* v *Agafiței and ors*, judgment of 7 July 2011, not yet reported. The Court of Justice may, but need not, call upon the referring court to explain (provide 'clarification') why it requires an answer to the questions referred in order to resolve the dispute before it; RP Court of Justice, art. 101; see e.g., *Interflora and anor* v *Marks and Spencer and anor* [2010] EWHC 925 (Ch), [2010] All ER (D) 216, in which Arnold J says (at para. 7) that he 'regard[s] the request for clarification as a helpful step in the dialogue between the Court of Justice and the national courts', but also recorded (at paras 8–9) that the Court of Justice could be more helpful in the documents and information it provides.

779 Cases C-338 etc./04 *Criminal proceedings against Placanica and ors* [2007] ECR I-1891, at para. 34; Case C-42/07 *Liga Portuguesa de Futebol Profissional and anor* v *Departamento de Jogos da Santa Casa da Misericórdia de Lisboa* [2009] ECR I-7633, at para. 40 (with slight differences). For earlier formulations to the same effect see Case C-320/90 *Telemarsicabruzzo* v *Circostel* [1993] ECR I-393; Case C-157/92 *Pretore di Genova* v *Banchero* [1993] ECR I-1085; Case C-386/92 *Monin Automobiles – Maison du Deux-Roues* (No. 1) [1993] ECR I-2049; Case C-378/93 *La Pyramide* [1994] ECR I-3999; Case C-176/96 *Lehtonen and anor* v *Fédération Royale Belge des Sociétés de Basket-ball* [2000] ECR I-2681; Case C-190/02 *Viacom Outdoor* v *Giotto Immobilier* [2002] ECR I-8289. The requirement is of particular importance in the area of competition in which legal and factual situations are often complex (Case C-250/06 *United Pan-Europe Communications Belgium and ors* v *État belge* [2007] ECR I-11135, at para. 20) and in which it is 'essential ... to impose particularly stringent criteria'; Case C-231/03 *Consorzio Aziende Metano* v *Comune di Cingia de' Botti* [2005] ECR I-7287, *per* A-G Stix-Hackl at para. 16 of her opinion.

Notwithstanding a presumption of relevance of a question of interpretation,[780] **5.134** the Court rejects (as inadmissible, by reasoned opinion) unsubstantiated references increasingly and is increasingly terse in doing so. It is therefore prudent to follow the (useful) guidance issued by the Court as to the form of a reference.[781] An issue of inadmissibility arises most frequently in references seeking interpretative assistance from the Court, but the criteria apply equally, *mutatis mutandis*, in references on the validity of a Union measure,[782] even though it may be a question upon which, depending upon the answer, the Court alone has jurisdiction to rule.[783] As this may result in a *déni de justice*, presumably it would be slower to reject such a reference. Whilst it is thought generally desirable that questions of fact are agreed or settled prior to a reference being made, which may have relevance for both its interpretation and admissibility, this may not always be possible, for example where national procedural rules require the national court to assess questions of evidence and of law simultaneously at the stage of deliberation, and a reference will not be rebuffed on that ground alone.[784] Cases turned away by the Court for inadmissibility sometimes, 'like a boomerang', come back to it.[785]

Generally a member state may adopt no rule which would limit the absolute **5.135** discretion of any court to seek a reference. Thus, the '*Rheinmühlen I* principle': a national rule that lower courts are bound on points of law by judgments of a superior court cannot deprive the former of power to refer to the Court of Justice questions on the interpretation of Union law involving such judgments;[786] and its corollary: the lower court must be free to depart from them when it finds, in light of a ruling of the Court of Justice, that the superior court is wrong as a matter of Union law.[787] This constitutes 'an important endorsement of the normative force of European Union law, ... thereby endowed ... with the capacity to take precedence over a judgment of a superior court whose case-law was binding on inferior courts'.[788] This is the reason for the express

---

780   Cases C-94 etc./04 *Cipolla and ors* v *Fazari and ors* [2006] ECR I-11421, at para. 26; Case C-379/05 *Amurta* v *Inspecteur van de Belastingdienst/Amsterdam* [2007] ECR I-9569, at para. 64; Case C-158/08 *Agenzia Dogane Ufficio delle Dogane di Trieste* v *Pometon* [2009] ECR I-4695, at para. 13.

781   Information Note on References by National Courts for a Preliminary Ruling [2011] OJ C160/1, paras 20–5.

782   Case C-344/04 *R (International Air Transport Association and anor)* v *Department for Transport* [2006] ECR I-403, at paras 24–5.

783   See 5.140 below.

784   Case C-52/09 *Konkurrensverket* v *TeliaSonera Sverige* [2011] ECR I-527.

785   Cases C-468 etc./06 *Sot. Lélos Kai Sia and ors* v *Glaxosmithkline Farmakeftikon Proïonton* [2008] ECR I-7139, *per* A-G Ruiz-Jarabo Colomer, at para. 1 of his opinion.

786   Case 166/73 *Rheinmühlen-Düsseldorf* v *Einfuhr- und Vorratsstelle für Getreide und Futtermittel* [1974] ECR 33.

787   Case C-173/09 *Elchinov* v *Natsionalna zdravnoosiguritelna kasa*, [2010] ECR I-8889, at para. 32; Case C-396/09 *Interedil* v *Fallimento Interedil and anor*, judgment of 20 October 2011, not yet reported.

788   Case C-173/09 *Elchinov*, *ibid.*, *per* A-G Cruz Villalón at para. 20 of his opinion.

statutory authority and direction in the United Kingdom to do so,[789] lower courts otherwise being bound by a strict rule of obedience to (bad) precedent. The principle extends to precluding a procedural rule requiring a reference to a constitutional court for consideration of constitutional compatibility of a national law insofar as any priority nature adhering to that procedure would have the effect of hindering, even temporarily, any other national court from referring, as it sees fit, the (Union elements of the) case to the Court of Justice.[790]

5.136 The courts in some member states have found the discretion of all national courts so unfettered that a decision to refer cannot in any circumstances be reviewed.[791] However, article 267 does not of itself preclude the availability, if it exists in national law, of a remedy by which a decision to refer may be varied or set aside by a superior court. But, once launched, the referring court alone has the power to recall or modify the reference:

> [I]t is for the referring court to draw the proper inferences from a judgment delivered on an appeal against its decision to refer and, in particular, to come to a conclusion as to whether it is appropriate to maintain the reference for a preliminary ruling, or to amend it or to withdraw it.[792]

It may therefore persevere with the reference even in the face of disapproval of a superior court and irrespective of any national rule to the contrary – this a proposition, it must be said, which makes light of the serious difficulties to which it inevitably gives rise[793] – for it is an autonomous jurisdiction conferred upon it by the Treaties,[794] and the Court of Justice, in the interests of clarity and legal certainty,[795] remains seised of the case. Still, the applicability of national procedural remedies creates a degree of variable geometry in the use of article 267. In *Cartesio*, for example, the issue was the law of civil procedure in

---

789   European Communities Act 1972, s. 3.
790   Cases C-188 and 189/10 *Melki and Abdeli* [2010] ECR I-5667.
791   See, in Italy: owing to l. 13 marzo 1958, no. 204, sulla ratifica dei Protocolli sui privilegi ed immunità e sullo Statuto della Corte di Guistizia, art. 3 and Codice di Procedura Civile, art. 279; in Germany (for the financial courts): BFH, 27. Januar 1981, BStBl. 1981 II S. 324; in Ireland: *Campus Oil Ltd* v *Minister for Industry and Energy* [1983] IR 82 (SC); in Belgium: Cour d'appel de Bruxelles, arrêt du 5 mars 1999, no. 322/96. In Austria it, or a native litigiousness, may explain in part a remarkable enthusiasm for art. 267 references; see Table 5.1.
792   Case C-210/06 *CARTESIO Oktató és Szolgáltató* [2008] ECR I-9641, at para. 96. *CARTESIO* is a more sophisticated gloss on *Rheinmühlen II* (Case 146/73 *Rheinmühlen-Düsseldorf* v *Einfuhr- und Vorratsstelle für Getreide und Futtermittel* [1974] ECR 139) which suggested that an order for reference could not be contested.
793   See e.g., *Højesteret*, dom af 11. februar 2010 (*Skatteministeriet mod Lady & Kid m.fl.*), U2010.1389H, finding the *CARTESIO* rule depriving an appellate court of the power to set aside or modify a judgment of a lower court with binding effect to be incompatible with the Danish system of judicial redress and hierarchy – implicitly, that it deprives an appeal of its very substance and purpose.
794   Case C-210/06 *CARTESIO*, n. 792 above, at para. 95.
795   *Ibid.* at paras 89, 97. This is now codified in RP Court of Justice, art. 100.

Hungary, which provides a general right of appeal against a decision to refer but permits appeal against a decision dismissing a request for a reference only from a second instance court or, exceptionally and by leave, an appeal on a point of law to the *Legfelsőbb Bíróság* (supreme court).[796] In England the Court of Appeal has set aside an order of the High Court making a reference because, there being no reasonable doubt as to the correct interpretation of Community law (which could be determined 'with complete confidence'), it was unnecessary to seek a ruling from the Court of Justice;[797] it said subsequently that if a provision of Community law is 'perfectly clear, ... it is not only not necessary but also inappropriate to trouble the ECJ with it'[798] and, stronger still, where 'the European jurisprudence gives only one answer ... I do not think that a reference is required, or permissible';[799] following *Cartesio*, the references would now remain alive unless and until recalled by the High Court. In Scotland, the decision of a sheriff to refer may be set aside on appeal but only if his exercise of discretion was 'plainly wrong';[800] even then if he disagrees he may (again, *Cartesio*) decline to withdraw it. The very existence of an appeal or review procedure creates (variable) time constraints: in Italy, for example, a court having determined to make a reference, it is transmitted to the Court of Justice 'immediately',[801] whilst in the United Kingdom it must wait (sometimes a considerable period of time) until an application to appeal is refused or time-barred, or the appeal determined.[802] In fact it is not clear beyond argument that the appellate jurisdiction of a higher court is *Cartesio*-disabled (the judgment referring to 'whether it is appropriate *to maintain* the reference ... or to withdraw it')[803] where the appeal is determined (and, say, the lower court decision to refer set aside) before the reference is lodged with the Court of Justice.

A reference may be withdrawn, in whole or in part,[804] without objection or even scrutiny from the Court of Justice,[805] but only by the referring court. In **5.137**

---

796   1952. évi III. törvény a Polgári perrendtartásról szóló, 155/A. §-ának (3), 249/A. § and 270. §.

797   *R v International Stock Exchange of the United Kingdom and the Republic of Ireland, ex parte Else* [1993] 1 All ER 420; cf. *Boehringer Ingelheim and anor v Swingward and ors* [2000] EuLR 660 (CA).

798   *Liu and ors v Secretary of State for the Home Department* [2007] EWCA Civ 1275, [2007] All ER (D) 381, *per* Buxton LJ at para. 27.

799   *Poole and ors v HM Treasury* [2007] EWCA Civ 1020, [2008] 1 All ER (Comm) 1132, *per* Buxton LJ at para. 56.

800   *Procurator Fiscal, Elgin v Cowie and Wood* 1991 SLT 401 (J). See also *Pigs Marketing Board (Northern Ireland) v Redmond* [1978] NI 73, in which the Northern Ireland Court of Appeal refused (on case stated) to interfere with a decision of a resident magistrate to refer a case to the Court of Justice.

801   L. 13 marzo 1958, no. 204, n. 791 above, art. 3.

802   CPR, r. 68.3(3); Criminal Procedure Rules, r. 75.3(2)(b); RC 65.5(2); Act of Adjournal (Consolidation) 1988, s. 6.5(2)(c); Sheriff Court Ordinary Cause Rules, r. 68.5(2).

803   Case C-210/06 *CARTESIO*, n. 792 above, at para. 96 (emphasis added).

804   Case C-3/90 *Bernini v Minister van Onderwijs en Wetenschappen* [1992] ECR I-1071, at para. 11.

805   Case 106/77 *Amministrazione delle Finanze dello Stato v Simmenthal* [1978] ECR 629, at para. 10.

England the authority is that this power should be exercised only when it is manifest that the reference no longer has (or ever had) any useful purpose, and only if the court is (re)constituted as that which originally referred the question;[806] if the law has been made clear by a supervening judgment of the Court of Justice such that the question asked could now be resolved by the national judge 'with complete confidence', this might extend to a duty to withdraw the reference.[807] The High Court has considered whether it has the power (under CPR r. 3.1(7)) to vary an order for reference once sealed, did not say unequivocally that it does not, but clearly set its heart against it.[808] Where a reference has (according to one of the parties) become devoid of purpose the Court will still respond so long as it is not withdrawn by the referring court and so long as the main proceedings remain alive.[809]

5.138 The absolute discretion of a court to refer is subject to two exceptions only.

5.139 First, where a question of interpretation or validity is at issue before a national court or tribunal from which there is no appeal, that court or tribunal *must* refer the question to the Court of Justice.[810] The purpose of this duty is to seek to ensure that no authoritative body of national case law which is not in accordance with Union law comes into existence in any member state;[811] there is debate as to exactly which courts or tribunals it applies.[812] The duty is tempered by a recognition by the Court of Justice that it ceases to apply where the matter in question has already been decided by the Court of Justice (*acte éclairé*)[813] or the correct interpretation of Union law is so obvious as to leave no scope for any

---

806 *Royscot Leasing* v *Commissioners of Customs and Excise* [1999] 1 CMLR 903 (CA).

807 *R* v *Secretary of State for Defence, ex parte Perkins* [1998] IRLR 508 (QBD).

808 *SAS Institute* v *World Programming* [2010] EWHC 3012 (Ch), [2010] All ER (D) 243.

809 Case C-148/10 *Express Line* v *Belgisch Instituut voor Postdiensten Telecommunicatie*, judgment of 13 October 2011, not yet reported; RP Court of Justice, art. 100.

810 TFEU, art. 267, 3rd para.

811 Case 107/86 *Hoffmann-La Roche* v *Centrafarm* [1977] ECR 957; Case C-337/95 *Parfums Christian Dior* v *Evora* [1997] ECR I-6013.

812 That is, whether it applies only to courts against whose decision there is *never* a right of recourse (the 'abstract theory'), or also to courts against whose decision there is no (or there is unlikely to be) right of recourse in the instant case (the 'concrete theory'). Lord Denning MR (and British courts generally) clearly favour the former approach (*Bulmer* v *Bollinger* [1974] Ch. 401 at 420 (CA)), the Court of Justice implicitly the latter (Case 6/64 *Costa* v *ENEL* [1964] ECR 585). Where there exists a possibility of final appeal to the highest national court by (discretionary) leave of that court, the lower/intermediate court is not bound by an obligation to refer (Case C-99/00 *Criminal proceedings against Lyckeskog* [2002] ECR I-4839; Case C-210/06 *CARTESIO Oktató és Szolgáltató* [2008] ECR I-9641); but implicitly the highest court is bound to grant leave if it is sought, and it will in its turn be bound to refer (*Lyckeskog*). Owing to the urgency of the proceedings, the duty to refer does not extend to interlocutory proceedings for an interim order; Case 107/76 *Hoffmann-La Roche* v *Centrafarm* [1977] ECR 957.

813 Cases 28–30/62 *da Costa en Schaake and ors* v *Nederlandse Belastingadministratie* [1963] ECR 31.

reasonable doubt (*acte clair*).[814] This licence is necessary for practical reasons: were, for example, the German *Bundesfinanzhof* alone, never mind all federal courts, to cleave loyally to the letter of article 267, the Court of Justice would be swamped with references. It is for the national court alone to determine whether the correct application of Union law is *acte clair* and so elect to refrain from referring to the Court of Justice a question concerning the interpretation of Union law which has been raised before it,[815] but, in accordance with the *CILFIT* criteria, it is a discretion to be used sparingly; as Lord Hoffmann said in the House of Lords:

> I think [a proposed outcome] is correct. But we have been shown two contrary opinions which must be entitled to respect ... [I]n the light of these two observations, I find it impossible to say that the view which I would otherwise have formed is *acte clair*.[816]

Latterly there has developed (in some member states at least) a convention that courts of final instance declining to submit a reference to the Court of Justice justify that decision.[817] There are problems where the national system recognises a final instance remedy residing in the constitutional court but the

---

814   Case 283/81 *CILFIT* v *Ministero della Sanità* [1982] ECR 3415, in which the Court set out the questions a national judge ought to ask before satisfying him or herself that the matter is *clair*; Case C-495/03 *Intermodal Transports* v *Staatssecretaris van Financiën* [2005] ECR I-8151.

815   Case C-340/99 *TNT Traco* v *Poste Italiane and ors* [2001] ECR I-4109, at para. 35; Case C-495/03 *Intermodal Transports*, *ibid.*, at para. 37.

816   *Marks & Spencer* v *HM Commissioners of Customs and Excise* [2005] UKHL 53, [2005] All ER (D) 442, at paras 11 and 13 of his speech. For other *dicta* from the Supreme Court on when it is (in its view) absolved from the duty to refer, because the issue of Union law is either *éclairé* or *clair* (or both), see *Henn and Darby* v *DPP* [1981] AC 850; *Garland* v *British Rail Engineering* [1983] 2 AC 751; *Freight Transport Assn and ors* v *London Boroughs Transport Committee* [1991] 1 All ER 915, *per* Lord Templeman at 927–8 (notwithstanding overruling a unanimous Court of Appeal on the Community law point); *Consorzio del Prosciutto di Parma* v *Asda Stores and ors* [2001] UKHL 7, [2001] 1 CMLR 1103; *Optident and anor* v *Secretary of State for Trade and Industry and anor* [2001] UKHL 32, [2001] All ER (D) 320; *Three Rivers District Council and ors* v *Governor and Company of the Bank of England (No. 3)* [2003] 2 AC 1, *per* Lord Hope at 219 (notwithstanding dissent below); *Percy* v *Board of National Mission of the Church of Scotland* [2005] UKHL 73, [2006] 2 AC 28, *per* Lord Hope at para. 135; *Inntrepreneur Pub Company and ors* v *Crehan* [2006] UKHL 38, [2007] 1 AC 333, *per* Lord Hoffmann at para. 70; *Sempra Metals* v *HM Commissioners of Inland Revenue and anor* [2007] UKHL 34, [2008] 1 AC 561, *per* Lord Nicholls at para. 131 and Lord Walker at paras 159–61; *R (Countryside Alliance and ors)* v *HM Attorney General and anor* [2007] UKHL 52, [2008] 1 AC 719, per Lord Bingham at paras 31, 35, Lord Hope at paras 66–73, 82–3, 85–8 and Lord Brown at para. 165; *Office of Fair Trading* v *Abbey National and ors* [2009] UKSC 6, [2010] 1 AC 689, *per* Lord Walker at paras 48–50, Lord Mance at paras 115–17 and Lord Neuberger at para. 120 (overruling a unanimous Court of Appeal); *R (ZO (Somalia))* v *Secretary of State for the Home Department* [2010] UKSC 36, [2010] 4 All ER 649, *per* Lord Kerr at paras 50–1; *Patmalniece* v *Secretary of State for Work and Pensions* [2011] UKSC 11, [2011] 3 All ER 1, *per* Lord Walker at para. 81; *Bloomsbury International and ors* v *Sea Fish Industry Authority and anor* [2011] UKSC 25, [2011] 4 All ER 721, *per* Lord Mance at para. 51. On the view of the High Court of Justiciary see *Orru and Stewart* v *HM Advocate* 1998 SCCR 59; *Jardine* v *Crowe (PF Hamilton)* 1999 SCCR 52. For the federal courts in Germany see BVerfG, 9. Januar 2001 (*Nichtvorabentscheidungsersuchen des BVerwG*), NJW 2001, 1267; for the Irish Supreme Court, *Martin* v *An Bord Pleanála* [2007] IESC 23, [2008] 1 IR 336.

817   In the United Kingdom a 2003 practice direction requires that, if leave to appeal is sought from the Supreme Court in a petition which includes a contention that Union law is involved, and is refused, the Court must give

constitutional court is barred from making a reference because, owing to peculiarities in its jurisdiction, it is not a court or tribunal within the meaning of article 267.[818]

5.140   Secondly, where the question concerns the validity of a Union act, the Court of Justice alone has jurisdiction definitively to declare that act invalid[819] – a 'prerogative [which] is an integral part of the competence of the Court of Justice'.[820] This is because the requirement of uniformity which is the corner-stone of article 267

> is particularly vital where the validity of an act of European Union law is in question. Differences between courts of the Member States as to the validity of acts of European Union law would be liable to jeopardise the very unity of the European Union legal order and to undermine the fundamental requirement of legal certainty.[821]

In consequence, a national court (*any* national court, not only a court of final instance) may satisfy itself that the act is lawful and so refuse to refer the plea of

---

additional reasons; House of Lords, Practice Directions and Standing Orders applicable to Civil Appeals, 2007–08 edition, direction 34.2; see Appellate Committee, 38th Report (2002–03): Petitions for leave to appeal: reasons for the refusal of leave (HL Paper 89); and now Supreme Court Rules 2009, rule 42(1). Following the initiation of enforcement proceedings against Sweden owing to an alleged lack of enthusiasm on the part of the the supreme courts (*Högsta domstolen* and *Regeringsrätten* (now *Högsta förvaltningsdomsto-len*)) for art. 267 (see n. 305 above), the rules of judicial procedure were amended so as to require that reasons be given where the court dismisses an appeal without referring to the Court of Justice when a party has sought it; Lag (2006:502) med vissa bestämmelser om förhandsavgörande från Europeiska unionens domstol. The Austrian, Czech and German constitutional courts have all set aside judgments of courts of last instance (respectively the *Bundesvergabeamt*, the *Nejvyšší správní soud* (supreme administrative court)) and the *Bundesarbeitsgericht* for failure to refer questions to the Court of Justice, having failed to consider the duty to do so and having failed to justify not doing so, as a denial of the right to a 'statutory judge' (*gesetzlicher Richter/zákonného soudce*) as guaranteed by their respective constitutions (art. 83(2) B-VG; § 101 I GG) or, for the Czechs, a Charter of Fundamental Rights; see VfGH, 11. Dezember 1995, B2300/95, VfSlg 14390/1995; II. ÚS 1009/08 ze dne 8. leden 2009 (*Obecne Soudy – Řízení o předběžné otázce*); BVerfG, 25. Februar 2010, NJW 2010, 1268.

818   See e.g., Corte Cost., 15 dicembre 1995, n. 536 (*Massagero Servizi ed altri c. Ufficio del registro di Padova*), Giur.Cost. 1995, 4459; Pl ÚS [České Republiky] 50/04 ze dne 17. března 2006, (*kvót v odvět cukru*), at Part A-1, paras 1–3. The difficulty in Italy at least seems now to have been overcome, the Corte Costituzionale having lodged its first reference with the Court of Justice in 2008 and the latter not objecting: Case C-169/08 *Presidente del Consiglio dei Ministri* v *Regione autonoma della Sardegna* [2009] ECR I-10821. Long thought to be unenthusiastic and never having requested a ruling, the *Bundesverfassungsgericht* seems to be prepared to do so at least where the question of the validity of a Directive is before it; BVerfG, 2. März 2010 (*Telekommuni-kationsverkehrsdaten*), BVerfGE 125, 260

819   Case 314/85 *Foto-Frost* v *Hauptzollamt Lübeck-Ost* [1987] ECR 4199. This was made clear in the ECSC Treaty (art. 41) but not in the EC, the Euratom or the present Treaties.

820   Court of Justice, Discussion document on certain aspects of the accession of the EU to the ECHR, 5 May 2010, unpublished, para. 8.

821   Case C-366/10 *R (Air Transport Association of America and ors)* v *Secretary of State for Energy and Climate Change*, judgment of 21 December 2011, not yet reported, at para. 47.

illegality raised before it;[822] but if it cannot or does not – if it 'has doubts about the validity of a Community measure';[823] if it 'considers that one or more arguments for invalidity ... are well founded';[824] if the issue is one which 'I cannot at present with complete confidence resolve myself. I have a real doubt about it';[825] or if there is 'a serious issue concerning the validity of' a Directive[826] – it must refer the question in order to trigger the exclusive jurisdiction of the Court to determine whether the act under review is unlawful. It should set out in the order for reference the reasons why it considers the reference to be appropriate.[827] Having referred, or having resolved to refer, a question on validity of a Union act, the national court may suspend *ad interim* national implementing measures based upon it, provided certain conditions are met;[828] a cross-undertaking or caution in damages may be ordered where appropriate.[829] Interim relief is the preserve of the courts: without judicial authority a national administrative body may not suspend the application of a Union measure.[830] The question of whether a member state may be restrained by injunction from introducing legislation giving effect to a Directive pending judgment in an invalidity reference, and if so whether Union or national tests ought to be applied, was discussed by the House of Lords in the United Kingdom[831] but not

---

822 Case C-344/04 *R (International Air Transport Association (IATA) and anor)* v *Department for Transport* [2006] ECR I-403, at paras 28–9.

823 Case 314/85 *Foto-Frost*, n. 819 above, *per* A-G Mancini at para. 9(1) of his opinion.

824 Case C-344/04 *IATA*, n. 822 above, at para. 30. The referring national court (the English High Court) had asked expressly which test or threshold ought to be applied, but the Court of Justice supplied no answer.

825 *Booker Aquaculture* v *Secretary of State for Scotland* 2000 SC 9, *per* the Lord President (Rodger) at 27.

826 *R (SCPM and ors)* v *Secretary of State for the Environment, Food and Rural Affairs* [2007] EWHC 2610 (Admin), [2008] EuLR 250, at para. 23.

827 Case C-344/04 *IATA*, n. 822 above. There is no guidance as to the correct course for a national court a validity reference from which has been rebuffed by the Court of Justice for vagueness or inadequate background, although it may be assumed that the Court of Justice would hesitate long before doing so. A related problem lies in the inadmissibility of a reference from a court of a non-member state (see 5.129 above): if the application of a Union act is a matter before such a court, and a question of its validity is raised, presumably the court could find it to be unlawful (applying Union tests) or inapplicable (applying its own public policy tests), and make an appropriate declaration. The Union could not object to the exercise of such a jurisdiction, but would not be required to recognise the declaration, which would be limited to the territorial jurisdiction of the court. In this context there is also an evident risk of divergence between the Court of Justice and the EFTA Court of Justice.

828 Cases 143/88 and C-92/89 *Zuckerfabriken Süderdithmarschen und Soest* v *Hauptzollämter Itzehoe und Paderborn* [1991] ECR I-415; Case C-465/93 *Atlanta Fruchthandelsgesellschaft and ors* v *Bundesamt für Ernährung und Forstwirtschaft* [1995] ECR I-3761.

829 Case C-465/93 *Atlanta, ibid.*, at para. 45; Cases C-453 etc./03 *R (ABNA and ors)* v *Secretary of State for Health and ors* [2005] ECR I-10423, at para. 107; for an English example see *R (ABNA Ltd)* v *Secretary of State for Health and anor* [2003] EWHC 2420 (Admin), [2004] EuLR 88.

830 Cases C-453 etc./03 *ABNA, ibid.*

831 *R* v *Secretary of State for Health and ors, ex parte Imperial Tobacco and ors* [2001] 1 All ER 850. In that case an interim injunction had been pronounced by the High Court ([1999] All ER (D) 1185 (QBD)) but quashed by the Court of Appeal ([2000] 1 All ER 572); no definitive answer was required of the House of Lords because shortly after an appeal was lodged the Directive was annulled in parallel proceedings raised under art. 263 (Case C-376/98 *Germany* v *Parliament and Council* (Tobacco Advertising) [2000] ECR I-8419).

referred to the Court of Justice and so not authoritatively answered. It nevertheless appears that a court is competent to make a reference as to the validity of a
Union act and restrain its implementation *ad interim* even if it has yet to
produce legal effects (a Regulation which is not yet in force,[832] or a Directive
the time limit for implementation of which having not yet passed,[833] even
where no national legislation, even in draft, has been adopted)[834] if, according
to the English courts, 'the balance is in favour',[835] it is on balance 'just and
convenient' to do so[836] or there is 'significant risk [of] serious damage' to the
petitioner;[837] or, according to the Court of Justice, so long as there is a genuine
dispute in which the question of validity is competently raised.[838] This compares with a request for an interpretative ruling upon a Directive which, in the
absence of implementing measures and prior to final date for implementation,
is premature and so inadmissible.[839] The Court of Justice has no jurisdiction to
order interim measures in article 267 proceedings, that being a matter exclusively for the national court.[840]

(c)   Annulment (article 263 TFEU) and invalidity (article 267 TFEU) of Union legislation

5.141   As with article 277,[841] article 267 TFEU cannot be used to secure the
annulment (properly so-called) of a Union act, for it is immune from annulment
except under article 263 proceedings. A successful, indirect challenge to Union

---

832   Case C-306/93 *SMW Winzersekt v Land Rheinland-Pfalz* [1994] ECR I-5555; *R v Secretary of State for the Environment, Transport and the Regions, ex parte Omega Air* [2000] EuLR 254 (QBD); *R (International Air Transport Association (IATA) and anor) v Department of Transport* [2004] EWHC 1721 (Admin), [2004] EuLR 998.

833   Case C-491/01 *R v Secretary of State for Health, ex parte British American Tobacco* [2002] ECR I-11453; *R v Secretary of State for Health, ex parte Imperial Tobacco* [1999] EurLR 582 (QBD); *R (ABNA Ltd) v Secretary of State for Health and anor* [2003] EWHC 2420 (Admin), [2004] EuLR 88; *ABNA and ors v Scottish Ministers* [2004] EuLR 559 (OH); *IATA, ibid.*

834   Case C-491/01 *British American Tobacco, ibid.; Case C-308/06 R (International Association of Independent Tanker Owners (Intertanko) and ors) v Secretary of State for Transport [2008] ECR I-4057; Imperial Tobacco, ibid.*

835   *ABNA*, n. 833 above, at para. 77.

836   *Omega Air*, n. 832 above, at 260; *Imperial Tobacco*, n. 833 above, at 592.

837   *IATA*, n. 832 above, at 1000.

838   Case C-491/01 *British American Tobacco*, n. 833 above, at para. 40. In Case C-308/06 *Intertanko*, n. 834 above, it was accepted without qualification; para. 33.

839   Case C-165/98 *Mazzoleni v Inter Surveillance Assistance* [2001] ECR I-2189. The exception is where there exists legislation by which the member state makes it clear it intends the requirements of the Directive to be given effect; Cases C-261 and 299/07 *VTB-VAB and anor v Total Belgium and anor* [2009] ECR I-2949. But see Case C-119/09 *Société fiduciere nationale d'expertise comptable v Ministre du Budget, de Comptes publics et de la Fonction publique*, judgment of 5 April 2011, not yet reported, in which the Court considered whether an interpretative reference was premature in the light of the likelihood of the national law in force seriously compromising the effectiveness of a Directive's implementation come the time limit for it (as to which see 6.73 below), concluded that this was not likely, yet found the reference admissible because it, the Court, was not entitled to ask that question.

840   E.g., Case C-186/01R *Dory v Bundesrepublik Deutschland* [2001] ECR I-7823.

841   See 5.104 above.

legislation under article 267 (which, unlike article 263, may be made without limit of time) results rather in a declaration of 'invalidity' of the act. This means that it cannot be applied in the main proceedings, and creates a duty for the relevant institution to amend or repeal or otherwise correct the (invalid) act:

> [A]ny determination by the Community courts that a Community measure is unlawful, even when not made in the exercise of their jurisdiction under Article [263] to annul measures, is inherently liable to have repercussions on the conduct required of the institution that adopted the measure in question.

> Thus, in particular, it is settled case-law that when the Court rules, in proceedings under Article [267], that a measure adopted by a Community authority is invalid, its decision has the legal effect of requiring the competent Community institutions to take the necessary measures to remedy that illegality, as the obligation laid down in Article [266] in the case of a judgment annulling a measure applies in such a situation by analogy.[842]

But until the erring institution does so the act remains in existence and, **5.142** technically, applicable to other persons and circumstances. However, the Court of Justice has found that a declaration of invalidity in a preliminary ruling under article 267 has effect *erga omnes*,[843] and so may be relied upon by other persons and in other proceedings. In light of this, the practical difference between annulment (article 263) and invalidity (article 267) lies in the means by which the issue is raised rather than in the legal outcome. However, the full licence recognised in *CILFIT*[844] for interpretative references carries over no further into questions of validity: a national court may not determine a Union act to be invalid even if very similar to one invalidated by the Court in other proceedings.[845] As the purpose of its jurisdiction of invalidation under article 267 is to protect the rights of parties unable to seek redress under article 263, the Court has found it to be an abuse of process for a party which had *clear* title and interest to raise an action of annulment against a Union act under article 263, but failed to do so, subsequently to challenge its validity in national proceedings, and a reference made to assist in this purpose will be inadmissible,[846] even

---

842 Cases C-120 and 121/06P *Fabbrica italiana accumulatori motocarri Montecchio and anor* v *Council and Commission* [2008] ECR I-6513, at paras 122–3.

843 Case 66/80 *International Chemical Corporation* v *Amministrazione delle Finanze dello Stato* [1981] ECR 1191. Great care should be taken with this judgment, as the English text is misleading on this point.

844 Case 283/81 *CILFIT* v *Ministero della Sanità* [1982] ECR 3415; see 5.139 above.

845 Case C-461/03 *Gaston Schul* v *Minister van Landbouw, Natuur en Voedselkwaliteit* [2005] ECR I-10513. The question, and answer, were phrased so as to apply to courts of final instance, but must logically apply to all courts contemplating invalidation of a Union act.

846 Case C-188/92 *TWD Textilwerke Deggendorf* v *Germany* [1994] ECR I-833; Case C-178/95 *Wiljo* v *Belgium* [1997] ECR I-585; Case C-239/99 *Nachi Europe* v *Hauptzollamt Krefeld* [2001] ECR I-1197; Case C-241/01 *National Farmers' Union* v *Secrétariat Général du Gouvernement* [2002] ECR I-9079; Cases C-261 and 262/01 *Belgium* v *van Calster and ors* [2003] ECR I-12249, *per* A-G Jacobs at paras 52–9 of his opinion. But the party must have been 'undoubtedly' entitled (*TWD*; Case C-343/07 *Bavaria and Bavaria Italia* v *Bayerischer Brauerbund* [2009] ECR I-5491, at para. 40), 'obviously' entitled (Case C-241/95 *R* v *Intervention Board for*

though this requires the Court to pierce the veil of the reference. This would appear to bar a public authority from pleading the invalidity of a Union measure in any national proceedings, member states being privileged applicants under article 263 in all circumstances.

(d)   Temporal limitation of a preliminary ruling

5.143   As a general rule, a judgment of the Court under article 267 (upon either interpretation or validity) applies *ex tunc*:

> [T]he interpretation which, in the exercise of the jurisdiction conferred upon it by Article [267], the Court gives to a rule of Community law clarifies and defines, where necessary, the meaning and scope of that rule as it must be, or ought to have been, understood and applied from the time of its coming into force. In other words, a preliminary ruling does not create or alter the law, but is purely declaratory, with the consequence that in principle it takes effect from the date on which the rule interpreted entered into force.[847]

But the Court has borrowed (generously) from article 264 to assert the power, in an interpretative ruling, to limit its retrospective effect.[848] Such temporal limitation can be made only in the judgment making the ruling[849] and will be pronounced only in exceptional circumstances,

> where there was a risk of serious economic repercussions owing in particular to the large number of legal relationships entered into in good faith on the basis of rules considered to be validly in force and where it appeared that both individuals and national authorities had been led into adopting practices which did not comply with Community legislation by reason of objective, significant uncertainty regarding the

---

Agricultural Produce, ex parte Accrington Beef and ors [1996] ECR I-6699, at para. 15) or enjoy standing 'clear beyond doubt' (*Van Calster, per* A-G Jacobs at paras 53, 54 of his opinion; Case C-550/09 *Criminal proceedings against E and F* [2010] ECR I-6213, at para. 48) to raise an action under art. 263 before being estopped from raising the plea of illegality in art. 267 proceedings. Logically a court may not apply a declaration of invalidity pronounced in another judgment (which normally is the case by virtue of the *erga omnes* effect it exerts) to the advantage of such a party, but there is no authority on this. Nor is there authority as to whether the rule applies to criminal courts, so that a defendant is estopped from raising the invalidity of a Union measure as a defence to a criminal charge when he had not sought to challenge it under art. 263 where he had standing to do so; if this is the case it is contrary to principles of English law: *Boddington* v *British Transport Police* [1999] 2 AC 143 (HL).

847   Case C-2/06 *Willy Kempter* v *Hauptzollamt Hamburg-Jonas* [2008] ECR I-411, at para. 35; also Case 61/79 *Amministrazione delle Finanze dello Stato* v *Denkavit Italiana* [1980] ECR 1205; Case C-453/00 *Kühne and Heitz* v *Productschap voor Pluimvee en Eieren* [2004] ECR I-837, at para. 21.

848   See e.g., Case 43/75 *Defrenne* v *SABENA* (No. 2) [1976] ECR 455; Case 24/86 *Blaizot* v *University of Liège* [1988] ECR 379; Case 292/88 *Barber* v *Guardian Royal Exchange* [1990] ECR I-1889; Case C-163/90 *Administration des Douanes et Droits Indirects* v *Legros and ors* [1992] ECR I-4625; Case C-437/97 *Evangelischer Krankenhausverein Wien and anor* v *Abgabenberufungskommission Wien and anor* [2000] ECR I-1157; Case C-292/04 *Meilicke and ors* v *Finanzamt Bonn-Innenstadt* [2007] ECR I-1835, *per* A-G Stix-Hackl.

849   Case 309/85 *Barra* v *Belgium* [1988] ECR 355; Case C-163/90 *Legros, ibid.*; Case C-57/93 *Vroege* v *NCIV Instituut voor Volkshuisvesting* [1994] ECR I-4541; Case C-292/04 *Meilicke, ibid.*

implications of Community provisions, to which the conduct of other Member States or the Commission may even have contributed.[850]

Thus 'two essential elements must be fulfilled, namely that those concerned acted in good faith and there is a risk of serious difficulties'.[851] Applying article 264 'by analogy' and more aptly, if the question is one of the validity of a Union act, the Court may, having found and declared it to be invalid, declare all or some of its provisions to be (or more commonly, thitherto to have been: *ex nunc erga omnes*) operative.[852]

(e) Applying the ruling

A preliminary ruling delivered under article 267 is binding for the referring **5.144** national court, which must apply it in disposing of the main proceedings;[853] it 'conclusively determines a question or questions of Community law and is binding on the national court for the purposes of the decision to be given by it in the main proceedings'.[854] A court may re-refer the same question if it encounters difficulties in understanding or applying the ruling, where the factual or legal context of the dispute in the main proceedings has undergone significant changes or where other circumstances have come to light which might lead the Court of Justice to decide the matter differently.[855] However, there is

---

850 Case C-184/99 *Grzelczyk* v *Centre public d'aide sociale d'Ottignies-Louvaine-la-Neuve* [2001] ECR I-6193, at para. 53; Case C-209/03 *R (Bidar)* v *London Borough of Ealing and anor* [2005] ECR I-2119, at para. 69. Cf. Cases C-290 and 333/05 *Nádasdi and anor* v *Vám- és Pénzügyőrség Észak-Alföldi Regionális Parancsnoksága* [2006] ECR I-10115; Case C-292/04 *Meilicke*, n. 848 above. In *Meilicke* oral procedure was re-opened for consideration of the question of temporal effect, the case referred to the Grand Chamber and a second A-G's opinion sought; A-G Stix-Hackl considered the question at length, recommended that no temporal limitation be pronounced, and the Court followed her peremptorily. It is worth noting that the redoubtable Mr Meilicke has rejoined the fray yet again from beyond the grave: Case C-262/09 *Meilicke and ors* v *Finanzamt Bonn-Innenstadt*, judgment of 30 June 2011, not yet reported.

851 Case C-73/08 *Bressol and Chaverot and ors* v *Gouvernement de la Communauté française* [2010] ECR I-2735, at para. 91 and case law cited.

852 Case 109/79 *Maïseries de Beauce* v *ONIC* [1980] ECR 2883 (but see n. 857 below and accompanying text); Case 112/83 *Société des Producteurs de Maïs* v *Administration des Douanes* [1985] ECR 719; Case C-228/92 *Roquette Frères* v *Hauptzollamt Geldern* [1994] ECR I-1445; Cases C-92 and 93/09 *Volker and Markus Schecke and anor* v *Land Hessen*, [2010] ECR I-11063. For a useful overview of circumstances in which the Court has found justification see Case C-475/03 *Banca Popolare di Cremona* v *Agenzia Entrate Ufficio Cremona* [2006] ECR I-9373, *per* A-G Stix-Hackl at paras 132–4 of her opinion.

853 Case 52/76 *Benedetti* v *Munari* [1977] ECR 163; Case 69/85 *Wünsche Handelsgesellschaft* v *Germany* [1986] ECR 947; Case C-173/09 *Elchinov* v *Natsionalna zdravnoosiguritelna kasa*, [2010] ECR I-8889, at para. 29; Case C-396/09 *Interedil* v *Fallimento Interedil and anor*, judgment of 20 October 2011, not yet reported, at para. 36.

854 Case 69/85 *Wünsche, ibid.*, at para. 13.

855 Case 69/85 *Wünsche*, n. 853 above; Case C-466/00 *Kaba* v *Secretary of State for the Home Department* [2003] ECR I-2219; *Boehringer Ingelheim and ors* v *Dowelhurst and ors* [2004] EWCA Civ 129, [2004] EuLR 757, the response in Case C-348/04 *Boehringer Ingelheim and ors* v *Swingward and anor* [2007] ECR I-3391; *Marks & Spencer* v *HM Commissioners of Customs and Excise* [2005] UKHL 53, [2005] STC 1254, the response in Case C-309/06 *Marks & Spencer* v *HM Commissioners of Customs and Excise* [2008] ECR I-2283; Case C-478/07 *Budějovický Budvar* v *Rudolf Ammersin* [2009] ECR I-7221, at para. 50.

sometimes (wilful?) delay in applying a ruling[856] and there are still (rare) instances in which, in the view of the referring national court, the Court of Justice misapplied or exceeded its jurisdiction, so absolving it of the obligation to apply it. For example, in a series of references from French administrative courts on the validity of a number of 1976 agricultural Regulations, the Court of Justice found them to be invalid *and* limited the temporal effect of that declaration;[857] the referring courts refused to apply the second limb of the ruling because, not having asked the question, the Court of Justice had, in their view, no jurisdiction to give it, and they certainly no obligation to follow it.[858] They were upheld by the *Conseil d'Etat*.[859] More recently, the High Court in England refused to apply a preliminary ruling on the interpretation of a Directive on the ground that the Court of Justice had strayed into findings of fact (and findings inconsistent with those of the national court), had therefore exceeded its jurisdiction under article 267, and the High Court was, as a consequence, relieved of the obligation to apply the ruling.[860] And in 2012 the Czech *Ústavní Soud* (constitutional court) set aside a judgment of the *Nejvyšší správní soud* (supreme administrative court) which had reversed previous case law in accordance with a preliminary ruling it had requested from the Court of Justice – the *Ústavní Soud* finding that by refusing to hear submissions from it (the *Ústavní Soud*) in the course of its proceedings, the Court of Justice had abandoned the principle *audiatur et altera pars*, and the ruling was therefore *ultra vires*.[861]

5.145 This does not happen often – and in fact the High Court was overturned by the Court of Appeal.[862] Nor are these the only instances in which the Court takes a generous view of its own jurisdiction. For example, in *Brasserie du Pêcheur*:

> While, in the present cases, the Court cannot substitute its assessment for that of the national courts, which have sole jurisdiction to find the facts in the main proceedings

---

856 For example in 2004 the Court delivered a series of judgments on milk levies (Cases C-231 etc./00 *Cooperative Lattepiù and ors* v *Azienda di Stato per gli interventi nel mercato agricolo* [2004] ECR I-2869 and Cases C-480 etc./00 *Azienda Agricola Ettore Ribaldi and ors* v *Azienda di Stato per gli interventi nel mercato agricolo* [2004] ECR I-2949) which were referred by the *Tribunale amministrativo regionale del Lazio* but which, at the time of writing, appears still not to have decided the cases.

857 Case 109/79 *Maïseries de Beauce* v *ONIC* [1980] ECR 2883. On temporal limitation of preliminary rulings see immediately above.

858 E.g, Tribunal Administratif, Orléans, 23 février 1982, Rec p. 471. Other lower administrative courts did likewise.

859 CE, Sec, 26 juillet 1985 (*Office National Interprofessionnel des Céréales c/ Maïseries de la Beauce*), Rec p. 233.

860 *Arsenal Football Club* v *Reed* [2002] EWHC 2695 (Ch), [2003] 1 All ER 137; refusing to apply Case C-206/01 *Arsenal Football Club* v *Reed* [2002] ECR I-2219.

861 Pl. ÚS 5/12 ze dne 31. leden 2012 (*Slovenských Dúchochů*).

862 *Arsenal Football Club* v *Reed* [2003] EWCA Civ 696, [2003] 3 All ER 865.

and decide how to characterize the breaches of Community law at issue, it will be helpful to indicate a number of circumstances which the national courts might take into account.[863]

Alternatively,

the Court may, in a spirit of cooperation with national courts, provide it with all the guidance that it deems necessary.[864]

In the view of the Court this is legitimate in order to provide 'guidance'[865] or a 'satisfactory', 'helpful' or 'useful' answer to the referring court,[866] extending on occasion, but with increasing frequency, to consideration of Union law not addressed in the question[867] – even to the extent of saying, unabashedly,

[t]he fact that the national court has, formally speaking, worded the question referred for a preliminary ruling with reference to certain provisions of Community law does not preclude the Court from providing to the national court all the elements of interpretation which may be of assistance in adjudicating on the case pending before it, whether or not that court has referred to them in its questions,[868]

and so interpreting provisions of the Euratom Treaty when the referring court had asked only about the EC Treaty. Bolder, or more casual, still, when asked a simple question about the interpretation of article 49 TFEU in the context of Swiss lessors to an Austrian hunting lease, so nothing to do with article 49 and manifestly nothing to do with Union law, the Court replied:

---

863 Cases C-46 and 48/93 *Brasserie du Pêcheur* v *Germany* and *R* v *Secretary of State for Transport, ex parte Factortame* [1996] ECR I-1029, at para. 58.

864 Case C-49/07 *Motosykletistiki Omospondia Ellados (MOTOE)* v *Elliniko Dimosio* [2008] ECR I-4863, at para. 30; Case C-142/05 *Åklagaren* v *Mickelsson and Roos* [2009] ECR I-4273, at para. 41.

865 Case C-438/05 *International Transport Workers' Federation* v *Viking Line* [2007] ECR I-10779, at para. 85; Case C-49/07 *MOTOE, ibid.*; Case C-142/05 *Mickelsson and Roos, ibid.*

866 E.g., Case 20/87 *Ministère public* v *Gauchard* [1987] ECR 4879, at para. 5; Case C-6/01 *Associação Nacional de Operadores de Máquinas Recreativas and ors* v *Estado português* [2003] ECR I-8621, at para. 37; Case C-49/07 *MOTOE*, n. 864 above; Case C-349/07 *Sopropré – Organizações de Calçado* v *Fazenda Público* [2008] ECR I-10369, at para. 43; Case C-142/05 *Mickelsson and Roos*, n. 864 above; Case C-382/08 *Neukirchinger* v *Bezirkshauptmannschaft Grieskirchen*, [2011] ECR I-139, at para. 30.

867 Case 35/85 *Procureur de la République* v *Tissier* [1986] ECR 1207; Case C-265/01 *Criminal proceedings against Pansard and ors* [2003] ECR I-683; Case C-420/06 *Jager* v *Amt für Landwirtschaft Bützow* [2008] ECR I-1315, at para. 47; Case C-205/07 *Criminal proceedings against Gysbrechts and Santurel Inter* [2008] ECR I-9947; Case C-544/07 *Rüffler* v *Dyrektor Izby Skarbowej we Wrocławiu Ośrodek Zamiejscowy w Wałbrzychu* [2009] ECR I-3389; Case C-420/07 *Apostolides* v *Orams and Orams* [2009] ECR I-3571. The clearest example, which gave rise to the principle of exhaustion of intellectual property rights under art. 34 when no such question was asked (see 10.80 below), is probably Case 78/70 *Deutsche Grammophon* v *Metro* [1971] ECR 487. For a good example of the Court in effect overruling the national court on questions of fact see Case C-418/93 *Semeraro Casa Uno* v *Comune di Erbusco* [1996] ECR I-2975.

868 Case C-115/08 *Land Oberösterreich* v *ČEZ* [2009] ECR I-10265, at para. 81.

[T]he Treaty provisions on freedom of establishment cannot apply to a national of a non-member country such as the Swiss Confederation.

However, in order to provide the referring court with elements of interpretation which may be of use to it, the Court can consider provisions of the European Union legal order which the national court has not referred to in the question submitted for a preliminary ruling,[869]

and took it upon itself to interpret the provisions of the 1999 Swiss-Community agreement on the free movement of persons. This auto-generosity to respond to questions not asked, if in *its* view an answer is required in order for the referring court to resolve the dispute in the main proceedings, is said now by the Court to be a duty,[870] but it erodes the basic principle that it is for the national court to delimit and define the scope of the reference and so to bind the Court. It must therefore be for the referring court to decide whether or not the provisions thus interpreted are applicable to the instant case.[871] Yet in virtually all cases the national courts apply the ruling without murmur. The rare exception may be taken as a shot across the Court's bow, an occasional warning of the limits of its jurisdiction and a (re-)assertion of that of the national court.

(f) Exceptional preliminary ruling procedures

5.146 From the start the Euratom Treaty provided for preliminary rulings to the Court of Justice in terms identical to article 177 EEC;[872] with Lisbon article 267 is itself carried over to 'apply' to Euratom.[873] The ECSC Treaty contained an equivalent provision but on its text restricted to references on the validity of Community acts,[874] extended nonetheless (*contra legem?*) by the Court of Justice in 1990 to include questions on their interpretation,[875] yet, owing to the executive nature of the ECSC Treaty, little used. In addition, the Treaty of Amsterdam introduced two exceptional procedures applicable in the framework of one subject area.

5.147 First, the application of article 234 EC to seek preliminary rulings on the interpretation of, or the validity of acts adopted under, Title IV of that Treaty (visas, asylum, immigration and the free movement of persons) was moderated by article 68 EC: references could be made (and were required to be made) but only by national courts of final instance.[876] The formulation as to what was a

---

869 Case C-70/09 *Hengartner and Gasser* v *Landesregierung Vorarlberg* [2010] ECR I-7229, at paras 26, 27.
870 Case C-437/09 *AG2R Prévoyance* v *Beaudout Père et Fils*, judgment of 3 March 2011, not yet reported, at para. 26.
871 Case 35/85 *Tissier*, n. 867 above.
872 Euratom Treaty, art. 150 (repealed by Lisbon). See Case C-115/08 *ČEZ*, n. 868 above, at para. 84.
873 Euratom Treaty, art. 106a(1).
874 ECSC Treaty, art. 41.
875 Case 221/88 *European Coal and Steel Community* v *Acciaierie e Ferriere Busseni* [1990] ECR I-495.
876 EC Treaty, art. 68(1).

court of final instance was *verbatim* the same as that of article 234(3) and there is no indication that it ought to have meant something different, although where there was a dispute as to the finality of the jurisdiction of the referring court there seemed to be a presumption favouring admissibility.[877] A reference from a lower court was manifestly inadmissible.[878] This excluded articles 61–69 of the EC Treaty from the normal application of article 234, and may, it must be said, have led to real injustice.[879] Further, all jurisdiction of the Court was expressly ousted as regards any measure adopted under article 62(1) (concerning the abolition of controls of cross-frontier movement of persons) if it related to the maintenance of law and order and the safeguarding of internal security.[880] A question on interpretation or validity could be referred not only by (final) courts but by the Council, the Commission or a member state, any ruling so obtained not to apply to judgments of national courts which had become *res judicata*.[881]

Secondly, under article 35 of the pre-Lisbon TEU a national court could refer a **5.148** question on the validity or interpretation of certain measures adopted by authority of Title VI of that Treaty (police and judicial cooperation in criminal matters) or the validity or interpretation of any measure implementing them *but* only if and insofar as each member state expressly permitted its courts to do so.[882] Not only did this create a risk of differing interpretations of the measures amongst the member states, it had the effect of barring from judicial proceedings in a non-participating member state any plea of invalidity of these measures, for, as with Community legislation, that was a matter solely for the Court of Justice.[883] At the entry into force of the Lisbon Treaty declarations had been made by 19 member states,[884] of which one (Spain) had, as article 35 permitted, restricted the referral power to courts of final instance.[885] There was in no case a Treaty obligation to refer analogous to article 234(3) EC, but a declaration attached to the Amsterdam Final Act recognised the authority to

---

877 See e.g., Case C-175/06 *Tedesco v Tomasoni Fittings and anor* [2007] ECR I-7929, *per* A-G Kokott at paras 20–8 of her opinion; Case C-14/08 *Roda Golf & Beach Resort* [2009] ECR I-5439.

878 Case C-51/03 *Criminal proceedings against Georgescu* [2004] ECR I-3203; Case C-555/03 *Warbecq v Ryanair* [2004] ECR I-6041.

879 See e.g., Case C-45/03 *Commissario Generale di Polizia di Catania v Dem'Yanenko*, order of 18 March 2004, unreported, involving deportation of a suicidal third country national (so a Title IV matter) for failure to have applied timeously for a residence permit, the reference dismissed peremptorily for inadmissibility as coming from an inferior court (the *Tribunale di Catania*).

880 EC Treaty, art. 68(2).

881 *Ibid.* art. 68(3).

882 TEU (pre-Lisbon), art. 35(2)–(3).

883 See e.g., Case C-303/05 *Advocaten voor de Wereld v Leden van de Ministerraad* [2007] ECR I-3633.

884 That is, Belgium, Czech Republic, Germany, Greece, Spain, France, Italy, Cyprus, Latvia, Lithuania, Luxembourg, Hungary, the Netherlands, Austria, Portugal, Romania, Slovenia, Finland and Sweden. Thus of the 15 pre-2004 member states, only Denmark, Ireland and the United Kingdom did not allow for references.

885 TEU (pre-Lisbon), art. 35(3). Hungary did likewise originally, but amended its declaration subsequently.

make such provision in national law,[886] and 11 of the declaring member states did so – or at least reserved the right to do so.[887] Subject to any special provision, the jurisdiction of the Court under article 35 followed the system of article 234 EC.[888] From Amsterdam to the entry into force of Lisbon there were some dozen references under article 35, most dealing with the application of the *non bis in idem* rule in the context of criminal prosecutions.[889] A reference purported to be made under article 234 but which should have been made under article 35 was admissible so long as it fell otherwise properly within the jurisdiction of the Court.[890]

5.149   Both articles 68 EC and 35 EU introduced, in their different ways, a degree of judicial variable geometry, or 'different speed references' (*demandes préjudicielles à vitesse spécifique*) into the Court's jurisdiction.[891] Because of this the Commission proposed in 2006 that article 68 be scrapped,[892] but this came about only with Lisbon – as a result of which articles 68 and 35, and the problems they created, disappeared. The erstwhile Title IV EC was significantly restructured and the article 68 limitation to the jurisdiction of the Court removed, leaving it general jurisdiction in the area and restoring the normal dialogue with national courts, no limitation as to national courts which may refer questions to it under article 267 and, with one exception,[893] no limitation *ratione materiae* as to what may be asked, all from the date of the entry into force of the Treaty. So, for example, a reference from the *Tribunal de grande instance de Paris* on a Title IV EC matter, rejected by the Court of Justice for inadmissibility ten days before the entry into force of Lisbon,[894] was simply referred back by the same court

---

886   Declaration (No. 10) on Article 35 (formerly Article K.7) of the Treaty on European Union.

887   That is, Belgium, Czech Republic, Germany, Spain, France, Italy, Luxembourg, the Netherlands, Austria, Romania and Slovenia.

888   Case C-105/03 *Criminal proceedings against Pupino* [2005] ECR I-5285, at paras 19 and 28; Case C-296/08 PPU *Santesteban Goicoechea* [2008] ECR I-6307, at para. 36.

889   Cases C-187 and 385/01 *Criminal proceedings against Gözütok* and *Brügge* [2003] ECR I-1343; Case C-469/03 *Criminal proceedings against Miraglia* [2005] ECR I-2009; Case C-436/04 *van Esbroeck* v *Openbaar Ministerie* [2006] ECR I-2333; Case C-467/04 *Criminal proceedings against Gasparini and ors* [2006] ECR I-9199; Case C-150/05 *Van Straaten* v *Netherlands and Italy* [2006] ECR I-9327; Case C-288/05 *Staatsanwaltschaft Augsburg* v *Kretzinger* [2007] ECR I-6441; Case C-367/05 *Criminal proceedings against Kraaijenbrink* [2007] ECR I-6619; Case C-297/07 *Staatsanwaltschaft Regensburg* v *Bourquain* [2008] ECR I-9425; Case C-491/07 *Criminal proceedings against Turanský* [2008] ECR I-11039; Case C-261/09 *Criminal proceedings against Mantello* [2010] ECR I-11477.

890   Case C-296/08 PPU *Santesteban Goicoechea*, n. 888 above.

891   Case C-14/08 *Roda Golf & Beach Resort* [2009] ECR I-5439, *per* A-G Ruiz-Jarabo Colomer, at para. 25 of his opinion.

892   COM(2006) 346; the Council had power to do so under art. 67(2) EC to 'adapt … the provisions [of Title IV] relating to the powers of the Court of Justice'.

893   TFEU, art. 276; n. 149 above and accompanying text.

894   Case C-278/09 *Martínez and Martínez* v *MGN* [2009] ECR I-11099.

some weeks later.[895] As regards Title VI TEU (pre-Lisbon), it too was drawn into general Union law, the article 267 jurisdiction of the Court becoming binding and available to any national court, no longer subject to national whim. However, full jurisdiction will apply only five years after Lisbon's entry into force,[896] that is in December 2014; even then one member state (the United Kingdom) may continue to hold out.[897]

(g) Preliminary rulings and extra-Treaty instruments

There were a number of conventions between the member states drawn up in **5.150** accordance with the procedures of the EC Treaty or of the Treaty on European Union[898] which conferred upon the Court of Justice a reference jurisdiction analogous to article 267 for their interpretation.[899] Many of them allowed the member states the discretion to decide that certain, all or none of their courts may, or must, refer such questions. Other than a significant number (more than 150) of references made under the 1968 Brussels Convention (which is now defunct)[900] and three references under the 1980 Rome Convention (also defunct),[901] none has ever been used.

---

895 Case C-161/10 *Martínez and Martínez* v *MGN*, judgment of 25 November 2011, not yet reported. In light of this the Court then found that the principle of procedural economy requires that it hear and respond to a reference lodged by an inferior court 'shortly before' the entry into force of Lisbon (shortly before being, respectively, on 17 July 2009, only a week and a half after, and on 6 July 2009, the same day as, the initial, inadmissible, reference in *Martínez & Martínez*) where examination of the case occurs only after that date; Case C-283/09 *Weryński* v *Mediatel 4B spółka*, judgment of 17 February 2011, not yet reported; Case C-396/09 *Interedil* v *Fallimento Interedil and anor*, judgment of 20 October 2011, not yet reported.

896 Protocol (No. 36) on Transitional Provisions, art. 10. The powers of the Court are to remain, transitionally, as previously with respect to acts falling within Title VI EU and adopted before Lisbon's entry into force.

897 Protocol (No. 36) on Transitional Provisions, art. 10(4); see 11.197 below.

898 See 11.169 below.

899 E.g., the Brussels Convention (see 11.169), First (or 'Luxembourg') Protocol ([1998] OJ C27/28); the Rome Convention (see 11.169), First and Second Protocols ([1998] OJ C27/47 and 52); Convention on Community Patents ([1989] OJ L401/1), not yet in force, art. 3; Convention on Insolvency ([1996] ILM 1225), not yet in force, art. 43; Protocol to the Convention on the Establishment of a European Police Office (Europol Convention) [1996] OJ C299/2, Protocol on the Jurisdiction of the Court of Justice in matters related to the Europol Convention, art. 2a, not yet in force; Protocol on the Customs Information System Convention [1997] OJ C151/16; Protocol to the Convention on the Protection of Essential Financial Interests (Fraud Convention) [1997] OJ C151/2; Convention on the Fight against Corruption involving Officials of the European Communities (Corruption Convention) [1997] OJ C195/2, art. 12(3–4).

900 Under the Brussels Convention references were admissible only from higher (appeal) courts or certain named courts of first instance; as Regulation 44/2001 (which replaced the Convention for the most part; see 11.169 below) was adopted by authority of art. 61(c) of the EC Treaty references became restricted to courts of final instance. Treaties between the Community/Union and Denmark necessitated by that country's peculiar status in these matters usually contain a provision granting the Court of Justice interpretative reference jurisdiction; see 11.178 below, n. 113.

901 Case C-133/08 *Intercontainer Interfrigo* v *Balkenende Oosthuizen and anor* [2009] ECR I-9687; Case C-384/10 *Voogsgeerd* v *Navimer*, judgment of 15 December 2011, not yet reported; Case C-29/10 *Koelzsch* v *Grand-Duché de Luxembourg*, judgment of 15 March 2011, not yet reported. The Rome Protocols entered into force only in August 2004 and are spent (except for Denmark and situations in which the Convention continues to apply *ratione temporis*) with the entry into application of Regulation 593/2008 [2008] OJ L177/6 ('Rome I') as of December 2009.

(h) EEA Agreement

5.151 The Treaty establishing the European Economic Area (EEA) provides the Court with two heads of jurisdiction. First, a dispute concerning provisions of the EEA Agreement which are 'identical in substance to corresponding rules of the [Community] Treat[ies]' may, failing settlement, be referred by the contracting parties to the Court of Justice.[902] Secondly, the contracting parties may agree to confer upon the Court limited jurisdiction to provide 'advisory rulings' to requesting national courts of EFTA states on the interpretation of the Agreement.[903] They have not done so.

(i) Popularity of preliminary references

5.152 The 'reception' of article 267 varies significantly from member state to member state – to compare, 13 references from Scottish courts (and only seven on other than fishing) in 40 years to 410 from Austrian courts in 18 years; or, a 1:70 ratio of Scottish to Austrian references. This is a function of a number of factors, amongst them the frequency and intensity of appropriate litigation, methods of national incorporation of Union law and the points of friction to which they may give rise, the tangency and familiarity (and enthusiasm) of the courts with and for Union law, and judicial culture generally. Table 5.1 provides an indication of its use. Doubtless the frequency will increase as the habit is acquired by the courts of 13 new(er) member states.

5. Opinions

5.153 The Court of Justice may be called upon by the Parliament, the Council, the Commission or a member state to give an opinion (*avis*) on the compatibility with the Treaties of a proposed association agreement between the Union and a third state, group of states or international organisation.[904] The purpose, drawn from French constitutional procedure,[905] is to forestall complications which would result from the introduction into Union law of international obligations incompatible with it,[906] which could provoke serious consequences not only for Union law but for international relations.[907] An opinion may be sought even if a convention to which the Union proposes to accede is still in draft form.[908] Uniquely amongst matters before the Court, the hearing is normally held in

---

902 EEA Agreement, art. 111(3).
903 EEA Agreement, Protocol 34.
904 TFEU, art. 218(11) (ex art. 300(6) EC).
905 Constitution of the Fifth Republic, art. 54.
906 Opinion 2/94 *Re Accession to the ECHR* [1996] ECR I-1759, at para. 3; Opinion 1/08 *Re GATS Special Commitments* [2009] ECR I-11129, at para. 107.
907 Opinion 3/94 *Re Framework Agreement on Bananas* [1995] ECR I-4577, at para. 17.
908 Opinion 1/09 *Re the European Patent Convention*, opinion of 8 March 2011, not yet reported.

Table 5.1 Requests to the Court of Justice for preliminary rulings*

	BE	BG	CZ	DK	DE	EE	EI	EL	ES	FR	IT	CY	LV	LT	LU	HU	MT	NL	AT	PL	PT	RO	SI	SK	FI	SE	UK	Total
1961	–	–	–	–	–	–	–	–	–	–	–	–	–	–	–	–	–	1	–	–	–	–	–	–	–	–	–	1
1962	–	–	–	–	–	–	–	–	–	–	–	–	–	–	–	–	–	5	–	–	–	–	–	–	–	–	–	5
1963	–	–	–	–	–	–	–	–	–	–	–	–	–	–	1	–	–	5	–	–	–	–	–	–	–	–	–	6
1964	–	–	–	–	–	–	–	–	–	–	2	–	–	–	–	–	–	4	–	–	–	–	–	–	–	–	–	6
1965	–	–	–	–	4	–	–	–	–	2	–	–	–	–	–	–	–	1	–	–	–	–	–	–	–	–	–	7
1966	–	–	–	–	–	–	–	–	–	–	–	–	–	–	–	–	–	1	–	–	–	–	–	–	–	–	–	1
1967	5	–	–	–	11	–	–	–	–	3	–	–	–	–	1	–	–	3	–	–	–	–	–	–	–	–	–	23
1968	1	–	–	–	4	–	–	–	–	1	1	–	–	–	–	–	–	2	–	–	–	–	–	–	–	–	–	9
1969	4	–	–	–	11	–	–	–	–	1	–	–	–	–	1	–	–	–	–	–	–	–	–	–	–	–	–	17
1970	4	–	–	–	21	–	–	–	–	2	2	–	–	–	1	–	–	3	–	–	–	–	–	–	–	–	–	32
1971	1	–	–	–	18	–	–	–	–	6	5	–	–	–	–	–	–	6	–	–	–	–	–	–	–	–	–	37
1972	5	–	–	–	20	–	–	–	–	1	4	–	–	–	1	–	–	10	–	–	–	–	–	–	–	–	–	40
1973	8	–	–	–	37	–	–	–	–	4	5	–	–	–	1	–	–	6	–	–	–	–	–	–	–	–	–	61
1974	5	–	–	–	15	–	–	–	–	6	5	–	–	–	–	–	–	7	–	–	–	–	–	–	–	–	1	39
1975	7	–	–	1	26	–	–	–	–	15	14	–	–	–	1	–	–	4	–	–	–	–	–	–	–	–	1	69
1976	11	–	–	–	28	–	1	–	–	8	12	–	–	–	–	–	–	14	–	–	–	–	–	–	–	–	1	75
1977	16	–	–	1	30	–	2	–	–	14	7	–	–	–	–	–	–	9	–	–	–	–	–	–	–	–	5	84
1978	7	–	–	3	46	–	1	–	–	12	11	–	–	–	–	–	–	38	–	–	–	–	–	–	–	–	5	123
1979	13	–	–	1	33	–	2	–	–	18	19	–	–	–	1	–	–	11	–	–	–	–	–	–	–	–	8	106

Table 5.1 Continued

	BE	BG	CZ	DK	DE	EE	EI	EL	ES	FR	IT	CY	LV	LT	LU	HU	MT	NL	AT	PL	PT	RO	SI	SK	FI	SE	UK	Total
1980	14	–	–	2	24	–	3	–	–	14	19	–	–	–	–	–	–	17	–	–	–	–	–	–	–	–	6	99
1981	12	–	–	1	41	–	–	–	–	17	11	–	–	–	4	–	–	17	–	–	–	–	–	–	–	–	6	108
1982	10	–	–	1	36	–	–	–	–	39	18	–	–	–	–	–	–	21	–	–	–	–	–	–	–	–	4	129
1983	9	–	–	4	36	–	2	–	–	15	7	–	–	–	–	–	–	19	–	–	–	–	–	–	–	–	6	98
1984	13	–	–	2	38	–	1	–	–	34	10	–	–	–	–	–	–	22	–	–	–	–	–	–	–	–	9	129
1985	13	–	–	–	40	–	2	–	–	45	11	–	–	–	6	–	–	14	–	–	–	–	–	–	–	–	8	139
1986	13	–	–	4	18	–	4	2	1	19	5	–	–	–	1	–	–	16	–	–	–	–	–	–	–	–	8	91
1987	15	–	–	5	32	–	2	17	1	36	5	–	–	–	3	–	–	19	–	–	–	–	–	–	–	–	9	144
1988	30	–	–	4	34	–	–	–	1	38	28	–	–	–	2	–	–	26	–	–	1	–	–	–	–	–	16	179
1989	13	–	–	2	47	–	1	2	2	28	10	–	–	–	1	–	–	18	–	–	2	–	–	–	–	–	14	139
1990	17	–	–	5	34	–	4	2	6	21	25	–	–	–	4	–	–	9	–	–	3	–	–	–	–	–	12	141
1991	19	–	–	2	54	–	2	3	5	29	36	–	–	–	2	–	–	17	–	–	1	–	–	–	–	–	14	186
1992	16	–	–	3	62	–	–	1	5	15	22	–	–	–	1	–	–	18	–	–	3	–	–	–	–	–	18	162
1993	22	–	–	7	57	–	1	5	7	22	24	–	–	–	1	–	–	43	–	–	1	–	–	–	–	–	12	204
1994	19	–	–	4	44	–	2	–	13	36	46	–	–	–	1	–	–	13	–	–	3	–	–	–	–	–	24	203
1995	14	–	–	8	51	–	3	10	10	43	58	–	–	–	2	–	–	19	2	–	5	–	–	–	–	6	20	251
1996	30	–	–	4	66	–	–	4	6	24	70	–	–	–	2	–	–	10	6	–	6	–	–	–	3	4	21	256
1997	19	–	–	7	46	–	1	2	9	10	50	–	–	–	3	–	–	24	35	–	2	–	–	–	6	7	18	239
1998	12	–	–	7	49	–	3	5	55	16	39	–	–	–	2	–	–	21	16	–	7	–	–	–	2	6	24	264
1999	13	–	–	3	49	–	2	3	4	17	43	–	–	–	4	–	–	23	56	–	7	–	–	–	4	5	22	255
2000	15	–	–	3	47	–	2	3	5	12	50	–	–	–	–	–	–	12	31	–	8	–	–	–	5	4	26	224**
2001	10	–	–	5	53	–	1	4	4	15	40	–	–	–	2	–	–	14	57	–	4	–	–	–	3	4	21	237
2002	18	–	–	8	59	–	–	7	3	8	37	–	–	–	4	–	–	12	31	–	3	–	–	–	7	5	14	216
2003	18	–	–	3	43	–	2	4	8	9	45	–	–	–	4	–	–	28	15	–	1	–	–	–	4	4	22	210
2004	24	–	–	4	50	–	1	18	8	21	48	–	–	–	1	2	–	28	12	–	1	–	–	–	4	5	22	249

Year																											
2005	21	–	1	4	51	–	2	11	10	17	18	–	–	–	2	3	–	36	15	1	2	–	–	–	4	11	12	221
2006	17	–	3	3	77	–	1	14	17	24	34	–	–	1	1	4	–	20	12	2	3	–	–	1	5	2	10	251
2007	22	1	2	5	59	2	2	8	14	26	43	–	–	1	–	2	–	19	20	7	3	1	1	1	5	6	16	265
2008	24	–	1	6	71	2	1	9	17	12	39	1	3	3	4	6	–	34	25	4	1	–	–	–	4	7	14	288
2009	35	8	5	3	59	2	–	11	11	28	29	1	4	3	–	10	1	24	15	10	3	1	2	1	2	5	28	302***
2010	37	9	3	10	71	–	4	6	22	33	49	–	3	2	9	6	–	24	15	8	10	17	1	5	6	6	29	385
2011	34	22	5	6	83	1	7	9	27	31	44	–	10	1	2	13	–	22	24	11	11	14	1	3	12	4	26	423
2012	27	16	7	8	63	6	6	1	16	15	63	–	5	2	7	15	1	44	23	6	14	8	–	8	3	8	16	389
Total	**712**	**56**	**27**	**149**	**1948**	**13**	**68**	**161**	**287**	**862**	**1163**	**2**	**25**	**13**	**83**	**61**	**2**	**833**	**410**	**49**	**102**	**41**	**4**	**19**	**79**	**99**	**547**	**7817**

Notes:

* includes references under art 41 ECSC, art 177 EEC, art 150 Euratom, art 234 EC, art 35 (pre-Lisbon) TEU, the first protocol to the 1968 Brussels Convention, the first and second protocols to the 1980 Rome Convention and art 267 TFEU.

** includes a case referred by the Benelux Court of Justice.

*** includes a case referred by the Complaints Board of the European Schools.

closed session, normally by the full Court, and all eight Advocates-General are 'heard'. If the Court finds the agreement to be inconsistent with the Treaties, the Union may proceed only if the agreement is altered in order to overcome the Court's objections or the Treaties are amended to remove the incompatibility.[909] The jurisdiction may be invoked not only to identify (if it exists) a Treaty bar to participation but also to determine whether the Union has exclusive or shared (or no) competence to enter into the agreement.[910] It is not a common procedure, to date only 17 opinions being delivered by the Court. If opinions are a 'class of action or proceeding', the Treaties allow jurisdiction to give them to be conferred upon the General Court;[911] but given their high constitutional import and sensitivity it is very unlikely.

5.154 There was a procedure under the ECSC Treaty for securing an opinion from the Court on the compatibility with that Treaty of proposed amendments to the powers of the High Authority,[912] which was used three times.[913] The Court has no power equivalent to article 218(11) TFEU under the Euratom Treaty but may be called upon to give a 'ruling' (*une délibération*) upon the compatibility with that Treaty of agreements entered into by a member state[914] or by a private person[915] with a third state, international organisation or third country private persons within the field of application of Euratom. Only one ruling has been sought and given.[916]

---

909   *Ibid.* For examples see 14.72 below, n. 416.
910   See e.g., Opinion 1/94 *Re the World Trade Organisation* [1994] ECR I-5267; Opinion 2/00 *Re the Convention on Biological Diversity* (Cartagena Protocol) [2001] ECR I-9713; Opinion 1/03 *Re the Lugano Convention* [2006] ECR I-1145; Opinion 1/08, n. 906 above.
911   TFEU, art. 256 (1) (ex art. 225(1) EC).
912   ECSC, art. 95. This was a specific amendment procedure applicable to 'adapt[ation of] the rules for the High Authority's exercise of its powers' which required the positive approval of the Court to proceed; it was not available under the other two Community treaties.
913   Opinion 1/59 *Re Amendment of the ECSC Treaty* [1959] ECR 259; Opinion 1/60 *Re Amendment of the ECSC Treaty* [1960] ECR 39; Opinion 1/61 *Re Amendment of the ECSC Treaty* [1961] ECR 243.
914   Euratom Treaty, art. 103, 3rd para.
915   *Ibid.* art. 104, 3rd para.
916   Ruling 1/78 *Re the IAEA Draft Convention on the Physical Protection of Nuclear Materials, Facilities and Transports* [1978] ECR 2151.

Part C

THE SOURCES, NATURE AND METHODS
OF EUROPEAN UNION LAW

6

THE SOURCES, NATURE AND METHODS OF EUROPEAN UNION LAW

A. SOURCES OF UNION LAW

The sources of European Union law may be categorised as follows: **6.01**

(1) Treaties:

    (a) (i) 'the Treaties', being the Treaty on European Union and the Treaty on the Functioning of the European Union;

          (ii) the Treaty establishing the European Atomic Energy Community (Euratom) which, whilst remaining distinct from the

   Union, predates it, conducts its business in the Community way (long before the Union did) and and is governed by the Union institutions;

  (iii) Treaties amplifying, modifying or amending the founding Community Treaties insofar as they are still in force;

  (iv) the various treaties of accession (and accompanying acts of accession) providing for the admission of new member states to the Communities/Union;

  (v) Protocols, conventions, and acts ancillary to the Treaties, the founding Treaties and/or the amending/accession Treaties;

  (vi) Declarations ancillary to the Treaties, the founding Treaties and/or the amending/accession Treaties;

 (b) (i) Agreements with third countries and multilateral conventions into which the Community/Union has entered;

  (ii) Agreements with third countries and multilateral conventions into which the member states have entered, to which obligations the Community/Union has succeeded.

(2) The EU Charter of Fundamental Freedoms, itself having a source outside the Treaties but recognised by them and accorded the same legal value.

(3) Legislation:

 (a) legislative acts and lawfully binding decisions of the Union institutions or other bodies acting under the powers conferred upon them by the Community Treaties (1952–2009) or by the Treaties (2009–);

 (b) legislative acts and lawfully binding decisions of the governments of the member states 'meeting in the European Council' or 'meeting in the Council' and acting under the powers conferred upon them by the Treaties;

 (c) acts of the institutions acting under powers conferred upon them by the Treaties, which, in accordance with those provisions, take effect upon ratification by the member states;

 (d) 'non-legislative acts' and binding decisions of a Union institution acting under powers lawfully conferred upon it by another institution ('secondary' or 'delegated' legislation);[1]

 (e) acts adopted by the institutions acting by authority conferred upon them by the pre-Lisbon Treaty on European Union which continue in force post-Lisbon.

---

1 By another convention, legislation adopted by the institutions by direct Treaty authority is 'secondary' legislation (or *droit dérivé*), the 'primary' rules (*droit primaire*) considered to reside in the Treaties themselves. As to non-legislative acts (a term of art introduced by the Lisbon Treaty), see 6.86 below.

(4) Case law: judgments of the Court of Justice of the European Union insofar as they are binding on the parties and upon the courts and tribunals of the member states, and more generally the case law of the Court insofar as it states or applies principles of Union law or provides an interpretation of the Treaties or of legislative provisions in cases involving different parties.

(5) 'General principles of law' derived (largely) from sources extraneous to the Treaties but absorbed by Union law and recognised to form principles by which it is administered.

There are also 'parallel agreements', conventions amongst the member states which are distinct from, but foreseen by and concluded within the context of, the founding Treaties,[2] most notably the 1968 Brussels Judgments Convention.[3] Others exist but have not entered into force,[4] still others were not foreseen in the Treaties but came into being through agreement amongst (some) member states, such as the 1980 Rome Contracts Convention,[5] the 1985 Schengen Agreement[6] and the 1990 Dublin Convention.[7] A new generation of such instruments ('conventions') were introduced by the Maastricht Treaty to be used in the area of police and judicial cooperation in criminal matters.[8] All of these lay technically outwith Union competences and operate outside the Union machinery, but they existed alongside, complemented and were highly integrated with it. Since changes made by the Treaty of Amsterdam the existing conventions have been largely (but not wholly) replaced by, and some draft conventions adopted in the form of, Community, now Union, instruments, as described in 3(a) and (e) above,[9] and both articles 293 EC and 34(2)(d) TEU disappeared with Lisbon. But it does not mean that the member states cannot continue to cooperate in related fields by means of extra-Union treaties, so long as addressing matters which remain within their competence

---

2   See EEC Treaty, art. 220 (art. 293 EC); repealed by Lisbon.
3   (Brussels) Convention of 27 September 1968 on Jurisdiction and Enforcement of Judgments in Civil and Commercial Matters, consolidated version at [1998] OJ C27/3.
4   E.g., conventions on recognition of companies (*Bulletin EC*, Supplement 2/69, 7). Of agreements foreseen by art. 220 only the Brussels Convention and the Convention of 23 July 1990 on the elimination of double taxation in connection with the adjustment of profits of associated undertakings [1990] OJ L225/10 came into force.
5   (Rome) Convention of 19 June 1980 on the Law Applicable to Contractual Obligations, consolidated version at [1998] OJ C27/34.
6   (Schengen) Agreement of 14 June 1985 on the gradual abolition of checks at their common borders [2000] OJ L239/13.
7   (Dublin) Convention of 15 June 1990 determining the state responsible for examining applications for asylum lodged in one of the Member States of the European Communities [1997] OJ 1997 C254/1. Other such conventions which never came into force are those on a Community patent ([1989] OJ L401/1) and on insolvency ([1996] ILM 1225).
8   TEU (pre-Amsterdam), art. K.3(2)(c) (art. 34(2)(d) TEU post-Amsterdam).
9   See 6.90–6.95 below.

(even if shared with the Union) and respecting the obligations of sincere cooperation with the Union.

6.02 There are other materials which, although 'soft' law, may be invoked as offering guidance to the interpretation and application of Union law. They include:

- declarations, communiqués and resolutions of the institutions;
- guidelines, notices and other statements of policy, such as green and white papers, issued by the Commission;
- answers to parliamentary questions in the European Parliament;
- learned opinion, such as academic writing (*la doctrine* being a respected guide to law in a number of member states) and other respected reports.

6.03 Two other sources of law may be identified. First, the Union and its law may be said to float within a matrix of public international law, which is, after all, the medium and means through which it was created. Union law is, moreover, a monist legal system, and so recognises rules of public international law, both customary and treaty, as a part of it. Thus is the Court able to observe:

> [T]he principle of good faith is a rule of customary international law the existence of which has been recognised by the Permanent Court of International Justice ..., and subsequently by the International Court of Justice and which, consequently, is binding ... on the Community,[10]

and able to enforce directly a bilateral treaty or multinational convention into which the Union has entered, which is an integral part of the Union legal order[11] and prevails over inconsistent Union legislation.[12] As a result, that legislation may be set aside by the Court of Justice where the agreement is binding upon the Union, its nature and broad logic do not preclude it, and the

---

10   Case T-231/04 *Greece* v *Commission* [2007] ECR II-63, at para. 85; also Case T–115/94 *Opel Austria* v *Council* [1997] ECR II-39, at para. 90. See also Case C-286/90 *Ankalgemyndigheden* v *Poulsen* [1992] ECR I-6019; Cases C-46 and 48/93 *Brasserie du Pêcheur* v *Germany* and *R* v *Secretary of State for Transport, ex parte Factortame (No. 3)* [1996] ECR I-1029, *per* A-G Tesauro at para. 38 of his opinion; Case C-27/96 *Danisco Sugar* v *Allmänna Ombudet* [1997] ECR I-6653; Case C-162/96 *Racke* v *Hauptzollamt Mainz* [1998] ECR I-3655; Case C-470/03 *AGM-COS.MET* v *Suomen valtio and anor* [2007] ECR I-2749, *per* A-G Kokott at para. 84 of her opinion; Case C-308/06 *R (International Association of Independent Tanker Owners (Intertanko) and ors)* v *Secretary of State for Transport* [2008] ECR I-4057, at para. 51; Case C-386/08 *Brita* v *Hauptzollamt Hamburg-Hafen* [2010] ECR I-1289, at para. 42.

11   Case C-459/03 *Commission* v *Ireland* (MOX) [2006] ECR I-4635; Case C-308/06 *Intertanko, ibid.*

12   Case C-61/94 *Commission* v *Germany* (International Dairy Arrangement) [1996] ECR I-3989; Case C-286/02 *Bellio F.lli* v *Prefettura di Treviso* [2004] ECR I-3465; Case C-311/04 *Algemene Scheeps Agentuur Dordrecht* v *Inspecteur der Belastingdienst–Douanedistrict Rotterdam* [2006] ECR I-609; Case C-308/06 *Intertanko*, n. 10 above, at para. 42; Cases C-402 and 415/05P *Kadi and Al Barakaat* v *Council and Commission* (Kadi II) [2008] ECR I-6351, at para. 307.

provisions in issue are unconditional and sufficiently precise.[13] Even where convention terms lack the precision necessary to be enforced directly (in EU terms, they are not 'directly effective'):[14]

> Community legislation must, so far as possible, be interpreted in a manner that is consistent with international law, in particular where its provisions are intended specifically to give effect to an international agreement concluded by the Community.[15]

This applies also to rules of customary international law, save that as they generally lack the precision of a provision of an international agreement, review is limited to the question of whether the Union institutions have made manifest errors of assessment concerning the conditions for applying them.[16] The Union is now, post-Lisbon, bound to contribute to 'the strict observance and the development of international law'.[17]

However it is clear is that whilst international obligations may flow into Union **6.04** law, they are made effective subject to its mandatory rules. So obligations created by or under the United Nations Charter (of which the Union is not a member[18] but by which it is bound by virtue of the member states' UN membership) prevail, from the standpoint of international law, over every other obligation of domestic law or of international treaty law.[19] But this does not mean that the Union legal order will 'bow to that rule with complete acquiescence and apply it unconditionally', for:

> [t]he relationship between international law and the Community legal order is governed by the Community legal order itself, and international law can permeate that legal order only under the conditions set by the constitutional principles of the Community.[20]

---

13 Case C-308/06 *Intertanko*, n. 10 above, at para. 45; Cases C-120 and 121/06P *Fabbrica italiana accumulatori motocarri Montecchio and anor* v *Council and Commission* [2008] ECR I-6513, at para. 110; Case C-366/10 *R (Air Transport Association of America and ors)* v *Secretary of State for Energy and Climate Change*, judgment of 21 December 2011, not yet reported, at paras 53–4.
14 See 6.13–6.15 below.
15 Case C-284/95 *Safety Hi-Tech* v *S & T* [1998] ECR I-4301, at para. 22. See also the extensive discussion of A-G Kokott in Case C-308/06 *Intertanko*, n. 10 above, at paras 34–112 of her opinion.
16 Case C-366/10 *Air Transport Association of America*, n. 13 above, at paras 107–10.
17 TEU, art. 3(5).
18 The EEC was accorded observer status in the General Assembly in 1974 (A/RES/3208 (XXIX)) to which the Union succeeded, the Union accorded the right to speak (but not vote) in the General Assembly in 2011 (A/RES/65/276)). It enjoys limited participation rights in some UN agencies.
19 See Charter of the United Nations, art. 103: 'In the event of a conflict between the obligations of the Members of the United Nations under the present Charter and their obligations under any other international agreement, their obligations under the present Charter shall prevail'.
20 Cases C-402 and 415/05P *Kadi and Al Barakaat* v *Council and Commission* [2008] ECR I-6351 (Kadi II), *per* A-G Poiares Maduro at para. 24 of his opinion.

So whilst it is not for the Court of Justice to control the legality of a Security Council resolution, it must nevertheless ensure the review, 'in principle the full review', of the lawfulness of a Union measure designed to give effect to any such resolution for compliance with the 'constitutional principles' of the Treaties, and in particular respect for fundamental rights.[21] This may unsettle public international lawyers and, it will become clear, is a courtesy which Union law does not extend to the national legal orders, even the constitutional legal orders, of the member states.[22]

6.05 Second, although in only one place did the original Treaty expressly recognise national law as a source of law – from the general principles of which are to be distilled the rules on non-contractual liability of the Union and its institutions[23] – its influence cannot be avoided elsewhere, for it nurtured those who drew up the Treaties and those charged with its interpretation and application. It is especially true for national conceptions of public law. In the early (European Coal and Steel Community, ECSC) cases it was recognised more readily: for example, that reference is to be had to the law of the different member states 'which is of decisive importance in the interpretation of our Community law',[24] and:

> [a]s regards the sources of that [Community] law, there is obviously nothing to prevent them being sought, where appropriate, in international law, but normally and in most cases they will be found rather in the internal law of the Member States.[25]

Later, the common constitutional and legal traditions of the member states were recognised as the inspiration, source and catalyst for the development of the general principles which form part of, and bind, the Union legal order.[26] But as early Community law developed and matured it cast off its reliance upon national law; in its detail it is now rarely cited, intentionally so, yet it necessarily

---

21 Cases C-402 and 415/05P *Kadi II, ibid.*, at paras 285, 326; Cases C-399 and 403/06P *Hassan and Ayadi* v *Council* [2009] ECR I-11393, at para. 71; Case T-85/09 *Kadi* v *Commission* (Kadi III), [2010] ECR II-5177. This compares with the view of the General Court which found that Security Council resolutions must, in accordance with art. 25 of the UN Charter, be given effect within the Union legal order and are immune from judicial control of the Court of Justice except insofar as they might, highly exceptionally, constitute an infringement of a peremptory norm of public international law (*jus cogens*); Case T-306/01 *Yusuf and Al Barakaat* v *Council and Commission* [2005] ECR II-3533, at para. 282; Case T-315/01 *Kadi* v *Council and Commission* (Kadi I) [2005] ECR II-3649, at para. 231.

22 See 6.16 below.

23 EEC Treaty, art. 215, 2nd para (art. 340, 2nd para. TFEU); see 5.94 above.

24 Case 6/54 *Netherlands* v *High Authority* [1954–56] ECR 103, *per* A-G Roemer at 118.

25 Case 8/55 *Fédération Charbonnière de Belgique* v *High Authority (Fédéchar)* [1954–56] ECR 245, *per* A-G Lagrange at 277.

26 TEU, art. 6; see 6.101 below.

informs Union law throughout. It might be described otherwise simply as custom, or the common European legal culture.

1. Relationship of the Treaties with other treaties

For clarity, the TFEU provides that treaty obligations between one or more **6.06** member states, on the one hand, and one or more third countries, on the other, which existed prior to its entry into force (or, for accession member states, prior to the date of their accession) 'shall not be affected by the provisions of the Treaties'.[27] This is simply articulation of a principle recognised in international law,[28] and in law generally, that a contractual obligation cannot be avoided by a party entering subsequently into a different obligation with an unconnected party which is inconsistent with the first:

> [T]he purpose of that provision is to make it clear, in accordance with the principles of international law, that application of the EC Treaty does not affect the duty of the Member State concerned to respect the rights of third countries under a prior agreement and to perform its obligations thereunder.[29]

If a matter falls properly within article 351 – which arises of course only where there is some incompatibility between the two treaty orders[30] – it justifies derogation for the relevant member state(s) from even primary (Treaty) law.[31] However, the Treaties impose upon the member states an obligation to 'take all appropriate steps' to do away with any irregularities to which pre-existing treaties give rise ('eliminate the incompatibilities established').[32] Presumably this extends to an obligation to denounce an inconsistent treaty obligation where that possibility exists[33] and, where it does not, to seek to negotiate its termination. The (excessive?) breadth of this obligation was made clear in three

---

27 TFEU, art. 351 (ex art. 307 EC).
28 Vienna Convention on the Law of Treaties, art. 30.
29 Case C-216/01 *Budejovický Budvar* v *Rudolf Ammersin* [2003] ECR I-13617, at para. 145 (substituting 'earlier' for 'prior'); Case T-306/01 *Yusuf and Al Bakaraat*, n. 21 above, at para. 236; Case T-315/01 *Kadi I*, n. 21 above, at para. 186; Case C-205/06 *Commission v Austria* [2009] ECR I-1301, at para. 33 (substituting 'is not to' for 'does not'); Case C-249/06 *Commission v Sweden* [2009] ECR I-1335, at para. 34 (substituting 'is not to' for 'does not'); Case C-118/07 *Commission v Finland* [2009] ECR I-10889, at para. 27 (substituting 'is not to' for 'does not' and omitting 'EC' and 'thereunder'). The Court recognised this principle to operate from the other side of the fence, saying it would breach art. 4(3) TEU (as well as public international law) were a member state now to enter into an international commitment with a third country which would affect or alter the scope of Union rules; Case C-523/04 *Commission v Netherlands* (Open Skies) [2007] ECR I-3267.
30 Case C-45/07 *Commission v Greece* [2009] ECR I-701, at para. 35.
31 Case C-124/95 *R, ex parte Centro-Com* v *HM Treasury and anor* [1997] ECR I-81, at paras 56–61; Cases C-402 and 415/05P *Kadi II*, n. 20 above, at para. 301; Case T-85/09 *Kadi III*, n. 21 above, at para. 119.
32 TFEU, art. 351, 2nd para.
33 See Case C-84/98 *Commission v Portugal* [2000] ECR I-5215; Case C-203/03 *Commission v Austria* [2005] ECR I-935.

2009 judgments of the Court of Justice which held that even where there was no present incompatibility, securing the immediate effectiveness of Union provisions required member states to denounce adherence to the obligations of a prior treaty which would make it difficult for them to comply with Union legislation which *might* be adopted in the future, if the treaty contained no opt out provision for a Union member state nor adduced rules of public international law which would make that possible.[34] If necessary the member states are to assist each other to the ends of article 351 and, where appropriate, adopt a common attitude.[35] Material amendment to a pre-existing treaty with a third country is deemed to be a new treaty, not enjoying the protection of article 351.[36]

6.07 Article 351 applies to bilateral or multilateral treaties with third countries, but if multilateral and involving two or more member states it does not apply as between or amongst them:[37]

> By virtue of the principles of international law, by assuming a new obligation which is incompatible with rights held under a prior treaty a state *ipso facto* gives up the exercise of these rights to the extent necessary for the performance of its new obligations ... In matters governed by the EEC Treaty, that Treaty takes precedence over agreements concluded between Member States before its entry into force.[38]

In other words, *lex (pacti) posterior derogat priori*: the more recent (Union) obligations displace prior obligations *inter se* where the interests of third countries (or persons in third countries), which it is the purpose of article 351 to protect, are not in issue. Thus, for example, the Union Treaties override any incompatible provision of the EEA Agreement for an EFTA state newly joining the Union so long as it does not impinge upon the rights of a non-EEA EFTA state.[39] This 'cannot be criticized by third countries since [it] does not interfere with the rights held by third counties under agreements still in force'.[40]

6.08 But the submission, as amongst the member states, of the *pactum prius* to the *posterius* is not a universal rule. Exceptions to it are:

---

34   Case C-205/06 *Commission v Austria*, n. 29 above, at paras 36–37; Case C-249/06 *Commission v Sweden*, n. 29 above, at paras 37–38; Case C-118/07 *Commission v Finland*, n. 29 above, at paras 30–31.

35   TFEU, art. 351, 2nd para.

36   Case C-523/04 *Commission v Netherlands* (Open Skies), n. 29 above.

37   Case 10/61 *EEC Commission v Italy* [1962] ECR 1; Case C-473/93 *Commission v Luxembourg* [1996] I-3207; Case C-147/03 *Commission v Austria* [2005] ECR I-5969; Case C-301/08 *Bogiatzi v Deutscher Luftpool and ors* [2009] ECR I-10185.

38   Case 10/61 *EEC Commission v Italy*, n. 37 above, at 10.

39   Case C-524/07 *Commission v Austria* [2008] ECR I-187*.

40   Case 10/61 *EEC Commission v Italy*, n. 37 above, at 11.

- the United Nations Charter, to which all member states (save Germany) were contracting parties prior to their Community/Union membership.[41] It is apparent that the Charter has priority over Union law even as amongst the member states simply as a function of the primacy it claims (and is generally accorded) within the hierarchy of public international law,[42] in which respect a declaration attached to the Final Act of the Lisbon IGC 'stresses that the European Union and its Member States will remain bound by the provisions of the Charter of the United Nations and, in particular, by the primary responsibility of the Security Council and of its Members for the maintenance of international peace and security'.[43] However, immunity from the jurisdiction of the Court of Justice 'as a corollary of the principle of the primacy at the level of international law' of Charter obligations has no basis in the Treaties,[44] and the Court reserves the authority to set aside measures implementing Security Council resolutions if they offend Union treaty (constitutional) principles.[45] Inversely, Advocate-General Poiares Maduro would extend the duty of article 351 to compel the member states, particularly those belonging to the Security Council, to prevent, as far as possible, the adoption of UN measures liable to enter into conflict with a core principle of the Union legal order;[46] as it is, the Treaties require members of the Security Council merely to 'defend the positions and the interests of the Union'.[47] Yet the Court has, post-Lisbon, begun to use language of which Mr Poiares Maduro would approve;[48]
- the North Atlantic Treaty,[49] which forms the foundation of collective defence for those member states party to it, and with which measures giving effect to the Union's Common Security and Defence Policy must be consistent;[50]

---

41 The Federal Republic and the Democratic Republic were both admitted to the United Nations, following long and complex legal and political debate, only in 1973: GA Resolution 3050 (XXVIII), 18 September 1973; membership of the Democratic Republic lapsed with its dissolution in 1990.

42 Case C-124/95 *R, ex parte Centro-Com* v *HM Treasury and anor* [1997] ECR I-81; Case T-306/01 *Yusuf and Al Bakaraat* v *Council and Commission* [2005] ECR II-3533, at paras 231–58; Case T-315/01 *Kadi* v *Council and Commission* (Kadi I) [2005] ECR II-3649, at paras 181–204. But the latter two judgments must be read in the light of Cases C-402 and 415/05P *Kadi and Al Bakaraat* v *Council and Commission* (Kadi II) [2008] ECR I-6351, which overturned them.

43 Declaration (No. 13) concerning the Common Foreign and Security Policy.

44 Cases C-402 and 415/05P *Kadi II*, n. 42 above, at para. 300.

45 Cases C-402 and 415/05P *Kadi II*, n. 42 above; Cases C-399 and 403/06P *Hassan and Ayadi* v *Council* [2009] ECR I-11393.

46 Cases C-402 and 415/05P *Kadi II*, n. 42 above, at para. 32 of his opinion.

47 TEU, art. 34(2) (ex art. 19(2) TEU (pre-Lisbon)).

48 See in particular Case C-246/07 *Commission* v *Sweden* [2010] ECR I-3317; 14.75 below.

49 Treaty of 4 April 1949, 34 UNTS 241.

50 TEU, art. 42(7).

- the treaties founding the Belgium–Luxembourg economic union (BLEU)[51] and the Benelux economic union,[52] which are ring-fenced from the application of the Union Treaties (they 'shall not preclude the existence or completion of [those] regional unions') insofar as 'the[ir] objectives ... are not attained by the application of the Treaties'.[53] Thus article 350 saves a BLEU and/or Benelux rule if it pursues a legitimate objective of the union, serves a more advanced degree of integration than the equivalent Union rule[54] and is necessary for that purpose.[55] In practice there has been little friction between the BLEU and/or the Benelux and the Community/Union, the latter following in the trail of BLEU/Benelux initiatives but gradually catching up and replacing them on the larger Community/Union stage; ultimately Union integration ought to render both regional unions – and with them article 350 – redundant. In the meanwhile they serve still as a useful laboratory, or 'advance party', for Union integration and of practical variable geometry;
- the Euratom Treaty, a *lex (pacti) specialis* from which the provisions of the Union Treaties 'shall not derogate'.[56] In the same way the priority of the EC and Euratom Treaties themselves were preserved over the Treaty on European Union,[57] the purpose being to safeguard, and safeguard the continuing development of, the *acquis communautaire*.[58] This continued so long as the Community/Union constitutional structure subsisted and so disappeared with Lisbon, the Union now founded upon two Treaties with

---

51 Convention du 25 juillet 1921 établissant une Union économique entre le Grand-Duché de Luxembourg et la Belgique, 9 LNTS 223 ; in force 1 May 1922. Concluded for a period of 50 years without right of unilateral denunciation (art. 29), it was from 1972 extended for successive periods of 10 years and replaced in 2005; see Protocole du 18 décembre 2002 portant modification de la Convention coordonnée instituant l'Union économique belgo-luxembourgeoise et de la nouvelle Convention coordonnée instituant l'Union économique belgo-luxembourgeoise en résultant, JO du G-D de Luxembourg du 17 juin 2004, p. 1515; in force 16 January 2005.

52 Traité du 5 février 1958 instituant l'Union économique Benelux, 381 UNTS 165, in force 1 November 1960; replacing the Benelux customs union (Convention douanière néerlando-belgo-luxembourgeoise du 5 septembre 1944, 32 UNTS 143, in force 1 January 1948).

53 TFEU, art. 350 (ex art. 306 EC). In the same way the Benelux Treaty (art. 94(1)) permits derogation for the BLEU in terms almost identical; and the 1972 Accession Treaty (art. 48) permitted similar, if more limited and now spent, derogation from the EEC Treaty for obligations arising from the 1965 Free Trade Agreement between Ireland and the United Kingdom.

54 Case 105/83 [1984] *Pakvries v Minister van Landbouw en Visserij* [1984] ECR 2101; Case C-473/93 *Commission v Luxembourg* [1996] ECR I-3207.

55 Case 56/75 *Elz v Commission* [1976] ECR 1097.

56 Euratom Treaty, art. 106a(3) (ex art. 305(2) EC). There was a similar saving provision for the ECSC Treaty in art. 305(1) EC which died with the European Coal and Steel Community and disappears from the present Treaties.

57 TEU (pre-Lisbon), art. 47: 'Nothing in this Treaty shall affect the Treaties establishing the European Communities or the subsequent Treaties and Acts modifying or supplementing them'.

58 Case C-91/05 *Commission v Council* (Small Arms Weapons) [2008] ECR I-3651, at para. 59.

'the same legal value',[59] any contradiction a matter internal to the Treaties no longer resolved by recourse to Treaty hierarchy.

The problematic case remains the co-application of the Union Treaties and the European Convention on Human Rights, to which all member states (save France) were signatories prior to Community/Union accession, and all requirements of which the Union purports to respect.[60] There is also the issue of the 'fiscal compact' agreed amongst 25 member states in Spring 2012, created by a treaty to exist independently of the Union framework: doubtless the relationship between the two Treaties is carefully circumscribed in the new treaty, yet should it enter into force the two could encounter significant complexities in their co-application, particularly as amongst the member states party to it and any member state(s) which stay(s) outside.

2. Languages

Something must be said of the (unique) language regime which governs the **6.09** Union, and the polyglot nature of the sources of Union law. The ECSC Treaty was drawn up in French and French was its sole authentic language text; other language versions remained official ('verified') translations only. Otherwise all Treaty texts exist now in 23 language versions (Bulgarian, Spanish, Czech, Danish, German, Estonian, Greek, English, French, Irish, Italian, Latvian, Lithuanian, Hungarian, Maltese, Dutch, Polish, Portuguese, Romanian, Slovak, Slovene, Finnish and Swedish) all equally authentic.[61] Croatia joins the list upon accession.[62] The only 'national' languages without this Treaty status are therefore Luxembourgish and Turkish, the latter recognised as an (equal) official language of Cyprus by the 1960 constitution[63] which is still technically in force, even if many of its provisions are inoperative. As for 'lesser' languages, many of which have some official status in parts of the various member states (and some spoken more extensively within the Union than several official languages), the Charter of Fundamental Rights provides that '[t]he Union shall respect cultural, religious and linguistic diversity'[64] and the Union provides some financial support for their protection and promotion, but they are otherwise unrecognised. With Lisbon the Treaties provide that they, the Treaties, may be translated into any other language with official status in a

---

59   TEU, art. 1, 3rd para; TFEU, art. 1(2).
60   See 6.109–6.112 below.
61   Lisbon Treaty, art. 7; TEU, art. 55; TFEU, art. 358. This is the order in which the languages normally appear – in (Roman) alphabetical order by the name of the language each in its own language ('Spanish' being Castellano). A similar convention exists in official listing of the member states.
62   2011 Act of Accession, arts 14 and 54.
63   Constitution of 16 August 1960, art. 3(1).
64   EU Charter of Fundamental Rights, art. 22; as to the Charter see 6.114–6.118 below.

member state or in any part of its territory and will be deposited in the archives of the Council, but accord them no official status.[65]

6.10 The 23 Treaty languages are also official languages and working languages of the institutions.[66] All legislative acts are adopted in all official languages,[67] each text equally authentic;[68] administrative acts addressed to particular member state(s) or person(s) are adopted in the language(s) of the addressee(s) and are authentic in that/those language(s) alone. There is a general principle that, in administrative dealings with the institutions, a person is entitled to use, and can be bound only by, a language he or she understands.[69]

6.11 If the lawyer's art turns upon the meaning of words, the challenge of dealing with words which exist in 23 different versions, with all the nuance and shading which that may bring, becomes apparent. The means of dealing with it is discussed below.

B. NATURE AND ENFORCEMENT OF UNION LAW

1. Status of EU law

6.12 The Union is created by international treaties, from which it derives its personality and authority. It also drew inspiration from the legal systems of the member states which were party to its creation, but constituted their own legal system independent of them[70] – a principle known as the autonomy of Union

---

65 TEU, art. 55(2).
66 Regulation 1 [1958] JO 385, art. 1, as amended; see Part B, Introduction above.
67 Regulation 1; 2003 Act of Accession, art. 58; 2005 Act of Accession, art. 58. The (slight) exceptions are: (a) Irish: since becoming an (equal) official and working language of the institutions in 2007 Union legislation is drafted in Irish and published in an Irish version of the *Official Journal* (*Iris Oifigiúil*), except transitionally this applies only to Regulations adopted jointly by the Parliament and the Council, the derogation to be reviewed every five years (and now extended to 2017, Regulation 1257/2010 [2010] OJ L343/5) and may be ended by a unanimous Council (Regulation 920/2005 [2005] OJ L156/3); (b) those (rare) legislative acts which do not have universal application, and so are not authentic in the language(s) of member state(s) in which they do not apply; and (c) owing primarily to recruitment difficulties not all acts were drafted and published in Maltese for a three-year period following accession (see Regulation 930/2004 [2004] OJ L169/1). A backlog of important legislation has been largely (but not fully) made up. Measures adopted by the ordinary legislative procedure are translated into Catalan/Valencian, Basque and Galician under an administrative agreement between the Council and Spain, but these versions have no legal force, even in Spain. Existing legislation still in force will be drawn up in Croatian prior to accession; 2011 Act of Accession, art. 52.
68 Regulation 1; Case C-296/95 *R v Commissioners of Customs and Excise, ex parte EMU Tabac and ors* [1998] ECR I-1605.
69 See 6.135 below.
70 See e.g., Case 9/65 *Acciaierie San Michele v High Authority* [1967] ECR 1; Case 28/67 *Mölkerei-Zentrale Westfalen/Lippe v Hauptzollamt Paderborn* [1968] ECR 143; Case 34/73 *Variola v Amministrazione Italiana delle Finanze* [1973] ECR 981.

law. On any view the Community Treaties were from the beginning international treaties different from most, and created an international organisation different from any other – so much so that the Court of Justice was able to observe in 1991 that the EEC Treaty, 'albeit concluded in the form of an international agreement, none the less constitutes the constitutional charter of a Community based on the rule of law'.[71] Why this is so is a product, first, of the special nature of the Treaties, but second, the principles more implicit than explicit in it which have been developed by the Court of Justice in discharging its task of 'ensur[ing] that … the law is observed'.[72] The product of 50 some years of this work may be characterised as an effective and coherent legal system, resting upon three fundamental pillars: the direct effect of Union law, the primacy of Union law, and a law of obligations comprising a right in reparation for persons unlawfully deprived of a Union law right. These were principles developed within and for the legal system created by the Community Treaties, to which the Union succeeded in 2009.

2. Direct effect

From the start the Treaties set out mechanisms by which the failure of a **6.13** member state to comply with a Community obligation may be brought before the Court of Justice by the Commission or by another member state.[73] It therefore supplied its own means of enforcement – and a compulsory and exclusive jurisdiction of the Court[74] – above and beyond such mechanisms as make international law effective. But judicial protection of Treaty rights was soon to be taken significantly further. In the early case of *van Gend en Loos*,[75] only the second referred to the Court under the preliminary ruling procedure of

---

71 Opinion 1/91 *Re the EEA Agreement* [1991] ECR I-6079, at para. 21. In 1986 the Court had referred to judicial review of Community legislation for 'conformity with the basic constitutional charter, the Treaty'; Case 294/83 *Parti Ecologiste 'Les Verts' v European Parliament* [1986] ECR 1339, at para. 23; repeated recently ('the basic constitutional charter') in Cases C-402 and 415/05P *Kadi and Al Bakaraat v Council and Commission* (Kadi II) [2008] ECR I-6351, at para. 281 and Case C-236/09 *Association Belge des Consummateurs Test-Achats and ors v Conseil des ministres*, judgment of 1 March 2011, not yet reported, *per* A-G Kokott at para. 26 of her opinion. The *Bundesverfassungsgericht* attributed this quality to the Treaty as early as 1967 ('Der EWG-Vertrag stellt gewissermaßen die Verfassung dieser Gemeinschaft dar'); BVerfG, 18. Oktober 1967, BVerfGE 22, 293 (296). Back further still, in only the tenth judgment of the (ECSC) Court A-G Lagrange said 'although the Treaty which the Court has the task of applying was concluded in the form of an international treaty and although it unquestionably is one, it is nevertheless, from a material point of view, the charter of the Community'; Case 8/55 *Fédération Charbonnière de Belgique v High Authority* (Fédéchar) [1954–56] ECR 245, at 277. He also said the ECSC was created 'on a model which is more closely related to a federal than to an international organization'.
72 TEU, art. 19(1) (ex art. 220 EC).
73 EEC Treaty, arts 169, 170 (arts 258, 259 TFEU); see 5.48–5.65 above.
74 EEC Treaty, art. 219 (art. 344 TFEU), which binds the member states 'not to submit a dispute concerning the interpretation of this Treaty to any method of settlement other than those provided for therein'.
75 Case 26/62 *Algemene Transport- en Expeditie Onderneming van Gend en Loos v Nederlandse Administratie der Belastingen* [1963] ECR 1.

article 177 EEC (article 267 TFEU), the Dutch government had attempted to impose, in 1961 as part of a customs protocol agreed within the Benelux union in 1958 (after the entry into force of the EEC Treaty), a higher duty than previously upon a consignment of industrial goods imported from Germany. The decision was challenged before the *Tariefcommissie*, a Dutch administrative court for customs and excise matters, on the ground that the increase was contrary to article 12 of the Treaty. Much of the argument centred upon the exact, technical meaning of, and so the nature of the obligation imposed by, the text of article 12 ('Member States shall refrain [*Les États membres s'abstiennent*; *De Lid-Staten onthouden zich*] from introducing ... any new customs duties ... and from increasing those which already apply'). But it was also argued that, whatever the meaning may be, the sole means by which a member state could be brought to book was by the enforcement procedure set out in the Treaty: that, whilst the EEC Treaty imposed obligations upon the signatory states, a failure to comply with them could be put right only by that procedure, and that those obligations conferred upon natural or legal persons no right by which they could enforce them directly in the only courts to which they had access – that is, in their national courts. Upon the case being referred to it, the Court of Justice disagreed. In what has become the best known passage in EU law, out of which all subsequent developments grew,[76] it said that

> the Community constitutes a new legal order of international law for the benefit of which the states have limited their sovereign rights, albeit within limited fields, and the subjects of which comprise not only Member States but also their nationals. Independently of the legislation of Member States, Community law therefore not only imposes obligations on individuals but is also intended to confer upon them rights which become part of their legal heritage.[77]

And so in the *dispositif*:

> Article 12 of the Treaty establishing the European Economic Community produces direct effects [*produit des effets immediats*; *heeft direkte werking*] and creates individual rights which national courts must protect.

---

76 See F. Mancini and D. Keeling, 'Democracy and the European Court of Justice' (1994) 57 MLR 175 at 183: '[I]f the European Community still exists 50 or 100 years from now, historians will look back on *Van Gend en Loos* as the unique judicial contribution to the making of Europe'.

77 Case 26/62 *van Gend en Loos*, n. 75 above, at 12. 'Legal heritage' is an inadequate translation of *patrimoine juridique*; 'patrimonial rights' might be a more meaningful translation, and in a subsequent formulation 'legal assets' was substituted; Case C-453/99 *Courage* v *Crehan* [1991] ECR I-6297, at para. 19. It is well to note that the formula contained in the first sentence cited was reiterated by the Court in a 1991 opinion and subsequently *verbatim*, except substituting 'albeit within limited fields' with 'in ever wider fields'; Opinion 1/91 *re the EEA Agreement* [1991] ECR I-6079, at para. 21; also Cases T-27 etc./03 *SP and ors* v *Commission* [2007] ECR II-4331, at para. 70; Case T-24/07 *ThyssenKrupp Stainless* v *Commission* [2009] ECR II-2309, at para. 63; Opinion 1/09 *Re the European Patent Convention*, opinion of 8 March 2011, not yet reported, at para. 65.

Hence the doctrine of 'direct effect', a quality adhering to Union law which is of itself capable of creating rights and obligations enforceable before national courts. As developed and refined by the Court of Justice,[78] it applies where a provision of Union law (that is, a provision of the Treaties, of legislation or of any other law-making measure):

- is clear and precise;
- creates an unconditional and unqualified obligation; and
- requires or admits of no further implementing measure on the part of any Union or national authority.

The third criterion may be, and soon was, absorbed by the second, 'unconditional' having come to mean setting forth an obligation which is not qualified by any condition, or subject, in its implementation or effects, to the taking of any measure either by the Union institutions or by those of the member states.[79] In these circumstances the provision is said to have direct effect, and is to be enforced by the appropriate national court or tribunal. In a simpler formulation, such provision is directly effective if it may

> be construed as establishing … a precise and unconditional principle which is sufficiently operational to be applied by a national court and which is therefore capable of governing the legal position of individuals.[80]

Alternatively,

> It is well established in the Court's case-law that certain Treaty articles are clear, precise and sufficiently unconditional to be invoked before national courts by a natural or legal person without the need for further implementing provisions – they are directly effective.[81]

A provision which meets the test is an immediate source of rights and obligations for all concerned, whether member states or individuals who are parties to legal relationships under Union law, the full effect of which must be

---

78 See e.g., Case 28/67 *Molkerei-Zentrale Wetfalen/Lippe* v *Hauptzollamt Paderborn* [1968] ECR 143; Case 2/74 *Reyners* v *Belgian State* [1974] ECR 631; Case 41/74 *Van Duyn* v *Home Office* [1974] ECR 1337; Case 148/78 *Pubblico Ministero* v *Ratti* [1979] ECR 1629; Case 271/82 *Auer* v *Ministère Public (No. 2)* [1983] ECR 2727; Case C-72/95 *Kraaijeveld* v *Gedeputeerde Staten van Zuid-Holland* [1996] ECR I-5403; Case C-435/97 *World Wildlife Fund* v *Autonome Provinz Bozen* [1999] ECR I-5613.

79 Case 28/67 *Molkerei-Zentrale, ibid.; Case C-236/92 Comitato di coordinamento per la Difesa della Cava and ors v Regione Lombardia and ors [1994] ECR I-483.*

80 Case C-63/99 *R* v *Secretary of State for the Home Department, ex parte Gloszczuk and anor* [2001] ECR I-6369, at para. 38; Case C-235/99 *R* v *Secretary of State for the Home Department, ex parte Kondova* [2001] ECR I-6427, at para. 39; Case C-268/99 *Jany and ors* v *Staatssecretaris van Justitie* [2001] ECR I-8615, at para. 26.

81 Case C-512/08 *Commission* v *France* [2010] ECR I-8833, *per* A-G Sharpston at para. 42 of her opinion.

deployed, in a uniform manner in all member states, as from its entry into force and throughout the duration of its validity.[82] The fact that the Treaties supply autonomous enforcement mechanisms, themselves serving to overcome the inertia and resistance of the member states,[83] is immaterial:

> The vigilance of individuals concerned to protect their rights amounts to an effective supervision in addition to the supervision entrusted … to the diligence of the Commission and of the Member States.[84]

On one view both issue and result are wholly unremarkable. Judge Pescatore called it an 'infant disease' of Community law[85] and wondered at the fuss created when it is 'the normal condition of any rule of law'[86] and 'nothing but the ordinary state of the law'.[87] But at the time it was, at least for those member states still wedded to a dualist approach to international law in general, and treaty law in particular, revolutionary. Adaptation to it was to cause constitutional difficulties in some member states and practical difficulties in many.

6.14 The Court of Justice has held a number of articles of the Treaties to have direct effect. It has also recognised over the years as directly effective a great mass of Community legislation which implements and/or expands upon Treaty principles, rights and obligations which are not themselves directly effective. The principle now applies, where the necessary conditions are present, across all spheres of Union law. In British statutory terms, rights created by directly effective Union law are 'enforceable EU rights' to be applied and enforced as part of the law of the United Kingdom.[88] Care should be taken not to confuse direct effect with direct applicability, which in Community law came to mean something different;[89] it is a slip to which even the Court is not immune.[90]

---

82 Case C-409/06 *Winner Wetten* v *Bürgermeisterin der Stadt Bergheim* [2010] ECR I-8015, at para. 54.

83 Case 20/59 *Italy* v *High Authority* [1960] ECR 325 at 339; Case 25/59 *Netherlands* v *High Authority* [1960] ECR 355 at 374.

84 Case 26/62 *van Gend en Loos*, n. 75 above, at 13. A good example illustrating this is enforcement actions initiated by the Commission in 2007 against Austria and Belgium for limiting access of foreign students to higher education (see 11.66 below, n. 419) but suspended for five years owing to, it is thought, a political deal done with those member states; disgruntled French students nonetheless took up the cudgels relying upon the direct effect of arts 12 and 18 EC (now arts 18 and 21 TFEU) and forced the matter of the Belgian Decree before the Court of Justice; see Case C-73/08 *Bressol and Chaverot and ors* v *Gouvernement de la Communauté française* [2010] ECR I-2735.

85 P. Pescatore, 'The Doctrine of "Direct Effect": An Infant Disease of Community Law' (1983) 8 *ELRev.* 155.

86 *Ibid.* at 155.

87 *Ibid.* at 177.

88 European Communities Act 1972, s. 2(1).

89 As to direct applicability see 6.59 below.

90 See Case 2/74 *Reyners* v *Belgium* [1974] ECR 631, at para. 32; Case 1/78 *Kenny* v *Insurance Officer* [1978] ECR 1489, at para. 12; Case 12/86 *Demirel* v *Stadt Schwäbisch Gmünd* [1987] ECR 3719, at para. 14; Case 157/86 *Murphy and ors* v *An Bord Telecom Eireann* [1988] ECR 673, at paras 7 and 11; and Case C-268/06 *Impact* v *Minister for Agriculture and Food and ors* [2008] ECR I-2483, *per* A-G Kokott at para. 96 of her opinion, in

There is a distinction to be drawn between provisions of Union law upon which **6.15** the individual may rely as against public authorities ('vertical direct effect') and those upon which he may rely as against other natural or legal persons ('horizontal direct effect'). This is a function less of the addressee of the right than of the addressee of the obligation. As much of Union law is concerned with obligations of the state (in all its manifestations), vertical direct effect is, perhaps, the 'normal' rule. But increasingly Union obligations are addressed, if sometimes indirectly, to private persons, so increasing the instances of horizontal direct effect. And this gives rise to particular problems.[91]

3. Primacy

The issue of inconsistency between Community law and national law first arose **6.16** frontally in 1964 in *Costa* v *ENEL*,[92] an apparently straightforward (and trifling) dispute involving a refusal by Mr Costa to pay an electricity bill of 1,925 *lire* to the newly privatised Italian monopoly (ENEL), his argument being that the formation of ENEL in 1961 was prohibited by the EEC Treaty and the company itself therefore a nullity. The case came to a Milanese *giudice conciliatore*,[93] before whom it was argued that in the event of incompatibility between Community law, made effective in Italy by means of an ordinary law,[94] and another ordinary law (such as the privatisation law) adopted subsequently in time to that which made EEC law effective in Italy, an Italian court was bound, in accordance with normal Italian rules of statutory construction (*lex posterior derogat priori*, or implied repeal), to give preference to the latter. In accordance with Italian judicial procedures, the question was referred by the judge for preliminary consideration to the Corte Costituzionale, which agreed with the argument.[95] Not convinced of the correctness of this response, the judge then referred the question to the Court of Justice under article 177 EEC (article 267 TFEU), which did not:

---

which the Court (and the A-G) refers, respectively, to art. 52 of the EEC Treaty as 'a directly applicable provision' (*rechtstreeks toepasselijk is*); to art. 7 EEC as 'directly applicable'; to a provision of an agreement with a third country as 'directly applicable' (*unmittelbar anwendbare*); to art. 119 EEC as 'directly applicable'; and to the provisions of a Directive having 'direct applicability' (*unmittelbare Anwendung*), when it clearly means directly effective.

91 See 6.77–6.81 below.

92 Case 6/64 *Costa* v *Ente Nazionale Energia Elettrica (ENEL)* [1964] ECR 585.

93 The *giudice conciliatore* was a magistrate (*magistrato onorario*) with jurisdiction in minor criminal matters, small civil claims and property disputes. The office was replaced in 1994 by the *giudice di pace*; l. 21 novembre 1991, no. 374, GU no. 278 del 27 novembre 1991.

94 L. 14 ottobre 1957, no. 1203, GU no. 317 del 23 dicembre 1957. This is the only constitutional means available in Italian law for this purpose; as in the United Kingdom, a treaty cannot be entrenched as a higher norm.

95 Corte Cost., 7 marzo 1964, no. 14, 9 Giur Cost 129.

The integration into the laws of each Member State of provisions which derive from the Community, and more generally the terms and spirit of the Treaty, make it impossible for the states, as a corollary, to accord precedence to a unilateral and subsequent measure over a legal system accepted by them on a basis of reciprocity …

The obligations undertaken under the Treaty establishing the Community would not be unconditional, but merely contingent, if they could be called in question by subsequent legislative acts of the signatories …

It follows from all these observations that the law stemming from the Treaty, an independent source of law, could not, because of its special and original nature, be overridden by domestic legal provisions, however framed, without being deprived of its character as Community law and without the legal basis of the Community itself being called into question.

The transfer by the States from their domestic legal system to the Community legal system of the rights and obligations arising under the Treaty carries with it a permanent limitation of their sovereign rights, against which a subsequent unilateral act incompatible with the concept of the Community cannot prevail.[96]

This principle – which is simply a practical articulation of the doctrine that *pacta sunt servanda* – is known as the doctrine of the primacy or supremacy,[97] very occasionally 'precedence' (although still *primauté*),[98] of Community (and now Union) law. It is a principle recognised in and for public international law,[99] if not always fully effective in that sphere, and a doctrine well known in the context of federal systems wherein, in the event of conflict within concurrent fields of jurisdiction, the law of the federal authority will normally take precedence over the law of the regional authorities. Also characteristic of federal systems, it neither requires nor results (of itself) in the nullity or non-existence of the national law,[100] merely that it be 'disapplied' (*écartée* or *laissée inappliquée*) to the extent of the inconsistency[101] (and only to that

---

96 Case 6/64 *Costa*, n. 92 above, at paras 10, 11, 13, 14. Mr Costa lost nevertheless, for the Court found no impediment in the EEC Treaty to the privatisation and formation of ENEL.

97 In its opinion on the compatibility of the Treaty establishing a Constitution for Europe and the Spanish Constitution the *Tribunal Constitucional* distinguished between the primacy (*primacía*) and supremacy (*supremacía*) of the EU legal order; TC, Declaración 1/2004 de 13 de diciembre de 2004 (BOE núm. 3, de 4 de enero de 2005). It is an interesting construct but has not attracted a wider currency, the two terms used elsewhere synonymously.

98 Case 106/77 *Amministrazione delle Finanze dello Stato* v *Simmenthal* [1978] ECR 629, at para. 17; Case C-409/06 *Winner Wetten* v *Bürgermeisterin der Stadt Bergheim* [2010] ECR I-8015, at para. 53.

99 See Vienna Convention on the Law of Treaties, arts 26–7; advisory opinion of the International Court of Justice in the *PLO Observer Mission Case* [1988] ICJ Rep. 12, at para. 57.

100 See especially Cases C-10 etc./97 *Ministero delle Finanze* v *IN.CO.GE.'90 and ors* [1998] ECR I-6307, at para. 21: 'It cannot … be inferred from the judgment in *Simmenthal* that the incompatibility with Community law of a subsequently adopted rule of national law has the effect of rendering that rule of national law non-existent'.

101 Cases C-10 etc./97 *IN.CO.GE.'90*, ibid. (*écarté*); Case C-208/05 *ITC Innovative Technology Centre* v *Bundesagentur für Arbiet* [2007] ECR I-181, in the *dispositif*,; Case C-432/05 *Unibet (London) and anor* v

extent)[102] – although national law may itself provide that primacy produces that effect.[103] As developed by the Court of Justice, primacy means that an enforceable right deriving from Union law in all its forms has priority over *any* inconsistent national law, which must in the event be set aside (disapplied) by a national court, if necessary on its own initiative.[104] This is so even where the national law embodies a fundamental constitutional principle or procedure.[105]

The issue of primacy has relevance logically only in areas in which law-making **6.17** authority is shared between the Union and the member states, that is in fields of 'concurrent' jurisdiction; where law-making authority is exclusive, either Union or national, it does not arise. This is another dichotomy familiar in federal

---

Justitiekanslern [2007] ECR I-2271, at para. 60; Case C-115/08 *Land Oberösterreich* v *ČEZ* [2009] ECR I-10265, at para. 140 and Case C-555/07 *Kücükdeveci* v *Swedex* [2010] ECR I-365, at paras 51, 52, 53, 54, 55, 56 and in the *dispositif* (*laissé inappliqué*); Cases C-188 and 189/10 *Melki and Abdeli* [2010] ECR I-5667 (both *laissé inappliqué* (paras 43, 57 and the *dispositif*) and *écarté* (para. 44)). Occasionally the formula is 'hold inapplicable' (*laisser inapplicable*) (Case 157/86 *Murphy and ors* v *An Bord Telecom Eireann* [1988] ECR 673, at para. 11); 'refrain from applying' (*écarté*) (Case C-443/03 *Leffler* v *Berlin Chemie* [2005] ECR I-9611, at para. 51); or 'setting aside' (*laissant inappliqué*) (Case C-144/04 *Mangold* v *Helm* [2005] ECR I-9981, at paras 77, 78). 'Disapplied' is the term of art adopted for normal use in UK courts; e.g., *Imperial Chemical Industries* v *Colmer (Inspector of Taxes)* [2000] 1 All ER 129 (HL), *per* Lord Nolan at 133, 134; *R (Junttan OY)* v *Bristol Magistrates' Court* [2003] UKHL 55, [2004] 2 All ER 555, *per* Lord Nicholls at 563; *Autologic Holdings* v *Inland Revenue Commissioners* [2005] UKHL, [2006] 1 AC 118, *per* Lord Nicholls at 127 ('disapplied or moulded to the extend needed'); *Fleming* v *HM Revenue and Customs Commissioners* [2008] UKHL 2, [2008] 1 All ER 1061, *per* Lord Walker at 1075; *McGeogh* v *Electoral Registration Officer, Dumfries and Galloway and ors* [2011] CSOH 65, at paras 20 and 21. But there are sometimes variations: 'To the extent that the primary legislation in play in this case is incompatible with [a] Directive, it is thereby rendered void and this court can and should so declare'; *Gough and anor* v *Chief Constable of the Derbyshire Constabulary* [2002] EWCA Civ 351, [2002] QB 1213, *per* Lord Phillips at 1230–1; '[t]he … issue … is whether the [UK] levy constitutes a charge having equivalent effect to customs duty [*sic*] (a 'CEE') in respect of imports … contrary to TFEU articles 28 and 30. If it is a CEE, then it is in relation to such imports void'; *Bloomsbury International and ors* v *Sea Fish Industry Authority and anor* [2011] UKSC 25, [2011] 4 All ER 721, *per* Lord Mance at para. 22. The power to disapply national law is the preserve of the national court, the Court of Justice has no power to do so.

102 E.g., Case C-212/06 *Government of the French Community and Walloon Government* v *Flemish Government* [2008] ECR I-1683.

103 For example, an Act of the Scottish Parliament or of the Northern Ireland or Welsh Assemblies, if incompatible with Union law, 'is not law'; Scotland Act 1998, s. 29(1), (2)(d); Northern Ireland Act 1998, ss. 6(2)(d), 24(1)(b); Government of Wales Act 2006, s. 94(2), (6)(c). It has a considerable effect upon the thinking and conduct of these bodies when they deal with (what might be) Union matters.

104 See Case 106/77 *Amministrazione delle Finanze dello Stato* v *Simmenthal* [1978] ECR 629; Case C-358/95 *Morellato* v *Unità Sanitaria Locale No. 11, Pordenone* [1997] ECR I-1431; Cases C-10 etc./97 *IN.CO.GE. '90*, n. 100 above; Case C-119/05 *Ministero dell'Industria, del Commercio e dell'Artigianato* v *Lucchini Siderurgica* [2007] ECR I-6199.

105 Case 11/70 *Internationale Handelsgesellschaft mbH* v *Einfuhr- und Vorratsstelle für Getreide und Futtermittel* [1970] ECR 1125; Case C-213/89 *R* v *Secretary of State for Transport, ex parte Factortame* [1990] ECR I-2433; Case C-473/93 *Commission* v *Luxembourg* [1996] ECR I-3207; Case C-118/08 *Transportes Urbanos y Servicios Generales* v *Administración del Estado* [2010] ECR I-635; Cases C-188 and 189/10 *Melki and Abdeli*, n. 101 above; Case C-271/08 *Commission* v *Germany* [2010] ECR I-7087; Case C-409/06 *Winner Wetten* v *Bürgermeisterin der Stadt Bergheim* [2010] ECR I-8015; Case C-173/09 *Elchinov* v *Natsionalna zdravnoosiguritelna kasa* [2010] ECR I-8889; Case C-208/09 *Sayn-Wittgenstein* v *Landeshauptmann von Wien* [2010] ECR I-13693; Case C-571/10 *Kamberaj* v *Istituto Per l'Edilizia Sociale della Provincia autonoma di Bolzano and ors*, judgment of 24 April 2012, not yet reported.

constitutions, although because Union authority is achieved by a fluid process of gradual accretion, it is perhaps better characterised in this context as a wholly occupied field. If exclusive Union competences exist it means that the member states have surrendered all authority to legislate in the relevant fields, and an attempt to do so is invalid not because a purported national rule cannot coexist with a Union rule of higher authority (primacy), but because the member state has no authority to make law in that field. The EC Treaty alluded to fields of exclusive Community competence *en passant*[106] but in fact made only one such provision expressly, the (exclusive) right conferred upon the European Central Bank to authorise the issue of euro banknotes.[107] The Court of Justice made reference to them from time to time,[108] but failed (satisfactorily) to define them. A stab at doing so was made by Lisbon, setting out areas of 'exclusive [Union] competence' and areas of 'shared competence'.[109] Because of the dynamic nature of Union authority these areas may grow and consolidate over time; but in any event generally Union competences exist in concurrent fields, in which the issue of primacy necessarily arises.

6.18 Notwithstanding the assured approach of the Court of Justice to it, it must be observed that issues adhering to primacy give rise to serious constitutional questions in some member states, and some have never entirely acquiesced in the principle of the absolute primacy of Union law over, in particular, national constitutional law. Indeed, a critic would say the Court has never rigorously, or adequately, identified its precise source, and its bluntness or lack of suppleness or nuance sits ill with the flexibility the Court requires of national courts in giving effect to Union law. It has engendered much doctrinal debate, particularly in Germany,[110] but so far no serious defiance there, and a long-running

---

106 EC Treaty, art. 5, 2nd para.: 'In areas which do not fall within its exclusive competence, the Community shall take action'.

107 *Ibid.* art. 106(1).

108 Case 22/70 *Commission* v *Council* (ERTA) [1971] ECR 263; Opinion 1/75 *Re Export Credit Guarantee* [1975] ECR 1355; Cases 3 etc./76 *Cornelius Kramer* [1976] ECR 1279; Case 804/79 *Commission* v *United Kingdom* (Fishery Conservation Measures) [1981] ECR 1045; Opinion 1/08 (Re GATS Special Commitments) [2009] ECR I-11129.

109 TFEU, arts 3, 4; see 7.06–7.09 below.

110 The lengthy (and thus far largely doctrinal/academic) debate as to the correct course to follow in the event of a clash between a Union right and the fundamental rights guarantees and/or the inviolable core of the German Basic Law can be traced in the case law of the *Bundesverfassungsgericht* from its seminal *Solange I* judgment in 1974, BVerfG, 29. Mai 1974, BVerfGE 37, 271, through BVerfG, 25. Juli 1979 (*Vielleicht*), BVerfGE 52, 187; BVerfG, 22. Oktober 1986 (*Solange II*), BVerfGE 73, 339; BVerfG, 12. Oktober 1993 (*Maastricht*), BVerfGE 89, 155; BVerfG, 7. Juni 2000 (*Bananenmarktordnung* or *Solange III*), BVerfGE 102, 147; BVerfG, 30. Juni 2009 (*Lissabon-Vertrag*), BVerfGE 123, 267; to the most recent BVerfG, 6. Juli 2010 (*Honeywell*), BVerfGE 126, 286. It should be noted that both the *Maastricht* and the *Lisbon* judgments, particularly the latter, contained extensive discussion as to limits imposed by the Basic Law upon the accretion of (future) Union authority. In *Honeywell* the *Bundesverfassungsgericht* set out the circumstances in which it would (and would be required to) reassume its constitutional duty to test Union legislation against the fundamental rules of the Basic Law; see n. 324 below.

spat with the French administrative courts seems now finally to be settled.[111] Each adapts in accordance with its constitution and habits. In the United Kingdom the constitutional difficulty stems from the doctrine of parliamentary supremacy, according to which there are no entrenched laws and the provisions of an Act adopted by the Queen in Parliament, of which there is no higher authority, will 'impliedly' repeal any prior rule of law (which might include Union rules, made effective by the European Communities Act 1972) with which they are inconsistent. The most authoritative judicial consideration of the meaning and breadth of the 1972 Act, and so UK compliance with the constitutional requirements of Union law, is to be drawn from the speech of Lord Bridge in *Factortame* (1991):

> If the supremacy within the European Community of Community law over national law was not always inherent in the EEC Treaty, it was certainly well established in the jurisprudence of the European Court of Justice long before the United Kingdom joined the Community. Thus, whatever limitations of its sovereignty Parliament accepted when it enacted the European Communities Act 1972 was entirely voluntary. Under the terms of the Act of 1972 it has always been clear that it was the duty of a United Kingdom court, when delivering final judgment, to override any rule of national law found to be in conflict with any directly enforceable [= directly effective] rule of Community law.[112]

Subsequently in the High Court in England:

> All the specific rights and obligations which EU [*sic*] law creates are by the 1972 Act incorporated into our domestic law and rank supreme: that is, anything in our substantive law inconsistent with any of these rights and obligations is abrogated or must be modified in order to avoid the inconsistency. This is true even where the inconsistent municipal provision is contained in primary legislation.[113]

---

111 Owing to a fundamental principle of French constitutional law (*acte clair*) the administrative courts long resisted the proposition that a Directive could confer direct effect so as to serve as a basis for a complaint against an individual administrative act. The gauntlet was thrown down in CE, Ass, 22 décembre 1978 (*Ministre de l'Intérieur* c. *Cohn-Bendit*), Rec Lebon 524; as to the general proposition see 6.74–6.76 below. The *Conseil d'Etat* slowly chipped away at the rule (see e.g., Ass, 30 octobre 1989 (*Nicolo*) Rec Lebon 190; Ass, 24 septembre 1990 (*Boisdet*), Rec Lebon 251) and following constitutional amendment in 1992 (see loi constitutionnelle no. 92–554 du 25 juin 1992 ajoutant à la Constitution un titre 'Des Communautés européennes et de l'Union européenne', JO du 26 juin 1992, 8406) and subsequently which took express notice of Community membership it finally yielded, partially in CE, Ass, 8 février 2007 (*Société Arcelor Atlantique et Lorraine e.a.* c. *Président de la République e.a.*), Rec Lebon 56 ('un véritable Waterloo' according to *Le Monde*, 9 February 2007), then fully in CE, Ass, 30 octobre 2009, *Perreux* c. *Ministère de la justice et des libertés*, [2010] Rec Dalloz, 553.

112 *R* v *Secretary of State for Transport, ex parte Factortame* [1991] 1 AC 603 at 658–9 (HL).

113 *Thoburn* v *Sunderland City Council* [2002] EWHC 195 (Admin), [2003] QB 151, *per* Laws J at para. 69.

Laws J attributed this pre-eminence to the fact that the 1972 Act is a 'constitutional statute' and recognised as such by the common law of England,[114] although authority for this unknown class of statute is elusive. Whatever the legal basis, constitutional difficulties which, according to Lord Bridge, were in any event 'based on a misconception',[115] appear to be settled: the European Communities Act is, almost uniquely, resistant to implied repeal.[116] Resistance to *express* repeal is a proposition utterly at variance with conventional (Diceyan) English constitutional theory, and various *dicta* from English courts hold that Union law (or part of it) could be overridden, or made ineffective in the United Kingdom, by an Act of Parliament which provided intentionally and expressly that it should do so:[117] 'by express words ..., or by words so specific that the inference of an actual determination to effect the result contended for [is] irresistible'.[118] Certainly on the Diceyan view Parliament remains free to alter, or repeal, the 1972 Act which continues to underpin the authority of Union law in the United Kingdom. In an aside from the High Court,

> I am here ignoring the ... point that Parliament has chosen to subordinate itself to European law, because that is an artefact of our membership of the European Union and Parliament could change that tomorrow.[119]

This ultimate reliance upon a statutory basis for 'the means by which ... European Union law has effect in the United Kingdom'[120] was, for greater certainty (and political expedience), reiterated in 2011 by Act of Parlament:

> Directly applicable or directly effective EU law (that is, the rights, powers, liabilities, obligations, restrictions, remedies and procedures referred to in section 2(1) of the European Communities Act 1972) falls to be recognised and available in law in the United Kingdom only by virtue of that Act or where it is required to be recognised and available in law by virtue of any other Act.[121]

---

114 *Ibid.*

115 *Factortame*, n. 112 above, at 658.

116 *Macarthys Ltd* v *Smith* [1979] 3 All ER 325, *per* Denning MR at 329; *Thoburn*, n. 113 above, at paras 37–70. Another statute which is said to enjoy this privileged status is the Human Rights Act 1998.

117 *Felixstowe Dock and Railway Co.* v *British Transport Docks Board* [1976] 2 CMLR 655, *per* Denning MR at 664–5; *Macarthys Ltd* v *Smith*, *ibid.*; *Thoburn*, n. 113 above. The constitutional issues have yet to be fully addressed by the courts in Scotland (but for an early foray see *Gibson* v *Lord Advocate* 1975 SC 136 (OH)) and in Northern Ireland.

118 *Thoburn*, n. 113 above, *per* Laws J at para. 63.

119 *Oakley* v *Animal and ors* [2005] EWHC 210 (Ch), [2005] EuLR 657 at 680.

120 European Union Act 2011, long title.

121 *Ibid.* s. 18.

Of course, these views are not restricted to the United Kingdom. Although **6.19** labouring under a republican constitution rather than a constitutional monarchy and navigating a complex theory of the state, in 2009 the *Bundesverfassungsgericht* nevertheless betrayed, in the final analysis, a similar approach:

> [A]n extensive autonomy of political authority conferred upon the European Union … can, in German constitutional law, come about only as a function of the freedom of action of the self-determining [German] people. According to the constitution, such integration steps … must, in principle, be revocable.[122]

Shortly after accession the Czech *Ústavní Soud* (constitutional court) cross-bred the Czech constitution and the earlier *Solange* case law of the *Bundesverfassungsgericht* and of the *Corte Costituzionale* and said, in a manner which reflects the experience of first brush with Union law in several member states:

> This conferral of a part of its [the Czech state's] powers [to the EU institutions] is of course a conditional conferral, as the original bearer of sovereignty, as well as the powers flowing therefrom, remains still the Czech Republic.[123]

It betrayed similar sentiments in the (principal) judgment by which it in turn approved Czech ratification of the Lisbon Treaty.[124] More forthright still are the views of the *Trybunał Konstytucyjny*, for whom the Treaty commitment to the principle of conferral is a (re-)affirmation of the sovereignty of the member states:[125] it says that, should it arise, an 'irreconcilable contradiction' (*nieusuwalnej sprzeczność*) between Union law and a Polish constitutional norm which cannot be resolved by a process of sympathetic interpretation, cannot be resolved by attributing primacy to the former, and would leave the nation (or the state authority speaking for it), as sovereign, with a choice of securing an alteration of the Union provisions, amending the constitution or, ultimately, quitting the Union.[126] Yet other supreme courts have adjusted to constitutional subservience without murmur.[127] Of course, that the constitutional courts of the 2004 intake should show sensitivity to a *Grundnorm* is not surprising, for,

---

122 BVerfG, 30. Juni 2009 (*Lissabon-Vertrag*), BVerfGE 123, 267 (350) ('[E]ine weitgehende Verselbständigung politischer Herrschaft für die Europäische Union … kann aus der Sicht des deutschen Verfassungsrechts allein aus der Handlungsfreiheit des selbstbestimmten Volkes heraus geschehen. Solche Integrationsschritte müssen von Verfassungs … prinzipiell widerruflich sein').

123 Pl. ÚS 50/04 ze dne 17. března 2006 (*kvót v odvěí cukru*), at Part B, para. 4 ('Toto propůjčení části pravomocí je ovšem … propůjčením podmíněným, neboť originálním nositelem suverenity a z ní vyplývajících pravomocí nadále zůstala ČR').

124 Pl. ÚS 19/08 ze dne 26. listopadu 2008 (*Lisabonská smlouva*).

125 K 32/09, Wyrok z dnia 24 listopada 2010 r. (*Traktat z Lizbony*), 2010 Nr 229, poz. 1506, at part 2.2.

126 K 18/04, Wyrok z dnia 11 maja 2005 r. (*Traktat akcesyjne*), 2005 Nr 5, poz. 49, at parts 6.3–6.4.

127 E.g., Riigikohus, 11 mai 2006. aasta otsus kohtuasjas 3–4–1–3–06; 26 juuni 2008. aasta otsus kohtuasjas 3–4–1–5–08.

for six of the ten, they are defending a sovereignty and a constitutional order (re)gained only in the previous 15 years.[128] Further points of constitutional friction in the new member states have yet fully to be explored.[129] It remains that in few member states has the pure view of the Court of Justice on primacy been wholly accepted.

6.20 Like direct effect, primacy was a principle developed and applied in and for Community law; it was *not* recognised (any more so than a requirement of public international law) as applying to (1993–2009) Union law as a whole, although it may be said to have slowly been seeping into it. This serves to contrast the (relatively) rudimentary legal order of the Union (its 'partial legal order characterised by international law')[130] with that of the Community: where national laws giving effect to the framework decision on the European arrest warrant[131] (that is, a legal act adopted by authority of Title VI of the pre-Lisbon Treaty on European Union which by express Treaty terms cannot confer directly effective rights)[132] were struck down by the *Trybunał Konstytucyjny*, the Ανώτατο Δικαστήριο (supreme court) and the *Bundesverfassungsgericht* for incompatibility with the Polish constitution, the Cypriot constitution and the German Basic Law respectively,[133] it resulted in serious

---

128 See e.g., Satversmes tiesa, 2009 gada 7. aprīļa spriedums lietā Nr 2008–35–1 (*Lisabonas līgum*) at para. 2, for evocative submissions urging rejection of Lisbon as incompatible with Latvian principles of democratic participation (art. 101 of the Constitution) by characterising relations with the Council and Parliament as not befitting a modern democratic state but more akin to those between the Latvian State Council and the state Duma in tsarist Russia.

129 The *Alkotmánybíróság* (constitutional court) in Hungary had an early encounter involving surplus agricultural stocks and, peripherally, the relationship between Community and Hungarian constitutional law, addressing the latter only indirectly; see 17/2004 (V. 25.) AB *határozat*. More worrying was a judgment of the Slovak *Ústavný Súd* (Pl. ÚS 8/04, 18 októbra 2005 (*Antidiskriminačný Zákon*)), in which it annulled part of the Slovak law implementing a Community Directive on non-discrimination (Directive 2000/43 [2000] OJ L180/22; see 14.45 below), determining its provisions on positive action to counter disadvantages linked to racial or ethnic origin to be incompatible with art. 12 of the Constitution on equal treatment before the law. However the judgment was based primarily upon the drafting of the Slovak law, broad, inspecific and disproportionate to derogation from the principle of equal treatment; there was no intervention from the Commission to seek rectification, and a subsequent law (Zákon č. 85/2008 Z. z. ktorým sa mení a dopĺňa zákon č. 365/2004 Z. z. o rovnakom zaobchádzaní a doplnení niektorých zákonov (antidiskriminačný zákon)) seems to have put matters right.

130 See 2.05 above, n. 21.

131 Framework Decision 2002/584 [2002] OJ L190/1.

132 TEU (pre-Lisbon), art. 32(4)(b); see 6.94 below.

133 P1/05, Wyrok z dnia 27 kwietnia 2005 r. (*Europejski Nakazi Aresztowania*), 2010 Nr 4, poz. 42; Ap. 294/2005, απόφασι της 7 Νοεμβρίου 2005, Γενικός Εισαγγελέας κατά Κωνσταντινίδου; BVerfG, 18. Juli 2005 (*Europäischer Haftbefehl-Beschluß*), BVerfGE 113, 273. However, the *Bundesverfassungsgericht* annulled the implementing legislation because the federal parliament did not use the discretion it enjoyed under the framework decision in a manner in conformity with the Basic Law, it did not impugn the legality of the framework decision itself as a function of the Basic Law. Judge Gerhardt nonetheless entered a strong dissent from the majority, very much regretting that the Court thus declined constructively to collaborate towards 'European solutions', so injuring the effectiveness of the framework decision, and the one-sided emphasis upon a national perspective rather than a balance between the requirements of national and European law ('Ich

political – and some legal (principally reciprocity, or *exceptio non adimpleti contractus*) – difficulties in the uniform prosecution of a Union programme; senior courts in Spain[134] and Greece,[135] for example, refused to give effect to arrest warrants issued in Germany owing to the latter's refusal to give the framework decision full effect there. The problem is made starker, but not resolved, where the framework decision itself is found unobjectionable by the Court of Justice.[136] These are issues which frequently trouble relations governed by public international law, as those of the Union essentially were; with the Lisbon *communautairisation* the Community/Union anomaly disappears. The question is then simply one of Union primacy, and a constitutional crisis should the principle be challenged. The Slovak *Ustavný Súd* came close with the (partial) setting aside of a national law giving effect to a Community directive, apparently a slip now put right.[137] But a gauntlet has now been thrown down by their Czech colleagues, in 2012 the *Ústavni Soud (in plenum)* asserting the supremacy of the material core of the constitution over the provisions of a Regulation as interpreted by the Court of Justice:[138]

> ... based on the principle explicitly stated by the Constitutional Court ..., we cannot do other than state, in connection with the effects of the ECJ judgment of 22 June 2011, Case C-399/09, an analogous cases, that in that case there were excesses on the part of a European Union body, that a situation occurred in which an act by a European body exceeded the powers that the Czech republic transferred to the European Union under Art. 10a of the Constitution; it exceeds the scope of the transferred powers, and is *ultra vires*.[139]

The fallout is yet to be assessed.

---

bedauere sehr, dass der Senat sich insoweit einer konstruktiven Mitarbeit an europäischen Lösungen verweigert ... [B]etont er einseitig die nationale Perspektive, statt einen Ausgleich zwischen den Bindungen des nationalen und des europäischen Rechts herzustellen' (342)).

134 Audiencia Nacional, Pleno de la Sala de lo penal, acuerdo no jurisdiccional de 13 de septiembre de 2005.

135 Άρειος Πάγος, Ποινικό τμήμα 6, απόφασι της 20 Δεκεμβρίου 2005.

136 Case C-303/05 *Advocaten voor de Wereld* v *Leden van de Ministerrad* [2007] ECR I-3633. The validity of the framework decision was considered upon grounds only of (EU) Treaty *vires* and principles of legality of criminal offences and penalties and of equality and non-discrimination. The compatability of its operation with fundamental rights guarantees of Union law was put to the Court subsequently but the Court found it unnecessary to answer; Case C-306/09 *IB* v *Conseil des ministers* [2010] ECR I-10341.

137 See n. 129 above.

138 The case was a constitutional complaint seeking the annulment of a judgment of the *Nejvyšší správní soud* (supreme administrative court) which had sought, and applied, a reference from the Court of Justice in Case C-399/09 *Landtová* v *Česká správa sociálního zabezpečení*, judgment of 22 June 2011, not yet reported.

139 Pl. ÚS 5/12 ze dne 31.leden 2012 (*Slovenských Důchochů*), at part VII ('... a vycházeje z principu explicitně vysloveného Ústavním Soudem ..., nelze než v souvislosti s dopady rozsudku ESD ze dne 22.6.2011 č.C-399/09 na obdobné případy konstatovat, že v jeho případě došlo k excesu unijního orgánu, k situaci, v níž akt orgánu Evropské unie vybočil z pravomocí, které Česká republika podle čl. 10a Ústavy na Evropskou unii překročení rozsahu svěřených kompetencí, k postupu *ulta vires*.')

6.21 The primacy of Union law was expressly codified in the Treaty establishing a Constitution for Europe.[140] In order to defuse what was seen by some to be its inflammatory language the provision did not appear in the text of the Lisbon Treaty. Instead, the Lisbon intergovernmental conference 'recalls that, in accordance with well settled case law of the EU [*sic*] Court of Justice, the Treaties and the law adopted by the Union [*sic*] on the basis of the Treaties have primacy over the law of Member States' and so attached to the Final Act of the IGC the following 'Opinion of the Council Legal Service of 22 June 2007' (that being the second day of the Brussels summit at which the mandate for the IGC was agreed):

> It results from the case-law of the Court of Justice that primacy of EC law is a cornerstone principle of Community law. According to the Court, this principle is inherent to the specific nature of the European Community. At the time of the first judgment of this established case law (*Costa/ENEL*, 15 July 1964, Case 6/64) there was no mention of primacy in the treaty. It is still the case today. The fact that the principle of primacy will not be included in the future treaty shall not in any way change the existence of the principle and the existing case-law of the Court of Justice.[141]

This 'opinion' is unambitious (it notes but does not seek to entrench primacy and it is accorded no Treaty authority) but might arguably be the wiser course as creating no hostage to fortune.

6.22 Taken together, direct effect and primacy 'in particular' constitute 'the essential characteristics of the Community legal order'.[142] Simple propositions, they nevertheless ensure the viability of an effective and uniform system of law thus: direct effect seeks to ensure that rights accruing from Union law are available to the individual, whilst primacy ensures that such rights are applied uniformly and in their entirety throughout the territory of the Union, immune from derogation the result of any unilateral act of a member state. So far as Union law is concerned, the obligations imposed upon the member state and their courts is clear, and are best stated still in the *Simmenthal* judgment in 1978:

---

140 Treaty establishing a Constitution for Europe, art. I-6. There was some debate as to exactly how far the formula adopted ('The Constitution and the law adopted by the institutions of the Union ... shall have primacy over the law of the Member States') extended.

141 Final Act of the Intergovernmental Conference, reproduced at [2007] OJ C306/231, Declaration No. 17 concerning Primacy. There is at 'Case 6/64' a direction to a footnote, the footnote containing a passage from the judgment in *Costa*.

142 Opinion 1/91 *Re the EEA Agreement* [1991] ECR I-6079, at para. 21; Opinion 1/09 *Re the European Patent Convention*, opinion of 8 March 2011, not yet reported, at para. 65 (substituting 'European Union' for 'Community').

[I]n accordance with the principle of the precedence of Community law, the relationship between provisions of the Treaty and directly applicable measures of the institutions on the one hand and the national law of the Member States on the other is such that those provisions and measures ... render automatically inapplicable any conflicting provisions of current national law ... [and] preclude the valid adoption of new national legislative measures to the extent to which they would be incompatible with Community provisions ...

[E]very national court must, in a case within its jurisdiction, apply Community law in its entirety and protect rights which the latter confers on individuals and must accordingly set aside any provision of national law which may conflict with it, whether prior or subsequent to the Community rule.

Accordingly, any provision of a national legal system and any legislative, administrative or judicial practice which might impair the effectiveness of Community law by withholding from the national court having jurisdiction to apply such law the power to do everything necessary at the moment of its application to set aside national legislative provisions which might prevent Community rules from having full force and effect are incompatible with those requirements which are the very essence of Community law.[143]

4. Interpretation of Union law

Whilst any judge or lawyer must be alive to the fact that the methods of **6.23** interpretation to be deployed in Union law are in some measure different from that to which he or she is accustomed in the national forum, a particular comment is called for to address the concerns of the common lawyer, many of whom profess to find the Union approach especially peculiar, and in some sense 'continental'. This is true to the extent that the Court of Justice, in discharging its function as authoritative arbiter of Union law, does not adopt the literal method of interpretation customarily adopted by common law courts in construing statutes, and that judgments of the Court of Justice do not constitute binding precedent the effect of which can be altered only by legislation.[144] In other respects the suggestion is based upon a misconception as to the nature of the sources of Union law. The Treaties themselves are not legislative acts but international agreements. They state the purposes for which they have been concluded and create reciprocal rights and obligations for the signatory states and (uncommonly) their nationals. Common law courts are accustomed to interpreting contracts in such a way as to give them business efficacy and, where the parties have expressly stated the purpose of the contract, in such a way as to give effect to that purpose. The approach of the Court of Justice to the

---

143   Case 106/77 *Amministrazione delle Finanze dello Stato* v *Simmenthal* [1978] ECR 629, at paras 17, 21, 22. For issues similar to *Simmenthal* again before the Court of Justice see Cases C-188 and 189/10 *Melki and Abdeli* [2010] ECR I-5667.
144   See immediately below.

interpretation of provisions of the Treaties and of Union legislation is not materially different, is reflected in its frequent reference to the *effet utile* of Union law, and is entirely consistent with the cardinal rule of international law that 'a treaty shall be interpreted in good faith in accordance with the ordinary meaning to be given to the terms of the treaty in their context and in the light of its object and purpose'.[145] The approach to the interpretation of legislative and other binding acts of the institutions, all of which are designed to further Treaty aims (and must recite how and why),[146] is equally understandable in the context.

6.24 Interpretation of Union law is, of course, made more complex by its polyglot sources. Each Treaty version and each language version in which legislation exists is equally authentic.[147] The traditional response of international law to bi- or multilingual treaty texts was interpretation sometimes by the language of least burden, sometimes by that of the original text, and sometimes each contracting party bound by its own language version; more recently it prefers adopting 'the meaning which best reconciles the texts, having regard to the object and purpose of the treaty'.[148] The challenge facing Union law is of a different order: 23 equally authentic language versions across multiple treaties and voluminous legislation – at the beginning of 2011 there were some 8,400 Regulations and nearly 2,000 Directives in force.[149] The burdens of the task were summarised by the Court of Justice thus:

> To begin with, in must be borne in mind that Community legislation is drafted in several languages and that the different language versions are all equally authentic. An interpretation of a provision of Community law thus involves a comparison of the different language versions.
>
> It must also be borne in mind, even when the different language versions are entirely in accord with one another, that Community law uses terminology which is peculiar to it. Furthermore, it must be emphasized that legal concepts do not necessarily have the same meaning in Community law and in the law of the various member states.
>
> Finally, every provision of Community law must be placed in its context and interpreted in the light of the provisions of Community law as a whole, regard being had to the

---

145   Vienna Convention on the Law of Treaties, art. 31.
146   TFEU, art. 296, 2nd para. (ex art. 253 EC); see 6.43–6.45 below.
147   See 6.09 above.
148   Vienna Convention on the Law of Treaties, art. 33(4).
149   *28th Annual Report on Monitoring the Application of EU Law (2010)*, COM(2011) 588 final, para. 2.2. At the end of 2006, when more extensive data were accessible, the figures were 7,349 Regulations (2,056 adopted by the Council or Council/Parliament, 5,293 by the Commission) and 1,930 Directives; *A Europe of Results – Applying Community Law*, COM(2007) 502 final.

objectives thereof and to its state of evolution at the date on which the provision in question is to be applied.[150]

Therefore

> it follows from the need for uniform application of European Union law and from the principle of equality that the terms of a provision of that law ... must normally be given an autonomous and uniform interpretation throughout the Union, having regard to the context of the provision and the objective pursued by the legislation in question.[151]

In the event of discrepancy, real or apprehended, the Court will therefore have recourse to all versions, within the context of the purpose and general scheme of the rules of which they form part, in order to determine their correct (and uniform) meaning.[152] To assist it will also have recourse to *travaux préparatoires* (of legislation – none exists for the original Treaties) to a much greater extent than is normally the case in national law. For these reasons if for no other, a literal interpretation of Union law texts is inappropriate.

5. Precedent

In the United Kingdom the courts are directed by statute to take notice of **6.25** judgments of the Court of Justice on the meaning or effect of the Treaties and of Union legislation.[153] The purpose of this was to recognise and 'import' the Court of Justice case law as a source of law and to allow lower courts to depart from higher domestic authority, which they otherwise cannot do, in the event of

---

150 Case 283/81 *CILFIT* v *Ministero della Sanità* [1982] ECR 3415, at paras 18–20.
151 Case C-174/08 *NCC Construction Danmark* v *Skatteministeriet* [2009] ECR I-10567, at para. 24 and case law cited; Case C-396/09 *Interedil* v *Fallimento Interedil and anor*, judgment of 20 October 2011, not yet reported, at para. 42.
152 For examples see Case C-64/95 *Konservenfabrik Lubella Friedrich Büker* v *Hauptzollamt Cottbus* [1996] ECR I-5105, at para. 17 and cases cited therein; Case C-457/05 *Schutzverband der Spirituosen-Industrie* v *Diageo Deutschland* [2007] ECR I-8075, at paras 17–18, and cases cited therein; Case T-411/07R *Aer Lingus Group* v *Commission* [2008] ECR II-411, at paras 85–92; Cases C-261 and 348/08 *Zurita García and Choque Cabrera* v *Delegado del Gobierno en la Región de Murcia* [2009] ECR I-10143, at paras 54–7; Case C-340/08 *R (M and ors)* v *Her Majesty's Treasury* [2010] ECR I-3913, at para. 44. See also the general discussion of A-G Stix-Hackl in Case C-265/03 *Simutenkov* v *Ministerio de Educación y Cultura and anor* [2005] ECR I-2579, at paras 14–27 of her opinion. The Court will sometimes give preference to the linguistic versions forming a majority if the resulting interpretation is consistent with the objectives pursued; e.g., Case 55/87 *Moksel Import und Export* v *Bundesanstalt für Landwirtschaftliche Marktordnung* [1988] ECR 3845; Case C-64/95 *Konservenfabrik Büker*, above. If a legislative measure contains provisions which apply to one member state only (and is thererefore authentic in that language alone), it is legitimate to give greater weight to the terms in the language of that member state; Case E-9/97 *Sveinbjörnsdóttir* v *Government of Iceland* [1998] EFTA CR 95, at paras 23–33.
153 European Communities Act 1972, s. 3.

inconsistencies.[154] But it is still important to understand precisely what the principle requires. A declaratory judgment in an action raised under article 258 has the force of *res judicata* and is binding for a defaulting member state and its courts; a preliminary ruling under article 267 binds the referring court in relation to the case in which the reference has been made; and in cases where a successful appeal to the Court of Justice is remitted back to the General Court (or equally, an appeal to the General Court remitted back to the Civil Service Tribunal) the latter is bound by the former's judgment on points of law. These are the only circumstances in which a judgment of the Court of Justice is formally 'binding' in the sense that another court must comply with and follow it. But, of course, all legal systems strive for uniformity, cohesion and legal certainty. The admissibility of references seeking the interpretation of a previous judgment of the Court, even though article 267 makes no express provision for it,[155] implies in some measure a recognition of the authority of case law.

Further, the Court has found a national court of final instance to be absolved of the duty imposed by article 267(3) to refer to the Court of Justice a question of interpretation of Union law where 'the Community provision in question has already been interpreted by the Court of Justice'[156] and it has adopted a policy of disposing of a reference by reasoned order if the 'question referred … is identical to a question on which [it] has already ruled'.[157] In fact this goes back to the beginning, the Court ruling in the third case referred to it under article 267 (*da Costa en Schaake*)[158] that it was unnecessary to respond as the answer had been provided in the second case referred to it (*van Gend en Loos*),[159] so that it sufficed for the referring court simply to be referred to the previous judgment.[160] It has also said that a declaration of invalidity of a particular measure under article 267 may be relied upon by any national court[161] and that a determination of validity renders it 'unnecessary' to reply to a subsequent reference on the same point.[162] These *dicta* imply that a previous judgment on the validity or interpretation of a specific legislative provision can, for practical purposes, be treated as binding. It has been accepted by the Supreme Court in the United Kingdom: 'I recognise that this Court must follow the judgment of

---

154 See e.g., *R (Countryside Alliance and ors) v HM Attorney General and anor* [2006] EWCA Civ 817, [2007] QB 305, *per* Sir Anthony Clarke MR, at para. 171.

155 See 5.122 above, n. 738.

156 Case 283/81 *CILFIT v Ministero della Sanità* [1982] ECR 3415, in the *dispositif*; see 5.139 above.

157 RP Court of Justice, art. 99; see 5.32 above.

158 Cases 28–30/62 *da Costa en Schaake and ors v Nederlandse Belastingadministratie* [1963] ECR 31.

159 Case 26/62 *Algemene Transport- en Expeditie Onderneming van Gend en Loos v Nederlandse Administratie der Belastingen* [1963] ECR 1.

160 Cases 28–30/62 *da Costa en Schaake*, n. 158 above, at 39.

161 Case 66/80 *International Chemical Corporation v Amministrazione delle Finanze dello Stato* [1981] ECR 1191; see 5.142 above.

162 Case C-120/08 *Bavaria v Bayerischer Brauerbund* [2010] ECR I-13393, at para. 34.

the Court of Justice in [a related case], even if some of us do not fully understand its reasoning',[163] but this may simply be betraying its habits. More telling, it is a proposition to which even the French *Conseil d'Etat* has now submitted.[164]

Further, the Court makes frequent reference to the 'consistent', 'well-established' or 'settled' case law (*jurisprudence constante* or *jurisprudence (bien) établie*) of the Court, implying that a series of decisions in the same sense upon an issue of principle can be treated as binding authority. The civilian may prefer to recognise and characterise it as an *arrêt de principe*, but the practical consequences are much the same. This (tacit) recognition of precedent goes to the creation of a hierarchical relationship between the Court of Justice and national courts which was not (necessarily) created by the Treaties, and an entrenchment of the place of the Court as a 'constitutional' court of the Union. It has been recognised and emphasised by the General Court, in a case involving previous authority of the Court of Justice which was not formally binding upon it:

> The General Court ... takes the view that ... the appellate principle itself and the hierarchical judicial structure which is its corollary generally advise against the General Court revisiting points of law which have been decided by the Court of Justice. That is *a fortiori* the case when, as here, the Court of Justice was sitting in Grand Chamber formation and clearly intended to deliver a judgment establishing certain principles. Accordingly, if an answer is to be given to the questions raised by the institutions, Member States and interested legal quarters following the judgment of the Court of Justice ..., it is for the Court of Justice itself to provide that answer in the context of future cases before it ...
>
> The General Court considers that in principle it falls not to it but to the Court of Justice to reverse precedent in that way.[165]

Yet, as in any case law-based system – even in the zenith of the species, the law of England[166] – the Court may depart from, or modify, its previous case law in the light of new factors or conditions, and has on three occasions expressly

---

163   *Patmalniece* v *Secretary of State for Work and Pensions* [2011] UKSC 11, *per* Lord Walker at para. 73.

164   CE, Ass, 11 décembre 2006 (*Soc de Groot en Slot Allium* v *Soc Bejo Zaden*), 2007 Rec Lebon 512, at para. 4: '[M]ême qu'elle ne faisait pas l'objet du renvoi préjudiciel, cette interprétation du traité et des actes communautaires, que la Cour était compétente pour donner en vertu du a) et du b) de l'article 234 du traité CE, s'impose au Conseil d'Etat.'

165   Case T-85/09 *Kadi* v *Commission* (Kadi III) [2010] ECR II-5177, at paras 121, 123.

166   The House of Lords had long considered itself strictly bound by its own precedent, for to do otherwise would be to usurp the power of Parliament. But it said in 1966 that it would depart from its own previous case law 'when it appears right to do so' (practice statement on behalf of the Lords of Appeal delivered by Lord Gardiner LC, [1966] 3 All ER 77), and has done so on a number of occasions since.

reversed (or 'reconsidered') previous judgments.[167] It is therefore always open to a party or to a referring national court to invite the Court of Justice to reconsider a previous decision or line of case law.[168]

C. ENFORCEMENT OF UNION RIGHTS

1. Court of Justice

6.26 The Treaties provide for judicial review of acts (and of failure to act) of the Union institutions and for damages for loss caused by the Union and its institutions. In all these actions the Court of Justice of the Union has original and exclusive jurisdiction. They are discussed above.[169]

2. National courts

6.27 Since the day-to-day administration of most substantive aspects of Union law lies with national authorities, since in accordance with the doctrine of direct effect Union law gives rise to rights and obligations enforceable by national courts, and since it is they to which the 'vigilant individual' must normally turn to seek protection of his rights, the availability of appropriate and satisfactory national remedies is an essential element in the proper application and enforcement of Union law. It is in this context that national courts (*all* national courts) may be, and have been, characterised as 'the courts of general jurisdiction in Community law' (*juge communautaire de droit commun*)[170] or the 'ordinary'

---

167 Case C-10/89 *CNL-Sucal* v *HAG* (Hag II) [1990] ECR I-3711; Cases C-267–8/91 *Criminal Proceedings against Keck and Mithouard* [1993] ECR I-6097; Case C-127/08 *Metock and ors* v *Minister for Justice, Equality and Law Reform* [2008] ECR I-6241. In Case T-177/01 *Jégo-Quéré et Cie* v *Commission* [2002] ECR II-2365 the Court of First Instance disregarded the self-restraint it was to articulate subsequently in *Kadi III* (n. 165 above) and boldly took it upon itself to 'reverse' previous authority (going back to 1963) on standing to raise annulment proceedings under art. 263, but was slapped down by the Court of Justice implicitly within ten weeks in an unrelated case (Case C-50/00P *Unión de Pequeños Agricultores* v *Council* [2002] ECR I-6677) and in due course, directly (Case C-263/02P *Commission* v *Jégo-Quéré et Cie* [2004] ECR I-3425). See 5.79 above.

168 See e.g., Cases C-267 and 268/95 *Merck* v *Primecrown* (Merck II) [1996] ECR I-6285, in which the English High Court expressly called upon the Court of Justice to reconsider its earlier judgment in Case 187/80 *Merck* v *Stephar* (Merck I) [1981] ECR 2063 which, in the view of the High Court, ought to be 'overturned'; the Court did reconsider, but declined the invitation to overturn. See also Case C-202/04 *Macrino and anor* v *Meloni* [2006] ECR I-11421, in which the Commission expressly invited the Court to reverse well-established case law on the duties of member states under arts 4(3), 101 and 102, but again the Court declined; and Case C-99/00 *Criminal proceedings against Lyckeskog* [2002] ECR I-4839, in which Denmark urged the Court to reformulate its *CILFIT* criteria on the duty of courts of final instance to seek a preliminary ruling from the Court of Justice (see the opinion of A-G Tizzano at para. 51 ff.), to no avail.

169 See 5.48–5.102 above.

170 Case C-555/07 *Kücükdeveci* v *Swedex* [2010] ECR I-365, *per* A-G Bot at para. 55 of his opinion.

courts within the European Union legal order' (*juges de 'droit commun' de l'ordre juridique de l'Union*).[171] They are the violins, the workhorses, of Union law.

Where a person wishes to enforce a Union right before a national court, the **6.28** basic principle is that, in the absence of relevant Union rules (and none has been adopted), national remedies and procedures are to apply:

> [I]n the absence of Community rules on this subject, it is for the domestic legal system of each Member State to designate the courts having jurisdiction and to determine the procedural conditions governing actions at law intended to ensure the protection of the rights which citizens have from the direct effect of Community law.[172]

This is consistent with principles of 'judicial autonomy' or 'procedural autonomy',[173] an application of subsidiarity: Union law does not, need not and ought not to interfere in matters of national judicial organisation, procedures and remedies,[174] nor does it require that member states provide for a freestanding action by which national provisions may be challenged for incompatibility with Union law.[175] However, existing national procedures and remedies are required to meet minimum standards necessary and sufficient for the protection of Union rights: first, a member state bears a duty of ensuring that there is in place a system of legal remedies adequate to effective judicial protection. This was recognised in the case law of the Court of Justice[176] and injected expressly into the Treaties by Lisbon.[177] It may require a degree of innovation, or flexibility, from the national judge: in the words of the English Court of Appeal:

> the national court is required to give a remedy, whether by way of restitution or as compensation, in respect of the breach of Community law. It is not open to the national court to deny restitution or compensation on the ground that no remedy would lie

---

171 Opinion 1/09 *Re the European Patent Convention*, opinion of 8 March 2011, not yet reported, at para. 80.

172 Case 33/76 *Rewe-Zentralfinanz and anor v Landwirtschaftskammer für das Saarland* [1976] ECR 1989, at para. 5; also Case C-312/93 *Peterbroeck v Belgium* [1995] ECR I-4599; Case C-224/01 *Köbler v Austria* [2003] ECR I-10239; Case C-233/08 *Kyrian v Celní úřad Tábor* [2010] ECR I-177; Cases C-317 etc./08 *Alassini and ors v Telecom Italia and ors* [2010] ECR I-2213, at para. 47.

173 For recognition of national procedural autonomy see Case C-212/04 *Adeneler and ors v Ellinikos Organismos Galaktos* [2006] ECR I-6057, at para. 95; Case C-180/04 *Vassallo v Azienda Ospedaliera Ospedale San Martino di Genova e Cliniche Universitarie Convenzionate* [2006] ECR I-7251, at para. 37; Case C-268/06 *Impact v Minister for Agriculture and Food and ors* [2008] ECR I-2483, *per* A-G Kokott at paras 45–53 of her opinion.

174 See e.g., Cases C-10 etc./97 *Ministero delle Finanze v IN.CO.GE.'90 and ors* [1998] ECR I-6307.

175 Case C-432/05 *Unibet (London) and anor v Justitiekanslern* [2007] ECR I-2271.

176 Case C-50/00P *Unión de Pequeños Agricultores v Council* [2002] ECR I-6677, at para. 41.

177 TEU, art. 19(1), 2nd para.; carried over from the Treaty establishing a Constitution for Europe, art. I-29(1), 2nd para.

under domestic law. If necessary, Community law demands an autonomous remedy in respect of the breach of Community law which has occurred.[178]

Or, as put since by the Court of Justice:

It is for the national court to the full extent of its discretion under national law, to interpret and apply domestic law in accordance with the requirements of Community law and, to the extent that such an interpretation is not possible in relation to the EC Treaty provisions conferring rights on individuals which are enforceable by them and which the national courts must protect, to disapply any provision of domestic law which is contrary to those provisions.[179]

Second, the remedies by which a Union right is to be protected are required to be:

- no less favourable than those relating to similar domestic actions (a principle of equivalence); and
- not such as to render virtually impossible the exercise of the Union right (a principle of effectiveness).[180]

Equivalence and effectiveness embody the general obligation for member states to ensure the effective judicial protection of an individual's Union law rights and apply to both the designation of the courts competent to hear and determine actions based in Union law and the procedural rules under which they operate.[181] However, it appears generally that it is a requirement of neither equivalence nor effectiveness that a national court raise of its own motion a point of Union law not raised by the parties.[182] Nor does effectiveness render improper a requirement of national law that parties to a dispute have recourse to a compulsory out-of-court settlement procedure prior to resorting to litigation,

---

178 *Sempra Metals* v *Commissioners of Inland Revenue and anor* [2005] EWCA Civ 389, [2006] QB 37, *per* Chadwick LJ at 48.

179 Case C-208/05 *ITC Innovative Technology Centre* v *Bundesagentur für Arbeit* [2007] ECR I-181, in the *dispositif*.

180 See e.g., Case 199/82 *Amministrazione delle Finanze dello Stato* v *San Giorgio* [1983] ECR 3595; Case C-208/90 *Emmott* v *Minister for Social Welfare and Attorney General* [1991] ECR I-4269; Case C-312/93 *Peterbroeck* v *Belgium* [1995] ECR I-4599; Cases C-430 and 431/93 *van Schijndel* v *Stichting Pensioenfonds voor Fysiotherapeuten* [1995] ECR I-4705; Case C-126/97 *Eco Swiss China Time* v *Benetton International* [1999] ECR I-3055; Case C-432/05 *Unibet (London)*, n. 175 above; Case C-268/06 *Impact*, n. 173 above, and in particular the discussion of A-G Kokott at paras 51–80 of her opinion; Case C-118/08 *Transportes Urbanos y Servicios Generales* v *Administración del Estado* [2010] ECR I-635, and in particular the discussion of A-G Poiares Maduro.

181 Case C-268/06 *Impact*, n. 173 above, at paras 47–8; Case C-63/08 *Pontin* v *T-Comalux* [2009] ECR I-10467, at para. 44; Cases C-317 etc./08 *Alassini*, n. 172 above, at para. 49.

182 Cases 222 etc./05 *van der Weerd and ors* v *Minister van Landbouw, Natuur en Voedselkwaliteit* [2007] ECR I-4233; Case C-2/06 *Willy Kempter* v *Hauptzollamt Hamburg-Jonas* [2008] ECR I-411; Case C-455/06 *Heemskerk and anor* v *Productschap Vee en Vlees* [2008] ECR I-8763.

provided a number of conditions are satisfied.[183] That the principle of equivalence may in some measure result in Union rights being applied differently from member state to member state is recognised, and tolerated, by the Court of Justice.[184]

(a) Public law remedies

Since it is the member states which bear most of the obligations set out in the Treaties for the attainment of the goals of the Union, it is against a public authority a person would normally seek to assert a Union right before the courts and remedies founded in public law by which he or she would do so.[185] The remedies must, of course, accord with fundamental Union law on direct effect and primacy, and be applied in manner which complies with the requirements of equivalence and effectiveness. But the constraints go further, requiring that any substantive or procedural rule of national law which denies or has the effect of limiting the right, even temporarily, be set aside:

6.29

> Any provision of a national legal system and any legislative, administrative or judicial practice which might impair the effectiveness of EU law by withholding from the national court having jurisdiction to apply such law the power to do everything necessary at the moment of its application to set aside national legislative provisions which might prevent European Union rules from having full force and effect are incompatible with those requirements which are the very essence of EU law.[186]

---

183   Cases C-317 etc./08 *Alassini*, n. 172 above, at paras 54–66.

184   Cases C-392 and 422/04 *i-21 Germany and anor* v *Bundesrepublik Deutschland* [2006] ECR I-8559.

185   In the United Kingdom therefore a person would normally seek judicial review (injunction/interdict, prohibition, suspension, mandatory order or declaratory relief) and/or damages as appropriate. Examples are legion. For only the most recent and/or widely recognised judgments see *R* v *Secretary of State for Transport, ex parte Factortame* [1990] 2 AC 85 (HL) (injunction); [1991] 1 AC 603 (HL); *R* v *Secretary of State for Employment, ex parte Equal Opportunities Commission* [1995] 1 AC 1 (HL) (injunction); *R* v *Secretary of State for Employment, ex parte Seymour-Smith* [1996] All ER (EC) 1 (CA) (declaratory relief); *Millar and Bryce* v *Keeper of the Records of Scotland* 1997 SLT 1000 (OH) (interdict, order *ad factum praestandum*); *Booker Aquaculture* v *Secretary of State for Scotland* 2000 SC 9 (1st Div) (declarator); *R (ABNA Ltd)* v *Secretary of State for Health and anor* [2003] EWHC 2420 (Admin), [2004] EuLR 88 (injunction); *ABNA Ltd and ors* v *Scottish Ministers* 2004 SLT 176 (OH) (interim suspension); *R (Watts)* v *Secretary of State for Health* [2004] EWCA Civ 166, [2004] All ER (D) 349 (injunction, *mandamus* and declaratory relief); *R (Infant and Dietetic Foods Association)* v *Secretary of State for Health* [2008] EWHC 575 (Admin), [2008] All ER (D) 452 (interim stay); *R (Partridge Farms)* v *Secretary of State for Environment, Food and Rural Affairs* [2008] EWHC 1645 (Admin), [2008] All ER (D) 165 (declaration) (but overturned in *R (Partridge Farms)* v *Secretary of State for Environment, Food and Rural Affairs* [2009] EWCA 284, [2009] All ER (D) 3); *Downs* v *Secretary of State for Environment, Food and Rural Affairs* [2008] EWHC 2666 (Admin), [2008] All ER (D) 145 (declaration) (but overturned in *Secretary of State for Environment, Food and Rural Affairs* v *Downs* [2009] EWCA 664, [2009] All ER (D) 71); *Axa General Insurance* v *Lord Advocate and ors* [2011] UKSC 46 (declarator and reduction). In Scotland a pursuer proceeds by ordinary action unless necessary to invoke the supervisory jurisdiction of the Court of Session; see, by analogy, *WM Fotheringham and Son* v *British Limousin Cattle Society* 2004 SLT 485 (Extra Div). As interdict cannot be mandatory (*Grosvenor Developments (Scotland)* v *Argyll Stores* 1987 SLT 738 (Extra Div.)) the remedy for a positive order is probably a petition for an order under the Court of Session Act 1988, s. 45(b); see also *Millar and Bryce*, above. As to damages, see 6.34–6.40 below.

186   Cases C-188 and 189/10 *Melki and Abdeli* [2010] ECR I-5667, at para. 44.

Examples of such provisions abound:

- a requirement that a national law may be disapplied for inconsistency with Union law only after a declaration of unconstitutionality by a constitutional court (with sole jurisdiction to make that declaration);[187]
- more generally, any procedural disadvantages deriving from the division of jurisdiction amongst national courts and tribunals;[188]
- the immunity of the Crown against injunction;[189]
- a construction which admits an enforceable right only if based in 'customary law' (*Gewohnheitsrecht*) of prolonged and consistent recognition and use, so excluding (recent) Union law;[190]
- an irrebuttable legal presumption of national law;[191]
- a fixed (and inadequate) statutory limit on the quantum of damages;[192]
- a rule that (compound) interest is not exigible in a restitutionary claim.[193]

6.30 A time limit for bringing a claim is in principle not inconsistent with the effective protection of a Union right – time bars being known to every legal system – but it must allow sufficient time.[194] It might be argued that the maximum of three months permitted in England to raise an action for judicial review[195] fails to pass muster, but it is unlikely it would be found to be so as a matter of Union law, the Treaty itself allowing only two months for review of

---

187   Case 106/77 *Amministrazione delle Finanze dello Stato* v *Simmenthal* [1978] ECR 629; Case C-555/07 *Kücükdeveci* v *Swedex* [2010] ECR I-365; Cases C-188 and 189/10 *Melki and Abdeli, ibid.*; Case C-457/09 *Chartry* v *Etat belge*, order of 1 March 2011, not yet reported (in which the Court managed to repeat the principle even whilst rejecting an art. 267 request for a preliminary ruling for inadmissibility).

188   Case C-268/06 *Impact* v *Minister for Agriculture and Food and ors* [2008] ECR I-2483.

189   *R* v *Secretary of State for Transport, ex parte Factortame* [1990] 2 AC 55 (HL); found incompatible with Community law in Case C-213/89 *R* v *Secretary of State for Transport, ex parte Factortame* [1990] ECR I-2433, applied in *R* v *Secretary of State for Transport, ex parte Factortame* (1991), n. 185 above; also *Millar and Bryce*, n. 185 above. The rule has since been reversed in English law in *M* v *Home Office* [1993] 3 All ER 537 (HL) and, after some prevarication, in Scots law: *Davidson* v *Scottish Ministers* [2005] UKHL 74, 2006 SC (HL) 41.

190   Case C-91/08 *Wall* v *Stadt Frankfurt am Main and anor* [2010] ECR I-2815, at paras 66–71.

191   Case 222/84 *Johnston* v *Chief Constable of the RUC* [1986] ECR 1651.

192   Case C-271/91 *Marshall* v *Southampton and South West Hampshire Area Health Authority* (No. 2) [1993] ECR I-4367.

193   *Sempra Metals* v *HM Commissioners of Inland Revenue and anor* [2007] UKHL 34, [2007] 4 All ER 657.

194   There is authority (Case C-208/90 *Emmott* v *Minister for Social Welfare and Attorney General* [1991] ECR I-4269) to the effect that where the Union right derives from a Directive, time cannot start to run until the provisions of the Directive have been fully and clearly transposed into national law. But the Court has taken pains to distinguish the judgment and it should now be treated with caution: Case C-338/91 *Steenhorst-Neerings* v *Bedrijfsvereniging voor Detailhandel, Ambachten en Huisvrouwen* [1993] ECR I-5475 and the cases cited in n. 180 above; Case C-445/06 *Danske Slagterier* v *Bundesrepublik Deutschland* [2009] ECR I-2119 ('the solution adopted in *Emmott* was justified by the particular circumstances of that case'; para. 54); Case C-452/09 *Iaia and ors* v *Ministero dell'Istruzione, dell'Università e della Ricerca and ors*, judgment of 19 May 2011, not yet reported.

195   RSC Ord. 53, r. 4.

Union legislation.[196] Interim relief must be available and granted if necessary to ensure the full effectiveness of the Union right;[197] the criteria are a matter for national law applicable to the relevant national court, subject to the twin requirements of equivalence and effectiveness.[198] In criminal proceedings a defence may be raised that the (criminal) conduct proscribed is in fact the legitimate exercise of a Union law right; if the argument proves well founded, a conviction cannot be entered. This is the so-called 'Euro-defence', used notably in England in attempts to circumvent Sunday trading legislation,[199] and by patrons of cross-Channel and Gulf of Finland 'booze cruises' seeking to avoid UK or Finnish excise duties on French-, Belgian- or Estonian- (or ferry-) bought tobacco and alcohol.[200] In the formulation of the English Court of Appeal, where the argument succeeds the courts must respond 'by treating [the national legislation creating the offence] as not being part of the law of England'.[201]

Where a person can establish an enforceable Union right against another person or persons ('horizontal direct effect'), which arises most frequently under Union employment legislation[202] and the rules on competition[203] (but increasingly in other areas),[204] the national court must enforce the right. Where both a private law and a public law remedy may be available (for example in matters of employment or contracts with public authorities, where remedies may be available before an employment tribunal/in civil or ordinary action[205] or in judicial review), it would appear that the private law action pre-empts, or at

---

196 TFEU, art. 263(5); see 5.67 above. See also Case C-126/97 *Eco Swiss China Time* v *Benetton International* [1999] ECR I-3055 in which the Court said (at para. 45) that a three-month time limit for challenging an arbitration award (for compatibility with Community law) in Dutch law 'does not seem excessively short' and 'does not render excessively difficult or virtually impossible the exercise of rights conferred by Community law'; and Case C-30/02 *Recheio – Cash and Carry* v *Fazenda Pública/Registro Nacional de Pessoas Colectivas* [2004] ECR I-6051, in which it found a 90-day time limit on annulment proceedings in Portuguese law equally unobjectionable. In Case C-349/07 *Sopropré – Organizações de Calçado* v *Fazenda Público* [2008] ECR I-10369, the Court found the period of 8 to 15 days allowed by Portuguese law to claim recovery of a customs debt also unobjectionable, provided the national court is satisfied that a proper hearing was thus obtainable.

197 Case C-213/89 *R* v *Secretary of State for Transport, ex parte Factortame* [1990] ECR I-2433; Case C-432/05 *Unibet (London) and anor* v *Justitiekanslern* [2007] ECR I-2271.

198 Case C-432/05 *Unibet (London)*, ibid.

199 Case 145/88 *Torfaen Borough Council* v *B&Q* [1989] ECR 3851; Case C-169/91 *Stoke on Trent City Council* v *B&Q* [1992] ECR I-6635; see 10.46 below.

200 See e.g., *R (Hoverspeed and ors)* v *Customs and Excise Commissioners* [2002] EWCA Civ 1804, [2003] QB 1041.

201 *Searby and anor* v *R* [2003] EWCA Crim 1910, [2003] EuLR 819 at 827.

202 See 14.47–14.49 below.

203 See 13.116–13.117 below.

204 See e.g. in the environmental sphere 14.62–14.64 below.

205 Civil Procedure Rules (England and Wales), Part 7.

least must precede, judicial review, which is the normal rule in English law,[206] notwithstanding arguments that judicial review may afford more effective protection of the Union law right.[207]

(b) Article 4(3) obligations

6.31 The second and third paragraphs of article 4(3) of the Treaty on European Union call for particular comment. They provide:

> The Member States shall take any appropriate measure, general or particular, to ensure fulfilment of the obligations arising out of the Treaties or resulting from the acts of the institutions of the Union.

> The Member States shall facilitate the achievement of the Union's tasks and refrain from any measure which could jeopardise the attainment of the Union's objectives.

From the beginning until Lisbon this was a self-standing Treaty article;[208] Lisbon bundled it into article 4 on relations between the Union and the member states generally, so alongside a statement of the principle of conferral (article 4(1)), an obligation of the Union to respect the equality of member states, their essential functions and territorial integrity (article 4(2)) and the obligation of 'sincere cooperation' (article 4(3), 1st paragraph). The terms of the second and third paragraphs might be read simply as a statement of *pacta sunt servanda*, and the (imprudent, perhaps) Lisbon reorientation may cause them to fade somewhat. But they, and particularly the third paragraph, were long co-opted by the Court as a means of identifying substantial duties for the member states '[i]n all the areas corresponding to the objectives of the Treaty'.[209] It is from these provisions that the Court first developed the duty of sincere cooperation,[210] and by virtue of article 4(3) that member states must ensure the effective judicial protection of Union law rights[211] and bear a general obligation to make Union law effective. So

---

206 E.g., *R v Secretary of State for Employment, ex parte Equal Opportunities Commission* [1995] 1 AC 1 (HL); *R v Secretary of State for Employment, ex parte Seymour-Smith* [1997] 2 All ER 273 (HL); *Cookson & Clegg v Minister of Defence* [2005] EWHC 38 (Admin), [2005] EuLR 517 (upheld on appeal, *R (Cookson & Clegg) v Minister of Defence and anor* [2005] EWCA Civ 811, [2005] All ER (D) 83). It is also the normal rule in Scotland: *National Union of Public Employees v Grampian Regional Council*, judgment of the Outer House of 11 March 1993, unreported; *McGeogh v Electoral Registration Officer, Dumfries & Galloway and ors* [2011] CSOH 65.

207 *Cookson and Clegg, ibid.* A further problem here is the short time bars for judicial review; the High Court implicitly countered this by saying that a case in judicial review could come to no different answer than a private action, but with no argument supporting the conclusion.

208 EEC Treaty, art. 5 (art. 10 EC).

209 Case C-246/07 *Commission v Sweden* [2010] ECR I-3317, at para. 69.

210 See 2.22 above.

211 Case C-50/00P *Unión de Pequeños Agricultores v Council* [2002] ECR I-6677; Case C-432/05 *Unibet (London) and anor v Justitiekanslern* [2007] ECR I-2271.

[w]here Community legislation does not specifically provide any penalty for an infringement or refers for that purpose to national laws, regulations and administrative provisions, Article [4(3)] of the Treaty requires the Member States to take all measures necessary to guarantee the application and effectiveness of Community law.

For that purpose, whilst the choice of penalties remains within their discretion, they must ensure in particular that infringements of Community law are penalised under conditions, both procedural and substantive, which are analogous to those applicable to infringements of national law of a similar nature and importance and which, in any event, make the penalty effective, proportionate and dissuasive.

Moreover the national authorities must proceed, with respect to infringements of Community law, with the same diligence as that which they bring to bear in implementing corresponding national laws.[212]

This applies equally to ensuring the effectiveness of substantive Union rights:

Article [34] therefore requires the Member States not merely themselves to abstain from adopting measures or engaging in conduct liable to constitute an obstacle to trade but also, when read with Article [4(3)] of the Treaty, to take all necessary and appropriate measures to ensure that the fundamental freedom is respected on their territory.[213]

Originally it was applied in tandem with other Treaty provisions – for example, with article 34 as here in the *Spanish Strawberries* case; or national law which frustrated or made ineffective the competition rules of articles 101 and 102 TFEU would be condemned as a breach of articles 101 and 102 'read in conjunction with' article 4(3);[214] or by seeking to settle a dispute in manner not envisaged in the Treaties 'Ireland has failed to fulfil its obligations under Articles [4(3)] and [344]'.[215] This was because it is 'worded so generally that there can be no question of applying it autonomously when the situation concerned is governed by a specific provision of the Treaty'.[216] But latterly it is recognised to constitute a free-standing obligation, so that, for example, a member state failing to cooperate actively and in good faith with Commission inquiries in the context of article 258 enforcement proceedings breaches article 4(3) *simpliciter*.[217] As a *lex generalis*, it is of itself applicable only where there is a

---

212 Case C-68/88 *Commission v Greece* [1989] ECR 2965, at paras 23–5.

213 Case C-269/95 *Commission v France* (Spanish Strawberries) [1997] ECR I-6959, at para. 32.

214 Case C-2/91 *Criminal proceedings against Meng* [1993] ECR I-5751, at para. 14; see 13.18 below.

215 Case C-459/03 *Commission v Ireland* (MOX Plant) [2006] ECR I-4635, in the *dispositif*.

216 Case C-18/93 *Corsica Ferries Italia v Corpo dei Piloti del Porto di Genova* [1994] ECR I-1783, at para. 18.

217 Case 192/84 *Commission v Greece* [1985] ECR 3967; Case C-478/01 *Commission v Luxembourg* [2003] ECR I-2351; Case C-82/03 *Commission v Italy* [2004] ECR I-6635; Case C-494/01 *Commission v Ireland* [2005] ECR I-3331; Case C-221/08 *Commission v Ireland* [2010] ECR I-1669. Cf. on the substance of cooperation Case C-232/05 *Commission v France* [2006] ECR I-10071, *per* A-G Ruiz-Jarabo Colomer at paras 91–9 of his opinion.

failure to comply with a Union obligation over and above infringement of a more specific provision.[218]

6.32   Because Union law does not differentiate amongst the various institutions of a member state, the obligations of article 4(3) apply to any and all of them which enjoy the necessary (internal) authority to make Union law effective.[219] They may, for example, in circumstances apply to the police[220] or the prosecuting authorities,[221] which may encounter difficulties stemming from the independence attributed to them by national (constitutional) law. Even more problematic, they apply also to the courts. It is thus article 4(3) which requires a national court to set aside any substantive or procedural impediment in national (or constitutional) law which would render the exercise of a Union right ineffective,[222] to interpret and apply national procedural rules governing the exercise of rights of action in a manner which ensures optimal judicial protection from the Union institutions[223] and to interpret substantive national law in a manner which best complies with non-directly effective Union law (the duty of *interprétation conforme*).[224] These are burdens which the national judge cannot always discharge easily.

6.33   It is also from article 4(3) that the Court of Justice drew and fashioned the rules on a right in reparation.

(c)   Reparation

6.34   Where a Union right is articulated in a manner which is not directly effective, the right is not, as such, enforceable in the national courts. However, the Court of Justice has drawn from article 4(3) two principles which enable the indirect enforcement of such rights, or, if not, at least a degree of satisfaction: the first is the *interprétation conforme* of national law, which is discussed below,[225] the second a right in reparation against public authorities, as follows.

---

218   Case C-374/89 *Commission* v *Belgium* [1991] ECR I-367, at paras 13–16; Case C-470/03 *AGM-COS.MET* v
       Suomen valtio and anor [2007] ECR I-2749, *per* A-G Kokott at para. 110 of her opinion.
219   Case C-453/00 *Kühne & Heitz* v *Productschap voor Pluimvee en Eieren* [2004] ECR I-837, at para. 20; Case
       C-2/06 *Kempter* v *Hauptzollamt Hamburg-Jonas* [2008] ECR I-411, at para. 34; Case C-91/08 *Wall* v *Stadt
       Frankfurt Main and anor* [2010] ECR I-2815, at para. 69.
220   Case C-269/95 *Spanish Strawberries*, n. 213 above.
221   Case T-193/04 *Tillack* v *Commission* [2006] ECR II-3995; Cases F-5 and 7/05 *Violetti and Schmit* v
       Commission, judgment of 28 April 2009, not yet reported.
222   See 6.29 above.
223   Case C-263/02P *Commission* v *Jégo-Quéré et Cie* [2004] ECR I-3425, at paras 30–2; Case C-15/06P *Regione
       Siciliana* v *Commission* [2007] ECR I-2591, at para. 39.
224   See 6.79 below.
225   See 6.79 below.

(i) Francovich *and* Brasserie du Pêcheur *liability*

There is a wide disparity in national law of public tort liability and so a risk that   **6.35**
the right to damages as a means of protecting a Union right will vary from
member state to member state. Very generally, the civilian systems have tended
to provide easy access to damages against public authorities, whilst the common
law jurisdictions, with a narrower view of public tort liability, have not. As for
the Community, the Court of Justice said, *obiter*, as early as 1960 that where a
national legislative or administrative measure is found to be contrary to
(ECSC) Community law the member state is obliged to rescind the measure
and 'to make reparation for any unlawful consequences which may have
ensued'.[226] It then remained silent on the matter for 30 years. It returned to it in
1991 in *Francovich*,[227] finding that where a member state has failed timeously to
implement into national law the requirements of a Directive,[228] so giving rise to
loss on the part of an individual who would have acquired rights had the
Directive been properly implemented, a remedy in damages lies against the
defaulting member state. This is so, said the Court:[229]

- where the purpose of the Directive was to create rights for individuals;[230]
- the content of the rights is identifiable in its provisions; and
- there is a causal link between the failure of the state and the loss.

Francovich, considered by the Court of Justice and reaffirmed in a number of   **6.36**
subsequent cases,[231] therefore establishes the principle of a right in reparation
from the state for loss caused by complete, or improper, failure timeously to
implement the provisions of a Directive which are intended to create rights for
the individual. It was taken further five years later in *Brasserie du Pêcheur/*

---

226   Case 6/60 *Humblet* v *Belgian State* [1960] ECR 559 at 569.
227   Cases C-6 and 9/90 *Francovich and Bonifaci* v *Italy* [1991] ECR I-5357.
228   As to directives see 6.63–6.81 below.
229   Cases C-6 and 9/90 *Francovich*, n. 227 above, at para. 40.
230   That is, derived from German principles of *Schutznormtheorie*; see 5.96 above, n. 604. It should not be read too
        broadly: see e.g., Case C-222/02 *Peter Paul and ors* v *Bundesrepublik Deutschland* [2004] ECR I-9425; *Poole and
        ors* v *Her Majesty's Treasury* [2007] EWCA Civ 1021, [2008] Lloyd's Rep. IR, 134.
231   Case C-334/92 *Wagner Miret* v *Fondo de Garantía Salarial* [1993] ECR I-6911; Case C-91/92 *Faccini Dori* v
        Recreb [1994] ECR I-3325; Cases C-178 etc./94 *Dillenkofer* v *Germany* [1996] ECR I-4845; Cases C-283
        etc./94 *Denkavit Internationaal* v *Bundesamt für Finanzen* [1996] ECR I-5063; Case C-127/95 *Norbrook
        Laboratories* v *Ministry of Agriculture, Fisheries and Food* [1998] ECR I-1531; Case C-319/96 *Brinkmann
        Tabakfabriken* v *Skattemimisteriet* [1998] ECR I-5255; Case C-140/97 *Rechtberger* v *Austria* [1999] ECR
        I-3499; Case C-424/97 *Haim* v *Kassenzahnärtzliche Vereinigung Nordrhein* [2000] ECR I-5123; Case
        C-63/01 *Evans* v *Secretary of State for the Environment, Transport and the Regions* [2003] ECR I-14447; C-397
        etc./01 *Pfeiffer and ors* v *Deutsches Rotes Kreuz, Kreisverband Waldshut* [2004] ECR I-8835; Case C-278/05
        Robins and ors v *Secretary of State for Work and Pensions* [2007] ECR I-1053; Case C-470/03 *AGM-COS.MET*
        v *Suomen valtio and anor* [2007] ECR I-2749; Case C-445/06 *Danske Slagterier* v *Bundesrepublik Deutschland*
        [2009] ECR I-2119.

Factortame III,[232] in which the Court found that a member state is liable in reparation where it deprives an individual of a Community law right even where the right can be enforced through directly effective provisions – *in casibus* rights flowing from the Treaty provisions on free movement of goods[233] and right of establishment.[234] It had been argued that damages was an ancillary remedy only, to fill a lacuna and to be made available only where there is no other means – direct effect – of enforcing the Community right. The Court disagreed: in the absence of direct effect damages may be a 'particularly indispensable' remedy,[235] but reparation is not pre-empted by direct effect, it is a natural corollary of it.

6.37   According to the *Brasserie du Pêcheur* (re-)formulation, a member state is liable in reparation where:

- the rule of Union law breached is intended to create rights for the individual;
- the breach is 'sufficiently serious'; and
- there is a direct causal link between the breach of the obligation borne by the state and the damage suffered.[236]

The Court also said that the principles regulating liability of the member states ought, as much as possible, to be the same as those applying to the liability of the Union and its institutions.[237] The *Brasserie du Pêcheur* rules, and particularly the parameters of 'sufficiently serious' (*suffisament caractérisé*), the major development beyond the *Francovich* criteria, have been reconsidered, and so given some substance, on a number of occasions.[238] The deprivation of a Union right is sufficiently serious when, borrowing from the tests developed under article 340 TFEU, the Union right (which is by definition a superior rule of law) is one intended for the benefit of the individual and the national authority responsible has acted in a manner which manifestly and gravely exceeds its margin of discretion. The factors to be considered therefore include, 'in particular': the degree of clarity and precision of the rule infringed; whether the infringement

---

232   Cases C-46 and 48/93 *Brasserie du Pêcheur* v *Germany* and *R* v *Secretary of State for Transport, ex parte Factortame* (No. 3) [1996] ECR I-1029.
233   TFEU, art. 34 (ex art. 28 EC) (*Brasserie du Pêcheur*).
234   TFEU, art. 49 (ex art. 43 EC) (*Factortame III*).
235   Cases C-6 and 9/90 *Francovich*, n. 227 above, at para. 34.
236   Cases C-46 and 48/93 *Brasserie du Pêcheur* and *Factortame III*, at para. 74.
237   See 5.96 above.
238   Case C-192/94 *El Corte Inglés* v *Blázquez Rivero* [1996] ECR I-1281; Case C-392/93 *R* v *HM Treasury, ex parte British Telecommunications* [1996] ECR I-1631; Case C-5/94 *R* v *Minister of Agriculture, Fisheries and Food, ex parte Hedley Lomas* [1996] ECR I-2553; Cases C-178 etc./94 *Dillenkofer*, Cases C-283 etc./94 *Denkavit Internationaal*, Case C-127/95 *Norbrook Laboratories*, Case C-319/96 *Brinkmann Tabakfabriken*, Case C-140/97 *Rechtberger*, Case C-424/97 *Haim*, Case C-63/01 *Evans*, Case C-278/05 *Robins*, Case C-470/03 *AGM-COS.MET* and Case C-445/06 *Danske Slagterier*, n. 231 above.

was intentional; whether the error of law was excusable or inexcusable;[239] and the position taken, if any, by a Union institution. The infringement will in any event be sufficiently serious where the decision concerned was made in manifest breach of the relevant case law of the Court in the matter.[240] This is so *a fortiori* if, and once, the conduct has been condemned by the Court in enforcement proceedings raised under article 258, but reparation is not made conditional upon such prior finding: that 'is admittedly an important factor, but is not indispensable when verifying that the condition that the breach of Community law must be sufficiently serious is met'.[241] A time bar in national law for raising proceedings (*in casu* three years from the date the injured party knew of it)[242] 'appears to be reasonable' and is not inconsistent with the principle,[243] as is an obligation for him to show reasonable diligence in limiting the extent of the injury.[244] Exemplary damages are available if (as in England and Ireland), and in the same manner as, they are available in a claim founded in national law[245] – an application of the principle of equivalence. For sake of completeness it can be recorded that Factortame succeeded in its action for damages, Brasserie du Pêcheur did not.[246]

Because Union law does not distinguish amongst the various authorities of the **6.38** member states, their liability extends to the deprivation of a Union right by a

---

239 For example, in Case C-392/93 *British Telecommunications*, n. 238 above, the faulty implementation of a Directive in the United Kingdom was not sufficiently serious because the Directive was 'imprecisely worded and was reasonably capable of bearing ... the interpretation given to it by the United Kingdom in good faith and on the basis of arguments which are not entirely devoid of substance. That interpretation, which was also shared by other Member States, was not manifestly contrary to the wording of the directive or to the objective pursued by it' (para. 43). According to Collins J the erroneous construction of a Directive results in a sufficiently serious breach of Union law only if 'entirely devoid of merit'; *R (Negassi) v Secretary of State for the Home Department* [2011] EWHC 386 (Admin), at para. 18. As to excusable judicial error see immediately below.

240 Cases C-46 and 48/93 *Brasserie du Pêcheur* and *Factortame III*, at para. 57.

241 Case C-445/06 *Danske Slagterier*, n. 231 above, at para. 38.

242 § 852 I BGB.

243 Case C-445/06 *Danske Slagterier*, n. 231 above, at para. 32. Note that the equivalent rule under art. 340 TFEU is five years; Statute of the Court of Justice, art. 46.

244 Cases C-46 and 48/93 *Brasserie du Pêcheur* and *Factortame III*, at paras 84–5; Case C-445/06 *Danske Slagterier*, at paras 60–1.

245 Cases C-46 and 48/93 *Brasserie du Pêcheur* and *Factortame III*, at para. 89.

246 Damages of some £55 million plus interest and costs were eventually agreed by the Secretary of State at the close of the epic *Factortame* litigation (see *Factortame and ors v Secretary of State for the Environment, Transport and the Regions* [2002] EWCA Civ 22, [2002] 2 All ER 838). Brasserie du Pêcheur (which had sought DM 1.8 million) was required to show 'legislative default' (*legislatives Unrecht*) on the part of the federal parliament and, for the breach identified by the Court of Justice as sufficiently serious, a direct and 'necessary and sufficient' (the '*Adäquanztheorie*') causal link to the injury suffered, a test it failed to meet; BGH, 24 Oktober 1996 (*Brasserie du Pêcheur*), BGHZ 134, 30.

judgment of a national court.[247] This sits uncomfortably with the principle of the independence of the judiciary, recognised not only in national law but by both the European Convention[248] and the Charter of Fundamental Rights.[249] Mere judicial error is not sufficiently serious, it applies in the 'exceptional case' in which a court of final instance[250] 'manifestly infringed [*a méconnu*] the applicable law':[251]

> Such manifest infringement is to be assessed, *inter alia*, in the light of a number of criteria, such as the degree of clarity and precision of the rule infringed, whether the infringement was intentional, whether the error of law was excusable or inexcusable, and the non-compliance by the court in question with its obligation to make a reference for a preliminary ruling under the third paragraph of Article [267 TFEU]; it is in any event presumed where the decision involved is made in manifest disregard of the case-law of the Court on the subject.[252]

So broad is the discretion normally afforded judges, they may have to get it quite astonishingly wrong before meeting the necessary standard.[253]

---

247 Case C-224/01 *Köbler v Austria* [2003] ECR I-10239; Case C-173/03 *Traghetti del Mediterraneo v Italy* [2006] ECR I-5177; Opinion 1/09 *Re the European Patent Convention*, opinion of 8 March 2011, not yet reported, at para. 86.

248 European Convention on Human Rights, art. 6(1).

249 EU Charter of Fundamental Rights, art. 47, 2nd para.

250 The judgments in both *Köbler* and *Traghetti del Mediterraneo* were restricted to consideration of courts of final instance because that was the issue at hand – Austrian liability for a judgment of the *Verwaltungsgerichtshof* (VwGH, 24. Juni 1998, Zl. 97/12/0421) and Italian liability for a judgment of the *Corte Suprema di Cassazione* (sentenza del 19 aprile 2000, n. 5087); they do not speak directly to the conduct of lower courts. This is consistent with the enforcement proceedings raised by the Commission against Sweden in 2004 owing to its dissatisfaction with the conduct of the supreme courts there; see 550 above, n. 305 above. It may therefore be that it is the conduct of courts of last instance alone which, owing to their special status as the 'keystone of judicial cooperation between the Court of Justice and its national counterparts' (Case C-173/09 *Elchinov v Natsionalna zdravnoosiguritelna kasa* [2010] ECR I-8889, *per* A-G Cruz Vallalón at paras 23–4 of his opinion), can engage the liability of the member states.

251 *Köbler*, n. 247 above, at para. 53; *Traghetti del Mediterraneo*, n. 247 above, at paras 32, 42.

252 *Traghetti del Mediterraneo*, at para. 43 (paraphrasing *Köbler*, paras 53–6).

253 In *Köbler*, for example, the Court of Justice seemed to go to some lengths to justify, and exonerate, the *Verwaltungsgerichtshof* judgment. (It may have had an indirect interest in doing so, for it had induced the court to withdraw a reference it had made under art. 267, leading then to the erroneous judgment.) It appeared less enthusiastic to exonerate the *Corte Suprema di Cassazione*. In *Traghetti del Mediterraneo* the Court was asked whether Italian law which limits liability to cases in which a judge acts with intentional fault or serious misconduct (*dolo o colpa grave*) was acceptable, to which the Court replied in effect that the Italian formula must be read in a manner harmonious with the *Köbler* test, which coupled with the standard *Brasserie du Pêcheur* requirements of individual rights and causation, was necessary and sufficient to the task. In the light of the *Corte Suprema di Cassazione* continuing to adhere to the (stricter) Italian standard the Court repeated the admonition in the context of enforcement proceedings under art. 258: Case C-379/10 *Commission v Italy*, judgment of 24 November 2011, not yet reported. In one (but only one) case so far, the Commission raised enforcement proceedings against a member state for a national law being 'construed and applied by the administrative authorities and a substantial proportion of the courts ... in such a way that the exercise of [a Community right] is made excessively difficult', and the Court of Justice found the case made out: Case

In the United Kingdom an action in damages therefore now lies (in England) **6.39** against the Attorney-General[254] or the appropriate Minister of the Crown;[255] this is so even if the injury is occasioned by an Act of Parliament, as was the case, in part, in *Factortame*. However unlikely the occurrence, if the injury is one which is claimed to stem from a judgment of the Supreme Court, presumably the appropriate defendant is the Secretary of State for Justice. An action lies elsewhere against the Crown (in Scotland against the Lord Advocate or the Advocate General for Scotland),[256] the appropriate UK minister and, in devolved matters, the Scottish/Welsh/Northern Irish Ministers. In all cases the Crown Proceedings Act 1947 must now be read and applied in this new light. Damages ought to be available also from local authorities where, acting within their powers in a Union sphere, they cause injury which meets the *Brasserie du Pêcheur* tests.[257] In England the subsisting cause of action appears to be breach of statutory duty,[258] although it has been suggested (but never followed up) that an innominate tort would be more appropriate;[259] it may be compared with the position in Ireland, where the High Court has recognised a new head of tort of 'actionable breach of a Directive'.[260] The matter has not been authoritatively settled in England; the most recent (and not wholly helpful) *dictum* from the Supreme Court on the matter recognises that the prohibitions of articles 101 and 102 TFEU (the major part of the Union's competition rules) 'create a new

---

C-129/00 *Commission v Italy* [2003] ECR I-14637; in such circumstances continued judicial obstruction might well result in liability of the state in damages. See also Case C-154/08 *Commission v Spain* [2009] ECR I-187*.

254 See *R v Secretary of State for Employment, ex parte Equal Opportunities Commission* [1995] 1 AC 1 (HL) *per* Lord Keith at 32.

255 It will be noted that the action for damages in *Factortame* was part of a claim lodged originally in judicial review proceedings of a Secretary of State.

256 See the Crown Suits (Scotland) Act 1857.

257 See Case 103/88 *Fratelli Costanzo v Comune di Milano* [1989] ECR 1839; Case C-302/97 *Konle v Austria* [1999] ECR I-3099; Case C-424/97 *Haim v Kassenzahnärtzliche Vereinigung Nordrhein* [2000] ECR I-5123; *Coppinger v Waterford County Council* [1998] 4 IR 220 (Irish HC). However there is authority (*obiter*) in England that where a local authority acts unlawfully, at least when discharging a statutory duty, so as to give rise to *Brasserie du Pêcheur* damages, liability lies with central government; *Kirklees Municipal Borough Council v Wickes Building Supplies Ltd* [1993] AC 227 (HL) *per* Lord Goff at 282 ('the United Kingdom … would properly be the party so liable'); *Nabadda v Westminster City Council* [2000] ICR 951 (CA).

258 *Sempra Metals v HM Commissioners of Inland Revenue and anor* [2007] UKHL 34, [2008] 1 AC 561, *per* Lord Nicholls at para. 69 ('a breach of the art. 43 EC [art. 49 TFEU] prohibition is characterised in English law as a breach of statutory duty'). See also *R v Secretary of State for Transport, ex parte Factortame* (No. 5) [1997] EuLR 475 (QBD); (No. 7) [2000] All ER (D) 2082 (QBD); *Phonographic Performance Ltd v Department of Trade and anor* [2004] EWHC 1795 (Ch), [2004] All ER (D) 437. The original source of this, upon which Lord Nicholls relied, is (although a private law action) *obiter dicta* in *Garden Cottage Foods v Milk Marketing Board* [1984] AC 130 (HL). In *Bourgoin v Minister of Agriculture, Fisheries and Food* [1985] 3 All ER 585, the Court of Appeal said that a tortious claim would require (and be satisfied by) misfeasance in public office, but the judgment was appealed to the House of Lords and settled before judgment. In any event *Bourgoin* is, in the light of *Francovich* and *Brasserie du Pêcheur*, dangerously unsafe.

259 *Application des Gaz v Falks Veritas* [1974] Ch 381 *per* Denning MR at 396.

260 *Coppinger v Waterford County Council* [1998] 4 IR 220.

tort of breach of statutory duty in respect of cartel agreements'.[261] In Scotland the general rules on availability of remedies in delict mean that the question (and difficulty) does not arise, but there is as yet no authority.

6.40 *Francovich* and *Brasserie du Pêcheur* principles apply to reparation from public authorities. Consistent with the law of delict as it exists in most member states, the Court of Justice is clear that the purpose of the action is not deterrence or punishment but compensation for loss or injury caused by the conduct of a member state;[262] it is thus a distinct but parallel and mutually compatible remedy with the deterrent penalties which may be imposed upon a member state by the Court under article 260.[263] Reparation from private persons is a different matter, for it addresses necessarily the rarer instances in which they bear Union law obligations. However, as such obligations seep into private law relationships they bring with them delictual liability, and in 2009 the Swedish Labour Court applied *Brasserie du Pêcheur* principles in awarding Kr 550,000 (plus costs) against a trade union for frustrating a Latvian firm's right to provide services there.[264] The law on damages in what is clearly a private law area, competition law, developed differently, and is discussed below.

D. UNION LEGISLATION

1. General

6.41 The forms of Union legislation which may be adopted by the institutions in accordance with the procedures discussed in Chapter 3,[265] or by the European Central Bank within its sphere of competence, are set out in article 288 TFEU:

> To exercise the Union's competences, the institutions shall adopt regulations, directives, decisions, recommendations and opinions.
>
> A regulation shall have general application. It shall be binding in its entirety and directly applicable in all Member States.
>
> A directive shall be binding, as to the result to be achieved, upon each Member State to which it is addressed, but shall leave to the national authorities the choice of form and methods.

---

261 *Norris* v *Government of the United States of America and ors* [2008] UKHL 16, [2008] 1 AC 920, *per curiam* at para. 32.
262 Case C-470/03 *A.G.M.-COS.MET* v *Suomen valtio and anor* [2007] ECR I-2749, at para. 88.
263 See 5.58 above.
264 Arbetsdomstolen, dom nr 89 den 2 december 2009; see 11.145 below.
265 See 3.60–3.65 above.

A decision shall be binding in its entirety. A decision which specifies those to whom it is addressed shall be binding only on them.

Recommendations and opinions shall have no binding force.

Notwithstanding proposals through the years for modification, sometimes very significant, the description of these legislative acts has survived unchanged since 1958 save that Lisbon altered the quality of decisions, providing for the first time the option of adopting a decision which has no addressee.[266] Article 288 is carried over to 'apply' to the Euratom Treaty.[267] From 1993 to 2009 the Treaty on European Union provided for other, different and less effective instruments for the pursuit of non-Community Union matters.

The difference amongst the various forms of act lies not in any hierarchical **6.42** ordering but in their scope and effect. In brief, Regulations and decisions have immediate legal effect; Directives require further implementing measures. Regulations are of the nature of general legislation, decisions more particular in their application; to draw (cautiously) an analogy perhaps most widely recognisable, Regulations are laws, decisions decrees. In any event the simplicity of these distinctions has become blurred, and the Court of Justice will always consider the substance of an act rather than its form in order to determine its legal effects.

The Union legislative process is subject to procedural requirements, discussed **6.43** in chapter 3. It is also subject to substantive requirements. First and foremost the Union and its institutions are expressly required to act within the limits of the powers conferred upon them by the Treaties.[268] The institutions may legislate (or adopt other binding acts with legislative effect) only when acting pursuant to express (or implied) Treaty authority, which normally (but not always) prescribes the form of legislative act to be adopted; where it does not the institutions may choose upon a case by case basis 'in compliance with the applicable procedures and with the principle of proportionality'.[269]

---

266 Prior to Lisbon the fourth paragraph of art. 189 EEC/249 EC (= art. 288 TFEU) read: 'A decision shall be binding in its entirety upon those to whom it is addressed'.

267 Euratom Treaty, art. 106a(1). It should be noted that under the ECSC Treaty (art. 14) 'decisions' and 'recommendations' corresponded respectively to Regulations and Directives adopted under the EC and Euratom Treaties.

268 TEU, arts 5(2) (the Union) and 13(2) (the institutions). See Opinion 2/94 *Re Accession to the ECHR* [1996] ECR I-1759, at para. 23: 'It follows from Article 3b of the [EEC] Treaty [now art. 5(2) TEU] ... that the Community ... has only those powers which have been conferred upon it'. Nor may the institutions by legislation extend the rules of the Treaties; Case C-240/90 *Germany* v *Commission* [1992] ECR I-5383.

269 TFEU, art. 296, 1st para.

6.44 Because the Treaties form its constituent norm, Union legislation is always subject to any substantive limitations imposed in and by them, either expressly – for example, the Treaty 'fundamentals' of subsidiarity[270] and proportionality[271] – or implicitly – limitations imposed by the general principles of Union law.[272] Further, all Union acts are required to state 'the reasoning on which they are based'; put more clearly, they must be 'reasoned'.[273] This is both an express Treaty requirement and a matter of public policy which must therefore be considered by the Court of Justice of its own motion if need be.[274] The statement of reasons must appear in the act itself,[275] and 'a failure to state the reasons cannot be remedied by the fact that the person concerned learns the reasons for the decision during the proceedings before the Court'.[276] This is the reason for the (sometimes extensive) preamble (or statement of reasons) in all Union legislation.

6.45 The Court of Justice has found it necessary not only to state reasons but to state sufficient and correct reasons:

> The statement of reasons required by ... the Treaty must explain clearly and unambiguously the reasoning followed by the Community institution which has adopted the ... act.[277]

It:

> must be appropriate to the act at issue and must disclose in a clear and unequivocal fashion the reasoning followed by the institution which adopted the measure in

---

270 TEU, art. 5(3); see 2.28–2.31 above.

271 *Ibid.* art. 5(4); see 2.32 above.

272 See 6.101–6.103 below.

273 The Treaties provide (art. 296 TFEU) that acts 'shall state the reasons on which they are based', but the French (and most other languages) prefer, simply and more clearly, '*sont motivés*'.

274 Case C-367/95P *Commission* v *Sytraval and Brink's France* [1998] ECR I-1719; Case C-265/97P *Coöperatieve Vereniging de Verenigde Bloemenveilingen Aalsmeer* v *Florimex and ors* [2000] ECR I-2061; Case T-102/03 *Centro informativo per la collaborazione tra le imprese e la promotione degli investimenti in Sicilia* v *Commission* [2005] ECR II-2357; Case C-171/05P *Piau* v *Commission* [2006] ECR I-37*; Cases C-89/08P *Commission* v *Ireland, France and Italy* [2009] ECR I-11245.

275 Case C-291/98P *Sarrió* v *Commission* (Cartonboard) [2000] ECR I-9991. It must also be adopted by the author of the act; Case C-137/92P *Commission* v *BASF and ors* (PVC) [1994] ECR I-2555. Derogation from this rule is possible only exceptionally; Case T-390/08 *Bank Melli Iran* v *Council* [2009] ECR II-3967.

276 Case 195/80 *Michel* v *Parliament* [1981] ECR 2861, at para. 22; Case T-228/02 *Organisation des Modjehedines du peuple d'Iran* v *Council* [2006] ECR II-4665, at para. 139, substituting 'act' for 'decision' and 'Community judicature' for 'Court'; Case T-185/06 *L'Air Liquide* v *Commission*, judgment of 16 June 2011, not yet reported, at para. 81; similarly, Case T-86;11 *Bamba* v *Council*, judgment of 8 June 2011, not yet reported, at paras 38–40.

277 Case C-351/98 *Spain* v *Commission* [2002] ECR I-8031, at para. 82.

question in such a way as to enable the persons concerned to ascertain the reasons for the measure and to enable the competent Community Court to exercise its power of review.[278]

However, the adopting institution

is not required to go into every relevant point of fact and law … [T]he question of whether a statement of reasons satisfies the requirements must be assessed with reference not only to the wording of the measure but also to the context and to the whole body of legal rules governing the matter in question. If the contested measure clearly discloses the essential objective pursued by the institution, it would be excessive to require a specific statement of reasons for each of the technical choices made by the institution.[279]

An act which is insufficiently or incorrectly reasoned is an infringement of an essential procedural requirement within the meaning of article 263[280] and so liable to annulment (article 263) or invalidation (article 267).[281] It extends to a subjective element: if a Union measure is adopted upon the basis of justification which 'no reasonable decision-maker could have honestly entertained', it may be annulled.[282] The preamble is also important in that the Court will frequently make reference to it as an aid to interpretation of the substantive provisions which follow, which are 'indissociably linked' to it.[283] However, it should be noted that

---

278   Case C-487/06P *British Aggregates Association* v *Commission* [2008] ECR I-10505, at para. 172; also Case C-89/08P *Commission* v *Ireland, France and Italy*, n. 274 above, *per* A-G Bot at para. 116 of his opinion.

279   Case C-210/03 *R (Swedish Match AB and anor)* v *Secretary of State for Health* [2004] ECR I-11893, at paras 63–4; also the opinion of A-G Bot in Case C-89/08P *Commission* v *Ireland, France and Italy*, n. 274 above.

280   The Court has said that the absence, or inadequacy, of reasons goes to infringement of an essential procedural requirement (Case C-367/95P *Commission* v *Sytraval and Brink's France* [1998] ECR I-1719; Case C-265/97P *Verenigde Bloemenveilingen Aalsmeer* [2000] ECR I-2061; Case C-378/00 *Commission* v *Parliament and Council* (LIFE) [2003] ECR I-937; Case T-168/01 *GlaxoSmithKline Services* v *Commission* [2006] ECR II-2969, at para. 54; Cases T-60 etc./06 *Ireland and ors* v *Commission* [2007] ECR II-172*, at para. 47) rather than infringement of the Treaties (that is, of art. 296).

281   See e.g., Case 158/80 *Rewe Handelsgesellschaft Nord* v *Hauptzollamt Kiel* [1981] ECR 1805; Case C-41/93 *France* v *Commission* [1994] ECR I-1829; Case C-360/92P *Publishers Association* v *Commission* [1995] ECR I-23; Cases C-289 etc./96 *Denmark and ors* v *Commission* [1999] ECR I-1541; Case C-351/98 *Spain* v *Commission*, n. 277 above; Case C-378/00 *Commission* v *Parliament and Council* (LIFE), *ibid.*; Case C-76/01P *Eurocoton and ors* v *Council* [2003] ECR I-10091; Case T-306/00 *Conserve Italia* v *Commission* [2003] ECR II-5705; Case T-327/03 *Stichting Al-Aqsa* v *Council* [2007] ECR II-79*; Case T-229/02 *Ocalan (on behalf of the Kurdistan Workers' Party (PKK))* v *Council* [2008] ECR II-45*; Case T-264/06 *DC-Hadler Networks* v *Commission* [2008] ECR II-199*. A large number of competition cases, in which the reasoning component of a decision is (and must be) very extensive, are raised under art. 263 in this context.

282   Case T-256/07 *People's Mojahedin Organization of Iran* v *Council* [2008] ECR II-3019, at para. 180. The British analogy is annulment of an administrative measure for '*Wednesbury* unreasonableness', derived from *Associated Provincial Picture Houses* v *Wednesbury Corporation* [1948] 1 KB 223.

283   Case C-298/00P *Italy* v *Commission* [2004] ECR I-4087, at para. 97; Cases C-402 and 432/07 *Sturgeon and ors* v *Condor Flugdienst and anor* [2009] ECR I-10923, at para. 42.

the preamble to a Community act has no binding legal force and cannot be relied on either as a ground for derogating from the actual provisions of the act in question or for interpreting those provisions in a manner clearly contrary to their wording.[284]

A Commission proposal for legislation (most commonly, important Regulations and Directives) will often be accompanied by an 'explanatory memorandum' of the Commission's devising. It is a species of *travaux préparatoires* and is helpful in understanding why and how the proposal came about, but it has 'self evidently ... no legally binding effect'.[285]

6.46 The three main political institutions have adopted a number of interinstitutional agreements upon the style, structure, clarity, quality and 'codification' of Union legislation.[286] They have limited, if any, legal effect.[287] Some would say they have limited, if any, practical effect. In 2006 the Parliament called for a new interinstitutional impetus towards 'better regulation':

> based on a core set of regulatory principles, namely subsidiarity, proportionality, accountability, consistency, transparency and targeting; stress[ing] that this approach cannot bypass the rights of social consultation and must respect the principles of participative [*sic*] democracy,[288]

and this was followed up by a Commission 'strategic review of better regulation in the European Union'.[289] Identifiable fruits of these initiatives have yet to appear.

6.47 The technical format of legislation is set out in the Council's Rules of Procedure.[290]

---

284 Case C-136/04 *Deutsches Milch-Kontor* v *Hauptzollamt Hamburg-Jonas* [2005] ECR I-10095, at para. 32. But in Cases C-402 and 432/07 *Sturgeon, ibid.*, the Court arguably did just that.

285 Case C-28/08P *Commission* v *Bavaria Lager* [2010] ECR I-6055, *per* A-G Sharpston at para. 110 of her opinion.

286 E.g., interinstitutional agreements on working methods for official codification of texts ([1996] OJ C102/2); on common guidelines for the quality of drafting of Community legislation ([1999] OJ C73/1); on a more structured use of the recasting technique for legal acts ([2002] OJ C77/1); and on better law-making ([2003] OJ C321/1). See also the 'Joint Practical Guide' drawn up by the legal services of the three institutions for persons involved in the drafting of legislation within the Community institutions, published in 2003. Care is required here: these various instruments speak sometimes of the 'recasting' (*refonte* or *Neufassung*) of legislation but normally its 'codification' (*codification*; *Kodifizierung*) which to the English speaker is a misleading *faux ami*: it means consolidation and should be called that. But isn't.

287 One (but only one) is stated expressly not to be binding; see the 1999 Agreement on the quality of drafting, recital 7.

288 'The implementation, consequences and impact of the internal market legislation in force', P6 TA(2006) O 204, para. 1.

289 COM(2006) 689 final.

290 RP Council, Annex VI.

(a) Legal base

'Related to' the duty to state reasons[291] is the Treaty authority for the adoption **6.48** of a measure: it thus extends to include an obligation to cite in all legislation that authority (the 'Treaty base' or 'legal base') under which the adopting institution is acting. It anchors a legislative measure in the Treaties and is a practical application of the principle of conferral which underpins all Union authority. The choice of the appropriate legal base therefore 'has constitutional significance'.[292] The standard formula at the head of the preamble to all Union measures[293] is now, for example, where the ordinary legislative procedure applies:

> The European Parliament and the Council of the European Union,
>
> Having regard to the Treaty on the Functioning of the European Union, and in particular Article x thereof ...

where article x is the Treaty provision conferring upon those institutions the necessary legislative competence in the field. Equally, where adopting 'non-legislative' (that is, delegated or implementing) acts the Commission (or other authorised institution or body) will cite the enabling legislation authorising it to act, and it must act within the four corners of that legislation.[294] Identification of the legal base must, owing to the principle of legal certainly, normally be express.[295] Identification of the *correct* legal base is an objective, not subjective, test, to be determined by analysis of the pith and substance, or 'object [or aim] and content', of the measure.[296] If the measure has a twofold purpose or twofold component but one of these is identifiable as pre-eminent and the other merely incidental, the act must be based upon the sole, primary legal base.[297] But if it pursues several objectives, indissociably linked, and no one is secondary or

---

291 Case C-370/07 *Commission* v *Council* (CITES) [2009] ECR I-8917, at para. 38.

292 Opinion 2/00 *Re the Convention on Biological Diversity* (Cartagena Protocol) [2001] ECR I-9713, at para. 5; Case C-370/07 *CITES, ibid.* at para. 47.

293 Styles are set out in the Joint Practical Guide for persons involved in the drafting of legislation within the Community institutions, 2003.

294 See e.g., Case C-240/90 *Germany* v *Commission* [1992] ECR I-5383. As to non-legislative acts see 6.86 below.

295 E.g., Case C-325/91 *France* v *Commission* [1993] ECR I-3283, at para. 26; Case C-370/07 *CITES*, n. 291 above, at para. 39.

296 See e.g., Case C-300/89 *Commission* v *Council* (Titanium Dioxide) [1991] ECR I-2867; Case C-295/90 *Parliament* v *Council* (Students) [1992] ECR I-4193; Case C-155/91 *Commission* v *Council* (Waste Disposal) [1993] ECR I-939; Case C-376/98 *Germany* v *Parliament and Council* (Tobacco Advertising) [2000] ECR I-8419; Opinion 2/00 *Re the Cartagena Protocol*, n. 292 above; Cases C-453 etc./03 *R (ABNA and ors)* v *Secretary of State for Health and ors* [2005] ECR I-10423; Case C-217/04 *United Kingdom* v *Parliament and Council* (Network and Information Security Agency) [2006] ECR I-3771.

297 Case C-42/97 *Parliament* v *Council* (Linguistic Diversity) [1999] ECR I-869; Case C-491/01 *R* v *Secretary of State for Health, ex parte British American Tobacco and ors* [2002] ECR I-11453; Cases C-154 and 155/04 *R (Alliance for Natural Health and ors)* v *Secretary of State for Health and anor* [2005] ECR I-6451; Case C-411/06 *Commission* v *Parliament and Council* (Shipment of Waste) [2009] ECR I-7585.

incidental in relation to another, then a multiple legal base is appropriate, indeed mandatory.[298] Adoption of such a measure becomes complex where the various legal bases require different legislative procedures. To make matters more complex still because it goes to the jurisdiction of the Court of Justice, latterly there were a number of challenges to legislation in which the dispute was between provisions in the EC or EU Treaty as the correct legal base,[299] an issue alive still at the frontier between Common Foreign and Security Policy (under Title V TEU) and general Union competences. Recitation of incorrect legal base(s) is an infringement of an essential procedural requirement or of the Treaties (the Court has never made it clear which), so leaving the measure liable to annulment or invalidation. However, the Court has come to find that it is a 'purely formal defect', and annulment or invalidation follows only if it gives rise to an irregularity in, or 'vitiates', the procedure appropriate to the adoption of the measure;[300] alternatively, an incorrect legal base does not result in annulment if (in administrative proceedings) it 'did not deprive the applicants of the procedural guarantees laid down by the relevant rules of procedure and did not have any adverse effect on their legal position'.[301] If the choice of Treaty base is an attempt intentionally to evade a particular legislative procedure it is a misuse of powers within the meaning of article 263.[302]

6.49 The (appropriate) legal base of a measure must be in force at the moment of its adoption.[303]

---

298 Case 165/87 *Commission v Council* (Nomenclature of Goods) [1988] ECR 5545; Opinion 2/00 *Re the Cartagena Protocol*, n. 292 above; Case C-91/05 *Commission v Council* (Small Arms Weapons) [2008] ECR I-3651; Case C-155/07 *Parliament v Council* [2008] ECR I-8103; Case C-166/07 *Parliament v Council* (International Fund for Ireland) [2009] ECR I-7135. See e.g., Regulation 178/2002 [2002] OJ L31/1 on food safety, which cites four legal bases for there are distinct elements of each in it: arts 37 EC (the legal base for agricultural legislation), 95 EC (harmonisation in the internal market), 133 EC (common commercial policy) and 152(4)(b) EC (veterinary and phytosanitary inspection to protect public health). For an extreme example see the decision (Decision 2008/429 [2008] OJ L151/33) to adopt a protocol to a partnership and cooperation agreement with a third state (Armenia), which owing to the breadth of the subject matter of the agreement required as its legal base 'Article 44(2), the last sentence of Article 47(2) and Articles 55, 57(2), 71, 80(2), 93, 94, 133 and 181a, in conjunction with the second sentence of Article 300(2) and the first subparagraph of Article 300(3)' EC.

299 Case C-176/03 *Commission v Council* [2005] ECR I-7879 (the contested bases being arts 29, 31(e), 34 and 47 TEU (pre-Lisbon) or art. 175 EC); Case C-440/05 *Commission v Council* [2007] ECR I-9097 (arts 31(1)(e), 34 and 47 TEU (pre-Lisbon) or art. 80(2) EC); Case C-91/05 *Small Arms Weapons, ibid.* (art. 14 TEU (pre-Lisbon) or art. 179 EC); Case C-301/06 *Ireland v Parliament and Council* [2009] ECR I-593 (arts 30, 31(1)(c) and 34(2)(b) TEU (pre-Lisbon) or art. 95 EC).

300 Case C-491/01 *British American Tobacco*, n. 297 above, paras 98–111; also Case C-210/03 *R (Swedish Match AB and anor) v Secretary of State for Health* [2004] ECR I-11893.

301 Case T-213/00 *CMA CGM and ors v Commission* [2003] ECR II-913, at para. 103.

302 Case 331/88 *R v Minister for Agriculture, Fisheries and Food, ex parte FEDESA* [1990] ECR I-4023; Case C-210/03 *Swedish Match*, n. 300 above.

303 Case C-269/97 *Commission v Council* [2000] ECR I-2257, at para. 45; Case C-512/99 *Germany v Commission* [2003] ECR I-845; Case T-310/00 *MCI v Commission* [2004] ECR II-3253, paras 78–114; Cases T-27

Identification of a legal base is often the subject of disagreement amongst the **6.50** institutions, each as a general rule favouring that which gives it greatest authority over the procedure for adoption of the measure. It is not infrequently the subject of infighting amongst the various Directorates-General even before it leaves the Commission. In this the advice of the Legal Service is especially useful and relied upon heavily.

The direct effect (or otherwise) of a Union measure is wholly unrelated to its **6.51** legal base, that depending rather upon whether it meets the requisite standard tests.[304]

(b) Article 352 and implied powers

Because Union competence is one of conferral the exercise of powers must be **6.52** founded in Treaty authority; all else ('residual powers') remains with the member states. This is common to most, but not all, federal constitutions, implicit in the previous Treaties and made express by Lisbon.[305] But having said that, the legislative competence conferred upon the Union, and its institutions, by the Treaties is very broad. This is a function not only of numerous Treaty articles constituting legal bases in a wide variety of fields, but in particular the breadth of one of them, article 352 TFEU:

> If action by the Union should prove necessary, within the framework of the policies defined in the Treaties, to attain one of the objectives set out in the Treaties, and the Treaties have not provided the necessary powers, the Council, acting unanimously on a proposal from the Commission and after obtaining the consent of the European Parliament, shall adopt the appropriate measures.[306]

Called by the Germans the 'flexibility clause' (*Flexibilitätsklausel*), sometimes the 'general enabling power', this is an extraordinary device to find in a federal constitution, never mind an international treaty. Article 352 is a residual legislative authority, to 'fill the gap'[307] and be used only where there is no other, sufficient legal base in the Treaties but Union action is nonetheless necessary in order that it carry out its proper functions;[308] it was therefore deployed

---

etc./03 *SP and ors v Commission* [2007] ECR II-4331, at para. 118; Cases C-113 etc./10 *Zuckerfabrik Jülich and ors v Hauptzollamt Aachen and ors*, pending.

304   Case C-319/97 *Criminal proceedings against Kortas* [1999] ECR I-3143, at para. 22.

305   TEU, arts 4(1), 5(2).

306   Prior to Lisbon the Parliament's consent was not necessary, it required only to be consulted; art. 308 EC. The words 'within the framework of the policies defined in the Treaties' were added in order more firmly to anchor the power to a Treaty basis.

307   Case C-166/07 *Parliament v Council* (International Fund for Ireland) [2009] ECR I-7135, at para. 41.

308   Case C-295/90 *Parliament v Council* (Students) [1992] ECR I-4193, at para. 11; Opinion 2/94 *Re Accession to the ECHR* [1996] ECR I-1759, at para. 29; Case C-84/94 *United Kingdom v Council* (Working Time Directive) [1996] ECR I-5755, at para. 48; Case C-166/07 *International Fund for Ireland*, *ibid.*

sparingly in the early years, and came into its own only as the Community advanced into new, perhaps unforeseen, areas. It comes very close, if not quite getting there, to *Kompetenz-Kompetenz*, an authority of the Union to determine the limits of its own competences; to the *Bundesverfassungsgericht* it 'relaxes' the principle of conferral[309] and makes possible substantial alteration of Treaty fundamentals without the participation of national parliaments.[310] The only (adequate?) lines of defence were that action be 'necessary' to obtain a Community objective, a requirement of unanimity (of governments) in the Council[311] and acquiescence of the Court of Justice, which, it is worthwhile recalling, has annulled a Community act for exceeding Community competences exceptionally rarely (and never in the context of an article 352 measure).[312] Lisbon has fortified them by adding the consent of the Parliament and a requirement that national parliaments be informed by the Commission of article 352 proposals so that they may monitor compliance with the principle of subsidiarity,[313] but at the same time extended the reach of the article beyond action necessary 'in the course of the operation of the common market' (as previously)[314] to that necessary 'within the framework of the policies defined in the Treaties'. Expressly barred are only harmonisation of national law in areas in which the Treaties exclude such harmonisation[315] and the objectives of the Common Foreign and Security Policy (CFSP).[316]

6.53 There are nevertheless limits to article 352. In an advisory opinion on whether the Community possessed the constitutional authority to accede to the European Convention on Human Rights the Court said:

> That provision, being an integral part of an institutional system based upon the principle of conferred powers, cannot serve as a basis for widening the scope of Community powers beyond the general framework created by the provisions of the

---

309 BVerfG, 30. Juni 2009 (*Lissabon-Vertrag*), BVerfGE 123, 267 (394) ('Art. 352 AEUV ... lockert ... das Prinzip der begrenzten Einzelermächtigung').

310 *Ibid.* at (395).

311 Since 2011 a statutory bar is in place whereby a UK minister may support an art. 352 measure in the Council only with prior approval by Act of Parliament, prior approval by both Houses without amendment where in the minister's opinion urgency justifies it, or if he certifies the draft measure as falling within an 'exempt purpose'; European Union Act 2011, s. 8.

312 It is commonly averred that the Court has done so only once, in Case C-376/98 *Germany v Parliament and Council* (Tobacco Advertising) [2000] ECR I-8419. But this is too simplistic a view: the Court can be said to have done so also (partly) in Case C-84/94 *Working Time*, n. 308 above, (obliquely) in Case C-440/05 *Commission v Council* [2007] ECR I-9097, and (indirectly) in Case C-91/05 *Commission v Council* (Small Arms Weapons) [2008] ECR I-3651.

313 TFEU, art. 352(2); Protocol (No. 2) on the Application of the Principles of Subsidiarity and Proportionality.

314 EC Treaty, art. 308.

315 TFEU, art. 352(3).

316 *Ibid.* art. 352(4).

Treaty ... On any view, Article [352] cannot be used as the basis for the adoption of provisions whose effect would, in substance, be to amend the Treaty ...

[Accession to the ECHR] would be of constitutional significance and would therefore be such as to go beyond the scope of Article [352].[317]

Nor could it be used as a legal base for Community legislation to serve an objective of the pre-Lisbon Union (for example, the CFSP), for that too would widen the scope of Community powers beyond the permissible limits of the EC Treaty.[318]

But even within its proper limits, circumscribed by article 5 TEU, article 352 **6.54** poses serious and difficult questions for the Union legal order and its relationship with those of the member states. For example, the Danish constitution provides that state authority may be 'entrusted' (*overlade*) to international bodies but 'to an extent specified by statute' (*ved lov i nærmere bestemt omfang*).[319] It was therefore argued in the Danish courts that article 235 EEC (= article 352 TFEU) made the limits of Community competences so elastic that it was impossible to specify their 'extent', so that the Danish law of accession to the Community was incompatible with the constitution. The *Højesteret* dismissed the petition, but added that should the '*ekstraordinære situation*' arise in which a Community act finds no objection in the Court of Justice but exceeds the surrender of sovereignty foreseen by the law of accession, the Danish courts would be bound to declare it 'inapplicable' (*uanvendelig*) in Denmark.[320] It is a principle which applies more widely when Union law is viewed through the prism of national/constitutional law: the Czech *Ústavní Soud*, for example, declared that

should one of the [constitutional] conditions for the transfer of powers cease to be fulfilled, that is, should developments in the EC, or the EU, threaten the very essence of state sovereignty of the Czech Republic or the essential attributes of a democratic state governed by the rule of law, it would be necessary for the state bodies of the Czech Republic to reassume those powers.[321]

---

317 Opinion 2/94 *Re Accession to the ECHR*, n. 308 above, at paras 30, 35.
318 Cases C-402 and 415/05P *Kadi and Al Barakaat v Council and Commission* [2008] ECR I-6351, at para. 308; now codified in TFEU, art. 352(4).
319 Grundlov, § 20.
320 *Højesteret*, dom af 6 april 1998 (*Carlsen m.fl. mod Statsminister*), U1998.800H. The 'inapplicability' of Union law adverted to here is a mirror (reverse) image of the inapplicability of national law which is a requirement of the primacy of Union law.
321 Pl. ÚS 50/04 ze dne 17. března 2006 (*kvót v odvěí cukru*), at Part B, para. 4 ('Pokud by jedna z těchto podmínek realizace přenosu pravomocí nebyla naplněna, tj. pokud by vývoj v ES, resp. EU, ohrožoval samotnou podstatu státní svrchovanosti ČR nebo podstatné náležitosti demokratického právního státu, bylo by třeba trvat na tom, aby se těchto pravomocí opětovně ujaly vnitrostátní orgány ČR'). See also *Satversmes tiesa*, 2009. gada 7. aprīļa spriedums lietā Nr 2008–35–1 (*Lisabonas līgum*), at para. 18.3: a 'transfer of competence ... which is acceptable

Equally doctrinaire was its response to the Lisbon Treaty, in which it said that any (purported) transfer by a Czech law to the Union of power of the character of 'constitutional *Kompetenz-Kompetenz*' (*ústavní kompetenční kompetence*) would infringe the constitution,[322] although in a later judgment it declined, when invited to do so, to define the substantive limits to the transfer of competences beyond which Czech ratification would be thus unconstitutional.[323] Not to be outdone, the *Bundesvefassungsgericht* likewise found the member states not to have yielded (*eingeräumt*) *Kompetenz-Kompetenz* to the Union under Lisbon and declared that any German law doing so would be impermissible under the Basic Law.[324] Moreover an expansive interpretation of Union law by the Court of Justice which which took the Union beyond that which was legitimately conferred upon it (to be determined by the *Bundesverfassungsgericht*) would be an 'inadmissible autonomous Treaty amendment' (*unzulässige autonome Vertragsänderung*) and of no force in Germany.[325] The Polish *Trybunał Konstytucyjny* followed suit, citing both the *Bundesverfassungsgericht* and the *Højesteret* with approval.[326]

6.55 The Court of Justice also recognises a doctrine of implied powers in its more conventional sense of necessarily incidental:

> The Community acts ordinarily on the basis of specific powers which, as the Court has held, are not necessarily the express consequence of specific provisions of the Treaty but may also be implied from them.[327]

---

only if EU law is compatible with a democratic State' ('kompetenču nodošana … kas ir pieņemami vienīgi tādā gadījumā, ja ES tiesības ir savietojamas ar demokrātiskas valsts').

322 Pl. ÚS 19/08 ze dne 26 listopadu 2008 (*Lisabonská smlouva*).

323 Pl. ÚS 29/09 ze dne 3 listopadu 2009 (*Lisabonská smlouva II*).

324 BVerfG, 30. Juni 2009 (*Lissabon-Vertrag*), BVerfGE 123, 267 (324, 349, 395). Yet a year later the *Bundesverfassungsgericht* was nothing if not emollient, setting out in the latest chapter of the *Solange* saga the circumstances in which it would (and would be required to) reassume its constitutional duty to test a Union measure (*in casu* a Directive afforded a very broad interpretation by the Court of Justice) against a fundamental rule of the Basic Law; that is, only if there is an invasion of the inviolable core of the Basic Law (§ 79 III GG) by the Union institutions which is expressly protected from Union incursion by the *Europa-Artikel* (§23 I Abs 1 GG) introduced in anticipation of Maastricht in 1992), a manifest transgression of competence (*ersichtliche Kompetenzüberschreitungen*) or a violation of the principle of conferral which is sufficiently serious (*hinreichend qualifiziert*), which is the case when it exceeds its authority in a manner which is obvious (*offensicht*) and the measure in question leads to a structurally significant shift in the division of competences at the expense of member state competences; BVerfG, 6. Juli 2010 (*Honeywell*), BVerfGE 126, 286 (302, 304, 309).

325 BVerfG, 30. Juni 2009 (*Lissabon-Vertrag*), *ibid.*, (400). Also BVerfG, 6. Juli 2010 (*Honeywell*), *ibid.*, (302). In the former it set out in a (non-exhaustive) enumeration five sensitive areas in which further integration is to be tightly circumscribed: criminal law, the use of force by the police (internally) and the military (externally), fundamental fiscal questions, living conditions in a social state and decisions of particular cultural importance such as family law, education, language, media and religion (357–63); there is of course no mention of monetary policy which would normally be regarded as a core issue of national sovereignty.

326 K 18/04, Wyrok z dnia 11 maja 2005 r. (*Traktat akcesyjny*), 2005 Nr 5, poz. 49, at part 4.5. Also K 32/09, Wyrok z dnia 24 listopada 2010 r. (*Traktat z Lizbony*), 2010 Nr 229, poz. 1506, at part 2.1.

327 Opinion 2/94 *Re Accession to the ECHR*, n. 308 above, at para. 25.

So:

> [w]here an article of the EEC Treaty … confers a specific task on the Commission it must be accepted, if that provision is not to be rendered wholly ineffective, that it confers on the Commission necessarily and *per se* the powers which are indispensable in order to carry out that task.[328]

This is an application of the public international law doctrine of effectiveness (*ut res magis valeat quam pereat*) and is a principle common to constitutional law in federations, which allows the centre and the regions each to trench upon the constitutional competences of the other where it is necessary in order that areas properly within their competences be governed effectively.[329] It is one little developed in the Union context.

(c) Criminal law

The pre-Lisbon Community had little authority in the sphere of criminal law, **6.56** which remained a matter essentially for the member states:[330] 'as a general rule, neither criminal law nor the rules of criminal procedure fall within in the Community's competence'.[331] Even provisions of the EC Treaty addressing customs cooperation and the protection of the Community's financial interests, areas normally regulated in a national context by means of criminal law, excluded Community measures which trenched upon 'the application of national criminal law or the national administration of justice'.[332] The Council created and conferred upon the Commission the power to impose (sometimes swingeing) fines for breaches of the competition rules, but these are carefully circumscribed to be non-criminal penalties ('shall not be of a criminal law nature'; '*n'ont pas un caractère pénal*').[333] In giving effect to a Directive a member state may, in discharging its duty, express or otherwise, to make the Directive effective, prohibit certain conduct with criminal sanctions, but that is a choice of the member state – if one which may give rise to internal difficulties[334] – and

---

328 Cases 281 etc./85 *Germany and ors* v *Commission* [1987] ECR 3203, at para. 28. See also Case 8/55 *Fédération Charbonnière de Belgique* v *High Authority* [1954–56] ECR 245; Case 22/70 *Commission* v *Council* (ERTA) [1971] ECR 263.

329 However there is in the Union no recognised principle of implied powers in the other direction; rather it may be said to reside in the various derogation clauses permitting member states to depart from Union rules in the interest of, for example, public policy or public morality; these are discussed below.

330 See e.g., Case 203/80 *Criminal proceedings against Casati* [1981] ECR 2595, at para. 27; Case C-226/97 *Criminal proceedings against Lemmens* [1998] ECR I-3711.

331 Case C-176/03 *Commission* v *Council* [2005] ECR I-7879, at para. 47; Case C-440/05 *Commission* v *Council* [2007] ECR I-9097, at para. 66.

332 EC Treaty, arts 135, 280(4).

333 Regulation 1/2003 [2003] OJ L 1/1, art. 23(5); in German the fines are *Geldbußen* (roughly, administrative fines), not *Geldstrafen* (criminal fines). See 13.99 below.

334 See e.g., *Browne* v *Attorney General and ors* [2003] 3 IR 205 in which Irish attempts to adopt serious (indictable) criminal penalties for breach of various Community fisheries Regulations were found by the

is consistent with subsidiarity. Criminal matters were of course frequently the subject of deliberation and action under Title VI of the pre-Lisbon TEU (Police and Judicial Cooperation in Criminal Matters), but not in a way which led to direct control of criminal law or procedure by the (then) Union.

6.57 Even before Lisbon the ground was shifting. In 2003 the Council adopted a Union framework decision by authority of Title VI requiring each member state 'to establish as criminal offences under its domestic law' various acts which, intentionally or negligently, caused environmental damage.[335] In 2005 the Court of Justice annulled it, finding it to have been adopted by an incorrect legal base:

> [O]n account of both their aim and their content, Articles 1 to 7 of the framework decision have as their main purpose the protection of the environment and they could have been properly adopted on the basis of Article 175 EC [article 192 TFEU] ... [T]he entire framework decision ... infringes Article 47 EU as it encroaches on the powers which Article 175 EC confers on the Community.[336]

This judgment was hailed by the Commission as a breakthrough, recognition of an authority in the EC Treaty to adopt, or at least compel the adoption of, criminal sanctions.[337] According to the Court, the Community's lack of *vires* in the criminal sphere

> does not prevent the Community legislature, when the application of effective, proportionate and dissuasive criminal penalties by the competent national authorities is an essential measure for combating serious environmental offences, from taking measures which relate to the criminal law of the Member States which it considers necessary in order to ensure that the rules which it lays down on environmental protection are fully effective.[338]

In a subsequent judgment involving a framework decision on criminal penalties for ship-source pollution it confirmed this position but limited Community action to the general rather than the specific: where the Community purported to determine the type and level of applicable criminal penalties which member

---

Supreme Court to be *ultra vires* as the *Oireachtas* had not in clear and plain language conferred adequate powers upon the government to do so.

335 Framework Decision 2003/80 [2003] OJ L29/55, arts 2 and 3. On the nature of framework decisions see 6.92 below.

336 Case C-176/03 *Commission v Council*, n. 331 above, at paras 51, 53.

337 Commission Communication to the European Parliament and the Council on the implications of the Court's judgment of 13 September 2005 (Case C-176/03 Commission v Council), COM(2005) 583 final.

338 Case C-176/03 *Commission v Council*, n. 331 above, at para. 48.

states must impose, it is exceeding its jurisdiction.[339] According to the Commission, Community action in criminal matters was now legitimate when based upon implicit powers associated with a specific legal basis, where there was a clear need to combat serious shortcomings in the implementation of Community objectives, and where two conditions – necessity (essentially a proportionality test) and consistency (measures adopted must respect the overall consistency of the Union's system(s) of criminal law, whether adopted on the basis of the first (Community) or the third pillar) – were met.[340] Whether the Commission was correct in its interpretation of the judgment and, if so, how far the principle could be stretched into other areas of Union law – the free movement of goods, persons, services and capital, or competition law, for example (and Advocate-General Mazák was clear that 'there is … no sound basis for regarding the power to provide for criminal measures' as limited to environmental protection)[341] – were, and are, unknown. There was also the practical matter of securing Council support for any such measure: the framework decision annulled by the Court in its 2005 judgment started life as a Commission proposal for a Community Directive by (what turned out to be the correct) authority of article 175 EC (requiring the co-decision (now ordinary legislative) procedure) but it was unable to muster the necessary qualified majority in the Council, whereupon it was proposed by a member state to be adopted as a framework decision under article 34(2)(b) of the Treaty on European Union (which required Council unanimity) – and, perversely, was adopted on that basis. Following annulment, a Directive to replace it was adopted only after three years of haggling.[342]

Yet the ice broken, the Council may be acquiring the habit: it had little difficulty in adopting (under article 63(3)(b) EC on illegal immigration and residence) a Directive prohibiting employment of illegally staying third country nationals and quite clearly requiring that infringement of the prohibition be made a criminal offence where it is (a) intentional and (b) continuing or persistently repeated, involving a significant number of illegally staying third country nationals, accompanied by particulary exploitative working conditions, or involving a minor or an individual known to be trafficked.[343] Additional insight was expected with a Directive requiring the creation of criminal sanctions for infringement of various intellectual property rights ('IPRED2'), proposed by

---

339   Case C-440/05 *Commission* v *Council* [2007] ECR I-9097. In this case the correct legal base for action (except for the specificity of the penalties) was art. 80(2) EC, part of the common transport policy.
340   Commission Communication, n. 337 above, at paras 7, 11–13.
341   Case C-440/05 *Commission* v *Council*, n. 339 above, at para. 92 of his opinion.
342   Directive 2008/99 [2008] OJ L328/28.
343   Directive 2009/52 [2009] OJ L168/24, art. 9.

the Commission in 2006,[344] but much contested and in the face of Council resistance withdrawn in 2010.[345] These issues remain live under the post-Lisbon Treaties, coupled with the clear Union authority in criminal matters necessary to attain the area of freedom, security and justice.[346]

(d) Publication and entry into force

6.58 All legislative acts and all non-legislative acts in the form of a Regulation, a Directive addressed to all member states or a decision addressed to no one, are required to be published in the *Official Journal*.[347] Failure to do so deprives a measure of any legal obligation for individuals it would otherwise have produced.[348] Measures enter into force on the date specified in them or, in the absence thereof, on the twentieth day following that of publication.[349] Other measures (Directives addressed to only some member states, decisions with an addressee) need not be published but require to be notified to those to whom they are addressed, and take effect upon notification.[350]

2. Forms of Union legislation

(a) Regulations

6.59 A Regulation is comparable to statute, or ordinary, law: it is, in accordance with article 288, of 'general application [and] binding in its entirety and directly applicable in all Member States'. 'Direct applicability' – to be distinguished carefully from direct effect[351] – means that a Regulation produces, of itself, immediate legal effect; it requires, in principle, no implementation or further action in the member states. Indeed, a member state may not even attempt to adopt implementing measures which might have the consequence of limiting or altering the effects of a Regulation which must be enforced as it stands.[352] Constitutional difficulties in some member states – for example, a constitutional prohibition of recognising or giving effect to a law the source of which

---

344 COM(2006) 168 final; see 10.79 below. Originally proposed as a Union framework decision (COM(2005) 276 final) but altered to a Directive (under art. 95 EC) in light of the judgment (two months later) in Case C-176/03 *Commission* v *Council*, n. 331 above.

345 [2010] OJ C252/9. The Commission then launched a new public consultation exercise; Report on the Application of Directive 2004/48, COM(2010) 779 final.

346 See 11.173–11.175 below.

347 TFEU, art. 297 (ex art. 254 EC).

348 Case C-345/06 *Heinrich* [2009] ECR I-1659; see n. 809 below. As for failure to publish in all languages see n. 803 below and accompanying text.

349 TFEU, art. 297.

350 *Ibid.* art. 297(2).

351 See J.A. Winter, 'Direct Applicability and Direct Effect: Two Distinct and Different Concepts in Community Law' (1972) 9 *CMLRev.* 425.

352 See e.g., Case 40/69 *Hauptzollamt Hamburg* v *Bollmann* [1970] ECR 69; Case 93/71 *Leonesio* v *Ministry of Agriculture and Forestry* [1972] ECR 287.

lies outwith the state[353] – are set aside, so far as the Union is concerned, by application of the primacy of Union law (that is, here, article 288).

A provision of a Regulation may or may not have direct effect, depending upon whether it fulfils the necessary criteria.[354]   **6.60**

(b)   Decisions

A decision is, like a Regulation, 'binding in its entirety'.[355] But it is generally of more limited and specific application than a Regulation: if a Regulation can be likened to a statute, then a decision is analogous to an executive or administrative act: **6.61**

> [T]he criterion for distinguishing between a regulation and a decision must be sought in the general application or otherwise of the measure in question. The essential characteristics of a decision arise from the limitation of the persons to whom it is addressed, whereas a regulation, being essentially of a legislative nature, is applicable to objectively determined situations and entails legal effects for categories of persons regarded generally and in the abstract.[356]

If a decision has an addressee – either a member state or a natural or juristic person (or several) – it is binding for it/him/her/them, and, as the text of article 288 makes clear, only for them.[357] Prior to Lisbon a decision always had an addressee, and it took effect upon notification.[358] It therefore had immediate legal effect for its addressee. But it could also create rights for third parties: where, for example, a decision was addressed to a member state and the decision fulfilled the criteria of direct effect, in the event of failure to comply the decision could be relied upon by third parties as against the state.[359]

---

353   E.g., Constitution of Ireland, art. 15.2.1°. It is worth noting that the Irish adapted by express constitutional amendment (now art. 29.4.6°) but the Italians resolved similar issues by means of judicial interpretation of the Constitution (see Corte Cost., 27 dicembre 1973, n. 183 (*Frontini* v *Ministero delle Finanze*), 18 Giur Cost I 2401; 30 ottobre 1975, n. 232 (*ICIC* v *Ministero Commercio Estero*), 20 Giur Cost I 2211; 8 guigno 1984, n. 170 (*Granital c/ Amministrazione delle Finanze dello Stato*), 29 Giur Cost I 1098). Some of the 2004 intake followed the Irish example with express constitutional amendment in order to avoid constitutional difficulties: to choose one example, the Lithuanian Constitution would seem to create formidable hurdles to Union membership in vesting supreme sovereign power in the state (art. 4) which may be restricted or diminished by no authority (art. 3) and permitting membership of international organisations only if compatible with the independence of the state (art. 136); the Gordian knot was cut by the adoption of a 'constitutional act' on membership (2004 m. liepos 13 d. Konstitucinis aktas „Dėl Lietuvos Respublikos narystės Europos Sąjungoje") as an integral part (*sudedamąja dalimi*) of the Constitution; see now art. 150.
354   See 6.13 above.
355   TFEU, art. 288, 4th para.
356   Case T-306/01 *Yusuf and Al Bakaraat* v *Council and Commission* [2005] ECR II-3533, at para. 185.
357   Case C-327/09 *Mensch und Natur* v *Freistaat Bayern*, judgment of 14 April 2011, not yet reported.
358   EC Treaty, art. 254(3).
359   Case 9/70 *Grad* v *Finanzamt Traunstein* (Leberpfennig) [1970] ECR 825.

6.62   Even prior to Lisbon the Council would from time to time adopt a 'decision' which had no addressee and was not a decision within the meaning of article 249 EC (article 288 TFEU); the confusion to which this gave rise was avoided in some other languages.[360] Such measure was characterised as an 'innominate decision' or a 'decision *sui generis*'; it did not have the law-making quality of an article 249 decision, and its effects (and validity) depended upon authority elsewhere in or under the Treaties.[361] For example, it was by a 'decision' that the heads of state and government provided certain 'legal guarantees and assurances' in order (successfully, in the event) to entice the Irish electorate to vote 'yes' in the second referendum on the Lisbon Treaty,[362] 'declared' by them to provide a 'legal guarantee' and that 'the [d]ecision is legally binding';[363] it was therefore a measure adopted by a body without Treaty authority making promises it had in any event no power to keep. Lisbon draws these decisions *suorum generum* into article 288 by providing for the adoption of decisions without an addressee,[364] still 'binding in [their] entirety' but without specifying for whom. But they will still have to find authority elsewhere in the Treaties in order to adopt them, the legal effects they produce (if any) a function of that authority.

(c)   Directives

6.63   The problematic legislative act is the Directive. A Directive is addressed – always – to member states. In principle, it prescribes a particular result to be achieved by a particular date, leaving it to the member states, in accordance with their own constitutional rules, to determine how and by whom it should be implemented in, or 'transposed' into, national law. Directives fulfil many functions but their staple is a comprehensive area of national law in a field of shared competences (tax, employment law, company law, environmental law, consumer protection, for example) which the Union has no power – or inclination – to displace or pre-empt, but which requires a degree of 'fine tuning' in order that impediments to the internal market the result of disparities in national law be ironed out; they therefore normally have as their purpose the adjustment ('approximation' or 'harmonisation') of national laws, regulations or

---

360   For example, in Danish, German, Dutch and Slovene a 'decision' within the meaning of art. 249 EC was, respectively, a *beslutning*, an *Entscheidung*, a *beschikking* or an *odločba* whilst a 'decision' adopted in other contexts was normally an *afgørelse*, a *Beschluß*, a *besluit* or a *sklep*.

361   As to the legal nature of decisions *suorum generum* and the conditions adhering to them (for example the obligation to give reasons) see Case C-370/07 *Commission* v *Council* (CITES) [2009] ECR I-8917, and the extensive discussion of A-G Kokott.

362   Decision of the Heads of State or Government of the 27 Member States of the EU, meeting within the European Council, on the concerns of the Irish people on the Treaty of Lisbon; attached to Brussels European Council, 18/19 June 2009, Presidency Conclusions, *Bulletin EU* 6–2009, 8, Annex I.

363   Presidency Conclusions, point 5(i) and (iii).

364   Interestingly, the Danish, German, Dutch and Slovene versions of an art. 288 decision is now an *afgørelse*, a *Beschluß*, a *besluit* and a *sklep* – the terms used previously to describe only a decision *sui generis*.

administrative provisions.[365] A Directive may seek to achieve 'exhaustive', 'partial' or 'minimal' harmonisation: exhaustive where it does seek substantially to occupy an aspect of a field and so pre-empt any national discretion thereafter; minimal where little is harmonised; and partial anywhere in between. This has importance for the residual adoption or application of national law and the availability to the member state of various safeguard provisions of the Treaties.[366] As a general rule and perhaps a nod to national sensitivities and subsidiarity, exhaustive harmonisation, never common, is falling further out of favour.

(i) Implementation

According to article 288, Directives are to be implemented by 'national authorities'. *Which* national authorities varies amongst the legislative, executive, national, regional or local authorities of each member state depending upon the constitutional structure, and a Directive may require anywhere from 40 to over 300 implementing measures across the Union.[367] But this is quite immaterial to the Union: so far as Union law is concerned, the obligation to implement fully and timeously rests with the member state as such, and the member state cannot excuse its failure to do so upon the ground of (internal) constitutional difficulties.[368] One of the reasons Italy has such an impressive record of censure by the Court of Justice for failure to implement Directives is that, for many years, primary legislation was required; Italian law provided no alternative means of implementation.[369] Nor may a member state excuse a failure to implement by reference to the serious social (even violent) unrest it would cause.[370] In all circumstances, and by whichever appropriate authority, the member state should, within the bounds of freedom it enjoys under article 288, choose the most appropriate form and method of incorporation in order to ensure the effectiveness of the Directive in light of its objective[371] and 'the provisions of directives must be implemented with unquestionable binding force, and the

6.64

---

365 See TFEU, arts 113 and 114 and 10.68–10.77 below.

366 See 10.77 below.

367 *A Europe of Results: Applying Community Law*, COM(2007) 502 final, p. 2.

368 See e.g., Cases C-1 and 176/90 *Aragonesa de Publicidad Exterior* v *Departmento de Sanidad y Securidad Social de la Generalitat de Cataluña* [1991] ECR I-4151; Case C-274/98 *Commission* v *Spain* [2000] ECR I-2823; Case C-387/97 *Commission* v *Greece* [2000] ECR I-5047; Case C-388/01 *Commission* v *Italy* (Museum Admission) [2003] ECR I-721. This is, of course, also a rule of public international law; Vienna Convention on the Law of Treaties, art. 27.

369 This was cured significantly by the device, first used in 1991, of adopting enabling legislation (annually) which delegates to the government (or the regions) significant authority to give effect to Directives. See most recently l. 15 dicembre 2011, no. 217 (Disposizioni per l'adempimento di obblighi derivanti dall'appartenenza dell'Italia alle Comunità europee (Legge comunitaria per il 2010)), GU no. 1 del 2 gennaio 2012.

370 Case C-121/07 *Commission* v *France* [2008] ECR I-9159, at para. 72.

371 E.g., Case 48/75 *Royer* [1976] ECR 4397, at para. 75; Case C-212/04 *Adeneler and ors* v *Ellinikos Organismos Galaktos* [2006] ECR I-6057, at para. 93.

specificity, precision and clarity necessary to satisfy the requirements of legal certainty'.[372] Mere administrative practices, which by their nature are alterable at will by the authorities and are not given the appropriate publicity,[373] or the possibility of judicial interpretation to make national law conform,[374] are insufficient. Of course it may be unnecessary for a member state to take positive action to implement a Directive in the case where national law in force already embodies all its requirements.[375] Thus 'the existence of general principles of constitutional or administrative law'[376] or 'an existing legal framework'[377] may suffice; but in all cases the law must meet the necessary standards. The obligation borne by the member states is best summed up by A-G Tizzano and is worth citing at length:

> [T]he established position [is] that [a]lthough [Article 288] leaves Member States to choose the ways and means of ensuring that the directive is implemented, that freedom does not affect the obligation imposed on all the Member States to which the directive is addressed, to adopt, in their national legal systems, all the measures necessary to ensure that the directive is fully effective, in accordance with the objective which it pursues ... [T]o that end, the Member States must define a specific legal framework in the sector concerned which ensures that the national legal system complies with the provisions of the directive in question. That framework must be designed in such a way as to remove all doubt or ambiguity, not only as regards the content of the relevant national legislation and its compliance with the directive, but also as regards the authority of that legislation and its suitability as a basis for regulation of the sector. Thus, for example, for the purposes of transposing a directive correctly into national law, mere administrative practice or ministerial circulars are not sufficient. In contrast with proper legislative measures, these offer no safeguards in terms of consistency, binding authority and publicity. Consequently, given that the Member State concerned is required to ensure the full and exact application of the provisions of any directive, it falls short of its obligations so long as it has not completely complied with [the directive], even if that [domestic] law has to a large extent already secured the objectives of the directive.
>
> ... [T]he Court has also acknowledged that for these purposes specific implementing measures are not indispensable, still less legislative action. That is so particularly when the relevant legislation already in force in the State concerned is sufficiently precise and clear, that is to say, when it is such that the persons concerned are made fully aware of

---

372   Case C-225/97 *Commission v France* [1999] ECR I-3011, at para. 37; Case C-159/99 *Commission v Italy* [2001] ECR I-4007, at para. 32.

373   E.g., Case 29/84 *Commission v Germany* [1985] ECR 1661; Case C-315/98 *Commission v Italy* [1999] ECR I-8001; Case C-159/99 *Commission v Italy, ibid.*

374   E.g., Case C-338/91 *Steenhorst-Neerings v Bedrijfsvereniging voor Detailhandel, Ambachten en Huisvrouwen* [1993] ECR I-5475, at paras 32–34.

375   Case C-365/93 *Commission v Greece* [1995] ECR I-499, at para. 9; Case C-144/99 *Commission v Netherlands* [2001] ECR I-3541, at para. 17; Case C-3/07 *Commission v Belgium* [2007] ECR I-154*, at para. 6.

376   Case 29/84 *Commission v Germany* [1985] ECR 1661, at para. 23.

377   Case C-190/90 *Commission v Netherlands* [1992] ECR I-3265, at para. 17.

their rights, and, where appropriate, afforded the possibility of relying on them before the national courts. However, it should be noted that such cases constitute an exception ... [I]t is not enough that the national legislation should, generally speaking, be compatible with the directive: the relationship between the two must be one of clear and precise conformity.

... [T]here are [therefore] two paramount requirements in such a situation: the directive must be fully and correctly applied within the Member States and, in consequence, any rights conferred by that directive must be guaranteed full protection. On the latter point, in particular, regard must be had to the Court's consistent concern to ensure that the existing national legislation leaves no doubt as to the effects of the directive upon the legal position of individuals.[378]

Yet it remains that because the (appropriate) national authorities enjoy a degree of discretion in transformation, a Directive may legitimately produce effects which vary as between member states, provided that the implementing authority has properly or fairly exercised its margin of appreciation.[379] Given that the subject matter of a Directive may fall within the constitutional competences of a region in a federal/devolved member state and so be implemented by the appropriate authorities there, there may be differing rules even as within a member state ('differentiated implementation'), and this too is (latterly) tolerated by Union law within limits;[380] it may give rise to a degree of discrimination but it is 'not ... discrimination contrary to Community law'.[381] It is also consistent with the principle of subsidiarity which, in its post-Lisbon incarnation, voices sensitivity and support for regional and local authorities.[382]

Implementation of Directives in the social sphere may, at the joint request of **6.65** the social partners (that is, in English style, management and labour), be entrusted to them, subject to a right (and duty) of legislative override should it be necessary to guarantee the results imposed by the Directive.[383]

In order that it be properly policed, a Directive normally requires the member **6.66** states to notify the Commission of the instruments by which they (purport to)

---

378 Case C-144/99 *Commission v Netherlands* [2001] ECR I-3541, at paras 15–17 of his opinion (internal quote marks omitted).

379 E.g., Case C-441/99 *Riksskaatterverket v Gharehveran* [2001] ECR I-7687; Case C-491/06 *Danske Svineproducenter v Justitsministeriet* [2008] ECR I-3339.

380 Case C-88/03 *Portugal v Commission* (Azores) [2006] ECR I-7115; Case C-428/07 *R (Horvath) v Secretary of State for Environment, Food and Rural Affairs* [2009] ECR I-6355; Case C-212/06 *Government of the French Community and Walloon Government v Flemish Government* [2008] ECR I-1683; Cases C-428 etc./06 *Unión General de Trabajadores de La Rioja and ors v Juntas Generales del Territorio Histórico de Vizcaya and ors* [2008] ECR I-6747.

381 Case C-428/07 *Horvath, ibid.*, at para. 58 and in the *dispositif*.

382 See 2.29 above.

383 TFEU, art. 153(3).

give it effect. Since Lisbon a failure to do so may attract specific enforcement procedure and penalties.[384]

(ii) Implementation in the United Kingdom

6.67 Some of the difficulties with Directives are universal, some unique to one member state or another, owing to constitutional, or perhaps elected, quirk. To illustrate, there follows a consideration of issues of implementation in the United Kingdom, which may, or may not, have a wider currency.

6.68 In the United Kingdom Directives are implemented (if centrally) invariably by regulations made by the Secretary of State, acting usually (but not always) by authority of section 2(2) of the European Communities Act 1972. Section 2(2) constitutes authority conferred by Parliament upon the Crown or a minister to make any order, rule, regulation or scheme 'for the purpose of implementing any EU obligation of the United Kingdom'. It is *'sui generis'*,[385] and the authority it confers very broad, including the power to vary, repeal or amend primary legislation (a so-called 'Henry VIII clause'):

> [I]t is clear that the combined effect of s. 2(2) and (4) is to enable the executive, in appropriate circumstances, to make legislation with all the force of an Act of Parliament, and even to amend an existing or future Act of Parliament.[386]

Further, an implementing measure made under section 2(2) may, if necessary or expedient, provide that reference therein to the Union instrument it is implementing is to be construed as a reference to it as amended from time to time;[387] called an 'ambulatory reference' to a Directive, this means that any future amendment to the directive requires no further UK action for its implementation, rather it is automatically incorporated into, and given effect by, the existing implementing measure.

6.69 However, whilst the authority conferred by section 2(2) is very broad, it is not limitless. As it authorises measures 'for the purpose of implementing any EU obligation in the United Kingdom', a statutory instrument which went beyond the reasonable margin of discretion afforded member states necessary to do so (or, put another way, the effect of which was 'to widen the scope of the Directive

---

384   *Ibid.* art. 260(3); see 5.62 above.
385   *Oakley v Animal and ors* [2005] EWCA Civ 1191, [2006] Ch 337, *per* Waller J at para. 19.
386   *Oakley v Animal and ors* [2005] EWHC 210 (Ch), [2005] EuLR 657 at 679.
387   European Communities Act 1972, Sch. 2, para. 1A; added by the Legislative and Regulatory Reform Act 2006.

which it is seeking to implement')[388] or was in some other manner inconsistent with the Directive[389] would be (to that extent) *ultra vires*; severance, if possible (if the terms are 'substantially severable'), is permissible.[390] Similarly, should a Directive be found to be unlawful by the Court of Justice, national legislation giving it effect – if adopted by authority of section 2(2) – would necessarily fall:

> The applicants say that the … Directive is invalid; it is, consequently, incapable of creating any Community obligation; accordingly no Community obligation existed which could activate the Minister's power to act under section 2(2) of the Act of 1972; and the Statutory Instrument which purports to give effect to the … Directive is, therefore, *ultra vires* and void.[391]

Since a Directive requires transformation as of a specified date the obligation arises only upon that date, and the courts will normally set aside a section 2(2) regulation which (unnecessarily) purports to have effect before that date.[392] Thus United Kingdom practice is to implement a Directive, if on time, only from the required date.

The High Court once sought from the Court of Justice guidance upon the legality, as a matter of (then) Community law, of a UK regulation which gave effect to a Directive but was adopted by other statutory authority (the Consumer Protection Act 1987) which does not depend upon the existence of an obligation to implement the Directive, in the event that the Directive itself is found to be unlawful;[393] but the Court of Justice found it unnecessary to provide an answer.[394] Similarly, in the 'metric martyrs' case[395] the Directive in issue was implemented by authority not of section 2(2) but of a provision of the Weights and Measures Act 1985; amongst the welter of arguments made on Mr Thoburn's behalf, no attention was paid to that issue. There was also authority

6.70

---

388 *Perth and Kinross Council* v *Donaldson and ors* [2004] ICR 667 (EAT(S)), at para. 7. On the breadth (and limitations) of s. 2(2) see also *R* (*Orange Personal Communications Ltd*) v *Secretary of State for Trade and Industry* [2001] 3 CMLR 781 (Admin); *Oakley* (CA), n. 385 above. For an instructive comparison with Irish law, which must adhere to a constitutional reservation of all legislative authority to the *Oireachtas* yet still musters a broad law-making power to the government where necessitated by the requirements of Union law, see *Browne* v *Attorney General and ors* [2003] 3 IR 205 (SC), especially the judgment of Keane CJ.

389 See e.g., *R* (*Infant and Dietetic Foods Association*) v *Secretary of State for Health* [2008] EWHC 575 (Admin), [2008] All ER (D) 452; cf. *Infant and Dietetic Foods Association and ors* v *Scottish Ministers* [2008] CSOH 18, 2008 SLT 137 (interim suspension refused on balance of convenience test).

390 *Oakley* (Ch), n. 386 above, at 700.

391 *R* v *Minister for Agriculture, Fisheries and Food, ex parte FEDESA and ors* [1988] 3 CMLR 207 at 209 (QBD).

392 *R* (*Infant and Dietetic Foods Association*), n. 389 above; *Infant and Dietetic Foods Association and ors* v *Scottish Ministers* [2008] CSOH 87, 2008 SLT 723. This may be characterised as an inarticulate expression of the principle of legal certainty.

393 *R* (*Swedish Match AB and anor*) v *Secretary of State for Health*, order of the QBD of 2 April 2003, unreported.

394 Case C-210/03 *R* (*Swedish Match AB and anor*) v *Secretary of State for Health* [2004] ECR I-11893.

395 *Thoburn* v *Sunderland City Council* [2002] EWHC 195 (Admin), [2003] QB 151.

from the High Court that where a Directive confers upon member states the option to derogate from the general rule of the Directive, but does not require it, it is not 'a[n EU] obligation', so that whilst implementation of the Directive may be *intra vires* section 2(2), seeking to exercise the option of derogation is not;[396] but this was overturned by the Court of Appeal as 'illogical',[397] 'logically possible but practically absurd'[398] and 'depend[ing] on such literalism and lead[ing] to such an absurd conclusion that it must be wrong',[399] without shedding much light on the proper limits of section 2(2).[400]

6.71 In many member states Directives are implemented in a fairly straightforward manner, by which the competent national authority provides that, for example, an annex to a law or decree 'is to be law' or 'is to have the force of law', and the annex reproduces the operative terms of the Directive more or less *verbatim*. In the United Kingdom the habit is different, transformation being very detailed and precise – indeed laborious – in a process known informally (and by its supporters) as 'gold plating' the Directive. But it is also a function of a perceived need to 'translate' Union terminology into normal statutory language, and this can give rise to serious difficulties:

> The drafting process [of the implementing measure] is so complex that there is a good chance that vital mistakes may be made. It must also be very time-consuming.
>
> The method is dangerous. A European directive means whatever the ECJ says it means – eventually. Whoever tries to re-express a directive in British statutory terminology runs the risk of getting it wrong. It happens quite often.
>
> There is no need for this rigamarole.[401]

In addition, a Directive may be implemented not by self-standing statutory instruments but by amendments to Acts of Parliament – good examples being the Employment Rights Act 1996, the Companies Act 2006 and the Equality Act 2010 which are riddled with sections giving effect to various Union Directives in their respective fields. It is important to take note of the Union 'inspiration' of national measures for purposes of their interpretation (or challenge), and 'individuals must ... have the possibility of determining the

---

396   *Oakley* (Ch), n. 386 above.
397   *Oakley* (CA), n. 385 above, *per* Waller J at para. 28.
398   Per May J at para. 44.
399   Per Jacobs J at para. 55.
400   These issues, and *Oakley*, were discussed subsequently in *R (Parker)* v *Bradford Crown Court* [2006] EWHC 3212 (Admin), [2007] RTR 369; *Risk Management Partners* v *Council of the London Borough of Brent and ors* [2008] EWHC 1094 (Admin), [2008] All ER (D) 226.
401   *Oakley* (Ch), n. 386 above, at 669.

[Union] source of the national measures';[402] to this end a Directive will frequently require that measures transposing it make express reference to it at the time of their official publication. But in cases of implementation by statutory amendment that source may be obscured.[403]

Devolution has done nothing to diminish section 2(2). Powers to give effect to **6.72** Directives continue to be enjoyed in devolved matters by the UK Parliament and government, but they are shared with the Scottish Parliament and Executive, the Northern Ireland Assembly and Ministers and the Welsh Assembly and Welsh Ministers, as the case may be.[404] No provision is made for precedence in the event of a clash between implementing measures, the smooth operation of which is now (hoped to be) governed by a 'concordat' amongst the various governments.[405] Directives may also require distinct implementing legislation in and for Gibraltar for which the United Kingdom bears Union liability.[406] Issues of *Francovich* liability[407] have yet to be met in this context, and will likely be considered upon a case by case basis. These are problems which of course obtain in other federal/devolved member states, addressed and overcome with varying degrees of success.

(iii) Sperrwirkung

Although a Directive requires no action until a given date, member states must, **6.73** prior to that date, refrain from adopting any measure liable seriously to compromise or frustrate its object.[408] This is consistent with similar rules of public international law,[409] and is sometimes called the 'blocking effect' (*Sperrwirkung*), or prohibition of frustrating the objective (*Frustrationsverbot*), of a

---

402 Case C-345/06 *Heinrich* [2009] ECR I-1659, at para. 46.

403 Some assistance may be had from the notes in *Current Law Statutes* which will normally identify British enactments which (are intended to) give effect to Directives. The Explanatory Memorandum annexed to statutory instruments will identify any Union measure upon which subordinate legislation is based.

404 Scotland Act 1998, ss. 53, 57(1); Northern Ireland Act 1998, s. 27; Government of Wales Act 1998, s. 29(1)–(2); Government of Wales Act 2006, ss. 59(1)–(2), 80.

405 Memorandum of Understanding and Supplementary Agreements between the UK Government, the Scottish Ministers, the Welsh Ministers and the Northern Ireland Executive Committee, March 2010, Part B4.16–21.

406 See e.g., Case C-30/01 *Commission v United Kingdom* [2003] ECR I-9481; Case C-349/03 *Commission v United Kingdom* [2005] ECR I-7321; Case C-505/04 *Commission v United Kingdom*, judgment of 20 October 2005, unreported; on the status of Gibraltar see 10.05 below.

407 Cases C-6 and 9/90 *Francovich and Bonifaci v Italy* [1991] ECR I-5357; see 6.35–6.37 above.

408 Case C-129/96 *Inter-Environnement Wallonie v Région Wallonne* [1997] ECR I-7411; Cases T-172 etc.98 *Salamander and ors v Parliament and Council* [2000] ECR II-2487; Case C-144/04 *Mangold v Helm* [2005] ECR I-9981; Case C-212/04 *Adeneler and ors v Ellenikos Organismos Galaktos* [2006] ECR I-6057; Cases C-261 and 299/07 *VTB-VAB and anor v Total Belgium and anor* [2009] ECR I-2949; Cases C-378–80/07 *Angelidaki and ors v Organismos Nomarchiadi Aftodiikisi Rethimnis and anor* [2009] ECR I-3071.

409 Vienna Convention on the Law of Treaties, art. 18.

Directive. The duty springs more particularly from article 4(3) TEU in conjunction with article 288, and applies to all national authorities,[410] even to national courts, which 'must refrain as far as possible from interpreting domestic law in a manner which might [come] seriously [to] compromise, after the period for transposition has expired, attainment of the objectives pursued by [a] directive'.[411] There is a thesis, supported particularly by Advocate-General Kokott, that relevant national legislation must be interpreted so as to accord with the terms of a Directive even prior to the deadline for its adoption into national law,[412] but she has failed to persuade the Court:

> [B]efore the period for transposition of a directive has expired, Member States cannot be reproached for not having yet adopted measures implementing it in national law.
>
> Accordingly, where a directive is transposed belatedly, the general obligation owed by national courts to interpret domestic law in conformity with the directive exists only once the period for its transposition has expired.[413]

However, it has found it legitimate to require a purposive interpretation of national law prior to expiry of that period where the competent national authorities have made it clear that that law (*in casu* a pre-existing measure) is the one by which the member state intends the requirements of the Directive to be given effect.[414]

(iv) Vertical direct effect

6.74 Whilst a Directive imposes a duty of implementation upon the member state, so far as the individual is concerned rights and obligations are brought into being, *in principle*, by the national implementing measures, and not by the Directive itself. According to the Court of Justice:

> [I]n all cases in which a directive has been properly implemented its effects reach individuals through the implementing measures adopted by the Member States concerned. The question whether [a Directive provision] may be relied upon before a national court therefore has no purpose since it is established that the provision has been put into effect in national law.[415]

---

410 Case C-212/04 *Adeneler*, n. 408 above, at para. 122 and case law cited.

411 *Ibid.* at para. 123.

412 Case C-313/02 *Wippel* v *Peek & Kloppenburg* [2004] ECR I-9483, *per* A-G Kokott at paras 60–3 of her opinion; Case C-212/04 *Adeneler*, n. 408 above, at paras 42–54 of her opinion; Case C-268/06 *Impact* v *Minister for Agriculture and Food and ors* [2008] ECR I-2483, at paras 126–32 of her opinion.

413 Case C-212/04 *Adeneler*, n. 408 above, at paras 114–15. Support for A-G Kokott's view may be identified in the earlier Case C-144/04 *Mangold* v *Helm* [2005] ECR I-9981, but its reliability is suspect, and undermined implicitly by the Court in Case C-427/06 *Bartsch* v *Bosch und Siemens Hausgeräte (BSH) Altersfürsorge* [2008] ECR I-7245, and directly by A-G Sharpston in her opinion in that case.

414 Cases C-261 and 299/07 *VTB-VAB*, n. 408 above.

415 Case 222/84 *Johnston* v *Chief Constable of the RUC* [1986] ECR 1651, at para. 51.

However, this general rule is subject to important exceptions which stem from the peculiar nature of Directives, the (all too common) failure of member states to do what is required by the Directive completely, accurately and/or time-ously[416] and the threat to the effectiveness and uniformity of Union law which that entails.

First, where the Directive imposes upon the member state a clear, precise and **6.75** unconditional obligation intended to create rights for individuals, then even if the member state has failed to implement it, individuals may nonetheless rely upon it as against the defaulting member state.[417] A Directive may therefore, depending upon its terms, have (vertical) direct effect. This would seem to fly in the face of the third criterion necessary for direct effect (no transformation required – transformation *always* being required of Directives), but the Court has said that where the Directive requirements are so clear and precise that transformation admits of no discretion and becomes a mere formality, it may be relied upon as against the state – again, so long as the time period provided for implementation has passed.[418] 'The state' includes any public authority and any 'emanation of the state', which is read very broadly[419] in order that Directives enjoy maximum possible effectiveness (*effet utile*). An individual may rely upon an unimplemented (but directly effective) Directive against a public authority not only in the context of the public obligations it discharges but in unrelated, private law matters.[420] Reliance upon the direct effect of a Directive extends to one properly implemented in national law but applied or enforced inadequately:

> [T]he adoption of national measures correctly implementing a directive does not exhaust the effects of the directive. Member States remain bound actually to ensure full application of the directive even after the adoption of those measures. Individuals are therefore entitled to rely before national courts, against the State, on the provisions of a

---

416 It ought to be noted that failure properly to implement a Directive may be in perfectly good faith; the Directive may come to be interpreted by the Court of Justice in a manner (with which the national implementing legislation must accord) which was reasonably unforeseen. But in the majority of cases the failure is less excusable. The good faith or otherwise of inadequate implementation may go to a finding of liability in damages.

417 Case 41/74 *Van Duyn v Home Office* [1974] ECR 1337; Case 148/78 *Pubblico Ministero v Ratti* [1979] ECR 1629; Case 152/84 *Marshall v Southampton and South West Hampshire Area Health Authority* (No. 1) [1986] ECR 723.

418 Case 148/78 *Ratti*, *ibid.*; Case C-316/93 *Vaneetveld v Le Foyer* [1994] ECR I-763.

419 See in particular, Case C-188/89 *Foster v British Gas* [1990] ECR I-3313; Case C-343/98 *Collino and Chiappero v Telecom Italia* [2000] ECR I-6659; Case C-356/05 *Farrell v Whitty and ors* [2007] ECR I-3067; Case C-282/10 *Dominguez v Centre informatique du Centre Ouest Atlantique and anor*, judgment of 24 January 2012, not yet reported. For various UK and Irish examples, *Doughty v Rolls Royce* [1992] 1 CMLR 1045 (CA); *Griffin and ors v South West Water Services* [1995] IRLR 15 (Ch); *National Union of Teachers v Governing Body of St Mary's Church of England (Aided) Junior School* [1997] IRLR 242 (CA); *R v Durham County Council, ex parte Huddleston* [2000] All ER (D) 297 (CA); *Farrell v Whitty and ors* [2008] IEHC 124, [2008] EuLR 603.

420 Thus Ms Marshall could rely upon a Directive as against her employer (an area health authority) in matters of her contract of employment; Case 152/84 *Marshall I*, n. 417, above.

directive which appear, so far as their subject matter is concerned, to be unconditional and sufficiently precise whenever the full application of the directive is not in fact secured, that is to say, not only where the directive has not been implemented or has been implemented incorrectly, but also where the national measures correctly implementing the directive are not being applied in such a way as to achieve the result sought by it.

... [I]t would be inconsistent with the Community legal order for individuals to be able to rely on a directive where it has been implemented incorrectly but not to be able to do so where the national authorities apply the national measures implementing the directive in a manner incompatible with it.[421]

6.76 However because the legal reasoning by which the Court of Justice recognises the vertical direct effect of Directives is based primarily upon estoppel or bar (*nemo auditur propriam turpitudinem allegans*), it means that vertical direct effect lies in one direction only: a national authority may not seek to enforce against an individual a provision of a Directive which has not been implemented as it should have been.[422] This will acquire particular sensitivity and complexity as the Union ventures increasingly – invariably by Directive – into fields of criminal law.

(v) Horizontal direct effect

6.77 Second, and owing equally to the logic of estoppel, a Directive cannot of itself have 'horizontal direct effect', creating rights enforceable as against private persons;[423] were it to be otherwise it would effectively destroy the Treaty distinction between regulations (which *may* produce horizontal direct effects) and Directives.[424] Advocate-General Bot suggested that Directives intended to counteract discrimination be regarded as a special class of Directives, so horizontally directly effective,[425] but the Court took a different tack.[426]

---

421 Case C-62/00 *Marks & Spencer* v *HM Commissioners for Customs and Excise* [2002] ECR I-6325, at paras 27–8.

422 Case 148/78 *Pubblico Ministero* v *Ratti* [1979] ECR 1629; Case 80/86 *Officier van Justitie* v *Kolpinghuis Nijmegen* [1987] ECR 3969; Case C-226/97 *Criminal proceedings against Lemmens* [1998] ECR I-3711; Cases C-387 etc./02 *Criminal proceedings against Berlusconi and ors* [2005] ECR I-3565. *Nemo auditur propriam turpitudinem allegans* is, apparently, the most frequently cited adage by the Court and Advocates-General: Cases C-89 and 96/10 *Q-Beef and anor* v *Belgische Staat and ors*, judgment of 8 September 2011, not yet reported, *per* A-G Jääskinen at note 3 of his opinion.

423 Case 152/84 *Marshall I*, n. 417 above; reconfirmed in Case C-91/92 *Faccini Dori* v *Recreb* [1994] ECR I-3325; Case C-192/94 *El Corte Inglés* v *Blázquez Rivero* [1996] ECR I-1281; Case C-80/06 *Carp* v *Ecorad* [2007] ECR I-4473; and most recently, Case C-555/07 *Kücükdeveci* v *Swedex* [2010] ECR I-365; Case C-227/09 *Accardo and ors* v *Comune di Torino* [2010] ECR I-10273 and Case C-282/10 *Dominguez* v *Centre informatique du Centre Ouest Atlantique and anor*, judgment of 24 January 2012, not yet reported.

424 Case C-91/92 *Faccini Dori, ibid.*

425 Case C-555/07 *Kücükdeveci*, n. 423 above, at paras 67–85 of his opinion.

426 See 14.49 below.

The constitutional (Treaty) incapacity of a Directive to create horizontal direct **6.78** effects gives rise to self-evident difficulties: it means that a Directive may apply differently from member state to member state depending upon the precision (or not) with which it has been implemented in national law, and may vary even within a member state, where it is subject to regional (mis)implementation and depending upon whether it is being relied upon against a public or a private person. This offends a fundamental rule of (Union) law, that it apply uniformly to all. In order to mitigate the problem the Court has developed four 'pallia-tives',[427] as follows.

(vi) Uniform interpretation

Even where civil litigation is raised against private parties involving the subject **6.79** matter of a Directive, where there is a divergence between national law and the requirements of the Directive (which ought to be, but are not, implemented) the national measures must, 'if it is possible to do so', be interpreted and applied by the national court so as to give effect to the Directive.[428] Put most clearly,

> Where a directive is transposed belatedly into a Member State's domestic law and the relevant provisions of the directive do not have direct effect, the national courts are bound to interpret domestic law so far as possible, once the period for transposition has expired, in the light of the wording and the purpose of the directive concerned with a view to achieving the results sought by the directive, favouring the interpretation of the national rules which is the most consistent with that purpose in order thereby to achieve an outcome compatible with the provisions of the directive.[429]

Thus the Directive may produce 'indirect effect'. This interpretative duty, called variously uniform, consistent, sympathetic or conforming interpretation (*inter-prétation conforme*), is derived from article 4(3) TEU, is inherent in the system of the Treaties as a means of ensuring the full effectiveness of Union law[430] and, according to the Court of Justice, applies even where the Directive remains

---

427 Case C-555/07 *Kücükdeveci*, n. 423 above, *per* A-G Bot at paras 59–65 of his opinion (identifying the first three palliatives).

428 Case 14/83 *von Colson and Kamann* v *Land Nordrhein-Westfalen* [1984] ECR 1891; Case 106/89 *Marleasing* v *La Comercial Internacional de Alimentación* [1990] ECR I-435; Case C-334/92 *Wagner Miret* v *Fondo de Garantía Salarial* [1993] ECR I-6911; Case C-421/92 *Habermann-Beltermann* v *Arbeiterwohlfahrt Bezirks-verband* [1994] ECR I-1657; Case C-91/92 *Faccini Dori* v *Recreb* [1994] ECR I-3325; Case C-456/98 *Centrolsteel* v *Adipol* [2000] ECR I-6007; Case C-343/98 *Collino and Chiapparo* v *Telecom Italia* [2000] ECR I-6659; Case C-160/01 *Mau* v *Bundesanstalt für Arbeit* [2003] ECR I-4791; Case C-555/07 *Kücükdeveci*, n. 423 above; Case C-282/10 *Dominguez*, n. 423 above.

429 Case C-212/04 *Adeneler and ors* v *Ellenikos Organismos Galaktos* [2006] ECR I-6057, in the *dispositif*. See also the useful statement of the present law by A-G Bot in Case C-555/07 *Kücükdeveci*, n. 423 above, at paras 54–66 of his opinion.

430 Case C-268/06 *Impact* v *Minister for Agriculture and Food and ors* [2008] ECR I-2483, at para. 99; Cases C-378–80/07 *Angelidaki and ors* v *Organismos Nomarchiadi Aftodiikisi Rethimnis and anor* [2009] ECR I-3071; Case C-282/10 *Dominguez*, n. 423 above.

unimplemented and even where the national rule in question existed prior in time to the adoption of the Directive.[431] However it recognises that there are countervailing principles at issue, particularly those of legal certainty and non-retroactivity, and that in no event can the principle compel a national judge to interpret national law *contra legem*.[432] It therefore imposes a difficult task upon national judges, and in the United Kingdom the Supreme Court has hitherto been prepared to comply with it only partially.[433] It also produces a situation whereby the same statutory provision is to be interpreted in one manner in a case in which a Union right is at issue, and in another in a case where it is not. This produces arguably perverse results, but it is the course followed by the Supreme Court:[434] 'although at first sight this may seem strange, any other solution would be even stranger'.[435] Owing perhaps to these difficulties, uniform interpretation seems to be falling slowly out of favour even with the Court of Justice.[436]

---

431   See in particular Case 106/89 *Marleasing* v *La Comercial Internacional de Alimentación* [1990] ECR I-435 – probably the high water mark of *interprétation conforme*, which is therefore sometimes called the *Marleasing* doctrine.

432   Case C-111/97 *EvoBus Austria* v *Niederösterreichische Verkehrsorganisations* [1998] ECR I-5411; Case C-212/04 *Adeneler*, n. 429 above, at para. 110; Case C-268/06 *Impact*, n. 430 above, at para. 100; Cases C-378–80/07 *Angelidaki*, n. 430 above, at para. 199.

433   The House of Lords held that where the government has acted to implement a Directive, it is proper for the courts to give a 'purposive' interpretation to the implementing national law in order that it accords with the provisions of the Directive (*Pickstone* v *Freemans* [1989] AC 66; *Litster* v *Forth Dry Dock Ltd* 1989 SC (HL) 96), although it has said more recently (in a case which involved implementing measures) that '[t]he rule is that the domestic court must seek to interpret national law to achieve the same result as that intended by the relevant provision of EU [*sic*] law, *where it is reasonably possible to do so*' (*Robb* v *Salamis (M&I) Ltd* [2006] UKHL 56, 2007 SC (HL) 71, *per* Lord Hope at para. 14 of his speech (emphasis added); Lord Clyde indicated, *obiter*, that a UK provision limiting liability for 'reasonable foreseeability' could be interpreted in a manner consistent with the provision of the Directive it implemented imposing liability except in 'unusual and unforeseeable circumstances' only with difficulty; para. 47 of his speech). In the absence of any action by any national authority the Supreme Court generally refused to construe (or 'distort') British legislation so as to conform with Directive provisions (*Duke* v *GEC Reliance Ltd* [1988] AC 618; *Finnegan* v *Clowney Youth Training Programme* [1990] 2 AC 407) – although it did so on occasion in which existing and relevant UK legislation easily bore the Directive-friendly interpretation (*Webb* v *EMO Air Cargo (UK) Ltd* [1995] 4 All ER 577). The test seems to be that purposive interpretation must 'go with the grain of the legislation' (*Ghaidan* v *Godin-Mendoza* [2004] UKHL 30, [2004] 2 AC 557, *per* Lord Rodger at para. 121) or not be inconsistent with a fundamental or cardinal feature of the legislation, otherwise it would cross the boundary between interpretation and amendment (per Lord Nicholls at para. 33; Lord Rodger at paras 110–13; although a human rights and not an EU case, the same principles apply and are discussed, and *Ghaidan* provides an excellent exposition of the issues and the Supreme Court's approach to them). Implicit in their Lordships' view is that there is a limit beyond which British courts cannot go in seeking to ensure UK compliance with a Directive; beyond that limit responsibility lies with parliaments and/or governments. For a useful discussion of the case law see *Vodaphone 2* v *Revenue and Customs Commissioners* [2009] EWCA Civ 446, [2010] Ch 77.

434   *R (Hurst)* v *Commissioner of Police of the Metropolis* [2007] UKHL 13, [2007] 2 AC 189.

435   Ibid. *per* Lord Rodger at para. 13.

436   See Case C-168/95 *Criminal proceedings against Arcaro* [1996] ECR I-4705; Case C-235/03 *QDQ Media* v *Omedas Lecha* [2005] ECR I-1937.

(vii) 'Incidental' effect

The general rule that a Directive can have no direct effect horizontally is subject **6.80**
to one important exception, and a second palliative. This applies where a
Directive is a measure not for the adjustment of national laws (the normal case)
but rather (a) lays down a control mechanism which requires member states to
notify the Commission prior to introducing certain national measures, or
(b) lays down a procedure for authorisation of a course of action by a national
regulatory authority. Where a measure as in (a) is introduced without notification, an individual may rely upon that (national) failure as against another
individual and have the national measure set aside by a competent national
court;[437] in the circumstances of (b) an individual may compel a national
authority to adopt a measure even where it is directly linked to the performance
of an obligation by a third party and has adverse repercussions for that party.[438]
In both cases it is sometimes called the 'incidental' or 'substitution' direct effect
of Directives, or the application of direct effect in 'triangular situations'. In all
events the meaning and application are undeveloped and unclear, and the scope
limited.

(viii) Francovich damages

In the third palliative, where an individual has suffered injury or loss in **6.81**
consequence of a member state failure to implement a Directive, which is not,
or cannot be, remedied by uniform interpretation of national law, the individual
may, by application of *Francovich* principles, be able to claim damages from the
state. It is discussed above.[439] And this, perhaps far more than any legal
admonishment, serves as an effective spur to member states otherwise inclined
to implementing lethargy.

(ix) Direct effect of general principles

A fourth palliative was articulated by the Court in *Kücükdeveci* itself. Partially in **6.82**
response to the knots in which it had tied itself in a previous judgment
(*Mangold*),[440] the Court recognised that a general principle of Union law may
adhere to a Directive, in which case the two taken together may apply in a
horizontal legal situation, and do so to the exclusion of incompatible national

---

437   See Case C-194/94 *CIA Securities International* v *Signalson* [1996] ECR I-2201; Case C-226/97 *Criminal
      proceedings against Lemmens* [1998] ECR I-3711; Case C-443/98 *Unilever Italia* v *Central Food* [2000] ECR
      I-7535; Case C-390/99 *Canal Satélite Digital* v *Administración General del Estado* [2002] ECR I-607; Case
      C-159/00 *Sapod Audic* v *Eco-Emballages* [2002] ECR I-5031; Case C-20/05 *Criminal proceedings against
      Schwibbert* [2007] ECR I-9447.
438   Case C-201/02 *R (Wells)* v *Secretary of State for Transport, Local Government and the Regions* [2004] ECR
      I-723; Cases C-152–154/07 *Arcor and ors* v *Bundesrepublik Deutschland* [2008] ECR I-5959.
439   See 6.35–6.40 above.
440   Case C-144/04 *Mangold* v *Helm* [2005] ECR I-9981; see 14.49 below.

law.[441] This is new, and faces formidable logical and practical obstacles. As it arises (thus far) in the context of one provision of one Directive, it will be discussed below in consideration of that Directive.[442]

6.83 In all events, these rules, particularly the embryonic *Kücükdeveci* rule, are still evolving and their full implications are not yet known. It is always of first importance that the practitioner develop antennae to detect the Union 'inspiration' of national legislation,[443] and also be aware of directives which, although not properly implemented, or not implemented at all, may nevertheless give rise to rights against the state and be used to interpret (apparently untouched) national legislation.

(d)   Recommendations and opinions

6.84 The institutions (in practice the Council and the Commission) have a general power to adopt recommendations, in accordance with the procedures regulating the subject area at issue;[444] the Commission and the European Central Bank may adopt recommendations when specifically authorised to do so under the Treaties.[445] According to article 288, recommendations and opinions have no binding force. This means that a *true* recommendation or opinion cannot create an enforceable right. However, the Court of Justice will consider whether an act in the form of a recommendation or opinion is in substance a different type of act which is intended to create and capable of creating such rights.[446] Even if it is not, a national court is bound to take notice of them, in particular where they cast light upon the interpretation of other provisions of national or Union law, where national measures are adopted in order to implement them or where they are designed to supplement binding provisions of Union law.[447]

(e)   Other binding acts

6.85 The list of legislative measures prescribed in article 288 of the Treaty is not exhaustive. The Union institutions may create legally binding acts – and therefore acts capable of creating enforceable rights, and capable of being annulled for that reason – by means other than those mentioned in article 288: for example through a decision *sui generis* (pre-Lisbon),[448] a resolution,[449]

---

441   Case C-555/07 *Kücükdeveci* v *Swedex* [2010] ECR I-365.
442   See 14.49 below.
443   See n. 403 above.
444   TFEU, art. 292.
445   *Ibid.*
446   Case 322/88 *Grimaldi* v *Fonds des Maladies Professionnelles* [1989] ECR 4407.
447   Case 322/88 *Grimaldi, ibid.*; Cases C-317 etc./08 *Alassini and ors* v *Telcom Italia and ors* [2010] ECR I-2213, at para. 40.
448   See 6.62 above.

through administrative memoranda[450] or by entering into a treaty or agreement with third states[451] – providing always there is authority to do so somewhere in the Treaties.

(f) Legislative and non-legislative acts

From time to time proposals have been made to change the nature and **6.86** nomenclature of legislative acts. Early proposals at the Maastricht IGC came to naught,[452] wholesale change written into the Treaty establishing a Constitution for Europe, introducing not only new types of acts but for the first time a formal hierarchy amongst them,[453] died with it. Lisbon's changes are more subtle, retaining the existing measures but introducing a new dimension to them. The Union institutions may adopt the same nominate measures as always, but they are now divided into 'legislative acts' and 'non-legislative acts' (*Rechtsakte ohne Gesetzescharakter*).[454] A legislative act is a Regulation, Directive or decision adopted by legislative procedure;[455] a non-legislative act is one adopted by authority of power delegated by a legislative act to the Commission[456] in order to supplement or amend certain non-essential elements of the legislative act.[457] The 'essential elements' of an area (*un domaine, ein Bereich*) are reserved to legislative acts,[458] which must define the objectives, content, scope and duration of any delegated authority.[459] They may set conditions to which the delegated authority is subject, being (a) the possibility of revocation by the Parliament (by a majority of its component members) or the Council (by qualified majority) and/or (b) the delegated act may enter into force only absent objection by the Parliament or Council (by the same majorities) within a set period.[460] The Commission measure must specify 'delegated' in its title.[461]

A distinction is to be drawn between delegated measures and 'implementing' **6.87** measures. Member states are bound to 'adopt all measures of national law'

---

449   See Case 22/70 *Commission* v *Council* (ERTA) [1971] ECR 263; Case 230/81 *Luxembourg* v *Parliament* [1983] ECR 255; Cases 213/88 and C-39/89 *Luxembourg* v *Parliament* [1991] ECR I-5643.
450   Case 366/88 *France* v *Commission* [1990] ECR I-3571.
451   Case C-327/91 *France* v *Commission* [1994] ECR I-3641; Case C-29/99 *Commission* v *Council* (Nuclear Safety Convention) [2002] ECR I-11221; on the force of treaties in Union law see 14.78–14.81 below.
452   See the 'Luxembourg "non-paper"' of 30 April 1991, unpublished, provisions on art. 189, which did not survive into the final text. The Maastricht IGC called for the hierarchy of Community acts to be revisited at the ensuing IGC (Declaration (No. 16) on the Hierarchy of Community Acts), but this too came to naught.
453   See Treaty establishing a Constitution for Europe, arts I-33–37.
454   TFEU, arts 289, 290.
455   *Ibid.* art. 289(3).
456   *Ibid.* art. 290(1).
457   *Ibid.*
458   *Ibid.*
459   *Ibid.*
460   *Ibid.* art. 290(2).
461   *Ibid.* art. 290(3).

necessary to implement legislative or non-legislative measures ('legally binding Union acts').[462] Where the uniform conditions for implementing them requires Union action, authority to do so is to be conferred upon the Commission (unless it is retained by the Council, either for good and stated reasons or in the area of Common Foreign and Security Policy (CFSP)), in accordance with conditions and general principles set out in advance.[463] An implementing measure must (since 2009) specify 'implementing' in its title.[464]

6.88 The type of act to be adopted is set out in the Treaty base (or enabling legislative act) or, if not, is to be selected by the institutions(s) upon a case-by-case basis in compliance with applicable procedures and the principle of proportionality.[465] The European Central Bank may propose ('recommend') the adoption of legislative acts[466] and autonomously adopt such measures necessary to carry out its tasks.[467]

(g) Regulatory acts

6.89 Lisbon introduced (indirectly) a new creature, the 'regulatory act', which goes to the standing by which it may be challenged before the Court of Justice. This is discussed below.[468]

(h) Legislation under the pre-Lisbon Treaty on European Union

6.90 The legislative authority conferred upon the institutions under Titles V and VI of the pre-Lisbon Treaty on European Union was of a fundamentally different quality than that which applied to the Community Treaties. It is necessary to consider it briefly, not only as an historical curiosity, but because the legal effects of such legislation are 'preserved' post-Lisbon as they were until such time as it is repealed, annulled or amended 'in implementation of' the Treaties.[469]

6.91 Under the original TEU the (non-Community) Union was competent to act in a number of different ways. Under Title VII the institutions could adopt 'decisions' establishing enhanced cooperation in Titles V and VI matters.[470] They never did so, so Title VII need not concern us further. Otherwise the (non-Community) Union was competent to adopt, in CFSP ('second pillar', or Title V) matters:

---

462 *Ibid.* art. 291(1).
463 *Ibid.* art. 291(2),(3).
464 *Ibid.* art. 291(4).
465 *Ibid.* art. 296, 1st para.
466 *Ibid.* art. 289(4).
467 *Ibid.* art. 282(4); also art. 292.
468 See 6.99 below.
469 Protocol (No. 36) on transitional provisions, art. 9.
470 TEU (pre-Lisbon), arts 27e, 40b, 43b.

- common strategies;
- joint actions;
- common positions; and
- decisions.[471]

Common strategies were the preserve of the European Council; they set out the objectives, duration and means provided by the Union and the member states in areas in which common interests were shared.[472] Joint actions were the means by which the Council implemented a common strategy to a specific situation, defining the objectives, scope and means of Union action[473] and committed the member states to it.[474] A common position was a measure adopted by the Council which defined the approach of the Union to a particular matter of a geographic or thematic nature.[475] A decision defined and implemented joint actions or common positions.[476]

Under Police and Judicial Cooperation in Criminal Matters ('third pillar', or **6.92** Title VI) the Union could adopt:

- common positions;
- framework decisions;
- decisions; and
- conventions.[477]

Any of these measures could be proposed by the Commission or by a member state;[478] this is to be compared with second pillar matters which remained wholly within Council (or European Council) initiative. Subject only to a duty of prior consultation with the Parliament,[479] each was solely Council competence. A common position defined the Union approach to a certain matter. Framework decisions provided for the approximation of national laws, decisions for any purpose other than approximation which is consistent with Justice and Home Affairs (JHA) objectives.[480] As such they were analogous to Community Directives: they were binding upon the member states but left to them the means of implementation. Conventions were 'established' by the

---

471   *Ibid.* arts 12, 13.
472   *Ibid.* art. 13(2).
473   *Ibid.* art. 14(1).
474   *Ibid.* art. 14(3).
475   *Ibid.* art. 15.
476   *Ibid.* art. 13.
477   *Ibid.* art. 34.
478   *Ibid.* art. 34(2).
479   *Ibid.* art. 39(1).
480   *Ibid.* art. 34(2)(b–c).

Council, which then proposed their adoption by the member states; once adopted by at least half the member states they entered into force for those member states unless the convention provided otherwise.[481]

6.93 As with Community legislation, there was no hierarchical ordering amongst the various instruments which might be adopted under the Treaty on European Union, and the Council had a choice amongst several in order to address the same subject matter.[482]

6.94 Because Union legislation was reserved effectively to the Council, and for the most part required unanimity, it was intergovernmental in character (as opposed to 'the Community method') and entrenched the pre-eminence of national governments. None of these measures produced law in the sense of the enforceable rights and obligations which could flow from Community measures; the only possible exceptions were framework decisions and decisions under Title VI, but although binding upon the member states in a manner analogous to Directives, they expressly did *not* entail direct effect;[483] such was the justification for the absence of democratic (and judicial) control of the Council under Titles V and VI. However, as with Directives, a framework decision imposed an obligation upon authorities of the state to interpret national law, if at all possible, in conformity with it.[484] This gave rise to difficulties in dualist member states which did not directly recognise the Union or its law; chief amongst them was the United Kingdom, yet the House of Lords, perhaps surprisingly, cleaved to this interpretative obligation (at least where there existed national legislation intending to give effect to a framework decision) without murmur.[485]

6.95 In any event, Council activity under the Union Treaty was often followed up by legislation which *did* create binding law, either by the Community or by the member states, as appropriate, and so subject to the democratic checks and balances applicable thereto. The EC Treaty made express provision for the Council to take the necessary measures to give effect to a CFSP common

---

481 *Ibid.* art. 34(2)(d).

482 Case C-303/05 *Advocaten voor de Wereld* v *Leden van de Ministerrad* [2007] ECR I-3633.

483 TEU (pre-Lisbon), art. 34(2)(b–c).

484 Case C-105/03 *Criminal proceedings against Pupino* [2005] ECR I-5285.

485 *Dabas* v *High Court of Justice, Madrid* [2007] UKHL 6, [2007] 2 AC 31. The House of Lords here broke new ground in faithful application of *Pupino* principles when under no obligation under s. 3 of the European Communities Act 1972 to do so, and so afforded the framework decision at least some recognition in UK law. Perversely this is a more generous disposition than appears to apply to uniform interpretation in light of a Community Directive; see n. 433 above.

position or joint action interrupting or reducing economic relations with one or more third countries.[486]

(i) Common Foreign and Security Policy

The Common Foreign and Security Policy is now, post-Lisbon, 'implemented' **6.96** by the European Council and the Council and 'put into effect' by the High Representative for Foreign Affairs and Security Policy and by the member states, using Union and national resources.[487] In order to do so the European Council and the Council may adopt 'decisions' but these are not decisions within the meaning of article 288 TFEU, and care must be taken to distinguish their force and effect. Where the Council adopts a decision defining the approach of the Union to a particular matter of a geographical or thematic nature, the member states must ensure that national policy conforms with the Union position.[488] Where it adopts decisions when 'the international situation requires operational action' which lay down the objective, scope and means,[489] they commit (*engagent*, *sind bindend*) the member states in the positions and conduct they adopt.[490] Member states are required to support the Union's external and security policy 'actively and unreservedly in a spirit of loyalty and mutual solidarity',[491] comply with Union action in the area[492] and consult within the European Council and the Council prior to taking any action or entering into any commitment which could affect the Union's interests;[493] diplomatic and consular missions of the member states and of the Union in third countries must cooperate in support of Union positions and actions.[494] In international fora their action is to be coordinated (organised by the High Representative) and the Union position upheld.[495] Member states members of the UN Security Council must concert (*stimmen sich*), keep other member states and the High Representative fully informed, and defend there the position and interests of the Union.[496]

All Common Security and Defence Policy decisions are taken by the Council, **6.97** acting (almost always) by unanimity on a proposal from the High Representative.[497] Where implementation of a task is entrusted to a group of member

---

486   EC Treaty, art. 301.
487   TEU, arts 24(1), 2nd para., 26(3).
488   *Ibid.* art. 29.
489   *Ibid.* art. 28(1).
490   *Ibid.* art. 28(2).
491   *Ibid.* art. 24(3).
492   *Ibid.*
493   *Ibid.* art. 32.
494   *Ibid.* art. 35(1).
495   *Ibid.* art. 34(1).
496   *Ibid.* art. 34(2).
497   *Ibid.* art. 42(4).

states they are to agree amongst themselves the management of the task in association with the High Representative.[498] Approval of the establishment of permanent structured cooperation is for the Council acting by qualified majority,[499] decisions thereafter for the Council comprising participating member states (by qualified majority thereof).[500]

E. JUDICIAL REVIEW OF LEGISLATION

6.98 The means by which legislative and administrative acts of the Union institutions may be challenged before the Court of Justice are discussed above.[501] It will be observed that a natural or legal person long found it virtually (but not quite) impossible to challenge a true Regulation under article 230 EC (article 263 TFEU) owing to the necessity of showing individual concern;[502] he may do so now without difficulty so long as at issue is a regulatory act of direct concern to him which does not entail implementing measures.[503] He still finds it virtually (but not quite) impossible to challenge a Directive owing to the necessity of showing direct concern;[504] for these he will normally have access to judicial review only indirectly via articles 267 or (exceptionally) 268 TFEU.[505] True recommendations and opinions are expressly barred from review by the Court of Justice under article 263, but because they may have relevance for the interpretation of Union or national legislation, they may properly be the subject of an interpretative preliminary reference under article 267.[506]

6.99 Lisbon introduced the new term of art, the 'regulatory act' (*acte règlementaire*; *Rechtsakte mit Verordnungscharakter*) but not via article 288, rather indirectly by article 263, in providing for a means of judicial review of 'a regulatory act which … does not entail implementing measures'.[507] The term appears nowhere else in the Treaties. In fact it grew out of a package of new legislative instruments to

---

498 *Ibid.*

499 *Ibid.* art. 46(2).

500 *Ibid.* art. 46(3).

501 See 5.66–5.85 above.

502 Exceptionally a true Regulation could be the subject of annulment proceedings raised by a non-privileged applicant; see 5.77 above. It was easier where a Regulation was in fact, on its true construction, a 'bundle of decisions'; Cases 16–17/62 *Confédération Nationale des Producteurs des Fruits et Légumes* v *EEC Council* [1962] ECR 471.

503 TFEU, art. 263, 4th para.; see 5.79 above.

504 In one instance only (Case T-420/05 *Vischim* v *Commission* [2009] ECR II-3841 and Case T-380/06 *Vischim* v *Commission* [2009] ECR II-3911) the Court found the requisite direct concern in a Directive justifying the admissibility of an annulment action raised by a non-privileged applicant; see 5.78 above.

505 See 5.121 above.

506 Case 322/88 *Grimaldi* v *Fonds des Maladies Professionnelles* [1989] ECR 4407.

507 TFEU, art. 263, 4th para. See 5.79 above.

be created by the Constitutional Treaty;[508] shorn of that context it is an orphan and makes little sense. All we have so far is recognition from the General Court that the relationship between a regulatory act and a legislative act and the circumstances in which a regulatory act does not require implementing measures are 'issues ... of some legal complexity',[509] yet with the rather simplistic determination that regulatory act covers 'all acts of general application apart from legislative acts'.[510] Further clarity from the Court is needed, and expected.[511]

As a general rule the Court of Justice had no power to review measures adopted **6.100** by authority of the pre-Lisbon Treaty on European Union.[512] The situation was described by the Court of Justice thus:

> [A]s regards the Union, the treaties have established a system of legal remedies in which ... the jurisdiction of the Court is less extensive under Title VI of the Treaty on European Union than it is under the EC Treaty. It is even less extensive under Title V.[513]

Or starker still,

> under the EU Treaty ... the powers of the Court of Justice are exhaustively listed in Article 46 EU. That article makes no provision for any jurisdiction of the Court in respect of the provisions of Title V of the EU Treaty.[514]

The exceptions to the rule made for some (variable) complexity, much (but not all) of which disappeared with Lisbon. However, the jurisdiction of the Court is still excluded over (a) most of the Common Foreign and Security Policy and (b) one area within the freedom, security and justice (*justice, liberté, securité*, JLS) field; and the rules which applied to review of JLS measures adopted pre-Lisbon generally continue to apply post-Lisbon for a transitional period of five years. This is considered above.[515]

---

508   Treaty establishing a Constitution for Europe, art. I-33; note especially the 'European regulation'.
509   Case T-18/10R *Inuit Tapiriit Kanatami and ors* v *Parliament and Council* [2010] ECR II-75*, at para. 46.
510   Case T-18/10 *Inuit Tapiriit Kanatami and ors* v *Parliament and Council*, order of 6 September 2011, not yet reported, at para. 56. Further (at paras 57–65), and also simplistic, a 'legislative act' is one adopted by the ordinary legislative procedure.
511   And may be forthcoming in Case T-526/10 *Inuit Tapiriit Kanatami and ors* v *Parliament and Council*, pending, challenging the first (legislative) act's implementing Regulation.
512   TEU (pre-Lisbon), art. 46 ; see Case T-338/02 *Segi and ors* v *Council* [2004] ECR II-1647; Case T-228/02 *Organisation des Modjahedines du peuple d'Iran* v *Council* [2006] ECR II-4665.
513   Case T-338/02 *Segi, ibid.*, at para. 50.
514   Case T-231/04 *Greece* v *Commission* [2007] ECR II-63, at para. 73.
515   See 5.29 and 5.149 (art. 35 EU) above.

F. GENERAL PRINCIPLES OF UNION LAW

1. General

6.101   As in other legal systems, but of especial importance in a developing legal order, the Court of Justice came over the years to develop legal principles of general application to assist in applying the law and to temper its rigidities. Authority to do so lay in the task assigned the Court by the Treaties, to 'ensure that … the law is observed'[516] – 'the law' in this context being *ius*, not *lex*, and signifying more than simply the written law of the Treaties and of legislation. The principles developed by the Court are 'general principles common to the law of the member states', the shared tradition of the member states being seen as a source of law prior to the Treaties. However, the Court has not limited itself to principles found in the law of every member state; rather it has adopted and moulded those which seemed best adapted to the Community/Union system. Since significant components of Union law are administrative law, some of the most important principles have been taken from the highly developed administrative law of Germany and France. But the Court has looked elsewhere – for example, embracing principles of natural justice as developed in the United Kingdom. Generally the Court cleaves to rules which possess, and are amenable to broad application by virtue of, a 'general comprehensive character … naturally inherent in general principles of law'.[517] A general principle of law, properly identified, is recognised to have an overriding authority, superior to that of 'ordinary' Union law. Put otherwise, it 'ha[s] constitutional status'.[518]

6.102   The general principles are addressed first and foremost to the Union institutions in the discharge of their legislative and executive competences.[519] But they apply also to the authorities of the member states when acting within the scope of Union law – when they are implementing, applying, obliged to implement or apply,[520] or, significantly, seeking to justify derogation from,[521]

---

516   TEU, art. 19(1) (ex art. 220 EC); see 5.01 above.
517   Case C-101/08 *Audiolux and ors* v *Groupe Bruxelles Lambert and ors* [2009] ECR I-9823, at para. 42.
518   *Ibid.* at para. 63.
519   Case C-354/04P *Gestoras Pro Amnistía and ors* v *Council* [2007] ECR I-1579, at para. 51; Case C-303/05 *Advocaten voor de Wereld* v *Leden van de Ministerrad* [2007] ECR I-3633, at para. 45.
520   See Case 5/88 *Wachauf* v *Germany* [1989] ECR 2609; Case C-2/92 *R* v *Ministry of Agriculture, Fisheries and Food, ex parte Bostock* [1994] ECR I-955; Cases C-80–82/99 *Flemmer and ors* v *Council, Commission and Bundesanstalt für Landwirtschaft und Ernährung* [2001] ECR I-7211; Case C-313/99 *Mulligan and ors* v *Minister for Agriculture and Food* [2002] ECR I-5719; Case C-62/00 *Marks & Spencer* v *Commissioners of Customs and Excise* [2002] ECR I-6325; Cases C-20 and 64/00 *Booker Aquaculture and anor* v *Scottish Ministers* [2003] ECR I-7411; Case C-275/06 *Productores de Música de España* v *Telefónica de España* [2008] ECR I-271, at para. 68. The general principle at least of human rights protection may also be called into aid in order to challenge a Union measure which authorises a member state to adopt contrary legislation; Case C-540/03 *Parliament* v *Council* (Family Reunification) [2006] ECR I-5769.

Union rules. They may also apply in (the much rarer) circumstances in which an individual bears an obligation under Union law, and so horizontally – here the Court of Justice now breaking new ground of wide constitutional significance.[522] They have no direct bearing upon, or relevance for, the member states outwith the sphere of Union law.[523]

> Specifically, national measures can be reviewed on the basis of their compliance with such general principles only if they fall within the scope of Community law. For that to be the case, the provision of national law at issue must in general fall into one of three categories. It must implement EC law (irrespective of the degree of the discretion the Member State enjoys and whether the national measure goes beyond what is strictly necessary for implementation). It must invoke some permitted derogation under EC law. Or it must otherwise fall within the scope of Community law because some specific substantive rule of EC law is applicable to the situation.[524]

Advocate-General Sharpston posits a logic by which Union fundmental rights could be extended, partially, into the purely national realm,[525] does not counsel the Court to accept it, and suggests it is a 'question [which] can be put off for the moment, but probably not for all that much longer'.[526] In any event it is thought that principles considered and applied by national judges within the Union context may by habit 'haemorrhage' into the purely national sphere – for example, reception of, and now casual and comfortable reference to, principles of proportionality and legitimate expectation in English administrative law.

The Court may engage in extensive discussion of general principles, only to find **6.103** that they do not apply to the facts of the case before it. Even where they may apply, rights deriving from them are not absolute, and they may, as with rights

---

521 See Case 260/89 *Elliniki Radiophonia Tiléorasi* v *Dimotiki Etairia Pliroforissis* [1991] ECR I-2925; Case C-60/00 *Carpenter* v *Secretary of State for the Home Department* [2002] ECR I-6279; Case C-112/00 *Eugen Schmidberger, Internationale Transporte und Planzüge* v *Austria* [2003] ECR I-5659; Case C-36/02 *Omega Spielhallen- und Automatenaufstellungs* v *Oberbürgermeisterin der Bundesstadt Bonn* [2004] ECR I-9609; Case T-385/07 *FIFA* v *Commission*, [2011] ECR II-205; Case T-55/08 *UEFA* v *Commission* [2011] ECR II-271; Case T-68/08 *FIFA* v *Commission*, [2011] ECR II-349 at paras 138, 179 and 142, respectively.

522 See 14.49 below.

523 See e.g., Case C-299/95 *Kremzow* v *Austria* [1997] ECR I-2629; Cases C-465/00 and 138–9/01 *Rechnungshof and ors* v *Österreichischer Rundfunk and ors* [2003] ECR I-4989; Case C-324/04 *Criminal proceedings against Vajnai* [2005] ECR I-8577; Case C-361/07 *Polier* v *Najar*, order of 16 January 2008, unreported; Case C-287/08 *Savia and ors* v *Ministero dell'Istruzione, dell'Università e della Ricerca and ors* [2008] ECR I-136*; Case C-339/10 *Estov and ors* v *Ministerski savet na Republika Bulgaria* [2010] ECR I-11465; Case C-457/09 *Chartry* v *État belge*, judgment of 1 March 2011, not yet reported.

524 Case C-427/06 *Bartsch* v *Bosch und Siemens Hausgeräte (BSH) Altersfürsorge* [2008] ECR I-7245, *per* A-G Sharpston at para. 69 of her opinion.

525 Case C-34/09 *Ruiz Zambrano* v *Office national de l'emploi*, judgment of 8 March 2011, not yet reported, at paras 151–77 of her opinion.

526 *Ibid.* at para. 177.

generally, be restricted or limited for the benefit of the general interest. In the terms of the EU Charter of Fundamental Rights:

> Any limitation on the exercise of the rights and freedoms recognised by this Charter must be provided for by law and respect the essence of those rights and freedoms ... [L]imitations may be made only if they are necessary and genuinely meet objectives of general interest recognised by the Union or the need to protect the rights and freedoms of others.[527]

So, where a fundamental right is not absolute, it

> must be viewed in relation to its social purpose. Consequently, the exercise of those rights may be restricted, provided that the restrictions in fact correspond to objectives of general interest and do not, taking account of the aim of the restrictions, constitute disproportionate and unacceptable interference, impairing the very substance of the right guaranteed ...
>
> In those circumstances, the interest involved must be weighed having regard to all the circumstances of the case in order to determine whether a fair balance was struck between those interests.[528]

Whether or not this is so will depend upon the margin of appreciation afforded the law-making authority, which will turn, *inter alia*, upon the importance adhering to the right and the nature of the measure (legislative or administrative) alleged to compromise it. Nevertheless, where the exercise of a fundamental right meets these tests, it will override even fundamental provisions of the Treaties.[529] And as 'higher' principles of law for the protection of the individual, their breach may trigger the non-contractual liability of the Union or of the member states, as the case may be.

6.104 The general principles are a mixed bag and come from different sources and in different guises. Advocate-General Trstenjak has noted that

> the terminology is inconsistent both in legal literature and in case-law. To some extent there are differences only in the choice of words, such as where the Court of Justice and the Advocates-General refer to a 'generally-accepted rule of law', a 'principle generally

---

527 EU Charter, art. 52(1); as to the Charter see below.
528 Case C-112/00 *Schmidberger*, n. 521 above, at paras 80–1.
529 See e.g. Case C-112/00 *Schmidberger*, n. 521 above, at para. 74; Case C-36/02 *Omega Spielhallen*, n. 521 above, at para. 35; Case C-438/05 *International Transport Workers' Federation* v *Viking Line* [2007] ECR I-10779, at para. 45; Case C-341/05 *Laval un Partneri* v *Svenska Byggnadsarbetareförbundet and ors* (Vaxholm) [2007] ECR I-11767, at para. 93.

accepted', a 'basic principle of law', a 'fundamental principle', 'a principle', a 'rule', or a 'general principle of equality which is one of the fundamental principles of EU law'.[530]

The most important of them can be grouped into four broad, interconnecting categories:

- fundamental (human) rights;
- constitutional rights;
- social and economic rights; and
- procedural rights,

as follows.

2. Fundamental rights

In the pantheon of the general principles of Union law, respect for fundamental **6.105** (human) rights is *primus inter pares* – 'a condition of the lawfulness of all European Union acts'.[531] The Treaty on European Union now provides at the outset, in article 2:

> The Union is founded on the values of respect for human dignity, freedom, democracy, equality, the rule of law and respect for human rights, including the rights of persons belonging to minorities. These values are common to the Member States in a society in which pluralism, non-discrimination, tolerance, justice, solidarity and equality between women and men prevail.

And in article 6(3):

> Fundamental rights, as guaranteed by the European Convention for the Protection of Human Rights and Fundamental Freedoms and as they result from the constitutional traditions common to the Member States, shall constitute general principles of the Union's law.

Prior to 1999 this was exhortatory only, any jurisdiction of the Court of Justice to apply it being expressly ousted.[532] But Amsterdam extended the authority of the Court to supervision of compliance with article 6(3) insofar as it may apply

---

530 Case C-282/10 *Dominguez v Centre informatique du Centre Ouest Atlantique and anor*, judgment of 24 January 2012, not yet reported, at para. 92 of her opinion (internal footnotes omitted).

531 Case C-236/09 *Association Belge des Consummateurs Test-Achats and ors v Conseil des ministres*, judgment of 1 March 2011, not yet reported, *per* A-G Kokott at para. 27 of her opinion.

532 TEU (pre-Amsterdam), art. L.

to 'action of the institutions' falling within the Court's power of review;[533] adherence to ('respect of') the principles of article 2 was made a precondition of accession to the Union;[534] and in the event of 'a clear risk of a serious breach' or 'a serious and persistent breach' of those principles, sanctions may now be adopted against a defaulting member state by the European Council and the Council[535] – although subject to pretty fierce procedural hurdles.[536] The closest the Union has come to deploying sanctions was in 1999, in protest against the (minor) participation in the Austrian federal government of the *Freiheits Partei Österreich*,[537] but there was no formal recourse, and the events cannot be taken as action adopted pursuant to article 7. Nor was action taken under article 7 following the 2003 invasion of Iraq against the member states party to it, notwithstanding war of aggression being identified by the European Parliament as 'a clear risk of a breach … or an actual breach' of article 2,[538] or in the light of 'extraordinary rendition flights' in and through a number of member states – *refoulement* prohibited (absolutely,[539] and probably with the force of *jus*

---

533 TEU (pre-Lisbon), art. 46(d); that is, the Court appeared to have jurisdiction to apply art. 6(2) TEU (pre-Lisbon) (= art. 6(3) now) to the institutions when they acted by authority of the EC Treaty (except where expressly excluded) or by authority of the TEU in those (narrow) instances in which the jurisdiction of the Court was recognised. Article 46, and the complexity it brought, became otiose with Lisbon restructuring and disappeared from Treaty texts.

534 TEU, art. 49; see 2.72 above.

535 *Ibid.* art. 7.

536 Action taken under art. 7 now takes two forms: first (a Nice innovation), upon a 'reasoned proposal' from the Parliament, the Commission or one-third of the member states, and with the consent of the Parliament (acting by a two-thirds majority vote representing a majority of MEPs; TFEU, art. 354), the Council may by a majority of four-fifths of its members determine that there is a 'clear risk of a serious breach' of art. 2 and address appropriate recommendations (but no more) to the errant member state (art. 7(1)). Second, upon a proposal from the Commission or one-third of the member states, and with the (same weighted) consent of the Parliament, the European Council may by unanimity (excepting the vote of the errant member state(s); TFEU, art. 354) determine the existence of a 'serious and persistent breach' of art. 2, after which the Council may by qualified majority suspend 'certain of' the member state's Treaty rights, including Council voting rights (art. 7(2)–(5)).

537 In the 1999 election the FPÖ won 27 per cent of the popular vote, making it the second largest party in the *Nationalrat*, and agreed to form a collation government with the *Österreichische Volkspartei* (ÖVP). This led to weekly protests (the *Donnerstagsdemonstrationen*) in Vienna and the boycott measures adopted by the other member states. The 'Statement of the XIV' said this state of affairs would last 'as long as necessary', but crumbled after seven months. A subsequent report (*Report on the Austrian Government's Commitment to the Common European Values, in particular concerning the rights of Minorities, Refugees and Immigrants, and the Evolution of the Political Nature of the FPÖ* ('Wise Men Report') (2001) 40 *International Legal Materials* 102) exonerated Austria of human rights abuses of any kind. The affair raises the interesting question of whether the boycott itself was consistent with the art. 2 commitment to (Austrian) democracy and if, and how, Austria (or an Austrian) might have challenged the conduct of the Fourteen on that ground.

538 European Parliament, Committee on Constitutional Affairs, *Report on the Commission Communication on Article 7 of the Treaty on European Union: Respect for and Promotion of the Values on which the Union is Based* (1 April 2004) A5–0227/2004, p. 11.

539 *Chahal* v *United Kingdom* (1997) 23 EHRR 413; *Saadi* v *Italy* (2008) 47 EHRR 427.

cogens) in international law[540] and under both the European Convention[541] and the EU Charter of Fundamental Rights[542] – and of related torture in some member states.[543]

As for rendition through the Union, the Parliament 'deplore[d]' the inability of the Council to act 'due to the opposition of certain Member States',[544] 'denounce[d] the lack of cooperation of many Member States' with the temporary committee of inquiry set up to consider the issue[545] and expressed 'outrage' at certain proposals of the Council presidency by way of response,[546] yet no action was taken. This is of course the major weakness of article 7 – the bar is set so high for a measure to be adopted: if member states work together to a common purpose, or at least in mutual contempt of fundamental rights, sufficient support in the Council for effective action is unlikely to be mustered. Once action *is* taken it is subject to only very limited review by the Court of Justice.[547]

The fealty to fundamental rights was not always so. The original Treaties made **6.106** no mention of fundamental human rights and the Court of Justice originally repelled any argument that Community action ought to be made subject to them[548] – a view sometimes attributed now to the 'sins of youth'. In the early 1970s, and it is thought at least partially in response to fear of rebellion from the *Bundesverfassungsgericht*, the Court of Justice began to develop what could be called an implied bill of rights, and has held consistently since that 'respect for fundamental human rights forms an integral part of the general principles of

---

540 UN (Geneva) Convention of 28 July 1951 Relating to the Status of Refugees, 189 UNTS 150, art. 33(1); UN Convention of 10 December 1984 against Torture and Other Cruel, Inhuman or Degrading Treatment or Punishment, 1465 UNTS 85, art. 3.

541 ECHR, art. 3.

542 EU Charter, art. 19(2). See also Regulation 343/2003 [2003] OJ L50/1 (Dublin Regulation), Preamble, 2nd recital; Directive 2008/115 [2008] OJ L348/98 on returning illegally staying third country nationals, which requires member states to 'respect' (arts 4(b), 5) and 'fully [to] respect' (preamble, 8th recital) the principle of *non-refoulement*. Post-Lisbon, art. 78 TFEU on asylum and protection of third country nationals requires that the Union 'ensur[e] compliance with the principle of *non-refoulement*'.

543 See the 'Marty Reports': Council of Europe, Parliamentary Assembly, Committee on Legal Affairs and Human Rights, *Alleged Secret Detentions and Unlawful Inter-state Transfers of Detainees involving Council of Europe Member States* (7 June 2006) AS/Jur (2006) 16 and *Secret Detentions and Illegal Transfer of Detainees involving Council of Europe Member States: Second Report* (7 June 2007) AS/Jur (2007) 36. Also the European Parliament's *Report on the Alleged Use of European Countries by the CIA for the Transportation and Illegal Detention of Prisoners* (30 January 2007), A6–0020/2007; *El-Masri v Former Yugoslav Republic of Macedonia* (Application No. 39630/09), pending.

544 Report A6–0020/2007, *ibid.*, Motion for a Resolution, point 7.

545 *Ibid.* point 13.

546 *Ibid.* point 25.

547 The Court may review the procedural propriety, but not the substance, of a determination under art. 7 and solely at the request of the member state(s) concerned; TFEU, art. 269. See 5.87 above.

548 Case 1/58 *Stork v High Authority* [1959] ECR 17; Cases 36 etc./59 *Präsident Ruhrkohlen-Verkaufsgesellschaft and ors v High Authority* [1960] ECR 423.

law protected by the Court of Justice'[549] – so much so that reference to them and their constraining authority is now almost casual: here is Advocate-General Sharpston in 2010:

> I shall not waste time or space on a lengthy exegesis of the importance of fundamental rights in the legal order of the European Union. Fundamental rights have been an essential part of that legal order for many years … I regard it as inconceivable that EU secondary legislation that contravened fundamental rights in general, or the ECHR or the Charter in particular, could be upheld as valid by the Court.[550]

They have of course acquired a far greater relevance and sensitivity since Amsterdam and the increasing Union forays into freedom, security and justice matters in which the personal freedoms, and the very liberty, of the individual may be at stake.

(a)   Sources of fundamental rights

6.107   The fundamental rights recognised and applied by Union law are derived now from three distinct (but not mutually exclusive) sources.

(i)   Constitutional traditions common to the member states

6.108   This is the source first, and since consistently, cited by the Court, and it is now formally recognised as such by article 6(3). 'Common' does not mean universal: legitimate expectation (*Vertrauenschutzprinzip*) is recognised to be a general principle of Union law[551] even though it derives essentially (and fully formed) from the law of only one member state. Generally the Court claims to look to, and distil, a high standard of protection rather than the lowest common denominator[552] and one moulded, and best suited, to the requirements of Union law:

> Although the Court of Justice must certainly be guided by the most characteristic provisions of the systems of domestic law, it must above all ensure that it adopts a solution appropriate to the needs and specific features of the Community legal system. In other words, the Court has the task of drawing on the legal traditions of the Member States in order to find an answer to similar legal questions arising under Community law that both respects those traditions and is appropriate to the context of the Community legal order.[553]

---

549   Case 11/70 *Internationale Handelsgesellschaft mbH* v *Einfuhr- und Vorratsstelle für Getreide und Futtermittel* [1970] ECR 1125, at para. 4.

550   Cases C-92 and 93/09 *Volker und Markus Schecke and anor* v *Land Hessen* [2010] ECR I-11063 at para. 64 of her opinion.

551   See 6.134 below.

552   The exception is confidentiality of communications between lawyer and client, in which context the Court adopted the principle only insofar as it was shown to be common to all member states: see n. 660 below.

553   Cases C-120 and 121/06P *Fabbrica italiana accumulatori motocarri Montecchio and anor* v *Council and Commission* [2008] ECR I-6513, *per* A-G Poiares Maduro at para. 55 of his opinion.

(ii)   International treaties

In 1974 – shortly after France (the last then member state to do so) ratified the   **6.109**
European Convention on Human Rights and recognised the right of individual
petition to the European Court of Human Rights – the Court first took notice
of international treaties for the protection of human rights on which the
member states have collaborated or of which they are signatories as a source of
fundamental rights recognised by Community law.[554] The most important of
the international treaties is, of course, the European Convention on Human
Rights, which is now formally recognised (and codified) as such in article 6 of
the Treaty on European Union. The standard formula adopted by the Court
became:

> [I]t is settled case law that fundamental rights form an integral part of the general
> principles of Community law whose observance is ensured by the Community judica-
> ture. For that purpose, the Court of Justice and the Court of First Instance draw
> inspiration from the constitutional traditions common to the Member States and from
> the guidelines supplied by international treaties for the protection of human rights on
> which the Member States have collaborated and to which they are signatories. The
> Convention has special significance in this respect.[555]

And it is a principle which extended beyond Community law to apply also to
the conduct of the Union:

> [I]n accordance with Article 6(2) EU, the Union must respect fundamental rights, as
> guaranteed by the European Convention for the Protection of Human Rights and
> Fundamental Freedoms … The Framework Decision must thus be interpreted in such a
> way that fundamental rights, including in particular the right to a fair trial as set out in
> Article 6 of the Convention and interpreted by the European Court of Human Rights,
> are respected.[556]

However, the Court was long careful to 'draw inspiration' from the Convention,   **6.110**
and not apply it directly. Hence, it would say, for example:

> Article 6(1) of the EHRC [*sic*] provides that in the determination of his civil rights and
> obligations or of any criminal charge against him, everyone is entitled to a fair and
> public hearing within a reasonable time by an independent and impartial tribunal

---

554   Case 4/73 *Nold* v *Commission* [1974] ECR 491.
555   Case T-112/98 *Mannesmannröhren-Werke* v *Commission* [2001] ECR II-729, at para. 60. For essentially
      identical constructions see Opinion 2/94 *Re Accession to the ECHR* [1996] ECR I-1759, at para. 33; Case
      C-299/95 *Kremzow* v *Austria* [1997] ECR I-2629, at para. 14; Case C-94/00 *Roquette Frères* v *Directeur
      Général de la Concurrence* [2002] ECR I-9011, at para. 23; Case C-112/00 *Schmidberger, Internationale
      Transporte und Planzüge* v *Austria* [2003] ECR I-5659, at para. 71; Case C-229/05P *Ocalan* v *Council* [2007]
      ECR I-439, at para. 76.
556   Case C-105/03 *Criminal proceedings against Pupino* [2005] ECR I-5285, at paras 58, 59.

established by law. The general principle of Community law that everyone is entitled to a fair legal process … is inspired by those fundamental rights.[557]

Alternatively,

[various provisions of a Community Directive] are not invalid by reason of infringement of Article 6(2) EU, read in the light of Article 8 of the ECHR and Article 1 of the First Protocol thereto;[558]

and,

[r]espect for that presumption [of innocence] is required of the Commission … by virtue of the fact that it is a fundamental right guaranteed by the ECHR and therefore a general principle of Community law pursuant to Article 6(2) EU and the settled case-law of the Community Courts.[559]

This is because the Community was not party to the Convention, and so, notwithstanding reference to respect of fundamental rights 'as guaranteed by the European Convention' in article 6 of the TEU (pre-Lisbon), it was not (and is not) 'as such' part of Community (or Union) law;[560] and under the pre-Lisbon Treaty the Community (and certainly not the Union) had no constitutional power to accede to it.[561]

6.111 However, the Court edged gradually ever closer to an embrace with the Convention – for example, Advocate-General Jacobs in 1996:

Although the Community itself is not a party to the Convention … and although the Convention may not be formally binding upon the Community, nevertheless for practical purposes the Convention can be regarded as part of Community law and can be invoked as such both in this court and in national courts.[562]

And in 2004 the Court, for the first time, applied the Convention directly: citing case law of the Court of Human Rights which found the refusal of English law to recognise gender reassignment to breach a transsexual's right to

---

557 Case C-185/95P *Baustahlgewebe* v *Commission* [1998] ECR I-8417, at paras 20–21.
558 Cases C-154 and 155/04 *R (Alliance for Natural Health and ors)* v *Secretary of State for Health and anor* [2005] ECR I-6451, at para. 130.
559 Cases T-22 and 23/02 *Sumitomo Chemical Co.* v *Commission* [2005] ECR II-4065, at para. 69.
560 Case T-112/98 *Mannesmannröhren-Werke* v *Commission* [2001] ECR II-729, at para. 59.
561 Opinion 2/94 *Re Accession to the ECHR* [1996] ECR I-1759.
562 Case C-85/94 *Bosphorus Hava Yollari Turizm ve Ticaret* v *Minister for Transport, Ireland* [1996] ECR I-3953, *per* A-G Jacobs, at para. 53 of his opinion.

marry under article 12 of the Convention,[563] it found it also to infringe a Community right to a spouse's pension rights, and so said:

> Article 141 EC, in principle, precludes legislation, such as that at issue before the national court, which, in breach of the European Convention for the Protection of Human Rights and Fundamental Freedoms, prevents [the enjoyment of a Community law right].[564]

More recently, in a case involving pre-Lisbon Union (not Community) legislation, it said:

> [I]n accordance with Article 6(2) EU, the Union must respect fundamental rights, as guaranteed by the European Convention … The Framework Decision must thus be interpreted in such a way that fundamental rights, including in particular the right to a fair trial as set out in Article 6 of the Convention and interpreted by the European Court of Human Rights, are respected.[565]

And back to the Community sphere:

> The obligations [imposed upon lawyers] of information and of cooperation with the authorities responsible for combating money laundering, laid down in [a Directive], do not infringe the right to a fair trial as guaranteed by Article 6 of the Convention for the Protection of Human Rights and Fundamental Freedoms and Article 6(2) EU.[566]

Yet it still continued, sometimes, to keep the Convention at arm's length. Here **6.112** is the General Court in mid-2008:

> It should be pointed out … that the Court has no jurisdiction to assess the lawfulness of an investigation under competition law in the light of provisions of the ECHR, inasmuch as those provisions do not as such form part of Community law. That said, the fact remains that the Community judicature is called upon to ensure the observance of the fundamental rights which form an integral part of the general principles of law and, for that purpose, it draws inspiration from the constitutional traditions common to the Member States and from the guidelines supplied by international instruments for the protection of human rights, on which the Member States have collaborated and to which they are signatories. In that regard, the ECHR has special significance;[567]

and the Court of Justice in early 2009:

---

563 *Goodwin* v *United Kingdom* (2002) 35 EHRR 447; *I* v *United Kingdom* (2003) 36 EHRR 967.
564 Case C-117/01 *K.B.* v *National Health Service Pensions Agency* [2004] ECR I-541, in the *dispositif*.
565 Case C-105/03 *Criminal proceedings against Pupino* [2005] ECR I-5285, at paras 58–9.
566 Case C-305/05 *Ordre des barreaux francophones et germanophone* v *Conseil des Ministres* [2007] ECR I-5305, in the *dispositif*.
567 Case T-99/04 *AC-Treuhand* v *Commission* [2008] ECR II-1501, at para. 45.

> [T]he fundamental right guaranteed under Article 3 of the ECHR forms part of the general principles of Community law, observance of which is ensured by the Court, and while the case-law of the European Court of Human Rights is taken into consideration in interpreting the scope of that right in the Community legal order, it is, however, Article 15(b) of the Directive which corresponds, in essence, to Article 3 of the ECHR. By contrast, Article 15(c) of the Directive is a provision, the content of which is different from that of Article 3 of the ECHR, and the interpretation of which must, therefore, be carried out independently, although with due regard for fundamental rights, as they are guaranteed under the ECHR.[568]

The Court nevertheless seems now to have acquired the taste for, at the least, more direct reference to the Convention.[569] It may, or may not, be relevant that four of the ten judges appointed upon the 2004 accessions had served previously as judges of the Court of Human Rights.[570] How far formal accession will lead to significant change in the application of these principles in Union law is a matter of spirited debate. But it is incontestable that because Union conduct is not directly subject to the jurisdiction of the European Court of Human Rights, and even if the Court of Justice 'pays the greatest heed to',[571] 'systematically takes into consideration'[572] or attaches 'particular significance and high importance to'[573] the case law of the European Court of Human Rights, there will inevitably be fissures between Strasbourg case law (on the Convention) and Luxembourg case law (on Union law inspired by it).[574] However, Strasbourg appears now to have stepped back, recognised Luxembourg to provide a standard of protection of fundamental rights 'equivalent' to the Convention system, and so even in those areas in which it has jurisdiction to intervene, a disinclination to do so.[575] The fissures may narrow with the new, institutionalised cooperation between, on the one hand, the EU Agency for Fundamental Rights, established in 2007 to provide the institutions and the member states

---

568 Case C-465/07 *Elgafaji & Elgafaji v Staassecretaris van Justitie* [2009] ECR I-921, at para. 28.
569 See e.g., Case C-432/04 *Commission v Cresson* [2006] ECR I-6387, at para. 112; Case T-279/02 *Degussa v Commission* [2006] ECR II-897.
570 That is, Judges Kūris, Levits, Lõhmus and Makarczyk.
571 Case C-466/00 *Kaba v Secretary of State for the Home Department* [2003] ECR I-2219, *per* A-G Ruiz-Jarabo Colomer at para. 89 of his opinion.
572 Cases C-411 and 493/10 *R (NS) and ME and ors v Secretary of State for the Home Department and ors*, judgment of 21 December 2011, not yet reported; *per* A-G Trstenjak at para. 147 of her opinion.
573 *Ibid.* at para. 148 of her opinion.
574 To give one example, the Strasbourg view of privilege against self-incrimination (derived from art. 6 of the ECHR) is, arguably, far wider than that recognised in Union law; compare *Funke v France* (1993) 16 EHRR 297 and *Saunders v United Kindom* (1997) 23 EHRR 313 with Case 374/87 *Orkem v Commission* [1989] ECR 3283 and Case T-112/98 *Mannesmanröhren-Werke v Commission* [2001] ECR II-729. See also Case C-94/00 *Roquette Frères v Directeur Général de la Concurrence* [2002] ECR I-9011, in which the Court was required to re-assess its previous case law on the inviolability of premises in the light of intervening judgments of the Court of Human Rights.
575 *Bosphorus Hava Tollari Turizm v Ireland* (2006) 42 EHRR 1.

with assistance and expertise relating to fundamental rights,[576] and on the other the Council of Europe,[577] which takes advantage of and borrows from the latter's 'extensive experience and expertise … in the field of human rights'.[578]

The Treaties now, post-Lisbon, require the Union to accede to the Conven- **6.113** tion,[579] so removing the previous Treaty bar. The Convention itself, long open to accession to member states of the Council of Europe only, was amended in 2010 to permit Union accession;[580] but it will still require formidable institutional problems to be settled, principally issues of Union representation on the Court and (perhaps) in the Council's Committee of Ministers and some form of accommodation on the judicial geometry between Luxembourg and Strasbourg, which must 'make provision for preserving the specific characteristics of the Union and Union law'[581] and which may, or may not, be permissible under the Treaties;[582] then both a unanimous Council and ratification by all member states (on the Union side)[583] and the consent, presumably, of two-thirds of the members of the Council of Europe.[584] The Treaties also purport to reserve a (small) number of Union matters from Convention rights,[585] which is permissible under the Convention[586] but may not impress the Committee of Ministers much.

(iii) Charter of Fundamental Rights

At the Nice Summit in December 2000 the Parliament, the Council and the **6.114** Commission adopted by 'solemn proclamation' the Charter of Fundamental Rights of the European Union.[587] The Charter is the fruit of long debate within the Union on the nature of fundamental rights: the rights which ought to be embraced; whether they ought to be legally binding, and if so how, whether they

---

576 Regulation 168/2007 [2007] OJ L53/1.
577 Agreement of 18 June 2008 between the European Community and the Council of Europe on Cooperation between the EU Agency for Fundamental Rights and the Council of Europe [2008] OJ L186/7.
578 Preamble, 4th indent.
579 TEU, art. 6(2).
580 ECHR, art. 59(2); as amended by Protocol No. 14, art. 17, which came into force with (belated) Russian ratification in June 2010.
581 Protocol (No. 8) relating to Article 6(2) of the TEU on the Accession of the Union to the ECHR, art. 1.
582 See Opinion 1/91 *Re the EEA Agreement* [1991] ECR I-6079, wherein the Court of Justice found the original EEA Agreement to be incompatible with the EEC Treaty owing to the authority which was to be conferred upon the proposed EEA Court diminishing that of the Court of Justice. It is not clear that the simple declaration of art. 6(2) that '[t]he Union shall accede to the European Convention' will be sufficient to overcome similar issues which arise here – *a fortiori* as it goes on to provide that 'accession shall not affect the Union's competences as defined in the Treaties'.
583 TFEU, art. 218(8).
584 Statute of the Council of Europe, arts 4 and 20.c.
585 Protocol (No. 8), n. 581 above.
586 ECHR, art. 64.
587 For the text see [2000] OJ C364/1.

ought to be incorporated into Treaty texts or simply 'declared', and if so by whom; whether they ought to bind (if anyone) the Community/Union institutions only, the member states acting within Community/Union spheres, the member states in areas unrelated to Community law, and so on. In the event, the Charter is a fairly comprehensive codification of essentially personal rights 'recognised' by the Union[588] – 54 articles divided into seven chapters, addressing dignity, freedoms, equality, solidarity, citizens' rights, justice, and a final chapter on general provisions. It is unique amongst international instruments in the breadth of its subject matter. However it does *not* form part of the Treaty and was originally adopted, however 'solemnly', not by the constituent authorities of the Treaties (the *'Herren der Verträge'*) but by the three political institutions. This they had done once before, admittedly far less ambitiously,[589] and to limited effect. At Nice the member states least enthusiastic of fundamental rights initiatives secured a victory of sorts. Article 51 of the Charter (within the chapter on general provisions, defining the 'Scope' of the Charter) provides:

1. The provisions of this Charter are addressed to the institutions and bodies of the Union with due regard for the principle of subsidiarity and to the Member States only when they are implementing Union law. They shall therefore respect the rights, observe the principles and promote the application thereof in accordance with their respective powers.
2. This Charter does not establish any new power or task for the Community or the Union, or modify powers and tasks defined by the Treaties.

There is concern that the application of the Charter to the conduct of the member states 'only when they are implementing [*uniquement lorsqu'ils mettent en œuvre*] Union law' is a backward step, a narrower jursidiction than 'within the field of application of Community law' (as prior case law has it) and excluding judicial control over national measures which derogate from Union rules. However the commentary ('explanations') on the Charter notes that 'it follows unambiguously from the case-law ... that the requirement to respect fundamental rights ... is only binding on the Member States when they act in the scope [*lorsqu'ils agissent dans le champ d'application*] of Union law',[590] which, if followed, will nullify the fear. The Court of Justice appears now to favour that course.[591]

---

588 Preamble, 7th indent.
589 Joint Declaration on Fundamental Rights of the European Parliament, the Council and the Commission of 5 April 1977 [1977] OJ C103/1. See also the Community Charter of the Fundamental Rights of Workers, adopted by 11 of the then 12 heads of state or government in 1989 (discussed at 14.32 below), elements of which surface in the Charter.
590 Explanations relating to the Charter of Fundamental Rights [2007] OJ C303/17; Explanation on [*sic*] Article 51. As to which see immediately below.
591 Cases C-411 and 493/10 *R (NS) and ME and ors* v *Secretary of State for the Home Department and ors*, judgment of 21 December 2011, not yet reported, at paras 64–9. The Court's reasoning was terse and may be limited to

Even existing outside the Treaties, the Charter yielded useful precision to those **6.115** rights already recognised as forming part of Community law. It was cited, with approbation, by an Advocate-General as an aid to interpretation of a social policy Directive within two months of its adoption[592] and has been referred to by Advocates-General (Mr Poiares Maduro and Ms Kokott especially) many times since. According to the General Court, '[a]lthough this document does not have legally binding force, it does show the importance of the rights its sets out in the Community legal order',[593] and according to Advocate-General Kokott it could 'be referred to as a source of inspiration with regard to the protection of fundamental rights at Union level'.[594] The Court of Justice took proper notice of it but infrequently,[595] and in most cases as a reflection, restatement or re-affirmation of an existing rule deriving from constitutional traditions of or international obligations common to the member states.

Its significance is now greater still. At the outset '[t]he Commission con- **6.116** sider[ed] that the Charter, by reason of its content, its tight drafting and its high political and symbolic value, ought properly to be incorporated in the Treaties sooner or later'.[596] It was in the event (intended to be) incorporated into the Treaties sooner, by the Treaty establishing a Constitution for Europe, comprising Part II (of its four Parts). There were minor, if significant, differences between the text of the original Charter and the text adopted in the Constitution, but essentially they were the same thing; there was, however, a substantial declaration supplying 'explanations' as to the meaning of the Charter,[597] which carried the authority of the Praesidium of the Constitutional Convention, but were recognised 'not as such [to] have the status of law', yet purported to be 'a valuable tool of interpretation intended to clarify the provisions of the Charter'.[598] So, had that Treaty been ratified, the Charter would have acquired

---

the interpretation of a particular Directive provision rather than wider national powers of derogation. Further clarification may come with Case C-617/10 *Åklagaren* v *Åkerberg Fransson*, pending.

592 Case C-173/99 *R* v *Secretary of State for Trade and Industry, ex parte Broadcasting, Entertainment, Cinematographic and Theatre Union* [2001] ECR I-4881, *per* A-G Tizzano, at paras 26–8 of his opinion.

593 Cases T-377 etc./00 *Philip Morris International* v *Commission* [2003] ECR II-1, at para. 122.

594 Case C-236/09 *Association Belge des Consummateurs Test-Achats and ors* v *Conseil des ministres*, judgment of 1 March 2011, not yet reported, at para. 28 of her opinion.

595 Case C-540/03 *Parliament* v *Council* (Family Reunification) [2006] ECR I-5769; Case C-303/05 *Advocaten voor de Wereld* v *Leden van de Ministerrad* [2007] ECR I-3633; Case C-438/05 *International Transport Workers' Federation* v *Viking Line* [2007] ECR I-10779; Case C-341/05 *Laval un Partneri* v *Svenska Byggnadsarbetareförbundet and ors* (Vaxholm) [2007] ECR I-11767; Case C-275/06 *Productores de Música de España* v *Telefónica de España* [2008] ECR I-271; Case C-450/06 *Varec* v *Belgian State* [2008] ECR I-581; Case C-385/07 *Der Grüne Punkt – Duales System Deutschland* v *Commission* [2009] ECR I-6155; Case C-403/09PPU *Detiček* v *Sgueglia* [2009] ECR I-12193.

596 EC Commission, Communiqué on the Legal Nature of the Charter of Fundamental Rights of the European Union, COM (2000)644 final, para. 11.

597 Declaration (No. 12) concerning the Explanations relating to the Charter of Fundamental Rights.

598 *Ibid.*, 2nd para.

'constitutional' status, and its place within the Union hierarchy of norms would be much clearer. With the Constitutional Treaty abandoned, the solution adopted by Lisbon was, rather than Treaty incorporation, that the Union 'recognises the rights, freedoms and principles set out in the Charter ... *which shall have the same legal value as the Treaties*'[599] and which has 'legally binding force'.[600] This is a half-way house, designed primarily not to frighten the (British) horses; but the result is that the Charter has, albeit through the back door, gained 'legal' force and 'Treaty' force, put otherwise 'the status of primary law',[601] is 'classifie[d] ... as EU primary law'[602] or 'is thus binding primary law'.[603] In anticipation of this the Charter was 'adapted' (or 'adjusted')[604] – that is, in the Constitutional Treaty version – and 'solemnly proclaim[ed]' in Strasbourg the day before the signature of the Lisbon Treaty,[605] and it is this version which replaced the 2000 text when Lisbon entered into force and, thereafter, which the Union recognises.[606] The new legal status of the Charter ('the same legal value as the Treaties') was duly 'noted' by the Court of Justice within two months of Lisbon's entry into force[607] and it was being applied, more or less directly, within six months[608] and more boldly thereafter: in the first 14 months it was cited in some 30 judgments of the Court,[609] making it 'the reference text and the starting point' in its assessment of fundamental rights;[610] put otherwise the Charter is now, according to the Commission, 'the compass of all EU policies, provid[ing] for a binding core of rules that protects

---

599   TEU, art. 6(1) (emphasis added).

600   Declaration (No. 1) concerning the Charter of Fundamental Rights of the European Union.

601   Case C-69/10 *Diouf* v *Ministre du Travail, de l'Emploi et de l'Immigration*, pending, *per* A-G Cruz Villalón at para. 1 of his opinion ('con rango de Derecho originario').

602   Cases C-411 and 493/10 *R (NS) and ME and ors* v *Secretary of State for the Home Department and ors*, judgment of 21 December 2011, not yet reported, *per* A-G Trstenjak at para. 70 of her opinion.

603   Cases C-628/10 and 14/11P *Alliance One International and ors* v *Commission*, judgment of 19 July 2012, not yet reported, *per* A-G Kokott at para. 96 of her opinion.

604   Cases C-317 etc./08 *Alassini and ors* v *Telecom Italia and ors* [2010] ECR I-2213, at para. 4.

605   The Lisbon IGC 'declare[d]' that the version of the Charter agreed in the 2004 IGC, and so forming Part II of the Treaty establishing a Constitution for Europe, was to be 'solemnly proclaimed' by the three political institutions on the date of signature of the Lisbon Treaty and prepared a Treaty declaration to that effect (Declaration on the Proclamation of the Charter by the European Parliament, the Council and the Commission), but it disappeared from the final text. In the event it was solemnly proclaimed the day before. The 'explanatory' declaration is preserved. For the text of the adapted Charter see [2007] OJ C303/1, reproduced at [2010] OJ C83/389; for the explanatory declaration see [2007] OJ C303/17.

606   TEU, art. 6(1).

607   Case C-555/07 *Kücükdeveci* v *Swedex* [2010] ECR I-365, at para. 22.

608   Case C-407/08P *Knauf Gips* v *Commission*, [2010] ECR I-6371, at paras 91–2, the Court setting aside a (pre-Lisbon, 2008) judgment of the General Court for inconsistency with 'fundamental principles of the rule of law' and 'moreover' art. 47 of the Charter; Case C-271/08 *Commission* v *Germany*, [2010] ECR I-7087, at paras 37, 38, recognising the right to bargain collectively as 'is apparent' from art. 28 of the Charter read in conjunction with art. 52(6).

609   Court of Justice, Joint Communication from Presidents Costa and Skouris, 24 January 2011, unpublished, para. 1.

610   *Ibid.*

citizens'.[611] By the end of 2011 the Court had directly set aside Union measures for Charter incompatibility on three occasions.[612] Yet tepid enthusiasm surfaces still ('[a]s regards fundamental rights, it is important, since the entry into force of the Lisbon Treaty, to take account of the Charter'[613]), and in *Dereci* (2011) the Court recognised the limits set by article 51 of the Charter and applied an (unexpectedly narrow?) interpretation to respect for family life in the context of removal of third country nationals from Austria.[614] It is therefore perhaps still too early to draw firm conclusions as to the changes which will transpire; but it is more than likely that significant change there will be. And it is no risk to predict increasing appearance of the Charter in pleadings and an acceleration in the development of fundamental rights as the Union ventures deeper into JLS activity. It is likely also to displace the Convention (and perhaps the general principles)[615] as the focus of human rights deliberations of the Court, for whilst the Union is still bound by the Convention and the Charter is presumed and required to be compatible with it (and its provisions which correspond to Convention provisions are to have the same meaning and scope)[616] and must afford protection 'no less than [that] granted by the ECHR',[617] in many respects Charter rights are broader than those of the Convention.

Another question which will inevitably arise is whether Charter terms are of **6.117** themselves sufficiently clear as to give rise to directly enforceable rights – a sword rather than a shield – and, given its status as primary law, whether they may be invoked in a horizontal legal context. It is true that the language of the Charter is of a general nature and generally without the necessary precision, but

---

611   COM(2011) 573 final, at p. 4.

612   Cases C-92 and 93/09 *Volker und Markus Schecke and anor* v *Land Hessen*, [2010] ECR I-11063, invalidating provisions of a Regulation for inconsistency with arts 7 (right to private life) and 8 (protection of personal data); Case C-236/09 *Association belge des Consummateurs Test-Achats and ors* v *Conseil des ministres*, judgment of 1 March 2011, not yet reported, invalidating provisions of a Directive on equal treatment in access to goods and services for incompatiblity with arts 21 (non-discrimination) and 23 (equality between men and women); and Cases C-411 and 493/10 *R (NS) and ME and ors* v *Secretary of State for the Home Department and ors*, judgment of 21 December 2011, not yet reported, setting aside a presumption set out in a Regulation on asylum for inconsistency with art. 4 (prohibition of inhuman or degrading treatment). In the latter judgment the Court also (at para. 113 and in the *dispositif*) directed that the conduct of national authorities, including the courts, would, if executed in a certain manner, infringe art. 4 of the Charter.

613   Case C-279/09 *DEB Deutsche Energiehandels- und Beratungsgesellschaft* v *Bundesrepublik Deutschland* [2010] ECR I-13849, at para. 30.

614   Case C-256/11 *Dereci and ors* v *Bundesministerium für Inneres*, judgment of 15 November 2011, not yet reported; especially at paras 70–2.

615   But see Case C-40/11 *Iida* v *City of Ulm*, pending, in which the Court has been asked to clarify whether and the manner in which the general principles of Union law on fundamental rights continue to apply autonomously and independently of the Charter.

616   EU Charter, art. 52(3) (the 'homogeneity clause'); Case C-400/10 PPU *JMcB* v *LE* [2010] ECR I-8965, at para. 53; Case C-279/09 *DEB Deutsche Enrgiehandels- und Beratungsgesellschaft*, n. 613 above, at para. 35.

617   Cases C-411 and 493/10 *NS and ME*, n. 612 above, *per* A-G Trstenjak at paras 145 and 148 of her opinion. Whether or not the Court delivered in its judgment is contestible.

the Court has occasionally found direct effect in less; and if a general principle of Union law can have horizontal direct effect (as it can in not yet fully explored circumstances),[618] it is no great leap to attribute that quality to a Charter right. Advocate-General Trstenjak has broached the question, analysed the issues and advised against it, at least in the context of the case at hand.[619] The Court, by silence, agreed, but it is an issue unlikely to go away.

6.118 It must be noted that the Charter is not to apply, in full, to Poland and the United Kingdom. As (part of) the price of consent to the Lisbon Treaty the UK government insisted upon a (partial) opt-out from the Charter; the Irish and the Poles reserved the right to do likewise, but the Irish came to think better of it and for their part abandoned the idea. The opt-out is thus embodied in a Treaty protocol in the following terms:

1. The Charter does not extend the ability of the Court of Justice of the European Union, or any court or tribunal of Poland or of the United Kingdom, to find that the laws, regulations or administrative provisions, practices or action of Poland or of the United Kingdom are inconsistent with the fundamental rights, freedoms and principles that it reaffirms.
2. In particular, and for the avoidance of doubt, nothing in Title IV of the Charter creates justiciable rights applicable to Poland or the United Kingdom except in so far as Poland or the United Kingdom has provided for such rights in its national law …

To the extent that a provision of the Charter refers to national laws and practices, it shall only apply to Poland or the United Kingdom to the extent that the rights or principles that it contains are recognised in the law or practices of Poland or of the United Kingdom.[620]

In order to coax final ratification of Lisbon from the Czechs, a promise was made by the heads of state and government to extend the application of the Protocol to the Czech Republic 'at the time of the conclusion of the next Accession Treaty'.[621] Thus the Lisbon Treaty has introduced and may introduce still yet more Treaty-entrenched variable geometry. The 'next Accession Treaty' (with Croatia) did nothing to meet this promise and alternative efforts to do so now stalled,[622] so it is not clear if the Czechs will gain the benefits of the Protocol, such as they are. The emphasis upon Title IV of the Charter

---

618 See 14.49 below.
619 Case C-282/10 *Dominguez* v *Centre informatique du Centre Ouest Atlantique and anor*, judgment of 24 January 2012, not yet reported.
620 Protocol (No. 30) on the Application of the Charter of Fundamental Rights to Poland and to the United Kingdom, arts 1 and 2.
621 Brussels European Council, 29–30 October 2009, Presidency Conclusions, para. I.2 and Annex I; see 2.66 above.
622 See 2.66 above.

('Solidarity' rights) marks the traditional British antipathy to Community authority in these areas, akin to the opt-out of the Social Protocol and Agreement the United Kingdom 'enjoyed' from 1993 to 1998,[623] although this is wholly at variance with the Polish position[624] which was motivated more by concern over real property rights. It is possible that the opt-out may be read down to that extent. Alternatively, its purpose was merely political, an 'insurance policy' that the Charter must not invade or permeate purely national spheres. Otherwise it is difficult to predict how the glutinous terminology will fare before the Court of Justice, and whether it will result in any practical difference at all. The Court of Appeal in England sought 'clarification' of the content and scope of the Protocol,[625] in response to which the Court found article 1(1) neither to call into question the applicability of the Charter in the United Kingdom (or Poland) nor exempt it from the obligation to comply with it nor prevent a national court from ensuring that compliance, reserving only the question of article 1(2) and rights arising under Title IV which, not in issue, required no interpretation;[626] all of which suggest the practical effect of the Protocol to be limited at best.

(b) Substance of the fundamental rights

Fundamental rights identified and considered by the Court of Justice include the following. Reference will be made to the relevant provisions of the European Convention on Human Rights ('Convention') and the EU Charter of Fundamental Rights ('Charter'), as appropriate. **6.119**

(i) Fair legal process

The right to fair legal process 'constitutes a fundamental right which the European Union respects as a general principle under Article 6(2) EU'.[627] This embraces a myriad of things. First and foremost, it requires that there be effective judicial protection – 'a general principle of EU law to which expression is now given by Article 47 of the Charter of Fundamental Rights'[628] – against all acts of the Union institutions[629] and an effective means of judicial review of **6.120**

---

623   See 14.34–14.35 below.
624   See Declaration (No. 62) by the Republic of Poland concerning the Protocol on the Application of the Charter of Fundamental Rights of the EU in relation to Poland and the United Kingdom. For the Czech concerns see 2.66 above, n. 290.
625   Cases C-411 and 493/10 *NS and ME*, n. 612 above, *per* A-G Trstenjak at para. 5 of her opinion.
626   *Ibid.* at paras 116–22 of the judgment.
627   Case C-305/05 *Ordre des barreaux francophones et germanophone and ors* v *Council* [2007] ECR I-5305, at para. 29; Case C-308/07P *Gorostiage Atxalandabaso* v *Parliament* [2009] ECR I-1059, at para. 41.
628   Case C-69/10 *Samba Diouf* v *Ministre de Travail, de l'Emploi et de l'Immigration*, judgment of 28 July 2011, not yet reported, at para. 49.
629   Convention, art. 6; Charter, art. 47, 1st para. Case T-177/01 *Jégo Quéré et Cie* v *Commission* [2002] ECR II-2365; Case T-54/99 *max.mobil* v *Commission* [2002] ECR II-313; Cases T-377 etc./00 *Philip Morris International* v *Commission* [2003] ECR II-1; Case C-432/05 *Unibet (London) and anor* v *Justitiekanslern*

any and all national measures adopted in the Union sphere.[630] In both cases the protection must be afforded by a fair and public hearing within a reasonable time by an independent and impartial tribunal (both subjectively and objectively)[631] established by law;[632] it must be said that, when its own or a Union institution's conduct is in question, the Court has taken a very generous view as to what constitutes a reasonable period of time,[633] but this is something now in flux.[634] The principle also requires that various procedural guarantees must be

---

[2007] ECR I-2271; Cases C-402 and 415/05P *Kadi and Al Barakaat* v *Council and Commission* [2008] ECR I-6351; Case T-284/08 *People's Mojehadin Organization of Iran* v *Council* [2008] ECR II-3487; Case T-390/08 *Bank Melli Iran* v *Council* [2009] ECR II-3967; Cases C-399 and 403/06P *Hassan and Ayadi* v *Council* [2009] ECR I-11393; Case T-85/09 *Kadi* v *Commission* (Kadi III) [2010] ECR II-5177 Case C-336/09 P *Commission* v *Poland*, judgment of 26 June 2012, not yet reported (a principle which is 'the very foundation' of the Union). Hence the concern expressed by A-G Jacobs in Case C-50/00P *Unión de Pequeños Agricultores* v *Council* [2002] ECR I-6677 that the difficulties encountered by natural or legal persons in meeting the rules on standing under art. 263 TFEU may be insufficient to satisfy this principle; see 5.79 above. Availability of a 'plea of illegality' is provided expressly in the Treaties (see 5.103 above) but is also recognised to be a general principle of law in this context; Case 92/78 *Simmenthal* v *Commission* [1979] ECR 777.

630   Case 222/84 *Johnston* v *Chief Constable of the RUC* [1986] ECR 1651; Case 222/86 *Union nationale des entraineurs et cadres techniques professionnels du football (Unectef)* v *Heylens* [1987] ECR 4097; Case C-97/91 *Borelli* v *Commission* [1992] ECR I-6313; Case C-50/00P *Unión de Pequeños Agricultores, ibid.*; Case C-229/05P *Ocalan* v *Council* [2007] ECR I-439, at para. 109; Case C-268/06 *Impact* v *Minister for Agriculture and Food and ors* [2008] ECR I-2483, at para. 43; Cases C-317 etc./08 *Alassini and ors* v *Telecom Italia and ors* [2010] ECR I-2213, at para. 61; Case C-279/09 *DEB*, n. 613 above, at para. 29.

631   Cases C-341 and 342/06P *Chronopost and La Poste* v *UFEX and ors* [2008] ECR I-4777, at para. 54; Case C-308/07P *Gorostiage Atxalandabaso*, n. 627 above, at para. 46.

632   Convention, art. 6; Charter, art. 47, 2nd para.

633   See Cases T-213/95 and 18/96 *Stichting Certificatie Kraanverhuurbedrijf* v *Commission* [1997] ECR II-1739; Cases C-238 etc./99P *Limburgse Vinyl Maatschappij* v *Commission* (PVC II) [2002] ECR I-8375, at paras 164–235; Cases C-120 and 121/06P *Fabbrica italiana accumulatori motocarri Montecchio (FIAMM) and anor* v *Council and Commission* [2008] ECR I-6513; Case C-322/07P *Papierfabrik August Koehler and ors* v *Commission* [2009] ECR I-7191; Case T-57/01 *Solvay* v *Commission* [2009] ECR II-4621; Case T-58/01 *Solvay* v *Commission* [2009] ECR II-4781; Case T-66/01 *Imperial Chemical Industries* v *Commission* (Soda Ash) [2010] ECR II-2631.

634   In only three pre-Lisbon cases did the Court find the temporal principle infringed: in Case C-185/95P *Baustahlgewebe* v *Commission* [1998] ECR I-8417 it remedied the breach by knocking €50,000 off a €3 million Commission fine as 'reasonable satisfaction' for the inordinate delay in proceedings before the Court of First Instance (this being 'for reasons of economy of procedure and in order to ensure an immediate and effective remedy regarding a procedural irregularity of that kind' (Cases C-120 and 121/06P *FAIMM*, n. 633 above, at para. 208)); in Case C-105/04P *Nederlandse Federatieve Vereniging voor de Groothandel op Elektrotechnisch Gebied* v *Commission* [2006] ECR I-8725 it found 'excessive duration, imputable to the Commission, of the entire administrative procedure' (at para. 51) but found no injury occasioned thereby; and in Case C-385/07P *Der Grüne Punkt – Duales System Deutschland* v *Commission* [2009] ECR I-6155 it found excessive time (almost six years) taken in proceedings before the Court of First Instance but that it would result in the setting aside of the judgment only if there was an indication that the excessive length of proceedings affected the outcome, there was none, and, *pace Baustahlgewebe*, the remedy was to be found in an action for damages under art. 288 EC (art. 340 TFEU). In Cases T-57/01 and T-58/01 *Solvay, ibid.*, both decided (on 17 December 2009) weeks after the entry into force of Lisbon, the General Court sustained Commission fines imposed by a decision in 2000 (and for conduct which ceased in 1989), the proceeding before it lasting a marathon eight years nine months, without blenching; the issue was raised on appeal (Case C-109/10P *Solvay* v *Commission* and Case C-110/10P *Solvay* v *Commission*, judgments of 25 October 2011, not yet reported) but not considered, the Commission measures set aside on other grounds. Subsequent to its 2009 *Solvay* judgments, the Commission having uncovered a cartel in the Dutch beer market, the General Court found an excessive and unjustified

respected throughout any prior administrative procedure.[635] The burden of ensuring compliance with these principles falls in the first instance to the national courts:

[T]he Member States – including the domestic courts – are ... required to ensure judicial protection of an individual's rights under Community law. It is for the Member States to ensure in each case that those rights are effectively protected. That reflects the principle of effective judicial protection which, according to settled case-law, is a general principle of Community law and forms part of the fundamental principles protected by the Community legal order;[636]

and ultimately to the Court of Justice:

[I]t is vitally important that the Court should seek to bring about a state of legal affairs not susceptible of any justified criticism with reference to the European Convention for the Protection of Human Rights. At all events, within the framework formed by the existing body of rules and the judgments handed down hitherto it must therefore be sought to ensure that legal protection within the Community meets the standard otherwise regarded as reasonable in Europe.[637]

Within an overarching principle of fair legal process may be found various **6.121** penumbrae:

- *Presumption of innocence:* '[A] fundamental right'[638] 'which [is] enforced by the Community judicature',[639] everyone is presumed innocent of wrongdoing until proven guilty according to law.[640] A measure deleterious to a person's interest may be adopted only after evidence is adduced (and notified to him) which may justify it,[641] albeit to differing standards of

---

lapse of time in Commission procedure (65 months from notification of an investigation to sending a statement of objections, 20 months thence to adoption of a decision), that this did not justify annulment of the decision as rights of defence were not jeopardised, but that a unilateral Commission reduction of €100,000 in the fines was inadequate recompense, so knocked a further 5 per cent (€1.1 million and €11 million, respectively) off the (readjusted) fines: Case T-235/07 *Bavaria* v *Commission* and Case T-240/07 *Heineken Nederland and anor* v *Commission*, judgments of 16 June 2011, not yet reported. It is unclear if the Lisbon-enhanced Charter had any bearing on this, it was not mentioned in the judgments.

635 See below.

636 Case C-268/06 *Impact*, n. 630 above, *per* A-G Kokott at paras 48–9 of her opinion.

637 Case T–1/89 *Rhône-Poulenc* v *Commission* (Polypropylene) [1991] ECR II-867, *per* acting A-G Vesterdorf at paras 885–6 of his opinion.

638 Cases T-37 and 323/07 *El Morabit* v *Council* [2009] ECR II-131*, at para. 39; Case T-49/07 *Fahas* v *Council* [2010] ECR II-5555, at para. 63.

639 Case T-49/07 *Fahas, ibid.*

640 Convention, art. 6(2); Charter, art. 48(1). Case C-235/92P *Montecatini* v *Commission* (Polypropylene) [1999] ECR I-4539; Cases T-22 and 23/02 *Sumitomo Chemical Co. and anor* v *Commission* [2005] ECR II-4065; Case T-474/04 *Pergen Hilfsstoffe für industrielle Prozesse* v *Commission* [2007] ECR II-4225; Cases T-37 and 323/07 *El Morabit*, n. 638 above; Case T-49/07 *Fahas*, n. 638 above.

641 Case T-228/02 *Organisation des Modjahedines du peuple d'Iran* v *Council* [2006] ECR I-4665.

proof depending upon the circumstances. The Court is (or claims to be) particularly resolute in circumstances in which a Union institution may impose punitive measures upon a person:

> In the latter situation, it is necessary to take account of the principle of the presumption of innocence resulting in particular from Article 6(2) of the European Convention for the Protection of Human Rights and Fundamental Freedoms, one of the fundamental rights which, according to the case-law of the Court of Justice and as reaffirmed in Article 6(2) EU, are general principles of Community law. Given the nature of the infringements in question and the nature and severity of the ensuing penalties, the principle of the presumption of innocence applies in particular to the procedures relating to infringements of the competition rules applicable to undertakings that may result in the imposition of fines or periodic penalty payments.
>
> Thus, the Commission must show precise and consistent evidence in order to establish the existence of the infringement and to support the firm conviction that the alleged infringements constitute appreciable restrictions of competition within the meaning of Article 81(1) EC.[642]

However, in the quasi-administrative, quasi-judicial proceedings which mark competition law, once a course of conduct is shown which is 'manifestly' at variance with prescribed rules the burden of proof may be reversed and it is for the accused party to show why that conduct should be exculpated.[643] The leaking to the media by the Commission of details of an impending decision and fine prior to its adoption by the college of Commissioners was found by the General Court to breach the principle, but whilst criticising the Commission roundly, it did not annul the measure since it was not established that the result would (note, not might) otherwise have been different.[644]

- *Nullum crimen, nulla poena sine lege (certa):* '[O]ne of the general legal principles underlying the constitutional traditions common to the Member States and … a specific expression of the general principle of legal certainty',[645] criminal offences and penalties for them must rest upon a

---

642 Case T-36/05 *Coats Holdings* v *Commission* [2007] ECR II-110*, at paras 70–1.

643 Case T-305 etc./94 *Limburgse Vinyl Maatschappij* v *Commission* (PVC II) [1999] ECR II-931; Case C-199/92P *Hüls* v *Commission* (Polypropylene) [1999] ECR I-4287.

644 Case T-62/98 *Volkswagen* v *Commission* [2000] ECR II-2707: 'It is settled case-law that an irregularity of the type found above may lead to annulment of the decision in question if it is established that the content of that decision would have differed [*ladite décision aurait eu un contenu différent*] if that irregularity had not occurred' (at para. 283).

645 Case C-308/06 *R (International Association of Independent Tanker Owners (Intertanko) and ors)* v *Secretary of State for Transport* [2008] ECR I-4057, at para. 70.

clear, unambiguous and lawful basis;[646] this applies also to penalties of a non-criminal nature (such as under competition rules) but with less absolute vigour. The principle is of great importance and growing application to Union activities in JLS matters which frequently touch upon criminal spheres.

- *Non-retroactivity*: A function of the principle of legal certainty,[647] a legal provision ought to apply only to situations existing after its entry into force, and the law (generally) ought not to be altered with retrospective effect. So national legislation may not retroactively curtail the available period for reclaiming sums paid in breach of a Directive,[648] and even in order to be read in conformity with an unimplemented Directive, it may not be interpreted in a manner which determines or aggravates the criminal liability of a person acting in conformity with the national law.[649] The principle applies with greatest vigour to the (purported) creation of criminal offences: 'the principle of non-retroactivity of criminal laws, enshrined in Article 7 of the ECHR as a fundamental right, constitutes a general principle of Community law which must be observed';[650] it applies less rigorously outwith the sphere of criminal law.[651] But even then, derogation is permissible only where the objective to be achieved requires it and then only upon condition that the legitimate expectations of all relevant parties are respected.[652] Nor may a heavier penalty be imposed than that which was applicable at the time of the offence; but if a penalty is lightened between commission and conviction of an offence,

---

646 Convention, art. 7; Charter, art. 49; Case 117/83 *Karl Könecke v Bundesanstalt für Landwirtschaftliche Marktordnung* [1984] ECR 3291; Case C-172/89 *Vandemoortele v Commission* [1990] ECR I-4677; Case C-198/01 *CIF Consorzio Industrie Fiammiferi v Autorità Grante della Concorrenza e del Mercato* [2003] ECR I-8055; Cases C-182 etc./02P *Dansk Rørindustri and ors v Commission* [2005] ECR I-5425, at paras 189–233; Case C-248/04 *Koninklijke Coöperatie Cosun and ors v Minister van Landbouw, Natuur en Voedselkwaliteit* [2006] ECR I-10211, at para. 80; Case C-303/05 *Advocaten voor de Wereld v Leden van Ministerrad* [2007] ECR I-3633; Case C-266/06P *Evonik Degussa v Commission* [2008] ECR I-81*, at paras 36–63; Case C-308/06 *Intertanko*, n. 646 above; Case T-99/04 *AC-Treuhand v Commission* [2008] ECR II-1501.

647 See 6.134 below.

648 Case C-62/00 *Marks and Spencer v Commissioners of Customs and Excise* [2002] ECR I-6325.

649 Case 80/86 *Officier van Justitie v Kolpinghuis Nijmegen* [1987] ECR 3969; Case C-168/95 *Criminal proceedings against Arcaro* [1996] ECR I-4705; Cases C-387 etc./02 *Criminal proceedings against Berlusconi and ors* [2005] ECR I-3565.

650 Cases C-189/02P *Dansk Rørindustri and ors v Commission* [2005] ECR I-5425, at para. 202; Case T-59/02 *Archer Daniels Midland v Commission* [2006] ECR II-3627, at para. 41; see Convention, art. 7; Charter, art. 49(1); Case 63/83 *R v Kirk* [1984] ECR 2689; Case C-550/09 *Criminal proceedings against E and F* [2010] ECR I-6213, at paras 58–62.

651 See e.g., Case 331/88 *R v Minister for Agriculture, Fisheries and Food, ex parte FEDESA* [1990] ECR I-4023; Case C-147/01 *Weber's Wine World and ors v Abgabenberufungskommission Wien* [2003] ECR I-11365; Case C-459/02 *Gerekens and anor v Luxembourg* [2004] ECR I-7315; Case C-413/04 *Parliament v Council (Estonian Energy)* [2006] ECR I-11221.

652 Case 98/78 *Racke v Hauptzollamt Mainz* [1979] ECR 69; Case C-110/97 *Netherlands v Council* [2001] ECR I-8763; Case T-251/00 *Lagardère and Canal+ v Commission* [2002] ECR II-4825; Case C-189/02P *Dansk Rørindustri*, n. 650 above.

the lighter penalty should apply – the principle of 'retroactive application of the more lenient penalty', or *lex mitior*, which forms part of the constitutional traditions common to the member states[653] and 'must be considered to be one of the general principles of Community law'.[654]

- *Non bis in idem:* The principle of *non bis in idem,* 'a fundamental principle of Community law'[655] requires that a person should not be subject to proceedings a second time for conduct in respect of which it has been declared not liable by a previous (final) judgment of a competent court, and should not be penalised twice for the same material offence.[656] Therefore, at least within the Schengen area, where a public prosecutor discontinues criminal proceedings, absent the direct involvement of a court, upon the accused meeting certain conditions, other courts are barred from proceeding with a prosecution for the same offence.[657] Whilst this is a principle applied rigorously in criminal law, it too appears to admit of a degree of porousness in the sphere of administrative proceedings and sanctions.[658]

- *Right to legal assistance:* A person is entitled to be advised, represented and defended by a lawyer when his legal rights are in issue.[659] This leads in turn to two further principles: (a) that the lawyer is entitled to see all relevant documents, and (b) that communications between lawyer and client are confidential.[660] In certain circumstances the right of access to

---

653 Case C-61/11 *Criminal proceedings against El Dridi,* judgment of 28 April 2011, not yet reported, at para. 61.

654 Case C-420/06 *Jager v Amt für Landwirtschaft Bützow* [2008] ECR I-1315, at para. 59; also Cases C-387 etc./02 *Berlusconi,* n. 649 above, at paras 66–9. It appears in the Charter, art. 49(1). In Cases T-101 and 111/05 *BASF and UCB v Commission* [2007] ECR II-4949 the Court of First Instance refused to apply the *lex mitior* rule in the competition field, but the Court of Justice subsequently noted it with approval in that context: Case C-17/10 *Toshiba Corporation and ors v Úřad pro ochranu hospodářské soutěže,* judgment of 14 February 2012, not yet reported, at para. 64.

655 Case T-24/07 *ThyssenKrupp Stainless v Commission* [2009] ECR II-2309, at para. 178.

656 Convention, Protocol 7, art. 4; Charter, art. 50; Cases 18 and 35/65 *Gutmann v Euratom Commission* [1966] ECR 103; Case 14/68 *Wilhelm v Bundeskartellamt* [1969] ECR 1; Case 7/72 *Boehringer Mannheim v Commission* [1972] ECR 1281; Cases C-238 etc./99P *Limburgse Vinyl Maatschappij v Commission* (PVC II) [2002] ECR I-8375, at paras 54–68; Case T-224/00 *Archer Daniels Midland v Commission* [2003] ECR II-2597, especially the opinion of A-G Tizzano at paras 86–118; Cases T-236 etc./01 *Tokai Carbon Co. Ltd and ors v Commission (Graphite Electrodes)* [2004] ECR II-1181, at paras 119–51; Cases C-205 etc./02P *Dansk Rørindustri and ors v Commission* [2005] ECR I-5425, at para. 202; Case C-17/10 *Toshiba,* n. 654 above, at para. 94; Case C-617/10 *Åklagaren v Åkerberg Fransson,* pending.

657 Cases C-187 and 385/01 *Criminal proceedings against Gözütok & Brügge* [2003] ECR I-1345.

658 See e.g., Cases C-238 etc./99P *Limburgse Vinyl Maatschappij,* n. 656 above; Case T-59/02 *Archer Daniels Midland v Commission* [2006] ECR II-3627, at paras 61–73; Decision 2003/2 (*Vitamins*) [2003] OJ L6/1, at paras 769–74.

659 Charter, art. 47, 2nd para.; Cases 46/87 and 227/88 *Hoechst v Commission* [1989] ECR 2859.

660 See e.g., Case 155/79 *AM&S Europe v Commission* [1982] ECR 1575; Case C-550/07P *Akzo Nobel Chemicals and anor v Commission* [2010] ECR I-8301. In Union law this applies only to 'outside' legal advice, and not to communications from 'enrolled in house lawyers' (*abhängig beschäftigter Syndikusanwalt,* the term favoured by A-G Kokott, *Akzo Nobel,* at para. 1 of her opinion) within a firm's legal department. This was reaffirmed in *Akzo Nobel,* despite spirited urging to the contrary, the reasoning being (at para. 45) that the in house lawyer does not enjoy the same degree of independence from his or her employer and is less able to deal effectively

the courts and to legal advice and representation may entail a right to legal aid.[661]

- *Protection from self-incrimination:* Whilst a person may be required to supply information and documents to a 'prosecuting' Union authority, even if the information supplied would incriminate him,[662] he cannot be compelled to answer leading questions where those answers would themselves constitute an admission of unlawful conduct, that being for the Union authority to establish;[663] this is 'acknowledged [as] one of the general principles of Community law'.[664]

- *Inviolability of premises:* The inviolability of the home is a fundamental right;[665] premises of juristic persons enjoy lesser protection but cannot be subjected to arbitrary and disproportionate intervention by public authorities.[666] Intervention may be subject to a requirement of prior judicial authority – that is, a warrant – in order to safeguard the principle.[667]

- *Audi alteram partem* and other rights of defence.[668]

The Court has recognised other fundamental rights unconnected with fair legal **6.122** process and with less frequent tangency with Union law. They include:

- *Respect for human life and dignity:* The Union legal order 'undeniably strives' to ensure respect for human life and dignity as a general principle

---

with conflicts between professional obligations and employer's interests. It is not certain the Union view could withstand a challenge under the Convention. The Court is far more generous with the Union institutions, finding that public policy requires the advice of their legal services to be afforded confidentiality, even to the extent that the advice of the Council legal service, obtained unofficially by an applicant, must be removed from the case file and any direct reference to it deleted from the application (*requête*); Case T-18/10R *Inuit Tapiriit Kanatami v Parliament and Council* [2010] ECR II-75*. However, it has said recently that advice to the Council Commission from their legal services is not necessarily privileged and they must make the case that it meets the necessary tests if they wish to withhold it; Cases L-39 and 52/05P *Sweden and Turko v Council* [2008] ECR I-4723; Case C-506/08P *Sweden v MyTravel and Commission*, judgment of 21 July 2011, not yet reported; Case T-529/09; *in't Veld v Council*, judgment of 4 May 2012, not yet reported.

661 Case C-279/09 *DEB Deutsche Energiehandels- und Beratungsgesellschaft v Bundesrepublik Deutschland* [2010] ECR I-13849.

662 Case C-301/04P *Commission v SGL Carbon* [2006] ECR I-5915.

663 See Case 374/87 *Orkem v Commission* [1989] ECR 3283; Case T-112/98 *Mannesmanröhren-Werke v Commission* [2001] ECR II-729; cf. Case C-60/92 *Otto v Postbank* [1993] ECR I-5683. As for the Strasbourg view see *Funke v France* (1993) 16 EHRR 297; *Saunders v United Kindom* (1997) 23 EHRR 313.

664 Cases T-125 and 253/03 *Akzo Nobel and anor v Commission* [2007] ECR II-3523, at para. 262.

665 Convention, art. 8(1); Charter, art. 7; Cases 46/87 and 227/88 *Hoechst v Commission* [1989] ECR 2859.

666 Cases 46/87 and 227/88 *Hoechst, ibid.*; Cases C-238/99P *Limburgse Vinyl Maatschappij and ors v Commission* (PVC II) [2002] ECR I-8375, at paras 236–57; Case C-94/00 *Roquette Frères v Directeur Général de la Concurrence* [2002] ECR I-9011.

667 *Ibid.*, especially Case C-94/00 *Roquette Frères*. The case law on entry to commercial premises indicates that a warrant may be necessary *if* national law requires it; the basic Regulation on enforcement of EU competition law (see 13.92 below), provides for a right of entry to private premises but makes prior authorisation by judicial warrant compulsory; Regulation 1/2003 [2003] OJ L1/1, art. 21.

668 See 6.138 below.

of law;[669] 'respect for human dignity does, in any event, constitute an integral part of the general legal tenets of Community law and a criterion and requirement of the legality of acts under Community law'.[670] Where called upon to consider the patentability of the processing of human embryonic stem cells the Court implicitly did so in a manner consistent with greatest respect for human dignity.[671] 'Closely related' to human dignity is respect for the fundamental rights of the child[672] and the protection of young people, 'a legitimate interest which, in principle, justifies a restriction on a fundamental freedom guaranteed by the Treaty'.[673]

- *Respect for family life:* Respect for family life 'is among the fundamental rights which ... are protected in Community law'.[674] It is a principle furthest developed, and with greatest relevance, in the context of admission, residence and/or expulsion from a member state of family members of individuals there by virtue of a Union law right,[675] but has a growing application in the context of the rights of Union citizenship[676] and Union intrusion into judicial cooperation in matrimonial matters.[677] However the Court's most recent (and unexpected?) contribution to the issue is a determination that the Treaty rights of citizenship do not extend to a right of residence for third country family members of home nationals.[678] Yet as

---

669 Convention, arts 1–4; Charter, arts 1–2; Case C-377/98 *Netherlands* v *Parliament and Council* (Biotechnological Inventions) [2001] ECR I-7079, at paras 69–81; Case C-36/02 *Omega Spielhallen- und Automatenaufstellungs* v *Oberbürgermeisterin der Bundesstadt Bonn* [2004] ECR I-9609, at para. 34.

670 Case C-36/02 *Omega Spielhallen, ibid., per* A-G Stix-Hackl at para. 90 of her opinion.

671 Case C-34/10 *Brüstle* v *Greenpeace*, judgment of 18 October 2011, not yet reported. The Advocate-General was more forceful.

672 Charter, art. 24; Case C-403/09 PPU *Detiček* v *Sgueglia* [2009] ECR I-12193.

673 Case C-244/06 *Dynamic Medien Vertriebs* v *Avides Media* [2008] ECR I-505, at para. 42.

674 Case C-441/02 *Commission* v *Germany* [2006] ECR I-3449, at para. 109; Case C-540/03 *Parliament* v *Council* (Family Reunification) [2006] ECR I-5769, at para. 52. Also Convention, art. 8; Charter, art. 7; Case C-60/00 *Carpenter* v *Secretary of State for the Home Department* [2002] ECR I-6279; Case C-109/01 *Secretary of State for the Home Department* v *Akrich* [2003] ECR I-9607; Case C-127/08 *Metock and ors* v *Minister for Justice, Equality and Law Reform*, order of 17 April 2008, unreported, at para. 14.

675 E.g., Case C-60/00 *Carpenter, ibid.*; Case C-459/99 *Mouvement contre le racisme, l'antisémitisme et la xénophobie* v *Belgian State* [2002] ECR I-6591; Case C-200/02 *Zhu and Chen* v *Secretary of State for the Home Department* [2004] ECR I-9925; Case C-291/05 *Minister voor Vreemdelingenzaken en Integratie* v *Eind* [2007] ECR I-10719; Case C-127/08 *Metock and ors* v *Minister for Justice, Equality and Law Reform* [2008] ECR I-6241; Case C-145/09 *Land Baden-Württemberg* v *Tsakouridis* [2010] ECR I-11979.

676 E.g, Case C-413/99 *Baumbast and R* v *Secretary of State for the Home Department* [2002] ECR I-7091; Case C-200/02 *Zhu and Chen* v *Secretary of State for the Home Department* [2004] ECR I-9925; Case C-34/09 *Ruiz Zambrano* v *Office national de l'emploi*, judgment of 8 March 2011, not yet reported.

677 See e.g., Case C-195/08 PPU *Rinau* [2008] ECR I-5271; Case C-403/09 PPU *Detiček* v, n. 672 above; Case C-211/10 PPU *Povse* v *Alpago* [2010] ECR I-6669; Case C-400/10 PPU *JMcB* v *LE* [2010] ECR I-8965; Case C-491/10 PPU *Aguirre Zarraga* v *Pelz* [2010] ECR I-14247; Case C-497/10 PPU *Mercredi* v *Chaffe* [2010] ECR I-14309.

678 Case C-256/11 *Dereci and ors* v *Bundesministerium für Inneres*, judgment of 15 November 2011, not yet reported.

a means of personal identification and a link to family, it extends to a right to a name, generally of the individual's choosing.[679]

- *Respect for private life:* Everyone has the right to respect for private life.[680] It extends to a duty to protect personal data,[681] the protection of privacy being a fundamental right.[682] But the case law here has been patchy. It includes 'notably' a right to keep the state of one's health a secret[683] but the right can be overridden by a public (or Union) authority where justified,[684] and whilst a person cannot be compelled to undergo medical examination in order to reveal the state of his health prior to taking up a post in a Union institution, refusal to consent to a test objectively necessary for discharging the tasks of the post will justify a refusal to employ him.[685] Various benefits in employment can be denied homosexuals[686] and lesbians,[687] but not transsexuals;[688] however, these cases were determined upon a basis of sex discrimination rather than respect for private life. It is anticipated that legislation which came into force in 2003 will right some of this imbalance.[689]

- *Freedom of expression and of assembly:* Freedom of expression is recognised as a fundamental right[690] and its exercise may legitimately hinder that of even fundamental Treaty rights.[691] Although less developed, freedom of assembly enjoys similar protection.[692] Freedom of expression extends to the maintenance of pluralism in the media, which can justify derogation from Treaty rules.[693] As regards servants of the Union institutions, freedom of expression is a fundamental right which the Court must ensure

---

679 Case C-208/09 *Sayn-Wittgenstein* v *Landeshauptmann von Wien* [2010] ECR I-13693, at para. 52.

680 Convention, art. 8; Charter, art. 7.

681 See TFEU, art. 16; Charter, art. 8; Case F-46/09 *V* v *Parliament*, judgment of 5 July 2011, not yet reported.

682 Case C-275/06 *Productores de Música de España* v *Telefónica de España* [2008] ECR I-271; Case C-73/07 *Tietosuojavaltuutettu* v *Satakunnan Markkinapörssi and anor* [2008] ECR I-9831,at paras 54–5.

683 Case C-404/92P *X* v *Commission* [1994] ECR I-4737; Case F-46/09 *V* v *Parliament*, judgment of 5 July 2011, not yet reported.

684 Case F-46/09 *V*, *ibid.*, at para. 113.

685 Case C-404/92P *X*, n. 683 above.

686 Cases C-122 and 125/99P *D* v *Council* [2001] ECR I-4319.

687 Case C-249/96 *Grant* v *South-West Trains* [1998] ECR I-621.

688 Case C-13/94 *P* v *S and Cornwall County Council* [1996] ECR I-2143; Case C-117/01 *KB* v *National Health Service Pensions Agency and anor* [2004] ECR I-541.

689 See Case C-147/08 *Römer* v *Freie und Hansestadt Hamburg*, judgment of 10 May 2011, not yet reported; as for the legislation see 14.45 below.

690 Convention, art. 10; Charter, art. 11; Case C-260/89 *Elliniki Radiophonia Tiléorassi and anor* v *Dimotiki Etairia Pliroforissis and ors*; Case C-250/06 *United Pan-Europe Communications Belgium and ors* v *État belge* [2007] ECR I-11135; Case C-73/07 *Markkinapörssi*, n. 682 above, at paras 54–55.

691 Case C-112/00 *Eugen Schmidberger, Internationale Transporte und Planzüge* v *Austria* [2003] ECR I-5659; Case C-250/06 *United Pan-Europe Communications*, *ibid.*

692 Convention, art. 11; Charter, art. 12; Case C-112/00 *Schmidberger*, *ibid.*

693 Protocol (annexed to the EC Treaty) on the system of public broadcasting in the Member States; Case C-288/89 *Stichting Collectieve Antennevoorziening Gouda and ors* v *Commissariaat voor de Media* [1991] ECR I-4007; Case C-250/06 *United Pan-Europe Communications Belgium*, n. 690 above.

is respected in Union law, overriding any duty of allegiance owed to the employer institution.[694] But having established the principle, it has since been honoured primarily in the breach.[695] Freedom of expression must be respected by the member states acting in the Union sphere but, as permitted by Strasbourg, may be limited where justified, and proportionate, in the general interest or by a pressing social need.[696]

6.123 Yet further rights, sometimes characterised as fundamental rights, include a right to property and a right to pursue a trade or profession; they are considered below.

3. Constitutional rights

6.124 The Treaty, of course, creates a great many substantive rights, but also other rights which are of the nature of general principles, and different from those generally recognised to be fundamental rights. Some predate the Treaties and have been codified subsequently, some are inherent in the Community/Union systems, and some are there by choice. They are as follows.

(a) Equal treatment or non-discrimination

6.125 The general principle of equality forms 'part of the foundations' of the Union,[697] now 'enshrined in Articles 20 and 21 of the Charter of Fundamental Rights'.[698] Put concisely, the principle of equal treatment, or non-discrimination, requires that equal, comparable, or similar situations not be treated differently, and different situations not be treated alike, unless there is in

---

694 Case 100/88 *Oyowe and Traore* v *Commission* [1989] ECR 4285.

695 Case C-274/99P *Connolly* v *Commission* [2001] ECR I-1611. Two other high profile whistleblowers exposing improprieties within the Commission (Mr van Buitenen and Miss Andreasen) were reprimanded and disciplined – and, in one of the Prodi Commission's final acts, Miss Andreasen eventually sacked. She challenged her dismissal unsuccessfully; Case T-17/08P *Andreasen* v *Commission*, judgment of 9 September 2010, not yet reported. It is worth noting that Mr van Buitenen was elected an MEP from the Netherlands (Verts/ALE) in 2004, Miss Andreasen in 2009, standing for the UK Independence Party (UKIP) – an impressive achievement for an Argentine-Spaniard resident in Barcelona. Nor has the Tillack affair (as to which see 4.16 above, n. 85) covered the institutions with glory.

696 Case C-368/95 *Vereinigte Familiapress* v *Heinrich Bauer Verlag* [1997] ECR I-3689; Case C-112/00 *Schmidberger*, n. 691 above; Case C-71/02 *Herbert Karner Industrie Auktionen* v *Troostwijk* [2004] ECR I-3025.

697 Cases 117/76 and 17/77 *Ruckdeschel and anor* v *Hauptzollamt Hamburg-St. Annen* [1977] ECR 1753, at para. 7 ('one of the fundamental principles of Community law'); Case C-17/05 *Cadman* v *Health & Safety Executive* [2006] ECR I-9583; Case C-427/06 *Bartsch* v *Bosch und Siemens Hausgeräte (BSH) Altersfürsorge* [2008] ECR I-7245, *per* A-G Sharpston at para. 42 of her opinion; Case C-101/08 *Audiolux* v *Groupe Bruxelles Lambert and ors* [2009] ECR I-9823, *per* A-G Trstenjak at para. 50 of her opinion.

698 C-550/07P *Akzo Nobel Chemicals and anor* v *Commission* [2010] ECR I-8301, at para. 54. Cases 117/76 and 17/77 *Ruckdeschel and anor* v *Hauptzollamt Hamburg-St. Annen* [1977] ECR 1753, at para. 7 ('one of the fundamental principles of Community law'); Case C-17/05 *Cadman* v *Health & Safety Executive* [2006] ECR I-9583; Case C-427/06 *Bartsch, ibid., per* A-G Sharpston at para. 42 of her opinion; Case C-101/08 *Audiolux ibid., per* A-G Trstenjak at para. 50 of her opinion.

either case objective justification for doing so.[699] The principle found expression in the original EEC Treaty in three specific areas: a prohibition of discrimination based upon nationality, both general ('[w]ithin the scope of application of thisTreaty')[700] and specific to a number of subject areas;[701] a prohibition of discrimination amongst producers and consumers in the common organisation of agricultural markets[702] ('merely a specific expression of the general principle of equal treatment');[703] and a prohibition of discrimination between men and women in the area of pay in employment.[704] The prohibition of discrimination on grounds of nationality remains fundamental to Union development and the *ne plus ultra* in the field: 'of all the grounds for discrimination prohibited by European Union law that based on nationality is particularly serious'.[705] It was re-emphasised by its inclusion by Lisbon in Part Two of the TFEU alongside Union citizenship.[706] But it is a principle equally applicable elsewhere. So, discrimination between agricultural sectors is impermissible even where not expressly proscribed by the Treaty;[707] rules on the transfer of pension rights to a Union scheme (for employees of the institutions) cannot discriminate between employed and self-employed persons;[708] an author or performer claiming copyright (or similar) protection afforded by the law of a member state cannot be subject to distinguishing criteria based upon the

699   E.g. Case 106/83 *Sermide* v *Cassa Conguaglio Zucchero and ors* [1984] ECR 4209; Case C-280/93 *Germany* v *Council* (Bananas) [1994] ECR I-4973; Case C-354/95 *R* v *Minister for Agriculture, Fisheries and Food, ex parte National Farmers' Union and ors* [1997] ECR I-4559; Case C-180/96 *United Kingdom* v *Commission* (BSE) [1998] ECR I-2265; Case T-311/94 *BPB de Eendracht* v *Commission* (Cartonboard) [1998] ECR II-1129; Cases C-27 and 122/00 *R* v *Secretary of State for the Environment, Transport and the Regions, ex parte Omega Air* [2002] ECR I-2569; Case T-213/00 *CMA CGM and ors* v *Commission* [2003] ECR II-913, at paras 405–32; Case C-210/03 *R (Swedish Match AB and anor)* v *Secretary of State for Health* [2004] ECR I-11893; Cases C-453 etc./03 *R (ABNA and ors)* v *Secretary of State for Health and ors* [2005] ECR I-10423; Case C-313/04 *Franz Egenberger* v *Bundesanstalt für Landwirtschaft und Ernährung* [2006] ECR I-6331; Case C-127/07 *Société Arcelor Atlantique et Lorraine and ors* v *Premier ministre and ors* [2008] ECR I-9895, at para. 23; Case C-236/09 *Association belge des Consummateurs Test-Achats and ors* v *Conseil des ministres*, judgment of 1 March 2011, not yet reported, at para. 28.
700   EEC Treaty, art. 7; see 8.02 below.
701   E.g., *ibid.* art. 37(1) (adjustment of commercial monopolies); art. 48(2) (workers); art. 52 (establishment, implicitly; Case 2/74 *Reyners* v *Belgian State* [1974] ECR 631); arts 60, 2nd para. and 65 (services); art. 67(1) (capital); art. 79(1) (transport rates and conditions); art. 221 (participation in the capital of companies or firms).
702   *Ibid.* art. 40(3).
703   Case C-313/04 *Franz Egenberger* v *Bundesandtalt für Landwirtschaft und Ernährung* [2006] ECR I-6331, at para. 33.
704   EEC Treaty, art. 119; see 14.38 below.
705   Case C-47/08 *Commission* v *Belgium*, Case C-51/08 *Commission* v *Luxembourg*, Case C-52/08 *Commission* v *Portugal*, Case C-53/08 *Commission* v *Austria*, Case C-54/08 *Commission* v *Germany* and Case C-61/08 *Commission* v *Greece*, judgments of 24 May 2011 (the 'Notaries judgments'), not yet reported, *per* A-G Cruz Villalón at para. 129 of his opinion.
706   See 8.01 below.
707   Cases 117/76 and 16/77 *Ruckdeschel* v *Hauptzollamt Hamburg-St Annen* [1977] ECR 1753; Case C-315/93 *Flip et Verdegem* v *Belgium* [1995] ECR I-913.
708   Case C-37/89 *Weiser* v *Caisse Nationale des Barreaux Français* [1990] ECR I-2395.

member state of origin of the protected work;[709] where financial penalties are imposed upon persons they must, in the absence of objective justification for doing otherwise, be determined and computed by the same method;[710] and a reduction in penalty afforded parties for compliance with a (clear) leniency policy must be equal where the degree of compliance is the same[711] and greater for a party which can show a greater degree of compliance.[712] The prohibition applies equally to both direct and indirect (or covert) discrimination,[713] although neither has been defined by the Court of Justice and the distinction between the two lacks precision.[714] But there is an important difference between them, for a national measure which discriminates indirectly upon grounds of, for example, nationality may be justified by reference to objective considerations independent of the nationality of the individuals concerned and proportionate to their legitimate aim,[715] whilst directly discriminatory measures cannot. In order that it be effective the right to equal treatment may give rise to a duty of transparency (it is 'a concrete and specific expression of the principle of equal treatment'[716]) which may be enforceable of itself where absent.[717]

6.126 There is, of course, a raft of legislation applying the principle in greater detail in a specific context – for example, a prohibition of discrimination amongst migrant workers in access to the labour market and ancillary rights.[718]

6.127 The Treaty of Amsterdam added an integration clause to the EC Treaty, providing that the Community 'aim to eliminate inequalities, and ... promote equality, between men and women' across all its activities,[719] and the EU

---

709   Cases C-92 and 326/92 *Phil Collins* v *Imtrat* [1993] ECR I-5145.

710   Case C-280/98P *Weig* v *Commission* [2000] ECR I-9757; Case C-291/98P *Sarrió* v *Commission* [2000] ECR I-9991; Case T-354/94 *Stora Kopparbergs Bergslags* v *Commission* [2002] ECR II-843 (all *Cartonboard* cases).

711   Case T-13/03 *Nintendo and anor* v *Commission* [2009] ECR II-975.

712   Case T-31/99 *ABB Asea Brown Boveri* v *Commission* [2002] ECR II-1881.

713   Case C-137/09 *Josemans* v *Burgemeester van Maastricht*, [2010] ECR I-13019, at para. 58 and case law cited.

714   For optimal clarification see the opinion of A-G Sharpston in Case C-73/08 *Bressol and Chaverot and ors* v *Gouvernement de la Communauté française* [2010] ECR I-2735 – cited by the UK Supreme Court as 'a lengthy, scholarly and closely-reasoned discussion' of the issues; *Patmalniece* v *Secretary of State for Work and Pensions* [2011] UKSC 11, [2011] 3 All ER 1, *per* Lord Walker at para. 63. The judgment of the Court failed to shed further light, which Lord Walker met with 'regret'; para. 64.

715   Case C-138/02 *Collins* v *Secretary of State for Work and Pensions* [2004] ECR I-2703; Case C-209/03 *R (Bidar)* v *London Borough of Ealing and anor* [2005] ECR I-2119; Case C-73/08 *Bressol and Chaverot, ibid.*

716   Case C-91/08 *Wall* v *Stadt Frankfurt am Main and anor* [2010] ECR I-2815, *per* A-G Bot at para. 34 of his opinion.

717   Case C-324/98 *Telaustria Verlags and anor* v *Telekom Austria* [2000] ECR I-10745; Case C-458/03 *Parking Brixen* v *Gemeinde Brixen and anor* [2005] ECR I-8585; Case C-91/08 *Wall, ibid.*

718   Case C-17/05 *Cadman* v *Health & Safety Executive* [2006] ECR I-9583, at para. 28.

719   EC Treaty, art. 3(2); now TFEU, art. 8.

Charter now provides for equality before the law,[720] a prohibition of discrimination based upon nationality[721] and upon 'any ground such as sex, race, colour, ethnic or social origin, genetic features, language, religion or belief, political or any other opinion, membership of a national minority, property, birth, disability, age or sexual orientation',[722] and equality between men and women 'in all areas'.[723] Thus '[t]he Court has consistently stressed the fundamental importance of the principle of equal treatment for men and women'[724] and 'the right not to be discriminated against on grounds of sex is one of the fundamental human rights the observance of which the Court has a duty to ensure'.[725] It is an important aspect of Union social policy, and is discussed below in that context.[726]

The EC Treaty was amended by the Single European Act to enable the Council **6.128** to adopt legislation to combat discrimination based upon nationality[727] and by Amsterdam to adopt legislation to combat discrimination based upon sex, racial or ethnic origin, religion or belief, disability, age or sexual orientation,[728] this being 'an expression of the commitment of the Community legal order to the principle of equal treatment and non-discrimination'.[729] Three Directives (the 'anti-discrimination Directives') have been adopted by the latter authority,[730] a fourth ('the Directive on Equal Treatment') proposed and, at the time of writing, before the Council.[731] They too are an aspect of Union social policy and of the rapidly growing social dimension of European citizenship, and are considered in greater detail below.[732]

(b) Proportionality, subsidiarity, democracy

The rubric of constitutional rights would extend to the principles of: **6.129**

---

720 Charter, art. 20.
721 *Ibid.* art. 21(2).
722 *Ibid.* art. 21(1).
723 *Ibid.* art. 23.
724 Case C-236/09 *Association Belge des Consummateurs Test-Achats and ors* v *Conseil des ministres*, judgment of 1 March 2011, not yet reported, *per* A-G Kokott at para. 31 of her opinion.
725 Case C-423/04 *Richards* v *Secretary of State for Work and Pensions* [2006] ECR I-3585, at para. 23.
726 See 14.37–14.43 below.
727 EC Treaty, art. 12, 2nd para; see e.g., Directive 93/96 [1993] OJ L317/59 on right of residence for students.
728 EC Treaty, art. 13; now TFEU, art. 19.
729 Case C-303/06 *Coleman* v *Attridge Law and anor* [2008] ECR I-5603, *per* A-G Poiares Maduro at para. 8 of his opinion.
730 Directive 2000/43 [2000] OJ L180/22 on equal treatment of persons irrespective of racial or ethnic origin; Directive 2000/78 [2000] OJ L303/16 on equal treatment in employment and occupation; Directive 2004/113 [2004] OJ L373/37 on equal treatment between men and women in access to and supply of goods and services.
731 Proposal for a Council Directive implementing the principle of equal treatment between persons irrespective of religion or belief, disability, age or sexual orientation, COM(2008) 426 final.
732 See 14.45–14.46 below.

- proportionality, long a general principle of Community law, incorporated into the Treaties expressly by Maaastricht;
- subsidiarity, not necessarily inherent in the Treaties but a principle embraced by the drafters of the Maastricht Treaty and incorporated into the Treaties thereby; and
- democracy, come late to the Treaties (expressly) with Lisbon.

Each is now elevated to near the head of the TEU, proportionality and subsidiarity amongst the common provisions of Title I governing the use of Union competences,[733] democratic principles meriting a Title of their own.[734] Each is of significant and increasing importance in the operation of the Union institutions. They are discussed above.[735]

4. Social and economic rights

(a) Right to property

6.130 Everyone is entitled to the peaceful enjoyment of his possessions, and no one may be deprived of them except in the public interest and subject to the conditions provided for by law.[736] The right has been expressly recognised by the Court of Justice as a general principle:[737] it is 'certainly one of the fundamental rights whose observance is ensured by the Court'.[738] Since the creation and definition of property rights is a matter reserved largely and primarily to the member states,[739] the normal point of tangency between a property right and Union law is the commercial use to which property is, or may be, put; it is a tension which has particular resonance in Germany.[740] But in all member states, including Germany, there are limitations to such rights imposed and regulated by law. Therefore a property right may in Union law be made subject to restrictions, sometimes 'to a considerable degree',[741] provided that

---

733 TEU, art. 5(3), (4). Subsidiarity could be said to be recognised also in art. 1, 2nd para.
734 TEU, Title II. Democracy is also one of the values upon which the Union is founded, art. 2 TEU.
735 See 2.28–2.32 and 2.37–2.39 above.
736 Convention, Protocol 7, art. 1; Charter, art. 17.
737 Case 4/73 *Nold* v *Commission* [1974] ECR 491; Case 44/79 *Hauer* v *Land Rheinland-Pfalz* [1979] ECR 3727; Case 5/88 *Wachauf* v *Germany* [1989] ECR 2609; Case C-84/95 *Bosphorus Hava Yollari Turizm ve Ticaret* v *Minister for Transport, Energy and Communications* [1996] I-3953; Cases C-20 and 64/00 *Booker Aquaculture and anor* v *Scottish Ministers* [2003] ECR I-7411; Cases C-154 and 155/04 *R (Alliance for National Health and ors)* v *Secretary of State for Health and anor* [2005] ECR I-6451; Cases C-120 and 121/06P *Fabbrica italiana accumulatori motocarri Montecchio (FIAMM) and anor* v *Council and Commission* [2008] ECR I-6513, at para. 183; Case T-16/04 *Arcelor* v *Parliament and Council* [2010] ECR II-211, at para. 153.
738 Case C-22/94 *Irish Farmers Association and ors* v *Minister for Agriculture, Food and Forestry* [1997] ECR I-1809, at para. 27; Case T-390/08 *Bank Melli Iran* v *Council* [2009] ECR II-3967, at para. 70.
739 TFEU, art. 345 (ex art. 295 EC); see 10.78–10.80 below.
740   See BVerfG, 7. Juni 2000 (*Bananenmarktordnung* or *Solange III*), BVerfGE 102, 147.
741 Case T-390/08 *Bank Melli Iran*, n. 738 above, at para. 71.

they in fact correspond to objectives of general interest pursued by the Union and do not constitute, with regard to their aim, disproportionate and intolerable interference undermining the very substance of the right.[742] This extends to the impounding of aircraft (as a function of UN Security Council sanctions),[743] the freezing of an individual's assets (in a non-arbitrary manner),[744] and even to a finding that a Directive compulsorily requiring the destruction of property (*in casu* 'farmed' fish with, or subject to a risk of, a viral disease) does not give rise to a duty to compensate the owner.[745] In only one area (in a rapidly growing number of directly related cases) has the Court found the right to be unfairly restricted.[746]

(b)   Right to pursue a trade or profession

In much the same way (and based, again, upon German inspiration) the Court **6.131** has recognised a basic right to pursue a trade or profession.[747] Rules alleged to inhibit this right arise most frequently, in Union law, in the context of quotas and levies fixed under a common organisation of an agricultural market.[748] But like and in the same manner as the right to property – and the two are sometimes pleaded in tandem[749] – the right can be restricted in the public

---

742   Case 5/88 *Wachauf* v *Germany* [1989] ECR 2609; Case C-177/90 *Kühn* v *Landwirtschaftskammer Weser-Ems* [1992] ECR I-35, at para. 16; Cases C-154 and 155/04 *Alliance for Natural Health*, n. 737 above, at para. 126; Cases C-120 and 121/06P *FIAMM*, n. 737 above, at para. 184; Case C-548/09P *Bank Melli Iran* v *Council*, judgment of 16 November 2011, not yet reported, at para. 114.

743   Case C-84/95 *Bosphorus*, n. 737 above.

744   Case C-117/06 *Möllendorf and Möllendorf-Niehuus* [2007] ECR I-8361.

745   Cases C-20 and 64/00 *Booker Aquaculture and anor* v *Scottish Ministers* [2003] ECR I-7411. However if legislation does provide for compensation for the destruction of some property it may be a breach of the principle of non-discrimination not to provide it for other property; Case C-315/93 *Flip et Verdegem* v *Belgium* [1995] ECR I-913.

746   Cases C-402 &and415/05P *Kadi and Al Barakaat* v *Council and Commission* [2008] ECR I-6351; Case T-318/01 *Othman* v *Council and Commission* [2009] ECR II-1627; Cases C-399 and 403/06P *Hassan &andAyadi* v *Council* [2009] ECR I-11393; Case C-550/09 *Criminal proceedings against E and F* [2010] ECR I-6213; Cases T-135 etc./06 *Al-Faqih and ors* v *Council,* [2010] ECR II-208*; Case T-85/09 *Kadi* v *Commission* (Kadi III) [2010] ECR II-5177; Case T-86/11 *Bamba v Council*, judgment of 8 June 2011, not yet reported; Case T-341/07 *Sison* v *Council* (Sison III), judgment of 23 November 2011, not yet reported; Case C-376/10P *Tay Za* v *Council*, judgment of 13 March 2012, not yet reported. They all involve restrictive measures and freezing of assets adopted by the Council and/or Commission in implementation of UN Security Council resolutions. Some seven dozen like cases have been raised before the General Court in 2011.

747   Charter, art. 15(1); Case 44/79 *Hauer* v *Land Rheinland-Pfalz* [1979] ECR 3727; Case 265/87 *Schräder* v *Hauptzollamt Gronau* [1989] ECR 2237; Case C-280/93 *Germany* v *Council* (Bananas) [1994] ECR I-4973; Cases C-184 and 223/02 *Spain and Finland* v *Parliament and Council* [2004] ECR I-7789; Case C-210/03 *R (Swedish Match AB and anor)* v *Secretary of State for Health* [2004] ECR I-11893; Cases C-120 and 121/06P *FIAMM*, n. 737 above; Case T-390/08 *Bank Melli Iran*, n. 738 above; Case T-16/04 *Arcelor* v *Parliament and Council* [2010] ECR II-211, at para. 153.

748   See e.g., Case 230/78 *Eridania Zuccherifici nazionale* v *Minister of Agriculture and Forestry* [1979] ECR 2749; Case 5/88 *Wachauf* v *Germany* [1989] ECR 2609.

749   See e.g., Cases C-154 and 155/04 *R (Alliance for National Health and ors)* v *Secretary of State for Health and anor* [2005] ECR I-6451; Cases C-120 and 121/06P *FIAMM*, n. 737 above; Case T-390/08 *Bank Melli Iran*, n. 738 above.

interest. Even Strasbourg takes a fairly generous view of the breadth of permissible limitations.[750] There is no case of the Court finding the right infringed.

6.132 In employment, there is a basic right to paid annual leave. It is recognised by both the Charter of Fundamental Rights[751] and the European Social Charter,[752] and whilst not (yet) recognised by the Court of Justice as a 'fundamental' right, it is 'a particularly important principle of Community social law',[753] and the right of every worker[754] from which there can be no derogations.[755]

(c) Collective rights

6.133 The Court of Justice has recognised as fundamental the individual right to form and join an association and the right to take action collectively.[756] Giving the general propositions more substance, according to Advocate-General Jacobs the Union legal order protects the right to form and join trade unions and employers' associations which is at the heart of freedom of association and the right to take collective action in order to protect occupational interests in so far as it is indispensable for the enjoyment of that freedom;[757] this has hardened latterly, perhaps a function of the elevation of the Charter to Treaty value, into a fundamental right to bargain collectively.[758] The Court has also said 'the right to take collective action, including the right to strike, must ... be recognised as a fundamental right which forms an integral part of the general principles of Community law',[759] but refused to permit it to be exercised in order to hinder a firm from relocating in another member state (the right of establishment).

Social and economic rights would also embrace:

---

750 See e.g., *Pinnacle Meat Processors* v *United Kingdom* (1998) 27 EHRR CD 217.
751 Charter, art. 31(2).
752 Social Charter, art. 2(3).
753 Cases C-350 and 520/06 *Schultz-Hoff* v *Deutsche Rentversicherung Bund* and *Stringer and ors* v *Her Majesty's Revenue and Customs* [2009] ECR I-179, at paras 22, 54.
754 *Ibid.* at para. 54.
755 *Ibid.* at para. 22.
756 Charter, arts 12(1), 28; European Social Charter, art. 6(4); Case 175/73 *Union syndicale – Service public européen – Bruxelles and ors* v *Council* [1974] ECR 917; Cases C-193 and 194/87 *Maurissen and European Public Service Union* v *Court of Auditors* [1990] ECR I-95; Case C-415/93 *Union Royale Belge des Sociétés de Football Association ASBL* v *Bosman* [1995] ECR I-4921; Case C-438/05 *International Transport Workers' Federation* v *Viking Line* [2007] ECR I-10779; Case C-341/05 *Laval un Partneri* v *Svenska Byggnadsarbetareförbundet and ors* (Vaxholm) [2007] ECR I-11767; Case C-271/08 *Commission* v *Germany* [2010] ECR I-7087.
757 Case C-67/96 *Albany International* v *Stichting Bedrijfspensioenfonds Textielindustrie* [1999] ECR I-5751, at paras 132–64 of his opinion.
758 Case C-271/08 *Commission v Germany*, n. 756 above, at paras 37, 38.
759 Case C-438/05 *Viking Line*, n. 756 above, at para. 44.

(d) Legal certainty

The principle of legal certainty is 'a fundamental principle of Community **6.134** law'.[760] The basic premise is that rules imposing obligations on persons ought to be clear and precise so that they may know without ambiguity their rights and obligations, and so take steps accordingly.[761] The rule applies equally (it 'also must be observed, and have the same consequences') to national legislation which gives effect to Community/Union legislation,[762] which must therefore be implemented with unquestionably binding force and with specificity, precision and clarity.[763] Thus, unpublished legislation of general application is of no legal effect,[764] and a person is not bound by any obligation contained even in directly applicable Union legislation (a Regulation) if he could not reasonably have known of it.[765] More generally, the principle requires that application of the law to a specific situation ought to be predictable. Where a rule of law imposes an obligation upon an individual, 'strict observance of the requirements flowing from the principle of legal certainty and the protection of the individual is naturally of particular importance'.[766] Non-retroactivity of legislation is a natural consequence,[767] and *nullum crimen, nulla poena sine lege (certa)* a corollary[768] or a specific expression,[769] of legal certainty. The Court of Justice applies the principle also when it declares the provisions of a measure it has annulled to be operative[770] and when, exceptionally, it limits the temporal effects of an interpretative judgment which is new, genuinely unforeseen and likely to give rise to significant difficulty.[771] Nor ought national law to be disapplied by reference to a Union rule where adherence to the former was compulsory and its disapplication would result in persons bound by it being exposed to serious

---

760 Case C-308/06 *R (International Association of Independent Tanker Owners (Intertanko) and ors)* v *Secretary of State for Transport* [2008] ECR I-4057, at para. 69; Case C-158/07 *Förster* v *Hoofddirectie van de Informatie Beheer Groep* [2008] ECR I-8507, *per* A-G Mazák at para. 140 of his opinion.

761 Case 169/80 *Administration des Douanes* v *Gondrand Frères* [1981] ECR 1931; Case C-108/01 *Consorzio del Prosciutto di Parma* v *Asda Stores and anor* [2003] ECR I-5121; Case C-236/02 *Slob* v *Productschap Zuivel* [2004] ECR I-1861; Cases T-22 and 23/02 *Sumitomo Chemical Co and anor* v *Commission* [2005] ECR II-4065; Case C-308/06 *Intertanko, ibid.*; Case C-345/06 *Heinrich* [2009] ECR I-1659.

762 Case C-345/06 *Heinrich, ibid.*, at para. 45.

763 Case C-313/99 *Mulligan and ors* v *Minister for Agriculture and Food* [2002] ECR I-5719.

764 Case C-345/06 *Heinrich*, n. 761 above; Case C-313/99 *Mulligan, ibid.*.

765 Case C-108/01 *Consorzio del Prosciutto di Parma and anor* v *Asda Stores and anor* [2003] ECR I-5121.

766 Case C-158/07 *Förster* v *Hoofddirectie van de Informatie Beheer Groep* [2008] ECR I-8507, *per* A-G Mazák at para. 141 of his opinion.

767 See 6.121 above.

768 Cases C-74 and 129/95 *Criminal proceedings against X* [1996] ECR I-6609, at para. 25. A further corallary is that any penalty imposed must have a proper and clear basis in law; Case T-279/02 *Degussa* v *Commission* [2006] ECR II-897, at para. 66.

769 Case C-308/06 *Intertanko*, n. 760 above, at para. 70.

770 See 5.83 above.

771 See 5.143 above.

penalties.[772] Time bars serve legal certainty – they are 'an application of the fundamental principle of legal certainty'[773] – on the flip side of the coin. Thus it is that an administrative act addressed to several persons remains binding for those who failed timeously to raise review proceedings, even if it is annulled subsequently in proceedings raised by others,[774] here legal certainly overriding the principle of legality. The same precedence is accorded the principle of *res judicata*,[775] one common to the law of the member states[776] and of which the Court of Justice 'has recognised the fundamental importance'.[777] So fundamental are these principles that they may override even the primacy of Union law: where a national administrative measure is confirmed by a judgment of last instance, but that judgment shown subsequently to have erred owing to a later judgment of the Court of Justice, Union law does not require that the original judgment be re-opened.[778] This recognises the force of *res judicata* and 'contributes to such legal certainty'.[779] It applies also to the judgment of a lower court which has hardened into *res judicata*:

> Community law does not require a national court to disapply domestic rules of procedure conferring finality on a decision, even if to do so would enable it to remedy an infringement of Community law by the decision at issue.[780]

Of course, the aggrieved party may have a remedy in damages.[781]

6.135 From the general principle of legal certainty spring other principles:

- *Legitimate expectation:* Drawn from German administrative law (*Vertrauensschutzprinzip*), a 'corollary of the principle of legal certainty'[782] and 'one of the fundamental principles of the Community',[783] legitimate expectation means that a person is entitled to act (and conduct his

---

772   Case C-198/01 *CIF Consorzio Industrie Fiammiferi* v *Autorità Grante della Concorrenza e del Mercato* [2003] ECR I-8055.

773   Case C-327/00 *Santex* v *Unità Socio Sanitaria Locale n. 42 di Pavia* [2003] ECR I-1877, at para. 52.

774   Case C-310/97P *Commission* v *AssiDomän Kraft Products* [1999] ECR I-5363.

775   Case C-234/04 *Kapferer* v *Schlank & Schick* [2006] ECR I-2585; Case C-2/06 *Willy Kempter* v *Hauptzollamt Hamburg-Jonas* [2008] ECR I-411.

776   Case T-341/07 *Sison* v *Council* (Sison III), judgment of 23 November 2011, not yet reported, at para. 23.

777   Case T-24/07 *ThyssenKrupp Stainless* v *Commission* [2009] ECR II-2309, at para. 112.

778   Case C-453/00 *Kühne & Heitz* v *Productschap voor Pluimvee en Eieren* [2004] ECR I-837. But Union law does not preclude it, if certain conditions are satisfied; see para. 28.

779   Case C-453/00 *Kühne & Heitz*, *ibid.*, at para. 24.

780   Case C-234/04 *Kapferer*, n. 775 above, at para. 21; applied in *R* v *Budomir and anor* [2010] EWCA Crim. 1486, [2010] 2 Cr. App. Rep. 310.

781   See 6.38 above.

782   Case C-63/93 *Duff and ors* v *Minister for Agriculture and Food* [1996] ECR I-569, at para. 20; Case C-562/07 *Commission* v *Spain* [2009] ECR I-9553, at para. 18.

783   Case 112/80 *Dürbeck* v *Hauptzollamt Frankfurt am Main-Flughafen* [1981] ECR 1095, at para. 48; Case C-310/04 *Spain* v *Council* [2006] ECR I-7285, at para. 81.

business) in the reasonable expectation that the law as it exists will continue to apply. A prohibition of legislation having retroactive effect, and the specific principle *nulla poena sine lege*,[784] are clear facets of the rule. Further, no measure can be applied to a person if it has been inadequately publicised, so that the person has had no reasonable opportunity to acquaint himself with it;[785] and where a measure takes effect upon publication in the *Official Journal*, publication cannot be backdated.[786] But it is necessary to be wary of it as a broad principle, for it could lead to legislative paralysis. Therefore a trader cannot have a legitimate expectation that an existing situation which is capable of being altered by the Union institutions in the exercise of their discretion will be maintained:

> [A]ny economic operator on whose part an institution has promoted reasonable expectations may rely on the principle of the protection of legitimate expectations. However, if a prudent and circumspect operator could have foreseen that the adoption of a Community measure is likely to affect his interests, he cannot plead that principle if the measure is adopted ... [E]conomic operators are not justified in having a legitimate expectation that an existing situation which is capable of being altered by the Community institutions in the exercise of their discretionary power will be maintained, particularly in an area ... the objective of which involves constant adjustment to reflect changes in economic circumstances.[787]

Whilst as a general rule, in the absence of transitional provisions new rules apply immediately to the future effects of a situation which arose under the old rules,[788] even in the face of legislative change a trader may rely upon a legitimate expectation that goods in transit to the Union will not be turned away upon arrival by application of new law, save for reasons of overriding public interest.[789] On the administrative plane, it

> is one of the fundamental principles of the Community [and] extends to any individual in a situation where it is clear that the Community administration has, by giving him precise assurances, led him to entertain reasonable expectations.[790]

---

784   See 6.121 above.
785   Case 98/78 *Racke* v *Hauptzollamt Mainz* [1979] ECR 69; Case C-108/01 *Consorzio del Prosciutto di Parma* v *Asda Stores and anor* [2003] ECR I-5121; see especially paras 116–45 of A-G Alber's opinion.
786   Case 98/78 *Racke, ibid.*; Case T-115/94 *Opel Austria* v *Council* [1997] ECR II-39.
787   Case C-310/04 *Spain* v *Council*, n. 783 above, at para. 81; see also Case 350/88 *Delacre and ors* v *Commission* [1990] ECR I-395; Case T-31/99 *ABB Brown Boveri* v *Commission* [2002] ECR II-1881; Cases C-154 and 155/04 *R (Alliance for Natural Health and ors)* v *Secretary of State for Health and anor* [2005] ECR I-6451, at para. 128.
788   Case C-162/00 *Land Nordrhein-Westfalen* v *Pokrzeptowicz-Meyer* [2002] ECR I-1049; Case C-512/99 *Germany* v *Commission* [2003] ECR I-845.
789   Case 152/88 *Sofrimport* v *Commission* [1990] ECR I-2477; Case C-183/95 *Affish* v *Rijksdienst voor de Keuring van Vee en Vlees* [1997] ECR I-4315.
790   Case T-471/04 *Karatzoglou* v *European Agency for Reconstruction* [2006] ECR-SC II-A-2-157, at para. 33. See also Case T-76/98 *Hamptaux* v *Commission* [1999] ECR-SC II-303, at para. 47; Case T-266/97 *Vlaamse*

To be reliable the assurances ought to be precise, unconditional and consistent ('preconditions for establishing the existence of a legitimate expectation')[791], and from authorised, reliable sources.[792] Yet they may be explicit or implicit – for example, long established practice,[793] notices or other soft law devices,[794] tacit acquiescence[795] or other form of inducement to a course of conduct. Where they exist, a Union institution is estopped from behaving in a contrary manner.[796] A legitimate expectation may exist in a procedural right as well as a substantive right.[797] But the principle cannot be relied upon by a party which has committed a flagrant infringement of the rules in force.[798] Breach of the principle is actionable in damages.[799]

A logical inversion of legitimate expectation, '[i]t is clear beyond doubt that it is a general principle of European Union law that abuse of rights is prohibited'.[800] In other words, an enforceable EU right can neither derive from fraudulent or abusive conduct nor be used for fraudulent or abusive ends;[801] nor may a person take advantage, improperly or fraudulently, of Union law in order to escape the effects of national laws.[802]

Televisie Maatschappij v *Commission* [1999] ECR II-2329, at para. 71; Case T-65/98 *Van den Bergh Foods* v *Commission* [2003] ECR II-4653, at para. 192.

791 Case T-471/04 *Karatzoglou* v *European Agency for Reconstruction*, judgment of 2 December 2008, not yet reported, at para. 41.

792 Case T-203/97 *Forvass* v *Commission* [1999] ECR-SC II-705, at para. 70; Case T-20/03 *Kahla/Thüringen Porzellan* v *Commission* [2008] ECR II-2305, at para. 146; Case T-13/03 *Nintendo and anor* v *Commission* [2009] ECR II-975, at paras 203 and 208.

793 Case T-310/00 *MCI* v *Commission* [2004] ECR II-3253.

794 See e.g., Notice on agreements of minor importance [2001] OJ C368/13, para. 4; Notice on immunity from fines and reduction of fines in cartel cases [2006] OJ C298/17, para. 38: 'The Commission is aware that this notice will create legitimate expectations on which undertakings may rely'.

795 Case 223/85 *Rijn-Schelde-Verolme* v *Commission* [1987] ECR 4617. But not all silence, 'however regrettable it may be', constitutes tacit acquiescence; Case T-123/89 *Chomel* v *Commission* [1990] ECR II-131.

796 See Case 74/74 *Comptoir National Technique Agricole* v *Commission* [1975] ECR 533; Case 120/86 *Mulder* v *Minister for Agriculture and Fisheries* [1988] ECR 2321; Case T-81/95 *Interhotel* v *Commission* [1997] ECR II-1265.

797 Case T-6/99 *ESF Elbe-Stahlwerke Feralpi* v *Commission* [2001] ECR II-1523.

798 Case T-126/97 *Sociedade Nacional de Segurança* v *Commission* [1999] ECR II-2793; Cases T-141 etc./99 *Vela and ors* v *Commission* [2002] ECR II-4547.

799 Case C-104/89 *Mulder* v *Council and Commission* [1992] ECR I-3061.

800 Case C-303/08 *Land Baden-Württemberg* v *Bozkurt* [2010] ECR I-13445, *per* A-G Sharpston at para. 58 of her opinion.

801 See e.g., Case C-367/96 *Kefalas and anor* v *Elliniko Dimosio and anor* [1998] ECR I-2843; Case C-373/97 *Diamantis* v *Elliniko Dimosio and anor* [2000] ECR I-1705; and Case C-16/05 *Tum and Dari* v *Secretary of State for the Home Department* [2007] ECR I-7415, at para. 64.

802 Case C-212/97 *Centros* v *Erhvervs- og Selskabsstyrelsen* [1999] ECR I-1459, at para. 24 and case law cited; Case C-63/99 *R* v *Secretary of State for the Home Department, ex parte Gloszczuk and Gloszczuk* [2001] ECR I-6369; Case C-200/02 *Chen and Zhu* v *Secretary of State for the Home Department* [2004] ECR I-9925, *per* A-G Tizzano at paras 108–29 of his opinion.

- *Respect for acquired rights:* A legal right, once acquired (*droit acquis*), should not, without reason and stated justification, be withdrawn. Further, a case ought to be judged in the light of the law as it stood at the time of the events in question, not as it may have been changed or developed subsequently;[803] Union rules apply to situations existing before their entry into force only insofar as it follows clearly from their terms, their object-ives or their general scheme that such effect ought to be given them.[804]

- *Identifiability of act, author and persons affected:* An act of an institution which produces (or is intended to produce) legal effects must be definitive, in particular as regards its author and content,[805] and the addressee of such a decision must be clearly identified or identifiable.[806]

- *Prescription:* An act cannot be declared unlawful, a penalty exacted or performance of an obligation required after an excessive lapse of time.[807]

- *Understandable language:* A decision must be communicated to a person affected by it in a language he understands,[808] and a Union legislative measure cannot be enforced against a person in a member state prior to its publication in the *Official Journal* in the language of that state, even if he could (constructively) have understood it.[809] Every citizen of the Union is entitled to write to any Union institution in any of the 23 Treaty languages and receive an answer in that language[810] – but there appears to be no duty borne by the Union to venture beyond those 23. Union legislation provides that documents sent to a member state or a person 'subject to the jurisdiction of a Member State' are to be in an official language of that state,[811] and service of enforcement orders in the context of a Union Directive in a language not an official language of the member state in

---

803 See e.g., Case 12/71 *Henck v Hauptzollamt Emmerich* [1971] ECR 743; see also Case 80/86 *Officier van Justitie v Kolpinghuis Nijmegen* [1987] ECR 3969.

804 Case 21/81 *Openbaar Ministerie v Bout* [1982] ECR 381; Case C-162/00 *Land Nordrhein-Westfalen v Pokrzeptowicz-Meyer* [2002] ECR I-1049.

805 Case C-286/95P *Commission v ICI* [2000] ECR I-2341; Cases C-287 and 288/95P *Commission v Solvay* [2000] ECR I-2391 (Soda Ash).

806 Case T-38/92 *All Weather Sports Benelux v Commission* [1994] ECR II-211; Case T-354/94 *Stora Kopparbergs Bergslags v Commission* (Cartonboard) [1998] ECR II-2111.

807 See e.g., Case 48/69 *ICI v Commission* [1972] ECR 619; Case C-185/95P *Baustahlgewebe v Commission* [1998] ECR I-8417; Case T-213/00 *CMA CGM and ors v Commission* [2003] ECR II-913; Case T-307/01 *François v Commission* [2004] ECR II-1669; Cases T-22 and 23/02 *Sumitomo Chemical Co. and anor v Commission* [2005] ECR II-4065; Case C-105/04P *Nederlandse Federatieve Vereniging voor de Groothandel op Elektrotechnisch Gebied v Commission* [2006] ECR I-8725.

808 See Case 66/74 *Farrauto v Bau-Berufsgenossenschaft Wuppertal* [1975] ECR 157; Cases T-25 etc./94 *Cimenteries CBR and ors v Commission* (Cement) [2000] ECR II-491; also Regulation 1/58 [1958] JO 385, art. 2.

809 Case 160/84 *Oryzomyli Kavallas and ors v Commission* [1986] ECR 1633; Case C-161/06 *Skoma-Lux v Celní ředitelství Olomouc* [2007] ECR I-10841; Case C-560/07 *Balbiino v Põllumajandusminister and anor* [2009] ECR I-4447.

810 TFEU, art. 24(4) (ex art. 21, 3rd para. EC).

811 Regulation 1/58 [1958] JO 385, arts 3, 8; if a choice, it is governed by the general rules applicable within the member state; see Case C-233/08 *Kyrian v Celní úřad Tábor* [2010] ECR I-177.

which it is served constitutes a fatal defect to it, if that is what national law provides.[812] No provision is made for a situation in which the person cannot understand the official language. Further, it also appears that, in direct dealings with the administration of a Union institution (primarily the Commission), a person has no right to a translation of all relevant documents into a language of his choice, or even one he necessarily understands;[813] measures adopted in breach of the principle (and in breach of Regulation 1/58) are 'regrettable' but merit annulment only if harmful consequences can be shown[814] or 'if, it were not for that irregularity, the procedure could have led to a different result'.[815] Certain notices published by a Union institution need not always be in all languages, but in such circumstances there must be notice drawn to the notice in all languages, otherwise they are (indirectly) discriminatory.[816]

5. Procedural rights

6.136 Procedural rights may be viewed as a subset of the general principle of fair legal process which apply in particular to the conduct of administrative procedures in or under Union law. They include the following.

(a) Good administration

6.137 There is a general principle of good, or sound, administration, that is a duty in administrative proceedings of a competent institution to examine carefully, impartially, fairly and with requisite discretion all relevant aspects of an individual case.[817] It can be said to embrace elements of fairness, good faith, transparency, consistency. It also embraces the duty to act when an institution is under a legal obligation to act,[818] and to do so within a

---

812 Case C-233/08 *Kyrian, ibid.*

813 Case T-148/89 *Tréfilunion* v *Commission* [1995] ECR II-1063; Cases T-25 etc./94 *Cimenteries CBR and ors* v *Commission* (Cement) [2000] ECR II-491, at paras 627–36; Case C-108/01 *Consorzio del Prosciutto di Parma* v *Asda Stores and anor* [2003] ECR I-5121, *per* A-G Alber at paras 133–45 of his opinion.

814 Cases T-25 etc./94 *Cement, ibid.*, at paras 642–45.

815 Cases C-465 and 466/02 *Germany and Denmark* v *Commission* (Feta) [2005] ECR I-9115, at para. 37.

816 Case T-185/05 *Italy* v *Commission* [2008] ECR II-3207.

817 Charter, art. 41; Case T-44/90 *La Cinq* v *Commission* [1992] ECR II-1; Case T-7/92 *Asia Motor France* v *Commission* [1993] ECR II-669; Cases T-528 etc./93 *Métropole Télévision* v *Commission* [1996] ECR II-649; Case T-62/98 *Volkswagen* v *Commission* [2000] ECR I-2707; Case T-54/99 *max.mobil* v *Commission* [2002] ECR II-313; Case T-31/99 *ABB Asea Brown Boveri* v *Commission* [2002] ECR II-1881; Case T-196/01 *Aristoteleio Panepistimio Thessalonikis* v *Commission* [2003] ECR II-3987; Case T-395/04 *Air One* v *Commission* [2006] ECR II-1343.

818 Cases T-344 and 345/00 *CEVA Santé Animal and Pharmacia* v *Commission* [2003] ECR II-229.

reasonable period of time.[819] Breach of the principle may give rise to damages.[820]

(b) Rights of defence

In contentious proceedings before an administrative authority, rights of defence **6.138** are 'guaranteed';[821] they constitute 'a fundamental principle of Community law which must be observed in all circumstances'.[822] The purpose is to promote equality of arms in contentious proceedings, and therefore has greatest application in staff and competition cases. More precisely:

- a person must be informed of any evidence adduced against them.[823] In competition cases therefore, the 'statement of objections' must be in terms sufficiently clear, containing the essential elements of the conduct libelled, such as the facts, the characterisation of those facts and the evidence upon which the Commission relies, that the party may identify the conduct complained of and in order properly to defend himself;[824] it must also specify unequivocally the legal person upon whom a penalty is proposed to be imposed and be addressed to that person;[825]

---

819 Cases T-213/95 and 18/96 *Stichting Certificatie Kraanverhuurbedrijf* v *Commission* [1997] ECR II-1739; Case T-54/99 *max.mobil*, n. 817 above, at paras 47–63; Cases C-238 etc./99P *Limburgse Vinyl Maatschappij* v *Commission* (PVC II) [2002] ECR I-8375, at paras 164–235; Case C-334/99 *Germany* v *Commission* [2003] ECR I-1139; Case T-213/00 *CMA CGM and ors* v *Commission* [2003] ECR II-913; Case T-196/01 *Aristoteleio Panepistimio Thessalonikis*, n. 817 above, at paras 227–40; Case T-307/01 *François* v *Commission* [2004] ECR II-1669; Case C-105/04P *Vereniging op Elektroteknisch Gebeid*, n. 807 above; Case T-145/06 *Omya* v *Commission* [2009] ECR II-145, at para. 84; Case T-66/01 *Imperial Chemical Industries* v *Commission* (Soda Ash), [2010] ECR II-2631.

820 Cases T-344 and 345/00 *CEVA Santé Animal*, n. 818 above (overturned on appeal as Case C-198/03P *Commission* v *CEVA Santé Animale and Pfizer Enterprises* [2005] ECR I-6357, but not on the point of principle). See e.g., Case 145/83 *Adams* v *Commission* [1985] ECR 3539, in which the plaintiff was awarded damages against the Commission (in a sum to be agreed) for breaching a duty of confidentiality owed him; Case T-19/07 *Systran & Systran Luxembourg* v *Commission* [2010] ECR II-6083, in which the claimants were awarded damages of €12 million for the Commission having improperly divulged their know-how.

821 Charter, art. 48(2).

822 Cases T-45 and 47/98 *Krupp Thyssen Stainless* v *Commission* [2001] ECR II-3757, at para. 56; Case T-17/99 *Ke Kelit Kunststoffwerk* v *Commission* [2002] ECR II-1647, at para. 63, inserting 'and' between 'law' and 'which' and substituting 'respected' for 'deserved'. To the same effect, Cases C-322 etc./07P *Papierfabrik August Koehler and ors* v *Commission* [2009] ECR I-7191, at para. 34; Case C-109/10P *Solvay* v *Commission* and Case C-110/10P *Solvay* v *Commission*, judgments of 25 October 2011, not yet reported, at paras 52 and 47 respectively.

823 Cases C-402 and 415/05P *Kadi and Al Barakaat* v *Council and Commission* [2008] ECR I-6351; Cases C-399 and 403/06P *Hassan and Ayadi* v *Council* [2009] ECR I-11393; Case T-85/09 *Kadi* v *Commission* (Kadi III) [2010] ECR I-5177.

824 Case 48/69 *ICI* v *Comission* (Dyestuffs) [1972] ECR 6198; Cases 89 etc./85 *Åhlström and ors* v *Commission* (Woodpulp) [1993] ECR I-1307; Case T-352/94 *Mo och Domsjö* v *Commission* (Cartonboard) [1998] ECR II-1989; Cases T-25 etc./95 *Cimenteries CBR and ors* v *Commission* (Cement) [2000] ECR II-491; Case T-310/01 *Schneider Electric* v *Commission* [2002] ECR II-4071; Cases C-322 etc./07P *August Koehler*, n. 822 above, at para 36.

825 Case C-176/99P *ARBED* v *Commission* [2003] ECR I-10687, at para 21; Cases C-322 etc./07P *August Koehler*, n. 822 above, at para. 38.

- if an inspection is carried out at the premises of an undertaking pursuant to Union law the inspecting authority must indicate its purpose, the essential characteristics of the suspected offence and some reasoning as to why it is suspected;[826]

- there is a general right to be heard (*audi alteram partem*) – it is 'a fundamental principle of Community law and forms, in particular, part of the rights of the defence'[827] – in all proceedings initiated against a person liable to culminate in a measure adversely affecting his interests, even where no such right is expressly provided.[828] It 'means, as a rule, that the parties have a right to a process of inspecting and commenting on the evidence and observations submitted to the court and, moreover, that that basic principle of law is infringed where a judicial decision is founded on facts and documents which the parties, or one of them, have not had an opportunity to examine and on which they have therefore been unable to comment'.[829] It may, in circumstances, require that proceedings be reopened.[830] The right applies not just to persons but extends to member states[831] and Union institutions;[832]

- disciplinary proceedings must be initiated within a reasonable time following the conduct libelled, must be conducted with due diligence and each procedural step therein is required to be taken within a reasonable period following the previous step;[833]

---

826   Case T-339/04 *France Télécom v Commission* [2007] ECR II-521, at paras 58–60.

827   Case C-413/06P *Bertelsman and anor v Independent Music Publishers and Labels Association* [2008] ECR I-4951.

828   See e.g., Case 17/74 *Transocean Marine Paint Association v Commission* [1974] ECR 1063; Case 85/76 *Hoffmann-La Roche v Commission* [1979] ECR 461; Case 322/81 *Michelin v Commission* [1983] ECR 3461; Case 49/88 *Al-Jubail Fertiliser Company v Council* [1991] ECR I-3187; Case C-135/92 *Fiskano v Commission* [1994] ECR I-2885; Case C-32/95P *Commission v Lisrestal and ors* [1996] ECR I-5373; Case T-348/94 *Enso Española v Commission* (Cartonboard) [1998] ECR II-1875; Cases T-186 etc./97 *Kaufring and ors v Commission* [2001] ECR II-1337; Case C-304/02 *Commission v France* [2005] ECR I-6263, *per* A-G Geelhoed in his (second) opinion; Case T-228/02 *Organisation des Modjahedines du peuple d'Iran v Council* [2006] ECR II-4665; Case T-170/06 *Alrosa v Commission* [2007] ECR II-2601; Cases C-402 and 415/05P *Kadi and Al Barakaat v Council and Commission* [2008] ECR I-6351; Case T-284/08 *People's Mojehadin Organization of Iran v Council* [2008] ECR II-3487; Case T-390/08 *Bank Melli Iran v Council* [2009] ECR II-3967; Cases C-399 and 403/06P *Hassan and Ayadi v Council* [2009] ECR I-11393; Case C-89/08P *Commission v Ireland, France and Italy* [2009] ECR I-11245. For a general discussion of the right to be heard see the opinion of A-G Sharpston in Cases C-439 and 454/05P *Land Oberösterreich and Austria v Commission* [2007] ECR I-7141.

829   Cases C-89/08P *Commission v Ireland, France and Italy, ibid.*, at para. 52.

830   See 5.70 above.

831   Cases C-48 and 66/90 *Netherlands and PTT Nederland v Commission* [1992] ECR I-565; Case C-288/96 *Germany v Commission* [2000] ECR I-8237.

832   Cases C-89/08P *Commission v Ireland and ors*, n. 828 above; Case C-197/09RX-II *M v European Medicines Agency* [2009] ECR I-12033.

833   Case T-549/93 *D v Commission* [1995] ECR-SC II-43; Case T-307/01 *François v Commission* [2004] ECR II-1669. Extensive argument on the issue was put to, and considerable guidance anticipated from, the Court of

- written communications between an undertaking and its (outside) lawyers are protected by confidentiality, as 'an essential corollary of the full exercise of the rights of the defence';[834]
- access to the institution's file, excepting confidential information, business secrets and internal administrative documents, must be made available;[835] infringement of the right leads to annulment of the measure at issue,[836] the interested party required to show only that the documents could have been useful to its defence;[837] it cannot be remedied at the judicial stage;[838]
- no decision can be based upon facts or documents of which a party has been unable to take cognisance and in relation to which he has therefore been unable to state a view;[839]
- an act of an institution must state the reasons upon which it is based,[840] so that a person may know the grounds and reasoning behind it and so have something concrete to challenge, and the Court has something concrete to review; generally, in staff or competition cases in which serious sanctions (loss of employment or related rights, heavy fines) are at issue, the reasoning must be particularly comprehensive;
- there must always be access to a judicial remedy;[841] and
- unjust enrichment: implicit but thinly articulated in the early case law of the Court of Justice on repayment of duties unlawfully levied[842] is a principle of unjust enrichment (*de in rem verso*). It has now been recognised by the Court of Justice as one common to the laws of the member states (*enrichissement sans cause, ungerechtsfertigte Bereicherung*)[843] but it remains underdeveloped at Union level. Since *San Giorgio*, a national authority which has imposed a levy or charge in breach of Union law must repay it unless it can show that the cost was passed on in its entirety to

---

Justice in Case C-109/10P *Solvay* v *Commission* and Case C-110/10P *Solvay* v *Commission*, judgments of 25 October 2011, not yet reported, but none forthcoming.

834 Cases T-125 and 253/03 *Akzo Nobel and anor* v *Commission* [2007] ECR II-3523, at para. 77.

835 Charter, art. 42; Case T-30/91 *Solvay* v *Commission* (Soda Ash) [1995] ECR II-1775; Case C-51/92P *Hercules Chemicals* v *Commission* (Polypropylene) [1999] ECR I-4235; Cases T-25 etc./95 *Cimenteries CBR and ors* v *Commission* (Cement) [2000] ECR II-491, at paras 140–44; Case T-23/99 *LR AF 1998* v *Commission* [2002] ECR II-1705. Access may be had to internal documents only if exceptional circumstances require it, which it is for the applicant to show; Cases 142 and 156/94 *BAT and Reynolds* v *Commission* [1986] ECR 1899, at para. 11; Cases T-45 and 47/98 *Krupp Thyssen Stainless and anor* v *Commission* [2001] ECR II-3757, at para. 34.

836 Cases C-109/10P and C-110/P *Solvay*, n. 833 above, at paras 55 and 50, respectively.

837 Case C-199/99P *Corus UK* v *Commission* [2003] ECR I-11177, at para. 128; Case C-110/P *Solvay*, n. 833 above, at para. 52.

838 Cases C-109/10P and C-110/P *Solvay*, n. 833 above, at paras 56 and 51, respectively.

839 Case C-480/99P *Plant and ors* v *Commission* [2002] ECR I-265; cf. Case C-497/99P *Irish Sugar* v *Commission* [2001] ECR I-5333, at para. 24; Cases C-109/10P and C-110/P *Solvay*, n. 833 above.

840 See 6.44–6.45 above.

841 Considered at 6.120 above.

842 Case 199/82 *Amministrazione delle Finanze dello Stato* v *San Giorgio* [1983] ECR 3595.

843 Case C-47/07P *Masdar (UK)* v *Commission* [2008] ECR I-9811.

someone else, for example a subsequent buyer.[844] But the principle applies generally to a national measure which would otherwise result in its unjust enrichment.[845] A Union institution which has, without lawful authority, imposed (and been paid) a financial penalty must repay the principal amount and also the amount of any enrichment or benefit it has obtained as a result.[846] As a related matter a principle of *negotiorum gestio* may be applicable as appropriate,[847] although this is even less developed.[848]

6.139 Very generally (for there has been much prevarication), it appears now that if a Union act is adopted in the face of a procedural requirement which is 'essential', it is not necessary for a party seeking its annulment or invalidation to show harm.[849] Otherwise infringement of a procedural right results in annulment or invalidation only if it can be established that, but for the irregularity, the outcome of the procedure might have been different[850] – or, put otherwise, if there had been 'any – even a small – chance of altering the outcome',[851] or 'whether the irregularity ... was capable of actually compromising the applicant's rights of defence'.[852] This is consistent with British administrative law.[853]

---

844 Case 199/82 *San Giorgio*, n. 842 above; Case C-192 etc./95 *Société Comateb and ors* v *Directeur Général des Douanes et Droits Indirects* [1997] ECR I-165; Case C-147/01 *Weber's Wine World and ors* v *Abgabenberufungskommission Wien* [2003] ECR II-11365; Case C-129/00 *Commission* v *Italy* [2003] ECR I-14637.

845 Case C-309/06 *Marks & Spencer* v *Commissioners of Customs and Excise* [2008] ECR I-2283.

846 Case T-171/99 *Corus UK* v *Commission* [2001] ECR II-2967; Case T-135/02 *Greencore Group* v *Commission* [2005] ECR II-31*. Cf. Case C-310/97 *Commission* v *AssiDomän Kraft Products* [1999] ECR I-5363.

847 Case C-47/07P *Masdar (UK)*, n. 843 above.

848 But see the full discussion of the General Court at first instance, Case T-333/03 *Masdar (UK)* v *Commission* [2006] ECR II-4377.

849 Case C-286/95P *Commission* v *ICI* [2000] ECR I-2341; Cases C-287 and 288/95P *Commission* v *Solvay* [2000] ECR I-2391 (Soda Ash).

850 Case 90/74 *Deboeck* v *Commission* [1975] ECR 1123; Cases 209 etc./78 *van Landewyck* v *Commission* (FEDETAB) [1980] ECR 3125; Case 142/87 *Belgium* v *Commission* [1990] ECR I-959.

851 Cases T-25 etc./94 *Cimenteries CBR and ors* v *Commission* (Cement) [2000] ECR II-491, at para. 247; see 5.68 above.

852 Case T-99/04 *AC-Treuhand* v *Commission* [2008] ECR II-1501, at para. 58.

853 *Malloch* v *Aberdeen Corporation* 1971 SC (HL) 85, *per* Lord Wilberforce at 118.

Part D

SUBSTANTIVE LAW

INTRODUCTION

Almost all of the substantive law of the Union is found in the Treaty on the Functioning of the European Union. It consists of a Preamble and seven Parts, as follows:

Part One   Principles
Part Two   Non-Discrimination and Citizenship of the Union
Part Three   Union Policies and Internal Action
Part Four   Association of the Overseas Countries and Territories
Part Five   External Action by the Union
Part Six   Institutional and Financial Provisions
Part Seven   General and Final Provisions.

The text is laid out as a complex of diminishing sections, comprising parts, within which are titles, within which chapters, within which sections, within which articles. This is especially so in the extensive Part Three in which the bulk of substantive rules are to be found; so, for example, the prohibition of cartels is to be found in Part Three ('Union policies and internal actions'), Title VII ('Common rules on competition, taxation and approximation of laws'), Chapter I ('Rules on competition'), section 1 ('Rules applying to undertakings'), article 101. The 358 articles of the TFEU are nevertheless numbered consecutively, and might equally be read as a narrative.

The scheme is to progress from the general to the specific. So, the Union is created by the Treaty on European Union which sets out its aim, creates the institutions (and 'institutional framework') through which it is to be achieved and sets out its fundamental (or constitutional) rules. These are provisions which used to be in Part One (the 'Principles' = *Grundsätze*) of the EC Treaty, now migrated to the TEU. What remains sets out the rules on allocation of authority and basic rules of general application in the light of which the remainder of the Treaty is to be interpreted and applied. The substantive rules follow in Part Three. Some of these are of themselves sufficiently clear, precise and unconditional so as to be directly effective, and much of the early interpretative work of the Court was directed towards determining which were so; others are not, and require to be given effect by legislation adopted by the institutions within the parameters and in accordance with the procedures set out in the Treaty bases scattered throughout Part Three for that purpose.

Annexed to the TFEU are 37 protocols (all also annexed to the TEU, some to the Euratom Treaty); annexed to the Final Act of the Lisbon Inter-governmental Conference (and previous IGCs) are a large number of declarations 'concerning provisions of the Treaties'. Their legal relevance is discussed above.[1] Annexed only to the TFEU are two Annexes which supplement particular Treaty articles, listing agricultural products for purposes of the common agricultural policy (Annex I) and those overseas countries and territories which enjoy 'association' status with the Union (Annex II);[2] they are thus similar to a schedule such as may be found in a UK Act of Parliament and treated as an integral part of the Treaty.

The substantive Treaty law of which it is necessary to be aware is almost all contained in Part Three (Union policies and internal actions), Titles I–VI (prior to Maastricht called the 'Foundations of the Community') and Title VII (the 'Common rules'), although significant substantive rules have now been adopted also under the (much revamped) economic and monetary (Title XIII), social (Title X) and environment (Title XX) provisions. But care must be taken to be alive to the technique of interpretation of the Court of Justice, that it will have recourse to the context in which those provisions are embedded, the Treaties as a whole, particularly the general provisions of the TEU, the TFEU principles (articles 1–17) and general principles, and including even the Treaty Preambles, as an aid to interpretation of a particular provision.

The scheme of this part of the book is to adhere to the Treaty narrative and consider the provisions of Part Three (more or less) sequentially. This has the advantage of seeing the substantive rules of Union law unfold in the manner in which those who drafted the Treaty approached the task and following the logic they bred into it.

---

1 See 2.17 above.
2 The present Annexes I and II were originally Annexes II and IV of the EEC Treaty; the original Annex I (an extensive list of tariff headings relevant to the progressive establishment of the common customs tariff) and Annex III (a list of invisible transactions subject to a standstill provision in the area of current payments) were spent by the end of the transition period and removed ('deleted') by the Treaty of Amsterdam.

7

THE PRINCIPLES

The EEC Treaty set out at the top – naturally enough, being then the starting **7.01** point of the Economic Community – its creation (article 1) and, in general terms, the economic, social and political 'task' (*mission*; *Aufgabe*) which it had been created to perform (article 2). That task is even now worth reproducing in full, for it constituted the cornerstone of Community endeavour for 50 years and its purpose holds important sway still:

> The Community shall have as its task, by establishing a common market and progressively approximating the economic policies of Member States, to promote throughout the Community a harmonious development of economic activities, a continuous and balanced expansion, an increase in stability, an accelerated raising of the standard of living and closer relations between the States belonging to it.

It will be apparent that the Treaty sets out the achievement of goals by economic means – '*by* establishing a common market' – which in turn is to be read in the light of the preamble, in which the signatories 'determined to lay the foundations of an ever closer union among the peoples of Europe' and 'resolved to ensure the economic and social progress of their countries by common action to eliminate the barriers which divide Europe'.[1] This was to be confirmed by the Court of Justice: the Treaty 'aim[ed] to achieve economic integration', but the relevant provisions, 'far from being an end in themselves, are only means for attaining th[e] objectives' of 'concrete progress towards European unity'.[2] Nevertheless the immediate task was the achievement of these means, first and

---

1 EEC Treaty, Preamble, 1st and 2nd indents.
2 Opinion 1/91 *Re the EEA Agreement* [1991] ECR I-6079, at paras 17, 18.

foremost the establishment of a 'common market', in accordance with a design which was, and is still at its core, an economic blueprint.

7.02 There followed in article 3, under 11 heads (which by 2009 had grown over successive Treaty amendments to 21), the 'activities' (*l'action*; *die Tätigkeit*) of the Community by which it was to achieve its task ('[f]or the purposes set out [*aux fins énoncées*] in Article 2'). The list of activities was, in essence, the programme for Part Three of the Treaty (Community Policies) and was set out more or less in the sequence in which they were addressed in the detail which there followed. They addressed essentially the fields which go into the making of a common market, the immediate nuts and bolts of achieving and maintaining it, and the flanking measures necessary to make it effective.

7.03 The common market addressed all forms of economic activity except those governed by the European Coal and Steel Community (ECSC) and Euratom Treaties.[3] There was no definition of a common market in the Treaty, but the Court of Justice said:

> The concept of a common market ... involves the elimination of all obstacles to intra-Community trade in order to merge the national markets into a single market bringing about conditions as close as possible to those of a genuine internal market.[4]

Subsequently there developed the concept of the 'internal market', the two existing alongside each other but the difference never satisfactorily clarified. With Lisbon the common market disappeared, the term (where surviving) abandoned and the Treaties now referring to the internal market throughout.[5]

7.04 In 1993 article 2 was amended by Maastricht so as to add to the Community's task the establishment of economic and monetary union. As this requires a very high degree of economic convergence, a new article 4 imposed upon both the Community and the member states significant financial discipline: they were required to comply with 'guiding principles' of stable prices, sound public finance and monetary conditions and a sustainable balance of payments, all conducted in accordance with the principle of an open market economy with

---

3 EEC Treaty, art. 232 (now art. 106a(3) Euratom). Aspects of these sectors in which the ECSC and Euratom Treaties were silent fell within the domain of the EEC Treaty; see e.g., Opinion 1/94 *Re the World Trade Organisation* [1994] ECR I-5267. With the end of the European Coal and Steel Community in 2002, all coal and steel activity was subsumed into the general EC regime.
4 Case 15/81 *Gaston Schul* v *Inspecteur der Invoerrechten en Accijnzen* [1982] ECR 1409, at para. 33.
5 Lisbon Treaty, art. 2(3)(g).

free competition. Article 4 thus 'establish[ed] the fundamental principles of economic policy of the Community system';[6] according to Dr Ehlermann it, in combination with the subsequent Treaty provisions on competition, meant that 'the Community has the most strongly free-market oriented constitution in the world'.[7]

THE TFEU

The Treaty on the Functioning of the European Union is different. It remains **7.05** the successor treaty to the E(E)C Treaty, but save the preamble which survives Lisbon unaltered it is shorn of ambition and purpose for the Union, those provisions transplanted to the TEU. Part One of the TFEU remains 'the Principles' but no longer recites the task of the Union. Rather it begins prosaically (and in stilted English):

> This Treaty organises [*regelt*] the functioning of the Union and determines [*legt fest*] the areas of, delimitation [*Abgrenzung*] of, and arrangements [*modalités*] for exercising its competences.[8]

It then reiterates article 1 of the TEU by providing that the Union is founded upon the two Treaties, they have the same legal value, and they are 'the Treaties'.[9] Two Titles follow.

1. Categories and areas of Union competence

The first Title addresses not activities (as previously) but 'categories and areas **7.06** [*domaines*] of Union competence' and comprises a recitation of Union competences, much as a federal constitution or devolution instrument would do, but for the first time seeking to slot them, at constitutional level, into three categories: those in which the Union exercises exclusive authority; contrasting those fields with others in which it enjoys concurrent authority with the member states; and giving form to a new category in which it has supporting authority. They might equally have found a home in the TEU, but as they go to substantive matters are more closely connected with the functioning of the Union and so left in the TFEU. They are also an aspect of the post-Lisbon emphasis upon a Union which enjoys authority and competences by virtue of conferral only.

---

6 Case C-451/03 *Servizi Ausiliari Dottori Commercialisti* v *Calafiori* [2006] ECR I-2941, at para. 20.
7 C.-D. Ehlermann, 'The Contribution of EC Competition Policy to the Single Market' (1992) 29 *CMLRev.* 257 at 273.
8 TFEU, art. 1(1).
9 *Ibid.* art. 1(2).

7.07 The Union has 'exclusive competence' in the areas of:

- the customs union;
- the establishing of the competition rules necessary for the functioning of the internal market;
- monetary policy for the member states whose currency is the euro;
- the conservation of marine biological resources under the common fisheries policy;
- common commercial policy; and
- the conclusion of an international agreement when its conclusion is provided for in a legislative act of the Union or is necessary to enable the Union to exercise its internal competence, or insofar as its conclusion may affect common rules or alter their scope.[10]

Some of this is self-evidently tautological, and much of it is codification of case law of the Court of Justice which recognised fields of Community activity which over time became wholly occupied by Community rules. Presumably other fields of concurrent Union activities may follow suit. Member state competence in these fields is excluded, except that they may act if and only insofar as authorised by the Union to do so or in order to implement Union measures.[11] This is common and consistent with the practice in federations marked by a degree of 'cooperative federalism', such as Germany, but it is constitutionally impermissible in others as fundamentally inconsistent with the federal principle.[12]

7.08 The fields (the 'principal areas') of concurrent competences ('shared competence'; *compétences partagées*) are:

- the internal market;
- social policy, for the aspects defined in the TFEU;
- economic, social and territorial cohesion;
- agriculture and fisheries, excluding the conservation of marine biological resources;
- environment;
- consumer protection;
- transport;
- trans-European networks;
- energy;
- the area of freedom, security and justice;

---

10   *Ibid.* art. 3.
11   *Ibid.* art. 2(1).
12   See *Aty-Gen Nova Scotia* v *Aty-Gen Canada* (Nova Scotia Interdelegation) [1951] SCR 31.

- common safety concerns in public health matters, for the aspects defined in the TFEU;
- research, technological development and space; and
- development cooperation and humanitarian aid,[13]

provided the exercise of this authority does not trench upon matters falling within articles 3 (exclusive competence) or 6 (supporting competence).[14] Concurrent competence is therefore constructed as the default category. Some of these have been Community activities from the beginning, others added over time; none is entirely new, and activity in the final two fields (research, technological development and space, and development cooperation and humanitarian aid) 'shall not result in Member States being prevented from exercising their [competences]',[15] which, uniquely in the Treaties, confers a (presumptive) primacy upon national law. As flanking measures the member states are to coordinate their economic policies within the Union in accordance with broad guidelines set by the Council,[16] and the Union is to take measures to ensure coordination of their employment policies[17] and may take measures to ensure coordination of their social policies.[18]

Article 2(2) seeks to set out the nature of concurrent jurisdiction thus: **7.09**

> When the Treaties confer on the Union a competence shared with the Member States in a specific area, the Union and the Member States may legislate and adopt legally binding acts in that area. The Member States shall exercise their competence to the extent that the Union has not exercised its competence. The Member States shall again exercise their competence to the extent that the Union has decided to cease exercising its competence.

Given that the Community operated in concurrent fields for over 50 years and survived quite happily without this (trite) guidance, the necessity of it is not immediately apparent. It is buttressed by a protocol which adds little to it:

> With reference to Article 2(2) of the Treaty on the Functioning of the European Union on shared competence, when the Union has taken action in a certain area, the scope of

---

13   TFEU, art. 4(2), (3), (4).
14   *Ibid.* art. 4(1).
15   *Ibid.* art. 4(3), (4).
16   *Ibid.* art. 5(1).
17   *Ibid.* art. 5(2).
18   *Ibid.* art. 5(3).

this exercise of competence only covers those elements governed by the Union act in question and therefore does not cover the whole area,[19]

and a declaration[20] which adds less.

7.10 The Union has ancillary competences, to carry out actions to support, co-ordinate or supplement at European level national action, but without super-seding (*remplacant*) the member states' competences,[21] in the areas of:

- protection and improvement of human health;
- industry;
- culture;
- tourism;
- education, vocational training, youth and sport;
- civil protection;
- administrative cooperation.[22]

Harmonisation of national law in these fields is expressly excluded.[23] All of them save sport were pre-Lisbon Community 'activities', albeit ancillary to national action. Some may be said to be downgraded by Lisbon by formal Treaty recognition of that status and the re-affirmation of national pre-eminence in the fields. Gone is any express mention of economic and social cohesion, the promotion and the strengthening of which had been a Community task and activity since Maastricht;[24] instead the promotion of economic, social and territorial cohesion has become a Union aim[25] and is provided for in a later TFEU Title.[26]

2. Provisions having general application: the integration clauses

7.11 Many of the principles of Part One of the EC Treaty migrated to the TEU at Lisbon. What is left is Title II of Part One of the TFEU, 'provisions having general application', and is essentially a recitation of a series of 'integration' (or 'comprehensive') clauses (*Querschnittsklauseln*). Integration clauses were first introduced (for environmental protection) in 1987 by the Single European Act, and represent one solution to the problem of Treaty adaptation to new social or

---

19 Protocol (No. 25) on the Exercise of Shared Competences.
20 Declaration (No. 18) in relation to the Delimitation of Competences.
21 TFEU, art. 2(5), 1st para.
22 *Ibid.* art. 6.
23 *Ibid.* art. 2(5), 2nd para.
24 EC Treaty, arts 2 and 3(j) respectively (pre-Amsterdam).
25 TEU, art. 3, 3rd para.
26 TFEU, Title XVIII, arts 174–8.

other demands. They provide, in varying terms and intensity, that their subject matter is to be taken into account across, and woven into, all fields of Union activity, as appropriate. The TFEU now provides a general obligation (or a 'super-integration clause')[27] that the Union ensure consistency in its policies and activities, taking all of its objectives into account and in accordance with the principle of conferral of powers.[28] There then follow seven integration clauses addressing specific areas. These too might be expected to appear in the TEU. In fact some do: the requirement of article 9 TEU that '[i]n all its activities, the Union shall observe the equality of its citizens' is of the nature of an integration clause. But they remain in the TFEU presumably because they are more directly related to the substantive (or functional, as the name suggests) as compared to the constitutional nature of Union activity as typical of that Treaty.

The integration clauses are as follows.   7.12

(a) Sex equality

The Community provided from the beginning a principle of equal pay for equal   7.13
work as between the sexes.[29] The rule evolved and expanded over the years as part of Community social policy. Amsterdam added a general integration clause[30] which was re-absorbed by Lisbon as the first (and so principal) provision having general application, thus: 'In all its activities, the Union shall aim to eliminate inequalities, and to promote equality, between men and women'.[31]

(b) Employment, social protection and social exclusion, education and training, human health

Also absorbed over time as part of the accretion and development of social   7.14
concerns in Community law, Maastricht was able to write the promotion of a high level of employment and social protection into the Community's task,[32] to introduce education and thus differentiate vocational training[33] and to provide for a Community contribution towards a high level of public health.[34] Article 9 TFEU now provides that in defining and implementing its policies and activities the Union is to take into account the promotion of high levels of employment, education, training and protection of human health; of adequate social protection; and combating social exclusion.

---

27   H. Vedder, 'The Treaty of Lisbon and European Environmental Law and Policy' (2010) 22 *JEnv.L* 285 at 289.
28   TFEU, art. 7.
29   EEC Treaty, art. 119.
30   EC Treaty, art. 3(2).
31   TFEU, art. 8.
32   EC Treaty, art. 2.
33   *Ibid.* arts 3(p), 126 and 127 (pre-Amsterdam).
34   *Ibid.* arts 3(o) and 129.

(c) Discrimination based upon sex, racial or ethnic origin, religion or belief, disability, age or sexual orientation

7.15 Amsterdam authorised the adoption (by unanimous Council) of 'appropriate action' to combat discrimination based upon sex, racial or ethnic origin, religion or belief, disability, age or sexual orientation, provided it is acting always 'within the limits of the powers conferred by [the Treaty] upon the Community'.[35] Such authority remains,[36] but Lisbon additionally drew this into a principle of general application, so that the Union must now aim to combat discrimination (above and beyond discrimination based upon nationality and sex, provided for elsewhere) in defining and implementing its policies and activities.[37]

(d) Environmental protection

7.16 A product of the mid-1950s, the original EEC Treaty was silent as to environmental concerns of any sort. But the environment had moved to centre stage by the mid-1980s, and environmental protection was added to the EEC Treaty by the Single European Act in the form of its first integration clause.[38] It has been 'upgraded' in turn by Maastricht (also bolstered by authority for the adoption of 'a policy in the sphere of the environment')[39], by Amsterdam (to a Part One principle,[40] further bolstered by inclusion as part of the Community's task)[41], and by Nice. It is now a provision having general application, in the following terms:

> Environmental protection requirements must be integrated into the definition and implementation of the Union policies and activities, in particular with a view to promoting sustainable development.[42]

Detailed provisions on policy are set out in Part Three.[43]

(e) Consumer protection

7.17 A Community contribution to a high level of consumer protection, in both harmonisation legislation and supporting and supplementing national action,

---

35 EC Treaty (post Amsterdam), art. 13(1). Nice added authority for the adoption of incentive measures contributing to the achievement of these objectives by co-decision (now ordinary legislative procedure); art. 13(2).
36 TFEU, art. 19; see immediately below.
37 *Ibid.* art. 10.
38 EEC Treaty, art. 130r(2).
39 EC Treaty (pre-Amsterdam), art. 3(k).
40 EC Treaty (post Amsterdam), art. 6.
41 *Ibid.* art. 2: 'to promote ... a high level of protection and improvement of the quality of the environment'.
42 TFEU, art. 11 (ex art. 6 EC).
43 Title XX, arts 191–3; see 14.54–14.66 below.

was written into the Treaty by Maastricht.[44] Its requirements are now to be taken into account in defining and implementing 'other' (presumably other than consumer protection, which remains a concurrent competence) Union policies and activities.[45]

(f) Animal welfare

A declaration was made and attached to the Final Act of the Maastricht IGC **7.18** which called upon the Community and the member states 'when drafting and implementing Community legislation on the common agricultural policy, transport, the internal market and research, to pay full regard to the welfare requirements of animals'.[46] It could probably be characterised as a 'soft' integration clause. It was upgraded by Amsterdam to a Treaty Protocol in its existing terms[47] and again by Lisbon into the Treaties proper, the TFEU now providing:

> In formulating and implementing the Union's agriculture, fisheries, transport, internal market, research and technological development and space policies, the Union and the Member States shall, since animals are sentient beings, pay full regard to the welfare requirements of animals, while respecting the legislative or administrative provisions and customs of the Member States relating in particular to religious rites, cultural traditions and regional heritage.[48]

In its previous guise it was probably the least effective of the integration clauses. Its upgrading by Lisbon into a Part One provision having general application, combined with a final clause its critics view as emasculating it, may, or may not, enhance its standing. It remains in all events anaemic when compared with similar provision which may be found elsewhere.[49]

(g) Commitment to services of general (economic) interest

Services of general economic interest – those provided universally in the public **7.19** interest, including, for example, but not limited to, utilities, transport and communications services – are addressed under the competition rules, but the rules have been applied, in the view of some, in a manner which diminishes their utility. They are provided by firms which are often, but not always, in public ownership, and may be a means by which (some) member states direct

---

44 EC Treaty (pre-Amsterdam), art. 129a.
45 TFEU, art. 12.
46 Declaration (No. 24) on the Protection of Animals.
47 Protocol on Protection and Welfare of Animals.
48 TFEU, art. 13.
49 Compare, for example, the situation in Switzerland where 'the dignity of the creature' (*Die Würde der Kreatur*) has constitutional and significant legislative protection; Constitution, art. 120(2); Tierschutzgesetz vom 16. Dezember 2005; Bundesgericht, 7 Oktober 2009 (*Tierexperimente Forschung*), 2C_421/2008 E.4.3.4.

economic policy. At largely French insistence, the Treaty of Amsterdam buttressed their position in economic planning and service provision with a new
integration clause which now provides (in unacceptably flabby English):

> [G]iven the place occupied by services of general economic interest in the shared values
> of the Union as well as their role in promoting social and territorial cohesion, the Union
> and the Member States, each within their respective powers and within the scope of
> application of the Treaties, shall take care [*veillent; Sorge tragen*] that such services
> operate on the basis of principles and conditions, particularly economic and financial
> conditions, which enable them to fulfil their missions [*missions; Aufgaben*].[50]

A new Lisbon protocol extols the virtues of services of general interest
(omitting 'economic')[51] so according them, perhaps, further special treatment
under the Treaties. As the tangency with the Treaties of both provisions is
primarily in the area of competition, they are discussed in that context.[52]

(h) Other integration clauses

7.20 Title II of Part One goes on to provide generally for transparency of the work of
the institutions and public access to documents,[53] protection of personal data,[54]
and Union respect for the status under national law of churches, religious
associations or communities and non-confessional organisations.[55] Further
integration clauses appear later in the relevant substantive provisions of the
TFEU, on matters of:

- culture;[56]
- public health;[57]
- industry;[58] and
- economic, social and territorial cohesion.[59]

Most contain an (unnecessary) express prohibition of harmonisation of national
law in the relevant area.[60] Gone is a previously existing integration clause in the

---

50 TFEU, art. 14 (ex art. 16 EC). Note that *mission* and *Aufgabe* were the terms used for the Community's 'task' as
    set out in art. 2 EEC/EC.
51 Protocol (No. 26) on Services of General Interest.
52 See 13.142–13.147 below.
53 TFEU, art. 15; see Part B, Introduction above.
54 *Ibid.* art. 16.
55 *Ibid.* art. 17.
56 *Ibid.* art. 167(4).
57 *Ibid.* art. 168(1). See also EU Charter of Fundamental Rights, art. 35.
58 *Ibid.* art. 173(3).
59 *Ibid.* art. 175, 1st para.
60 *Ibid.* arts 167(5), 168(5), 173(3) – unnecessary because they are areas of ancillary Union competence (art. 6) so
    subject to the general bar of art. 2(5); but it is not the case for economic, social and territorial cohesion which is
    an area of concurrent jurisdiction (art. 4).

field of development cooperation,[61] now subsumed within the more specific rules on the Union's external action. Irrespective of where they appear in the Treaties they are thought all to apply in a like manner. However their exact status – whether they are superior norms or general principles of law, whether depending upon their terms some are of a higher status and application than others, whether they are justiciable, or whether they are merely policy guidelines for the political institutions – is elusive and has never been clearly pinned down.

---

61   EC Treaty, art. 178.

8

NON-DISCRIMINATION AND CITIZENSHIP OF THE UNION

A. NON-DISCRIMINATION	8.02	Rights of citizenship	8.11
B. CITIZENSHIP OF THE UNION	8.05		

8.01 Part Two of the TFEU creates and provides for 'citizenship of the Union'. Introduced in 1993 by Maastricht, it marked the first express recognition *in the Treaties* of the individual as a person deriving rights and obligations directly from them. Of course with recognition of direct effect in *van Gend en Loos*[1] persons became able to claim the benefits of a large number of Community rights, but this was the first Treaty provision expressly to say so. In contrast to the 'rights of the individual' which fall to be protected by recourse to direct effect, the citizenship provisions of the TFEU apply necessarily (in accordance with Treaty definitions) only to individuals properly so-called, that is natural (or physical) persons. Lisbon severed from the Principles of Part One of the EC Treaty two articles of fundamental application to Community law and transferred them to Part Two. They continue to have general application but their new place in the Treaties aligns them with the rights of citizenship, which may (or may not) produce very significant change to the latter.[2]

A. NON-DISCRIMINATION

8.02 Article 18 TFEU, which was in the EEC Treaty amongst the Part One Principles since the beginning, is an articulation of one of the most important principles affecting the rights of individuals:

> Within the scope of application the Treaties, and without prejudice to any special provisions contained therein, any discrimination on grounds of nationality shall be prohibited.

---

1 Case 26/62 *Algemene Transport- en Expeditie Onderneming van Gend en Loos* v *Nederlandse Administratie der Belastingen* [1963] ECR 1; see 6.13 above.
2 See 11.96–11.106 below.

It is reproduced, effectively *verbatim*, in the Charter of Fundamental Rights.[3] However even a cursory reading of the case law reveals that it does not mean what it says: it is not a general prohibition of discrimination on grounds of nationality, it applies (for the most part) only to nationals of a member state. Thus closer to the mark is the (new) TEU general provision on democratic principles:

> In all its activities, the Union shall observe the principle of the equality of its citizens, who shall receive equal attention from its institutions, bodies, offices and agencies.[4]

Discrimination against third country nationals is not prohibited. It is presumed, and indeed expected, that they will be treated differently.

The effect of article 18 is, for practical purposes, to require the member states to **8.03** be 'nationality blind' and to ensure equality of treatment for all Union individuals (in its Union law sense of both natural and juristic persons) in any sphere of Union activity. More specific non-discrimination rules are provided in particular contexts in subsequent Treaty provisions; where this obtains it pre-empts the application of article 18 (for it operates 'without prejudice to any special provisions contained [elsewhere in the Treaties]'), which may therefore be of independent application but only to situations which fall within a sphere of Union activity but are subject to no more specific rules.[5] It is a general principle of Union law, a breach, a 'particularly serious' affront to principles of equal treatment,[6] and informs everything the Union does. As with anti-discrimination measures generally, there may be discrimination upon grounds of nationality which is direct or indirect. The former is always prohibited, subject to specific derogation provided for in the Treaties or in (Treaty compatible) legislation; the latter may seek, and be permitted, wider justification. The issues are considered in detail both above and below.[7]

---

3   EU Charter of Fundamental Rights, art. 21(2).

4   TEU, art. 9.

5   Case C-179/90 *Merci Convenzionali Porto di Genova* v *Siderurgica Gabrielli* [1991] ECR I-5889; Case C-18/93 *Corsica Ferries Italia* v *Corpo dei Piloti del Porto di Genova* [1994] ECR I-1783; Case C-131/96 *Mora Romero* v *Landesversicherungsanstalt Rheinprovinz* [1997] ECR I-3659; Case C-387/01 *Weigel and Weigel* v *Finanzlandesdirektion für Vorarlberg* [2004] ECR I-4981, at paras 57–9; Case C-40/05 *Lyyski* v *Umeå universitet* [2007] ECR I-99; Case C-341/05 *Laval un partneri* v *Svenska Byggnadsarbetareförbundet and ors* (Vaxholm) [2007] ECR I-11767.

6   Case C-47/08 *Commission* v *Belgium*, Case C-51/08 *Commission* v *Luxembourg*, Case C-52/08 *Commission* v *Portugal*, Case C-53/08 *Commission* v *Austria*, Case C-54/08 *Commission* v *Germany* and Case C-61/08 *Commission* v *Greece*, judgments of 24 May 2011 (the 'Notaries judgments'), not yet reported, *per* A-G Cruz Villalón at para. 129 of his opinion.

7   See 6.125–6.128 and 11.112–11.117.

8.04 The Single European Act amended (the predecessor of) article 18 to provide a Treaty basis for the adoption of legislation to combat discrimination based upon nationality.[8] Since the power is limited, as always, to discrimination falling '[w]ithin the scope of application of the Treaties', it ought in theory to be unnecessary, any discrimination sought to be remedied caught by the general application of article 18. But it has utility in enabling the adoption of measures which provide greater precision and depth.[9] There is no equivalent authority in the Euratom Treaty, but because 'equal treatment … is one of the fundamental legal provisions of the Community' and '[a]rticle [18] … is a specific expression of the general principle of equality, which itself is one of the fundamental principles of Community law', discrimination on grounds of nationality can be no more tolerated within the scope of application of the Atomic Energy Community.[10] A new article was added to the EC Treaty by Amsterdam authorising the adoption, by a unanimous Council, of 'appropriate action' to combat discrimination based upon sex, racial or ethnic origin, religion or belief, disability, age or sexual orientation, provided it is acting always 'within the limits of the powers conferred by [the Treaties] upon the Union'.[11] This goes well beyond what was originally thought necessary to secure the internal market and is an aspect of the rapidly growing social dimension of European citizenship. Three such measures (the 'non-discrimination Directives') have been adopted, a fourth is in the pipeline. They are discussed below.[12]

B. CITIZENSHIP OF THE UNION

8.05 Citizenship of the Union was created by Maastricht, although the relevant provisions made part not of the Union Treaty, as might perhaps be expected, but of the EC Treaty. It now bestrides both Treaties. Article 20 TFEU provides:

> 1. Citizenship of the Union is hereby established. Every person holding the nationality of a Member State shall be a citizen of the Union. Citizenship of the Union shall be additional to [*s'ajoute à*; previously 'complement'] and not replace national citizenship.[13]

---

8 TFEU, art. 18, 2nd para. (ex art. 12, 2nd para. EC).

9 For discussion see Case C-295/90 *Parliament* v *Council* (Students) [1992] ECR I-4193 and the ensuing Directive 93/96 [1993] OJ L317/59.

10 Case C-115/08 *Land Oberösterreich* v *ČEZ* [2009] ECR I-10265, at paras 88–90.

11 TFEU, art. 19(1) (ex art. 13(1) EC). The Treaty of Nice added a second paragraph (art. 19(2)) which provides that any incentive measures contributing to the achievement of these objectives are to be adopted (now) by ordinary legislative procedure.

12 See 14.45–14.46 below.

13 The third sentence of art. 20(1) was added by the Treaty of Amsterdam.

2. Citizens of the Union shall enjoy the rights and be subject to the duties provided for in the Treaties,

whilst the second and third sentences of paragraph 1 appear also in the TEU, as a provision on democratic principles.[14]

Two points will immediately be apparent: first, Union citizenship is, like **8.06** Roman citizenship long before it and that of the German Empire less remote,[15] multilayered: it is 'additional to', and co-exists with, national citizenship. Second, it is *not* an independent status, rather it is one derived wholly from (or parasitic upon) the fact of nationality of a member state: the Treaties confer upon the Union no competence as to citizenship or naturalisation, that remains firmly within the sphere of national sovereignty.[16] The nationality laws of all member states confer that status by reference to place of birth (*jus soli*), to blood (*jus sanguinis*), or to a variety of combinations of the two; each also provides for acquisition of nationality by those not having it at birth by, for example, marriage, adoption or naturalisation, and its loss – again, in varying fashion and degree. In this they are completely unfettered, certainly by Union law as it now stands;[17] there is an occasionally quoted *dictum* from the Court that any decision as to conditions of acquisition or loss of nationality should be taken 'having due regard to Community law',[18] but this imposes (as yet) no identifiable burdens.

So, for example, if the nationality law of the Federal Republic conferred German citizenship, and so by extension citizenship of the Union, upon citizens of the Democratic Republic and upon ethnic Germans from Eastern Europe (the 'Volga Germans'), as it did;[19] if that of Ireland confers Irish citizenship upon persons by virtue of birth in (part of) another member state, as

---

14 TEU, art. 9; the wording of the first sentence is slightly different.
15 See Gesetz vom 16. April 1871, betreffend die Verfassung des Deutschen Reiches (Die Bismarcksche Reichsverfassung), RGBl. 1871 S. 63, Art. 4.
16 See Case C-369/90 *Micheletti and ors v Delegación del Gobierno en Cantabria* [1992] ECR I-4239; Case C-179/98 *Belgian State v Mesbah* [1999] ECR I-7955, at para. 29; Case C-192/99 *R v Secretary of State for the Home Department, ex parte Kaur* [2001] ECR I-1237; Case C-200/02 *Zhu and Chen v Secretary of State for the Home Department* [2004] ECR I-9925; European Convention of 6 November 1997 on Nationality, CETS No. 166, art. 3; in force 1 November 2000.
17 Case C-135/08 *Rottmann v Freistaat Bayern* [2010] ECR I-1449, at para. 39; Case C-34/09 *Ruiz Zambrano v Office national de l'emploi*, judgment of 8 March 2011, not yet reported, at para. 40. Some minimal limitations are imposed by public international law, both customary (see *Liechtenstein v Guatemala* ('Nottebohm case') [1955] ICJ Rep. 4) and conventional (see e.g., Convention of 30 August 1961 on the Reduction of Statelessness, 989 UNTS 175; European Convention on Nationality, *ibid.*).
18 Case C-369/90 *Micheletti*, n. 16 above, at para. 10; Case C-179/98 *Mesbah*, n. 16 above, at para. 29.
19 § 116 GG; Reichs- und Staatsangehörigkeitsgesetz (RuStAG) vom 22. Juli 1913, RBGl. 1913 S. 583; now significantly amended (and renamed the Staatsangehörigkeitsgesetz (StAG)) in the light of reunification by the Gesetz zur Reform des Staatsangehörigkeitsgesetz vom 15. Juli 1999, BGBl. 1999 I S. 1618.

it does;[20] if that of Romania confers a right to 'regain' Romanian citizenship upon (potentially millions of) Moldovans who have a pre-partition (1940) Romanian great-grandparent, as it is doing;[21] or if that of Hungary provides a means of acquiring its citizenship upon the ethnic Hungarians resident in (and for the most part citizens of) Romania (around 1.5 million, the 'Transylvanian Hungarians'), Slovakia (0.5 million), Serbia (0.3 million) and Ukraine (150,000, the 'transCarpathian Hungarians') as it has just done,[22] these are matters solely, and determinatively, for Germany, Ireland, Romania and Hungary – although it may invite serious political repercussions.[23] Even though it brings to the bearer substantial benefits in, and so creates burdens for, a host member state, nationality conferred by one member state cannot be called into question by another.[24] It follows that a Union citizen, perhaps one having exercised the rights of citizenship in another member state over many years, who loses the nationality of a member state which underpins it (e.g., by marriage, by naturalisation in a third country, by renunciation), as Union law now stands ceases to be a Union citizen. In the one case in which the Court considered potential limits to member state discretion by reference to Union law it found a member state (Germany) not barred from revoking citizenship obtained by intentional deception, even if the result deprived the individual of (*inter alia*) Union citizenship and its associated rights – in fact, left him

---

20 Until 2005 Irish law conferred Irish citizenship upon anyone born in the island of Ireland, so including Northern Ireland, as an absolute right; Irish Nationality and Citizenship Act, 1956 (No. 26 of 1956), s. 6(1); see Case C-200/02 *Zhu and Chen*, n. 16 above. There is still no distinction between north and south but now a person born (anywhere) in Ireland of non-Irish parents is an Irish citizen only if the parents can show a 'genuine link' to Ireland; s. 6A (as amended by the Irish Nationality and Citizenship Act, 2004 (No. 38 of 2004)).

21 NVD Nr. 36/2009, *Monitorul Oficial* nr. 259, din 21 aprilie 2009.

22 2010 évi XLIV. törvény a magyar állampolgárságról szóló 1993. évi LV. törvény módosításáró; in force 1 January 2011. Of course except for the Serbian and Ukrainian Hungarians who may benefit from this law, this (as in the Irish case) does not generally result in the (indirect) conferral of Union citizenship upon someone who would not otherwise have it.

23 For example, Slovakia responded immediately to the 2010 Hungarian law with a change to its own nationality law which strips of Slovak nationality anyone obtaining the citizenship of another country having actively ('by an explicit expression of will': *na základe výslovného prejavu vole*) sought it; Zákon č. 250/2010 ktorým sa mení a dopĺňa Zákon č. 40/1993 Z. z. o štátnom občianstve; in force 17 July 2010. The law may be unconstitutional as a matter of Slovak law. Slovakia also amended the language law restricting the public use of languages other than Slovak (Zákon č. 652/2009 ktorým sa mení a dopĺňa Zákon č. 270/1995 Z. z. o štátnom jazyku; in force 1 September 2009) and banned an unofficial visit to the (ethnically Hungarian) border town of Komárno by the Hungarian president; see Case C-364/10 *Hungary* v *Slovakia*, judgment of 16 October 2012, not yet reported. The contentious 2011 Hungarian Basic Law (Magyarország Alaptörvénye, in force 1 January 2012) in turn speaks of 'a nation torn apart in the storms of the last century' (Preamble, 7th indent), of a 'unified Hungarian nation' (D) §), and requires Hungary to 'bear a responsibility for the destiny of Hungarians beyond its borders' (D) §).

24 Case C-369/90 *Micheletti and ors*, n. 16 above; Case C-148/02 *Garcia Avello* v *Belgian State* [2003] ECR I-11613; Case C-200/02 *Zhu and Chen*, n. 16 above; *Mendes Machado* v *Secretary of State for the Home Department* [2005] EWCA Civ 597, [2005] All ER (D) 289. Nor may a member state treat Union nationals differently according to the time at which or the manner in which they acquired their nationality; Case 136/78 *Ministère Public* v *Auer* (No. 1) [1979] ECR 437, at para. 28.

stateless.[25] The result might be different with an individual less unsavoury. There exists no mechanism by which a citizen of a member state may repudiate the status of citizen of the Union which comes with it, should he or she wish to do so.

For absolute certainty a declaration of the intergovernmental conference was **8.07** attached to the Final Act of the Maastricht IGC, as follows:

> [W]herever in the Treaty establishing the European Community reference is made to nationals of the Member States, the question whether an individual possesses the nationality of a Member State shall be settled solely by reference to the national law of the Member State concerned. Member States may declare, for information, who are to be considered their nationals for Community purposes by way of a declaration lodged with the Presidency and may amend any such declaration when necessary.[26]

This has two additional components absent from substantial Treaty texts. First, it recognises an exclusive authority for the member states each to determine who is a national of each *and* who is a national 'for Union purposes'. It thus posits a bifurcated status, that of citizen and that of citizen for Union purposes, to be determined at the whim (by 'declaration') of each member state; the status of citizen of a member state but not of the Union is rare, but does exist.[27] Second, it authorises each member state unilaterally to alter that status, as, for example, the United Kingdom did in 1983 when its current nationality law entered into force.[28] But it should be borne in mind that this is a conference declaration only, and whilst it probably accurately states the situation, it does not have the force of the Treaties themselves. If, however, a member state were to attempt, by simple declaration, unilaterally to deprive some or all of its citizens of the status of citizen of the Union (admittedly an unlikely occurrence), this might be open to challenge before the Court of Justice.

Because Union citizenship, and Union rights generally, adhere to citizens of the **8.08** member states, it leaves rights of third country nationals untouched and in principle subject solely to national regulation. So a third country national working, resident or merely present in a member state is there by grace of the

---

25 Case C-135/08 *Rottmann* v *Freistaat Bayern* [2010] ECR I-1449. It must be considered whether the decision to revoke citizenship is, insofar as the consequences it entails, proportionate. The Court declined to answer, as premature, the question put as to whether the member state of original nationality (Austria) was required automatically to reinstate that status.

26 Declaration (No. 2) on Nationality of a Member State.

27 See 8.10 below.

28 See, in light of the British Nationality Act 1981, Declaration by the United Kingdom replacing the (1972) Declaration on the Definition of the Term 'Nationals' [1983] OJ C23/1; see now the 'reiterated' Declaration (No. 63) by the United Kingdom of Great Britain and Northern Ireland on the Definition of the Term 'Nationals' annexed to the Final Act of the Lisbon IGC.

law of that member state, and his or her presence goes unnoticed and unaffected (and unhindered) by Union law. This is true in principle, but developments with the purpose of ensuring the free movement of persons have begun to chip away at the rule.

8.09 It will also be noted that the Treaties conflate the terms 'nationality' and 'citizenship', the TFEU itself creating 'citizenship' of the Union upon a basis of 'nationality', and article 20(1) referring consecutively to 'nationality of a Member State' and 'national citizenship'. This may spring in part from previous Treaty usage, from the beginning referring to prohibition of 'discrimination on grounds of [based on] nationality'[29] and to 'nationals of a Member State'.[30] The co-mingling of the two terms is an old habit in the English speaking jurisdictions in the Union[31] but it is not restricted to English: Treaty terms are rendered similarly in many other official languages (e.g., *nationalité/citoyenneté*, and the bearer commonly called in the case law a *ressortissant*; *Staatsangehörigkeit/Bürgerschaft*). However in some member states, and particularly in the Baltic states, there are very important distinctions between nationality and citizenship, and the Treaty versions in Estonian, Latvian and Lithuanian are therefore careful to refer only to citizens and citizenship.[32]

8.10 Absolute privilege afforded the member states gives rise to other anomalies. As a general (but not universal) constitutional rule both territory and citizenship are indivisible: Greenland is as much a part of Denmark as is Jutland,[33] and a Dutch citizen born and resident in Aruba or Curaçao is no less a citizen for that reason that the resident of Amsterdam.[34] But the territory of the member states

---

29 EEC Treaty, arts 7, (48(2)).

30 *Ibid.* arts 52, 59, 213(1).

31 In the United Kingdom the term 'citizen' was unknown in law before 1949; it was introduced by the British Nationality Act 1948, prior to which there existed only British subjects (a status enjoyed without distinction throughout the Commonwealth) and aliens. Citizenship (*sic*) has since then been regulated by a series of nationality (*sic*) laws (currently the British Nationality Act 1981), and those having that status are normally called 'British nationals' (see e.g., the opinion of A-G Kokott in Case C-434/09 *McCarthy v Secretary of State for the Home Department*, judgment of 5 May 2011, not yet reported ('*britische Staatsangehörigen*'); as she reports (in note 1) she is following the style of the order for reference), which is legally meaningless. In Ireland the Irish Nationality and Citizenship Act, 1956 creates the status of citizen (*saoránach*) but other than the title makes no further mention of nationality. The relevant Maltese legislation (Att dwar iċ-Ċittadinanza Maltija, Att XXX ta' 1-1965) adheres strictly to citizen (*ċittadin*) and citizenship.

32 That is, *kodakondsus*, *pilsonība* and *pilietybė*, respectively. Thus many of the 1 million plus ethnic Russian (or other Soviet) 'nationals' (properly so-called), many of them born and resident in the Baltic states, do not have citizenship there (because Estonian/Latvian/Lithuanian law declines them that status, regarding them as having 'undefined citizenship' (*kodakondsuseta isik*) or as 'non-citizens' or 'aliens' (*nepilsoņi*)), and are therefore not citizens of the Union.

33 Constitution of Denmark, § 1.

34 Wat van 28 october 1954 (Statuut van het Koninkrijk der Nederlanden), stb. 1954 503; Wet van 19 december 1984 (Rijkwet op het Nederlanderschap), stb. 1984, 628.

and the territory of the Union are not entirely coterminous.[35] Thus neither the Færoes nor Greenland is part of the Union; however the Færoese are Danish citizens but not Danish citizens 'for Union purposes', and therefore are not citizens of the Union,[36] yet Greenlanders (probably) are. Arubans, Curaçaoans and French inhabitants of both the overseas *départements* and the 'overseas collectivities' are fully citizens of the Union. Channel Islanders and Manxmen are not,[37] Gibraltarians are,[38] and there are categories of British citizens, although fewer than previously, who enjoy no right of admission or residence ('right of abode') in the United Kingdom and are not Union citizens.[39]

Rights of citizenship

The rights accruing to citizenship of the Union are set out twice, generally in **8.11** article 20 and then again, in somewhat greater detail, in the articles which follow. There is no explanation (or logic) as to why, or for the (slightly) different construction, particularly as regards the rights of movement and residence.[40] They are:

(1)   the right to move and reside freely within the territory of the Union subject to the limitations and conditions laid down;[41] the institutions may adopt any measure 'necessary to attain this objective' even if authority is not provided elsewhere in the Treaties;[42]

(2)   the right to vote and stand as a candidate in municipal and European elections (but not for election to national parliaments) in another member state ('in a Member State of which he is not a national') in which he or she resides;[43]

---

35   As to the territory of the Union see 10.05–10.06 below.

36   Protocol No. 2 (annexed to the 1972 Accession Treaty) on the Faroe Islands, art. 4; they will become so 'only from the date on which [the Treaties] become applicable to those islands', which they have not.

37   Protocol No. 3 on the Channel Islands and the Isle of Man, art. 2.

38   British Nationality Act 1981, ss. 15 ff., 50(1), Sch. 6; Declaration by the United Kingdom replacing the (1972) Declaration on the Definition of the Term 'Nationals'[1983] OJ C23/1; 'reiterated' at the Lisbon IGC, Declaration (No. 63) by the United Kingdom of Great Britain and Northern Ireland on the Definition of the Term 'Nationals'. This was so even though Gibraltarians were not, at the time, British citizens.

39   That is, British overseas territories citizens (previously British dependent territories citizens), British overseas citizens, British subjects, British nationals (overseas) and British protected persons; see now the British Nationality Act 1981, ss. 15–38. Since 2002, some, but not all, British overseas territories citizens are, either automatically or subsequently by naturalisation or registration, also British citizens (British Overseas Territories Act 2002, s. 3). The other categories are residual, remnants of the Empire, and will lapse with time.

40   See 11.97 below, n. 598.

41   TFEU, arts 20(2)(a) and 21(1) (ex art. 18(1) EC).

42   TFEU, arts 21(2) (added by the Treaty of Nice; ex art. 18(2) EC) and 21(3) (added by Lisbon); see 11.97 below.

43   TFEU, arts 20(2)(b) and 22 (ex art. 19 EC); for detailed implementation for European parliamentary elections see Directive 93/109 [1993] OJ L329/34, for municipal elections Directive 94/80 [1994] OJ L368/38. This is reflected in and consistent with the Charter of Fundamental Rights (drafted after these provisions), which

(3)   the right to diplomatic representation by the diplomatic or consular authorities of another member state in the territory of a third country where the state of which he or she is a national is not represented;[44]

(4)   the right to petition the European Parliament on a matter which comes within the Union's fields of activity;[45] and

(5)   new with Lisbon, the right to participate in the democratic life of the Union,[46] including a right to 'invite' the Commission to formulate proposals for legislation.[47]

Other rights, such as a right of complaint to the Ombudsman[48] and a right of access to Union documents,[49] are sprinkled throughout the Treaties.

8.12   The creation of a Union citizenship – 'a European *status civitatis*'[50] – was both ambitious and perilous, if for no other reason than it is a concept which resonates very deeply in some member states whilst in others it is met with indifference. There is a view abroad that it was not intended to provide much by way of substantial rights beyond those already in existence; to Professor Weiler, it was 'little more than a cynical exercise in public relations'.[51] Certainly in comparison with a catalogue of rights (and duties) normally adhering to 'citizenship', this is pretty thin gruel. The right to petition the Parliament (article 24) may be useful, and the right of diplomatic and consular representation (article 23) is doubtless of significant practical use to unfortunate citizens of particularly the smaller member states, which may have a limited consular presence in many third countries. The Commission has adopted a Green Paper on the diplomatic and consular protection of Union citizens in third countries[52] and has urged that the text of article 23 be reproduced in all Union passports;[53] it is an aspect of Union citizenship which is likely to gain prominence as the Union's External Action Service develops.

---

refers to a right of Union citizens to vote (and stand for election) in European (art. 39) and municipal (art. 40) elections 'in the Member State in which he or she resides, under the same conditions as nationals of that State'.

44   TFEU, arts 22(2)(c) and 23 (ex art. 20 EC).

45   TFEU, arts 20(2)(d) and 24 (ex art. 21 EC).

46   TEU, art. 10(3).

47   TEU art. 11(4); see 3.74 above.

48   TFEU, art. 228.

49   TFEU, art. 15.

50   Case C-258/04 *Office national de l'emploi* v *Ioannidis* [2005] ECR I-8275, *per* A-G Ruiz-Jarabo Colomer at para. 46 of his opinion.

51   J.H.H. Weiler, *The Selling of Europe: The Discourse of European Citizenship in the IGC 1996*, Harvard Jean Monnet Working Paper 3/96 (1996).

52   [2007] OJ C30/8.

53   Recommendation 2008/355 [2008] OJ L118/30.

The electoral rights conferred by article 22 *do* bite into national sovereignty, the **8.13** right to vote traditionally restricted to citizens and this frequently preserved in the constitution,[54] and they add some democratic legitimacy to the exercise of citizens' rights. Yet here too there are anomalies. First, the Treaties provide a right to vote in European and 'municipal' elections. The term is not defined, and there is a huge variety amongst the member states in the manner in which sub-national government is organised. Thus non-national Union residents may vote in 'county' elections (that is, a tier of regional government between the commune and the national level) in Denmark (elections to the *amt*), Hungary (the *megye*), Slovakia (the *kraj*) and Sweden (the *län*), even up to elections for devolved regional parliaments (the Scottish Parliament, the Northern Ireland and Welsh Assemblies) in the United Kingdom;[55] but this is not so in other member states.[56] The determining factor seems to be a political culture in which regional elections are regarded as a part of local government and not an exercise of national sovereignty. Even at what is indisputably local (commune) level there is a permitted degree of variable geometry[57] and a dilution of the right in that in a number of member states the right to vote locally is conferred upon all residents, irrespective of nationality.[58]

---

54 E.g., Constitution of Spain, art. 13; Constitution of France, art. 3; thus both constitutions were required to be amended prior to ratification of Maastricht in order to accommodate (what is now) art. 22 TFEU.

55 See e.g., for the Scottish Parliament, Representation of the People Act 1983, s. 2(1)(c) in combination with Scotland Act 1998, s. 11(1); and see *McGeogh* v *Electoral Registration Officer, Dumfries and Galloway and ors* [2011] CSOH 65.

56 See e.g., for the German and Austrian *Landtage*, Gesetz über die Landtagswahlen (Landtagswahlengesetz – LWG) vom 15. April 2005, GBl. S. 384, § 7 I (Baden-Württemberg); Gesetz über die Wahlen zum Abgeordnetenhaus und zu den Bezirksverordnetenversammlungen (Landeswahlgesetz) vom 25. September 1987, GVBl. S. 300, § 1 I (as amended) (Berlin); Verfassungsgesetz über die Verfassung des Landes Vorarlberg (Landesverfassung – LV) LGBl. Nr 9/1999, § 13(2). Resident Union citizens may vote only in elections to district councils (*Gemeindesämte, Bezirkesämte* and similar); e.g., Berlines Landeswahlgesetz, § 22a. It should be noted that it is clear in German that an art. 19 right to vote in '*Kommunalwahlen*' extends no higher. Nor may non-Spanish Union citizens vote in elections to the Basque/Catalan/Galician parliaments; arts 13(2) and 23(1) of the Spanish Constitution.

57 Directive 94/80 [1994] OJ L368/38, art. 12(1) permits member states in which the proportion of non-nationals amongst the resident population of voting age exceeds 20 per cent (that is, Luxembourg, Estonia (probably just) and Latvia) to require a residence period, and art. 12(2) permits Belgium to do the same as regards 'a limited number of local government units' simply upon selection. Voting in the Åland Islands requires a period of residency which is required also for Finns who do not have right of domicile (*hembygdsrätt*) there, and this appears to have the Union's acquiescence; Directive 96/30 [1996] OJ L122/14, preamble, 3rd recital.

58 See e.g., in Belgium, loi fédérale du 19 mars 2004 à octroyer le droit de vote aux elections communales à des étrangers, MB du 23 avril 2004, p. 24188. An attempt to provide similar privileges in Schleswig-Holstein and Hamburg was struck down by the *Bundesverfassungsgericht* for inconsistency with the Basic Law; BVerfG, 31. Oktober 1990, BVerfGE 83, 37 (Schleswig-Holstein) and 60 (Hamburg). Usually a period of residence for non-Union citizens is required. The Council of Europe has promulgated a convention in the area (Convention of 5 February 1992 on the Participation of Foreigners in Public Life at Local Level (CETS No. 144)) but it has met with limited enthusiasm; it is in force in five member states (Denmark, Italy, the Netherlands, Finland and Sweden).

8.14 Second, the (limited) right to vote is in a host member state of residence, otherwise the Treaties are silent. The French overseas *départements* are part of the Union, the overseas collectivities are not, yet voting in elections to the European Parliament is organised throughout these territories in accordance with French electoral law.[59] In other non-European territories of the member states they are not, and the Court of Justice has held that whilst a member state *may* (as France does) organise elections to the Parliament there, it is under no Treaty obligation to do so.[60] European elections are held in Gibraltar, but only from the 2004 elections following censure by the European Court of Human Rights for having failed previously so to provide.[61] This was challenged by Spain owing to the peculiarity of UK electoral law which grants full voting rights to all resident (so including non-British) Commonwealth citizens,[62] so enfranchising (some 100) non-citizens of the Union resident in Gibraltar and so, according to Spain, infringing the Treaties; the Court disagreed, finding Union law not to preclude a member state from enfranchising third country nationals 'who have close links to [it]'.[63] There are yet further irregularities, for electoral law in some member states confer upon its citizens a right to vote irrespective of residence, whilst others do not. In UK electoral law, for example, a British citizen may vote in all elections (local, devolved, national, European) while absent the country – or the continent – for a period of up to 15 years, provided he or she was entered on a UK electoral register before departing.[64] This means that a UK citizen, as well as his Dutch neighbour,[65] resident in, say, Melbourne, enjoy a right to vote in European elections, whilst their Greek

---

59   Loi no. 77–729 du 7 juillet 1977 relative à l'élection des représentants au Parlement européen, JO du 8 juillet 1977, p. 3579, art. 2; code électoral, livre 1er, titre 1er.

60   Case C-300/04 *Eman and Sevinger v College van Burgemeester en Wethouders van Den Haag* [2006] ECR I-8055. However the outcome of the case, raised by two disenfranchised and disgruntled Dutch citizens resident in Aruba, turned on a peculiarity of Dutch electoral law which grants the right to vote in European elections to Dutch citizens wherever in the world they may be *except* if resident in Aruba or the (then) Netherlands Antilles (Wet van 28 september 1989 (Kieswet), stb. 1989, 423, arts B1, Y3). This, said the Court, was an unjustified breach of the principle of equal treatment. The anomalous result is (a) that the Dutch authorities are under no obligation to organise elections in Aruba, yet (b) must now afford a vote to Dutch residents there. Aruba being outwith the territorial scope of the Treaties, it is not clear if they must do likewise for other Union citizens – which would turn (a) on its head.

61   *Matthews v United Kingdom* (1999) 26 EHRR 361. The necessary provision was made by the European Parliament (Representation) Act 2003.

62   European Parliamentary Elections Act 1978, s. 3C(1),(2) in combination with Representation of the People Act 1983, s. 1(c).

63   Case C-145/04 *Spain v United Kingdom* [2006] ECR I-7917, at para. 78. Presumably this applies equally to the anomaly of over 1 million Commonwealth citizens resident in the United Kingdom who are not Union citizens but (have the right to) vote in European elections. And it raises a distinct question of discrimination amongst non-national Union citizens, and whether UK law may, as it does, confer full voting rights upon resident Cypriot, Maltese and (a historical residue) Irish citizens but not upon other Union citizens. As to special privileges afforded Irish but not other EU citizens in a different context see *Patmalniece v Secretary of State for Work and Pensions* [2011] UKSC 11, [2011] 3 All ER 1, *per* Lord Hope.

64   Representation of the People Act 1985, s. 1 (as amended).

65   See n. 60 above.

neighbour – for Greek electoral law makes no similar provision[66] – does not. The electoral law in some member states (that is Belgium, Greece, Italy, Cyprus and Luxembourg) makes voting compulsory[67] (although enforcement of the obligation is usually relaxed), and this generally carries over for Union citizens if they appear (for which they must apply in these member states) on the electoral roll.

Ironically perhaps, it is the first enumerated right of citizenship, the right to move and reside freely within the territory of the Union subject to the limitations and conditions laid down in the Treaties and by legislation,[68] which seems to add nothing to what was already there, yet has been interpreted by the Court of Justice so as to augment substantially, maybe fundamentally, the rights of citizens. As most of these developments arose, and continue to arise, against a backdrop of the movement and residence of persons, they are best understood in that context, and so will be discussed in later chapters.[69] **8.15**

---

66 A Greek citizen may vote for Greek candidates in European elections (or of course for candidates in a member state in which he is resident) but only if resident within the European Union; Νόμος 1427/84 για την άσκηση των εκλογικών δικαιωμάτων από Έλληνες που κατοικούν στην ΕΕ, ΦΕΚ Α' 40.

67 E.g., Decreto del 30 marzo 1957, n. 361, GURI no. 139 del 3 juni 1957, art. 4 ; Loi électorale du 18 février 2003, JO du G-DL du 21 février 2003, p. 446, art. 89. Voting was compulsory in various Austrian *Länder* but this was abandoned over time, the last *Land* to do so (Vorarlberg) in 2004.

68 TFEU, art. 21(1).

69 See 11.96–11.106 below.

9

UNION POLICIES AND INTERNAL ACTIONS: INTRODUCTION

A. GENERAL

9.01 Part Three of the TFEU, comprising articles 26–197 and arranged under 24 Titles, is entitled 'Union Policies and Internal Actions'. Previously simply 'Community Policies', the reorientation serves to contrast, and emphasise, the new, post-Lisbon provisions on external action. Some of the 24 Titles are of course more important than others, and especial emphasis must be laid upon the first and third, the free movement of goods (Title II) (within which agriculture and fisheries is a *lex specialis* (Title III)) and the free movement of persons, services and capital (Title IV) which go directly to the internal market.

9.02 The original Treaty was different. Part Two of the EEC Treaty was called 'the Foundations of the Community' and embraced what is essentially the present Titles II to IV of Part Three; thereafter the original Part Three addressed 'Policy [*sic*] of the Community', being precursors (some fully fledged, some rudimentary) of the present Titles VII–XXIV. This led the Court to give priority to the foundations – which came informally but universally to be known as the 'four freedoms', that is of goods, persons, services and capital – as the core of Community business; and this was, of course, in consonance with a primary task of the Community of establishing the common market. Part Three of the Treaty was regarded as ancillary and/or complementary to its more important task. But Maastricht married the original Community 'foundations' and 'policy' into a single Part III on 'Community Policies'. This had a significant, and possibly unintended, effect upon Treaty interpretation; no longer did the free movement of goods enjoy a higher Treaty stature than any of the remaining 16 titles, and the Court faced the new task of balancing possibly competing policy claims which had come to enjoy equal Treaty standing.[1] Yet as a counterweight, the meaning of much of (the present) articles 26–100 (except for articles 67–89, new with Amsterdam and significantly amended by Lisbon) came to be established during the 30-odd years they enjoyed Treaty pre-eminence, and the Court has shown no great enthusiasm to depart significantly from this established authority.

B. THE COMMON/INTERNAL MARKETS

From the beginning the Community had as a task the creation of a common **9.03** market, which was undefined in the EEC Treaty but, according to the Court of Justice, 'involves the elimination of all obstacles to intra-Community trade in order to merge the national markets into a single market bringing about conditions as close as possible to those of a genuine internal market'.[2] Put simply, a common market is a customs union-plus: a customs union is concerned with the free movement of goods, a common market is concerned traditionally with the free movement of goods *and* the free movement of the factors of their production, that is, capital and labour. In its more modern incarnation it usually also embraces the unimpeded provision and availability of services.

The EEC Treaty laid down a timetable for the progressive establishment of a **9.04** common market within a transitional period of 12 years,[3] so ending on 31 December 1969. It was in significant measure (most obviously with the customs union), but not comprehensively, achieved. In 1985 Lord Cockfield, then Commissioner with responsibility for the internal market, produced his White Paper ('the Cockfield White Paper'),[4] which identified the remaining barriers to trade within the Community, grouping them within three principal categories: physical barriers, technical barriers and fiscal barriers. The White Paper then set out some 300 items of legislation which, it argued, would be both

---

1   See e.g., Case C-379/98 *PreussenElektra* v *Schleswag* [2001] ECR I-2099, in which the Court of Justice was required to weigh in the balance (and ultimately preferred the latter) the competing interests of the free movement of goods and the concerns of environmental policy. In the same manner the Court of First Instance can be said to have favoured environmental objectives over the state aids rules in Case T-210/02 *British Aggregates* v *Commission* [2006] ECR II-2789 and Case T-233/04 *Netherlands* v *Commission* (NOx Emissions) [2008] ECR II-951 (although both judgments were set aside on appeal: Case C-487/06P *British Aggregates Association* v *Commission* [2008] ECR I-10505; Case C-279/08P *Commission* v *Netherlands* (NOx Emissions), judgment of 8 September 2011, not yet reported).
2   Case 15/81 *Gaston Schul* v *Inspecteur der Invoerrechten en Accijnzen* [1982] ECR 1409, at para. 33.
3   EEC Treaty, art. 8.
4   *Completing the Internal Market*, COM(85) 310.

necessary and sufficient to eliminate those barriers. As a means of implementing the Cockfield proposals the Single European Act amended the EEC Treaty
to include a new definition of 'the internal market' as 'an area without internal
frontiers in which the free movement of goods, persons, services and capital is
ensured in accordance with the provisions of this Treaty',[5] new timetable for its
completion by 31 December 1992[6] – hence the '1992 programme' – and specific
legislative procedures to assist in achieving it.[7] Between 1985 and 1993 some
500 internal market measures were adopted, and much (but not all) of the
programme was completed by the end of 1992.

9.05 The question then begged was the difference between the common market and
the internal market. In principle the latter appeared to be a subset of the former:
it was concerned with the four freedoms and the technical means of achieving
them, in other words the abolition of the physical, fiscal and technical barriers
to the four freedoms identified by the Cockfield White Paper. The common
market reaches further into the necessary flanking fields of, for example,
competition, economic and monetary and social policy. Yet confusion
abounded. The internal market was sometimes called the single market, or
'single internal market', and both were frequently used interchangeably for
common market. The Court clarified in *Gaston Schul* the meaning of common
market as the replication of a 'genuine internal market', and other case law
spoke of the fusion of national markets 'into a single market having the
characteristics of a domestic market'.[8] According to Advocate-General Tesauro
'[t]he concept of "internal market" [is based] on that of the "common market"'.[9]
If competition policy is a function of a common market it makes sense that a
Community activity be 'the institution of a system ensuring that competition in
the common market is not distorted', as it was from the start;[10] yet this was
altered to 'a system ensuring that competition in the *internal* market is not
distorted',[11] and not by the Single European Act by which the internal market
was introduced but subsequently, by stealth, by Maastricht. Conversely, another
Community activity remained the approximation of national laws 'to the extent
required for the functioning of the common market',[12] yet in its operative Part
Three the Treaty provided for the approximation of national laws 'which have as

---

5   EEC Treaty, art. 7a, 2nd para. (now art. 26(2) TFEU).
6   EEC Treaty, art. 7a, 1st para.
7   *Ibid.* art. 100a (now art. 114 TFEU). There was another provision (EEC Treaty, art. 100b) enabling the Council
    to declare provisions in force in a member state to be equivalent to those in force in another before the end of
    1992; the power was never used, and the provision was repealed (*sic*) by Amsterdam.
8   Case 270/80 *Polydor* v *Harlequin* [1982] ECR 329, at para. 16.
9   Case C-300/89 *Commission* v *Council* (Titanium Dioxide) [1991] ECR I-2867, at para. 10(8) of his opinion.
10 EEC Treaty, art. 3(f).
11 EC Treaty, art. 3(g) (pre-Amsterdam) (emphasis added).
12 *Ibid.* art. 3(h).

their object' (national laws generally) and 'to the extent ... necessary to ensure' (tax laws specifically) 'the establishment and functioning of the internal market'.[13] Imprecision abounded. Therefore in general, and even in authoritative texts, the terms common, single and internal market were used interchangeably.

Lisbon abandoned all reference to the common market: instead, '[t]he Union **9.06** shall establish an internal market',[14] there is a new Title I of Part Three entitled 'The Internal Market' and the Union is authorised to 'adopt measures with the aim of establishing or ensuring the functioning of the internal market',[15] the definition remaining as it was,[16] and the term 'common market' wherever found in the Treaties replaced with 'internal market'.[17]

It is worth noting that in 2007 the Commission published its 'review pack- **9.07** age',[18] the fruit of an 18-month review initiated by its 2006 'vision paper' (*sic*) which the review 'translates ... into action'.[19] It is intended (and purports) to set out 'a new approach to the single market'.[20] Extensive discussion by the European Council and others was promised but has yet to occur. In 2010 the Commission produced a plan it called 'Towards a Single Market Act'[21] with a view to retrenching and relaunching the single market as a highly competitive social market economy, and outlines 50 'proposals' to that end to be pursued over 2011/12. Progress has not been swift.

C. THE FOUR FREEDOMS

Scheme of the Treaties

The original Treaty divided the four freedoms across four Titles, but which do **9.08** not coincide precisely: the free movement of goods (now Title II); agriculture, being a species of good to which special rules were to apply (Title III); free movement of persons, services and capital (Title IV); and transport, being a

---

13 *Ibid.* arts 95(1), 93.
14 TEU, art. 3(3).
15 TFEU, art. 26(1).
16 *Ibid.* art. 26(2).
17 Lisbon Treaty, art. 2(3)(g).
18 *A Single Market for 21st Century Europe*, COM(2007) 724 final. See also the staff working papers accompanying the review, SEC(2007) 1521 (review of single market achievements); SEC(2007) 1518 (modernisation instruments); SEC(2007) 1517 (implementing new methodology); SEC(2007) 1519 (external dimension); and SEC(2007) 1520 (retail financial services).
19 *A Single Market for 21st Century Europe*, n. 18 above, at p. 3.
20 *Ibid.* at p. 4.
21 COM(2010) 608 final.

species of service to which special rules were to apply (Title VI). Title IV blurs especially into four chapters: workers, right of establishment, services and capital, the movement of 'persons' falling across the first three. But for the addition of a new Title introduced by the Treaty of Amsterdam on visas, asylum, immigration and related matters[22] which is an added gloss upon the free movement of persons, the original scheme has survived essentially intact into present Treaties.

9.09 Of the four freedoms the Treaties characterise only establishment as a 'right', the rest are 'freedoms',[23] but this varies slightly amongst the various language versions and nothing ought to be read into it. The Court does not distinguish a hierarchy amongst them, rather it accords them the same (pre-eminent) stature within the Treaties: the free movement of goods is a 'fundamental freedom',[24] a 'fundamental right',[25] a 'fundamental principle',[26] 'one of the foundations[27] or 'one of the fundamental principles of the Community'[28] or 'of the Treaty';[29] the free movement of workers is a 'fundamental right',[30] a 'fundamental freedom',[31] 'one of the essential aspects'[32] and 'one of the foundations of the Community';[33] the right of establishment and freedom to provide services are 'fundamental

---

22   EC Treaty, Title IV, being arts 61–9; now TFEU, Title V, being arts 67–89.

23   Thus the TFEU speaks variously of 'free movement of goods' (Title II); 'freedom of movement for workers' (art. 45(1)); both 'right of establishment' (Title IV, chapter 2) and 'freedom of establishment' (art. 49); 'freedom to provide services' (art. 56); and merely the 'movement of capital' (art. 63).

24   Case C-265/95 *Commission v France* (Spanish Strawberries) [1997] ECR I-6959, at para. 32; Case C-394/97 *Criminal proceedings against Heinonen* [1999] ECR I-3599, at para. 38; Case C-112/00 *Eugen Schmidberger Internationale Transporte Planzüge v Austria* [2003] ECR I-5659, at para. 59; Case C-244/06 *Dynamic Medien Vertriebs v Avides Media* [2008] ECR I-505, at para. 42.

25   Case C-228/98 *Dounias v Ypourgio Oikonomikon* [2000] ECR I-577, at para. 64.

26   Case C-320/03 *Commission v Austria* [2005] ECR I-9871, at para. 63; Case C-82/05 *Commission v Greece* ('Bake-off' Products) [2006] ECR I-93*, at para. 19; Case C-170/04 *Rosengren and ors v Riksåklagaren* [2007] ECR I-4071, at para. 31; Case C-143/06 *Ludwigs-Apotheke München Internationale Apotheke v Juers Pharma Import-Export* [2007] ECR I-9623, at para. 25; Case C-421/09 *Humanplasma v Republik Österreich* [2010] ECR I-12869 at para. 25; Case C-28/09 *Commission v Austria*, judgment of 21 December 2011, not yet reported, at para. 111.

27   Case C-433/05 *Åklagaren v Sandström* [2010] ECR I-2885, at para. 42.

28   Case C-112/00 *Schmidberger*, n. 24 above, at para. 51; Case C-65/05 *Commission v Greece* (Electronic Games) [2006] ECR I-10341, at para. 25; Case C-110/05 *Commission v Italy* [2009] ECR I-519, *per* A-G Bot at para. 48 of his opinion.

29   Case C-265/95 *Commission v France* [1997] ECR I-6959, at para. 24; Case C-320/03 *Commission v Austria* [2005] ECR I-9871, at para. 63; Case C-65/05 *Commission v Greece* [2006] ECR I-10341, at para. 25; Case C-28/09 *Commission v Austria*, n. 26 above, at para. 113.

30   Case 152/82 *Forcheri v Belgium* [1983] ECR 2323, at para. 11; Regulation 492/2011 [2011] OJ L141/1, Preamble, 4th indent.

31   Case 66/85 *Lawrie-Blum v Land Baden-Württemberg* [1986] ECR 2121, at para. 16; Case C-415/93 *Union Royale Belge des Sociétés de Football Association and ors v Bosman and ors* [1995] ECR I-4921, at para. 78; Case C-281/98 *Angonese v Cassa di Risparmio di Bolzano* [2000] ECR I-4139, at para. 35; Case C-94/07 *Raccanelli v Max-Planck-Gesellschaft zur Förderung der Wissenschaften* [2008] ECR I-5939, at para. 44.

32   Case C-371/08 *Ziebell v Land Baden-Württemberg*, judgment of 8 December 2011, not yet reported, at para. 55.

33   Case C-344/95 *Commission v Belgium* [1997] ECR I-1035, at para. 14.

freedoms',[34] 'fundamental principles',[35] a 'fundamental rule'[36] and 'one of the fundamental provisions of Union law';[37] the free movement of capital a 'fundamental principle'[38] and 'one of the fundamental freedoms of the Community';[39] collated, the 'freedom of movement or freedom to move services, goods or capital as well as [the] freedom to reside or to set up the seat of their activities in the Community [are] fundamental freedoms'[40] and '[a]ccording to the Court's case-law, the articles of the Treaty relating to the free movement of goods, persons, services and capital are fundamental Community provisions'.[41] It does, however, view the four freedoms as sealed (although not hermetically so) compartments. So, for example, where a national measure is argued to have the effect of restricting both the free movement of goods and the freedom to provide services, the Court will in principle examine it in relation to only one of those fundamental freedoms where it is shown that, in the circumstances of the case, one of them is secondary in relation to the other and may be considered together with it.[42]

---

34 Case C-55/94 *Gebhard* v *Consiglio dell'Ordine degli Avvocati e Procuratore di Milano* [1995] ECR I-4165, at para. 37; Case C-193/05 *Commission* v *Luxembourg* [2006] ECR I-8673, at para. 39 (establishment only); Case C-438/05 *International Transport Workers' Union* v *Viking Line* [2007] ECR I-10779, at para. 59 (establishment only – which is also 'one of the fundamental principles of the Community' (para. 68)); Case C-446/05 *Procureur du Roi* v *Doulamis* [2008] ECR I-1377, *per* A-G Bot at para. 76 of his opinion; Case C-346/06 *Rüffert* v *Land Niedersachsen* [2008] ECR I-1989, at para. 36 (services only); Case C-371/10 *National Grid Indus* v *Inspecteur van de Belastingdienst Rijnmond/kantoor Rotterdam*, judgment of 29 November 2011, not yet reported, at para. 26 (establishment only).

35 Case 81/87 *R* v *HM Treasury and Commissioners of Inland Revenue, ex parte Daily Mail and anor* [1988] ECR 5483, at para. 15 (establishment); Case C-341/05 *Laval un Partneri* v *Svenska Byggnadsarbetareförbundet and ors* (Vaxholm) [2007] ECR I-11767, at para. 101 (services); Cases C-261 and 299/07 *VTB-VAB and anor* v *Total Belgium and anor* [2009] ECR I-2949, *per* A-G Trstenjak at para. 124 of her opinion (services).

36 Case C-451/03 *Servizi Ausiliari Dottori Commercialisti* v *Calafiori* [2006] ECR I-2941, at para. 45 (establishment); Case C-438/08 *Commission* v *Portugal* [2009] ECR I-10219, at para. 34 (establishment).

37 Case C-157/09 *Commission* v *Netherlands*, judgment of 1 December 2011, not yet reported, at para. 50 (establishment) (*une des dispositions fondamentales, een van de basisbepalingen*; no English version yet available).

38 Case C-315/02 *Lenz* v *Finanzlandesdirektion für Tirol* [2004] ECR I-7–63, at para. 26; Case C-562/07 *Commission* v *Spain* [2009] ECR I-9553, at para. 42.

39 Case C-203/80 *Criminal proceedings against Casati* [1981] ECR 2595, at para. 8.

40 Cases C-158 and 159/04 *Alfa Vita Vassilopoulos and anor* v *Elliniko Dimosio* [2006] ECR I-8135, *per* A-G Poiares Maduro, at para. 51 of his opinion.

41 Case C-212/06 *Government of the French Community and Walloon Government* v *Flemish Government* [2008] ECR I-1683, at para. 52.

42 Case C-275/92 *HM Customs and Excise* v *Schindler* [1994] ECR I-1039; Case C-368/95 *Vereinigte Familiapress Zeitungsverlag* v *Heinrich Bauer Verlag* [1997] ECR I-3689; Case C-390/99 *Canal Satélite Digital* v *Administración General del Estado* [2002] ECR I-607; Case C-71/02 *Herbert Karner Industrie-Auktionen* v *Troostwijk* [2004] ECR I-3025; Case C-36/02 *Omega Spielhallen- und Automatenaufstellungs* v *Oberbürgermeisterin der Bundesstadt Bonn* [2004] ECR I-9609; Case C-20/03 *Openbaar Ministerie* v *Burmanjer and ors* [2005] ECR I-4133; Case C-42/07 *Liga Portuguesa de Futebol Profissional and anor* v *Departamento de Jogos da Santa Casa da Misericórdia de Lisboa* [2009] ECR I-7633; Case C-137/09 *Josemans* v *Burgemeester van Maastricht* [2010] ECR I-13019. Where not the case the rules of both chapters are to be considered and applied concurrently; see e.g., Case C-452/04 *Fidium Finanz* v *Bundesanstalt für Finanzdienstleistungsaufsicht* [2006] ECR I-9521 (provision of loans and credit both capital and services); Cases C-261 and 299/07 *VTB-VAB*, n. 35 above, *per* A-G Trstenjak at paras 96–109 of her opinion (a breakdown service combined with sale of fuel both services and goods); Case C-531/06 *Commission* v *Italy* [2009] ECR I-4103 (buying into the management of Italian

9.10   Articles 45, 49 and 56 too, although all dealing with movement of persons, are, in principle (if not always in practice), 'mutually exclusive'.[43] This applies also within a freedom, so that, for example, in the Treaty prism an impediment to the movement of goods may be a tariff barrier, a fiscal barrier, or a technical barrier, but cannot be more than one of these things at the same time. Having said that, it may not result in a great deal of practical difference, for the Court has developed principles which apply across all four freedoms, and in fact some implementing legislation applies irrespective of under which of the Treaty chapters an activity falls. This is a very important characteristic of the principles developed by the Court of Justice, and so of the law of the internal market, a cross-fertilisation amongst the four freedoms. Thus Advocate-General Kokott: 'restrictions on the fundamental freedoms must, as a rule, be justified by reference to the same principles'.[44] Put another way, a principle which emerges for the application of one of the four freedoms is very likely to resurface in the context of another.

9.11   The Treaty establishing a Constitution for Europe proposed a reconfiguration of the four freedoms into five, recognising the free movement of persons, services, goods and capital, and a distinct freedom of establishment, to be 'fundamental freedoms' which are 'guaranteed',[45] and reordered the sequence in which they appeared, moving persons and services ahead of goods;[46] Lisbon did not follow suit, reverting to the existing construction.

9.12   The approach of the Treaties to the achievement of the common market was similar across the four freedoms. Most were, under the original EEC Treaty, subject to a 'standstill' clause, that is a prohibition upon the introduction of any new measure having the object or effect of creating conditions more restrictive of free movement than those already in force, effective immediately.[47] Thereafter those measures which were in force were gradually to be abolished in accordance with a timetable (the three stage 'transitional period') set out in the Treaty. This does not mean that the common market was achieved in a uniform manner across the four freedoms. As it will be seen, the free movement of goods within the Union, for example, has been driven, and achieved, largely through

---

pharmacies both establishment and capital); Case C-108/09 *Ker-Optika* v *ÀNTSZ Dél-dunántúli Regionális Intézete* [2010] ECR I-12213 (Internet sale of contact lenses and optician/opthalomologist prescription/checks both goods and services).

43   Case C-55/94 *Gebhard*, n. 34 above, at para. 20.

44   Cases C-403 and 429/08 *Football Association Premier League* v *QC Leisure and ors* and *Murphy* v *Media Protection Services*, judgment of 4 October 2011, not yet reported, at para. 183 of her opinion.

45   Constitution establishing a Constitution for Europe, art. I-4.

46   *Ibid.* arts III-133–50 (persons and services), arts III-151–5 (goods).

47   EEC Treaty, arts 12 and 31 (goods), 53 (establishment), 62 (services), 71 (capital; but not compulsory) and 76 (transport).

the case law of the Court of Justice, working with the bare (but sufficient) bones of the Treaty: obligations and timetable provisions so clear as to stand on their own (or which were, in language not yet then adopted, 'directly effective'). Capital, by comparison, came to be freed up only with legislative intervention, following the original scheme of the Treaty. Persons and services fell somewhere in between the two, some (blunt) operative provisions drawn by the Court directly from the Treaty but the finesse of implementing legislation required in some of their wider or more complex amplifications.

However the rules developed, they are now largely directly effective. They are **9.13** uncontentiously 'vertically' directly effective: they are obligations addressed, expressly or implicitly,[48] to, and so enforceable against, the member states – 'member states' being all public authorities, the national, regional and local authorities of the state which through legislative, administrative or other means (even judicial means) use public power to hinder, directly or indirectly, intentionally or otherwise, the free flow of goods, persons, services and capital. But this is no longer exclusively so: latterly the Court has recognised that the obligations of these provisions bear not only upon the member states but also upon individuals ('horizontal direct effect'). This is a profound development in Union law, and it is not yet clear how or how far the principle applies. The Court has so far recognised it unequivocally only in the area of the free movement of workers,[49] but the principle is slowly haemorrhaging into other of the freedoms. This will be considered in due course.

In all events the common market was to be established within 12 years.[50] And **9.14** that, at some risk of excessive oversimplification, is it. It is important to bear in mind that, with the exceptions of agriculture and transport, the Treaty is not *dirigiste*. The four freedoms were to be achieved by the dismantling and prohibition of measures by which states traditionally obstruct them; thus it is that the primary enforcement mechanism laid down in the Treaties to ensure compliance with Treaty obligations – articles 258 and 259 – is available against the member states only. Thereafter it was left to the free market – subject to the (presumably light, proportionate) regulatory touch of legislation implementing the common market – and the self-interest of market operators to make it work. This was implicit in the original Treaty and made explicit by Maastricht,

---

48 Some provisions were expressly addressed to the member states ('Member States shall refrain from introducing' new customs duties (EEC Treaty, art. 12); 'Member States shall progressively abolish ... restrictions on the movement of capital' (art. 67)); others were not ('[q]uantitative restrictions on imports and all measures having equivalent effect shall ... be prohibited' (art. 30); '[f]reedom of movement for workers shall be secured' (art. 48(1)); and some were originally addressed to the member states but, owing to Treaty amendment, are no longer ('[c]ustoms duties on imports and exports ... shall be prohibited' (TFEU, art. 30 (ex art. 25 EC))).
49 Case C-281/98 *Angonese* v *Cassa di Risparmio di Bolzano* [2000] ECR I-4139; see 11.140–11.144 below.
50 EEC Treaty, art. 8.

providing that Community activities included an economic policy 'conducted in accordance with the principle of an open market economy with free competition',[51] and is why the competition rules which follow in a later chapter are so pivotal to the success of the Treaty endeavour.

---

51   EC Treaty (pre-Amsterdam), art. 3b.

10

THE FREE MOVEMENT OF GOODS

At its core the Union is a customs union: 'The Union shall comprise [previously, **10.01** "shall be based upon"] a customs union which shall cover all trade in goods',[1] and the Treaties now number the customs union amongst the fields of exclusive Union competence.[2] But it is in fact a sophisticated variant thereof. Title II of Part Three of the TFEU addresses the free movement of goods, and is divided into three chapters, 'the customs union' *simpliciter* (articles 30–2), customs cooperation (article 33) but also 'prohibition of quantitative restrictions between Member States' (articles 34–7), so addressing, first, the tariff barriers and second, other, non-tariff barriers by which the movement of goods across frontiers is traditionally hindered. Subsequent provisions make possible the harmonisation of national non-tariff barriers which persist in having that effect. Because it is not merely a free trade area, the Treaty provisions apply 'to products

---

1   TFEU, art. 28(1) (ex art. 23(1) EC).
2   TFEU, art. 3.

originating in Member States and to products coming from third countries which are in free circulation in Member States'.[3] Goods coming from third countries are in free circulation, in effect, as soon as they are subject to no further control by customs authorities.[4] Once in free circulation, they are to be accorded treatment identical to that of Union produced goods – they are 'definitively and wholly assimilated to products originating in Member States'.[5]

10.02 Whilst they provide for the free movement of goods, 'goods' are defined neither in the Treaties[6] nor in legislation. The Court of Justice has said that 'by goods … there must be understood products which can be valued in money and which are capable, as such, of forming the subject of commercial transactions'.[7] The category is therefore of very broad application. A good is normally (but not exclusively) corporeal moveable property. It is not restricted to consumer goods, articles of general use or ordinary merchandise, and may extend, to cite only a few peripheral examples, to products banned, with criminal sanction, in some or all member states,[8] to bees,[9] to a human kidney,[10] to coinage which is no longer legal tender,[11] to pet animals (not the subject of commercial trade),[12] to non-recyclable waste (with a negative economic value),[13] to electricity, noth-withstanding being incorporeal.[14] It does not, however, extend to things of

---

3   TFEU, art. 28(2) (ex art. 23(2) EC).
4   TFEU, art. 29 (ex art. 24 EC).
5   Case 41/76 *Donckerwolcke* v *Procureur de la République* [1976] ECR 1921, at para. 17.
6   Confusingly, the English text of the TFEU refers in turns to 'goods' (art. 28(1)) and to 'products' (arts 28(2), 29, 110), as do most language texts (excepting Bulgarian, German, Danish and Swedish, which use the same word throughout). No distinction is to be drawn between the two terms.
7   Case 7/68 *Commission* v *Italy* (Art Treasures) [1968] ECR 423 at 428.
8   E.g., narcotic drugs: Case 289/86 *Happy Family* v *Inspecteur der Omzetbelasting* [1988] ECR 3655; see also Case C-158/98 *Staatssecretaris van Financiën* v *Coffeeshop 'Siberië'* [1999] ECR I-3971; but customs duties are not exigible upon the importation of narcotics which are by law required to be seised and destroyed; Case 50/80 *Horvath* v *Hauptzollamt Hamburg-Jonas* [1981] ECR 385, and whilst goods, they may enjoy special restrictive treatment under Treaty rules; see 10.27–10.31 below. In Case C-137/09 *Josemans* v *Burgemeester van Maastricht* [2010] ECR I-13019, the Court of Justice said that a Dutch coffeeshop selling cannabis (a 'soft' narcotic drug) outwith strictly controlled lawful channels (for medical/scientific purposes), although the trade was tolerated as a matter of public policy, could not rely upon Treaty rights, without fully explaining why. See further cases on pornography (Case 34/79 *R* v *Henn and Darby* [1979] ECR 3795) and 'counterfeit' perfumes (Case C-3/97 *R* v *Goodwin and Unstead* [1998] ECR I-3257).
9   Case C-67/97 *Criminal proceedings against Bluhme* [1998] ECR I-8033.
10 Case C-203/99 *Veedfald* v *Århus Amtskommune* [2001] ECR I-3569.
11 Case 7/78 *R* v *Thompson* [1978] ECR 2247.
12 This derived from, e.g., Regulation 998/2003 [2003] OJ L146/1 on the non-commercial movement of pet animals; adopted by authority of art. 37 EC (art. 43 TFEU), so making pets 'agricultural products'.
13 Case C-2/90 *Commission* v *Belgium* (Walloon Waste) [1992] ECR I-4431; Case C-221/06 *Stadtgemeinde Frohnleiten and anor* v *Bundesminister für Land- und Forstwirtschaft, Umwelt und Wasserwirtschaft* [2007] ECR I-9643.
14 Case C-393/92 *Gemeente Almelo* v *Energiebedrijf IJsselmij* [1994] ECR I-1477; Case C-158/94 *Commission* v *Italy* [1997] ECR I-5789. In this the Court appears to have been influenced by the classification of electricity as

economic value which fall properly within other of the four freedoms, notwithstanding that they can be valued in money and may be the subject of market transactions. Thus the physical transfer of coins and banknotes which are legal tender[15] and of shares, bonds and other securities[16] involves not goods but falls within the later chapter on capital; so too donations in kind made to a charitable body.[17] Lottery tickets,[18] angling permits,[19] hunting leases[20] and decoding devices used for reception of encrypted pay-to-view broadcasts[21] are not goods but ancillary to the services they effect, although games of chance appearing in and forming an integral part of a magazine are subsumed within the good which is the magazine.[22] Sound records, film apparatus and other products used for the diffusion of television signals, insofar as they consist of tangible objects, are goods, but television broadcasting itself is a service.[23] When fruit or other electronic games machines are bought and sold they are goods, but their operation, hire, licensing, franchising and/or maintenance is a service.[24] Equally, consultation which may follow the Internet sale of contact lenses is a service but the original sale is dissociable from it, and falls under the provisions on goods.[25] Intellectual property rights may be bought and sold but are not goods, rather they are a *res sui generis* which nevertheless fall within the scope of application of the Treaties.[26]

Throughout both chapters on goods, the nationality of the owner, seller or buyer is wholly irrelevant.[27] **10.03**

---

a good under the common customs tariff and in various national laws. According to A-G Fennelly this may 'appear surprising' and is a 'specific case'; Case C-97/98 *Jägerskiöld* v *Gustafsson* [1999] ECR I-7319, at para. 20 of his opinion.

15   Case 7/78 *R* v *Thompson*, n. 11 above; Cases C-358 and 416/93 *Ministerio Fiscal* v *Bordessa and ors* [1995] ECR I-361.

16   Case C-222/97 *Trummer and Mayer* [1999] ECR I-1661.

17   Case C-318/07 *Persche* v *Finanzamt Lüdenscheid* [2009] ECR I-359.

18   Case C-275/92 *HM Customs and Excise* v *Schindler* [1994] ECR I-1039.

19   Case C-97/98 *Jägerskiöld*, n. 14 above.

20   Case C-70/09 *Hengartner and Gasser* v *Landesregierung Vorarlberg* [2010] ECR I-7229.

21   Cases C-403 and 429/08 *Football Association Premier League* v *QC Leisure and ors* and *Murphy* v *Media Protection Services*, judgment of 4 October 2011, not yet reported.

22   Case C-368/95 *Vereinigte Familiapress Zeitungsverlag* v *Heinrich Bauer Verlag* [1997] ECR I-3689.

23   Case 155/73 *Giuseppe Sacchi* [1974] ECR 409; Case C-23/93 *TV10* v *Commissariat voor de Media* [1994] ECR I-4795.

24   Case C-124/97 *Läärä and ors* v *Kihlakunnansyyttäjä (Jyväskylä) and anor* [1999] ECR I-6067; Case C-36/02 *Omega Spielhallen- und Automatenaufstellungs* v *Oberbürgermeisterin der Bundesstadt Bonn* [2004] ECR I-9609; Case C-452/03 *RAL (Channel Islands) and ors* v *Commissioners of Customs and Excise* [2005] ECR I-3947; Case C-65/05 *Commission* v *Greece* (Electronic Games) [2006] ECR I-10341.

25   Case C-108/09 *Ker-Optica* v *ÁNTSZ Dél-dunátúli Regionális Intézete* [2010] ECR I-12213.

26   Cases C-92 and 326/92 *Phil Collins and ors* v *Imtrat Handelsgesellschaft and anor* [1993] ECR I-5145; see 10.80–10.82 below.

27   Cases 2 and 3/69 *Sociaal Fonds voor de Diamantarbeiders* v *Brachfeld & Sons and anor* [1969] ECR 211.

A. THE CUSTOMS UNION

10.04 In order to create the customs union the Treaties set out, first, to abolish all customs and other charges on the movement of goods across an internal Union frontier, and second, to establish a uniform customs tariff for goods from a third country entering the Union via any member state. As to the first, the scheme adopted in the original EEC Treaty was to freeze existing customs duties (the 'standstill' clause)[28] and provide for their gradual elimination over the 12-year transitional period.[29] The uniform customs tariff ('Common Customs Tariff', CCT) too was to be introduced over the course of the transitional period by a gradual approximation of the four existing customs tariffs (the three Benelux states already comprising a single customs territory).[30] In the event the timetable was 'accelerated', the customs union coming into being[31] and the CCT adopted and in place[32] 18 months early, on 1 July 1968. The complex provisions governing the transition timetable became otiose thereafter, and were repealed in 1999 as part of the Amsterdam spring clean of the Treaties.

1. Territory of the customs union

10.05 The territory of the customs union is set out in the Treaties[33] and in legislation.[34] Generally, the customs union incorporates the territory, the territorial sea and the air space of all the member states, including those European territories for whose external relations a member state is responsible. There are, however, significant anomalies. The customs territory does not include the Færoe Islands[35] or Greenland,[36] which are outside the territorial scope of the Treaties. It does include the Azores, Madeira, the Canary Islands, the French

---

28   EEC Treaty, art. 12 – being the provision which led to recognition of the principle of direct effect; see 6.13 above.

29   *Ibid.* arts 13–16.

30   *Ibid.* arts 18–29. The Benelux customs union came into being on 1 January 1948 (Traité de 5 septembre 1944 instituant l'Union douanière de Benelux, 32 UNTS 143). It has since mutated into a full economic union (Traité de 3 février 1958 instituant l'Union économique Benelux (the Hague Treaty), 381 UNTS 165, in force 1 January 1960), concluded for a period of 50 years but automatically renewed for ten-year periods absent renunciation from one of the signatories (art. 99). With the passing of the 50 year mark on 1 January 2009 there is no indication of an intention to renounce it. In significant measure the Benelux served and serves as a mini-laboratory for Community/Union development.

31   Council Decision 66/532 [1966] JO 2971 (the 'Acceleration Decision').

32   Regulation 950/68 [1968] JO L172/1.

33   TEU, art. 52; TFEU, art. 355 (ex art. 299 EC).

34   Regulation 2913/92 [1992] OJ L302/1 (Community Customs Code), art. 3 as amended; implementing rules in Regulation 2454/93 [1993] OJ L253/1; Regulation 450/2008 [2008] OJ L145/1 (Modernised Customs Code, which is being phased in between 2009 and 2013), art. 3.

35   TFEU, art. 355(5)(a). Nor are the Færoese Danish nationals within the meaning of the Treaties; see 8.10 above.

36   See 1.20 above.

overseas *départements* (other than Mayotte) and Saint-Martin,[37] parts of the Union but owing to their 'structural, social and economic situation ... compounded by their remoteness, insularity, small size, different topography and climate' are 'outermost regions' (OMRs) entitled to various derogations (particularly in customs (within limits) and fiscal matters) from the full rigour of the Treaties;[38] the erstwhile Netherlands Antilles of Bonaire, Saba and Sint Eustatius are outside the Union but thought likely to be absorbed into it, as OMRs, in 2015;[39] and the Union, and the customs territory, includes the Åland Islands subject to special provisions.[40] The French 'overseas collectivities' (other than Saint-Martin),[41] New Caledonia and the 'southern territories' (*Terres Australes et Antarctiques Françaises*) are not part of the Union but they are subject to Euratom.[42] Monaco, an independent state, is part of the customs

---

37 TFEU, art. 355(1). The Canary Islands were originally outwith the customs territory but absorbed into it in 1991; Regulation 1911/91 [1991] OJ L171/1. The *départements d'outre-mer* are Guadeloupe, Guyane, Martinique, Mayotte and Réunion; originally the Treaty applied there only in part (see EEC Treaty, art. 227(2)) but was made fully applicable by the Treaty of Amsterdam (EC Treaty, art. 299(2): 'The provisions of this Treaty shall apply to the French overseas departments'). This does not yet apply to Mayotte which became a *département* only in 2011 (previously a *collectivité d'outre-mer*) and retains temporarily its pre-2011 status as an overseas country or territory (OCT) outwith the Union until absorbed into it as an OMR with effect from January 1914 (Decision 2012/419 [2012] OJ L204/131). Saint-Martin and Saint-Barthélemy were part of Community territory, ceased to be in 2007, reassumed the status with Lisbon in 2009, Saint-Barthélemy abandoning it again in 2012; see 2.75 above. The Treaties now (post-Lisbon) have a mechanism whereby the status in Union law of various of these territories (Danish, Dutch and French but not British) can be altered by the European Council (by unanimity) without need of Treaty amendment, TFEU, art. 355(6); it used this power in 2010 to transform Saint-Barthélemy from an OMR within the Union to an OCT outwith it, with effect from January 2012 (Decision 2010/718 [2010] OJ L325/4) and again in 2012 to settle the Union status of Mayotte.
38 See TFEU, art. 349 (ex art. 299(2) EC).
39 Prior to 2010 the Netherlands Antilles (Curaçao, Bonaire, Sint Maarten, Saba and Sint Eustatius) and Aruba (which had seceded in 1986) were both 'countries' ((*autonome*) *landen*) of the Kingdom of the Netherlands but not part of the Union. The Netherlands Antilles were dissolved in 2010 (Rijkswet van 7 september 2010 tot wijziging van het Statuut voor het Koninkrijk der Nederlanden in verband met de wijziging van de staatkundige hoedanigheid van de eilandgebieden van de Nederlandse Antillen, stb 2010, 333; in force 10 October 2010), Curaçao and Sint Maarten each becoming a *land* within the kingdom in its own right with a status similar to that of Aruba, so still outwith the Union and retaining (indefinitely) the OCT status accorded the Netherlands Antilles. Bonaire, Saba and Sint Eustatius ('the BES islands', or *Caribisch Nederland*) were (re-)integrated into *land Nederland* (the European part of the Kingdom) but not (as anticipated) as municipalities (*gemeenten*) within a mainland province, rather as public bodies (*openbare lichamen*) – yet as part of *land Nederland* properly part of the (territory of the) Union but still recognised by the Treaties as OCTs; and the Dutch government has resolved to preserve that status for a transitional period of five years, after which it will be reassessed. As to their likely future status see Declaration (No. 60) by the Kingdom of the Netherlands on Article 355 of the TFEU.
40 TFEU, art. 355(4). The scheme of the 1994 Accession Treaty was that the islands remained outside the Union unless they opted in. The Finnish-wide referendum on accession attracted the support of only 51 per cent of Ålanders, but, following the Finnish (and Swedish) 'yes', a referendum on the islands alone supported Åland accession under the special terms negotiated (see Protocol No. 2 (annexed to the 1994 Accession Treaty) on the Åland islands) by a 74–26 per cent majority; the Finnish government then deposited the necessary declaration.
41 The French *collectivités d'outre-mer* (prior to 2003 *territoires d'outre-mer*) are Saint-Pierre-et-Miquelon, Polynésie (Française), Wallis-et-Futuna, Saint-Martin and Saint-Barthélemy. The status of the (uninhabited) Ile de la Passion (Clipperton) is unclear.
42 Euratom Treaty, art. 198 ('Save as otherwise provided, this Treaty shall apply to the European territories of Member States and to non-European territories under their jurisdiction'). Expressly excluded are the Færoe

447

territory,[43] San Marino was, is no longer, but has entered into a customs union with the Union;[44] Andorra is in partial customs union with the Union.[45] Ceuta and Melilla are part of the Union[46] but not part of the customs territory.[47] Heligoland too is part of the Union but excluded from the customs union, as are Büsingen am Hochrhein and Campione d'Italia, respectively German and Italian enclaves in, and in customs union with, Switzerland; Livigno is part of the customs union but retains its special tax-free status. The Saimaa Canal and Maly Vysotskiy, under long lease to Finland but still part of Russian territory,[48] are not. The Crown dependencies of the Channel Islands and the Isle of Man are not part of the Union but are part of its customs territory[49] and for those purposes, as a rule, to be regarded as part of the United Kingdom.[50] Conversely, Gibraltar is part of the Union but is treated as being outside the customs territory,[51] and not all Union law applies there.[52] However Gibraltarians are citizens of the Union, although Channel Islanders and Manxmen are not.[53] Other British Overseas Territories lie entirely outwith the Union.

Islands, Greenland, Curaçao and Sint Maarten (according to the Dutch government), the UK sovereign base areas in Cyprus, the British overseas territories listed in Annex II to the Treaties and, to the same extent as the TFEU, the Channel Islands and the Isle of Man.

43   Regulations 2913/92 and 450/2008, art. 3(2)(a); see Case C-291/09 *Francesco Guarnieri & Cie* v *Vandevelde Eddy VOF*, judgment of 7 April 2011, not yet reported.

44   Agreement of 16 December 1991 on Cooperation and Customs Union between the European Economic Community and the Republic of San Marino [2002] OJ L84/43; in force May 2002.

45   Exchange of letters of 28 June 1990 [1990] OJ L374/14; in force 1 July 1991. But Monaco, San Marino and the Vatican are, and Andorra will be, in monetary union with the Union; see 14.11 below.

46   Act of Accession annexed to the 1985 Accession Treaty, art. 25.

47   Protocol No. 2 (annexed to the 1985 Accession Treaty) concerning the Canary Islands and Ceuta and Melilla, art. 1(2); Regulations 2913/92 and 450/2008, art. 3(1).

48   Sopimus 27 päivänä syyskuuta 1962 Suomen Tasavallan ja Sosialististen Neuvostotasavaltain Liiton kesken Saimaan kanavan Neuvostoliitolle kuuluvan osan ja Malyj Vysotskij-saaren vuokraamisesta Suomen Tasavallalle. The present lease expires in 2013, the lease on the canal to be renewed (and the rent quadrupled) for a further 50 years; sopimus 27 päivänä toukokuuta 2010 (Saimaan kanavan vuokrasopimus).

49   TFEU, art. 355(5)(c); Protocol No. 3 (annexed to the 1972 Accession Treaty) on the Channel Islands and the Isle of Man; Regulations 2913/92 and 450/2008, art. 3(1). On the application of the Treaties in the Channel Islands and the Isle of Man see Case C-355/89 *Department of Health and Social Security* v *Barr and Montrose Holdings Ltd* [1991] ECR I-3479, especially the opinion of A-G Jacobs; C-171/96 *Pereira Rocque* v *HM Lieutenant Governor of Jersey* [1998] ECR I-4607; Case C-293/02 *Jersey Produce Marketing Organisation* v *States of Jersey* [2005] ECR I-9543; Case C-491/04 *Dollond & Aitchison* v *Commissioners of Customs and Excise* [2006] ECR I-2129; *Manx Ices* v *Department of Local Government* [2001] EuLR 650 (IoM High Court of Justice).

50   Case C-293/02 *Jersey Produce Marketing Organisation, ibid.*

51   1972 Act of Accession, art. 28 and Annex I, section I, point 4; Regulations 2913/92 and 450/2008, art. 3(1) (by silence); Case C-30/01 *Commission* v *United Kingdom* [2003] ECR I-9481.

52   In particular Union legislation on harmonisation of turnover taxes does not apply there; 1972 Act of Accession, art. 28. But see Cases C-106 and 107/09P *Commission* v *Gibraltar and United Kingdom*, judgment of 15 November 2011, not yet reported (Gibraltarian tax legislation offending Union state aid rules). On the status of Gibraltar in Union law generally see Case C-30/01 *Commission* v *United Kingdom, ibid.* and the opinion of A-G Tizzano; Case C-349/03 *Commission* v *United Kingdom* [2005] ECR I-7321; Case C-145/04 *Spain* v *United Kingdom* [2006] ECR I-7917.

53   See 8.10 above.

Most important, Union law does not apply – it is 'suspended' – in the northern **10.06** part of Cyprus, the so-called Turkish Republic of Northern Cyprus, being Cypriot territory 'in which the Government of the Republic of Cyprus does not exercise effective control';[54] nor therefore, being under UN and not Cypriot jurisdiction, does it appear to apply to the buffer zone between the two communities. This is a situation very similar to that which obtained in the (non-)application of Community law to the territory of the German Democratic Republic prior to reunification in 1990,[55] and awaits a political solution to the division of the island, in which event the Council may, acting unanimously, assert Union jurisdiction over the northern part.[56] The United Kingdom Sovereign Base Areas of Akrotiri and Dhekelia are not part of the Union but are, now, part of the customs territory;[57] the Cypriot enclaves within Dhekelia (Xylotýmvou and Ormídheia) are fully part of the Union.

2. Customs duties and charges of equivalent effect

The EEC Treaty provided for the elimination over the transitional period of **10.07** customs duties and 'charges having equivalent effect' upon imports (articles 12 and 13) and exports (article 16) within the Community customs territory. That having been achieved, the operative provision is now article 30 TFEU, much simplified by the Treaty of Amsterdam:

 Customs duties on imports and exports and charges having equivalent effect shall be prohibited between Member States.

It is well to note from the beginning that this is language commonly used in the Treaties, speaking frequently of 'effects'. The significance is that (and it applies even where it is not stated) they address the substance of what is done – what actually happens and what is its practical effect – rather than the form or method by which it is done. Obstacles to the achievement of Treaty goals are, following this fashion and across the four freedoms (and beyond), sometimes accorded 'effects-based definitions'. The prohibition of article 30 is rigorously applied, and even in its previous form was directly effective as regards exports

---

54 Protocol No. 10 (annexed to the 2003 Accession Treaty) on Cyprus, art. 1(1). See Case C-420/07 *Apostolides* v *Orams and Orams* [2009] ECR I-3571 (confirming the duty of a court in another member state to enforce, as a matter of Union law, a civil judgment pronounced in a (southern) Cypriot court relating to title to land in the northern area).

55 See Protocol (annexed to the EEC Treaty) on German Internal Trade and Connected Problems (repealed by the Treaty of Amsterdam) which referred to 'the German territories subject to the Basic Law ... and the German territories in which the Basic Law does not apply'.

56 Protocol No. 10 on Cyprus, art. 1(2).

57 TFEU, art. 355(5)(b); Protocol No. 3 (annexed to the 2003 Accession Treaty) on the sovereign base areas; Regulations 2913/92 and 450/2008, art. 3(2)(b). Prior to Cypriot accession in 2004 they were not.

from the end of the first transition period[58] and as regards imports from the end of the final transitional period.[59]

10.08 Customs duties are such a straightforward matter there has been little difficulty in member states faithfully complying with their prohibition. More problematic are other forms of financial costs exigible at the point of importation or export, for example, inspection charges, licence fees, compulsory contributions to export marketing bodies and the like which are not customs duties properly so-called but nevertheless hinder the movement of goods by increasing (indirectly) their cost. Thus it is that article 30 prohibits also 'charges having equivalent effect' to a customs duty. A charge having equivalent effect to a customs duty (CEE) is an objective legal concept of Union law, defined by the Court of Justice as

> any pecuniary charge, however small, and whatever its designation and mode of application, which is imposed unilaterally on domestic or foreign goods by reason of the fact that they cross a frontier, and which is not a customs duty in the strict sense, ... even if it is not imposed for the benefit of the State, is not discriminatory or protective in effect and if the product on which the charge is imposed is not in competition with any domestic product.[60]

At issue was a 'statistical levy' imposed by Italian law of 10 *lire* per quintal or tonne of imported and exported goods for purposes of collecting trade statistics, a sum so trifling even the Advocate-General accepted that it 'scarcely has an appreciable effect on the movement of goods between Member States'.[61] It was nevertheless a CEE. Thus article 30 admits of no *de minimis* defence, it applies where a charge is imposed without discrimination, without protectionist purpose or effect, irrespective of the purpose for which it was introduced and the destination of the revenue raised.[62] Given the centrality of the customs union to Union purpose, it is not surprising the Court adheres to such a rigorous view.[63] The prohibition applies even if a charge is imposed also upon goods entering a region from another part of the same member state (for example the imposition of 'dock dues' (*octroi de mer*) upon the importation of goods from metropolitan

58 Case 63/74 *Cadsky* v *Instituto nationale per il Commercio Estero* [1975] ECR 281.
59 Case 33/70 *SACE* v *Ministero delle Finanze* [1970] ECR 1213.
60 Case 24/68 *Commission* v *Italy* [1969] ECR 193, at para. 9.
61 *Ibid.* per A-G Roemer at 208.
62 Case C-72/03 *Carbonati Apuani* v *Comune di Carrere* [2004] ECR I-8027, at para. 31; Case C-173/05 *Commission* v *Italy* [2007] ECR I-4917, at para. 42.
63 Repeated consistently, e.g., Cases 2 and 3/69 *Sociaal Fonds voor de Diamantarbeiders* v *Brachfeld* [1969] ECR 211; Case 29/72 *Marimex* v *Ministero delle Finanze* [1972] ECR 1309; Case 39/73 *Rewe-Zentralfinanz* v *Direktor der Landwirtschaftskammer Westfalen-Lippe* [1973] ECR 1039; Case C-426/92 *Germany* v *Deutsches Milch-Kontor* [1994] ECR I-2757.

France into Réunion),[64] and is imposed even upon a good crossing an internal frontier – 'despite the fact that [it] is imposed also on goods the final destination of which is within the Member State'[65] – which goes to the overall integrity of the internal market. Amongst the free movement provisions of the Treaty this is unique: in all other respects (except, partially, for article 35)[66] Treaty rights do not adhere to the movement of goods, persons, services or capital when that movement is restricted wholly to the territory of a single member state – the 'wholly internal rule', which is in some of those fields coming under increasing strain.[67]

There are three exceptions to the general rule. A charge imposed upon importation (or export) of a good is not a CEE, and so escapes the prohibition of article 30 altogether, if: **10.09**

(a) it is one for compulsory inspection of the goods which is required by Union law or international agreement, it does not exceed the true cost, and the scheme of which it is part promotes the free movement of goods (that is, neutralises a threat of unilateral national action which might be justified under article 36);[68]

(b) it is payment for a service provided by public authorities for the specific benefit of an individual trader; put otherwise, it is 'consideration for a specific benefit actually and individually conferred'[69] or 'consideration for a service actually rendered to the importer and … of an amount commensurate with that service'.[70] Examples which suggest themselves are inspection services outwith normal hours or provision of special warehousing or bonding facilities. The Court has recognised that this exception to the general rule exists, but in no case has applied it;[71]

---

64 Case C-163/90 *Administration des Douanes et Droits Indirects* v *Legros and ors* [1992] ECR I-4625.

65 Case C-72/03 *Carbonati Apuani*, n. 62 above, at para. 35; also Case C-293/02 *Jersey Produce Marketing Organisation* v *States of Jersey* [2005] ECR I-9543.

66 See 10.53 below.

67 See 11.90–11.95 below.

68 Case 46/76 *Bauhuis* v *Netherlands State* [1977] ECR 5; Case 86/76 *Commission* v *Netherlands* [1977] ECR 1355; Case 18/87 *Commission* v *Germany* [1988] ECR 5427. As to art. 36 see 10.27–10.31 below.

69 Case 63/74 *Cadsky* v *Instituto nationale per il Commercio Estero* [1975] ECR 281, at para. 8.

70 Case 132/82 *Commission* v *Belgium* [1983] ECR 1649, at para. 8.

71 E.g., Case 87/75 *Bresciani* v *Amministrazione Italiana delle Finanze* [1976] ECR 129; Case 132/82 *Commission* v *Belgium*, ibid.; Case 340/87 *Commission* v *Italy* [1989] ECR 1483; Cases C-277 etc./91 *Ligur Carni and ors* v *Unità Sanitaria Locale n. XV di Genova and ors* [1993] ECR I-6621. In one case (Case 170/88 *Ford España* v *Estado Español* [1989] ECR 2305) the Court appears to have accepted that a service (customs clearance on the importer's premises) met the required tests of a genuine service for the specific benefit of the individual trader, but declared it unlawful as the fee imposed was disproportionate. In Case 39/82 *Donner* v *Netherlands State* [1983] ECR 19 the Court said the test might be satisfied and left it to the referring national court to determine whether this was so, but (unlike A-G Rozès) it did not seem wholly convinced. The case may be assumed to have been well argued, the Mr Donner who bristled at the imposition of a 'customs clearance charge' and

(c) it 'relates to a general system of internal dues [*redevances*] applied systematically and in accordance with the same criteria to domestic products and imported products alike'.[72] In this case it is not a CEE but a function of a member state's system of internal taxation, and falls for consideration not under article 30 but under article 110, which deals with that field.[73] The two categories are mutually exclusive: a charge levied upon a good crossing a frontier may fall under article 30 or article 110, but cannot fall under both.[74]

A fourth category and a frontal assault upon the the principles of the customs union was the CAP system of 'compensatory payments' levied upon agricultural products crossing a frontier designed to correct currency fluctuations, but these have been abolished.[75]

10.10 Duties or charges which have been unlawfully levied are recoverable unless the importer/trader can be shown to have passed the cost on to subsequent buyers (and so would be unjustly enriched by recovery).[76] In 2010 the Council adopted a Directive on mutual assistance for the recovery in one member state of claims relating to taxes, duties and similar measures levied in another.[77]

3. Common Customs Tariff

10.11 Because the Union is based upon a customs union and not a mere free trade area, it was necessary to create a uniform tariff wall so that goods from third countries are subject to the same duty upon importation irrespective of where it

---

'commission' totalling *f* 85.30 for the completion of VAT forms on consignments of imported books having been a judge at the Court of Justice from 1958 to 1969 and its first president, from 1958 to 1964. See also Case 132/82 *Commission v Belgium* [1983] ECR 1649, in which A-G Mancini found the operation of certain warehousing facilities to constitute a specific benefit, but the Court disagreed. 'Specific services' are defined in Union customs legislation (applicable to charges upon imports from third countries) as 'in particular' attendance, where requested, by customs staff outside official office hours or at premises other than customs premises; analyses or expert reports on goods and postal fees for the return of goods to an applicant; examination or sampling of goods for verification purposes, or the destruction of goods; and exceptional control measures, made necessary by the nature of the goods or potential risk; Regulation 450/2008 [2008] OJ L145/1, art. 30(1).

72 Case 132/78 *Denkavit v French State (Customs Authorities)* [1979] ECR 1923, at para. 7. The English text in ECR reads 'supplied' rather than 'applied', but applied (the authentic version is *apprehendant systematiquement*) is probably more correct, and is used in later cases which cite *Denkavit* with approval; e.g., Case 18/87 *Commission v Germany* [1988] ECR 5427, at para. 6.

73 See 10.16–10.20 below.

74 See 10.17 below.

75 See n.632 below.

76 E.g., Case 199/82 *Amministrazione delle Finanze dello Stato v San Giorgio* [1983] ECR 3595. There has been significant litigation on this point. National law which makes it practically impossible to rebut a presumption that this was the case is inconsistent with this rule. It is a principle with which the Italian authorities have had significant difficulty in complying; see Case C-129/00 *Commission v Italy* [2003] ECR I-14637.

77 Directive 2010/24 [2010] OJ L84/1; required to be implemented by January 2012.

may occur. The EEC Treaty therefore provided for the progressive establishment of a Common Customs Tariff (CCT), which was fully in place by 1969.[78] A customs tariff comprises two essential parts, a comprehensive and systematic classification of goods (the 'nomenclature') and the rates of duty (normally *ad valorem*), if any, they attract upon entry into the customs territory. As reorganised in 1987, the CCT is classified now by means of the Integrated Community Tariff ('Taric', from *TARif Intégré Communautaire*), which is based upon a Combined Nomenclature ('CN').[79] The detail is amended frequently by the Commission in accordance with the comitology examination (previously management) procedure,[80] and each year the Commission adopts a hefty (915 pages in 2013) 'complete version of the Combined Nomenclature together with the corresponding autonomous and conventional rates of duty of the Common Customs Tariff, as it results from measures adopted by the Council or by the Commission'[81] which is published in the *Official Journal*.[82] The fixing of the duties themselves is reserved to the Council.[83] Since the coming into force of the CCT member states are no longer competent to impose any autonomous duties upon goods from third countries,[84] and the Treaties now formally recognise the customs union to be an area of exclusive Union competence.[85]

A raft of Community legislation was adopted in order to provide for common **10.12** customs rules so that goods from third countries undergo uniform valuation

---

78 EEC Treaty, arts 18–29; Regulation 950/68 [1968] JO L172/1.

79 Regulation 2658/87 [1987] OJ L256/1. There is an accompanying integrated system for the statistical classification of products 'by activity' (CPA) which regulates customs statistics for Union purposes and may be adopted by the relevant national authorities for their own; Regulation 451/2008 [2008] OJ L145/65.

80 Regulation 2658/87, arts 9, 10; as to comitology and the examination procedure, see 3.27 above.

81 *Ibid*. art. 12. Extensive 'expanatory notes' (CNEN) to the CN are also adopted and published by the Commission; see [2011] OJ C137/1. They are an important aid to interpretation of the scope of the various tariff headings but have no legally binding force; Case C-250/05 *Turbon International* v *Oberfinanzdirektion Koblenz* [2006] ECR I-10531, at para. 16.

82 For the most recent version (for 2013) see [2012] OJ L304/3. See also Regulation 1255/96 [1996] OJ L158/1 (and its frequent (biannual) amendment) which temporarily suspends any autonomous CCT duties upon goods which are not produced, or are produced in small quantities, within the Union. From time to time the Court of Justice is asked via art. 267 references from national courts competent in customs adjudication to interpret the minutiae of the CCT – for example whether imported Thai nightdresses were 'women's, girls' and infants' ... nightdresses' (CCT subheading 60.04 B IV b 2 bb) or 'dresses ... of synthetic textile fibres [CCT subheading 60.05 A II b 4 cc 22] which on the basis of their appearance are intended mainly, but not exclusively, to be worn in bed' (Case C-338/95 *Wiener* v *Hauptzollamt Emmerich* [1997] ECR I-6495); or whether vegetables (garlic bulbs) dried to some degree, but from which not all, or not almost all, of the moisture has been removed are garlic (CN 0703 20 00) or dried vegetables (CN 0712 90 90) (Case C-423/09 *Staatssecretaris van Financiën* v *X* [2010] ECR I-10821). In *Wiener* A-G Jacobs argued with feeling that highly technical questions of customs classification such as this were an abuse of art. 267 and ought to be rebuffed, but the Court supplied a ruling without disapproval or comment. The risk is, of course, that important cases can grow out of customs classification disputes – of which there can be no better example than *van Gend en Loos*.

83 TFEU, art. 31 (ex art. 26 EC).

84 Cases 37–38/73 *Sociaal Fonds voor de Diamantarbeiders* v *Indiamex* [1973] ECR 1609.

85 TFEU, art. 3(1)(a).

and procedures upon entry into the Community, irrespective of where. The legislation was consolidated in 1992 in the Community Customs Code[86] and now simplified, streamlined and replaced ('modernised') by the 'Modernised Customs Code' which is being phased into operation between 2009 and 2013.[87] The Code regulates in detail:

- definition of the Union's customs territory;
- origin of goods;
- value of goods for customs purposes;
- entry, presentation, unloading, temporary storage and release of goods;
- warehousing;
- inward processing;
- outward processing;
- free zones and warehouses;
- transit;
- security and recovery of customs duties.

10.13 Duties recovered under the CCT are Union 'own resources',[88] that is they are autonomous Union revenues accruing to the general budget of the Union. In 2012 net CCT revenues were about €19 thousand million.[89] The duties are collected by the competent national authorities, which act here in effect as agents of the Union, for which collection and other costs they keep 25 per cent,[90] presumably intended to persuade the member states to take the task seriously and maintain in place the necessary infrastructure. Nevertheless 'such a percentage must contemplate a surprising level of inefficiency if it is intended to cover no more than actual collection costs',[91] and the Commission now proposes a return to 10 per cent (as it had been prior to 2001) from 2014.[92] The Parliament and Council may adopt measures to strengthen customs cooperation between the member states and between the member states and the Commission.[93] The mutual assistance directive on recovery of claims in one

---

86 Regulation 2913/92 [1992] OJ L302/1; in force 1 January 1994. See also Regulation 1186/2009 [2009] OJ L324/23 on relief from customs duties for, for example, settlers' effects, trousseaux, inherited property, school accountrements and academic, scientific and educational materials, small consignments of non-commercial nature or negligible value.

87 Regulation 450/2008 [2008] OJ L145/1.

88 Decision 2007/436 [2007] OJ L163/17, art. 2(1)(a).

89 More accurately, €19,171,200,000 projected: definitive adoption of the general budget of the European Union for the financial year 2012 [2012] OJ L56, I/22; this excludes agricultural duties and sugar levies, and represents some 15 per cent of total budget revenues.

90 Decision 2007/436, art. 2(3).

91 Cases C-113 etc./10 *Zuckerfabrik Jülich and ors* v *Hauptzollamt Aachen and ors*, judgment of 25 September 2012, not yet reported, *per* A-G Sharpston at para. 134 of her opinion.

92 COM(2011) 510 final.

93 TFEU, art. 33 (ex art. 135 EC). Article 135 EC excluded areas of national criminal law or the administration of justice, art. 33 TFEU does not.

member state for duties levied in another applies equally to those levied on behalf of the Union, including CCT duties and agricultural levies.[94]

The CCT is one facet, and tool, of the Common Commercial Policy (CCP) **10.14** called for by the Treaties in commercial relations with third countries – for example the Union may, and does, confer preferential tariff treatment, so long as it does so in compliance with international trade law. The CCP is now itself an aspect of the Union's external action, is the subject of a separate Treaty Title within that context, and is discussed below.[95]

B. INTERNAL TAXATION

Although they appear in later provisions of the TFEU dealing with competi- **10.15** tion, taxation and harmonisation of laws,[96] the Treaty rules on internal taxation have greatest nexus with, and are best considered alongside the prohibition of, article 30. This resonates with the Cockfield analysis, which identified fiscal barriers as one of the three means, and with customs duties one of the two means involving payment of money, by which the movement of goods is impeded.

Article 110 provides: **10.16**

> No Member State shall impose, directly or indirectly, on the products of other Member States any internal taxation of any kind in excess of that imposed directly or indirectly on similar domestic products.
>
> Furthermore, no Member State shall impose on the products of other Member States any internal taxation of such a nature as to afford indirect protection to other products.

Articles 111 and 112 prohibit repayment upon export to another member state of internal taxation (article 111) or any other equivalent charge (article 112) in excess of that actually imposed (and so amounting to an export subsidy).

Article 30 addresses financial barriers to the movement of goods which occur at **10.17** a frontier, article 110 with financial barriers which exist within the internal ordering of a member state's laws. The former are banned, the latter regulated.

---

94 Directive 2010/24, n. 77 above, art. 2; as to agricultural levies see 10.105 below.
95 See 14.68–14.113 below.
96 That is, Part Three, Title VII, arts 101–18, of which the 'tax provisions' comprise Chapter 2 (of three), arts 110–13. Given the scheme of the original Treaty (see 9.02 above), this would suggest a subordination of these provisions to those on the free movement of goods, at least until homogenised as 'Community Policies' by Maastricht.

It is not the intention of the Treaties to deprive the member states of the power to levy taxes for the purpose of raising public revenues; but in order that the movement of goods is not impeded by distortion stemming from that power it is necessary for the member states to be fiscally neutral. The Court of Justice said early on that the purpose of article 110 is to 'fill in any loop-hole' (*colmater les brèches*) which a taxation scheme could open up in the prohibition of customs duties and like measures.[97] Alternatively, article 110 'supplements' (*constitue ... un complément de*) article 30:[98]

> Its aim is to ensure free movement of goods between the Member States in normal conditions of competition by the elimination of all forms of protection which may result from the application of internal taxation that discriminates against products from other Member States. Thus Article [110] must guarantee the complete neutrality of internal taxation as regards competition between domestic products and imported products.[99]

As indicated above, the two categories are mutually exclusive:

> [A]s regards the scope of Articles [30] and [110], it is settled case-law that provisions relating to charges having equivalent effect and those relating to discriminatory internal taxation cannot be applied together, with the result that, under the system established by the Treaty, the same charge cannot belong to both categories at the same time.[100]

This is a logical necessity, for the two are mutually incompatible: article 30 provides for an absolute prohibition, article 110 bites only where a tax has a discriminatory and/or protective purpose or effect, absent which there is no breach.[101] It may therefore be necessary to examine whether a given charge is a CEE or a function of taxation. A charge adhering to a good upon importation

> constitutes internal taxation within the meaning of Article [110], rather than a charge having an effect equivalent to a customs duty, if it relates to a general system of internal dues applied systematically to categories of products in accordance with objective criteria irrespective of the origin or destination of the products.[102]

---

97 Cases 2 and 3/62 *EEC Commission* v *Belgium and Luxembourg* (Gingerbread) [1962] ECR 425 at 431.

98 Cases C-290 and 333/05 *Nádasdi and anor* v *Vám- és Pénzügyőrség Észak-Alföldi Regionális Parancsnoksága* [2006] ECR I-10115, at para. 45; Case C-221/06 *Stadtgemeinde Frohnleiten and anor* v *Bundesminister für Land- und Forstwirtschaft, Umwelt und Wasserwirtschaft* [2007] ECR I-9643, at para. 30.

99 Case 252/86 *Bergandi* v *Directeur général des impôts* [1988] ECR 1343, at para. 24.

100 Case C-383/01 *De Danske Bilimportører* v *Skatteministeriet and ors* [2003] ECR I-6065, at para. 33; effectively identical construction in Case C-221/06 *Stadtgemeinde Frohnleiten*, n. 98 above, at para. 26; first established in Case 94/74 *Industria Gomma Articoli Vari, IGAV* v *Ente nazionale per la Cellulosa e per la Carta, ENCC* [1975] ECR 699.

101 E.g., Case 27/67 *Fink-Frucht* v *Hauptzollamt München-Landsbergerstraße* [1968] ECR 223; Case 31/67 *August Stier* v *Hauptzollamt Hamburg-Ericus* [1968] ECR 235.

102 Case C-234/99 *Nygård* v *Svineafgiftsfonden* [2002] ECR I-3675, at para. 19; Case C-517/04 *Visserijbedrijf Koornstra & Zn* v *Productschap Vis* [2006] ECR I-5015, at para. 16.

However it *is* a CEE, and so falls within article 30, if the revenue from that charge is used to finance activities which benefit only the domestic products intended for the national market and the advantages stemming from the use of the revenue from that charge fully offset the burden borne by those products.[103] If the burden is only partially offset the charge remains one to be dealt with under article 110, and the (limited) financial advantage extended the home producers may fall for consideration under the Treaty provisions on state aids.[104]

In the same way articles 30 and 110 are a (financial) subspecies of obstacles to **10.18** the movement of goods addressed more generally in article 34 ('Article [110] … is a *lex specialis* as opposed to [*par rapport à*] the general prohibition on barriers to trade, laid down in Article [34]'),[105] and are in principle applied to its exclusion:

> The Court has consistently held that the scope of Article [34] does not extend to the obstacles covered by other, specific provisions of the Treaty and that the obstacles which are of a fiscal nature or have an effect equivalent to customs duties and are covered by Articles [30] and [110] of the Treaty do not fall within the prohibition laid down in Article [34].[106]

A problem arises here where a tax is levied upon imported products for which there are no similar or competing goods produced within the member state of importation (and so lacks any discriminatory or protective effect). Such a tax is compatible with Union law so long as it remains within the general framework of the national system of taxation of which the tax in question is an integral part.[107] But the Court has indicated *obiter* that there may be circumstances in which such a tax escapes the prohibition of article 110 and is 'of such an amount' as to constitute a measure having equivalent effect to a quantitative restriction and so fall under article 34.[108] No case has yet been found.

---

103 Case C-234/99 *Nygård*, n. 102 above; Case C-517/04 *Koornstra, ibid.* Cf. the earlier, different, and slightly more burdensome formulation in Case 105/76 *Interzuccheri* v *Ditta Rizzano e Cavassa* [1977] ECR 1029.

104 See 13.163–13.169 below.

105 Case C-383/01 *De Danske Bilimportører* v *Skatteministeriet and ors* [2003] ECR I-6065, at para. 30.

106 Cases C-78 etc./90 *Compagnie Commerciale de l'Ouest and ors* v *Receveur principal des douanes de la Pallice-Port* [1992] ECR I-1847, at para. 20; also Cases C-34 etc./01 *Enirisorse* v *Ministero delle Finanze* [2003] ECR I-14243, at para. 56.

107 Case 31/67 *August Stier* v *Hauptzollamt Hamburg-Ericus* [1968] ECR 235; Case 90/79 *Commission* v *France* [1981] ECR 283.

108 Case 31/67 *August Stier, ibid.*, at 241; Case 47/88 *Commission* v *Denmark* [1990] ECR I-4509, at paras 12–13; Case C-383/01 *De Danske Bilimportører*, n. 105 above, at paras 32–42. In this context there has been, and continues to be, extensive consideration of the power of member states which do not produce them to impose tax provisions to (imported) motorcars: Case 47/88 *Commission* v *Denmark*; Case 132/88 *Commission* v *Greece* [1990] ECR I-1567; Case C-375/95 *Commission* v *Greece* [1997] ECR I-5981; Case C-383/01 *De*

10.19   Article 110, first paragraph[109] prohibits discriminatory taxation 'of any kind' upon imported goods which are 'similar', article 110, second paragraph (which 'is complementary to the first [paragraph]')[110] upon imported goods in a manner which affords indirect protection to domestic goods. 'Similar' is not defined. To find similarity the Court looks first to common treatment of products under fiscal, customs (such as the CCT) and/or statistical classification,[111] but will consider on a case by case basis a battery of objective characteristics such as origin, composition, method of production, and generally whether goods are (seen to be) interchangable from a consumer's point of view.[112] This latter characteristic is capable of some elasticity – the Commission, for example, takes the view that ouzo, gin, vodka, whisky, rum, tequila and arak are all 'similar' products[113] – and comes close to the tests for article 110, second paragraph, which is essentially a (generous) variation of the competition law tests of product substitutability or cross-elasticity of demand.[114] For the second paragraph to be joined it is necessary also that home product enjoy some advantage denied, and so is 'indirectly protected' as against, the imported product. So, for example, a member state is free to impose high excise duties[115] upon wine and low excise duties upon beer, so long as home vintners and brewers, on the one hand, and those in an exporting member state, on the other, suffer the tax burdens equally. But if the member state in fact produces no, or an insignificant amount of, wine, *and* if wine and beer are competing products (as they are for purposes of article 110), then the typically home-produced product (beer) is indirectly protected against the typically imported product (wine) – put another way, the 'fiscal levy is likely to discourage imports of goods originating

---

Danske Bilimportører, Cases C-290 and 333/05 *Nádasdi and anor* v *Vám- és Pénzügyőrség Észak-Alföldi Regionális Parancsnoksága* [2006] ECR I-10115; Case C-313/05 *Brzeziński* v *Dyrektor Izby Celnej w Warszawie* [2007] ECR I-513; Case C-426/07 *Krawczyński* v *Dyrektor Izby Celnej w Białymstoku* [2008] ECR I-6021; Case C-10/08 *Commission* v *Finland* [2009] ECR I-39*.

109   The first and second paragraphs of art. 110 are frequently cited as arts 110(1) and 110(2), sometimes by the Court, frequently in the literature, when in fact they are not numbered. The original art. 95 EEC contained a third paragraph which required member states to abolish national provisions inconsistent with the first two paragraphs, but it proved to be a damp squib and less pressing with the advent of direct effect (art. 95 EEC being directly effective from the end of the first stage) Case 57/65 *Alfons Lütticke* v *Hauptzollamt Saarelouis* [1966] ECR 205 (art. 95, 1st para); Case 27/67 *Fink-Frucht* v *Hauptzollamt München-Landsbergerstraße* [1968] ECR 223 (art. 95, 2nd para.)), and was repealed by the Treaty of Amsterdam.

110   Case 27/67 *Fink-Frucht,* n. 109 above, at para. 3(b) of the *dispositif.*

111   E.g., Case 27/67 *Fink-Frucht, ibid.*; Case 28/69 *Commission* v *Italy* [1979] ECR 187; Case 45/75 *Rewe-Zentrale des Lebensmittel-Großhandels* v *Hauptzollamt Landau-Pfalz* [1976] ECR 181.

112   E.g., Case 169/78 *Commission* v *Italy* [1980] ECR 385; Case 216/81 *Cogis (Compagnia Generale Interscambi)* v *Amministrazione delle Finanze dello Stato* [1982] ECR 2701; Case 243/84 *John Walker & Sons* v *Ministeriet for Skatter og Afgifter* [1986] ECR 875; cf. Case 184/85 *Commission* v *Italy* [1987] ECR 2013.

113   Case C-475/01 *Commission* v *Greece* (Ouzo) [2004] ECR I-8923.

114   See 13.21 below.

115   Nothing should be read into the absence in art. 110, 2nd para. of reference to taxation 'of any kind', as is present in art. 110, 1st para.: the two apply equally to the panoply of the state's taxing power.

in other Member States to the benefit of domestic production'[116] – and article 110 is breached.[117] And because the prohibition applies to discriminatory taxation of competing products, there must logically be, again unlike article 30, a *de minimis* element: so, Belgian VAT of 25 per cent on wine (typically, in Belgium, an imported product) and 19 per cent on beer is not incompatible with article 110 because of insignificant (or at least subject to statistical margin of error – 'they do not show with any certainty') impact on the comparative price of or demand for the products,[118] and a similar differential in Sweden upon the taxation of 'strong beer' (*starköl*) and of 'intermediate category' (*mellanklassen*) wine, found to be competing products, is so slight that it cannot be said to influence consumer behaviour or produce any protective advantage for the beer.[119] Here then is a material difference between the two paragraphs of article 110: in a situation in which a tax upon an imported product is greater than the tax upon domestic product but not so great as to afford indirect protection, if the products are similar, article 110 first paragraph is breached, if not, there is no breach of article 110 second paragraph. And owing to its clarity the former may be applied with greater precision. So article 110, first paragraph is infringed where the taxation on the imported product and that on the similar domestic product are calculated in a different manner on the basis of different criteria – for example the latter at a different taxable event at stages of production, the former upon the finished (worth more, so attracting a higher rate of *ad valorem* tax) imported product – which lead, if only in some cases, to higher taxation being imposed on the imported product;[120] and any tax relief afforded home producers, even for good (for example, to encourage best environmental practice in production) reasons, must be extended to imported goods.[121]

Notwithstanding the literal limitation of article 110 to 'products of other **10.20** Member States', the Court of Justice held that it applies to discriminatory

---

116 Case 252/86 *Bergandi* v *Directeur général des impôts* [1988] ECR 1343, at para. 25.
117 Case 170/78 *Commission* v *United Kingdom* (Wine and Beer) [1980] ECR 417, [1983] ECR 2265. This case also stands for the proposition that art. 110, 2nd para. extends to potential as well as actual competition. See also Case 184/85 *Commission* v *Italy* [1987] ECR 2013 and Case 193/85 *Cooperativa Co-Frutta* v *Amministrazione delle Finanze dello Stato* [1987] ECR 2085 (Italian 'consumption' tax on bananas where domestic production insignificant).
118 Case 356/85 *Commission* v *Belgium* (Wine and Beer) [1987] ECR 3299, at para. 20.
119 Case C-167/05 *Commission* v *Sweden* (Wine and Beer) [2008] ECR I-2127.
120 Case 45/75 *Rewe-Zentrale des Lebensmittel-Großhandels* v *Hauptzollamt Landau/Pfalz* [1976] ECR 181; Case 127/75 *Bobie Getränkevertrieb* v *Hauptzollamt Aachen-Nord* [1976] ECR 1079; Case C-375/95 *Commission* v *Greece* [1997] ECR I-5981.
121 E.g., Case 148/77 *Hansen* v *Hauptzollamt Flensberg* [1978] ECR 1787; Case 21/79 *Commission* v *Italy* [1980] ECR 1; Case C-375/95 *Commission* v *Greece*, *ibid.*

taxation upon *any* products, whatever their origin, which are in free circulation.[122] And in keeping with general toleration of reverse discrimination, article 110 does not prohibit the imposition on national products of internal taxation in excess of that imposed upon imported products.[123]

Harmonisation of taxation

10.21 So long as schemes, methods and rates of taxation vary amongst the member states there will continue to be impediments to the free movement of goods, identified in the Cockfield White Paper as tax disequilibrium and the frontier controls and equalisation charges necessary to deal with it – the 'effectiveness of fiscal supervision' being recognised as a mandatory requirement justifying impediments to the free movement of goods under the general prohibition of article 34.[124] Righting this disequilibrium – in the jargon, the abolition of fiscal frontiers – was a key component of the 1992 programme. Article 99 EEC (now article 113 TFEU), beefed up by the Single European Act for this purpose, therefore provided for the harmonisation of national legislation on turnover taxes, excise duties and other forms of indirect taxation 'to the extent that such harmonization is necessary to ensure the establishment and functioning of the internal market within the time-limit laid down in Article 7a'.[125] Because article 110 is fundamental, no legislation adopted under article 113 may depart or derogate from it.[126] Article 113 allows the adoption of 'provisions' so, perhaps surprisingly, leaving the form of legislation to the Council, but Directives are the much preferred choice. Significant progress, particularly in the fields of turnover taxes (VAT),[127] capital duty[128] and (to a lesser extent) consumption

---

122 Case 193/85 *Cooperativa Co-Frutta* v *Amministrazione delle Finanze dello Stato* [1987] ECR 2085. However the Court limited the application of art. 110 to 'all products coming from Member States, including products originating in non-member countries which are in free circulation in the Member States' (para. 29), so excluding direct imports from third countries and so giving rise to limited trade deflection; confirmed in Case C-130/92 *OTO* v *Ministero delle Finanze* [1994] ECR I-3281; Cases C-114 and 115/95 *Texaco and anor* v *Middelfart Havn and ors* [1997] ECR I-4263.

123 Case 86/78 *Grandes Distilleries Peureux* v *Directeur des Services Fiscaux de la Haute-Saône et du territoire de Belfort* [1979] ECR 89.

124 See 10.40 below.

125 Previously art. 99 EEC had read a woolly 'harmonised in the interest of the common market'. The new phraseology (which survives, excepting that 'within the time-limit laid down by Article 7a' is replaced by 'and to avoid distortion of competition') means that art. 113, like art. 114 (see 10.72 below), cannot be used to adopt harmonisation for harmonisation's sake, but must be fixed to, and 'necessary' for, the internal market.

126 Case 21/79 *Commission* v *Italy* [1980] ECR 1; Case 15/81 *Gaston Schul* v *Inspecteur der Invoerrechten en Accijnzen* [1982] ECR 1409.

127 See Directive 2006/112 [2006] OJ L347/1, being the 'recasting' of Directive 77/388 [1977] OJ L145/1 ('Sixth VAT Directive'), as (extensively) amended; also Regulation 282/2011 [2011] OJ L77/1 implementing Directive 2006/112.

128 E.g., Directive 69/335 [1969] JO L249/25 ('Capital Duty Directive'; now replaced by Directive 2008/7 [2008] OJ L46/11).

taxes on personal property[129] and excise duties,[130] was made by 1993. Since then there has been further significant progress on taxation of energy products[131] and cooperation amongst the administrative authorities of the member states competent in matters of VAT,[132] of excise duties[133] and of other taxes.[134] However, unlike the general enabling provision on harmonisation of laws for the functioning of the internal market[135] a measure adopted by authority of article 113 requires unanimity in the Council, and some member states view tax harmonisation as overly intrusive, a prerogative of the state in defence of which 'a line in the sand' must be drawn. An example: in 2011 the Commission proposed the adoption of a harmonised financial transaction tax (FTT) with a view to raising €57 thousand million of Union own resources annually as a means of redressing in part the financial sector's contribution to the economic and financial crisis;[136] it was generally well received but is unlikely ever to see the light of day (except perhaps as an enhanced cooperation measure) owing to UK opposition in the costs of such a tax it perceives to the City of London. It is one example only; until there is agreement across the range of indirect taxes there will continue to be an imperfect internal market:

> [T]he realisation of an area without internal frontiers has still not led to the abolition of administrative formalities and checks ... upon crossing intra-Community national frontiers. The continuing existence of frontiers in terms of the checks which are carried out is explained by the fact that the Community legislature has still not achieved harmonisation, within the Community, of the rate of national excise duties.[137]

---

129 Directive 83/183 [1983] OJ L105/64 (now replaced by Directive 2009/55 [2009] OJ L145/36).

130 E.g., Directive 2008/118 [2008] OJ L9/12 (general arrangements for excise duty); Directive 92/80 [1992] OJ L316/10 ((partial) approximation of taxes on manufactured tobacco); Directive 92/83 [1992] OJ L316/21 (harmonisation of structures of excise duty on alcohol and alcoholic beverages). Directive 2008/118 (replacing Directive 92/12 [1992] OJ L76/1) is the most widely recognised, for it provides for duty free importation of goods 'acquired by a private individual for his own use and transported ... by him' (as to which see Case C-5/05 *Staatssecretaris van Financiën* v *Joustra* [2006] ECR I-11075) if excise duty was paid in the member state of purchase (art. 32) so giving rise to tax travel, 'booze cruises' and significant loss of revenue in high tax member states, but excepting goods 'held for commercial purposes' (again, Case C-5/05 *Joustra*) upon which excise duty is exigible (art. 33(1)), for which member states may lay down 'guide levels, solely as a form of evidence' (art. 32(3)); there is concern that these provisions are far too vague, especially as tax evasion is a matter for criminal law and subject to very heavy penalties. Duty free imports in travel from third countries are regulated by other legislation, Regulation 1186/2009 [2009] OJ L324/23, art. 41 (customs duties) and Directive 2007/74 [2007] OJ L346/6 (excise duties).

131 Directive 2003/96 [2003] OJ L283/51.

132 Regulation 904/2010 [2010] OJ L268/1 (recasting Regulation 1798/2003 [2003] OJ L264/1).

133 Regulation 389/2012 [2012] OJ L121/1 (replacing Regulation 2073/2004 [2004] OJ L359/1).

134 Directive 2011/16 [2011] OJ L64/1 (replacing Directive 77/799 [1977] OJ L336/15); to be implemented by 1 January 2013.

135 TFEU, art. 114; see 10.68–10.77 below.

136 COM(2011) 594 final.

137 Case T-170/00 *Förde-Reederie* v *Council and Commission* [2002] ECR II-515, at para. 51.

10.22   As for direct taxation the Treaties are almost silent, in fact quieter now than in 1958.[138] Some Directives adopted under article 114 in the field of company law, and some more generally, have a bearing upon direct taxation[139] but that is not, and cannot be, their primary purpose. Yet direct taxation cannot be levied in a manner which is inconsistent with various rights under the Treaties, and latterly the Court of Justice has cut significantly into the taxing power of the member state in ensuring the free movement of workers, establishment, services and capital.[140]

C. QUANTITATIVE RESTRICTIONS AND MEASURES HAVING EQUIVALENT EFFECT

10.23   The TFEU declares quantitative restrictions upon imports (article 34) and exports (article 35) between member states and all measures having equivalent effect to be prohibited. Although the Treaty does not say so, the rule applies equally to goods in transit.[141] It is a general prohibition, a consequence of which is that where a national measure falls within it and another (more specific) Treaty provision, articles 30 or 110 for example, it will governed by the latter.[142] The exception is the rules on state aids: a national measure which constitutes a state aid falls within separate Treaty provisions which address that matter but is not wholly immunised from, and may fall also within, the prohibition of article 34.[143]

10.24   Article 34 in particular is of very wide application and there is a rich body of case law on it. But the principles can be stated quite simply.

1. Quantitative restrictions

10.25   Quantitative restrictions – generally, set limits, or quotas, on the physical amounts of particular commodities which may be imported or exported during

---

138   The EEC Treaty, art. 220 (art. 293 EC) required that the member states negotiate between themselves 'with a view to securing for the benefit of their nationals' agreements for the abolition of double taxation within the Community, but this was repealed by Lisbon. The Treaties require now only that there be no arbitrary discrimination in the taxation of the movement of capital and payments; TFEU, art. 65(3) (ex art. 58(3) EC).

139   See 11.51 below.

140   See 11.132–11.138 below.

141   Case C-320/03 *Commission v Austria* [2005] ECR I-9871; Case C-173/05 *Commission v Italy* [2007] ECR I-4917; Case C-28/09 *Commission v Austria*, judgment of 21 December 2011, not yet reported, *per* A-G Trstenjak at para. 59 of her opinion.

142   Cases C-78 etc./90 *Compagnie Commerciale de l'Ouest and ors v Receveur principal des douanes de la Pallice-Port* [1992] ECR I-1847; Case C-383/01 *De Danske Bilimportører v Skatteministeriet and ors* [2003] ECR I-6065; see 10.18 above.

143   See 13.169 below.

a specified period of time, measured usually by volume or weight, sometimes by value – are seen to be blunter, and more injurious, barriers to the movement of goods than tariff or fiscal barriers, for the latter will hinder but not prevent imports: goods will still be imported so long as they are price competitive enough to overcome the tariff or fiscal disadvantage they bear; with quantitative restrictions the door is shut, irrespective of price competitiveness. In Union law a quantitative restriction is a measure 'which amounts to a total or or partial restraint of, according to the circumstances, imports, exports or goods in transit'.[144] Thus a complete ban, even if not expressly so-called (for example criminal interdiction of possession or marketing of a good), being 'the most extreme form of prohibition', is a quantitative restriction,[145] as is a ban upon private individuals importing goods from other member states other than by personally transporting them.[146]

(a) Measures having effect equivalent to a quantitative restriction: Dassonville

Much more supple, and complex, are measures of equivalent effect. Just as article 30 prohibits charges having equivalent effect to a customs duty, so articles 34 and 35 prohibit measures having equivalent effect to a quantitative restriction (MEQRs). According to the Commission, 'measures' within the meaning of articles 34 and 35 embraces laws, regulations, administrative provisions, administrative practices, and all instruments issuing from a public authority, including recommendations.[147] As to when any such measure constitutes an MEQR, the ice was broken in 1974 in *Dassonville*,[148] a criminal case involving the importation of whisky from France into Belgium, the importer/retailer (the Dassonvilles) having forged the official certificate of origin required by Belgian law attesting to the right of the product to the (protected) designation 'Scotch whisky'. In considering whether it was competent for Belgium to require such certification upon importation in the face of article 34, the Court of Justice declared that: **10.26**

> All trading rules enacted by Member States which are capable of hindering, directly or indirectly, actually or potentially, intra-Community trade are to be considered as measures having an effect equivalent to quantitative restrictions.[149]

---

144 Case 2/73 *Geddo* v *Ente nazionale Risi* [1973] ECR 865, at para. 7(3).
145 Case 34/79 *R* v *Henn and Darby* [1979] ECR 3795, at para. 12.
146 Case C-170/04 *Rosengren and ors* v *Riksåklagaren* [2007] ECR I-4071.
147 Directive 70/50 [1970] JO L13/29, preamble, 2nd recital; further, 'administrative practices' means any standard and regularly followed procedure of a public authority, and 'recommendations' means any instruments issuing from a public authority which, while not legally binding upon the addressees thereof, cause them to pursue a certain conduct; 3rd recital. On breach of art. 34 by means of administrative practices see Case 21/84 *Commission* v *France* [1985] ECR 1355; Case C-192/01 *Commission* v *Denmark* [2003] ECR I-9693.
148 Case 8/74 *Procureur du Roi* v *Dassonville* [1974] ECR 837.
149 *Ibid.* at para. 5.

This '*Dassonville* formula', cited consistently (indeed, persistently) by the Court, is the categorical definition of an MEQR. The terms 'all legislation' (*toute réglementation*),[150] 'all measures'[151] or 'all rules'[152] have latterly (but not consistently)[153] been substituted for 'all trading rules', which only expands upon a notion of MEQRs which is, according to Advocate-General Bot, already 'very broad'.[154] As if to remove any lingering doubt, the Court has now added that

> [a]ny legal provision of a Member State prohibiting goods which have not been previously authorised from being marketed, acquired, offered, put on display or sale, kept, prepared, transported, sold, disposed of for valuable consideration or free of charge, imported or used, constitutes a measure having an effect equivalent to a quantitative restriction within the meaning of Article [34];[155]

and

> [a]ny other measure which hinders access of products originating in other Member States to the market of a Member State is also covered by that concept.[156]

The breadth will become apparent in the following discussion.

(b) Exception: Article 36

10.27 Owing to that breadth, and their capacity to intrude upon the exercise of public authority in areas of vital, or very important and legitimate public interest, the prohibitions of articles 34 and 35 are not absolute. Article 36 provides that:

> [t]he provisions of Articles 34 and 35 shall not preclude prohibitions or restrictions on imports, exports or goods in transit justified on grounds of:

---

150 Case C-143/06 *Ludwigs-Apotheke München Internationale Apotheke* v *Juers Pharma Import-Export* [2007] ECR I-9623, at para. 26; Case C-265/06 *Commission* v *Portugal* [2008] ECR I-2245, *per* A-G Trstenjak at para. 37 of her opinion; Case C-170/07 *Commission* v *Poland* [2008] ECR I-87*, at para. 43; Case C-249/07 *Commission* v *Netherlands* [2008] ECR I-174*, at para. 25; Case C-100/08 *Commission* v *Belgium* [2009] ECR I-140*, at para. 80; Case C-421/09 *Humanplasma* v *Republik Österreich* [2010] ECR I-12869, at para. 26.

151 Case C-366/04 *Schwarz* v *Bürgermeister der Landeshauptstadt Salzburg* [2005] ECR I-10139, at para. 28; Case C-319/05 *Commission* v *Germany (Garlic Preparation)* [2007] ECR I-9811, at para. 80; Case C-524/07 *Commission* v *Austria* [2008] ECR I-187*, at para. 28; Case C-88/07 *Commission* v *Spain* [2009] ECR I-1353, at para. 82.

152 Case C-265/06 *Commission* v *Portugal*, n. 150 above, at para. 31.

153 E.g., Case C-110/05 *Commission* v *Italy* [2009] ECR I-519, Case C-108/09 *Ker-Optika* v *ÀNTSZ Dél-dunántúli Regionális Intézete* [2010] ECR I-12213 and Case C-291/09 *Francesco Guarnieri & Cie* v *Vandevelde Eddy VOF*, judgment of 7 April 2011, not yet reported, which revert (at paras 33, 47 and 15, respectively) to 'all trading rules'.

154 Case C-110/05 *Commission* v *Italy*, *ibid.*, at para. 56 of his opinion.

155 Case C-219/07 *Nationale Raad van Dierenkwekers en Liefhebbers en Andibel* v *Belgische Staat* [2008] ECR I-4475, at para. 22.

156 Case C-110/05 *Commission* v *Italy*, n. 153 above, at para. 37; Case C-142/05 *Åklagaren* v *Mickelsson and Roos* [2009] ECR I-4273, at para. 24.

[●] public morality, public policy or public security;

[●] the protection of health and life of humans, animals or plants;

[●] the protection of national treasures possessing artistic, historic or archaeological value; or

[●] the protection of industrial and commercial property.

Two points ought immediately to be noted: first, it is a closed list, article 36 providing exhaustively the permitted grounds for derogation from articles 34 and 35; second, because it constitutes an exception to a basic Treaty freedom, it must be interpreted restrictively.[157] Further, article 36 may be invoked to save national measures which would otherwise fall foul of articles 34 or 35 only so long as they:

- are not 'a means of arbitrary discrimination or a disguised restriction on trade between Member States';[158]
- are not pre-empted by Union legislation;[159]
- are objectively justified and appropriate; and
- are proportionate.

Some see objective justification as an integral component of a proportionality test, others see them as two distinct tests; the Court sometimes prevaricates in its analysis, yet in either case the practical result is the same.

In the very first case it was considered, the Court said that article 36 'is directed **10.28** to eventualities of a non-economic kind'.[160] This indicates the character of the permitted derogations and is an important limitation thereto, for otherwise member states could (and certainly would) seek to justify restrictions on any number of important economic concerns which could fall within the (elastic) ambit of public policy – an unsatisfactory rendering of *ordre public/öffentliche Ordnung*, which have well established and extensive meanings in member states which use the terms. It should be apparent, but bears noting, that the exceptions of article 36 apply to set aside the prohibitions of articles 34 and 35 only: a

---

157   See e.g., Case 4/75 *Rewe Zentralfinanz* v *Landwirtschaftskammer* [1975] ECR 843; Case 46/76 *Bauhuis* v *Netherlands State* [1977] ECR 5. For successful instances of member states justifying breaches of art. 34 by reference to public policy, see Case 7/78 *R* v *Thompson and ors* [1978] ECR 2247; to public morality, Case 34/79 *R* v *Henn and Darby* [1979] ECR 3795 (cf. Case 121/85 *Conegate* v *HM Customs and Excise* [1986] ECR 1007); to public security, Case 72/82 *Campus Oil and ors* v *Minister for Industry and Energy and ors* [1984] ECR 2727. Public security here includes the external security of a member state; Case C-367/89 *Criminal proceedings against Richardt and Les Accessoires Scientifiques SNC* [1991] ECR I-4621; Case C-83/94 *Criminal proceedings against Leifer and ors* [1995] ECR I-3231. A distinction between public/internal security and public policy has never been clearly drawn.

158   TFEU, art. 36, final sentence.

159   See 10.77 below.

160   Case 7/61 *EEC Commission* v *Italy* [1961] ECR 317, at 329.

member state may not protect national treasures of artistic, historic or archaeo-logical value by imposing export duties (a matter for article 30),[161] nor may it seek to justify differential excise duties (article 110) upon tobacco products on grounds of health protection.[162]

10.29 A national rule constitutes an arbitrary or disguised restriction when adopted ostensibly for a legitimate purpose permitted by article 36 but in truth to prevent or discourage imports[163] or when it has the effect of excluding goods alleged to endanger, for example, public morality but the law does not at the same time provide rules which effectively inhibit domestic production and sale of the goods in question.[164] It is not enough to escape the reach of article 34, or to bring a measure within the scope of article 36, that the national rule-making body claims it to be, or even genuinely and honestly thinks it to be, necessary; it must be shown to be necessary, and appropriate (that is, it genuinely reflects a concern to attain that objective in a consistent and systematic manner), for the purpose it purports to achieve;[165] the burden of proof is for the national authority which made the rule.[166] However

> [w]hilst it is true that it is for a Member State which invokes an imperative requirement as justification for the hindrance to free movement of goods to demonstrate that its rules are appropriate and necessary to attain the legitimate objective being pursued, that burden of proof cannot be so extensive as to require the Member State to prove, positively, that no other conceivable measure could enable that objective to be attained under the same conditions.[167]

10.30 The national rule must also be proportionate, that is it will be justified only if there are no other means less disruptive to trade which will achieve the same ends as the measure in question. Put another way, the public authority must show that the benefits to the (legitimate) interest to be protected justify the

---

161 Case 7/68 *Commission* v *Italy* (Art Treasures) [1968] ECR 423.

162 Case C-302/00 *Commission* v *France* [2002] ECR I-2055.

163 E.g., Case 34/79 *R* v *Henn and Darby* [1979] ECR 3795; Case 40/82 *Commission* v *United Kingdom* (Newcastle Disease) [1982] ECR 2793; Case 40/82 *Commission* v *United Kingdom* (Poultry Imports) [1984] ECR 283.

164 Case 121/85 *Conegate* v *HM Customs and Excise* [1986] ECR 1007.

165 E.g., Case 120/78 *Rewe Zentrale* v *Bundesmonopolverwaltung für Branntwein* (Cassis de Dijon) [1979] ECR 649; Case 178/84 *Commission* v *Germany* (Reinheitsgebot) [1987] ECR 1227.

166 Case 251/78 *Denkavit Futtermittel* v *Minister für Ernährung, Landwirtschaft und Forsten des Landes Nordrhein-Westfalen* [1979] ECR 3369; Case C-510/99 *Criminal proceedings against Tridon* [2001] ECR I-7777; Case C-14/02 *ATRAL* v *Belgian State* [2003] ECR I-4431; Case C-249/07 *Commission* v *Netherlands* [2008] ECR I-174*.

167 Case C-110/05 *Commission* v *Italy* [2009] ECR I-519, at para. 66.

costs exacted upon the free movement of goods.[168] This is not to say that a national measure may not significantly disrupt free movement: the member states retain significant discretion in determining the level of protection to be afforded the protection of life and health,[169] and a measure adopted to that end may have effects which are draconian so long as it remains proportionate. Thus a complete ban upon the export of bovines, bovine meat and derived products from the United Kingdom produced very serious effects upon agricultural trade but, following the outbreak there of bovine spongiform encephalopathy (BSE), the Court sustained a ban, saying:

> Since the most likely explanation of this fatal disease [Creutzfeldt-Jacob disease] is exposure to BSE, there can be no hesitation. Whilst acknowledging the economic and social difficulties caused by the Commission's decision in the United Kingdom, the Court cannot but recognize the paramount importance to be accorded to the protection of health,[170]

although this is coloured by the proposition that the protection of human life and health is (without Treaty authority) given highest priority, 'rank[ing] first among the property [foremost amongst the assets] or [and] interests protected by Article 36 [of the Treaty]'.[171] Equally the requirement of an import licence or authorisation, normally a clear breach of article 34 even if only a formality,[172] may be justified for the marketing of (some) foodstuffs, and the fact that not all member states elect to adopt such a rule does not render unlawful the choice of

---

168 See e.g., Case 124/81 *Commission v United Kingdom* (UHT Milk) [1983] ECR 203; Case 261/85 *Commission v United Kingdom* (Pasteurised Milk) [1988] ECR 547; Case C-333/08 *Commission v France* [2010] ECR I-757.

169 Case C-265/06 *Commission v Portugal* [2008] ECR I-2245, *per* A-G Trstenjak at para. 58 of her opinion and cases there cited; Case C-141/07 *Commission v Germany* [2008] ECR I-6935, at para. 51; Cases C-171 and 172/07 *Apothekerkammer des Saarlandes and ors v Saarland, Ministerium für Justiz, Gesundheit und Soziales* [2009] ECR I-4171, art para. 19; Case C-108/09 *Ker-Optika v ÀNTSZ Dél-dunántúli Regionális Intézete* [2010] ECR I-12213, at para. 58.

170 Case C-180/96R *United Kingdom v Commission* [1996] ECR I-3903, at para. 93; also Case 104/75 *de Peijper* [1976] ECR 613. The BSE ban was in fact imposed by the Commission, not by a member state, but the same principles apply; see 10.59 below.

171 Case 104/75 *de Peijper, ibid.*, at para. 15; Case C-320/93 *Ortscheit v Eurim-Pharm Arzneimittel* [1994] ECR I-5243, at para. 16; Case C-170/04 *Rosengren and ors v Riksåklagaren* [2007] ECR I-4071, at para. 39; Case C-143/06 *Ludwigs-Apotheke München Internationale Apotheke v Juers Pharma Import-Export* [2007] ECR I-9623, at para. 27; Case C-108/09 *Ker-Optika*, n. 169 above, at para. 58; Case C-421/09 *Humanplasma v Republik Österreich* [2010] ECR I-12869, at para. 32. The words in square paraentheses appear in the last four judgments. A-G Tesauro once said (Case C-157/96 *R v Ministry of Agriculture, Fisheries and Food, ex parte National Farmers' Union and ors* [1998] ECR I-2211, at para. 20 of his opinion) that the protection of health 'constitutes a priority objective which the Treaty itself endows with an autonomous, ultimately higher degree of validity' but doesn't say how or why.

172 Cases 51 etc./71 *International Fruit Company and ors v Produktschap voor Groenten en Fruit* [1971] ECR 1107; Case 251/78 *Denkavit Futtermittel*, n. 166 above; Case C-235/91 *Commission v Ireland* [1992] ECR I-5917; Case C-249/07 *Commission v Netherlands* [2008] ECR I-174*.

a member state which does.[173] This admits of an element of variable geometry: the member states remain competent to determine the level of protection they wish to attach to human life and health, and lack of uniformity in substance or application does not of itself exclude the availability of an article 36 defence. Strict import licensing may, for example, be justified if there is no equally effective way of addressing the apparent Finnish propensity for strong (+80 per cent alcohol) spirits.[174] Even so, in all circumstances

> national rules or practices likely to have a restrictive effect, or having such an effect, on imports are compatible with the Treaty only to the extent to which they are necessary for the effective protection of health and life of humans. A national rule or practice cannot benefit from the derogation provided for in Article [36] if the health and life of humans may be protected just as effectively by measures which are less restrictive of intra-Community trade.[175]

Proportionality is therefore a test which is applied differently from that of appropriateness:

> Whilst it is true that a Member State seeking to justify a restriction on a fundamental Treaty freedom must establish both its appropriateness and its proportionality, that cannot mean, as regards appropriateness, that the Member State must establish that the restriction is the most appropriate of all possible measures to ensure achievement of the aim pursued, but simply that it is not inappropriate for that purpose. As regards proportionality, however, it is necessary to establish that no other measures could have been equally effective but less restrictive of the freedom in question.[176]

So a complete British ban upon milk imports[177] or a requirement of testing which replicates that to which it was already subject in the exporting member state;[178] the systematic health and œnological French inspection of imports of Italian table wines, ostensibly to protect health and life from unhygienic practices;[179] and subjecting the importation of technological adjuvants and foodstuffs in the preparation of which they were used to a scheme of prior

---

173 Case C192/01 *Commission* v *Denmark* [2003] ECR I-9693, at para. 42; Case C-446/08 *Solgar Vitamin's France and ors* v *Ministre de l'Économie, des Finances et de l'Emploi and ors* [2010] ECR I-3973, at para. 35.

174 Case C-434/04 *Ahokainen and Leppik* v *Virallinen Syyttäjä* [2006] ECR I-9171. The retail sale of such spirits is also prohibited, but this is an 'indistinctly applicable measure' (see below); its (lawful) commercial use is restricted to industrial purposes or as a raw material.

175 Case C-170/04 *Rosengren*, n. 171 above, at para. 43. To much the same effect, Case C192/01 *Commission* v *Denmark*, n. 173 above, at para. 46; Case C-446/08 *Solgar Vitamin's France* v, n. 173 above, at para. 54.

176 Case C-400/08 *Commission* v *Spain*, judgment of 24 March 2011, not yet reported, *per* A-G Sharpston at para. 89 of her opinion (although dealing with right of establishment and not free movement of goods). For an especially good discussion of the various elements of proportionality in the context of arts 34/36 see the opinion of A-G Poiares Maduro in Case C-434/04 *Ahokainen and Leppik*, n. 174 above, at paras 23–7.

177 Case 261/85 *Commission* v *United Kingdom* (Pasteurised Milk) [1988] ECR 547.

178 Case 124/81 *Commission* v *United Kingdom* (UHT Milk) [1983] ECR 203.

179 Case 42/82 *Commission* v *France* [1983] ECR 1013.

authorisation with no allowance for mutual recognition,[180] were disproportionate. Inherent in the test, the lesser the importance to the public interest the lower may be the degree of tolerance to the interference with free movement. Accordingly, the systematic German inspection of composition and quality of skimmed milk powder seeking to qualify for export refunds was disproportionate, but random checks, justified in the interests of combating fraud, were not;[181] and even spot checks of individual travellers at British ports of entry for evasion of excise duties were found to be an excessive restraint upon free movement.[182] But again it is important to bear in mind that member states are allowed a margin of appreciation in protecting the interests set out in article 36, so that the fact that one member state imposes rules less strict than another does not mean (of itself) that the latter's rules are disproportionate.[183]

It appears (but no more) that there are territorial limitations to article 36,[184] so **10.31** that it may not be invoked to prevent the importation of, for example, the products of animals which have been subject to brutal treatment in another member state or a third country.[185] A stronger case could be made in the context

---

180   Case C-333/08 *Commission* v *France* [2010] ECR I-757.

181   Case C-426/92 *Germany* v *Deutsches Milch-Kontor* [1994] ECR I-2757.

182   *R (Hoverspeed and ors)* v *Customs and Excise Commissioners* [2002] EWCA Civ 1804, [2003] QB 1041. Inspection was justified only where there were 'reasonable grounds to suspect' incidents of tax evasion.

183   Case C-219/07 *Nationale Raad van Dierenkwekers en Liefhebbers and Andibel* v *Belgische Staat* [2008] ECR I-4475, at para. 31; Case C-110/05 *Commission* v *Italy* [2009] ECR I-519, at para. 65; Case C-100/08 *Commission* v *Belgium* [2009] ECR I-140*, at para. 95; Case C-421/09 *Humanplasma* v *Republik Österreich* [2010] ECR I-12869, at para. 40.

184   See Case C-5/94 *R* v *Minister of Agriculture, Fisheries and Food, ex parte Hedley Lomas* [1996] ECR I-2553, *per* A-G Léger at para. 31: 'a Member State can rely on Article 36 only in order to ensure protection of an interest safeguarded by that article within its own national territory', and case law there discussed.

185   Case C-169/89 *Criminal proceedings against Gourmetterie van den Burg* [1990] ECR I-2143; Case C-265/01 *Criminal proceedings against Pansard and ors* [2003] ECR I-683. This notwithstanding (a) a protocol attached to the EC Treaty required the Community and the member states '[i]n formulating and implementing the Community's ... policies [to] pay full regard to the welfare requirements of animals' (Protocol on the Protection and Welfare of Animals), which may be taken to be an integration clause, and (b) there has been an acknowledgment of the protection of the health and life of animals as 'a fundamental requirement recognised by Community law' (Case C-219/07 *Nationale Raad van Dierenkwekers en Liefhebbers*, n. 183 above, at para. 28; Case C-100/08 *Commission* v *Belgium*, n. 183 above, at para. 92). It also ignores the possibility that it may be contrary to public policy or public morality in member state X that animals are mistreated in member state Y – support for which proposition may be had from a preambular reference in the Services Directive (Directive 2006/123 [2006] OJ L376/36, as to which see 11.45–11.48 below; preamble, recital 41) identifying animal welfare to be amongst a number of fields which 'in particular' fall within public policy for its purposes. If true it leaves the member states powerless, as regards goods in free circulation, to comply with obligations under international conventions such as, for example, the CITES (Convention of 3 March 1973 on International Trade in Endangered Species of Wild Fauna and Flora, 993 UNTS 243) unless all member states are party (which they are in this case, 16 of them prior to Union accession which may give CITES priority over the Treaty in those 16 in accordance with art. 351 TFEU) and enforce it fully and uniformly. The Union itself labours under no such limitation, banning, for example, the importation of the pelts of harp seal pups in response to public outrage (Directive 83/129 [1983] OJ L91/30; Regulation 1007/2009 [2009] OJ L286/36, extending to all pinnipeds) and the fur of cats and dogs and products made therefrom, as '[i]n the perception of EU citizens, cats and dogs are considered to be pet animals and therefore it is not acceptable to use their fur or

of article 35 for the prevention of export of animals – for example, the export of live sheep to another member state where the normal method of slaughter is systematically and demonstrably objectionable,[186] or the export of calves to another member state to be reared (briefly) in veal crates, the practice banned in the exporting member state[187] – because the animals meriting protection are still within the jurisdiction of the protecting state. But the relevant cases have been decided upon the basis of recourse to article 36 being pre-empted by Union measures exhaustively harmonising national law, and there is as yet no clear authority.

2. Serious internal disturbances and international tension

10.32 A later provision of the TFEU, a derogation clause of general application across the whole of the operation of the internal market, but with significant relevance to the free movement of goods, permits the member states to adopt measures which they are 'called upon to take' in the event of serious internal disturbances affecting the maintenance of law and order, in the event of war, serious international tension constituting a threat of war, or in order to discharge obligations they have accepted for the purpose of maintaining peace and international security.[188] Should any such measure distort the conditions of competition in the internal market the Commission and the relevant member state(s) are to 'examine how [it] can be adjusted' to be made Treaty compliant,[189] and the Commission is afforded a fast-track procedure to the Court of Justice where it considers a member state to be making 'improper use' of this licence.[190] Yet barred from review of the validity or proportionality of police (or similar) operations for the maintenance of law and order and internal security[191] it is not clear how far the Court's inquiry into misuse can extend.

---

products containing such fur' (Regulation 1523/2007 [2007] OJ L343/1, preamble, 1st recital). It also implements the CITES even though not a party to it (for CITES does not, yet, permit accesson by non-states); Regulation 338/97 [1997] OJ L61/1. The upgrading by Lisbon of the animal welfare protocol to the Treaties proper (art. 13 TFEU), as a provision having general application, may have a salutary influence upon the applicable law here.

186 Case C-5/94 *Hedley Lomas*, n. 184 above.
187 Case C-1/96 *R v Minister of Agriculture, Fisheries and Food, ex parte Compassion in World Farming* [1998] ECR I-1251. As to the export of animals to an unpleasant end being hindered not by public authorities but by organised individual protest see 10.63 below.
188 TFEU, art. 347 (ex art. 297 EC).
189 TFEU, art. 348, 1st para. (ex art. 298, 1st para. EC).
190 TFEU, art. 348, 2nd para.
191 *Ibid.* art. 276.

There is in any event little case law on it. As for serious internal disturbances **10.33** affecting the maintenance of law and order, the Court said in *Johnston* (involving not goods but social policy: rules on equal treatment in employment,[192] the discriminatory treatment of woman police constables in Northern Ireland who were not to be armed or trained in the use of firearms, and the reservation of 'general policing duties' to armed male constables), that article 347 addresses 'a wholly exceptional situation',[193] to be compared with circumstances which permit a derogation under article 36 which are (merely) 'exceptional'.[194] Advocate-General Jacobs took the view that

> [w]hen Article [347] speaks of 'serious internal disturbances affecting the maintenance of law and order', it must in my view be read as envisaging a breakdown of public order on a scale much vaster than the type of civil unrest which might justify recourse to Article 36. What seems to be envisaged is a situation verging on a total collapse of internal security, for otherwise it would be difficult to justify recourse to a sweeping derogation which is capable of authorizing the suspension of all of the ordinary rules governing the common market.[195]

Yet having regard to the requirements of public safety in the context of the Northern Irish 'Troubles' the Court found implicitly in *Johnston* that the Chief Constable had not exceeded his margin of discretion. The matter was discussed in later cases involving the exclusion of women entirely from service in the Royal Marines[196] and from military service in the *Bundeswehr* except as medics and bandswomen,[197] but the Court waffled and drew no firm conclusions, although Advocate-General La Pergola was not so sure that article 347 ought to be applied to military service in peacetime, perhaps it being reserved to temporary and non-permanent situations 'which are at the same time crisis situations, in the full and true sense, the occurrence of which represents a grave danger for vital interests, if not the very existence, of a Member State'.[198]

As for war or serious international tension constituting a threat of war, the **10.34** question 'is far more complex'[199] and raises even starker issues of justiciability. As Yugoslavia collapsed Greece sealed off its northern frontier to the movement of goods except those vital for humanitarian purposes (food and medicines)

---

192 See 14.41–14.42 below.

193 Case 222/84 *Johnston v Chief Constable of the Royal Ulster Constabulary* [1986] ECR 1651, at para. 27.

194 Case C-120/94 *Commission v Greece* (Macedonia) [1996] ECR I-1513, *per* A-G Jacobs at para. 46 of his opinion; Case C-273/97 *Sirdar v Army Board and anor* [1999] ECR I-7403, *per* A-G La Pergola, at para. 21 of his opinion.

195 Case C-120/94 *Macedonia, ibid.*, at para. 47 of his opinion.

196 Case C-273/97 *Sirdar*, n. 194 above.

197 Case C-285/98 *Kreil v Bundesrepublik Deutschland* [2000] ECR I-69.

198 Case C-273/97 *Sirdar*, n. 194 above, at para. 21 of his opinion.

199 Case C-120/94 *Macedonia*, n. 194 above, *per* A-G Jacobs at para. 50 of his opinion.

owing to growing tension, real or apprehended, with Macedonia. The Commission regarded it a breach of various of the rules regulating the Common Commercial Policy and raised an enforcement action under article 258. It never came to judgment as the turn of events caused the Commission to withdraw it, but Advocate-General Jacobs said it was not open to the Court to adopt a view on the merits, for 'Greece could have had some basis for considering, from its own subjective point of view, that the strained relations between itself and the Former Yugoslav Republic of Macedonia (FYROM) could degenerate into armed conflict',[200] and 'I do not think that it can be said that Greece is acting wholly unreasonably by taking the view that the tension between itself and FYROM bears within it the threat – even if it may be long-term and remote – of war'.[201] This indicates essentially a hands-off approach to judicial interference in the field.

10.35 Even more so with issues genuinely of international security, which is consistent with the exclusion (uniquely in the Treaties) of the supervisory jurisdiction of the Court of Justice over the validity and proportionality of operations carried out by police or other law enforcement services of a member state and the exercise of the responsibilities of a member state to maintain law and order and safeguard internal security[202] and with Strasbourg case law.[203] However article 347 cannot be understood as authorising derogation from 'foundation' principles of the Union[204] and the the Court of Justice will review Union law, even law giving effect to a UN Security Council resolution designed to combat terrorism, for compliance with those principles, and in particular respect for fundamental rights.[205] As for obligations accepted for the purpose of maintaining peace and international security, increasingly these are matters taken up by the Union's external action, and, if applied uniformly, create no distortion to the internal market, so are no concern of article 348.

3. Distinctly and indistinctly applicable measures: *Cassis de Dijon*

10.36 Non-tariff barriers to trade may take a virtually infinite variety of forms. Some are overtly protectionist, discriminating directly against imported products by prescribing rules which apply only to them; put another way, they are discriminatory on the face of the measure. Others have no protectionist intent and apply

---

200 *Ibid.* para. 54.
201 *Ibid.* para. 56.
202 TFEU, art. 276; see 11.197 below.
203 E.g., *Ireland* v *United Kingdom* (1978) 2 EHRR 25.
204 Cases C-402 and 415/05P *Kadi and Al Barakaat* v *Council and Commission* (Kadi II) [2008] ECR I-6351, at para. 303.
205 Cases C-402 and 415/05P *Kadi II, ibid.,* at para. 285; Cases C-399 and 403/06P *Hassan and Ayadi* v *Council* [2009] ECR I-11393, at para. 71; Case T-85/09 *Kadi* v *Commission* (Kadi III) [2010] ECR II-5177.

without distinction to imported and domestic products, they are a function simply of the manner in which the composition and marketing of goods is, and frequently has long been, regulated; but they nevertheless constitute barriers to the free movement of goods, by, for example, requiring exported goods to be produced differently, or imported goods to be repackaged, in order to meet the requirements extant in the importing member state, so incurring additional costs which even if passed on to the buyer may act as a disincentive to trade.[206] To illustrate: Spanish and Italian law regulate the cocoa content of, and ban the use of other vegetable fats in, chocolate. This is in principle a blameless thing to do. But it had the effect of preventing the sale, in Spain or Italy, of a product called 'chocolate' produced from vegetable fats in other member states wholly in conformity with applicable laws there; more accurately, that product could be sold but not by the name *chocolate* (in Spain) or only as '*surrogato de cioccolato*' ('chocolate substitute', in Italy).[207] The most robust of marketing departments might quail at the commercial challenge of marketing *surrogato de cioccolato* in Rome in competition with *cioccolato* or, even more difficult, marketing some Spanish formulation of 'vegetable fat based sweetmeat' in Madrid in competition with *chocolate*. In a similar but more widely known case, there was in German law a 'purity decree' (*Reinheitsgebot*), its origins found in a 1516 Bavarian decree, which prohibited the production and sale of beer as beer ('*Bier*') which contained ingredients other than malted barley, hops, yeast and water.[208] Brewers in other member states which used other ingredients could therefore (a) forego the (thirsty) German market, (b) produce, at additional cost, beer in a manner which complied with the *Reinheitsgebot*, as some did, or (c) market their product there as something different: Guinness, for example, was available without legal hindrance in Germany, but not sold as, and never represented to be, *Bier*.

These are but three examples of which the number is legion. Such rules may **10.37** have the effect of precluding absolutely the importation of products originating in other member states, but even if not they are likely to make their marketing

---

206 See e.g., Case 261/81 *Walter Rau Lebensmittelwerke* v *de Smedt* [1982] ECR 3961; Case C-315/92 *Verband Sozialer Wettbewerb* v *Clinique Laboratoires and anor* [1994] ECR I-317; Case C-470/93 *Verein gegen Unwesen in Handel und Gewerbe Köln* v *Mars* [1995] ECR I-1923.

207 Case C-12/00 *Commission* v *Spain* (Chocolate) [2003] ECR I-459; Case C-14/00 *Commission* v *Italy* (Chocolate) [2003] ECR I-513. In fact the composition of 'chocolate' has now been harmonised, by Directive 2000/36 [2000] OJ L197/19.

208 Case 178/84 *Commission* v *Germany* (Reinheitsgebot) [1987] ECR 1227; also the contemporaneous, and often ignored, similar Case 176/84 *Commission* v *Greece* [1987] ECR 1193, an equivalent law having been introduced in Greece by Otto, first king of the Hellenes and formerly a Bavarian prince. In fact the original *Reinheitsgebot* made no reference to yeast, its role in fermentation unknown until the time (and work) of Louis Pasteur.

more difficult and thus impede the free movement of goods;[209] they thus have the effect, even if genuinely unintended, of providing a degree of protection to home producers. In the jargon, a national measure which is discriminatory on its face is called a 'distinctly applicable measure'; a national measure such as these which applies without distinction to domestic and imported products but nevertheless has the effect of inhibiting the movement of goods, or put otherwise subjects imported goods to the same burdens in law but different burdens in fact, is an 'indistinctly applicable measure'.[210] A national rule may be indistinctly applicable even if imported goods and domestic goods are subject to different enactments, so long as the treatment to which they are subjected is, on the facts, equivalent.[211]

10.38 The *Dassonville* formula is applicable to both distinctly and indistinctly applicable measures. However, distinctly applicable measures fall directly under articles 34 and 35 and are prohibited unless they can be justified under article 36;[212] indistinctly applicable measures require to be analysed more closely to see whether they are struck at. Indeed, it was not at the outset wholly clear that they fell within articles 34 and 35 at all, or whether discrimination and/or protectionism was a necessary component of a breach. In an early attempt to grapple with the issue, the Commission identified measures governing the marketing of products which deal 'in particular' with shape, size, weight, composition, presentation, identification or putting up, which are equally applicable to domestic and imported products, yet ought to be 'abolished' for inconsistency with article 34.[213] However the Court of Justice stole a march on the Commission, and cut the Gordian knot, in *Cassis de Dijon*.[214]

10.39 *Cassis de Dijon* involved a German company (Rewe) seeking authorisation from the federal spirits monopoly (the *Bundesmonopolverwaltung für Branntwein*) to import into Germany a consignment of the French blackcurrant liqueur Cassis

---

209 See e.g., Case 182/84 *Criminal proceedings against Miro* [1985] ECR 3731, at para. 22; Case C-448/98 *Criminal proceedings against Guimont* [2000] ECR I-10663, at para. 26; Case C-12/00 *Commission* v *Spain*, n. 207 above, at para. 79; Case C-14/00 *Commission* v *Italy*, n. 207 above, at para. 75.

210 The terms are not used by the Court of Justice, which prefers, for indistinctly applicable measures, 'rules apply[ing] without distinction to all products'; e.g., Cases C-267 and 268/91 *Criminal proceedings against Keck and Mithouard* [1993] ECR I-6097, at para. 15.

211 Cases C-447 and 448/08 *Criminal proceedings against Sjöberg and Gerdin* [2010] ECR I-6917, at paras 55–6. This is a case involving the provision of services but the logic applies equally to the free movement of goods.

212 Case 113/80 *Commission* v *Ireland* (Irish Souvenirs) [1981] ECR 1625; re-affirmed in Case 434/85 *Allen and Hanburys* v *Generics (UK)* [1988] ECR 1245; Cases C-1 and 176/90 *Aragonesa de Publicidad Exterior and anor* v *Departamento de Sanidad y Seguridad Social de la Generalitat de Cataluña* [1991] ECR I-4151.

213 Directive 70/50 [1970] JO L13/29, art. 3.

214 Case 120/78 *Rewe-Zentrale* v *Bundesmonopolverwaltung für Branntwein* [1979] ECR 649.

de Dijon;[215] the authorisation was refused because, owing to provisions in German law on minimum alcohol content, in order to be marketed as such a fruit liqueur (such as Cassis de Dijon) was required to have an alcohol content of at least 25 per cent, that of Cassis being 15–20 per cent. The measure otherwise bore no more heavily upon imported goods than upon domestic products, so was indistinctly applicable.

In its judgment the Court established two principles fundamental to the **10.40** operation of article 34. First, it set out the general rule that where a product has been lawfully produced and marketed in one member state, it must, in principle, be allowed to be traded unhindered throughout the Union. The effect of this was summarised subsequently by the Court thus:

> It is established by the case-law beginning with 'Cassis de Dijon' ... that, in the absence of harmonization of legislation, obstacles to the free movement of goods which are the consequence of applying, to goods coming from other Member States where they are lawfully manufactured[216] and marketed, rules that lay down requirements to be met by such goods (such as those relating to designation, form, size, weight, composition, presentation, labelling, packaging) constitute measures of equivalent effect prohibited by article [34]. This is so even if those rules apply without distinction to all products.[217]

This is an inarticulate application of a principle of equivalence or mutual recognition, a presumption that a good produced in one member state in accordance with relevant rules on manufacture or production will satisfy those required in another. But second, the Court recognised that some disparities in national rules have to be accepted even if their effect constitutes a barrier to trade, where 'their application can be justified by a public-interest objective taking precedence over the free movement of goods'.[218] This is the case, said the Court in *Cassis de Dijon*, where the rules are necessary to satisfy the 'mandatory requirements' (a miserable translation of '*exigences impératives*' – imperative/ overriding needs, sometimes now rendered 'overriding requirements')[219] of, for example:

---

215 Normally the mere requirement of authorisation would be a distinctly applicable breach of art. 34, but because marketing of the relevant products was, and is, administered by a public monopoly in Germany, special considerations apply; see 10.96–10.98 below.

216 This is a misleading formulation, as goods need not be produced in a member state to fall within the the field of art. 34, they need only be in free circulation; see 10.01 above and Case C-184/96 *Commission v France* (Foie Gras) [1998] ECR I-6197, *per* A-G La Pergola at n. 26 of his opinion. It is useful to recall here that at the time of the events giving rise to *Dassonville*, whisky was the product of a third country.

217 Cases C-267–68/91 *Criminal proceedings against Keck and Mithouard* [1993] ECR I-6097, at para. 15.

218 *Ibid.*

219 Case C-320/03 *Commission v Austria* [2005] ECR I-9871, at para. 70; Case C-366/04 *Schwarz v Bürgermeister der Landeshauptstadt Salzburg* [2005] ECR I-10139, at para. 30; Case C-88/07 *Commission v Spain* [2009] ECR I-1353, *per* A-G Mazák at para. 47 of his opinion; Case C-108/09 *Ker-Optika v ÀNTSZ Dél-dunántúli Regionális Intézete* [2010] ECR I-12213, at para. 57.

- the effectiveness of fiscal supervision;
- public health;
- the fairness of commercial dealings; and
- defence of the consumer.[220]

These four categories were expressly cited but it was clear that, unlike article 36, the intention was not to provide an exhaustive list ('provisions ... necessary in order to satisfy mandatory requirements relating *in particular* to ...').[221] Advocate-General Trstenjak has characterised article 36 and the *Cassis de Dijon* exceptions as, respectively, the written and unwritten justifications for inhibitions of the movement of goods.[222] The Court has (so far) recognised as fields in which mandatory requirements analysis applies:

- the improvement of working conditions;[223]
- the promotion of national (and presumably regional) culture;[224]
- protection of the environment;[225]
- protection of national or regional 'socio-cultural characteristics';[226]
- press diversity;[227]
- the preservation and financial balance of social security systems;[228]
- the maintenance of biodiversity;[229]

---

220 Case 120/78 *Cassis de Dijon*, n. 165 above, at para. 8(2). 'Defence of the consumer' must be understood more broadly than that English term suggests, extending, in German eyes, to the extensive body of law characterised as *Verbraucherschutz*.

221 *Ibid.* (emphasis added).

222 Case C-28/09 *Commission v Austria*, judgment of 21 December 2011, not yet reported, at para. 78 of her opinion.

223 Case 155/80 *Oebel* [1981] ECR 1993.

224 Cases 60–61/84 *Cinéthèque v Fédération National des Cinemas Français* [1985] ECR 2605; Case C-17/92 *Federación de Distribuidores Cinematográficos v Estado Español and anor* [1993] ECR I-2239.

225 Case 302/86 *Commission v Denmark* (Returnable Bottles) [1988] ECR 4607; Case C-2/90 *Commission v Belgium* (Walloon Waste) [1992] ECR I-4431; Case C-463/01 *Commission v Germany* [2004] ECR I-11705; Case C-309/02 *Radlberger Getränkegesellschaft and anor v Land Baden-Württemberg* [2004] ECR I-11763; Case C-320/03 *Commission v Austria* [2005] ECR I-9871; Case C-219/07 *Nationale Raad van Dierenkwekers en Liefhebbers and Andibel v Belgische Staat* [2008] ECR I-4475, at para. 29; Case C-28/09 *Commission v Austria*, judgment of 21 December 2011, not yet reported. The status of environmental protection as a mandatory requirement has only been enhanced by its subsequent inclusion as a Community task (EC Treaty, art. 2) and an integration clause (TFEU, art. 11), which 'emphasises the fundamental nature of that objective and its extension across the range of those policies and activities'; Case C-176/03 *Commission v Council* [2005] ECR I-7879, at para. 42; Case C-320/03 *Commission v Austria*, at para. 74. The Court has recently admitted a degree of variable geometry by recognising that environmental protection may take account of the particular geographical circumstances of a member state; Case C-142/05 *Åklagaren v Mickelsson and Roos* [2009] ECR I-4273, at para. 36.

226 Case 145/88 *Torfaen Borough Council v B & Q* [1989] ECR 3851, at para. 14. This was part of the series of cases dealing with Sunday trading, and the relevance of 'socio-cultural characteristics' may have faded with subsequent case law; see 10.46 below.

227 Case C-368/95 *Vereinigte Familia Press v Heinrich Bauer Verlag* [1997] ECR I-3689.

228 Case C-120/95 *Decker v Caisse de maladie des employés privés* [1998] ECR I-1831.

229 Case C-67/97 *Criminal proceedings against Bluhme* [1998] ECR I-8033; Case C-249/07 *Commission v Netherlands* [2008] ECR I-174*; Case C-100/08 *Commission v Belgium* [2009] ECR I-140*.

- the effective exercise of fundamental rights;[230]
- the protection and promotion of road safety;[231] and
- the protection of books as cultural objects.[232]

But again, it is only a measure which is indistinctly applicable that may thus escape the reach of article 34;[233] and as with article 36, a mandatory requirement will not be permitted to serve aims of an economic nature,[234] and the national rule must be objectively justified and proportionate. So, a national measure which has the effect of barring from or hindering access to the market of imported weak liqueur (*Cassis de Dijon*), 'impure' beer (*Reinheitsgebot*) or vegetable fat-based chocolate (Spanish and Italian chocolate) infringes article 34; it may (because it is indistinctly applicable) be justified on grounds of protection of the consumer, but only if there exists no means less disruptive of trade which could serve the interests of the consumer to the same standard. In all of these cases, and generally, the Court has found that a requirement of labelling would be more proportionate, and adequate to the needs of the consumer.[235]

---

230 Case C-112/00 *Eugen Schmidberger, Internationale Transporte und Planzüge* v *Austria* [2003] ECR I-5659.

231 Case C-297/05 *Commission* v *Netherlands* [2007] ECR I-7467; Case C-170/07 *Commission* v *Poland* [2008] ECR I-87*; Case C-110/05 *Commission* v *Italy* [2009] ECR I-519; Case C-438/08 *Commission* v *Portugal* [2009] ECR I-10219. Distinctly applicable national rules 'so far as they are necessary for road safety reasons' may fall also within art. 36; Case C-406/85 *Procureur de la République* v *Gofette and Gilliard* [1987] ECR 2525, at para. 7. Also Case C-54/05 *Commission* v *Finland* [2007] ECR I-2473; Case C-265/06 *Commission* v *Portugal* [2008] ECR I-2245.

232 C-531/07 *Fachverband der Buch- und Medienwirtschaft* v *LIBRO Handelsgesellschaft* [2009] ECR I-3717.

233 Case 113/80 *Commission* v *Ireland* (Irish Souvenirs) [1981] ECR 1625; Case 434/85 *Allen and Hanburys* v *Generics (UK) Ltd* [1988] ECR 1245; Case C-2/90 *Commission* v *Belgium* (Walloon Waste) [1992] ECR I-4431. Care is to be taken with *Walloon Waste*, for the Court found the measures at hand to be non-discriminatory and therefore amenable to environmental considerations, when this was clearly a legal fiction.

234 Case C-254/98 *Schutzverband gegen unlauteren Wettbewerb* v *TK-Heimdienst Sass* [2000] ECR I-151, at para. 33.

235 There is serious criticism of this, for the Court posits a 'reasonable' or reasonably diligent and discerning consumer (see e.g., Case C-210/96 *Gut Springenheide and anor* v *Oberkreisdirektor des Kreises Steinfurt – Amt für Lebensmittelüberwachung* [1998] ECR I-4657, at para. 31; Case C-457/05 *Schutzverband der Spirituosen-Industrie* v *Diageo Deutschland* [2007] ECR I-8075, at para. 27) but provides no evidence that he or she exists; many studies would indicate the opposite. Moreover a number of products considered here (draught beer, loose chocolates, for example) are sold generally without labels, to which the Court's solution that 'a system of consumer information may operate perfectly well ... when the requisite information must appear on the casks or the beer taps' (Case 178/84 *Reinheitsgebot*, n. 208 above, at para. 36) is at least contestable. For rare exceptions to the general trend see Case 382/87 *Buet and anor* v *Ministère Public* [1989] ECR 1235 and Case C-446/08 *Solgar Vitamin's France and ors* v *Ministre de l'Économie, des Finances et de l'Emploi and ors* [2010] ECR I-3973, in which the Court tolerated limitations to the free movement of goods justified for the protection of particularly vulnerable consumers (respectively, canvassing and selling education material at private homes and vitamin supplements in children's foodstuffs). As to the extent to which a member state may require (re-)labelling in specific languages see Case 27/80 *Criminal proceedings against Fietje* [1980] ECR 3839; Case C-369/89 *Piageme and ors* v *Peeters* [1991] ECR I-2971; Case C-51/93 *Meyhui* v *Schott Zwiesel Glaswerke* [1994] ECR I-3879; Case C-33/97 *Colim* v *Bigg's Continent Noord* [1999] ECR I-3175. There is some harmonisation of labelling of foodstuffs; e.g. Directive 2000/13 [2000] OJ L109/29 (replaced by Regulation 1169/2011 [2011] OJ L304/18 from December 2014).

10.41   *Cassis de Dijon* constituted a huge boost to the fluidity of the movement of
goods, by the simple expedient of generating a rule that, in principle, producers
need comply with one layer of regulation only; put otherwise, the 'dual burden'
borne normally by imported goods (but not domestically produced goods)
disappeared. According to Advocate-General Jacobs:

> The importance of the 'Cassis de Dijon' principle cannot be overstated: if a Member
> State were allowed to prevent the importation and sale of products lawfully manufac-
> tured in another Member State, simply because they were not made in the manner
> prescribed by the law of the importing State, there would be no such thing as a common
> market.[236]

The reverse side of the coin is that it may lead to a deregulatory spiral or the
'race to the bottom', but this seems not to have happened to an extent necessary
to cause alarm. The mandatory requirements doctrine is sometimes called the
rule of reason, the term borrowed from competition law, but it does not best
describe the logic of *Cassis de Dijon* and is better left to its original purpose.

4. Technical barriers

10.42   There remains another, distinct type of hindrance to the free movement of
goods which has little to do with article 36 or mandatory requirements, those a
product of technical barriers in a more widely understood sense, simple
differences in technical specifications (sometimes 'standards') a product of long
habit and tradition, or law, in the various member states. There is, for example,
no legal impediment to the marketing in continental member states of a British
or Irish three pin electric plug, yet no one would buy one because it is useless
there. There are a host of like differences, to which the only solution is
harmonisation (indeed many such measures were introduced and developed for
just that purpose in efforts to knit together nineteenth century national
markets). There is some progress in their elimination, sometimes in accordance
with standards promulgated internationally, for example within the World
Trade Organization.[237] But it is slow, and frequently in the teeth of vested
interests and huge inertia. Indeed the problem is sometimes insurmountable:
doubtless efficiencies could be gained were all motorcars intended for the
Union market designed, engineered and built to be driven on the same side of
the road; but achieving that would require massive expenditure in road redesign
and rebuilding for four (or 23) member states, and it will not happen. The
technique of harmonisation is discussed below.[238]

---

236   Case C-412/93 *Edouard Leclerc-Siplec* v *TF1 Publicité and anor* [1995] ECR I-179, at para. 25 of his opinion.
237   See e.g., the TBT (technical barriers to trade) Agreement of 15 April 1994, in force 1 January 1995.
238   See 10.68–10.77 below.

(a) Directive 98/34

In an exercise of proaction rather than reaction, a 1998 Directive (the 'Technical **10.43** Standards Directive')[239] lays down a requirement that any draft technical specifications, regulations, standards or other requirements, defined very broadly,[240] be notified 'immediately' to the Commission[241] in order that they can be measured for likelihood of impeding the free movement of goods. There is in all cases a three-month standstill period following notification,[242] extended another three months if a member state or the Commission objects (by means of a 'detailed opinion')[243] or a further nine months if the Commission proposes the adoption of harmonising measures.[244] An amendment made to a draft technical regulation already notified which is 'not significant' and relaxes the conditions set (and therefore reduces their possible impact upon the movement of goods) need not be renotified.[245] Member states are sometimes comically inefficient at notifying[246] and there are serious constitutional difficulties on the rights of affected individuals in circumstances in which new specifications are introduced without notification.[247] A similar scheme is in place requiring Commission approval for the introduction of new national measures on the labelling, presentation and advertising of foodstuffs.[248]

(b) 2008 'Goods Package'

In 2008 the Parliament and the Council adopted a 'fourth generation' of **10.44** measures intended to remove yet further technical barriers to the free movement of goods. The so-called 'goods package' includes measures: setting out the requirements for accreditation and market surveillance relating to the marketing of products;[249] laying down procedures relating to the application of certain technical or other national rules (on quality, performance, safety, testing,

---

239 Directive 98/34 [1998] OJ L204/37, being a consolidation of earlier legislation first adopted in 1983 (Directive 83/189 [1983] OJ L109/8); as to the horizontal (or 'triangular') effect of which see Case 194/94 *CIA Security International* v *Signalson and anor* [1996] ECR I-2201; Case C-226/97 *Criminal proceedinga against Lemmens* [1998] ECR I-3711; Case C-443/98 *Unilever Italia* v *Central Food* [2000] ECR I-7535.

240 Directive 98/34, art. 1.

241 *Ibid.* art. 8.

242 *Ibid.* art. 9(1).

243 *Ibid.* art. 9(2).

244 *Ibid.* art. 9(3), (4).

245 Case C-433/05 *Åklagaren* v *Sandström* [2010] ECR I-2885.

246 For example, several provisions of the Video Recordings Act 1984 requiring to be notified under Directive 83/189 were notified only in 2009. They were therefore unenforceable against individuals (vertically and horizontally) for 26 years. The remedy was (eventual) notification (September 2009), a three-month wait, then repeal and revival of the relevant provisions; see the Video Recordings Act 2010. But convictions secured under the unnotified provisions of the 1984 Act in ignorance (on all sides) of their unenforceability and then appealed out of time were safe; *R* v *Budomir and anor* [2010] EWCA Crim 1486, [2010] 2 Cr App. Rep. 310.

247 See 6.80 above.

248 Directive 2000/13 [2000] OJ L109/29, arts 19, 20.

249 Regulation 765/2008 [2008] OJ L218/30.

and the like) to products lawfully marketed in another member ⟩n mutual assistance amongst national administrative authorities and mission to ensure the correct application of the law on customs and al matters;[251] and on a common framework for the marketing of ____.[252] They continue to rely upon mutual recognition but shift the burden of proof to the importing member state and increase transparency and legal certainty on market entry, assisted by administrative cooperation between member states.

(c) Schengen

10.45 The 1990 Schengen Convention,[253] which deals primarily with the free movement of persons,[254] addresses peripherally the free movement of goods, contracting parties undertaking 'jointly [to] ensure that their laws, regulations or administrative provisions do not unjustifiably impede the movement of goods at internal borders'.[255] But this was intended primarily to ensure that the free movement of persons is not hindered by technical rules on the goods they carry, otherwise little has come directly of it, and it, and the provisions which follow, may be taken as statements of political goodwill. Whatever it means, it does not bind Ireland or the United Kingdom.[256]

5. 'Certain selling arrangements': Keck

10.46 So deeply does article 34, fortified by *Cassis de Dijon*, bite that it came to be applied in a manner which interfered (with benefit of hindsight) unnecessarily in matters legitimately of local regulation. This came to the fore in a number of cases involving national laws which, in varying degees, prohibited Sunday trading[257] – cases which Advocate-General Tesauro was later to say had 'nothing to do with trade, still less with the integration of the markets'.[258] Because it had been allowed to overreach its proper limits the Court of Justice did something it does only rarely, it reversed itself:

---

250 Regulation 764/2008 [2008] OJ L218/21.
251 Regulation 766/2008 [2008] OJ L218/48.
252 Regulation 768/2008 [2008] OJ L218/82.
253 Convention of 19 June 1990 implementing the Schengen Agreement of 14 June 1985 on the gradual abolition of checks at their common borders [2000] OJ L239/19.
254 See 11.182–11.196 below.
255 Schengen Convention, art. 120(1).
256 See 11.189–11.190 below.
257 See Case C-145/88 *Torfaen Borough Council* v *B & Q* [1989] ECR 3851; Case C-312/89 *Union Déparmentale des Syndicats CGT de l'Aisne* v *Conforama* [1991] ECR I-997; Case C-332/89 *Criminal proceedings against Marchandise and ors* [1991] ECR I-1027; Case C-169/91 *Stoke-on-Trent City Council* v *B & Q* [1992] ECR I-6635.
258 Case C-292/92 *Hünermund* v *Landesapothekerskammer Baden-Württemberg* [1993] ECR I-6787, at para. 24 of his opinion.

In view of the increasing tendency of traders to invoke Article [34] of the Treaty as a means of challenging any rules whose effect is to limit their commercial freedom even where such rules are not aimed at products from other Member States, the Court considers it necessary to re-examine and clarify its case-law on this matter.[259]

This was *Keck*, a case waiting to happen,[260] and leavens the byproduct of *Cassis de Dijon* as a charter for deregulation. *Keck* involved criminal prosecutions for reselling products in Alsacian supermarkets in an unaltered state at prices lower than their actual purchase price ('resale at a loss'), contrary to French law. The Court was asked (expansively) whether the French law was compatible with the principles of the free movement of goods, services and capital, free competition and non-discrimination on grounds of nationality as laid down in the Treaties. In response the Court restricted itself to article 34 and in a terse (19 paragraph) judgment, drew it back:

> [C]ontrary to what has previously been decided, the application to products from other Member States of national provisions restricting or prohibiting certain selling arrangements is not such as to hinder directly or indirectly, actually or potentially, trade between Member States within the meaning of the *Dassonville* judgment, so long as those provisions apply to all relevant traders operating within the national territory and so long as they affect in the same manner, in law and in fact, the marketing of domestic products and of those from other Member States.

> Provided that those conditions are fulfilled, the application of such rules to the sale of products from another Member State meeting the requirements laid down by that State is not by nature such as to prevent their access to the market or to impede access any more than it impedes the access of domestic products. Such rules therefore fall outside the scope of Article [34] of the Treaty.[261]

This formulation was unnecessarily elaborate; it could have been, and subsequently was, stated by the Court with greater precision and clarity:

> According to [*Keck*], the application to products from other Member States of national provisions restricting or prohibiting, within the Member State of importation, certain selling arrangements is not such as to hinder trade between Member States so long as, first, those provisions apply to all relevant traders operating within the national territory

---

259 Cases C-267 and 268/91 *Criminal proceedings against Keck and Mithouard* [1993] ECR I-6097, at para. 14. The Court has expressly reversed itself on only one other occasion, in Case C-10/89 *CNL-Sucal v Hag* (Hag II) [1990] ECR I-3711.

260 The Court clearly seised upon *Keck* as an opportunity of an *arrêt de principe*. The case was originally remitted to and heard by the second chamber (of three judges), A-G van Gerven provided a terse (11 paragraph) and unremarkable opinion, but it was then referred to the full court, the parties were invited to submit further observations and Mr van Gerven a second opinion. In fact it is likely the *Keck* judgment borrows much from the prescient opinion of A-G Tesauro in *Hünermund* (n. 258 above), the judgment in which was delivered three weeks after *Keck*, but Mr Tesauro's opinion delivered four weeks before.

261 Cases C-267 and 268/91 *Keck*, n. 259 above, at paras 16, 17.

and, secondly, they affect in the same manner, in law and in fact, the marketing of domestic products and of those from other Member States. The reason is that the application of such provisions is not such as to prevent access by the latter to the market of the Member State of importation or to impede such access more than it impedes access by domestic products.[262]

10.47 A number of points are to be made. The judgment refers to 'certain' selling arrangements but there has been no clarification as to what this means; in the absence of contradiction it seems safe to assume it applies to all selling arrangements (also undefined). This (invented) category is formalistic, certainly in comparison with the normal approach of the Court to look for effects which inhibit free movement irrespective of a category to which they may be ascribed. They are then to be 'contrast[ed]' with 'rules that lay down requirements to be met by [imported] goods'[263] (in the new shorthand, 'product characteristics'), the two categories apparently mutually exclusive; this has been criticised by Advocate-General Jacobs as too rigid a distinction and 'unsatisfactory',[264] taking inadequate account of the impact a selling arrangement may have upon market access. As it stands, *Keck* applies even if the measure is likely to limit the total volume of sales, so the volume of imports from other member states,[265] which goes against earlier case law (primarily the Sunday trading case law) which seemed to accept that article 34 was breached by any rule the effect of which was to limit in any way the number or amount of imported goods sold on the national market. The second of the two tests for *Keck* compliance (affecting in the same manner, in law and in fact, the marketing of imported and domestic products) re-introduces the issue of discrimination which had been sidelined by *Cassis de Dijon*. And the first (universality) test must be read with some caution. Taken literally it would disqualify for *Keck* consideration any rule emanating from a regional authority; after all, the Sunday trading legislation in the United Kingdom which was a catalyst for *Keck* and which it indirectly addressed did not 'apply to all relevant traders operating within the national territory', it applied only to traders in England and Wales.

10.48 Notwithstanding criticism (Advocate-General Bot notes that it 'caused puzzlement. Many commentators regretted the contradictions contained in it and its lack of reasoning and of clarity'),[266] *Keck* has for the most part been welcomed, as drawing article 34 back within its proper limits and dispelling any notion that it is the source of a general right to trade unhindered and unregulated. With

---

262 Case C-384/93 *Alpine Investments* v *Minister van Financiën* [1995] ECR I-1141, at para. 37.
263 *Keck*, n. 259 above, at paras 16, 15.
264 Case C-412/93 *Edouard Leclerc-Siplec* v *TF1 Publicité and anor* [1995] ECR I-179, at para. 38 of his opinion.
265 *Keck*, n. 259 above, at para. 13.
266 Case C-110/05 *Commission* v *Italy* [2009] ECR I-519, at para. 77 of his opinion.

Keck, according to the Commission, 'the Court has completed its case law' on the free movement of goods.[267]

Various measures adopted by the member states which have been found to be **10.49** *Keck* selling arrangements include: a prohibition on advertising in chemists;[268] limiting the opening hours of petrol stations;[269] prohibitions of Sunday trading[270] and regulation of shop opening hours generally;[271] restriction of the sale of baby milk to chemists;[272] price controls;[273] bans on various types of advertising;[274] a requirement that partially baked bread be separately pre-packaged and labelled;[275] a ban on notice for the sale of goods that they originated in an insolvent estate;[276] the itinerant sale of newspapers and magazines on a public highway;[277] the itinerant selling of jewellery and home 'jewellery parties';[278] and 'combined offers', being the sale of one product tied to another.[279] If the tests are met, the rule escapes the prohibition of article 34 altogether, and so any need of further analysis for objective justification and proportionality. There have, of course, been a number of cases in which a party has argued for *Keck* release but failed to persuade the Court, either because (a) the measure at issue was not a 'selling arrangement' – generally any practical requirement to alter the packaging or the labelling of imported products goes to 'product characteristics'

---

267 Communication to the Council and the Parliament [1993] OJ C353/4, at point 22.

268 Case C-292/92 *Hünermund v Landesapothekerkammer Baden-Württemberg* [1993] ECR I-6787.

269 Cases C-401 etc./92 *Criminal proceedings against Tankstation 't Heukske and Boermans* [1994] ECR I-2199.

270 Cases C-69 and 258/93 *Punto Casa v Sindaco del Commune di Capena* [1994] ECR I-2355; Cases C-418 etc./93 *Semeraro Casa Uno and ors v Sindaco del Comune di Erbusco and ors* [1996] ECR I-2975.

271 Cases C-418 etc./93 *Semeraro Casa Uno, ibid.*; Case C-393/08 *Sbarigia v Azienda USL RM/A and ors*, [2010] ECR I-6333, *per* A-G Jääskinen at para. 81 of his opinion.

272 Case C-391/92 *Commission v Greece* [1995] ECR I-1621.

273 Case C-63/94 *Groupement National des Négociants en Pommes de Terre de Belgique (Balgapom) v ITM Beligum and anor* [1995] ECR I-2467. There is earlier case law which provides that price controls may breach art. 34 where they have the effect of making the marketing of imported goods impossible or more difficult (Case 13/77 *GB-Inno-BM v Association des détaillants en tabac (ATAB)* [1977] ECR 2115; Case 82/77 *Openbaar Ministerie v van Tiggele* [1978] ECR 25; Cases 16 etc./79 *Openbaar Ministerie v Danis* [1979] ECR 3327; Case 231/83 *Cullet and anor v Centre Leclerc* [1985] ECR 305), which presumably survives *Keck*. See now Case C-531/07 *Fachverband der Buch- und Medienwirtschaft v LIBRO Handelsgesellschaft* [2009] ECR I-3717; Case C-197/08 *Commission v France* [2010] ECR I-1599; Case C-198/08 *Commission v Austria* [2010] ECR I-1645; Case C-221/08 *Commission v Ireland* [2010] ECR I-1669. The issue is likely to be re-visited with Scottish attempts to introduce minimum pricing in order to discourage alcohol consumption.

274 See immediately below.

275 Case C-416/00 *Morellato v Comune di Padova* [2003] ECR I-9343.

276 Case C-71/02 *Herbert Karner Industrie-Auktionen v Troostwijk* [2004] ECR I-3025.

277 Case C-20/03 *Openbaar Ministerie v Burmanjer and ors* [2005] ECR I-4133.

278 Case C-441/04 *A-Punkt Schmuckhandels v Schmidt* [2006] ECR I-2093; re-referred for clarification but the reference withdrawn, Case C-315/07 *A-Punkt Schmuckhandels v Schmidt*, order of 30 May 2008, unreported.

279 Cases C-261 and 299/07 *VTB-VAB and anor v Total Belgium and anor* [2009] ECR I-2949, *per* A-G Trstenjak at paras 110–19 of her opinion (the Court found the field occupied by a Directive and so did not consider the point).

and will disqualify them as *Keck* selling arrangements;[280] or (b) because they provided for inequality of treatment, in law or in fact, as between imports and domestic products.[281] There then followed standard article 36/mandatory requirements analysis. It is now suggested that *Keck* principles be transferred to apply also to national rules comprising conditions for use of goods.[282]

10.50 *Keck* was a product of, intended to resolve a problem in the context of, and applies first and foremost to, article 34. Yet although 'the distinction laid down in *Keck and Mithouard* is undoubtedly difficult to transpose into the context of

---

280 See e.g., Case C-315/92 *Verband Sozialer Wettbewerb* v *Clinique Laboratoires and anor* [1994] ECR I-317 (prohibition of marketing cosmetic products using names attributing to them properties they do not possess); Case C-470/93 *Verein gegen Unwesen in Handel und Gewerbe Köln* v *Mars* [1995] ECR I-1923 (prohibition of publicity markings on external packaging); Case C-33/97 *Colim* v *Bigg's Continent Noord* [1999] ECR I-3175 (labelling requirements); Case C-12/00 *Commission* v *Spain* (Chocolate) [2003] ECR I-459 (fat content of chocolate).

281 E.g., Case C-320/93 *Ortscheit* v *Eurim-Pharm Arzneimittel* [1994] ECR I-5243 (prohibition of advertising medicinal products); Case C-254/98 *Schutzverband gegen unlauteren Wettbewerb* v *TK-Heimdienst Sass* [2000] ECR I-151(selling on rounds within an administrative district (*Verwaltungsbezirk*) restricted to bakers, butchers and grocers with a permanent establishment in that or in an adjacent district); Case C-322/01 *Deutscher Apothekerverband* v *0800 DocMorris and anor* [2003] ECR I-14887 (prohibition on sale of medicinal products by mail order); Case C-463/01 *Commission* v *Germany* [2004] ECR I-11705 and Case C-309/02 *Radlberger Getränkegesellschaft and anor* v *Land Baden-Württemberg* [2004] ECR I-11763 (global compulsory packaging recovery system); Case C-366/04 *Schwarz* v *Bürgermeister der Landeshauptstadt Salzburg* [2005] ECR I-10139 (prohibition of the sale of unwrapped sugar confectionary from vending machines); Cases C-158 and 159/04 *Alfa Vita Vassilopoulos and ors* v *Elliniko Dimosio and ors* [2006] ECR I-8135 (requirement that 'bake-off' products be sold only by fully equipped bakeries); Case C-244/06 *Dynamic Medien Vertriebs* v *Avides Media* [2008] ECR I-505 (prohibition of sale by mail order of image storage media which have not been examined and classified by a competent authority as to suitability for viewing by children); Case C-141/07 *Commission* v *Germany* [2008] ECR I-6935 (provision of pharmaceutical medicines to hospitals restricted to nearby chemists); Case C-110/05 *Commission* v *Italy* [2009] ECR I-519 (restriction of the towing of trailers by vehicles other than motorcars, trolleybuses and tractors, so banning mopeds, motorcycles, three-wheeled and other four-wheeled '*motoveicoli*'); Case C-531/07 *Fachverband der Buch- und Medien-wirtschaft* v *LIBRO Handelsgesellschaft* [2009] ECR I-3717 (fixing of retail prices of books); Case C-142/05 *Åklagaren* v *Mickelsson and Roos* [2009] ECR I-4273 and Case C-433/05 *Åklagaren* v *Sandström* [2010] ECR I-2885 (restrictions on the use of recreational personal watercraft (jet-skis)); Case C-108/09 *Ker-Optica* v *ÁNTSZ Dél-dunátúli Regionális Intézete* [2010] ECR I-12213 (restriction of the sale of contact lenses to specialist medical accessory shops).

282 Case C-142/05 *Mickelsson and Roos*, *ibid.*, *per* A-G Kokott, at para. 47 of her opinion: 'I suggest excluding arrangements for use in principle from the scope of Article [34], in the same way as selling arrangements, where the requirement set out by the Court in *Keck and Mithouard* is met'. The Court could have adopted this approach in Case C-110/05 *Commission* v *Italy*, *ibid.*, in *Mickelsson and Roos* or in Case C-433/05 *Sandström*, *ibid.*, but did not. The former turned upon Italian impediments to importing 'trailers which are specially designed to be towed by motorcycles and are legally produced and marketed in [other] Member States' (para. 54), the latter two upon Swedish rules which 'have the effect of preventing users of personal watercraft from using them for the specific and inherent purposes for which they were intended or of greatly restricting their use' (*Mickelsson and Roos*, para. 28), which could be characterised as differential treatment in fact. The *Keck* door is therefore not necessarily closed. Although *Mickelsson and Roos* and *Sandström* recognise a wide discretion enjoyed by national authorities, they were applied by the *Højesteret* to quash a conviction for riding a 'water scooter' in territorial waters contrary to a Danish ministerial order, the order being a breach of art. 34 for disproportionality; *Højesteret*, dom af 19. november 2010 (*Rigsadvokaten mod T*), U2011.539H.

the other freedoms of movement',[283] *Keck* principles have begun to inform other of the Treaty freedoms.

Advertising

Advertising may play a key role in furthering the goals of the internal market. It **10.51** can be ancillary to the activity of marketing goods (or services),[284] or it can itself constitute a service;[285] in some circumstances the two aspects may collide.[286] Where it is ancillary to the cross-frontier movement of goods (that is, goods advertised and not only the advertising crosses a frontier) it is often characterised as a *Keck* selling arrangment and so beyond the scope of article 34.[287] But this is to ignore the link between advertising and market access/penetration,[288] where 'legislation which restricts or prohibits certain forms of advertising and certain means of sales promotion ... affects marketing opportunities'.[289] It is possible now to detect in the case law a differentiation between total bans upon advertising and restrictions applying to form and content,[290] the former more likely to fall within article 34 (but may be justified by reference to article 36),[291] the latter likely to constitute a *Keck* selling arrangment. The matter may become much clearer as the Audiovisual Media Services Directive (AVMSD, or 'Audiovisual Without Frontiers II')[292] beds in.

6. Restrictions upon exports

Article 35 TFEU prohibits quantitative restrictions and all measures having **10.52** equivalent effect on exports. There is relatively scant case law on it. Its wording (identical to article 34 save substituting 'exports' for 'imports') and its place in

---

283   Cases C-158 and 159/04 *Alfa Vita Vassilopoulos*, n. 281 above, *per* A-G Poiares Maduro at para. 50 of his opinion.

284   See e.g., for goods, Case 286/81 *Criminal proceedings against Oosthoek's Uitgeversmaatschappij* [1982] ECR 4575; Case C-126/91 *Schutzverband gegen Unwesen in der Wirtschaft* v *Yves Rocher* [1993] ECR I-2361.

285   See 11.129 below.

286   E.g., Cases C-34 etc./95 *Konsumentombudsmannen* v *De Agostini (Svenska) Förlag* [1997] ECR I-3843; Case C-405/98 *Konsumentombudsmannen* v *Gourmet International Products* [2001] ECR I-1795.

287   Case C-292/92 *Hünermund and ors* v *Landesapothekerskammer Baden-Württemberg* [1993] ECR I-6787; Case C-412/93 *Edouard Leclerc-Siplec* v *TF1 Publicité and anor* [1995] ECR I-179; Cases C-34 etc./95 *De Agostini (Svenska)*, *ibid.*; Case C-405/98 *Gourmet International Products, ibid.*

288   See the discussion of A-G Jacobs in Case C-412/93 *Leclerc-Simplec, ibid.*

289   Cases C-1 and 176/90 *Aragonesa de Publicidad Exterior SA and anor* v *Departamento de Sanidad y Seguridad Social de la Generalitat de Cataluña* [1991] ECR I-4151, at para. 10.

290   E.g., Case C-254/98 *Schutzverband gegen unlauteren Wettbewerb* v *TK-Heimdienst Sass* [2000] ECR I-151; Case C-71/02 *Herbert Karner Industrie-Auktionen* v *Troostwijk* [2004] ECR I-3025.

291   E.g., Case C-320/93 *Ortscheit* v *Eurim-Pharm Arzneimittel* [1994] ECR I-5243; Case C-405/98 *Gourmet International Products*, n. 286 above; Case C-143/06 *Ludwigs-Apotheke München Internationale Apotheke* v *Juers Pharma Import-Export* [2007] ECR I-9623.

292   Directive 2007/65 [2007] OJ L332/27. The Directive amended significantly the 1989 'Television without Frontiers' Directive (Directive 89/552 [1989] OJ L298/23). It was required to be implemented by the end of 2009.

the Treaty suggest that it be interpreted and applied in the same manner as article 34. But it is not. Quantitative restrictions themselves are accorded a parallel definition,[293] and include a complete ban on exports.[294] But measures having equivalent effect are defined much more restrictively under article 35 than under article 34. Initially the Court spliced the *Dassonnville* formula to article 35.[295] But thereafter it narrowed the scope, restricting measures having equivalent effect to

> national measures which have as their specific object or effect the restriction of patterns of exports and thereby the establishment of a difference in treatment between the domestic trade of a Member State and its export trade in such a way as to provide a special advantage for national production or for the domestic market of the state in question, at the expense of the production or of the trade of other Member States;'[296]

in other words, to translate from article 34, distinctly applicable measures. The (unstated) reason is surely that article 35 would otherwise catch a raft of national regulation far removed from issues of interstate movement of goods, areas of regulation in which the Treaty ought not to interfere – 'a very large number of measures, … [i]n practice … all production conditions and restrictions, all measures which increase production costs in any manner whatsoever and measures concerning working conditions, for example'.[297] It resonates, tacitly, with the principle of subsidiarity.

10.53 The *Groenveld* test has three interdependent limbs:

- the object or effect of the measure is the restriction specifically of patterns of exports;
- the measure gives rise to a difference in treatment between domestic trade and export trade; and
- by virtue of the measure, a particular advantage is provided for national

---

293 Case 2/73 *Geddo* v *Ente Nazionale Risi* [1973] ECR 865, at para. 7.

294 Case C-5/94 *R* v *Minister of Agriculture, Fisheries and Food, ex parte Hedley Lomas* [1996] ECR I-2553; Case C-1/96 *R* v *Minister of Agriculture, Fisheries and Food, ex parte Compassion in World Farming* [1998] ECR I-1251.

295 Case 53/76 *Procureur de la République, Besançon* v *Les Sieurs Bouhelier and ors* [1977] ECR 197, at para. 16.

296 Case 15/79 *Groenveld* v *Produktschap voor Vee en Vlees* [1979] ECR 3409, at para. 7 ('the *Groenveld* test'); confimed many times since: Case 155/80 *Oebel* [1981] ECR 1993, at para. 15; Cases 141 etc./81 *Holdijk* [1982] ECR 1299, at para. 11; Case 237/82 *Jongeneel Kaas and ors* v *Netherlands and anor* [1984] ECR 483, at para. 22; Case C-108/01 *Consorzio del Prosciutto di Parma and anor* v *Asda Stores and anor* [2003] ECR I-5121, at para. 54; Case C-293/02 *Jersey Produce Marketing Organisation* v *States of Jersey* [2005] ECR I-9543, at para. 73. In all judgments following *Groenveld* there is a comma after 'export trade'; *Jersey Produce Marketing Organisation* substitutes 'particular' for 'special' in the penultimate clause.

297 Case C-205/07 *Criminal proceedings against Gysbrechts and Santurel Inter* [2008] ECR I-9947, *per* A-G Trstenjak at para. 54 of her opinion.

production or for the domestic market of the state in question, at the expense of the trade or production of other member states.

It will therefore catch, for example, a requirement of an export licence[298] or export dependent upon compulsory registration or management agreement with a public body.[299] The prohibition applies even if the restriction is imposed upon the movement of goods to another part of the same member state, for it is likely to constitute an obstacle to subsequent export to other member states.[300]

In 2008 Advocate-General Trstenjak queried the continued application of **10.54** *Groenveld*, noted that the movement of exports remained alone amongst the fundamental freedoms in which the Court persisted in requiring different treatment in order for the Treaty prohibition to be joined and, finding no justification for it, proposed 'modifying' the case law, transposing *Dassonville* to article 35 but excluding measures having an effect upon exports which is 'too uncertain and too indirect' and fashioning an adapted *Keck* test.[301] The Court met her half way. It referred to the *Groenveld* test with apparent approval, considered the measure at issue (a Belgian law on consumer protection which prohibited in distance selling a trader requiring of a buyer (a) a deposit or payment prior to the end of the prescribed cooling off period and (b) provision of his payment card number), determined that their consequences 'are generally more significant in cross-border sales made directly to consumers',[302] and so found that

> even if a prohibition such as that at issue in the main proceedings is applicable to all traders active in the national territory, its actual effect is none the less greater on goods leaving the market of the exporting Member State than on the marketing of goods in the domestic market of that Member State. It must therefore be held that a national measure, such as that at issue in the main proceedings … constitutes a measure having equivalent effect to a quantitative restriction on exports.[303]

It then proceeded to consider whether consumer protection could serve as justification for the bans on advance payment (which it could) and requirement of a buyer's payment card number (which it could not).

---

298   Cases 51 etc./71 *International Fruit Company and ors* v *Produktschap voor Groenten en Fruit* [1971] ECR 1107; Case 68/76 *Commission* v *France* [1977] ECR 515.

299   Case 83/78 *Pigs Marketing Board* v *Redmond* [1978] ECR 2347; Case C-293/02 *Jersey Produce Marketing Organisation*, n. 296 above.

300   Case C-293/02 *Jersey Produce Marketing Organisation*, n. 296 above; Case C-161/09 *Kakavetsos-Frangopoulos AE Epexergasias kai Emporias Stafidas* v *Nomarchiaki Aftodioikisi Korinthias*, judgment of 3 March 2011, not yet reported. This is analogous to a similar prohibition under art. 30; see n. 65 above and accompanying text.

301   Case C-205/07 *Gysbrechts*, n. 297 above at paras 42–65 of her opinion.

302   Judgment of the Court, at para. 42.

303   *Ibid.* at paras 43–44.

10.55   It is difficult to say whether the Court intends *Gysbrechts* to be a re-tooling of or a break with *Groenveld*. There is no recognition in the judgment of a change of tack, but change there is; if nothing else the Court applied considerations of consumer protection, a mandatory requirement (or an overriding requirement of public interest)[304] which in the context of article 34 may serve to justify indistinctly applicable measures only. More is now needed before a rule can be identified with confidence.

7. De minimis

10.56   Just as the prohibition of article 30 is applied rigourously, so it is for articles 34. It is immaterial that a restriction to the movement of goods affects only part of a member state[305] (so that an argument that imported goods suffer no greater burdens than those of (most of) the importing member state is immaterial) or that it does so minimally: to give only the best known example, a Danish ministerial order prohibiting the importation onto the island of Læsø and its neighbouring islands of living bees and reproductive material for domestic bees which were not Læsø brown bees (*apis mellifera mellifera*) – Læsø being an island in the Kattegat of 114 km² (0.26 per cent of the territory of metropolitan Denmark) with a population of 2,365 souls (0.04 per cent of the Danish total) and some 300 brown bee colonies – was caught by article 34, although it was justified under article 36 in order to protect and preserve the species.[306] Subsequently Austria argued that local regulation of motorway traffic (in order to decrease air pollution) had produced no significant economic consequences and had effects, if any, which were 'too uncertain or indirect to be regarded as being capable of hindering trade between Member States';[307] the 'too uncertain or indirect' test is one which is applied to the other Treaty freedoms[308] but here the Court peremptorily ignored it.[309] Advocate-General Jacobs suggested on more than one occasion that article 34 apply only to 'substantial restriction' to

---

304   *Ibid.* at para. 45; Case C-161/09 *Frangopoulos*, n. 300 above, at para. 51.

305   E.g., Case 21/88 *Du Pont de Nemours Italiana v Unità sanitaria locale No. 2 di Carrara* [1990] ECR I-889; Cases C-1 and 176/90 *Aragonesa de Publicidad & Publivía v Departamento de Sanidad* [1991] ECR I-4151; Cases C-277 etc./91 *Ligur Carni and ors v Unità Sanitaria Locale No XV di Genova and ors* [1993] ECR I-6621.

306   Case C-67/97 *Criminal proceedings against Bluhme* [1998] ECR I-8033; the Læsø size and population data are provided at para. 9 of the judgment, the bee population taken from Danmarks Biavlerforening, Læsøbierne. See also Case 16/83 *Criminal proceedings against Prantl* [1984] ECR 1299, at para. 20 ('For there to be a breach of [art. 34] … [i]t is not necessary that [the national measure] should have an appreciable effect on intra-Community trade'); Case C-184/96 *Commission v France* (Foie Gras) [1988] ECR I-6197, at paras 14–17; Case C-309/02 *Radlberger Getränkegesellschaft and anor v Land Baden-Württemberg* [2004] ECR I-11763, at para. 68 ('a measure capable of hindering imports must be classified as a measure having equivalent effect to a quantitative restriction even though the hindrance is slight and even though it is possible for the products to be marketed in other ways').

307   Case C-28/09 *Commission v Austria*, judgment of 21 December 2011, not yet reported, at para. 86.

308   See 11.127 and 12.09 below.

309   Case C-28/09 *Commission v Austria*, n. 307 above, at paras 113–17.

market access – admitting that 'it would of course amount to introducing a *de minimis* test' into article 34[310] – but has not been followed by the Court, and Advocate-General Kokott has noted:

> With regard to the delimitation of the broad scope of Article [34] when the *Dassonville* formula is applied, the Court has attempted from time to time to exclude national measures whose effects on trade are too uncertain and too indirect from the scope of Article [34]. However, an argument against these criteria is that they are difficult to clarify and thus do not contribute to legal certainty …

> In this respect it is not only rules which result in complete exclusion, such as a general prohibition on using a certain product, that are to be regarded as preventing access to the market. A situation where only a marginal possibility for using a product remains because of a particularly restrictive rule on use is to be regarded as preventing access to the market.[311]

De minimis is therefore unknown, or unknown yet, in article 34, at least formally; for it remains that there is a small number of cases which are difficult to understand unless they were determined – tacitly – upon *de minimis* reasoning,[312] and it is arguably just possible to detect the embryo of *de minimis* in fleeting case law.[313]

As for article 35, the Court has appeared more readily to recognise a remoteness test: **10.57**

> It is true that the effect of the national provision [at issue] is to subject traders to different procedural rules according to whether they supply goods within the Member State concerned or export them to other Member States. However, … the possibility that nationals would therefore hesitate to sell goods to purchasers established in other Member States is too uncertain and indirect for that national provision to be regarded as liable to hinder trade between Member States.[314]

---

310 Case C-412/93 *Edouard Leclerc-Siplec* v *TF1 Publicité and anor* [1995] ECR I-179, at para. 42 of his opinion; see also his opinion in Case C-112/00 *Eugen Schmidberger Internationale Transporte und Planzüge* v *Austria* [2003] ECR I-5659, at para. 67.

311 Case C-142/05 *Åklagaren* v *Mickelsson and Roos* [2009] ECR I-4273, at paras 46 and 67 of her opinion.

312 E.g., Case C-69/88 *Krantz* v *Ontvanger der Directe Belastingen and anor* [1990] ECR I-583; Case C-169/91 *Stoke-on-Trent City Council and anor* v *B & Q* [1992] ECR I-6635. Both are pre-*Keck* cases, and it may be that *Keck* has removed much of the need for unspoken *de minimis* gymnastics.

313 Case C-93/92 *CMC Motorradcenter* v *Baskiciogullari* [1993] ECR I-5009, at para. 12; Case C-379/92 *Criminal proceedings against Peralta* [1994] ECR I-3453, at para. 24; Cases C-140 etc./94 *DIP and ors* v *Comune di Bassano del Grappa and ors* [1995] ECR I-3257, at para. 29; Case C-20/03 *Openbaar Ministerie* v *Burmanjer and ors* [2005] ECR I-4133, at para. 31; and especially Case C-291/09 *Francesco Guarnieri & Cie* v *Vandevelde Eddy VOF*, judgment of 7 April 2011, not yet reported, at para. 17.

314 Case C-412/97 *ED* v *Italo Fenocchio* [1999] ECR I-3845, at para. 11; implicit in Case C-12/02 *Criminal proceedings against Grilli* [2003] ECR I-11585.

This is in keeping with the traditional relatively gentler touch of article 35. The development of *Gysbrechts*[315] may bring welcome light to this area too.

8. Horizontal direct effect of article 34

10.58 Articles 34 and 35 have long been recognised to produce direct effect in all of their facets (quantitative restrictions and MEQRs on both imports and exports).[316] But this is now too simplistic. There is a serious question now to be considered of against *whom* they are directly effective.

(a) Member states

10.59 Although neither article has a formal addressee ('[q]uantitative restrictions … and all measures having equivalent effect shall … be prohibited between Member States'), the member states are the clear and primary target of articles 34 and 35. This is consistent with the early view of the Commission on the nature of 'measures' articulated in Directive 70/50[317] and with the *Dassonville* formula of MEQRs being 'trading rules enacted *by Member States*'. In all its guises – national, sub-national, local governments – and through all means by which they act, legislative or administrative activities and practices, even the exercise of police and judicial authority, the state is caught by the prohibitions. Equally caught are commercial monopolies which may be private persons in law, subject to article 37,[318] private companies set up and controlled by government to serve its ends,[319] and, in some circumstances, (semi-)private bodies to which a member state has delegated powers normally the preserve of the state, for example the regulation and discipline of a profession or the certification of products necessary prior to marketing, which may be exercised in a manner such as to impede imports.[320]

(b) The Union

10.60 The prohibitions appear also to apply to the Union and its institutions:

---

315 Case C-205/07 *Criminal proceedings against Gysbrechts and Santurel Inter* [2008] ECR I-9947; see immediately above.
316 First considered and recognised in Case 13/68 *Salgoil* v *Italian Ministry for Foreign Trade* [1968] ECR 453.
317 [1970] JO L13/29; see n. 147 above.
318 See 10.96–10.98 below.
319 Case 249/81 *Commission* v *Ireland* (Buy Irish) [1982] ECR 4005; Case C-325/00 *Commission* v *Germany* (CMA) [2002] ECR I-9977.
320 Cases 266 and 267/87 *R* v *Royal Pharmaceutical Society of Great Britain, ex parte Association of Pharmaceutical Importers* [1989] ECR 1295; Case C-292/92 *Hünermund* v *Landesapothekerskammer Baden-Württemberg* [1993] ECR I-6787; Case C-171/11 *Fra.bo* v *Deutsche Vereinigung des Gas- und Wasserfaches- Technisch-Wissenschaftlicher Verein*, judgment of 12 July 2012, not yet reported.

It is settled case-law that the prohibition of quantitative restrictions and of all measures having equivalent effect applies not only to national measures but also to measures adopted by the Community institutions.[321]

But this is too broad a proposition. The Union legislature will frequently adopt legislation which distorts the free movement of goods. That on agricultural regulation is a primary offender. Another is harmonisation legislation adopted under articles 114 or 115 in order to cure impediments to the free movement of goods.[322] Indeed, all harmonisation prohibits trade in goods which do not meet the harmonised standard; it may extend even to an absolute ban of trade in a product[323] and so constitute a quantitative restriction *simpliciter*. Given no *de minimis* escape from article 34 the Union measure therefore itself constitutes an impediment to the movement of goods, albeit one (presumably) less disruptive than those it seeks to cure. To this the Court points out simply that 'all secondary legislation [must] be interpreted in the light of the Treaty rules on the free movement of goods',[324] and Advocate-General Fennelly said:

> Community legislation is adopted pursuant to the Treaty; it must respect the basic rules of the Treaty and ... must be interpreted in harmony with the Treaty ... Even if Community secondary law may, as the occasion demands, itself lead to an incidental restriction of trade, this should result from a considered balancing of objectives.[325]

Or, as the Court said for other purposes but might be prayed in aid here:

> The free movement of goods is ... one of the objectives of those directives, which, through the elimination of the differences existing between the Member States ..., are designed to encourage intra-Community trade. The right conferred by Article [34] is thus defined and given concrete expression by those directives.[326]

In all events it is an underdeveloped area of the law.

---

321 Case C-220/98 *Estée Lauder Cosmetics* v *Lancaster Group* [2000] ECR I-117, *per* A-G Fennelly at para. 22 of his opinion; Case C-169/99 *Schwarzkopf* v *Zentrale zur Bekämpfung unlauteren Wettbewerbs* [2001] ECR I-5901, at para. 37; Case C-108/01 *Consorzio del Prosciutto di Parma and anor* v *Asda Stores and anor* [2003] ECR I-5121, at para. 53; Case C-210/03 *R (Swedish Match and anor)* v *Secretary of State for Health* [2004] ECR I-11893, at para. 59; the words 'of all' do not appear in the third or fourth judgments; the words 'laid down by Articles 28 EC and 29 EC' appear in the fourth judgment between 'effect' and 'applies'.
322 See 10.68–10.77 below.
323 Case C-210/03 *Swedish Match*, n. 321 above (Swedish '*snus*' oral tobacco); Regulation 1523/2007 [2007] OJ L343/1 (ban of the sale of cat and dog fur); Regulation 1007/2009 [2009] OJ L286/36 ((virtual) ban of seal products).
324 Case C-315/92 *Verband Sozialer Wettbewerb* v *Clinique Laboratoires and anor* [1994] ECR I-317, at para. 12.
325 Case C-3/99 *Cidrerie Ruwet* v *Cidre Stassen and anor* [2000] ECR I-8749, at para. 26 of his opinion.
326 C-445/06 *Danske Slagterier* v *Bundesrepublik Deutschland* [2009] ECR I-2119, at para. 23.

(c)   The individual

10.61   Once far-fetched, and probably unintended, it seems now quite possible that article 34 imposes obligations upon the individual, especially in light of a like finding for article 45 in the area of free movement of workers,[327] now spilling over into articles 49 and 56 on right of establishment and freedom to provide services.[328]

10.62   In one respect the individual is clearly a subject of article 34, that is where the proprietor of an intellectual property right seeks to exercise an exhausted right in a manner which impedes the movement of goods.[329] *Why* this is a matter falling within article 34 has never been adequately explained by the Court.[330] An intellectual property right is, after all, a property right and its exploitation a private law right; compare the exercise of a right in contract – also a private right derived from national (contract) law, necessarily reliant upon it and enforced by the courts – by a private person in a manner argued to hinder the free movement of goods:

> [T]hat … obligation arises out of a private contract between the parties to the main proceedings. Such a contractual provision cannot be regarded as a barrier to trade for the purposes of Article [34] since it was not imposed by a Member State but agreed between individuals.[331]

But whatever the logic (or lack thereof), it is now firmly established that article 34 applies, at least this far, to the conduct of individuals.

---

327   Case C-281/98 *Angonese* v *Cassa di Risparmio di Bolzano* [2000] ECR I-4139; see 11.140–11.144 below.

328   Respectively, Case C-438/05 *International Transport Workers' Federation and anor* v *Viking Line* [2007] ECR I-10779 and Case C-341/05 *Laval un Partneri* v *Svenska Byggnadsarbetareförbundet and ors* (Vaxholm) [2007] ECR I-11767; see 11.145–11.146 below.

329   Case 78/70 *Deutsche Grammophon* v *Metro-SB-Großmärkte* [1971] ECR 487; see 10.82 below.

330   The question was raised subsequently to *Deutsche Grammophon* (Case 15/74 *Centrafarm and de Pijper* v *Sterling Drug* [1974] ECR 1147) but not satisfactorily considered by the Court, although it fashioned a Delphic judgment in terms of the exercise of an intellectual property right 'which [the proprietor] enjoys under the legislation of a Member State' (at para. 15); see also Cases C-403 and 429/08 *Football Association Premier League* v *QC Leisure and ors* and *Murphy* v *Media Protection Services*, judgment of 4 October 2011, not yet reported, at para. 88. The justification seems to be that it is not the exercise of the private law right which offends art. 34, but rather the necessary reliance upon the national statute which creates it and provides it with legal protection – so bringing into the measure which inhibits the free movement of goods the imprimatur and the exercise of state power. Alternatively, it is the reliance upon the courts to give effect to the right which brings it within the ambit of art. 34; this is a practical application of a principle recognised in some jurisdictions of *unmittelbare Drittwirkung*, or 'indirect horizontal effect'.

331   Case C-159/00 *Saphod Audic* v *Eco-Emballages* [2002] ECR I-5031, at para. 74.

Otherwise it does not.[332] But this is now witnessing stages of early erosion. The   **10.63**
'*Strawberries*' (or '*Spanish Strawberries*') case[333] involved protests, often violent,
waged by French farmers against imported agricultural products: the intercep-
tion ('*contrôle*') of lorries transporting them, destruction of their loads, menaces
and violence against drivers, wholesalers and shops selling imported produce;
and all over an extended period (more than a decade) and met, it was claimed,
with indifference or tacit acquiescence on the part of the French authorities.
Schmidberger[334] involved peaceful protest by environmental campaigners proceeding with the approval of the Austrian authorities (it being a lawful protest
in Austrian law) which temporarily halted heavy motor traffic through the
Brenner Pass. According to Advocate-General Lenz in *Spanish Strawberries*,

> [t]here can be no doubt in this case that the conduct of private individuals in question
> would constitute an infringement of the principle of the free movement of goods *if* it
> could be attributed to the French Republic.[335]

But it couldn't, or couldn't readily; this was not the French state, it was
rampaging French farmers. *But*, it was argued, they rampaged with the com-
plicity of the authorities of the French state. Equally, the environmental
campaigners in the Brenner Pass acted with the express permission of competent authorities of the Austrian state. In the former the Court said:

> As an indispensable instrument for the realization of the market without internal
> frontiers, Article [34] therefore does not prohibit solely measures emanating from the
> State which, in themselves, create restrictions on trade between Member States. It also
> applies where a Member State abstains from adopting the measures required in order to
> deal with obstacles to the free movement of goods which are not caused by the State.

> The fact that a Member State abstains from taking action or, as the case may be, fails to
> adopt adequate measures to prevent obstacles to the free movement of goods that are
> created, in particular, by actions of private individuals on its territory aimed at products
> originating in other Member States is just as likely to obstruct intra-Community trade
> as is a positive act.

---

332   There is one rogue judgment of the Court (sitting in a chamber of three) in Case 58/80 *Dansk Supermarked* v
    Imerco [1981] ECR 181 which holds individuals responsible for breaches of art. 34, but it involved the Danish
    law on unfair competition so was thought to rely too much upon *Deutsche Grammophon* logic, and is now
    thought not to be good law. There is also a judgment in which the Court says quite clearly that art. 35 'may be
    relied on by individuals … in disputes against other individuals' (Case C-47/90 *Établissements Delhaize Frères*
    and anor v *Promalvin and anor* [1992] ECR I-3669, in the *dispositif*), but this is misleading, a function of
    sloppy drafting; what the Court *meant* was that art. 35 may be relied upon in disputes between individuals as a
    means of assessing the compatability with Union law of national public measures which are relevant to the
    dispute, a point made more clearly by A-G Gulmann.
333   Case C-265/95 *Commission* v *France* [1997] ECR I-6959.
334   Case C-112/00 *Eugen Schmidberger, Internationale Transporte und Planzüge* v *Austria* [2003] ECR I-5659.
335   Case C-265/95 *Commission* v *France*, n. 333 above, at para. 13 of his opinion (emphasis in original).

Article [34] therefore requires the Member States not merely themselves to abstain from adopting measures or engaging in conduct liable to constitute an obstacle to trade but also, when read with Article [4(3) TEU], to take all necessary and appropriate measures to ensure that the fundamental freedom is respected on their territory.[336]

France was therefore in breach of article 34 in combination with article 4(3), not for impeding imports but for failing to prevent the thuggery on the part of individuals which did so.[337] Acknowledging the existence of a fundamental right to protest and considering its margin of discretion, the Court found in *Schmidberger* that Austria was not.[338]

10.64 This opens a potentially very broad new avenue, the extent to which a member state must ensure the adequacy of movement of goods within its frontiers in the face of private conduct which would thwart it. France was found wanting, Austria was not. But neither case stands for the proposition that article 34 imposes obligations upon individuals – or at least, does so directly. Although it was individuals, literally in this case, acting collectively, who impeded the free movement of goods, the issue was the duty of the state to ensure that they should or could not do so. Article 34 therefore goes still to the burdens of the member state, hence the necessary reference in both cases to article 4(3). Whether the Court will advance article 34 further still remains to be seen. An opportunity to do so presented itself in 2001 with yet more restive French farmers, this time addressing a crisis in the French beef market occasioned by incidents of BSE and foot and mouth disease, but the disruption orchestrated by a number of trade associations and unions. Just as the horizontal direct effect of article 45 began with private bodies which regulated 'access to employment in a collective manner', it is perhaps not stretching that principle too far to see it applied to article 34 and private bodies which may regulate the movement of goods in a collective manner – in other words, a trade union. The Commission intervened *but* under the competition rules, found that the associations/unions had infringed article 101(1) TFEU by suspending imports of beef into France

---

336 *Ibid.* at paras 30–32 of the judgment.

337 The case also led to the adoption of Regulation 2679/98 [1998] OJ L337/8 (the 'Strawberry Regulation'), intended to enable speedy action by the Commission to prevent repetition of similar breaches of art. 34. As to the application of the Strawberry Regulation see Resolution of the Council and of the representatives of the governments of the Member States meeting in the Council [1998] 1998 L337/10 and Case C-320/03 *Commission* v *Austria* [2005] ECR I-9871.

338 In this the judgment was very like that of the House of Lords in the United Kingdom which had earlier come to a similar conclusion, on the matter of policing protests at English ports from which live veal calves were to be exported (before the trade was banned owing to BSE); *R* v *Chief Constable of Surrey, ex parte International Trader's Ferry Ltd* [1999] 2 AC 418.

and price fixing, and fined them almost €17 million.[339] It did *not* seek or find a breach of article 34. It would therefore appear that – for now – the Commission at least considers horizontal direct effect of article 34 a bridge too far. The subsequent finding of the Court that article 49 is capable of producing effects enforceable as against union action which hinders the right of establishment,[340] and the comment, *obiter*, therein in which the Court cites *Spanish Strawberries* and *Schmidberger* as

> the case-law on the Treaty provisions on the free movement of goods, from which it is apparent that restrictions may be the result of actions by individuals or groups of such individuals rather than caused by the State,[341]

suggests that the span is narrowing.

In a 2007 judgment the Court said that statements by an individual which had **10.65** the effect of hindering imported goods (*in casu* widely disseminated statements of an official of a national ministry which had a bearing upon the safety of the goods) could constitute a breach of article 34,[342] but this applied where, by reason of their form and circumstances, the persons to whom they were addressed reasonably formed the view that they were not personal opinions but official positions attributable to the state[343] – thus again, the conduct of individuals, but again going (vicariously) to the obligations of the member state in order to attract the application of article 34. Yet the Court then muddied the water by saying that:

> Community law does not preclude an individual [*un sujet de droit*] other than a Member State from being held liable, in addition to the Member State itself, for damage caused to individuals by measures which that individual has taken in breach of Community law.[344]

This may have been a function of a peculiarity of Finnish law on the personal liability of a public official, but it is an odd construction which requires state action to find an infringement of article 34 yet at the same time holds the

---

339 Decision 2003/600 (French Beef) [2003] OJ L209/12; upheld essentially on review as Cases T-217 and 245/03 *Fédération nationale de la coopération bétail et viande* v *Commission* [2006] ECR II-4987. As to the competition rules and their enforcement see Chapter 13.

340 Case C-438/05 *International Transport Workers' Federation and anor v Viking Line* [2007] ECR I-10779; see 11.145 below.

341 *Ibid.* at para. 62.

342 Case C-470/03 *A.G.M.-COS.MET* v *Suomen valtio and anor* [2007] ECR I-2749. More accurately, they could constitute a breach of a Directive which had exhaustively harmonised the relevant field.

343 *Ibid.* at para. 66.

344 *Ibid.* at para. 98.

individual liable in damages (or more accurately, permits him to be held liable)[345] for 'measures which [he] has taken in breach of Community law'.

9. Reverse discrimination

10.66 Application of *Cassis de Dijon* may have the effect of discriminating against home producers, to the (greatest) benefit of producers in the member state of light(est) regulatory burden. Thus, where national rules regulate the production of goods in a manner more stringent than the rules which obtain in other member states, article 34 will normally require that goods produced in those other member states have access to the home market, but the home producer, bound by the domestic rules, will be operating at a cost or other comparative disadvantage. A German brewer, for example, may not lade his beer with maize, manioc, rice, soya, caramel, sulphur dioxide, tannin, propylene glycol alginate and isinglass as brewers elsewhere can and do, and an Italian chocolatier cannot use (cheap) vegetable fats. It was argued that this offends the general Union principle of non-discrimination, so that a home producer ought to be exempt from the national rules to the same extent as competitors who have access to the home market. The Court of Justice disagreed, finding reverse discrimination not to be prohibited by the Treaties, and so (more burdensome) national rules applicable to domestic producers and sellers.[346] A (peculiar) justification was offered by the Court in *Jongeneel Kaas*:

> Article [34] does not prevent the adoption of national rules which, whilst leaving imported products unaffected, have as their purpose to improve the quality of domestic production so as to make it more attractive to consumers. A measure of that kind complies with the requirement of sound and fair competition laid down by the Treaty.[347]

But an unstated reason seems more likely to be that a prohibition of reverse discrimination would have the effect of reducing all national rules to the lowest common denominator.[348] It is sometimes called the 'purely national measures' or 'wholly internal' rule; it does not apply (uniquely) to article 30 and has greatest resonance in the context of the free movement of persons, where it is

---

345 *Ibid.* at para. 99.

346 See e.g., Case 286/81 *Criminal proceedings against Oosthoek's Uitgeversmaatschappij* [1982] ECR 4575; Case 237/82 *Jongeneel Kaas and ors* v *State of the Netherlands and anor* [1984] ECR 483; Case 355/85 *Commissaire du Police, Thouars* v *Cognet* [1986] ECR 3231; Case 98/86 *Ministère Public* v *Methot* [1987] ECR 809; but cf. Cases C-321 etc./94 *Criminal proceedings against Pistre and ors* [1997] ECR I-2343.

347 Case 237/82 *Jongeneel Kaas, ibid.*, at para. 20.

348 A related fear is that member states, under pressure from their own producers, may reduce standards, resulting in a race to the bottom. But there is not much evidence that this occurs.

now under siege.[349] The problem lapses in the event of legislative intervention which harmonises national rules or otherwise directs the member states, so creating a legal obligation upon which the individual may rely even against his own member state.

Article 35 occupies a peculiar half-way house. If article 35 catches a national **10.67** measure which, directly or indirectly, actually or potentially, affects exports provided that it exerts different treatment as between products destined for export and those sold domestically, it would prohibit *any* national marketing rule in the member state of export which, by definition, does not apply in other member states. Article 35 therefore applies only to measures which restrict exports. But since *Frangopoulos* it can appy to measures which restrict export to another part of the same member state, so relaxing in part the wholly internal rule.

10. Harmonisation of technical barriers to trade

Where national measures which impede trade can be justified by recourse to **10.68** article 36 or to the mandatory requirements, or where the impediment is a function of varying mandatory/voluntary technical standards, it can be resolved only by changes to the national rules and standards at issue. This was foreseen in the original EEC Treaty, which provided authority for the adoption of

> directives for the approximation of such provisions laid down by law, regulation or administrative action in Member States as directly effect the establishment or functioning of the common market.[350]

However this approximation, or more commonly 'harmonisation', of national laws required unanimity in the Council,[351] and progress was slow. The Single European Act therefore amended the EEC Treaty so as to create a simpler means of achieving the same task, authorising the Council, by the new cooperation procedure (so abandoning the veto), to

> adopt the measures for the approximation of the provisions laid down by law, regulation or administrative action in Member States which have as their object the establishment and functioning of the internal market[352]

Whilst articles 100 and 100a applied to harmonisation measures for the common/internal market respectively, and so to all of the four freedoms, they

---

349 See 11.90–11.95 below.
350 EEC Treaty, art. 100 (now art. 115 TFEU *mutatis mutandis*).
351 *Ibid.*
352 EEC Treaty, art. 100a (now art. 114(1) TFEU).

have been used for the most part in order to smooth away technical barriers to the free movement of goods. They will therefore be considered here. Notwithstanding the concept of 'common market' disappearing with Lisbon the two provisions remain distinct.

10.69 Article 100a EEC (article 114 TFEU) was adopted, as part of the 1992 programme, as the means of breaking up the logjam which had hindered progress in the completion of the common market. In large measure it worked, and a raft of harmonising Directives were adopted. But because measures adopted under article 114 circumvent the national veto it is hedged with safeguards for the benefit of the member states which do not exist under article 115:

- specifically excluded from the ambit of article 114 are fiscal provisions and provisions relating to the free movement of persons and to the rights of employed persons;[353]
- in proposing measures related to health, safety and environmental and consumer protection the Commission is bound to take as a base a 'high level of protection';[354]
- harmonising measures may, 'in appropriate cases', include safeguard clauses expressly permitting 'provisional' derogation by reference to the criteria of article 36;[355] this, combined now with a provision (introduced by the Single European Act) amongst the Treaty principles and applying to internal market legislation generally,[356] marked the beginning of variable geometry;
- even absent a derogation clause, a member state which 'after the adoption … of a harmonisation measure … deems it necessary to maintain national provisions on grounds of major needs [*exigences importantes*] referred to in Article 36, or relating to protection of the environment or the working environment' may, in effect, opt out of the measure by notification to the

---

353   TFEU, art. 114(2). Harmonisation the pith and substance of which is fiscal is reserved to art. 113 (as to which see 10.21 above), that relating to free movement of persons and rights in employment to art. 115; both require Council unanimity. For examples see Directive 2003/48 [2003] OJ L157/38 (taxation of savings income); Directive 2003/49 [2003] OJ L157/49 (taxation of interest and royalties); Directive 2003/123 [2004] OJ L7/41 (taxation of parent companies and subsidiaries in different member states); the extension of 'Social Agreement' Directives to the United Kingdom, as to which 14.35 below. As for art. 114 measures trenching upon fiscal provisions see Case C-533/03 *Commission* v *Council* [2006] ECR I-1025.
354   *Ibid.* art. 114(3).
355   *Ibid.* art. 114(10).
356   EEC Treaty, art. 7c (now art. 27 TFEU): in proposing internal market legislation the Commission 'shall take into account the extent of the effort that certain economies showing difference in development will have to sustain'; if derogation is permitted it 'must be of a temporary nature and must cause the least possible disturbance to the functioning of the internal market'.

Commission[357] and thereafter maintain (presumably existing) higher standards and exclude goods which do not meet them; this eases significantly the process of political agreement in the Council, but the provision is cited frequently as the most confusing, and the most poorly drafted, in the Treaties.

With Maastricht the legislative procedure of article 114 was altered from **10.70** cooperation to co-decision. Then the Treaty of Amsterdam made two important changes: first, it made express reference to the possibility of introduction, post-harmonisation, of new national measures in the light of new scientific evidence;[358] this had the effect of creating two bifurcated categories: the maintenance of existing national provisions, which must be justified on grounds of the major needs referred to in article 36 or relating to the protection of the environment or the working environment, and the introduction of new national provisions, which can serve only protection of the environment or working environment (so not article 36 criteria) and must be based on new scientific evidence upon grounds of a problem specific to that member state, arising after the adoption of the harmonisation measure.[359] In all events it is for the requesting member state to provide the grounds which justify the maintenance/introduction of the derogating national measure and show that the necessary conditions have been met,[360] but the Commission is required to respond with fair and adequate analysis of the relevant scientific evidence.[361] Second, Amsterdam introduced a requirement for the Commission to respond to a notification for derogation within six months (extendable to one year where justified by the complexity of the matter and absent a danger to human health),

---

357 TFEU, art. 114(4). The Commission is to verify that the national measure is not a means of arbitrary discrimination or disguised restriction to trade (art. 114(6)); whatever it decides, the response must be properly reasoned, Case C-41/93 *France* v *Commission* [1994] ECR I-1829. Where a member state is alleged to be making improper use of derogation, 'fast track' enforcement proceedings could be raised by the Commission or another member state circumventing the administrative phase of art. 258 (art. 114(9)). In an indirectly related instrument, new technical standards in areas not regulated by harmonisation are required to be notified to the Commission for vetting, and cannot be introduced for a period of time; see 10.43 above.

358 TFEU, art. 114(5).

359 For reasons underpinning this two tier approach see Cases C-439 and 454/05P *Land Oberösterreich and Austria* v *Commission* [2007] ECR I-7141, *per* A-G Sharpston at para. 41 of her opinion.

360 Case C-512/99 *Germany* v *Commission* [2003] ECR I-845; Case C-3/00 *Denmark* v *Commission* [2003] ECR I-2643; Cases T-366/03 and 235/04 *Land Oberösterreich and Austria* v *Commission* [2005] ECR II-4005. For good examples of (successful) applications to maintain existing measures see Decisions 2002/398 and 2002/399 [2002] OJ L15 and 25 (cadmium content of fertilisers in Finland and Sweden) and Decision 2008/448 [2008] OJ L157/98 (nitrite additives in meat in Denmark); and to introduce new national measures, Decision 2002/884 [2002] OJ L308/30 (importation of creosote-treated wood into the Netherlands). For an unsuccessful example of the latter see Decision 2008/62 [2008] OJ L16/16 (GMOs in Poland).

361 Case C-405/07P *Netherlands* v *Commission* [2008] ECR I-8301.

failing which the national provision is deemed to be approved.[362] The requesting member state enjoys no right to be heard.[363]

10.71   Since article 115 was the appropriate legal base for harmonisation to assist the common market, and article 114 that for harmonisation to assist the internal market, the former was appropriate only in those (undefined) areas of lacuna which were common, but not internal, market, or those which were expressly excluded from the reach of article 114. This combined with the fact that, not requiring unanimity and allowing the possibility of derogation, it is much easier to reach Council agreement under article 114, means that it has been, since 1987, the much preferred option of the two. With Lisbon the common/internal market conundrum disappeared with the disappearance of the common market from the Treaties,[364] both articles now directed towards serving the internal market.[365] The remaining distinction is therefore (a) article 115 continues to apply in those areas excuded from article 114; and (b) whilst article 115 permits the adoption of Directives only, article 114 provides for the adoption of 'measures': Directives remain the preferred choice for a task appropriate to harmonisation, but other forms of legislation (Regulations) are therefore permissible, 'depending on the general context and the specific circumstances of the matter to be harmonised, as regards the method of approximation most appropriate for achieving the desired result, in particular in fields with complex technical features'.[366] It must be observed that the institutions sometimes elect to adopt a Regulation where there are no complex technical features yet with little or no justification for choice of that instrument.[367] It is also permissible to use article 114 to establish a Union regulatory body, so long as the tasks

---

362   TFEU, art. 114(6) (ex art. 95(6) EC). Prior to the entry into force of this provision in 1999 a member state could apply derogating provisions only after having obtained a Commission decision authorising them (Case C-41/93 *France* v *Commission* [1994] ECR I-1829); this was so even if the Commission took an undue length of time – or failed utterly – to adopt it (Case C-319/97 *Criminal proceedings against Kortas* [1999] ECR I-3143). The suggested remedy was an action under art. 265 TFEU for failure to act. But this availed the affected individual little, for he lacked standing to raise proceedings under art. 265, and probably could not recover damages for any injury from the Commission as the Commission decision which ought to have been adopted was probably one for the general good, so failing to meet the individual rights test of art. 340.

363   Case C-3/00 *Denmark* v *Commission*, n. 360 above; Cases C-439 and 454/05P *Land Oberösterreich and Austria*, n. 359 above.

364   Lisbon Treaty, art. 2(3)(g).

365   *Nota bene* for the avoidance of confusion, Lisbon reversed the ordering of arts 94 and 95 EC, that is, the present art. 114 TFEU was art. 95 EC, and the present art. 115 TFEU was art. 94 EC.

366   Case C-217/04 *United Kingdom* v *Parliament and Council* (Network and Information Security Agency) [2006] ECR I-3771, at para. 43; Case C-58/08 *R (Vodafone and ors)* v *Secretary of State for Business, Enteprise and Regulatory Reform* [2010] ECR I-4999, at para. 35.

367   E.g., Regulation 1007/2009 [2009] OJ L286/36; under (indirect) review in Case T-526/10 *Inuit Tapiriit Kanatami and ors* v *Commission*, pending.

conferred upon it are 'closely linked to the subject-matter of the acts approximating the laws, regulations and administrative provisions of the Member States'.[368]

Articles 114 and 115 do *not* vest in the institutions a general power to regulate the common/internal market, that is beyond Union authority.[369] Nor is the mere existence of disparities between national rules sufficient to justify recourse to harmonisation measures.[370] But legislative intervention *is* justified **10.72**

> where there are differences between the laws, regulations or administrative provisions of the Member States which are such as to obstruct the fundamental freedoms and thus have a direct effect on the functioning of the internal market.[371]

Then

> [a]rticle [114] empowers the Community legislature to adopt measures to improve the conditions for the establishment and functioning of the internal market and they must genuinely have that object, contributing to the elimination of obstacles to the economic freedoms guaranteed by the Treaty.[372]

Put otherwise:

> As regards the scope of the legislative powers laid down in Article [114] it must be observed that ... that provision is used as a legal basis only where it is actually and objectively apparent from the legal act that its purpose is to improve the conditions for the establishment and functioning of the internal market.[373]

It is legitimate to use article 114 even where hindrances to the free movement of goods do not exist, but are likely to do so in the future:

> [R]ecourse to Article [114] as a legal basis is possible if the aim is to prevent the emergence of future obstacles to trade resulting from multifarious development of national laws [so long as] the emergence of such obstacles [is] likely and the measure in question [is] designed to prevent them ...

---

368 Case C-217/04 *Network and Information Security Agency*, n. 366 above, at para. 45.
369 Case C-376/98 *Germany* v *Parliament and Council* (Tobacco Advertising) [2000] ECR I-8419, at para. 83.
370 *Ibid.*, at para. 84.
371 Case C-210/03 *R (Swedish Match and anor)* v *Secretary of State for Health* [2004] ECR I-11893, at para. 29; Cases C-154 and 155/04 *R (Alliance for Natural Health and ors)* v *Secretary of State for Health and anor* [2005] ECR I-6451, at para. 28.
372 Case C-436/03 *Parliament* v *Council* (SCE) [2006] ECR I-3733, at para. 38.
373 Case C-66/04 *United Kingdom* v *Parliament and Council* (Smoke Flavouring) [2005] ECR I-10553, at para. 44; Case C-217/04 *Network and Information Security Agency*, n. 366 above, at para. 42.

It follows ... that when there are obstacles to trade, or it is likely that such obstacles will emerge in the future, because the Member States have taken, or are about to take, divergent measures with respect to a product or a class of products, which bring about different levels of protection and thereby prevent the product or products concerned from moving freely within the Community, Article [114] authorises the Community legislature to intervene by adopting appropriate measures.[374]

This is why proposals for new technical regulations must be notified to the Commission and their introduction suspended for a time.[375] But once action is justified the legislature enjoys significant discretion in determining what is appropriate. Contrary to popular perception, article 114 is not a charter for deregulation: 'the ... case-law does not require [it] to be interpreted as a kind of liberal charter, entailing harmonisation towards the lowest standard or even towards some sort of mean of the pre-existing national standards'.[376] Rather '[a]rticle [114] can, indeed, provide the basis for an intensification of regulation in addition to deregulatory measures. This is, in principle, to be decided by the political process'.[377] The Union legislature will, as always, be subject to considerations of subsidiarity and proportionality,[378] and it is the subject area in which the Court appears most disposed seriously to consider issues of subsidiarity; but it nevertheless allows the legislature a wide leeway. Its discretion here too extends to embracing non-economic considerations (banning the sale of cosmetic products which have been tested on animals)[379] and even to banning the marketing of a product altogether (Swedish '*snus*' oral tobacco;[380] cat and dog fur and products made therefrom;[381] seal products).[382] Advocate-General Poiares Maduro took the view that article 114 may be used to cure by

---

374 Case C-210/03 *Swedish Match*, n. 371 above, at paras 30, 33; Cases C-154 and 155/04 *Alliance for Natural Health*, n. 371 above, at paras 29, 32.
375 Directive 98/34 [1998] OJ L204/37; see 10.43 above.
376 Case C-376/98 *Germany v Parliament and Council* (Tobacco Advertising) [2000] ECR I-8419, *per* A-G Fennelly at para. 85 of his opinion.
377 Case C-58/08 *R (Vodafone and ors) v Secretary of State for Business, Enteprise and Regulatory Reform* [2010] ECR I-4999, *per* A-G Poiares Maduro at para. 9 of his opinion.
378 See the discussion of A-G Poires Maduro, *ibid.*, at paras 27–44 of his opinion.
379 Case C-244/03 *France v Parliament and Council* (Cosmetic Products) [2005] ECR I-4021.
380 Case C-210/03 *Swedish Match*, n. 371 above. But Sweden itself is exempted indefinitely from the prohibition (Directive 2001/37 [2001] OJ L194/26, art 8) in accordance with a derogation secured in the 1994 Act of Accession, art 151 and Annex XV, X.(9).
381 Regulation 1523/2007 [2007] OJ L343/1.
382 Regulation 1007/2009 [2009] OJ L286/36, subject to limited derogation for traditional Inuit hunting. The Regulation was nevertheless challenged directly in Case T-18/10 *Inuit Tapiriit Kanatami and ors v Parliament and Council*, judgment of 6 September 2011, not yet reported (unsuccessfully, the applicants lacking direct concern and/or individual concern) and indirectly (via its implementing Regulation) in Case T-526/10 *Inuit Tapiriit Kanatami and ors v Commission*, pending. Whatever the merits of the ban it marks an impressive display of hypocrisy, the Commission having spent €300,000 through Interreg III (part of regional development funding) on creating markets for (European) seal products, including a cookery book extolling gastronomic potential, published (only) in Swedish, Norwegian and Finnish: Svenska Jägareförbundet, *Säl hylje sel: Sälen i det moderna köket* (2006).

harmonisation impediments to the internal market not only those a product of of law, regulation or administrative action in the member states but also those resulting from the actions of private persons;[383] this is perhaps odd, for article 113 speaks of fiscal harmonisation 'to avoid distortions of competition' and article 116 speaks of the adoption of Directives 'necessary' to eliminate distortions to competition a product of national laws, regulations or administrative actions, but article 114 says nothing of competition. Yet the Court did not repudiate the proposition, and perhaps agreed *sotto voce*.[384]

The Parliament and Council have now adopted a common framework of general principles and reference provisions for drawing up harmonising legislation[385] and, as a 'complement' to it, rules on accreditation, whether compulsory or voluntary, of conformity assessment.[386] The Commission has now adopted a recommendation for best practices in 'the correct and timely transposition into national law of directives affecting the internal market'.[387] It appears to have met with limited success. **10.73**

There is a latent constitutional difficulty with harmonisation, springing from the fact that articles 114 and 115 permit legislation only where there exist impediments to the common/internal market resulting from disparities in national law: given this, logic dictates that where a Directive had harmonised national law in a given field and so had removed those impediments, it would be *ultra vires* the Council to act again – not least, to amend that Directive. But the logic does not impress the Court: it is based upon an **10.74**

> erroneous premiss that complete harmonisation in a particular field is incompatible with the fact that such harmonisation is in a state of continuing evolution. [Existing exhaustive harmonsation] in no way means that the Community legislature cannot amend or adapt those rules or, if necessary, introduce new ones so as better to attain the objectives [of the original measure].[388]

Were it otherwise it would disable the Union legislature of power to remedy defects in a harmonisation measure or adapt it to changed circumstances, which

---

383   Case C-58/08 *Vodafone*, n. 377 above, at paras 19–24 of his opinion.
384   *Ibid.* at paras 38, 46 and 47 of the judgment.
385   Decision 768/2008 [2008] OJ L218/82. The institutions may depart from the framework if 'appropriate' owing to the specificity of a sector; art. 2, 2nd para.
386   Regulation 765/2008 [2008] OJ L218/30; quality of 'complementary' to Decision 768/2008 from the Preamble, 3rd recital. Thus member states are required to establish a (not for profit) single national accreditation body; art. 4.
387   Recommendation 2005/309 [2005] OJ L98/47.
388   Case C-374/05 *Gintec International Import-Export* v *Verband Sozialer Wettbewerb* [2007] ECR I-9517, at para. 29; see also Case C-58/08 *Vodafone*, n. 377 above, at para. 34.

would, according to Advocate-General Poiares Maduro, be 'absurd and undemocratic'.[389]

10.75 There is frequently overlap between the subject matter of a harmonisation Directive and substantive Treaty provisions. A measure for the harmonisation of legislation may well trench upon, for example, the social provisions (articles 151–61 TFEU), the provisions on public health (article 168), on consumer protection (article 169) or on the environment (articles 191–3). There are therefore frequent disputes as to whether article 114 or 115 is the appropriate legal base for legislation adopted, in which case the Court is required to consider whether the measure at issue is in truth one for the benefit of the internal market, or whether it is in pith and substance one for the regulation of the substantive field which only incidentally harmonises market conditions.[390] An additional difficulty is that some subsequent Treaty provisions expressly bar harmonisation of national law in certain spheres, for example in the protection and improvement of human health.[391] This 'does not mean that harmonising measures adopted on the basis of other provisions of the Treaty cannot have any impact on the protection of human health';[392] this is so even if public health protection,[393] or equally, consumer protection,[394] is a decisive factor in the choices made in the Directive. However, article 114 'may not ... be used as a legal basis in order to circumvent the express exclusion of harmonisation laid down [elsewhere in] the Treaty'.[395]

10.76 If a harmonisation measure imposes administrative burdens (for example, inspections) upon a member state upon import or export of goods, the member

---

389 Case C-58/08 *Vodafone*, n. 377 above, at para. 11 of his opinion.

390 E.g., Case C-300/89 *Commission v Council* (Titanium Dioxide) [1991] ECR I-2867 (art. 115 or environmental protection); Case C-84/94 *United Kingdom v Council* (Working Time Directive) [1996] ECR I-5755 (art. 115 or health and safety of workers); Case C-269/97 *Commission v Council* (Bovines) [2000] ECR I-2257 (art. 114 or agricultural legislation); Case C-376/98 *Germany v Parliament and Council* (Tobacco Advertising No. 1) [2000] ECR I-8419 (art. 114 or public health); Case C-377/98 *Netherlands v Parliament and Council* (Biotechnological Inventions) [2001] ECR I-7079 (art. 114 or research and technological development); Case C-533/03 *Commission v Council* [2006] ECR I-1025 (art. 114 or art. 115 or tax harmonisation); Case C-301/06 *Ireland v Parliament and Council* (Data Retention) [2009] ECR I-593 (art. 114 or EU criminal matters); Case T-526/10 *Inuit Tapiriit Kanatami and ors v Commission*, pending (art. 114 or animal welfare).

391 TFEU, art. 2(5), 2nd para.; subject to the exception of art. 168(4).

392 Case C-376/98 *Tobacco Advertising No. 1*, n. 390 above, at para. 78. Were it otherwise the integration clauses of arts 9 and 168(1) TFEU would be rendered impotent.

393 Case C-491/01 *R v Secretary of State for Health, ex parte British American Tobacco (Investments) and ors* [2002] ECR I-11453, at para. 62; Cases C-154 and 155/04 *R (Alliance for Natural Health and ors) v Secretary of State for Health and anor* [2005] ECR I-6451, at para. 30; Case C-380/03 *Germany v Parliament and Council* (Tobacco Advertising No. 2) [2006] ECR I-11573, at para. 39.

394 Case C-58/08 *Vodafone*, n. 377 above, at para. 36.

395 Case C-376/98 *Tobacco Advertising No. 1*, n. 390 above, at para. 79.

state may impose a charge upon traders for their use without offending article 30 (or 34), provided the charge does not exceed the true cost.[396]

It is frequently important to determine whether a given measure harmonises **10.77** the law minimally, partially or exhaustively. Where an article 115 Directive harmonises exhaustively and coherently, it occupies the field and pre-empts the adoption of any autonomous national rules, so excluding any possibility of invoking article 36 or mandatory requirements.[397] As a corollary, where a matter has been exhaustively harmonised, any national measure relating to it is to be assessed in light of the provisions of the harmonising measure and not of articles 34 and 36.[398] In the event exhaustive harmonisation is a legislative technique falling out of favour. More commonly a Directive harmonises only partially or minimally, in both cases, *a fortiori* the latter, recourse to article 36 and the mandatory requirements surviving in areas not harmonised. This applies equally to article 114 except that it is more supple, allowing derogation under article 114(4) and 114(5) with Commission approval. Some Directives themselves, 'in appropriate cases', permit derogation by their own express terms.[399]

11. Intellectual property rights

The Treaties mention intellectual property in five articles, one of which has no **10.78** relevance here.[400] Lisbon added two of them, express authority for the creation of European intellectual property rights and provision of uniform protection[401] (which had been undertaken anyway by authority of the flexibility clause of article 352) and authority to confer jurisdiction upon the Court of Justice over

---

396 See 10.09 above.

397 See e.g., Case 5/77 *Tedeschi* v *Denkavit Commerciale* [1977] ECR 1555; Case C-169/89 *Criminal proceedings against Gourmetterie van den Burg* [1990] ECR I-2143; Case C-52/92 *Commission* v *Portugal* [1993] ECR I-2361; Case C-5/94 *R* v *Minister of Agriculture, Fisheries and Food, ex parte Hedley Lomas* [1996] ECR I-2553; Case C-1/96 *R* v *Minister of Agriculture, Fisheries and Food, ex parte Compassion in World Farming* [1998] ECR I-1251; Case C-1/00 *Commission* v *France* [2001] ECR I-9989; Case C-241/01 *National Farmers' Union* v *Secrétariat Général du Gouvernement* [2002] ECR I-9079; Case C-470/03 *A.G.M.-COS.MET* v *Suomen valtio and anor* [2007] ECR I-2749.

398 Case C-323/93 *Société Civile Agricole du Centre d'Insémination de la Crespelle* v *Coopérative d'Elevage et d'Insémination Artificielle du Département de la Mayenne* [1994] ECR I-5077, at para. 31; Case C-180/96 *United Kingdom* v *Commission* (BSE) [1998] ECR I-2265, at para. 63; Case C-322/01 *Deutscher Apothekerverband* v *DocMorris and anor* [2003] ECR I-14887, at para. 64; Case C-309/02 *Radlberger Getränkegesellschaft and anor* v *Land Baden-Württemberg* [2004] ECR I-11763, at para. 53; Case C-470/03 *A.G.M.-COS.MET* v *Suomen valtio and anor* [2007] ECR I-2749.

399 TFEU, art. 114(10); see e.g., Case 4/75 *Rewe-Zentralfinanz* v *Landwirtschaftskammer* [1975] ECR 843; Cases C-96 and 97/03 *Tempelman and anor* v *Directeur van de Rijksdienst voor de keuring van Vee en Vlees* [2005] ECR I-1895.

400 TFEU, art. 207 (ex art. 133 EC), introduced originally by the Treaty of Amsterdam, extends the application of the Common Commercial Policy expressly to cover intellectual property; see 14.70 below.

401 *Ibid.* art. 118.

disputes arising therefrom.[402] But the pivotal provisions have been in the Treaties since the beginning. The first, article 345, reserves, or appears to reserve, the field to the member states, thus: 'The Treaties shall in no way prejudice the rules in Member States governing the system of property owner-ship'; clearer perhaps is the German, whereby the Treaties 'leave untouched' (*lassen unberührt*) the national regimes of property ownership. Second, article 36 provides that a breach of article 34 or article 35 may be justified 'on grounds of … the protection of industrial or commercial property'. These provide little clarity to the place which intellectual property rights were to enjoy under Union law.

Problems could be eased very considerably by the adoption of uniform rules valid throughout the Union, for example, a single patent, a single trade mark, a single copyright law, and so on. But this has proved a course difficult to pursue. There has been some legislative intervention, on two fronts. First, the Council has created (by authority of article 352) Union-wide species of intellectual property rights in some areas: thus, the Community trade mark[403] and the Community design,[404] whereby a single trade mark or a single design may be registered at the Office for Harmonisation in the Internal Market (Trade Marks and Designs) in Alicante, and is thereafter valid throughout the territory of the Union; the Community plant variety right,[405] whereby, equally, a plant variety may be registered at the Community Plant Variety Office in Angers and is thereafter protected throughout the Union; and the draft EU Patent Regu-lation (EUPR), which proposes similar treatment for a Union-wide patent to be granted by the European Patent Office in Munich.[406] Each is a complete and

---

402 *Ibid.* art. 262.
403 Regulation 207/2009 [2009] OJ L78/1 (a consolidated version replacing Regulation 40/94 [1994] OJ L11/1). In 2004 the Community acceded to the Madrid Protocol on the international registration of marks (for the text see [2003] OJ L296/22) under the umbrella of the World Intellectual Property Organisation (WIPO) and so is now governed by its applicable rules.
404 Regulation 6/2002 [2002] OJ L3/1.
405 Regulation 2100/94 [1994] OJ L227/1.
406 Draft Proposal for a Council Regulation on the European Union Patent, Council doc. 16113/09. The Regulation was first proposed in 2000 (COM(2000) 412 final), amended repeatedly, and now deadlocked in the Council owing primarily to linguistic issues (the Treaty base (art. 118 TFEU) requiring Council unanimity to establish the language arrangements of European IPRs). Owing to the deadlock it is now proposed to be adopted under the enhanced cooperation procedure, so applicable in only some member states; see 2.46 above. It is not to be confused with the Community Patent Conventions of 1975 ([1976] OJ L17/1) and 1989 ([1989] OJ L401/9), independent of (but buttressing) Union law, neither of which ever entered into force, nor with the (pan-)European Patents Convention (EUPC) of 1973, TS 16 (1982). Alongside the EUPC, in 2008 a draft agreement (Draft Agreement on the European and EU Patent Court and Draft Statute, Council doc. 14970/08) was drawn up which would 'integrate' or 'unify' the patent and patent litigation system across Europe within the EPO structure to which the Union would accede, but the Court of Justice found it to be incompatible with both the TEU and the TFEU owing to the proposed judicial structure (Opinion 1/09 *Re the European Patent Convention*, opinion of 8 March 2011, not yet reported) so barring Union participation and perhaps giving new urgency to the EUPR.

self-contained regime of property ownership, with rules on definition, capacity, application, registration, duration, renewal, extinction, assignment, enforcement, and so on. They exist alongside, and do not replace, their national equivalents.[407]

Second, the Council has adopted a number of Directives for the purpose of **10.79** harmonising national intellectual property law,[408] most on substantive provisions but an importat instrument of general application in a 2004 Directive for the enforcement of intellectual property rights (the 'First Intellectual Property Rights Enforcement Directive', sometimes IPRED), which requires all member states to adopt and apply effective, dissuasive and proportionate remedies and penalties for infringement of any right created by Union and/or national law and covered by the Directive.[409] A second enforcement Directive ('IPRED2') was proposed by the Commission to 'supplement' the first, requiring the creation of criminal sanctions for infringement of various intellectual property rights,[410] but it was much contested and in the face of Council antipathy the proposal was withdrawn in 2010,[411] the Commission then launching a new public consultation.[412] The Court of Justice approved the creation of Union intellectual property rights by authority of article 352[413] (now displaced by the express authority of article 118) and, notwithstanding the Treaty imperative that national law in the field be 'left untouched', appears, incidentally, not to object to harmonisation of national laws under articles 114 and 115.[414]

---

407   Therefore a mark, design or plant variety cannot be registered in the face of an existing identical or potentially confusing national mark or design. Because this is a relative, not absolute, ground for refusal each instrument makes provision for an opposition procedure; see e.g., Regulation 207/2009, arts 7, 8.

408   See e.g., Directive 87/54 [1987] OJ L24/36 (semiconductor topographies); Directive 93/83 [1993] OJ L248/15 (copyright and cable retransmission of satellite broadcasting); Directive 96/9 [1996] OJ L77/20 (databases); Directive 98/44 [1998] OJ L213/13 (biotechnological inventions); Directive 98/71 [1998] OJ L289/28 (designs); Directive 2001/29 (copyright) [2001] OJ L167/10; Directive 2006/115 [2006] OJ L376/28 (rental and lending rights; consolidation of Directive 92/100 [1992] OJ L346/61); Directive 2006/116 [2006] OJ L372/12 (duration of copyright; consolidation of Directive 93/98 [1998] OJ L290/9); Directive 2008/95 [2008] OJ L299/25 (trade marks; consolidation of Directive 89/104 [1989] OJ L40/1); Directive 2009/24 [2009] OJ L111/16 (computer programs; consolidation of Directive 91/250 [1991] OJ L122/42). Directive 89/104 (and 2008/95) has bitten deeply into national trade mark law; see e.g., Case C-355/96 *Silhouette International Schmied* v *Hartlauer* [1998] ECR I-4799; Case C-414/99 *Zino Davidoff* v *A & G Imports* [2001] ECR I-8691; Case C-59/08 *Copad* v *Christian Dior Couture and ors* [2009] ECR I-3421.

409   Directive 2004/48 [2004] OJ L157/45. According to a Commission statement ([2005] OJ L94/37) the Directive covers 'at least' copyright, rights related to copyright, *sui generis* rights of a database maker, rights of creators of topographies of semiconductor products, trade mark rights, design rights, patent rights, geographic indictions, utility model rights, plant variety rights and trade names.

410   COM(2006) 168 final.

411   [2010] OJ C252/9.

412   Report on the Application of Directive 2004/48, COM(2010) 779 final.

413   Opinion 1/94 *Re the World Trade Organisation* [1994] ECR I-5267.

414   *Ibid.*; but this was *obiter* only, the question of (in)consistency with art. 345 neither raised nor argued.

10.80   But the intellectual property Regulations do not (and cannot) displace national rules, and generally the Directives achieve partial harmonisation only. For the most part intellectual property rights continue to derive from national law, and whilst they are not themselves goods (albeit they are property, and capital assets),[415] they have a character *sui generis* which can have the effect of hindering the free movement of goods (and of other Treaty freedoms).[416] Therefore the use of various privileges traditionally adhering to intellectual property may fall under article 34. The basic rule was recognised and set out in *Deutsche Grammophon* thus:

> [T]he essential purpose of the Treaty, which is to unite national markets into a single market ... could not be attained if, under [*aufgrund*] the various legal systems of the Member States, nationals of those States were able to partition the market and bring about arbitrary discrimination or disguised restrictions on trade between Member States.[417]

As to the application of articles 345 and 36 in the context, the Court said, first, that whilst article 345 reserves to the member states authority to create and define the subject matter of an intellectual property right (the *existence* of the right), the *exercise* of the right nevertheless falls within the field of the application of the Treaties. This existence/exercise dichotomy, whilst perhaps facile and questionable, has been followed since. Its ramifications were stated more clearly in a subsequent case:

> Article [345] according to which the Treaty in no way prejudices the rules in Member States governing the system of property ownership, cannot be interpreted as reserving to the national legislature, in relation to industrial and commercial property, the power to adopt measures which would adversely affect the principle of the free movement of goods within the common market as provided for and regulated by the Treaty.[418]

Second, it said that article 36 does shield the exercise of an intellectual property right from the full vigour of article 34, but only insofar as it is necessary for the protection of the 'specific subject matter' of the right. Beyond that the right is 'exhausted', and cannot be relied upon by the proprietor in a manner which inhibits the free movement of goods. This then is the trade off between the mutually incompatible interests of protection of rights and the free movement of goods; the proprietor continues to enjoy certain of the monopoly privileges accruing to the former, but the principle of exhaustion of rights cuts into the

---

415   Directive 88/361 [1988] OJ L178/5, art. 1, Annex I; see 12.06 below.
416   Cases C-92 and 326/92 *Phil Collins* v *Imtrat* [1993] ECR I-5145.
417   Case 78/70 *Deutsche Grammophon* v *Metro-SB-Großmärkte* [1971] ECR 487, at para. 12(2).
418   Case C-30/90 *Commission* v *United Kingdom* (Compulsory Patent Licences) [1992] ECR I-829, at para. 18.

monopoly profits which he was previously able to wield in the commercialisation of his right in various member states to his maximum advantage.

The specific subject matter of the right, its *objet spécifique* or *spezifischer* **10.81** *Gegenstand*, of which it is a bad translation – its pith and substance, its essence, which justifies its anticompetitive effects which are tolerated by Union law as in national law – therefore lies at the heart of the protection of intellectual property rights in Union law. It varies somewhat from right to right depending upon the subject matter, but most of the applicable principles are common to all intellectual property rights. The specific subject matter embraces the essence of the right, the monopoly right to the process, the article, the work or the mark in question. These are either not touched by article 34, or, insofar as they are, they are saved by article 36 as part of their specific subject matter. Article 34 comes into play only when the proprietor seeks commercially to exploit the protected article through sale or trade. Even then, the specific subject matter of the right has been held by the Court to extend, across all forms of intellectual property, to conferring upon the proprietor the exclusive right to place the product on a market where the right exists for the first time, the right of first marketing. It is then, and only then, that the right is exhausted. Thereafter the proprietor cannot object to a third party – usually a parallel trader seeking to frustrate official distribution networks by buying in a 'grey market' in order to undercut its prices – (re-)importing his protected goods from any member state in which he has marketed them into another in which the right is exhausted. But he remains competent to oppose the importation into a member state in which he enjoys protection from another member state in which goods which would infringe his right are marketed by an unrelated third party who may, or may not, be exercising an identical right there.

This is the basic rule. A number of points are required to be borne in mind. **10.82**

- In order to be joined article 34 requires a restriction, however generously defined, upon the movement of goods between member states. Therefore opposition of a proprietor of an intellectual property right to the importation of a protected good into a member state from a third country, even if the right is in common ownership and it has been exhausted in each, is not prohibited by article 34.[419] This is so even if a free trade agreement exists with the third country in question.[420] But there is a counter exception for

---

419 Case 51/75 *EMI* v *CBS* [1976] ECR 811; Case C-355/96 *Silhouette International Schmied* v *Hartlauer* [1998] ECRI-4799; Cases C-414 etc./99 *Zino Davidoff and ors* v *A & G Imports and ors* [2001] ECR I-8691.
420 Case 270/80 *Polydor* v *Harlequin Records* [1982] ECR 329.

the European Economic Area, exhaustion of rights being expressly written into the EEA Agreement;[421] a proprietor may therefore no longer oppose the importation of his protected goods from Iceland, Liechtenstein or Norway (or from the Union into those countries) where the right has been exhausted, for to do so would breach article 11 of the Agreement (= article 34 TFEU).

- Thus exhaustion of the right applies to those specific goods which have been marketed by the proprietor within the Union. The marketing within the Union of, for example, a batch of goods protected by a trade mark exhausts the proprietor's marketing rights in respect of that batch but not in respect of an identically marked batch marketed by him in a non-Union country, importation of which he may continue to oppose.[422]

- This is so even in member states which traditionally recognised a principle of 'international exhaustion', that is, the proprietor of a mark exhausted his right to oppose importation of marked goods once he had marketed them anywhere in the world. The Court of Justice found that a proper construction of the 1989 Trade Mark Directive abolished the principle of international exhaustion in any member state which thitherto adhered to it.[423] This applies equally to the 2001 Copyright Directive.[424]

- From the beginning the Court stressed that the specific subject matter of the right is exhausted following first marketing by the proprietor or with his consent. So article 34 cannot be circumvented by licensing: if the process is worked or the product marketed in any member state by licence from the proprietor, even where the licensee is an unconnected, independent undertaking, the right is as exhausted as if he had done so himself. This principle came subsequently to be refined by the Court to require that it be the proprietor's *free* consent. So, a proprietor may continue to oppose the importation of his protected goods from another member state where they are marketed by him by virtue of a legal obligation to do so[425] or by a third party by virtue of a compulsory licence.[426] There is a substantial case law on the circumstances in which consent may be implicit or implied.[427]

---

421 EEA Agreement, Protocol 28, art. 2.

422 Case C-173/98 *Sebago* v *GB-Unic* [1999] ECR I-4103. The right does not extend to opposition to transit across territory in which the right is held unless the goods are subject to the act of a third party which necessarily entails their being put on the market in the member state of transit; Case C-281/05 *Montex Holdings* v *Diesel* [2006] ECR I-10881.

423 Case C-355/96 *Silhouette*, n. 419 above; Case C173/98 *Sebago, ibid.*; Cases C-414 etc./99 *Zino Davidoff*, n. 419 above.

424 Case C-479/04 *Laserdisken* v *Kulturministeriet* [2006] ECR I-8089.

425 Cases C-267–268/95 *Merck* v *Primecrown* (Merck II) [1996] ECR I-6285.

426 Case 19/84 *Pharmon* v *Hoechst* [1985] ECR 2281.

427 Cases C-414 etc./99 *Zino Davidoff*, n. 419 above (cf. the judgment of the English High Court in *Zino Davidoff* v *A & G Imports* [1999] 3 All ER 711); Case C-244/00 *Van Doren + Q* v *Lifestyle sports + sportswear*

- However, the principle of exhaustion applies as regards imports from a member state in which the proprietor has marketed his goods but in which no intellectual property protection is granted or recognised – and so, strictly speaking, no right has been exhausted for none there exists. This arose primarily in the context of sale of pharmaceutical products in the Mediterranean member states which, historically and for public policy reasons, did not grant them patent protection. Where the proprietor of a right in another member state nevertheless elects freely, and in full knowledge of all relevant circumstances, to market the protected goods in the unprotected market, he must accept the consequences and cannot oppose their re-importation[428] – although he can oppose the importation of goods marketed there, unhindered as he is, by another party proprietor of an analogous right in another member state or by a domestic manufacturer.[429]

- As it is no breach of article 34 to oppose the importation of goods which infringe the proprietor's right from another member state in which they are produced and/or marketed by an unconnected third party, it follows that this situation may be recreated as between two member states in which the one proprietor holds the relevant right if he assigns his right in one or more of them to a third party.[430]

Finally it is important to note that this discussion relates to the rules on the free **10.83** movement of goods, in particular the application of articles 34 and 36. It is possible that the exercise of an intellectual property right may *also* fall for consideration under the competition rules of articles 101 and 102; or, conversely, that conduct which escapes the prohibition of article 34 – opposition of imports from third countries or from another member state following assignment of a right, for example – may well result in an infringement of article 101 or of article 102.[431]

Handelsgesellschaft and anor [2003] ECR I-3051; Case C-324/08 *Makro Zelfbedieningsgroothandel and ors* v *Diesel* [2009] ECR I-10019.

428   Case 187/80 *Merck* v *Stephar* (Merck I) [1981] ECR 2063. The English High Court subsequently urged the Court of Justice to reconsider the *ratio* in *Merck I*, but the Court declined to do so; Cases C-267–8/95, *Merck II*, n. 425 above.

429   Case 24/67 *Park, Davis* v *Probel* [1968] ECR 55.

430   Case C-9/93 *IHT Internationale Heiztechnik* v *Ideal Standard* [1994] ECR I-2789. This was not always so. For trade marks at least the Court once recognised a principle of 'common origin' which precluded a proprietor from opposing the importation of marked goods marketed by a third party in another member state if the mark had once been in common ownership; Case 192/72 *van Zuylen Frères* v *Hag* [1974] ECR 731. But, in the first case it ever expressly did so, the Court reversed itself on this point; Case C-10/89 *CNL Sucal* v *HAG* (Hag II) [1990] ECR I-3711 and the *coup de grâce* delivered in *IHT*.

431   See 13.149–13.153 below.

Repackaging/relabelling

10.84 A particular question arises in the area of trade marks. A parallel trader wishing to buy up goods marked and marketed by the proprietor of a trade mark in one member state in order to undercut the price offered by the latter in another member state may be required, or wish, to repackage or relabel the goods, either because he must do so by virtue of national law – simply a requirement, for example, that any external instructions be in the language(s) of the member state – or he may see some advantage in doing so from his view of the attractiveness of the packaging to the consumer. Yet the purpose – and specific subject matter – of a trade mark includes a guarantee to the consumer that all products which bear it have been manufactured under the control of an undertaking to which responsibility for its quality may be attributed,[432] and therefore a proprietor may oppose any use of the trade mark which is liable to impair this guarantee of origin.[433] In some cases the packaging may be an essential part of the image upon which the proprietor trades, so that removing or altering it may harm the image and so the reputation of the mark.[434] Where this is not the case repackaging and/or relabelling by a third party is permissible, even to the extent of replacing the trade mark used in the member state of export with that used in the member state of import if it is objectively necessary in order to be marketed in the latter,[435] but only under restricted conditions:

> [A]ccording to the case-law of the Court Article 36 does not permit the owner of the trade mark to oppose the reaffixing of the mark where such use of his trade mark rights contributes to the artificial partitioning of the markets between Member States and where the reaffixing takes place in such a way that the legitimate interests of the trade mark owner are observed. Protection of those legitimate interests means in particular that the original condition of the product inside the packaging must not be affected, and that the reaffixing is not done in such a way that it may damage the reputation of the trade mark and its owner.

> It follows that under Article 36 of the Treaty the owner of trade mark rights may rely on those rights to prevent a third party from removing and then reaffixing or replacing labels bearing the trade mark, unless:
> - it is established that the use of the trade mark rights by the owner to oppose the marketing of the relabelled products under that trade mark would contribute to the artificial partitioning of the markets between Member States;
> - it is shown that the repackaging cannot affect the original condition of the product; and

---

432 Case 102/77 *Hoffmann–La Roche* v *Centrafarm* [1978] ECR 1139.
433 *Ibid.*; Cases C-427 etc./93 *Bristol-Meyers Squibb* v *Paranova* [1996] ECR I-3457.
434 Case C-324/09 *L'Oréal and ors* v *eBay International and ors*, judgment of 12 July 2011, not yet reported.
435 Case C-379/97 *Pharmacia & Upjohn* v *Paranova* [1999] ECR I-6927.

- the presentation of the relabelled product is not such as to be liable to damage the reputation of the trade mark and its owner.[436]

For pharmaceutical products, in which context so much of the case law has arisen, the Court has supplied a different formulation ('the *Bristol-Meyers Squibb* conditions'): the proprietor may legitimately oppose the further marketing of a repackaged pharmaceutical product unless:

- it would contribute to the artificial partitioning of the markets between member states;
- the repackaging cannot have affected the original condition of the product inside the packaging;
- the new packaging clearly states who repackaged the product and the name of the manufacturer;
- the presentation of the repackaged product is not such as to be liable to damage the reputation of the trade mark and of its owner; thus, the packaging must not be defective, of poor quality, or untidy; and
- the importer gives notice to the trade mark owner before the repackaged product is put on sale, and, on demand, supplies him with a specimen of the repackaged product.[437]

12. Protected origin

A species of intellectual property, recognised as such by the 1883 Paris **10.85** Convention, is 'indications of source or appellations of origin'.[438] They are closely bound to consumer protection and the repression of unfair competition which are part of the purpose of intellectual property rights. Following the models which exist in a number of (but not all) member states, the best known being the French system of *Appellation d'origine contrôlée* for wine and, since 1990, other agricultural products, the Union has developed a system of protected names by which agricultural products and foodstuffs may be marketed (by the name) throughout the Union only if they comply with strict production or similar rules. Legislation was first introduced in 1992[439] and replaced in

---

436 Case C-349/95 *Frits Loendersloot* v *George Ballantine & Sons* [1997] ECR 6227, at paras 28, 29.
437 Cases C-427 etc./93 *Bristol-Meyers Squibb*, n. 433 above. See also Case 1/81 *Pfizer* v *Eurim-Pharm* [1981] ECR 2913; Case C-232/94 *MPA Pharma* v *Rhône-Poulenc Pharma* [1996] ECR I-3671; Case C-379/97 *Pharmacia & Upjohn*, n. 435 above; Case C-143/00 *Boehringer Ingelheim and anor* v *Swingward and ors* (Boehringer I) [2002] ECR I-3759; Case C-348/04 *Boehringer Ingelheim and ors* v *Swingward and anor* (Boehringer II) [2007] ECR I-3391.
438 Paris Convention of 20 March 1883 for the Protection of Industrial Property, 828 UNTS 305, art. 1(2).
439 Regulation 2081/92 [1992] OJ L208/1; Regulation 2082/92 [1992] OJ L208/9.

2006.[440] It does not apply to wines (except wine vinegar) and spirits, which are subject to their own legislation.[441] It is otherwise exhaustive in nature, so supplanting any other system of protection laid down by national law or agreement between member states.[442]

10.86 There are three categories of protection, the first two similar so governed by the one Regulation, the third by another:

- *Protected designation of origin* (PDO): the term used to describe foodstuffs with a defined character and which are produced, processed and prepared in a defined region, place or country and owe their quality or characteristics to that environment, either physical or human.[443] The Court of Justice recognises that the requirement that all these steps take place in the one region in order to qualify for a PDO (so barring further processing or preparation in another member state) constitutes an MEQR on exports within the meaning of article 35, but equally that it is justified in order to uphold the reputation of the product (so invoking the protection of intellectual property).[444] Examples of widely recognised PDOs include Roquefort, gorgonzola,[445] Parmigiano Reggiano[446] and feta[447] cheese (some five dozen French and two dozen Greek cheeses are so protected), some two dozen German spring (*Quelle*) waters, a dozen Portuguese honeys, prosciutto di Parma,[448] prosciutto di Modena, pesto alla Genovese and basilico Genovese, Kalamata olives and Siteia and Selino olive oil, Corinth and Zakynthou currants,[449] Jersey royal potatoes, Cornish

---

440   Regulation 509/2006 [2006] OJ L93/1; Regulation 510/2006 [2006] OJ L93/12. See also Regulation 1898/2006 [2006] OJ L369/1 laying down detailed rules (and the necessary forms) for the implementation of Regulation 510/2006.

441   See, for wine, Regulation 479/2008 [2008] OJ L148/1, arts 45–56 (and its implementing Regulation (in this respect) 607/2009 [2009] OJ L193/60); this is the general Regulation on the common organisation of the market in wine, which absorbs and expands upon rules for the protection of quality wines produced in a specific region first introduced in 1987 (Regulation 823/87 [1987] OJ L84/59). For spirits see Regulation 110/2008 [2008] OJ L39/16 (replacing a 1989 predecessor), which permits and protects 'reserved names' which may be accompanied by a geographic designation ('composite' or 'compound' designation) regulated by the member state of production; hence, for example, Scotch whisky, Irish whiskey, Cassis de Dijon.

442   Case C-478/07 *Budějovický Budvar* v *Rudolf Ammersin* [2009] ECR I-7221.

443   Regulation 510, art. 2(1)(a).

444   Case C-108/01 *Consorzio del Prosciutto di Parma and anor* v *Asda Stores and anor* [2003] ECR I-5121; Case C-161/09 *Kakavetsos-Frangopoulos AE Epexergasias kai Emporias Stafidas* v *Nomarchiaki Aftodioikisi Korinthias*, judgment of 3 March 2011, not yet reported, at para. 30.

445   See Case C-87/97 *Consorzio per la tutela del formaggio Gorgonzola* v *Käserei Champignon Hofmeister and anor* [1999] ECR I-1301.

446   See Case C-132/05 *Commission* v *Germany* (Parmigiano Reggiano) [2008] ECR I-957.

447   See Cases C-465 and 466/02 *Germany and Denmark* v *Commission* (Feta) [2005] ECR I-9115.

448   See Case C-108/01 *Consorzio del Prosciutto di Parma*, n. 444 above.

449   See Case C-161/09 *Frangopoulos*, n. 444 above.

(but not Devon) clotted cream, Pomme du Limousin, Noix de Périgord, Azafrán de La Mancha, Sidra de Asturias and the like.

- *Protected geographical indication* (PGI): a category similar to PDO but broader, the defining characteristic(s) being not inherent in geographic origin, but in the product's quality or reputation.[450] The essential difference between a PDO and a PGI is therefore, first, the latter lacks the 'inherent' quality necessary for the former, and second, the former requires that a product be produced, processed *and* prepared in the region,[451] the latter only that it be produced, processed *or* prepared there.[452] Examples of PGIs include another raft of cheeses (boerenkaas, edam, gouda, de Valdeón, Danablu, Hessischer Handkäse, Saaremae and similar), Scottish wild salmon, Arbroath smokies, Cornish pasties, Melton Mowbray pies (after some dispute),[453] Fraise de Périgord, M(i)el de Galicia, Cidre de Bretagne, České pivo, (Česko)budějovické pivo,[454] Brněnské/Starobrněnské pivo, Černá Hora, Newcastle Brown Ale (but no longer),[455] Kölsch, Münchener Bier, Hallertau hops and many more.

- *Traditional speciality guaranteed* (TSG): refers not to origin but highlights traditional defined character, either in the composition or means of production, 'traditional' being proven usage in a Union market over generations, or at least 25 years.[456] There have been relatively few applications for TSGs, but a variety of Belgian beers are now so protected.

A PDO, PGI or TSG is secured by registration, for which only groups may **10.87** apply.[457] A name which has become generic is ineligible for registration as a PDO or PGI.[458] An application for registration is scrutinised for eligibility in the first instance by competent authorities of a member state in which the geographic area lies,[459] and, if favourable, is then forwarded by them to the

---

450 Regulation 510, art. 2(1)(b).
451 *Ibid.* art. 2(1)(a), 3rd indent.
452 *Ibid.* art. 2(1)(b), 3rd indent.
453 See *R (Northern Foods)* v *Secretary of State for Environment, Food and Rural Affairs* [2006] EWCA Civ 337, [2006] EuLR 929; Regulation 566/2009 [2009] OJ L168/20.
454 See Case C-478/07 *Budějovický Budvar* v *Rudolf Ammersin* [2009] ECR I-7221.
455 See n. 469 below.
456 Regulation 509, art. 2(1). For implementing rules on TSGs see Regulation 1216/2007 [2007] OJ L275/3.
457 Regulation 510, art. 5(1); Regulation 509, art. 7(1).
458 Regulation 510, art. 3(1). See Cases C-465 and 466/02 *Germany and Denmark* v *Commission* (Feta) [2005] ECR I-9115.
459 Regulation 510, art. 5(4)–(10); Regulation 509, art. 7(4)–(8). Transfrontier applications are subject to special rules; Regulation 1898/2006 [2006] OJ L369/1, art. 12. In accordance with TRIPs rules the 2006 Regulations introduced the possibility of application from third countries (Regulation 510/2006, art. 5(9); Regulation 509/2006, art. 7(7)), either through competent national authorities (if they exist) or directly to the Commission. The first non-Union product so recognised was Café de Colombia, granted PGI status in 2007. It appears that a name need not be rendered in a Union language (or alphabet), 龙口粉丝 (longkou fen si) being granted PGI status in 2010.

Commission for further scrutiny;[460] it may be opposed at both levels[461] and the determination of a national authority must be subject to review/appeal.[462] Approval of an application is published in the *Official Journal*,[463] and the Commission is required to keep up-to-date Registers of PDOs/PGIs and TSGs.[464] A registered PDO/PGI is protected against commercial use of the name in respect of products not covered insofar as it would constitute passing off and any misuse, imitation or evocation,[465] provision being made for honest concurrent use;[466] a TSG is to be protected against misuse or misleading use.[467] Where a product ceases to comply with the conditions of specification the Commission will cancel its registration;[468] any person with a legitimate interest may request cancellation of a PDO or a PGI.[469] Whilst member states are required to have in place mechanisms which ensure adequate legal protection against misuse or misleading use of PDOs/PGIs and TSGs,[470] they are not themselves bound to proceed on their own initiative against it.[471]

10.88 The Union scheme was extended to, by reciprocal arrangement with, Switzerland[472] and Liechtenstein[473] in 2011.

10.89 It may appear odd that a non-edible product may be considered an agricultural product or foodstuff but a few (gum, hay, essential oils) have gained protection, including a PDO for 'native Shetland wool', so that a movement afoot to secure similar status for the 'Scottish kilt' may not be that far-fetched. A scheme similar to PDO/PGI/TSG exists for the production and labelling of organic foodstuffs.[474]

---

460 Regulation 510, art. 6; Regulation 509, art. 8. The Commission has appointed a panel of scientific experts ('the group') which it may consult; Decision 2007/71 [2007] OJ L32/177.

461 Regulation 510, arts 5(5), 7; Regulation 509, arts 7(5), 9.

462 Regulation 510, art. 5(5), 4th para; see e.g., *Northern Foods*, n. 453 above.

463 Regulation 510, art. 7(4), (5); Regulation 509, art. 9(4), (5).

464 Regulation 510, art. 7(6); Regulation 509, art. 3.

465 Regulation 510, art. 13(1); thus expression of the name with 'style', 'type', 'method', 'imitation' is prohibited.

466 Regulation 510, art. 13(4).

467 Regulation 509, art. 17.

468 Regulation 509, art. 10; Regulation 510, art. 12(1).

469 Regulation 510, art. 12(2). See e.g., Regulation 952/2007 [2007] OJ L210/26, cancelling Newcastle Brown Ale's PGI upon the brewery's relocation to Gateshead, across the River Tyne from Newcastle. The brewery itself petitioned for the cancellation, otherwise it would have been barred from using the name.

470 Regulation 509, art. 17; Regulation 510, art. 13.

471 Case C-132/05 *Commission v Germany* (Parmigiano Reggiano) [2008] ECR I-957.

472 Agreement of 17 May 2011 between the European Union and the Swiss Confederation on the Protection of Designations of Origin and Geographical Indications for Agricultural Products and Foodstuffs [2011] OJ L297/3.

473 Agreement of 17 May 2011 between the European Union, the Swiss Confederation and the Principality of Liechtenstein on the Accession of Liechtenstein to the Agreement *ibid.*, [2011] OJ 297/49.

474 Regulation 834/2007 [2007] OJ L189/1; Regulation 889/2008 [2008] OJ L250/1.

At the end of 2010 the Commission proposed the adoption of a new 'Agricul- **10.90**
tural Product Quality Schemes Regulation', a consolidation designed to
reinforce the PDO and PGI schemes, amend the TSG scheme and provide a
framework for the development of 'optional quality terms' regarding terms such
as, for example, 'free range' and 'first cold pressing'.[475]

13. Public procurement

Falling for consideration under the free movement of both goods and services, **10.91**
and even when the former are not strictly speaking a matter for article 34 (or at
least not always),[476] the Cockfield White Paper identified the continued
partitioning of national markets in public procurement, and the universal
tendency to 'buy national', as one of the most evident barriers to the achievement of a genuine internal market.[477] It is also a very significant proportion of
economic activity, in 2010 accounting for some 17 per cent of the Union's
GDP.[478] In 1971 the Council began a piecemeal approach to addressing the
field (starting with public works contracts),[479] the 'principal objective' of which
is 'the free movement of services and the opening-up [of public procurement] to
undistorted competition in all the Member States'.[480] The ensuing bundle of
Community measures was consolidated in 2004 into a general Directive
governing public works, public supply and public service contracts in general, or
'classical', sectors[481] and a specialist Directive in the utilities (water, energy,
transport and postal services) sectors;[482] they are sometimes distinguished
(inaccurately) as the 'Public Contracts Directive' and the 'Utilities Directive'.
Both are extensive, detailed and complex. Additional measures have been
adopted with a view to developing a 'common procurement vocabulary' (CPV)
of standardised nomenclature in references to the subjects of a contract.[483] The
rules are now extended expressly to 'defence and security' procurement but

---

475   COM(2010) 733.
476   It may be if laid down (as it frequently is) as a statutory duty of public authorities in legislative, administrative
       or other instruments; it is a moot point if art. 34 applies to a free choice upon a case by case basis.
477   Completing the Internal Market, COM(85) 310, para. 81.
478   COM (2010) 546 final, p. 16.
479   Directive 71/305 [1971] JO L185/5. There followed Directive 77/62 [1977] OJ L13/1 (public supply
       contracts); Directive 90/531 [1990] OJ L297/1 (utilities contracts); Directives 93/36, 93/37 and 93/38 [1993]
       OJ L199/1, 54 and 84 (coordination of procedures for the award of contracts).
480   Case C-26/03 *Stadt Halle and anor* v *Arbeitsgemeinschaft Thermische Restabfall- und Energieverwertungsanlage
       TREA Leuna* [2005] ECR I-1, at para. 44.
481   Directive 2004/18 [2004] OJ L134/114.
482   Directive 2004/17 [2004] OJ L134/1.
483   Regulation 2195/2002 [2002] OJ L340/1.

subject to special rules.[484] A mixed contract of part military and part non-military scope is regulated by the latter Directive.[485]

10.92 Generally the Directives apply to:

- *public works contracts*: contracts, including concessions and design contests, which have as their object either the execution, or both the design and execution, of building or civil engineering works which fulfil an economic or technical function;
- *public supply contracts*: contracts which are not public works contracts and have as their object the purchase, lease, rental or hire purchase, with or without option to buy, of products;
- *public service contracts*: contracts other than public works or supply contracts having as their object the provision of services;[486] and
- military and sensitive works and services, military and sensitive equipment and works, supplies and services directly related thereto[487]

which involve pecuniary interest,[488] are in writing, and are awarded to an 'economic operator' (a contractor, supplier or service provider, as appropriate)[489] by a 'contracting authority', that is the state, a regional or local authority, a body governed by public law, an association formed by one or several of such authorities or one or several of such bodies governed by public law.[490] Excluded are:

- contracts below prescribed thresholds: that is, contracts to the value, exclusive of VAT, of:
  - €5,000,000 for public works contracts;[491]

---

484 Directive 2009/81 [2009] OJ L216/76; required to be implemented by August 2011.
485 *Ibid.* art. 3.
486 Directive 2004/18, art. 1(2); Directive 2004/17, art. 1(2).
487 Directive 2009/81, art. 2.
488 As to which see Case C-119/06 *Commission* v *Italy* [2007] ECR I-168; *R (Chandler)* v *Secretary of State for Children, Schools and Families and ors* [2009] EWCA Civ 1101, [2009] All ER (D) 115.
489 Directive 2004/18, art. 1(8); Directive 2004/17, art. 1(7).
490 Directive 2004/18, art. 1(9); Directive 2004/17, art. 1(8). Contracting authorities include 'central purchasing bodies'; Directive 2004/18, art. 1(10); Directive 2004/17, art. 1(8). A body governed by public law is any body established for the specific purpose of meeting needs in the general interest, having legal personality, and financed, for the most part, by the state, regional or local authorities, or other bodies governed by public law; or subject to management supervision by those bodies; Directive 2004/18, art. 1(9). An extensive (48 pages in length) but non-exhaustive list of bodies which fulfil these criteria are set out in Annex III of the Directive.
491 Directive 2004/18, art. 7(c). The thresholds are reviewed every two years and may be revised by the Commission: Directive 2004/18, art. 78; Directive 2004/17, art. 69. Those provided, lowered significantly from original thresholds in order to comply with a Uruguay Round agreement on public procurement, are those with effect from 1 January 2012.

- €130,000 or €200,000 (depending upon the awarding body) for general public supply and service contracts;
- €400,000 for supply and service contracts in the utilities sectors;[492] and
- €400,000 for defence and security supply and service contracts;[493]

the method of calculating the estimated value of contracts is supplied;[494]

- certain (broadly defined) contracts involving military and security measures;[495]
- contracts for the acquisition or rental of land, arbitration and conciliation services, financial services and research and development;[496]
- service concessions;[497] and
- utilities concessions[498] and utilities contracts carried out in third countries.[499]

However, the Court has said that even where the Directives do not apply, public authorities are bound by the fundamental rules of the Treaties in general and the principle of non-discrimination on grounds of nationality in particular, so that public contracts ought at all events to be open to competition, transparent and subject to some (unspecified) form of tendering.[500] To assist, the Commission adopted an 'interpretative communication' detailing best practices in the field.[501] But even this is inapplicable to 'in-house' contracts, for the rules are addressed to agreements between two distinct persons: a contracting authority and an economic operator. A contract awarded to a legally distinct economic operator remains in-house if the authority exercises over the operator a control which is similar to that which it exercises over its own departments and, at the same time, the operator carries

---

492 Directive 2004/18, arts 8, 7; Directive 2004/17, art. 16.
493 Directive 2009/81, art. 8.
494 Directive 2004/18, art. 9; Directive 2004/17, art. 17; Directive 2009/81, art. 9; for clarification see Case C-220/05 *Auroux and ors* v *Commune de Roanne* [2007] ECR I-385.
495 Directive 2009/81, art. 13. In any event defence and security contracts continue to be subject to the general exclusionary application of art. 346 TFEU on essential security interests, expressly saved by art. 2.
496 Directive 2004/18, art. 16; Directive 2004/17, art. 24.
497 Directive 2004/18, art. 17; see Case C-458/03 *Parking Brixen* v *Gemeinde Brixen and anor* [2005] ECR I-8585; Case C-231/03 *Consorzio Aziende Metano* v *Comune di Cingia de' Botti* [2005] ECR I-7287; Case C-91/08 *Wall* v *Stadt Frankfurt am Main and anor* [2010] ECR I-2815.
498 Directive 2004/17, art. 18.
499 *Ibid.* art. 20.
500 Case C-458/03 *Parking Brixen*, n. 497 above; Case C-195/04 *Commission* v *Finland* [2007] ECR I-3351; Case T-258/06 *Germany* v *Commission* [2010] ECR II-2027.
501 Commission interpretative communication on the Community law applicable to contract awards not or not fully subject to the provisions of the Public Procurement Directives [2006] OJ C179/2.

out the essential part of its activities with the authority (the '*Teckal* exemption').[502] This gives rise to complex questions of the application of the rules in the context of public–private partnerships.[503]

10.93 Where the Directives apply, contracting authorities are obliged to give notice of a contract they intend to award,[504] providing information[505] and time limits[506] in accordance with prescribed form, which is then published in the *Official Journal* in prescribed format.[507] Because technical specifications may have the effect (intentional or otherwise) of favouring certain makes or sources of contract goods or services,[508] there are rules on their formulation seeking that they be rendered as neutrally as possible.[509] In awarding contracts economic operators are to be treated equally and non-discriminatorily (*sic*),[510] and contracting authorities are to act in a transparent manner.[511] A contract is awarded in accordance with prescribed procedures, one of:

- open procedure: any interested economic operator may submit a tender;
- restricted procedure: any economic operator may request to participate and only those economic operators invited by the contracting authority may submit a tender; or
- negotiated procedure: the contracting authorities consult economic operators of their choice and negotiate the terms of contract with one or more of them.[512]

---

502 Case C-107/98 *Teckal* v *Comune di Viano and anor* [1999] ECR I-8121; Case C-458/03 *Parking Brixen*, n. 497 above; Case C-340/04 *Carbotermo and anor* v *Comune di Busto Arsizio and anor* [2006] ECR I-4137; Case C-295/05 *Asociación Nacional de Empresas Forestales (Asemfo)* v *Transformación Agraria (Tragsa) and anor* [2007] ECR I-2999; Case C-220/06 *Asociación Profesional de Empresas de Reparto y Manipulado de Correspondencia* v *Administración del Estado* [2007] ECR I-12175.

503 See Case C-196/08 *Acoset* v *Conferenza Sindaci e Presidenza Prov. Reg. ATO Idrico Ragusa and ors* [2009] ECR I-9913.

504 Directive 2004/18, art. 35 ff.; Directive 2004/17, art. 41 ff.; Directive 2009/81, art. 30 ff.

505 Directive 2004/18, art. 36 and Annex VII; Directive 2004/17, art. 44 and Annexes XIII–XVI; Directive 2009/81, art. 32 and Annex VI.

506 Directive 2004/18, art. 38; Directive 2004/17, art. 45; Directive 2009/81, art. 33.

507 Directive 2004/18, arts 36(2–8), 58(3), 64(3), 70(2), Annex VIII; Directive 2004/17, arts 41–4; Directive 2009/81, art. 32(2–4). The notice is submitted to the Union's publication office and then published as an invitation to tender in the 'S' (for 'Supplement') series of the *Official Journal*. The notices are also available at http://ted.europa.eu ('ted' being tenders electronic daily). The Union institutions are probably not bound by the Directives (unless they are contracting authorities by virtue of being 'bodies established by public law' and bound by private law contracts in accordance with the law of the member state in which they are based), but public contracts for Union institutions and bodies are in any event advertised in the 'S' series.

508 See e.g., Case 45/87 *Commission* v *Ireland* [1988] ECR 4929.

509 Directive 2004/18, art. 23 and Annex VI; Directive 2004/17, art. 34; Directive 2009/81, art. 18 and Annex III.

510 Directive 2004/18, art. 2; Directive 2004/17, art. 10; Directive 2009/81, art. 4 (but 'in a non-discriminatory manner').

511 *Ibid.*

512 Directive 2004/18, art. 1(11); Directive 2004/17, art. 1(9); Directive 2009/81, art. 1(19)(20).

Provision is also made in the general and defence Directives for a 'competitive dialogue' whereby any economic operator may request to participate, the contracting authority conducts a dialogue with the candidates admitted to that procedure, with the aim of developing one or more suitable alternatives capable of meeting its requirements, and on the basis of which the candidates chosen are invited to tender.[513] This is appropriate for 'particularly complex' contracts in which the contracting authority is not objectively able to define the technical means or specify the legal and/or financial make-up of a project. A contract is to be awarded applying one of only two citeria, either:

(a)   the most economically advantageous (applying acceptable criteria which are specified in the notice); or

(b)   the lowest price only.[514]

Provision is made for dealing with abnormally low tenders.[515]

In order to prevent circumvention of the rules through the means of publicly **10.94** owned operations there is a 'Transparency Directive' which requires the member states to make the books of those undertakings available to Commission inspection.[516] In order to ensure the Directives are complied with and contracts selected and awarded openly, fairly and in a transparent manner generally,[517] there are two 'Remedies Directives'.[518] They require that member states adopt review procedures;[519] that interlocutory relief be available such that any decision taken prior to conclusion of a contract may be set aside;[520] that contracts awarded in a manner inconsistent with the rules be rescinded;[521] and that damages may be awarded to persons injured by infractions.[522] Where there is a

---

513   Directive 2004/18, arts 1(11)(c), 29; Directive 2009/81, arts 1(21), 27.
514   Directive 2004/18, art. 53; Directive 2004/17, art. 55(1); Directive 2009/81, art. 47(1). The criteria permitted for determining the 'most economically advantageous' tender are, 'for example' (so presumably permitting others which can be objectively justified), quality, price, technical merit, aesthetic and functional characteristics, running costs, cost-effectiveness, after-sales service and technical assistance, delivery date and delivery period or period of completion.
515   Directive 2004/18, art. 55; Directive 2009/81, art. 49.
516   Directive 2006/111 [2006] OJ L318/17 (being a consolidation of Directive 80/723 [1980] OJ L195/35).
517   As to selection and award of a contract, and the distinction between the two, see Case C-532/06 *Lianakis and ors* v *Dimos Alexandroupolis and ors* [2008] ECR I-251.
518   Directive 89/665 [1989] OJ L395/33 (for the 'classical' sectors); Directive 92/13 [1992] OJ L176/14 (in the utilities (water, energy, transport and telecommunications) sectors). The review provisions are self-contained in the Defence and Security Directive; Directive 2009/81, arts 55–64.
519   Directive 89/665, art. 1(3); Directive 92/13, art. 1; Directive 2009/81, arts 55–6.
520   Directive 89/665, art. 2; Directive 92/13, art. 2; Case C-81/98 *Alcatel Austria and ors* v *Bundesministerium für Wissenschaft und Verkehr* [1999] ECR I-7671.
521   *Ibid.*; see Case C-503/04 *Commission* v *Germany* [2007] ECR I-6153.
522   *Ibid.* For an example see *Aquatron Marine* v *Strathclyde Fire Board* [2007] CSOH 185.

'clear and manifest infraction' the Commission may intervene directly.[523] Amendments to each require the introduction (from the end of 2009) of a short (10–15 calendar days) standstill period before contracts may be concluded, so allowing the opportunity of swift, effective review by unsuccessful tenderers and extension of the circumstances in which contracts concluded in a manner inconsistent with various aspects of the Directives are to be declared 'ineffective' (*absent d'effets*; *unwirksam*).[524]

10.95 At the time of writing the public procurement rules are undergoing re-evaluation and public consultation with a view to streamlining.[525]

14. State monopolies of a commercial character

10.96 Article 37 TFEU deals with the special situation of 'state monopolies of a commercial character', that is those enjoying exclusive rights under national law in the procurement, distribution and/or retail of goods. They are created for a variety of reasons, chief amongst which are public policy (e.g., public safety in the distribution or marketing of dangerous or medicinal products; control of prices and consumption for the protection of health; ensuring equitable and universal supply of a given (vital) product); and revenue raising. Less common than they were in the past, the best known modern example is probably *Systembolaget* in Sweden. Article 37 applies to the movement of goods and not to a monopoly in the provision of services,[526] except insofar as a monopoly service provider might indirectly influence trade in goods in a manner which discriminates against imported, in preference to domestic, products.[527] Its requirements are, from the end of the transitional period, directly effective.[528]

10.97 The Treaties require that state monopolies be

> adjust[ed] ... so as to ensure that ... no discrimination regarding the conditions under which goods are procured and marketed exists between nationals of Member States.[529]

---

523 Directive 89/665, art. 3; Directive 92/13, art. 8. However it should be noted that an enforcement action raised under art. 258 in the field is, if a contract in dispute has been completely performed, inadmissible; Case C-362/90 *Commission* v *Italy* [1992] ECR I-2353; Case C-237/05 *Commission* v *Greece* [2007] ECR I-8203.

524 Directive 2007/66 [2007] OJ L335/31 (New Remedies Directive); also Directive 2009/81, arts 57, 60.

525 See Green Paper on the Modernisation of EU Public Procurement Policy: Towards a More Efficient European Procurement Market, COM(2011) 15 final.

526 Case 30/87 *Bodson* v *Pompes funèbres des regions libérées* [1988] ECR 2479; Case C-6/01 *Associação Nacional de Operadores de Máquinas Recreativas (Anomar) and ors* v *Estado português* [2003] ECR I-8621.

527 Case 30/87 *Bodson*, n. 526 above.

528 Case 59/75 *Pubblico Ministero* v *Manghera and ors* [1976] ECR 91.

529 TFEU, art. 37(1) (ex art. 31(1) EC).

Article 37 addresses discrimination 'between nationals of Member States'; it refers to traders and not to goods. It therefore differs from article 34 in being limited to discrimination and protecting not the free movement of goods but traders who participate in the free movement of goods. However there is no indication in the Treaty that article 37 is to allow derogation from the fundamental rules of articles 34–36. Article 37 applies only to those activities connected intrinsically with the functioning of the monopoly and not other severable national rules;[530] put otherwise, it applies to rules relating to 'the existence and operation' of a monopoly, but 'the effect on intra-Community trade of the other provisions of the domestic legislation, which are separable from the operation of the monopoly although they have a bearing upon it, must be examined with reference to Article [34]'.[531] It must be read not only with article 34 but also with later provisions of the Treaties relating particularly to the application of the competition rules to public undertakings, and to state aids.[532]

Although it would be one way, and it was argued the best way, of adjusting them **10.98** to this end, article 37 does not require the abolition of commercial monopolies; rather it requires them to be adjusted in such a way as to ensure that no discrimination regarding the conditions under which goods are procured and marketed exists between nationals of member states.[533] An exclusive right of importation conferred upon the monopoly cannot but result in discrimination, and, if it exists, its 'adjustment' requires its prohibition.[534] Otherwise

> [t]he purpose of Article 37 of the Treaty is to reconcile the possibility for Member States to maintain certain monopolies of a commercial character as instruments for the pursuit of public interest aims with the requirements of the establishment and function-ing of the common market. It aims at the elimination of obstacles to the free movement of goods, save, however, for restrictions on trade which are inherent in the existence of the monopolies in question.[535]

Thus a monopoly must not be allowed to conduct its activities in such a way as to put at a disadvantage, in law or in fact, trade in goods from other member states as compared with trade in domestic goods. It is therefore necessary, upon a case by case basis, to determine whether the way in which a monopoly is organised and operates is liable to place products from other member states at a

---

530 Case 86/78 *Grandes Distilleries Peureux v Directeur des Services Fisceaux* [1979] ECR 897.

531 Case C-170/04 *Rosengren and ors v Riksåklagaren* [2007] ECR I-4071, at paras 17, 18.

532 See 13.142–13.147 and 13.163–13.181 below.

533 Case 59/75 *Manghera*, n. 528 above; Case 91/78 *Hansen v Hauptzollamt Flensburg* [1979] ECR 935.

534 Case 59/75 *Manghera*, n. 528 above; Case E-1/94 *Ravintoloitsijain Liiton Kustannus Restamark v Helsingen Piiritullikamari* [1994–95] EFTA CR 15.

535 Case C-189/95 *Criminal proceedings against Franzén* [1997] ECR I-5909, at para. 39; Case C-438/02 *Åklagaren v Hanner* [2005] ECR I-4551, at para. 35.

disadvantage, or whether in fact it does so in practice. As to the first limb, the Court of Justice said in the context of *Systembolaget* that it is necessary to consider three points:

- the selection system of a sales monopoly must be based on criteria that are independent from the origin of the products and must be transparent by providing both for an obligation to state reasons for decisions and for an independent monitoring procedure;
- the retail network must be organised in such a way that the number of sales outlets is not limited to the point of compromising consumers' procurement of supplies; and
- marketing and advertising measures must be impartial and independent of the origin of the products and must endeavour to make known new products to consumers.[536]

As to the second limb, standard *Dassonville* analysis applies. So, in *Franzén*, the right of importation being restricted to holders of a production or wholesale licence, a licence requiring significant background, a substantial application fee (Kr 25,000) and annual subscription fee (up to Kr 323,750), and being issued almost entirely to traders established in Sweden, taken together constituted a breach of article 34. The continuing prohibition of third parties to import alcoholic beverages at the request or on behalf of private individuals[537] was found subsequently not to be bound up with *Systembolaget*'s existence and operating system and constituted a breach of article 34, not saved by article 36.[538]

D. AGRICULTURE AND FISHERIES

10.99 A particular subset of goods is agricultural goods, for which the Treaties provide special and very complex rules. Agriculture is in varying degrees an important part of the economy of all member states, and enjoys subsidy, again in varying degrees, in each. Certainly in no country is agriculture a matter left wholly to the free market. Further, in the aftermath of the 1939–45 war and the lean years which followed, self-sufficiency in food was regarded as an important and praiseworthy objective. The Treaties therefore provided from the start a separate Title making distinct provisions for agriculture, in two ways: first, by making special rules for trade in agricultural products, and second, by providing

---

536   Case C-189/95 *Franzén*, n. 535 above, at paras 44–62.
537   2 § Alkohollag, SFS 1994:1738.
538   Case C-170/04 *Rosengren and ors* v *Riksåklagaren* [2007] ECR I-4071; Case C-186/05 *Commission* v *Sweden* [2007] ECR I-129*.

for the development of a Common Agricultural Policy (CAP). Alone in the Treaties, *dirigisme* prevails. The workings of the CAP are beyond the scope of this book. But there can be no real understanding of the Union without a passing familiarity with the basics of the rules on agriculture and their history, for, whilst it is unsophisticated, the view of many is that in practice the Union *is* the CAP. Certainly it has occupied much of the time of the Court of Justice, agricultural disputes traditionally being the most frequent source of litigation before the Court,[539] and the vast case law produced informs many other areas of Union law: for example, being a closely regulated system, many of the general principles of Union law were first recognised, and came to be developed, in the context of the CAP. The following general points form its core.

1. The Treaty provisions

The original Treaty 'extended' the common market to agriculture and trade in agricultural products.[540] This was a rarity, many international treaties by which states pursue economic integration – the European Free Trade Association (partially)[541] and the European Economic Area,[542] for example – excluding agriculture and agricultural trade. But according to the Spaak Report it was inconceivable that the Community should go down that route.[543] The Treaty therefore called for 'the adoption of a common policy in the sphere of agriculture'[544] which was a necessary corollary of inclusion of the field: 'the operation and development of the common market for agricultural products must be accompanied by the establishment of a common agricultural policy'.[545]   **10.100**

The objectives of the CAP were, and are: **10.101**

    (a) to increase agricultural productivity by promoting technical progress and by ensuring the rational development of agricultural production and the optimum utilisation of the factors of production, in particular labour; thus to ensure a fair standard of living for the agricultural community, in particular by increasing the individual earnings of persons engaged in agriculture;

    (c) to stabilise markets;

---

539 Perusal of the statistics provided in *Court of Justice of the European Union: Annual Report* indicates agricultural issues to have been the most frequent subject matter of cases before the Court, although recently questions relating to environment and consumer protection have overtaken it. The other pre-eminent issues are competition and taxation.

540 EEC Treaty, art. 38(1).

541 EFTA Convention (Consolidated ('Vaduz') version, 2001), art. 8 and Annex C.

542 EEA Agreement, art. 8. But the contracting parties undertake to work towards progressive liberalisation of agricultural trade; art. 19(2).

543 See Chapter 1, n. 15.

544 EEC Treaty, art. 3(d).

545 *Ibid.* art. 38(4).

(d) to assure the availability of supplies;

(e) to ensure that supplies reach consumers at reasonable prices.[546]

With the gradual integration of environmental protection, 'one of the essential objectives of the Community', into the Treaties, it too 'must be regarded as an objective which also forms part of the common agricultural policy',[547] and by virtue of other integration clauses the protection of animal and public health 'forms an integral part of the common agricultural policy'.[548] The institutions are afforded a wide margin of appreciation in giving greater weight to one or another of these objectives as the economic circumstances of the day may dictate.[549] Artice 43(2) TFEU authorises the Council, by the ordinary procedure, to adopt Regulations, Directives, decisions and/or recommendations, as it sees fit, in order to 'work ... out and implement ... the common agricultural policy'. Article 43 is therefore the principal legal base for legislation in the agricultural field – so that, for example, measures for the harmonisation of national law in agricultural sectors fall properly under article 43, not articles 114 and 115,[550] and neither significant public health[551] nor environmental protection[552] components to legislation negate article 43 as the correct legal base. But significant legislative competence in the field, and certainly the day-to-day administration of the CAP, has been delegated by the Council to the Commission, which in turn enjoys a wide measure of discretion in discharging that task.[553] It is assisted by the Management Committee of the Common Organisation of Agricultural Markets and acts in accordance with the management procedure set out in the comitology decision.[554]

2. Agricultural products

10.102 The CAP applies to 'agricultural products', which are 'the products of the soil, of stockfarming and of fisheries and products of first-stage processing directly related to these products'.[555] Products falling within the CAP are listed in an

---

546 TFEU, art. 39(1) (ex art. 33(1) EC).
547 Case C-428/07 *R (Horvath) v Secretary of State for Environment, Food and Rural Affairs* [2009] ECR I-6355, at para. 29; as to environmental protection see 14.58–14.66 below.
548 Case C-180/96 *United Kingdom v Commission* (BSE) [1998] ECR I-2265, at para. 119.
549 See e.g., *Balkan-Import-Export v Hauptzollamt Berlin-Packhof* [1973] ECR 1091, at para. 24; Case C-189/01 *Jippes and ors v Minister van Landbouw, Natuurbeheer en Visserij* [2001] ECR I-5689, at paras 80–101.
550 Case 69/86 *United Kingdom v Council* (Hormones) [1988] ECR 855; Case 131/86 *United Kingdom v Council* (Battery Hens) [1988] ECR 905.
551 Case C-180/96 *United Kingdom v Commission* (BSE) [1998] ECR I-2265; Case C-269/97 *Commission v Council* (Bovines) [2000] ECR I-2257.
552 Case C-428/07 *Horvath* , n. 547 above, at para. 29.
553 Case C-180/96 *BSE*, n. 551 above, at para. 60.
554 Regulation 1234/2007 [2007] OJ L299/1, arts 4, 195.
555 TFEU, art. 38(1).

Annex to the TFEU.[556] The list is exhaustive: a product not included cannot be considered an agricultural product.[557] 'First stage processing' however is defined purposively and broadly as

> implying a clear economic interdependence between basic products and products resulting from a productive process, irrespective of the number of operations involved therein ... [T]he number of operations necessary to obtain a processed product is not the criterion for determining its classification as a product of first-stage processing.[558]

The Treaties provide that 'save as otherwise provided ..., the rules laid down for **10.103** the establishment of the internal market shall apply to agricultural products'.[559] This means that agriculture is a *lex specialis*, and agricultural goods are isolated from the application of general Treaty rules only insofar as required by special provisions of the CAP. This is true, but it does not provide an accurate picture. According to the Court of Justice

> It follows from Article [38(2) TFEU] that the provisions of the Treaty relating to the common agricultural policy have precedence, in case of any discrepancy, over the other rules relating to the establishment of the Common Market.[560]

However, the rules on free movement and on agriculture are set neither against each other nor in order of precedence, 'but on the contrary combined';[561] in order for agricultural rules to be allowed derogation from the general rules on free movement of goods 'it is necessary to find in Articles [38] to [44] a provision which either expressly or by necessary implication provides for or authorizes [it]'.[562] Yet there is a vast field of CAP regulation – quantitative restrictions, quotas, price fixing, intervention, subsidies, levies, licensing, inspections, fees, compensatory payments – that involves disruption to free movement, which would clearly be impermissible if adopted by a member state, or by the Union (or even by private producers) in another sphere, but is allowed under the CAP. It is also (self-) evident that the link between agriculture and human/animal/plant health means that much of the case law on article 36, and

---

556 Annex I (originally Annex II, but renumbered by the Treaty of Amsterdam with the deletion of the original Annex I, on computation of the common customs tariff); the Annex was supplemented in 1960 (Regulation 7a/59 [1961] JO 71) and thereafter immune from legislative change (EEC Treaty, art. 38(3)). Although not listed, cotton was made effectively an agricultural product by the 1979 Athens Accession Treaty, protocol 4.

557 Cases 2 and 3/62 *Commission v Belgium and Luxembourg* (Gingerbread) [1962] ECR 425.

558 Case 185/73 *Hauptzollamt Bielefeld v König* [1974] ECR 607, at paras 13, 14. Hence dilute ethyl alcohol (*König*) and ginned cotton (Case C-310/04 *Spain v Council* [2006] ECR I-7285, *per* A-G Sharpston) are products of first stage processing. But there is scarce case law on the point.

559 TFEU, art. 38(2).

560 Case 83/78 *Pigs Marketing Board v Redmond* [1978] ECR 2347, at para. 37.

561 Cases 80 and 81/77 *Ramel v Receveur des douanes* [1978] ECR 927, at para. 19.

562 *Ibid.* at para. 26.

on mandatory requirements, arises in the context of trade in agricultural goods. Perhaps even more striking, the competition rules apply in principle to the agricultural sector,[563] yet the CAP is itself nothing if not a pan-European cartel; therefore article 101 is excluded from any anticompetitive practice which forms an integral part of a national market organisation or is necessary for attainment of the objectives set out in article 39.[564] So even if 'common organisation of the markets in agricultural products are ... not a competition-free zone'[565] and the derogation from the general rule of article 101 is to be interpreted narrowly,[566] the rules are applied with a lightness of touch[567] and where the objectives of the CAP come up against those of competition it is often the former which prevail, for the latter 'must ... be applied having regard to the aims of the common agricultural policy, whose precedence over the application of the Treaty provisions relating to competition is enshrined in the Treaty itself, in Article [42]'.[568] Generally however, at least in post-production trade and marketing, agricultural products do fall subject to general Treaty rules. The state aids rules apply as from January 2008[569] but with limited exemption.[570]

3. Common organisation of agricultural markets

10.104 The EEC Treaty required that 'a common organisation of agricultural markets' be established[571] but left it to the Community institutions to determine the means, and form, by which this was to be achieved. The choices were three: (a) common rules on competition; (b) compulsory coordination of the various

---

563 Regulation 1184/2006 [2006] OJ L214/7 (replacing Regulation 26/62 [1962] JO 1962 993), art. 1a; Regulation 1234/2007 [2007] OJ L299/1, art. 175. But for agricultural goods not falling within Annex I (and so not 'agricultural products') the competition rules apply normally: Case C-250/92 *Gøttrup-Klim v Dansk Landbrugs Grovvareselskab* [1994] ECR I-5461.

564 Regulation 1184/2006, art. 2(1); Regulation 1234/2007, art. 176.

565 Case C-137/00 *R v Competition Commission and ors, ex parte Milk Marque and National Farmers' Union* [2003] ECR I-7975, at para. 61.

566 Case C-399/93 *Oude Luttikhuis and ors v Verenigde Coöperatieve Melkindustrie Coberco* [1995] ECR I-4515, at para. 23; Cases T-217 and 245/03 *Fédération nationale de la coopération bétail et viande v Commission* [2006] ECR II-4987, at para. 199.

567 See e.g., Regulation 1184/2006, art. 2, which excludes from the prohibition of art. 101 agreements, decisions and practices of farmers, farmers' associations or associations of such associations in a single member state which concern the production or sale of agricultural products or the use of joint facilities for the storage, treatment or processing of agricultural products, so long as they include no obligation to charge identical prices and do not result in an exclusion of competition.

568 Case T-82/96 *Associação dos Refinadores de Açúcar Portugueses and ors v Commission* [1999] ECR II-1899 (confirmed in Case C-321/99 *Associação dos Refinadores de Açúcar Portugueses and ors v Commission* [2002] ECR I-4287); see also Case 139/79 *Maizena v Council* [1980] ECR 3393, at para. 23; Case C-137/00 *Milk Marque*, n. 565 above, at para. 81.

569 Regulation 1184/2006, art. 3 (as amended); Regulation 1234/2007, art. 180.

570 Regulation 1234/2007, art. 180; Regulation 3/2008 [2008] OJ L3/1, art. 13(6); Regulation 479/2008 [2008] OJ L148/2, art. 127(2).

571 EEC Treaty, art. 34(1) (now art. 40(1) TFEU).

national market organisations; or (c) a European market organisation.[572] In the event it was the third option which was chosen. At the 1961/62 marathon at which the CAP was born the agricultural Council produced common organisations of the market for six products: cereals,[573] pigmeat,[574] eggs,[575] poultrymeat,[576] fruit and vegetables,[577] and wine.[578] Others followed. There are now common organisations for the original six and for bananas,[579] live trees and floriculture, dried fodder, processed fruit and vegetables, hops, olive oil and table olives, flax and hemp, milk and milk products, rice, seeds, sugar, raw tobacco, beef and veal, and sheepmeat and goatmeat, all subject to substantial regulation as laid down in each measure. There was also a 1968 Regulation creating a residual common market organisation for a number of miscellaneous products but subject to only rudimentary market control;[580] cotton is not recognised as having a common market organisation but is subject to regulation (the 'cotton support scheme') as if it had;[581] and the Council had adopted Regulations providing specific rules, but not creating a common market organisation, for ethyl alcohol, apiculture and silkworms. Agricultural products produced in any quantity within the Union but not (yet) regulated are therefore potatoes (other than starch potatoes), grain legumes and cork. Water is not an agricultural product. Pet animals apparently are.[582] As a function of simplifying CAP regulation,[583] in 2007 the Council adopted a Regulation bringing all market organisations within the umbrella of a single measure ('Single CMO Regulation'),[584] which was brought into force by stages (according to product) across 2008.

---

572 *Ibid.* art. 34(2).
573 Regulation 19/62 [1962] JO 933.
574 Regulation 20/62 [1962] JO 945.
575 Regulation 21/62 [1962] JO 953.
576 Regulation 22/62 [1962] JO 959.
577 Regulation 23/62 [1962] JO 965.
578 Regulation 24/62 [1962] JO 989.
579 Regulation 404/93 [1993] OJ L47/1. It was the adoption of this Regulation which led to a political, and a threat of a constitutional, crisis in Germany; see Case C-280/93 *Germany v Council* (Bananas) [1994] ECR I-4973; BVerfG, 7. Juni 2000 (*Bananenmarktordnung* or *Solange III*), BVerfGE 102, 147.
580 Regulation 827/68 [1968] JO L51/16, including, for example, various live animals; the meat of horses, asses, mules and hinnies; offal; guts, bladders and stomachs; nuts; dates and figs; tea; spices; seaweed.
581 Regulation 73/2009 [2009] OJ L30/16, Title IV, Chap. 1, Sec. 6.
582 Regulation 998/2003 [2003] OJ L146/1; on the non-commercial movement of pet animals, based partly upon art. 43 TFEU.
583 As part of a Commission policy launched in 2005. See Commission Communication on simplification and better regulation for the Common Agricultural Policy (CAP), COM(2005) 509 final; *A Simplified CAP for Europe – A Success for All*, COM(2009) 128 final.
584 Regulation 1234/2007 [2007] OJ L299/1. Excluded were the CMOs in the midst of substantial policy reform; fruits and vegetables, processed fruit and vegetables and certain citrus fruits (Regulation 361/2008 [2008] OJ L121/1) and wine (Regulation 491/2009 [2009] OJ L154/1) were subsequently incorporated into the Single CMO.

10.105   The detailed rules governing the common organisation of markets vary from product to product, but generally when originally adopted they provided for, and conformed to the following pattern:

- a *reference price*, sometimes target, basic or guide price: a price set annually by the Council which it thinks a given product ought ideally to attract;
- robust protection from imported goods through *import levies*, or 'agricultural levies'.[585] These are the difference between the world price of an agricultural good (normally c.i.f. Rotterdam) and the *threshold price* (or sluicegate price), calculated from the reference price and being the mimimum price at which goods may be imported into the Union. The threshold price is set annually by the Council but the import levies vary with world prices, so are computed daily. In the view of the Union import levies are not customs duties, rather they are charges regulating external trade intended to protect and stabilise the common price policy.[586] They are therefore distinct from, and in addition to, the Common Customs Tariff;
- an *intervention price* (sometimes 'buying in' price), being the price at which intervention bodies in the member states are required to buy in agricultural products. The intervention price is set at or lower than the reference price, but forms a guaranteed price. An intervention body is required to release goods it holds back onto the market should prices stabilise and rise above the intervention price. This has given rise to significant commodity speculation. Under the Single CMO Regulation intervention is now applicable to common wheat, durum wheat, barley, maize and sorghum; paddy rice; white or raw sugar (within quota); fresh or chilled beef and veal; butter from pasteurised cream; skimmed milk powder; and pig-meat;[587]
- export refunds: world market prices are normally lower than the intervention price, never mind reference prices. Therefore export refunds are paid in order to enable Union produce to be sold on the world market.[588] In the view of the Union export refunds are not subsidies, rather they are price stabilisers. It is a view widely derided outside the Union;

---

585   See now Regulation 1234/2007, arts 170–92 and Regulation 612/2009 [2009] OJ L186/1.

586   Case 17/67 *Neumann* v *Hauptzollamt Hof/Saale* [1968] ECR 441; Case 113/75 *Frecasseti* v *Amministrazione delle Finanze dello Stato* [1976] ECR 983.

587   Regulation 1234/2007 [2007] OJ L299/1, art. 10. For implementation see Regulation 1272/2009 [2009] OJ L349/1.

588   Agricultural levies, or agricultural duties, were abandoned as a distinct customs classification in 2007 in compliance with Uruguay Round agreement, now subsumed within 'other duties'; Decision 2007/436 [2007] OJ L163/17.

- export levies, now export taxes: on those (very rare) occasions in which the Union price is lower than the world market price, export is discouraged by imposition of export levies;
- production quotas: some products (milk and milk products, sugar) are subject to a production quota; production in excess of the quota attracts a surplus levy;
- aid: direct subvention is available in a number of sectors for, for example, processing (fodder, flax, milk and milk products), operator organisations (olive oil and table olives) and general assistance (beekeeping, silkworm rearing). Significant amounts are available to assist in rural development (the CAP 'second pillar').[589]

Much of this has been, or is in the process of being, dismantled or reformed.[590]

The creation of a common organisation of a market has the effect of depriving **10.106** the member states of the power to take any measure which might undermine the operation of the market mechanisms or machinery,[591] and in some circumstances may deprive them of recourse to article 36.[592] For an agricultural product not made subject to a common organisation, normal Treaty rules apply.[593]

4. Fisheries

Whilst calling originally for a common policy 'in the sphere of agriculture', the **10.107** EEC Treaty definition of agricultural products included 'the products of … fisheries', Annex I includes 'fish, crustaceans and molluscs' and it was therefore apparent that fish and fisheries were to fall within, and considered to be an aspect of, the CAP.[594] Maastricht identified as a Community activity 'a common policy in the sphere of agriculture and fisheries'[595] and Lisbon reframed the heading of Title II to 'Agriculture and Fisheries' and provides that all

---

589 See below.
590 See below.
591 See e.g., Case 51/74 *Van der Hulst's Zonen* v *Produktschap voor Siergewassen* [1975] ECR 79; Case 111/76 *Officier van Justitie* v *van den Hazel* [1977] ECR 901; Case 83/78 *Pigs Marketing Board* v *Redmond* [1978] ECR 2347; Case 148/85 *Direction générale des impôts and anor* v *Forest and anor* [1986] ECR 3449; Case C-1/96 *R* v *Minister of Agriculture, Fisheries and Food, ex parte Compassion in World Farming* [1998] ECR I-1251; Case C-428/99 *van den Bor* v *Voedselvoorzieningsin- en verkoopbureau* [2002] ECR I-127; Case C-283/03 *Kuipers* v *Produktschap Zuivel* [2005] ECR I-3761.
592 Case C-462/01 *Criminal proceedings against Hammarsten* [2003] ECR I-781.
593 Case 48/74 *Charmasson* v *Minister for Economic Affairs and Finance (Paris)* [1974] ECR 1383; Case 288/83 *Commission* v *Ireland* [1985] ECR 1761; Case C-293/02 *Jersey Produce Marketing Organisation* v *States of Jersey and ors* [2005] ECR I-9543.
594 Confirmed in Case 141/78 *France* v *United Kingdom* [1979] ECR 2923.
595 EC Treaty, art. 3(e) (pre-Amsterdam).

references to agriculture 'shall be understood as also referring to fisheries, having regard to the specific characteristics of this sector'.[596] But of course fishing is unlike agricultural activity generally, and a distinct set of rules has evolved to govern it. Relevant legislation was first adopted in 1970[597] which grew into a recognisable Common Fisheries Policy (CFP) in 1983.[598] Since 1992 the CFP has been recognised to include aquaculture.[599] Fisheries generally remain a sector of significant economic (the Union is the world's third largest producer, after China and Peru), regional and social importance.

10.108   The CFP covers 'conservation, management and exploitation of living aquatic resources, aquaculture, and the processing and marketing of fishery and aquatic products' within the Union or by Union flagged vessels.[600] It is governed now by:

- a common organisation of the markets in fishery and aquaculture products, which (uniquely) remains distinct from the Single CMO Regulation;[601] and
- specific rules on conservation and sustainable exploitation.[602]

To this end measures are adopted with a view to comprehensive regulation of conservation, management and exploitation; limitation of environmental impact of fishing; conditions of access to waters; structural policy and management of fleet capacity; control and enforcement; aquaculture; common organisation of the markets; and international relations.[603] The general rule is that 'Union fishing vessels' (fishing vessels flying the flag of a member state *and* registered in the Union) have equal access to all Union maritime (but not inland)[604] waters, that is the 200 nautical mile exclusive economic zone (EEZ)

---

596   TFEU, art. 38(1).

597   Regulation 2141/70 [1970] JO L236/1 (common structural policy); Regulation 2142/70 [1970] JO L236/5 (common organisation of the market).

598   The 1972 Act of Accession, arts 100–1, permitted derogation from the principle of equal access as regards the accession member states for a period of ten years, whilst art. 103 committed the (nine) member states to the adoption of a CFP by and for January 1983. This obligation, adopted on the eve of Community waters more than trebling in size (quintupling with Greenland), is thought to be a principal reason for the Norwegian 'no' to accession in 1973. Agreement was reached in January 1983 (three weeks late, as to the importance of which see Case 63/83 *R v Kirk* [1984] ECR 2689) and given effect by the adoption of Regulations 170/83, 171/83 and 172/83 [1983] OJ L24/1, 14 and 30.

599   Regulation 3760/92 [1992] OJ L389/1.

600   Regulation 2371/2002 [2002] OJ L358/59, art. 1(1).

601   Regulation 104/2000 [2000] OJ L17/22.

602   Regulation 2371/2002; implementing Regulation 1013/2010 [2010] OJ L293/1; also Regulation 734/2008 [2008] OJ L201/8 (protection of the marine ecosystem of the high seas).

603   Regulation 2371/2002, art. 1(2).

604   This because the 1972 Act of Accession, art. 102 refers to fishing and conservation 'of the biological resources of the sea' only, and the first structural policy measure (Regulation 2141/70, n. 597 above) laid down rules 'for fishing in maritime waters' (art. 1). But the CFP applies to aquaculture in inland waters.

asserted now by most littoral member states,[605] except that until the end of 2012 (likely to be extended) a member state may restrict fishing in waters up to 12 nautical miles from the baseline to fishing vessels which traditionally fish in those waters from ports on the adjacent coast.[606] Within Union maritime waters each member state is allocated a quota ('total allowable catch', TAC) which ensures for 'each Member State relative stability of fishing activities for each stock or fishery'.[607] Because TACs are set by the Council (by qualified majority)[608] they are thought frequently to err on the side of generosity, not conservation; so jealously do the member states guard this prerogative that, contrary to the general duty to confer implementing authority upon the Commission,[609] the power (of 'the fixing and allocation of fishing opportunities') was reserved by the Lisbon Treaty to the Council.[610] The allocation to individual fishing vessels within the national fleet is for each member state.[611] Notoriously weak surveillance and enforcement mechanisms, intended to combat not only improper fishing operations themselves but national connivance and/or indifference to them, were beefed up in 2002[612] and 2008,[613] a Community Fisheries Control Agency created in 2005 to organise and coordinate national efforts,[614] a 'Community control system' for control, inspection and enforcement introduced in 2009,[615] and in 2011 the Union ratified a 2009 FAO Agreement on greater port control over illegal, unreported and unregulated fishing,[616] but it is not yet clear if these steps have resulted in

---

605 However the EEZ is outside the customs territory of the Union which includes only the territorial sea of each member state; Regulation 2913/92 [1992] OJ L302/1, art. 3(3); Regulation 450/2008 [2008] OJ L145/1, art. 3(1). There are no EEZs in the Mediterranean, national sovereignty extending only to the territorial seas. Fish taken in the EEZ (or on the high seas) are deemed to originate in the fishing vessel's flag state; Regulation 2913/92, art. 23(2)(f); Regulation 450/2008, art. 133. In the event of joint operations fish are taken by the vessel responsible for the 'essential part of the operation', not necessarily that which actually draws them from the sea; Case 100/84 *Commission* v *United Kingdom* [1985] ECR 1169.

606 Regulation 2371/2002, art. 17(1), (2). The Commission proposes that the derogation be extended to 2022: Proposal for a Regulation on the CFP, COM (2011) 425 final, art. 6(2).

607 *Ibid.* art. 20(1). For the most recent (2012) TACs see Regulations 43/2012 and 44/2012 [2012] OJ L25/1 and 55. But this advantage is diluted by the fact that a Union national has a Treaty right (a right of establishment; see 11.06 below) to own and operate fishing vessels in any other member state (Case C-48/93 *R* v *Secretary of State for Transport, ex parte Factortame and ors* [1996] ECR I-1029), so permitting fishing interests in one member state, their quotas having been exhausted, to buy into those of another – a practice known as 'quota hopping'.

608 Regulation 2371/2002, art. 20(1).

609 TFEU, art. 291(2); see 3.26 above.

610 *Ibid.* art. 43(3).

611 Regulation 2371/2002, art. 20(3).

612 *Ibid.* arts 21–8.

613 Regulation 1005/2008 [2008] OJ L286/1, establishing a Community system to prevent, deter and eliminate illegal, unreported and unregulated fishing; for implementation see Regulation 1010/2009 [2009] OJ L280/5.

614 Regulation 768/2005 [2005] OJ L128/1.

615 Regulation 1224/2009 [2009] OJ L343/1; see also its implementing Regulation 404/2011 [2011] OJ L112/1.

616 Agreement of 22 November 2009 on Port State Measures to Prevent, Deter and Eliminate Illegal, Unreported and Unregulated Fishing [2011] OJ L191/3.

significant improvement; an extensive Commission working paper produced (but not published) in 2008, described informally as the 'Frankenstein Report',[617] paints a bleak picture. A seemingly ineluctable problem is a direct product of TACs, the elimination of 'discards', for total allowable catches are, in practice, total allowable landings, where most monitoring and control takes place; this leads to extensive discarding into the sea of 'bycatch' (juveniles, unintended species) or, worse, 'high grading', fish in the hold jettisoned in favour of later, more valuable (fresher, more valuable species) catches in order to stay within quota. At the time of writing the Commission promises change to address the problem. Since 2007 a European Fisheries Fund (EFF) assists in providing aid for processing and marketing but also for decommissioning, retraining and early retirement, 'green tourism' and regeneration of fishing communities, and new gear which limits environmental damage.[618]

10.109   It should be noted that the CFP is a high profile aspect of the Union's external action. Conservation of marine resources was recognised as an exclusive Community competence in 1976,[619] formally confirmed by Lisbon,[620] and to this end it is party to, and enforces the provisions of, various international conventions on maritime conservation.[621] The Union is a contracting party to the 1982 Convention on the Law of the Sea (UNCLOS)[622] and the accompanying Convention on the conservation and management of straddling and migratory fish stocks.[623] Union competence is recognised by third states in negotiating (reciprocal or otherwise) access to respective fishing grounds – in, for example, the agreements with Norway,[624] the Færoe Islands,[625] Canada,[626] Iceland,[627]

---

617   *A Diagnosis of the EU Fisheries Sector* (September 2008).
618   Regulation 1198/2006 [2006] OJ L223/1; detailed implementing rules in Regulation 498/2007 [2007] OJ L120/1. The Regulation provides for support for inland fisheries even though not part of the CFP; arts 1, 4(c), 13, 33. The EFF has a projected expenditure of almost €5 thousand million for 2007–13; art. 12(1).
619   Cases 3 etc./76 *Cornelius Kramer* [1976] ECR 1279.
620   TFEU, art. 3(1)(d).
621   E.g., Convention of 24 October 1978 on Future Multilateral Cooperation in the Northwest Atlantic Fisheries (Ottawa Convention) [1978] OJ L378/2, to which the EEC acceded in 1978; Convention of 18 November 1980 on Future Multilateral Cooperation in the North-East Atlantic Fisheries [1981] OJ L227/22, to which the EEC acceded in 1981.
622   Convention of 10 December 1982 on the Law of the Sea, 1833 UNTS 3.
623   Convention on the Law of the Sea of 10 December 1982 relating to the Conservation and Management of Straddling Fish Stocks and Highly Migratory Fish Stocks ('the 1995 Fish Stock Agreement') (1995) 34 ILM 1542. The Union is also party to 'area' conventions under the Agreement, e.g., the Southern Indian Ocean Fisheries Agreement (SIOFA) of 7 July 2006 [2006] OJ L196/15; Convention of 26 July 2010 on the Conservation and Management of High Seas Fisheries Resources in the South Pacific Ocean, not yet published or in force.
624   Agreement on Fisheries between the EEC and the Kingdom of Norway [1989] OJ L226/48.
625   Agreement on Fisheries between the EEC and the Government of Denmark and the Home Government of the Færoe Islands [1980] OJ L226/11.
626   Agreement on Fisheries between the EEC and the Government of Canada [1981] OJ L379/54.
627   Agreement on Fisheries and the Marine Environment between the EEC and Iceland [1993] OJ L161/2.

Greenland[628] and Russia.[629] Less honourable are the agreements (in latter incarnation 'fisheries partnership agreements') by which a struggling over-capacity Union fleet is afforded access to the waters of African, Caribbean and Pacific (ACP), and particularly African, countries, a policy traditionally of 'pay, fish and leave'. Rules on authorisation for fishing activities of Union fishing vessels outside Union waters and the access of third country vessels to Union waters are set out in Regulations.[630]

5. Reform

The open-ended price guarantee and commitment to intervention, combined **10.110** with technological advance, the advent of intensive farming techniques and promiscuous use of fertilisers came to produce huge surpluses (the grain, beef and butter mountains, the milk and wine lakes) which could be stored (at vast expense), further processed (e.g., skimmed milk powder, industrial alcohol), given away (free food schemes), dumped on world markets, or destroyed. In all its aspects the CAP entailed extensive environmental costs. Pressure for reform from within, based primarily upon the huge cost of intervention support and export subvention, and from without – criticism within the GATT, subsequently the WTO, of both impenetrable Union barriers and disruption in other markets the result of dumped Union overproduction – became irresistible. Tentative efforts were made in the 1980s, first with the introduction of levies and 'superlevies' on milk production[631] and subsequently with 'stabilisers' put in place for a number of products, penalising increases in production (diminishing support where it exceeded previous 'reference quantities'). But there are three identifiable stages in the process of radical reform:

- the 'MacSharry reforms' (after Mr Ray MacSharry, the Commissioner responsible for agriculture at the time), set in motion in 1992; coincided with the closing negotiations of the Agreement on Agriculture within the Uruguay Round; introduced a gradual reduction in prices, the (very) slow phasing out of target and intervention prices, withdrawal of land from production ('set aside'), compensation to counteract price reduction, and

---

628 Fisheries Partnership Agreement between the EC and the Governments of Denmark and the Home Government of Greenland [2007] OJ L172/4. The Treaties now provide for free trade in fishery products with Greenland subject to 'satisfactory' Union access to Greenland waters; Protocol (No. 34) on Special Arrangements for Greenland.

629 Agreement between the EC and the Russian Federation on Cooperation in Fisheries and the Conservation of the Living Marine Resources in the Baltic Sea [2009] OJ L129/2.

630 Regulation 1006/2008 [2008] OJ L286/33; Regulation 201/2010 [2010] OJ L61/10.

631 Regulation 864/84 [1984] OJ L90/10. Levies remain in milk production, governed now by Regulation 1234/2007 [2007] OJ L299/1, arts 78–84.

direct payment to farmers to encourage best practices; and the 'agri-monetary' financial mechanisms were abolished;[632]

- Agenda 2000: the 1992 reforms were reiterated by the Berlin Summit in 1999 and became part of Agenda 2000.[633] The 1992 reforms were to be 'deepened and widened' with further reductions in price support and increasingly greater reliance upon compensation and direct payments; the concepts of a first pillar (market expenditure, direct aid to producers) and a second pillar (rural development) of the CAP were introduced, rural development measures were brought within a single legal/institutional framework[634] and increased resources allocated to them. To an unprecedented extent powers were devolved from the Community to the local level, so allowing for differentiation of measures in accordance with national or local needs. The background was one of impending accessions and the cost to the CAP of absorbing Polish, and to a lesser extent Hungarian, agriculture;

- significant agreement in 2003 on the next stage of the MacSharry reforms. Progress consisted principally in:

    - a Regulation establishing common rules for direct support schemes for farmers across all sectors ('the Horizontal Regulation').[635] This generally 'decoupled' subsidy from production and established the framework for direct income support for farmers ('the single payment scheme') subject to standards of food safety, environmental protection, animal health and welfare and best agricultural practices (the 'cross compliance system'), the purpose being to afford farmers greater freedom to determine the most effective use of their land whilst at the same time guaranteeing a minimum income.[636] Member States may choose whether single payments are to be made to

---

632 In order to address the problem of a single price system coexisting with fluctuating currencies in the wake of the collapse of the Bretton Woods system, in 1971 the Community introduced a system of 'agri-monetary compensatory payments' whereby sums ('monetary compensatory amounts' (MCAs)) computed upon the basis of nominal representative rates ('green rates') were paid out or levied (depending upon the relative strength of the two currencies) upon agricultural goods subject to a common organisation of the market crossing a frontier. The system was abandoned in 1992 as part of the internal market programme (Regulation 3813/92 [1992] OJ L387/1). With prices now set in euros the problem of currency fluctuation has disappeared, at least in trade between member states within the eurozone; for trade with the 'outs' it is the producer who now bears the exchange risk.

633 Berlin European Council, Conclusions of the Presidency, *Bulletin EU* 3–1999, 7–12.

634 Regulation 1257/1999 [1999] OJ L160/80; see now Regulation 1698/2005 [2005] OJ L2771 and Regulation 1974/2006 [2006] OJ L368/25.

635 Regulation 1782/2003 [2003] OJ L270/1 and implementing Regulation 972/2007 [2007] OJ L216/3; now replaced by Regulation 73/2009 [2009] OJ L30/16.

636 Regulation 1782/2003, Preamble, recital 28.

individual producers (based upon reference periods 2000–02) or upon a regional basis. Decoupling is only partial in some sectors (arable crops, sheepmeat and goatmeat, beef and veal), and single farm payments came on line in the milk sector only in 2008. The Regulation also introduced a number of quality premiums for, e.g., durum wheat, protein crops, biofuel and biomass;

– upgrading support for rural development, encouraging diversification and restructuring of rural areas and economies and transferring further resources from first to second pillar spending.[637] These measures 'accompany' the 1992 reforms and support (a) early retirement, 'agri-environment' and afforestation, and the less favoured areas; and (b) modernisation, investment, training, conversion of land from agriculture to other use;

– significant market reforms in a number of sectors.[638]

All of this is a work in progress.

In 2009 the Commission published a Green Paper on reform of the common fisheries policy,[639] public consultation was intitiated,[640] and a 'reform package' of not much detail put forward in 2011,[641] quickly running aground. **10.111**

6. Financing the CAP

In terms of the budget the CAP has been the Union's most important policy for more than 40 years; in 1984 it accounted for more than 71 per cent of expenditure and it is currently thought to stand at approximately 40 per cent,[642] still the largest single item. The first instrument for financing the CAP was adopted in 1962,[643] creating the European Agricultural Guidance and **10.112**

---

637 Regulation 1783/2003 [2003] OJ L270/70, amending Regulation 1257/1999 (n. 634 above). For detailed rules on implementation see Regulation 817/2004 [2004] OJ L153/30. See also the Council's strategic guidelines for rural development 2007–13 [2006] OJ L55/20.

638 That is, the common organisation of the market in cereals, rice, dried fodder and milk; Regulations 1784–1787/2003 [2003] OJ L270/78, 96, 114 and 121. Olive oil and olives followed in 2004 (Regulation 865/2004 [2004] OJ L161/97), sugar in 2006 (Regulation 318/2006 [2006] OJ L58/1) and wine in 2008 (Regulation 479/2008 [2008] OJ L148/1). At the time of writing a new regime for bananas is still in the pipeline; see MEMO/06/335.

639 COM(2009) 163 final.

640 See Commission Staff Working Document, *Synthesis on the Consultation on the Reform of the CFP*, SEC(2010) 428 final.

641 COM(2011) 417 final.

642 Cases C-92 and 93/09 *Volker und Markus Schecke and anor v Land Hessen* [2010] ECR I-11063, *per* A-G Sharpston at para. 1 of her opinion.

643 Regulation 25/62 [1962] JO 991.

Guarantee Fund (EAGGF, but more commonly known as FEOGA, from *Fonds Européen d'Orientation et de Garantie Agricole*). In 1964 FEOGA was split into two,[644] the guarantee section, concerned essentially with intervention buying and export assistance, and the guidance section, concerned with rural development measures. Fundamental change, the first since the CAP was established, was made in 2005 with a new Regulation on financing the CAP,[645] so that since October 2006 there are two distinct agricultural funds:

- a European Agricultural Guarantee Fund (EAGF, but preferably FEAGA, *Fonds européen agricole de garantie*), concerned primarily with market expenditure (continuing intervention, export refunds), income support for farmers and information and promotion, otherwise the first pillar of the CAP; and
- a European Agricultural Fund for Rural Development (EAFRD, or FEADER, *Fonds européen agricole pour le développement rural*), concerned with second pillar rural development measures.[646]

Both come under the general Union budget.[647] There is now an annual ceiling to FEAGA expenditure set by agreement amongst the three political institutions in accordance with the 2006 interinstitutional agreement on budgetary discipline,[648] and budgetary discipline is written into the Regulation.[649] FEADER spending comes out of this sum but is set by the Commission.[650] FEAGA payments are made monthly by the Commission to national 'paying agencies',[651] FEADER payments made annually to 'the member state'.[652] There are provisions on 'irregularities' and recovery of sums paid out in irregular circumstances[653] and national authorities are obliged systematically to scrutinise both payment and receipt transactions,[654] but there remains a significant amount of fraud in CAP spending, which occupies much of the efforts of the Court of Auditors, of OLAF and, with varying degrees of assiduity, of competent national authorities. Detailed provisions have been laid down by the

---

644   Regulation 17/64 [1964] JO 586.
645   Regulation 1290/2005 [2005] OJ L209/1.
646   *Ibid.* arts 2(1), 3, 4.
647   *Ibid.* art. 2(2).
648   *Ibid.* art. 12(1). On the interinstitutional agreement see [2006] OJ C139/1.
649   *Ibid.* arts 18–21.
650   *Ibid.* art. 12(2).
651   *Ibid.* arts 15–17.
652   *Ibid.* arts 22–9.
653   *Ibid.* arts 32–3.
654   Regulation 485/2008 [2008] OJ L143/1.

Commission.[655] There are also express rules establishing the agrimonetary arrangements for the euro within the CAP.[656]

The Common Fisheries Policy is regulated by separate financial instruments.[657]   **10.113**

---

655   Regulation 1848/2006 [2006] OJ L355/56.
656   Regulation 2799/98 [1998] OJ L349/1 and Regulation 1913/2006 [2006] OJ L365/52.
657   Regulation 861/2006 [2006] OJ L160/1 and Regulation 2003/2006 [2006] OJ L379/49.

11

THE FREE MOVEMENT OF PERSONS
AND SERVICES

A. INTRODUCTION

The essential feature distinguishing a common market from a customs union is **11.01** the free movement within the territory not only of goods but of persons and capital. The economic underpinning is that these are factors of production, movement of which must be fluid in any effectively integrated market. As for persons, the bargain creating the common market may take just such a narrow view, addressing only those who are economically active and ignoring those who are not. This was in fact the approach of the original Treaty. But subsequent developments – legislative intervention, case law of the Court of Justice and Treaty amendment – have progressively elevated the status of persons far beyond that of mere labour or service providers. It is also well to reflect from the outset upon the fundamental nature and the legal and political ramifications of the (joint, reciprocal) undertaking into which the member states have entered, in which context the House of Lords noted in 2004 that the power to admit, exclude and expel aliens was amongst the earliest and most widely recognised powers of the sovereign state.[1]

The provisions of the Treaties on freedom of movement for persons are, as the **11.02** Court of Justice asserts frequently, designed to facilitate the pursuit by Union citizens of occupational activities of all kinds throughout the Union.[2] But the consequent Treaty approach to the relevant two of the four freedoms, persons and services, is not straightforward. Persons and services spans three chapters of Title IV of Part Three of the TFEU, which address 'workers' (articles 45–8), the 'right of establishment' (articles 49–55) and 'services' (articles 56–62). The distinction is confusing since 'free movement of persons' would normally be taken to imply the right of individuals to move from one country to another, whether temporarily or permanently, whilst 'free movement of services' would be taken to imply the more abstract concept of an unrestricted right to provide or receive services in any part of the Union. But that is not how the Treaties approach the matter. The situation of a Union citizen who moves to another member state in order there to pursue an economic activity is governed by the chapter of the TFEU on the free movement of workers, or the chapter on the

---

1 *R (European Roma Rights Centre)* v *Immigration Officer at Prague Airport* [2004] UKHL 55, [2005] 2 AC 1, *per* Lord Bingham at para. 11 of his speech.
2 E.g., Case 143/87 *Stanton and anor* v *Institut national d'assurances sociales pour travailleurs indépendants* [1988] ECR 3877, at para. 13; Case C-415/93 *Union royale belge des sociétés de football association ASBL* v *Bosman* [1995] ECR I-4921, at para. 94.

right of establishment or the chapter on services, depending upon the circumstances – in fact the chapter on services may be activated where there is no physical transfrontier movement of persons at all – and the three are in principle mutually exclusive.[3] Additional complexity came with Maastricht and Union activity in the third pillar sphere of Justice and Home Affairs (JHA), intended in large measure to complement Community rules on free movement of persons; and again with Amsterdam and the break up of JHA matters into part-Community and part-Union competences, hence the introduction in the EC Treaty of a new Title IV addressing 'visas, asylum, immigration and other policies related to the free movement of persons' which overlaps with and has a bearing across all other provisions on the movement of persons. With its creation in 1993 by Maastricht, Union citizenship too has coloured the applicable rules. Probably a function of the growing importance of Union citizenship, the Treaty establishing a Constitution for Europe altered the order in which these provisions appear in the Treaty, giving the free movement of persons and services sequential priority over the free movement of goods;[4] but Lisbon reverted to the previous (and present) construction.

1. Clarification of the distinction

(a) Workers

11.03 The chapter on workers is concerned with enabling individual wage or salary earners (*personnes* or *travailleurs salariés*) to pursue employment within the context of the economic operations of an actual or potential employer. It applies therefore only to individuals (properly so-called) who are (or wish to be) in a contract of employment, and is not concerned with the freedom of employers to conduct their operations. Although not defined in the Treaties or in Union legislation, the term 'worker' has (as it must) a specific Union law meaning.[5] It covers anyone pursuing or wishing to pursue in a member state other than that of his or her nationality effective and genuine employment (that is, under the direction of and remunerated by an employer), even if part time, so long as the work is not so infinitesimal as to be disregarded as such (it is 'real and genuine'), for consideration, even if at a rate lower than a minimum guaranteed wage:[6]

---

3 Case C-55/94 *Gebhard v Consiglio dell'Ordine degli Avvocati e Procuratori di Milano* [1995] ECR I-4165, at para. 20.

4 Treaty establishing a Constitution for Europe, arts III-133–150 (persons and services), arts III-151–155 (goods).

5 Case 75/63 *Unger v Bestuur der Bedrijfsvereniging voor Detailhandel en Ambachten* [1964] ECR 177; Case C-1/97 *Birden v Stadtgemeinde Bremen* [1998] ECR I-7747.

6 Case 53/81 *Levin v Staatssecretaris van Justitie* [1982] ECR 1035; Case 139/85 *Kempf v Staatssecretaris van Justitie* [1986] ECR 1741; Case 66/85 *Lawrie-Blum v Land Baden-Württemberg* [1986] ECR 2121; Case C-444/93 *Megner and Scheffel v Innungskrankenkasse Vorderpfalz* [1995] ECR I-4741; Case C-1/97 *Birden, ibid.*; Case C-188/00 *Kurz v Land Baden-Württemberg* [2002] ECR I-10691.

In order to be treated as a worker, a person must pursue an activity which is genuine and effective, to the exclusion of activities on such a small scale as to be regarded as purely marginal and ancillary. The essential feature of an employment relationship is that for a certain period of time a person performs services for and under the direction of another person in return for which he receives remuneration. By contrast, neither the *sui generis* nature of the employment relationship under national law, nor the level of productivity of the person concerned, the origin of the funds from which the remuneration is paid or the limited amount of the remuneration can have any consequence in regard to whether or not the person is a worker for the purposes of Community law.[7]

Therefore a trainee teacher who gives lessons under the direction and supervision of the school authorities for only a few hours a week in return for remuneration below the salary of a starting teacher is nonetheless a worker,[8] as is any trainee similarly engaged;[9] labours (on top of devotions) in a religious community in exchange for board, lodging and pocket money constitute 'work' for these purposes;[10] odd-jobbing 'interrupted by periods of prolonged unemployment' may be work;[11] and an '*au pair*' will 'as a rule' have the status of a worker.[12] However, paid activity carried out as a means of rehabilitation or reintegration within the framework of a social programme does not qualify the participant as a worker,[13] and board and lodging in a Salvation Army hostel and some pocket money in return for various jobs for about 30 hours a week as part of a personal socio-occupational reintegration programme is (probably) not work.[14] Nor is any economic activity not carried out in the context of a relationship of subordination,[15] which is to be classified as self-employment falling under article 49 (or article 56).[16] The expression 'self-employed worker' is therefore, in this context, an oxymoron,[17] even if let slip by the Court from

---

7 Case C-188/00 *Kurz, ibid.*, at para. 32.
8 Case 66/85 *Lawrie-Blum*, n. 6 above.
9 Case 197/86 *Brown v Secretary of State for Scotland* [1988] ECR 3205; Case C-3/90 *Bernini v Minister van Onderwijs en Wetenschappen* [1992] ECR I-1071. This applies to legal trainees (*Rechtsreferendare*) on a subsistence allowance: Case C-109/04 *Kranemann v Land Nordrhein-Westfalen* [2005] ECR I-2421; Case C-345/08 *Peśla v Justizministerium Mecklenberg-Vorpommern* [2009] ECR I-11677.
10 Case 196/87 *Steymann v Staatssecretaris van Justitie* [1988] ECR 6159.
11 Cases C-482 and 493/01 *Orfanopoulos and ors v Land Baden-Württemberg* [2004] ECR I-5257, at para. 24.
12 Case C-294/06 *R (Payir and ors) v Secretary of State for the Home Department* [2008] ECR I-203, *per* A-G Kokott at para. 22 of her opinion.
13 Case 344/87 *Bettray v Staatssecretaris van Justitie* [1989] ECR 1621.
14 Case C-456/02 *Trojani v Centre public d'aide sociale de Bruxelles* [2004] ECR I-7573.
15 Case C-107/94 *Asscher v Staatssecretaris van Financiën* [1996] ECR I-3089, considering whether a company director works under direction, and so is a worker; also Case C-232/09 *Danosa v LKB Līzings* [2010] ECR I-11405.
16 Case C-268/99 *Jany and ors v Staatssecretaris van Justitie* [2001] ECR I-8615; Cases C-151 and 152/04 *Criminal proceedings against Nadin and ors* [2005] ECR I-11203.
17 According to Sedley LJ the term 'self-employed' is itself an oxymoron: 'It is, first of all, an oxymoron: you cannot in law or in common sense be employed by yourself'; *R (Tilianu) v Secretary of State for Work and Pensions* [2010] EWCA Civ 1397, at para. 8.

time to time.[18] But it means that an individual may, contrary to the general rule, fall under both chapters varying with his activities – if he is, for example, in paid employment in another member state but also a part-time independent contractor there.

11.04 It is important to note that these criteria go to the definition of a worker for purposes of article 45. The term has a different meaning under article 48 (rules on social security)[19] and may have a different meaning under various measures adopted in the field of social policy.[20]

11.05 As the Union rights of a worker are triggered only when he or she seeks to exercise them,[21] the term 'migrant worker' (or migrant Union worker) is sometimes used to describe a worker in a member state other than that of his or her nationality, and so entitled to Treaty rights. The domicile of the employer is irrelevant: a Dutch employee of a Dutch company posted (briefly) in the United Kingdom (the employer itself therefore exercising article 56 rights) is still a migrant worker.[22] That state is in turn the 'host member state', being a member state 'to which a Union citizen moves in order to exercise his/her right of free movement and residence'.[23] A migrant worker who was but is no longer in work now retains the status of a worker in the host member state (but not elsewhere) where he or she:

(a) is temporarily unable to work through illness or accident;

(b) is, after at least one year in work, duly recorded as involuntarily unemployed and has registered as a job seeker;

(c) is, after less than one year in work on a fixed term contract, duly recorded as involuntarily unemployed and has registered as a job seeker, but in this case the status of worker can lapse after six months; or

---

18 Cases C-151 and 152/04 *Nadin*, n. 16 above, at para. 34 ff. and in the *dispositif*, more egregiously, in Case C-306/09 *IB* v *Council of Ministers* [2010] ECR I-10341, A-G Cruz Villalón refers (at para. 16 of his opinion) to 'an independent worker established in Belgium' (*una trabajadora autónoma establecida en Bélgica*) – although he is citing the order for reference, so the source of the imprecision may lie elsewhere. The confusion is avoided in some other languages, e.g., *Arbeiter, Arbeitnehmer* (a worker) and *Selbständiger* (a self-employed) – so, Mr Cruz Villalón's 'independent worker' is rendered '*in Belgien als Selbständige niedergelassen*' in German.

19 So, art. 48 provides for rules on social security benefits for 'employed and self-employed migrant workers' (*zu- und abwandernden Arbeitnehmern und Selbstständigen*); as to which see 11.24–11.29 below.

20 See 14.51 below.

21 See 11.90 below.

22 Case C-18/95 *Terhoeve* v *Inspecteur van de Belastingdienst Particulieren/Ondernemingen buitenland* [1999] ECR I-345; also Case C-385/00 *de Groot* v *Staatssecretaris van Financiën* [2002] ECR I-11819.

23 Directive 2004/38 [2004] OJ L158/77, art. 2(3).

(d) embarks upon a course of vocational training, which, except in the case of involuntary unemployment, must be related to his or her previous employment.[24]

Under previous case law a member state was held entitled to remove a prospective worker from another member state who had failed to find employment within a reasonable period of time,[25] but this no longer obtains in the case of a worker no longer in work, but with at least a year of active employment to his or her credit, whose status presumably now subsists indefinitely so long as he or she remains a job seeker. The duration of the employment is not of itself determinative: a migrant worker does not lose the status of worker after a period of employment lasting only two and a half months[26] or one which was 'brief and inadequate to sustain livelihood' or 'lasted barely more than one month' so long as it was real and genuine.[27] Unavailability on the employment market owing to a term of imprisonment does not as a general rule break the link, provided the worker secures another job within a reasonable time after his or her release.[28]

(b) Establishment and services

A person seeking to exercise economic activity under the Treaties in a capacity **11.06** other than employment must rely upon the chapters on establishment and services which apply to independent, or self-employed, economic operators (*personnes non-salariées*; *Selbständigen*), whether natural or juristic persons, pursuing economic activities in their own names beyond the frontiers of their home member state. They can be distinguished from workers by the fact that they operate independently, in their own name and, more importantly, under their own liability. As between them, the difference between establishment and services is not always clear-cut. Establishment 'allows all types of self-employed activity to be taken up and pursued on the territory of any other Member State, undertakings to be formed and operated, and agencies, branches or subsidiaries

---

24 *Ibid.* art. 7(3); the latter criterion in (d) is codification of earlier case law; see Case 39/86 *Lair* v *Universität Hannover* [1988] ECR 3161; Case C-357/89 *Raulin* v *Minister for Education and Science* [1992] ECR I-1027. The family of a worker falling within (c) enjoys rights of residence more limited than the norm; *ibid.* art. 7(4).

25 Case C-292/89 *R* v *Immigration Appeal Tribunal, ex parte Antonissen* [1991] ECR I-745 ; see n. 99 below and accompanying text.

26 Case C-413/01 *Ninni-Orasche* v *Bundesminister für Wissenschaft, Verkehr und Kunst* [2003] ECR I-13187.

27 Cases C-22 and 23/08 *Vatsouras and Koupatantze* v *Arbeitsgemeinschaft Nürnberg 900* [2009] ECR I-4585, at paras 25, 30. The English in the first phrase is rendered 'brief minor professional activity engaged in [which] did not ensure him a livelihood', which makes an unnecessary meal of the original '*kurze und nicht existenzsichernde geringfügige*'.

28 Case C-340/97 *Nazli and ors* v *Stadt Nürnberg* [2000] ECR I-957, at para. 40; Cases C-482 and 493/01 *Orfanopoulos and ors* v *Land Baden-Württemberg* [2004] ECR I-5257, at para. 50. Of course the conduct which gave rise to the term of imprisonment may in circumstances justify expulsion of the worker; see 11.114–11.116 below. *Quaere* whether prison work is 'work' for purposes of art. 45.

to be set up'.[29] It entails 'the actual pursuit of an economic activity through a fixed establishment in another Member State for an indefinite period'[30] and implies domiciliation (strongly suggested by the German term *Niederlassung*) and permanent or at least durable integration into economic life there. It is therefore entirely possible to be established in two or more member states; companies frequently are so when they exercise their Treaty right to set up agencies, branches or subsidiaries in another member state,[31] and even an individual may in circumstances be established in two member states coterminously.[32]

11.07   Services, by comparison, implies the provision or enjoyment of economic activity in another member state upon a temporary basis. The clearest demarcation between the two is set out in *Gebhard*, involving a question of whether a German *Rechtsanwalt* and member of the Stuttgart Bar who lived and maintained a legal office (*studio legale*) in Milan (and there representing himself to be an *avvocato*) was established or providing services in Italy:

> The concept of establishment within the meaning of the Treaty is … a very broad one, allowing a Community national to participate, on a stable and continuous basis, in the economic life of a Member State other than his State of origin and to profit therefrom, so contributing to economic and social interpenetration within the Community in the sphere of activities as self-employed persons. In contrast, where the provider of services moves to another Member State, the provisions of the chapter on services, in particular the third paragraph of Article [57], envisage that he is to pursue his activity there on a temporary basis …

> [T]he temporary nature of the activities in question has to be determined in the light, not only of the duration of the provision of the service, but also of its regularity, periodicity or continuity. The fact that the provision of services is temporary does not mean that the provider of services within the meaning of the Treaty may not equip himself with some form of infrastructure in the host Member State (including an office, chambers or consulting rooms) in so far as such infrastructure is necessary for the purposes of performing the services in question.[33]

The chapter on services will generally therefore apply where the the provider and the recipient of a service are established, or normally resident, in two

---

29   Case C-55/94 *Gebhard* v *Consiglio dell'Ordine degli Avvocati e Procuratori di Milano* [2005] ECR I-4165, at para. 23.

30   Case C-221/89 *R* v *Secretary of State for Transport, ex parte Factortame* [1991] ECR I-3905, at para. 20.

31   TFEU, art. 49.

32   Case 107/83 *Ordre des avocats au Barreau de Paris* v *Klopp* [1984] ECR 2971; Case C-55/94 *Gebhard*, n. 29 above, at para. 24.

33   Case C-55/94 *Gebhard*, n. 29 above, at paras 25–7.

different member states.[34] In the Treaty scheme services were envisaged to be subordinate to establishment: the provisions of the chapter apply 'only if those relating to the right of establishment do not apply'.[35] They embrace 'in particular' activities of an industrial character, activities of a commercial character, activities of craftsmen and activities of the professions[36] but this is intended to show breadth of application rather than limit it. They must be 'normally provided for remuneration',[37] which means for reasonable consideration,[38] but it does not require that the service be paid for by the recipient.[39]

If services was presumed to be the weak cousin of the triumvirate (or 'the Cinderella freedom'), subsequent developments were to make it otherwise. In particular, **11.08**

(a) the Court recognised that the chapter on services covers not only a right to provide them in another member state, as a reading of article 56 might suggest, but also a right to receive them there[40] – sometimes called passive provision of services. The rights of article 56 are therefore for the benefit of, and may be claimed by, both provider and recipient of services.[41] Combined with a liberal view of what may constitute a 'service' – for example, tourism[42] (abetted now by the exponential growth of low-cost air travel), health care,[43] (private) education,[44] attendance at a sporting event,[45] procuring an abortion[46] or, ironically, insemination[47] – it means that the chapter on services applies to virtually any

---

34 Case 205/84 *Commission v Germany* (Insurance and Co-Insurance) [1986] ECR 3755, at para. 18; Case C-55/94 *Gebhard*, n. 29 above, at para. 22 (both citing art. 56(1) TFEU, which refers (laboriously) to 'nationals of Member States who are established in a State other than that of the person for whom the services are intended').

35 Case C-55/94 *Gebhard*, n. 29 above, at para. 22. This is drawn from art. 57(1) which defines services as services 'insofar as they are not governed by the provisions relating to freedom of movement for goods, capital and persons'.

36 TFEU, art. 57 (ex art. 50 EC).

37 *Ibid.*

38 Case 263/86 *Belgium v Humbel and Edel* [1988] ECR 5365; Case C-157/99 *Geraets-Smits and Peerbooms v Stichting Ziekenfonds VGZ and Stichting CZ Groep Zorgverzekeringen* [2001] ECR I-5473.

39 Case 352/85 *Bond van Adverteerders and ors v Netherlands State* [1988] ECR 2085; Case C-157/99 *Geraets-Smits and Peerbooms, ibid.*; Case C-372/04 *R (Watts) v Bedford Primary Care Trust and anor* [2006] ECR I-4325.

40 Cases 286/82 and 26/83 *Luisi and Carbone v Ministero del Tesoro* [1984] ECR 377; Case 186/87 *Cowan v Trésor Public* [1989] ECR 195.

41 Case C-42/07 *Liga Portuguesa de Futebol Profissional and anor v Departamento de Jogos da Santa Casa da Misericórdia de Lisboa* [2009] ECR I-7633, at para. 51; Case C-153/08 *Commission v Spain* [2009] ECR I-9735, at para. 29.

42 Cases 286/82 and 26/83 *Luisi and Carbone*, n. 40 above; Case 186/87 *Cowan*, n. 40 above.

43 Cases 286/82 and 26/83 *Luisi and Carbone*, n. 40 above; Case C-372/04 *Watts*, n. 39 above.

44 Case C-76/05 *Schwartz and Gootjes-Schwartz v Finanzamt Bergisch Gladbach* [2007] ECR I-6849; see 11.65 below.

45 *Gough and anor v Chief Constable of the Derbyshire Constabulary* [2002] EWCA Civ 351, [2002] QB 1213.

46 Case C-159/90 *Society for the Protection of Unborn Children v Grogan* [1991] ECR I-4685.

47 *R v Human Fertilisation and Embryology Authority, ex parte Blood* [1997] 2 All ER 687 (CA).

situation in which a Union citizen finds him or herself lawfully but temporary present in another member state: 'Article [56] ... covers all nationals of Member States who, independently of other freedoms guaranteed by the Treaty, visit another Member State where they intend or are likely to receive services'.[48]

(b) Moreover, with advances in technology unforeseen and unforeseeable in 1957, there are a host of services provided across frontiers which involve no movement of persons – broadcasting, telecommunications, financial services, internet services, e-commerce for example, put otherwise, 'disembodied services' – to which the chapter applies. It is thus triggered more easily, or less laboriously, than the chapters on workers and establishment in that it requires no movement of persons,[49] merely an intention to deal with a person in another member state. Here the temporal presumption of service provision is set aside: mutual economic relations may be indefinite, even permanent, but are governed nonetheless by the chapter on services if provided (or received) across a frontier. And unlike the normal application of the rules on workers and establishment, it may be relied upon as against the home state by any person (natural or juristic) resident or established there wishing to do so but hindered in that intent;[50] it may extend even to a right of residence for a third country national in the home state of her Union citizen spouse (which is not normally the case)[51] if her childminding and homecare activities there are necessary to enable the spouse effectively to provide services from time to time in another member state.[52] The general rule is that any national legislation which, without objective justification,[53] impedes or makes more difficult a provider of a service from exercising the right to do so infringes article 56,[54] or, put otherwise, it precludes the application of any national rule which has the effect of making the provision of a service between member states more difficult than the provision of services purely within a member state.[55]

---

48   Case 274/96 *Criminal proceedings against Bickel and Franz* [1998] ECR I-7637, at para. 15.
49   E.g., Case C-243/01 *Criminal proceedings against Gambelli and ors* [2003] ECR I-13031; Case C-65/05 *Commission* v *Greece* (Electronic Games) [2006] ECR I-10341.
50   Case C-18/93 *Corsica Ferries Italia* v *Corpo dei Piloti del Porto di Genova* [1994] ECR I-1783; Case C-384/93 *Alpine Investments* v *Minister van Financiën* [1995] ECR I-1141; Case C-405/98 *Konsumentombudsmannen* v *Gourmet International Products* [2001] ECR I-1795.
51   See 11.90–11.91 below.
52   Case C-60/00 *Carpenter* v *Secretary of State for the Home Department* [2001] ECR I-6279, *per* A-G Stix-Hackl; the point was not fully canvassed in the judgment of the Court.
53   See 11.126–11.128 below.
54   Case C-288/89 *Stichting Collectieve Antennevoorziening Gouda* v *Commissariat voor de Media* [1991] ECR I-4007; Case C-381/93 *Commission* v *France* (Maritime Transport) [1994] ECR I-5145.
55   Case C-118/96 *Safir* v *Skattemyndigheten i Dalarnas Län* [1998] ECR I-1897; Case C-157/99 *Geraets-Smits and Peerbooms* v *Stichting Ziekenfonds VGZ and Stichting CZ Groep Zorgverzekeringen* [2001] ECR I-5473; Case C-444/05 *Stamatelaki* v *NPDD Organismos Asfaliseos Eleftheron Epangelmation* [2007] ECR I-3185.

In all events it matters increasingly little in practical terms under which of the **11.09**
three chapters an economic activity falls. The Court of Justice long treated them
as particular aspects of a uniform system and, unless concerned with the specific
rules of a particular chapter, construed them in the same manner. This in fact is
an interpretative tool deployed by the Court across the four freedoms, but the
cohesion of the provisions on free movement of persons and services, being
'human' freedoms as opposed to the 'non-human' freedoms of articles 34
(goods) and 63 (capital), makes it particularly apposite. Latterly, legislation
which gives greater clarity to these freedoms, adopted originally upon a
chapter-by-chapter basis, was threaded into one.[56] Furthermore events have
moved on, so that Union citizens now enjoy rights of movement and residence,
within limits, even if they are not economically active.

2. Beneficiaries

The primary subjects, or beneficiaries, of the Treaty provisions on the free **11.10**
movement of persons and services are:

(a) nationals of a member state as defined by the nationality laws of that state.
     Such persons were long described as 'Community nationals' even though
     that term had no meaning in law; they are now called, variously, Union
     nationals (still meaningless) or Union citizens/citizens of the Union;[57]
(b) for purposes of the chapters on establishment and services only,
     (i)   companies or firms (*sociétés*; *Gesellschaften*) – that is, a company or
           firm constituted under civil or commercial law, a cooperative society
           or another legal person governed by public or private law, unless
           non-profit-making[58] – formed in accordance with the law of a
           member state and having their registered office, central administra-
           tion or principal place of business within the Union;[59] for these
           purposes they are to be 'treated in the same way as natural persons
           who are nationals of Member States';[60] and
     (ii) juristic persons created under Union law.[61]

Third country nationals enjoy very limited rights under Union law *unless*
indirect beneficiaries of 'derivative' (or 'parasitic') rights; for example: those
vested in the family members of Union citizens in the exercise of the latter's

---

56 Directive 2004/38 [2004] OJ L158/77; see 11.11 below.
57 See 8.05–8.09 above.
58 TFEU, art. 54 (ex art. 48 EC).
59 TFEU, arts 54, 62 (ex arts 48, 55 EC).
60 TFEU, art. 54.
61 See 11.60–11.64 below.

Union law rights;[62] third country nationals employed by a Union company or firm posted to another member state in the context of the employer firm providing services there;[63] and a third country national established in one member state, chairman and beneficial owner of a company there, enjoys a right to enter another member state in order to transact the business of the company there.[64] The Treaties authorise the Council to extend the benefits of the chapter on services to third country nationals established in a member state[65] (this being the only mention of third country nationals in the original EEC Treaty)[66] but it has not done so.[67] Advocate-General Léger invited the Court to apply article 56 to a situation in which the recipient of a (passive) service was a Union national but the provider a citizen of a third country resident in another member state, for it would otherwise require the service recipient systematically to obtain and check information concerning the nationality of his trading partners established in another member state, but the Court declined.[68] Non-natural legal persons (companies, primarily) based in third countries bear the same disability as third country citizens and, generally, derive no rights from the Treaties:

> the chapter regulating the freedom to provide services does not contain any provision which enables service providers in non-member countries and established outside the European Union to rely on those provisions … [T]he objective of the latter chapter is to secure the right to provide services for nationals of Member States. Therefore, Article [56] et seq. cannot be relied on by a company established in a non-member country.[69]

Notwithstanding, slow inroads in the direct conferral of rights upon third country nationals, at least natural persons, are finally in train.[70]

---

62 See immediately below.
63 Case C-113/89 *Rush Portuguesa* v *Office National de l'Immigration* [1990] ECR I-1417; Case C-43/93 *Vander Elst* v *Office des Migrations Internationales* [1994] ECR I-3803; Case C-244/04 *Commission* v *Germany* [2006] ECR I-855; Case C-168/04 *Commission* v *Austria* (EU Posting Confirmation) [2006] ECR I-9041; Case C-219/08 *Commission* v *Belgium* [2009] ECR I-9213.
64 *R (Loutchansky and anor)* v *First Secretary of State* [2005] EWHC 1779 (Admin), [2005] 3 CMLR 413.
65 TFEU, art. 56, 2nd para. (ex art. 49, 2nd para. EC).
66 EEC Treaty, art. 59, 2nd para.
67 A Directive to that purpose was proposed by the Commission for the first time in 1999 ([1999] OJ C67/17) but has not been adopted by the Council.
68 Case C-290/04 *FKP Scorpio Konzertproduktionen* v *Finanzamt Hamburg-Eimsbüttel* [2006] ECR I-9461.
69 Case C-452/04 *Fidium Finanz* v *Bundesanstalt für Finanzdienstleistungsaufsicht* [2006] ECR I-9521, at para. 25.
70 See 11.26–11.28 (on social security) and 11.167 below.

The rights of free movement conferred by articles 45, 49 and 56 are (in large **11.11** measure) of themselves directly effective[71] but they have been amplified, 'strengthened' (*renforcé*)[72] or given greater precision by a series of legislative measures adopted over the course of a number of years and, to a lesser extent, by the case law of the Court of Justice. In 2004 the core of these rights was codified, consolidated and further developed in a single instrument applying across all three chapters, Directive 2004/38 on the right of citizens of the Union and their families to move and reside freely within the territory of the member states (the Residency Directive, sometimes the Citizens' Directive, or Citizens' Rights Directive).[73] It is to be interpreted expansively.[74]

Families

Persons entitled to free movement within the Union would (presumably) be less **11.12** inclined to exercise that freedom if they were required to leave their families behind. Union legislation therefore provides that the rules on entry and residence for Union citizens seeking to work, establish themselves or provide or receive a service apply, irrespective of their nationality, also to 'family members', that is:

(a) their spouses: a 'spouse' exists only by virtue of a lawfully contracted marriage.[75] That is a matter to be determined by the relevant law of each member state; another member state cannot question the existence of a marriage, although its recognition is a matter of international private law and it may, in circumstances, rely upon public policy in order to refuse to accord marriage rights for spouses of (lawful) marriages of which it disapproves, for example polygamous or homosexual marriages;[76]

---

71 E.g., Case 41/74 *van Duyn* v *Home Office* [1974] ECR 1337 (art. 45); Case 2/74 *Reyners* v *Belgium* [1974] ECR 631 (art. 49); Case 33/74 *van Binsbergen* v *Bestuur van de Bedrijfsvereniging voor de Metaalnijverheid* [1974] ECR 1299 (art. 56).

72 Case C-256/11 *Dereci and ors* v *Bundesministerium für Inneres*, judgment of 15 November 2011, not yet reported, at para. 50.

73 Directive 2004/38 [2004] OJ L158/77; required to be implemented by 30 April 2006. The Directive repealed its predecessors, Directives 64/221 [1964] JO 850 (expulsion on grounds of public policy, public security or public health); 68/360 [1968] JO L257/13 (abolition of restrictions on movement and residence for workers); 72/194 [1972] JO L121/32 (extending Directive 64/221 to workers remaining in a member state); 73/148 [1973] OJ L172/14 (abolition of restrictions on movement and residence for establishment and services); 75/34 [1975] OJ L14/10 (right to remain after establishment); 75/35 [1975] OJ L14/14 (extending Directive 64/221 to persons coming under Directive 75/34); 90/364 [1990] OJ L180/26 (general right of residence); 90/365 [1990] OJ 180/28 (pensioners' right of residence); and 93/96 [1993] OJ L317/59 (students' right of residence). It left in operation (but amended) the basic Regulation on equal treatment for workers, Regulation 1612/68 [1968] JO L257/2, the latter now consolidated as Regulation 492/2011 [2011] OJ L141/1.

74 Case C-127/08 *Metock and ors* v *Minister for Justice, Equality and Law Reform* [2008] ECR I-6241.

75 Case 59/85 *Netherlands* v *Reed* [1986] ECR 1283. But the status of spouse continues so long as the marriage survives, even if the spouses are separated and divorce proceedings are in progress; Case 267/83 *Diatta* v *Land Berlin* [1985] ECR 567; Case C-370/90 *R* v *Immigration Appeal Tribunal and Singh, ex parte Secretary of State for the Home Department* [1992] ECR I-4265.

76 See 11.113–11.115 below.

(b)   their partners if the product of a registered partnership in a member state and if the host member state recognises a registered partnership as equivalent to marriage;

(c)   their own and their spouses'/partners' direct descendants who are either under 21 years of age or are dependants; and

(d)   dependent direct relatives in the ascending line of both spouses/partners.[77]

Admission and residence of 'other' family members who do not fall within heads (a) to (d) (in UK terms, 'extended family members')[78] must be 'facilitated' (*favorisé; erleichtert*) in accordance with national legislation if they are dependent upon the Union citizen exercising his or her right of entry and residence or there exist serious health grounds which strictly require the latter's personal care.[79] Equally to be facilitated is entry and residence of an (unregistered) partner with whom the Union citizen has a 'durable relationship, duly attested'.[80] A host member state may refuse entry and residence to extended family members and partners only after an 'extensive examination' and with justification.[81] Family members (*sic*) of a Union citizen working or established in another member state have the right, irrespective of nationality, to work there.[82] This applies even in a regulated profession, provided the family member has the requisite qualifications.[83] The Union citizen's children have a right, if resident in the host member state, to its general educational, appenticeship and vocational training programmes under the same conditions as home nationals, and are to be encouraged by it to enable the children to exercise the right under

---

77   Directive 2004/38, art. 2(2).

78   Immigration (European Economic Area) Regulations 2006, SI 2006/1003, reg. 8.

79   Directive 2004/38, art. 3(2)(a). There is no definition of 'facilitated', but it should be read in the light of a preambular direction (recital 6) that, whilst a matter for national law, the relationship with the Union citizen and any other circumstances, such as financial or physical dependence, ought to be taken into consideration. Member states have a wide latitude but are required to subject an application to an 'extensive examination' of the personal circumstances, justify any refusal, and make available judicial review of its decision; Case C-83/11 *Secretary of State for the Home Department* v *Rahman and ors*, judgment of 6 September 2012, not yet reported. For further discussion see *KG (Sri Lanka) and AK (Sri Lanka)* v *Secretary of State for the Home Department* [2008] EWCA Civ 13, [2008] All ER (D) 285.

80   Directive 2004/38 art. 3(2)(b). Prior to this provision a long-term partner was afforded a right (or privilege) of residence only if the host member state extended such right to long-term partners of its own citizens; this was a 'social advantage' (see 11.21 below) to which the Community national was entitled upon an equal footing with home nationals; Case 59/85 *Netherlands* v *Reed*, n. 75 above. Presumably this rule survives, so that where a host member state affords its own nationals such right, entry into and residence in a host member state of a Union citizen's partner must be assured, and not merely facilitated.

81   Directive 2004/38 art. 3(2)(b).

82   *Ibid.* art. 23. This expands upon the previous right under Regulation 1612/68, art. 11 (repealed by Directive 2004/38) which extended only to spouse and children. According to case law, the non-national spouse (or child, presumably) enjoyed a right to work only in that member state in which the Union citizen was employed (Case C-10/05 *Mattern and Cikotic* v *Ministre du Travail et de l'Emploi* [2006] ECR I-3145), and this appears to be reflected in art. 23.

83   Case 131/85 *Gül* v *Regierungspräsident Düsseldorf* [1986] ECR 1573.

the best possible conditions.[84] This is so even where the primary right holder has ceased to exercise his or her Treaty rights and has quit the host member state, in which event, provided that they 'installed' themselves there during a period of the exercise of those rights, the children may stay on (lawfully residing) and complete their education in the host member state, irrespective of whether they have adequate resources to do so.[85] The text of neither Regulation nor Directive extends the right to the spouse's or partner's children, but it may perhaps be inferred from case law.[86]

All these rights may be withheld or withdrawn in the event of abuse of rights or fraud 'such as marriages of convenience'.[87] **11.13**

3. Substantive rights

(a) Right of exit

A Union citizen, and his or her family members if third country nationals, has **11.14** the right to leave the territory of a member state in order to travel to another member state.[88] No exit visa may be required,[89] only a valid identity card or passport,[90] which member states are required to provide in accordance with their laws.[91]

(b) Right of entry and residence

Equally, leave to enter the territory of another member state is to be granted **11.15** upon production of a valid identify card or passport.[92] No further formality may be required of a Union citizen.[93] Their family members nationals of third

---

84 Regulation 492/2011, art. 10.
85 Case C-413/99 *Baumbast and R* v *Secretary of State for the Home Department* [2002] ECR I-7091; Case C-310/08 *London Borough of Harrow* v *Ibrahim and Secretary of State for the Home Department* [2010] ECR I-1065; Case C-480/08 *Teixeira* v *London Borough of Lambeth and Secretary of State for the Home Department* [2010] ECR I-1107. This entails a further (parasitic) right of the primary carer of the child(ren) to reside in the host member state (*Baumbast*; Case C-200/02 *Zhu and Chen* v *Secretary of State for the Home Department* [2004] ECR I-9925), again irrespective of adequate resources and/or comprehensive sickness insurance (*Ibrahim*; *Teixeira*) and notwithstanding neither parent being in work on the date on which the child started in education (*Teixeira*), which survives until the child(ren) reach(es) the age of majority or so long as the care (and residence) of the parent is reasonably required in order to allow the child to pursue and complete his or her education (*Teixeira*). There rights are a reflection of the status of citizen of the Union, as to which see 11.96–11.106 below.
86 Case C-413/99 *Baumbast*, *ibid.*
87 Directive 2004/38, art. 35; Case C-109/01 *Secretary of State for the Home Department* v *Akrich* [2003] ECR I-9607; Case C-285/95 *Kol* v *Land Berlin* [1997] ECR I-7415.
88 Directive 2004/38 art. 4(1); see generally Case C-33/07 *Ministerul Administrației și Internelor – Direcția Generală de Pașapoarte București* v *Jipa* [2008] ECR I-5157.
89 Directive 2004/38 art. 4(2).
90 *Ibid.*
91 *Ibid.* art. 4(3).
92 *Ibid.* art. 5(1).
93 *Ibid.*; Case 157/79 *R* v *Pieck* [1980] ECR 2171.

countries may be required to obtain a visa if the third country is one the nationals of which are required by Union law to have them,[94] but member states are required to grant such persons 'every facility' to obtain the necessary visa[95] and cannot turn them away without affording them every reasonable opportunity to obtain the necessary documentation within a reasonable period of time or show by other means that they are entitled to admission.[96]

11.16 The Treaties provide a migrant worker the right to accept 'offers of employment actually made', to move freely throughout the territory of and to stay (*séjourner, verbleiben*) within the member states for that purpose, and to remain there after employment.[97] Notwithstanding the apparent limitation to entry predicated upon an offer of employment, the Court of Justice recognised that effective access to labour markets would require more, and so extended the provision to a right to enter a member state in order to look for work,[98] even if unemployed and without an offer of work, so long as the intention was genuine. The period for which an intending worker might do so was not defined. The Court said only that it must be a 'reasonable period',[99] generally understood to be a minimum of three months (a time scale which seems likely to have informed Directive 2004/38). The United Kingdom (which allows six months)[100] was held to be entitled to remove a Belgian migrant who had failed to find work during that six-month period (and had been convicted of minor drug offences), unless he could show that he was continuing to look for work and had a genuine chance of becoming engaged.[101] This has now been codified and simplified by Directive 2004/38 which provides Union citizens (and their families) with a right of residence in another member state for a period of up to three months 'without any conditions or any formalities other than the requirement to hold a valid identity card or passport'[102] – although this is without prejudice to any

---

94 Directive 2004/38 art. 5(2). As to the uniform visa requirements see Regulation 539/2001 [2001] OJ L81/1 and n. 998 below and accompanying text.
95 *Ibid.*
96 *Ibid.* art. 5(4).
97 *Ibid.* art. 39(1).
98 See e.g., Case 53/81 *Levin v Staatssecretaris van Justitie* [1982] ECR 1035; Case C-85/96 *Martínez Sala v Freistaat Bayern* [1998] ECR I-2961, at para. 32; Case C-138/02 *Collins v Secretary of State for Work and Pensions* [2004] ECR I-2703.
99 Case C-292/89 *R v Immigration Appeal Tribunal, ex parte Antonissen* [1991] ECR I-745, at para. 16; Case C-344/95 *Commission v Belgium* [1997] ECR I-1035, at paras 16, 17; Case C-138/02 *Collins*, n. 98 above, at para. 37.
100 Immigration Rules, rule 23A. It was proposed at the end of 2007 that this be reduced to three months but no change has been effected.
101 Case C-292/89 *Antonissen*, n. 99 above. Confirmed in Case C-344/95 *Commission v Belgium*, n. 99 above (automatic expulsion after three months impermissible); Case C-138/02 *Collins*, n. 98 above.
102 Directive 2004/38, art. 6(1). Note (n. 94 and accompanying text) that family members nationals of third states may be required to have a visa to gain admission; but the requirement is waived if in possession of a 'residence card of a family member of a European citizen' to which they are entitled after six months residence (art. 10).

more favourable treatment accorded job seekers by virtue of applicable case law.[103] During that period the Union citizen may well seek work but, now, needn't; thereafter he or she (and they), unless able to rely upon some other provision of Union law,[104] may be shown the door unless satisfying the *Antonissen* criteria, now codified in Directive 2004/38, 'for as long as [he or she] can provide evidence that [he or she is] continuing to seek employment and [has] a genuine chance of being engaged'.[105]

Until 1992 a person was required to show an economic nexus with his or her **11.17** movement, falling under one of the three Treaty chapters;[106] if he or she could not, he or she enjoyed no right of entry, let alone residence. But in 1990 three Directives were adopted, providing a right of residence for retired Union nationals ('employees and self-employed persons who have ceased their occupational activity'),[107] a right of residence for students for the duration of their studies[108] and a general right of residence[109] (in each case including also their families) *provided* they had sufficient resources (through, for example, a pension, a student grant, sickness insurance in respect of all risks, simply financial assets) to avoid becoming a burden on the social assistance system of the host member state during their period of residence.[110] For the first time the link of free movement rights with the economically active was broken. This was carried over into Directive 2004/38, so that Union citizens, and their families, have a right of residence of greater than three months in any member state if they:

---

103 Preamble, recital 9.
104 Case C-466/00 *Kaba* v *Secretary of State for the Home Department* (No. 2) [2003] ECR I-2219, at para. 47; Cases C-482 and 493/01 *Orfanopoulos and ors* v *Land Baden-Württemberg* [2004] ECR I-5257, at para. 49.
105 Directive 2004/38, art. 14(4)(b).
106 See e.g., Case 48/75 *Royer* [1976] ECR 497, at para. 31; Case C-363/89 *Roux* v *Belgian State* [1991] ECR 273, at para. 9; Case C-413/99 *Baumbast and R* v *Secretary of State for the Home Department* [2002] ECR I-7091, at para. 81.
107 Directive 90/365 [1990] OJ L180/28. This was a right already enjoyed by a Community national who had worked or been established in another member state and so had (after completing a prescribed period of residence) acquired a permanent right of residence there without further condition (Regulation 1251/70 [1970] JO L142/23 (workers), Directive 75/35 [1975] OJ L14/10 (establishment)), but these measures were repealed in 2006 and replaced with the general provisions of Directive 2004/38. Of course a retired person who works in another member state post-retirement is nonetheless a worker with all the rights that entails; but a person having worked entirely in his home member state, now retired in another with no intention to work there, is not a worker: Case C-520/04 *Turpeinen* [2006] ECR I-10685; Case C-544/07 *Rüffler* v *Dyrektor Izby Skarbowej we Wrocławiu Ośrodek Zamiejscowy w Wałbrzychu* [2009] ECR I-3389.
108 Directive 90/366 [1990] OJ L180/30. The Directive was annulled for incorrect legal base (Case C-295/90 *Parliament* v *Council* [1992] ECR I-4193) and replaced by Directive 93/96 [1993] OJ L317/39. Students are discussed in greater detail at 11.65–11.68 below.
109 Directive 90/364 [1990] OJ L180/26 (the 'Playboy' or 'Layabouts' Directive).
110 Directive 90/365, art. 1(1); Directive 90/364, art. 1(1); Directive 93/96, art. 1.

(a)   are workers or self-employed in the host member state or providing or receiving a service there (so exercising 'traditional' free movement rights); if not,

(b)   they have sufficient resources for themselves and their family so that they do not become a burden on the social assistance system of the host member state during their period of residence and have comprehensive sickness insurance cover (in UK terms, they are 'self-sufficient persons');[111] or

(c)   are students (in futher education or vocational training), duly registered as such, have comprehensive sickness insurance cover and assure the competent national authority (through declaration or other means) that they have sufficient resources for themselves and their family so that they do not become a burden on the social assistance system of the host member state during their period of residence.[112]

Looked at a different way, the Directive articulates a right of residence for up to three months conditional upon possession of nothing other than a valid identity card or passport, the right extended thereafter so long as the Union citizen and his or her family do not become a burden upon the host member state's social assistance system.[113] It follows that a Union citizen lawfully resident in a host member state by virtue of (b) or (c) loses the right, and so may be removed, should his or her means be lost or dissipated and so he or she does become dependent upon social assistance.[114] Even then the Directive refers to an 'unreasonable' burden upon social assistance,[115] provides that removal should not be the 'automatic consequence' of recourse to it[116] and invites the member states to examine whether it is a case of temporary difficulty and to take into account the duration of residence and other personal circumstances in order to determine whether the burden is unreasonable.[117] The uncertainty lapses after five years of lawful residence.[118]

---

111   Immigration (European Economic Area) Regulations 2006, SI 2006/1003, reg. 4(1)(c).
112   Directive 2004/38, art. 7. 'Sufficient resources' may not be a fixed amount but must take into account personal circumstances, and may be no higher than the threshold below which home nationals become eligible for social assistance; art. 8(4). As to students see 11.65–11.68 below.
113   Cases C-424 and 425/10 *Ziolkowski and Szeja* v *Land Berlin*, judgment of 21 December 2011, not yet reported, at para. 39.
114   See e.g., Case C-456/02 *Trojani* v *Centre public d'aide sociale de Bruxelles* [2004] ECR I-7573, at para. 45; *Barnet London Borough Council* v *Ismail and anor* [2006] EWCA 383, [2007] 1 All ER 202.
115   Directive 2004/38, art. 14(1).
116   *Ibid.* art. 14(3).
117   Preamble, recital 16.
118   See n. 131 below and accompanying text.

It is for the Union citizen to show that these criteria are satisfied – that, for **11.18** example, he or she has the Union nationality claimed,[119] that a relationship with his or her partner is 'durable',[120] that, if economically inactive, he or she has the requisite financial resources,[121] or that, if a third country national mother-in-law claiming right of residence in a host member state to which she is entitled if dependent upon her son and his Union citizen spouse there,[122] she is in fact dependent.[123] But in all cases it must be possible to furnish the necessary evidence by any reasonable means, and any penalty imposed for failure to do so must be proportionate. Having entered a host member state the Union citizen (and his or her family) may be required to report his/her/their presence within a reasonable and non-discriminatory period of time,[124] and once (lawfully) resident there he or she (and they) may be required to register with the competent authorities (but no sooner than three months from date of arrival),[125] at which point the Union citizen is entitled to a 'registration certificate' (*attestation d'enregistrement; Anmeldebescheinigung*), issued immediately;[126] his or her family members are also entitled to a registration certificate if themselves Union citizens,[127] if not they are entitled to be issued with a 'residence card of a family member of a Union citizen' within a period of six months, valid for five years or for the envisaged period of residence of the Union citizen if shorter.[128] These documents are not constitutive but declaratory, so that one issued in error gives rise to no rights.[129] Once legally resident for a period of five years (or three years immediately prior to reaching pensionable age if in work for the previous 12 months)[130] a Union citizen and his or her family (if resident lawfully with him or her in the host member state for that period) gain a right, without condition, of permanent residence in the host member state.[131] It is lost only by absence for a period exceeding two

---

119 Case C-215/03 *Oulane* v *Minister voor Vreemdelingenzaken en Integratie* [2005] ECR I-1215.

120 Directive 2004/38, arts 3(2)(b), 8(5)(f).

121 Case C-408/03 *Commission* v *Belgium* [2006] ECR I-2647. A member state may not set a minimum term of residence and require resources for that term; Case C-398/06 *Commission* v *Netherlands* [2008] ECR I-56*.

122 Directive 2004/38, art. 2(2)(d).

123 Case C-1/05 *Jia* v *Migrationsverket* [2007] ECR I-1.

124 Directive 2004/38, art. 5(5); failure to comply may attract only non-discriminatory and proportionate penalties.

125 *Ibid.* art. 8.

126 *Ibid.* art. 8(2).

127 *Ibid.* art. 8(5).

128 *Ibid.* arts 10–11. Member states may (as some do) require non-nationals always to carry their cards, and punish failure to do so, only if they impose equivalent obligations upon home nationals; art. 26.

129 Case C-325/09 *Secretary of State for the Home Department* v *Dias*, judgment of 21 July 2011, not yet reported.

130 Directive 2004/38, arts 17, 18.

131 *Ibid.* art. 16. They are entitled to permanent residence certificates (Union citizens) or cards (third country nationals) attesting to that status (arts 19, 20). 'Permanent residence' is a right new with Directive 2004/38. As the Directive predicates a residence period 'in compliance with the conditions laid down in this Directive' (Preamble, recital 17) rather than 'on the basis of the Directive', it covers residence periods completed (even wholly) prior to the date of effective operation of the Directive (Case C-162/09 *Secretary of State for Work and*

consecutive years.[132] A right of residence in principle covers the whole territory of the host member state; restrictions limiting access to/residence in only part of it may be imposed only where they may be applied also to home nationals.[133] The right of residence of third country national family members is, as always, limited to the member state in which the Union citizen resides.[134] Whilst Directive 2004/38 provides the right of entry and residence to family members 'who accompany or join' the Union citizen in the host member state,[135] the Court has said the right of residence must extend even to (future) family members already there; that is, a third country national in a Union member state, even illegally, acquires a right of residence there upon marriage to a migrant Union citizen, the latter him or herself having taken up residence there.[136]

11.19 Because theirs are parasitic rights, issues of fairness arose as to the fate of family members, themselves either economically inactive or third country nationals, long resident in a host member state but then severed – through, for example, death or separation/annulment/divorce/abandonment – from the prop of the primary right holder upon which they relied. Directive 2004/38 therefore breaks new ground by providing for retention of a right of residence:

(a) for family members who are Union nationals in the event of death or departure of, or divorce, annulment of marriage or termination of registered partnership with, the Union citizen;[137] but this does not lead to a right of permanent residence, which must be earned independently;[138]

Pensions v *Lassal* [2010] ECR I-9217) but only if the conditions set out, in particular those of art. 7(1), were met during that period; Case C-325/09 *Dias*, n. 129 above; Cases C-424 and 425/10 *Ziolkowski and Szeja* v *Land Berlin*, judgment of 21 December 2011, not yet reported. A national of a new member state may count towards the five years a residence period prior to accession (*Ziolkowski and Szeja*); it is not clear if this extends to a right of permanent residence for an individual who has only recently acquired Union citizenship by naturalisation but has nonetheless met the five year lawful/in accordance with the conditions of art. 7(1) residency test in a host member state.

132 Directive 2004/38 art. 16(4).
133 *Ibid.* art. 22; codifying Case 36/75 *Rutili* v *Minister of the Interior* [1975] ECR 1219. In Case C-100/01 *Ministre de l'Intérieur* v *Oteiza Olazabal* [2002] ECR I-10981 the Court suggested a moderation of this view; art. 22 may therefore be an attempt to overrule *Oteiza Olazabal* and reinstate the *Rutili* rule. Yet there is good logic, grounded in proportionality, which might justify a territorial restriction in a given case as a better alternative to outright removal.
134 Case C-291/05 *Minister voor Vreemdelingenzaken en Integratie* v *Eind* [2007] ECR I-10719.
135 Directive 2004/38, arts 3(1), 6(2), 7(2).
136 Case C-127/08 *Metock and ors* v *Minister for Justice, Equality and Law Reform* [2008] ECR I-6241. This reverses previous authority (Case C-109/01 *Secretary of State for the Home Department* v *Akrich* [2003] ECR I-9607) which required lawful residence in another member state prior to entry into the host member state in order for a third country national to gain a right of residence there. In the event of unlawful entry prior to marriage the member state may impose 'other penalties' but removal is disproportionate; *Metock*, at para. 97.
137 Directive 2004/38, arts 12(1) and 13(1).
138 *Ibid.* arts 12(1), 2nd para. and 13(1), 2nd para.

(b) for family members who are not Union nationals who:

    (i) in the event of death of the Union citizen have resided as family members in the host member state for at least a year and are themselves workers or self-employed or have resources sufficient not to become a burden on social assistance;[139]

    (ii) in the event of departure of the Union citizen are children or the parent with custody of the children who are enrolled at an educational establishment, until completion of studies;[140] or

    (iii) in the event of divorce from, annulment of marriage or termination of registered partnership with the Union citizen have, prior to the initiation of such proceedings, been married or in a registered partnership for at least three years, including one year in the host member state, or have agreed custody of the Union citizen's children or right of access to a minor child in the host member state, and are themselves workers or self-employed or have resources sufficient not to become a burden on social assistance.[141]

These provisions are stated to pay due regard to family life and human dignity,[142] protection of which is recognised to be a general principle of Union law.[143]

(c) Equal treatment

The Treaties lay down a general prohibition against discrimination based upon nationality in article 18 TFEU, which has greatest resonance for the free movement of persons and services and has been accorded extensive reach by the Court of Justice:

      11.20

> In so far as it prohibits 'any discrimination on grounds of nationality', Article [18] of the Treaty requires persons in a situation governed by Community law and nationals of the Member State concerned to be treated absolutely equally.[144]

In fact it doesn't go quite so far as absolute equality, otherwise member states would be barred from removing Union citizens in any circumstances owing to the prohibition in international law against expulsion of the state's own

---

139   *Ibid.* art. 12(2).

140   *Ibid.* art. 12(3). This is codification of earlier case law, Case C-413/99 *Baumbast and R* v *Secretary of State for the Home Department* [2002] ECR I-7091.

141   Directive 2004/38 art. 13(2).

142   *Ibid.* Preamble, recital 15.

143   See 6.122 above.

144   Case C-323/95 *Hayes and Hayes* v *Kronenberger* [1997] ECR I-1711, at para. 18.

citizens.[145] The principle is amplified – it is 'given specific expression and effect'[146] – in each of the chapters on workers, establishment and services,[147] which largely displace the application of article 18[148] and seek to ensure equal treatment of all Union nationals (including, for establishment and services, companies and firms incorporated in a member state) wherever they may be within the Union and whatever the nature of the economic activity they wish to pursue.

11.21 A 1968 Regulation,[149] re-adopted in consolidated form in 2011,[150] 'on the free movement of workers within the Union' seeks to guarantee to migrant workers the right to take up employment with the same priority and employment law protection as home nationals. Thus any form of limitation of employment to home nationals, recruitment procedures designed specifically for them, restrictive advertising and eligibility limited to conditions which other Union nationals cannot reasonably meet are prohibited,[151] and any clause of a collective agreement which lays down or authorises discriminatory treatment is null and void.[152] The prohibition applies not only to direct discrimination but also to rules and practices which produce a similar effect (i.e., covert or indirect discrimination).[153] The only exceptions are language requirements (which are likely to exert an indirectly discriminatory effect) where, given the nature of the employment, there is objective justification for them;[154] and discriminatory tax

---

145 This is a rule originally not of customary international law but of Convention (e.g., UN Covenant on Civil and Political Rights, 999 UNTS 171, art. 12(4); ECHR, Protocol 4, art. 3) which may now have hardened into customary law. It is recognised by the Court of Justice as 'a principle of international law … which European Union law cannot be assumed to disregard'; Case 11/74 *van Duyn* v *Home Office* [1974] ECR 1337, at para. 22 (substituting 'EEC Treaty' for 'European Union law'); Case C-174/96 *Pereira Roque* v *His Excellency the Lieutenant Governor of Jersey* [1998] ECR I-4607, at para. 38 ('EC Treaty'); Case C-434/09 *McCarthy* v *Secretary of State for the Home Department*, judgment of 5 May 2011, not yet reported, at para. 29.

146 Case C-341/05 *Laval un partneri* v *Svenska Byggnadsarbetareförbundet and ors* (Vaxholm) [2007] ECR I-11767, at para. 55.

147 TFEU, art. 45(2) (workers); art. 49, as interpreted in, e.g., Case 2/74 *Reyners* v *Belgian State* [1974] ECR 631 and Case C-221/89 *R* v *Secretary of State for Transport, ex parte Factortame and ors* [1991] ECR I-3905 (establishment); art. 56, as interpreted in, e.g., Case C-22/98 *Criminal proceedings against Becu and ors* [1999] ECR I-5665 and Case C-55/98 *Skatteministeriet* v *Vestergaard* [1999] ECR I-7641 (services).

148 Article 18 has residual application to persons insofar as their situation is not covered by any specific subsequent provision; see 8.03 above.

149 Regulation 1612/68 [1968] JO L257/2.

150 Regulation 492/2011 [2011] OJ L141/1.

151 Regulation 492/2011, arts 3–4.

152 *Ibid.* art. 7(4); see e.g., Case C-15/96 *Schöning-Kougebetopoulou* v *Freie und Hansestadt Hamburg* [1998] ECR I-47.

153 E.g., Case 152/73 *Sotgiu* v *Deutsche Bundespost* [1974] ECR 153; Case C-209/03 *R (Bidar)* v *London Borough of Ealing and anor* [2005] ECR I-2119; Case C-147/03 *Commission* v *Austria* [2005] ECR I-5969. But neither direct nor indirect discrimination has been properly defined by the Court of Justice; see n. 714 above and accompanying text.

154 Regulation 492/2011, art. 3(1); see Case 379/87 *Groener* v *Minister for Education and anor* [1989] ECR 3967; Case C-281/98 *Angonese* v *Cassa di Risparmio di Bolzano* [2000] ECR I-4139.

rules for which there is, again, objective justification.[155] There is a machinery for vacancy clearing and a European Coordination Office to assist.[156] Once in employment (but not before), a migrant worker gains an additional series of rights ('section 2 rights'):[157] he has, on the same footing as home nationals, a right to vocational training,[158] to trade union membership and activity[159] and to housing[160] and social and tax advantages.[161] 'Social advantages' has been read particularly broadly by the Court: it cannot be made subject to completion of a given period of employment[162] and it is not restricted to such fields obviously and directly related to employment as a guaranteed minimum income,[163] a job seeker's allowance[164] or a 'tideover allowance' (*allocation d'attente*) to assist in obtaining first employment following completion of secondary study;[165] rather it extends to

> advantages ... which, whether or not linked to a contract of employment, are generally granted to national workers primarily because of their objective status as workers or by virtue of the mere fact of their residence on the national territory,[166]

and so includes, for example, study maintenance grants (for both the worker[167] and his or her children), saver cards for railway travel for large families,[168] an interest free 'childbirth loan' (*Geburtsdarlehen*) to encourage the national birth rate[169] and a child-raising allowance (*Erziehungsgeld*),[170] a right to elect the language of proceedings when answering criminal charges for brawling after a

---

155 See 11.132–11.138 below.
156 Regulation 492/2011, ch. I, section 2.
157 Regulation 492/2011, ch. I, section 1 ('eligibility for employment') is concerned with equal treatment in access to the labour market and applies to job seekers; section 2 ('employment and equality of treatment') is concerned largely with equal treatment of workers and associated rights, and applies only to those in work (Case C-138/02 *Collins* v *Secretary of State for Work and Pensions* [2004] ECR I-2703) or those previously in work who retain the status of a worker.
158 Regulation 492/2011, art. 7(3).
159 *Ibid.* art. 8; see e.g., Case C-213/90 *Association de Soutien aux Travailleurs Immigrés* v *Chambre des Employés Privés* [1991] ECR I-3507.
160 *Ibid.* art. 9.
161 *Ibid.* art. 7(2).
162 Case 157/84 *Frascogna* v *Caisse des dépôts et consignations* [1985] ECR 1739.
163 Case C-299/01 *Commission* v *Luxembourg* [2002] ECR I-5899.
164 Case C-138/02 *Collins* v *Secretary of State for Work and Pensions* [2004] ECR I-2703; Cases C-22 and 23/08 *Vatsouras and Koupatantze* v *Arbeitsgemeinschaft Nürnberg 900* [2009] ECR I-4585.
165 Case C-224/98 *D'Hoop* v *Office national de l'emploi* [2002] ECR I-6191.
166 Case 207/78 *Ministère public* v *Even and anor* [1979] ECR 2019, at para. 22.
167 Case 39/86 *Lair* v *Universität Hannover* [1988] ECR 3161. This presupposes study coterminous with work or the student having prior status as a worker. See 11.67–11.68 below.
168 Case 32/75 *Cristini* v *Société nationale des chemins de fer français* [1975] ECR 1085.
169 Case 65/81 *Reina* v *Landeskreditbank Baden-Württemberg* [1982] ECR 33.
170 Case C-212/05 *Hartmann* v *Freistaat Bayern* [2007] ECR I-6303.

pub crawl[171] and a right of residence for a worker's non-Union unmarried (and unregistered) partner.[172]

Notwithstanding the limitations of section 2 rights to existing employment, the Court found that, as a matter of article 45(2) TFEU, an ex-worker who was (but is no longer) in employment of such short duration as to deprive him of the status of worker, is nevertheless entitled to financial benefits intended to facilitate access to employment (that is, a job seeker's allowance) so long as he or she can show a 'real link' with the labour market of the host member state;[173] the existence of a real link is to be determined 'in particular' by establishing that he or she has, for a reasonable period, in fact genuinely sought work there[174] – a criterion which, in logic, may be satisfied even without a previous period of employment.

11.22 The right of equal treatment does not, of course, extend to a right of entry and residence for Union nationals in a third country for these are beyond Union authority to grant, but a migrant worker enjoys various rights in employment (primarily prohibition of discrimination in contract or related terms) even where the work is carried out partly[175] or wholly[176] abroad, so long as the bond of employment is formed within the Union and is governed by the law of a member state.

11.23 All of these developments were overtaken in a general cutting of the Gordian knot in Directive 2004/38:

> Subject to such specific provisions as are expressly provided for in the Treaty and secondary law, all Union citizens residing on the basis of this Directive in the territory of the host Member State shall enjoy equal treatment with the national of that Member State within the scope of the Treaty.[177]

It extends this benefit to family members not Union citizens if resident or permanently resident.[178]

---

171   Case 137/84 *Ministère public* v *Mutsch* [1985] ECR 2681.
172   Case 59/85 *Netherlands* v *Reed* [1986] ECR 1283.
173   Cases C-22 and 23/08 *Vatsouras and Koupatantze* v *Arbeitsgemeinschaft Nürnberg 900* [2009] ECR I-4585, at para. 38.
174   at para. 39.
175   Case 36/74 *Walrave and Koch* v *Association Union cycliste internationale and ors* [1974] ECR 1405.
176   Case C-214/94 *Boukhalfa* v *Bundesrepublik Deutschland* [1996] ECR I-2253.
177   Directive 2004/38, art. 24(1). The exception is entitlement to social assistance during the first three months of residence and to a study maintenance grant prior to acquisition of a right of permanent residence; art. 24(2).
178   *Ibid.*

4. Social security

Persons entitled to free movement within the Union would be disinclined to **11.24** exercise that freedom if by so doing they were to jeopardise any accrued entitlements to social security benefits – the most obvious example being pension rights. The TFEU therefore provides authority for the adoption of 'such measures in the field of social security as are necessary to provide freedom of movement for workers' and 'to secure for employed and self-employed migrant workers [*sic*] and their dependants' access to social security protection.[179] In 1971 the Council therefore adopted Regulation 1408/71 'on the application of social security schemes to employed persons, to self-employed persons and to members of their families moving within the Union'[180] in order to coordinate (but not harmonise)[181] the various existing national social security schemes so as to ease the transferability of benefit entitlement for Union nationals exercising free movement rights.

In 2004 the Parliament and Council adopted a new Regulation 'on the **11.25** coordination of social security systems',[182] the purpose being to retire Regulation 1408/71 and consolidate, simplify and clarify the rules as 'essential to achieve the aims of the free movement of persons';[183] it constitutes now the new reference measure (or 'the basic Regulation')[184] in the field. It does not differ substantially from Regulation 1408/71 save that added were paternity[185] and 'pre-retirement'[186] benefits. Regulation 883/2004 came into operation with the entry into force of its implementing Regulation[187] in May 2010,[188] save that Regulation 1408/71 continues to govern the social security rights of migrant workers from and in Greenland, and all relevant agreements with EEA member states and Switzerland until they are replaced.[189]

Regulation 883/2004 covers (a) employed or self-employed individuals who are **11.26** or have been subject to the social security legislation of one or more member

---

179 TFEU, art. 48 (ex art. 42 EC).
180 Regulation 1408/71 [1971] JO L149/1; implemented by Regulation 574/72 [1972] JO L74/1. Both were amended hundreds of times, and so were updated and consolidated from time to time, most recently in Regulation 118/97 [1997] OJ L28/1, Annex A.
181 Case C-211/08 *Commission* v *Spain* [2010] ECR I-5267, at para. 61.
182 Regulation 883/2004 [2004] OJ L166/1. It too is subject to frequent change, so it may be safest to consult the online ('though unofficial) version.
183 Preamble, 3rd recital.
184 Regulation 987/2009 [2009] OJ L284/1, art. 1(1)(a).
185 Regulation 883/2004, art. 3(1)(b).
186 *Ibid.* art. 3(1)(i); defined in art. 1(x).
187 *Ibid.* art. 91; Regulation 987/2009, n. 184 above.
188 Regulation 987/2009, art. 97.
189 Regulation 883/2004, art. 90; Regulation 987/2009, art. 96.

states and who are Union nationals, stateless or refugees residing in a member state, and their families and survivors; and (b) survivors of employed or self-employed individuals who have been subject to the legislation of one or more member states irrespective of the latters' nationality but the survivors being Union nationals, stateless or refugees residing in a member state.[190] It has been extended to apply to third country nationals (lawfully) resident in a member state who can show personal circumstances which are not confined in all respects within a single member state.[191] Employment and self-employment are defined not by reference to these concepts as understood by articles 45, 49 or 56 TFEU but in terms of activities or equivalent treated as such for purposes of the social security legislation of the member state in which it takes place.[192] 'Families' are defined not in terms of Regulation 2004/38 but so as to cover any person defined, recognised or designated a member of the family or of the household by the applicable national legislation under which benefits are provided, as defined by that legislation.[193]

11.27 Regulation 883/2004 applies to all legislation dealing with:

(a)   sickness benefits;
(b)   maternity and equivalent paternity benefits;
(c)   invalidity benefits;
(d)   old-age benefits;
(e)   survivors' benefits;
(f)   benefits in respect of accidents at work and occupational diseases;
(g)   death grants;
(h)   unemployment benefits;
(i)   pre-retirement benefits;
(j)   family benefits;
(k)   all general and special social security schemes, whether contributory or non-contributory, and schemes concerning employers' (or shipowers') liability in respect of the benefits listed in (a) to (j); and
(l)   special non-contributory cash benefits which are provided under legislation which, because of its personal scope, objectives and/or conditions for entitlement has characteristics both of the social security legislation in (a)

---

190   Regulation 883/2004, art. 2.
191   Regulation 1231/2010 [2010] OJ L344/1. No rights accrue from circumstances prior to the entry into force of the Regulation's predecessor (Regulation 859/2003 [2003] OJ L124/1), that is 1 June 2003.
192   Regulation 883/2004, art. 1(a), (b).
193   *Ibid.* art. 1(i).

to (j) and of social assistance.[194] It does not apply to medical or social assistance or to benefit schemes for victims of war or its consequences.[195]

The general scheme of the Regulation is that an individual to whom it applies is **11.28** made subject to the legislation of one member state only (the 'competent state'),[196] rules for the determination of which are set out.[197] Normally it is the member state in which he or she is employed or carries out self-employed activity, irrespective of where he or she resides or the seat of his or her employer,[198] with special rules for persons employed in one member state and self-employed in another, posted workers, civil servants, diplomats and mariners. Affiliation is therefore quite independent of nationality. Subject to any special provisions, he or she (and they) is subject to the same obligations and enjoys the same benefits as home nationals ('equality of treatment').[199] Generally entitlement to benefits accrued anywhere within the Union is 'aggregated', so that affiliation in another member state must be taken into account in the disbursement of benefits by the competent institution.[200] Some benefits (e.g., pensions)[201] are 'apportioned' so that a competent institution bears only a share of the financial burden, in others (e.g., unemployment benefits)[202] (part) reimbursement may be claimed from a previous competent state. There may be a time limit to entitlement (e.g., to unemployment benefits, limited to three months).[203] Detailed (and complex) rules for each category ('chapter') of benefit are provided.[204] There are provisions on overlapping of benefits[205] but generally both the Regulation and relevant national law are to be interpreted in such a way as to maximise the entitlement of claimants.[206] Not surprisingly there is a vast case law on it.

Social security legislation post-Lisbon is by ordinary procedure, save that a **11.29** member state which takes the view that a proposal would affect important aspects of its social security system, including scope, cost and financial structure

---

194 *Ibid.* art. 3.
195 *Ibid.* art. 3(5).
196 *Ibid.* art. 11(1).
197 *Ibid.* arts 11–16.
198 *Ibid.* art. 11(3).
199 *Ibid.* art. 4.
200 *Ibid.* art. 6.
201 *Ibid.* art. 52.
202 *Ibid.* art. 65(6).
203 *Ibid.* art. 64(1)(c).
204 *Ibid.* arts 17–70.
205 *Ibid.* art. 10 and detailed provisions in some chapters.
206 See e.g., Case 7/75 *Mr and Mrs F* v *Belgium* [1975] ECR 679; Case 24/75 *Petroni* v *Office nationale des pensions pour travailleurs salariés* [1975] ECR 1149; Case C-165/91 *van Munster* v *Rijksdienst voor Pensioenen* [1994] ECR I-4661.

and balance, may by 'declaring' that fact cause it to be referred to the European Council, which may, by consensus,[207] refer it back to the Council, the ordinary procedure re-established by that act; or do nothing or request the Commission to submit a new proposal, in either case the original proposal dying.[208]

B. ESTABLISHMENT AND SERVICES: SPECIFIC ISSUES

11.30   It will be observed that the guarantee of equal treatment, secured originally for workers in the detailed provision of Regulation 1612/68[209] (now Regulation 492/2011)[210] applies now to all those exercising rights of residence on the basis of Directive 2004/38,[211] and therefore both to workers and to the self-employed. But equal treatment for those exercising rights of establishment or providing (but not receiving) services in access to those activities is a more complex question. At the outset it was presumed that both rights would require substantial legislative intervention in order to be made effective. The Treaty plan was:

(1)   the prohibition of any new restrictions on the right of establishment of, or provision of services by, nationals of other member states ('the stand-still');[212]

(2)   the abolition of any restriction on the ground of nationality by the end of the transitional period and the prohibition of any such restriction after that date;[213]

(3)   the implementation of 'General Programmes' for the abolition of (further) existing restrictions on the freedom of establishment and the freedom to provide services within the Union;[214] and

(4)   the adoption of Directives '[i]n order to make it easier for persons to take up and pursue activities as self-employed persons'.[215]

---

207   See Declaration (No. 23) on the second paragraph of Article 48 of the TFEU.
208   TFEU, art. 48, 2nd para.
209   Regulation 1612/68 [1968] JO L257/2.
210   Regulation 492/2011 [2011] OJ L141/1; see n. 73 above.
211   Directive 2004/38, art. 24(1).
212   EEC Treaty, arts 53 (establishment) and 62 (services); repealed by the Treaty of Amsterdam.
213   *Ibid.* art. 52 (as interpreted in Case 2/74 *Reyners* v *Belgian State* [1974] ECR 631) (establishment); arts 59 (as interpreted in Case 33/74 *van Binsbergen* v *Bestuur van de Bedrijfsvereniging voor de Mataalnijverheid* [1974] ECR 1299) and 65 (services).
214   EEC Treaty, arts 54 (establishment) and 63 (services). Programmes were adopted in 1961; see General Programme for the abolition of restrictions on the freedom of establishment [1962] JO 36; General Programme for the abolition of restrictions on freedom of services [1962] JO 32.
215   EEC Treaty, arts 57 (establishment) and 66 (services).

It will be observed that key to both articles 49 and 56 is the abolition/prohibition of 'restrictions', interpreted subsequently by the Court of Justice to cover all measures which prohibit, impede or render less attractive the freedom of establishment or the freedom to provide services.[216] Phases (1) and (2) related solely to the prohibition and removal of restrictions which amount, directly or indirectly, to restrictions on grounds of nationality. The relevant provisions are of themselves (from the end of the transition period) directly effective.[217] Phases (3) and (4) required the institutions to act. Phase (3), as the language of article 54 EEC made clear, is concerned with the *abolition* of restrictions, whilst phase (4) is concerned not so much with abolition of restrictions as with positive measures to secure mutual recognition and coordination of the national regulatory regimes. The Treaties do not call for or require the creation of a market for professional or other services which is 'free' in the sense of being unregulated. Nor are they a manifesto for deregulation. Some of the measures adopted may have that effect, but that is in part a matter of political choice, and in part a consequence of the developed rules on competition which complement the rules on the internal market. In the event, some of it became unnecessary because of the manner in which the Court of Justice has interpreted the breadth of articles 49 and 56, splicing to them principles developed in the free movement of goods.

1. Regulation of self-employment

The two major barriers to the free movement of a self-employed person are (a) admission to and (b) regulation and supervision of the economic activity he or she wishes to pursue.[218] First, there are frequently qualifications which a person must hold in order to be admitted to a regulated profession or trade – 'regulated' here meaning governed by law, regulation or administrative provision such that an activity is expressly reserved to those who fulfil certain conditions and access to it barred to those who do not.[219] It applies not only to the (obvious) higher professions but to *any* trade or activity for which a qualification is legally

11.31

---

216 Case C-55/94 *Gebhard* v *Consiglio dell'Ordine degli Avvocati e Procuratori di Milano* [2005] ECR I-4165, at para. 37; Case C-442/02 *CaixaBank France* v *Ministère de l'Économie, des Finances et de l'Industrie* [2004] ECR I-8961, at para. 11; Case C-465/05 *Commission* v *Italy* [2007] ECR I-11091, at para. 17; Case C-389/05 *Commission* v *France* [2008] ECR I-1057, at para. 52.

217 Case 6/64 *Costa* v *ENEL* [1964] ECR 585; Case 2/74 *Reyners*, n. 213 above.

218 The issue may arise also in the context of workers: a migrant worker may require professional or other qualifications – many practising doctors are, for example, employees of a national health service – yet fall for Treaty consideration nonetheless under art. 45. But it adheres most commonly to the self-employed.

219 Case C-164/94 *Aranitis* v *Land Berlin* [1996] ECR I-135; Case C-285/01 *Burbaud* v *Ministre de l'Emploi et de la Solidarité* [2003] ECR I-8219; Case C-586/08 *Rubino* v *Ministero dell'Università e della Ricerca* [2009] ECR I-12013.

required – extending, for example, to football trainers in France,[220] tourist guides in France,[221] Italy[222] and Greece,[223] photographers in Austria,[224] ski monitors (*maestri di sci*) in Italy,[225] snowboarding instructors in France[226] and operators of hot air balloons in Austria.[227] It is a significant impediment to the right of establishment and the freedom to provide (although not receive) services, for qualifications required in one member state permitting access to a given trade or profession are likely to be different, sometimes very significantly so, to those obtained in another. The problem is compounded by the fact that the lines of demarcation between different trades and professions in the member states are not always the same.[228] Second, trades and professions and standards of conduct therein are commonly regulated by a public or semi-public authority (the 'competent authority') for the general good – normally called 'prudential supervision'. This too has the effect of impeding free movement, not simply in the regulation itself and a requirement of authorisation (which equivalent rule is normally not tolerated in the free movement of goods) but in the fact that standards vary from member state to member state, from very strict to non-existent, and are not always mutually compatible. In addition the means of exerting authority may vary as between establishment and services: the Union national establishing him or herself in another member state presumptively submits to the regulation and discipline of the competent authority in the host member state, but the provider of services *ex hypothesi* does not. To sum up,

> the taking-up and pursuit of certain self-employed activities may be conditional on complying with certain provisions laid down by law, regulation or administrative action justified by the general good, such as rules relating to organization, qualifications, professional ethics, supervision and liability. Such provisions may stipulate in particular that pursuit of a particular activity is restricted to holders of a diploma, certificate or other evidence of formal qualifications, to persons belonging to a professional body or to persons subject to particular rules or supervision, as the case may be. They may also lay down the conditions for the use of professional titles.[229]

---

220 Case 222/86 *Union nationale des entraîneurs et cadres techniques professionnels du football (Unectef) v Heylens and ors* [1987] ECR 4097.
221 Case C-154/89 *Commission v France* [1991] ECR I-659.
222 Case C-180/89 *Commission v Italy* [1991] ECR I-709.
223 Case C-198/89 *Commission v Greece* [1991] ECR I-727.
224 Case C-184/03 *Fröschl v Republik Österreich*, order of 1 April 2004, unreported.
225 Case C-142/01 *Commission v Italy* [2002] ECR I-4541.
226 Case C-200/08 *Commission v France*, removed from the register; opinion of A-G Sharpston delivered 16 July 2009.
227 Case C-382/08 *Neukirchinger v Bezirkshautpmannschaft Grieskirchen* [2011] ECR I-139.
228 See 11.43 below.
229 Case C-55/94 *Gebhard v Consiglio dell'Ordine degli Avvocati e Procuratori di Milano* [2005] ECR I-4165, at para. 35.

There is an inbuilt imbalance, for some member states will regulate a given **11.32** trade or profession, others will not. In cases where an activity is unregulated and imposes no burdens upon the practitioner, the Union migrant encounters no let or hindrance:

> In the event that the specific activities in question are not subject to any rules in the host State, so that a national of that Member State does not have to have any specific qualification in order to pursue them, a national of any other Member State is entitled to establish himself on the territory of the first State and pursue those activities there.[230]

As a general rule the requirement (and rigour) of qualifications protects the consumer of services in the member state(s) of highest standards. As a corollary advantage, individuals qualified there will enjoy maximum free movement elsewhither, but the freedom unreciprocated. And the concern of these member states in the face of Union incursion is always a dilution of the standards to which they adhere (again, the deregulatory spiral or the race to the bottom).

One method of addressing the problem is legislative harmonisation of qualifi- **11.33** cations. In the early days the Community pursued this route, the Council adopting normally by (combined) authority of articles 49 (for workers), 57 (establishment) and 66 (services) EEC Directives in a number of sectors harmonising, or setting minimum standards to, national rules on educational or professional qualifications, so enabling a person duly qualified in one member state to work, establish him or herself or provide a service in a regulated activity in any other member state. These early 'coordination' and/or 'mutual recognition' Directives covered various trades (for example, the wholesale trade,[231] retail trade,[232] mining and quarrying,[233] and horticulture[234] and the electricity, gas, water and sanitary sectors)[235] and a number of professions (physicians,[236] veterinarians,[237] dentists,[238] general care nurses,[239] midwives,[240] pharmacists[241] and architects).[242] The legal professions proved particularly problematic, not

---

230 C-55/94 *Gebhard, ibid.* at para. 34.
231 Directive 64/223 [1964] JO 863.
232 Directive 68/363 [1968] JO L260/1.
233 Directive 64/428 [1964] JO 1871.
234 Directive 65/1 [1965] JO 1.
235 Directive 66/162 [1966] JO 584.
236 Directives 75/362 and 75/363 [1975] OJ L167/1, 14; Directive 93/16 [1993] OJ L165/1.
237 Directives 78/1026 and 78/1027 [1978] OJ L362/1, 7.
238 Directives 78/686 and 78/687 [1978] OJ L233/1, 10.
239 Directives 77/452 and 77/453 [1977] OJ L176/1, 8.
240 Directives 80/154 and 80/155 [1980] OJ L33/1, 8.
241 Directives 85/432 and 85/433 [1985] OJ L253/34, 37.
242 Directive 85/384 [1985] OJ L223/15.

surprisingly as they often differ significantly, in terms of supervision if not more, even within the confines of a single member state; the best that could be achieved was the Lawyers' Services Directive (1977),[243] providing lawyers qualified in one member state with a right to represent a client in, and a right of audience in the courts of, another member state but within tightly controlled limits, and in no circumstances extending beyond the temporary nature of service provision. The free movement of notaries and judges is not even seriously contemplated. There may also be an issue of ancillary or secondary qualification – whether, for example, an individual successfully established in a host member state as, say, a plumber is entitled to have his home driving licence recognised there, and whether this varies with whether he requires (or merely chooses) to drive as part of his business operations or wishes merely to drive for pleasure or other personal purposes which have no connection with his professional activities.[244] The same could be said of a tax disc, or even a television licence, with still some months to run on them.

11.34 This process of sectoral harmonisation proved in many cases to be excessively time-consuming – the Architects' Directive, a fairly straightforward matter, was 18 years in the making – and, in the more difficult sectors in which national traditions vary widely, impossible. The Court of Justice had in the meanwhile identified and developed a principle of 'equivalence' of qualifications.[245] It means that the member states still retain the authority to regulate qualifications and professional or academic titles,[246] but that, even absent harmonisation or coordinated standards – for it is a right stemming directly from article 49[247] (or

---

243   Directive 77/249 [1977] OJ L78/17.

244   See e.g., Case C-193/94 *Criminal proceedings against Skanavi and Chryssanthakopoulos* [1996] ECR I-929. In fact recognition of driving licences is now regulated by legislation, Directive 2006/126 [2006] OJ L403/18, which sets out harmonised standards, mutual recognition and a system of registration and exchange. A licence obtained autonomously in one member state in order to circumvent suspension of a licence in another need not be recognised in the latter; Cases C-329 and 343/06 *Wiedemann and Funk* v *Land Baden-Württemberg and anor* [2008] ECR I-4635; Cases C-334 etc./06 *Zerche and ors* v *Landkreis Mittweida and anor* [2008] ECR I-4691; Case C-1/07 *Criminal proceedings against Weber* [2008] ECR I-8571; Case C-419/10 *Hofmann* v *Freistaat Bayern*, judgment of 26 April 2012, not yet reported. This may apply equally to the acquisition of a licence in a member state other than that of the driver's normal residence in any circumstances; Case C-184/10 *Grasser* v *Freistaat Bayern*, judgment of 19 May 2011, not yet reported.

245   The principle of equivalence ('*Cassis de Dijon* for establishment and services', although it came first) can be traced through Case 71/76 *Thieffry* v *Conseil de l'ordre des avocats à la Cour de Paris* [1977] ECR 765; Case 11/77 *Patrick* v *Ministre des Affaires Culturelles* [1977] ECR 1199; Case 222/86 *Union nationale des entraineurs et cadres techniques professionnels du football (Unectef)* v *Heylens and ors* [1987] ECR 4097; Case C-340/89 *Vlassopoulou* v *Ministerium für Justiz, Bundes- und Europaangelegenheiten Baden-Württemberg* [1991] ECR I-2357; Case C-319/92 *Haim* v *Kassenzahnärtzliche Vereinigung Nordrhein* [1994] ECR I-428; Case C-234/97 *Fernández de Bobadilla* v *Museo Nacional del Prado and ors* [1999] ECR I-4773; Case C-313/01 *Morgenbesser* v *Consiglio dell'Ordine degli avvocati di Genova* [2003] ECR I-13467; Case C-345/08 *Peśla* v *Justizministerium Mecklenberg-Vorpommern* [2009] ECR I-11677.

246   See e.g., Case C-19/92 *Kraus* v *Land Baden-Württemberg* [1993] ECR I-1663.

247   Case C-39/07 *Commission* v *Spain* [2008] ECR I-3435, at para. 37.

article 45 or 56, as the case may be) – a person seeking to work, establish him or herself or provide a service in a regulated trade or profession in another member state has the right to have such qualifications as he or she may possess taken into account towards that end. The competent supervisory authorities of the host member state are under a duty to consider whether those qualifications, even if different, are 'equivalent' to those required of home nationals, and may refuse authorisation only if they decide on reasonable grounds that they are inadequate. In carrying out this comparative assessment a degree of flexibility is required lest mutual recognition become merely notional, but the authorities are not required to lower standards, even slightly.[248] A refusal must be reasoned, and subject always to a right of review/appeal by an independent (judicial) authority.[249] Where the existing qualifications are equivalent in some aspects but not in others, the person is entitled to pursue further training to make up the difference, and can be required to do no more. Even where a profession is not technically regulated, in that formal qualification is not strictly necessary, but access to a post turns upon selection based upon a comparative assessment of candidates, national authorities must ensure that qualifications obtained in other member states are accorded their proper value and are duly taken into account.[250] The broad effect is that a requirement of educational, technical or professional qualifications can inhibit the right of a Union national to work, establish him or herself or provide a service in another member state only where he or she has no qualifications from his or her own state or where they are demonstrably deficient or demonstrably different compared to those required of home nationals. Perhaps surprisingly this simple formula proved sufficient to ease the free movement of lawyers to an extent.[251]

The case law of the Court of Justice led to a policy shift from harmonisation to **11.35** equivalence as part of the 1992 single market programme. In 1988 the Council adopted the Mutual Recognition Directive, creating a *general* system for the mutual recognition of higher education diplomas.[252] Equivalence was presumed, and (very broadly) member states were required to give the fullest

---

248   Case C-345/08 *Peśla*, n. 245 above.
249   Case 222/86 *Heylens*, n. 245 above; Case C-506/04 *Wilson* v *Ordre des avocats du barreau de Luxembourg* [2006] ECR I-8613.
250   Case C-586/08 *Rubino* v *Ministero dell'Università e della Ricerca* [2009] ECR I-12013.
251   See e.g., Case 71/76 *Thieffry*, n. 245 above (a Belgian Diplôme de Docteur en Droit recognised as equivalent to a French Licence en droit); *Bloomer and ors* v *Incorporated Law Society of Ireland and ors* [1995] 3 IR 14 (HC) (an LLB degree from a UK university (Queen's, Belfast) materially equivalent to an LLB degree from an Irish university for purposes of admission to a solicitors' vocational training course; *quaere* whether an LLB from an English university would meet the test). Cf. Case C-345/08 *Peśla*, n. 245 above.
252   Directive 89/48 [1989] OJ L19/16. A higher education diploma is, in principle, one which requires at least three years' tertiary education evidenced by a degree or comparable award; art. 1(a). It must attest to genuine education or training covered by the education system of the awarding member state and to examination taken

possible recognition to university and similar qualifications gained in other member states. In 1992 the Council adopted a second Directive to 'supplement' the first, providing similar rules ('in essence, identical to those of Directive 89/48')[253] for post-secondary training or education of one to three years' duration.[254] Both applied in all areas not subject to harmonisation by specific sectoral Directives.[255] Minor amendments to these measures were made in in 1999,[256] more significant change in 2005 with the adoption of Directive 2005/36 'on recognition of professional qualifications'[257] which replaced both previous general mutual recognition measures, and altered several of the sectoral measures. In substance it consolidated rather than altered the existing system and applies across all three chapters on free movement, but with the rules on services differing from the other two.

2. Directive 2005/36

11.36 The Directive applies to all Union nationals wishing to pursue a regulated trade or profession in a member state other than that in which they obtained their professional qualifications, on either an employed or self-employed basis.[258] Generally it provides access in a host member state to the same profession as that for which he or she is qualified elsewhere, and the right to pursue it in the host member state under the same conditions as its home nationals, if the activities covered are 'comparable'.[259] But it is well to note that the general systems for recognition of qualifications does not concern the choice of selection and recruitment procedures for filling posts: it does not constitute a basis for a right actually to be recruited.[260]

11.37 For establishment (and workers required to invoke professional or other qualifications), the directive sets out a general system for mutual recognition of

---

and/or professional experience acquired there; Case C-311/06 *Consiglio Nazionale degli Ingegneri* v *Ministero della Guistizia and anor* [2009] ECR I-415.

253   Case C-151/07 *Chatzithanasis* v *Ypourgos Ygeias kai Koinonikis Allilengyis and anor* [2008] ECR I-9013, at para. 33.

254   Directive 92/51 [1992] OJ L209/25.

255   Directive 89/48, art. 2, 2nd para; Directive 92/51, art. 2, 2nd para.

256   Directive 1999/42 [1999] OJ L201/77.

257   [2005] OJ L255/22.

258   Directive 2005/36, art. 2(1). Thus the Directive does not apply to (nor does it hinder) first recognition of qualifications obtained in a non-Union country, that remaining a matter for national law (art. 2(2)), although the Council previously recommended (Recommendation 89/49 [1989] OJ L19/24) that third country diplomas otherwise falling within Directive 89/48 be recognised. But third country qualifications recognised by the competent authority of one member state must be recognised by that of another following completion by the holder of three years' certified professional experience in the former; art. 3(3).

259   Directive 2005/36, art. 4.

260   Case C-285/01 *Burbaud* v *Ministère de l'Emploi et de la Solidarité* [2003] ECR I-8219; Case C-586/08 *Rubino* v *Ministero dell'Università e della Ricerca* [2009] ECR I-12013.

qualifications and evidence of training (the 'general system'). It sets out, first, 'levels of qualification', on a scale from general primary or secondary education to a degree/diploma attesting to post-secondary study of at least four years' duration.[261] Generally, where a profession is regulated in the host member state, admission to it contingent upon possession of specific professional qualifications, the competent authorities there are required to permit access to and pursuit of the profession, under the same conditions as apply to home nationals, to any applicant possessing the evidence of formal qualification or attestation of competence required in the member state in which he or she is qualified for access to and pursuit of that profession there,[262] so long as they satisfy the conditions set out in the Directive, essentially attesting to a level of qualification equivalent to no more than one level lower on the level of qualification scale than that required in the host member state.[263] However the host member state may require completion of an adaptation period of up to three years or an aptitude test ('compensation (or compensatory) measures'):

- if the duration of the training of which the applicant provides evidence is at least one year shorter than that required by the host member state;
- if it covers substantially different matters than those covered by the evidence of formal qualifications required in the host member state; or
- the regulated profession in the host member state comprises one or more regulated professional activities which do not exist in the corresponding profession in the applicant's home member state and the difference is of specific training required which covers substantially different matters from those the applicant offers.[264]

'Substantially different matters' means matters of which knowledge is essential for pursuing the profession and with regard to which the training received by the migrant shows important differences in terms of duration or content from the training required by the host member state.[265] Compensatory measures must be restricted to cases in which they would be proportionate[266] and a competent authority ought to take into account any professional or other practical experience the applicant has undergone.[267] The choice between

---

261 Directive 2005/36, art. 11.
262 *Ibid.* art. 13(1), (2).
263 *Ibid.* art. 13(1), 2nd para, (2), 2nd and 3rd paras.
264 *Ibid.* art. 14(1).
265 *Ibid.* art. 14(4).
266 Case C-330/03 *Colegio de Ingenieros de Caminos, Canales y Puertos* v *Administración del Estado* [2006] ECR I-801, at para. 24; Case C-197/06 *Confederatie van Immobiliën-Beroepen van België and anor* v *van Leuken* [2008] ECR I-2627, at para. 39.
267 Directive 2005/36, arts 16–19; Case C-340/89 *Vlassopoulou* v *Ministerium für Justiz, Bundes- und Europa-angelegenheiten Baden-Württemberg* [1991] ECR I-2357; Case C-234/97 *Fernández de Bobadilla* v *Museo*

adaptation period and aptitude test is for the applicant[268] save for (a) professions the pursuit of which requires precise knowledge of national law and in respect of which the provision of advice and/or assistance concerning national law is an essential and constant aspect of the professional activity[269] and (b) the pursuit of certain medical activities.[270] In both cases the member state must justify to the Commission the derogation from the general rule, and the Commission may object ('ask the Member State to refrain').[271] Where admission to or pursuit of a regulated activity is contingent upon possession of general, commercial or professional knowledge and aptitudes, the host member state must recognise previous pursuit of the activity in another member state (over given lengths of time, varying with the activity at issue)[272] as sufficient proof thereof.[273] Finally, there are specific provisions on recognition of minimum training conditions of and use of professional titles by doctors, general care nurses, dental practitioners (specialised or otherwise), veterinary surgeons, midwives, pharmacists and architects.[274]

11.38 For services the burdens are lighter. A member state cannot restrict the free provision of services 'for any reason relating to professional qualifications' by a service provider from another member state where he or she is established for the purpose of pursuing the same profession,[275] and must exempt him or her from any requirement of authorisation by, registration with or membership of a relevant professional organisation or body or public social security body.[276] The exception is where there is a substantial difference between the professional qualifications of the service provider and the training required in the host member state, to the extent that that difference is such as to be harmful to public health or safety; in that case the host member state must allow the service provider the opportunity to show, in particular by means of an aptitude test, that he or she has acquired the knowledge or competence lacking.[277] In all cases it

---

Nacional del Prado and ors [1999] ECR I-4773; Case C-313/01 *Morgenbesser* v *Consiglio dell'Ordine degli avvocati di Genova* [2003] ECR I-13467; Case C-345/08 *Peśla* v *Justizministerium Mecklenberg-Vorpommern* [2009] ECR I-11677; Cases C-422 etc./09 *Vandorou and ors* v *Ipourgos Ethnikis Pedia kai Thriskevmaton* [2010] ECR I-12411.

268   Directive 2005/36, art. 14(2).
269   Directive 2005/36, art. 14(3). This is not limited to the legal professions, but to any activity in which a knowledge of the law is reasonably required; see e.g., Case C-149/05 *Price* v *Conseil des ventes volontaires de meubles aux enchères publiques* [2006] ECR I-7691 (auctioneers required by French law to have adequate knowledge of all relevant law).
270   Directive 2005/36, art. 14(3), 2nd para.
271   *Ibid.* art. 14(2), 3rd para.
272   *Ibid.* arts 17–19.
273   *Ibid.* art. 16.
274   *Ibid.* arts 21–52.
275   *Ibid.* art. 5(1).
276   *Ibid.* art. 6.
277   *Ibid.* art. 7(4), 3rd para.

may require that he or she furnish to the relevant competent authority in the host member state in advance of (first) arrival a declaration of insurance or other cover for professional liability, renewed annually if appropriate,[278] and proof of nationality, attestation of establishment, evidence of qualifications and, if it is required of home nationals, evidence of no criminal convictions.[279] The service provider holds him or herself out under his or her home professional title.[280] But there remains a well established general rule that a person may not, in order to evade the professional rules of conduct in one member state, establish himself in another and then rely upon the Treaties in order to provide services in the former; if that is his sole or primary purpose he will be deemed to be established in the former state and subject to its supervisory rules,[281] and this rule presumably survives the adoption of Directive 2005/36. However, the acquisition of a qualification in one member state for the purpose of pursuing the relevant profession or trade in another (in which the path to qualification may be more arduous) is not, of itself, abusive.[282]

For both establishment and services, just as a worker may be required to have **11.39** adequate linguistic ability where objectively justified,[283] persons seeking to exercise rights under the Directive 'shall have a knowledge of languages necessary for practising the profession in the host Member State'.[284]

(a) Lawyers

Like its predecessors, Directive 2005/36 does not apply where there exist other **11.40** specific measures for a given regulated profession.[285] This means that lawyers and the legal professions fall partly within and partly without the Directive. Services continue to be regulated by the 1977 Lawyers' Services Directive, establishment (and workers) by a 1998 Directive 'to facilitate practice of the profession of lawyer on a permanent basis in a Member State other than that in which the qualification was obtained' (the Lawyers' Home Title Directive).[286]

---

278 *Ibid.* art. 7(1).

279 *Ibid.* art. 7(2). See Case C-564/07 *Commission v Austria* [2009] ECR I-100*.

280 *Ibid.* art. 7(3).

281 Case 33/74 *van Binsbergen v Bestuur van de Bedrijfsvereniging voor de Mataalnijverheid* [1974] ECR 1299; Case 292/86 *Gullung v Conseil de l'ordre des avocats du barreau de Colmar et de Saverne* [1988] ECR 111; Case 61/89 *Bouchoucha* [1990] ECR I-3551; Case C-148/91 *Vereniging Veronica Omroep Organisatie v Commissariat voor de Media* [1993] ECR I-487; Case C-23/93 *TV10 v Commissariat voor de Media* [1994] ECR I-4795; Case C-286/06 *Commission v Spain* [2008] ECR I-8025, at paras 69–70.

282 Case C-311/06 *Consiglio Nazionale degli Ingegneri v Ministero della Giustizia and Cavallera* [2009] ECR I-415, *per* A-G Poiares Maduro at paras 43–58 of his opinion; Case C-118/09 *Koller* [2010] ECR I-13627, especially the opinion of A-G Trstenjak at paras 80–6.

283 Regulation 492/2011, art. 3(1); see n. 154 above and accompanying text.

284 Directive 2005/36, art. 53.

285 *Ibid.* art. 2(3).

286 Directive 98/5 [1998] OJ L77/36.

But these measures apply to recognition of a lawyer's authorisation to practise rather than his or her qualifications,[287] which are a matter for Directive 2006/36. Under the Lawyers' Home Title Directive, a lawyer qualified in one member state has the right to pursue in another, under his or her home country professional title, the activities of a lawyer and advise on the law of his home member state, Union law, international law and the law of the host member state.[288] He or she may act for a client in court proceedings, but, where the law of the host member state reserves right of audience to lawyers practising under the professional title of that state, only in conjunction with such a lawyer who would, where necessary, be answerable to the court.[289] The activities of a notary are excepted,[290] and notaries are excluded from Directive 2006/36.[291] In all cases he or she must register with the competent authority in the host member state,[292] abide by its rules of professional conduct[293] and be subject to its disciplinary procedures.[294] He or she may enter into salaried practice as a lawyer if the host member state permits it of its own lawyers.[295]

11.41 Should a migrant lawyer wish to go wholly native, he or she may, after at least three years of 'effectively and regularly pursu[ing] … an activity in the host Member State in the law of that State including Community law', apply to be admitted to the legal profession there.[296] It is for the applicant to show he or she satisfies the test,[297] rejection by the competent authority must be reasoned and subject to appeal under domestic law.[298] A lawyer satisfying the test is entitled to be admitted and is exempted from requalification by successful completion of the compensation measures (adaptation period or aptitude test) of Directive 2005/36, although those provisions survive and it is always open to a lawyer with less than three years' practice (or, indeed, no practice) in a host member

---

287 See Case C-313/01 *Morgenbesser* v *Consiglio dell'Ordine degli avvocati di Genova* [2003] ECR I-13467, at para. 45.

288 Directive 98/5, arts 2, 1st para., 5(1).

289 *Ibid.* arts 2, 1st para., 5(3).

290 *Ibid.* art. 5(2).

291 Case C-47/08 *Commission* v *Belgium*, Case C-51/08 *Commission* v *Luxembourg*, Case C-52/08 *Commission* v *Portugal*, Case C-53/08 *Commission* v *Austria*, Case C-54/08 *Commission* v *Germany* and Case C-61/08 *Commission* v *Greece*, judgments of 24 May 2011, not yet reported.

292 Directive 98/5, art. 3.

293 *Ibid.* art. 6.

294 *Ibid.* art. 7.

295 *Ibid.* art. 8.

296 *Ibid.* arts 2, 2nd para., 10(1). 'Effective and regular pursuit' means actual exercise of the activity without any interruption other than that resulting from the events of everyday life; art. 10(1). A lawyer practising for three years but less than three years in the law of the host member state may make up the difference by evidence of experience and further education pursued; art. 10(3). It appears that an element of Community (*sic*) law is a necessary component of practice, which may create difficulties for integration via a provincial practice in which little or no Union law may be encountered.

297 *Ibid.* art. 10(1), 2nd para. Bare bones guidance is supplied; arts 10(1), 2nd para. (a)–(b) and 10(3)(a)–(b).

298 *Ibid.* art. 10(1), final para.

state to go that route.[299] The two Directives therefore 'complement one another' and provide two distinct means of gaining admission to the profession in another member state.[300] The lawyer who successfully requalifies may use both home country and host country professional titles.[301]

None of these Directives, nor the equivalence principles generally, has any **11.42** bearing upon recognition of qualifications as within a member state, that being a wholly internal matter.[302]

(b) Partial access

Not directly addressed by Directive 2005/36 are the problems which arise **11.43** where the lines of demarcation between different trades and professions – definition of their exercise remaining a matter, barring harmonisation, within national competence – are materially different as between the member states. Examples would include a holder of a British diploma in osteopathy seeking to establish himself in France[303] or a German *Heilpraktiker* (lay health practitioner) wishing to practise in Austria,[304] in which countries the functions of the osteopath and the *Heilpraktiker* are reserved to fully qualified medical doctors; a holder of an Italian hydraulic engineering qualification seeking access to the profession of civil engineer in Spain, the latter profession (*ingeniero de caminos, canales y puertos*) being significantly broader, requiring six years of specific post-secondary education and covering design and construction of hydraulic installations, land, sea and inland waterway transport infrastructures, conservation of beaches and town and country planning;[305] or German and British qualified snowboard instructors being barred from admission to teaching that sport in France where the necessary (and sole) qualification (*brevet d'Etat d'enseignement du ski alpin*) covers training to teach alpine skiing (on and off piste, freeride, freestyle, acrobatic, crosscountry, telemark and 'vélo' skiing), snowboarding, snowshoeing and relevant first aid.[306] In such cases the two

---

299 *Ibid.* arts 2, 2nd para., 10(2). Article 10(2) continues to refer to qualifications 'recognised in accordance with Directive 89/48/EEC' even though Directive 89/48 was repealed by Directive 2005/36, but this is to be understood as referring to the latter; Directive 2005/36, art. 62.

300 Case C-359/09 *Ebert* v *Budapesti Ügyvédi Kamara* [2011] ECR I-269, at para. 35.

301 *Ibid.* art. 10(6).

302 Yet, for lawyers in the United Kingdom at least, Directive 89/48 served as inspiration for Parliament to adopt a similar scheme for transferability of legal qualifications amongst the three UK jurisdictions; see the Courts and Legal Services Act 1990, s. 60 (for England and Wales) and the Law Reform (Miscellaneous Provisions) (Scotland) Act 1990, s. 30 (for Scotland). On the 'wholly internal' rule see 11.90–11.95 below.

303 Case C-61/89 *Bouchoucha* [1990] ECR I-3551.

304 Case C-294/00 *Deutsche Paracelsus Schulen für Naturheilverfahren* v *Gräbner* [2002] ECR I-6515.

305 Case C-330/03 *Colegio de Ingenieros de Caminos, Canales y Puertos* v *Administración del Estado* [2006] ECR I-801.

306 Case C-200/08 *Commission* v *France*, removed from the register; but see the opinion of A-G Sharpston, delivered 16 July 2009.

extreme options are full recognition of the former qualification as means of unconditional access to the latter profession or total exclusion from it. The *via media* is some form of 'restricted recognition' or partial access to the profession.

11.44 Where ('first scenario') the degree of similarity between the professions in the home and host member states is such that the two may be regarded as effectively the same, the applicant is to be accorded full recognition, subject only to material shortcomings which can be made up through compensatory measures.[307] However in the 'second scenario', where the differences between the fields of activity are so great that in reality the full programme of education and training is reasonably required, it will result in dissuasion for an individual to pursue in another member state an activity for and from which he or she is qualified but barred.[308] In that case if the activity in question may objectively be separated from the rest of the activities covered by the profession in the host member state, it is not inconsistent with Directive 2005/36 that the latter allow partial take-up of the profession only. Moreover, a refusal to do so is a disproportionate breach of articles 49 and/or 56 ('the dissuasive effect caused by the preclusion of any possibility of partial recognition … is too serious to be offset by the fear of potential harm to recipients of services [who may be protected] through less restrictive means'),[309] although the Court leaves open the door that such refusal might be justified by overriding reasons in the general interest which are suitable and proportionate.[310] Presumably this does not apply where the various activities in the host member state cannot, objectively, be dissociated one from another.

3. Services Directive

11.45 The importance of services to the internal market had been noted as part of the 1992 programme,[311] but well after that deadline had passed the Commission observed that serious impediments to the free provision of services remained still.[312] This was, in its view, particularly injurious to the internal market because services 'constitute the engine of economic growth' and account for 70 per cent of GDP and employment in most member states.[313] Small and

---

307 Case C-330/03 *Colegio de Ingenieros de Caminos, Canales y Puertos*, n. 305 above, at para. 34.
308 *Ibid.* at para. 35.
309 *Ibid.* at para. 38; implicit in Case C-102/02 *Beuttenmüller* v *Land Baden-Württemberg* [2004] ECR I-5405; Case C-200/08 *Commission* v *France*, n. 306 above.
310 Case C-330/03 *Colegio de Ingenieros de Caminos, Canales y Puertos*, n. 305 above, at para. 39.
311 *The European Challenge 1992: The Benefits of a Single Market* (Cecchini Report), 1988, Part I.6.
312 See *An Internal Market Strategy for Services*, COM(2000) 888; *The State of the Internal Market for Services*, COM(2002) 441 final.
313 Proposed Directive on services in the internal market, COM(2004) 2 final, Preamble, 3rd recital; survived into adopted Directive, n. 315 below, Preamble, 4th recital.

medium sized enterprises (SMEs) faced particular difficulties yet 'predominate' in the field of services.[314] In order to cut the Gordian knot, in 2004 the Commission proposed a Directive 'on services in the internal market', also known as the Bolkestein Directive after the responsible Commissioner and so, to its (witty) critics, the Frankenstein Directive. It was adopted by the Parliament and Council in 2006[315] and required to be implemented by the end of 2009.[316]

The Services Directive is in fact a misnomer: it applies to both services (in its **11.46** Treaty sense) and the establishment in other member states of service providing firms (and individuals), although creating a different regulatory regime for each. It therefore covers 'services' in a meaning more aligned to that of the WTO General Agreement on Trade in Services (GATS), and hence its double Treaty base in articles 53(2) and 62. The original proposal was nothing if not bold. The key (and revolutionary) element for services *stricto sensu* was, with some exceptions, 'home country control' or the 'country of origin principle', whereby member states were to 'ensure that [service] providers are subject only to the national provisions of their Member State of origin' and that member state was to 'be responsible for supervising the provider and the services provided by him, including services provided by him in another Member State'.[317] This marked a presumption of equivalence, would have removed the 'double burden' regulation facing service providers and constituted a pure *Cassis de Dijon* approach for services. It was of course what inspired such hostility to the proposal, a perceived threat to social service provision (and protection) in a number of member states and dilution to the lowest common demoninator; given its timing, it is believed to be a major reason for the French rejection of the constitutional Treaty. In the event it was watered down significantly, especially by the Parliament, probably because in the absence of their being traded they had no champion(s) to fight their cause, and the revolutionary aspects largely neutered. First, a host of service activities (services of general (non-economic) interest, financial services, electronic communications services and networks, transport services, temporary work agencies, health care services, audiovisual services, gambling, services connected with the exercise of official authority, a number of social services, private security services and the services of notaries and bailiffs) are excluded;[318] other matters (service monopolies, liberalisation,

---

314 Proposed Directive, Preamble, 2nd recital; adopted Directive, Preamble, 3rd recital.
315 Directive 2006/123 [2006] OJ L376/36.
316 *Ibid.* art. 44. It is reported to have been fully implemented by that date in only nine member states (Czech Republic, Denmark, Germany, Estonia, Hungary, the Netherlands, Finland, Sweden and United Kingdom); Eurochambres, *Mapping the Implementation of the Services Directive in EU Member States* (February 2010).
317 Draft proposal cited in n. 313 above, art. 16(1) and (3).
318 *Ibid.* art. 2(2). In the original proposal only financial services, electronic communications and networks and transport services were excluded.

definition, organisation and financing of services of general economic interest, criminal and labour law)[319] are declared not to be affected by it. In the event of conflict with another Union measure on a specific sector or profession, the latter is to prevail.[320] Second, the country of origin principle was abandoned (or severely restricted); instead there is set out a general principle of free movement of services ('[t]he Member State in which [a] service is provided shall ensure free access to and free exercise of a service activity within its territory')[321] and a prohibition of restrictions thereto *but* accompanied by a complex and confusing list of permissible contrary principles and requirements.[322] Much of it is codification of existing case law. The main innovation, and utility, of the Directive lies in the adoption of rules of 'smooth administration' comprising:

- *administrative simplification* (Chapter II), most notably the requirement of a 'point of single contact' through which a service (in the Treaty sense) provider may complete 'all procedures and formalities needed for access to his service activities, in particular, all declarations, notifications or applications necessary for authorisation from the competent authorities, including applications for inclusion in a register, a roll or a database, or for registration with a professional body or association [and] any applications for authorisation needed to exercise his service activities';[323] any information necessary for both provision and receipt of services must be 'easily accessible' from the point of single contact; and
- *freedom of establishment for service providers* (Chapter III), with extensive provisions on authorisation and prohibition of common impediments and requirements, so providing service firms with rules on establishment eased somewhat in comparison with other firms. Much of the latter is of the nature of horizontal cross-sector recognition of qualifications as embodied now in Directive 2006/36.[324]

There is also a prohibition of measures which might inhibit passive provision of services.[325]

11.47 The Services Directive confers no rights upon third country nationals established in a member state.

---

319 *Ibid.* art. 1.
320 *Ibid.* art. 3.
321 Directive 2006/123, art. 16(1), 2nd para.
322 *Ibid.* art. 16(1), 3rd para. and 16(2)–(3). See also art. 17, setting out an extensive list of exempted fields.
323 *Ibid.* art. 6(1).
324 Directive 2005/36 [2005] OJ L255/22; see 11.36–11.39 above.
325 Directive 2006/123, arts 19–21; for example, an obligation to obtain authorisation, discrimination upon grounds of nationality or place of residence; combined with the new duty to provide information and assistance from the point of single contact.

A product of a triangular squabble amongst the Commission, the Council and **11.48** the Parliament, in terms of precision, clarity and legal certainty the Services Directive cannot be counted amongst the Union draughtsman's successes. It creates further confusion in muddying the waters of derogation permissible by reference to the general good.[326] It will doubtless become a focus of spirited litigation.

Posted workers

A firm which is providing services in a host member state is entitled to install **11.49** and use its own workforce necessary to that end. This applies irrespective of the nationality of the worker(s) affected,[327] and so is one of the few areas in which third country nationals enjoy (derivative) rights under the Treaties. In order to provide for the protection of workers in such a situation, a 1996 Directive (the Posted Workers Directive)[328] requires member states to ensure that, irrespective of the law governing their contract of employment, posted workers enjoy (for the most part) the same terms and conditions as to hours, wages (including overtime), holidays and health, safety and hygiene at work as are guaranteed by law or collective agreement in the host member state.[329] However the Court of Justice noted that this undercuts the competitive advantage a service providing firm may have by virtue of the lower wage (and related) costs which obtain in the home member state.[330] Therefore

> by requiring undertakings performing public works contracts and, indirectly, their subcontractors to apply the minimum wage laid down by [a sectoral] collective agreement, a law [doing so] may impose on service providers established in another Member State where minimum rates of pay are lower an additional economic burden that may prohibit, impede or render less attractive the provision of their services in the host Member State. Therefore, a measure such as that at issue in the main proceedings is capable of constituting a restriction within the meaning of Article [56],[331]

and the posted workers directive must be interpreted in that light.[332] An alternative view is that it has been turned on its head. The Court is quick to add

---

326 See 11.130 below.
327 Case C-113/89 *Rush Portuguesa v Office National de l'Immigration* [1990] ECR I-1417; Case C-43/93 *Vander Elst v Office des Migrations Internationales* [1994] ECR I-3803; Case C-168/04 *Commission v Austria* (EU Posting Confirmation) [2006] ECR I-9041. But the host member state may check so as to ensure that third country nationals do not abuse this right, for example that they are in lawful and regularised residence in the member state of establishment and in the lawful employment of the service provider; Case C-244/04 *Commission v Germany* [2006] ECR I-855; Case C-219/08 *Commission v Belgium* [2009] ECR I-9213.
328 Directive 96/71 [1997] OJ L18/1.
329 *Ibid.* art. 3.
330 Case C-346/06 *Rüffert v Land Niedersachsen* [2008] ECR I-1989, at para. 14.
331 *Ibid.* at para. 37.
332 *Ibid.* at para. 43. See now a proposed Directive intended to give Directive 96/71 greater teeth, COM(2012) 131 final.

that there may be justification in the measure which serves an imperative reason in the public interest (the protection of workers, the prevention of social dumping), but is slow to apply it.[333] This is not cured by the general principle of non-discrimination.[334]

4. Companies

11.50 The rights of establishment and services are extended to companies or firms formed in accordance with the laws of a member state.[335] To give the provision its widest possible amplitude, and in tacit recognition of the difficulties arising from variations in company law from member state to member state, it is then enough that the company has its registered office, its central administration, *or* its principal place of business within the Union.[336] It is a relatively straight-forward matter when a company (or a natural person) establishes an agency, a branch or a subsidiary in another member state, a right expressly provided by article 49; in these cases the agencies, branches or subsidiaries are created (unhindered) in, and made subject to, the law of the host member state. Matters are more difficult in the provision of cross-frontier services, in which rules on prudential supervision are met frontally, or where a company may wish to decamp completely to another member state.

11.51 The EEC Treaty anticipated difficulties as a result of variations in national company law. To iron them out it required the member states to enter into negotiations to secure

> so far as is necessary … the mutual recognition of companies or firms within the meaning of the second paragraph of Article 58, the retention of legal personality in the event of transfer of their seat from one country to another, and the possibility of mergers between companies or firms governed by the laws of different countries.[337]

In 1968 the member states entered into such an extra-Community Convention on the mutual recognition of companies,[338] but it has never been ratified and

---

333 E.g., Case C-165/98 *Mazzoleni* v *Inter Surveillance Assitance* [2001] ECR I-2189; Case C-341/05 *Laval un Partneri* v *Svenska Byggnadsarbetareförbundet and ors* (Vaxholm) [2007] ECR I-11767; Case C-346/06 *Rüffert*, n. 330 above; Case C-515/08 *Procureur du Roi* v *Santos Palhota and ors* [2010] ECR I-10413.

334 See 8.03 below.

335 TFEU, arts 49, 54 (ex arts 43, 48 EC).

336 TFEU, art. 54.

337 EEC Treaty, art. 220; repealed by Lisbon.

338 Convention of 29 February 1968 on the Mutual Recognition of Companies and Bodies Corporate, *Bulletin EC*, Supplement 2/69, 7.

must be considered a dead letter. Yet articles 56 and 63 have been afforded significant breadth in this context, and the Union has, from the beginning, had power

> by coordinating to the necessary extent the safeguards which, for the protection of the interests of members and other, are required by Member States of companies or firms within the meaning of the second paragraph of Article 54 with a view to making such safeguards equivalent throughout the Union[339]

and has used it to address the regulatory framework of companies structure, capitalisation and management of companies in order to ensure that companies incorporated in one member state can operate freely in another. These are the Directives on:

- disclosure of company data for the protection of company members (the First Company Law Directive);[340]
- safeguards for members in the formation of public limited companies and maintenance and alteration of capital (the Second Directive);[341]
- mergers[342] and scission (or 'de-merger')[343] of public limited liability companies (the Third and Sixth Directives);
- accounts (the Fourth and Seventh Directives)[344] and statutory auditing of accounts (the Eighth Directive);[345]
- cross-border mergers (the CBM or Tenth Directive);[346]
- disclosure requirements in respect of subsidiaries (the Eleventh Directive);[347]
- single member private limited liability companies (the Twelfth Directive);[348]

---

339 TFEU, art. 50(2)(g) (ex art. 42(2)(g) EC).
340 Directive 2009/101 [2009] OJ L258/11 (consolidation of the original Directive 68/151 [1968] JO L65/8).
341 Directive 77/91 [1977] OJ L26/1.
342 Directive 2011/35 [2011] OJ L110/1 (being a consolidation of Directive 78/855 [1978] OJ L295/36).
343 Directive 82/891 [1982] OJ L378/47.
344 Directive 78/660 [1978] OJ L222/11 (annual accounts) (Fourth Directive); Directive 83/349 [1983] OJ L193/1 (consolidated accounts) (Seventh Directive); also Directive 86/635 [1986] OJ L372/1 (annual and consolidated accounts of banks and other financial institutions); Directive 91/674 [1991] OJ L374/7 (annual and consolidated accounts of insurance undertakings). International accounting standards have been adopted: Regulation 1606/2002 [2002] OJ L243/1; set out in Regulation 1126/2008 [2008] OJ L320/1, Annex.
345 Directive 2006/43 [2006] OJ L157/87.
346 Directive 2005/56 [2005] OJ L310/1; also Directive 2009/133 [2009] OJ L310/34 on a common system of taxation applicable to mergers, divisions, transfer of assets and exchange of shares of companies in different member states (replacing Directive 90/434 [1990] OJ L225/1 on taxation applicable to mergers (Fiscal Merger Directive)).
347 Directive 89/666 [1989] OJ L395/36.
348 Directive 2009/102 [2009] OJ L258/20 (consolidation of the original Directive 89/667 [1989] OJ L395/40).

- takeover bids (the Thirteenth Directive);[349] and
- shareholders' rights.[350]

A draft proposal for a Directive on the transfer of the company seat (the Fourteenth Directive)[351] has, following public consultation and an impact assessment study in 2007,[352] been shelved by the Commission, and requests from the Parliament 'swiftly' to kick start it back into life[353] have gone unheeded. More venerable proposals for Directives on worker participation, or co-determination/*Mitbestimmung* (the Fifth, or Vredeling, Directive)[354] and on the structure of groups (or pyramids) of companies, or *Unternehmensgruppe* (the Ninth Directive),[355] both based upon the German models, have gone cold.

11.52 The single most difficult issue in company law for many years has been the right of a company formed under the law of one member state to exercise a freedom of establishment in – more particularly, to move operations to – another. The Court of Justice established in the *Daily Mail* case in 1988 that, should it be prohibited (or otherwise made subject to restriction) in the company law of the member state of incorporation, article 52 EEC (49 TFEU) did not confer upon a company incorporated and having its registered office (*siège statutaire*) there the right to transfer its central (or effective) management and control (its 'real seat'; *siège réel* or *siège social; siège de direction effective*) to another member state ('outbound conversion') whilst maintaining its original registered office.[356] This is because

> unlike natural persons, companies are creatures of the law and, in the present state of Community law, creatures of national law. They exist only by virtue of the varying national legislation which determines their incorporation and functioning.[357]

The proposed operation would amount to the winding-up of the company, effectively its extinguishing (or its '*mort civile*'), so losing the legal personality and breaking the connecting factor upon which it relied in order to avail itself of article 49 rights to establish itself elsewhere.

---

349 Directive 2004/25 [2004] OJ L142/12.
350 Directive 2007/36 [2007] OJ L184/17.
351 IP/03/716. It never reached the stage of a formal proposal.
352 SEC(2007) 1707.
353 P6_TA(2009)0086; A7–0008/2012.
354 Proposed in 1980, [1980] OJ C297/33. But related legislation has been adopted under the social provisions of the Treaties; see 14.44 below.
355 The NinthDirective has never been formally proposed or published; a draft text may be found in ZGR 1985, S. 446.
356 Case 81/87 *R v HM Treasury and Commissioners of Inland Revenue, ex parte Daily Mail and anor* [1988] ECR 5483.
357 *Ibid.* at para. 19.

But the principle then entered a period of flux, a result of a trio of key judgments **11.53** in 1999–2003. They were the following.

In *Centros* (1999),[358] an English private limited company was refused registra- **11.54** tion of a Danish branch as it was a 'pseudo-foreign company': it had two shareholders, a husband and wife both Danes living in Denmark, had never traded in the United Kingdom, and had been incorporated in England and Wales as a vehicle for avoiding the minimum capital requirements imposed by Danish law (Kr 200,000, as opposed to £100 in England, which was kept in a cash box in the shareholders' home). The Court of Justice said this was a use, not abuse, of article 49:

> [T]he refusal of a Member State to register a branch of a company formed in accordance with the law of another Member State in which it has its registered office on the grounds that the branch is intended to enable the company to carry on all its economic activity in the host State, with the result that the secondary establishment escapes national rules on the provision for and the paying-up of a minimum capital, is incompatible with Articles [49] and [54] of the Treaty, in so far as it prevents any exercise of the right freely to set up a secondary establishment which Articles [49] and [54] are specifically intended to guarantee.[359]

Danish protests that the Danish rules were necessary in order to protect creditors met with little sympathy.

In *Überseering* (2002),[360] it was held that a member state may not deny legal **11.55** capacity to a company formed in a member state but having moved its central place of administration to another member state, and generally, that a company established under the law of one member state must be recognised in any other member state, irrespective of its real seat.

Inspire Art (2003),[361] like *Centros*, involved an English private limited company **11.56** with its registered office there but its sole director domiciled in the Netherlands where it traded; its registration in the commercial register (*Handelregister*) gave no indication that it was a 'formally foreign company' (*formeel buitenlandse vennootschap*) as required by Dutch law of a company formed elsewhere and trading entirely or almost entirely in the Netherlands. The Court said:

---

358   Case C-212/97 *Centros v Ervehrs- og Selskabsstyrelsen* [1999] ECR I-1459.
359   *Ibid.* at para. 30.
360   Case C-208/00 *Überseering v Nordic Construction Baumanagement* [2002] ECR I-9919.
361   Case C-167/01 *Kamer van Koophandel en Fabrieken voor Amsterdam v Inspire Art* [2003] ECR I-10155.

[T]he fact that the company was formed in a particular Member State for the sole purpose of enjoying the benefit of more favourable legislation does not constitute an abuse even if that company conducts its activities entirely or mainly in that second State ... the fact that Inspire Art was formed in the United Kingdom for the purpose of circumventing Netherlands company law which lays down stricter rules with regard in particular to minimum capital and the paying-up of shares does not mean that that company's establishment of a branch in the Netherlands is not covered by freedom of establishment as provided for by Articles [49] and [54].[362]

11.57 A fourth case (*de Lastyrie du Sallaint* (2004))[363] was thought to alter some of the tax avoidance issues which had arisen in *Daily Mail* but dealt with a natural rather than juristic person, so one not depending upon the legal order of his home member state for his existence; and a fifth (*SEVIC Systems* (2005))[364] shed a little more light on recognition in the member state of incorporation of a company of an establishment operation carried out by it in another member state by means of a cross-border merger. None of these overruled *Daily Mail* and the Court was careful to distinguish it throughout, but they (in *Überseering* in particular) chipped away at it. It was anticipated by some that the Court would engineer a root and branch change in *Cartesio* (2008).[365] Advocate-General Poires Maduro recommended doing so, abandoning *Daily Mail*, finding the prohibition in Hungarian company law of a limited partnership transferring its *siège réel* to Italy whilst retaining its incorporation in Hungary to breach articles 49 and 54: '[o]therwise, Member States would have *carte blanche* to impose a "death sentence" on a company constituted under its laws just because it had decided to exercise the freedom of establishment'.[366] The Court declined to follow him. In what is an uncommonly unnavigable judgment it cited *Daily Mail* at length, expressly distinguished *Centros*, *Überseering*, *Inspire Art* and *SEVIC Systems* as 'situation[s] fundamentally different from the circumstances at issue in the case which gave rise to *Daily Mail*',[367] found the problem created by the differences in national law still extant and not resolved by articles 49 and 54 but required to be dealt with by future legislation (such as the Fourteenth Company Law Directive, still in the long grass) or Conventions,[368] absent which a company's right to freedom of establishment 'is a preliminary matter which, as Community law now stands, can only be resolved by the applicable national law'.[369] Where a company transfers its real seat from one member state to another but that transfer does *not* affect its status as a

---

362 *Ibid.* at paras 96, 98.
363 Case C-9/02 *de Lasteyrie du Saillant* v *Ministère de l'Économie, des Finances et de l'Industrie* [2004] ECR I-2409.
364 Case C-411/03 *SEVIC Systems* [2005] ECR I-10805.
365 Case C-210/06 *CARTESIO Oktató és Szolgáltató* [2008] ECR I-9641.
366 *Ibid.* at para. 31 of his opinion.
367 *Ibid.* at para. 122 of the judgment.
368 *Ibid.* at para. 108.
369 *Ibid.* at para. 109.

company in the former, article 49 may apply to the (tax) rules which would hinder it so doing.[370] And national law which permits conversion of a company internally but which imposes a blanket ban ('in a general manner') upon that possibility for companies from another member state infringes article 49, but a requirement of compliance with national rules, for example, on strict legal and economic continuity between the predecessor company and the converted successor company or on the provision of evidence for the registration procedure (subject to fair account taken of documents from the member state of origin), does not.[371] Otherwise the choice of international private law doctrine in each member state, either real seat or incorporation theory, thus continues to distort, asymmetrically, the right of establishment for companies.

The increasing freedom of company movement has yet to produce a significant 'Delaware effect'. **11.58**

Banks, insurance companies and other providers of financial services are 'persons' enjoying right of free movement under the Treaties. But the Court of Justice has recognised that special rules are legitimate in these fields for the protection of the consumer.[372] There are a number of Directives designed to ease the process of mutual recognition[373] and in 2005 the Commission published a White Paper on financial services.[374] But any possible progress towards liberalisation has now been dashed by the 2008 (and ongoing) financial crisis. **11.59**

---

370   *Ibid.* at paras 111–12 (*obiter*); Case C-371/10 *National Grid Indus* v *Inspecteur van de Belastingdienst Rijnmond/kantoor Rotterdam*, judgment of 29 November 2011, not yet reported. In the latter the rules in question infringed art. 49 but were (for the most part) justified as overriding requirements in the general interest.

371   Case C-378/10 VALE *Építési*, judgment of 12 July 2012, not yet reported.

372   E.g., Case 205/84 *Commission* v *Germany* (Insurance and Co-Insurance) [1986] ECR 3755.

373   See e.g., in the insurance sector, Directive 64/225 [1964] JO 878 (reinsurance and retrocession); Directive 73/239 [1973] OJ L228/3 (non-life direct insurance); Directive 78/473 [1978] OJ L151/25 (co-insurance); Directive 87/344 [1987] OJ L185/77 (legal expenses insurance); Directive 88/357 [1988] OJ L172/1 (second non-life direct insurance); Directive 92/49 [1992] OJ L228/1 (third non-life direct insurance); Directive 98/78 [1998] OJ L330/1 (supplementary supervision on insurance undertakings in an insurance group); Directive 2001/17 [2001] OJ L110/28 (reorganisation and winding up on insurance undertakings); Directive 2002/83 [2002] OJ L345/1 (life assurance); Directive 2002/92 [2003] OJ L9/3 (insurance mediation); Directive 2005/68 [2005] OJ L323/1 (reinsurance); all of these Directives are consolidated and replaced with effect from November 2012: Directive 2009/138 [2009] OJ L335/1 (Solvency II Directive). For banking, Directives 2006/48 [2006] OJ L177/1 and 2006/49 [2006] OJ L177/201 (Capital Adequacy Directives). For financial instruments, Directive 2004/39 [2004] OJ L145/1 (Markets in Financial Instruments, or MiFI, Directive; to be replaced by the proposed Alternative Investment Fund Managers (AIFM) Directive, COM(2009) 207).

374   COM(2005) 629 final.

EU juristic persons

11.60 Alongside companies or firms formed in accordance with the law of a member state, there are now three juristic persons which may be created by authority of Union law. They are:

- the European Economic Interest Grouping (EEIG), the first corporate structure created by Community law, which enables companies or firms in various member states to undertake joint ancillary activities without need for capitalisation;[375]
- the European Company (*Societas Europæa*, SE), envisaged in the 1950s, first formally proposed in 1970[376] and the rules for its formation finally adopted in 2001;[377] and
- the European Cooperative Society (*Societas Cooperativa Europæa*, SCE), a form of incorporation based upon democratic participation and equitable profit sharing amongst its members.[378]

An EEIG is in the nature of a joint venture. It is formed by contract amongst companies, firms or other juristic persons and/or natural persons who provide professional or other services, at least two of them required to have their central administration/to carry on their principal activities in two different member states.[379] Its purpose is to facilitate or develop the activities of its members and to improve or increase the results of those activities; its own activities must be related to those of its members, must not be more than ancillary to them, and is not to make profits for itself.[380] It has the capacity to have rights and obligations, to make contracts and to sue and be sued, but does not necessarily have legal personality, that to be determined by the member state in which it is registered.[381]

11.61 Longer in coming but closer in nature are the European Company and the European Cooperative Society. An SE is formed not *ex nihilo* but from other, constituent companies, by: a merger of public limited liability companies from at least two member states; the formation of a holding SE of public or private limited liability companies from at least two member states; formation of a

---

375 Regulation 2137/85 [1985] OJ L199/1.
376 COM(70) 600 final.
377 Regulation 2157/2001 [2001] OJ L294/1 ('on the Statute for a European company').
378 Regulation 1435/2003 [2003] OJ L207/1 ('on the Statute for a European Cooperative Society').
379 Regulation 2137/85, art. 4.
380 *Ibid.* art. 3.
381 *Ibid.* art. 1(2), (3).

subsidiary SE by an existing company, firm or other juristic person; or conversion of an existing public limited liability company into an SE.[382] By contrast, an SCE may be formed *de novo*, by five or more natural persons resident in at least two member states or by five or more natural persons and/or juristic persons formed and resident in, or governed by the law of, at least two different member states; it may also be formed by companies, firms or other juristic person governed by the law of at least two different member states, by a merger between existing cooperatives at least two of which are governed by the law of different member states, and by conversion of an existing cooperative.[383] Both require a minimum prescribed capital (€120,000 for an SE, €30,000 for an SCE),[384] both have legal personality.[385] Each is governed by its respective Statute, otherwise by the law on public limited liability companies/cooperatives of the member state in which it has its registered office.[386] They adhere to the real seat theory, and registered office and head office are required to be located in the same member state.[387] The office may be transferred to another member state without winding up the existing company/cooperative or creating a new legal person,[388] but it results in a change in the applicable law.[389] There is no Union-wide register: an SE is registered in the companies register(s) of the member state in which it has its head office,[390] publication of SCE documents and particulars effected in the manner laid down in the member state of its registered office,[391] although each registration is published for information in the *Official Journal*.[392] Employees' rights are laid down in separate instruments, one for each.[393]

Although not formed in accordance with the law of a member state (as **11.62** otherwise required by article 54 TFEU), both an SE and an SCE are to be 'treated in every Member State as if it were a public limited-liability company [cooperative] formed in accordance with the law of the Member State in which

---

382 Regulation 2157/2001, art. 2.
383 Regulation 1435/2003, art. 2(1).
384 Regulation 2157/2001, art. 4; Regulation 1435/2003, art. 3.
385 Regulation 2157/2001, art. 1(3); Regulation 1435/2003, art. 1(5).
386 Regulation 2157/2001, art. 15; Regulation 1435/2003, art. 17(1).
387 Regulation 2157/2001, art. 7; Regulation 1435/2003, art. 6. National law requiring the two to be in the same place is permissible. It is possible that these provisions are unlawful for incompatibility with arts 49/54 TFEU as interpreted in Case C-208/00 *Überseering* v *Nordic Construction Baumanagement* [2002] ECR I-9919; see 11.55 above.
388 Regulation 2157/2001, art. 8; Regulation 1435/2003, art. 7.
389 Regulation 2157/2001, art. 9(1)(c)(ii)(iii); Regulation 1435/2003, art. 8(1)(c)(ii)(iii).
390 Regulation 2157/2001, art. 12.
391 Regulation 1435/2003, art. 12.
392 Regulation 2157/2001, art. 14; Regulation 1435/2003, art. 13.
393 Directive 2001/86 [2001] OJ L294/22 (for SEs); Directive 2003/72 [2003] OJ L207/25 (for SCEs).

it has its registered office',[394] so entitled to the panoply of rights conferred by articles 49 and 56.

11.63 As at September 2012 there were 1,379 registered SEs but only 217 of them 'normal', that is with employees and conducting business, the remainder 'empty' or 'shelf' (or 'UFO') SEs.[395] Most (864) are based in the Czech Republic, most normal SEs (103) in Germany. The number is (unexpectedly) low, perhaps because cross-border mergers, facilitation of which was a major purpose of the SE,[396] have been eased by other means, the adoption of the Cross-border Mergers Directive[397] and the *SEVIC* judgment of the Court of Justice.[398] The SCE has proved even less attractive, by mid-2010 the Commission able to count only 17 established in the Union, none having a significant number of employees.[399]

11.64 2008 the Commission proposed a Statute on the European Private Company (*Societas Privata Europæa*, SPE),[400] intended to cater for smaller, less ambitious companies – the proposed minimum share capital being €1.[401] An SPE is to be created *ex nihilo* or by the transformation, merger or division of existing companies[402] and is to be governed by the Statute and otherwise by the law of the member state in which it has its registered office,[403] a branch by the law where it is located.[404]

5. Special sectors

(a) Students

11.65 A Union national wishing to pursue studies in another member state falls uncomfortably into the Treaty prism. Except insofar as it is ancillary to other Treaty rights (for example, schooling for a worker's family, albeit taken generously by the Court of Justice)[405] education fell largely outwith the original Treaties. As article 57 does not require that a service be paid for by the

---

394   Regulation 2157/2001, art. 10; (Regulation 1435/2003, art. 9).
395   ETUI SE Factsheet, Overview of current state of SE founding in Europe, 26 August 2012.
396   Regulation 2157/2001, Preamble, 10th indent.
397   Directive 2005/56 [2005] OJ L310/1 (CBM or Tenth Company Law Directive).
398   Case C-411/03 *SEVIC Systems* [2005] ECR I-10805; see 11.57 above. *SEVIC* recognised cross-border mergers to fall within the scope of arts 49/54 TFEU and applies to any company, society or partnership, not simply limited companies as does the SE Statute.
399   COM(2010) 481 final.
400   COM(2008) 396/3, proposing 'a Statute on the European private company'.
401   *Ibid.* art. 19.
402   *Ibid.* art. 5.
403   *Ibid.* art. 4.
404   *Ibid.* art. 13.
405   See 11.12 above.

recipient,[406] migrant students might have fallen within the chapter on services as (passive) recipients thereof. But they do not. When it was first suggested the Court responded:

> The first paragraph of Article [57] … provides that only services 'normally provided for remuneration' are to be considered to be 'services' within the meaning of the Treaty … The essential characteristic of remuneration thus lies in the fact that it constitutes consideration for the service in question, and is normally agreed upon between the provider and the recipient of the service. That characteristic is, however, absent in the case of courses provided under the national education system. First of all, the State, in establishing and maintaining such a system, is not seeking to engage in gainful activity but is fulfilling its duties towards its own population in the social, cultural and educational fields. Secondly, the system in question is, as a general rule, funded from the public purse and not by pupils or their parents.[407]

Education is therefore not a service if, as is normally the case, it is offered by establishments forming part of the system of public education and is financed, in whole or in part, by public funds. Private education in another member state which is financed 'essentially' by private funds, even if that funding comes from sources other than the pupil or his or her parents, is a service,[408] but this represents only a tiny fraction of the context in which education is pursued.[409]

Having said that, higher (that is, tertiary and technical) education, being a form **11.66** of education which 'prepare[s] for a qualification for a particular profession, trade or employment or provide[s] the necessary training and skills for such a profession, trade or employment',[410] is recognised to fall within the rubric of vocational training, which *is* and has always been a concern of the Treaties,[411] so that conditions of access to higher education (so defined) fall within the scope of Union law.[412] It is possible that higher education pursued for the sole purpose of an improvement in general knowledge may not so qualify,[413] but the

---

406 Case 352/85 *Bond van Adverteerders and ors* v *Netherlands State* [1988] ECR 2085; Case C-157/99 *Geraets-Smits and Peerbooms* v *Stichting Ziekenfonds VGZ and Stichting CZ Groep Zorgverzekeringen* [2001] ECR I-5473; Case C-372/04 *R (Watts)* v *Bedford Primary Care Trust and anor* [2006] ECR I-4325.

407 Case 263/86 *Belgium* v *Humbel and Edel* [1988] ECR 5365, at paras 15–18; confirmed in Case C-109/92 *Wirth* v *Landeshauptstadt Hannover* [1993] ECR I-6447, at para. 15.

408 Case C-76/05 *Schwartz and Gootjes-Schwartz* v *Finanzamt Bergisch Gladbach* [2007] ECR I-6849.

409 For a general discussion of education in Union law, including an extensive historial overview, see the opinion of A-G Ruiz-Jarabo Colomer in Cases C-11 and 12/06 *Morgan and Bucher* v *Bezirksregierung Koln and anor* [2007] ECR I-9161.

410 Case 24/86 *Blaizot* v *University of Liège and ors* [1988] ECR 379, at para. 19.

411 This because of EEC Treaty, art. 118: 'The Commission shall have the task of promoting close cooperation between Member States in the social field, particulary in matters relating to … basic and advanced vocational training'. See now TFEU, art. 166.

412 Case 293/83 *Gravier* v *Ville de Liège* [1985] ECR 593; Case 24/86 *Blaizot*, n. 410 above; Case C-65/03 *Commission* v *Belgium* [2004] ECR I-6427; Case C-147/03 *Commission* v *Austria* [2005] ECR I-5969.

413 See Case 293/85 *Commission* v *Belgium* [1988] ECR 305, *per* A-G Slynn at 335–8.

Court has never developed the point. The Maastricht Treaty introduced a Community policy on education (properly so-called), essentially a supporting role for 'quality' education[414] and including an aim of encouraging the mobility of students (and teachers),[415] but this has not caused the Court to redefine higher education as different from previously. Nor does it require saying (although the Court says it anyway)[416] that the content of syllabus and the organisation of education systems remain matters exclusively for the member states, and Lisbon confirmed education and vocational training to be areas in which the Union enjoys support, coordinating or supplementary competences only.[417] The net result of these provisions is that

- First, admission to study must be upon an equal footing, and any additional burden for students who are of another nationality or have completed their secondary education in another member state, so that they bear a disadvantage when compared to home (educated) students, is contrary to articles 18, 165 and 166 TFEU.[418] This of course carries with it a (rebuttable) presumption of equivalence of secondary education. The open playing field is a cause for concern in member states the universities and colleges of which are, for various reasons, attractive to students from other member states (notably Belgium, Denmark, Austria, United Kingdom), and Austria is thought to have secured from the Commission as a price of its agreement to the Lisbon Treaty a five-year moratorium upon enforcement action on the question of its quotas for admission to medical schools.[419] The Court has said that differential treatment may be justified if based upon objective considerations independent of the nationality of the students concerned and proportionate to the legitimate aim of the national provisions[420] but has not indicated what this might encompass. A *numerus clausus* for admission of non-Belgian students (more accurately, non-residents of the Communauté française de Belgique) to medical and related courses adopted by parliamentary decree in the Communauté was

---

414 TFEU, art. 165(1) (ex art. 149(1) EC).
415 TFEU, art. 165(2), 2nd indent.
416 Cases C-11 and 12/06 *Morgan and Bucher* v *Bezirksregierung Köln and anor* [2007] ECR I-9161, at para. 24.
417 TFEU, art. 6(e).
418 Case C-147/03 *Commission v Austria* [2005] ECR I-5969.
419 In January 2007 the Commission sent art. 258 letters of formal notice to Austria (for failure to comply with the judgment of the Court in Case 147/03 *Commission* v *Austria, ibid.*) and Belgium (for adoption of a *numerus clausus* by the Communauté française on admission to higher education (Décret régulant le nombre d'étudiants dans certains cursus de premier cycle de l'enseignement supérieur, MB du 6 juillet 2006, p. 34055)), but in November 2007 suspended both proceedings for a period of five years. The Belgian rules were then taken on directly by Mr Bressol and Ms Chaverot, n. 421 below.
420 Case C-147/03 *Commission v Austria*, n. 418 above, at para. 48. The Austrian government claimed justification in the interests of safeguarding the homogeneity and financial equilibrium of the higher or university education system but without success, possibly through failure to produce any data supporting the argument.

found not to be justified by reference to financial burden but it could be justified, even though discriminating (indirectly) on grounds of nationality, if necessary to ensure the provision of adequate public health services.[421] An inability adequately to understand the language of instruction is (indirect) discrimination on grounds of nationality, but is, *mutatis mutandis*, a legitimate ground for limiting rights of free movement of workers,[422] establishment and services,[423] so doubtless applies and is justified equally here, although there is no case law on it.

- Next, owing to the prohibition of discrimination in article 18, a member state may not impose upon students from other member states fees higher than those exigible from home students.[424] A fee structure based upon domicile rather than nationality – such as obtains in the United Kingdom[425] – is compatible with this; so, a migrant student who has resided outwith the Union (the rule cannot be outside the United Kingdom, for that would result in indirect discrimination) for a period of time (three years) may be required to pay higher ('overseas') fees so long as a British national in the same circumstances is subject to the same burden.

- Thirdly, a student in higher education has a right of residence for the duration of his or her studies.[426] The Citizens' Rights Directive permits member states to require incoming students to have comprehensive sickness insurance cover and to assure the relevant national authority that they have sufficient resources for themselves (and their family members, if applicable) not to become a burden on the social assistance system of the

---

421 Case C-73/08 *Bressol and Chaverot and ors* v *Gouvernement de la Communauté française* [2010] ECR I-2735; applied by the Supreme Court in the United Kingdom (without benefit of a preliminary ruling from the Court of Justice) to deny a Latvian pensioner resident in the United Kingdom a 'state pension credit' in order to protect the social security system against benefit or social tourism: *Patmalniece* v *Secretary of State for Work and Pensions* [2011] UKSC 11, [2011] 3 All ER 1.

422 Regulation 492/2011 [2011] OJ L141/1, art. 3(1).

423 Directive 2005/36 [2005] OJ L255/22, art. 53.

424 Case 293/83 *Gravier* v *Ville de Liège* [1985] ECR 593; Case 24/86 *Blaizot* v *University of Liège and ors* [1988] ECR 379. Tolerance of reverse discrimination (or the 'wholly internal' rule, as to which see 11.90–11.95 below) may have (financially) significant application here. For example: Scottish students studying for first degrees at Scottish universities pay no fees (more accurately, their assessed fees are paid by the government (the Student Awards Agency for Scotland)), and this entitlement is shared (as it must be) with students from other Union member states; but students from other parts of the United Kingdom are required to pay a substantial 'variable tuition fee' which discrimination is not remedied by Union law so long as the wholly internal rule persists (and so long as the United Kingdom remains a single member state).

425 Education (Fees and Awards) Regulations 1997, SI 1997/1972 (for England and Wales).

426 Case C-357/89 *Raulin* v *Minister for Education and Science* [1992] ECR I-1027; Directive 2004/38 [2004] OJ L158/77, art. 7(c). This right derives directly from the Treaty, the codification in Directive 2004/38 therefore having utility only in that it grants a right of residence also to a student's family (art. 7(d)). The right of residence is restricted to those in further education or vocational training, however generously defined, art. 7(c) providing a right of residence to students 'enrolled … for the principal purpose of following a course of study, including vocational training'. It therefore does not apply to children of school age and primary or secondary (non-vocational) education.

host Member State during their period of study;[427] but a student may satisfy this test by means of a declaration or by any such equivalent means as he or she may choose,[428] and is entitled to rely upon other sources of support, such as a spouse's (or other family member's) earnings.[429]

11.67 As for the financial subvention frequently made available to students, the Treaties originally required that subsistence grants paid to home students be provided to a migrant student from another member state only if he or she had previously been a migrant worker in the host member state and became unintentionally unemployed, there was a link between the previous work and the course of education he or she wished to pursue, or the purpose of further study was to improve his or her prospects in the labour market.[430] But in 2001 the Court first linked entitlement to financial support to citizenship of the Union,[431] in light of which, combined with the introduction (by Maastricht) of Treaty provisions on education and vocational training, and notwithstanding the express provision in the (then operative) Students' Movement Directive that it was not to establish any entitlement to a maintenance grant from the host member state,[432] the Court was able to say in 2005:

> In view of those developments since the judgments in *Lair* and *Brown*, it must be considered that the situation of a citizen of the Union who is lawfully resident in another Member State falls within the scope of application of the Treaty within the meaning of the first paragraph of Article [18 TFEU] for the purposes of obtaining assistance for students, whether in the form of a subsidised loan or a grant, intended to cover his maintenance costs.[433]

However, owing to concerns of a connection between the (parent or student) taxpayer and the benefit and ensuring that the grant of assistance to cover the maintenance costs of students from other member states does not become an unreasonable burden and so imperil the overall level of assistance coming from public funds, it is legitimate that such assistance be restricted to students who have demonstrated 'a certain degree of integration into the society of' the host member state.[434] For these purposes the member state cannot require a link

---

427 Directive 2004/38, *ibid.*, art. 7(1)(c), 2nd indent.

428 *Ibid.*

429 Case C-408/03 *Commission* v *Belgium* [2006] ECR I-2647.

430 Case 39/86 *Lair* v *Universität Hannover* [1988] ECR 3161; Case 197/86 *Brown* v *Secretary of State for Scotland* [1988] ECR 3205; Case C-357/89 *Raulin*, n. 426 above; now codified in Directive 2004/38, art. 7(3)(d) .

431 Case C-184/99 *Grzelczyk* v *Centre public d'aide sociale d'Ottignies-Louvain-la-Neuve* [2001] ECR I-6193; see 11.101 below.

432 Directive 93/36 [1993] OJ L317/59, art. 3.

433 Case C-209/03 *R (Bidar)* v *London Borough of Ealing and anor* [2005] ECR I-2119, at para. 42.

434 Case C-209/03 *Bidar*, *ibid.*, at para. 57; Cases C-11 and 12/06 *Morgan and Bucher* v *Bezirksregierung Köln and anor* [2007] ECR I-9161, at para. 43.

with the labour market (which is a legitimate precondition to entitlement to various social allowances),[435] and the requisite degree of integration may be established by (lawful) residence 'for a certain length of time'.[436] Mr Bidar (a French national) had lived in the United Kingdom (completing his secondary education) for three years prior to embarking upon a university degree course and seeking assistance for maintenance costs; he was thus 'lawfully resident and ... received a substantial part of his secondary education in the host Member State and has consequently established a genuine link with the society of that State'.[437] Directive 2004/38 seeks to set a minimum period, providing that, by way of derogation from the principle of equal treatment, a host member state is not obliged to grant maintenance aid for study to incoming students prior to their acquisition of a right of permanent residence[438] – that is, for five years. The question is, whether it falls within the Union legislator's legitimate discretion in ensuring a certain degree of integration to define 'a certain length of time', and do so in excess of that which applied to Mr Bidar (the Directive adopted prior to *Bidar* but *Bidar* decided prior to the deadline for its implementation). The Court of Justice appears to think so.[439]

A student who works alongside his or her studies is to be classified as a worker **11.68** (with all the benefits that status entails), unless, in keeping with general principles, that activity is one that is purely marginal and ancillary.[440] The recipient of a scholarship in order to pursue full time doctoral research is not a worker unless some of his or her activity is performed for a period of time under the direction of the awarding body for which the scholarship can be character-ised as payment.[441] There is an argument to be derived from the judgment in *Bettray*[442] that paid work which is wholly or essentially ancillary to study and its

---

435 Case C-224/98 *D'Hoop* v *Office national de l'emploi* [2002] ECR I-6191; Case C-138/02 *Collins* v *Secretary of State for Work and Pensions* [2004] ECR I-2703; Cases C-22 and 23/08 *Vatsouras and Koupatantze* v *Arbeitsgemeinschaft Nürnberg 900* [2009] ECR I-4585.

436 Case C-209/03 *Bidar*, n. 433 above, at para. 59.

437 *Ibid.* at para. 63.

438 Directive 2004/38, art. 24(2).

439 Case C-158/07 *Förster* v *Hoofddirectie van de Informatie Beheer Groep* [2008] ECR I-8507; cf. the opinion of A-G Mazák, who proposed (at paras 123–35) that a student must be able to rely upon other factors, and demonstrate them by appropriate means, in order to indicate a substantial degree of integration into the society of the host member state. In Case C-542/09 *Commission v Netherlands*, judgment of 14 June 2012, not yet reported, the Court accepted that the Dutch '3 out of 6 years' residence requirement for migrant workers' children in order to gain entitlement to funding for foreign study could be objectively justified, but that the Dutch government had failed to show it to be proportionate.

440 Case C-184/99 *Grzelczyk* v *Centre public d'aide sociale d'Ottignies-Louvain-la-Neuve* [2001] ECR I-6193, especially the opinion of A-G Alber at paras 65–74 of his opinion; Case C-294/06 *R (Payir and ors)* v *Secretary of State for the Home Department* [2008] ECR I-203.

441 Case C-94/07 *Raccanelli* v *Max-Planck-Gesellschaft zur Förderung der Wissenschaften* [2008] ECR I-5939. It is submitted that supervision of a thesis is not 'under direction' for these purposes.

442 Case 344/87 *Bettray* v *Staatssecretaris van Justitie* [1989] ECR 1621; see n. 13 above and accompanying text.

educational purpose (tutoring, for example) would be insufficient to meet the test, but it appears that the Court might distance itself from *Bettray* in this context.[443]

(b)   Health care

11.69   Health care shares a number of characteristics with education. As with education, it was recognised (but earlier, in 1984) that receipt of private medical care in another member state is a passive provision of services falling within article 56 TFEU.[444] But just as with education, much health care is provided not privately but by the state. It will be recalled that the Court of Justice said of education:

> First of all, the State, in establishing and maintaining such a system, is not seeking to engage in gainful activity but is fulfilling its duties towards its own population ... Secondly, the system in question is, as a general rule, funded from the public purse and not by pupils or their parents.[445]

Substutite 'patients' for 'pupils' and there is no immediately apparent reason why this could not or should not apply equally to medical care. But it does not: the two follow different paths.

11.70   In fact the Community first intruded into the field of medical care in 1971. Regulation 1408/71 on social security (and Regulation 883/2004 which replaced it in 2010)[446] was (is) concerned primarily with the coordination of national social security schemes so as to ease the transferability of benefit entitlement;[447] in this it 'helps to facilitate the free movement of persons covered by social insurance'.[448] In order to do so it includes a chapter on sickness and maternity benefits which provides for a person so covered ('affiliated'), and his or her family, emergency medical cover during a temporary stay in a member state other than his or her competent state (under the European Health Insurance Card (EHIC) scheme, previously the E111 (or similar) scheme).[449] It was thus concerned primarily with health care for individuals

---

443   See Case C-1/97 *Birden* v *Stadtgemeinde Bremen* [1998] ECR I-7747, at para. 31; Case C-294/06 *Payir*, n. 440 above, *per* A-G Kokott at paras 35–8 of her opinion.

444   Cases 286/82 and 26/83 *Luisi and Carbone* v *Ministero del Tesoro* [1984] ECR 377.

445   Case 263/86 *Belgium* v *Humbel and Edel* [1988] ECR 5365, at para. 18; cited at greater length at 11.65 above.

446   See 11.25 above.

447   See 11.24–11.28 above.

448   Case C-368/98 *Vanbraekel and ors* v *Alliance nationale des mutualités chrétiennes* [2001] ECR I-5363, at para. 32.

449   Regulation 883/2004, art. 20 (ex Regulation 1408/71, art. 22(1)). Prior to 2006 when it was replaced with the EHIC a person might rely instead upon a E110 (international road hauliers), E111 (tourists), E119 (unemployed, job seekers) or E128 (students, temporary workers) form. The EHIC scheme applies also in the EEA and in Switzerland.

ancillary to their exercise of rights of free movement, for example a migrant worker resident in, or a tourist visiting, a member state other than that of his or her affiliation. But it also provides for receipt of health care in a member state other than his or her competent state or state of residence where authorisation may be, or alternatively must be, granted.[450] As a general rule authorisation for such treatment is required to be sought from the competent institution of the member state of affiliation,[451] but it cannot be refused where the treatment is amongst the benefits provided in the member state of residence but cannot be provided within a time limit which is medically justifiable, taking into account the patient's current state of health and the probable course of the illness.[452] The patient is entitled to reimbursement from the competent health authorities of the member state of affiliation of the costs of treatment, other benefits in kind standard in the member state of treatment and necessary upon medical grounds, and any cash benefits provided under the legislation it applies.[453]

It was long assumed that public health care is not a service, and that the relevant **11.71** chapter of Regulation 1408/71 exhausted Community interest in the field. But in 1998 the Court of Justice found the public provision in another member state of 'extra-mural' (*in casu*, dental) health care to fall within article 56,[454] and extended it in 2001 to intra-mural (hospital) care.[455] So health care is not in the event special: or rather its 'special nature ... does not remove [it] from the ambit of the fundamental principle of freedom of movement'.[456] Article 56 therefore provides for benefits alongside those of Regulation 883/2004. The Court did not overlay the rule of Regulation 1408/71 with article 56, rather it married the two: article 22 'helps to facilitate the free movement of persons'[457] *and* 'to the same extent, the cross-border provision of medical services between Member States'.[458] Therefore

> the applicability of Article 22 of Regulation No. 1408/71 ... does not mean that Article [56 TFEU] cannot apply at the same time. The fact that national legislation may be in conformity with Regulation No. 1408/71 does not have the effect of removing that legislation from the scope of the provisions of the [Treaties].[459]

The two are therefore to be integrated and interpreted harmoniously.

---

450 Regulation 883/2004, art. 20 (ex Regulation 1408/71, art. 22(1)).
451 Regulation 883/2004, art. 20(1) (ex Regulation 1408/71, art. 22(1)(c)).
452 Regulation 883/2004, art. 20(2) (ex Regulation 1408/71, art. 22(2)).
453 Regulation 883/2004, arts 17–21 (ex Regulation 1408/71, arts 22(1)(a) and (c), 36).
454 Case C-158/96 *Kohll* v *Union des Caisses de Maladie* [1998] ECR I-1931.
455 Case C-157/99 *Geraets-Smits and Peerbooms* v *Stichting Ziekenfonds VGZ and anor* [2001] ECR I-5473.
456 Case C-158/96 *Kohll*, n. 454 above, at para. 20.
457 Case C-368/98 *Vanbraekel*, n. 448 above, at para. 32.
458 Case C-56/01 *Inizan* v *Caisse primaire d'assurance maladie des Hauts-de-Seine* [2003] ECR I-12403, at para. 21.
459 Case C-211/08 *Commission* v *Spain* [2010] ECR I-5267, at para. 45.

11.72 Yet there are compelling arguments that health *is* a special case, and the Court appears so to recognise it from time to time.[460] It is a facet of social cohesion which is a Union objective and the subject of a Treaty integration clause[461] and is recognised by the Charter of Fundamental Rights in forthright language:

> Everyone has the right of access to preventive health care and the right to benefit from medical treatment under the conditions established by national laws and practices. A high level of human health protection shall be ensured in the definition and implementation of all Union policies and activities,[462]

which was emphasised by Advocate-General Ruiz-Jarabo Colomer in 2007:

> [A]lthough the case-law takes as the main point of reference the fundamental freedoms established in the Treaty, there is another aspect which is becoming more and more important in the Community sphere, namely the right of citizens to health care, proclaimed in Article 35 of the Charter …, since, 'being a fundamental asset, health cannot be considered solely in terms of social expenditure and latent economic difficulties'. This right is perceived as a personal entitlement, unconnected to a person's relationship with social security, and the Court of Justice cannot overlook that aspect.[463]

11.73 Health care having been drawn within article 56, a prior authorisation procedure (as prescribed by Regulation 883/2004) became an infringement of the right to provide (and receive) services, which would require objective justification (*inter alia*) in order to survive.[464] Such justification could, by reference to imperative reasons in the general interest, be found in a risk of seriously undermining the financial balance of a social security system[465] or by reference to article 62 TFEU (the protection of public health)[466] in order to maintain a balanced medical and hospital service open to all, insofar as it contributes to the attainment of a high level of health protection,[467] and treatment capacity or

---

460 E.g., Case C-322/01 *Deutscher Apothekerverband* v *0800 DocMorris and anor* [2003] ECR I-14887; Case C-531/06 *Commission* v *Italy* [2009] ECR I-4103, at para. 36; Cases C-171 and 172/07 *Apothekerkammer des Saarlandes and ors* v *Saarland, Ministerium für Justiz, Gesundheit und Soziales (Doc Morris)* [2009] ECR I-4171.
461 TFEU, art. 175, 1st para.
462 EU Charter of Fundamental Rights, art. 35.
463 Case C-444/05 *Stamatelaki* v *NPDD Organismos Asfaliseos Eleftheron Epangelmation* [2007] ECR I-3185, at para. 40 of his opinion.
464 See 11.122–11.128 below.
465 Case C-158/96 *Kohll*, n. 454 above, at para. 41; Case C-157/99 *Geraets-Smits and Peerbooms*, n. 455 above, at para. 72; Case C-385/99 *Müller-Fauré and anor* v *Onderlinge Waarborgmaatschappij OZ Zorgverzekeringen UA and anor* [2003] ECR I-4503, at para. 73; Case C-372/04 *R (Watts)* v *Bedford Primary Care Trust and anor* [2006] ECR I-4325, at para. 103; Case C-444/05 *Stamatelaki*, n. 463 above, at para. 30.
466 See 11.118, 11.128 below.
467 Case C-158/96 *Kohll*, n. 454 above, at para. 50; Case C-157/99 *Geraets-Smits and Peerbooms*, n. 455 above, at para. 73; Case C-385/99 *Müller-Fauré*, n. 465 above, at para. 67; Case C-372/04 *Watts*, n. 465 above, at para. 104; Case C-444/05 *Stamatelaki*, n. 463 above, at para. 31.

medical competence within the national territory essential for public health.[468] Thus hospital waiting lists which manage the supply of treatment and set priorities upon the basis of available resources and capacity are in principle legitimate.[469]

Whilst there is no legal distinction to be drawn between hospital and non- **11.74** hospital treatment,[470] generally a scheme of prior authorisation cannot be justified for non-hospital treatment[471] for its absence will not undermine the financial equilibrium of a social security system, so long as reimbursement remains within the limits of cover to be met by the member state of affiliation;[472] there are exceptions.[473] It can more easily be justified in the case of hospital treatment,[474] but then not always.[475] Different considerations may apply as between scheduled and unscheduled treatment.[476] If authorisation is refused the patient may proceed nonetheless and, if he or she can show that it was improperly refused, recover reimbursement in the amount which would ordinarily have been paid had authorisation been properly granted.[477] Normally reimbursement is to the level the treatment would cost if provided in the member state of affiliation but higher costs may be recovered (by virtue of article 56, not of Regulation 883/2004) where certain criteria (the *Vanbraekel* criteria) are met.[478]

Cross-Border Health Care Directive

Owing to the potential cost to social security systems and the risk of 'health **11.75** tourism' the cases involving article 56 and health care have normally attracted spirited intervention from (and the disquiet of) the governments of the

---

468 Case C-158/96 *Kohll*, n. 454 above, at para. 51; Case C-157/99 *Geraets-Smits and Peerbooms*, n. 455 above, at para. 74; Case C-385/99 *Müller-Fauré*, n. 465 above, at para. 67; Case C-372/04 *Watts*, n. 465 above, at para. 105; Case C-444/05 *Stamatelaki*, n. 463 above, at para. 32.
469 Case C-372/04 *Watts*, n. 465 above, at para. 67.
470 Case C-157/99 *Geraets-Smits and Peerbooms*, n. 455 above, at para. 53; Case C-8/02 *Leichtle* v *Bundesamt für Arbeit* [2004] ECR I-2641, at para. 28; Case C-372/04 *Watts*, n. 465 above, at para. 86; Case C-444/05 *Stamatelaki*, n. 463 above, at para. 19.
471 E.g., Case C-158/96 *Kohll*, n. 454 above,; Case C-385/99 *Müller-Fauré*, n. 465 above.
472 COM(2008) 414, para. 7.1.
473 Case C-512/08 *Commission* v *France* [2010] ECR I-8833 (involving treatment by 'major medical equipment': scintillation camera, nuclear magnetic resonance imaging or spectrometry apparatus, medical scanner, hyperbaric chamber, cyclotron).
474 Case C-157/99 *Geraets-Smits and Peerbooms*, n. 455 above; Case C-56/01 *Inizan*, n. 458 above; Case C-8/02 *Leichtle* v, n. 470 above; Case C-385/99 *Müller-Fauré*, n. 465 above; Case C-372/04 *Watts*, n. 465 above.
475 E.g., Case C-368/98 *Vanbraekel*, n. 448 above; Case C-444/05 *Stamatelaki*, n. 463 above; Case C-173/09 *Elchinov* v *Natsionalna zdravnoosiguritelna kasa* [2010] ECR I-8889.
476 Case C-211/08 *Commission* v *Spain* [2010] ECR I-5267.
477 Case C-368/98 Vanbraekel, n. 448 above; Case C-372/04 *Watts*, n. 465 above; Case C-173/09 *Elchinov*, n. 475 above.
478 Case C-368/98 *Vanbraekel*, n. 448 above, at para. 53.

member states. The results have been 'controversial'.[479] In order to regain some control the political institutions took a hand. The 2006 Services Directive had expressly excluded health care services 'whether or not they are provided via healthcare facilities, and regardless of the ways in which they are organised and financed at national level or whether they are public or private'.[480] But in 2008 the Commission proposed a Directive on the application of patients' rights in cross-border health care,[481] it was adopted by the Parliament and Council in 2011[482] and is to be implemented by 25 October 2013.[483]

11.76 The primary aims of the Directive are codification of the case law of the Court on cross-border health care[484] ('to achieve a more general, and also effective, application of the principles developed by the Court of Justice on a case-by-case basis')[485] and clarification of its interplay with Regulation 883/2004[486] and of the right to reimbursement for health care received in another member state.[487] It applies to cross-border health care, being a health service, including the prescription, dispensation and provision of medicinal products and devices, provided by or under the supervision of a health professional (doctor, nurse, dentist, pharmacist) in the exercise of his or her profession in a member state other than that in which the patient is affiliated (within the meaning of Regulation 883/2004),[488] 'regardless of how it is organised, delivered and financed'.[489] The care is to be provided in accordance with the legislation, standards and guidelines of the member state of treatment.[490]

11.77 Regulation 883/2004 is not displaced, rather it applies to the exclusion of the Directive where it obliges the authorisation of treatment in another member state,[491] otherwise the Directive prevails.[492] Costs are to be reimbursed (or paid

---

479 Case C-512/08 *Commission v France*, n. 473 above, *per* A-G Sharpston at para. 1 of her opinion.
480 Directive 2006/123 [2006] OJ L376/36, art. 2(2)(f).
481 Proposal for a Directive on the application of patients' rights in cross-border health care, COM(2008) 414 final. See also *A Community Framework on the Application of Patients' Rights in Cross-border Healthcare*, COM(2008) 415 final.
482 Directive 2011/24 [2011] OJ L88/45.
483 *Ibid.* art. 21.
484 COM(2008) 415, para. 4.
485 Directive 2011/24, Preamble, 8th indent.
486 *Ibid.* art. 1(1).
487 COM(2008) 414, para. 2.
488 Directive 2011/24, art. 3(a), (b), (e), (f).
489 *Ibid.* art. 1(2). The Directive excised the closing words 'or whether it is public or private' from the Commission proposal.
490 *Ibid.* art. 4(1). In the case of 'telemedicine' the member state of treatment is that in which the provider is established; art. 3(d).
491 *Ibid.* arts 3(m), 7(1); Preamble, 46th indent. Article 3(m) also accords priority to a number of other Union measures.
492 This was much clearer under the Commission proposal (COM(2008) 414, art. 3(2)), it must be inferred from the Directive.

directly by the member state of affiliation) if the health care in question is amongst the benefits to which the patient is entitled in the member state of affiliation,[493] up to the level which it would have assumed had the health care been provided there, without exceeding the actual cost incurred.[494] If the costs are higher the competent authority 'may nevertheless' reimburse them[495] and other related costs such as accommodation and travel in accordance with national legislation[496] (the latter not an entitlement under Regulation 883/2004). It is not clear if this will displace the *Verbraekel* case law requiring recovery of higher costs.

A member state (of affiliation) may impose a requirement of prior authorisation **11.78** for reimbursement of the cost of health care in another member state if (and only if) the treatment:

- is made subject to planning requirements for ensuring adequacy and efficiency of the home service and requires:
  - overnight hospital accommodation; or
  - the use of highly specialised and cost-intensive medical infrastructure or medical equipment;
- presents a particular risk for the patient or the population; or
- is provided by a health care provider which upon a case by case basis could give rise to specific and serious concerns relating to quality or safety of care.[497]

These treatments defined 'hospital care' under the Commission proposal[498] but the distinction was dropped from the Directive. Authorisation for these must be granted when the patient is entitled to the health care in question (as set out in article 7) and when it cannot be provided at home within a time limit which is medically justifiable, based upon an objective medical assessment of the patient's medical condition, the history and probable course of his or her illness, the degree of pain and/or the nature of the disability at the time when the request for authorisation was made (or renewed).[499] It may nevertheless be refused in some cases, as set out in the Directive.[500] Conditions for eligibility and regulatory and administrative formalities may be imposed if they apply to

---

493   Directive 2011/24, arts 5(a), 7(1).
494   *Ibid.* art. 7(4).
495   *Ibid.* art. 7(4), 2nd para.
496   *Ibid.* art. 7(4), 3rd para.
497   *Ibid.* arts 7(8), 8(2).
498   COM(2008) 414, n. 492 above, art. 8.
499   Directive 2011/24, art. 8(5).
500   *Ibid.* art. 8(6), (7).

home health care.[501] A gatekeeper system (for example, access to a specialist only upon referral by a general practitioner) is therefore compatible with the Directive so long as it produces no discrimination and does not inhibit the movement of patients, services or goods.[502] If the conditions set out in Regulation 883/2004 are met authorisation must be granted.[503] There are specific rules for prescriptions for medicinal products to be dispensed in another member state[504] and provision for the development of 'eHealth' services.[505]

11.79 Reimbursement may be limited in order to protect overriding reasons of general interest (planning requirements relating to the aim of ensuring sufficient and permanent access to a balanced range of high-quality treatment or to the wish to control costs and avoid, as far as possible, any waste of financial, technical and human resources) so long as it is necessary and proportionate.[506] Costs for care following authorisation must be met.[507]

11.80 Member states are required to designate one or more national 'contact points' which liaise with contact points in other member states and provide information to (prospective) patients seeking treatment, both home (seeking treatment in another member state) and abroad (seeking treatment there).[508] There is to be mutual assistance and cooperation amongst member states and national contact points, including at regional and local level.[509]

(c) Sport

11.81 Participation in sport is of course normally gratuitous, and its organisation serves a social or recreational purpose which has nothing to do with Union law. However,

> [i]t should be borne in mind ... that any activity consisting in offering goods or services on a given market is an economic activity. Provided that that condition is satisfied, the fact that an activity has a connection with sport does not hinder the application of the rules of the Treaty.[510]

---

501 *Ibid.* art. 7(7).
502 *Ibid.*
503 *Ibid.* art. 8(3).
504 *Ibid.* art. 11.
505 *Ibid.* art. 14.
506 *Ibid.* art. 7(9), (11).
507 *Ibid.* art. 7(8).
508 *Ibid.* arts 4(2)(a), 5(b), 6.
509 *Ibid.* art. 10.
510 Case C-49/07 *Motosykletistiki Omospondia Ellados* v *Elliniko Dimosio* [2008] ECR I-4863, at para. 22.

More particularly, where a sporting activity takes the form of paid employment or a provision of remunerated service, it falls within the scope of article 45 or article 56, respectively.[511] Given the growth and economic importance of professional sport – its popularity, ubiquity, high wages, telediffusion of fixtures, gaming thereon, associated marketing rights – it is surprising that the Court of Justice came only late to be troubled by it. It was in 1974 (*Walrave and Koch*) that the Court first encountered it, and another 20 years (*Bosman*) before the breadth of Community intrusion in the sphere became apparent.

Mr Bosman was a Belgian footballer seeking a transfer from his club RC Liège **11.82** (in Belgium) to US Dunkerque (France). But he encountered two problems: first, the rules on nationality adopted by the *Fédération Internationale de Football Association* (FIFA) and enforced by national football associations, according to which the number of foreign players (as defined by FIFA regulations) whose names may be included on the team-sheet may be restricted to not more than three per team, plus two players who have played in the country in question for five years uninterruptedly (the '3+2 rule'); second, Liège sought (as it was entitled to do, in accordance with FIFA regulations) a transfer fee (of BFr 6 million) from Dunkerque, although Mr Bosman was out of contract. The 3+2 rule, which limited the number of players fielded by nationality, was a clear breach of article 45 (provided of course the affected players were Union nationals). With hindsight it is curious that it took the Court so long to be asked. But *Bosman* is more important in two other respects: first, the transfer fee was nationality blind: that is, a fee was exigible irrespective of Mr Bosman's nationality and irrespective of the member state in which the club wishing to employ him was located, yet it nevertheless hindered him in his intention to work in another member state. It was thus analogous to an indistinctly applicable rule in the free movement of goods, and so invites (and imports into article 45) justification based upon *Cassis de Dijon* reasoning or, in language more common to article 56, imperative reasons in the general interest. The Court considered such justification but dismissed it in *Bosman*;[512] in a subsequent footballer's case (*Olympique Lyonnais*) it was persuaded that a compulsory compensation scheme could be justified in the interests of recruitment and training of young players, so long as it was effective and proportionate.[513]

---

511   Case 36/74 *Walrave and Koch v Association Union cycliste internationale and ors* [1974] ECR 1405, at para. 5; Case C-415/93 *Union Royale Belge des Sociétés de Football Association and ors v Bosman and ors* [1995] ECR I-4921, at para. 73; Case C-325/08 *Olympique Lyonnais v Bernard and Newcastle United FC* [2010] ECR I-2177, at para. 28. Matters involving team sports tend to fall under art. 45, those involving sports in which individual athletes participate art. 56.

512   Case C-415/93 *Bosman, ibid.* at paras 105–14. Much more extensive consideration was given the issue by A-G Lenz (at paras 214–52 of his opinion), but he too ultimately failed to be convinced.

513   Case C-325/08 *Olympique Lyonnais*, n. 511 above; also the more extensive analysis of A-G Sharpston at paras 44–58 of her opinion.

Second, the rules in question were adopted not by a member state but by a private person (FIFA), a private association (*Verein*) formed in Swiss law, so giving rise to the issue of the horizontal direct effect of article 45. This is discussed below.[514] But it has serious practical ramifications for international sport, which is, increasingly, organised and governed globally. Here, the FIFA rules can be neutered insofar as they apply within the Union; but the Union cannot touch the rule itself, so, unless altered, it continues to govern sporting activities in other countries and, owing to the wholly internal rule,[515] within a member state – so that if Mr Bosman had been seeking to sign with, say, Galatasaray (Istanbul) or Anderlecht (Brussels), the Treaties would have been (and are) silent.[516] In the meanwhile a Brazilian teammate remains unaffected by all this except insofar as his (or her) club is engaged in an international fixture, in which case the employer club is entitled to field him – in another member state, but not in a home fixture – as a function of its provision of a service there;[517] and then only if the Brazilian is an employee of his (her) club and not there under a contract for services. This creates a complex new type of variable geometry, peculiar to professional sport. The second leg was provisionally scheduled as a result of FIFA's stated intention to introduce a new '6+5 rule' in 2012/13[518] but the plan was abandoned in 2010 owing to Commission disapproval. It is thought to be no better disposed to proposals from the French *Ligue nationale de rugby* that, from 2013/2014, 'home-grown players' (*joueurs issus des filières de formation: JIFF*) must comprise 60 per cent of the roster of top flight clubs, home-grown meaning having been licensed (*licencié*) by the

---

514 See 11.140–11.144 below.

515 See 11.90–11.95 below.

516 However, the prohibition of discrimination on grounds of nationality has been extended to professional sportsmen from third countries with which the Union has entered into an association (or similar) agreement, provided the player is in lawful employment, a precondition of the agreements for entitlement to equal treatment; see Case C-265/03 *Simutenkov v Ministerio de Educación y Cultura and anor* [2005] ECR I-2579 (on the partnership agreement with Russia); Case C-152/08 *Real Sociedad de Fútbol and Kahveci v Consejo Superior de Deportes and anor* [2008] ECR I-6291 (the association agreement with Turkey).

517 This by virtue of the *Rush Portuguesa* case law (Case C-113/89 *Rush Portuguesa v Office National de l'Immigration* [1990] ECR I-1417); see n. 327 above and accompanying text.

518 See Resolution adopted by the FIFA Congress in Sydney on 29–30 May 2008. The 6+5 rule (to be introduced in stages, 4+7 in 2010/11, 5+6 in 2011/12, 6+5 in 2012/13) required that at the beginning of each match, each club must field at least six players eligible to play for the national team of the club's country; but there was no restriction upon the number of non-eligible players under contract or upon use of substitutes (leaving open the possibility of a 3+8 configuration at the end of the match). The rule was defended as countering the fruits of *Bosman*, the loss of clubs' national identity, an increase in inequality and widening financial and sporting gap amongst them, and a reduction in competitiveness and increasing predictability of results; and promoting the education and training of young players, training clubs and the values of effort and motivation in football, particularly for young players. In light of what *Bosman* has wrought, this new (and more proportionate) rule might, or might not, have passed muster with the Court of Justice.

Fédération Française de Rugby for five seasons before the age of 21 or having attended a French rugby academy for three years between the ages of 16 and 21.[519]

The absorption by sport of Union law may be summed up thus: **11.83**

> [T]he prohibitions laid down by those provisions of the Treaty apply to the rules adopted in the field of sport which concern the economic aspect which sporting activity can present ... [T]he rules providing for the payment of fees for the transfer of professional players between clubs (transfer clauses) or limiting the number of professional players who are nationals of other Member States which those clubs may field in matches (rules on the composition of club teams), or fixing, without objective reasons concerning only the sport or justified by differences in the circumstances between players, different transfer deadlines for players coming from other Member States (clauses on transfer deadlines) fall within the scope of those provisions of the Treaty and are subject to the prohibitions which they enact.[520]

However, the regulation of the sport itself, 'the rules of the game' in the strict **11.84** sense, on, for example, the duration of a match or the number of players on the field, exist because sport can exist and be practised only in accordance with specific rules. Those which relate to the particular nature and context of sporting events and are inherent in the organisation and proper conduct of sporting competition cannot be regarded as constituting a restriction on the free movement of workers and the freedom to provide services.[521] Into this category falls the rules on the composition of national teams, which are frontally discriminatory on grounds of nationality, but are purely sporting rules ('a question of purely sporting interest and ... nothing to do with economic activity')[522] and so outwith the scope of articles 45 and 56. With the passing of amateurs in international sport this is transparently a fiction but one with overwhelming popular support; notwithstanding the claim that Union law applies to 'rules on the composition of club teams',[523] it is difficult to see why the same rule does not apply (or indeed, must apply) equally to sub-national teams, for example, cricket at county level.[524] In the same vein rules relating to

---

519 Règlements généraux de la Ligue Nationale de Rugby, Saison 2011/2012, art. 24.
520 Case T-313/02 *Meca-Medina and Majcen* v *Commission* [2004] ECR II-3291, at para. 40, citing previous authority.
521 Case 36/74 *Walrave and Koch*, n. 511 above; Case 13/76 *Donà* v *Mantero* [1976] ECR 1333; Case C-49/07 *Motosykletistiki Omospondia Ellados* v *Elliniko Dimosio* [2008] ECR I-4863.
522 Case 36/74 *Walrave and Koch* v, n. 511 above, at para. 8; also Case 13/76 *Donà, ibid.*, at para. 14.
523 Case T-313/02 *Meca-Medina and Majcen*, n. 520 above, the passage quoted immediately above.
524 For many years Yorkshire County Cricket Club famously required its players to have been born within the 'historic county boundaries' of Yorkshire. This excluded cricketers of other nationalities (and other English players) but there is no apparent reason why it would or could be treated any differently from the 'question of purely sporting interest' which is the selection of a national side and so immune from arts 45 and 56. The rule

the selection by (national) sports federations of those of their members who may participate in competitions constitute purely sporting rules beyond the scope of articles 45 and 56.[525] But this immunisation from the Treaties of certain aspects of sport is restricted to those which remain within their proper objective[526] – put otherwise, 'as long as [the rule] derives from a need inherent in the organisation of such a competition'.[527] *Lehtonen*, for example, involved a deadline imposed by the *Fédération internationale de basket-ball* (FIBA) after which basketball teams could not include a player who had played for another team in the same season; Mr Lehtonen wished to play (temporarily) for a Belgian club following the conclusion of the Finnish season, the FIBA rule clearly restricted him from so doing, but was legitimate in ensuring the 'regularity' of sporting competitions[528] – that is, preventing a club from distorting the tables (especially during playoffs for promotion) by swamping the side with 'ringers' bought in as the season closed. 'Transfer windows' might fall into this category but would be more difficult to justify. A case was put to the Court of Justice on the question of whether FIFA rules on the compulsory release of club players for international duty (without compensation) is such a rule, but it was subsequently withdrawn.[529] Some of these rules – anti-doping rules adopted by a regulatory body, for example[530] – may have the effect of hindering competition and so may fall foul of the Union rules on competition, to which different considerations apply.[531]

11.85 In the meanwhile, the Treaties say little about sport. They were until Lisbon silent on it save for a declaration annexed to the Amsterdam IGC[532] which emphasises its social significance and encourages the institutions to heed the views of sporting associations where questions of sport are at issue, with special consideration given to the particular characteristics of amateur sport. The 'considerable social importance' adhering to sporting activities was recognised

---

was never challenged for inconsistency with Community law (by any, say, budding Dutch or Corfiot cricketer), and was abandoned in 1992.

525 Cases C-51/96 and 191/97 *Deliège* v *Ligue Francophone de Judo and ors* [2000] ECR I-2549, at para. 64.

526 Case 36/74 *Walrave and Koch*, n. 511 above, at para. 9; Case 13/76 *Donà*, n. 521, above, at para. 15; Case C-415/93 *Bosman*, n. 511 above, at paras 76 and 127; Cases C-51/96 and 191/97 *Deliège, ibid.*, at para. 43; Case C-176/96 *Lehtonen and anor* v *Fédération royale belge des sociétés de basket-ball* [2000] ECR I-2681, at para. 34.

527 Cases C-51/96 and 191/97 *Deliège*, n. 525 above, at para. 69.

528 Case C-176/96 *Lehtonen*, n. 526 above, at para. 53. The Court did find differentials in the deadline varying as between clubs within the jurisdiction of the same national governing body and other clubs unjustified.

529 Case C-243/06 *Sporting du Pays de Charleroi and anor* v *Fédération internationale de football association (FIFA)*, order of 25 November 2008, unreported.

530 Case C-519/04P *Meca-Medina and Majcen* v *Commission* [2006] ECR I-6991.

531 See 13.85 below.

532 Declaration (No. 29) on sport.

by the Court of Justice,[533] but this says little, and certainly does nothing to modify the application of the Treaties to sport. The role of sport in society, and its specific nature, were recognised by the European Council in 2000 (the 'Nice declaration').[534] In 2007 the Commission adopted a White Paper on Sport,[535] setting out a 'Pierre de Coubertin action plan' addressing strategic orientation on the role of sport in the Union, encouraging debate on specific problems, enhancing the visibility of sport in policy-making, raising awareness of the needs and specificities of the sector, and identifying the appropriate level of further action at Union level. With Lisbon sport has joined education, vocational training and youth as an ancillary Union competence, an area in which it may carry out 'actions to support, coordinate or supplement the actions of the Member States'.[536] It is to contribute to the promotion of European sporting issues (undefined) whilst taking account of the specific nature of sport, its structures based upon voluntary activity and its social and educational function,[537] with a view to developing the European dimension of sport by promoting fairness and openness in sporting competitions and cooperation between responsible bodies and by protecting the physical and moral integrity of sportsmen and women, especially the youngest.[538] But there remains no general exemption of sport, as has sometimes been urged, from the operation of Treaty rules.

(d) Transport

The provision of transport services is a *lex specialis*, falling not within the **11.86** chapter on services but within Title VI TFEU on transport, so subject to the development of the common transport policy.[539] This is so even in a sphere unoccupied by appropriate rules adopted under the CTP.[540] But the rules regulating a transport undertaking with a permanent establishment in another member state are properly those of the chapter on establishment.[541]

---

533 Case C-415/93 *Bosman*, n. 511 above, at para. 106; also Cases C-51/96 and 191/97 *Deliège*, n. 525 above, at para. 41.
534 Declaration on the Specific Characteristics of Sport and its Social Function in Europe, *Bulletin EU*, 12–2000, 27.
535 COM(2007) 391 final.
536 TFEU, art. 6.
537 *Ibid.* art. 165(1), 2nd para.
538 *Ibid.* art. 165(2).
539 *Ibid.* art. 58(1) (ex art. 51(1) EC); Case 4/88 *Lambregts Transportbedrijf* v *Belgian State* [1989] ECR 2583, at para. 9; Case 49/89 *Corsica Ferries France* v *Direction générale des douanes françaises* [1989] ECR 4441, para. 10 and case law cited; Case C-467/98 *Commission* v *Denmark* (Open Skies) [2002] ECR I-9519, at para. 123; see 11.199 below.
540 Case C-382/08 *Neukirchinger* v *Bezirkshauptmannschaft Grieskirchen* [2011] ECR I-139.
541 Case C-338/09 *Yellow Cab Verkehrsbetriebs* v *Landeshauptmann von Wien* [2010] ECR I-13927.

(e) Intellectual property

11.87 There is little case law on intellectual property rights in the context of services. Services differ from goods in that normally they cannot be re-used: with its provision the economic value of a service is realised and it cannot thereafter be passed on as such. Therefore there is limited scope for an 'exhaustion' of an intellectual property right in the service in the same way as there is with goods.[542] Nevertheless the principles of exhaustion of rights apply *mutatis mutandis* so that, for example, a restriction on the satellite transmission of football matches from one member state (where they are lawfully broadcast by the right holder) to another is an infringement of article 56.[543]

(f) Public procurement

11.88 The rules on public procurement apply to procurement not only of goods but similarly (and increasingly) to cross-frontier provision of services. They are discussed above.[544]

(g) Services of general economic interest

11.89 There are special rules, and limited immunity from Treaty discipline, on services of universal provision, or 'services of general (economic) interest'. Their closest Treaty tangency is with the competition rules, and they are discussed below in that context.[545]

C. MATTERS PURELY INTERNAL TO A MEMBER STATE: 'REVERSE DISCRIMINATION'

11.90 The language and technique of the Treaties reveal that the rules on free movement are concerned essentially with ensuring rights for the Union citizen in other member states. For example, the right of establishment is one which adheres to 'nationals of a Member State in the territory of another Member State'[546] and the beneficiaries of the Citizens' Rights Directive are 'all Union citizens who move to or reside in a Member State other than that of which they are a national'.[547] They betray an implicit (although inaccurate) presumption that member states confer upon their own citizens rights at least to the standard

---

542 Cases C-403 and 429/08 *Football Association Premier League* v *QC Leisure and ors* and *Murphy* v *Media Protection Services*, judgment of 4 October 2011, not yet reported, *per* A-G Kokott at para. 184 of her opinion. As to free movement of goods and exhaustion of rights see 10.81 above.

543 *Ibid.*

544 See 10.91–10.95 above.

545 See 13.142–13.147 below.

546 TFEU, art. 49, 1st para; see n. 564 below.

547 Directive 2004/38 [2004] OJ L158/77, art. 3(1).

to which the Treaties and their implementing law strive. A product of this approach is that where a person's affairs are restricted to the confines of a member state (or of a member state and any variety of third countries), they involve no 'appreciable Union element', are 'wholly internal' or 'purely internal' matters, and Union law will not apply. It is a rule which applies partly to the free movement of goods, to articles 34 and 35 (quantitative restrictions and measures having equivalent effect)[548] but not article 30 (customs duties and measures having equivalent effect).[549] But the issue has arisen most frequently in the context of persons, for example workers (or their families) seeking to invoke in their home member states free movement, residence, employment or social rights under article 45, Regulation 492/2011, Directive 2004/38 and/or Regulation 883/2004. Cases of it abound: a British citizen entering England (from Northern Ireland) in contravention of an English court's 'binding over' order;[550] Dutch nationals laying claim to a Union right of residence in Amsterdam for their dependent Surinamese parents[551] and Austrian nationals for their Turkish/Nigerian/Sri Lankan/Yugoslav and Serbian spouses and children in Austria;[552] an Ivoirian son of a French national claiming a Union social advantage in Paris;[553] a German national claiming unlawful discrimination at the hands of his German employer;[554] Belgians seeking to exercise Union linguistic rights in an action against the (Belgian) *Office national des pensions*[555] or equal access rights to a Flemish care insurance scheme;[556] an Italian seeking to compel an Italian employer to recognise the equivalence of his qualifications;[557] and a British national seeking to exercise a Treaty right to vote in UK municipal elections.[558] In all cases Union law avails them not.

The rule applies equally under the other freedoms: a Portuguese driving instructor restricted in his trade to the Minicípio of Lisbon;[559] an Austrian wishing to set up a driving school but whose Austrian qualifications are not **11.91**

---

548 See 10.66–10.67 above.

549 See 10.08 above.

550 Case 175/78 *R* v *Saunders* [1979] ECR 1129.

551 Cases 35 and 36/82 *Morson and Jhanjen* v *Netherlands* [1982] ECR 3723. Mrs Morson and Mrs Jhanjen had of course been themselves Dutch nationals until losing that status seven years earlier, by virtue of Toescheidings-overeenkomst van 25 november 1975 inzake nationaliteiten tussen het Koninkrijk der Nederlanden en de Republiek Suriname, Trb 1975, nr 132.

552 Case C-256/11 *Dereci and ors* v *Bundesministerium für Inneres*, judgment of 15 November 2011, not yet reported.

553 Case C-206/91 *Koua Poirrez* v *Caisse d'allocations familiales de la région parisienne* [1992] ECR I-6685.

554 Case C-332/90 *Steen* v *Deutsche Bundespost* [1992] ECR I-341.

555 Case C-153/91 *Petit* v *Office national des pensions* [1992] ECR I-4974.

556 Case C-212/06 *Government of the French Community and Walloon Government* v *Flemish Government* [2008] ECR I-1683.

557 Case C-281/98 *Angonese* v *Cassa di Risparmio di Bolzano* [2000] ECR I-4139; see 11.140–11.144 below.

558 *McGeogh* v *Electoral Registration Officer, Dumfries and Galloway and ors* [2011] CSOH 65.

559 Case C-60/91 *Criminal proceedings against Batista Morais* [1992] ECR I-2085.

recognised by the competent Austrian authorities as adequate to the purpose;[560] French firms seeking to circumvent planning rules in Calvados[561] or in Brittany;[562] and hairdressers defending themselves against a criminal charge of unlawful operation of *salons de coiffure* in the French Ardennes,[563] cannot plead that they infringe Union rules on the right of establishment.[564] Equally, neither the validity of a contract relating to a German nominated by a German recruitment consultant[565] nor the propriety of an arrangment for the subcontracting of services between two Italian firms in Italy[566] nor Belgian rules on the recovery of a social security debt by a Belgian principal contractor from its Belgian subcontractors[567] attract the Treaty provisions on services; nor may a Roman dispensing chemist challenge Italian laws on holiday closing hours[568] or a Finn the entitlements of an angling permit of a Finn angling in a Finnish lake[569] on the ground that they impede article 56 rights. This results in the peculiar situation whereby, for example, a plumber established in Luxembourg may, when contracting for a job in Trier (45 km distant), Arlon (50 km) or Metz (100 km), challenge any German, Belgian or French (or Luxembourg) law which inhibits him in that purpose. But he cannot do so when contracting for a job in Luxembourg – unless, of course, he is a non-Luxembourger.

11.92 Closer to home, because it is immaterial to article 45 that an employer is an international organisation governed by a special statute under international law, the employee nonetheless being a migrant worker,[570] it means that *référendaires* or *fonctionnaires* (indeed, the judges) at the Court of Justice are workers entitled

---

560 Case C-104/08 *Kurt v Bürgermeister der Stadt Wels* [2008] ECR I-97*.

561 Case 20/87 *Ministère public v Gauchard* [1987] ECR 4879.

562 Case 204/87 *Bekaert v Procureur de la République, Rennes* [1988] ECR 2036.

563 Cases C-29 etc./94 *Criminal proceedings against Aubertin and ors* [1995] ECR I-301.

564 In the context of establishment this is in part a product of the Treaties themselves, which define the right as one for 'nationals of a Member State in the territory of another Member State' (art. 49, 1st para. TFEU). The Court of Justice interpreted this to mean than art. 49 cannot be relied upon against a person's home member state even in the presence of an appreciable Union element until there exists Union legislation intended to implement the right; see Case 115/78 *Knoors v Secretary of State for Economic Affairs* [1979] ECR 399; Case 136/78 *Ministère Public v Auer* (No. 1) [1979] ECR 437 (cf. the opinion of A-G Warner, who argued against the proposition, and so the clear language of art. 49); following legislative intervention, Case 271/82 *Auer v Ministère Public* (No. 2) [1983] ECR 2727; Case C-274/05 *Commission v Greece* [2008] ECR I-7969; Case C-286/06 *Commission v Spain* [2008] ECR I-8025. In one case the Court required assessment of a home national's foreign country qualification absent any applicable legislative intervention (Case C-19/92 *Kraus v Land Baden-Württemberg* [1993] ECR I-1663, involving a German with a degree from a Scottish university seeking to use in Germany the title thus acquired) without explaining a departure from previous authority; the issue seems unlikely to arise again following the adoption of Directive 2005/36; see 11.36–11.39 above.

565 Case C-41/90 *Höfner and Elser v Macrotron* [1991] ECR I-1979.

566 Case 134/95 *Unità Socio-Sanitaria Locale no. 47 di Biella (USSL) v Istituto nazionale per l'assicurazione contro gli infortuni sul lavoro (INAIL)* [1997] ECR I-195.

567 Case C-245/09 *Omalet v Rijksdienst voor Sociale Zekerheid* [2010] ECR I-13771.

568 Case C-393/08 *Sbarigia v Azienda USL RM/A and ors* [2010] ECR I-6333.

569 Case C-97/98 *Jägerskiöld v Gustafsson* [1999] ECR I-7319.

570 Cases C-389 and 390/87 *Echternach and Moritz v Minister van Onderwijs en Wetenschappen* [1989] ECR 723.

to the exercise and protection of article 45 rights – all except the Luxembourg-ers.[571] This is the irony, that Treaty rights, and so the rights and privileges of Union citizenship, may be claimed in any member state other than that of which the individual is actually a citizen. It is illustrated in sharp relief in the well-known English case of Mrs Blood, who wished to be inseminated with her husband's sperm held in storage by a competent statutory body (the Human Fertilisation and Embryology Authority); the Authority refused to release it because in British law to do so required the husband's written consent, which, he being comatose (and subsequently deceased), could not be obtained. She was refused any relief by the High Court,[572] but as soon as she made ready to seek the necessary treatment in Belgium, the Court of Appeal found the refusal to release and authorise the export of her husband's sperm made that treatment impossible, constituted an infringement of article 56, and so set aside the Authority's decision.[573] The case also points to what is perhaps most inequitable and most troubling, that the fundamental rights recognised as part of Union law cannot, as such, be invoked in a national court by a home national in the absence of an appreciable Union law element.[574]

There are growing fissures in the principle which may, ultimately, render it untenable. In the vanguard is *Singh*, involving a British citizen, having worked in Germany, returning to the United Kingdom in order to (re-)'establish' herself there in a self-employed capacity.[575] In those circumstances her Indian husband must be afforded a (Union) right of residence in the United Kingdom, otherwise she may be deterred from exercising her right to go to another member state as a worker; she would 'in particular be deterred from so doing if [her] spouse and children were not also permitted to enter and reside in the territory of [her] Member State of origin under conditions at least equivalent to those granted them by Community law in the territory of another Member State'.[576] The principle may be stated as follows: **11.93**

---

571 Whether or not this applies to a judge at the Court turns upon whether he or she is a worker (as to which see the related Case C-393/10 *O'Brien v Ministry of Justice*, judgment of 1 March 2012, not yet reported), otherwise art. 49 or 56 would presumably apply to produce the same result.

572 *R v Human Fertilisation and Embryology Authority, ex parte Blood* [1996] 3 WLR 1176 (QB).

573 *R v Human Fertilisation and Embryology Authority, ex parte Blood* [1999] Fam 191. Cf. *L v Human Fertilisation and Embryology Authority and anor* [2008] EWHC 2149 (Fam), [2009] EuLR 107.

574 E.g. Case C-299/95 *Kremzow v Austria* [1997] ECR I-2629; Cases C-465/00 and 138–9/01 *Rechnungshof and ors v Österreichischer Rundfunk and ors* [2003] ECR I-4989; *Criminal proceedings against Vajnai* [2005] ECR I-8577; on fundamental rights see 6.105–6.123 above.

575 Case C-370/90 *R v Immigration Appeal Tribunal and Singh, ex parte Secretary of State for the Home Department* [1992] ECR I-4265. The judgment refers throughout to 'establishment' of a Union national in her home member state although, in the technical Treaty sense, this is not possible; see n. 564 above.

576 *Ibid.* at para. 20.

It is settled case-law that the Treaty rules governing freedom of movement for persons and measures adopted to implement them cannot be applied to activities which have no factor linking them with any of the situations governed by Community law and which are confined in all respects within a single Member State.

However ... any Community national who, irrespective of his place of residence and his nationality, has exercised the right to freedom of movement for workers and who has been employed in another Member State falls within the scope of the aforesaid provisions ... [T]herefore ... Article [45] of the Treaty and Article 7 of Regulation No. 1612/68 may be relied on by a worker against the Member State of which he is a national where he has resided and been employed in another Member State.[577]

It extends to a right of residence for family members where the Union citizen, having been a migrant worker, returns to his home member state and unemployment[578] and the availability against his home member state of a social benefit (a child-raising allowance) under Regulation 492/2011 to a frontier worker, having relocated his residence to another member state for reasons wholly unconnected with his employment but remaining in that employment in his home member state.[579] It extends even to a right of residence in the United Kingdom for Mrs Carpenter, a Philippina married to a British citizen who had never resided outside the United Kingdom but who travelled from time to time to other member states in order to sell advertising space in a British journal (and so provide services), if necessary to enable him to do so;[580] and it applies to a German living and working in Germany as regards his German tax allowances on the maintenance he pays to his ex-wife living in Austria, although no intra-Union movement of goods or services was involved.[581]

11.94 Mr Terhouve could claim article 45 and Regulation 1612/68 rights in the Netherlands because he had previously 'resided and been employed in another Member State',[582] if for only ten months and as a result of being posted there by his Dutch employer. Would his situation be different if he had resided there but not been employed? What if he had visited and taken afternoon tea in a café? What if he had never left the Netherlands but watched Flemish television occasionally, or Dutch soap operas transmitted on RTL Nederland from Luxembourg?

---

577 Case C-18/95 *Terhoeve* v *Inspecteur van de Belastingdienst Particulieren/Ondernemingen buitenland* [1999] ECR I-345, at paras 26–9.
578 Case C-291/05 *Minister voor Vreemdelingenzaken en Integratie* v *Eind* [2007] ECR I-10719.
579 Case C-212/05 *Hartmann* v *Freistaat Bayern* [2007] ECR I-6303.
580 Case C-60/00 *Carpenter* v *Secretary of State for the Home Department* [2002] ECR I-6279; see 11.08 above.
581 Case C-403/03 *Schempp* v *Finanzamt München V* [2005] ECR I-6421.
582 Case C-18/95 *Terhoeve*, n. 577 above.

Even the governments of a number of member states find the consequences **11.95** 'unjustified'.[583] More thoughtfully, Advocate-General Sharpston finds the situation 'deeply paradoxical',[584] 'paradoxical (to say the least)'[585] and the result 'strange and illogical'.[586] She is not alone. In 2007 she presented a cogent case for its abandonment[587] but the Court did not take up the challenge, responding instead with a straight bat:

> In this respect, it must be borne in mind that it is settled case-law that the Treaty rules governing freedom of movement for persons and the measures adopted to implement them cannot be applied to activities which have no factor linking them with any of the situations governed by Community law and which are confined in all relevant respects within a single Member State.[588]

Rebuffed but unbowed she tried again in 2010, this time sweetening the pill by proposing alteration to the rule only in the presence of certain conditions.[589] The Court responded this time by allowing a few (ill-defined) worms from the can.[590] Yet two months later it reverted to type and denied a dual British/Irish national seeking to secure for her Jamaican husband a residence permit (so invoke Directive 2004/38) a right to do so, for her situation was, notwithstanding her dual nationality, confined to the United Kingdom and had no factor linking it to Union law.[591] No change yet, then. But it is nevertheless widely thought that the wholly internal rule must some day give way. If and when it does, it will probably yield to the rights adhering to the evolving status of citizenship of the Union. To which we now turn.

D. FREE MOVEMENT AND CITIZENSHIP OF THE UNION

Intended or not, the Maastricht provisions on citizenship of the Union intro- **11.96** duced a wild card into the free movement rights of Union nationals, at least those of individuals properly so called to whom the status adheres. There was already an extensive case law on free movement, to a significant extent knitted

---

583 Case C-127/08 *Metock and ors v Minister for Justice, Equality and Law Reform* [2008] ECR I-6241, at para. 76.
584 Case C-212/06 *Government of the French Community and Walloon Government v Flemish Government* [2008] ECR I-1683, at para. 116 of her opinion.
585 Case C-34/09 *Ruiz Zambrano v Office national de l'emploi*, judgment of 8 March 2011, not yet reported, at para. 84 of her opinion.
586 *Ibid.* at para. 86.
587 Case C-212/06 *French Community and Walloon Government*, n. 584 above, at paras 116–57 of her opinion.
588 *Ibid.* at para. 33 of the judgment.
589 Case C-34/09 *Ruiz Zambrano*, n. 585 above.
590 See immediately below.
591 Case C-434/09 *McCarthy v Secretary of State for the Home Department*, judgment of 5 May 2011, not yet reported. See immediately below.

together into common principles irrespective of a particular Treaty chapter relied upon. But this was different:

> The rights which are connected with each category of free movement differ, although in the course of the years a certain degree of convergence has been attained in the interpretation of the Treaty provisions on workers, establishment and services and there is greater homogeneity in the manner in which these provisions are applied. The Treaty provisions on citizenship, by contrast, remain a distinct category and the rights which may be derived from this status, though evolving, are restricted by comparison to those which flow from the economic freedoms.[592]

11.97 Citizenship of the Union is created and defined by article 20 TFEU. The rights accruing to it are (for some reason) set out twice, generally in article 20 and in somewhat more detail in the articles which follow. They are:

- voting rights;[593]
- the right to diplomatic representation;[594]
- the right to petition the European Parliament;[595] and
- a right of participatory democracy.[596]

These are discussed above.[597] The remaining (sequentially the first) right of citizenship is 'the right to move and reside [*séjourner, aufzuhalten*] freely within the territory of the Member States', either 'in accordance with the conditions and limits defined by' or 'subject to the limitations and conditions laid down in' the Treaties and by the measures adopted (thereunder) to give them effect.[598] Since Maastricht article 21 has been amended twice, authorising:

- the Parliament and Council to adopt, by ordinary legislative procedure, any measure 'necessary to attain this objective' (of article 21(1)) even if authority is not provided elsewhere in the Treaties;[599] and

---

592 Case C-212/05 *Hartmann* v *Freistaat Bayern* [2007] ECR I-6303, *per* A-G Geelhoed at para. 34 of his opinion.

593 TFEU, arts 20(2)(b) and 22 (ex art. 19 EC).

594 TFEU, arts 20(2)(c) and 23 (ex art. 20 EC).

595 TFEU, arts 20(2)(d) and 24 (ex art. 21 EC).

596 TEU, arts 10(3), 11(4).

597 See 8.11–8.14 above.

598 Citizens of the Union have 'the right to move and reside freely within the territory of the Member States … exercised in accordance with the conditions and limits defined by the Treaties and by the measures adopted thereunder' (TFEU, art. 20(2)) and/or 'subject to the limitations and conditions laid down in the Treaties and by the measures adopted to give them effect' (art. 21(1)). There is explanation neither for this approach nor for the (slightly) different construction.

599 TFEU, art. 21(2) (ex art. 18(2) EC) (added by Nice).

- the Council, by unanimity, to do likewise in the spheres of social security and social protection.[600]

This is, uniquely in the Treaties, the express provision to one area of the general enabling power of article 352 TFEU; put otherwise, mini-flexibility clauses. The requirement of Council unanimity in the spheres of social security and protection is unsurprising, a reflection of high costs and the financial burdens borne by the state; prior to Lisbon Community inroads into them were expressly excluded.[601] Unlike article 352 consent of the Parliament is not required. No measure has been adopted under either provision.

The 1990 Directives on rights of residence for students, pensioners and **11.98** 'playboys'[602] went some way in homogenising rights of residence, for the first time extending them beyond, and disengaging them from, the strict Treaty approach of workers, establishment or services. Yet these additional rights of movement required financial self-sufficiency, mirrored later in the terms of the Citizens' Rights Directive.[603] Citizenship (in any meaningful sense of the word) surely goes further, decoupling Treaty rights from economic activity, elevating the citizen to more than a *Marktbürger*, or wealth. It was put clearly by Advocate-General Mazák: 'the concept of Union citizenship ... marks a process of emancipation of Community rights from their economic paradigm';[604] and elegantly by Advocate-General Sharpston:

> From the moment that the Member States decided to add, to existing concepts of nationality, a new and complementary status of 'citizen of the Union', it became impossible to regard such individuals as mere economic factors of production. Citizens are not 'resources' employed to produce goods and services, but individuals bound to a political community and protected by fundamental rights.[605]

Yet the rights continued to be fenced in by the requirement of their enjoyment in accordance with, or subject to, the conditions and limit(ation)s laid down in the Treaties and by the measures adopted (thereunder). The rights of citizenship are, like that of non-discrimination in article 18 (the two now bound together in Part Two of the TFEU), residual rights: it is only when an individual

---

600 *Ibid.* art. 21(3) (added by Lisbon).
601 EC Treaty, art. 21(3). Also excluded were provisions on passports, identity cards, residence permits or any other such document.
602 See 11.17 above.
603 Directive 2004/38 [2004] OJ L158/77; see 11.17 above.
604 Case C-158/07 *Förster* v *Hoofddirectie van de Informatie Beheer Groep* [2008] ECR I-8507, at para. 54 of his opinion.
605 Case C-34/09 *Ruiz Zambrano* v *Office national de l'emploi*, judgment of 8 March 2011, not yet reported, at para. 127 of her opinion.

finds no assistance otherwise in the Treaties or in legislation 'adopted to give them effect' that article 21 comes into play.[606] From this basis citizenship of the Union could therefore add a great deal – inspire an 'evolution ... both coherent and inevitable', according to Advocate-General Sharpston[607] – or could add very little, to rights which existed before.

11.99 For a number of years following Maastricht articles 20 and 21 lay fallow. They were first applied seriously in 1998 in *Martínez Sala*,[608] involving a Spaniard resident in Germany since 1968 who had worked there irregularly (mostly prior to, and for only a six-week period after, Spanish accession), ceased employment in 1989, and in 1993 applied for a child-raising allowance (*Erziehungsgeld*). The allowance is a non-contributory benefit available to any person permanently or ordinarily resident in Germany who has a dependent child in the household, looks after and brings up the child, and is not in full-time employment.[609] The Court refused to answer the questions (expressly put by the referring court) of whether Ms Martínez retained the status of a worker or fell within the provisions of Regulation 1408/71 on social security, having been 'provide[d in]sufficient information' by that court to do so.[610] Instead it put decisive store by the fact that she was, and had been recognised as, lawfully resident in Germany *as a matter of German law*.[611] Then,

> [a]s a national of a Member State lawfully residing in the territory of another Member State, the appellant in the main proceedings comes within the scope *ratione personae* of the provisions of the Treaty on European citizenship. Article [20(2) TFEU] attaches to the status of citizen of the Union the rights and duties laid down by the Treaty, including the right, laid down in Article [18], not to suffer discrimination on grounds of nationality within the scope of application *ratione materiae* of the Treaty. It follows that a citizen of the European Union, such as the appellant in the main proceedings, lawfully resident in the territory of the host Member State, can rely on Article [18] in all situations which fall within the scope *ratione materiae* of Community law.[612]

---

606   Case C-92/01 *Stylianakis v Elliniko Dimosio* [2003] ECR I-1291; Case C-76/05 *Schwartz and Gootjes-Schwartz v Finanzamt Bergisch Gladbach* [2007] ECR I-6849; Case C-137/09 *Josemans v Burgemeester van Maastricht* [2010] ECR I-13019.

607   Case C-34/09 *Ruiz Zambrano*, n. 605 above, at para. 125 of her opinion.

608   Case C-85/96 *Martínez Sala v Freistaat Bayern* [1998] ECR I-2691.

609   Gesetz vom 6. Dezember 1985 über die Gewährung von Erziehungsgeld und Erziehungsurlaub (BErzGG), BGBl. 1989 I S. 1550.

610   Case C-85/96 *Martínez Sala*, n. 608 above, at para. 45.

611   There was also an issue arising from the fact that entitlement for non-Germans to the allowance turned upon possession of a residence entitlement (*Aufenthaltsberechtigung*) or a residence permit (*Aufenthaltserlaubnis*), and the first instance social court had dismissed Ms Martínez's claim because she could produce no residence permit (although she had had one previously) but only proof of having applied for an extension of one.

612   Case C-85/96 *Martínez Sala*, n. 608 above, at paras 61–3.

So Ms Martínez, lacking any other Treaty right, was able to call upon article 20 (not the free movement rights of article 21) to underpin a (citizenship) right to equal treatment with home nationals even though her presence in Germany was not a function of Union law.

The second case involved (the unpronounceable) Mr Grzelczyk,[613] a French **11.100** student in the fourth year of a diploma programme at the Catholic University of Louvain (Louvain-La-Neuve) in Belgium. He had subvented the costs of his upkeep, accommodation and studies during his first three years with part-time work and arranging credit facilities, but found his fourth year to be more demanding, requiring that he redouble his efforts at study and abandon his outside employment. He therefore applied for the 'minimex' (*minimum de moyen d'existence*), the Belgian social assistance allowance.[614] The minimex was at first granted but after four months withdrawn.

The Court accepted that Mr Grzelczyk was not a worker (the referring court **11.101** having so decided); that its own case law[615] held student maintenance grants to fall outwith the scope of the Treaties, but 'at that stage in the development of Community law';[616] in the interim the status of Union citizenship, a new Treaty chapter on education and vocational training, and the Students' Residence Directive had been introduced; that Mr Grzelczyk's residence was, unlike that of Ms Martínez, a product of Union law (the Students Directive); that the Directive expressly excluded a right to a maintenance grant (so arguably a limitation laid down in a measure adopted to give the Treaties effect) *but* 'there are no provisions in the directive that preclude those to whom it applies from receiving social security benefits';[617] so that Mr Grzelczyk was, like Ms Martínez, entitled to the protection of article 18, and so the minimex on the same conditions as home nationals, by virtue of article 21:

> As the Court held in ... *Martínez Sala*, ... a citizen of the European Union, lawfully resident in the territory of a host Member State, can rely on Article [18] of the Treaty in all situations which fall within the scope *ratione materiae* of Community law. Those situations include those involving the exercise of the fundamental freedoms guaranteed by the Treaty and those involving the exercise of the right to move and reside freely in another Member State, as conferred by Article [21].[618]

---

613 Case C-184/99 *Grzelczyk* v *Centre public d'aide sociale d'Ottignies-Louvain-la-Neuve* [2001] ECR I-6193.
614 Loi du 26 mai 2002 concernant le droit à l'intégration sociale, MB du 31 juillet 2002, p. 33610; so called now *le revenu d'intégration* but still, informally, the minimex.
615 Case 197/86 *Brown* v *Secretary of State for Scotland* [1988] ECR 3205.
616 Case C-184/99 *Grzelczyk*, n. 613 above, at para. 34. The law has since further evolved; see 11.67 above.
617 *Ibid.* at para. 39.
618 *Ibid.* at paras 32–33.

11.102   Halfway into *Grzelczyk* the Court casually dropped a (slow fuse) bombshell:

> Union citizenship is destined to be the fundamental status of nationals of the Member States, enabling those who find themselves in the same situation to enjoy the same treatment in law irrespective of their nationality, subject to such exceptions as are expressly provided for.[619]

It has been repeated many times since, sometimes in full, sometimes only the first clause;[620] sometimes to emphasise the status of citizenship whilst deciding a case upon other, traditional grounds, sometimes applying it as a status standing alone. And it led Advocate-General Sharpston to the rather breath-taking:

> The consequences of that statement are, I suggest, as important and far-reaching as those of earlier milestones in the Court's case-law. Indeed, I regard the Court's description of citizenship of the Union in *Grzelczyk* as being potentially of similar significance to its seminal statement in *Van Gend en Loos* that 'the Community constitutes a new legal order of international law for the benefit of which the States have limited their sovereign rights... and the subjects of which comprise not only Member States but also their nationals'.[621]

11.103   From the case law emerges (opaquely) a number of principles:

- Article 21(1) constitutes a self-standing, directly effective right, at last insofar as it accords the citizen a right of residence in any member state. This was first expressly recognised in *Baumbast*[622] but was implicit in other cases before and since.
- The fact of citizenship extends the application of article 18 beyond the exercise of express Treaty rights. So long as the individual falls within the scope of application *ratione materiae* of the Treaties, he or she can suffer no disadvantage by virtue of his or her nationality. So, citizens who would

---

619   *Ibid.* at para. 31.
620   E.g., Case C-224/98 *D'Hoop* v *Office national de l'emploi* [2002] ECR I-6191, at para. 28; Case C-413/99 *Baumbast and R* v *Secretary of State for the Home Department* [2002] ECR I-7091, at para. 82; Case C-148/02 *Garcia Avello* v *Belgian State* [2003] ECR I-11613, at para. 22; Case C-138/02 *Collins* v *Secretary of State for Work and Pensions* [2004] ECR I-2703, at para. 61; Case C-200/02 *Zhu and Chen* v *Secretary of State for the Home Department* [2004] ECR I-9925, at para. 25; Case C-209/03 *R (Bidar)* v *London Borough of Ealing and anor* [2005] ECR I-2119, at para. 31; Case C-403/03 *Schempp* v *Finanzamt München V* [2005] ECR I-6421, at para. 15; Case C-76/05 *Schwartz and Gotojes-Schwartz* v *Finanzamt Bergisch Gladbach* [2007] ECR I-6849, at para. 86; Case C-34/09 *Ruiz Zambrano* v *Office national de l'emploi*, judgment of 8 March 2011, not yet reported, at para. 41; Case C-434/09 *McCarthy* v *Secretary of State for the Home Department*, judgment of 5 May 2011, not yet reported, at para. 47; Case C-256/11 *Dereci and ors* v *Bundesministerium für Inneres*, judgment of 15 November 2011, not yet reported, at para. 62.
621   Case C-34/09 *Ruiz Zambrano, ibid.*, at para. 68 of her opinion.
622   Case C-413/99 *Baumbast and R* v *Secretary of State for the Home Department* [2002] ECR I-7091, at paras 84, 94.

otherwise fall through the Treaty net have an entitlement to admission to study in another member state[623] and (within limits) to a study maintenance grant;[624] to social assistance (the minimex);[625] and to other social benefits or advantages.[626] The case law normally speaks of rights accruing to Union citizens *lawfully* resident in another member state,[627] but even this may be tempered somewhat by the judgment in *Metock*.[628]

- Citizenship confers rights against a home member state in another member state or once returned: any 'national legislation ... which places at a disadvantage certain of its nationals simply because they have exercised their freedom to move and to reside in another Member State is a restriction on the freedoms conferred by Article [21(1) TFEU] on every citizen of the Union'.[629]

- Most contentiously, in a number of cases the Court has held that articles 20/21 prohibit certain non-discriminatory rules. In other words, it is not necessary for the purposes of articles 20/21 to show that a national measure adversely affects a national of another member state *more* than it does home nationals, merely that it affects him or her adversely.[630] It is best considered in the context of a number of cases involving the autonomous right of residence in a member state for infants/children, themselves Union citizens but clearly not workers or otherwise economically active so as to attract the traditional rights of movement/residence, nor themselves possessed of resources adequate to maintain themselves; and trickier still, the derivative rights of other family members. The first

---

623 Case C-147/03 *Commission* v *Austria* [2005] ECR I-5969. The right was based upon arts 18, 165 and 166 TFEU (see ... above) but the rights of citizenship prayed in support; at para. 45.

624 Case C-209/03 *R (Bidar)* v *London Borough of Ealing and anor* [2005] ECR I-2119; Case C-76/05 *Schwartz and Gootjes-Schwartz*, n. 620 above; Cases C-11 and 12/06 *Morgan and Bucher* v *Bezirksregierung Köln and anor* [2007] ECR I-9061. See 11.67 above.

625 Case C-184/99 *Grzelczyk*, n. 613 above; C-456/02 *Trojani* v *Centre public d'aide sociale de Bruxelles* [2004] ECR I-7573.

626 Case C-85/96 *Martínez Sala*, n. 608 above (a German child-raising allowance (*Erziehungsgeld*)); Case C-274/96 *Criminal proceedings against Bickel and Franz* [1998] ECR I-7637 (the right to use German in judicial and administrative proceedings in Trentino-Alto Adige (Italy), a privilege afforded only German-speaking Italians resident in the province; thus, an extension to citizenship of the principles of Case 137/84 *Ministère public* v *Mutsch* [1985] ECR 2681, n. 171 above); Case C-224/98 *D'Hoop*, n. 620 above and Case C-258/04 *Office national de l'emploi* v *Ioannidis* [2005] ECR I-8275 (a Belgian tideover allowance (*allocations d'attente*) following studies but pending employment); Case C-138/02 *Collins*, n. 620 above (a British job seeker's allowance; but refusal justified); Case C-192/05 *Tas-Hagen and Tas* v *Raadskamer WUBO van de Pensioen- en Uitkeringsraad* [2006] ECR I-10451 (benefits for civilian victims of war).

627 See especially Case C-109/01 *Secretary of State for the Home Department* v *Akrich* [2003] ECR I-9607.

628 Case C-127/08 *Metock and ors* v *Minister for Justice, Equality and Law Reform* [2008] ECR I-6241; the issue re-visited in Case C-256/11 *Dereci*, n. 620 above.

629 Case C-406/04 *De Cuyper* v *Office national de l'emploi* [2006] ECR I-6947, at para. 39; almost *verbatim*: Case C-499/06 *Nerkowska* v *Zakład Ubezpieczeń Społecznych Oddział w Koszalinie* [2008] ECR I-3993, at para. 32; Case C-353/06 *Grunkin and Paul* v *Standesamt Niebüll* [2008] ECR I-7639, at para. 21.

630 See Case C-224/02 *Pusa* v *Osuuspankkien Keskinäinen Vakuutusyhtiö* [2004] ECR I-5763, *per* A-G Jacobs at para. 18 of his opinion.

involved school-age children with German and French nationality having lived in the United Kingdom as family members of their migrant worker (and Union citizen) fathers, the fathers subsequently quitting the country to work elsewhere (for a German firm in China and Lesotho) or divorcing the mother, the children now wishing to stay in the United Kingdom with their third country national (Columbian and American) mothers who were their primary carers, but not their dependants within the meaning of Directive 2004/38 – quite the opposite.[631] In both cases the families were covered by comprehensive sickness insurance and had adequate resources to prevent them from becoming burdens upon the state. And in both cases they prevailed. Where a child of a Union citizen is 'installed' (*installé*; *voher seinem Wohnsitz ... hatte*)[632] in the host member state whilst the latter was there as a migrant worker and had during that time begun his schooling (a right accorded by Regulation 1612/68)[633] he was entitled to stay in order to complete it,[634] and his primary carer was, irrespective of her nationality, entitled to reside with him, 'during his studies',[635] in order to facilitate the exercise of that right.[636] In two subsequent cases the Court extended the right by dismissing the need for the carer to have sufficient resources and comprehensive sickness insurance, they being requirements of Directive 2004/38 and, so long as the child was installed (although not yet necessarily in education) in the host member state at a time when a Union citizen parent was a worker there, these rights deriving from Regulation 1612/68 alone;[637] articles 20/21 TFEU were not considered.

---

631   Case C-413/99 *Baumbast and R v Secretary of State for the Home Department* [2002] ECR I-7091.

632   Case C-413/99 *Baumbast, ibid.*, at para. 63. The German formulation comes from later cases (Case C-310/08 *London Borough of Harrow v Ibrahim and Secretary of State for the Home Department* [2010] ECR I-1065, at para. 34; Case C-480/08 *Teixeira v London Borough of Lambeth and Secretary of State for the Home Department* [2010] ECR I-1107, at para. 45); the original in *Baumbast* was *die in einem Mitgliedstaat seit einem Zeitpunkt wohnen*.

633   Regulation 1612/68 [1968] JO L257/2, art. 12; now Regulation 492/2011 [2011] OJ L141/1, art. 10; see 11.21 above.

634   Case C-413/99 *Baumbast*, n. 631 above. It was not clear when such education is 'completed', the judgment referring to a child's right 'to attend general educational courses' (at para. 63) and 'to pursue ... his education' (at para. 73). In a subsequent case (Case C-480/08 *Teixeira*, n. 632 above) the Court said the right of residence of the primary carer parent ends when the child reaches the age of majority, unless he or she continues to need the presence and care of that parent in order to be able to pursue and complete his or her education. In Cases C-147 and 148/11 *Secretary of State for Work and Pensions v Czop and Punakova*, judgment of 6 September 2012, not yet reported, the Court confirmed that these rights stem from Regulation 492/2011 and so are available to workers but not the self-employed.

635   Case C-413/99 *Baumbast*, n. 631 above, at para. 73.

636   The Court went on to find implicity that the rule applied even if the child was not a Union citizen (at para. 74) and, oddly, that Baumbast *père*, who no longer resided in the United Kingdom, enjoyed a right of residence there by direct application of art. 21(1) (at para. 94).

637   Case C-310/08 *Ibrahim*, n. 632 above; Case C-480/08 *Teixeira*, n. 632 above.

But a father has no right to reside in the member state of his children's nationality when they are not dependent upon him for their subsistence.[638]

Next up was a case in which neither parent was a Union citizen. *Zhu and* **11.104** *Chen*[639] involved an infant daughter of Chinese parents but of Irish nationality by virtue of her birth in Northern Ireland – so raising the very peculiar situation in which a child born in one member state does not acquire the nationality of that state at birth, but does, by the fact and place of that birth, acquire that of another[640] – wishing to reside in the United Kingdom with her mother, the latter applying for indefinite leave to remain. Not yet of school-age herself, the young Miss Zhu in turn enjoyed a right of residence in the United Kingdom by virtue of article 21 TFEU (and the Playboy Directive) for an 'indefinite period',[641] and her mother an ancillary right to reside there with her for the duration of that residence in order that Miss Zhu's right not be 'deprive[d] … of any useful effect' (*de tout effet utile*).[642] The Court accepted that the mother had come to the United Kingdom in order to circumvent China's 'one child policy' and that there was no reason for Miss Zhu's birth in Belfast other than, via her Irish nationality, to acquire a right of residence in the United Kingdom, but this was not (it 'is clearly distinguishable from')[643] an abuse of rights. As previously in *Baumbast* the Court borrowed from the conditions of Directive 2004/38 (even though it did not apply) and put significant store by the fact of adequacy of financial resources and health insurance from the parent/carer. There is now English authority that these conditions cannot be met through the (third country national) carer's income if he or she cannot work owing to unlawfulness of his or her presence,[644] or although in employment, it is too precarious.[645]

A clearer and cleaner illustration of rights accruing to citizenship may be had **11.105** from the progressive recognition of a different (perhaps surprising) right, that

---

638 Case C-256/11 *Dereci and ors* v *Bundesminister für Inneres*, judgment of 15 November 2011, not yet reported; see 11.108 below.

639 Case C-200/02 *Zhu and Chen* v *Secretary of State for the Home Department* [2004] ECR I-9925.

640 Prior to 1983 British law adhered to an absolute *ius soli*, founded originally in common law (and natural law) pre-dating the union of the Crowns as a necessary entitlement of a natural born subject of the King; see *Calvin's Case* (1608) 7 Co. Rep. 1a. Now a person born in the United Kingdom acquires British citizenship only if either parent is a citizen or is 'settled' there, so withholding it from the infant Zhu; British Nationality Act 1981, s. 1(1). Nor did she have Chinese nationality. Changes to Irish law made in 2005 (see 8.10 above, n. 20 above) would now deprive her also of her Irish nationality.

641 Case C-200/02 *Zhu and Chen*, n. 639 above, at para. 41.

642 *Ibid.* at para. 45.

643 Case C-34/09 *Ruiz Zambrano* v *Office national de l'emploi*, judgment of 8 March 2011, not yet reported, *per* A-G Sharpston at para. 104 of her opinion.

644 *W (China) and anor* v *Secretary of State for the Home Department* [2006] EWCA Civ 1494, [2007] 1 WLR 1514.

645 *Lui and ors* v *Secretary of State for the Home Department* [2007] EWCA Civ 1275, [2007] All ER (D) 381.

to a name of the individual's choosing. In the early 1990s a Greek established in Germany had his name transliterated grotesquely by the German authorities (from Χρίστος Κωνσταντινίδης to Hrēstos Kōnstantinidēs) in accordance with a system promulgated by an International Organization for Standardization, to which Germany (and Greece) adhered; Advocate-General Jacobs (maybe influenced by the signature, although not yet the entry into force, of Maastricht) thought he ought to have a right to his name as he chose it as a matter of dignity, that is, in accordance with a common code of fundamental values which ought to be his, as a European citizen, by right,[646] but the Court found that this would be so only if the mistransliteration affected deleteriously his economic activities (so hindering his rights of establishment).[647] Subsequently, as Article 21 bedded in, the Court came to find that a dual national has a right, accruing from Union citizenship, to an (additional) matronymic surname in one member state of nationality if it accords with the law and traditions of the other member state[648] and that a Union citizen has a choice of surname, enforceable even against his member state of (sole) nationality, as determined and registered in a second member state in which he has resided.[649] Coming full circle from Mr Konstantinidis (or Kōnstantinidēs), the Court has now considered the entertaining question of whether a member state may refuse to register a child born there but adopted in middle age in another member state, in accordance with a noble title acquired upon adoption and borne by her in the member state of her adoption;[650] and, most recently, has condemned as a breach of article 21 (provided certain tests are satisfied, which it left to the referring court) Lithuanian legislation which requires first names and surnames to be rendered in documents indicating civil status using only the Roman letters recognised in Lithuanian and without unrecognised diacritics and ligatures.[651]

11.106 These cases cement the dignity of the individual by a right accruing from citizenship, even absent an element of discrimination. The cases on right of residence are however confused and confusing; the reasoning of *Baumbast* is

---

646 Case C-168/91 *Konstantinidis* [1993] ECR I-1191, at para. 46 of his opinion.

647 Case C-168/91 *Konstantinidis, ibid.*

648 Case C-148/02 *Garcia Avello* v *Belgian State* [2003] ECR I-11613.

649 Case C-353/06 *Grunkin and Paul* v *Standesamt Niebüll* [2008] ECR I-7639. That is, a German child born in Denmark of German parents, the latter wishing to register the child, still in Denmark, in a German family register (*Familienbuch*) by his Danish (double barrelled) surname which was not permitted under German law.

650 Case C-208/09 *Sayn-Wittgenstein* v *Landeshauptmann von Wien* [2010] ECR I-13693. Ms (Fürstin von) Sayn-Wittgenstein's rights under art. 21 were restricted but the restriction justified by reference to public policy. She might have found support in *Konstantinidis*, for she was an estate agent specialising in the sale of castles and stately homes and might have argued that deprivation of her noble title would injure her in her occupation, but the Court addressed only art. 21, finding issues specific to the freedom to provide services to be excluded by the questions put by the referring court.

651 Case C-391/09 *Runevič-Vardyn and anor* v *Vilniaus miesto savivaldybės administraciją*, judgment of 12 May 2011, not yet reported.

particularly impenetrable. They are also coloured by the right to family life in article 8 of the European Convention and article 7 of the Charter of Fundamental Rights which is (in the Union context) developing still. There is an irresistible sense that the Court is making it up as it goes along. Yet it remains that, as things stand, the rights of citizenship may vary with the wealth of the citizen, which is surely an affront to any (modern, at least) understanding of the word. Certainly the status of citizenship adds to the rights of the holder, but precisely how it is too early to say; as it is too early to say whether Advocate-General Sharpston's confidence in the *dictum* from *Grzelczyk* is well placed.

Reverse discrimination

Already precarious, the existence of the wholly internal rule comes under **11.107** increasing strain with a slow totting up of rights of citizenship which are (anomalously?) beyond the reach of the home national. If and when it falls, it will probably yield to the developing rights of citizenship and the Treaty right of articles 20(2)(a) and 21(1) of every citizen 'to move and reside freely within the territory of the Member States', drawing no distinction between the member state of which he or she is a national and any other. A 2008 *dictum* from the Court seems to point in this direction.[652] The likelihood is only further enhanced by

- the marriage of the prohibition of discrimination on grounds of nationality and the provisions on citizenship in a single Part (Part Two) of the TFEU;
- a (Lisbon) provision on democractic principles which provides that '[i]n all its activities, the Union shall observe the principle of equality of its citizens' with no further qualification;[653] and
- the EU Charter, its stature enhanced by Lisbon, with a provision prohibiting discrimination on grounds of nationality[654] and another, also without qualification, that '[e]very citizen of the Union has the right to move and reside freely within the territory of the Member States'.[655]

The Court had a post-Lisbon opportunity to abandon the wholly internal rule **11.108** but refused – or skirted – the fence. *Ruiz Zambrano* involved two (child)

---

652 Case C-221/07 *Zablocka-Weyhermüller* v *Land Baden-Württemberg* [2008] ECR I-9029, at para. 30: 'By taking up residence in Poland [her country of citizenship], the claimant in the main proceedings ... exercised the right conferred by Article [21(1)] on every citizen of the Union to move and reside freely in the territory of the Member States'.

653 TEU, art. 9.

654 EU Charter of Fundamental Rights, art. 21(2).

655 *Ibid.* art. 45(1).

citizens of Belgium who had lived only in Belgium and whether they acquired a right of residence there by virtue of Union law (articles 18, 20 and 21 TFEU), which, following *Baumbast* and *Zhu and Chen*, would confer upon their (Columbian) father upon whom they were dependent and who (maybe) had resources sufficient to provide for the family (although Mr Ruiz had worked without authority, and paid social security contributions, he had become temporarily unemployed) an indirect right of residence and related social benefits.[656] An affirmative answer would require the abandonment of the wholly internal rule. Advocate-General Sharpston recommended just that course, recognition of the existence of a free-standing right of residence[657] uncoupled from any *Singh*-ish prior movement[658] or other 'appreciable Union element'. Mindful of the antipathy of (some members of) the Court she sugared the pill, recommending only incremental change, that 'Article 18 TFEU should be interpreted as prohibiting reverse discrimination' where there is a gap between the rights of article 21 and their enjoyment in national law, and then if, and only if, three conditions are met:

- the claimant is a citizen of the Union resident in his or her member state of nationality who has not exercised free movement rights, and so whose situation is comparable to that of other (non-home) Union citizens enjoying Union rights as would the claimant but for the toleration of reverse discrimination;
- the discrimination in issue entails violation of a fundamental right protected under Union law; and
- reliance upon article 18 is a subsidiary safeguard, national law alone affording inadequate protection of the fundamental right.[659]

She warned that a response from the Court to wider implications, on the cusp of constitutional change, 'can be put off for the moment, but probably not for all that much longer'.[660]

11.109 The Court stayed below the parapet. It found Directive 2008/34 not to apply; that article 20 TFEU precludes a national measure which deprives a (minor) citizen of the Union of the genuine enjoyment of the substance of the rights of citizenship; and that refusal to grant a right of residence (and a work permit, so as to ensure the children are not deprived of the genuine enjoyment of the right)

---

656 Case C-34/09 *Ruiz Zambrano v Office national de l'emploi*, judgment of 8 March 2011, not yet reported. See the similar *AN.O and ors v Minister for Justice, Equality and Law Reform* [2009] IEHC 531.

657 Case C-34/09 *Ruiz Zambrano, ibid.*, at para. 101 of A-G Sharpston's opinion.

658 Case C-370/90 *R v Immigration Appeal Tribunal and Singh, ex parte Secretary of State for the Home Department* [1992] ECR I-4265; see 11.93 above.

659 Case C-34/09 *Ruiz Zambrano*, n. 656 above, at paras 145–8 of A-G Sharpston's opinion.

660 *Ibid.* at para. 177.

to a third country national with dependent minor children in the member state where those children are nationals and reside has such an effect.[661] The judgment was perfunctory (10 operative paragraphs) and, it might be said, does little justice to the Advocate-General's meticulous analysis and suppleness. It did not address whether the children had a right of residence in their member state of nationality as a matter of Union law (other than passing reference to residence of the father 'in the Member State where those children are nationals and reside'),[662] there is no recognition that the wholly internal rule was in issue, and in truth we are left no wiser as to whether, and if so how, it survives.

Within two months the Court muddied the water further, finding a dual **11.110** British/Irish national, born in the United Kingdom and never having left it – in fact never having worked or been economically active there – entitled to rely upon article 21 against the United Kingdom:

> [H]owever … the situation of a Union citizen who, like Mrs McCarthy, has not made use of the right to freedom of movement cannot, for that reason alone, be assimilated to a purely internal situation …

> As a national of at least one Member State, a person such as Mrs McCarthy enjoys the status of a Union citizen under Article 20(1) TFEU and may therefore rely on the rights pertaining to that status, including against his Member State of origin, in particular the right conferred by Article 21 TFEU to move and reside freely within the territory of the Member States.[663]

But as she enjoyed an unconditional right of residence in the United Kingdom (by virtue of her British citizenship) she was not (the Court found) impeded in the enjoyment of her free movement rights: the refusal of the British authorities to accord her the rights of Union citizenship 'in no way affects her in her right to move and reside freely within the territory of the Member States, or any other right conferred on her by virtue of her status as a Union citizen';[664] her case 'has no factor linking it with any of the situations governed by European Union law and the situation is confined in all relevant respects within a single Member State'.[665] So she could rely upon article 21, but perversely, because she did not require to do so, she could not. The fact that Union law and Directive 2004/38 (which could not apply in accordance with a literal, teleological and contextual interpretation of its text)[666] would accord her a right to have her

---

661 *Ibid.* at at paras 36–45 of the judgment.
662 *Ibid.* at para. 43.
663 Case C-434/09 *McCarthy* v *Secretary of State for the Home Department*, judgment of 5 May 2011, not yet reported, at paras 46, 48.
664 *Ibid.* at para. 49.
665 *Ibid.* at para. 55.
666 *Ibid.* at para. 31.

husband reside there (which was the purpose of her claim), but that British law (unmodified by Union law) did not,[667] was ignored.

11.111   In its most recent consideration of the issues the Court confirmed the inapplicability of Treaty rules on free movement to 'situations which have no factor linking them with any of the situations governed by European Union law and which are confined in all relevant respects within a single Member State',[668] and that the Treaty rights of citizenship, although available against a home member state, do not preclude that member state (Austria) from removing family members (some present lawfully, some unlawfully) of Austrian nationals where it would not result in depriving the latter of the genuine enjoyment of the substance of the rights of citizenship. This would be the case (it 'refers to situations') where he or she 'has ... to leave' (*se voit obligé ... de quitter*) the territory of the Union[669] but not to the forced removal of his or her family members, for in none of the cases was the home national dependent upon the third country family member and, notwithstanding the 'desirability' of cohabitation as a family, for economic reasons or or in order to keep the family together within the Union, it is not such as to compel the Union citizen to leave.[670]

11.112   So, reverse discrimination is still not wholly abandoned and the ball is still in play. Should it eventually be jettisoned, whether with Advocate-General Sharpston's conditions or otherwise, there is over the horizon another question: citizenship traditionally brings with it not only rights but duties. The Treaties too provide that Union citizens are 'subject to the duties provided for in the Treaties',[671] but these are light to the point of non-existent. Not so for duties of citizenship in national law, which gives rise to an as yet unexplored (reverse) area of reverse discrimination: whether a Union citizen resident in a host member state by virtue of that status ought to be subject also to duties borne by home nationals – of which the most obvious (but certainly not the only) example is military service. It is a surface as yet unscratched.

---

667   A-G Kokott had ventured (at paras 59–60 of her opinion) that she also had such right by virtue of art. 8(1) of the European Convention on Human Rights (respect for family life); but this was, as she admitted, not a question of Union law.
668   Case C-256/11 *Dereci and ors* v *Bundesministerium für Inneres*, judgment of 15 November 2011, not yet reported, at para. 60.
669   *Ibid.* at para. 66.
670   *Ibid.* at para. 68.
671   TFEU, art. 20(2).

E. DEROGATION

As with the free movement of goods, the rights of free movement of persons are **11.113** not absolute. The Treaty recognises permissible limitations to those rights

- justified upon grounds of public policy, public security or public health;[672] and
- as regards employment in the public service and, for the self-employed, the exercise of official authority.[673]

The Court has crafted other limitations which serve the public interest and apply in certain circumstances.

1. Public policy, public security and public health

As with article 36, considerations of public policy,[674] public security and public **11.114** health permit exceptional derogation from fundamental Treaty rights which may not be invoked to serve economic ends,[675] must be interpreted restrictively,[676] and any limitation to the rights of free movement must be objectively justified, appropriate and proportionate. So whilst a member state 'essentially retain[s] the freedom to determine the requirements of public policy and public security in

---

672 *Ibid.* art. 45(3) (ex art. 39(3) EC) (workers), art. 52(1) (ex art. 46(1)) (establishment), art. 62 (ex art. 55) (services).

673 *Ibid.* arts 45(4) (workers) and 51, 1st para., 62 (establishment and services).

674 'Public policy' is a very unsatisfactory translation of *ordre public, öffentliche Ordnung, openbare orde* and *ordine pubblico*, all of which have well-established and specific meanings in the national law of other member states which are neither rendered by 'public policy' nor necessarily equivalent to the meaning to be given to the term in Union law. In this context 'public order' would probably be better than 'public policy', except that it comes laden with its own baggage in English. 'Social order', or perhaps 'public weal', probably conveys best what is meant, and maybe dovetails best with the outcome of the difficult issues in Case C-137/09 *Josemans* v *Burgemeester van Maastricht* [2010] ECR I-13019 (reducing drug tourism and the nuisance which attends it in Maastricht). A preambular reference in the Services Directive (Directive 2006/123 [2006] OJ L376/36, as to which see 11.45–11.48 above; preamble, recital 41) provides that the concept includes 'in particular' issues relating to human dignity, the protection of minors and vulnerable adults and animal welfare; and that the concept of public security includes issues of public safety. But see Case C-208/09 *Sayn-Wittgenstein* v *Landeshauptmann von Wien* [2010] ECR I-13693, in which public policy is stretched to include respect for and compliance with elements of constitutional and national identity.

675 Directive 2004/38 [2004] OJ L158/77, art. 27(1). An inhibition on the movement of a person for the purpose of recovery of a debt owed to a public authority does not (simply) serve economic ends: Case C-434/10 *Aladzhov* v *Zamestnik direktor na Stolichna direktsia na vatreshnite raboti kam Ministerstvo na vatreshnite raboti*, judgment of 17 November 2011, not yet reported.

676 E.g., Case 41/74 *van Duyn* v *Home Office* [1974] ECR 1337; Case 30/77 *R* v *Bouchereau* [1977] ECR 1999; Case C-36/02 *Omega Spielhallen- und Automatenaufstellungs* v *Oberbürgermeisterin der Bundesstadt Bonn* [2004] ECR I-9609; Case C-503/03 *Commission* v *Spain* [2006] ECR I-1097.

accordance with [its] national needs',[677] or 'in accordance with its own scale of values and in the form selected by it',[678] and which may therefore quite legitimately 'vary from one Member State to another and from one era to another',[679] it may invoke this privilege in order to deny a Union national the exercise of his or her Treaty rights only if his or her presence would constitute, in addition to the perturbation of the social order which any infringement of the law involves,[680] 'a genuine, present and sufficiently serious threat affecting one of the fundamental interests of society'.[681] A decision to bar or remove an individual must be justified by reference exclusively to his or her personal conduct;[682] it cannot be used as a general preventive device, that is, a means of deterrence.[683] As with article 36 again, a member state may not invoke grounds of public policy where it has adopted no measures (although not necessarily criminal) effectively to inhibit or combat the activities in question amongst its own nationals.[684]

11.115 Previous criminal convictions, even several,[685] are not in themselves sufficient justification[686] and 'can only be taken into account in so far as the circumstances which gave rise to that conviction are evidence of personal conduct constituting a present threat to the requirements of public policy'.[687] So

---

677 Case C-33/07 *Ministerul Administrației și Internelor – Direcția Generală de Pașapoarte București* v *Jipa* [2008] ECR I-5157, at para. 23; Case C-348/09 *Infusino* v *Oberbürgermeisterin der Stadt Remscheid*, judgment of 22 May 2012, not yet reported, at para. 23.

678 Case 121/85 *Conegate* v *HM Customs and Excise* [1986] ECR 1007, at para. 14.

679 Case C-36/02 *Omega Spielhallen*, n. 676 above, at para. 31 (substituting 'country' for 'Member State'); Case C-33/07 *Jipa*, n. 677 above, at para. 23; C-208/09 *Sayn-Wittgenstein*, n. 674 above, at para. 87; Case C-348/09 *Infusino* n. 677 above, at para. 23.

680 Case 30/77 *R* v *Bouchereau* [1977] ECR 1999, at para. 35; Cases C-482 and 493/01 *Orfanopoulos and ors* v *Land Baden-Württemberg* [2004] ECR I-5257, at para. 66.

681 Directive 2004/38, art. 27(2), 2nd para. This formula is codification of earlier case law; see Case 36/75 *Rutili* v *Minister of the Interior* [1975] ECR 1219, at para. 28 ('une ménace réelle et suffisamment grave pour l'ordre public'); Case 30/77 *Bouchereau*, n. 680 above. This construction is self-evidently infused with considerations of proportionality; see *Mendes Machado* v *Secretary of State for the Home Department* [2005] EWCA Civ 597, [2005] All ER (D) 289.

682 Directive 2004/38, art. 27(2), 1st para. Voluntary association with a group may be taken to indicate support for the group's policies or activities and, if they are objectionable, go fairly to personal conduct; Case 41/74 *van Duyn* v *Home Office* [1974] ECR 1337.

683 Directive 2004/38, art. 27(2), 2nd para; Case 67/74 *Bonsignore* v *Oberstadtdirektor der Stadt Köln* [1975] ECR 297; Case C-340/97 *Nazli and ors* v *Stadt Nürnberg* [2000] ECR I-957.

684 Cases 115 and 116/81 *Adoui and Cornuaille* v *Belgium* [1982] ECR 1665; Case C-268/99 *Jany and ors* v *Staatssecretaris van Justitie* [2001] ECR I-8615; Case C-100/01 *Ministre de l'Intérieur* v *Oteiza Olazabal* [2002] ECR I-10981. But see Case C-137/09 *Josemans* v *Burgemeester van Maastricht* [2010] ECR I-13019 in which the Court, not very convincingly, circumvented the principle.

685 Case C-349/06 *Polat* v *Stadt Rüsselheim* [2007] ECR I-8167, at para. 36.

686 Directive 2004/38, art. 27(2), 1st para.

687 Case C-348/96 *Criminal proceedings against Calfa* [1999] ECR I-11, at para. 24; Cases C-482 and 493/01 *Orfanopoulos*, n. 680 above, at para. 67 (substituting 'justify an expulsion only' for 'only be taken into account').

expulsion automatically following a criminal conviction,[688] or any national rules or procedures which apply to Union citizens general legislation relating to foreign nationals which which make it possible to establish a systematic and automatic connection between a criminal conviction and a removal order,[689] are impermissible. So far-reaching is the rule that it may extend, for example, to requiring the admission as a worker of a former terrorist[690] or the quashing of a removal order against a Union citizen convicted in the host member state of a 'particularly notorious and shocking' murder[691] but released after serving 12 years of an indefinite sentence (detained during Her Majesty's pleasure)[692] where both had, upon close analysis, ceased to constitute a 'present' threat to public policy. Competent authorities may from time to time identify conduct

> so heinous that the burden of [a migrant worker] to prove that her present and future conduct will not adversely affect the fundamental interests of our society is especially heavy,[693]

or

> as wholly repugnant to the generally accepted standards of morality, such that the continued presence of the offender after his release from prison is offensive to the public if it can be avoided and is contrary to the requirements of public policy.[694]

---

688 Case C-348/96 *Calfa, ibid.*; Case C-340/97 *Nazli*, n. 683 above; Case C-441/02 *Commission* v *Germany* [2006] ECR I-3449. In the United Kingdom a non-British citizen convicted of a (single) offence for which he or she is sentenced to a term of imprisonment of 12 months or more is now subject to 'automatic deportation' (United Kingdom Borders Act 2007, s. 32), which is declared to be conducive to the public good (s. 32(4)), a requirement of deportation under the Immigration Act 1971, s. 3(5)(b). However there is an exception provided where deportation would 'breach rights of the foreign criminal under the Community treaties' (s. 33(4)), with no further elaboration. There appears to be a presumption that a sentence of two years or more will justify deporation of a Union citizen: UK Border Agency, Enforcement Instructions and Guidelines, ch. 12.3. The introduction of automatic deportation has caused the English courts to cease making recommendations for deportation under the Immigration Act 1971, ss. 3(6) and 5(6) in cases to which the 2007 Act applies as 'no longer necessary or appropriate' (*R* v *Kluxen*; *R* v *Rostas and anor* [2010] EWCA Crim 1081, [2010] Crim LR 657, at para. 33) which may deprive the Union national of the judicial protection of Directive 2004/38. By way of comparison, German law provides for mandatory expulsion of a foreign national convicted of an 'intentional offence' (*eine vorsätzliche Straftat*) and sentenced to at least three years' imprisonment or youth custody; Gesetz über den Aufenthalt, die Erwerbstätigkeit und die Integration von Ausländern im Bundesgebiet vom 30. Juli 2004 (Aufenthaltsgesetz), BGBl. 2004 I S. 1950, §53 I.

689 Case C-50/06 *Commission* v *Netherlands* [2007] ECR I-4383.

690 *Proll* v *Entry Clearance Officer, Düsseldorf* [1988] 2 CMLR 387 (IAT).

691 *R (Chindamo)* v *Secretary of State for the Home Department* [2006] EWHC 3340 (Admin), [2006] All ER (D) 342, *per* Underhill J at para. 1.

692 *LC* v *Secretary of State for the Home Department* (No. IA/13107/2006), determination of the Asylum and Immigration Tribunal of 17 August 2007, unreported. The tribunal gave extensive weight to considerations of family life (at paras 91–103) as required by art. 28; see n. 698 below and accompanying text.

693 Determination of the immigration adjudicator in *Proll*, n. 690 above, quoted at 391.

694 *Goremsandu* v *Secretary of State for the Home Department* [1996] ImmAR 250, *per* Stuart-Smith LJ at 254 (involving a non-Union citizen).

This seems a legitimate facet of a proportionality test, and doubtless the revulsion occasioned by an offence is normally weighed in the balance. Yet under the rules a risk of reoffending is an obligatory component of the equation, absent which a member state may not remove a Union citizen however wicked or disruptive he or she may in the past have been. Even where an exclusion or removal order satisfies this battery of tests and is justified, the individual may apply to have it lifted after a 'reasonable period', and in any event after three years,[695] and must be afforded the opportunity to show that there has been a material change in the circumstances which justified the order.[696]

11.116 Directive 2004/38 introduced a new graduated (or 'enhanced')[697] scale of protection from expulsion. Before taking a decision to remove a person upon grounds of public policy or public security, the host member state must 'take account' of considerations 'such as' how long he or she has resided there, his/her age, state of health, family and economic situation, social and cultural integration into the host member state and the extent of the links with his or her country of origin.[698] This is articulation of a proportionality test,[699] that 'the greater the degree of integration of Union citizens and their family members in the host Member State, the greater the degree of protection against expulsion should be'.[700] It applies in all cases[701] but hardens into a higher threshold with accretion of time. Thus the Danes may, perhaps, remove Union citizens convicted of professional shop theft and 'distraction theft' (*tricktyveri*), the *Højesteret* satisfied (without referring to the Court of Justice) that this conduct was sufficiently repugnant to Danish social order, but material to the judgments a finding that none of the convicted had (other than their temporary presence) ties to Denmark,[702] whilst at the same time setting aside a removal order

---

695   Directive 2004/38, art. 32(1).
696   *Ibid.*
697   Case C-145/09 *Land Baden-Württemberg* v *Tsakouridis* [2010] ECR I-11979, *per* A-G Bot at para. 45 of his opinion.
698   Directive 2004/38, art. 28(1). These criteria are drawn from the case law of the European Court of Human Rights; see discussion of A-G Geelhoed in Case C-109/01 *Secretary of State for the Home Department* v *Akrich* [2003] ECR I-9607, at para. 46 of his opinion and cases there cited. The provision says expressly in all languages 'country of origin' rather than country of nationality. (It also says in most languages, including English, 'the' country of origin, but in others 'his' (or her) country of origin.) It is not clear whether it means the country from which the individual arrived in the host member state, the country in which he or she was born (as it suggests), his or her 'country' in the international private law sense or the country of his or her citizenship (as seems to make most sense, as it is the only country required to (re)admit him or her unconditionally). The Court subsequently used 'country of origin' (*Herkunftmitgliedstaat*) in a context in which it could mean only country of citizenship; Case C-145/09 *Tsakouridis, ibid.*, at para. 16; Case C-40/11 *Iida* v *Stadt Ulm* pending, *per* A-G Trstenjak.
699   Directive 2004/38, preamble, recital 23.
700   *Ibid.*, recital 24.
701   See e.g., *LC* v *Secretary of State for the Home Department*, n. 692 above.
702   Dom af 29. december 2008 (*Rigsadvokaten mod T*), U2009.813H; Dom af 19. oktober 2009 (*Rigsadvokaten mod T1 og T2*), U2010.250H.

imposed by a lower court upon a British national convicted of assault after noting that he had lived and worked in the country for three years (since his arrival) and his parents and elder brother lived there.[703] Once a Union citizen has acquired a permanent right of residence a member state may properly invoke public policy or public security to remove him or his third country national family member only if the grounds are 'serious' (*impérieuses*; *schwerwiegenden*)[704] – although it is difficult to project what might be 'serious' and not at the same time 'a genuine, present and sufficiently serious threat affecting one of the fundamental interests of society'. After ten years' residence the immunity from removal is 'considerably strengthen[ed]',[705] a Union citizen thereafter liable to expulsion upon 'imperative' grounds (*motives graves*; *zwingenden Gründen*) of public security only.[706] This is a construction which is 'considerably stricter' than serious grounds,[707] limited to 'exceptional circumstances'[708] where there is a threat to public security 'of a particularly high degree of seriousness'.[709]

There are difficulties in the (much rarer) case of a member state imposing, and **11.117** seeking to justify, a measure which prevents a Union national (normally a home national) from leaving, rather than entering, its territory. Whether Ireland may prevent an Irish citizen from leaving the state to procure (the service of) an abortion in another member state in order to protect Irish public policy has arisen but never been clearly resolved.[710] Requiring an individual charged with

---

703 Dom af 29. december 2008 (*Rigsadvokaten mod T*), U2009.809H.

704 Directive 2004/38, art. 28(2).

705 Case C-145/09 *Tsakouridis*, n. 697 above, at para. 28. As to meeting the ten-year residence period see paras 22–38. The Court of Appeal in England determined that (lengthy) terms of imprisonment do not count towards calculation of that period; *HR (Portugal)* v *Secretary of State for the Home Department* [2009] EWCA 371, [2010] 1 All ER 144.

706 Directive 2004/38, art. 28(3). *Silentio* this does not extend to third country national family members. A minor, however, appears to enjoy this level of immunity in all circumstances unless removal is in his or her best interests as provided for in the UN Convention on the Rights of the Child. Public security is to be defined by the member states. The Commission had proposed absolute immunity from expulsion after five years' residence ([2001] OJ C270E/150, art. 26(2)) but the Council, 'almost unanimously', would not wear it (Common Position No. 6/2004 [2004] OJ C54E/12, at 32).

707 Case C-145/09 *Tsakouridis*, n. 697 above, at para. 40. For initial consideration of the gap between 'serious grounds of public policy or public security' (justifying removal of a permanent resident) and 'imperative grounds of public security' (removal after ten years' residence) see *LG (Italy)* v *Secretary of State for the Home Department* [2008] EWCA Civ 190, [2008] All ER (D) 262; Carnwath J wonders (at para. 30), with reason, if the French qualifiers *impérieuses* and *graves* have been inadvertently transposed.

708 Case C-145/09 *Tsakouridis*, n. 697 above, at para. 40.

709 *Ibid.* at para. 41. Alternatively, commission of offences 'disclos[ing] particularly serious characteristics': Case C-348/09 *Infusino* v *Oberbürgermeisterin der Stadt Remscheid*, judgment of 22 May 2012, not yet reported, at para. 33. Both judgments contain extensive discussion of the meaning and breadth of imperative grounds of public security, as will Case 300/11 *ZZ* v *Secretary of State for the Home Department*, pending.

710 Case C-159/90 *Society for the Protection of Unborn Children Ireland* v *Grogan* [1991] ECR I-4685; *Attorney-General* v *X* [1992] 1 IR 1 (SC). Whether the situation would be any different in the case of a non-Irish citizen resident in Ireland has never been considered.

a criminal offence to surrender his or her passport as a condition of bail limits his or her Treaty right to travel to another member state, but is a reasonable and proportionate means of ensuring the accused does not abscond, so safeguarding criminal proceedings within the member state. The same may apply to family or civil proceedings – for example, a prohibition on leaving the (home) national territory of a director of a commercial company which owes an unpaid public law debt 'of a significant amount'[711] – although arguments that this is necessary and/or proportionate are diminished by increasing Union regulation of extra-territorial enforcement of judgments. Equally restrictive is a travel ban imposed by judicial order, upon, for example, an individual convicted of paedophile offences,[712] or a 'banning order' imposed upon a football supporter (and normally requiring him or her to report at a local police station at the time a 'designated' match, at home or in another member state, takes place).[713] Each may be justified in the case of an individual convicted previously of a paedophile offence or a (football) hooligan-related offence (this may be necessary in order to satisfy the 'personal conduct' test of Directive 2004/38) and there are reasonable grounds to believe that the orders will protect children or help to prevent violence or disorder at or in connection with a football match. But in both cases the disorder in question is (anticipated) to occur in another member state, an application of article 45(3) apparently not mirrored in the application of article 36.[714] Certainly, that member states 'should take all possible measures to prevent [home] citizens from participating in and/or organising public order disturbances in another country' has the support of the Council.[715] Yet the Court has said that 'a measure limiting the exercise of the right of free movement must ... be adopted in the light of considerations pertaining to the protection of public policy or public security in the Member State imposing the measure'.[716] This appears to mean that article 45(3) allows one member state to determine a question of the public policy of another by reference to its own. Alternatively, it cannot impose orders limiting movement of its home nationals

---

711 Case C-434/10 *Aladzhov v Zamestnik direktor na Stolichna direktsia na vatreshnite raboti kam Ministerstvo na vatreshnite raboti*, judgment of 17 November 2011, not yet reported; provided that the travel ban is not automatic, is proportionate, and the liability may be attributed to the personal conduct of the individual concerned as well as the threat his or her quitting the country would pose to public policy. The question is again before the Court, but involving a significant debt owed a private company, C-249/11 *Byankov v Glaven sekretar na Ministerstvo na vatreshnite raboti*, pending.

712 See e.g., in the United Kingdom, the Sexual Offences Act 2003, s. 114 ('foreign travel orders'). Presumably there requires at the same time to be in place effective repressive measures for the protection of children within the member state.

713 Football Spectators Act 1989, s. 14A. See *Gough and anor v Chief Constable of the Derbyshire Constabulary* [2002] EWCA Civ 351, [2002] QB 1213.

714 See 10.31 above.

715 Resolution of 6 December 2001 [2002] OJ C22/1, ch. 3.

716 Case C-33/07 *Ministerul Administraţiei şi Internelor – Direcţia Generală de Paşapoarte Bucureşti v Jipa* [2008] ECR I-5157, at para. 25.

(or any other Union citizen) to or in another member state. Most recently the Court has said that a member state may restrict (for a period of time prescribed by law for purposes of rehabilitation) the right of a home national, convicted previously of narcotic drug trafficking in a third country, to travel to another member state, provided (*inter alia*) that his 'personal conduct ... constitutes a genuine, present and sufficiently serious threat affecting one of the fundamental interests of society' without identifying that society.[717] Greater clarity or precision from the Court would be welcome.

As for derogation in the interests of the protection of public health, a member **11.118** state may limit the exercise of free movement rights of the individual on a basis that his or her presence constitutes a threat thereto only by reference to diseases with epidemic potential as defined by the relevant instruments of the World Health Organisation and to other infectious diseases or contagious parasitic diseases if they are the subject of protection provisions applying to nationals of the host member state.[718] A disease occurring (*survenant, auftreten*) more than three months after the date of arrival in the host member state cannot justify removal.[719] In the event of 'serious indications that it is necessary', a member state may require persons to undergo a medical examination within three months of arrival in order to determine whether they suffer from any of these diseases.[720] An examination may not be required as a matter of routine, and it must be free of charge.[721] Public health considerations may also legitimately inhibit free movement rights more broadly where national measures to that purpose are applicable without discrimination on grounds of nationality.[722]

2. Procedural safeguards

Directive 2004/38 lays down 'procedural safeguards' in order to ensure that **11.119** member states do not abuse their (exceptional) power to exclude or remove Union citizens and their families. The provisions are directly effective.[723] A decision restricting the freedom of movement and residence upon grounds of

---

717 Case C-430/10 *Gaydarov v Direktor na Glavna direktsia'Ohranitelna politsia' pri Ministerstvo na vatreshnite raboti*, judgment of 17 November 2011, not yet reported, at para. 42.

718 *Ibid.* art. 29(1). It is not clear in the English text whether the final criterion (application of protective provisions to home nationals) applies to both WHO-identified epidemic diseases *and* to other infectious or contagious diseases, or only to the latter; comparison with other language texts would indicate both.

719 *Ibid.* art. 29(2).

720 *Ibid.* art. 29(3).

721 *Ibid.*

722 See 11.128 below.

723 The Court of Justice said this first in relation to its predecessor in this respect (Directive 64/221 [1964] JO 850, which applied at first only to workers but was extended to other freedoms in 1975), found to be directly effective in Case 41/74 *van Duyn v Home Office* [1974] ECR 1337 – which sparked the constitutional debate as to the direct effect of Directives; see 6.74–6.78 above.

public policy, public security or public health must be notified in writing and in such a manner as imparts clearly its content and implications.[724] The grounds upon which the decision was taken must be disclosed precisely and in full unless contrary to the interest of state security,[725] and the court or administrative authority to which appeal lies specified, with time limits and time allowed to quit the member state, which except in duly substantiated cases of urgency must be no less than one month from the date of notification.[726] If a removal order is executed more than two years after it was issued (for example, following a term of imprisonment), the member state is bound to (re)assess whether the individual remains a threat ('currently and genuinely') to public policy or public security and assess whether there has been an intervening material change in circumstances.[727] The availability of a judicial (or administrative) redress procedure is mandatory;[728] it must allow for examination of the legality of the decision as well as of the facts and circumstances upon which it is based, and must in particular ensure the decision is not disproportionate.[729] A person may be excluded pending result of the redress procedure but if removed (as opposed to denied entry) must be allowed a right to present his or her defence in person unless it would cause serious troubles (*provoquer des troubles graves; ernsthalt gestört werden*) to public policy or public security.[730] Where he or she applies to have a (lawful) exclusion order lifted following accretion of time[731] there is no right of entry during consideration of the application[732] but it must be determined within six months.[733]

3. Public service/official authority

11.120 The Treaty permits member states to restrict to home nationals employment (article 45) 'in the public service'[734] and any self-employed activity (articles 49 and 56) 'connected, even occasionally, to the exercise of official authority'.[735] As for the latter several languages use words meaning 'the exercise of public power' (*Ausübung öffentlicher Gewalt; esercizio dei pubblici poteri; ejercicio del poder*

---

724 Directive 2004/38, art. 30(1).

725 *Ibid.* art. 30(2). See Case C-300/11 *ZZ v Secretary of State for the Home Department,* pending.

726 *Ibid.* art. 30(3).

727 *Ibid.* art. 33(2). This is codification of earlier case law, Case 131/79 *R v Secretary of State for Home Affairs, ex parte Santillo* [1980] ECR 1585; which, it might be noted, was sidestepped by the referring national court (and the Court of Appeal): *R v Secretary of State for the Home Department, ex parte Santillo* [1981] QB 778.

728 *Ibid.* art. 31(1).

729 *Ibid.* art. 31(3).

730 *Ibid.* art. 31(4).

731 *Ibid.* art. 32(1); see n. 695 above and accompanying text.

732 *Ibid.* art. 32(2).

733 *Ibid.* art. 32(1), 2nd para.

734 TFEU, art. 45(4) (ex art. 39(4) EC).

735 TFEU, arts 52, 1st para. and 62 (ex arts 46, 1st para. and 55 EC).

público; utövandet av offentlig makt) which perhaps convey more clearly what is meant:[736] it manifests itself in particular in the exercise of powers of constraint.[737] In any event, not only is the language potentially very broad, it raises serious risk to the uniform application of Union law, for the concept of public service, and who is employed in it, varies extensively from member state to member state. Adding to the complexity is that in some member states various duties are entrusted by statute to public authorities yet

> do not involve any association with tasks belonging to the public service properly so called[; this] would be to remove a considerable number of posts from the ambit of the principles set out in the Treaty and to create inequalities between Member States according to the different ways in which the State and certain sectors of economic life are organized,[738]

whilst conversely, private bodies, and even individuals, are called upon from time to time to discharge duties which fall fairly within the ambit of official authority.

11.121 The first serious consideration of article 45(4) arose in the context of a series of advertisements of job vacancies in the national and local railways and local councils in Belgium for, variously, shunters, loaders, drivers, plate-layers, signalmen, cleaners, painter's assistants, furnishers, coil-winders, canteen staff and workshop hands, as well as hospital nurses, children's and crèche nurses, nightwatchmen, plumbers, joiners, electricians, gardeners, architects and supervisors with the councils. Each stipulated a condition of eligibility to be Belgian nationality. The Commission raised enforcement proceedings under article 258.[739] To which the Court of Justice said:

> [Article 45(4)] removes from the ambit of Article [45](1) to (3) a series of posts which involve direct or indirect participation in the exercise of powers conferred by public law and duties designed to safeguard the general interests of the State or of other public authorities. Such posts in fact [*en effet*] presume on the part of those occupying them the existence of a special relationship of allegiance to the State [*un rapport particulier de solidarité à l'égard de l'État*] and reciprocity of rights and duties which form the foundation of the bond of nationality.[740]

---

736   See the extensive discussion of A-G Cruz Villalón in the *Notary* cases, n. 766 below.
737   Case C-114/97 *Commission v Spain* [1998] ECR I-6717, at para. 37.
738   Case 149/79 *Commission v Belgium* (Belgian Railways) (No. 1) [1980] ECR 3881, at para. 11.
739   Case 149/79 *Commission v Belgium* (Belgian Railways) (No. 1), *ibid.* and (No. 2) [1982] ECR 1845.
740   Case 149/79 *Belgian Railways No. 1*, n. 738 above, at para. 10.

Therefore '[t]he posts excluded are confined to those which, having regard to the tasks and responsibilities involved, are apt to display the characteristics of the specific activities of the public service in the spheres described above'.[741] And

> it is not sufficient for the duties inherent in the post at issue to be directed specifically towards public objectives which influence the conduct and action of private individuals. Those who occupy the post must don full battle dress: in non-metaphorical terms, the duties must involve acts of will which affect private individuals by requiring their obedience or, in the event of disobedience, by compelling them to comply. To make a list ... is practically impossible; but certainly the first examples which come to mind are posts which involve the exercise of powers relating to policing, defence of the State, the administration of justice and assessments to tax.[742]

Further useful guidance was drawn up by the Commission in 1988:

> On the basis of current Court of Justice rulings ... the derogation in Article [45](4) covers specific functions of the State and similar bodies such as the armed forces, the police and other forces for the maintenance of order, the judiciary, the tax authorities and the diplomatic corps. This derogation is also seen as covering posts in State Ministries, regional government authorities, local authorities and other similar bodies, central banks and other public bodies, where the duties of the post involve the exercise of State authority, such as the preparation of legal acts, the implementation of such acts, monitoring of their application and supervision of subordinate bodies.[743]

11.122 Each post is to be measured against the test on its merits. So, a provision of national (constitutional) law which reserves public service posts to home nationals (they 'alone are eligible for civil and military service' save where the law provided otherwise in an individual case) is, notwithstanding the opt in, a blanket refusal which is incompatible with article 45(4).[744] The same fate befell Greek law which in an impressive show of bravura had in force a blanket ban restricting to Greek nationals access to employment in the water, gas and electricity sectors; in the operational sectors of the public health service; to teachers from nursery schools to universities subject to the national education

---

741 Case 66/85 *Lawrie-Blum* v *Land Baden-Württemberg* [1986] ECR 2121, at para. 27.

742 Case C-307/84 *Commission* v *France* [1986] ECR 1725, *per* A-G Mancini at para. 5(2) of his opinion.

743 Notice on freedom of movement of workers and access to employment in the public service of the Member States [1988] OJ C72/2, at 3.

744 Case C-473/93 *Commission* v *Luxembourg* [1996] ECR I-3207. In light of this judgment the Constitution was amended in 1999, replacing '[S]euls [les luxembourgeois] sont admissibles aux emplois civils et militaires, sauf les exceptions' (art. 11(2)) with 'Ils sont admissibles à tous les emplois publics, civils et militaires; la loi détermine l'admissibilité des non-Luxembourgeois à ces emplois' (art. 10*bis*(2)); see now loi du 18 décembre 2009, JO du 22 décembre 2009], p. 4394. The reservation of public posts to home nationals by the Constitution is not unique to Luxembourg (see e.g., the Constitution of Spain, arts 13(2) and 23(2)) and if not, its reservation by law is the norm.

ministry; to posts in air and sea transport services and related companies or
organisations; in the railways and public city and inter-city transport services; to
posts for scientific and non-scientific staff in public establishments conducting
non-military research; to posts in the postal, telecommunications and radio and
television services; and to places in the Athens Opera and in municipal and local
orchestras.[745] Taken individually, Belgium is entitled to reserve some (but not
many) of the posts within the railways to home nationals;[746] the police may be
ring-fenced, but private security services may not;[747] nursing in public hospitals
does not constitute a public service post,[748] nor does secondary school[749] or
university[750] teaching. The management of a body which advises the state on
scientific and technical questions, and the post of advisor itself, can be protected,[751] as can a deputy chief fire officer.[752] Captains/masters and first
officers/chief mates of merchant vessels and fishing boats may be required to be
nationals of the flag state but only if the rights under powers conferred upon
them by public law are in fact exercised upon a regular basis and represent more
than a very minor part of their activities.[753]

Article 45(4) may justify exclusion from the public service, but not discrimin- **11.123**
ation in, for example, remuneration or other conditions of employment for a
Union citizen admitted to employment.[754] In a like vein, if national law (or a
collective agreement) requires previous experience in the public service for
recruitment[755] or promotion,[756] experience acquired in the public service of

---

745 Case C-290/94 *Commission* v *Greece* [1996] ECR I-3285.
746 Case 149/79 *Commission* v *Belgium* (Belgian Railways) (No. 2) [1982] ECR 1845; the posts were head
     technical office supervisor, principal supervisor, works supervisor, stock controller and nightwatchman with
     the municipality of Brussels and architects with the municipalities of Brussels and Auderghem.
747 Case C-114/97 *Commission* v *Spain* [1998] ECR I-6717; Case C-355/98 *Commission* v *Belgium* [2000] ECR
     I-1221; Case C-283/99 *Commission* v *Italy* [2001] ECR I-4363. Nor may a member state require a private
     security guard to swear an oath of allegiance to it; Case C-465/05 *Commission* v *Italy* [2007] ECR I-11091.
748 Case C-307/84 *Commission* v *France* [1986] ECR 1725.
749 Case 66/85 *Lawrie-Blum* v *Land Baden-Württemberg* [1986] ECR 2121; Case C-4/91 *Bleis* v *Ministère de
     l'Éducation Nationale* [1991] ECR I-5627.
750 Case C-195/98 *Österreichischer Gewerkschaftsbund, Gewerkschaft öffentlicher Dienst* v *Republik Österreich* [2000]
     ECR I-10497; Case C-178/04 *Marhold* v *Land Baden-Württemberg*, order of 10 March 2005, unreported;
     Case C-281/06 *Jundt and Jundt* v *Finanzamt Offenburg* [2007] ECR I-12231.
751 Case 225/85 *Commission* v *Italy* [1987] ECR 2625, at para. 9 (*obiter*).
752 *Re O'Boyle's and anor's application for Judicial Review* [1999] NI 126 (CA).
753 Case C-405/01 *Colegio de Oficiales de la Marina Mercante Española* v *Administración del Estado* [2003] ECR
     I-10391; Case C-47/02 *Anker and ors* v *Bundesrepublik Deutschland* [2003] ECR I-10447; Case C-89/07
     Commission v *France* [2008] ECR I-45*; Case C-94/08 *Commission* v *Spain* [2008] ECR I-160*; Case
     C-460/08 *Commission* v *Greece* [2009] ECR I-216*.
754 Case 152/73 *Sotgiu* v *Deutsche Bundespost* [1974] ECR 153; Case 225/85 *Commission* v *Italy* [1987] ECR
     2625; Cases 389 and 390/87 *Echternach and Moritz* v *Minister van Onderwijs en Wetenschappen* [1989] ECR
     723.
755 E.g., Case C-419/92 *Scholz* v *Opera Universitaria di Cagliari* [1994] ECR I-505; Case C-371/04 *Commission* v
     Italy [2006] ECR I-10257.
756 E.g. Case C-15/96 *Schöning-Kougebetopoulou* v *Freie und Hansestadt Hamburg* [1998] ECR I-47.

another member state must be taken into account, as it must in the context of an incremental pay scale which depends upon length of public sector service[757] and computation of pension rights.[758]

11.124 Whilst most of the cases involve access of workers to public service employment, the same considerations apply, *mutatis mutandis*, to establishment and services. In fact the nets are cast wider, for articles 49 and 56 apply also to juristic persons, and any reservation by the state to a public authority (or privileged private body) established within the state of various activities of involving the supply of services (in a non-Treaty sense) is likely seriously to impede the free provision of services (in a Treaty sense) there. Therefore whilst neither freedom extends to activities connected with the exercise of official authority,

> [i]n that regard, it must be remembered that, as derogations from the fundamental rule of freedom of establishment, Articles [51] and [62] must be interpreted in a manner which limits their scope to what is strictly necessary for safeguarding the interests which those provisions allow the Member States to protect. Thus, according to settled case-law, derogation under those articles must be restricted to activities which in themselves are directly and specifically connected with the exercise of official authority.[759]

Moreover, the derogation cannot justify exclusion from activities which are auxiliary and/or preparatory *vis-à-vis* an entity which effectively exercises public authority by, or are carried out under the active supervision of a competent public authority responsible ultimately for, taking final decisions.[760]

11.125 In one of the first cases in which the issue was considered the Court determined that the profession of *avocat* in Belgium fell outwith this category:

> [I]t is not possible to give this description, in the context of a profession such as that of *avocat*, to activites such as consultation and legal assistance or the representation and defence of parties in court, even if the performance of these activities is compulsory or there is a legal monopoly in respect of it.[761]

---

757 Case C-187/96 *Commission* v *Greece* [1998] ECR I-1095.

758 Case C-443/93 *Vougioukas* v *Idryma Koinonikon Asfalisseon* [1995] ECR I-4033.

759 Case C-451/03 *Servizi Ausiliari Dottori Commercialisti* v *Calafiori* [2006] ECR I-2941, at paras 45–6; first articulated in Case 2/74 *Reyners* v *Belgian State* [1974] ECR 631, at para. 45.

760 Case C-393/05 *Commission* v *Austria* [2007] ECR I-10195; Case C-404/05 *Commission* v *Germany* [2007] ECR I-10239; Case C-438/08 *Commission* v *Portugal* [2009] ECR I-10219.

761 Case 2/74 *Reyners*, n. 759 above, at para. 55. Here the Court sidestepped the issue of the course to be followed in situations in which, as is the case in various jurisdictions in the Union, a practising lawyer may be called upon (or required), from time to time, to perform functions in, for example, areas of criminal or public law which do fall within the rubric of official authority, saying that the legitimate ends of art. 51 are 'fully satisfied

Nor does it extend to the setting up an of and teaching in 'coaching establishments' (φροντιστήρια) and other private schools in Greece,[762] the office of 'approved commissioner' (*erkend commisaris*) in a Belgian public body which regulates the insurance sector,[763] private security services[764] or tax advice, including submission of annual returns.[765] In a clutch of judgments the Court has now determined that the reservation to home nationals of the profession of notary in Belgium, Germany, Greece, France, Luxembourg, the Netherlands and Austria exceeds the limits of article 51.[766]

4. Imperative reasons in the general interest

As the Court of Justice recognised that there may be non-discriminatory (or **11.126** 'indistinctly applicable') inhibitions to the free movement of goods, so it recognised that the same may apply to the free movement of persons and services. Thus it says, for example:

> According to settled case-law, Article [49] precludes any national measure which, even if applicable without discrimination on grounds of nationality, is liable to hinder or render less attractive the exercise by Union nationals of the freedom of establishment that is guaranteed by the Treaty,[767]

and

> Article [56] of the Treaty requires not only the elimination of all discrimination on grounds of nationality against providers of services who are established in another Member State, but also the abolition of any restriction, even if it applies without distinction to national providers of services and to those of other Member States, which

---

when the exclusion of nationals is limited to those activities which, taken on their own, constitute a direct and specific connection with the exercise of official authority' (para. 45) without addressing the practical difficulties to which it gives rise.

762 Case 147/86 *Commission v Greece* [1988] ECR 1637.
763 Case C-42/92 *Thijssen v Controledienst voor de verzekeringen* [1993] ECR I-4047.
764 Case C-114/97 *Commission v Spain* [1998] ECR I-6717; Case C-283/99 *Commission v Italy* [2001] ECR I-4363; Case C-465/05 *Commission v Italy* [2007] ECR I-11091.
765 Case C-451/03 *Calafiori*, n. 759 above.
766 Case C-47/08 *Commission v Belgium*, Case C-50/08 *Commission v France*, Case C-51/08 *Commission v Luxembourg*, Case C-53/08 *Commission v Austria*, Case C-54/08 *Commission v Germany* and Case C-61/08 *Commission v Greece*, judgments of 24 May 2011, not yet reported; Case C-157/09 *Commission v Netherlands*, judgment of 1 December 2011, not yet reported. A further ten member states (Bulgaria, Czech Republic, Estonia, Latvia, Lithuania, Hungary, Poland, Romania, Slovakia and Slovenia) intervened in support of the defendant member states, one (United Kingdom) in support of the Commission. The Court expressly did not address issues of the provision of notarial services, to which different considerations may apply.
767 Case C-384/08 *Attanasio Group v Comune di Carbognano* [2010] ECR I-2055, at para. 43.

is liable to prohibit, impede or render less advantageous the activities of a provider of services established in another Member State in which he lawfully provides similar services.[768]

For goods, it led to the development of the 'mandatory requirements' doctrine, first articulated in *Cassis de Dijon*,[769] and recognition of legitimate barriers, where certain conditions are met, to free movement beyond those expressly permitted in the Treaties. For persons and services it led to an equivalent doctrine, first stated formally in the *Insurance and Co-Insurance* judgments in 1986,[770] wherein it considered the extent to which national rules on prudential supervision of the insurance (and co-insurance) sector might legitimately frustrate a (co-)insurer in one member state from underwriting a policy in another — that is, providing insurance services there. For a time the principles were recognised in the context of services only,[771] the presupposition being that those seeking to exercise the right of establishment would 'go native' and submit wholly to the rules of prudential supervision in the host member state so long as they suffered no arbitrary or greater burdens that those faced by home nationals. But in *Gebhard* (1995) the Court extended the principles to establishment and made them uniform across both Treaty chapters thus:

> [N]ational measures liable to hinder or make less attractive the exercise of fundamental freedoms guaranteed by the Treaty must fulfil four conditions: they must be applied in a non-discriminatory manner; they must be justified by imperative requirements in the general interest; they must be suitable for securing the attainment of the objective which they pursue; and they must not go beyond what is necessary in order to attain it.[772]

---

768   Case C-76/90 *Säger* v *Dennemeyer* [1991] ECR I-4221, at para. 12 (where the *dictum* originated, in slightly less extensive form); Cases C-369 and 376/96 *Arblade and anor* v *Leloup and ors* [1999] ECR I-8453, at para. 33; Case C-164/99 *Proceedings against Portugaia Construções* [2002] ECR I-787, at para. 16 (transposing 'attractive' for 'advantageous').

769   Case 120/78 *Rewe-Zentrale* v *Bundesmonopolverwaltung für Branntwein* [1979] ECR 649; see 10.36–10.41 above.

770   Case 22/83 *Commission* v *France* [1986] ECR 3663; Case 252/83 *Commission* v *Denmark* [1986] ECR 3713; Case 205/84 *Commission* v *Germany* [1986] ECR 3755; Case 206/84 *Commission* v *Ireland* [1986] ECR 3817. Of the four the German case is considered definitive.

771   See e.g., Case C-154/89 *Commission* v *France* (Tourist Guides) [1991] ECR I-659; Case C-288/89 *Stichting Collectieve Antennevoorziening Gouda* v *Commissariat voor de Media* [1991] ECR I-4007; Case C-211/91 *Commission* v *Belgium* [1992] ECR I-6757; Case C-275/92 *HM Customs and Excise* v *Schindler* [1994] ECR I-1039.

772   Case C-55/94 *Gebhard* v *Consiglio dell'Ordine degli Avvocati e Procuratori di Milano* [1995] ECR I-4165, at para. 37. Repeated in essentially the same manner in Case C-424/97 *Haim* v *Kassenzahnärztliche Vereinigung Nordrhein* [2000] ECR I-5123, at para. 57 (establishment); Case C-243/01 *Criminal proceedings against Gambelli and ors* [2003] ECR I-13031, at para. 65 (establishment and services); Case C-500/06 *Corporación Dermoestética* v *To Me Group Advertising Media* [2008] ECR I-5785, at para. 35 (services).

In *Bosman*[773] the principle was carried over into the chapter on workers, although it has applied rarely in that context for it is uncommon for non-discriminatory measures to be challenged as a hindrance to the rights of article 45. But it is of course important that the principle apply, otherwise a raft of social legislation could be called into question by, for example, an employer minded to circumvent it.

Thus 'imperative (or overriding) reasons (or requirements) in the general (or public) interest'[774] is the equivalent, for the free movement of persons and services, of mandatory requirements for the free movement of goods; in fact the terms are now beginning to be applied to goods.[775] As with mandatory requirements, they cannot be used to serve purely economic ends[776] and are applicable only where the national rule applies independently of the nationality of persons concerned[777] (but, unlike article 34, tolerating a degree of indirect discrimination),[778] is objectively justified, genuinely reflects a concern to attain the legitimate end in a consistent and systematic manner,[779] due account is

11.127

---

773 Case C-415/93 *Union Royale Belge des Sociétés de Football Association and ors v Bosman and ors* [1995] ECR I-4921.

774 The formula has been rendered a number of ways in English. The French has used *raisons impérieuses d'intérêt général* consistently, of which 'overriding reasons in the general interest' is probably the closest equivalent.

775 E.g., Case C-265/06 *Commission v Portugal* [2008] ECR I-2245, *per* A-G Trstenjak at para. 59 of her opinion; Case C-110/05 *Commission v Italy* [2009] ECR I-519, at paras 59, 60; Case C-531/07 *Fachverband der Buch- und Medienwirtschaft v LIBRO Handelsgesellschaft* [2009] ECR I-3717, at para. 34; Case C-28/09 *Commission v Austria*, judgment of 21 December 2011, not yet reported, *per* A-G Trstenjak at para. 78 of her opinion; Regulation 764/2008 [2008] OJ L218/21, Preamble, 3rd recital.

776 Case C-109/04 *Kranemann v Land Nordrhein-Westfalen* [2005] ECR I-2421, at para. 34 (and case law cited there); Case C-96/08 *CIBA Speciality Chemicals Central and Eastern Europe Szolgáltató, Tanácsadó és Keresk-edelmi v Adó- és Pénzügyi Ellenőrzési Hivatal Hatósági Főosztály* [2010] ECR I-2911, at para. 48.

777 E.g., Case C-288/89 *Collectieve Antennevoorziening Gouda v Commissariaat voor de Media* [1991] ECR I-4007, at para. 11; Case C-490/04 *Commission v Germany* [2007] ECR I-6095, at para. 86. But they remain applicable where home and incoming services (for example) are subject to different enactments, so long as, on the facts, the two are subject to equal treatment and, if proscribed, prosecuted with the same diligence and subject to equivalent penalties; Cases C-447 and 448/08 *Criminal proceedings against Sjöberg and Gerdin* [2010] ECR I-6917.

778 See e.g., Case C-73/08 *Bressol and Chaverot and ors v Gouvernement de la Communauté française* [2010] ECR I-2735 ('a difference in treatment based indirectly on nationality may be justified by the objective of maintaining a balanced high-quality medical service open to all'; para. 62). Further, Case C-209/03 *R (Bidar) v London Borough of Ealing and anor* [2005] ECR I 2119; Case C-158/07 *Förster v Hoofddirectie van de Informatie Beheer Groep* [2008] ECR I-8507; Case C-103/08 *Gottwald v Bezirkhauptmannschaft Bregenz* [2009] ECR I-9117, cases involving social benefits which may be withheld by reference to residence. Were it otherwise, various rules justified by prudential supervision of, for example, the professions – requirements of linguistic ability or compulsory qualifications – which have an indirectly discriminatory effect could not be tolerated.

779 Case C-169/07 *Hartlauer Handelsgesellschaft v Wiener Landesregierung and Oberösterreichische Landesregierung* [2009] ECR I-1721, at para. 55 (establishment); Cases C-171 and 172/07 *Apothekerkammer des Saarlandes and ors v Saarland, Ministerium für Justiz, Gesundheit und Soziales* [2009] ECR I-4171, at para. 42 (establishment); Case C-42/07 *Liga Portuguesa de Futebol Profissional and anor v Departamento de Jogos da Santa Casa da Misericórdia de Lisboa* [2009] ECR I-7633, at para. 61 (services); Case C-384/08 *Attanasio Group v Comune di Carbognano* [2010] ECR I-2055, at para. 51 (establishment); Case C-325/08 *Olympique Lyonnais v Bernard*

taken of the standards and rules to which the provider of the service is subject in his home state (equivalence),[780] the restriction is proportionate and it is not pre-empted by Union legislative intervention. As with article 34, the fact that one member state imposes less strict rules than another does not mean (of itself) that the latter's rules are incompatible with the Treaties.[781] Unlike article 34 (but not article 35), there is an articulated remoteness test, applicable where the alleged impediment to free movement is 'too uncertain or indirect'[782] or 'hypothetical'.[783] So, here is Advocate-General Sharpston on Catalan planning rules claimed to inhibit the right of establishment (so 'market access' considerations):

> First, the case-law emphasises that market access restrictions should be significant in order to fall within Article [49] …

> Second, national measures which have too uncertain and indirect an effect on a fundamental freedom do not generally fall within the Treaty prohibitions.

> Third, from a logical and teleological point of view, there must be a threshold below which a national measure is not a restriction on freedom of establishment. Otherwise, even the most minor regulation would fall under Article [49].[784]

11.128 National measures which have been held to inhibit the exercise of the right of establishment and/or the freedom to provide services but may be saved by application of the imperative reasons rule include, first and foremost ('without doubt'),[785] public health: as with articles 34/36 (*mutatis mutandis*), public health is both a justification for discriminatory expulsion/refusal of admission of a Union national by virtue of articles 45(3), 52 and 62 and a mandatory requirement/imperative reason in the general interest, and

> the health and life of humans rank foremost among the assets and interests protected by the Treaty and […] it is for the Member States to determine the level of protection which they wish to afford to public health and the way in which that level is to be

---

and Newcastle United FC [2010] ECR I-2177, at para. 38 (workers); Cases C-570 and 571/07 *Blanco Pérez and Chao Gómez* v *Consejería de Salud y Servicios Sanitarios* [2010] ECR I-4629, at para. 94 (establishment).

780 E.g., Case C-458/08 *Commission* v *Portugal* [2010] ECR I-8219, at para. 100.

781 Cases C-570 and 571/07 *Blanco Pérez and Chao Gómez*, n. 779 above, at para. 68.

782 Case C-190/98 *Graf* v *Filzmoser Maschinenbau* [2000] ECR I-493, at para. 25; Case C-325/08 *Olympique Lyonnais*, n. 779 above, *per* A-G Sharpston at para. 39 of her opinion; Case C-211/08 *Commission* v *Spain* [2010] ECR I-5267, at para. 72 (substituting 'and' for 'or').

783 Case C-211/08 *Commission* v *Spain*, *ibid.*, at para. 73.

784 Case C-400/08 *Commission* v *Spain*, judgment of 24 March 2011, not yet reported, at paras 65–7 of her opinion.

785 Cases C-570 and 571/07 *Blanco Pérez and Chao Gómez*, n. 779 above, *per* A-G Poiares Maduro at para. 17 of his opinion.

achieved. Since the level may vary from one Member State to another, Member States must be allowed discretion.[786]

So, for example, Italian and German rules which restrict authorisation to open and/or operate a pharmacy to those with the professional qualification of *farmacista/Apotheker* (or, in Italy, a company composed exclusively of *farmacisti*)[787] and Spanish or Finnish rules which restrict the opening of pharmacies by reference to population size and propinquity between them or to statutory obligations borne by existing pharmacies[788] inhibit the right of establishment but are justified in the interests of ensuring the reliable provision of quality medicinal products to the community. Other legitimate inhibitions include many for the protection of the consumer;[789] a requirement of adequate linguistic knowledge in the host member state;[790] conservation of historical and artistic heritage[791] and protection and promotion of archaeological, historical, artistic and cultural heritage;[792] the protection of intellectual property;[793] restrictions on appointment and limitation of numbers and territorial jurisdiction of notaries;[794] a prohibition of 'cold calling' in order to protect investor confidence in national financial markets;[795] regulation of and a requirement of

---

786   Case C-531/06 *Commission v Italy* [2009] ECR I-4103, at para. 36; Cases C-171 and 172/07 *Apothekerkammer des Saarlandes*, n. 779 above, at para. 19; Cases C-570 and 571/07 *Blanco Pérez and Chao Gómez*, n. 779 above, at para. 44 (substituting '*should* be allowed *a measure of* discretion').

787   Case C-531/06 *Commission v Italy*, *ibid.*; Cases C-171 and 172/07 *Apothekerkammer des Saarlandes*, n. 779 above. Cf. Case C-140/03 *Commission v Greece* [2005] ECR I-3177 (Greek law prohibiting a qualified optician from operating more than one optician's shop and limiting authorisation for the establishment and operation of an optician's shop to a qualified optician holding at least half the company's share capital and participating at least to that extent in the profits and losses of the company a disproportionate breach of arts 49 and 56); Case C-356/08 *Commission v Austria* [2009] ECR I-108* (Oberösterreich regulation requiring doctors to have an account with a particular bank for purposes of payment of fees from the national medical insurance scheme a breach of art. 56, and probably arts 49 and 63).

788   Cases C-570 and 571/07 *Blanco Pérez and Chao Gómez*, n. 779 above; Case C-84/11 *Susisalo and ors v Helsingon yliopiston apteekki*, judgment of 21 June 2012, not yet reported.

789   Case 205/84 *Commission v Germany* (Insurance and Co-Insurance) [1986] ECR 3755; Case C-3/95 *Reisebüro Broede v Sandker* [1996] ECR I-6511; Cases C-261 and 299/07 *VTB-VAB and anor v Total Belgium and anor* [2009] ECR I-2949, per A-G Trstenjak at paras 125–32 of her opinion; Case C-564/07 *Commission v Austria* [2009] ECR I-100*; Case C-384/08 *Attanasio Group*, n. 779 above, at para. 50.

790   Case C-424/97 *Haim v Kassenzahnärztliche Vereinigung Nordrhein* [2000] ECR I-5123; Case C-506/04 *Wilson v Ordre des avocats du barreau de Luxembourg* [2006] ECR I-8613; Case C-193/05 *Commission v Luxembourg* [2006] ECR I-8673.

791   Case 180/89 *Commission v Italy* [1991] ECR I-709.

792   Case C-154/89 *Commission v France* [1991] ECR I-659; Case C-180/89 *Commission v Italy* [1991] ECR I-709; Case C-198/89 *Commission v Greece* (Tourist Guides) [1991] ECR I-727.

793   Case 62/79 *Coditel and ors v Ciné Vog Films and ors* (Cotidel I) [1980] ECR 881.

794   Case C-47/08 *Commission v Belgium*, Case C-50/08 *Commission v France*, Case C-51/08 *Commission v Luxembourg*, Case C-53/08 *Commission v Austria*, Case C-54/08 *Commission v Germany* and Case C-61/08 *Commission v Greece*, judgments of 24 May 2011, not yet reported, respectively at paras 97, 87, 97, 96, 98 and 97.

795   Case C-384/93 *Alpine Investments v Minister van Financiën* [1995] ECR I-1141.

authorisation for lotteries[796] and other gaming activities, areas in which 'there are significant moral, religious and cultural differences between the Member States',[797] as a function of, variously, fighting gambling addiction, consumer protection, social policy, protection against crime, protection against fraud, preservation of public order[798] – even to the extent of the creation of a national monopoly and so the exclusion of all private operators from the market,[799] although it may be necessary to show the member state is seeking genuinely and for good reason to ensure a particularly high level of protection;[800] a ban on electronic games which mimic killing for the protection of human dignity;[801] regulation of broadcast media for the maintenance and promotion of pluralism, (linguistic) culture and/or programme quality;[802] a requirement that candidates for teacher training courses be employed in schools within the member state in order to stem a shortfall in teachers (so promoting and protecting the education system);[803] the recruitment and training of young professional footballers[804] and, perhaps, of employees more generally;[805] social protection for victims of road traffic accidents;[806] town and country planning;[807] the soundness and

---

796   Case C-275/92 *HM Customs and Excise* v *Schindler* [1994] ECR I-1039; Case C-432/05 *Unibet (London) and anor* v *Justitiekanslern* [2007] ECR I-2271.

797   Case C-42/07 *Liga Portuguesa de Futebol Profissional and anor* v *Departamento de Jogos da Santa Casa da Misericórdia de Lisboa* [2009] ECR I-7633, at para. 57; Cases C-447 and 448/08 *Criminal proceedings against Sjöberg and Gerdin* [2010] ECR I-6917, at para. 37.

798   Case C-275/92 *Schindler*, n. 796 above; Case C-6/01 *Associação Nacional de Operadores de Máquinas Recreativas and ors* v *Estado português* [2003] ECR I-8621; Case C-243/01 *Criminal proceedings against Gambelli and ors* [2003] ECR I-13031; Cases C-338 etc./04 *Criminal proceedings against Placanica and ors* [2007] ECR I-1891; Case C-432/05 *Unibet*, n. 796 above; cf. Case C-65/05 *Commission* v *Greece* [2006] ECR I-10341; Case C-42/07 *Santa Casa da Misericórdia, ibid.*; Case C-203/08 *Sporting Exchange* v *Minister van Justitie* [2010] ECR I-4695; Case C-258/08 *Ladbrokes Betting and Gaming and anor* v *Stichting de Nationale Sporttotalisator* [2010] ECR I-4757; Cases C-447 and 448/08 *Sjöberg and Gerdin, ibid.*; Case C-409/06 *Winner Wetten* v *Bürgermeisterin der Stadt Bergheim,* [2010] ECR I-8015; Cases C-316 etc./07 *Stoß* v *Wetterankreis* [2010] ECR I-8069; Case C-46/08 *Carmen Media Group* v *Land Schleswig-Holstein and anor* [2010] ECR I-8149.

799   Case E-1/06 *EFTA Surveillance Authority* v *Norway* [2007] EFTA CR 7; Case C-42/07 *Santa Casa da Misericórdia,* n. 797 above; Case C-203/08 *Sporting Exchange, ibid.*; Cases C-316 etc./07 *Stoß, ibid.*; Case C-46/08 *Carmen Media Group, ibid.* But a member state cannot justify restricting gaming licences to undertakings established within its territory: Case C-64/08 *Criminal proceedings against Engelmann* [2010] ECR I-8219.

800   Case C-212/08 *Zeturf* v *Premier ministre,* judgment of 30 June 2011, not yet reported.

801   Case C-36/02 *Omega Spielhallen- und Automatenaufstellungs* v *Oberbürgermeisterin der Bundesstadt Bonn* [2004] ECR I-9609.

802   Case C-288/89 *Collectieve Antennevoorziening Gouda and ors* v *Commissariaat voor de Media* [1991] ECR I-4007; Case C-250/06 *United Pan-Europe Communications Belgium and ors* v *État belge* [2007] ECR I-11135; Case C-222/07 *Unión de Televisiones Comerciales Asociadeas* [2009] ECR I-1407.

803   Case C-40/05 *Lyyski* v *Umeå universitet* [2007] ECR I-99.

804   Case C-415/93 *Union Royale Belge des Sociétés de Football Association and ors* v *Bosman and ors* [1995] ECR I-4921, at para. 106; Case C-325/08 *Olympique Lyonnais* v *Bernard and Newcastle United FC* [2010] ECR I-2177. But encouraging the public to attend football matches appears to be uncompelling: Cases C-403 and 429/08 *Football Association Premier League* v *QC Leisure and ors* and *Murphy* v *Media Protection Services,* judgment of 4 October 2011, not yet reported.

805   See the opinion of A-G Sharpston in Case C-325/08 *Olympique Lyonnais, ibid.*, at paras 29–31.

806   Case C-518/06 *Commission* v *Italy* [2009] ECR I-3491.

safety of building construction, architectural heritage and the consumers and users of buildings;[808] various social measures to combat working 'on the black' (*travail dissimulé*)[809] and social dumping[810] or protect workers generally[811] and ensure independence in the organisation of working life by trade unions;[812] combating drug tourism and the accompanying public nuisance;[813] and a prohibition of privileges and designations pertaining to nobility.[814] Generally the administrative convenience of a member state cannot serve to justify derogations from articles 49 and 56.[815]

Particularly sensitive is advertising: advertising is a means of market penetra- **11.129** tion which may be ancillary to the free movement of goods,[816] may be ancillary to services,[817] or it may itself be a service 'as such'.[818] Yet it is an activity banned in some measure – for example in various member states in given sectors,[819] of given products[820] and/or by target market[821] – and elsewhere universally regulated, sometimes tightly, for the protection of the consumer. A ban on (or mere impediment to) cross-frontier advertising is a restriction prohibited by article 56 (or 34). However it may be justified by reference to public policy or

---

807 Case C-567/07 *Minister voor Wonen, Wijken en Integratie* v *Woningstichting Sint Servatius* [2009] ECR I-9021; Case C-400/08 *Commission* v *Spain*, judgment of 24 March 2011, not yet reported.

808 Case C-458/08 *Commission* v *Portugal* [2010] ECR I-8219, not yet reported, at para. 89.

809 Case C-255/04 *Commission* v *France* [2006] ECR I-5251.

810 Case C-165/98 *Criminal proceedings against Mazzoleni and anor* [2001] ECR I 2189; Case C-164/99 *Proceedings against Portugaia Construções* [2002] ECR I-787; Case C-438/05 *International Transport Workers' Federation and anor* v *Viking Line and anor* [2007] ECR I-10779; Case C-341/05 *Laval un partneri* v *Svenska Byggnadsarbetareförbundet and ors* (Vaxholm) [2007] ECR I-11767.

811 Cases C-369 and 376/96 *Criminal proceedings against Arblade and ors* [1999] ECR I-8453.

812 Case C-346/06 *Rüffert* v *Land Niedersachsen* [2008] ECR I-1989.

813 Case C-137/09 *Josemans* v *Burgemeester van Maastricht* [2010] ECR I-13019.

814 Case C-208/09 *Sayn-Wittgenstein* v *Landeshauptmann von Wien* [2010] ECR I-13693.

815 Cases C-369 and 376/96 *Arblade*, n. 811 above; Case C-58/98 *Corsten* [2000] ECR I-7919; Case C-356/08 *Commission* v *Austria* [2009] ECR I-108*.

816 See 10.51 above.

817 E.g., Case C-275/92 *HM Customs and Excise* v *Schindler* [1994] ECR I-1039; Case C-384/93 *Alpine Investments* v *Minister van Financiën* [1995] ECR I-1141; Case C-318/00 *Bacardi-Martini and anor* v *Newcastle United Football Co.* [2003] ECR I-905.

818 Case 155/73 *Sacchi* [1974] ECR 409, at para. 6.

819 E.g., Case C-320/93 *Ortscheit* v *Eurim-Pharm Arzneimittel* [1994] ECR I-5243 (the health sector); Case C-412/93 *Edouard Leclerc-Siplec* v *TF1 Publicité and anor* [1995] ECR I-179 (the distribution sector, on television); Case C-446/05 *Procureur du Roi* v *Doulamis* [2008] ECR I-1377 (a ban on advertising dental services).

820 Case C-405/98 *Konsumentombudsmannen* v *Gourmet International Products* [2001] ECR I-1795 (alcoholic beverages on radio and television); Case C-318/00 *Bacardi-Martini*, n. 817 above (tobacco and alcoholic beverages); Case C-421/07 *Anklagemyndigheden* v *Damgaard* [2009] ECR I-2629 (medicinal products).

821 Cases C-34 etc./95 *Konsumentombudsmannen* v *De Agostini (Svenska) Förlag* [1997] ECR I-3843 (television advertising directed at children).

public health (as the case may be) or, as a function of consumer protection, to overriding justification in the general interest.[822]

11.130 The Services Directive had a stab at identifying 'overriding reasons relating to the public interest' which may justify an inhibition to provide a service (and the right of establishment for service providers) to be those derived from the case law of the Court, and 'including': public policy; public security; public safety; public health; preserving the financial equilibrium of the social security system; the protection of consumers, recipients of services and workers; fairness of trade transactions; combating fraud; the protection of the environment and the urban environment; the health of animals; intellectual property; the conservation of the national historic and artistic heritage; social policy objectives and cultural policy objectives.[823] However, the 'requirements' which may justify an inhibition to the provision of a service activity (within the meaning of the Directive) are then listed as public policy, public security, public health, protection of the environment and rules on employment conditions[824] with no explanation as to the discrepancy between the two lists and the legal status of those interests included in the first but not the second. It adds yet more confusion by providing in a preambular recitation a third list of 'overriding reasons relating to the public interest … recognised in the case law of the Court of Justice' much more extensive than either of the other two.[825] This invites, and will doubtless receive, clarification from and the active intervention of the Court of Justice.

11.131 There have been some attempts to graft *Keck*[826] principles to the movement of persons, establishment and services,[827] but so far with limited success.

---

822 E.g., Case C-446/05 *Procureur du Roi* v *Doulamis* [2008] ECR I-1377. However, restriction of services to protect public health in one medium but not another is not justified; Case C-500/06 *Corporación Dermoestética* v *To Me Group Advertising Media* [2008] ECR I-5785.

823 Directive 2006/123 [2006] OJ L376/36, art. 4(8). As to the Services Directive see 11.45–11.48 above.

824 Directive 2006/123, art. 16(3).

825 Preamble, 40th recital: covering 'at least' public policy, public security and public health; the maintenance of order in society; social policy objectives; the protection of the recipients of services; consumer protection; the protection of workers, including the social protection of workers; animal welfare; the preservation of the financial balance of the social security system; the prevention of fraud; the prevention of unfair competition; the protection of the environment and the urban environment, including town and country planning; the protection of creditors; safeguarding the sound administration of justice; road safety; the protection of intellectual property; cultural policy objectives, including safeguarding the freedom of expression of various elements, in particular social, cultural, religious and philosophical values of society; the need to ensure a high level of education, the maintenance of press diversity and the promotion of the national language; the preservation of national historical and artistic heritage; and veterinary policy.

826 Cases C-267 and 268/91 *Criminal proceedings against Keck and Mithouard* [1993] ECR I-6097; see 10.46–10.50 above.

827 Case C-384/93 *Alpine Investments* v *Minister van Financiën* [1995] ECR I-1141 (services); Case C-415/93 *Union Royale Belge des Sociétés de Football Association and ors* v *Bosman and ors* [1995] ECR I-4921, *per* A-G Lenz at paras 204–13 of his opinion (workers); Cases C-51/96 and 191/97 *Deliège* v *Ligue francophone de judo and ors* [1999] ECR I-2549, *per* A-G Cosmas at paras 64–6 of his opinion (services); Case C-190/98 *Graf* v

5. Taxation

The manner in which indirect taxation is levied can distort the internal market, **11.132** so the member states' freedom of manoeuvre is limited to an extent (for goods) by article 110 TFEU and there is Treaty authority in article 113 for the harmonisation of national legislation to the extent 'necessary to ensure the establishment and functioning of the internal market and to avoid distortions to competition'.[828] Direct taxation, by contrast, is a field which remains resolutely within national competence. The original Treaty addressed it only to direct the member states to enter into negotiations with each other with a view to securing the abolition of double taxation within the Community.[829] This was exhortatory only, and any agreement concluded not part of Community law,[830] yet it has been largely successful, a skein of double taxation treaties amongst the member states now in place. Maastricht added a provision requiring that there be no arbitrary discrimination in the taxation of the movement of capital and payments.[831] Some Directives adopted under article 115 (it is a field expressly excluded from article 114)[832] in the field of company law,[833] and some more generally,[834] have a bearing upon direct taxation but that is not (and cannot be) their primary purpose.

Filzmoser Maschinenbau [2000] ECR I-493, *per* A-G Fennelly at paras 18–36 of his opinion (workers); Case C-98/01 *Commission* v *United Kingdom* [2003] ECR I-4641, at para. 34 (establishment); Case C-36/02 *Omega Spielhallen- und Automatenaufstellungs* v *Oberbürgermeisterin der Bundesstadt Bonn* [2004] ECR I-9609, *per* A-G Stix-Hackl at paras 34–8 of her opinion (services); Case C-400/08 *Commission* v *Spain*, judgment of 24 March 2011, not yet reported, *per* A-G Sharpston at para. 75 of her opinion (establishment); Case C-565/08 *Commission* v *Italy*, judgment of 29 March 2011, not yet reported (services; *Keck* thinking implicit).

828 See 10.21 above.
829 EEC Treaty, art. 220 (art. 293 EC; repealed by Lisbon).
830 Case C-298/05 *Columbus Container Services* v *Finanzamt Bielefeld-Innenstadt* [2007] ECR I-10451, at para. 47.
831 EC Treaty, art. 73d(3) (art. 65(3) TFEU).
832 TFEU, art. 114(2).
833 They are: Directive 77/799 [1977] OJ L336/1 (Mutual Assistance Directive), to be replaced by Directive 2011/16 [2011] OJ L64/1 from 1 January 2013; Directive 2009/133 [2009] OJ L310/34 (Fiscal Merger Directive), a consolidated version of Directive 90/434 [1990] OJ L225/1; Directive 2011/96 [2011] OJ L345/8 (Parent-Subsidiary Directive), a consolidated version of Directive 90/435 [1990] OJ L225/6; Directive 2003/48 [2003] OJ L157/38 (Savings Interest Directive); and Directive 2003/49 [2003] OJ L157/49 (Interest and Royalty Directive). There is also the extra-Treaty Convention of 23 July 1990 on the Elimination of Double Taxation in connection with the Adjustment of Profits of Associated Enterprises [1990] OJ L225/10 and the (soft law) Code of Conduct for Business Taxation [1998] OJ C2/2. See also *Report of the Committee of Independent Experts on Company Taxation* (1992) (Ruding Committee Report) which recommended further steps to be taken in order to eliminate remaining distortions to competition resulting from variations in direct taxation but which met with limited enthusiasm from the Commission; see Commission MEMO/01/335. Perhaps surprisingly, neither the European Company Statute nor the Statute on the SCE (as to which see 11.60–11.63 above) contains any provisions on tax.
834 See e.g., Case C-533/03 *Commission* v *Council* [2006] ECR I-1025.

11.133   But direct taxation too is capable in its own way of distorting the internal market, less as regards the movement of goods, more persons and capital. The act of moving, working, operating or investing across borders is to invite the operation of two (or more) sets of tax rules which may vary quite considerably. Treaty freedoms could be inhibited by the deployment of tax credits, allowances, relief, exemption and deductions on the basis of nationality (were it permitted), primary place of business or residence (which, to an extent, it is). Therefore although remaining a matter of national competence, direct taxation must be levied in a manner compatible with Union law,[835] in particular as regards the Treaty rights of movement and residence within the territory of the member states, and is therefore subject in principle to a prohibition on any overt or covert discrimination on the basis of nationality.[836] For a migrant worker this is codified in legislation, he or she, once in employment, being entitled to 'the same ... tax advantages as national workers'.[837]

11.134   It is worth recalling that the effectiveness of fiscal supervision was one of the original mandatory requirements recognised in *Cassis de Dijon*[838] for purposes of article 34 TFEU. This is carried over to the free movement of persons, the Court of Justice recognising that Treaty rights of free movement may legitimately be inhibited by reference to the effectiveness of the supervision of taxation, the prevention of tax avoidance and the cohesion of a national taxation system.[839] Justification is deployed either as a public policy exemption (in the sense of articles 45(3), 52 and 62) or an imperative reason in the general interest, but in all events the general tests for the application of the latter normally apply. Since a national tax system, the preservation of which is itself recognised to be a legitimate objective in Union law,[840] is often a very complex edifice, the maintenance of its cohesion will require some latitude. Reasonable, non-(directly) discriminatory and proportionate measures intended to counteract, for example, tax avoidance or the multiplication of tax reliefs will normally

---

835   Case C-279/93 *Finanzamt Köln-Altstadt* v *Schumacker* [1995] ECR I-225; Case C-80/94 *Wielocks* v *Inspecteur der Directe Belastingen* [1995] ECR I-2493; Case C-107/94 *Asscher* v *Staatssecretaris van Financiën* [1996] ECR I-3089.

836   Case C-279/93 *Schumacker, ibid.*, at paras 21 and 26; Case C-385/00 *De Groot* v *Staatssecretaris van Financiën* [2002] ECR I-11819, at para. 75.

837   Regulation 492/2011 [2011] OJ L141/1, art. 7(2).

838   Case 120/78 *Rewe-Zentrale* v *Bundesmonopolverwaltung für Branntwein* [1979] ECR 649.

839   See e.g., Case C-204/90 *Bachmann* v *Belgian State* [1992] ECR I-249 (cohesion of taxation system); Case C-386/04 *Centro di Musicologia Walter Stauffer* v *Finanzamt München für Körperschaften* [2006] ECR I-8203 (prevention of tax avoidance); Case C-150/04 *Commission* v *Denmark* [2007] ECR I-1163 (all three); Case C-318/07 *Persche* v *Finanzamt Lüdenscheid* [2009] ECR I-359 (effectivenss of fiscal supervision); Case C-250/08 *Commission* v *Belgium* and Case C-253/09 *Commission* v *Hungary*, judgments of 1 December 2011, not yet reported (cohesion of taxation system).

840   Case C-446/03 *Marks & Spencer* v *Halsey (HM Inspector of Taxes)* [2005] ECR I-10837, at para. 45; Case C-231/05 *AA* [2007] ECR I-6373 at para. 51.

pass muster. But a concern for budgetary cost or a reduction in tax receipts can serve neither as a public policy exception nor as an imperative reason in the public interest.[841] So, tax relief afforded contributions paid into domestic pension funds must be extended to contributions paid to foreign funds,[842] enabling a migrant worker to remain affiliated to home pension (or life insurance or sickness) schemes if he or she wishes without fiscal penalty; tax deductions available to fees for schooling must be extended to school fees in other member states;[843] where there is interest relief on mortgages with domestic banks it must be extended to interest paid to a bank established elsewhere in the Union;[844] and restricting exemption from tax on the transfer of immovable property to home nationals or persons already permanently resident in the member state,[845] or making exemption from capital gains tax on such transfer conditional upon the gains being reinvested in the purchase of real property situated in the member state,[846] is a breach of articles 18 and 45 or 49, as the case may be.

However, differential treatment based upon residence, although on one view **11.135** discriminatory, may be justified; in fact it is written expressly into Treaty provisions on the free movement of capital.[847] Generally it turns upon a direct link between the tax advantage concerned and the offsetting of that advantage by a particular tax levy.[848] So a national law which denies deduction of insurance premiums paid in another member state is not incompatible with the Treaties where the exemption of taxation of the premiums is offset by taxation of the pensions, annuities or capital sums paid out by the insurers;[849] this is legitimate to protect the cohesion of the tax system and satisfies the proportionality test as taxation of sums payable by insurers in another member state could not be guaranteed. A member state may restrict tax deductions on post-divorce

---

841 Case C-109/04 *Kranemann* v *Land Nordrhein-Westfalen* [2005] ECR I-2421; Case C-464/02 *Commission* v *Denmark* [2005] ECR I-7929; Case C-196/04 *Cadbury Schweppes* v *Inland Revenue* [2006] ECR I-7995; Case C-76/05 *Schwartz and Gootjes-Schwartz* v *Finanzamt Bergisch Gladbach* [2007] ECR I-6849.

842 Case C-150/04 *Commission* v *Denmark*, n. 839 above; Case C-522/04 *Commission* v *Belgium* [2007] ECR I-5701. Equivalent proceedings against seven other member states were terminated with compliance with the Commission's reasoned opinion.

843 Case C-76/05 *Schwartz and Gootjes-Schwartz*, n. 841 above.

844 Case C-484/93 *Svensson and Gustavsson* v *Ministre du Logement et de l'Urbanisme* [1995] ECR I-3955.

845 Case C-155/09 *Commission* v *Greece*, [2011] ECR I-65. Justification put forward based upon considerations of social policy or countering property speculation and tax avoidance met with little sympathy.

846 Case C-345/05 *Commission* v *Portugal* [2006] ECR I-10633.

847 TFEU, art. 65(1) (ex art. 58(1) EC); see 12.11 below.

848 Case C-204/90 *Bachmann*, n. 839 above; Case C-345/05 *Commission* v *Portugal*, n. 846 above; Case C-347/04 *Rewe Zentralfinanz* v *Finanzamt Köln-Mitte* [2007] ECR I-2647, at para. 62 and case law cited; Case C-250/08 *Commission* v *Belgium* and Case C-253/09 *Commission* v *Hungary*, judgments of 1 December 2011, not yet reported.

849 Case C-204/90 *Bachmann*, n. 839 above.

maintenance to that paid within the member state.[850] It may in principle tax the income of a worker employed but not resident in the state more heavily that it does a resident[851] for this is not comparing like with like, unless the worker derives the major part of his income from the member state in which he works and insufficient income in the member state of residence as to enable personal and family circumstances to be taken into account for tax purposes.[852] This is the case equally for individuals exercising a right of establishment under article 49,[853] and *mutatis mutandis* for students[854] and pensioners.[855]

11.136 As for juristic persons, each member state strives to strike a balance, as it sees fit, between lower (and so lower costs, increased foreign investment) and higher (to increase revenues) levels of corporate taxation. Private firms will not be slow to use Treaty freedoms (primarily the freedom of establishment they enjoy under article 49)[856] if they see fiscal advantage to be had from it. Member states may in turn wish to favour their 'home' companies, those with their registered office, central administration or principal place of business (within the meaning of article 54) there which links them to the legal system of a particular member state, 'like nationality in the case of natural persons',[857] a link preserved by *Daily Mail* and *Cartesio*,[858] and which presumably pay their full tax liabilities; this would offset the comparative advantage enjoyed by 'offshore' (re-)incorporated firms, and more generally correct the imbalance, or distortion, in the internal market created by the existence of different corporate tax rates. So, if Dutch law makes a company transferring its real seat to another member state immediately liable to taxation of the unrealised capital gains relating to the assets transferred, whereas such gains are not taxed should the company transfer its real seat elsewhither within the Netherlands, it is liable to deter a company from doing so, infringes, *prima facie*, article 49, but may be justified by reference to the preservation of the allocation of tax powers as between the member states.[859]

---

850   Case C-403/03 *Schempp* v *Finanzamt München V* [2005] ECR I-6421.
851   Case C-279/93 *Schumacker*, n. 835 above; Case C-391/97 *Gschwind* v *Finanzamt Aachen–Außenstadt* [1999] ECR I-5451.
852   Case C-279/93 *Schumacker*, n. 835 above.
853   Case C-80/94 *Wielocks*, n. 835 above; Case C-107/94 *Asscher*, n. 835 above.
854   Case C-169/03 *Wallentin* v *Riksskatteverket* [2004] ECR I-6443.
855   Case C-520/04 *Turpeinen* [2006] ECR I-10685.
856   See 11.50–11.59 above.
857   Case 270/83 *Commission* v *France* (Avoir Fiscal) [1986] ECR 273, at para. 18; Case C-231/05 *AA* [2007] ECR I-6373, at para. 30.
858   Case 81/87 *R* v *HM Treasury and Commissioners of Inland Revenue, ex parte Daily Mail and anor* [1988] ECR 5483; Case C-210/06 *CARTESIO Oktató és Szolgáltató* [2008] ECR I-9641. See 11.57 above.
859   Case C-371/10 *National Grid Indus* v *Inspecteur van de Belastingdienst Rijnmond/kantoor Rotterdam*, judgment of 29 November 2011, not yet reported. But to require the tax to be recovered immediately was disproportionate.

However, to permit a member state to wield differential tax treatment solely **11.137** because the 'nationality' of a company is situated in another member state would deprive article 49 of its substance.[860] Freedom of establishment is designed to guarantee the benefit of national treatment in the host member state, by prohibiting all discrimination upon that basis. Further, article 49 precludes tax advantages conferred upon domestic companies with domestic subsidiaries which are denied, or granted upon less favourable terms, to domestic companies with subsidiaries in other member states;[861] and equally, tax advantages may not be conferred upon subsidiaries of domestic companies whilst not extending them to those of foreign companies.[862] A member state may wish to counteract these 'artificial' advantages by means of 'controlled foreign company' (CFC) legislation.[863] It is legitimate here, as with natural persons, to adopt measures necessary to protect the coherence of the national taxation system.[864] But as the mere fact of establishment in another member state in order to benefit from a more favourable tax regime is not of itself an abuse,[865] to preclude the inclusion in the tax base of a domestic company of profits made by a CFC in another member state which are subject in the latter to a level of taxation lower than that of the former is a breach of article 49 unless its corporate arrangements are 'wholly artificial ... intended to escape the national tax normally payable'.[866]

The wholly internal rule applies to direct taxation, so that an individual or **11.138** company can avail itself of no Treaty rights absent a significant Union element in his, her or its operations.[867] To abandon the rule might have serious and unintended consequences here.

---

860 Case 270/83 *Avoir Fiscal*, n. 857 above; Case C-231/05 *AA*, n. 857 above.

861 Case C-251/98 *Baars* v *Inspecteur der Belastingen Particulieren/Ondernemingen Gorinchem* [2000] ECR I-2787; Case C-446/03 *Marks & Spencer* v *Halsey (HM Inspector of Taxes)* [2005] ECR I-10837; Case C-96/08 *CIBA Speciality Chemicals Central and Eastern Europe Szolgáltató, Tanácsadó és Kereskedelmi* v *Adó- és Pénzügyi Ellenőrzési Hivatal Hatósági Főosztály* [2010] ECR I-2911.

862 Case 270/83 *Avoir Fiscal*, n. 857 above (generally recognised to be the first judgment of the Court on direct taxation); Cases C-397 and 410/98 *Metallgesellschaft and ors* v *Commissioners of Inland Revenue and anor* [2001] ECR I-1727; Case C-231/05 *AA*, n. 857 above, at paras 30–43 and cases cited.

863 For example, in the United Kingdom, the Income and Corporation Taxes Act 1988, ss. 747–56; Finance Act 2011, s. 47, Sch. 12.

864 E.g., Case C-157/07 *Finanzamt für Körperschaften III in Berlin* v *Krankenheim Ruhesitz am Wannsee-Seniorenheimstatt* [2008] ECR I-8061.

865 Case C-196/04 *Cadbury Schweppes* v *Inland Revenue* [2006] ECR I-7995, at paras 34–8.

866 Case C-196/04 *Cadbury Schweppes*, *ibid.*, at para. 75. There is little guidance in the judgment as to what this is to mean. A-G Léger proposed an objective test, essentially whether the parent company has in truth established genuine operations in another member state as opposed to an abusive practice of setting up a 'letter-box' company. Also Case C-446/04 *Test Claimants in the FII Group Litigation* v *Commissioners of Inland Revenue* [2006] ECR I-11753.

867 Case C-112/91 *Werner* v *Finanzamt Aachen-Innenstadt* [1993] ECR I-429. This was so even though Mr Werner, a German, German-trained and German-established dentist was a long-term resident of the Netherlands.

6. Serious internal disturbances and international tension

11.139 As with the free movement of goods – in fact, across the whole of the application of the internal market – member states may restrict the movement of persons and services in the event of serious internal disturbances affecting the maintenance of law and order, in the event of war, serious international tension constituting a threat of war, or in order to discharge obligations they have accepted for the purpose of maintaining peace and international security.[868] This is discussed above.[869]

F. HORIZONTAL DIRECT EFFECT OF FREE MOVEMENT PROVISIONS: *ANGONESE; VIKING LINES; VAXHOLM*

11.140 As with the free movement of goods,[870] the obligations of articles 45, 49 and 56 are addressed first and foremost to the member states. But in 2000 in *Angonese*[871] the Court of Justice found article 45 to impose obligations not only upon the member states but upon private persons as well. This obtains most clearly to workers amongst the free movement provisions of the Treaties, but its repercussions are now being felt, and its applicability uncovered, in relation to other of the freedoms.

11.141 *Angonese* was in fact not the first time the issue had been touched upon. In *Walrave and Koch* (1974)[872] and *Bosman* (1995)[873] the Court had already confronted impediments to the movement of workers a function of rules adopted by the pan-European associations regulating the sports of, respectively, cycling and football. The Court found article 45 (and in *Walrave and Koch* also article 56, both articles being at issue) to apply in those situations because the relevant associations 'regulat[ed] gainful employment in a collective manner'.[874] Thus article 45 (and 56) catches not only the member state but private law associations which, as here, enjoy *de facto* authority to regulate access to employment across an entire sector. The principle was reapplied subsequently,

---

868 TFEU, art. 347 (art. 297 EC).
869 See 10.32–10.35 above.
870 See 10.59 above.
871 Case C-281/98 *Angonese* v *Cassa di Risparmio di Bolzano* [2000] ECR I-4139.
872 Case 36/74 *Walrave and Koch* v *Union Cycliste Internationale and ors* [1974] ECR 1405; also Case 13/76 *Donà* v *Mantero* [1976] ECR 1333.
873 Case C-415/93 *Union Royale Belge des Sociétés de Football Association and ors* v *Bosman and ors* [1995] ECR I-4921.
874 Case 36/74 *Walrave and Koch*, n. 872 above, at para. 27; Case C-415/93 *Bosman*, *ibid.* at para. 82.

to the same effect, in the context of regulation of the sports of judo,[875] basketball[876] and handball.[877]

Angonese goes further. It involved a rule adopted by a regional savings bank in **11.142** the trilingual (German, Italian, Ladin) autonomous Italian province of Trentino-Alto Adige which set out possession of a certificate of bilingualism in German and Italian (the '*patentino*') as a condition for admission to competitions for positions of employment at the bank. A *patentino* could be obtained only from the public authorities of the province after passing an examination, diets in which were held four times a year at a single examination centre in Bolzano. Mr Angonese, an Italian citizen born and raised in the province, was fluent in both languages but had no *patentino*, and was accordingly refused admission to a competition. He raised an action against the bank seeking, in effect, a declaration that evidence (which he claimed to possess) of bilingualism other than the *patentino* ought to suffice, and damages for loss of opportunity.

Amongst the many hurdles he required to overcome was the fact that the rule **11.143** which (he claimed) limited his rights of free movement was adopted not by an Italian or provincial authority but by a bank – by any definition, a private person. On this point the Court of Justice noted the prohibitions of article 45 were in general terms, and not addressed to the member states ('Freedom of movement for workers shall be secured within the Union ... [It] shall entail the abolition of any discrimination based on nationality').[878] It cited *Walrave* and *Bosman* with approval, and reiterated the *Walrave* concerns that rules governing access to employment may be a function of public or private regulation, and so a risk of inequality of application amongst member states. It then referred to *Defrenne II*, in which the Court had found 25 years previously that article 157 TFEU (which prohibited pay differentials based upon sex) conferred horizontal direct effect,[879] and said

> such considerations must, *a fortiori*, be applicable to Article [45 TFEU], which lays down a fundamental freedom and which constitutes a specific application of the general prohibition of discrimination contained in Article [18]. In that respect, like Article [157], it is designed to ensure that there is no discrimination on the labour market.

---

875   Cases C-51/96 and 191/97 *Deliège* v *Ligue francophone de judo et disciplines associées and ors* [2000] ECR I-2549, at para. 47.
876   Case C-176/96 *Lehtonen and anor* v *Fédération royale belge des sociétés de basket-ball* [2000] ECR I-2681, at para. 35.
877   Case C-438/00 *Deutscher Handballbund* v *Kolpak* [2003] ECR I-4135, at para. 37.
878   TFEU, art. 45(1), (2).
879   Case 43/75 *Defrenne* v *SABENA* [1976] ECR 455; see 14.47 below.

Consequently, the prohibition of discrimination on grounds of nationality laid down in Article [45] of the Treaty must be regarded as applying to private persons as well.[880]

11.144 There is much to criticise in *Angonese*, but the inescapable consequence is the horizontal direct effect of, and so burdens placed upon private persons by, article 45. It leaves us with significant intrusion into private law (labour law) matters, all private employers now bound to afford Union law standards to all migrant workers, presumably in both access to employment and in conditions of employment, but, so long as the wholly internal rule survives, not to home workers.[881] Or at least they must do so if to do otherwise would result in discrimination, for *Angonese* was limited to (indirectly) discriminatory measures; whether article 45 applies horizontally to non-discriminatory measures is not known. And wholly unexplored is the extent to which and manner in which a private employer may invoke the exclusionary provisions of article 45(3) or imperative reasons in the public interest and how objective justification might be pled.

11.145 The horizontal direct effect of article 45 has been confirmed, the (putative) employer this time being one of a complex of scientific research institutes in Germany (the Max Planck Institutes) forming an association in private law operating in the national interest.[882] A key question was then whether *Angonese* was going to spill over into other of the four freedoms. To an extent it has already done so in the freedom of establishment and the provision of services. In *Viking Line*,[883] a Finnish passenger ferry operator sought to re-flag one of its (Helsinki–Tallinn) ferries (which was operating at a loss) and register it in Estonia in order to take advantage of lower wages/labour costs there. The Finnish seamen's union threatened strike action and boycotts with a view to preventing the re-registration or compelling the ferry operator to enter into a collective agreement on any Estonia-flagged ship on Finnish terms. The Court decided that the conduct of the union, the 'collective action such as that at issue in the main proceedings',[884] fell within the scope of article 49:

> Article [49 TFEU] is to be interpreted as meaning that, in principle, collective action initiated by a trade union or a group of trade unions against an undertaking in order to

---

880   Case C-281/98 *Angonese*, at n. 871 above, paras 35, 36.
881   This was another hurdle facing Mr Angonese, his argument being that his situation fell within the scope of Community law because he had previously exercised Community rights in another member state; following extensive consideration A-G Fennelly was not convinced and would have refused to answer the questions on that ground (see paras 14–37 of his opinion), but the Court paid the issue scant attention (paras 17–20) and proceeded with judgment.
882   Case C-94/07 *Raccanelli v Max-Planck-Gesellschaft zur Förderung der Wissenschaften* [2008] ECR I-5939.
883   Case C-438/05 *International Transport Workers' Union and anor v Viking Line* [2007] ECR I-10779.
884   *Ibid.* at para. 36.

induce that undertaking to enter into a collective agreement, the terms of which are liable to deter it from exercising freedom of establishment, is not excluded from the scope of that article.[885]

Relying upon *Defrenne*, *Spanish Strawberries*[886] and *Schmidberger*[887] logic and authority, it then determined that article 49 'may be relied on by a private undertaking [is capable of conferring rights on a private undertaking which may be relied on] against a trade union or an association of trade unions',[888] and added strong 'guidance' that the referring court ought to think carefully before finding any justification for the threatened action.[889] At the same time, in *Vaxholm*[890] the Court found the 'blockade' by Swedish trade unions (including secondary action) of a building site (in Vaxholm, a town in the Stockholm archipelago) at which a Latvian firm was building a school and paying its (Latvian) workforce in accordance with agreed Latvian wages which were below those which obtained in Sweden, the blockade intended to compel the firm to negotiate and enter into a collective agreement which complied with Swedish rates, to constitute measures 'which [although] not public in nature ... are designed to regulate, collectively, the provision of services'[891] and so to fall within the prohibition of article 56, in a manner which could not be justified by reference to prevention of social dumping or other public policy. The principle was extended subsequently to rules adopted by an Austrian Land medical association (*Ärtzekammer*) which inhibited the provision of doctors' services from other member states.[892]

Neither *Viking Line* nor *Vaxholm* go quite so far as *Angonese*. Rather, both deal **11.146** with collective action (through trade unions) which impeded the exercise of a Union right – in *Vaxholm* they managed collectively to shut down the entirety of Laval's operations throughout Sweden.[893] They are thus analogous to the 'regulation of gainful employment in a collective manner' of *Walrave* and *Bosman*, and, at least for article 56, this was not entirely new.[894] But as *Angonese*

---

885   *Ibid.* at para. 55.
886   Case C-265/95 *Commission* v *France* [1997] ECR I-6959.
887   Case C-112/00 *Eugen Schmidberger, Internationale Transporte und Planzüge* v *Austria* [2003] ECR I-5659.
888   Case C-438/05 *Viking Line*, n. 883 above, at para. 61 [and para. 67].
889   *Ibid.* at paras 85–9.
890   Case C-341/05 *Laval un Partneri* v *Svenska Byggnadsarbetareförbundet and ors* (Vaxholm) [2007] ECR I-11767.
891   *Ibid.* at para. 98.
892   Case C-356/08 *Commission* v *Austria* [2009] ECR I-108*.
893   Case C-341/05 *Vaxholm*, n. 890 above, at para. 38. Laval eventually recovered Kr 550,000 in general damages (having sought Kr 2.8 million but awarded no damages for economic loss which it could not show) from the union; Arbetsdomstolen, dom nr 89 den 2 december 2009. The union was also required to pay Laval's costs of Kr 2.1 million. It is the first case in which a trade union has been found liable in damages for breach of EU law.
894   E.g., Case 36/74 *Walrave and Koch*, Case C-415/93 *Bosman*, Cases C-51/96 and 191/97 *Deliège* and Case C-176/96 *Lehtonen*, cited at nn. 872–6 above. It might be noted that the Commission seemed on one occasion

followed *Walrave* and *Bosman*, the application of articles 49 and 56 to the unilateral conduct of a single undertaking may not be far behind. It also marks a clarification of the application of these Treaty rights: there was an argument that the Court's generosity to individuals impeded in their economic endeavour by other persons was a (tacit) recognition of rights springing from their citizenship of the Union, for *Walrave, Bosman, Deliège, Lehtonen* and *Angonese* all involved the inhibition of Treaty rights of individuals properly so-called. But *Viking Line* and *Vaxholm* extend the principles seamlessly to juristic persons.

11.147 As to whether these provisions, most directly article 45, are binding upon the Union institutions, it must be noted that they (and the Commission in particular) discriminate (directly) in filling posts on grounds of nationality as a matter of course. The Commission was once challenged on this in litigation but managed to sidestep it.[895] This is either unlawful; or employment as a Commission *fonctionnaire* is not constitutive of '(migrant) worker' (*quaere* whether Belgian citizens could/must be treated differently owing to the wholly internal rule), or is employment in the public service (athough this is a privilege probably afforded the member states only), for purposes of article 45; or the policy goal of some sort of balance of nationalities working within the Commission services is an imperative reason in the public interest, justifying even direct discrimination on grounds of nationality (which normally cannot be prayed in aid of direct discrimination); or in some other way the Commission is above the law of these 'fundamental' free movement provisions of the Treaties which now bind everyone else. The Commission is not the sole erring institution: the Court of Justice itself requires that parties appearing before it have an address for services somewhere in Luxembourg,[896] but this apparent breach of article 56 has never been challenged.[897]

---

at least to disapprove: following a complaint that the anti-doping rules adopted by International Olympic Committee (IOC) and the *Fédération Internationale de Natation* (FINA) infringed the competition rules and art. 56, the Commission said: 'The complaint contains no details which could justify a finding that there exists an infringement of article [56] of the Treaty by a member state ... Indeed, there is no evidence of the responsibility of any authority of a member state for the adoption of measures which could prove contrary to the principle of the free movement of services' (Case COMP/38.158, *Meca Medina et Majken/CIO*, decision of 1 August 2002, unpublished, para. 71; translated by the author; challenged, unsuccessfully, in Case T-313/02 *Meca-Medina and Majcen* v *Commission* [2004] ECR II-3291 but with no direct consideration of this issue; upheld on appeal as Case C-519/04P *Meca-Medina and Majcen* v *Commission* [2006] ECR I-6991). Even at the time, but most certainly now, this must be regarded as an aberrant view.

895   In the early 1980s a German national refused admission to a Commission *concours* for a post as a *fonctionnaire* (a response to alleged over-representation of Germans working in rhe Commission services and an attempt at a better balance of nationalities therein) challenged the refusal on grounds of unlawful discrimination on grounds of nationality but the Commission evaded any censure of the Court by the expedient of abandoning the *concours*; settled in Case 89/82R *Wölker* v *Commission* [1982] ECR 1323.

896   RP General Court, art. 44(2); RP Civil Service Tribunal, art. 35(3). An equivalent rule for the Court of Justice was abandoned in 2012.

897   Nor has the requirement of the Statute of the Court (art. 14) that the judges, the Advocates-General and the Registrar reside in Luxembourg been challenged for incompatibility with art. 45 (if the judges are workers, as

G. TREATIES WITH THIRD COUNTRIES

The Community/Union has entered into a number of treaties with third **11.148** countries regulating their mutual relationships.[898] They are a very mixed bag, some extensive, some not. A number (but because of the sensitivity attached, a small number) of them contain provisions not only on trade and commercial matters but addressing the free movement of persons. They are as follows.

1. European Economic Area

The Treaty creating the European Economic Area[899] contains provisions on the **11.149** free movement of workers, right of establishment and services which are essentially carbon copies of the equivalent Union provisions.[900] Uniformity of meaning is buttressed by the adoption into EEA law of the *acquis communautaire* as at the date of signature of the Treaty insofar as EEA terminology is identical in substance to (then) existing Community provisions[901] (as much of it is). The rights of Icelanders, Liechtensteiners and Norwegians in the Union (and vice versa) are therefore for all intents and purposes, save those which derive solely from the status of Union citizenship, identical to those enjoyed by Union nationals. One measure of this is that the United Kingdom legislation which gives effect to Directive 2004/38[902] does not distinguish between Union citizens and citizens of other EEA member states. It might be noted that Liechtenstein imposes certain restrictions (by quota) upon the right of residence of Union workers, relying upon a provision of the EEA Agreement which permits unilateral safeguard measures which are 'strictly necessary' in order to remedy 'serious economic, societal or environmental difficulties of a sectorial [*sic*] or regional nature',[903] and Union authorities appear to accept this equably as legitimate given the size, small population and already high proportion of foreign nationals resident there; but this is not to say it could not be challenged by a disgruntled Union national and the EFTA Court would necessarily agree.

---

to which see Case C-393/10 *O'Brien* v *Ministry of Justice*, judgment of 1 March 2012, not yet reported) or art. 56 (if they are not). However, the Statute of the Court is based in a protocol, therefore has Treaty status (although is surely not a 'fundamental principle' as is art. 56), and so may survive a challenge. It may in any event be reasonable.

898   See 14.82–14.98 below.
899   Agreement of 2 May 1992 on the European Economic Area [1994] 1994 L1/3 ('EEA Agreement'). As to the EEA see 14.85–14.86 below.
900   EEA Agreement, arts 28–30 (workers), 31–5 (establishment), 36–9 (services).
901   *Ibid.* art. 6.
902   Immigration (European Economic Area) Regulations 2006, SI 2006/1003.
903   EEA Agreement, art. 112.

2. Switzerland

11.150 Following Swiss failure to ratify the EEA Agreement, in 1999 the Community (and the member states) and Switzerland entered into a series of agreements ('bilateral agreements I') covering various areas of cooperation.[904] Most ambitious is the agreement on the free movement of persons,[905] which provides for reciprocal access to labour markets, rights of establishment and services, equal treament, rights of entry and residence (also for the non-economically active if self-sufficient), recognition of qualifications and cross-border health care; it allows for quotas (lapsed in 2007), national priority (lapsed in 2004 for 'old' member states and Cyprus and Malta, in 2011 for the other 'new' member states) and special protective measures in the event of an excessive increase in immigration (lapses in 2014).[906] Following renewal (by referendum in Switzerland) in 2009, the agreement now continues indefinitely.[907]

3. Turkey

11.151 In 1963 a Treaty was signed creating an 'association' between the EEC and Turkey.[908] In 1980, in an effort to 'revitalise' and 'develop' the association, the Association Council created by the treaty adopted Decision 1/80. Oddly it has never been published in the *Official Journal*,[909] but this has never led the Court of Justice to question its force.

11.152 Decision 1/80 addresses a number of issues but predominant, and with teeth, are those on the movement of workers. Article 6(1) of the Decision provides:

> [A] Turkish worker duly registered as belonging to the labour force of a Member State:
>
> - shall be entitled in that Member State, after one year's legal employment, to the renewal of his permit to work for the same employer, if a job is available;
> - shall be entitled in that Member State, after three years of legal employment and subject to the priority to be given to workers of Member States of the Community, to respond to another offer of employment, with an employer of his choice, made under normal conditions and registered with the employment services of that State, for the same occupation;

---

904 See 14.87 below.

905 Agreement of 21 June 1999 between the European Community and its Member States and the Swiss Confederation on the Free Movement of Persons [2002] OJ L114/6; in force 1 June 2002.

906 *Ibid.* art. 10.

907 See 14.87 below.

908 Treaty of 12 September 1963 between the European Economic Community and its Member States and the Republic of Turkey creating an Association (Ankara Agreement) [1973] OJ C113/2.

909 The text is available in *EEC-Turkey Association Agreement and Protocols and Other Basic Texts*, Office for Official Publications of the European Communities (1992).

- shall enjoy free access in that Member State to any paid employment of his choice, after four years of legal employment.

According to the Court of Justice, the benefits of Decision 1/80 therefore accrue to a Turk meeting three objective conditions: he or she

- is (lawfully) a worker;
- is duly registered as belonging to the labour force in the host member state; and
- is in a stable and secure situation as a member of that labour force and so has an undisputed right of residence there.[910]

There is also a standstill provision prohibiting any new restrictions on the freedom of establishment and the freedom to provide services.[911]

Article 6(1) is directly effective.[912] The Decision does not touch upon the **11.153** competence retained by the member states to regulate both the entry of Turkish nationals and the conditions under which they may first take up employment, rather it is concerned with the situation of Turkish workers already in and integrated into the host member state (as defined by the Decision),[913] with a view progressively to consolidate their position there.[914] No further restrictions or conditions may be imposed by national authorities.[915] It is not necessary that he or she entered the host member state originally as a worker[916] or that the purpose for which he or she did so no longer exists,[917] and an expressed intention to return to Turkey cannot deprive him or her of the right, unless he or she had set out to deceive the competent authorities by making a false declaration with the sole intention of inducing them to authorise initial entry.[918] The Decision has no bearing on the rights of a Turkish worker in a

---

910   Case C-1/97 *Birden v Stadtgemeinde Bremen* [1998] ECR I-7747; Case C-188/00 *Kurz v Land Baden-Württemberg* [2002] ECR I-10691; Case C-294/06 *R (Payir and ors) v Secretary of State for the Home Department* [2008] ECR I-203. As to the concept of 'duly registered as belonging to the labour force' see *Birden* at paras 33–54; as for 'lawful employment' see Case C-192/89 *Sevince v Staatssecretaris van Justitie* [1990] ECR I-3461, at para. 30; Case C-434/93 *Bozkurt v Staatssecretaris van Justitie* [1995] ECR I-1475, para. 26; *Birden* at paras 55–68.
911   Association Agreement, Additional Protocol, art. 41(1).
912   Case C-192/89 *Sevince*, n. 910 above. So too is art. 41(1) of the Additional Protocol, Case C-16/05 *Tum and Dari v Secretary of State for the Home Department* [2007] ECR I-7415, at para. 46 and case law cited.
913   Case C-98/96 *Ertanir v Land Hessen* [1997] ECR I-5179.
914   Case C-230/03 *Sedef v Freie und Hansestadt Hamburg* [2006] ECR I-157.
915   Case C-36/96 *Günaydin v Freistaat Bayern* [1997] ECR I-5143; Case C-294/06 *Payir*, n. 910 above.
916   Case C-355/93 *Eroglu v Land Baden-Württemberg* [1994] ECR I-5133 (originally entered as a student); Case C-1/97 *Birden*, n. 910 above (no identifiable purpose); Case C-188/00 *Kurz*, n. 910 above (training as a plumber); Case C-294/06 *Payir*, n. 910 above (students).
917   Case C-14/09 *Genc v Land Berlin* [2010] ECR I-931.
918   Case C-36/96 *Günaydin*, n. 915 above, at paras 54 and 60; Case C-294/06 *Payir*, n. 910 above, at para. 40.

third member state, which are regulated by the general application of other legislation.[919]

11.154 In employment, Turkish workers are entitled to treatment equal to that accorded other Union nationals 'as regards conditions of work and remuneration'.[920] This extends to rules adopted by a sporting federation (the *Real Federación Española de Fútbol*) which would otherwise limit the fielding of a Turkish footballer on account of his nationality.[921] A Turk cannot be subjected to an administrative fee for regularising his situation (for example, for a residence permit) which is disproportionately higher than that imposed upon Union citizens in a like situation.[922] A Turkish worker's family (undefined; presumably, although not yet confirmed, the same as that in Directive 2004/38) is entitled to work after three year's lawful residence, subject to any priority afforded Union nationals, and without limit after five years;[923] so that this right of access to the labour market is not rendered ineffective, the family member enjoys a concomitant right of residence.[924] Once earned the right survives divorce[925] and appears to survive indefinitely, even if unexercised.[926] If the worker upon whom the family member relies had obtained his or her right of entry and residence upon falsehoods so that the right is withdrawn, the family member's rights survive if he or she had fulfilled the necessary conditions prior to the date of withdrawal.[927] They also survive the naturalisation of the (dual national) Turkish worker in the host member state if it would modify the rights accured under Decision 1/80.[928] A Turk may be removed where his or her presence constitutes a genuine and serious threat to public policy, public security or public health,[929] to be interpreted by analogy with the equivalent provisions of Directive 2004/38,[930] and although Decision 1/80 does not say so,

---

919 Principally Directive 2003/109 [2003] OJ L16/44; see 11.167 below.
920 Additional Protocol (to the EEC-Turkey Association Agreement) of 23 November 1970 [1973] OJ C113/18, art. 37.
921 Case C-152/08 *Real Sociedad de Fútbol and Kahveci v Consejo Superior de Deportes and anor* [2008] ECR I-6291.
922 Case C-92/07 *Commission v Netherlands* (Turkish Residence Permits) [2010] ECR I-3683.
923 Decision 1/80, art. 7; also directly effective, Case C-351/95 *Kadiman v Freistaat Bayern* [1997] ECR I-2133. There is no wait for a worker's child who has completed a course of vocational training in the host member state provided the worker has been legally employed there for at least three years.
924 Case C-329/97 *Ergat v Stadt Ulm* [2000] ECR I-1487; Case C-467/02 *Cetinkaya v Land Baden-Württemberg* [2004] ECR I-10895.
925 Case C-303/08 *Land Baden-Württemberg v Bozkurt* [2010] ECR I-13445.
926 Case C-453/07 *Er v Wetteraukreis* [2008] ECR I-7299.
927 Case C-337/07 *Altun v Stadt Böblingen* [2008] ECR I-10323.
928 Cases C-7 & 9/10 *Staatssecretaris van Justitie v Kahveci and Inan*, judgment of 29 March 2012, not yet reported.
929 Decision 1/80, art. 14(1).
930 Case C-303/08 *Bozkurt*, n. 925 above, at para. 55 and case law cited.

the procedural guarantees of Directive 2004/38 apply.[931] But the enhanced protection from expulsion it now provides Union citizens does not carry over.[932]

4. Europe Agreements

In the 1990s the Community (and the member states) entered into a 'Europe Agreement' with each of the candidate countries from central and eastern Europe (Cyprus and Malta followed a different path) which went on to join the Union in 2004 and 2007. As part of the 'pre-accession strategy', each provided to nationals of and companies formed in the contracting parties a right of establishment (in most sectors) and the freedom to provide services in each other's territory.[933] They did not extend to a general right of access to employment,[934] but they did provide (a) a right of employment in the host member state (or the host candidate country) for the 'key personnel' of companies (and only with those companies) exercising the right of establishment or providing a service there;[935] and (b) for workers nationals of each in lawful employment in a host state (by grace of that state), (i) equal treatment with home nationals as regards working conditions, remuneration and dismissal, and (ii) a right to work for their spouse and children.[936] These provisions died with the Europe Agreements of which they were part, but they may come to be adopted for future pre-accession arrangements.

11.155

5. Association agreements

Some other association agreements, such as the partnership and cooperation agreements with the former Soviet republics,[937] contain provisions on the movement of persons similar to those in the Europe Agreements, so providing for equality with home nationals as regards working conditions, remuneration

11.156

---

931 Case C-136/03 *Dörr and Ünal* v *Sicherheitsdirektion für die Bundesländer Kärnten und Vorarlberg* [2005] ECR I-4759.

932 Case C-371/08 *Ziebell* v *Land Baden-Württemberg*, judgment of 8 December 2011, not yet reported.

933 See e.g., the Agreement of 12 June 1995 establishing an Association between the European Communities and their Member States and the Republic of Latvia (that is, the Europe Agreement with Latvia) [1998] OJ L26/3, arts 44, 52. The ten European Agreements were essentially identical.

934 *Ibid.* art. 46(d)(i).

935 *Ibid.* arts 49, 52.

936 *Ibid.* art. 37. For consideration of the ambit of these provisions see Case C-63/99 *R* v *Secretary of State for the Home Department, ex parte Gloszczuk and anor* [2001] ECR I-6369; Case C-235/99 *R* v *Secretary of State for the Home Department, ex parte Kondova* [2001] ECR I-6427; Case C-268/99 *Jany and ors* v *Staatssecretaris van Justitie* [2001] ECR I-8615.

937 See 14.92 below.

or dismissal for those lawfully in employment,[938] most favoured nation treatment for the establishment of each others' companies and provision of services in their mutual territories,[939] movement of 'key personnel' to assist the right of establishment[940] and temporary movement of natural persons if necessary for the effective provision of services.[941]

H. THE AREA OF FREEDOM, SECURITY AND JUSTICE

11.157 Of the sequence of reforming treaties beginning with the Single European Act in 1986 and ending (for now) with the Lisbon Treaty, the least of them is probably the Treaty of Amsterdam, a primary purpose of which was to make institutional changes appropriate to looming enlargement, but that achieved only later with the Treaty of Nice. However in one particular Amsterdam marked a major change, that is a fundamental constitutional reorganisation of Title VI of the (then) Treaty on European Union, drawing some of its activities from the Union into the Community sphere – or, from the third into the first pillar – and creating treaty authority (primarily but not wholly within the first pillar) for the achievement of, in the new jargon, an 'area of freedom, security and justice', sometimes called JLS, for *justice, liberté et sécurité* (the name of the relevant Commission Directorate-General until split into two (D-G Home Affairs and D-G Justice) in 2010), which had thitherto been merely foreshadowed.[942] It is an adjunct, closely linked to the free movement of persons, and an attempt to adopt the rules necessary finally and fully to complete the internal market. The importance accorded this new Treaty construct is evident from the Lisbon Treaty which *communautairised* the whole and posits it at the outset as a cornerstone of the Union and the operation of (and even prior to) the internal market: 'The Union shall offer its citizens an area of freedom, security and justice without internal frontiers, in which the free movement of persons is ensured'.[943]

---

938   E.g., Agreement of 24 June 1994 on Partnership and Cooperation establishing a Partnership between the European Communities and their Member States and the Russian Federation [1997] OJ 1997 L327/1, art. 23(1); see Case C-265/03 *Simutenkov* v *Ministerio de Educación y Cultura and anor* [2005] ECR I-2579.
939   Agreement of 24 June 1994, arts 28, 36.
940   *Ibid.* art. 32.
941   *Ibid.* art. 37.
942   TEU (pre-Amsterdam), art. K.1.
943   TEU, art. 3(2).

From 1999 to 2009 the area of freedom, security and justice spanned the **11.158** Community/Union constitutional divide. This dictated significantly the manner in which it developed and bedded down, which it is necessary to review in order properly to understand it.

1. The Amsterdam scheme

(a) Community provisions

Title IV of the EC Treaty, created by Amsterdam, was entitled 'Visas, Asylum, **11.159** Immigration and Other Policies related to Free Movement of Persons' and provided authority, in order progressively to establish the area of freedom, security and justice, for the adoption of Community measures:

- to ensure the free movement of persons in accordance with article 14 EC (now article 26 TFEU), in conjunction with directly related flanking measures with respect to external border controls, asylum and immigration; in the fields of asylum, immigration and safeguarding the rights of nationals of third countries; in the field of judicial cooperation in civil matters (encompassing improvement and simplification of cross-border service of judicial and extrajudicial documents, cooperation in the taking of evidence and the recognition and enforcement of decisions in civil and commercial cases, promoting compatibility of the rules on conflict of laws and jurisdiction and eliminating obstacles to the effective functioning of civil proceedings); and to encourage and strengthen administrative cooperation;[944]
- to ensure, in compliance with article 14 EC, the absence of any controls on persons, irrespective of nationality, when crossing internal borders; as a corollary, measures on entry at external frontiers, such as standards and procedures in carrying out checks on persons, rules on visas (which third country nationals require a visa, procedures and conditions for issuing visas, uniform format and rules on a uniform visa); and the conditions under which third country nationals have the freedom to travel within the territory of the member states for a period of no more than three months;[945]
- on asylum and the status and treatment of refugees and displaced persons; on conditions of entry and residence and standards on procedures for the issue of long-term visas and residence permits; on illegal immigration and illegal residence, including repatriation; and on the rights and conditions

---

944   EC Treaty, arts 61, 65.
945   *Ibid.* art. 62.

under which nationals of third countries who are legally resident in one member state may reside in other member states;[946]

- to ensure cooperation between the relevant departments of the administrations of the member states in the areas covered by this title, as well as between those departments and the Commission.[947]

It will be noted from this recitation that, whilst the purpose of creating the area of freedom, security and justice is nominally to ensure that Union nationals enjoy fully and effectively the rights conferred upon them by the Treaties, much of its emphasis is in fact on issues relating to third country nationals, and a key element of JLS policy is the strengthening of external frontiers, the jargon now turning from 'border control' to 'border security'.

11.160 Appropriate measures were to be adopted within a period of five years from the entry into force of Amsterdam[948] (that is, by 1 May 2004) by the Council acting unanimously upon a proposal from the Commission or on the initiative of a Member State and after consulting the Parliament,[949] thereafter upon proposals from the Commission, which was bound to consider (but not necessarily follow up) any request made by a member state that it (the Commission) submit a proposal to the Council.[950] The Council was obliged at the close of the five-year period to decide (unanimously, after consulting the Parliament) which, if any, of the provisions of the Title would thenceforward be governed by the co-decision procedure.[951] This was one of three bridging clauses in the EC Treaty, probably its most contentious, and in the event the only one ever deployed. Following criticism from the Parliament for delay,[952] in late 2004 the Council adopted a decision extending the co-decision procedure to measures for the abolition of controls at internal frontiers, checks at external frontiers, travel of third country nationals for up to three months, sharing burdens of receiving refugees and displaced persons and illegal immigration and residence.[953]

---

946 *Ibid.* art. 63.
947 *Ibid.* art. 66.
948 *Ibid.* arts 61–3.
949 *Ibid.* art. 67(1); exceptions were some visa matters, to be adopted by qualified majority (art. 76(3)) and amending legislation on asylum, refugees and displaced persons (art. 76(5), 1st indent) and legislation of judicial cooperation in civil matters excepting aspects relating to family law (art. 76(5), 2nd indent), both to be adopted by co-decision.
950 *Ibid.* art. 67(2), 1st indent; exceptions were additional visa matters, to be adopted co-decision (art. 76(4)).
951 *Ibid.* art. 67(2), 2nd indent.
952 *Report on the Future of the Area of Freedom, Security and Justice,* A6–0010/2004 (Bourlanges Report).
953 Decision 2004/927 [2004] OJ L396/45.

(b)   Union provisions

Notwithstanding the transfer of a number of relevant third pillar matters to the   **11.161**
first pillar, flanking measures necessary to make the area of freedom, security
and justice fully effective remained still, in part, within the (narrowed) domain
of police and judicial cooperation in criminal matters, so Union competence.
Article 61 EC defining the area made express reference to appropriate third
pillar activities, being measures to prevent and combat crime 'in accordance
with the provisions of Article 31(e) of the Treaty on European Union'[954] and
measures in the field of police and judicial cooperation in criminal matters 'in
accordance with the provisions of the Treaty on European Union'.[955] Thus at
the heart of the third pillar lay the Union objective:

> Without prejudice to the powers of the European Community, ... to provide citizens
> with a high level of safety within an area of freedom, security and justice by developing
> common action among the Member States in the fields of police and judicial
> cooperation in criminal matters and by preventing and combating racism and xeno-
> phobia.[956]

The Union served these objectives by preventing and combatting crime,
organised or otherwise, in particular terrorism, trafficking in persons and
offences against children, illicit drug trafficking and illicit arms trafficking,
corruption and fraud, through:

- closer cooperation between police forces, customs authorities and other
  competent national authorities, both directly and through Europol;
- closer cooperation between judicial and other competent national authorities, including cooperation through Eurojust and the European Judicial
  Network; and
- approximation, where necessary, of rules on criminal matters.[957]

It is self-evident that these are areas attended by great legal and political
sensitivity – which is of course why they were reserved to the third pillar. Yet
there was a constitutional bridging clause here: any of these matters could have
been transferred to the first pillar by a unanimous Council decision, subsequently approved ('adopted') by each member state in accordance with constitutional requirements.[958] It was never used.

---

954   EC Treaty, art. 61(a).
955   *Ibid.* art. 61(e).
956   TEU (pre-Lisbon), art. 29.
957   *Ibid.*; further detail provided in arts 30–2.
958   *Ibid.* art. 42. This was an incarnation of the simplified Treaty amendment ('simplified revision') procedure
      adopted subsequently by Lisbon; see 2.62 above.

11.162   Shortly after the Treaty of Amsterdam entered into force a special meeting of the European Council (the 'Tampere Council') was convened for the purpose of mapping out the Community (and Union) approach to its new authority. It concluded that the creation of the area of freedom, security and justice ought to embrace four 'essential areas': a common asylum and immigration policy; better access to justice (including mutual recognition and enforcement of judicial decisions, increased convergence in procedural law); coordinated action against crime; and integrated external action.[959] The Tampere programme was revisited in 2004,[960] re-adopted by the European Council as the Hague Programme,[961] in achievement of which the Commission launched in 2005 a five-year 'Action Plan for Freedom, Justice and Security',[962] the 'cornerstone' of its strategic objectives for 2010. A Commission evaluation of the Hague Programme was published in summer 2009[963] and yet another action plan to replace it ('the Stockholm programme') adopted by the European Council in December 2009.[964] Support, and balance and coherence of the support, is now provided through general 'framework programmes' over the course of 2007–13.[965]

11.163   The substantive fruits of the Tampere/Hague/Stockholm programmes are many, varied and ongoing. Some measures pursue the approximation of national law, but the preferred approach is promotion of mutual recognition, the 'cornerstone of judicial cooperation in both civil and criminal matters'.[966] They are now effected through the filter of the Lisbon reorganisation of JLS which grasped the nettle and *communautairised* the whole field into a new Title V of

---

959   Tampere European Council, Presidency Conclusions, *Bulletin EU* 10–1999, 7 ff.

960   See *Area of Freedom, Security and Justice: Assessment of the Tampere Programme and Future Orientations*, COM(2004) 401 final.

961   Brussels European Council, 4–5 November 2004, Presidency Conclusions, Annex I, *Bulletin EU* 11–2004, 14 ff.

962   *The Hague Programme: Ten Priorities for the Next Five Years. The Partnership for European Renewal in the Field of Freedom, Security and Justice*, COM(2005) 184 final.

963   COM(2009) 263 final.

964   European Council, *The Stockholm Programme: An Open and Secure Europe Serving and Protecting Citizens* [2010] OJ C115/1.

965   There are three recognised framework programmes, covering (a) solidarity and management of migration flows (at its creation largely of Community concern), (b) security and safeguarding liberties and (c) fundamental rights and justice (largely of Union concern). Examples of support measures adopted include: under (a) a European Refugee Fund (Decision 573/2007 [2007] OJ L144/1), an External Border Fund (Decision 574/2007 [2007] OJ L144/22), a European Return Fund (Decision 575/2007 [2007] OJ L144/45) and a European Fund for Integration of Third Country Nationals (Decision 2007/435 [2007] OJ L168/16); under (b) prevention, preparedness and consequence management of terrorism and other security related risks (Decision 2007/124 [2007] OJ L58/1) and prevention and fight against crime (Decision 2007/125 [2007] OJ L58/7); under (c) criminal justice (Decision 2007/126 [2007] OJ L58/13), fundamental rights and citizenship (Decision 2007/252 [2007] OJ L110/33), violence against children, young people and women (Decision 779/2007 [2007] OJ L173/19), civil justice (Decision 1149/2007 [2007] OJ L257/16) and drug prevention and information (Decision 1150/2007 [2007] OJ L257/23).

966   Tampere European Council, Presidency Conclusions, n. 959 above, para. 33.

the TFEU on 'Area of Freedom, Security and Justice', comprising five distinct chapters on:

- general provisions;
- policies on border checks, asylum and immigration;
- judicial cooperation in civil matters;
- judicial cooperation in criminal matters; and
- police cooperation.[967]

At its core the Union 'constitute[s] an area of freedom, security and justice with respect for fundamental rights and the different legal systems and traditions of the Member States'[968] achieved by action across the five chapters. The strategic guidelines for legislative and operational planning are to be defined by the European Council.[969] Legislation is adopted by the ordinary legislative procedure, with exceptions and safeguards. It may be proposed not only by the Commission but uniquely in the Treaties, in judicial cooperation in criminal matters and police cooperation, by ('on the initiative of') a muster of one-quarter of the member states.[970] For certainty there is express provision for measures to be adopted, 'where necessary', for the freezing of funds, assets or economic gains in the context of preventing and combating terrorism and related activities,[971] an area in which the Community previously encountered constitutional difficulties. The member states remain free to treat with third countries in the subject areas of chapters 3–5 so long as they comply with Union law.[972]

2. Border checks, asylum and immigration

The Union   **11.164**

> ensure[s] the absence of internal border controls for persons and shall frame a common policy on asylum, immigration and external border control, based on solidarity between Member States, which is fair towards third-country nationals,[973]

---

967   TFEU, arts 67–89.
968   *Ibid.* art. 67(1).
969   *Ibid.* art. 68.
970   *Ibid.* art. 76. See e.g., Directive 2010/64 on rights to interpretation and translation in criminal proceedings [2010] OJ L280/1, Directive 2011/99 on the European Protection Order, and the proposal for a European Investigation Order (EIO) (Council Doc. 9145/10) [2011] OJ L338/2, 'initiated' by 13, 12 and eight member states, respectively.
971   *Ibid.* art. 75. The United Kingdom declared an intention to take part to the full in any such measures; Declaration (No. 65) by the United Kingdom on Article 75 of the TFEU.
972   Declaration (No. 36) on Article 218 of the TFEU concerning the negotiation and conclusion of international agreements by Member States relating to the area of freedom, security and justice.
973   TFEU, art. 67(2). 'Third country nationals' includes stateless persons.

all with a view to ensuring the absence of any controls on persons, irrespective of nationality, when crossing internal borders, to carrying out checks on persons and efficient monitoring of the crossing of external borders, and the gradual introduction of an integrated management system for external borders.[974] This is the province of the Schengen arrangements which will be considered below.[975] The Union is to develop a common policy on asylum[976] and a common immigration policy, ensuring the efficient management of migration flows, fair treatment of third country nationals residing legally in member states and the prevention of illegal immigration and trafficking in human beings.[977] The policies and measures adopted to implement them are to be governed by the principle of solidarity and a fair sharing of burdens, including financial implications, amongst the member states.[978] The nature and burdens of maintaining social security systems are to be duly taken into account.[979]

11.165 Much of this was achieved prior to Lisbon, indeed some of it prior to Amsterdam. In 1990 the member states had entered into a Convention setting out rules for determining which amongst them would examine and determine an application of any alien who applies at the border or in their territory to any one of them for asylum (the Dublin Convention).[980] As asylum was drawn squarely into Title IV EC,[981] the Dublin Convention was replaced by a Regulation in 2003 ('Dublin II').[982] Ancillary measures have been adopted addressing the establishment of a database (Eurodac) for fingerprint identification of asylum seekers[983] and four Directives on minimum standards adopted, for qualification and status of refugees[984] and the provision of temporary protection,[985] for reception of asylum seekers[986] and for procedures for granting

---

974   *Ibid.* art. 77(2).
975   See 11.182–11.196 below.
976   TFEU, art. 78(1).
977   *Ibid.* art. 79(1).
978   *Ibid.* art. 80.
979   Declaration (No. 22) on Articles 48 and 79 of the TFEU.
980   Convention of 15 June 1990 determining the State Responsible for Examining Applications for Asylum Lodged in one of the Member States of the European Communities [1997] OJ C254/1; in force 1 September 1997 (except for Austria and Sweden (1 October 1997) and Finland (1 January 1998)).
981   EC Treaty, art. 61(b).
982   Regulation 343/2003 [2003] OJ L50/1; detailed rules for application set out in Regulation 1560/2003 [2003] OJ L222/3. There are significant changes in the criteria for asylum between the Convention and the Regulation.
983   Regulation 2725/2000 [2000] OJ L316/1.
984   Directive 2011/95 [2011] OJ L337/9 (Qualification Directive) (a recast Directive 2004/83 [2004] OJ L304/12); for consideration see Cases C-175 etc./08 *Abdulla and ors v Bundesrepublik Deutschland* [2010] ECR I-1493; Cases C-57 and 101/09 *Bundesrepublik Deutschland v B and D* [2010] ECR I-10709.
985   Directive 2001/55 [2001] OJ L212/12.
986   Directive 2003/9 [2003] OJ L31/18 (Reception Directive).

and withdrawing refugee status.[987] 'Rapid border intervention teams' (RABITs) have been created to deal with urgent and exceptional pressure created by the influx of a large number of third country nationals.[988] The Dublin arrangements took a serious knock when the Court of Human Rights (Grand Chamber) found both Belgium and Greece to have infringed article 3 of the European Convention (prohibition of torture and inhuman or degrading treatment or punishment) and article 13 (effective remedy) in conjunction with article 3 by the former returning an asylum seeker to Greece (the 'Member State responsible') where his living conditions amounted to degrading and inhuman treatment.[989] But the Court of Justice takes a gentler view, perhaps in recognition of the disproportionate burden facing Greece as the point of entry for almost 90 per cent of the Union's illegal immigrants,[990] and says that the transfer of an asylum seeker thither is not rendered improper by a 'slight' infringement of Dublin II;[991] rather that would be the case where the sending member state

> *cannot be unaware* that *systemic* deficiencies in the asylum procedure and in the reception conditions of asylum seekers in that Member State amount to *substantial* grounds for believing that the asylum seeker would face a *real risk* of being subjected to inhuman or degrading treatment within the meaning of Article 4 of the Charter.[992]

The member states are themselves 'safe countries' for purposes of asylum so that a claim for asylum made by a citizen of a member state is inadmissible except in exceptional circumstances.[993] In 2007 the Commission published a Green Paper on the future common European asylum system.[994]

Determination of those third country nationals requiring a visa was, curiously, **11.166** made Community competence in 1993 by the Maastricht Treaty.[995] A uniform visa format was adopted in 1995.[996] Amsterdam having brought the whole visa field within the Community sphere, there followed legislation on uniform

---

987 Directive 2005/85 [2005] OJ L326/13 (Procedures Directive); parts annulled in Case C-133/06 *Parliament* v *Council* [2008] ECR I-3189.

988 Regulation 863/2007 [2007] OJ L199/30.

989 *MSS* v *Belgium and Greece* (2011) 53 EHRR 28. The Strasbourg court was not alone, asylum conditions in Greece being criticised by other courts; see e.g., VfGH, 7. Oktober 2010, Geschäftszahl U694/10. The Commission has initiated art. 258 proceedings against Greece (first letter of formal notice in November 2009, supplementary letter in June 2010) for infringement of various provisions of the asylum Directives.

990 Cases C-411 and 493/10 *R (NS) and ME and ors* v *Secretary of State for the Home Department and ors*, judgment of 21 December 2011, not yet reported, at para. 87.

991 *Ibid.* at para. 84.

992 *Ibid.* at paras 94 and 106 and in the *dispositif*, emphasis added.

993 Protocol (No. 24) on Asylum for Nationals of Member States of the European Union.

994 COM(2007) 301 final.

995 EC Treaty, art. 100c (repealed 1999).

996 Regulation 1683/95 [1995] OJ L164/1.

residence permit format for third country nationals,[997] identification of third country nationals requiring a visa[998] and conditions and procedures for issuing them ('Community Code on Visas').[999]

11.167 Unless exercising derivative rights, third country nationals traditionally went virtually unrecognised in Community law,[1000] and their movement within the Union has long served as justification for frontier controls on the movement of persons. The problem, and its solution, was identified by the Tampere Council:

> The European Union must ensure fair treatment of third-country nationals who reside legally on the territory of its Member States. A more vigorous integration policy should aim at granting them rights and obligations comparable to those of EU citizens ... The legal status of third-country nationals should be approximated to that of Member States' nationals,[1001]

this 'approximation' being the equalivant, for persons, of the 'definitive assimilation' afforded goods from third countries which are in free circulation.[1002] But progress has been slow. The one major substantial benefit now created and conferred upon a third country national is a right to 'long term resident status' if he or she has resided legally and continuously in a member state – by grace of the law of that member state, the measure itself confers no rights of entry or residence – for a period of five years[1003] and can show that he or she has, for him or herself and for dependent family members, adequate ('stable and regular') resources sufficient to maintain him or herself and his or her family members without recourse to social assistance.[1004] The status is permanent unless it was acquired fraudulently, the individual is lawfully expelled or he or she is absent from the territory of the Union for a period of 12 consecutive months.[1005] It

---

997 Regulation 1030/2002 [2002] OJ L157/1.

998 Regulation 539/2001 [2001] OJ L81/1.

999 Regulation 810/2009 [2009] OJ L243/1. The Regulation includes provisions on the issue of visas at the frontier (arts 35–6) and freedom of movement for those on long-stay visas, so replacing a previous measure dealing specifically with that (Regulation 415/2003 [2003] OJ L64/1).

1000 There were, and are, a few exceptions to this general rule: the right to petition the Parliament (TFEU, art. 227) and the Ombudsman (art. 228), the rules on access to documents (art. 15), the right to equal pay (art. 157) and many provisions of the Charter of Fundamental Rights apply to all persons resident in the Union irrespective of nationality. So do the rules on free movement of goods and capital, which are nationality-blind so far as their ownership is concerned. Thus a third country national resident in a member state may enjoy all the benefits of arts 30, 110, 34 and 63 TFEU, and when travelling may be controlled in his movement from one member state to another member state, but his goods and capital assets may not.

1001 Tampere European Council, Presidency Conclusions, *Bulletin EU* 10–1999, paras 18, 21.

1002 See 10.01 above.

1003 Directive 2003/109 [2004] OJ L16/44, art. 4.

1004 *Ibid.* art. 5(1)(a).

1005 *Ibid.* art. 9.

entitles the holder to a 'long-term resident's EC residence permit',[1006] equal treatment in the 'first member state' broadly similar to that provided by Directive 2004/38[1007] and a right of residence in another (a 'second') member state for purposes of employment or self-employment, pursuit of study or vocational training, or other purposes as defined by each member state,[1008] and to (more or less) equal treatment there.[1009] Measures have also been adopted on facilitation of family reunification;[1010] admission of third country nationals for purposes of scientific research[1011] and of study and training;[1012] mutual recognition of decisions on expulsion[1013] (and mutual assistance to that end);[1014] prohibition, with criminal sanctions, of employing illegally staying third country nationals[1015] and common standards and procedures for returning them to their home counties.[1016]

In 2005 and 2006 the Commission adopted policy papers on European migration;[1017] in 2009 the Council adopted a Union-wide employment permit for highly skilled incomers (the 'EU blue card'), enabling the holder (and his or her family) to reside and work in any member state[1018] and in 2011 a single application procedure and a single permit for third country national seeking work and residence workers and a common set of rights for those in work;[1019] in 2010 the Commission proposed a Directive on entry and residence for third

---

1006   *Ibid.* art. 8. An administrative charge may be made for the permit but it cannot be excessively or disproportionately expensive; Case C-508/10 *Commission* v *Netherlands*, judgment of 26 April 2012, not yet reported.

1007   *Ibid.* art. 11.

1008   *Ibid.* art. 14. Members of his or her family also have a right of residence but only if already constituted (*constitué, gevormd*) in the first member state (art. 16), otherwise Directive 2003/86 (n. 1010 below) applies. But this must now be read in the light of Case C-127/08 *Metock and ors* v *Minister for Justice, Equality and Law Reform* [2008] ECR I-6241, as to which see 11.103 above.

1009   Directive 2003/109, arts 14(3), (4) and 21.

1010   Directive 2003/86 [2003] OJ L251/13; challenged unsuccessfully (for inadequacy of compliance with a fundamental right to family life) in Case C-540/03 *Parliament* v *Council* (Family Reunification) [2006] ECR I-5769; for further consideration see Case C-578/08 *Chakroun* v *Minister van Buitenlandse Zaken* [2010] ECR I-1839. The Directive applies only to reunification of third country families, family members of Union citizens are expressly excluded; art. 3(3).

1011   Directive 2005/71 [2005] OJ L289/15.

1012   Directive 2004/114 [2004] OJ L375/12.

1013   Directive 2001/40 [2001] OJ L149/34.

1014   Directive 2003/110 [2003] OJ L321/26.

1015   Directive 2009/52 [2009] OJ L168/24; required to be implemented by July 2011.

1016   Directive 2008/115 [2008] OJ L348/98. The Directive has been roundly criticised by human rights groups, and may prove to be inconsistent with the ECHR. For consideration of it see Case C-357/09 PPU *Kadzoev* v *Direktsia 'Migratsia' pri Ministerstvo na vatreshnite raboti* [2009] ECR I-11189; Case C-61/11 PPU *Criminal proceedings against El Dridi*, judgment of 28 April 2011, not yet reported; Case C-329/11 *Achughbabian* v *Préfet du Val-de-Marne*, judgment of 6 December 2011, not yet reported.

1017   *Policy Plan on Legal Migration*, COM(2005) 669 final; *The Global Approach to Migration One Year On: Towards a Comprehensive European Migration Policy*, COM(2006) 735 final.

1018   Directive 2009/50 [2009] OJ L155/17; required to be implemented by June 2011.

1019   Directive 2011/98 [2011] OJ L343/1; required to be implemented by December 2013.

country nationals for purposes of seasonal employment.[1020] All form 'part of the EU's efforts to develop a comprehensive immigration policy',[1021] in pursuit of which in 2008 the Commission adopted a 'communication'[1022] and the European Council the 'EU Immigration Pact' (European Pact on Immigration and Asylum),[1023] which has no legal force but is intended to inform developments over the following five years. With Lisbon's express mandate to 'develop' a common immigration policy, efforts are expected to be stepped up.

3. Judicial cooperation in civil matters

11.168 The Union 'facilitate[s] access to justice' through mutual recognition of judicial and extrajudicial decisions in civil matters[1024] and develops cooperation in that context where there are cross-border implications.[1025] Measures may be adopted 'particularly when necessary for the proper functioning of the internal market' in order to ensure the mutual recognition and enforcement between member states of judgments and of decisions in extrajudicial cases; cross-border service of judicial and extrajudicial documents; compatibility of national rules of international private law and of jurisdiction; cooperation in the taking of evidence; effective access to justice; elimination of obstacles to the proper functioning of civil proceedings; development of alternative methods of dispute settlement; support for the training of the judiciary; and to address matters of family law with cross-border implications.[1026]

> [T]he principles which underlie judicial cooperation in civil and commercial matters in the European Union [are] ... free movement of judgments in civil and commercial matters, predictability as to the courts having jurisdiction and therefore legal certainty for litigants, sound administration of justice, minimisation of the risk of concurrent proceedings, and mutual trust in the administration of justice in the European Union. Observance of each of those principles is necessary for the sound operation of the internal market.[1027]

1020   COM(2010) 379 final.
1021   Proposal for a Council Directive on the conditions of entry and residence of third country nationals for the purposes of highly qualified employment, COM(2007) 637 final, p. 1; COM(2010) 379, p. 1.
1022   *A Common Immigration Policy for Europe: Principles, Actions and Tools*, memo 08/402.
1023   Council Doc. 13440/08.
1024   TFEU, art. 67(4).
1025   *Ibid.* art. 81(1).
1026   *Ibid.* art. 81(2), (3).
1027   Case C-533/08 *TNT Express Nederland* v *AXA Versicherung* [2010] ECR I-4107, at paras 49–50.

In taking action the ordinary legislative procedure applies[1028] save in family law matters which require a unanimous Council having consulted the Parliament, subject to a (mini-)bridging clause to the ordinary procedure.[1029]

Here much has already been achieved. Prior to Amsterdam a number of **11.169** Conventions had been drawn up addressing issues of international private law in, primarily, the commercial arena. The Treaty had proposed that these were matters into which the member states might wish to enter into agreement 'so far as is necessary',[1030] but any such agreement was of the nature of a public international law treaty amongst the member states, complementary to, but not part of, Community law. The best known, and of widest application, were:

- the 1968 Convention on Jurisdiction and Enforcement of Judgments in Civil and Commercial Matters (Brussels Convention),[1031] addressing identification of the proper forum, jurisdiction, *lis pendens*, recognition, enforcement and appeal of judgments in civil and commercial (so excluding revenue, customs and administrative) disputes, entailing extensive amendment to those areas of international private law in all member states and comprising the cornerstone of cross-frontier dispute settlement; and
- the 1980 Convention on the Law Applicable to Contractual Obligations (the Rome, or Contracts, Convention).[1032]

Immediately the Treaty of Amsterdam entered into force the subject matter of these Conventions was drawn into Community competences under the Treaty rubric of measures in the field of judicial cooperation in civil matters[1033] (informally, the 'common judicial area'), including improvement and simplification of cross-border service of judicial and extrajudicial documents, cooperation in the taking of evidence and the recognition and enforcement of decisions in civil and commercial cases, promotion of compatibility of the rules of international private law and jurisdiction and elimination of obstacles to the effective functioning of civil proceedings.[1034] As a result the Brussels Convention was replaced in 2001, in substance essentially unchanged, by a Council

---

1028   TFEU, art. 81(2).
1029   *Ibid.* art. 81(3). Thus it was that the failure to agree unanimously to common rules for divorce between couples of different Union nationalities ('Rome III') required recourse to the enhanced cooperation procedure for the first time; see 2.46 above.
1030   EEC Treaty, art. 220.
1031   Convention of 27 September 1968 on Jurisdiction and Enforcement of Judgments in Civil and Commercial Matters, in force 1 February 1973; consolidated version at [1998] OJ C27/3.
1032   Convention of 19 June 1980 on the Law Applicable to Contractual Obligations, in force 1 April 1991; consolidated version at [1998] OJ C27/34.
1033   EC Treaty, art. 61(c).
1034   *Ibid.* art. 65.

Regulation on recognition and enforcement of judgments in civil and commercial matters ('Brussels I' Regulation).[1035] In the same manner the Rome Convention has been replaced by a Regulation on the law applicable to contractual obligations ('Rome I');[1036] and in the event preceded by a Regulation on the law applicable to non-contractual obligations ('Rome II'), for which there was no Convention antecedent.[1037] There exist also a number of other legislative measures:

- ancillary to, and deepening and broadening, Brussels I;[1038]
- on the recognition and enforcement of judgments in matrimonial matters and matters of parental responsibility (now 'Brussels II *bis*');[1039]
- on succession ('Brussels IV');[1040]

1035   Regulation 44/2001 [2001] OJ L12/1.

1036   Regulation 593/2008 [2008] OJ L177/6. The Regulation applies from (and to contracts made after) 17 December 2009; prior to that the Rome Convention remained in force – the last subsisting international private law instrument of general application still in that form. There is also an action plan on A More Coherent European Contract Law ([2003] OJ C63/1) seeking to establish a 'common frame of reference', a non-binding reference 'toolbox' on principles, definitions and model rules for adopting and revising Union legislation in the sphere of contract law.

1037   Regulation 864/2007 [2007] OJ L199/40. It 'appl[ies] to events giving rise to damage which occur after its entry into force' (art. 31) but 'appl[ies]' from January 2009 (art. 32); to make sense of this opaque construction see Case C-412/10 *Homawoo* v *GMF Assurances*, judgment of 17 November 2011, not yet reported.

1038   E.g., rules on the service in the member states of judicial and extrajudicial documents in civil and commercial matters, Regulation 1393/2007 [2007] OJ L324/79 (replacing Regulation 1348/2000 [2000] OJ L160/37, which itself replaced a pre-Amsterdam JHA convention which never entered into force); cooperation between courts in the taking of evidence in civil and commercial matters, Regulation 1206/2001 [2001] OJ L174/1; the establishment of a European Judicial Network in civil and commercial matters, Decision 2001/470 [2001] OJ L174/25; a general Community framework of activities to facilitate the implementation of judicial cooperation in civil matters, Regulation 743/2002 [2002] OJ L115/1; access to justice in cross-border disputes by establishing minimum common rules relating to legal aid in civil and commercial matters, Directive 2003/8 [2003] OJ L26/41; enforcement orders for uncontested claims, Regulation 805/2004 [2004] OJ L143/15. Also the promotion in cross-border civil and commercial disputes, Directive 2008/52 [2008] OJ L136/3 (Mediation Directive). Many of these measures give rise to practical linguistic hurdles, as to which see Case C-14/07 *Ingenieurbüro Michael Weiss und Partner* v *Industrie- und Handelskammer Berlin* [2008] ECR I-3367; Case C-233/08 *Kyrian* v *Celní úřad Tábor* [2010] ECR I-177; Case C-283/09 *Weryński* v *Mediatel 4B Spółka*, [2011] ECR I-601.

1039   Regulation 2201/2003 [2003] OJ L338/1, replacing Regulation 1347/2000 [2000] OJ L160/19 ('Brussels II'); considered in Case C-195/08 PPU *Rinau* [2008] ECR I-5271; Case C-403/09 PPU *Detiček* v *Sgueglia* [2009] ECR I-12193; Case C-211/10 PPU *Povse* v *Alpago* [2010] ECR I-6669; Case C-400/10 PPU *JMcB* v *LE*, [2010] ECR I-8965 ; Case C-491/10 PPU *Aguirre Zarraga* v *Pelz* [2010] ECR I-14247; Case C497/10 PPU *Mercredi* v *Chaffe* [2010] ECR I-14309. There is also a French proposal for a Regulation (Community legislation to be proposed (from 1999 to 2004) by the Commission but also by ('on the inititative of') a member state; art. 67 EC), as yet unadopted, on the mutual enforcement of judgments on rights of access to children [2000] OJ L234/7; and (as yet unformulated) plans for measures on the harmonisation of rules on matrimonial property ('Brussels III').

1040   Regulation 650/2012 [2012] OJ L201/107 on jurisdiction, applicable law, recognition and enforcement of decisions and instruments in matters of succession; applying for the most part from August 2015 (art. 84).

- on common rules for divorce between couples of different Union nationalities ('Rome III');[1041]
- on jurisdiction, applicable law, recognition and enforcement of decisions and cooperation in matters relating to maintenance obligations;[1042]
- on insolvency proceedings;[1043]
- on a European order for payment procedure;[1044] and
- on a European small claims procedure.[1045]

The Union is also party to the Hague Conference on Private International Law (HCCH)[1046] and, within it, the Hague Convention on Choice of Court Agreements.[1047] Because these measures were adopted in the form of Community legislation (and not extra-Community instruments as previously), they attracted the political procedures which marked the Community way, the principles of Community law and, in essentially, if not completely, the normal manner, the supervisory jurisdiction of the Court of Justice.[1048] Because the existing provisions were fairly comprehensive and had met with significant success, the Lisbon Treaty tinkered little with them.

1041   Regulation 1259/2010 [2010] OJ L343/10; applies from June 2012. But adopted by enhanced cooperation and not applicable in all member states. The application of Regulation 2201/2003, n. 1039 above, is unaffected; art. 2.

1042   Regulation 4/2009 [2009] OJ L7/1; applicable (in two stages) from September 2010 and June 2011. In the context of this Regulation the Community acceded to the Hague Protocol of 23 November 2007 on the law applicable to maintenance obligations [2009] OJ L331/19.

1043   Regulation 1346/2000 [2000] OJ L160/1; regulating collective insolvency proceedings which entail the partial or total divestment of a debtor and the appointment of a liquidator.

1044   Regulation 1896/2006 [2006] OJ L399/1; to simplify, speed up and reduce the costs of litigation in cross-border cases concerning uncontested pecuniary claims and to permit the free circulation of European orders for payment without need of intermediate proceedings in the member state of enforcement prior to recognition and enforcement.

1045   Regulation 861/2007 [2007] OJ L199/1; simplifying and speeding up small claims (less than €2,000) litigation with a cross-frontier element; it is an alternative to, and does not replace, existing small claims procedures.

1046   Statute of 31 October 1951 of the Hague Conference on Private International Law, 220 UNTS 121. The Community acceded in 2006 (Decision 2006/719 [2006] OJ L297/1) after the Statute was amended (for the first time in over 50 years) in order to allow the participation of non-states.

1047   Convention of 30 June 2005 on Choice of Court Agreements [2009] OJ L133/3.

1048   See 11.197 below. The Court did have jurisdiction to hear preliminary references for interpretation of the Brussels Convention and the Rome Convention by virtue of protocols to them (Protocol on the Interpretation by the Court of Justice of the European Communities of the Convention of 27 September 1968 on Jurisdiction and Enforcement of Judgments in Civil and Commercial Matters [1998] OJ C27/28; First and Second Protocols on the Interpretation by the Court of Justice of the European Communities of the Convention of 19 June 1980 on the Law Applicable to Contractual Obligations [1998] OJ C27/47 and 52) but the validity of the provisions of each was unassailable. There were a considerable number of references seeking interpretation of the Brussels Convention over the years, only one for the interpretation of the Rome Convention.

11.170 The rules of the original Brussels Convention were extended to EFTA countries by agreement with them (Lugano Convention)[1049] in 1988; in light of the *communautairisation* of the matter by Brussels I,[1050] from 2009 Lugano was replaced by a new convention ('Lugano II') applying a Brussels I regime to Iceland, Norway and Switzerland (and Denmark).[1051]

4. Judicial cooperation in criminal matters and police cooperation

11.171 Chapters 4 and 5 of Title V are matters falling previously within the third pillar of Union activity, so suffer greatest bruising in their *communautairisation* by Lisbon and, once *communautairised*, remain JLS matters of greatest constitutional/political sensitivity.

11.172 Prior to Lisbon there was significant progress in the area of judicial cooperation in criminal matters, although progress here was 'comparatively slow',[1052] and always within the framework of Title VI TEU (pre-Lisbon) and so the gentler touch which measures adopted thereunder allowed. A common approach to crime prevention pre-dated Maastricht, starting with the Trevi Group, established in 1976 as a forum of intergovernmental collaboration amongst the (then) nine interior ministries in order to counter terrorism and coordinate policing in the Community. It took its place front and centre in the third pillar matters of police and judicial cooperation in criminal matters. In many cases third pillar action complemented, or buttressed, the achievements of Title IV EC: for example, whilst immigration fell within Community competences, the prevention of illegal immigration was in pith and substance a criminal, and so third pillar, matter, the Council adopting a framework decision on the strengthening of the penal framework in order to prevent the facilitation of unauthorised entry, transit and residence.[1053]

1049 Convention of 16 September 1988 on Jurisdiction and the Enforcement of Judgments in Civil and Commercial Matters [1988] OJ L319/9.

1050 See Opinion 1/03 *Re the Lugano Convention* [2006] ECR I-1145 which confirmed the subject matter to be exclusive Community competence.

1051 Convention of 30 October 2007 on Jurisdiction and the Recognition and Enforcement of Judgments in Civil and Commercial Matters [2009] OJ L147/5; in force for Norway and Denmark from 1 January 2010, for Switzerland 1 January 2011 and for Iceland 1 May 2011. Liechtenstein has not signed the Convention but is entitled to do so in future; arts 69–71. As to the peculiar, distinct participation of Denmark see 11.178–11.179 below.

1052 *Justice, Freedom and Security in Europe since 2005: An Evaluation of the Hague Programme*, COM(2009) 263 final, p. 14.

1053 Framework Decision 2002/946 [2002] OJ L328/1.

In 2000 the Council adopted a Title VI Convention on mutual assistance in **11.173** criminal matters[1054] and in 2001 established a European Crime Prevention Network (EUCPN)[1055] to promote crime prevention activities in the member states and provide a means through which valuable good practice in preventing crime, mainly 'traditional' crime, could be shared. Much of the day-to-day work of police and judicial cooperation lay, and lies, in the myriad activities of Europol and Eurojust respectively, and its success is often down to executive action as much as legislation. Having said that, harmonising/coordinating legislation was adopted in a number of fields, for example: combating fraud and counterfeiting of non-cash means of payment;[1056] combating organised crime;[1057] the standing of victims in criminal proceedings;[1058] of money laundering, identification, tracing, freezing, seizing and confiscation of instrumentalities and the proceeds of crime;[1059] combating terrorism;[1060] the creation of a European protection order,[1061] an (increasingly contentious) European arrest warrant (EAW),[1062] a European evidence warrant (EEW)[1063] and now a proposal for an even more contentious European investigation order (EIO);[1064] on combating trafficking in human beings;[1065] combating the sexual abuse and sexual exploitation of children;[1066] the protection of the environment through criminal sanctions;[1067] combating

---

1054 Convention of 29 May 2000 on Mutual Assistance in Criminal Matters between the Member States of the European Union [2000] OJ C197/1; in force 23 August 2005. This was the first art. 34 Convention to be adopted. See also the Protocol to the Convention [2001] OJ C326/1. Other Conventions have been adopted, not all of them yet in force.

1055 Decision 2001/427/JHA [2001] OJ L153/1; now Decision 2009/902/JHA [2009] OJ L321/44.

1056 Framework Decision 2001/413 [2001] OJ L149/1.

1057 Framework Decision 2008/841 [2008] OJ L300/42.

1058 Framework Decision 2001/220 [2001] OJ L82/1. More ambitious was a Community (*sic*) Directive adopted (by authority of art. 308 EC (art. 352 TFEU)) on compensation for the victims of crime; Directive 2004/80 [2004] OJ L261/2.

1059 Framework Decision 2001/500 [2001] OJ L182/1. Also Directive 2005/60 [2005] OJ L309/15 (Third Money Laundering Directive; adopted as a Community measure (under arts 47(2) and 95 EC) as it is directed towards the regulation of credit and financial institutions).

1060 Framework Decision 2002/475 [2002] OJ L164/3.

1061 Directive 2011/99 [2011] OJ L338/2; to be implemented by 11 January 2015. The United Kingdom, but not Ireland, participates in the Directive.

1062 Framework Decision 2002/584 [2002] OJ L190/1; validity confirmed in Case C-303/05 *Advocaten voor de Wereld* v *Leden van de Ministerraad* [2007] ECR I-3633, but attracting wariness from a number of national constitutional courts; see 6.19 above. See also Directive 2012/13 [2012] OJ L142/1 on the supply of information to persons subject to a EAW, and the accused in criminal proceedings more generally.

1063 Framework Decision 2008/978 [2008] OJ L350/72; required to be implemented by January 2011.

1064 See Council Doc. 9145/10. The Directive was proposed (initiated) in 2010 by eight member states (Belgium, Bulgaria, Estonia, Spain, Luxembourg, Austria, Slovenia and Sweden), using the power of initiative created by Lisbon (art. 76 TFEU). If adopted it will replace and extend the European evidence warrant (*ibid.*). The United Kingdom has indicated an intention to participate in the Directive.

1065 Directive 2011/36 [2011] OJ L101/1 (replacing Framework Decision 2002/629 [2002] OJ L203/1).

1066 Directive 2011/93 [2011] OJ L335/1 (replacing Framework Decision 2004/68 [2004] OJ L13/44).

1067 Framework Decision 2003/80 [2003] OJ L29/55; annulled by the Court of Justice for incorrect legal base, see 6.57 above.

private sector corruption;[1068] execution orders freezing property or evidence[1069] and confiscation of crime-related proceeds, instrumentalities and property;[1070] the exchange of information extracted from criminal records;[1071] mutual recognition of financial penalties[1072] and confiscation orders;[1073] and the exchange of DNA, dactyloscopic and national vehicle registration data, data relating to major (particularly sporting) events with a cross-border dimension and information to prevent terrorist offences, as well as stepping up cross-border police cooperation.[1074] In 2008 the Council adopted a framework decision on the application of the principle of mutual recognition to judgments in criminal matters imposing custodial sentences or other measures involving deprivation of liberty for the purpose of enforcement throughout the Union.[1075]

11.174 Alongside police and judicial cooperation in criminal matters, the Union identified prevention of and combatting racism and xenophobia to be pivotal to the area of freedom, security and justice.[1076] This was to be prosecuted across a broad front, conceived to embrace the promotion and protection of fundamental rights via the Charter of Fundamental Rights and other means, the anti-discrimination Directives adopted under article 13 EC (article 19 TFEU),[1077] other miscellaneous legislation on, for example, the investigation and prosecution of genocide, crimes against humanity and war crimes,[1078] the criminalisation of certain forms and expressions of racism and xenophobia[1079] and the work of the European Monitoring Centre on Racism and Xenophobia, created in 1997 and absorbed into the EU Agency for Fundamental Rights

---

1068   Framework Decision 2003/568 [2003] OJ L192/54.
1069   Framework Decision 2003/577 [2003] OJ L196/45.
1070   Framework Decision 2005/212 [2005] OJ L68/49; also Decision 2007/845 [2007] OJ L332/103 on cooperation between National Asset Recovery Agencies.
1071   Framework Decision 2009/315 [2009] OJ L93/23.
1072   Framework Decision 2005/214 [2005] OJ L76/16.
1073   Framework Decision 2006/783 [2005] OJ L328/59.
1074   Decision 2008/615/JHA [2008] OJ L210/1 ('Prüm decision'). This decision grew out, and absorbed much (but not all), of the Prüm Convention (sometimes called Schengen III) signed by seven member states (Belgium, Germany, Spain, France, Luxembourg, the Netherlands and Austria) in 2005 (Traité du 25 août 2005 relatif à l'approfondissement de la coopération transfrontalière, notamment en vue de lutter contre le terrorisme, la criminalité transfrontalière et la migration illégale, Council Doc. 10900/05) which was an instrument adopted not in the context or by the mechanisms of enhanced cooperation but simply by treaty amongst those member states; hence, another example of extra-Treaty initiative drawn subsequently into the Community/Union sphere. The Convention still exists, includes six more member states as party to it with a further five having applied to join.
1075   Framework Decision 2008/909 [2008] OJ L327/27; required to be implemented by December 2011.
1076   TEU (pre-Lisbon), art. 29 (now, slightly reformulated, in art. 67(3) TFEU).
1077   Directive 2000/43 [2000] OJ L180/22 on equal treatment of persons irrespective of racial or ethnic origin; Directive 2000/78 [2000] OJ L303/16 on equal treatment in employment and occupation; see 8.04 above and 14.45 below.
1078   Decision 2003/355 [2003] OJ L118/12.
1079   Framework Decision 2008/913 [2008] OJ L328/55.

upon its creation in 2007. Critics will say that this is merely sticking plaster over a nasty and growing phenomenon.

Lisbon strengthened the Union's hand, equipping it to venture in the Community way into sensitive areas previously preserved to national sovereignty by third pillar safeguards. Judicial cooperation in criminal matters is based upon the principle of mutual recognition of judgments and judicial decisions,[1080] and the Union may adopt rules: **11.175**

(a) to ensure recognition throughout the Union of all forms of judgments and judicial decisions, prevent and settle conflicts of jurisdiction, support judicial training and facilitate judicial cooperation amongst the appropriate authorities of the member states;[1081]

(b) for the mutual admissibility of evidence between member states, the rights of individuals in criminal procedure, the rights of victims of crime and any other specific aspects of criminal procedure indentified by a unamimous Council with the prior consent of the Parliament;[1082]

(c) concerning the definition of criminal offences and sanctions in the areas of particularly serious crime (terrorism, trafficking in human beings and sexual exploitation of women and children, illicit drug trafficking, illicit arms trafficking, money laundering, corruption, counterfeiting of means of payment, computer crime and organised crime; the so-called 'Euro crimes') with a cross-border dimension resulting from the nature or impact of such offences or from a special need to combat them on a common basis;[1083]

(d) with regard to the definition of criminal offences and sanctions in an area harmonised by Union law should it prove 'essential' to ensure its effective implementation;[1084] and

(e) to adopt measures necessary to prevent and fight against fraud affecting the financial interests of the Union.[1085]

1080 TFEU, art. 82(1).
1081 *Ibid.*
1082 *Ibid.* art. 82(1), (2).
1083 *Ibid.* arts 82(1), 83(1). The list may be may be extended in light of 'developments in crime' by a unanimous Council with the consent of the Parliament, but must 'meet the criteria specified', that is, be particularly serious crime with a cross-border dimension.
1084 *Ibid.* arts 82(1), 83(2).
1085 *Ibid.* art. 325(4). Relevant measures already exist: a (pre-Lisbon) TEU Title VI 'Convention' (Council Act of 26 July 1995 drawing up the Convention on the protection of the European Communities' financial interests,[1995] OJ C316/48) which calls for effective, proportionate and dissuasive criminal penalties where fraud is found, and a Regulation (Regulation 2988/95 [1995] OJ L312/1) which calls for 'administrative penalties' (*verwaltungsrechtliche Sanktionen*).

Union competence extends to the approximation, by Directive, of national laws,[1086] but only to the adoption of 'minimum' rules; this is rare, an express (beyond the constant principles of subsidiarity and proportionality) Treaty limitation to the degree of harmonisation permissible, and its justiciability a grey area. Even so, because these measures are subject to the ordinary legislative procedure yet intrude frontally in the most sensitive member state jurisidiction, there are two 'emergency brakes' (or 'alarm bells'), allowing a member state to cause discussion of proposals relating to:

- 'facilitat[ion of] mutual recognition of judgments and judicial decisions and police and judicial cooperation in criminal matters having a cross-border dimension',[1087] and
- the definition of criminal offences and sanctions in the areas of particularly serious crime with a cross-border dimension,[1088]

in both cases where they would affect fundamental aspects of its criminal justice system, to be suspended, referred to the European Council, and returned to the Council to be adopted only if the European Council opts to do so by consensus. It was these developments which exercised the *Bundesverfassungsgericht* and caused it to require changes to internal German parliamentary procedural rules prior to ratification of Lisbon in order that the emergency brakes could be effectively (and democratically) applied.[1089] Practical cooperation is achieved through the machinery of Eurojust and the European Judicial Network. A unanimous Council may with the Parliament's consent create from Eurojust a European Public Prosecutor's Office, competent to investigate and prosecute (in competent national courts) offences against the Union's financial interests,[1090] and, by authority conferred upon it by a unanimous European Council (again with the Parliament's consent), serious crimes having a cross-border dimension.[1091] In the light of the Lisbon changes the Commission has adopted a framework for the further development of an EU criminal policy,[1092] one which 'foster[s] citizens' confidence in the fact that they live in a Europe of freedom, security and justice, that EU law protecting their interests is fully implemented and enforced and ... in full respect of subsidiarity and proportionality and other basic Treaty principles'.[1093]

1086   TFEU, arts 82(1),(2), 83(1),(2).
1087   *Ibid.* art. 82(3).
1088   *Ibid.* art. 83(3).
1089   BVerfG, 30. Juni 2009 (*Lissabon-Vertrag*), BVerfGE 123, 267.
1090   TFEU, art. 86.
1091   *Ibid.* art. 86(4).
1092   COM(2011) 573 final.
1093   *Ibid.* at p. 2.

Police cooperation is to be 'established' by the Union.[1094] This embraces all **11.176** national competent authorities (police, customs and other specialised law enforcement services) involved in the prevention, detection and investigation of criminal offences.[1095] Legislation may be adopted by the ordinary procedure for the collection, storage, processing, analysis and exchange of relevant information; support for the training of staff, and cooperation on the exchange of staff, on equipment and on research into crime detection; common investigative techniques in relation to the detection of serious forms of organised crime;[1096] and by a unanimous Council for (a) operational cooperation amongst the competent authorities,[1097] a special enhanced cooperation procedure applying where the Council fails to reach unanimity;[1098] and (b) laying down conditions and limitations for the operation of the competent authorities in the territory of another member state, in liaison and in agreement with the authorities of that state.[1099] Determination of the structure, operation, field of action and tasks of Europol was assumed by the Union institutions;[1100] the tasks may include the collection, storage, processing, analysis and exchange of information, in particular that forwarded by the authorities of the member states or third countries or bodies, and the coordination, organisation and implementation of investigative and operational action carried out jointly with the national competent authorities or in the context of joint investigative teams, where appropriate in liaison with Eurojust,[1101] and its activities are to be subject to scrutiny by the Parliament 'together with' national parliaments.[1102]

5. Integrated external action

It should be noted that in the fourth of the Tampere areas for action, integrated **11.177** external action, not much of coherence has been achieved. Just as much of the area of freedom, security and justice touches upon sensitive areas internally, so it is for its external aspects in which by definition control passes in some measure out of Union hands; witness, for example, the legal tussle and political storm which attended an agreement between the Union and the United States on the transfer of passenger name record (PNR) data by air carriers to the Department

---

1094   TFEU, art. 87(1).
1095   *Ibid.*
1096   *Ibid.* art. 87(2).
1097   *Ibid.* art. 87(3).
1098   *Ibid.*
1099   *Ibid.* art. 89.
1100   *Ibid.* art. 88(2).
1101   *Ibid.*
1102   *Ibid.* art. 88(2), final para.

of Homeland Security.[1103] In 2005 the Council adopted a 'strategy' to promote progress in the area[1104] and the Commission published a progress report in 2006.[1105] With Lisbon it was drawn into the Union's external action[1106] which is likely to lead to greater coherence and progress.

6. Position of Denmark

11.178 It will be recalled that the Danes at first voted against the Maastricht Treaty,[1107] wary of its intrusion into matters of great political sensitivity even when shielded from the Community pillar. They were no more enthusiastic about Amsterdam's area of freedom, justice and security and, accordingly, wished, and were permitted, to opt out of any and all activities pursued in the field by authority of the EC Treaty,[1108] the privilege carried over into the TFEU. Denmark absents herself from Council meetings in which JLS matters are discussed, voting arithmetic recalibrated to take account of it,[1109] and is excused thoroughly from the field:

> None of the provisions of Title V …, no measure adopted pursuant to that Title, no provision of any international agreement concluded by the Union pursuant to that Title, and no decision of the Court of Justice of the European Union interpreting any such provision or measure or any measure amended or amendable pursuant to that Title shall be binding upon or applicable in Denmark; and no such provision, measure or decision shall in any way affect the competences, rights and obligations of Denmark; and no such provision, measure or decision shall in any way affect the Community or Union *acquis* nor form part of Union law as they apply to Denmark.[1110]

Title V therefore operates as a distinct species of enhanced cooperation and one which, unlike enhanced cooperation generally, is commonly in use. So, for example, the Brussels I Regulation does not apply in Denmark, its subject

---

1103   [2007] OJ L204/18. The agreement was signed originally in 2004 ([2004] OJ L183/84) but the Council decision concluding it was annulled by the Court of Justice for excess of jurisdiction; Cases C-317 and 318/04 *Parliament v Council and Commission* [2006] ECR I-4721. It was replaced ('superseded') by a new agreement in 2012, [2012] OJ L215/5.

1104   *Strategy for the External Dimension of the Area of Freedom, Security and Justice*, Council Doc. 14366/3/05 JAI 417 RELEX 628.

1105   *Progress Report on the Implementation of the Strategy for the External Dimension of JHA: Global Freedom, Security and Justice*, SEC(2006) 1498 final.

1106   See e.g., TEU art. 21(2)(a), (c).

1107   See 1.31 above, n. 56.

1108   By comparison, normal rules applied to Danish participation in Title VI TEU (pre-Lisbon) matters, they being subject to Union and not Community procedures and so less offensive to sensibilities of sovereignty, and Denmark frequently took part.

1109   Protocol (No. 22) on the position of Denmark, art. 1.

1110   *Ibid.* art. 2. The only exception is determination of third country nationals who require a visa and measures relating to visa format (art. 6), which was Community competence since introduced in 1993 (EC Treaty (pre-Amsterdam), art. 100c).

matter continuing to be governed by the Brussels Convention in and for Denmark (and so in and for any other member state as regards matters relating to Denmark) until superseded by other international instruments.[1111] Similarly the Dublin Convention continued in force for (and only for) Denmark, not displaced by the Dublin II Regulation, although it too is now replaced by a new treaty.[1112] Amendment of any existing instrument requires Danish agreement and implementation to be made effective there. These instruments are, for Denmark, not Union law and remain, for both Denmark and the Union, matters governed by public international law – but not beyond the jurisdiction of the Court of Justice, which by express provision is (partially) retained.[1113] Denmark bears no financial obligations for Title V matters (other than institutional administrative costs)[1114] and Title V legislation is published, but is not authentic, in Danish. Should a Title V matter arise for Council deliberation during a Danish presidency, the Dane may retain the chair or yield it to another member of the group holding the trio presidency, but of course cannot vote.[1115]

Pre-Lisbon Denmark was locked out of Title V activities, as described. Lisbon changed that, affording Denmark the opportunity unilaterally to opt out of the protocol in whole or in part ('inform the other Member States that it no longer wishes to avail itself of all or part of this Protocol') and so opt into Title V and 'apply in full all relevant measures … within the framework of the European Union'.[1116] Alternatively, it may by unilateral notification cause the protocol to be altered so that Denmark adopts rules equivalent to those which which apply to Ireland and the United Kingdom.[1117] It has done neither, and neither course seems likely. **11.179**

1111 Brussels I was extended to Denmark originally by a bilateral treaty (Agreement of 19 October 2005 between the European Community and Denmark on Jurisdiction and the Recognition and Enforcement of Judgments in Civil and Commercial Matters [2005] OJ L299/62; in force 1 July 2007) and extended further by Lugano II, to which Denmark is a distinct contracting party; see n. 1113 below. Other treaties extend various (but not all) of the Brussels I supporting Regulations (see 11.169 above) to Denmark.

1112 Agreement between the European Community and Denmark extending to Denmark the Provisions of Council Regulation (EC) No. 343/2003 [2006] OJ L66/38; in force 1 April 2006.

1113 See e.g., the Brussels I Treaty with Denmark (n. 1111 above), art. 7; the Dublin II treaty with Denmark (*ibid.*), art. 7. This does not apply to Lugano II which (owing to lack of willingness from its non-Union signatories) the Court has no jurisdiction to interpret, but its interpretation of the Brussels I Regulation is in some measure binding for the Convention; see Protocol 2 of Lugano II.

1114 Protocol (No. 22) on the Position of Denmark, art. 3.

1115 Prior to the introduction of the trio presidency; presidency was assumed temporarily by the next member state in rotation; but in 2012 the Danish minister of justice chaired JLS Councils. Presumably he would step aside for military/defence discussions in Relex Councils (as Denmark yielded to Greece in 2002).

1116 Protocol (No. 22) on the Position of Denmark, art. 7.

1117 *Ibid.* art. 8; Annex.

7. Ireland and the United Kingdom

11.180   Ireland and the United Kingdom share with Denmark a right to opt out of Title
V activities in accordance with a Treaty protocol containing operative provisions on Council voting and the non-application of Title V matters essentially
identical to those of the Danish protocol.[1118] However their reticence was less
doctrinaire than that of Denmark and so they did not bar themselves from the
field but reserved a right to opt in *à la carte*: by notification to the president of
the Council within three months of its proposal either or both may indicate a
wish to take part in the adoption and application a proposed Title V measure,
whereupon it or they are entitled to do so;[1119] if no agreement can be reached
which accommodates Irish and/or UK inclusion within a 'reasonable period',
the other member states may nevertheless proceed without them.[1120] Where
the Council determines that Irish and/or UK non-participation in the amended
version of an existing measure makes the application of the measure inoperable
for other member states or the Union it may urge them (*les engager; nachdrück-
lich ersuchen; een dringend verzoek richten*) to sign up, affording them a further
two months to do so.[1121] Absent notification the existing measure ceases to
apply to either or both as the case may be,[1122] and the Council may require them
to bear the direct financial consequences necessarily and unavoidably incurred
as a result.[1123] In all cases the Council is to hold a full discussion on the possible
implications and effects of non-participation.[1124] A Title V measure always
contains a preambular recitation to the effect that Ireland and/or the United
Kingdom are, or are not, taking part in its adoption and are, or not, bound by
and subject to its application (for certainty, even though it is always the case, it
also recites that Denmark is not participating in its adoption and is not bound
by it or subject to its application). Ireland or the United Kingdom may also 'at
any time after the adoption of a [Title V] measure' notify the Council and
Commission of an 'intention … that it wishes to accept that measure', in which
case the normal rules on accession to enhanced cooperation measures apply
mutatis mutandis.[1125] Both have in fact taken part from the beginning in most of
the measures on judicial cooperation in civil and commercial matters, but not so

---

1118   Protocol (No. 21) on the Position of the United Kingdom and Ireland in respect of the Area of Freedom,
Security and Justice, arts 1 and 2. Treaty solidarity is broken for the first time with Lisbon providing that
Ireland will not opt out of administrative measures on the freezing of assets to combat terrorism; art. 9.

1119   *Ibid.* art. 3(1).

1120   *Ibid.* art. 3(2).

1121   *Ibid.* art. 4a(2). This is new with Lisbon.

1122   *Ibid.* art. 4a(2), 2nd para.

1123   *Ibid.* art. 4a(3).

1124   Declaration (No. 26) on non-participation by a Member State in a measure based on Title V of Part Three of
the TFEU.

1125   Protocol No. (21), art. 4; that is, the procedure supplied in TFEU, art. 331; see 2.44 above.

those on the movement of persons, including those on third country nationals.[1126] Title V legislation is, since 2004, authentic in English even if neither Ireland nor the United Kingdom take part owing to its application in Malta.

Non-participation in a measure does not bar Ireland or the United Kingdom (or **11.181** presumably Denmark) from challenging its legality under article 263.[1127]

8. Schengen

An important aspect of the free movement of persons, expressly recognised as a **11.182** component of the area of freedom, security and justice,[1128] is, in the Lisbon jargon, 'border checks' (*contrôles aux frontières*; *Grenzkontrollen*): the abolition of controls on persons, irrespective of nationality, when crossing internal Union frontiers and concomitant common rules on entry at external borders. The free movement of persons is, of course, part of the internal market which was to be achieved by the end of 1992 after which 'the free movement of … persons … is ensured',[1129] and 'the right to move … freely within the territory of the Member States' is a fundamental right of Union citzenship.[1130] There was a brave attempt in 1993 by a Mr Wijsenbeek, a Dutch citizen (and MEP 1984–99) who upon landing at Rotterdam airport on a flight from Strasbourg (and Rotterdam serves no flights from outside the Union) refused to present his passport for inspection as required by Dutch law, relying instead directly upon articles 7a and 8a EC (articles 26 and 21 TFEU). The Court of Justice went against him, finding that, even post-1992, in the absence of common rules or harmonised law on controls at external frontiers and immigration, visa and asylum policy (as did not then exist), neither articles 7a or 8a precluded a member state from requiring a person, upon his entry into its territory from another member state, to establish his nationality, even under threat of (proportionate) criminal penalties.[1131] The adoption of rules necessary to achieve that falls now within Title V.

But here (some) member states had stolen a march on Amsterdam. In 1985 five **11.183** of them (Belgium, Germany, France, the Netherlands and Luxembourg) signed

---

1126   See below.
1127   Case C-77/05 *United Kingdom* v *Council* (Frontex) [2007] ECR I-11459 and Case C-137/05 *United Kingdom* v *Council* (Biometric Passports) [2007] ECR I-11593.
1128   TFEU, arts 67(2) and 77(1).
1129   EC Treaty, art. 14(2).
1130   *Ibid.* art. 18(1).
1131   Case C-378/97 *Criminal proceedings against Wijsenbeek* [1999] ECR I-6207. Mr Wijsenbeek was sentenced to a fine of ƒ65 or a day's imprisonment.

(on a ship on the Mosel(le) at Schengen, symbolically at the juncture of the German, French and Luxembourg frontiers) the 'Schengen Agreement'[1132] for the purpose of eliminating the remaining frontier controls on the movement of persons. Schengen marked a special and modified form of enhanced cooperation but established outwith the framework of the Treaties, and beyond the institutional scope of the (then) Community, by international treaties signed by (some) member states acting still in their capacity as states. The Schengen Agreement was essentially an agreement in principle, and was followed up by a much more comprehensive Convention amongst the five states signed (again in Schengen) in 1990 and providing detailed rules for its implementation;[1133] the adjustments to national law necessary for compliance made, the Convention came into operation in March 1995. The core of Schengen is, quite simply, that within the (metropolitan)[1134] territory of the contracting parties (the Schengen area, or informally 'Schengenland'), '[i]nternal borders may be crossed at any point without a[ny border] check[s] on persons[, irrespective of their nationality,] being carried out'.[1135] To make it effective, the Convention provided flanking rules on, *inter alia*:

1132 Agreement of 14 June 1985 on the Gradual Abolition of Checks at their Common Borders [2000] OJ L239/13. Schengen was signed at the tail-end of an Italian presidency, but Italy not (then) party to it, and Luxembourg about to assume the presidency. The depositary is the government of Luxembourg.

1133 Convention of 19 June 1990 implementing the Schengen Agreement of 14 June 1985 on the Gradual Abolition of Checks at their Common Borders [2000] OJ L239/19 (Schengen Convention; elsewhere sometimes called the Convention implementing the Schengen Agreement (CISA), the Schengen Implementation Convention (CIS), or Schengen II).

1134 Certain overseas territories (all French overseas territories, Aruba, Curaçao, Sint Maarten and *Caribisch Nederland*), Heligoland and Ceuta and Mililla are excluded from Schengen. Problems remain for Saint-Martin/Sint Maarten, both outwith Schengenland but Saint-Martin part of the Union so applying common Union rules on visas, Sint Maarten inclined to greater hospitality; the problem is addressed by bilateral treaty (Verdrag van 17 mei 1994 tussen het Koninkrijk der Nederlanden en de Franse Republiek inzake personencontrole op de luchthavens op Sint Maarten, Trb 1994, 144, in force 1 August 2007 but still not fully implemented). Greenland and the Færoes are both excluded from Schengen but are party to the Nordic Passport Union, so by virtue of the Danish Accession Treaty (Agreement of 19 December 1996 on the Accession of the Kingdom of Denmark to the 1990 Schengen Convention, art. 5(2)) there are no border checks on travellers to and from Schengen countries, border controls for (rare) arrivals from third countries carried out by Danish police. Schengen became binding for Büsingen am Hochrhein only with full Swiss accession in 2008. Owing to the (very) peculiar rules on the movement of persons which obtain there (and thought to be saved by Joint Declaration (No. 4) appended to the 1979 Athens Accession Treaty, Joint Declaration (No. 5) appended to the Agreement on Accession of Greece to the Schengen Agreement [2000] OJ L239/83, the Lisbon requirement that the Union respect the status of established churches (TFEU, art. 17) and/or the EU Charter), Mount Athos is considered to lie outwith the Schengen area, although there are no (official) frontier controls at Ouranópolis, admission being controlled by the (self-governing) monasteries.

1135 Schengen Convention, art. 2(1); Regulation 562/2006 [2006] OJ L105/1 (Schengen Borders Code), art. 20, the latter including the words in square parentheses.

- uniform principles on checks at external frontiers;
- a common visa policy and a uniform (short stay) visa[1136] valid for all of the Schengen area;
- responsibility for processing applications for asylum;
- police and security cooperation;
- hot pursuit;
- mutual assistance in criminal matters;
- *non bis in idem*;
- extradition;
- transfer of the enforcement of criminal judgments; and
- the establishment of a joint information system (the Schengen Information System, SIS), an automated search procedure available to the relevant authorities of each contracting party for the purpose of making and detecting 'alerts' on persons and property for the purpose of border checks and other police and customs checks.

The Convention also created an Executive Committee, comprising one member from each contracting party, with authority to adopt (by unanimity) measures 'for the purposes of implementing this Convention'.[1137]

Schengen was open to accession by any Community member state subject to **11.184** the agreement of the contracting parties,[1138] and the Convention was entered into subsequently by Italy (agreement in 1990; in force 1997), Spain and Portugal (1991; 1995), Greece (1992; 2000), Austria (1995; 1997) and Denmark, Finland and Sweden (1996; 2001).

The Treaty of Amsterdam re-opened all of these issues, emphasising the **11.185** abolition of controls upon persons crossing internal frontiers as a matter of Community concern,[1139] so trespassing frontally upon Schengen achievements. The Amsterdam solution was to draw Schengen into the Union (both Community and Union, for it spanned the first and third pillars) sphere, subject to special rules, by means of a separate protocol.[1140] With the entry into force of Amsterdam, both the Schengen Agreement and Convention therefore ceased

---

1136   A long stay visa (exceeding three months) remained national competence, but conferred upon the holder a right of transit through another contracting party; Schengen Convention, art. 18. As to the provisions on short stays see Cases C-261 and 348/08 *Zurita García and Choque Cabrera v Delegado del Gobierno en la Región de Murcia* [2009] ECR I-10143.

1137   Schengen Convention, art. 131.

1138   *Ibid.* art. 140.

1139   EC Treaty, art. 62(1).

1140   Protocol (annexed to the TEU (pre-Lisbon) and the EC Treaty) integrating the Schengen *acquis* into the Framework of the European Union; now Protocol (No. 19) on the Schengen *acquis* integrated into the Framework of the European Union (Schengen Protocol).

to exist as autonomous measures of international law. Immediately thereafter, as charged by the Schengen Protocol,[1141] the Council identified

- those provisions of law still operative within the Schengen framework, including decisions of the Executive Committee, and declared them to constitute the Schengen *acquis*;[1142] it was reproduced in the *Official Journal*[1143] and ran to 473 pages; and
- the legal base (Community or Union) for each measure comprising the *acquis*.[1144] The distinction, and the need for it, disappeared with Lisbon.

The provisions of the Schengen *acquis* were, and are, valid only if and insofar as they are compatible with Union and Community law,[1145] and any inconsistency must be determined in favour of the latter.[1146]

11.186 The operation of Schengen was incorporated into the Union's single institutional framework (the Council substituting for the Schengen Executive Committee[1147] and the Schengen Secretariat absorbed into the General Secretariat),[1148] the Council thereafter adopting measures which 'build upon the Schengen *acquis*', by authority of either the Community or the Union Treaty, as appropriate. Notably the uniform principles on checks at external frontiers have been supplemented and consolidated in the Schengen Borders Code,[1149] an equivalent for persons of the Community Customs Code, and there has been significant adjustment and development of the SIS, which 'constitute[s] an essential tool for the application of the provisions of the Schengen *acquis*',[1150] and without which the system would collapse. It was re-adopted in its 'second generation' ('SIS II'), requiring two separate instruments, one for Community matters,[1151] the other for Union

---

1141 Schengen Protocol (of 1999), art. 2(1), (2); now repealed.
1142 Decision 1999/435 [1999] OJ L176/1.
1143 [2000] OJ L239.
1144 Decision 1999/436 [1999] OJ L176/17.
1145 Schengen Protocol (of 1999), Preamble, 3rd recital. This condition had been written into the Schengen Convention (art. 134) but in 1999 acquired the force of Community law and, more importantly, took the matter into the jurisdiction of the Court of Justice, which thitherto had no jurisdiction to interpret the Convention. The provision was subsumed within art. 1 of the Schengen Protocol by Lisbon ('[Schengen] cooperation shall be conducted within the institutional and legal framework of the European Union and with respect for the relevant provisions of the Treaties').
1146 Case C-503/03 *Commission* v *Spain* [2006] ECR I-1097.
1147 Schengen Protocol, art. 2.
1148 Schengen Protocol (of 1999), art. 7; Decision 1999/307 [1999] OJ L119/49.
1149 Regulation 562/2006 [2006] OJ L105/1. Practical cooperation is assisted by the European Agency for the Management of Operational Cooperation at the External Borders (FRONTEX), established in 2004; Regulation 2007/2004 [2004] OJ L349/1.
1150 Regulation 1987/2006 [2006] OJ L381/4 and Decision 2007/533 [2007] OJ L205/63, Preamble, 1st recital of each; *acquis* is italicised only in the latter.
1151 Regulation 1987/2006, n. 1150 above.

matters,[1152] but nevertheless constituting a single information system and should operate as such.[1153] It will enter into operation (SIS I will 'migrate' to SIS II) on a date to be fixed by the Council, and no later than the end of 2013.[1154]

There remain territorial vagaries to Schengen, as follows.   **11.187**

(a) Denmark

Denmark signed the Schengen Convention in 1996 so is bound by it as it then **11.188** stood and progressed until 1999, at which point arose constitutional difficulties with the absorption of Schengen into the Community/Union and the special privileges enjoyed by Denmark as regards Title IV EC (Title V TFEU). This was recognised by the Schengen Protocol, which absolved Denmark from participation in any subsequent development of those provisions of the *acquis* which have a legal base in Title IV EC, even those which constitute a development of the Schengen *acquis*;[1155] but Denmark bore 'the same rights and obligations as other signatories to the Schengen agreements' as regards those provisions based in Title VI of the EU Treaty.[1156] Post-Lisbon, where the Council adopts a Title V (TFEU) measure building upon the Schengen *acquis* Denmark is to decide within six months whether it elects to implement it in Danish law; if it does so it creates an obligation between Denmark and individual Schengen states governed by public international law,[1157] as is the case for all Schengen arrangements so far as Denmark is concerned. If Denmark declines to implement the measure 'appropriate measures' are to be taken.[1158]

(b) Ireland and the United Kingdom

Ireland and the United Kingdom have enjoyed an ill-defined 'common travel **11.189** area' since partition in 1921/22. It has never been the subject of a legally binding treaty, but it provides for a *de facto* passport union and an absence of frontier controls on the movement of persons between the two countries (and the Isle of Man and the Channel Islands) and marks considerable practical cooperation between the immigration authorities of each. Neither signed the Schengen Convention, the United Kingdom long wary of 'relaxing' its frontier

---

1152   Decision 2007/533, n. 1150 above.
1153   Regulation 1987/2006 and Decision 2007/533, Preamble, 4th recital of each.
1154   Regulation 1987/2006, art. 55; Decision 2007/533, art. 71; Regulation 1104/2008 [2008] OJ L299/1, art. 19 (as amended); Decision 2008/839 [2008] OJ L299/43, art. 19 (as amended). An agency (the European Agency for the Management of Large-Scale IT Systems in the Area of Freedom, Security and Justice) was established in 2011 (fully operational in December 2012) for the operational management of SIS II.
1155   Schengen Protocol (of 1999), art. 3, 1st para; now repealed.
1156   *Ibid.* art. 3, 2nd para; now repealed.
1157   Protocol on the Position of Denmark, art. 4(1).
1158   *Ibid.* art. 4(2).

controls – 'an effective means of controlling immigration, and of combatting terrorism and other crime ... match[ing] both the geography and traditions of the country and ... ensur[ing] a high degree of personal freedom within the UK',[1159] and Ireland, although more amenable, unwilling to jeopardise its open frontier with Northern Ireland (which Irish constitutional law long recognised to be part of its territory).[1160] The United Kingdom secured additional safeguards at Amsterdam by an inclusion in the Treaty of a guarantee that notwithstanding article 14 EC (article 26 TFEU) or any other rule of Community or Union law, it would remain free to exercise such controls as 'it may consider necessary' in order to verify the right of Union (and other EEA) citizens entering the United Kingdom to do so, and to determine who otherwise would be allowed entry;[1161] the same privilege adheres to Ireland 'as long as they maintain [the common travel area]'.[1162] Schengen member states may (and do) maintain in force reciprocal controls (in accordance with the Schengen Border Code) on the movement of persons from the United Kingdom and Ireland.[1163]

11.190   The Schengen Protocol recognises that neither Ireland nor the United Kingdom is bound by the *acquis*,[1164] but that either may at any time 'request' to opt into it, subject to the unanimous consent of participating member states in the Council.[1165] The United Kingdom made three such requests in 1999, seeking

1159   *Fairer, Faster, Firmer: A Modern Approach to Immigration and Asylum* (1998 White Paper), Cmnd 4018, para. 2.9.

1160   The Constitution of 1937 provided that '[t]he national territory consists of the whole island of Ireland' (art. 2) but recognised that the national territory was provisionally incoherent (art. 3); the Supreme Court read these two provisions taken together to mean that the 're-integration' of the national territory was a 'constitutional imperative' towards which all institutions of the state were obliged to work; *McGimpsey* v *Ireland* [1990] 1 IR 110. As part of the 'Good Friday Agreement', art. 2 was amended in 1998 to the much more emollient '[i]t is the entitlement and birthright of every person born in the island of Ireland ... to be part of the Irish nation' and art. 3 to 'recognis[e] that a united Ireland shall be brought about only by peaceful means with the consent of a majority of the people, democratically expressed, in both jurisdictions in the island'.

1161   Protocol (No. 20) on the Application of Certain Aspects of Article 26 of the Treaty on the Functioning of the European Union to the United Kingdom and to Ireland, art. 1.

1162   *Ibid.* art. 2. This anomalous construction means that Ireland loses these privileges in the event of the dissolution of the common travel area but the United Kingdom does not. It is also one of very few legal instruments to recognise the common travel area.

1163   *Ibid.* art. 3.

1164   Schengen Protocol, art. 4. The Schengen Protocol takes priority over the general Protocol (No. 21 on the Position of the United Kingdom and Ireland) on opting out of Title V matters, the latter being 'without prejudice to the [Schengen] Protocol'; art. 7.

1165   Schengen Protocol, art. 4. The member states were to use 'best efforts' in allowing Ireland and the United Kingdom to take up the opportunity thus afforded (Declaration (No. 45) on Article 4 of the Schengen Protocol annexed to the Final Act of the Treaty of Amsterdam), but it remained for the Council to ensure that their participation 'must respect the coherence of the ... acquis'; Decision 2000/365 [2000] OJ L131/45, Preamble, 11th recital.

accession essentially to the 'compensatory measures' ancillary to the management of internal frontiers and common regulation of external frontiers, namely police and judicial cooperation in criminal matters, the fight against drugs and the Schengen Information System – an approach described as 'appearing to involve a total rejection of the free movement of persons without checks at internal borders, accompanied nevertheless by a wish to cooperate in the repressive part of the legal regime governing free movement'.[1166] The Council approved the request in 2000,[1167] and a subsequent Irish request covering much the same ground in 2002,[1168] subject to the necessary 'preconditions for the implementation of those provisions' being put into effect.[1169] It was achieved by the United Kingdom, and the operation of the (partial) *acquis* extended to it on 1 January 2005,[1170] save for the provisions on the SIS, for which the United Kingdom 'will continue to prepare'.[1171] As for measures adopted subsequently to the 1999 consolidation of the Schengen *acquis*, or '[p]roposals and initiatives to build upon the Schengen acquis', normal Treaty rules apply[1172] – that is, Ireland and the United Kingdom may take part, although they may do so only if participating in the prior element(s) of the *acquis* upon which the subsequent measure builds;[1173] if they decline to do so (and may withdraw a notification to that effect up until the last minute of its adoption)[1174] other member states may proceed upon a basis of enhanced cooperation; where either or both have failed to notify the president of the Council within a reasonable period of time that

---

1166 Case C-137/05 *United Kingdom* v *Council* [2007] ECR I-11593, *per* A-G Trstenjak, at para. 94 of her opinion (citing academic authors). It extends to a general UK (and perforce Irish) disinclination, permitted under art. 1 of the Protocol on certain aspects of Article 26, to take part in any of the legislation involving third country nationals.

1167 Decision 2000/365 [2000] OJ L131/45.

1168 Decision 2002/192 [2002] OJ L64/20. In Declaration (No. 56) by Ireland on Article 3 of the Protocol on the Position of the United Kingdom and Ireland in respect of the Area of Freedom, Security and Justice, Ireland declared that it intends to exercise its right to take part in Title V measures 'to the maximum extent it deems possible', presumably whilst maintaining the common travel area, participate 'in particular' to the maximum possible extent in police cooperation, and review the wisdom of the whole of the Irish opt-out within three years of Lisbon's entry into force.

1169 Decision 2000/365, art. 6; Decision 2002/192, art. 4; this to be determined by the Council by unanimity of the Schengen states plus the requesting state; arts 6(2)–(4) and 4(2)–(3), respectively.

1170 Decision 2004/926 [2004] OJ L395/70.

1171 *Ibid.* Preamble, 3rd recital. The problem lies in full integration with Schengen communication infrastructure (SISNET).

1172 Schengen Protocol, art. 5(1).

1173 Case C-77/05 *United Kingdom* v *Council* (Frontex) [2007] ECR I-11459; Case C-137/05 *United Kingdom* v *Council* (Biometric Passports) [2007] ECR I-11593; Case C-482/08 *United Kingdom* v *Council* (Visa Information System) [2010] ECR I-10413. Each contains useful discussion as to when a measure properly builds upon the Schengen *acquis*.

1174 Declaration (No. 44) on Article 5 of the Protocol on the Schengen *acquis* integrated into the Framework of the European Union. Again, the Council is to hold a full discussion on the possible implications of non-participation; Declaration (No. 45) on Article 5(2) of the Protocol on the Schengen *acquis* integrated into the Framework of the European Union.

they wish to take part, that will constitute the necessary authorisation required under the enhanced cooperation procedures for the others to proceed.[1175]

(c)   New member states

11.191   The Schengen *acquis* and other measures adopted within its scope are 'regarded as an *acquis* which must be accepted by all States candidates for admission' to the Union.[1176] The 2004 and 2007 accession member states are therefore bound by the *acquis* (as at their date of accession) and bound to participate thereafter subject to transitional and developmental measures provided in the respective Acts of Accession.[1177] All of the 2004 accession member states save Cyprus came on stream with the SIS in September 2007,[1178] and internal border controls between them, and between them and the older member states, were lifted at land and sea frontiers in December 2007, at airports in March 2008. Cyprus is hampered by its lack of infrastructure for 'separate gateways' at ports of entry and for movement across the ceasefire line and from the United Kingdom sovereign base territories, and intends to accede once the necessary arrangements (not least completion of the new Larnaca airport) are in place.[1179] Bulgaria and Romania are scheduled to become Schengen compatible in 2012/13, a projection which may prove optimistic.

(d)   Iceland and Norway

11.192   Together with Denmark, Finland and Sweden, Iceland and Norway belong to the Nordic passport union which abolished internal border checks in 1958.[1180] Sweden, Finland and Denmark acceded to Schengen in 1996. The Treaty post-Amsterdam provides that Iceland and Norway are to be 'associated' with the implementation, application and further development of the Schengen *acquis*,[1181] given effect by a 1999 agreement between the European Union, Iceland and Norway,[1182] and the *acquis* was formally extended to the whole of

---

1175   Schengen Protocol, art. 5(1); that is, the authorisation required by art. 329(1) TFEU.

1176   Schengen Protocol, art. 7.

1177   2003 Act of Accession, art. 3(1) and (2), and Annex I; 2005 Act of Accession, art. 4 and Annex II; 2011 Act of Accession, art. 4 and Annex II.

1178   Decision 2007/471 [2007] OJ L179/46.

1179   Movement of persons (and goods) across the green line are subject to special rules (Regulation 866/2004 [2004] OJ L161/128), close supervision and is heavily restricted (to some half dozen crossing points); even more restricted is movement across the green line directly into the Eastern Sovereign Base Area; see Protocol No. 3 (annexed to the 2003 Accession Treaty) on the Sovereign Base Areas, art. 5(2) and Annex, part 4.

1180   Överenskommelse av den 12 juli 1957 mellan Sverige, Danmark, Finland och Norge om upphävande av passkontrollen vid de internordiska gränserna, 322 UNTS 245; in force 1 May 1958. Iceland acceded in 1965, the Færoes in 1966. Nordic cooperation is recognised (or 'recorded') in Union law (see Joint Declaration (No. 28) on Nordic Cooperation attached to the 1994 Accession Treaty) but it appears to enjoy no privileged status; see Case C-435/06 *C* [2007] ECR I-10141.

1181   Schengen Protocol, art. 6.

1182   Agreement of 18 May 1999 between the European Union, the Republic of Iceland and the Kingdom of Norway concerning the latter's Association with the Implementation, Application and Development of the

the Nordic union in 2001.[1183] In practice the association takes the form of a joint committee outside the framework of the Union, comprising representatives from the Icelandic and Norwegian governments and members of the Council and the Commission. Procedures for notifying and accepting future measures or acts have been set out. Iceland and Norway also take part in common action in examination of requests for asylum[1184] and in extradition,[1185] and some provisions of Union JLS legislation apply there by (treaty) agreement on a case-by-case basis.

(e) Switzerland and Liechtenstein

An agreement was signed in 2002 between the European Union, the European Community and the Swiss Confederation and formally adopted in 2004,[1186] by virtue of which the latter became associated with the implementation, application and development of the Schengen *acquis* in much the same manner as Iceland and Norway. The proposal was approved by federal referendum in June 2005 and, following Swiss adoption of the necessary infrastructure and rules, it came fully into force for land frontiers in December 2008 and for air frontiers in March 2009. Switzerland is now party to the operation of Frontex.[1187] It also participates in a common asylum system.[1188]   **11.193**

With Swiss accession pending Liechtenstein took an interest, and in 2006 it was agreed the principality would accede to the Union/Community/Swiss   **11.194**

Schengen acquis [1999] OJ L176/36. Svalbard is excluded (art. 14; as it must be, owing to the internationally guaranteed status of the island, Svalbardtraktatet den 9 de februar 1920, NT 1 s. 409) but, by silence, it appears that Jan Mayen, Bouvetøya, Dronning Maud Land and Peter I Øy are not, however unlikely travel thence to another Schengen country.

1183   Decision 2000/777 [2000] OJ L309/24.

1184   Agreement of 19 January 2001 between the European Community and Iceland and Norway concerning the Criteria and Mechanisms for Establishing the State Responsible for Examining a Request for Asylum Lodged in a Member State or in Iceland or Norway [2001] OJ L93/40.

1185   Agreement (undated) between the European Union and Norway and Iceland on the Surrender Procedure between the Member States of the European Union and Norway and Iceland [2006] OJ L292/2.

1186   Agreement of 26 October 2004 between the European Union, the European Community and the Swiss Confederation on the Swiss Confederation's Association with the Implementation, Application and Development of the Schengen *acquis* [2008] OJ L53/52.

1187   'Arrangement' of 30 September 2009 between the European Community, the Swiss Confederation and the Principality of Liechtenstein on the Modalities of the Participation of those states in the European Agency for the Management of Operational Cooperation at the External Borders of the Member States of the European Union [2010] OJ L243/4.

1188   Agreement of 26 October 2004 between the European Community and the Swiss Confederation concerning the Criteria and Mechanisms for Establishing the State Responsible for Examining a Request for Asylum Lodged in a Member State or in Switzerland [2008] OJ L53/5; in force 1 March 2008.

agreement.[1189] A protocol achieving this result was signed in 2008[1190] but ratification by the Community/Union was held up for want of Swedish consent (withheld owing to concern over Liechtenstein as a tax haven). In the meanwhile the Swiss/Liechtenstein frontier had become an external Schengen frontier, so in principle requiring the re-establishment of the border controls abolished in 1923,[1191] but video surveillance plus additional mobile controls in the Swiss border area and Liechtenstein cooperation in Frontex appears to have been a satisfactory (and temporary) *modus vivendi*. Union agreement eventually secured, the 2008 Protocol entered into force, bringing Liechtenstein fully within the operation of Schengen, from April 2011. Liechtenstein also acceded to the Community/Swiss agreement on asylum so participates in a common asylum system.[1192]

(f) Other countries

11.195   The Vatican indicated an interest in Schengen accession alongside Liechtenstein but no significant progress has been made. Neither San Marino nor Monaco is party to Schengen but they have open borders with Italy and France, respectively. As none of these countries has an airport, there is only one (private, titchy) aerodrome (Torraccia, San Marino), three heliports (in the Vatican (for the Pope's use), Monaco and Borgo Maggiore (San Marino), all closed to flights from (and beyond the reach of) non-Schengen countries) and one train station (Monaco-Monte-Carlo), the sole concern is control of land frontiers, which are not extensive and not 'external' in the sense that the Schengen Border Code applies, and, for Monaco, the ports (Hercule and Fontvieille), at which French authorities carry out Schengen frontier checks. Andorra is not integrated into the Schengen zone and border controls remain.

11.196   There is provision for 'local border traffic', allowing non-visa entry of third country nationals into Schengen territory where that third country abuts a Schengen frontier and satisfactory details are agreed (upon a basis of reciprocity) between it and the relevant Union member state.[1193] The right is restricted

---

1189   Protocol (initalled in Brussels on 21 June 2006) on the Accession of Leichtenstein to the Agreement of 26 October 2004 between the European Union, the European Community and the Swiss Confederation, n. 1186 above.

1190   Protocol of 28 February 2008 between the European Union, the European Community, the Swiss Confederation and the Principality of Liechtenstein on the Accession of the Principality of Liechtenstein to the (2004 EC/EU/Swiss Agreement)[2011] OJ L160/3.

1191   Vertrag vom 29 März 1923 zwischen der Schweiz und Liechtenstein über den Anschluss des Fürstentums Liechtenstein an das schweizerische Zollgebiet (1924) 21 LNTS No. 545.

1192   Protocol of 28 February 2008 between the European Community, the Swiss Confederation and the Principality of Liechtenstein concerning the Criteria and Mechanisms for Establishing the State Responsible for Examining a Request for Asylum Lodged in a Member State or in Switzerland [2011] OJ L160/39; in force 1 May 2011.

1193   Regulation 1931/2006 [2006] OJ L405/1.

to the bearer of a 'local border traffic permit' who may enter and stay in the 'border area' (up to 30 kilometres from the common frontier) for the period agreed, up to a maximum of three months.[1194] There are five 'LBT agreements' in place, three between Ukraine and each of Hungary, Slovakia and Poland, one between Moldova and Romania[1195] and one between Russia (for Kaliningrad) and Poland (with, exceptionally, all of Kaliningrad oblast constituting the border area); a sixth, between Russia (for Kaliningrad) and Lithuania, is in the pipeline. Otherwise, two anomalies exist, one present, one future, forming larger but carefully controlled chinks in the Schengen frontier. First, by virtue of pre-accession treaties[1196] Croatians have the right to enter (all of) Italy, Hungary and Slovenia upon production of a Croatian identity card only, and this continues to be so (when accompanied by an 'entry and exit stamping card'). But if a Croat intends thence to enter another Schengen country he or she is required to have a passport, presented and stamped upon entry into Italy, Hungary or Slovenia, as the case may be. Immediately upon its accession to the Union Schengen is binding for Croatia, final implementation to be set out in a (unanimous) Council decision,[1197] so that anomaly will disappear. Secondly, a terminal is being built at Gibraltar airport on the southern side of the frontier (the British view) or the fence (the Spanish view) between La Línea de la Concepción and Gibraltar. When completed it will allow direct access to the terminal from La Línea, the terminal deemed for those passengers thus using it to be part of the Schengen area. So, a passenger on a flight from, say, Marseille to Gibraltar exiting the airport at La Línea will not have left the Schengen area and need comply with no entry formality even if, on the British view, entering Spain from UK territory.

9. Judicial control of the Area of Freedom, Security and Justice

It is to be recalled that the jurisdiction of the Court of Justice was, in a manner **11.197** unique in the EC Treaty, curtailed in JLS matters: all jurisdiction of the Court was expressly ousted as regards measures adopted under article 62(1) EC (abolishing controls on cross-frontier movement) *if* they related to the maintenance of law and order and the safeguarding of internal security,[1198] and preliminary rulings on the interpretation of Title IV EC (Title V TFEU) or on the validity of acts adopted under it could not be requested by lower courts (but

---

1194   *Ibid.* arts 3(2), 5, 7(2).
1195   This is so even though Romania remains outwith Schengen because it is subject to common EU visa rules; see 11.166 above.
1196   See e.g., Sporazum 28 travnje 1997. godine između Republike Hrvatske i Republike Slovenije o pograničnom prometu i suradnji (SOPS), *Narodne Novine* no 15/1997, 14 listopad 1997.
1197   2011 Act of Accession, art. 4.
1198   EC Treaty, art. 68(2).

conversely could be requested by the Council, the Commission or a member state),[1199] so excluding articles Title IV from the normal application of article 234 (article 267 TFEU). The purpose of the latter was understood to be the prevention of the Court being swamped by immigration and asylum references from lower courts or tribunals,[1200] although doubtless an antipathy to cede jurisdiction to the Court in such sensitive matters played a part. As for pre-Lisbon Union matters, most measures were wholly immune from review,[1201] and even where there was no immunity the authority of a national court to seek a preliminary ruling under article 35 TEU (pre-Lisbon), upon either validity or interpretation, was subject to the whim of governments.[1202] With Lisbon's *communautairisation* of JLS (most of) this disappears. The jurisdiction of the Court of Justice is extended to cover all JLS matters, save that in judicial cooperation in criminal matters and police cooperation it may review neither the validity or proportionality of operations carried out by police or other law enforcement services of a member state nor the exercise of the responsibilities of a member state to maintain law and order and safeguard internal security;[1203] the reservation of the reference power under article 267 to national courts of final instance disappears and the whole of Title V becomes subject to the normal application of article 267. However, the *status quo ante* is preserved in two respects: first, measures adopted by authority of Title VI TEU (pre-Lisbon) will continue in force until such time as they are repealed, annulled or amended, thus producing the (relatively anaemic) legal effects they were accorded under the provisions of that Title;[1204] the Lisbon IGC 'invited' the institutions to replace the lot with new instruments within five years,[1205] a target unlikely to be met. Secondly, for five years from the entry into force of Lisbon the Commission may raise no enforcement proceedings under article 258, and the jurisdiction of the Court is maintained transitionally as it was, 'with respect to acts of the Union in the field of police cooperation and judicial cooperation in criminal matters which have been adopted before [then]'.[1206]

Uniquely, the United Kingdom may notify the Council, at the latest six months prior to the expiry of the transitional period (that is, before June 2014), that it does not accept the powers of the institutions over those excepted matters, in which case they will cease to apply to and in the United Kingdom from the end

---

1199 *Ibid.* art. 68(1), (3); see 5.147 above; it never happened.
1200 See Case C-14/08 *Roda Golf & Beach Resort* [2009] ECR I-5439, *per* A-G Ruiz-Jarabo Colomer at paras 22–7 of his opinion.
1201 See 5.29 above.
1202 See 5.148 above.
1203 TFEU, art. 276.
1204 Protocol (No. 36) on Transitional Provisions, art. 9.
1205 Declaration (No. 50) concerning Article 10 of the Protocol on Transitional Provisions.
1206 Protocol (No. 36), art. 10.

of the transitional period.[1207] The Council may require the United Kingdom to bear the direct financial consequences necessarily and unavoidably incurred as a result[1208] and the United Kingdom may opt (back) in subsequently, with a view to re-establishing its widest possible measure of participation in the Union JLS *acquis* without jeopardising its practical operability, and respecting its coherence.[1209]

It should also be recalled that in a reference under article 267 in any JLS matter **11.198** in which a ruling is required as a matter of urgency a special urgent procedure (the ppu) may apply;[1210] it will in all cases apply (for the Court must 'act with the minimum of delay')[1211] in respect of a person in custody.

I. TRANSPORT

Transport is governed by its own Title in the TFEU, Title VI comprising **11.199** articles 90–100. As agriculture is a particular subset of goods made subject to special rules, so transport is a particular subset of services, specifically excluded from the general Treaty chapter and reserved and made subject to Title VI.[1212] More accurately, transport by rail, road and inland waterway is reserved to Title VI,[1213] but it applies to sea and air transport only if, and as far as, the Union legislature decides to make it so[1214] – which, largely, it has. Other general rules of the Treaties nonetheless apply subject to any specific rules to the contrary.[1215]

Also as with agriculture, the Treaties anticipated and posit not a free market but **11.200** a regulated market in transport, implemented 'within the framework of a common transport policy'.[1216] This was for two reasons: first, the variegated approach of the original six member states to transport, favouring variously and in different blends water, rail and road haulage and varying significantly in terms of public control and subvention, meant that a *laissez faire* approach

---

1207 *Ibid.* art. 10(4).
1208 *Ibid.*
1209 *Ibid.* art. 10(5).
1210 Statute of the Court of Justice, art. 23a; RP Court of Justice, arts 107–114. As to the ppu see 5.37–5.38 above.
1211 TFEU, art. 267, 4th para.
1212 *Ibid.* art. 58(1) (ex art. 51(1) EC).
1213 *Ibid.* art. 100(1) (ex art. 80(1) EC).
1214 *Ibid.* art. 100(2) (ex art. 80(2) EC).
1215 E.g., Case 167/73 *Commission* v *France* [1974] ECR 359, at para. 32 (application of art. 45 TFEU); Cases 209 etc./84 *Criminal proceedings against Asjes and ors* (Nouvelles Frontières) [1986] ECR 1425, at paras 40–5 (art. 101); Case C-476/98 *Commission* v *Germany* (Open Skies) [2002] ECR I-9855 (art. 49); Case C-382/08 *Neukirchinger* v *Bezirkshauptmannschaft Grieskirchen*, [2011] ECR I-139, at para. 21 (art. 18).
1216 TFEU, art. 90 (ex art. 70 EC).

would be unworkable and unacceptable; secondly, some (passenger, primarily) transport services remain viable only through public service obligations adhering to them, and these would be imperilled by a free market. It is in itself an important economic sector, accounting for 5 per cent of Union GDP,[1217] 13.4 per cent of household expenditure[1218] and employing directly around 10 million people,[1219] representing 4.4 per cent of all jobs.[1220] And it is fundamental to economic activity and a precondition to economic growth: the cost of infrastructure development alone to match (ever increasing) demand is estimated at €1.5 billion (thousand milliard) for 2010–30,[1221] and inefficiency, in the form of congestion, is thought to cost the Union €80 thousand million a year, or 1 per cent of GDP,[1222] projected to increase by 2050 to €200 thousand million.[1223] Above all transport is self-evidently core to Union endeavour, being the means by which the common market was and is to be effected. The reliance upon transport for the free movement of goods is self-evident, and the Treaty provisions betray a clear bias towards the carriage of goods;[1224] but it is a prerequisite for the proper functioning of a labour market and the provision and receipt of services too. It is also, for obvious reasons, closely bound up with Union environmental and energy policies (accounting for 32.6 per cent of EU energy consumption,[1225] of which oil and oil products account for 96 per cent[1226]), industrial policy, social policy, employment policy and regional policy.

11.201 Transport is also an important aspect of the Union's external policies. Indeed one of its major 'constitutional' judgments, and the starting point for the recognition of exclusive Community competences, involved external transport policy and Community capacity and procedure to enter into an international agreement on road transport,[1227] the Court of Justice deciding that the Community could exhaustively occupy a field and so exclude national competence to deal with third countries, and even pre-empt national competence in a field regulated but not occupied by Community rules in the interests of the unity of the common market and the uniform application of Community law.[1228] Sea

---

1217   2011 White Paper, n. 1243 below, para. 15.
1218   European Commission, 'EU Energy and Transport in Figures', *Statistical Pocketbook 2010*, p. 95.
1219   2011 White Paper, n. 1243 below, para. 15.
1220   'EU Energy and Transport in Figures', n. 1218 above, p. 95.
1221   2011 White Paper, n. 1243 below, para. 55.
1222   2001 White Paper, n. 1241 below, p. 8 (projected to 2010).
1223   Commission Working Document, SEC(2011) 358 final, para. 20.
1224   TFEU, art. 95 (ex art. 75 EC).
1225   'EU Energy and Transport in Figures', n. 1218 above, p. 36.
1226   2011 White Paper, n. 1243 below, para. 7.
1227   European Agreement of 1 July 1970 concerning the Work of Crews of Vehicles engaged in International Road Transport (AETR), 993 UNTS 14533.
1228   Case 22/70 *Commission* v *Council* (ERTA) [1971] ECR 263; see 14.71 below.

and air transport in particular invite an international approach and accommodation, for plain reasons.

1. Common Transport Policy

The Treaty provisions on transport have remained essentially unchanged since **11.202** 1958. They set out no general policy objectives for the Common Transport Policy (CTP) as they do for agriculture,[1229] rather they require only that account be taken of cases in which rules adopted might seriously affect the standard of living and level of employment in certain regions and the operation of transport facilities,[1230] that transport rates and conditions take account of the economic circumstances of the carrier,[1231] and that rules adopted ensure that users benefit from them to the full.[1232] The Court of Justice has now said that with the gradual integration of environmental protection ('one of the essential objectives of the Community') into the Treaties, it 'must be regarded as an objective which also forms part of the common transport policy'.[1233] It is also one of the areas (alongside telecommunications and energy) earmarked for infrastructure interconnection and interoperability through the promotion of 'trans-European networks', a concept introduced by Maastricht.[1234]

Notwithstanding (or maybe because of) the free hand afforded the institutions, **11.203** progress in development of the CTP was slow off the mark: it was to be agreed and in place by the end of the transitional period[1235] but was not, and in 1985 the Council was censured by the Court of Justice for desultory progress.[1236] Provisions on transport were included in the 1985 Cockfield White Paper[1237] and a number of measures were adopted as part of the 1992 programme. There followed a Commission White Paper on future development of the CTP (1992),[1238] a Green Paper (1995),[1239] another White Paper (1998),[1240] yet

---

1229   TFEU, art. 39(1) (ex art. 33(1) EC); see 10.101 above.
1230   TFEU, art. 91(2) (ex art. 71(2) EC).
1231   TFEU, art. 94 (ex art. 74 EC).
1232   TFEU, art. 95(3), 2nd para. (ex art. 75(3), 2nd para. EC).
1233   Case C-440/05 *Commission* v *Council* (Ship-Source Pollution) [2007] ECR I-9097, at para. 60.
1234   EC Treaty, arts 129b–129d (pre-Amsterdam) (arts 170–2 TFEU).
1235   EEC Treaty, art. 75(1), (2).
1236   Case 13/83 *Parliament* v *Council* [1985] ECR 1513.
1237   *Completing the Internal Market*, COM(85) 310, paras 44, 108–12.
1238   *The Future Development of the Common Transport Policy: A Global Approach to the Construction of a Community Framework for Sustainable Mobility*, COM(92) 494 final; *Bulletin EU*, Supplement 3/93.
1239   *Towards Fair and Efficient Pricing in Transport*, COM(95) 691.
1240   *Fair Payment for Infrastructure Use: a Phased Approach to a Common Transport Infrastructure Charging Framework in the EU*, COM(98) 466 final.

another (2001)[1241] with a mid-term review (2006),[1242] and one more (2011).[1243] The 2001 White Paper, on transport policy for the ensuing decade, proposed the adoption of some 60 measures to develop a transport system capable of shifting the balance between modes of transport, revitalising the railways, promoting transport by sea and inland waterway and controlling the growth in air transport. This, it claimed, was thus consistent with the sustainable development strategy adopted at the Göteborg Council in 2001.[1244] The 2011 White Paper is a 'roadmap' to 2020 and the creation of a single European transport area through the elimination of remaining residual barriers between modes of transport and national systems, innovation and coherent forward planning. In 2009 the Commission published a Green Paper on a fundamental review of (hoping to give fresh impetus to) the trans-European transport network (TEN-T).[1245]

11.204 Generally, legislation came in fits and starts, in series of 'packages' addressing, generally, market access, cabotage, operator tariffs, structural harmonisation, mutual recognition of qualifications, operators' licences, social conditions, technical and safety standards, type approval, and passengers' rights.

(a) Road

11.205 Road remains the principal means of transport in the Union for both goods and passengers, road haulage accounting for about 73 per cent of inland freight transport,[1246] one-third of which crosses a national frontier,[1247] passenger cars accounting for 73.6 per cent (in passenger/kilometres) of total passenger transport,[1248] buses and coaches another 8.2 per cent.[1249]

11.206 Community action focused primarily on controlling the multiple costs of road transport. The key legislation is now contained in three Regulations, on common rules on road transport operators,[1250] access to the international road

---

1241 *European Transport Policy for 2010: Time to Decide*, COM(2001) 370 final.
1242 *Keep Europe Moving: Sustainable Mobility for our Continent*, COM(2006) 314 final.
1243 *Roadmap to a Single European Transport Area: Towards a Competitive and Resource Efficient Transport System*, COM(2011) 144 final. Also the accompanying Commission Working Documents, SEC(2011) 358 final, SEC(2011) 359 final and SEC(2011) 391 final.
1244 European Council, 15–16 June 2001, Presidency Conclusions, *Bulletin EU* 6–2001, 10.
1245 *Toward a Better Integrated Transeuropean Transport Network at the Service of the Common Transport Policy*, COM(2009)44 final.
1246 European Commission, *Road Freight Transport Vademecum* (2009), p. 3.
1247 *Ibid.*
1248 European Commission, *Road Transport Policy: Open Roads Across Europe* (2006), p. 2. It is predicted to remain above two-thirds up to 2050; Commission Working Document, SEC(2011) 358 final, para. 18.
1249 *Ibid.*
1250 Regulation 1071/2009 [2009] OJ L300/51.

haulage market[1251] and access to the international market for coach and bus services,[1252] the latter two consolidations of previous legislation. Taxation of HGVs has been coordinated,[1253] rights of passengers in coach and bus transport established.[1254] There is a raft of legislation on technical standards and type approval of vehicles, fuel, emissions, and so on. As for road safety, the Commission adopted action programmes in 2003[1255] and in 2010 for the decade to come.[1256] There is yet more legislation on technical safety standards, and social legislation on working conditions for operators (essentially drivers),[1257] and the use, to make it effective, of recording equipment (tachographs) in road transport,[1258] which was stoutly resisted by the industry in some member states yet tachographs were made tamper-proof in 2006.[1259] There is a uniform driving licence[1260] and compulsory use of seatbelts.[1261] Common action on speed limits and alcohol/drug consumption continues to be resisted by the member states.

Throughout, the Commission seems to be unaware of the existence of the bicycle.   **11.207**

(b) Inland waterways

Transport by inland waterways is less developed. Some member states (Belgium, Germany, France, the Netherlands, Finland) have a relatively comprehensive network in at least some parts of the country, whilst elsewhere it is rudimentary (and then much of it given over to leisure craft) or non-existent. But it has potential: it is particularly suited to long distance haulage of bulk transport, it is underused, compared to saturated capacity in other sectors – for example, only 10 per cent of the capacity of the Danube is utilised[1262] – and its external costs, especially environmental and safety (and especially as regards shipment of dangerous goods), are low. The Commission therefore aims to promote and strengthen the competitive position of the inland waterway transport and integrate it better into into an 'intermodal logistic chain'. In 2006   **11.208**

1251   Regulation 1072/2009 [2009] OJ L300/72.
1252   Regulation 1073/2009 [2009] OJ L300/88.
1253   Directive 1999/62 [1999] OJ L187/42.
1254   Regulation 181/2011 [2011] OJ L55/1.
1255   *Road Safety Action Programme*, COM(2003) 311 final.
1256   *Towards a European Road Safety Area: Policy Orientations on Road Safety 2011–20*, COM(2010) 389 final.
1257   Regulation 561/2006 [2006] OJ L102/1; detailed rules in Directive 2002/15 [2002] OJ L80/35. The AETR (see n. 1227 above) is applied to road transport between the Union and a third country; Regulation 561/2006, art. 2(3).
1258   Regulation 3821/85 [1985] OJ L370/8.
1259   *Ibid.* art. 15.
1260   Directive 2006/126 [2006] OJ L403/18 (consolidating earlier legislation).
1261   Directive 91/671 [1991] OJ L373/26.
1262   2006 Action Programme, n. 1263 below, p. 3.

it launched an integrated action programme to 2013 for inland waterway transport[1263] called – in an exercise stretching acronyms to breaking point – the Naiades programme, from *N*avigation *A*nd *I*nland waterway *A*ction and *D*evelopment in *E*urope and the naiades (οι ναϊάδες), the Greek spring and river nymphs. A mid-term progress report was published in 2011.[1264] Achievement is still limited. There is relatively little legislation specific to inland waterway transport,[1265] but some of the measures on maritime transport, and some on transport more generally, apply.

(c)   Rail

11.209   Like inland waterways, the provision of rail services varies widely across the Union, from comprehensive to rudimentary to, in two member states (Cyprus and Malta), none.[1266] The 2001 White Paper called for a revitalisation of rail as part of a policy of sustainable mobility. It resulted in three packages adopted over the ensuing decade:

- *The first railway package* (2001), intended to kickstart the thitherto lumbering progress. It consisted primarily of four Directives, on development of the Community's railways,[1267] the licensing of railway undertakings,[1268] the allocation of infrastructure capacity and levying charges for its use[1269] and the interoperability of conventional rail systems.[1270]
- *The second railway package* (2004), intended to create a legally and technically integrated European railway area. It consisted of measures on railway safety,[1271] further interoperability of high speed and conventional railways,[1272] the liberalisation of national and international freight services (from 1 January 2007),[1273] the creation of the European Railway Agency to coordinate and promote safety and interoperability[1274] and a

---

1263   COM(2006) 6 final.

1264   SEC(2011) 453 final.

1265   Directive 87/540 [1987] OJ L322/20 (access to the occupation and mutual recognition of qualifications); Directive 91/672 [1991] OJ L373/29 (reciprocal recognition of national boatmasters' certificates); Directive 2006/87 [2006] OJ L389/1 (technical requirements for vessels); Regulation 1365/2006 [2006] OJ L264/1 (statistics); Directive 2009/30 [2009] OJ L140/88 (fuel and emission control for inland waterway vessels); Directive 2009/100 [2009] OJ L259/8 (reciprocal recognition of navigability licences).

1266   Thus the railway legislation normally includes a provision that it 'shall not apply to Cyprus and Malta for so long as no railway system is established within their territory'.

1267   Directive 2001/12 [2001] OJ L75/1 (significantly amending Directive 91/440 [1991] OJ L237/25, a then-rudimentary Directive on the development of Community railways).

1268   Directive 2001/13 [2001] OJ L75/26 (amending Directive 91/440).

1269   Directive 2001/14 [2001] OJ L75/29.

1270   Directive 2001/16 [2001] OJ L110/1; now consolidated as Directive 2008/57 [2008] OJ L191/1.

1271   Directive 2004/49 [2004] OJ L164/44 (Railway Safety Directive).

1272   Directive 2004/50 [2004] OJ L164/114 (amending Directives 96/48 and 2001/16, both now consolidated as Directive 2008/57).

1273   Directive 2004/51 [2004] OJ L164/164 (amending Directive 91/440).

1274   Regulation 881/2004 [2004] OJ L220/3.

decision that the Community should accede to the Intergovernmental Organisation for International Carriage by Rail (COTIF).[1275]

- *The third railway package* (2007) consists of measures on (further) allocation of infrastructure capacity and levying of charges for its use, envisaging liberalisation of the market for international passenger services to competition (from 1 January 2010);[1276] certification of train drivers and crews operating locomotives and of trains;[1277] and a minimum standard for rail passengers' rights and obligations, addressing, for example, insurance and ticketing and access for passengers with reduced mobility.[1278]

These measures have largely completed the regulatory framework for the internal market for rail services. Only some technical, administrative and legal obstacles remain. In 2010 the Commission proposed a Directive consolidating the first railway package legislation (and some of the second) in order to establish 'a single European railway area'.[1279]

(d) Maritime transport

A maritime package was first developed in 1986, consisting of measures on the **11.210** free provision of services,[1280] the application of the competition rules (with generous exemption) to the sector,[1281] the prohibition of unfair pricing[1282] and free access to cargoes in ocean trades (*sic*) (*au trafic transocéanique*);[1283] and subsequently rules on the transfer of ships from one register to another[1284] and a right of maritime cabotage.[1285] They still exist[1286] but have been polished and complemented over time.[1287] In 2009 the Commission adopted coterminously an action plan with a view to establishing a European maritime transport space

---

1275 Convention of 9 May 1980 concerning International Carriage by Rail (COTIF, Convention internationale sur le transport international ferroviaire) 1397 UNTS 3; now amended by the (Vilnius) Protocol of Modification of 3 June 1999; Union accession in force at 1 July 2011.

1276 Directive 2007/58 [2004] OJ L315/44 (amending Directives 91/440 and 2001/14). Excluded are solely urban, suburban and regional services, services between a member state and a third country and services transiting the Union.

1277 Directive 2007/59 [2004] OJ L315/51. Also Regulation 36/2010 [2010] OJ L13/1 on Community models for train driving licences.

1278 Regulation 1371/2007 [2004] OJ L315/14.

1279 COM(2010) 475 final.

1280 Regulation 4055/86 [1986] OJ L378/1.

1281 Regulation 4056/86 [1986] OJ L378/4.

1282 Regulation 4057/86 [1986] OJ L378/14.

1283 Regulation 4058/86 [1986] OJ L378/21.

1284 Regulation 613/91 [1986] OJ L68/1.

1285 Regulation 3577/92 [1986] OJ L364/7.

1286 Except that Regulation 4056/86 was repealed and Regulation 613/91 replaced by Regulation 789/2004 [2004] OJ L138/19.

1287 E.g., Directive 96/98 [1997] OJ L46/25 on the safety of maritime equipment; Directive 2008/106 [2008] OJ L323/33 on training of seafarers.

without barriers[1288] and a policy paper on development of maritime policy to 2018.[1289] Mirroring measures adopted in other sectors, in 2010 the Parliament and Council adopted a Regulation on passengers' rights which applies to both sea and inland waterway transport.[1290]

11.211 Three legislative packages on maritime safety have been proposed, two (Erika I and II) in 2000,[1291] a third in 2005;[1292] a European Maritime Safety Agency was set up in 2002 to provide technical and scientific assistance to ensure the proper application of Union legislation in the field of maritime safety, monitor its implementation and evaluate its effectiveness. In 2009 the Parliament and Council adopted a number of measures on safety of marine transport (the 'third maritime safety package'), including common rules and standards for ship inspection and survery organisations,[1293] accident investigation,[1294] carriers' liability in the event of accident,[1295] shipowners' insurance,[1296] penalties, including criminal penalties, for ship-source pollution[1297] and supervisory responsibilities (for safety and pollution) of flag states.[1298]

(e) Air

11.212 The Council adopted three packages in air transport, in 1987, 1990 and 1992. The third comprised three Regulations on granting and maintenance of carriers' operating licences,[1299] access to intra-Community routes[1300] and criteria and procedures applicable to fares and rates for carriage wholly within the Community.[1301] According to the Commission this established a complete set of common rules enabling the internal market in air transport, based upon the freedom to provide services, to be created.[1302] The three are now consolidated in a single instrument 'on common rules for the operation of air services in the

---

1288   COM(2009) 10.
1289   *Strategic Goals and Recommendations for the EU's Maritime Transport Policy until 2018*, COM(2009) 8 final.
1290   Regulation 1177/2010 [2010] OJ L334/1.
1291   Commission Communication on the safety of the seaborne oil trade (ERIKA I), COM(2000) 142 final; Commission Communication on a second set of Community measures on maritime safety following the sinking of the oil tanker Erika (ERIKA II), COM(2000) 802 final.
1292   Communication from the Commission: Third package of legislative measures on maritime safety in the European Union, COM(2005) 585 final.
1293   Regulation 391/2009 [2009] OJ L131/14; Directive 2009/15 [2009] OJ L131/47.
1294   Directive 2009/18 [2009] OJ L131/114.
1295   Regulation 392/2009 [2009] OJ L131/24 (Athens Regulation).
1296   Directive 2009/20 [2009] OJ L131/128.
1297   Directive 2009/123 [2009] OJ L280/52, amending Directive 2005/35 [2005] OJ L255/11.
1298   Directive 2009/21 [2009] OJ L131/132.
1299   Regulation 2407/92 [1992] OJ L240/1.
1300   Regulation 2408/92 [1992] OJ L240/8.
1301   Regulation 2409/92 [1992] OJ L240/15.
1302   Case C-476/98 *Commission* v *Germany* (Open Skies) [2002] ECR I-9855, at paras 86, 91.

Community'.[1303] Previous legislation on a code of conduct for computerised reservation systems (CRSs),[1304] on access to groundhandling[1305] and on common rules for slot allocation at Union airports[1306] remains. There are now common rules for levying airport charges.[1307]

(f) The Single European sky

The 'Single European sky' is a package of legislation on air traffic management **11.213** intended 'to enhance current safety standards and overall efficiency for general air traffic in Europe, to optimise capacity meeting the requirements of all airspace users and to minimise delays'.[1308] It consists of a framework Regulation[1309] and three technical Regulations on the provision of air navigation services Service Provision Regulation),[1310] organisation and use of the airspace (Airspace Regulation)[1311] and interoperability of the European air traffic management network (Interoperability Regulation).[1312] The institutions are assisted in this by the European Aviation Safety Agency, created in 2002,[1313] which develops and promotes common standards of safety and environmental protection in civil aviation. The measures address appropriate cooperation with Eurocontrol, within which a common charging scheme for air navigation services has been agreed;[1314] they do not apply to military operations but the member states undertake to enhance civil/military cooperation to the necessary extent. In 2006 the Parliament and the Council adopted a Directive on the Community air traffic controller licence,[1315] now subsumed within a broader Regulation on airworthiness of aircraft, pilots and air and cabin crews.[1316] In 2008 the scheme for greenhouse gas emission allowance trading was extended to aviation.[1317] There are also measures on common rules for civil aviation security[1318] and for compensation and assistance to passengers denied boarding

---

1303   Regulation 1008/2008 [2008] OJ L293/3.
1304   Regulation 80/2009 [2009] OJ L35/47 (replacing earlier legislation).
1305   Directive 96/67 [1996] OJ L272/36.
1306   Regulation 95/93 [1993] OJ L14/1.
1307   Directive 2009/12 [2009] OJ L70/11.
1308   Regulation 549/2004 [2004] OJ L96/1, art. 1(1).
1309   *Ibid.*
1310   Regulation 550/2004 [2004] OJ L96/10.
1311   Regulation 551/2004 [2004] OJ L96/20.
1312   Regulation 552/2004 [2004] OJ L96/26.
1313   Regulation 1592/2002 [2002] OJ L240/1.
1314   Regulation 1794/2006 [2006] OJ L341/3.
1315   Directive 2006/23 [2006] OJ L114/22.
1316   Regulation 216/2008 [2008] OJ L79/1 (as amended); detailed implementation in Regulation 748/2012 [2012] OJ L224/1 on airworthiness and environmental certifications of aircraft.
1317   Directive 2008/101 [2008] OJ L275/32, the validity of which was challenged unsuccessfully in Case C-366/10 *R (Air Transport Association of America and ors)* v *Secretary of State for Energy and Climate Change*, judgment of 21 December 2011, not yet reported.
1318   Regulation 300/2008 [2008] OJ L97/72 (replacing Regulation 2320/2002 [2002] OJ L355/1).

or inconvenienced by cancellation or long delay of flights.[1319] There is a list of carriers banned from operating, or made subject to specific operational restrictions, within the Union,[1320] which the Commission amends from time to time. The package is in the process of being updated and deepened by 'Single European Sky II' (SES II), a rolling programme already partly achieved.[1321] The Union has now entered into an agreement on enhanced cooperation with the ICAO.[1322]

11.214 One of the seven sectoral agreements with Switzerland signed in 1999 concerns air transport,[1323] as a result of which Switzerland is fully integrated into the Single European Sky. Owing to continuing dispute over the territory upon which it is situated (an issue distinct from that of sovereignty over the fortified town as it was in 1704), Gibraltar airport was, at Spanish insistence, long – and uniquely – excluded from any and all Community aviation measures. The dispute remains unresolved but the exclusion was lifted in 2006.[1324]

(g) Open skies agreements

11.215 With air transport with third countries long excluded from Community competence, there was a complex of international agreements between individual member states and third countries regulating mutual access of air services into and within their territories. A number of them with the United States (and the EU and US aviation markets accounting for about 60 per cent of global air traffic) were updated in a series of bilateral agreements in the 1990s – an exercise, to the cynic, of divide and conquer; but these were struck down by the Court of Justice in 2002 as *ultra vires* the member states for breach of article 10 EC (article 4(3) TFEU) and the Community legislation adopted in the

---

1319 Regulation 261/2004 [2004] OJ L46/1. The rights under the Directive are to be given an expansive interpretation (Cases C-402 and 432/07 *Sturgeon and ors* v *Condor Flugdienst and anor* [2009] ECR I-10923) and were tested to the full (in particular the defence in art. 5(3) which relieves carriers of the obligation to make compensation (but not reimbursement, assistance and free care entitlements) 'if … the cancellation is caused by extraordinary circumstances which could not have been avoided even if all reasonable measures had been taken') following the 2010 Eyjafjallajökull ash cloud; see Case C-12/11 *McDonagh* v *Ryanair*, pending.

1320 Regulation 2111/2005 [2005] OJ L344/15.

1321 Primarily by Regulation 1070/2009 [2009] OJ L300/34 (amending Regulations 549/2004, 550/2004, 551/2004 and 552/2004) 'to improve the performance and sustainability of the European aviation system', Regulation 1008/2009 [2009] OJ L309/51, and Regulation 1191/2010 [2010] OJ L333/6 (amending Regulation 1794/2006).

1322 Memorandum of Cooperation of 27 September 2010 between the European Union and the International Civil Aviation Organization [2011] OJ L232/2; provisionally in force from that date.

1323 Agreement of 21 June 1999 between the European Community and the Swiss Confederation on Air Transport [2002] OJ L114/73; in force 1 June 2002. As to the agreements see 14.87 below

1324 Ministerial Statement on Gibraltar airport agreed at Córdoba on 18 September 2006 ('Córdoba tripartite agreement').

field.[1325] Eventually the Community and the member states together signed an 'open skies' agreement with the United States in 2007[1326] which supplanted all existing bilateral agreements and entered into force in March 2008. This so-called 'first stage agreement' allows, in principle, unrestricted access for any and all Union and American flag carriers from their respective territories, via any intermediate point and to any point or points in the territory of the other and beyond ('behind, between and beyond rights'). But it is controversial for it is an unequal treaty: for all cargo service European carriers must operate to or from a point or points within the Union, but an American carrier need not operate from the United States, it may operate freely (point to point) within Europe.[1327] Further, foreign nationals may acquire no more than 25 per cent of the voting equity of an American airline, whilst American nationals may control up to 49 per cent of a Union airline.[1328] A second stage agreement, building upon the first, was signed in 2010;[1329] it is not yet ratified, waiting upon inter alia the (requisite)[1330] consent of the European Parliament, but has applied provisionally since its signature.[1331] An agreement on cooperation in the regulation of civil aviation safety between the the EU and the United States was signed in 2008 and entered into force in 2011.[1332] The exchange of passenger name records (PNR) data required by the American Department of Homeland Security has proved problematic.[1333] Compliance by American (and

---

1325 Case C-466/98 *Commission* v *United Kingdom* [2002] ECR I-9427; Case C-467/98 *Commission* v *Denmark* [2002] ECR I-9519; Case C-468/98 *Commission* v *Sweden* [2002] ECR I-9575; Case C-469/98 *Commission* v *Finland* [2002] ECR I-9627; Case C-471/98 *Commission* v *Belgium* [2002] ECR I-9681; Case C-472/98 *Commission* v *Luxembourg* [2002] ECR I-9741; Case C-475/98 *Commission* v *Austria* [2002] ECR I-9797; Case C-476/98 *Commission* v *Germany* [2002] ECR I-9855; and subsequently Case C-523/04 *Commission* v *Netherlands* [2007] ECR I-3267 ('Open Skies judgments').

1326 Air Transport Agreement of 25 (Brussels) and 30 (Washington) April 2007 [2007] OJ L134/4; in force 30 March 2008.

1327 *Ibid.* art. 3.

1328 *Ibid.* Annex 4.

1329 Air Transport Agreement of 24 June 2010 ('2010 Amending Protocol') [2010] OJ L223/3.

1330 TFEU, art. 218(6).

1331 In accordance with art. 9(1) of the Amending Protocol in conjunction with Decision 2010/465 [2010] OJ L223/1, art. 1(3).

1332 Agreement of 30 June 2008 between the United States and the European Community on Cooperation in the Regulation of Civil Aviation Safety [2011] OJ L291/3; in force 1 May 2011. A similar agreement exists with Canada: Agreement of 6 May 2009 on Civil Aviation Safety between the European Community and Canada [2009] OJ L153/11; in force 19 July 2011.

1333 The Council decision approving a 2004 agreement (Agreement between the European Community and and the United States on the Processing and Transfer of PNR Data by Air Carriers to the US Department of Homeland Security [2004] OJ L183/84) providing for the exchange of PNR data was annulled by the Court of Justice for lack of competence; Cases C-317 and 318/04 *Parliament* v *Council and Commission* (Passenger Name Records) [2006] ECR I-4721. Subsequent agreements (see now Agreement of 23 and 26 July 2007 between the United States and the European Union on the Processing and Tansfer of PNR Data by Air Carriers to the US Department of Homeland Security [2007] OJ L204/18, '2007 PNR Agreement') fared better. Equivalent agreements now exist with other countries. Sharing of PNR data amongst air carriers within the Union is regulated by Directive 2004/82 [2004] OJ L261/24; significant new rules are now proposed; see COM(2011) 32 final.

other) carriers with Union carbon emissions rules which begin to bite in 2012[1334] may prove more so.

11.216 Iceland and Norway acceded to the EU–United States agreement in 2011.[1335] Similar open sky agreements between the Union and a number of third countries (amongst them Canada (signed 2009, not yet in force), Brazil (signed 2011), Chile, Morocco, Indonesia, Australia and New Zealand) are in the pipeline.

2. Competition rules

11.217 Union competition rules apply to transport. Prior to 2004 the sector was excluded from the general operation of the competition rules of the EC Treaty[1336] which were applied to it by means of, and in accordance with, specific measures.[1337] In 2004 these were altered to bring transport within the general enforcement procedures of Regulation 1/2003.[1338] Tramp vessel services, maritime cabotage and commercial air transport between a Union airport and a third country were originally excluded[1339] but the exclusions were lifted in in 2004[1340] and 2006.[1341] Specific legislation therefore survives for rail, road and inland waterways only,[1342] which, owing to 'the distinctive features of transport' in those sectors,[1343] certain types of technical agreements (standardisation, pooling of staff and equipment, complementary or combined operations, single mode of transport on appropriate routes, coordination of timetables for connecting routes, grouping of single consignments, uniform rules of structure of tariffs and conditions of application)[1344] and certain agreements between small and medium sized undertakings[1345] are 'excepted' from the competition rules.

1334　See Directive 2008/101 and the unsuccessful (and ill-spirited) legal challenge to it by American and Canadian carriers in Case C-366/10 *R (Air Transport Association of America and ors)* v *Secretary of State for Energy and Climate Change*, judgment of 21 December 2011, not yet reported. In October 2011 the House of Representatives approved a bill (H.R. 2594: European Union Emissions Trading Scheme Prohibition Act of 2011) to bar American carriers from complying with the ETS; at the time of writing the Chinese Civil Aviation Administration (CAAC) is proposing to do the same.

1335　Agreement of 16 (Luxembourg) and 21 (Oslo) June 2011 [2011] OJ L283/3.

1336　Regulation 141/62 [1962] JO 2751.

1337　Regulation 1017/68 [1968] JO L175/1 (rail, road and inland waterways); Regulation 4056/86 [1986] OJ L378/4 (maritime transport; now repealed); Regulation 3975/87 [1987] OJ L374/1 (air transport; now repealed).

1338　Regulation 1/2003 [2003] OJ L1/1, arts 36, 38, 39. As to Regulation 1/2003 see 13.86–13.102 below.

1339　*Ibid.* art. 32 (now repealed).

1340　Regulation 411/2004 [2004] OJ L68/1 (air transport to third countries).

1341　Regulation 1419/2006 [2006] OJ L269/1 (tramp services, maritime cabotage).

1342　Regulation 169/2009 [2009] OJ L61/1, a consolidation of Regulation 1017/68, n. 1337 above.

1343　Regulation 169/2009, Preamble, 3rd indent.

1344　*Ibid.* art. 2.

1345　*Ibid.* art. 3.

There is a specialist block exemption for agreements within liner shipping consortia.[1346] The Commission has the power to adopt block exemptions in the air transport sector[1347] and has done so in the past, but none now exists, although general block exemption Regulations apply. The state aids rules apply as normally, except that the compatibility of aid for public service obligations is written into the Treaties,[1348] the normal ceiling of €200,000 (over three years) for automatic exemption from the exclusion on article 107 on *de minimis* grounds is lowered to €100,000 in the road transport sector[1349] and the exemption for subvention of services of general economic interest does not apply to land transport and applies only sparingly to maritime and air transport.[1350] Yet the Commission adopts a hands-on (and generous) approach to directing public intervention in transport, and guidelines are commonly adopted.[1351] The merger rules apply as normally, but it is perhaps worth noting that two of only three Commission prohibitions of a merger since the present rules entered into force in 2004 were in the field of air transport.[1352]

1346 Regulation 906/2009 [2009] OJ L256/31. See also Guidelines on the Application of Article 81 of the EC Treaty to Maritime Transport Services [2008] OJ C245/2. On block exemptions see 13.60–13.62 below.

1347 Regulation 487/2009 [2009] OJ L148/1, a consolidation of Regulation 3976/87 [1987] OJ L374/9.

1348 TFEU, art. 93 (ex art. 73 EC). As to public service obligations under the competition rules see 13.142–13.147 below.

1349 Regulation 1998/2006 [2006] OJ L379/5, art. 2(2). As to exemption in the sphere of state aids see 13.168 below.

1350 Decision 2012/21 [2012] OJ L7/3 on the application of article 106(2) of the TFEU to state aid in the form of public service compensation granted to certain undertakings entrusted with the operation of SGEIs; see 13.167 below.

1351 See e.g., Community Guidelines on State Aid to Maritime Transport [2004] OJ C13/3; Community Guidelines on State Aid for Railway Undertakings [2008] OJ C184/13.

1352 Case COMP/M.4439 *Ryanair/Aer Lingus* [2008] OJ C47/9 (summary publication); Case COMP/M.5830 *Olympic/Aegean Airlines*, decision of 26 January 2011, not yet published. As to merger control see 13.131–13.141 below.

12

THE FREE MOVEMENT OF CAPITAL

A. GENERAL	12.01	C. THE PROHIBITION	12.09
B. SCOPE	12.06	D. DEROGATION	12.11

A. GENERAL

12.01   The free movement of capital is an essential component of a single, integrated market, in (reciprocal) terms both of access to adequate capital to fuel investment and growth and of optimal (liberalised) conditions in which capital markets might wish to invest. This was recognised from the beginning, capital being one of the four freedoms at the core of the common market. Yet whilst the EEC Treaty addressed capital in much the same manner and language it did the other freedoms, its course was to develop very differently: and from a much slower start it has now, in ways, overtaken and surpassed the other freedoms.

12.02   Unlike the provisions on the free movement of goods, persons and services, the original Chapter of the EEC Treaty on capital (articles 67–73) produced, for practical purposes, no direct effect and could not be interpreted constructively otherwise at the end of the transitional period.[1] Even the standstill provision, used purposively by the Court of Justice for other Treaty freedoms to derive significant obligations for the member states, was uncommonly feeble ('Member States shall endeavour to avoid introducing ... any new exchange restrictions on the movement of capital ... and shall endeavour not to make existing rules more restrictive')[2] and created no directly effective rights.[3] Here the Court showed a deference to the member states it denied them with other Treaty freedoms, a function both of the cautious language of the Treaty and implicit recognition that the movement of capital is locked into economic and monetary policies, addressed (then rudimentarily) elsewhere in the Treaty,[4] and so could

---

1   Case 203/80 *Criminal proceedings against Casati* [1981] ECR 2595.
2   EEC Treaty, art. 71.
3   Case 203/80 *Casati*, n. 1 above.
4   EEC Treaty, arts 103–9.

be liberalised only as and when national policies began to knit together. It is also inextricably bound up with the economic and monetary union which would come later.

The movement of money may, however, be a function of the effective exercise of **12.03** another Treaty freedom. For example, the acquisition and disposal of immovable property on the territory of another member state by a non-resident is normally an investment, so to be governed by the rules on movement of capital.[5] But its acquisition and use in other circumstances may be a precondition,[6] or corollary,[7] of the right of establishment.[8] Equally a worker's right of residence extends (once in employment) to 'ownership of the housing he needs'.[9] Even acquisition of shareholdings in a foreign company, normally simply a financial investment,[10] is a matter for establishment if the purpose is to acquire a definite influence (*influence certaine*; *ein sicherer Einfluss*) over its activities and decision-making.[11] And, of course, a Treaty right to passive services would be meaningless were the recipient unable to take with him funds adequate to pay for them.[12] Where money is transferred to serve these purposes it is a case not of a capital movement but of a 'current payment' – consideration in support of the free movement of goods, persons or services, sometimes characterised as a fifth freedom. Payments were 'freed from all restrictions'[13] and addressed by a later provision of the Treaty[14] which *was* directly effective and so could not be impeded by exchange controls.[15] It was spliced to the chapter on capital by Maastricht, renamed 'Capital and Payments',[16] and so it remains today.[17]

---

5 Case C-302/97 *Konle* v *Republik Österreich* [1999] ECR I-3099, at para. 22; Case C-423/98 *Albore* [2000] ECR I-5965, at para. 14.
6 Case 203/80 *Casati*, n. 1 above, at para. 8.
7 Case C-302/97 *Konle*, n. 5 above, at para. 22.
8 See TFEU, art. 50 (the legal base for measures on establishment): in order to attain the freedom of establishment the Union is to 'enabl[e] a national of one Member State to acquire and use land and buildings situated in the territory of another Member State'.
9 Regulation 492/2011 [2011] OJ L141/1, art. 9(1).
10 Cases C-436 and 437/08 *Haribo Lakritzen Hans Riegel Betriebs and anor* v *Finanzamt Linz*, [2011] ECR I-305, at para. 35 and case law cited.
11 Case C-446/04 *Test Claimants in the FII Group Litigation* v *Commissioners of Inland Revenue* [2006] ECR I-11753, at para. 37.
12 Cases 286/82 and 26/83 *Luisi and Carbone* v *Ministero del Tesoro* [1984] ECR 377.
13 EEC Treaty, art. 67(2).
14 *Ibid.* art. 106.
15 Cases 286/82 and 26/83 *Luisi & Carbone*, n. 12 above. This was not necessarily to be so, the member states having by art. 106 merely 'undertake[n] to authorise ... payments' and 'undertake[n] not to introduce ... any new restrictions on transfers connected with ... invisible transactions'. The rule on payments applied to all four freedoms (goods, persons, services and capital) but became directly effective only with their 'liberalis[ation] pursuant to this Treaty'; the movement of capital, lagging behind the other three, was for a time the odd one out. For the distinction between arts 67 and 106 see Case 308/86 *Ministère public* v *Lambert* [1988] ECR 377.
16 EC Treaty (pre-Amsterdam), arts 67–73.
17 TFEU, arts 63–6.

12.04 As for capital within its Treaty meaning, following early, modest legislative forays,[18] a Directive was adopted in 1988 'for the implementation of Article 67 of the Treaty'[19] as part of the 1992 programme, which *was* directly affective and 'brought about the full liberalization of capital movements'.[20] Capital was therefore the only of the four freedoms to be achieved (albeit 20 years late) in the manner envisaged in the original Treaty, by means of a programme of legislation.

12.05 In light of this progress the chapter on capital was replaced completely by Maastricht with effect from 1 January 1994[21] (so allowing the Directive 88/361 dust to settle). Notwithstanding significant power of derogation afforded the member states[22] the new article 73b EC (article 63 TFEU) was of itself also directly effective.[23] Whilst *Sanz de Lera* involved criminal charges for leaving the country in possession of currency in banknotes beyond the amount permitted, and so (successful) reliance upon the vertical direct effect of article 63, there is nothing in the language of article 63 ('all restrictions on the movement of capital ... shall be prohibited') and nothing in *Sanz de Lera* which limits that direct effect. Nor is it difficult to envisage circumstances in which private persons – banks and other financial institutions certainly, or even individuals – could by unilateral conduct hinder the movement of capital. In the *Volkswagen Law* case[24] it was suggested that an agreement between the Volkswagen workforce and trade unions hindered the movement of capital in a manner contrary to article 63. The Court did not reject the argument outright, finding instead the agreement to have been homologated by the federal Parliament in the form of a law, the manifestation of state power *par excellence*,[25] and proceeded upon that basis. The horizontal direct effect of article 63 therefore remains an open question.

---

18 (First) Directive for the implementation of Article 67 of the Treaty [1960] JO 919; (Second) Directive 63/21 [1963] JO 62.

19 Directive 88/361 [1988] OJ L178/5, required to be implemented for the most part by 1 July 1990 but Spain, Greece, Ireland and Portugal were allowed extensions; arts 5 and 6(2). It was flanked by a Directive on credit institutions, Directive 89/646 [1989] OJ L386/1, the latter now replaced by Directive 2006/48 [2006] OJ L177/1.

20 Cases C-358 and 416/93 *Ministerio Fiscal* v *Bordessa and ors* [1995] ECR I-361, at para. 17.

21 EC Treaty (per-Amsterdam), arts 73a–73g.

22 See below.

23 Cases C-163 etc./ 94 *Criminal proceedings against Sanz de Lera and ors* [1995] ECR I-4821.

24 Case C-122/05 *Commission* v *Germany* [2007] ECR I-8995.

25 *Ibid.* at para. 27.

B. SCOPE

Like goods, what constitutes capital or payments is not defined in the Treaties. **12.06**
Directive 88/361 set out a 'classification' (or nomenclature)[26] of 'capital movements' upon which member states were required to abolish restrictions between
persons resident in member states,[27] as follows:

- direct investments:
  - establishment and extension of branches or new undertakings
    belonging solely to the person providing the capital, and the acquisi-
    tion in full of existing undertakings;
  - participation in new or existing undertaking with a view to estab-
    lishing or maintaining lasting economic links;
  - long-term loans with a view to establishing or maintaining lasting
    economic links;
  - reinvestment of profits with a view to maintaining lasting economic
    links;
- investment in immovable property;
- operations in securities (in both capital and money markets);
- operations in units of collective investment undertakings;
- operations in current and deposit accounts;
- credits related to commercial transactions or to provision of services;
- loans;
- sureties, guarantees, rights of pledge;
- transfers in performance of insurance contracts;
- personal capital movements:
  - loans, gifts and endowments, dowries, inheritances and legacies,
    settlement of debts, death duties, royalties;
- physical import and export of financial assets;
- other captital movements;
  - death duties, damages, refunds, royalties, patents, designs, trade
    marks, inventions and assignment thereof, miscellaneous.[28]

The list is exemplicative, is not exhaustive,[29] and although overtaken by article
63 TFEU it remains in the absence of Treaty definitions useful and may be
prayed in aid (it has 'indicative value') for the purpose of defining what

---

26 Case C-302/97 *Konle* v *Republik Österreich* [1999] ECR I-3099, at para. 22.
27 Directive 88/361, art. 1.
28 *Ibid.* art. 1 and Annex I.
29 E.g., Case C-35/98 *Staatssecretaris van Financiën* v *Verkooijen* [2000] ECR I-4071.

constitutes a capital movement.[30] In fact, some of it could be better characterised as payments, a distinction which loses much of its importance with the
Maastricht reorganisation.

12.07 Like other Treaty freedoms a wholly internal rule applies: article 63 does not
apply to capital movement absent a material effect upon the movement across
frontiers.[31] The determining factor is movement of capital assets between two
territories, neither residence nor nationality of the person making or receiving
the transfer of any relevance. So a migrant worker taking out a loan in his or her
host member state engages no Treaty rights (other than article 18 TFEU, if
necessary). But capital differs from the other freedoms (and here article 63
marks a significant advance on Directive 88/361) in that the rules apply not
only to the movement of capital between member states but to that between
member states and a third country. This was made express in the 1994 changes
('all restrictions on the movement of capital [payments] between Member
States and between Member States and third countries shall be prohibited')[32]
and confirmed straightaway by the Court, *Sanz de Lera*[33] involving in part the
physical export of *peseta* banknotes by individual travellers to Switzerland and
to Turkey. Thus the Union extends its extraterritorial reach to authority over the
movement of capital in ways in which in other freedoms it still strives (goods,
services) or has only scratched the surface (workers, establishment). It goes to
the integrity of the internal market so far as capital movements are concerned,
without which the credibility of the single currency would be undermined.

12.08 However, whilst in principle liberalised, movement of capital and payments to
and from third countries may be restricted by the institutions in a number of
ways which they cannot as regards movement within the Union. The Parliament and Council may adopt measures regulating the movement of capital to or
from third countries in respect of direct investment (including investment in
real estate), establishment, the provision of financial services and the admission
of securities to capital markets,[34] and the Council may across the field, by
unanimity, adopt measures which 'step backwards' from the liberalisation of
capital movement to and from third countries.[35] Where such movements cause
or threaten to cause, in exceptional circumstances, serious difficulties for the

---

30   Case C-222/97 *Trummer and Mayer* [1999] ECR I-1661; Case C-367/98 *Commission v Portugal* (Golden
     Shares) [2002] ECR I-4731; Case C-122/05 *Commission v Germany*, n. 24 above.
31   Case C-11/07 *Eckelkamp and ors v Belgische Staat* [2008] ECR I 6845, at para. 39; Case C-43/07 *Arens-Sikken v
     Staatssecretaris van Financiën* [2008] ECR I 6887, at para. 30; Case C-67/08 *Block v Finanzamt Kaufbeuren*
     [2009] ECR I-883, at para. 21.
32   EC Treaty, art. 73b(1) (73b(2)) (now art. 63(1) (63(2)) TFEU).
33   Cases C-163 etc./ 94 *Sanz de Lera*, n. 23 above; also Case C-101/05 *Skatteverket v A* [2007] ECR I-11531.
34   TFEU, art. 64(2).
35   *Ibid.* art. 64(3).

operation of economic and monetary union the Council may take such safe-guard measures as are 'strictly necessary' for a period not exceeding six months.[36] Authority to adopt sanctions in the sphere of capital movements and payments in order to prevent and combat terrorism was written into the Treaties by Amsterdam[37] and refined by Lisbon[38] as a specific subset of a more general power to adopt restrictive measures against third countries;[39] any such measure must include 'necessary' legal safeguards.[40] And there is some leeway permitted the member states still: national (or Community) measures on the movement of capital to and from third countries in the same categories as are subject to Parliament/Council regulation[41] which were in force on 31 December 1993 may remain in force,[42] and the Commission or Council (by unanimity, if the Commission has failed to act within three months) may at the request of a member state adopt a decision declaring a restrictive tax measure adopted by it concerning one or more third countries to be compatible with the Treaties insofar as justified by a Union objective and compatible with the proper functioning of the internal market.[43]

C. THE PROHIBITION

The original prohibition applied (however imperfectly) to 'restrictions on the movement of capital' belonging to Union residents and 'any discrimination based on the nationality or on the place of residence of the parties or on the place where such capital is invested'.[44] The Maastricht amendments abandoned the reference to discrimination, the prohibition now set out clearly and suc-cinctly in article 63 TFEU: **12.09**

1. Within the framework of the provisions set out in this Chapter, all restrictions on the movement of capital between Member States and between Member States and third countries shall be prohibited.

---

36 *Ibid.* art. 66.
37 EC Treaty, art. 60.
38 TFEU, art. 75. See 14.112 below.
39 *Ibid.* art. 215 (ex art. 301 EC); see 14.112 below.
40 *Ibid.* art. 75, 3rd para.
41 See n. 34 above and accompanying text.
42 TFEU, art. 64(1); for Bulgaria, Estonia and Hungary the date is 31 December 1999.
43 *Ibid.* art. 65(4).
44 EEC Treaty, art. 67.

2. Within the framework of the provisions set out in this Chapter, all restrictions on payments between Member States and between Member States and third countries shall be prohibited.

Notwithstanding the change, the Court followed the approach of the other freedoms and identified and categorised restrictions which, first, discriminate, directly or indirectly, upon the basis of nationality. This occurs more frequently than with other freedoms, for example the acquisition of immovable property, or of shares, limited in a variety of ways by reference to nationality (direct discrimination) or residence (indirect discrimination).[45] It is no longer possible to discriminate on the basis of a currency itself as amongst the 17 member states in the eurozone. Discrimination in matters of taxation is commonplace and, to an extent, lawful. But as with the rules on the free movement of goods, its direct effect requires that taxes levied in contravention of article 63 be recoverable[46] unless it is shown that they have already been passed on direct to a buyer.[47] Second, the Court has identified restrictions in national measurës which, although genuinely non-discriminatory, constitute nevertheless measures which impede, or may impede, the movement of capital or have, or are likely to have, a deterrent or dissuasive effect upon cross-frontier transactions.[48] This includes any home national measure likely to dissuade capital investment in another member state[49] – indeed, subject to legislative intervention to the contrary, anywhere offshore. There has been no recognition of a *de minimis* exception to article 63, but it seems more likely than not that in the case of an insubstantial or remote hindrance to movement of capital or payments the Court would apply the 'too uncertain or indirect' or 'hypothetical' exculpation it has recognised in the context of the right of establishment.[50]

---

45   E.g., Case C-302/97 *Konle v Republik Österreich* [1999] ECR I-3099; Case C-423/98 *Albore* [2000] ECR I-5965; Case C-367/98 *Commission v Portugal* (Golden Shares) [2002] ECR I-4731.

46   Cases C-397 and 410/98 *Metallgesellschaft and ors v Commissioners of Inland Revenue and anor* [2001] ECR I-1727; Case C-446/04 *Test Claimants in the FII Group Litigation v Commissioners of Inland Revenue* [2006] ECR I-11753.

47   Case C-398/09 *Lady & Kid and ors v Skatteministeriet*, judgment of 6 September 2011, not yet reported, at paras 18–26.

48   Case 157/85 *Brugnoni and Ruffinengo v Cassa di Risparmio de Genova e Imperia* [1986] ECR 2013; Case C-484/93 *Svensson and Gustavsson v Ministre du Logement et de l'Urbanisme* [1995] ECR I-3955; Case C-222/97 *Trummer and Mayer* [1999] ECR I-1661; Case C-35/98 *Staatssecretaris van Financiën v Verkooijen* [2000] ECR I-4071; Case C-478/98 *Commission v Belgium* [2000] ECR I-7587; Case C-436/00 *X and Y v Riksskatteverket* [2000] ECR I-10829; Case C-367/98 *Golden Shares*, n. 45 above; Case C-174/04 *Commission v Italy* [2005] ECR I-4933; Case C-531/06 *Commission v Italy* [2009] ECR I-4103.

49   Case C-319/02 *Manninen* [2004] ECR I-7477; Case C-292/04 *Meilicke and ors v Finanzamt Bonn-Innenstadt* [2007] ECR I-1835; Case C-271/09 *Commission v Poland*, judgment of 21 December 2011, not yet reported.

50   Case C-190/98 *Graf v Filzmoser Maschinenbau* [2000] ECR I-493, at para. 25 ('too uncertain or indirect'); Case C-211/08 *Commission v Spain* [2010] ECR I-5267, at para. 73 ('hypothetical'); see 11.27 above. A kernel of this approach to art. 63 may be detected in Case C-377/07 *Finanzamt Speyer-Germersheim v STEKO Industriemontage* [2009] ECR I-299.

The liberalisation of capital movements does not mean the area is wholly free **12.10** from regulation. At Union level particular note should be taken of measures adopted and designed to hinder those who would take advantage of it for less worthy ends. First and foremost is a 2005 Directive 'on the prevention of the use of the financial system for the purpose of money laundering and terrorist financing'[51] which applies to credit and financial institutions, prohibits anonymous accounts or passbooks and requires 'customer due diligence', reporting obligations, the keeping of records and the supervision and licensing of currency exchange offices (authorisation required for the movement of capital or payments normally being a breach of article 63).[52] It is bolstered by further Community measures on control of cash entering or leaving the Union[53] and information on the payer accompanying transfer of funds,[54] on payment services[55] and a number of measures adopted under the third (Justice and Home Affairs) pillar of the pre-Lisbon Treaty on European Union[56] which in due course will be rendered as article 288 instruments. Post-Lisbon, the areas of particularly serious crime with a cross-border dimension in which the Union may establish minimum rules concerning the definition of criminal offences and sanctions include money laundering and counterfeiting of means of payment,[57] and crimes affecting the financial interests of the Union are amongst those which may be made subject to the jurisdiction of the European Public Prosecutor's Office,[58] should that post ever come into being.

D. DEROGATION

The Treaties provide expressly for derogation from the prohibition of article 63 **12.11** in a manner like, yet unlike, those which qualify other freedoms. First, member states may for purposes of taxation distinguish between and treat differently taxpayers who are not in the same situation with regard to their place of residence or with regard to the place where their capital is invested,[59] but only if

---

51 Directive 2005/60 [2005] OJ L309/15. It replaced two earlier, feebler, measures, Directive 91/308 [1991] OJ L166/77 on money laundering (First Directive), substantially amended by Directive 2001/97 [2001] OJ L344/76 (Second Directive).
52 E.g., Cases C-358 and 416/93 *Ministerio Fiscal* v *Bordessa and ors* [1995] ECR I-361; Case C-302/97 *Konle* v *Republik Österreich* [1999] ECR I-3099.
53 Regulation 1889/2005 [2005] OJ L309/9.
54 Regulation 1781/2006 [2006] OJ L345/1.
55 Directive 2007/ 64 [2007] OJ 319/1 (Payment Services Directive).
56 Joint Action 98/699/JHA [1998] OJ L333/1 on money laundering; Framework Decision 2001/500/JHA [2001] OJ L182/1 on money laundering; Convention of 29 May 2000 on mutual assistance in criminal matters [2000] OJ C197/3.
57 TFEU, art. 83(1).
58 *Ibid.* art. 86(1).
59 *Ibid.* art. 65(1)(a).

the situation at hand is not objectively comparable[60] or if it can be justified by reference to overriding reasons in the general interest in relation to the coherence of the system of taxation or the effectiveness of fiscal supervision,[61] provided that a direct link be established between the tax advantage concerned and the offsetting of that advantage by a particular tax levy.[62] So, for example, a member state cannot tax dividends which go to another member state ('outbound dividends') at a rate higher than that of dividends which remain in the country ('domestic dividends') unless the other member state compensates for the higher taxation on the outbound dividends.[63] Similarly, a member state cannot tax dividends coming from another member state ('inbound dividends') at a higher rate or in any manner less favourably than domestic dividends.[64] The Commission has felt obliged to initiate more than 40 infringement proceedings against member states in this area.[65] Secondly, member states may 'take all requisite measures' (a) to prevent infringements of national law and regulations, 'in particular' in the field of taxation and the prudential supervision of financial institutions; (b) to lay down procedures for the declaration of capital movements for purposes of administrative or statistical information; or (c) which are justified on grounds of public policy or public security.[66] Further, any Treaty-compatible restriction on the right of establishment will set aside any impediment to capital movement which (reasonably) accompanies it.[67] In a clear echo of article 36, none of these measures and procedures may constitute either a means of arbitrary discrimination or a disguised restriction on the free movement of capital and payments.[68]

12.12 Although these are of a more open-ended texture than the derogation provisions of other Treaty freedoms, the Court has interpreted them restrictively

---

60 Case C-279/93 *Finanzamt Köln-Altstadt* v *Schumacker* [1995] ECR I-225.

61 Case C-204/90 *Bachmann* v *Belgian State* [1992] ECR I-249; Case C-319/02 *Manninen* [2004] ECR I-7477, at para. 42; Cases C-155 and 157/08 *X and Passenheim-van Schoot* v *Staatssecretaris van Financiën* [2009] ECR I-5093, at para. 45 and case law cited; Case C-233/09 *Dijkman and Dijkman-Lavaleije* v *Belgische Staat* [2010] ECR I-6645, at paras 54 and 58.

62 Case C-319/02 *Manninen, ibid.*, at para. 42; Case C-418/07 *Société Papillon* v *Ministère du Budget, des Comptes publics et de la Fonction publique* [2008] ECR I-8947, at para. 43 and case law cited; Case C-233/09 *Dijkman and Dijkman-Lavaleije, ibid.*, at para. 55.

63 Case C-487/08 *Commission* v *Spain* [2010] ECR I-4843.

64 Case C-35/98 *Staatssecretaris van Financiën* v *Verkooijen* [2000] ECR I-4071; Case C-446/04 *Test Claimants in the FII Group Litigation* v *Commissioners of Inland Revenue* [2006] ECR I-11753.

65 SEC(2010) 1576, pp. 7–8.

66 TFEU, art. 65(1)(b). The protection of public health falls within public policy; Case C-531/06 *Commission* v *Italy* [2009] ECR I-4103.

67 TFEU, art. 65(2).

68 *Ibid.* art. 65(3).

and in much the same manner.[69] In building its approach it has drawn heavily, transparently, and admittedly from the case law on the movement of persons:

> [W]hile Member States are still, in principle, free to determine the requirements of public policy and public security in the light of their national needs, those grounds must, in the Community context and, in particular, as derogations from the fundamental principle of free movement of capital, be interpreted strictly, so that their scope cannot be determined unilaterally by each Member State without any control by the Community institutions. Thus, public policy and public security may be relied on only if there is a genuine and sufficiently serious threat to a fundamental interest of society. Moreover, those derogations must not be misapplied so as, in fact, to serve purely economic ends. Further, any person affected by a restrictive measure based on such a derogation must have access to legal redress.

> Second, measures which restrict the free movement of capital may be justified on public-policy and public-security grounds only if they are necessary for the protection of the interests which they are intended to guarantee and only in so far as those objectives cannot be attained by less restrictive measures.[70]

In keeping with other Treaty freedoms, the Court has recognised that non-discriminatory impediments to the movement of capital and payments may be justified by overriding requirements in the general interest.[71] The overall result is one which, again, fits comfortably as an expression of permitted derogation in the context of any of the Treaty freedoms: **12.13**

> The free movement of capital, as a fundamental principle of the Treaty, may be restricted only by national rules which are justified by reasons referred to in Article [65(1)] of the Treaty or by overriding requirements of the general interest and which are applicable to all persons and undertakings pursuing an activity in the territory of the host Member State. Furthermore, in order to be so justified, the national legislation must be suitable for securing the objective which it pursues and must not go beyond what is necessary in order to attain it, so as to accord with the principle of proportionality.[72]

Whist article 63 liberalises intra- and extra-Union capital movement equally, the Court is more likely to find justification in national measures which affect

---

69 E.g., Case C-54/99 *Association Eglise de scientologie de Paris and anor* v *Premier Ministre* [2000] ECR I-1355; Case C-35/98 *Verkooijen*, n. 64 above; Case C-478/98 *Commission* v *Belgium* [2000] ECR I-7587.

70 Case C-54/99 *Association Eglise de scientologie de Paris and anor* v *Premier Ministre* [2000] ECR I-1355, at paras 17–18.

71 E.g., Cases C-163 etc./94 *Criminal proceedings against Sanz de Lera and ors* [1995] ECR I-4821; Case C-54/99 *Eglise de scientologie, ibid.*; C-503/99 *Commission* v *Belgium* [2002] ECR I-4809; Case C-101/05 *Skatteverket* v *A* [2007] ECR I-11531; Case C-531/06 *Commission* v *Italy* [2009] ECR I-4103.

72 Case C-367/98 *Commission* v *Portugal* (Golden Shares) [2002] ECR I-4731, at para. 49.

external capital movements, for the common rules and framework of cooperation amongst the member states (by which the Court often measures equivalence and proportionality) cannot be assured outside the Union.[73]

---

73 See e.g., Case C-101/05 *Skatteverket* v *X* [2007] ECR I-11531.

13

COMPETITION

A. GENERAL

13.01 Title VII of the TFEU is entitled 'Common Rules on Competition, Taxation and Approximation of Laws'. It is divided into three chapters:

(1) rules on competition (articles 101–9), in turn divided into two sections, on rules applying to undertakings and to aids granted by states;
(2) tax provisions (articles 100–3); and
(3) approximation of laws (articles 114–18).

The link between tax provisions and the rules on approximation (or harmonisation) of law, on the one hand, and competition, on the other, is an increasingly tenuous one. Certainly the former have acquired a far more direct nexus with the four freedoms, particularly that of goods, and are discussed above in that context.[1] The present chapter will consider the Union rules on competition only.

1. 'Competition law'

13.02 Article 3(f) of the original EEC Treaty prescribed as one of the activities of the Community 'a system ensuring that competition in the common market is not distorted'. 'Competition law' can, and does, have two distinct meanings, and it is important to understand which is here addressed. Competition law may comprise rules addressing 'unfair competition', that is, abusive marketing practices such as passing off (and other breaches of intellectual property rights), deception, use of substandard materials, misleading advertising or sales, generally deceptive or sharp practices which work to the direct injury of the buyer or consumer. Although addressed in the Preamble to the TFEU,[2] these fall only tangentially within Union activities, and generally in the context of rules adopted under articles 114/115 for the harmonisation of national legislation necessary for the functioning of the internal market.[3] In its more widely understood sense,

---

1 See 10.15–10.22 and 10.68–10.77 above.
2 The removal of existing obstacles which divide Europe 'calls for concerted action in order to guarantee... fair competition' (4th recital); for 'fair' other language versions use words (*loyauté*, *Redlichkeit*, *eerlijkheid*) which mean honest or upright.
3 E.g., harmonising Directives on general product safety (Directive 2001/95 [220] OJ L11/4), misleading and comparative advertising (Directive 2006/114 [2006] OJ L376/21), combating late payment in commercial transactions (Directive 2000/35 [2000] OJ L200/35; replaced by Directive 2011/7 [2011] OJ L48/1 from March 2013), consumer credit agreements (Directive 2008/48 [2008] OJ L133/66), civil liability and insurance in motoring (Directive 2009/103 [2009] OJ L263/11), injunctions for the protection of consumers' interests (Directive 2009/22 [2009] OJ L110/30) and consumer protection in 'off-premises' and 'distance' contracts (Directive 2011/83 [2011] OJ L304/64; 'Consumer Rights Directive', a consolidation of earlier Directives; to be implemented by June 2014). But see the important general Directive on unfair competition adopted in 2005: Directive 2005/29 [2005] OJ L149/22 (Unfair Commercial Practices Directive). Consumer protection is an

competition law addresses distortions of the market engineered by and amongst producers or suppliers for their economic benefit; these too work to the detriment of the buyer or consumer, but *also* to the detriment of the market itself, which, in the (neo-)liberal economics to which the Treaties are wedded, is the motive force which maximises consumer welfare. Here competition is not 'unfair', it is 'distorted' (*faussée; verfälscht*).[4] The fields are not unrelated, and both may be the subject of the same legislation: in Hungary[5] and Poland,[6] for example, the 'competition laws' address and regulate both; in Germany, Greece and Finland, by comparison, there are distinct statutes addressing 'unfair competition'[7] and 'restraints/protection of competition'.[8] But competition law in the Union is addressed to the latter: rules regulating distortions to the competitive forces of the free market.[9] It is a new discipline: in its modern incarnation it takes shape from the antitrust law promulgated in the United States in the 1890s, and, virtually unknown in Europe until the second half of the last century,[10] it has now been embraced and adopted not only by the Union but, applying concurrently with the Union rules, by the law of every European country. So universal has competition law become that China adopted equivalent legislation in 2007[11] and saw its so-called first competition case in 2009.[12]

---

area of shared Union/member state competences (TFEU, art. 4(2)(f)) but the Union's is essentially a supporting role (TFEU, art. 169 (ex art. 153 EC)) and little has come of it directly.

4   EEC Treaty, art. 3(f) (art. 3(1)(g) EC).

5   1996. évi LVII. törvény a tisztességtelen piaci magatartás és a versenykorlátozás tilalmáról.

6   Ustawa z dnia 16 lutego 2007 r. o ochronie konkurencji i konsumentów.

7   Gesetz gegen den unlauteren Wettbewerb vom 3. Juli 2004, BGBl. 2010 I S. 254, replacing the venerable Gesetz gegen den unlauteren Wettbewerb vom 7. Juni 1909, RGBl. 1909 S. 499; Νόμος 146/1914 περί αθεμίτου ανταγωνισμού; Kuluttajansuojalaki (38/1978).

8   Gesetz gegen Wettbewerbsbeschränkungen vom 27. Juli 1957, BGBl. 1957 I S. 1081; Neufassung vom 26. August 1998, BGBl. 2005 I S. 2114; hereinafter the 'GWB'; Νόμος 703/1977 περί ελέγχου μονοπωλίων και ολιγοπωλίων και προστασίας του ελευθέρου ανταγωνισμού, ΦΕΚ Α' 278; Kilpailulaki (948/2011), replacing Laki Kilpailunrajoituksista (480/1992).

9   A hybrid of the two spheres of competition law may be said to reside in Directive 2003/6 [2003] OJ L96/16 which prohibits insider dealing and market manipulation.

10 The pathbreakers were the Germans, if not wholly by choice. As part of the US-led 'decartelisation and decentralisation' programme, the three Western occupying powers introduced competition laws modelled on the Sherman Act in 1947 (Law No. 56 of 1947), *Military Government Gazette, Germany, US Zone* of 1 April 1947, p. 2; Military Government Ordinance No. 78 of 1947, *Military Government Gazette, Germany, British Zone of Control* No. 16, p. 412 (the two being identical, the American and British zones having been fused and 'treated as a single area for all economic purposes' from 1 January 1947; Memorandum of Agreement of 2 December 1946, Cmnd 6984, para. 2); l'ordonnance No. 96 du 9 juin 1947, *JO du Commandment en Chef Français en Allemagne* No. 2, p. 784. With the end of the occupation regime in 1955 they were homologated as federal law (Gesetz vom 24. März 1955 betreffend das Protokoll vom 23 Oktober 1954 über die Beendigung des Besatzungsregimes in der BRD, BGBl. 1955 II S. 213; in force 5 May 1955 (Souveränitätsstichtag)) and, then leavened with native ordoliberalism, significantly informed the GWB which replaced them and entered into force on 1 January 1958 – as did the Rome Treaties. With the zeal of the converted, it was the Germans who insisted most strongly upon inclusion of competition provisions in the EEC Treaty.

11 Antimonopoly Law (中华人民共和国反垄断法) of 30 August 2007; in force 1 August 2008.

12 *Tangshan Renren Information Service* v *Baidu*, Beijing No. 1 Intermediate People's Court, 18 December 2009; involving exclusionary abuse of market dominance in a computer search engine.

13.03   Competition law (in the Union context) is addressed in the Treaties for two distinct, and normally (but not always) complementary, reasons. First, the framers of the Treaties were alive to the fact that the creation of the common market would require not only a neutering of powers of the member states which could otherwise hinder the common market, but a contribution from private industry as well. Much of the Treaties is addressed to the member states and is concerned with the dismantling, and subsequent prohibition, of tariff, fiscal and technical barriers to the free movement of goods and services – put otherwise, the public law side of the single market. But if the Treaties did no more, the danger would be that private firms would step in to recreate the dismantled barriers for their own economic advantage and so frustrate the internal market by means of market power or private law (contractual) devices. The competition rules are therefore a necessary ancillary, a component part, of the internal market. This had been recognised in the Spaak Report,[13] and moved the Court of Justice to observe that the competition rules are 'so essential that without [them] numerous provisions of the Treaty would be pointless',[14] and subsequently:

> [A]ccording to [*conformément à; in overeenstemming met*] Article 3[(1)](g) of the EC Treaty ..., Article 81 ... constitutes a fundamental provision which is essential to the accomplishment of the tasks entrusted to the Community and, in particular, the functioning of the internal market.[15]

Later still, the 'implementation of the European competition rules ... [is] essential for the functioning of the internal market [and] without any doubt a fundamental aim of the Treaties'.[16] As such, the competition rules are accorded a shared primacy in the Union scheme; according to a past president of the Court, Judge Rodríguez Iglesias, 'the rules on free movement and competition ... constitute the core and best established layer of the Community legal order.'[17] This aspect of the competition rules is sometimes called their 'integration goals'.

---

13   Comité intergouvernemental créé par la conférence de Messine, Rapport des chefs de delegations aux ministres des Affaires étrangères , 21 avril 1956, p. 53 ff.

14   Case 6/72 *Europemballage and Continental Can* v *Commission* [1973] ECR 215, at para. 24.

15   Case C-126/97 *Eco Swiss China Time* v *Benetton International* [1999] ECR I-3055, at para. 36; also Case C-453/99 *Courage* v *Crehan* [2001] ECR I-6297, at para. 20; Cases T-217 and 245/03 *Fédération nationale de la coopération bétail et viande* v *Commission* [2006] ECR II-4987, at para. 97.

16   Case C-109/10P *Solvay* v *Commission* and Case C-110/10P *Solvay* v *Commission*, judgments of 25 October 2011, not yet reported, *per* A-G Kokott at paras 328 and 169 of her respective opinions.

17   GC Rodríguez Iglesias, inaugural address to the FIDE XX Congress, 2002, London.

At the same time they pursue 'economic goals': the Treaties are, for good or ill,   **13.04**
imbued with neo-liberal preconceptions. This was so implicitly from the
beginning, and expressly since Maastricht, the EC Treaty providing that

> the activities of the Member States and the Community shall include ... the adoption
> of an economic policy which is based on the close coordination of the Member States'
> economic policies, on the internal market and on the definition of common objectives,
> and *conducted in accordance with the principle of an open market economy with free
> competition*.[18]

This provision 'establish[ed] the fundamental principles of economic policy of
the Community system and set out the context of which the competition rules
... form part'.[19] The free market, of which competition (and now its regulation)
is a *leitmotif*, is therefore now a constitutional imperative.

This pre-eminence of competition has now suffered what many see as a   **13.05**
constitutional demotion. The Treaty establishing a Constitution for Europe
provided, at the outset, as a Union objective:

> The Union shall offer its citizens an area of freedom, security and justice without
> internal frontiers, and a single market where competition is free and undistorted,[20]

so placing competition formally at the very heart of the internal market.
However, the final clause was deleted from the Lisbon Treaty (controversially,
and at French insistence) and the successors to article 4 EC in the opening
provisions of both the TEU and the TFEU make no reference to competition;[21]
its text is reproduced lower down in title VII of Part Three and merely as a
component of economic and monetary policy.[22] Gone also is article 3(1)(g) EC
upon which the Court often relied as a basis for 'the general objectives of
European Community action',[23] banished from the Treaty proper to a new
protocol attached to both Treaties thus:

THE HIGH CONTRACTING PARTIES,

CONSIDERING that the internal market as set out in Article 3 of the Treaty on
European Union includes a system ensuring that competition is not distorted,

HAVE AGREED that:

---

18   EC Treaty, art. 3a (pre-Amsterdam), art. 4 (post-Amsterdam) (emphasis added).
19   Case C-451/03 *Servizi Ausiliari Dottori Commercialisti* v *Calafiori* [2006] ECR I-2941, at para. 20.
20   Treaty establishing a Constitution for Europe, art. I-3(2).
21   TEU, art. 3(3); TFEU, art. 5.
22   TFEU, art. 119(1).
23   Case C-202/07P *France Télécom* v *Commission* [2009] ECR I-2369, at para. 103.

to this end the Union shall, if necessary, take action under the provisions of the Treaties, including under Article 352 of the Treaty on the Functioning of the European Union.[24]

It is not easy to discern what exactly this means. There continues to be Treaty recognition of undistorted competition as an integral part of the internal market: the Court of Justice has now recognised this but said no more than 'it must be observed that [the] internal market …, in accordance with Protocol No. 27 …, is to include a system ensuring that competition is not distorted'.[25] The practical effect of its downgrading from a Community activity at the head of the EC Treaty to a preambular reference in a badly drafted protocol upon the intepretation of the competition provisions may be considerable, or it may be negligible, and remains to be seen.

2. The Treaty scheme

13.06 The 'rules on competition' (or in most language versions, the rules *of* competition) are contained articles 101–109 of the Treaty. The layout of these provisions is as follows.

(a) Articles 101 and 102 TFEU

13.07 Article 101 addresses anticompetitive accommodation between or amongst economic operators which compete, or ought to be competing, with one another. In a free market economy they are presumed and required to be in a state of competition. But as Adam Smith noted in *The Wealth of Nations*,[26] too often there is a tendency to recoil from competition: that the interests of producers, if not consumers, are better served if competition between or amongst them is curtailed in an effort jointly to build and profit from market power. Competition may also be diminished by an accommodation reached on the vertical plane – for example, by contracts between producers and distributors which contain various restrictive provisions. Article 101 strikes primarily at cartels, 'amongst the most serious violation of competition law',[27] but they are not its only target.

13.08 Article 102, on the other hand, addresses essentially the unilateral conduct of single operators which alone enjoy such market power that they are not subject to the normal forces of competition. There is a presumption that it is the motive force of competition between or amongst economic operators which will make

---

24 Protocol (No. 27) on the Internal Market and Competition.
25 Case C-52/09 *Konkurrensverket* v *TeliaSonera Sverige*, [2011] ECR I-527, at para. 20.
26 A. Smith, *An Inquiry into the Nature and Causes of the Wealth of Nations* (1776).
27 EC Commission, *Report on Competition Policy 2008*, COM(2009) 374 final, para. 5.

them efficient. But some will be so powerful, through either statutory privilege or some other advantage, legal or economic, that they are above the fray and can pursue strategies, policies and conduct irrespective of the moderating influence of their competitors (if any). This is the concern of article 102. And whilst it addresses first and foremost the conduct of monopolies, it applies also to other operators which enjoy substantial, but not monopolistic, market power.

This approach addressing, distinctly, (a) accommodation between or amongst **13.09** economic operators which ought to be competing with one another but by which they elect not to do so, and primarily, but not exclusively, cartels, and (b) the unilateral conduct of dominant operators with such market power that they need not trouble themselves with competition and primarily, but not exclusively, monopolies, derives originally from American antitrust law, specifically sections 1 and 2 of the Sherman Act 1890. It is now the gold standard in the formulation of rules intended to regulate competition: the operative parts of the national competition laws of Belgium,[28] Denmark,[29] Greece,[30] Ireland,[31] Italy,[32] Luxembourg,[33] the Netherlands,[34] Portugal,[35] Sweden[36] and the United Kingdom,[37] all of them (except the Greek law, and that in anticipation of accession) adopted since 1990, are all effectively carbon copies of articles 101 and 102. Those national laws which follow a different pattern have been amended to bring them more closely into line with the Community/Union approach.[38] And the member states joining in 2004, 2007 and 2013 were required to replicate the Treaty approach as part of the pre-accession strategy.[39]

---

28 Loi du 5 août 1991 sur la protection de la concurrence économique, 'coordonnée' le 15 septembre 2006, MB du 29 septembre 2006, p. 50613.

29 LBK nr. 1027 af 21 august 2007 om Konkurrenceloven.

30 Νόμος 703/1977, n. 8 above.

31 Competition Act, 2002 (No. 14 of 2002).

32 L. 10 ottobre 1990, no. 287, GU no. 240 del 13 ottobre 1990.

33 Loi du 17 mai 2004 relative à la concurrence, JO du G-DL du 26 mai 2004, p. 1112.

34 Wet van 22 mei 1997 (Mededingingswet), stb. 1997, 242.

35 Lei n.º 19/2012 de 8 de maio 2012 aprova o novo regime juridico de concorrêcia, DR de 8 de maio de 2012.

36 Konkurrenslaget, SFS 2008:579.

37 Competition Act 1998.

38 See e.g., Sechstes Gesetz zur Änderung des GWB vom 26. August 1998, BGBl. 1998 I S. 2521, which marks the most significant alteration of the GWB since its adoption in 1957, and Siebtes Gesetz zur Änderung des GWB vom 7. Juli 2005, BGBl. 2005 I S. 1954, both exercises in making it more 'Community compatible'. See also Laki kilpailunrajoituksista annetun lain muuttamisesta (318/2004); the (Austrian) Kartellgesetz (KartG) BGBl. I Nr. 2005/61 (hereinafter öKartG); Ley 15/2007, de 3 de julio, de Defensa de la Competencia, BOE de 4 de julio 2007; Ordonnance no. 2008-1161 du 13 novembre 2008 portant modernisation de la régulation de la concurrence, JO du 14 novembre 2008, p. 2427; and Νόμος 3784/2009 αναθεώρηση διατάξεων του ν. 703/1977, ΦΕΚ Α' 137.

39 See now the relevant laws in Bulgaria (Закон за защита нкуренцията, Обн., ДВ, бр. 102 от 28.11.2008 г.); the Czech Republic (Zákon č. 143/2001 Sb., o ochran č hospodářské soutěže); Estonia (Konkurentsiseadus, RT I 2001, 56, 332); Croatia (Zakon o zaštiti tržišnog natjecanja, OG 79/2099); Cyprus (Ο Περί της

13.10   Both articles 101 and 102 state principles – 'application[s] of the general objective of European Community action laid down by Article 3(1)(g) [EC]'[40] – and should not be construed as if they were statutory provisions. Nor are they mutually exclusive: an agreement or practice may in circumstances be caught by both.[41] They address the conduct or behaviour of economic operators; thus they are concerned primarily not with the structure of markets and the anti-competitive forces which may be a direct or indirect result of those structures, but with the manner in which operators conduct themselves in the market. The Treaty presumes an environment of stable markets and so workable competition:

> The requirement contained in Articles 3 and 85 [now 101 TFEU] of the EEC Treaty that competition shall not be distorted implies the existence on the market of workable competition, that is to say the degree of competition necessary to ensure the observance of the basic requirements and the attainment of the objectives of the Treaty, in particular the creation of a single market achieving conditions similar to those of a domestic market.[42]

Where competition is hindered not because market participants elect to make it so but because the very structure of the market is inimical to competition, articles 101 and 102 are in ways ill suited to it. This is especially so in addressing the problems of oligopolistic markets and mergers.[43]

13.11   Articles 101 and 102 apply to all economic activities falling within the application of the Treaties. They have been applied for the most part to the manufacture, production, distribution and sale of goods, but the prohibitions apply equally, and latterly more forcefully, to distortion in services markets. Competition in coal and steel markets was subject to specific rules under the Coal and Steel Treaty[44] but with its death in 2002 were subsumed wholly within

---

Προστασίας του Ανταγωνισμού Νόμος 207/89); Latvia (Konkurences Likums (04.10.2001)); Lithuania (Konkurencijos Įstatymas, 1999 m. kovo 23 d. Nr. VIII-1099); Hungary (1996. évi LVII. törvény a tisztességtelen piaci magatartás és a versenykorlátozás tilalmáról); Malta (Att dwar il-Kompetizzjoni, Att XXXI ta' l-1994); Poland (Ustawa z dnia 16 lutego 2007 r. o ochronie konkurencji i konsumentów); Romania (Legea nr. 21 din 10 aprilie 1996 Legea concurenței); Slovakia (Zákon č. 136/2001 Z. z. o ochrane hospodárskej súťaže); and Slovenia (Zakon o preprečevanju omejevanja konkurence – ZPOmK-1).

40   Case C-202/07P *France Télécom* v *Commission* [2009] ECR I-2369, at para. 103.

41   See e.g., Case 66/86 *Ahmed Saeed Flugreisen* v *Zentrale zur Bekämpfung Unlauteren Wettbewerbs* [1989] ECR 803; Case T-51/89 *Tetrapak* v *Commission* [1990] ECR II-309; Cases T-68 and 77–78/89 *Società Italiana Vetro* v *Commission (Flat Glass)* [1992] ECR II-1403.

42   Case 26/76 *Metro-SB-Großmärkte* v *Commission* (No. 1) [1977] ECR 1875, at para. 20.

43   See 13.125–13.141 below.

44   ECSC Treaty, arts 65–7.

the EC Treaty and its procedures.[45] Agriculture alone is immunised, to an extent, from the full rigour of the competition rules.[46]

Both articles 101 and 102 are directly effective.[47]   **13.12**

(b) Supporting provisions

The operative provisions of the competition rules are articles 101 and 102, those   **13.13**
which follow support them. They are:

- articles 103–105 address the enhancement and the enforcement of the competition rules. Article 103 serves as the Treaty base for legislation, the Council authorised to adopt any 'appropriate regulations or directives to give effect to the principles set out in Articles 101 and 102',[48] the primary purpose of which is to ensure observance of the prohibitions of articles 101 and 102 by the imposition of financial penalties and to define the role of the Commission in their application.[49] The Council has adopted a number of measures under article 103 giving flesh to the principles and effect to their enforcement. Articles 104 and 105 provide provisionally for the enforcement of the competition rules by, respectively, national competition authorities and the Commission. They are now largely spent, displaced by the implementing legislation adopted under article 103;
- article 106 is a *lex specialis* provision, addressing entities in public ownership and those to which member states 'grant special or exclusive rights' in order, first, to ensure that they comply with the competition rules (article 106(1)); and second, to provide a degree of immunity from the full vigour of articles 101 and 102 to entities (essentially state monopolies) which operate services 'of general economic interest' (article 106(2)). Article 106 has acquired increasing importance since the early 1990s, owing in part to the raft of privatisation of public utilities and services throughout a number of member states;
- articles 107–109 address state aids. They are therefore concerned directly not with the commercial conduct of economic operators but with

---

45 Case T-25/04 *González y Díez* v *Commission* [2007] ECR II-3121; Cases C-201 and 216/09P *ArcelorMittal Luxembourg and ors* v *Commission* and Case C-352/09 P *ThyssenKrupp Nirosta* v *Commission*, judgments of 29 March 2011, not yet reported. More accurately the substantive ECSC provisions continued to be applicable to conduct predating the death of that Community but the procedural law was that of the EC.
46 Regulation 1184/2006 [2006] OJ L214/7; see 10.103 above.
47 See 13.112 below.
48 TFEU, art. 103(1). Legislation is adopted not by ordinary legislative procedure but by qualified majority vote in the Council following a proposal from the Commission and consultation with the Parliament.
49 Case C-550/07P *Akzo Nobel Chemicals and anor* v *Commission* [2010] ECR I-8301, at para. 117.

distortions through the competitive advantage to be had from the allocation of public funds. There has now developed a significant body of case law on and distinct to articles 107–109, which is discussed below.

3. Concepts and principles common to articles 101 and 102 TFEU

(a) Undertakings

13.14 The competition rules are concerned with the conduct of, and impose obligations upon,'undertakings'. The term, borrowed from the more common German (*Unternehmer*) and Dutch (*onderneming*), is not defined in the Treaties, but is of very wide application, embracing, in the now standard formula, 'every entity engaged in an economic activity, regardless of the legal status of the entity and the way in which it is financed'.[50] The fact that the activity may be one primarily of cultural,[51] social[52] or sporting[53] pursuits, or that it may be non-profit making,[54] does not diminish its quality as an undertaking. It is not even necessary that it have legal personality[55] (hence careful use in the now standard formula of the word 'entity' in preference to '(legal) person'), so encompassing, for example, partnerships in English law.[56] Undertakings have therefore stretched to include: mutual associations;[57] agricultural cooperatives;[58] pension

---

50 Case C-41/90 *Höfner and Elser* v *Macrotron* [1991] ECR I-1979, at para. 21; repeated consistently since.

51 Cases 43 and 63/82 *Vereniging ter Bevordering van het Vlaamse Boekwezen* v *Commission* [1984] ECR 19.

52 Case C-70/95 *Sodemare* v *Regione Lombardia* [1997] ECR I-3395; Case C-67/96 *Albany International* v *Stichting Bedrijfspensioenfonds Textielindustrie* [1999] ECR I-5751.

53 Case C-415/93 *Union Royale Belge des Sociétés de Football Association* v *Bosman* [1995] ECR I-4921, *per* A-G Lenz; Decision 2000/12 (*1998 World Cup*) [2000] OJ L5/55; Decision 2005/396 (*Bundesliga Media Rights*) [2005] OJ L134/46; Case COMP/38.173 *FA Premier League Media Rights*, decision of of 22 March 2006, [2008] OJ C7/18 (summary publication).

54 Cases 209 etc./78 *van Landewyck* v *Commission* (FEDETAB) [1980] ECR 3125; Case C-70/95 *Sodemare*, n. 52 above; Case C-49/07 *Motosykletistiki Omospondia Ellados* v *Elliniko Dimosio* [2008] ECR I-4863, especially *per* A-G Kokott at paras 37–51 of her opinion; Case C-113/07P *SELEX Sistemi Integrati* v *Commission* [2009] ECR I-2207, at para. 116.

55 Confirmed in Cases C-189 etc./02P *Dansk Rørindustri and ors* v *Commission* [2005] ECR I-5425, at paras 103–15.

56 There is no authority on English partnerships but comparable legal associations in other member states, the *Kommanditgesellschaft* (KG) (Decision 73/323 (*William Prym-Werk KG*) [1973] OJ L296/24), the *société en nom collectif* (Decision 85/561 (*Breeders' Rights: Roses*) [1985] OJ L369/9) and the *vennootschap onder firma* (Decision 78/59 (*Centraal Bureau voor de Rijwielhandel*) [1978] OJ L20/18), have been found to be undertakings. See also Regulation 800/2008 [2008] OJ L214/3 (General Block Exemption Regulation, see 13.168 below), Annex I, art. 1, which includes partnerships (*sociétés de personnes*; *Personengesellschaften*) in the definition of 'enterprises' (*entreprises*; *Unternehmen*) for purposes of Union rules on state aids.

57 Decision 1999/329 (*P & I Clubs*) [1999] OJ L125/12.

58 Case 61/80 *Coöperatieve Stremsel- en Kleurselfabriek* v *Commission* [1981] ECR 851; Case C-250/92 *Gøttrup-Klim* v *Dansk Landbrugs Grovvarselskab* [1994] ECR I-5641.

funds;[59] association football clubs[60] and their national associations;[61] the International Olympic Committee and its affiliated international and national associations;[62] individuals (properly so-called) engaged in the liberal professions of intellectual property agents,[63] customs agents[64] and patent agents;[65] football players' agents;[66] medical specialists,[67] architects[68] and advocates;[69] farmers;[70] judoka[71] (individual practitioners of that martial art); and opera singers.[72] So elastic is the meaning of the term that there are only two general categories of economically active persons who fall beyond its embrace:

- *Employees:* Employees acting as such are not undertakings, rather they are deemed to form an 'economic unit' with their employer undertaking.[73] Advocate-General Jacobs considered whether an employee is an undertaking *vis-à-vis* his employer – that is, in matters of (negotiation of) his contract of employment – and determined he was not.[74] It is not abundantly clear this should not be so; but if it was, it would have very serious repercussions for contract negotiations and collective bargaining – even if, as Mr Jacobs recognised, that is protected in Union law.[75] Whether or not

---

59 Case C-67/96 *Albany International* v *Stichting Bedrijfspensioenfonds Textielindustrie* [1999] ECR I-5751. But some bodies which administer certain social security operations fall outwith the meaning of the term; see Case C-218/00 *Cisal di Battistello Venanzio and anor* v *Istituto nazionale per l'assicurazione contro gli infortuni sul lavoro (INAIL)* [2002] ECR I-691; Case C-350/07 *Kattner Stahlbau* v *Mashinenbau- und Metall-Berufsgenossenschaft* [2009] ECR I-1513.

60 Case C-415/93 *Union Royale Belge des Sociétés de Football Association* v *Bosman* [1995] ECR I-4921.

61 *Ibid.*; Case T-46/92 *Scottish Football Association* v *Commission* [1994] ECR II-1039; also Case C-49/07 *Motosykletistiki Omospondia Ellados* v *Elliniko Dimosio* [2008] ECR I-4863, for a national affiliate of the International Motorcyling Federation.

62 Case C-519/04P *Meca-Madina and Majcen* v *Commission* [2006] ECR I-6991.

63 Decision 95/188 (*Coapi*) [1995] OJ L122/37.

64 Case C-35/96 *Commission* v *Italy* [1998] ECR I-3851; Case T-513/93 *Consiglio Nazionale degli Spedizionieri Doganali* v *Commission* [2000] ECR II-1807.

65 Case T-144/99 *Institute of Professional Representatives before the European Patent Office* v *Commission* [2001] ECR II-1087.

66 Case T-193/02 *Piau* v *Commission* [2005] ECR II-209.

67 Cases C-180 etc./98 *Pavlov and ors* v *Stichting Pensioenfonds Medische Specialisten* [2000] ECR I-6451.

68 Case C-221/99 *Conte* v *Rossi* [2001] ECR I-9359.

69 Case C-309/99 *Wouters and ors* v *Algemene Raad van de Nederlandse Orde van Advokaten* [2002] ECR I-1577; Case C-250/03 *Mauri* v *Ministero della Giustizia* [2005] ECR.I-1267.

70 Cases T-217 and 245/03 *Fédération nationale de la coopération bétail et viande* v *Commission* [2006] ECR II-4987.

71 Cases C-51/96 and 191/97 *Deliège* v *Ligue Francophone de Judo* [2000] ECR I-2549, *per* A-G Cosmas.

72 Decision 78/516 (*RAI/Unitel*) [1978] OJ L157/39.

73 Cases 40 etc./73 *Coöperatieve Vereniging 'Suiker Unie'* v *Commission* [1975] ECR 1663; Case C-22/98 *Criminal proceedings against Becu* [1999] ECR I-5665.

74 Case C-67/96 *Albany International* v *Stichting Bedrijfspensioenfonds Textielindustrie* [1999] ECR I-5751. The issue was not seriously considered by the Court. See also Cases T-217 and 245/03 *Fédération nationale de la coopération bétail et viande*, n. 70 above, at paras 95–103.

75 Case C-67/96 *Albany International, ibid.*, at paras 132 ff. of his opinion; see also Case C-271/08 *Commission* v *Germany* [2010] ECR I-7087. This issue is sometimes addressed in national law by express exclusion of competition law from the field of labour relations; see e.g., 2 § Konkurrenslaget, SFS 2008:579; 2 § Kilpailulaki (948/2011).

employers are equally immune – for example, in collaboration on wages or recruitment – may logically follow, but it has not been considered by the Court. If they are not, the Union institutions themselves may be in the frame.[76]

- *End users:* In German competition law an individual purchasing a good or service for his or her personal consumption (an *Endverbraucher*) is not an undertaking.[77] It was long unconfirmed whether Community law shared this view. However, in 2003 the Court of First Instance vaulted the point, and determined that the Spanish Sistema nacional de salud (SNS) was not an undertaking:

> It is the activity consisting in offering goods and services in a given market that is the characteristic feature of an economic activity, not the business of purchasing as such … Consequently, an organisation which purchases goods – even in great quantity – not for the purpose of offering goods and services as part of an economic activity, but in order to use them …, does not act as an undertaking simply because it is a purchaser in a given market. Whilst an entity may wield very considerable economic power, even giving rise to a monopsony, it nevertheless remains the case that, if the activity for which the entity purchases goods is not an economic activity, it is not acting as an undertaking for purposes of Community competition law and is therefore not subject to the prohibitions laid down in Articles 81(1) EC and 82 EC.[78]

There is much economically (and legally) to criticise in this; faced with like situations and legislation the administrative authorities and courts in the Netherlands,[79] Germany[80] and the United Kingdom[81] concluded that their respective competition laws apply to public entity purchasing even if the subsequent use is non-economic. But on appeal the Court of Justice upheld the Court of First Instance,[82] and has since reiterated the principle.[83]

---

76 In 2002 the Secretaries-General of the Parliament, the Council, the Commission, the Court of Justice, the Court of Auditors, the Economic and Social Committee, the Committee of the Regions and the Ombudsman signed an agreement on common principles for a harmonised selection and recruitment policy and the principles for drawing from shortlists (Agreement of 25 July 2002, unpublished) by which they each work towards harmonised classification criteria in the recruitment of staff 'afin de guarantir le respect du principe de l'égalité de traitement et d'éviter la concurrence entre les institutions' (para. 4): an agreement (between undertakings?) the (stated) object of which is anticompetitive.

77 See e.g., Bundeskartellamt, *Jahresbericht* 1961, S. 61.

78 Case T-319/99 *Federación Nacional de Empresas de Instrumentación Científica, Médica, Técnica y Dental (FENIN)* v *Commission* [2003] ECR II-357.

79 NMa, Zaaknummer 181, besluit van 10 Maart 2000 (*Ontheffingsaanvraag Zorgkantoren*).

80 BGH, 12. November 2002 (*Einkaufsgemeinschaft von Gemeinden*), BGHZ 152, 347.

81 *BetterCare Group* v *Director General of Fair Trading* [2002] CompAR 299. But owing to statutory instruction to shadow the meaning given to equivalent Union law terms (Competition Act 1998, s. 60, the 'Europrinciples clause') the Office of Fair Trading has now adopted a preference for the *FENIN* view; *The Competition Act 1998 and Public Bodies*, Policy note 1/2004, OFT 443, August 2004.

82 Case C-205/03P *Federación Española de Empresas de Tecnología Sanitaria* v *Commission* [2006] ECR I-6295.

83 Case C-113/07P *SELEX Sistemi Integrati* v *Commission* [2009] ECR I-2207.

Beyond these two categories, there is now authority that certain bodies, public **13.15** or private, which operate various social insurance schemes (for example, insurance against accidents at work and occupational diseases, sectoral pension schemes, employers' liability insurance associations), are subject to (some) control by the state and operate in accordance with a principle of solidarity are not undertakings.[84]

Undertaking has the same meaning for both article 101 and article 102.[85] **13.16**

(b)   Economic entity doctrine

However, 'undertaking' is a construct of economic fact rather than legal **13.17** personality. Therefore where a company or other similar person has no real freedom to determine its own course of conduct – as is the case with a wholly owned and directly controlled subsidiary – Union law will view the group, independent legal personality of its component companies notwithstanding, as a single undertaking. Consequently, where the Treaties proscribe anticompetitive conduct *between* undertakings (article 101) it is addressing conduct between undertakings which are capable of and presumed to be competing with one another, and the prohibition therefore does not, and cannot, apply to agreements between parent and subsidiary or between or amongst subsidiaries part of the same corporate group:

> [I]n competition law the term 'undertaking' must be understood as designating an economic unit for the purposes of the subject-matter of the agreement in question even if in law the economic unit consists of several persons, natural or legal.[86]

And

> for the purposes of the application of the competition rules, the unified conduct on the market of the parent company and its subsidiaries takes precedence over the formal separation between those companies as a result of their separate legal personalities.

> It follows that … relations within an economic unit cannot amount to an agreement or concerted practice between undertakings within the meaning of Article [101](1) of the

---

84 Cases C-180 etc./98 *Pavlov* v *Stichting Pensioenfonds Medische Specialisten* [2000] ECR I-6451; Case C-218/00 *Cisal di Battistello Venanzio & C. Sas* v *Istituto nazionale per l'assicurazione contro gli infortuni sul lavoro* [2002] ECR I-691; Cases C-264 etc./01 *AOK Bundesverband and ors* v *Ichthyol-Gesellschaft Cordes and ors* [2004] ECR I-2493; Case C-350/07 *Kattner Stahlbau* v *Maschinenbau- und Metall-Berufsgenossenschaft* [2009] ECR I-1513; Case C-437/09 *AG2R Prévoyance* v *Beaudout Père et Fils*, judgment of 3 March 2011, not yet reported.

85 Cases T-66 etc./89 *Società Italiano Vetro* v *Commission* (Flat Glass) [1992] ECR II-1403.

86 Case 170/83 *Hydrotherm* v *Compact* [1984] ECR 2999, at para. 11.

Treaty ... Article [101](1) does not apply to the relationship between the subsidiary and the parent company with which it forms an economic unit.[87]

Whether there is control, and so the economic entity (or 'single entity') doctrine applies, is a matter of fact, taking into account criteria such as links between various undertakings as a result of share ownership and overlapping management which deprive the members of the group of the autonomy to determine its course of action on the market.[88] Where a parent/subsidiary is in issue two cumulative conditions must be met: the parent company must be in a position to exert decisive influence over its subsidiary, and it must actually assert that influence;[89] if the latter's share capital is wholly owned by the former the first test is met and there is a rebuttable presumption the second is met.[90] The importance lies not least in that where there is control the parent company (or companies) may be held jointly and severally liable for any financial penalty imposed upon its subsidiary (or subsidiaries).[91] Generally the economic entity doctrine applies also to an agency agreement, for the agent is deemed to be acting as an adjunct of the principal,[92] and so a true agency contract is not an agreement between undertakings within the meaning of article 101.[93]

(c) Obligations of the member states

13.18 It follows that 'undertaking' can include even the state insofar as it is 'engaged in an economic activity'. The state discharges various functions, many of which are

---

87 Case T-102/92 *Viho Europe* v *Commission* [1995] ECR II-17, at paras 50–1; upheld on appeal as Case C-73/95P *Viho Europe* v *Commission* [1996] ECR I-5457. See also Case T-198/98 *Micro Leader Business* v *Commission* [1999] ECR II-3989; Cases C-189 etc./02P *Dansk Rørindustri and ors* v *Commission* [2005] ECR I-5425.

88 Case 22/71 *Béguelin* v *GL Import Export* [1971] ECR 949; Case 48/69 *ICI* v *Commission* (Dyestuffs) [1972] ECR 619; Case 15/74 *Centrafarm* v *Sterling Drug* [1974] ECR 1147; Case 107/82 *AEG* v *Commission* [1983] ECR 3151; Case 30/87 *Bodson* v *Pompes Funèbres des Régions Libérées* [1988] ECR 2479; Case T-65/89 *BPB Industries and British Gypsum* v *Commission* [1993] ECR II-389; Cases C-182 etc./02P *Dansk Rørindustri, ibid.*, at paras 103–31; Case C-407/08P *Knauf Gips* v *Commission* [2010] ECR I-6371; Cases C-201 and 216/09P *ArcelorMittal Luxembourg and ors* v *Commission*, judgment of 29 March 2011, not yet reported, at paras 95–107.

89 Case 48/69 *Dyestuffs, ibid.*, at para. 137.

90 Case C-97/08P *Akzo Nobel and ors* v *Commission* [2009] ECR I-8237; Case C90/09P *General Química and ors* v *Commission*, [2011] CRCI-1.

91 See e.g., Case C-97/08P *Akzo Nobel* , *ibid.*, at para. 61; Case C90/09P *General Química* , *ibid.*, at para. 40.

92 EC Commission, Guidelines on Vertical Restraints attached to the Draft Commission Regulation on the Application of Articles 81(3) to Categories of Vertical Agreements and Concerted Practices [199] OJ C270/12, ch. II.2.

93 Cases 56 and 58/64 *Établissements Consten and Grundig-Verkaufs* v *EEC Commission* [1966] ECR 299, at 340; Case T-325/01 *Daimler Chrysler* v *Commission* [2005] ECR II-3319, at paras 87–120; Case C-217/05 *Confederación Española de Empresarios de Estaciones de Servicio* v *Compañía Española de Petróleos* [2006] ECR I-11987. However the agent must be tightly integrated into the organisation of the principal; if an independent trader, who assumes some risk (which must be more than negligible; *Confederación Española*), it is not true agency.

purely public and regulatory, and many of which fall under other provisions of the Treaties. But it also engages in various aspects of commercial activity and, in that context, is an undertaking and so subject to the competition rules:

> [T]he State may act either by exercising public powers or by carrying on economic activities of an industrial or commercial nature by offering goods and services on the market. In order to make such a distinction, it is therefore necessary in each case, to consider the activities exercised by the State and to determine the category to which those activities belong ...

> [T]he fact that a body has or has not, under national law, legal personality separate from that of the State is irrelevant in deciding whether it may be regard as a[n] ... undertaking.[94]

Furthermore a public body (or a private body acting under statutory duties and privileges) may be an undertaking in discharging some of its functions but not others.[95] So articles 101 and 102 have been applied to a great many instances of commercial activity of the state.[96] When not acting as an undertaking the state is not bound directly by the competition rules but it has a duty, drawn from articles 101 and 102 in conjunction with article 4(3) of the TEU,[97] not to introduce or maintain in force any national measure, even of a legislative or regulatory nature, which might render their application ineffective. More specifically, a member state may not (a) require or (b) favour the adoption of agreements, decisions or concerted practices contrary to article 101, (c) reinforce their effects or (d) deprive its own legislation of its official character by delegating to private traders responsibility for taking decisions affecting the economic sphere.[98]

---

94 Case 118/85 *Commission* v *Italy* [1987] ECR 2599, at paras 7, 11.
95 Case C-49/07 *Motosykletistiki Omospondia Ellados* v *Elliniko Dimosio* [2008] ECR I-4863; Case C-113/07P *SELEX Sistemi Integrati* v *Commission* [2009] ECR I-2207, at para. 119.
96 E.g., postal services (Case C-320/91 *Criminal proceedings against Corbeau* [1993] ECR I-2533; Decision 1999/695 (*REIMS II*) [1999] OJ L275/17); public service employment (Case C-41/90 *Höfner and Elser* v *Macrotron* [1991] ECR I-1979; Case C55/96 *Job Centre Coop* [1997] ECR I-7119); sectoral pension funds (Case C-67/96 *Albany International* v *Stichting Bedrijfspensioenfonds Textielindustrie* [1999] ECR I-5751); land registry (*Millar and Bryce* v *Keeper of the Registers of Scotland* 1997 SLT 1000 (OH)); civil aviation (Decision 1999/198 (*Ilmailulaitos/Luftfartsverket*) [1999] OJ L69/24); publicly financed research (Case C-237/04 *Enirisorse* v *Sotacarbo* [2006] ECR I-2843); 'banking foundations' (Case C-222/04 *Ministero dell'Economia e delle Finanze* v *Cassa di Risparmio di Firenze and ors* [2006] ECR I-289); and manufacture and sale of tobacco (Case C-280/06 *Autorità Garante della Concorrenza e del Mercato* v *Ente tabacchi italiana* [2007] ECR I-10893).
97 On art. 4(3) see 2.24 above. The Court also long drew upon art. 3(1)(g) EC which no longer exists.
98 See Case 311/85 *Vereniging van Vlaamse Reisebureaus* v *Sociale Dienst van de Plaatselijke en Gewestelijke Overheidsdiesten* [1987] ECR 3801; Case 267/86 *van Eycke* v *ASPA* [1988] ECR 4769; Case C-41/90 *Höfner* v *Macrotron* [1991] ECR I-1979; Case C-2/91 *Criminal Proceedings against Meng* [1993] ECR I-5751; Case C-185/91 *Bundesanstalt für den Güterfernverkehr* v *Gebrüder Reiff* [1993] ECR I-5801; Case C-245/91 *Criminal proceedings against Ohra Schadeverzekeringen* [1993] ECR I-5851 (the latter three, along with *Keck*, comprising the 'November revolution' on greater deference to national regulation); most recently, Cases C-94

4. Relevant market

13.19 Article 3(f) of the EEC Treaty required that competition not be 'distorted' (*fausée; in Vorfälschungen schützt*). As the competition rules address distortions to competition, it is always necessary to define, in any particular case, the market under consideration, or the 'relevant market'. This is fundamental to any understanding of competition law. Competition and competition law do not exist in a vacuum. If competition is to be distorted, it is necessary to ascertain how it is distorted, and for that it is necessary to ascertain the market in which it is (or might be) distorted in order to assess market power within it. As the Court of First Instance noted, 'the appropriate definition of the market in question is a necessary precondition of any judgment concerning allegedly anti-competitive behaviour'.[99] It is of clinical importance in the context of the rules governing monopoly behaviour (article 102) and mergers in particular.

13.20 The identification of a relevant market consists implicitly in identification of a product or service or group of products or services in which a hypothetical single producer or supplier could exercise market power. It has two essential elements: the product or service market in issue and the geographic market in issue.[100] Best assistance may be had from a very helpful and lucid notice adopted by the Commission in 1997 on definition of relevant market.[101]

(a) Relevant product or service market

13.21 According to the 1997 Commission notice,

> [a] relevant product market comprises all those products and/or services which are regarded as interchangeable or substitutable by the consumer, by reason of the products' characteristics, their price and their intended use.[102]

The primary tests to be applied are those of product/service substitutability or interchangeability and cross-elasticity of demand, that is the identification of a product or products or service(s) for which no other product(s) or service(s) can satisfactorily be substituted. If products or services can be differentiated by

---

and 202/04 *Cipolla and ors* v *Fazari and anor* [2006] ECR I-11421; Case C-531/07 *Fachverband der Buch- und Medienwirtschaft* v *LIBRO Handelsgesellschaft* [2009] ECR I-3717, *per* A-G Trstenjak at paras 109–96 of her opinion.

99   Cases T-66, 77 and 78/89 *Società Italiano Vetro* v *Commission* (Flat Glass) [1992] ECR II-1403, at para. 159.

100   A third characteristic may be a 'temporal' consideration since markets may change over time (e.g., with technological development or evolution of consumer demand) or there may be seasonal variations; see e.g., Case 27/76 *United Brands* v *Commission* [1978] ECR 207.

101   Commission Notice on the definition of relevant market for the purposes of Community competition law [1997] OJ C372/5.

102   *Ibid.* at para. 7.

various criteria but nonetheless satisfy the same essential consumer demand it is the wider market, comprising all products or services which are interchangeable with or substitutable for one another, which constitutes the relevant market for purposes of determining competition within it. If they do not the market is accordingly narrower. It is sufficient that there be an identifiable market in which the substitution of one product or service for another is more burdensome or less attractive, for whatever reason, to the consumer.[103] Put another way, a relevant market is defined by all products or services which generate a competitive restraint and so (ought to) prevent the exercise of market power.

To take some actual examples from the case law, bananas constitute their own, **13.22** distinct product market because of special characteristics – 'appearance, taste, softness, seedlessness, easy handing, a constant level of production which enable [them] to satisfy the constant needs of an important section of the population consisting of the very young, the old and the sick' – which distinguish them from fresh fruit generally.[104] Bottled water is a product market distinct from soft drinks[105] and cola drinks are distinct from other soft drinks;[106] roses are distinct from other ornamental cut flowers;[107] and, owing to the nature of consumer demand, catering ice cream, take-home ice cream and impulse ice cream are (in Ireland) all distinct product markets.[108] The same analysis applies for service markets: for example, in air travel the Commission normally defines the service market upon the basis of point of origin/point of destination ('O&D') pairs, any combination comprising a separate market from the point of view of demand owing to the inconvenience for a number of passengers of using other airline routes or other means of transportation.[109]

---

103 The methodology by which the economist would normally measure elasticity is the 'small but significant non-transitory increase in price' (SSNIP) test, that is identification of the narrowest range of products or services for which a hypothetical monopolist could permanently and profitably raise relative prices by a small but significant amount (say 5 per cent; hence also sometimes called the '5 per cent test'). The SSNIP test is considered in the 1997 notice, para. 17.

104 Case 27/76 *United Brands* v *Commission* [1978] ECR 207, at para. 31.

105 Decision 92/553 (*Nestlé/Perrier*) [1992] OJ L356/1.

106 Decision 97/540 (*Coca-Cola/Amalgamated Beverages GB*) [1997] OJ L218/15; Decision 2005/620 (*Coca-Cola*) [2005 OJ L253/21.

107 Decision 85/561 (*Breeders' Rights: Roses*) [1985] OJ L369/9.

108 Case T-65/98 *van den Bergh Foods* v *Commission* [2003] ECR II-4653. In Germany the relevant markets would be different; Case T-7/93 *Langnese-Iglo* v *Commission* [1995] ECR II-1533.

109 Case 66/86 *Ahmed Saeed Flugreisen* v *Zentrale zur Bekämpfung unlauteren Wettbewerbs* [1989] ECR 803; Decision 88/589 (*London European/Sabena*) [1988] OJ L317/47; Decision 92/213 (*British Midland/Aer Lingus*) [1992] OJ L96/34; Case COMP/M.3280 *Air France/KLM* [2004 OJ C60/5. However, Roissy-Charles-de-Gaulle and Paris-Orly are in some measure substitutable; *Air France/KLM*. Flights on the Paris–Amsterdam route are a service market distinct from existing fast train (Thalys) services at least for the 'time sensitive' passenger because they are quicker (three hours city centre to city centre as compared to 4 hours 9 minutes) but a reduction in the latter could meld them into a single product market; Case T-177/04 *easyJet* v *Commission* [2006] ECR II-1931.

(b)   Geographic market

13.23 The second limb of the tests to be applied in identifying a relevant market is that of the geographic market. This addresses that homogenous territory in which the product in question moves or the service in question is available. According to the Court of Justice the relevant geographic market is

> a clearly defined geographic area in which [the product or service] is marketed and where the conditions of competition are sufficiently homogenous for the effect of ... economic power ... to be able to be evaluated.[110]

And according to the 1997 Commission notice it is a territory involving the supply and demand of products or services

> in which the conditions of competition are sufficiently homogenous and which can be distinguished from neighbouring areas because the conditions of competition are appreciably different in those area [*sic*].[111]

The relevant geographic market therefore turns on questions of market homogeneity, identification of a geographic territory in which the objective conditions of competition are similar or sufficiently homogenous that it can be said to constitute a coherent but discrete territory in which competitive forces apply – in other words, a territory sufficiently isolated so that market power could be deployed insufficiently disturbed by the moderating influence of competitors from elsewhere. In the Union the gradual integration of markets ought to lead to the growth in size of geographic markets as conditions of homogeneity increase. Yet for a variety of reasons and in a variety of circumstances the relevant geographic market for purposes of the application of the competition rules remains that of a member state. It may in specific circumstances be smaller.

B.   ARTICLE 101 TFEU

13.24 Article 101 is divided into three parts:

(a)   *The prohibition*: Article 101(1) prohibits '[a]ll agreements between undertakings, decisions by associations of undertakings and concerted practices which may affect trade between Member States and which have as their object or effect the prevention, restriction or distortion of competition

---

110   Case 27/76 *United Brands*, n. 104 above, at para. 11.
111   1997 notice, at para. 8.

within the internal market'. This is a very closely worded, and great care ought to attend each twist and turn.

(b) *Civil consequences*: Article 101(2) provides that any agreement or decision which infringes article 101(1) is 'automatically void' (*nul de plein droit*). This has a bearing in particular for the enforcement of article 101 before national courts and the remedies there sought and provided.

(c) *Exemption*: So broad is the prohibition of article 101(1) that it was recognised from the start that it may catch agreements or practices which nevertheless produce economically beneficial effects. Provision was therefore made in article 101(3) for the 'exemption' of certain types of agreements and practices from the prohibition.

It is a complete, coherent package, or 'indivisible whole'. Article 101(3) in particular is part and parcel, and a necessary component, of the package.[112] Whilst it is necessary to consider first the nature of the prohibition as contained in article 101(1), an understanding of the prohibition cannot be complete without appreciation of the possibility of exemption and the manner in which it is applied, and that ought to be borne in mind throughout.

1. The prohibition

(a) *Agreements, decisions of associations of undertakings and concerted practices*

Article 101(1) applies to anticompetitive 'agreements between undertakings, **13.25** decision by associations of undertakings and concerted practices'. They are intended 'from a subjective point of view, to catch forms of collusion having the same nature which are distinguishable from each other only by their intensity and the forms in which they manifest themselves'.[113] The term 'restrictive practices' is sometimes used as shorthand to cover all three. Of the three, agreements and concerted practices merit equal, and closest, consideration.

(i) *Agreements and concerted practices*

Neither 'agreement' nor 'concerted practice' is defined in the Treaties or in **13.26** Union legislation. An agreement requires *consensus ad idem* but in a sense much wider and looser than that normally accorded by the law of contract – in the formula now adopted by the Court, a 'concurrence of wills ..., the form in

---

112 Cases 209 etc./84 *Ministère Public* v *Asjes* (Nouvelles Frontières) [1986] ECR 1425; Case 66/86 *Ahmed Saeed Flugreisen* v *Zentrale zur Bekämpfung unlauteren Wettbewerbs* [1989] ECR 803.

113 Case C-49/92P *Commission* v *Anic Partecipazioni* [1999] ECR I-4125, at para. 131; Case C-8/08 *T-Mobile Netherlands and ors* v *Raad van bestuur van de Nederlandse Mededingingsautoriteit* [2009] ECR I-4529, at para. 23. For an excellent discussion of the character and quality of agreements and concerted practices see the opinion of A-G Kokott in the latter case.

which it is manifested being unimportant so long as it constitutes the faithful expression of the parties' intention'.[114] According to the Commission,

> An agreement can be said to exist ... when the parties adhere to a common plan which limits or is likely to limit their individual commercial conduct by determining the lines [*Richtung, lignes*] of their mutual action or abstention from action in the market. While it involves joint decision-making and commitment to a common scheme, it does not have to be made in writing; no formalities are necessary, and no contractual sanctions or enforcement measures are required. The fact of agreement may be express or implicit in the behaviour of the parties.[115]

A concerted practice, on the other hand, is

> a form of coordination between undertakings which, without having reached the stage where an agreement properly so-called has been concluded, knowingly substitutes practical cooperation between them for the risks of competition.[116]

It:

> in no way require[s] the working out of an actual plan, [but] must be understood in the light of the concept inherent in the provisions of the Treaty relating to competition that each economic operator must determine independently the policy which he intends to adopt on the common market ...
>
> Although it is correct to say that this requirement of independence does not deprive economic operators of the right to adapt themselves intelligently to the existing and anticipated conduct of their competitors, it does however strictly preclude any direct or indirect contact between such operators, the object or effect whereof is either to influence the conduct on the market of an actual or potential competitor or to disclose to such a competitor the course of conduct which they themselves have decided to adopt or contemplate adopting on the market.[117]

Alternatively,

> conduct may fall under Article [101](1) as a concerted practice where the parties have not agreed or decided in advance among themselves what each will do in the market,

---

114 Case T-41/96 *Bayer* v *Commission* [2000] ECR II-3383, at para. 69.

115 Decision 1999/60 (*Pre-Insulated Pipes*) [1999] OJ L24/1, at para. 129. Similar formulations in Decision 94/815 (*Cement*) [1994] OJ L343/1; Decision 94/601 (*Cartonboard*) [1994] OJ L243/1; Decision 1999/210 (*British Sugar/Tate & Lyle/Napier Brown/James Budgett*) [1999] OJ L76/1.

116 Case 48/69 *ICI* v *Commission* (Dyestuffs) [1972] ECR 619, at para. 64; Cases 40 etc./73 *Coöperatieve Vereniging 'Suiker Unie'* v *Commission* [1975] ECR 1663, at para. 26; Case 172/80 *Zückner* v *Bayerische Vereinsbank* [1981] ECR 2021, at para. 12. *Suiker Unie* adds 'which leads to conditions of competition which do not correspond to the normal conditions of the market'.

117 Cases 40 etc./73 *Suiker Unie, ibid.*, at paras 174–4; also Cases T-305 etc./94 *Limburgse Vinyl Maatschappij* v *Commission* [1999] ECR II-931, at para. 720.

but knowingly adopt or adhere to some collusive device which encourages or facilitates the co-ordination of their commercial activity.[118]

The object of the Treaties in creating the concept of concerted practice 'was to forestall the possibility of undertakings evading the application of competition rules by colluding in an anti-competitive manner falling short of a definite agreement'.[119] It is clearly intended to catch collusive conduct between or amongst undertakings which is a product not of an agreement, however generously defined, but of a nod and a wink: not a concurrence of wills, but informal accommodation or an understanding. And such conduct is legion. However, concerted practice is not a 'subset' of agreement, or a device simply to lessen the evidential burden where the existence of an agreement cannot be shown or adduced, but a construct of independent scope and application. Having said that, it is one which resists precise definition.

The difficulty is, of course, one of proof. Undertakings consciously engaged in **13.27** anticompetitive conduct, be it by medium of agreement or of concerted practice, may go to great lengths to cover their tracks. Where there is no agreement it is much easier to do. In either case, it is the reason behind the adoption by the Commission of a policy of not imposing or of mitigating fines for cartel whistleblowers.[120] But assuming no breaking of ranks, it may not be an easy matter to show the existence of a concerted practice, which must in all events be based upon concrete evidence and not mere hypothesis.[121] The prime indicator, although not necessarily in itself constitutive of a concerted practice,[122] is parallel conduct – suspiciously uniform and contemporaneous price rises (price parallelism being in the first rank of concerted practices) or refusal to deal outwith established markets, for example. But this is inherently risky, as there may be a fine line between independent 'intelligent adaptation to market conditions', or 'innocent parallel behaviour', which is not objectionable, and the 'knowing substitution of practical cooperation', 'conscious parallelism', 'artificial certainty' or most commonly 'concertation', which is. It is an especially fine line in oligopolistic markets in which the 'normal conditions of the market' may be marked by price parallelism.[123] The Court of Justice has said that evidence must be 'sufficiently precise and coherent ... to justify the view that the parallel behaviour ... was the result of concerted action'[124] and that '[i]n the absence of a

---

118   Decision 1999/210 (*British Sugar/Tate & Lyle/Napier Brown/James Budgett*) [1999] OJ L76/1, at para. 69.
119   Decision 94/601 (*Cartonboard*) [1994] OJ L243/1, at para. 126.
120   See 13.100 below.
121   Cases T-374 etc./94 *European Night Services* v *Commission* [1998] ECR II-3141.
122   Case 48/69 *ICI* v *Commission* (Dyestuffs) [1972] ECR 619.
123   See 13.125–13.130 below.
124   Cases 29 and 30/83 *Compagnie Royale Asturienne des Mines* v *Commission* [1984] ECR 1679, at para. 20.

firm, precise and consistent body of evidence, it must be held that concertation ... has not been established'.[125] A simple formulation is whether the existence of concertation is necessarily to be inferred. Put another way, if parties alleged to be engaged in a concerted practice can show any one (persuasive) reason why their conduct can be attributable to other than concertation, a concerted practice cannot be found.[126] It may in particular be inferred from parallel conduct following contact between or amongst the parties. This is because a motive force of competition is uncertainty as to the conduct of competitors, and the exchange of commercially confidential information cannot but inform those taking part as to their future conduct, which is therefore of itself anticompetitive even if it cannot be shown that market conduct was as a result of this information adjusted in any way.[127] A single meeting of competitors may be enough to draw an inference of concertation in the market,[128] and it is for them to show they took no account of any information exchanged.[129] The narrower (more oligopolistic) the market the greater the sensitivity and value of information,[130] and so the greater the threat to competition.

13.28   Whilst agreement and concerted practice are independent and distinct concepts, there is no rigid dividing line between the two and they are not mutually exclusive to a given situation. Especially where there is a complex of cartel relationships amongst undertakings which contains elements of both and extends over a period of time, the Commission turned to finding a single infringement of article 101(1), and in this it has been supported by the General Court.[131]

(ii)   Decisions of associations of undertakings

13.29   The inclusion amongst the three classes of restrictive practices of 'decisions of associations of undertakings' was intended to catch anticompetitive conduct which might otherwise fall uncomfortably between the two stools of

---

125   Cases 89 etc./85 *Åhlström* v *Commission* (Woodpulp) [1993] ECR I-1307, at para. 127.

126   Cases 29 and 30/83 *Compagnie Royale Asturienne des Mines*, n. 124 above; Cases 89 etc./85 *Woodpulp, ibid.*; Case T-145/89 *Baustahlgewebe* v *Commission* [1995] ECR II-987.

127   Case T-1/89 *Rhône-Poulenc* v *Commission* (Polypropylene) [1991] ECR II-867; upheld, albeit upon slightly different reasoning, on appeal as Case C-199/92P *Hüls* v *Commission* (Polypropylene) [1999] ECR I-4287; Cases C-182 etc./02P *Dansk Rørindustri and ors* v *Commission* [2005] ECR I-5425, at paras 132–51.

128   Case C-8/08 *T-Mobile Netherlands and ors* v *Raad van bestuur van de Nederlandse Mededingingsautoriteit* [2009] ECR I-4529.

129   Case C-8/08 *T-Mobile Netherlands, ibid.*

130   Case T-34/92 *Fiatagri and New Holland Ford* v *Commission* [1994] ECR II-905; Case T-35/92 *John Deere* v *Commission* [1994] ECR II-957; Case C-8/08 *T-Mobile Netherlands*, n. 129 above.

131   Case T-1/89 *Rhône-Poulenc* v *Commission* (Polypropylene) [1991] ECR II-867; Cases T-354 etc./94 *Stora Kopparbergs Bergslags and ors* v *Commission* (Cartonboard) [1998] ECR II-2111; Cases T-141 etc./94 *Thyssen Stahl and ors* v *Commission* (Steel Beams) [1999] ECR II-347; Cases T-25 etc./95 *Cimentieries CBR and ors* v *Commission* (Cement) [2000] ECR II-491; Cases T-236 etc./01 *Tokai Carbon and ors* v *Commission* (Graphite Electrodes) [2004] ECR II-1181.

coordination between or amongst undertakings (article 101) and the unilateral conduct of a single undertaking (article 102). An association of undertakings is normally a trade association which is made up of separate undertakings, the purpose of which is to represent and defend the interests of its constituent members, although in the Union context it embraces other forms of association, most commonly agricultural cooperatives.[132] A trade union may be an association of undertakings but only if its members are independent economic operators (and so undertakings).[133]

Any direction of an association of undertakings which leads to price fixing, the **13.30** imposition of quotas amongst their members or the allocation of markets will breach article 101(1). An association may also engage in activities – exchange of information, collection of statistical and other data for example – which lead all too easily to a concerted practice amongst its members.[134] As a general rule, membership of an association necessarily means acceptance of its rules and conduct and implies awareness of its activities; so where an association issues instructions for a proposed course of action, whether or not all members are expected to take part, and the results of implementation of the instructions are subsequently communicated to all, an agreement involving all members exists even if they took no positive action.[135]

The inclusion in article 101(1) of the three classes of restrictive practices – **13.31** agreements, decisions of associations of undertakings and concerted practices – was intended as a comprehensive description of the devices by which independent undertakings could prevent, restrict or distort competition. Nevertheless, anticompetitive conduct must fall within one or another of them in order to be proscribed. Thus, where the Commission imputed the existence of anticompetitive agreements between a pharmaceutical manufacturer and wholesalers in a number of member states consisting in the former's restriction of supplies in order to discourage parallel exports, such conduct was plainly, and admittedly, anticompetitive; but it was not caught by article 101(1) because, however elastic its meaning, the Commission erred in finding the existence of an agreement.[136] But it will be few anticompetitive practices which slip through the net.[137]

---

132 Case 61/80 *Coöperatieve Stremsel- en Kleurselfabriek* v *Commission* [1981] ECR 851; Case C-250/92 *Gøttrup-Klim* v *Dansk Landbrugs Grovvarselskab* [1994] ECR I-5641.

133 Decision 2003/600 (*French Beef*) [2003] OJ L209/12.

134 E.g., Case T-29/92 *Vereniging van Samenwerkende Prijsregelende Organisaties in de Bouwnijverheid* v Commission [1995] ECR II-289; Decision 94/815 (*Cement*) [1994] OJ L343/1.

135 Decision 94/815 (*Cement*), *ibid.*, at para. 45(8).

136 Case T-41/96 *Bayer* v *Commission* [2000] ECR II-3383; upheld on appeal as Cases C-2 and 3/01P *Artzneimittel-Importeure and Commission* v *Bayer* [2004] ECR I-23.

137 For example, the Court has readily accepted that in the context of a selective distribution system, most common in the motor trade, a dealer may be presumed to comply with all terms adopted from time to time,

(b) Which may affect trade between Member States

13.32 In order that article 101(1) be joined, an anticompetitive agreement, decision or concerted practice must affect, or be capable of affecting, trade between member states – sometimes called informally the 'intra-Community clause'. So a restrictive practice, even a gross cartel, will not fall within the prohibition if its effects are limited to the territory of a single member state, and it will be governed, if at all, by the national competition rules there in force. This is entirely consistent with the principle of subsidiarity. Equally, a restrictive practice which affects trade between a member state and one or more non-member states will also escape the prohibition, for it does not affect trade *between* member states. The effect upon trade between member states, and the effect upon competition generally, is required also to be 'appreciable'.

13.33 The test for a restrictive practice which may affect trade between member states was first set out by the Court of Justice in *Société Technique Minière*:

> It is in fact to the extent that the agreement may affect trade between Member States that the interference with competition caused by that agreement is caught by the prohibitions of … Article [101], while in the converse case it escapes those prohibitions. For this requirement to be fulfilled it must be possible to foresee with a sufficient degree of probability on the basis of a set of objective factors of law or of fact that the agreement in question may have an influence, direct or indirect, actual or potential, on the pattern of trade between Member States.[138]

The normal test is consideration of the nature of the relevant market(s), supply, demand, cost and price structures, the place of the parties in the market (and in related markets) and assessment of the competition in question as it would occur in the absence of the agreement or practice in dispute.[139] It is not necessary to examine each clause individually in order to show an effect upon trade, it is enough if an agreement viewed in the round does so.[140] As is clear from the *Société Technique Minière* formulation which includes 'potential' effect, article 101(1) does not require that agreements or practices have actually affected trade between member states, only that they are capable of having that

---

apparently unilaterally, by the manufacturer, which will therefore go to the existence of an agreement between them. See e.g., Cases 25 and 26/84 *Ford Werke* v *Commission* [1985] ECR 2725; Case C-70/93 *Bayerische Motorenwerke* v *ALD Auto-Leasing* [1995] ECR I-3439; Case T-62/98 *Volkswagen* v *Commission* [2000] ECR II-2707; cf. Case T-208/01 *Volkswagen* v *Commission* [2003] ECR II-5141.

138 Case 56/65 *Société Technique Minière* v *Maschinenbau Ulm* [1966] ECR 235, at 249.

139 Case 56/65 *Société Technique Minière*, ibid.; Cases 209 etc./78 *van Landewycke* v *Commission* (FEDETAB) [1980] ECR 3125; Case 61/80 *Coöperatieve Stremsel- en Kleurselfabriek* v *Commission* [1981] ECR 851; Case T-34/92 *Fiatagri and New Holland Ford* v *Commission* [1994] ECR II-905.

140 Cases 25 and 26/84 *Ford Werke* v *Commission* [1985] ECR 2725; Case 193/83 *Windsurfing International* v *Commission* [1986] ECR 611.

effect.[141] Even where all parties to an agreement are situated in one member state, and so on its face it produces effects which are restricted to that state, article 101 is not necessarily excluded; especially where an agreement or practice extends throughout the territory of the state, it may have a tendency to inhibit real or potential competitors in other member states from entering or establishing themselves in the market and so

> by its very nature has the effect of reinforcing the compartmentalization of markets on a national basis, thereby holding up the economic interpenetration which the Treaty is designed to bring about and protecting domestic production.[142]

Once the test is satisfied the matter falls legitimately within Union jurisdiction; there is, as yet, no consideration or application of a (further) subsidiarity test.

Of course, even a remote overseas contract could have a *potential* effect upon **13.34** intra-Union trade because it may restrict resale of the contract goods outwith the contract territory and so in(to) the Union market. The relevant question in this context is the next test to be applied to an effect upon trade between member states, and that is whether competition is affected appreciably.

(i) De minimis

The Court of Justice said early on that not only must trade be affected between **13.35** member states, it – and competition generally – must be affected to an 'appreciable' extent.[143] In order to assist in determining when trade and competition are affected appreciably (or perceptibly), the Commission has adopted a series of notices on agreements 'of minor importance'. According to the current notice, adopted in 2001,[144] an agreement does not appreciably restrict competition, and so falls outwith the prohibition of article 101(1), if

(a)   in the case of horizontal agreements ('agreements between competitors'), the aggregate market share of all parties to it does not exceed 10 per cent of the relevant market; and

---

141   Case 19/77 *Miller* v *Commission* [1978] ECR 131; Case T-29/92 *Vereniging van Samenwerkende Prijsregelende Organisatie in de Bouwnijverheid* v *Commission* [1995] ECR II-289; Case C-219/95P *Ferriere Nord* v *Commission* [1997] ECR I-4411; Cases T-217 and 245/03 *Fédération nationale de la coopération bétail et viande* v *Commission* [2006] ECR II-4987, at para. 68.

142   Case 8/72 *Vereeniging van Cementhandelaren* v *Commission* [1972] ECR 977, at para. 29; Case 42/84 *Remia* v *Commission* [1985] ECR 2545, at para. 22; Case C-35/96 *Commission* v *Italy* [1998] ECR I-3851, at para. 48.

143   Case 56/65 *Société Technique Minière* v *Maschinenbau Ulm* [1966] ECR 235; Case 5/69 *Völk* v *Vervaecke* [1969] ECR 295; Case T-328/03 *O₂ (Germany)* v *Commission* [2006] ECR II-1231, at para. 68.

144   Notice on agreements of minor importance which do not appreciably restrict competition under article 81(1) of the Treaty establishing the European Community (de minimis) [2001] OJ C368/13. This is the fifth such notice, each replacing previous notices adopted, in turn, in 1970, 1977, 1986 and 1997.

(b) in the case of vertical agreements ('agreements between non-competitors'), the market share held by each of the parties does not exceed 15 per cent of any of the relevant markets affected by the agreement.

However, expressly excluded from the field of the notice are the 'hardcore restrictions' of horizontal price fixing, production quotas and market sharing[145] and, for vertical agreements, minimum price fixing and absolute territorial protection[146] – although this ought not to be taken to mean that hardcore restraints are beyond *de minimis* immunity, rather only that the notice is silent on them. The notice 'acknowledges' that agreements between small and medium-sized enterprises (SMEs) as defined by Union law[147] are 'rarely capable' of appreciably affecting trade between member states.[148] In the event of an agreement falling within the terms of the notice the Commission will not institute proceedings, and where parties erroneously but in good faith assumed this to be so, the Commission will impose no fines.[149] The notice is of general application.

(ii)   Networks of agreements

13.36 There is a particular problem with agreements which taken singly will benefit from the *de minimis* defence but form part of a larger whole which may not do so. For example, a tied lease between a brewer and a publican is an agreement within the meaning of article 101. It normally ties the hands of the publican in various ways which are anticompetitive and would offend article 101(1) *except* that any restrictive provisions of a single lease over one public house cannot possibly exert an appreciable effect upon intra-Union trade. But a large number of like leases with a major brewer taken cumulatively (and so a 'network' or 'bundle' of agreements) could do so.

13.37 The Court of Justice established early on the principle that it is necessary to consider agreements not in isolation but in the broader context of the general body of contracts of which they form part.[150] But the template was laid down

---

145   *Ibid.* para. 11(1).

146   *Ibid.* para. 11(2).

147   Commission recommendation 2003/361 [2003] OJ L124/36.

148   2001 notice on agreements of minor importance, n. 144 above, para. 3. However it is important to note that an SME caught up in a cartel involving larger players will not be exculpated by its size; e.g., Decision 85/206 (*Aluminium Imports from Eastern Europe*) [1985] OJ L92/1; Case T-56/99 *Marlines* v *Commission* [2003] ECR II-5225.

149   *Ibid.* para. 4. But see Case C-226/11 *Expedia v Autorité de la concurrence and ors*, pending, in which the Court is considering whether, and if so how far, national competition authorities are bound by the terms of the notice when they are enforcing both art. 101 and the equivalent national law.

150   Case 23/67 *Brasserie de Haecht* v *Wilkin* [1967] ECR 407.

subsequently in *Delimitis*,[151] in which the Court developed a twofold and cumulative test (the first and second *Delimitis* conditions, or *Delimitis 1* and *2*): first, will a network of agreements taken cumulatively and in their context foreclose the market or hinder significantly the access of producers in other member states to it ? If 'yes', second, does a particular bundle of agreements contribute significantly to that foreclosure? In the 2001 *de minimis* notice the Commission posits that a cumulative foreclosure effect is likely if more than 30 per cent of the relevant market is covered by parallel networks of agreements having similar effects, and a single supplier or distributor does not contribute significantly to that foreclosure if it has a market share of less than 5 per cent.[152]

(c) Which have as their object or effect

An agreement, decision or concerted practice may fall foul of article 101(1) if its **13.38** object *or* effect is to distort competition. '"[I]nfringements by object" [are] forms of collusion between undertakings [which] can be regarded, by their very nature, as being injurious to the proper functioning of normal competition'.[153] It is an objective, not subjective, test:

> [E]ven supposing it to be established that the parties to an agreement acted without any subjective intention of restricting competition, but with the object of remedying the effects of a crisis in their sector, such considerations are irrelevant for the purposes of applying [article 101(1)]. Indeed, an agreement may be regarded as having a restrictive object even if it does not have the restriction of competition as its sole aim but also pursues other legitimate objectives.[154]

They are not cumulative but alternative conditions.[155] Thus an agreement which is not intended to distort competition, but nevertheless does so, is caught,[156] as is an agreement the (objective) purpose of which is to distort competition but fails to produce the intended result. Put another way, if the

---

151 Case C-234/89 *Delimitis* v *Henninger Bräu* [1991] ECR I-935. See subsequently Case C-214/99 *Neste Markkinointi* v *Yötuuli* [2000] ECR I-11121; Case T-65/98 *van den Bergh Foods* v *Commission* [2003] ECR II-4653; for a British example, *Calor Gas* v *Express Fuels (Scotland) and anor* [2008] CSOH 13.

152 2001 Notice on agreements of minor importance, n. 144 above, para. 8.

153 Case C-209/07 *Competition Authority* v *Beef Industry Development Society and anor* [2008] ECR I-8637, at para. 17; also Case C-8/08 *T-Mobile Netherlands and ors* v *Raad van bestuur van de Nederlandse Mededinging-sautoriteit* [2009] ECR I-4529, at para. 29. This formula, from the Third Chamber (of five judges, four of them the same in the two cases), comes close to the '*per se* rule' recognised in US antrirust law. For an extensive discussion of an anticompetitive object being attributable to measures adopted in the (vertical) context of distribution of goods see the opinion of A-G Trstenjak in Cases C-501 etc./06P *GlaxoSmithKline Services Unlimited* v *Commission* [2009] ECR I-9291, at paras 89–137.

154 Case C-209/07 *Beef Industry Development Society, ibid.*, at para. 21. See also the lengthy discussion of the issue by A-G Trstenjak.

155 Case 56/65 *Société Technique Minière* v *Maschinenbau Ulm* [1966] ECR 235.

156 See Case 56/65 *Société Technique Minière, ibid.*; Case C-306/96 *Javico International* v *Yves Saint Laurent Parfums* [1998] ECR I-1983. See also Case T-328/03 *O₂ (Germany)* v *Commission* [2006] ECR II-1231, at paras 65–73.

object of an agreement can be shown to be anticompetitive, it is unnecessary to show that it produces that effect:[157]

> In any case, for Article [101](1) to be applicable, it is sufficient for there to have been the intention to restrict competition; it is not necessary for the intention to have been carried out, in full or only in part, that is to say, for the restriction of competition to have been put into effect.[158]

This applies inevitably to a cartel, where the Commission will identify its existence and look no further for the effects it produces. But it applies also to a less blatantly objectionable anticompetitive agreement (or part of an agreement) which was never put into force,[159] or one which has been suspended or is formally no longer in force, in which case it is sufficient to show that it continues to produce its effects after formal suspension or termination.[160] The fact that the object of the agreement cannot be achieved[161] or that a party to it never intended to comply[162] is irrelevant. Indeed, optimal benefit for the individual undertaking may be had from the formation of a cartel upon which it cheats. In other words, '[a]n undertaking which, despite colluding with its competitors, follows a policy that departs from that agreed on may simply be trying to exploit the cartel for its own benefit'[163] and is not exonerated.

(d)   *Prevention, restriction or distortion of competition within the internal market*

(i)   *Preliminary issues*

13.39   Agreements and concerted practices which may prevent, restrict or distort competition can be divided into two broad subsets, horizontal and vertical arrangements. Whilst the law of some jurisdictions sometimes formally distinguishes between the two,[164] article 101(1) does not. A horizontal agreement or practice is an agreement or practice between or amongst two or more undertakings at the same level of supply, at its most basic an agreement between direct

---

157   Cases 56 and 58/64 *Établissements Consten and Grundig-Verkaufs* v *EEC Commission* [1966] ECR 299; Case 277/87 *Sandoz Prodotti Farmaceutici* v *Commission* [1990] ECR I-45; Case C-219/95P *Ferriere Nord* v *Commission* [1997] ECR I-4411; Case C-199/92P *Hüls* v *Commission* (Polypropylene) [1999] ECR I-4287.

158   Decision 84/405 (*Zinc Producer Group*) [1984] OJ L220/27, at para. 71.

159   Case T-43/92 *Dunlop Slazenger* v *Commission* [1994] ECR II-441; Case T-77/92 *Parker Pen* v *Commission* [1994] ECR II-549.

160   Case 51/75 *EMI* v *CBS* [1976] ECR 811; Case 243/83 *Binon* v *Agence et Messageries de la Presse* [1985] ECR 2015.

161   Decision 89/515 (*Welded Steel Mesh*) [1989] OJ L260/1, upheld on review as Case T-148/89 *Tréfilunion* v *Commission* [1995] ECR II-1063.

162   Case T-141/89 *Tréfileurope Sales* v *Commission* [1995] ECR II-791, at para. 60; Case T-18/03 *CD-Contact Data* v *Commission* [2009] ECR II-1021, at para. 67.

163   Case T-18/03 *CD-Contact Data, ibid.*, at para. 67.

164   E.g., both German and Austrian law did so until 2005; see §§ 14–18 GWB (pre-2005) and §§ 30a–30e öKG 1988/600 (both repealed); also the Chinese Antimonopoly Law, n. 11 above, arts 13, 14.

competitors to fix prices or to share out markets – in other words, the meat and drink of the classic cartel. That horizontal cartel arrangements are the main target of article 101 is clear from the first three examples provided in article 101(1) which 'in particular' prevent, restrict or distort competition: price fixing, production quotas and market sharing. These, along with bid rigging, were recognised in 1998 by the OECD as the hardcore cartels which 'most egregiously' restrict competition.[165] These may be elements present in and given effect by vertical arrangements as well, but they are barest and most grievous in a cartel. In fact the application of article 101(1) to horizontal agreements is fairly straightforward, and becomes difficult only in the context of vertical agreements where the application is much more nuanced.

(ii)   Horizontal agreements

Price fixing agreements: the clearest and most transparent medium of competition is that of price. Agreements or practices aimed at restricting price competition are therefore a matter of 'indisputable gravity'.[166] There have been a large number of cases in which the Commission has pursued price fixing cartels,[167] many of which involved not only price fixing but also production quotas (almost necessarily, in order to sustain the extracompetitive prices) and market sharing. And these are only the cases involving large-scale cartels covering all or substantial parts of the Union; the Commission also pursues price fixing practices in which only two undertakings are involved.[168] Price fixing elements may also be present in vertical agreements. Whilst most of the cases have involved agreements amongst producers of goods, the prohibition applies equally to agreements amongst suppliers of services.   **13.40**

The prohibition applies not only to price fixing *simpliciter*, but to any agreement or practice the effect of which is to suppress price competition or to distort the normal formation of prices on the market, extending, for example, to   **13.41**

---

165   OECD Council Recommendation concerning effective action against hard core cartels, C(98)35/FINAL.
166   Decision 94/210 (*HOV SVZ/MCN*) [1994] OJ L104/34 ,at para. 259; Decision 1999/243 (*Transatlantic Conference Agreement*) [1999] OJ L95/1, at para. 591.
167   Pre-eminent are Decision 85/202 (*Woodpulp*) [1985] OJ L85/1; Decision 86/398 (*Polypropylene*) [1986] OJ L230/1; Decision 89/190 (*PVC I*) [1989] OJ L74/1; Decision 94/599 (*PVC II*) [1994] OJ L349/14; Decision 89/191 (*LdPE*) [1989] OJ L74/21; Decision 89/515 (*Welded Steel Mesh*) [1989] OJ L260/1; Decision 94/215 (*Steel Beams*) [1994] OJ L116/1; Decision 94/601 (*Cartonboard*) [1994] OJ L243/1; Decision 94/815 (*Cement*) [1994] OJ L343/1; Decision 1999/60 (*Pre-Insulated Pipes*) [1999] OJ L24/1; Decision 2002/271 (*Graphite Electrodes*) [2002] OJ L100/1; Decision 2002/742 (*Citric Acid*) [2002] OJ L239/18; Decision 2003/2 (*Vitamins*) [2003] OJ L6/1; Decision 2005/493 (*Sorbates*) [2005] OJ L182/20; Decision 2006/485 (*Copper Plumbing Tubes*) [2006 OJ L192/21; Case COMP/38.638 *Synthetic Rubber* [2008] OJ C7/11 (summary publication); Case COMP/38.899 *Gas Insulated Switchgear* [2008] OJ C5/7 (summary publication); Case COMP/38.823 *Lifts and Escalators* [2008] OJ C75/19 (summary publication).
168   E.g., Decision 2005/590 (*Christie's/Sotheby's*) [2005] OJ L200/92.

arrangements for pooling profits or indemnifying losses,[169] intervention buying[170] and joint prohibition of discounts or rebates.[171] Indeed, given the nature of a concerted practice an exchange of price information may in itself be (or more accurately, lead inexorably to) a breach of article 101(1).[172] It is irrelevant that prices agreed or concerted upon cannot be achieved,[173] that a party or parties to them had no intention of adhering to any accommodation made[174] or that it leads to an increase or decrease in price.[175] They are all hardcore breaches of article 101(1) and if detected by the Commission will attract censure and high fines.

13.42 Article 101(1) applies equally to price fixing on the demand side. There have been few cases of this except for instances of collusive tendering or bid rigging.[176] Bid rigging may well also attract the application of the criminal law in a number of member states.[177]

13.43 *Production quotas*: a quota agreement is a type of market sharing whereby competitors fix or limit the quantity of goods (or less commonly services) they each produce and/or market. It is an indirect means of, and goes hand in hand with, price fixing, its purpose being artificially to adjust supply to demand. As price is closely a function of supply, production quotas may directly, certainly indirectly, affect price competition.[178] Quota arrangements are frequently an ancillary to, and buttress, price fixing agreements or practices.[179] It is a classic form of market sharing and a hardcore breach of article 101(1), being expressly prohibited as a 'limit[ation] or control [of] production'.[180] However, it is not an easy cartel to engineer: it may be difficult to allocate quotas and it is difficult to

---

169 Decision 91/299 (*Soda Ash*) [1991] OJ L152/21; Cases T-213/95 and 18/96 *Stichting Certificatie Kraan-verhuurbedrijf* v *Commission* [1997] ECR II-1739; Decision 1999/60 (*Pre-Insulated Pipes*) [1999] OJ L24/1.
170 Decision 84/405 (*Zinc Producer Group*) [1984] OJ L220/27.
171 Cases 209 etc./78 *van Landewyck* v *Commission* (FEDETAB) [1980] ECR 3125; Cases T-68 etc./89 *Società Italiano Vetro* v *Commission* (Flat Glass) [1992] ECR II-1403.
172 See 13.26–13.27 above, and especially Case COMP/37.152 *Plasterboard*, decision of 27 November 2002, not yet published.
173 Decision 89/515 (*Welded Steel Mesh*) [1989] OJ L260/1.
174 Decision 86/399 (*Belgian Roofing Felt*) [1986] OJ L232/15.
175 Decision 86/398 (*Polypropylene*) [1986] OJ L230/1; Cases T-213/95 and 18/96 *Stichting Certificatie Kraan-verhuurbedrijf* v *Commission* [1997] ECR II-1739.
176 Cases 40 etc./73 *Coöperatieve Vereniging 'Suiker Unie'* v *Commission* [1975] ECR 1663; Case T-26/92 *Vereniging van Samenwerkende Prijsregelende Organisaties in de Bouwnijverheid* v *Commission* [1995] ECR II-289; Case COMP/38.899 *Gas Insulated Switchgear* [2008] OJ C5/7 (summary publication).
177 (UK) Enterprise Act 2002, s. 188; § 298 (deutsches) StGB; § 186b (öst.) StGB.
178 Decision 94/599 (*PVC II*) [1994] OJ L349/14, at para. 35.
179 E.g., Decision 94/601 (*Cartonboard*) [1994] OJ L243/1; Decision 94/815 (*Cement*) [1994] OJ L343/1; Decision 1999/60 (*Pre-Insulated Pipes*) [1999] OJ L24/1.
180 TFEU, art. 101(1)(b).

police. Of the classic cartels it is the least transparent and so the easiest upon which to cheat.

Market sharing: like price fixing, market sharing is normally a horizontal **13.44** accommodation which has the same effect, if prosecuted successfully, of eliminating or at least moderating price competition. Of the classic cartels it is the least difficult to engineer: the difficulties of actually agreeing on prices or quotas are avoided, and policing of cartel loyalty is easier. It is also less transparent a cartel than is price fixing, for it can be disguised by vertical selling arrangements and the allocation and exercise of intellectual property rights. It is seriously anticompetitive in itself – 'by [its] very nature restrict[s] competition within the meaning of Article [101](1)'[181] and a 'patent infringement [*infraction patente*, *offensichtliche Zuwiderhandlung*] of competition law'[182] – but particularly so in the Union context because it may (seek to) reinforce the isolation of national markets.

Other horizontal arrangements: there are some forms of horizontal cooperation **13.45** amongst undertakings which constitute no threat (or do so only remotely) to competition, and may be advantageous to small and medium-sized undertakings and to the consumer. Various 'cooperation agreements' fall within this category.[183] Other horizontal arrangements are less benign, but at the same time less offensive than the gross cartel. These include specialisation agreements and research and development agreements, which therefore enjoy the benefits of (block) exemption.[184] A hybrid of horizontal/vertical arrangements is the joint venture, which may or may not have anticompetitive qualities and which may fall for consideration – if at all – under article 101, article 102 if one of the parties enjoys market dominance, and the Merger Regulation.[185] Mergers and takeovers may be characterised as horizontal agreements when they are concerned with the fusion, or 'concentration', of competitors; they fall, if at all, under the Merger Regulation.[186]

(iii) Vertical agreements

Vertical agreements are those between undertakings at different levels on the **13.46** economic chain, such as, for example, between producer of raw materials and manufacturer, manufacturer and distributor, distributor and retailer, retailer and

---

181 Decision 1999/60 (*Pre-Insulated Pipes*) [1999] OJ L24/1, at para. 147.
182 Case C-534/07P *William Prym* v *Commission* [2009] ECR I-7415, at para. 68.
183 See the Commission notice on the applicability of article 81 of the EC Treaty to horizontal cooperation agreements [2001] OJ C3/2.
184 See 13.60–13.62 below.
185 The application of art. 101 to joint ventures is very complex and beyond the scope of this book. For some assistance see the Commission notice on the assessment of cooperative joint ventures [1993] OJ C43/2.
186 See 13.133–13.138 below.

customer or any variation within these distinctions. Primarily they address the contractual chain(s) between the original producer of a good or service and its eventual consumer. Their prime advantage is that they allow for net economic efficiency: they enable the producer to concentrate upon production and relieve it of the obligation of shifting the goods on the market, for that will be the concern of the (specialist) distributor who is better suited to the task. The consumer in turn is better served as the marketing of goods and services is devolved from their production and distinct efficiencies may thereby be produced at that level.

13.47 It was at the outset unclear if, and if so in what manner, article 101(1) applies to vertical agreements or practices, but the Court confirmed that it did so in 1966 in *Consten and Grundig*.[187] So article 101 is concerned not only with horizontal agreements which limit competition between competitors but also with vertical agreements which may encourage but nonetheless distort it. However, vertical arrangements are usually less objectionable than horizontal. The Court therefore views them with some equanimity, and has found article 101(1) not to be joined where an agreement can be said to restrain competition but does so only in certain contexts and minimally and justifiably.[188] This is sometimes said to recognise, and so import into Union law, a 'rule of reason', a construct of American antitrust law (with roots in the common law)[189] which permits agreements which are not *per se* anticompetitive to be saved by a balancing test from the prohibitions of the Sherman Act. But the term has never been used by the Court of Justice (except by Advocate-General Roemer in *Société Technique Minière*)[190] and the General Court has said:

> As regards [the] argument relating to application of the rule of reason in the present case, the Court would point out that the existence of such a rule in Community competition law is not accepted.[191]

---

187 Cases 56 and 58/64 *Établissements Consten and Grundig-Verkaufs* v *EEC Commission* [1966] ECR 299.
188 Case 56/65 *Société Technique Minière* v *Maschinenbau Ulm* [1966] ECR 235; Case 26/76 *Metro-SB-Großmärkte* v *Commission* (No. 1) [1977] ECR 1875; Case 75/84 *Metro-SB-Großmärkte* v *Commission* (No. 2) [1986] ECR 3021; Case 243/83 *Binon* v *Agence et Messageries de la Presse* [1985] ECR 2015; Case 258/78 *Nungesser* v *Commission* (Maize Seeds) [1982] ECR 2015; Case 161/84 *Pronuptia de Paris* v *Schillgalis* [1986] ECR 353; Case C-309/99 *Wouters* v *Algemene Raad van de Nederlandse Orde van Advokaten* [2002] ECR I-1577; Case C-519/04P *Meca-Medina and Majken* v *Commission* [2006] ECR I-6991; Case T-328/03 O_2 *(Germany)* v *Commission* [2006] ECR II-1231; Case C-271/08 *Commission* v *Germany* [2010] ECR I-7087, at para. 45.
189 See *Nordenfelt* v *Maxim Nordenfelt Guns & Ammunition Co.* [1894] AC 535, *per* Lord Macnaughten at 565.
190 Case 56/65 *Société Technique Minière*, n. 188 above, at 257: 'the introduction of such a rule of reason (let us give it that name) … '.
191 Case T-65/98 *van den Bergh Foods* v *Commission* [2003] ECR II-4653, at para. 106; repeated (in woeful English) in Case T-328/03 O_2 *(Germany)* v *Commission* [2006] ECR II-1231, at para. 69.

Yet it remains there are limits to the reach of article 101(1), applied hitherto to vertical arrangements and to anticompetitive restraints proportionate, objectively justifiable and ancillary to a legitimate commercial venture which is not hardcore anticompetitive; and it is sometimes called the rule of reason. But it is important to treat the term with great care both because of its foreign provenance, and because it is on any view of much narrower scope and application than its American progenitor.[192] Care should also be taken not to confuse it with the *de minimis* defence: both produce the same practical result, that the agreement in issue falls outwith the prohibition of article 101(1), but they do so for distinct reasons, the rule of reason because the restraints are minimal, proportionate and ancillary, *de minimis* because their effects are inappreciable. Both *de minimis* and rule of reason are also to be contrasted in turn with agreements which are exempted: those which offend article 101(1) but escape the prohibition because they are adjudged to meet the beneficial criteria provided in article 101(3), which applies to a number of aspects common to vertical agreements.

There are also practical differences between horizontal and vertical agreements, for whilst the standard of proof required for the purposes of establishing the existence of an anticompetitive agreement in the context of a vertical relationship is in principle no higher than that required in the context of a horizontal relationship,[193] it is in some respects not comparing like with like. Contact and information exchange between direct competitors is best avoided and may go to the existence of a concerted practice, but contact, exchange and indeed restraint between, for example, a supplier and a distributor is of course a necessary and blameless aspect of their contractual relationship. Further, distributors/dealers are dependent upon a supplier and are therefore in the weaker position; this may make it difficult for them to dissociate themselves from policies adopted (unilaterally?) by the latter and so to find acceptance of, or at least tacit acquiescence to, those policies which will form a 'concurrence of wills' to anticompetitive aspects of what is otherwise a wholesome relationship.[194] **13.48**

Common types of vertical agreements which fall to be considered under article 101 are the following. **13.49**

Exclusive distribution agreements: an efficient means of getting goods to the market, and of particular utility in the Union context, in which producers in one **13.50**

---

192 For particular consideration of transplantation of the rule of reason see the discussion of A-G Cosmas in Case C-235/92P *Montecatini* v *Commission* [1999] ECR I-4539, at paras 42–50.
193 Case C-260/09P *Activision Blizzard Germany* v *Commission*, [2011] ECR I-419, at para. 71.
194 Case C-260/09P *Activision Blizzard Germany*, *ibid.* See also the cases cited in n. 188 above.

member state now have access to 26 other markets but perhaps no long experience of dealing there, no knowledge of the market and no transport and marketing infrastructure there. The danger is that the exclusivity the distributor requires, and will demand, in order to combat free-riders and parallel traders may offend article 101(1). It is of particular sensitivity to Union competition law, given its integration goals, because of their tendency to seal off markets, particularly upon national lines. So minimum price fixing is a hardcore restraint,[195] as is, in Union law, exclusive territorial protection. An export ban is particularly to be reproached; as the General Court said of a series of motor dealership agreements which, by withholding bonuses from dealers, inhibited exports,

> the infringement had as its object the partitioning of the internal market. Such a patent infringement of competition law is, by its nature, particularly serious. It goes against the most fundamental aims of the Community and, in particular, the accomplishment of the internal market.[196]

Generally any measure which restricts parallel trade will have as its object the prevention or restriction of competition, but the presumption is rebuttable.[197] Some restraints which are less restrictive of competition may be saved by application of article 101(3).[198]

13.51 *Exclusive purchasing agreements*: the mirror image on the demand side of exclusive distribution agreements. Generally they improve distribution, assist market interpenetration, especially for small and medium-sized undertakings, and so increase consumer choice, and indirectly improve security of distribution systems and promotion of the contract product(s) at little or no cost to the retailer. As with any contract exclusivity they limit (voluntarily) the buyer's freedom of choice and run the risk of restricting competition and so breaching article 101(1), but they are generally less offensive to article 101(1) than are exclusive distribution agreements, for they do not confer upon the buyer/retailer an exclusive sales territory, and intra-brand competition is therefore not appreciably diminished; even where it is so, an exclusive purchasing agreement will often satisfy the criteria of article 101(3).

13.52 *Franchising*: franchising agreements are a specific type of distribution agreement marked by the additional element of licensing of the franchisor's know-how. Generally they are beneficial to competition, for they allow the franchisor

---

195   See 13.55 below.
196   Case T-368/00 *General Motors and Opel Nederland* v *Commission* [2003] ECR II-4491, at para. 191.
197   Case T-168/01 *GlaxoSmithKline Services* v *Commission* [2006] ECR II-2969, at paras 115, 116, 121.
198   See 13.56–13.62 below.

to penetrate new markets without set-up costs and allow the franchisee immediate start up upon the basis of the franchisor's methods and reputation. The application of article 101(1) to them is set out principally in the judgment of the Court of Justice in *Pronuptia*;[199] further restraints may fall within the ambit of article 101(3).

Selective distribution: a system in which a producer wishes to ensure that its **13.53** goods are sold at retail only in outlets which meet certain criteria laid down by the producer ('authorised dealers') and so sells only to them or imposes upon its distributors and/or wholesalers an obligation to do likewise and ensure the obligation is passed on in resale. The system is used normally for branded goods and found most commonly in the sale of technical equipment, luxury items and musical and film recordings, but it may be found elsewhere; and it is an inherent characteristic of the specialist motor trade. The selective nature of the system ensures on its face that the customer will have the advantage of, for example, knowledgeable sales staff and easy performance of a manufacturer's guarantee. But it also has the effect of limiting sales of goods to technical or 'posh' outlets when they could be sold more cheaply by less prepossessing retailers. By their nature they therefore restrict price competition. But because they are not a direct device for market sharing, and may actually assist interpenetration, the Court of Justice views them with a relatively benign eye, recognising as a 'rule of reason' criterion that of consumer protection.[200] A selective distribution system escapes article 101(1) entirely if outlets are selected upon qualitative criteria alone, such as staff training and technical and operation requirements of the outlet, which are related to and objectively justifiable given the nature of the goods (the 'principle of necessity'), proportionate and non-discriminatory (in which case it is a 'simple selective distribution' system), and assuming all the while that there remains a reasonable level of inter-brand competition. Other restrictions may be caught by article 101(1) but may qualify for exemption under article 101(3).

Licensing: a common and commonly vertical arrangement (although it may also **13.54** be addressed in specialisation and research and development agreements and joint ventures). Generally licensing agreements are pro-competitive: they permit a licensee to do something which would otherwise be unlawful and they allow the proprietor a reasonable return on his right whilst at the same time improving the efficiency of availability and distribution of goods and so promote market interpenetration. Many aspects of a licensing agreement are

---

199 Case 161/84 *Pronuptia de Paris* v *Schillgalis* [1986] ECR 353.
200 Case 26/76 *Metro-SB-Großmärkte* v *Commission* (No. 1) [1977] ECR 1875; Case 75/84 *Metro-SB-Großmärkte* v *Commission* (No. 2) [1986] ECR 3021; Case 107/82 *AEG-Telefunken* v *Commission* [1983] ECR 3151.

saved from article 101(1) because they fall within the specific subject matter of the right being licensed or enjoy the benefits of a rule of reason analysis or of exemption.

13.55 *Resale price maintenance*: a potential component of any vertical agreement is resale price maintenance. Depriving a buyer of the freedom to sell at a price of his choosing is an obvious restraint of competition, expressly prohibited by article 101(1) ('directly or indirectly fix[ing]… selling prices').[201] The prohibition applies not only at the retail level but throughout the producer–consumer chain.[202] Even in vertical arrangements price fixing is so objectionable that the relevant block exemption expressly discounts (minimum) resale price maintenance.[203] The setting of maximum retail prices or recommended retail prices appears to fall outwith the prohibition unless it amounts to a fixed resale price[204] or leads to concerted action.[205] Collective resale price maintenance (that is, a horizontal agreement amongst dealers, or a decision of their association of undertakings) is a clear breach of article 101(1).[206] Where resale price maintenance is a legal requirement in national law (this being less common than in the past, but it has not disappeared) the Commission may recognise that there may be a legitimate social aim pursued and will normally intervene only where there is a significant breach of article 101.

2. Exemption: article 101(3) TFEU

13.56 It was from the start recognised that so broad is the prohibition of article 101(1) that it may catch agreements or practices which might actually be beneficial in terms of competition or, alternatively, might produce benefits in other spheres which outweigh their anticompetitive effects. Article 101(3) therefore provides for the possibility of setting aside ('declaring inapplicable'), or exemption from, the prohibition provided a number of criteria are met. If exempt, an agreement or practice becomes valid and enforceable notwithstanding any breach of article 101(1). It is a benefit which applies only in the context of article 101, and not of article 102, conduct prohibited by which is always illegal without possibility of

---

201 TFEU, art. 101(1)(a).
202 E.g., Cases 209 etc./78 *van Landewyck* v *Commission* (FEDETAB) [1980] ECR 3125.
203 Regulation 2790/1999 [1999] OJ L336/21, art. 4(a); see immediately below. But cf. *Leegin Creative Leather Products* v *PSKS*, 551 US 877 (2007), in which the United States Supreme Court overturned almost 100 years of authority in finding that minimum resale price maintenance is not a *per se* breach of § 1 of the Sherman Act.
204 Follow-up to the Green Paper on vertical restraints [1998] OJ C365/3, section III.2.1.
205 Case 161/84 *Pronuptia de Paris* v *Schillgalis* [1986] ECR 353; Decision 85/616 (*Villeroy & Boch*) [1985] OJ L376/15; Decision 87/14 (*Yves Rocher*) [1987] OJ L8/49.
206 Cases 209 etc./78 FEDETAB, n. 202 above; Cases 43 and 63/82 *Vereniging ter Bevoerdering ven het Vlaamse Boekwezen* v *Commission* [1984] ECR 19; Cases 240 etc./82 *Stichting Sigarettenindustrie* v *Commission* [1985] ECR 3831; Case 45/85 *Verband der Sachversicherer* v *Commission* [1987] ECR 405.

exemption.[207] Exemption is available across all three categories of anticompetitive devices recognised by article 101 (agreements, decisions of associations of undertakings and concerted practices).

Exemption is available only if the agreement, decision or practice meets the **13.57** conditions set out in article 101(3), which are both positive and negative, two of each. The agreement must:

- positively, (1) contribute to 'improving the production or distribution of goods or to promoting technical or economic progress, while [2] allowing consumers a fair share of the resulting benefit'; and
- negatively, (3) neither 'impose on the undertakings concerned restrictions which are not indispensable to the attainment of these objectives' nor (4) 'afford such undertakings the possibility of eliminating competition in respect of a substantial part of the products in question'.

They are sometimes called, respectively, the efficiency test, the fair share for consumers test, the proportionality test and the elimination of competition test. It will be observed that they are purely economic in character; there is no provision for consideration of other criteria, such as cultural, environmental or social benefits or requirements.[208] It is for the undertaking(s) claiming the benefit of exemption to show that the agreement fulfils the four conditions,[209] and they must provide 'convincing arguments and evidence' to that purpose.[210] The four are cumulative and each must be met: an agreement or practice which fails to satisfy any one of the four does not qualify for exemption.[211] Each case must be examined carefully and impartially, in all its relevant aspects, to determine whether the benefit of article 101(3) applies.[212]

Prior to 2004 exemption was a matter exclusively for the Commission.[213] That **13.58** is, an anticompetitive agreement or practice caught by article 101(1) was presumptively unlawful, and enjoyed the benefit of exemption only if it was conferred by the Commission. Generally exemption was secured upon a case by case basis ('individual exemption') following 'notification' of the agreement or

---

207 Except by reference to art. 106(2); see 13.145 below.
208 But such considerations may be absorbed into exemption logic by reference to the various integration clauses scattered throughout the Treaty (see 7.11–7.20 above), although it seems rarely that they have done so.
209 Regulation 1/2003 [2003] OJ L1/1, art. 2.
210 Case T-168/01 *GlaxoSmithKline* v *Commission* [2006] ECR II-2969, at para. 235.
211 Case T-7/93 *Langnese-Iglo* v *Commission* [1995] ECR II-1533; Cases T-213/95 and 18/96 *Stichting Certificatie Kraanverhuurbedrijf* v *Commission* [1997] ECR II-1739; Case T-185/00 *Métropole Télévision and ors* v *Commission* [2002] ECR II-3805.
212 See e.g., Cases T-528 etc./93 *Métropole Télévision* v *Commission* [1996] ECR II-649.
213 Regulation 17/62 [1962] JO 204, art. 9.

practice to the Commission,[214] which, if satisfied the criteria of article 101(3) were met, would grant the exemption for a limited period of time. Alternatively, following authorisation by the Council,[215] the Commission adopted (starting in 1967)[216] a series of 'block exemptions' (exemption *de manière générale*) whereby an agreement or practice which satisfied all the criteria set out, and in particular offended none of the prohibited (informally, 'black list') criteria, was, without need for notification, automatically exempt from article 101(1).

13.59 The rules changed fundamentally in 2004. Instead of the (German) system of authorisation by administrative authority, a new 'directly applicable exemption system' – essentially the French approach of *exception légale*, or '*ex post* control' – was adopted, whereby the notification system was scrapped and article 101(3) made directly effective. Thus an anticompetitive agreement or practice is now valid from its formation provided that it satisfies the relevant tests for exemption. The change was implemented by Regulation 1/2003[217] which came into force in May 2004, by providing simply that:

> Agreements, decisions and concerted practices caught by Article 81(1) of the Treaty which satisfy the conditions of Article 81(3) of the Treaty shall not be prohibited, no prior decision to that effect being required.[218]

This places a great degree of faith in national courts, and in national competition authorities which are required – another innovation, part of Regulation 1/2003 – to play their part.[219] Indeed, there are fears that so vague, or arbitrary, are the four tests that article 101(3) cannot be, or ought not to be, treated as directly effective. In order to (seek to) ensure uniformity in the application of the re-fused article 101 in its entirety – applied now by the Commission, national administrative authorities and countless national civil and commercial courts – the Commission adopted a number of notices, of most direct importance here a notice providing extensive 'guidelines on the application of Article 101(3) of the Treaty'.[220] Other measures for the enforcement of articles 101 and 102 more generally, such as the establishment of a Network of Competition

---

214 The forms and procedures were laid down by Regulation 17, arts 4, 5 and Regulation 27/62 [1962] JO 1118.
215 There are five enabling Regulations authorising the adoption of block exemptions which apply to: vertical agreements (Regulation 19/65 [1965] JO 533); certain horizontal agreements (Regulation 2821/71 [1971] JO L285/46); liner conferences (Regulation 246/2009 [2009] OJ L79/1; a codification of Regulation 479/92 [1992] OJ L55/3); commercial air traffic agreements (Regulation 487/2009 [2009] OJ L148/1; a consolidation of Regulation 3976/87 [1987] OJ L374/9); and agreements in the insurance sector (Regulation 1534/91 [1991] OJ L143/1).
216 Regulation 67/67 [1967] JO 849 on exclusive dealing agreements; now repealed.
217 [2003] OJ L1/1.
218 *Ibid.* art. 1(2).
219 See 13.109–13.111 below.
220 [2004] OJ C101/97.

Authorities (NCAs) and cooperation between the Commission and national courts, will have a bearing upon the application of article 101(3); they are discussed below.[221]

Block exemptions

With the entry into force of Regulation 1/2003 block exemptions ought, in logic, to have become otiose. But they have been retained for greater certainty, the Treaties expressly recognise them for the first time with Lisbon[222] and the Commission will continue to adopt them. As at 1 September 2012 block exemptions are in force applicable in the following fields: **13.60**

- technology transfer;[223]
- agreements within liner shipping consortia;[224]
- agreements in the insurance sector;[225]
- vertical agreements;[226]
- the motor vehicle sector;[227]
- (horizontal) research and development agreements;[228] and
- (horizontal) specialisation agreements.[229]

The basic Regulations applying articles 101 and 102 to agriculture[230] and to transport by rail, road and inland waterway[231] contain provisions analogous to block exemption. There have been block exemptions in the past in the air transport sector, but none now in operation.

Since 1999 they were made more 'economic' (as opposed to 'form-based') in their approach. Thus the block exemption on vertical agreements, by far the **13.61**

---

221   See 13.109–13.118 below.
222   TFEU, art. 105(3).
223   Regulation 772/2004 [2004] OJ L123/11. See also Guidance on the Application of Article 81 of the EC Treaty to Technology Transfer Agreements [2004] OJ C101/2.
224   Regulation 906/2009 [2009] OJ L256/31. See also Guidelines on the Application of Article 81 of the EC Treaty to Maritime Transport Services [2008] OJ C245/2.
225   Regulation 267/2010 [2010] OJ L83/1. See also Communication from the Commission on the Application of Article 101(3) of the TFEU to the Insurance Sector [2010] OJ C82/2.
226   Regulation 330/2010 [2010] OJ L102/1 (replacing Regulation 2790/1999 [1999] OJ L336/21). See also the (very useful) Guidelines on Vertical Restraints [2010] OJ C130/1.
227   Regulation 461/2010 [2010] OJ L129/52. See also Supplementary Guidelines on Vertical Restraints in the Sale, Repair and Distribution for Motor Vehicles [2010] OJ C135/8.
228   Regulation 1217/2010 [2010] OJ L335/36. See also Guidelines on the Applicability of Article 101(3) of the TFEU to Horizontal Cooperation Agreements [2010] OJ C11/1.
229   Regulation 1218/2010 [2010] OJ L335/43. See also Guidelines, n. 228 above.
230   Regulation 1184/2006 [2006] OJ L214/7, art. 2; Regulation 1234/2007 [2007] OJ L299/1, art. 176; see 10.103 above.
231   Regulation 169/2009 [2009] OJ L61/1, arts 2, 3; see 11.217 above.

most widely applicable, exempts all vertical agreements[232] except those (a) between competing undertakings, although permitting certain non-reciprocal vertical agreements;[233] or involving (b) a supplier or a buyer which enjoys a market share exceeding 30 per cent of the relevant market;[234] or (c) an association of retailers including a member with an annual turnover exceeding €50 million.[235] The Regulation provides a 'black list' excluding certain hardcore restraints, principally the imposition of fixed or minimum resale prices,[236] certain resale conditions and forms of territorial protection (including passive (but not active) sales outwith the contract territory),[237] 'non-compete' clauses except of less than five years' duration,[238] restraints following termination of the agreement[239] and certain sales restrictions within a selective distribution system.[240] The Commission may declare the Regulation inapplicable where a relevant market is foreclosed to an extent by parallel networks of similar vertical restraints.[241] And, as with all block exemptions, both the Commission and national competition authorities may withdraw the benefits of exemption in a particular case where a vertical agreement falling within the Regulation nevertheless produces effects incompatible with article 101(3).[242]

13.62 The block exemptions continue to be of importance in securing legal certainty as to the validity of an agreement, but with the advent of a directly effective article 101(3) they are of less central importance. They still serve as a safe harbour: an agreement which falls within the terms of a block exemption is presumed to satisfy the four criteria for exemption, and parties to it are relieved of the onus of showing that it is so.[243] Nevertheless a national administrative authority or court may extend the benefits of article 101(3) beyond its terms if it is persuaded that it is justified in a particular case.

---

232 Regulation 330/2010; defined in art. 1(1)(a).

233 *Ibid.* art. 2(4). Previously there was an additional turnover threshold; Regulation 2790/1999, art. 2(4).

234 *Ibid.* art. 3. Previously the buyer's market share was taken into account only in the case of exclusive supply obligations. Market share is calculated in accordance with criteria provided in art. 7.

235 *Ibid.* art. 2(2). Annual turnover is to be calculated in accordance with criteria provided in art. 8.

236 *Ibid.* art. 4(a).

237 *Ibid.* art. 4(b), (c).

238 *Ibid.* art. 5(1)(a).

239 *Ibid.* art. 5(1)(b).

240 *Ibid.* arts 4(d), 5(1)(c).

241 *Ibid.* art. 6.

242 Regulation 1/2003, art. 29. But a national authority exercising this power must show that the territory of the member state, or a part of it, has characteristics of a distinct geographic market. The power has been expressly codified in most member states; see e.g., in the Netherlands, the Mededingingswet, art. 89a; in the United Kingdom, the Competition Act 1998 (Office of Fair Trading's Rules) Order 2004, SI 2004/2751, s. 13.

243 Notice on the application of Article 81(3) of the Treaty [2004] OJ C101/97, at para. 35.

C. ARTICLE 102 TFEU

1. General

Whilst article 101 is concerned with distortion to competition which is the **13.63** product of collaboration between or amongst undertakings, article 102 is concerned with the unilateral conduct of single undertakings which alone enjoy such market power that they are not bound by the discipline of competitive forces which (ought to) mark the play of the market. The natural target for regulation such as that laid down by article 102 is the monopoly. But it casts its nets wider than this, so bringing other undertakings within its discipline.

Article 102 is of a more straightforward construction than article 101. It **13.64** provides:

> Any abuse by one or more undertakings of a dominant position within the internal market or in a substantial part of it shall be prohibited as incompatible with the internal market in so far as it may affect trade between Member States.
>
> Such abuse may, in particular, consist in: …

and there follows a list of hardcore practices in which a monopoly producer or supplier might engage.

Article 102 therefore addresses expressly not monopolies, but rather undertak- **13.65** ings in a 'dominant position'. It does not outlaw monopolies as such: there is no 'recrimination' (reproche) attached to the existence of market dominance,[244] even monopolistic dominance. Rather it prohibits 'any abuse … of a dominant position', or, in words which more closely reflect other language versions of the Treaties, 'the abusive exploitation of a dominant position'. In any event the concepts are difficult to define. As with article 101(1) a series of examples of prohibited conduct is provided, and it will be seen that the list is exemplicative ('abuse may, *in particular*, consist in: …'), not exhaustive, and a host of infringements of article 102 have been found to exist beyond the examples given. It is also worth recalling that exemption is a benefit which applies only in the context of article 101, and not of article 102, conduct prohibited by which is always illegal without possibility of exemption.[245]

---

244 Case 322/81 *Michelin* v *Commission* [1983] ECR 3461, at para. 57.

245 See Case T-51/89 *Tetrapak* v *Commission* (Tetrapak I) [1990] ECR II-309. There is one exception to this rule, provided in art. 106(2); see 13.145 below. Of course it can be argued that art. 102 contains an implied exemption provision analogous to art. 101(3) in that conduct of a dominant undertaking which might benefit from an availability of exemption because of the economic benefits it brings may thereby cease to be abusive conduct and so fall outwith the prohibition. Cf. the defence of objective justification: 'If the behaviour of an

13.66 Abuse of a dominant position therefore has two consecutive components: market dominance, which is not prohibited, and abusive exploitation of that dominance, which is. A third hurdle necessary to bring article 102 into play is that the abusive conduct may affect trade between member states. It should be borne in mind that whilst most of the case law on article 102 has concerned dominance (and abuse thereof) in the manufacture, production, distribution and sale of goods, its prohibition applies equally – and recently with vigour – to the provision of services. It also applies – although this has seen limited play – to dominance on the demand side, that is in monopsonistic markets, in the purchase of goods and services.[246]

13.67 Article 102 prohibits abuse by one 'or more' undertakings of a dominant position. It is only latterly that the Commission has turned its guns on abusive conduct of undertakings which together enjoy joint or collective dominance. This will be considered below.[247]

2. Dominance

13.68 A dominant position within the meaning of article 102 is, put concisely:

> a position of economic strength enjoyed by an undertaking which enables it to prevent effective competition being maintained on the relevant market by affording it the power to behave to an appreciable extent independently of its competitors, its customers and ultimately of consumers. Such a position does not preclude some competition, which it does where there is a monopoly or quasi-monopoly, but enables the undertaking which profits by it, if not to determine, at least to have an appreciable influence on the conditions under which that competition will develop, and in any case to act largely in disregard of it so long as such conduct does not operate to its detriment.[248]

13.69 Dominance is, in other words, a position of market power in which an undertaking is not constrained in its conduct by competitive forces. Further,

> [t]he power to exclude effective competition is not however in all cases coterminous with independence from competitive factors but may also involve the ability to eliminate or seriously weaken existing competitors or to prevent potential competitors from entering the market.[249]

---

undertaking in a dominant position can be objectively justified, it is not an abuse'; Case C-49/07 *Motosykletistiki Omospondia Ellados* v *Elliniko Dimosio* [2008] ECR I-4863, *per* A-G Kokott at para. 89 of her opinion.

246   See e.g., Case T-219/99 *British Airways* v *Commission* [2003] ECR II-5917.
247   See 13.129–13.130 below.
248   Case 85/76 *Hoffmann–La Roche* v *Commission* [1979] ECR 461, at paras 38–9; reformulated in Case 322/81 *Michelin* v *Commission* [1983] ECR 3461, at para. 30 as 'enables it to *hinder the maintenance of effective competition* on the relevant market by *allowing it* to behave to an appreciable extent independently'.
249   Decision 85/609 (*AKZO*) [1985] OJ L374/1, at para. 67.

It may also therefore exist in the power an undertaking may exert not only in the market but upon the structure of the market. In order to determine whether an undertaking occupies a dominant position it is necessary to apply a two stage test: first, to identify the relevant market and second, to assess the market strength of an undertaking alleged to be dominant therein.

(a) Relevant market

Definition of the relevant market is of clinical importance in the context of **13.70** article 102, and is why a Commission decision in the field will contain many pages of economic analysis. It is a function essentially of identification of the correct product/service market and a geographic market. The means for doing so, and the economic tests to be applied of substititutability or interchangeability and cross-elasticity of demand, are considered above.[250] But it ought to be emphasised that whilst the Commission (or any party seeking to establish dominance) is sometimes cavalier in its market analysis under article 101, it has no such latitude under article 102; definition, and an economically correct definition, of the relevant market is absolutely essential – 'a necessary precondition'[251] – to determination of a breach of article 102, for it is axiomatic, if trite, that dominance cannot be assessed in the absence of market definition.

As to the relevant geographic market, article 102 applies to dominance within **13.71** the internal market 'or a substantial part of it'. 'Substantial' ought not to be taken as too high a hurdle: it may be the territory of a single member state[252] – even that of Luxembourg[253] – and may in circumstances be part of a member state.[254] Trade between member states must be affected (appreciably): as with article 101, it is necessary to foresee with a sufficient degree of probability, on the basis of a set of objective legal and factual elements, that the behaviour in question may have an influence, direct or indirect, actual or potential, on trade between member states in such a way as might hinder the attainment of the

---

250 See 13.20–13.23 above.
251 Cases T-66, 77 and 78/89 *Società Italiano Vetro* v *Commission* (Flat Glass) [1992] ECR II-1403, at para. 159.
252 See e.g., Case 322/81 *Michelin* v *Commission* [1983] ECR 3461; Case T-65/89 *BPB Industries and British Gypsum* v *Commission* [1991] ECR II-389; Case T-228/97 *Irish Sugar* v *Commission* [1999] ECR II-2969; Case C-49/07 *Motosykletistiki Omospondia Ellados* v *Elliniko Dimosio* [2008] ECR I-4863.
253 See the *dictum* of A-G Warner in Case 77/77 *BP* v *Commission* [1978] ECR 1513, at 1537.
254 E.g., Cases 40 etc./73 *Coöperatieve Vereniging 'Suiker Unie'* v *Commission* [1975] ECR 1663, in which a relevant geographic market was Bavaria, Baden-Württemberg and parts of Hesse. In Case C-179/90 *Merci Convenzionali Porto di Genova* v *Siderurgica Gabrielli* [1991] ECR I-5889 and Case C-18/93 *Corsica Ferries Italia* v *Corpo dei Piloti del Porto di Genova* [1994] ECR I-1783 port of Genoa and was held subject to the discipline of art. 102 owing to the volume of trade processed in the port which affected a significant part of the common market, and the Commission has applied art. 102 to airports by the same logic; Decision 98/190 (*Flughaven Frankfurt/Main*) [1998] OJ L72/30; Decision 1999/198 (*Ilmailulaitos//Luftfartsverket*) [1999] OJ L69/24. In Case C-209/98 *Entreprenørforeningens Affalds/Miljøsektion* v *Københavns Kommune* [2000] ECR I-3743 the commune of Copenhagen was a substantial part of the Community in the market for the recovery of non-hazardous waste.

single market;[255] and whilst it does not mean that the abuse must actually have affected trade, rather it is sufficient to establish only that the conduct is capable of having such an effect;[256] purely hypothetical or speculative effects are not enough.

(b) Market strength

13.72 Having identified the relevant product/service and geographic markets, the next step is to determine the strength in that market of an undertaking alleged to be dominant. Market strength constitutive of dominance within the meaning of article 102 can be as elusive as the product market. It turns upon a number of indicators, no one of which may necessarily be determinative; but the most obvious test is market share. As the Court of Justice said in Hoffmann-La Roche,

> The existence of a dominant position may derive from several factors which, taken separately, are not necessarily determinative but among these factors a highly important one is the existence of very large market shares.[257]

Where there is a monopoly – whether by virtue of statutory privilege or of simple market dominance – there is by definition no competition, and so necessarily dominance. Shy of monopoly, a very high market share (more than 85 per cent) is determinative of itself of a dominant position except in wholly exceptional circumstances.[258] A market share of 70–80 per cent is 'in itself, a clear indication of the existence of a dominant position',[259] and a market share of 50 per cent constitutes a dominant position except in exceptional circumstances.[260] Whether dominance can exist with a lesser market share depends upon the respective shares of the undertaking and its competitors; in *United Brands* a market share of 40–45 per cent was held to constitute dominance where the competition was highly fragmented,[261] and dominance was found in *British Airways* with a market share of just under 40 per cent, being 2.2 times the share of its four largest rivals combined.[262] There are no instances of lower market shares having been held to constitute dominance, but it cannot be ruled out.

---

255   Cases T-24 etc./93 *Compagnie Maritime Belge v Commission* [1996] ECR II-1201, at para. 201; Case C-475/99 *Ambulanz Glöckner v Landkreis Südwestpfalz* [2001] ECR I-8089, at para. 48.
256   Case C-41/90 *Höfner v Macrotron* [1991] ECR I-1979; Cases C-241 and 242/91P *RTE and ITP v Commission* [1995] ECR I-743.
257   Case 85/76 *Hoffmann-La Roche v Commission* [1979] ECR 461, at para. 39.
258   E.g., Case 85/76 *Hoffmann-La Roche*, *ibid.*; Case T-83/91 *Tetra Pak v Commission* (Tetra Pak II) [1994] ECR II-755; Case T-228/97 *Irish Sugar v Commission* [1999] ECR II-2969.
259   Case T-30/89 *Hilti v Commission* [1991] ECR II-1439, at para. 91.
260   Case 62/86 *AKZO v Commission* [1991] ECR I-3359.
261   Case 27/76 *United Brands v Commission* [1978] ECR 207.
262   Case T-219/99 *British Airways v Commission* [2003] ECR II-5917.

Considerations other than market share include the overall size and strength of **13.73** the undertaking, its financial and technical resources, its vertical integration (so distribution networks and ancillary services), its ownership of intellectual property rights, all of which may constitute barriers to market entry, and its very conduct on the market may all have a bearing. An important consideration may be the pressures of latent or potential competition (market contestability). The fact that an undertaking operates at a loss is not inconsistent with dominance.[263] Given that the various criteria are nebulous and potentially arbitrary, the most reliable indicator of dominance, notwithstanding its element of circularity, probably remains the Michelin test: a position of economic strength which enables an undertaking to hinder the maintenance of effective competition on the relevant market by allowing it to behave to an appreciable extent independently of its competitors and customers and ultimately of consumers.[264] Further, or alternatively, an undertaking holds a dominant position when it is able to hinder the emergence of any effective competition because actual or potential competitors are in a position of economic dependence upon it.[265] And it should be borne in mind that although article 102 is frequently applied to large multinational undertakings, it applies also to smaller undertakings so long as they enjoy dominance within a distinct, definable market.[266]

3. Abuse

Having established the existence of a dominant position, the next question is **13.74** whether an undertaking has abused that dominance. Abuse of a dominant position is

> an objective concept relating to the behaviour of an undertaking in a dominant position which is such as to influence the structure of the market where, as a result of the very presence of the undertaking in question, the degree of competition is weakened and which, through recourse to methods different from those which condition normal competition in products or services on the basis of the transactions of commercial operators, has the effect of hindering the maintenance of the degree of competition still existing in the market or the growth of that competition.[267]

---

263   Case 322/81 *Michelin* v *Commission* [1983] ECR 3461; Case T-228/97 *Irish Sugar* v *Commission* [1999] ECR II-2969.

264   Case 322/81 *Michelin*, *ibid.*

265   Cases C-241 and 242/91P *RTE and ITP* v *Commission* [1995] ECR I-743; Case T-229/94 *Deutsche Bahn* v *Commission* [1997] ECR II-1689.

266   See e.g., Case 22/78 *Hugin Kassaregister* v *Commission* [1979] ECR 1869; Case T-30/89 *Hilti* v *Commission* [1991] ECR II-1439.

267   Case 85/76 *Hoffmann–La Roche* v *Commission* [1979] ECR 461, at para. 91; effectively also in Case C-95/04P *British Airways* v *Commission* [2007] ECR I-2331, at para. 66.

It is therefore a supple concept and is permitted by the Court to have a wide application. And it imposes upon dominant undertakings burdens not shared by other undertakings, for whilst a dominant undertaking is not to be reproached for its dominance, 'irrespective of the reasons for which it has such a dominant position, [it] has a special responsibility not to allow its conduct to impair genuine undistorted competition on the common market'.[268] Put otherwise, dominant undertakings 'have specific obligations and may, accordingly, be deprived of the right to adopt courses of conduct which are not in themselves abuses and which would be acceptable if adopted by a non-dominant undertaking'.[269] This can be a fine line, and goes to a central issue of competition policy, the extent to which it ought, if at all, to draw the claws of the powerful for the advantage of the weak. The generally accepted view is that article 102 is to serve consumer welfare in its broader sense; as stated by Advocate-General Jacobs,

> the primary purpose of Article [102] is to prevent distortion of competition – and in particular to safeguard the interests of consumers – rather than to protect the position of particular competitors,[270]

and by Advocate-General Kokott:

> Article [102], like the other competition rules of the Treaty, is not designed only or primarily to protect the immediate interests of individual competitors or consumers, but to protect the *structure of the market* and thus *competition as such (as an institution)*, which has already been weakened by the presence of the dominant undertaking on the market. In this way, consumers are also indirectly protected.[271]

Thus as a general principle dominance cannot and should not deprive an undertaking of the right/obligation vigorously to compete in the marketplace. Yet

> [a]lthough it is true … that the fact that an undertaking is in a dominant position cannot disentitle it from protecting its own commercial interests if they are attacked, and that such an undertaking must be conceded the right to take such reasonable steps

---

268 Case 322/81 *Michelin* v *Commission* [1983] ECR 3461, at para. 57.

269 Case C-202/07P *France Télécom* v *Commission* [2009] ECR I-2369, at para. 17.

270 Case C-7/97 *Oscar Bronner* v *Mediaprint Zeitungs- und Zeitschriftenverlag* [1998] ECR I-7701, at para. 58 of his opinion. This applies generally to all of the competition provisions of the Treaties; Case C-8/08 *T-Mobile Netherlands and ors* v *Raad van bestuur van de Nederlandse Mededingingsautoriteit* [2009] ECR I-4529, at para. 38.

271 Case C-95/04P *British Airways* v *Commission* [2007] ECR I-2331, at para. 68 of her opinion (emphasis in original).

as it deems appropriate to protect its said interests, such behaviour cannot be countenanced if its actual purpose is to strengthen this dominant position and abuse it.[272]

The responsibility is especially onerous for a monopoly or for an undertaking which enjoys 'dominance approaching monopoly', 'superdominance' or 'overwhelming dominance verging on monopoly'[273] – so much so that there is a passage in one case involving a superdominant firm (Microsoft) in which the General Court suggests that merely acquiring a significant market share may be an abuse of a dominant position,[274] which would seem to turn article 102 on its head. A prudent dominant firm will therefore always be wary of its conduct in the market.

Abuse may be exploitative in character, deploying market power to lever **13.75** advantage from the (dependent) buyer; exclusionary in character, inhibiting the emergence or growth of competition; or both. Common types are as follows.

(a) Pricing

Freed from the constraints of competitive forces, a dominant undertaking may **13.76** incline towards charging excessively high prices for its goods or services. Hence, article 102(a) expressly provides that abuse may consist in 'directly or indirectly imposing unfair purchase or selling prices'. Perhaps surprisingly there have been very few cases in which the issue of excessive pricing arose,[275] and in the one case in which the Commission libelled its presence simpliciter[276] the finding was annulled by the Court of Justice.[277] The Court added obiter that 'charging a price which is excessive because it has no reasonable relation to the economic value of the product supplied is ... an abuse',[278] and in later cases that charging for services 'fees which are disproportionate to the economic value of the service provided' is abusive;[279] but it supplied no indication as to what might constitute an excessive/disproportionate profit margin/fee or a fair price, which is to be assessed by reference to the relationship between price and and the economic

---

272 Case 27/76 *United Brands* v *Commission* [1978] ECR 207, at para. 189; effectively also in Case C-202/07P *France Télécom* v *Commission* [2009] ECR I-2369, at para. 46.

273 Cases C-395 and 396/96P *Compagnie Maritime Belge* v *Commission* [2000] ECR II-1365, *per* AG Fennelly at paras 132, 137 of his opinion.

274 Case T-201/04 *Microsoft* v *Commission* [2007] ECR II-3601, at para. 664.

275 Case 26/75 *General Motors Continental* v *Commission* [1975] ECR 1367; Case 27/76 *United Brands* v *Commission* [1978] ECR 207; Case 226/84 *British Leyland* v *Commission* [1986] ECR 3263; Case C-52/07 *Kanal 5 and TV 4* v *Föreningen Svenksa Tonsättares Internationella Musikbyrå* [2008] ECR I-9275.

276 Decision 76/353 (*Chiquita*) [1976] OJ L95/1.

277 Case 27/76 *United Brands*, n. 275 above.

278 *Ibid.* at para. 250.

279 Case 226/84 *British Leyland* v n. 275 above, at para. 27; Case C-340/99 *TNT Traco* v *Poste Italiane and ors* [2001] ECR I-4109, at para. 46; Case C-385/07P *Der Grüne Punkt – Duales System Deutschland* v *Commission* [2009] ECR I-6155, at para. 142.

value of the good or service in question[280] and would require to be the product of a construction of the price obtainable under conditions of normal competition. Far more common is predatory pricing, an exercise by a dominant undertaking, with the wherewithal to sustain losses at least in the short term, of charging prices lower than production or supply costs in order to drive lesser, more vulnerable, competitors from the market.[281] In *AKZO*[282] the Court of Justice supplied a working definition of predatory pricing as prices set lower than average variable cost. This definition was reapplied subsequently in *Tetra Pak II*,[283] in which the Court added that predatory pricing was always abusive conduct, for it had 'no conceivable economic purpose other than elimination of a competitor'.[284] Finally, discriminatory pricing may be an abuse of 'applying dissimilar conditions to equivalent transactions with other trading parties, thereby placing them at a competitive disadvantage'.[285] However, article 102 does not impose upon dominant undertakings a duty to charge identical prices for all transactions; quantity discounts are, for example, normally unobjectionable. But any artificial price differences,[286] and certainly price discrimination based upon nationality of the buyer, is abusive conduct unless it can be objectively justified by, for example, differential in supply costs, variations in the conditions of marketing and intensity of competition.[287]

(b) Loyalty or fidelity rebates

13.77 Closely associated with discriminatory pricing are loyalty or fidelity rebates, whereby a dominant undertaking offers price rebates, bonuses or other form of payment in return for an undertaking from a buyer not to purchase from the former's competitors.[288] Unless it is one which is related to efficiencies (where, for example, greater volumes are in fact cheaper to produce and/or supply and the saving is passed on to the buyer) a rebate is not a quantity discount but is designed to secure loyalty (or 'tie' the buyer) at the expense of competing

---

280 Case 26/75 *General Motors Continental*, n. 275 above.

281 See e.g., Case 86/76 *Hoffmann–La Roche* v *Commission* [1979] ECR 461; Case T-340/03 *France Télécom* v *Commission* [2007] ECR II-107.

282 Case 62/86 *AKZO* v *Commission* [1991] ECR I-3359.

283 Case C-333/94P *Tetra Pak* v *Commission* [1996] ECR I-5951.

284 *Ibid.* at para. 41.

285 TFEU, art. 102(c); see e.g., Case 27/76 *United Brands* v *Commission* [1978] ECR 207; Case T-228/97 *Irish Sugar* v *Commission* [1999] ECR II-2969; Case T-219/99 *British Airways* v *Commission* [2003] ECR II-5917.

286 Case T-83/91 *Tetra Pak* v *Commission* (Tetra Pak II) [1994] ECR II-755; Decision 98/513 (*Alpha Flight Services/Aéroports de Paris*) [1998] OJ L230/10.

287 Case 27/76 *United Brands* v *Commission* [1978] ECR 207; Case T-83/91 *Tetra Pak II, ibid.*

288 See e.g., Cases 40 etc./73 *Coöperatieve Vereniging 'Suiker Unie'* v *Commission* [1975] ECR 1663; Case 85/76 *Hoffmann–La Roche* v *Commission* [1979] ECR 461; Case 322/81 *Michelin* v *Commission* [1983] ECR 3461; Case T-65/89 *BPB British Industries* v *Commission* [1993] ECR II-389; Case COMP/37.990 *Intel* [2009] OJ C227/13 (summary publication).

suppliers.[289] It applies equally to turnover or target related rebates and discounts, which will dissuade buyers from seeking alternative suppliers.[290] It is immaterial that the rebate or discount was granted at the buyer's request.[291] 'English clauses' or 'competition clauses', whereby a buyer may secure supplies from competing suppliers without losing the benefits of a fidelity rebate but only in circumstances in which the competing supplier offers more attractive terms which the dominant undertaking does not wish to meet, are less restrictive of competition than a fidelity rebate simpliciter, but are nonetheless abusive.[292] Loyalty secured by means other than rebates or discounts can fall foul of article 102: where a dominant undertaking insists upon long-term and exclusive supply contracts with its customers – perfectly reasonable and commonplace practice in the context of article 101 – it can be abusive if the effect is such as to hinder the emergence and development of competing suppliers.[293]

(c) Refusal to deal or supply

Whilst under article 101 freedom of contract is the general rule, article 102 **13.78** limits that freedom to an extent as part of the price of dominance in the market. There may be good commercial reasons for wishing not to deal: where, for example, a dominant undertaking becomes vertically integrated and so is now in direct competition with an erstwhile buyer. But if the buyer cannot, or cannot easily, obtain the goods from another supplier, the buyer is in a position of 'economic dependence' upon the dominant supplier (which goes to defining its dominance),[294] and it is an abuse for the latter to refuse to sell. This is so a fortiori where the buyer has previously been a regular customer.[295] As the Court said in *United Brands*:

> [An] undertaking in a dominant position for the purposes of marketing a product …
> cannot stop supplying a long standing customer who abides by regular commercial
> practice, if orders placed by that customer are in no way out of the ordinary.[296]

In service markets in particular (but not exclusively), article 102 may impose a duty upon dominant undertakings through the 'essential facilities' doctrine: where an undertaking controls (and so enjoys a dominant position in the

---

289   Cases 40 etc./73 *Suiker Unie, ibid.*; Decision 2003/7 (Soda Ash) [2003] OJ L10/33.
290   Case 322/81 *Michelin* v *Commission* [1983] ECR 3461; Case T-228/97 *Irish Sugar* v *Commission* [1999] ECR II-2969; Case T-219/99 *British Airways* v *Commission* [2003] ECR II-5917.
291   Case 85/76 *Hoffmann-La Roche* v *Commission* [1979] ECR 461.
292   Case 85/76 *Hoffmann-La Roche, ibid.*; Decision 2003/6 (*Soda Ash – Solvay*) [2003] OJ L10/10, at para. 112 ff.
293   *IRE/Nordion*, discussed in Commission press release IP(98) 647.
294   Cases C-241 and 242/91P *RTE and ITP* v *Commission* [1995] ECR I-743.
295   Cases 6 and 7/73 *Commercial Solvents* v *Commission* [1974] ECR 223; Case 27/76 *United Brands* v *Commission* [1978] ECR 207; Decision 78/68 (*Lipton/Hugin*) [1978] OJ L22/23 (annulled but on other grounds in Case 22/78 *Hugin* v *Commission* [1979] ECR 1869).
296   *Ibid.* at para. 182.

provision of) an essential facility – that is, a facility or infrastructure without access to which competitors cannot or cannot without difficulty provide complementary or ancillary services in a neighbouring or submarket – it may be abusive to reserve to itself and refuse competitors access to that facility. And this of course cuts across a principle of competition law which generally seeks to inhibit cooperation between or amongst undertakings which provides succour to competitors. In this context the Court of Justice has said

> an abuse within the meaning of Article [102] is committed where, without any objective necessity, an undertaking holding a dominant position on a particular market reserves to itself or to an undertaking belonging to the same group an ancillary activity which might be carried out by another undertaking as part of its activities on a neighbouring but separate market, with the possibility of eliminating all competition from such undertaking.[297]

The Commission applied (tacit) essential facilities reasoning in a number of cases in the 1990s involving port/airport facilities,[298] and it has been recognised in some courts.[299] But the dangers are that it risks neutralising a legitimate advantage enjoyed by a dominant competitor or serves as justification for seeking access to an infrastructure in which it may have invested heavily (and perhaps at high risk) to create. Therefore the Court has said that it (without formally recognising it) applies only in exceptional circumstances,[300] where there is no real or potential substitute,[301] or where, according to Advocate-General Jacobs, the dominant undertaking has 'a genuine stranglehold' on the upstream market.[302] Most of the cases on essential facilities have occurred in the context of compulsory licensing of an intellectual property right.[303]

13.79 In 2008 the Commission defined a series of priorities for the application of article 102 to abusive exclusionary conduct.[304]

---

297 Case 311/84 *CBEM* v *CLT and IPB* (Télémarketing) [1985] ECR 3261, at para. 27.

298 E.g., Decision 94/19 (*Sea Containers/Stena Sealink*) [1994] OJ L18/8; Decision 94/119 (*Rødby Havn*) [1994] OJ L55/52; Decision 98/190 (*Flughafen Frankfurt/Main*) [1998] OJ L72/30.

299 E.g., *Attheraces and anor* v *British Horse Racing Board and anor* [2005] EWHC 3015 (Ch), [2006] FSR 336; overturned on appeal (but not on that point), [2007] EWCA (Civ) 38, [2007] All ER (D) 26; *Albion Water* v *Water Services Regulation Authority* [2006] CAT 23, [2007] CompAR 22.

300 Cases C-241 and 242/91P *RTE and ITP* v *Commission* [1995] ECR I-743; Case C-418/01 *IMS Health* v *NDC Health* [2004] ECR I-5039.

301 Case T-504/93 *Tiercé Ladbroke* v *Commission* [1997] ECR II-923.

302 Case C-7/97 *Oscar Bronner* v *Mediaprint* [1998] ECR I-7701, at para. 65 of his opinion.

303 See 13.151–13.153 below.

304 Guidance on the Commission's Enforcement Priorities in Applying Article 82 EC Treaty to Abusive Exculsionary Conduct by Dominant Undertakings [2009] OJ C45/7.

(d) Tying

Related in turn to refusal to deal is tying, or bundling, by which a dominant **13.80** undertaking will supply a dependent buyer only if the buyer agrees also to buy another product or service (the 'tied' product or service) which the latter might otherwise be disinclined to do. This type of conduct is caught by article 102(d), which prohibits 'making the conclusion of contracts subject to acceptance of supplementary obligations which, by their nature or according to commercial usage, have no connection with the subject of such contracts'. So, if a dominant undertaking refuses to supply the tying product without purchases of the tied product,[305] or otherwise ties buyers, even if it does so at the latters' request and even if it is common commercial practice, by an obligation or promise to purchase all or most of their requirements from the former, it is abusive.[306]

A tying arrangement may be a more subtle form of inducement, for example, an **13.81** offer to corner shops of free ice cream freezers or drinks coolers upon condition they are used to stock only the supplier's ice cream or cola.[307] Notwithstanding the language of article 102(d), even where tied sales of two products are in accordance with normal commercial conduct or there is a natural link between the two products, tying is abusive, as usage which is acceptable in a competitive market ought not to be permitted in the case of a market in which competition is already restricted by the existence of a dominant undertaking. Tying may be permitted where it is objectively justified, but even then the tying clauses must be proportionate and cannot be intended to strengthen dominance by reinforcing economic dependence upon the dominant undertaking.[308]

(e) Mergers

An abuse of a dominant position may consist in a dominant undertaking **13.82** acquiring, or merging with, a competitor. This is discussed below.[309]

(f) Intellectual property rights

In certain circumstances the exercise of an intellectual property right by a **13.83** dominant undertaking may infringe article 102. This too is discussed below.[310]

---

305   Case T-30/89 *Hilti* v *Commission* [1991] ECR II-1439.
306   Case 85/76 *Hoffmann-La Roche* v *Commission* [1979] ECR 461; Case 62/86 *AKZO* v *Commission* [1991] ECR I-3359; Case T-201/04 *Microsoft* v *Commission* [2007] ECR II-3601.
307   Case T-65/98 *van de Bergh Foods* v *Commission* [2003] ECR II-4653; Decision 2005/620 (*Coca-Cola*) [2005] OJ L253/21.
308   Case T-83/91 *Tetra Pak* v *Commission* (Tetra Pak II) [1994] ECR II-755.
309   See 13.131 below.
310   See 13.151–13.153 below.

13.84   Much of the discussion and management of article 102 cases is organised by such categories of conduct as indicated. There is a view abroad that this 'form-based' approach should give way in the fullness of time, and a move to a more 'economic' effects-based approach is moving slowly through the pipeline.[311]

4. Sport

13.85   A (brief) special mention should be made of sport. Professional sport is not excluded from the Treaty rules on free movement of persons and services,[312] still less from the rules on competition.[313] Certainly association football clubs[314] and their national associations,[315] the International Olympic Committee and its affiliated international and national associations,[316] individual athletes[317] and their agents,[318] are all undertakings or associations of undertakings. Yet sport is wholly predicated upon, and is shot through with organisation and practices which clearly affect, 'competition'; and these might fall for consideration under article 101 or article 102 or both, yet sport is a phenomenon for which these were manifestly not designed. Sport suffers from its peculiar nature, in that assuming the economic success of the 'product' on offer is a function of its entertainment value to the spectator, competitors in professional sport, be they individuals or teams, find themselves in the abnormal position of mutual reliance upon each other in order to maintain the quality of the product;[319] '[s]uch a natural community of interests can probably be found in scarcely any other sector'.[320] The application of the competition rules to it is now being addressed by the Court of Justice, but gingerly.[321]

---

311   See Report of the Economic Advisory Group for Competition Policy (commissioned by the Commission), *An Economic Approach to Article 82* (July 2005).
312   See 11.81–11.85 above.
313   Case C-49/07 *Motosykletistiki Omospondia Ellados (MOTOE)* v *Elliniko Dimosio* [2008] ECR I-4863, at para. 22.
314   Case C-415/93 *Union Royale Belge des Sociétés de Football Association* v *Bosman* [1995] ECR I-4921.
315   Case C-415/93 *Bosman*, ibid.; Case T-46/92 *Scottish Football Association* v *Commission* [1994] ECR II-1039; also Case C-49/07 *MOTOE*, n. 313 above, for a national affiliate of the International Motorcyling Federation.
316   Case C-519/04P *Meca-Madina and Majcen* v *Commission* [2006] ECR I-6991.
317   Cases C-51/96 and 191/97 *Deliège* v *Ligue Francophone de Judo* [2000] ECR I-2549, *per* A-G Cosmas.
318   Case T-193/02 *Piau* v *Commission* [2005] ECR II-209.
319   Discussed at length by A-G Lenz in Case C-415/93 *Bosman*, n. 314 above, at paras 253–86 of his opinion.
320   *Ibid.* at para. 285.
321   Case C-415/93 *Bosman*, n. 314 above; Case C-519/04P *Meca-Madina and Majcen* v *Commission* [2006] ECR I-6991; Case C-171/05 *Piau* v *Commission* [2006] ECR I-37*; Case C-49/07 *MOTOE*, n. 313 above; Case T-273/09 *Associazione 'Giùlemanidallajuve'* v *Commission*, order of 19 March 2012, not yet reported.

D. ENFORCEMENT OF THE COMPETITION RULES

1. General

The EEC Treaty laid down mechanisms for the provisional enforcement of   **13.86**
articles 101 and 102 by national competition authorities[322] and by the Commission[323] pending the adoption of 'appropriate regulations or directives to give
effect to the principles' set out therein.[324] An appropriate measure was adopted
by the Council in 1962 in the form of Regulation 17,[325] the principal Regulation implementing articles 101 and 102, leaving the transitional measures
largely (but not entirely) spent. Regulation 17 was honourably retired and
replaced in 2004 by Regulation 1/2003,[326] which now governs the field.

The framers of neither the Treaties nor Regulation 17 necessarily foresaw the   **13.87**
development of direct effect, and those instruments presumed an administrative enforcement of the competition rules. But in 1974 the Court of Justice
declared both articles 101(1) and 102 to be directly effective;[327] and unlike
many Treaty articles, they are 'horizontally' directly effective,[328] which is no less
than reasonable – indeed, inevitable – for Treaty provisions the subject of which
are 'undertakings'. Articles 101 and 102 are therefore also enforced by national
courts, by authority not of enabling legislation but of their inherent direct
effect.[329]

Regulation 17 conferred upon the Commission autonomous and formidable   **13.88**
powers of investigation and enforcement of the competition rules, and it is this
which, alongside the exclusive power of exemption under article 101(3),[330]
endowed the Commission with pre-eminence in shaping the direction of
Community competition policy. From the mid-1960s it began to share honours
with the national courts. Commission pre-eminence is maintained by Regulation 1/2003, but it also charges administrative authorities in the various
member states with the duty of giving effect to articles 101 and 102, which must

---

322   EEC Treaty, art. 88.
323   *Ibid.* art. 89.
324   *Ibid.* art. 87.
325   Regulation 17/62 [1962] JO 204.
326   Regulation 1/2003 [2003] OJ L1/1.
327   Case 127/73 *Belgische Radio en Televisie* v *SABAM* [1974] ECR 51.
328   Confirmed expressly in Case C-282/95P *Guérin Automobiles* v *Commission* [1997] ECR I-1503, at para. 39.
329   Although the breadth of art. 103 probably extends to disabling arts 101 and 102 of direct effect, Regulation 17
       did nothing to do so, and Regulation 1/2003 provides expressly the contrary: 'National courts shall have the
       power to apply Articles 81 and 82 of the Treaty' (art. 6).
330   See 13.58 above.

ensure they are applied effectively in the general interest.[331] The provisions are therefore enforced polycephalously by the Commission, by national competition authorities, and by national courts. It is a system which, in a number of respects, is not given to harmony.

2. Enforcement by the Commission

(a) Complaints

13.89 The Commission may, upon its own initiative or upon a complaint from a member state or a natural or legal person who can show a legitimate interest,[332] launch an investigation of an alleged infraction of articles 101 or 102. A special form ('Form C') has been prepared by the Commission for the lodging of a complaint,[333] but its use is not obligatory. When a complaint is made, the Commission has a duty carefully and diligently (or 'attentively') to consider the issues raised in order to determine whether there exists conduct liable to distort competition and so which infringes the competition rules, and failure to do so may be the subject of proceedings against the Commission under article 265 of the TFEU for failure to act.[334] There is therefore a duty to respond to a complaint – an 'article 7 letter',[335] which, if followed up, may in circumstances be challenged by way of article 263 proceedings[336] – but beyond that no duty to adopt a decision regarding the existence or otherwise of a breach of articles 101 or 102 and no duty to pursue the complaint by means of an investigation; the Commission need only give adequate (and coherent) reasons for not doing so.[337]

---

331 Case C-439/08 *Vlaamse federatie van verenigingen van Brood- en Banketbakkers, Ijsbereiders en Chocoladebewerkers* v *Raad voor de Mededinging and anor* [2010] ECR I-12471, at para. 56.

332 Regulation 1/2003, art. 7(1).

333 Regulation 773/2004 [2004] OJ L123/18, Annex.

334 Case T-28/90 *Asia Motor France* v *Commission* [1992] ECR II-2285; Case C-282/95P *Guérin Automobiles* v *Commission* [1997] ECR I-1503; Case T-127/98 *UPS Europe* v *Commission* [1999] ECR II-2633; Case T-427/08 *Confédération européenne des associations d'horlogers-réparateurs (CEAHR)* v *Commission* [2010] ECR II-5865.

335 Regulation 773/2004 [2004] OJ L123/18, art. 7; previously it was an 'article 6 letter': Regulation 2842/98 [1998] OJ L354/18, replacing Regulation 99/63 [1963] JO 2268, art. 6 of each.

336 Case T-24/90 *Automec* v *Commission* (Automec II) [1992] ECR II-2223; Case T-74/92 *Ladbroke Racing Deutschland* v *Commission* [1995] ECR II-115; Case C-282/95P *Guérin Automobiles* v *Commission* [1997] ECR I-1503.

337 Case 125/75 *GEMA* v *Commission* [1979] ECR 3173; Case T-24/90 *Automec II, ibid.*; Case T-186/94 *Guérin Automobiles* v *Commission* [1995] ECR II-1753; Case T-387/94 *Asia Motor France* v *Commission* [1996] ECR II-961; Case T-198/98 *Micro Leader Business* v *Commission* [1999] ECR II-3989; Case T-154/98 *Asia Motor France and ors* v *Commission* [2000] ECR II-3453; Case C-425/07P *AEPI Elliniki Etaireia Prostasian tis Pnevmatikis Idioktisias* v *Commission* [2009] ECR I-3205. This is not so if a complaint is lodged by a member state, in which event the Commission has a duty to initiate an investigation; TFEU, art. 105(1) and Case T-24/90 *Automec II*, at para. 76. Legitimate reasons not to pursue a complaint may include other priorities (and the Commission enjoys a wide discretion to apply different degrees of priority to complaints and to concentrate its scarce resources where it sees fit; see especially *AEPI*), in particular insufficient 'Union interest'

Although the Commission no longer responds to notification for exemption **13.90** from the prohibition of article 101, it may, '[w]here the Community public interest … so requires' and on its own initiative, find by decision that article 101 is not applicable to a given agreement or practice, either because the conditions for the application of article 101(1) are not joined or because those of article 101(3) are satisfied.[338] This 'finding of inapplicability' is intended to assist consistency. To date it has not been used.

(b) Investigation

(i) Request for information

Having elected to proceed with an investigation, the Commission may seek to **13.91** obtain all 'necessary information' from the undertakings under investigation, from third parties, and from national competition authorities.[339] There is a compulsory two stage procedure: first, a simple request for information to which the addressee may, but need not, respond,[340] and second, a request by way of formal decision, to which it must.[341] In either case supplying incorrect information may result in a fine.[342] This power of investigation is very broad but it is not limitless.[343] Information obtained may be used 'only for the purpose for which it was acquired',[344] and so cannot be used by the Commission in order to make out another infraction different from that envisaged in the request (although the Commission may start a new investigation afresh).[345] Previously it could not be used by a national competition authority in order to make out an infringement of national competition rules[346] (but which authority could, of course, initiate its own investigation and proceedings), but this is no longer so if

and (now) that the matter has been, is being, or would be better dealt with by another (national) authority. For the correct approach to review of a Commission decision to refuse to initiate an investigation see Case T-427/08 *CEAHR* v *Commission*, n. 334 above.

338   Regulation 1/2003, art. 10.
339   *Ibid.* art. 18(1).
340   *Ibid.* art. 18(2); Case T-30/89 *Hilti* v *Commission* [1991] ECR II-1439; Cases T-305 etc./94 *Limburgse Vinyl Maatschappij* v *Commission* (PVC II) [1999] ECR II-931.
341   *Ibid.* art. 18(3).
342   *Ibid.* art. 23(1)(a), (b).
343   See Case 374/87 *Orkem* v *Commission* [1989] ECR 3283; Case C-60/92 *Otto* v *Postbank* [1993] ECR I-5683 (but cf. the judgments of the European Court of Human Rights in *Funke* v *France* (1993) 16 EHRR 297 and *Saunders* v *United Kingdom* (1997) 23 EHRR 313, which cast some doubt upon the *Orkem* judgment); Case T-112/98 *Mannesmannröhren-Werke* v *Commission* [2001] ECR II-729; Cases T-236 etc./01 *Tokai Carbon and ors* v *Commission* (Graphite Electrodes) [2004] ECR II-1181, at paras 401–12; Case C-301/04P *Commission* v *SGL Carbon* [2006] ECR I-5915; Case T-59/02 *Archer Daniels Midland* v *Commission* [2006] ECR II-3627.
344   Regulation 1/2003, art. 28(1).
345   Case 85/87 *Dow Benelux* v *Commission* [1989] ECR 3137.
346   Case C-67/91 *Dirección General de Defensa de la Competencia* v *Asociación Española de Banca Privada* [1992] ECR I-4785.

the national law 'is applied ... in parallel to Community competition law and does not lead to a different outcome'.[347]

(ii)   Inspection

13.92   Distinct and independent from but complementary to the power to require information,[348] the Commission is further empowered to authorise its officials to enter the premises of any undertaking, examine books and business records (in any medium), take copies therefrom, and demand oral explanations on the spot;[349] in 2004 the power was extended to the search of the homes and motorcars of officers of an undertaking.[350] Properly called an 'inspection' but known univerally as the 'dawn raid', it may be ordered by written authorisation ('the mandate')[351] or by formal decision,[352] and, as with requests for information, an undertaking is required to comply only if ordered by formal decision;[353] but unlike the former there is no need for a preliminary request: having consulted the competition authorities in the member state(s) in which it is to take place (a mandatory procedural requirement),[354] the Commission may proceed directly to an inspection and need provide no advance warning.[355] So as not to alert undertakings to its interest, and because it is an independent procedure, an inspection under article 20 may, and often does, precede any request for information under article 18. The Commission must notify the competition authorities of the relevant member state(s),[356] in some circumstances must hear from them,[357] and may request or require that they carry out the inspection;[358] they must in all circumstances actively assist the Commission to the extent necessary to make an inspection effective.[359] If national law requires judicial authority (a warrant) to enter premises – and in all cases of

---

347   Regulation 1/2003, art. 12(2).
348   Case 136/79 *National Panasonic* v *Commission* [1980] ECR 2033; Case 387/87 *Orkem* v *Commission* [1989] ECR 3283.
349   Regulation 1/2003, art. 20(1), (2). Some documents of the nature of legal advice from (outside) lawyers are privileged and cannot be viewed; this is of course attended by difficulties of who is to determine which documents are so privileged; see Case 155/79 *AM&S Europe* v *Commission* [1982] ECR 1575; Case C-550/07 *Akzo Nobel Chemicals* v *Commission* [2010] ECR I-8301.
350   *Ibid.* art. 21. But there must be a 'reasonable suspicion' that relevant documents or records are being kept there.
351   *Ibid.* art. 20(3).
352   *Ibid.* art. 20(4).
353   *Ibid.*
354   Regulation 1/2003, art. 20(4); the consultation may be informal: Case 5/85 *AKZO* v *Commission* [1986] ECR 2585.
355   Case 136/79 *National Panasonic* v *Commission* [1980] ECR 2033; Case 5/85 *AKZO, ibid.*
356   Regulation 1/2003, art. 20(3).
357   *Ibid.* art. 20(4).
358   *Ibid.* art. 22.
359   *Ibid.* art. 20(5); Cases 46/87 and 227/88 *Hoechst* v *Commission* [1989] ECR 2859. As to the (mutual) duties of sincere cooperation between Commission and national authorities see Case T-328/03 *O₂ (Germany)* v *Commission* [2006] ECR II-1231.

search of personal private premises – it is required to be obtained,[360] and judges are severely limited in their authority to refuse it.[361] If an inspection is ordered by formal decision, an undertaking is bound to 'submit' to it,[362] and refusal may attract a fine of up to 1 per cent of annual turnover[363] and a *per diem* penalty payment pending compliance.[364]

(c) Termination and fines

(i) Termination

Having completed its fact finding and/or investigation, the Commission may **13.93** proceed to the formal establishment of a breach of article 101 or of article 102. Before it does so it must comply with a number of procedural rights of defence intended to safeguard the interests of the party under investigation,[365] in particular hold an oral hearing conduced by a hearing officer who is a Commission official but acts 'in full independence';[366] it must consult the Advisory Committee on Restrictive Practices and Dominant Positions;[367] and it must in all events act within a 'reasonable' period of time.[368] Throughout the course of the proceedings the Commission may order appropriate interim remedial measures, either positive or negative, where there is a *prima facie* breach of articles 101 or 102 and urgency owing to a risk of serious and irreparable injury to competition.[369] Where it finds that a breach has occurred the Commission 'may by decision require the undertakings or associations of undertakings concerned to bring such infringement to an end'.[370] This consists usually in a decision (properly so-called) compelling undertakings simply to stop doing whatever they were doing which constituted the infringement, and sometimes includes an express prohibition of repetition or adoption of any similar ('any measure having the same or equivalent object or effect'),[371] offending conduct

---

360 Regulation 1/2003, arts 20(7), 21(3).
361 *Ibid.* arts 20(7), 21(3); Cases 46/87 and 227/88 *Hoechst*, n. 359 above; Case C-94/00 *Roquette Frères* v *Directeur Général de la Concurrence* [2002] ECR I-9011.
362 *Ibid.* art. 20(4).
363 *Ibid.* art. 23(1)(c).
364 *Ibid.* art. 24(1)(e). Of course, an undertaking which refuses entry to officials in possession of a warrant is also in contempt. Frequently an inspection ordered by warrant will be attended by police officers in order to enforce it.
365 *Ibid.* art. 27; Regulation 773/2004 [2004] OJ L123/18, arts 11–14. See D-G Competition, Draft Notice on best practices on the conduct of the proceedings concerning Articles 101 and 102 TFEU [2011] OJ C308/6.
366 *Ibid.* art. 14(1). See Decision 2011/695 [2011] OJ L275/39 on the function and terms of reference of the hearing officer in certain competition proceedings.
367 Regulation 1/2003, art. 14.
368 The Court of Justice is now reassessing what is 'reasonable' time; see 6.120 above, n. 634.
369 Regulation 1/2003, art. 8. See e.g., Case 792/79R *Camera Care* v *Commission* [1980] ECR 119; Case T-44/90 *La Cinq* v *Commission* [1992] ECR II-1.
370 *Ibid.* art. 7(1).
371 E.g., Decision 2003/2 (*Vitamins*) [2003] OJ L6/1, art. 2; Decision 2007/53 (*Microsoft*) [2007] OJ L32/23 (summary publication; full decision available at [2005] 4 CMLR 964), art. 4 (substituting 'act or conduct' for 'measure').

in the future. It also includes now the power to to impose 'any behavioural or structural remedies which are proportionate to the infringement committed and necessary to bring the infringement effectively to an end'.[372]

13.94 The Commission may, and frequently does, issue a decision declaring the existence of an infringement, even if it had already been brought to an end, in order to establish its existence or to clarify a point of law and so prevent future infractions or establish civil liability; this practice has been endorsed by the Court of Justice, provided the Commission has (and shows that it has) a legitimate interest in so doing.[373] It has, however, from time to time accepted an undertaking rather than proceed to a final decision.[374] Since 2004 it may accept 'commitments' from the relevant undertaking(s) and, by decision, make them binding.[375] Thereafter the case may be re-opened only if the decision was based upon incorrect information provided by an undertaking, there is a material change of circumstances, or an undertaking fails to honour its commitments;[376] in the latter event it may be fined.[377] Settlement of (non-cartel) cases by commitment is becoming commonplace.

(ii) Fines

13.95 If it finds a breach of article 101 or 102 which was intentional or negligent or if an undertaking breaches a binding commitment, the Commission may impose a fine of up to 10 per cent of an undertaking's worldwide annual turnover.[378] 'Intentional' does not require that an undertaking knew it was infringing the competition rules, rather it requires only that it could not have been unaware that its conduct would result in a distortion of competition.[379] The amount of a

---

372 Regulation 1/2003, art. 7(1). No such power was expressly included in Regulation 17 but the Court found it to be implied: Cases 6 and 7/73 *Commercial Solvents* v *Commission* [1974] ECR 223. The imposition of behavioural and structural remedies (the latter permissible only when the former will not be 'equally effective' (art. 7(1)) is normally appropriate only in the context of an infringement of art. 102. To date the Commission has not imposed structural remedies, but it has accepted structural changes as commitments; Case COMP/ 39.389 *E.ON* [2009] OJ C36/8; Case COMP/39.402 *RWE* [2009] OJ C133/10 (summary publication). The most contentious use of behavioural remedies has been in the *Microsoft* case; Decision 2007/53, *ibid.*, paras 994–1053.

373 Case 7/82 *Gesellschaft zur Verwertung von Leistungsschutzrechten* v *Commission* [1983] ECR 483; Cases T-22 and 23/02 *Sumitomo Chemical Co and anor* v *Commission* [2005] ECR II-4065. See now Regulation 1/2003, art. 7(1): 'If the Commission has a legitimate interest in doing so, it may … find that an infringement has been committed in the past'. As to what might constitute a legitimate interest see paras 119–22 of *Sumitomo*.

374 See e.g., Decision 87/500 (*BBI/Boosey & Hawkes*) [1987] OJ L286/36; Decision 94/19 (*Sea Containers/Stena Sealink*) [1994] OJ L15/8.

375 Regulation 1/2003, art. 9. On the scope of the Commission's power to adopt binding decision on commitments see Case C-441/07P *Commission* v *Alrosa* [2010] ECR I-5949.

376 Regulation 1/2003, art. 9(2).

377 *Ibid.* art. 23(2)(c).

378 *Ibid.* art. 24(2).

379 Case 19/77 *Miller* v *Commission* [1978] ECR 131; Case T-83/91 *Tetra Pak* v *Commission* [1994] ECR II-755.

fine is to be a function of the gravity and duration of the infringement,[380] yet the Commission enjoys a wide margin of discretion.[381] This discretion has been challenged from time to time as an affront to a general principle of certainty in relation to penal provisions (*nulla poena sine lege certa*) but it appears not to trouble the Court.[382] In 1998 and in 2006 the Commission published notices detailing various tariffs it uses and the consideration it will give to gravity ('minor', 'serious' and 'very serious' infractions), duration and aggravating and attenuating circumstances;[383] these guidelines are recognised as capable of producing legal effects.[384] Thus

> the Commission enjoys a wide discretion as regards the method used for calculating fines ...
>
> The exercise of that discretion is nevertheless constrained by rules of conduct that the Commission has imposed on itself by adopting the Guidelines. Although the latter do not constitute rules of law which the administration is always bound to observe, the Court nevertheless considers that the Commission cannot depart from those rules without being found to be in breach of the general principles of law, such as equal treatment or the protection of legitimate expectations.[385]

It is therefore increasingly careful to reason the amount of fines in the light of the guidelines. Although it is not a requirement of Regulation 1/2003, it is invariably Commission practice to find an infringment (if it exists) and impose a fine (if it is warranted) in a single decision.

Commission avarice has been increasing steadily over the years, up to record **13.96** fines imposed, for cartel infringements alone (which 'by reason of their very nature ... merit the severest fines'),[386] in/of:

2002   € 937 million
2003   € 416 million

---

380 Regulation 1/2003, art. 23(3). An increase in a fine by reference to duration is limited to circumstances in which there is a direct relation between duration and acute damage to the objectivers of the competition rules; Case T-203/01 *Michelin* v *Commission* [2003] ECR II-4071, at para. 278 and case law cited there.

381 E.g., Cases C-189 etc./02P *Dansk Rørindustri and ors* v *Commission* [2005] ECR I-5425, at para. 172; Case C-308/04P *SGL Carbon* v *Commission* [2006] ECR I-5977, at paras 207–8.

382 See Case C-266/06P *Evonik Degussa* v *Commission* [2008] ECR I-81*, at paras 36–63.

383 Guidelines on the Method of Setting Fines pursuant to Article 15(2) of Regulation No. 17 and Article 65(5) of the ECSC Treaty [1998] OJ C9/6; supplemented by Guidelines on the Method of Setting Fines pursuant to Article 23(2)(a) of Regulation No. 1/2003 [2006] OJ C210/2.

384 Case C-510/06P *Archer Daniels Midland* v *Commission* [2009] ECR I-1843, at para. 60.

385 Case C-76/06P *Britannia Alloys & Chemicals* v *Commission* [2007] ECR I-4405, *per* A-G Bot at paras 45–6 of his opinion. See also Cases C-189/02P *Dansk Rørindustri and ors* v *Commission* [2005] ECR I-5425, at para. 209.

386 Case T-127/04 *KME Germany and ors* v *Commission* [2009] ECR II-1167, at para. 64.

2004   € 388 million
2005   € 422 million
2006   € 1,850 million
2007   € 3,340 million
2008   € 2,238 million
2009   € 1,540 million
2010   € 3,056 million
2011   € 613 million
2012   € 1.876 million

13.97 To date the highest fine (2012) is €1,471 million in respect of a ten-year cartel amongst seven international groups of companies in the cathode ray tube (used in computer monitors and televisions) market.[387] The highest fine upon a single undertaking for a single infraction is €1,060 million imposed upon Intel (2009) for infringement of article 102 through fidelity rebates and direct payments to downstream manufacturers to halt or delay use of its (only effective) competitor's components.[388] The highest total fines imposed upon a single undertaking is €1,677 million, upon Microsoft, comprising a fine of €497 million in 2004 for two concurrent breaches of article 102 (refusal to license and bundling)[389] and a further €1,180 million for failure to comply with a behavioural remedy ordered by the Commission in the 2004 decision.[390] The highest fine imposed for a non-cartel breach of article 101, that is one involving vertical restraints, is €168 million.[391]

13.98 In order to ensure compliance with a decision the Commission may also impose a liquidate penalty ('periodic penalty payment') of up to 5 per cent of average daily turnover during the preceding business year per day for each day on which an undertaking, having been ordered to do so, fails to put an end to an

---

387   Case COMP/39.473 *Cathode Ray Tubes*, decision of 5 December 2012, not yet published. The total of €1,470,515,000 came after a reduction made under the Commission's leniency programme (as to which see immediately below); the fines were originally computed at €1,895,000,000. The previous highest fine (2008) was €1,384 million for a cartel in the automative glass sector (Case COMP/39.125 [2009] OJ C173/13 (summary publication), which included a fine for Saint-Gobain of Courbevoie of €896 million, the highest single fine imposed upon an undertaking for a cartel infraction anywhere in the world.

388   Case COMP/37.990 *Intel* [2009] OJ C227/13 (summary publication); under review as Case T-286/09 *Intel* v *Commission*, pending.

389   Decision 2007/53 (*Microsoft*) [2007] OJ L32/23 (summary publication; full decision available at [2005] 4 CMLR 965); upheld in Case T-201/04 *Microsoft* v *Commission* [2007] ECR II-3601.

390   In 2006 Microsoft was fined €280.5 million for failure to comply to June of that year (Case COMP/37.792 *Microsoft* [2006] OJ C138/10 (summary publication); in 2008 it was fined a further €889 million for continued failure to comply to October 2007, when it finally did so to the Commission's satisfaction ([2009] OJ C166/20 (summary publication); see Case T-167/08 *Microsoft* v *Commission*, judgment of 27 June 2012, not yet reported).

391   Decision 2003/675 (*Nintendo*) [2003] OJ L255/33, of which Nintendo was fined €149 million, the remainder imposed upon its (independent) European distributors; the €149 million was reduced to €119 million on review, Case T-13/03 *Nintendo and anor* v *Commission* [2009] ECR II-975.

infringement (including compliance with any remedy ordered by the Commission), fails to comply with a formal request for information, or refuses to submit to a formal investigation.[392]

Commission fines are subject to a prescription period of three years for **13.99** infringements of the provisions on requests for information and the conduct of investigations, five years for all other infringements.[393] They are, in the view of Union law, administrative, not criminal, penalties,[394] but it is a view coming increasingly under serious challenge.[395]

---

392 Regulation 1/2003, art. 24. This was a material change introduced by Regulation 1/2003, periodic penalty payments under Regulation 17 being limited to €1,000 per day, and is what enabled the Commission to fine Microsoft €1,180 million; if subject to Regulation 17 limits it could have been no more than €1.05 million.

393 *Ibid.* art. 25.

394 *Ibid.* art. 23(5); confirmed by the Court of Justice in Case 45/69 *Boehringer Mannheim* v *Commission* [1970] ECR 769.

395 For example, it is highly unlikely the European Court of Human Rights would agree: see *Société Stenuit* v *France* (1992) 14 EHRR 509; *Dubus* v *France* (Application No. 5242/04), judgment of 11 June 2009, not yet reported; and *Menarini Diagnostics* v *Italy* (Application No. 43509/08), judgment of 27 September 2011, not yet reported. Equivalent fines ('penalties') in UK law (Competition Act 1998, s. 36) are recognised to be criminal sanctions (*Napp Pharmaceuticals* v *Director General of Fair Trading* [2002] CompAR 13, at para. 91 ff. (CCAT)) and in Denmark a 'penalty' (*strafansvar*) imposed for infringements of the Konkurrenceloven is fixed by reference to the general rules of the Straffeloven (LBK nr. 1027 af 21. august 2007, § 23(3)). The closest the Court of Justice has come to agreeing is an observation by A-G Kokott that the Union regime of sanctions means that 'the area is at least akin to criminal law' ('es sich um einen dem Strafrecht zumindest verwandten Bereich handelt'), Case C-97/08P *Akzo Nobel and ors* v *Commission* [2009] ECR I-8237, at para. 39 of her opinion, whilst A-G Sharpston speaks of the 'de facto' and 'ongoing' '"criminalisation" of competition law', Case C-272/09P *KME Germany and ors* v *Commission*, judgment of 8 December 2011, not yet reported, at paras 46 and 51 of her opinion. It is an important distinction in some member states in which commission of a 'regulatory offence' (*Ordnungswidrigkeit*) does not inhibit an undertaking's capacity to carry on trading, and there is a natural antipathy to it in some member states in which only natural persons can commit a criminal offence. In all cases it has ramifications for the procedural safeguards afforded by art. 6 of the Convention, but which sets stricter standards in the criminal arena. This is recognised by the Court of Justice, which therefore developed various rights of the defence, and takes the view that its supervisory jurisdiction is adequate for the protection of the individual in this context; see e.g., Case C-137/92 *Commission* v *BASF* (PVC) [1994] ECR I-2555; Case T-30/91 *Solvay* v *Commission* (Soda Ash) [1995] II-1775; Case C-185/95P *Baustahlgewebe* v *Commission* [1998] ECR I-8417; Case T-352/94 *Mo och Domsjö* v *Commission* (Cartonboard) [1998] ECR II-1989; Cases T-305 etc./94 *Limburgse Vinyl Maatschappij* v *Commission* (PVC II) [1999] ECR II-931. But as A-G Sharpston allows (Case C-272/09P *KME Germany, supra*, at para. 51 of her opinion), '[t]he requirements a system of judicial review must meet to comply with Article 6(1) ECHR have yet to be fully clarified, but it is uncertain whether the existing system of EU competition law enforcement, including judicial review, meets those requirements'. With Lisbon the Union is required to accede to the Convention (TEU, art. 6(2)) and perhaps with this in mind there is now before the Court a number of challenges to the machinery and review of Commission fines. There were hopes in some quarters that the Court of Justice would take a robust stand in the *KME* cases (Case C-272/09P *KME Germany, supra* and Case C-389/10P *KME Germany and ors* v *Commission*, judgment of 8 December 2011, not yet reported) and in *Chalkor* (Case C-386/10P *Chalkor Epexergasias Metallon* v *Commission*, judgment of 8 December 2011, not yet reported) but they were dashed, the Court finding no affront to the right to effective judicial review. Recent indications from Strasbourg (*Menarini, supra*) suggest the Court of Human Rights might not disagree. There remain others in the pipeline (Case T-56/09 *Saint-Gobain Glass and ors* v *Commission* and Case T-286/09 *Intel* v *Commission*, both pending) but it is difficult to see how the General Court can now say otherwise. Yet there is still the occasional rattle of dissent: see e.g. the opinion of A-G Bot in Case C-89/11P *E.ON Energie* v Commission, pending, at paras 116–120.

13.100 In order better to detect and combat (or corrode) cartels, and inspired in part by the corporate leniency programme adopted by the authorities in the United States, the Commission has adopted a policy (the 'leniency policy') by which it undertakes to impose no fine upon an undertaking party to a hardcore cartel which 'shops' the existence of the cartel to the Commission, provided it is the first to break ranks, and to offer a significant reduction in fines to others which provide 'significant added value' to the evidence going to the establishment of the cartel.[396] As a 'self-imposed rule of practice'[397] it is bound by the terms of the notice (as it itself recognises)[398] and cannot depart from it[399] unless it can show adequate reasons.[400] There are serious questions raised as to the fairness of the practice, similar to those attending analogous accommodation in criminal prosecution, but the Commission considers that '[t]he interests of consumers and citizens in ensuring that secret cartels are detected and punished outweigh the interest in fining those undertakings that enable the Commission to detect and prohibit such practices' and that the policy is justified 'in the Community interest' and of 'intrinsic value',[401] and it appears to have borne significant fruit. In 2008 the Commission introduced a 'settlement package'[402] whereby parties to a cartel, having seen the evidence in the Commission file, admit involvement and liability (and so free up Commission resources) and are afforded a 10 per cent reduction in fines in return. The procedure was used for the first time in 2010[403] and six times in total to September 2012.

13.101 A Commission decision imposing a financial penalty is enforced by civil process.[404] In the United Kingdom it is registered by the High Court or the

---

396 Notice on immunity from fines and reduction of fines in cartel cases ('Leniency' or 'Whistleblowers' Notice) [2006] OJ C298/17. This is the third such notice, replacing the second ([2002] OJ C45/3) which significantly altered the first ([1996] OJ C207/4). The notice is limited to cartel activity ('[s]ecret cartels ... aimed at ... the fixing of purchase or selling prices or other trading conditions, the allocation of production or sales quotas, the sharing of markets including bid-rigging, restrictions of imports or exports'; para. 1) but Commission discretion extends to taking notice of cooperation in other contexts; see e.g., Case T-13/03 *Nintendo and anor* v *Commission* [2009] ECR II-975.

397 Case T-161/05 *Hoechst* v *Commission* [2009] ECR II-3555, at para. 99.

398 See para. 38: the Commission 'is aware that this notice will create legitimate expectations on which undertakings may rely'.

399 Case T-15/02 *BASF* v *Commission* [2006] ECR II-497, at para. 119.

400 Case C-397/03P *Archer Daniels Midland and anor* v *Commission* [2006] ECR I-4429, at para. 91; Case T-161/05 *Hoechst*, n. 397 above, at para. 99.

401 2006 notice, n. 396 above, paras 3, 3 and 4, respectively. Nor does the General Court appear to be impressed by these arguments: e.g., Case T-352/94 *Mo och Domsjö* v *Commission* (Cartonboard) [1998] ECR II-1989.

402 Regulation 622/2008 [2008] OJ L171/3 (amending Regulation 773/2004); Notice on the conduct of settlement procedures in cartel cases [2008] OJ C167/1.

403 Case COMP/38.511 *DRAMS Cartel* [2011] OJ C180/15 (summary publication); Case COMP/38.866 *Animal Feed Phosphates Cartel* [2011] OJ C111/19 (summary publication) – a 'hybrid' case, involving settlement with some but not all undertakings.

404 TFEU, art. 299 (ex art. 256 EC).

Court of Session as a 'European Community judgment'[405] and enforced in accordance with specific rules of court.[406] The Commission may (but need not)[407] agree – and frequently offers – to defer enforcing payment of a fine pending any judicial review of the decision upon condition that the undertaking will pay default interest if the action for review fails and provides bank guarantees as to eventual payment of principal, interest and any increase in the fine. As the provision of a bank guarantee is a matter of choice for the relevant undertaking(s), the (sometimes substantial) cost is not recoverable even if the Commission decision is eventually annulled.[408]

The Commission is required to publish any decision adopted under Regulation **13.102** 1/2003 whereby it finds an infringement, adopts interim measures, accepts a commitment, finds inapplicability or imposes a fine or periodic penalty payment.[409] But it may not make public any information 'covered by the obligation of professional secrecy'.[410] An undertaking may challenge a Commission failure to abide by this stricture,[411] and presumably recover damages for any loss caused.

(d) Judicial control of the Commission

Except for provisional steps in the course of an investigation, all measures **13.103** adopted by the Commission under the authority granted it by Regulation 1/2003 are decisions within the meaning of article 288 of the TFEU and so subject to judicial review under article 263.[412] Because most cases are brought by aggrieved undertakings they go to the General Court, which therefore now fashions much of the case law on procedural aspects. Any third (private) party not the addressee wishing to challenge a Commission decision must satisfy the tests laid down by article 263(4) that the decision affects it directly and individually, but whilst individual concern in particular is normally a very difficult test to meet,[413] the Court of Justice has been more lenient in the competition field than in more general areas of Union activity, so that a complainant, an undertaking participating or playing a significant role in a

---

405   European Communities (Enforcement of Community Judgments) Order 1972, SI 1972/1590.
406   Civil Procedure Rules, rule 74.19–74.26 (England and Wales), RC 62.18–62.25 (Scotland).
407   E.g., Case T-191/98R *DSR-Senator Lines* v *Commission* [1999] ECR II-2531.
408   Case C-282/05P *Holcim (Deutschland)* v *Commission* [2007] ECR I-2941; Case T-113/04 *Atlantic Container Line and ors* v *Commission* [2007] ECR II-171*.
409   Regulation 1/2003, art. 30. Latterly decisions are published in the *Official Journal* only in summary form; they are available in full (in a 'non-confidential' version, and only in their official language(s)) from the Commission or on the DG Competition website.
410   TFEU, art. 339 (ex art. 287 EC); Regulation 1/2003, art. 28.
411   E.g., Case T-474/04 *Pergan Hilfsstoffe für industrielle Prozesse* v *Commission* [2007] ECR II-4225.
412   See 5.66 above.
413   See 5.79 above.

Commission investigation, and sometimes others so long as they are appreciably affected, are recognised as being individually concerned by a Commission decision and so enjoy standing to challenge it.[414]

13.104 The normal grounds for annulment supplied by article 263 apply. Specifically to the field of competition, the Court will annul a Commission decision where it has failed to comply with an essential procedural requirement[415] or with any material aspect of a party's right of defence;[416] where it is insufficiently reasoned;[417] where the Commission has failed to adduce sufficient evidence to the requisite standard of proof,[418] it bearing the burden of showing the existence of an infringement;[419] or where it disagrees with the Commission's assessment or interpretation of the facts or of the law, or both.[420] Generally the discretion the Commission enjoys in competition matters results in a lighter touch in review; here is the General Court in *Microsoft*:

---

414 See e.g., Case 26/76 *Metro* v *Commission* (No. 1) [1977] ECR 1875; Case 75/84 *Metro* v *Commission* (No. 2) [1986] ECR 3021; Case T-19/92 *Leclerc* v *Commission* [1996] ECR II-1851; Cases T-528 etc./93 *Métropole Télévision* v *Commission* [1996] ECR II-649; Case T-177/04 *easyJet* v *Commission* [2006] ECR II-1931; Case T-170/06 *Alrosa* v *Commission* [2007] ECR II-2601; Case C-260/05P *Sniace* v *Commission* [2007] ECR I-10005.

415 Case C-137/92 *Commission* v *BASF* (PVC) [1994] ECR I-2555; Cases T-31 and 32/91 *Solvay* v *Commission* (Soda Ash) [1995] ECR II-1821 and 1825; Case 17/74 *Transocean Marine Paint Association* v *Commission* [1974] ECR 1063.

416 E.g., Cases T-30/91 *Solvay* v *Commission* (Soda Ash) [1995] ECR II-1775; Case T-353/94 *Postbank* v *Commission* [1996] ECR II-921; Cases T-191 etc./98 *Atlantic Container Lines and ors* v *Commission* [2003] ECR II-3275.

417 Cases 8–11/66 *Cimenteries CBR* v *EEC Commission* [1967] ECR 75; Cases 89 etc./85 *Åhlström* v *Commission* (Woodpulp) [1993] ECR I-1307; Case C-360/92P *Publishers Association* v *Commission* [1995] ECR I-23; Cases T-374 etc./94 *European Night Services* v *Commission* [1998] ECR II-3141; Case T-328/03 *O₂ (Germany)* v *Commission* [2006] ECR II-1231; Case T-613/97 *Française de l'Express and ors* v *Commission* [2006] ECR II-1531.

418 Cases 41, 44–5/69 *ACF Chemifarma* v *Commission* (Quinine) [1970] ECR 665; Case 6/72 *Continental Can* v *Commission* [1973] ECR 215; Cases 40 etc./73 *Coöperatieve Vereniging 'Suiker Unie'* v *Commission* [1975] ECR 1663; Cases T-68, 77–8/91 *Società Italiano Vetro* v *Commission* (Flat Glass) [1992] ECR II-1403; Case T-67/01 *JCB Services* v *Commission* [2004] ECR II-49; Case T-56/02 *Bayerische Hypo- und Vereinsbank* v *Commission* [2004] ECR II-3495; Case T-325/01 *Daimler Chrysler* v *Commission* [2005] ECR II-3319.

419 Regulation 1/2003, art. 2; Case C-185/95P *Baustahlgewebe* v *Commission* [1998] ECR I-8417. The Court has been reticent clearly to define the standard of proof required, but there is recent guidance in Case T-38/02 *Groupe Danone* v *Commission* [2005] ECR II-4407, at paras 214–18; Case T-168/01 *GlaxoSmithKline Services* v *Commission* [2006] ECR II-2969; Case T-36/05 *Coats Holdings* v *Commission* [2007] ECR II-110*, at paras 65–96; Case T-474/04 *Pergan Hilfsstoffe für industrielle Prozesse* v *Commission* [2007] ECR II-4225, at paras 75–81; and especially Case T-439/07 *Coats Holdings* v *Commission*, judgment of 27 June 2012, not yet reported, at paras 38–52.

420 Case 26/75 *General Motors* v *Commission* [1975] ECR 1367; Case 258/78 *Nungesser* v *Commission* (Maize Seeds) [1982] ECR 2015; Cases T-68 and 77–8/89 *Flat Glass*, n. 418 above; Cases 89 etc./85 *Woodpulp*, n. 417 above; Case T-77/94 *Vereniging van Groothandelaren in Bloemkwekerijprodukten* v *Commission* [1997] ECR II-759; Cases T-374 etc./94 *European Night Services* v *Commission* [1998] ECR II-3141; Case T-41/96 *Bayer* v *Commission* [2000] ECR II-3383; Case T-208/01 *Volkswagen* v *Commission* [2003] ECR II-5141; Case T-325/01 *Daimler Chrysler*, n. 418 above; Case T-328/03 *O₂ (Germany)* v *Commission* [2006] ECR II-1231.

[A]lthough as a general rule the Community Courts undertake a comprehensive review of the question as to whether or not the conditions for the application of the competition rules are met, their review of complex economic appraisals made by the Commission is necessarily limited to checking whether the relevant rules on procedure and on stating reasons have been complied with, whether the facts have been accurately stated and whether there has been any manifest error of assessment or a misuse of powers.

Likewise, in so far as the Commission's decision is the result of complex technical appraisals, those appraisals are in principle subject to only limited review by the Court, which means that the Community Courts cannot substitute their own assessment of matters of fact for the Commission's.[421]

It adds that this

does not mean that they [the Community Courts] must decline to review the Commission's interpretation of economic or technical data. The Community Courts must not only establish whether the evidence put forward is factually accurate, reliable and consistent but must also determine whether that evidence contains all the relevant data that must be taken into consideration in appraising a complex situation and whether it is capable of substantiating the conclusions drawn from it.[422]

Notwithstanding, the extensive powers of sanction enjoyed by the Commission under Regulation 1/2003 and the manner in which it is exercised gives pause for concern that this approach is unduly timid. Yet it has been reconfirmed (by the General Court) since *Microsoft*.[423] And in a 2010 (so post-Charter) judgment in which a commitment offered and accepted by the Commission was challenged on grounds of proportionality, the Court of Justice (Grand Chamber) said '[j]udicial review for its part relates solely to whether the Commission's assessment is manifestly incorrect'[424] and 'the Commission … committed a manifest error of assessment only if [its] conclusion was obviously unfounded'.[425]

13.105 Whilst the initiation of proceedings before the Court of Justice or the General Court has no automatic suspensory effect,[426] the Court may, upon application from a party to a case before it and 'if it considers that circumstances so require',

---

421 Case T-201/04 *Microsoft* v *Commission* [2007] ECR II-3601, at paras 87–8. The approach has been reconfirmed in Case T-301/04 *Clearstream Banking and Clearstream International* v *Commission* [2009] ECR II-3155, at paras 93–5.
422 Case T-201/04 *Microsoft, ibid.* at para. 89.
423 Case T-301/04 *Clearstream,* n. 421 above, at paras 93–5.
424 Case C-441/07P *Commission* v *Alrosa* [2010] ECR I-5949, at para. 42.
425 *Ibid.* at para. 63.
426 See 5.39 above.

suspend the operation of a contested decision.[427] It is not uncommon for a party to make the request, and not wholly uncommon for the Court to accede to it.[428]

13.106   Only those aspects vitiated by illegality will be annulled, provided they can be severed from the whole of the decision,[429] and this occurs frequently, the Court annulling one or more of several findings of a breach by the Commission but allowing the others to stand. Where a decision is annulled on procedural grounds or on grounds of insufficiency of reasoning or of proof, there is, other than the five-year time bar for the imposition of fines, nothing to prevent the Commission, its nose having been bloodied by the Court, from re-initiating proceedings.[430]

13.107   In contradistinction to the review jurisdiction the Court enjoys in the matter of finding an infringement of article 101 or 102, it has 'unlimited jurisdiction' (*une compétence de pleine juridiction*) to review Commission fines imposed under Regulation 1/2003.[431] Although necessarily raised in the context of annulment proceedings under article 263,[432] it is therefore not limited to review of legality but subject to a 'full merits review' and, if appropriate, a fine may be varied (cancelled, reduced or increased) even where the decision is not annulled.[433] A full review may in fact be a requirement of article 6 of the European

---

427   TFEU, art. 278 (ex art. 242 EC).

428   For good examples see Case T-395/94R *Atlantic Container Line* v *Commission* [1995] ECR II-595; Case T-41/96R *Bayer* v *Commission* [1996] ECR II-381; Case C-393/96P(R) *Antonissen* v *Council and Commission* [1997] ECR I-441; Case T-65/98R *van den Bergh Foods* v *Commission* [1998] ECR II-2641; Case T-201/04R(2) *Microsoft* v *Commission* [2004] ECR II-4463. The Court may also suspend the obligation to pay a fine or provide a bank guarantee in lieu; e.g., Case T-217/03R *Fédération nationale de la coopération bétail et viande* v *Commission* [2004] ECR II-239.

429   Cases 56 and 58/64 *Établissements Consten and Grundig-Verkaufs* v *EEC Commission* [1966] ECR 299. On partial annulment of competition decisions ('whose practical importance should not be underestimated'; para. 1) see the discussion of A-G Kokott in Case C-441/11P *Commission* v *Verhuizingen Coppens*, pending.

430   Cases T-305 etc./94 *Limburgse Vinyl Maatschappi and ors* v *Commission* (PVC II) [1999] ECR II-931; Decision 2003/6 (Soda Ash – Solvay) [2003] OJ L10/10; Decision 2003/7 (Soda Ash – ICI) [2003] OJ L10/33); Case COMP/37.956 *Concrete Reinforcing Bars*, decision of 30 September 2009, not yet published; Case COMP/36.212 *Carbonless Paper*, decision of 23 June 2010, not yet published. Time stands still during (sometimes lengthy) proceedings before the Court of Justice (Regulation 1/2003, art. 25(6); *PVC II*; Case T-57/01 *Solvay* v *Commission* [2009] ECR II-4621; Case T-58/01 *Solvay* v *Commission* [2009] ECR II-4781; Case T-66/01 *Imperial Chemical Industries* v *Commission* (Soda Ash) [2010] ECR II-2631) but only *inter partes*; Cases C-201 and 216/09P *ArcelorMittal Luxembourg and ors* v *Commission*, judgment of 29 March 2011, not yet reported. For a degree of deftness required by the Commission see Case C-109/10P *Solvay* v *Commission* and Case C-110/10P *Solvay* v *Commission*, judgments of 25 October 2011, not yet reported, at paras 70–2 and 67–9, respectively.

431   Regulation 1/2003, art. 31 (in accordance with TFEU, art. 261 (ex art. 229 EC)).

432   Case T-252/03 *Fédération nationale de l'industrie et des commerces en gros des viandes* v *Commission* [2004] ECR II-3795.

433   Cases C-238 etc./99P *Limburgse Vinyl Maatschappij and ors* v *Commission* (PVC II) [2002] ECR I-8375, at para. 692.

Convention.[434] Yet it is felt in some quarters that, notwithstanding the breadth of its jurisdiction, the Court is still unduly timid. It affords the Commission a margin of discretion in fixing fines, it is 'desirable' that the method used in their calculation be ascertainable from a decision,[435] and it will consider whether the amount is proportionate to the gravity and duration of the infraction, taking into account all relevant factors of the case.[436] Since the adoption of the 1998 notice on the method of setting fines the General Court has devoted increasing care to analysis of the Commission's adherence both to it and to the leniency notice.[437] However, its unlimited jurisdiction means that the Court may substitute its own appraisal for that of the Commission,[438] it is certainly not bound by the guidelines in the same way,[439] yet continues generally to show deference. The General Court has even suggested (wrongly) that its review jurisdiction is restricted to a finding of illegality.[440] It has cancelled and reduced fines in a number of cases but increased a fine once only, and that a product of mechanical recalculation rather than a reassessment of culpability.[441] In an appeal from the General Court on the matter of fines, the Court of Justice cannot substitute its own appraisal for that of the General Court,[442] but it may consider whether the latter has responded to a sufficient legal standard to the arguments raised for having the fine cancelled or reduced.[443]

There are concerns that the whole enforcement mechanisms of Regulation **13.108** 1/2003 – a single (political) body investigates the facts, prosecutes, determines guilt and imposes punishment, with no public hearing before a neutral authority – combined with the severity of fines which may be imposed and the gentleness with which the Court is said to view them is under serious strain: it is 'an issue which is time and again the subject of discussion and currently ... of

---

434 See *Compagnie des gaz de pétrole Primagaz* v *France* (Application No. 29613/08), judgment of the ECtHR of 21 December 2010, not yet reported.

435 Case T-148/89 *Tréfilunion* v *Commission* [1995] ECR II-1063.

436 Regulation 1/2003, art. 2; Case C-185/95P *Baustahlgewebe* v *Commission* [1998] ECR I-8417.

437 See e.g., Case T-23/99 *LR af 1998* v *Commission* [2002] ECR II-1705, at paras 223–391; Case T-224/00 *Archer Daniels Midland and anor* v *Commission* [2003] ECR II-2597; Cases T-236 etc./01 *Tokai Carbon and ors* v *Commission* (Graphite Electrodes) [2004] ECR II-1181; Case T-241/01 *Scandinavian Airlines System* v *Commission* [2005] ECR II-2917; Case T-38/02 *Groupe Danone* v *Commission* [2005] ECR II-4407; Case T-33/02 *Britannia Alloys & Chemicals* v *Commission* [2005] ECR II-4973; Case T-279/02 *Degussa* v *Commission* [2006] ECR II-897; Case C-308/04P *SGL Carbon* v *Commission* [2006] ECR I-5977.

438 Case C-3/06P *Groupe Danone* v *Commission* [2007] ECR I-1331, at para. 61.

439 Cases T-49–51/02 *Brasserie nationale and ors* v *Commission* [2005] ECR II-3033, at para. 169.

440 Case T-15/02 *BASF* v *Commission* [2006] ECR II-497, at para. 582.

441 Cases T-101 and 111/05 *BASF and UCB* v *Commission* [2007] ECR II-4949; cf. Cases T-259 etc./02 *Raiffeisen Zentralbank Österreich and ors* v *Commission* [2006] ECR II-5169 (rebuffing a Commission invitation to increase a fine).

442 Case C-320/92P *Finsider* v *Commission* [1994] ECR I-5697; Case C-310/93P *BPB Industries and British Gypsum* v *Commission* [1995] ECR I-867.

443 Case C-219/95P *Ferriere Nord* v *Commission* [1997] ECR I-4411.

increasing attention'[444] – not least in light of, and when measured against, the Charter of Fundamental Rights and, in the fullness of time, the European Convention. The former now elevated to Treaty status and the Union Treaty-bound to accede to the latter, there are cases (recent and pending) before the General Court and the Court of Justice which raise the issues, but, so far, the Court of Justice seems unimpressed.[445]

3. Enforcement by national competition authorities

13.109   From the beginning the Treaty authorised 'the authorities in Member States … in accordance with the law of their country'[446] to give effect to (the predecessors of) articles 101 and 102 pending entry into force of implementing legislation under article 103. 'Authorities' means administrative authorities for the enforcement of competition law, the primary model of which is the German *Bundeskartellamt*. Regulation 17 did nothing to disable this power: in fact it was expressly saved ('they shall remain competent in this respect'), except that the Commission would pre-empt any national enforcement proceedings once it had 'initiated [a] procedure'.[447] So, the appropriate national authorities retained the power to enforce articles 101 and 102 – if they existed and if there resided in national law authority for them to do so. By 2004 this was the case in nine of the then 15 member states.[448]

13.110   The 1999 White Paper on reform of articles 101 and 102[449] proposed changes not only to the application of article 101(3) but to enforcement of the competition rules more generally. This included implementation of a decentralisation policy, part of which is a requirement that articles 101 and 102 be enforced by national competition authorities (NCAs). No longer had a member state an option in the matter. Thus:

> The competition authorities of the Member States shall have the power to apply Articles [101] and [102] of the Treaty in individual cases … [T]hey may take the following decisions:

---

444   Cases C-628/10 and 14/11P *Alliance One International and ors* v *Commission*, judgment of 19 July 2012, not yet reported, *per* A-G Kokott at para. 95 of her opinion.
445   See n. 395 above.
446   EEC Treaty, art. 88 (art. 104 TFEU).
447   Regulation 17/62, art. 9(3). Initiating a procedure meant an authoritative act of the Commission evidencing an intention of taking a decision as to negative clearance, exemption or termination; Case 48/72 *Brasserie de Haecht* v *Wilkin-Janssen* [1973] ECR 77.
448   That is, those other than Ireland, Luxembourg, Austria, Finland, Sweden and the United Kingdom.
449   White Paper on Modernisation of the Rules Implementing Articles 85 and 86 of the EC Treaty, Commission Programme No. 99/027.

- requiring that an infringement be brought to an end,
- ordering interim measures,
- accepting commitments,
- imposing fines, periodic penalty payments or any other penalty provided for in their national law.[450]

The Regulation conferred not only the power, but an obligation: if and when an NCA applies its own competition law to a situation in which article 101 and/or article 102 is also joined, it is required to apply them as well.[451] Each member state was required to designate an authority for this purpose (and so create one if it didn't exist), and to adopt '[t]he measures necessary to empower those authorities to apply those Articles'.[452]

The decentralisation programme raises a number of issues, primarily that of the **13.111** uniformity of application of the Union rules by 28(-plus)[453] autonomous authorities. Efforts were therefore made to minimise the risks, primarily through a system of compulsory 'close cooperation' between Commission and NCAs,[454] information exchange,[455] a number of soft law devices[456] and the establishment of a 'Network of Competition Authorities' (or European Competition Network; ECN) addressing allocation of work and the provision of assistance to and from the Commission and amongst the NCAs themselves.[457]

---

450 Regulation 1/2003, art. 5. The list does not include the power to find and declare that art. 101 or 102 has *not* been infringed, as the Commission may do under art. 10 of Regulation 1/2003 (the 'finding of inapplicability'), and the Court has confirmed that an NCA does not have that power; Case C-375/09 *Prezes Urzędu Ochrony Konkurencji i Konsumentów* v *Tele2 Polska*, judgment of 3 May 2011, not yet reported.

451 Regulation 1/2003, art. 3(1). This is analogous to the Commission's (compulsory) practice since 1994 of applying in art. 101/102 proceedings also arts 53/54 of the EEA Agreement if the effects of conduct at issue extend to the EEA; see 13.160 below.

452 *Ibid.* art. 35. For the United Kingdom see the Competition Act 1998 and Other Enactments (Amendment) Regulations 2004, SI 2004/1261. The designated authority is the Office of Fair Trading and, within their powers under the Competition Act 1998, the sectoral regulators.

453 In the United Kingdom, for example, NCA duties are borne not only by the OFT but by a number of sectoral regulators, whilst in Germany each *Land* has its own competition authority (the *Landeskartellamtbehörden*) competent, within their jurisdiction, to enforce Union rules.

454 Regulation 1/2003, art. 11(1). See generally Case T-339/04 *O₂ (Germany)* v *Commission* [2006] ECR II-1231.

455 Regulation 1/2003, arts 11, 12. This jeopardises the confidentiality purported to be protected (art. 28) but was better protected under Regulation 17 – for example, the disappearance of the bar to using information provided the Commission to make out an infringement of national competition law; see n. 346 above and accompanying text. There is a growing problem on access to documents as between the Commisson and NCAs; see especially Case C-360/09 *Pfleiderer* v *Bundeskartellamt*, judgment of 14 June 2011, not yet reported.

456 Guidance on the Application of Article 81(3) of the Treaty [2004] OJ C101/97; Notice on informal guidance relating to novel questions concerning Articles 81 and 82 of the EC Treaty that arise in individual cases (guidance letters) [2004] OJ C101/78.

457 See Commission Notice on cooperation within the Network of Competition Authorities [2004] OJ C101/43. It is buttressed by a Notice on the handling of complaints by the Commission under Articles 81 and 82 of the EC Treaty [2004] OJ C101/65.

Member states have adopted specific legislation to make all this possible.[458]
One ineluctable issue is that in applying articles 101 and 102 the NCAs are
bound by the European Convention on Human Rights and subject to the
jurisdiction of the Court of Human Rights, whilst the Commission is not.

4. Enforcement by national courts

13.112 In 1974 the Court of Justice recognised articles 101 and 102 to be directly
effective,[459] and Regulation 1/2003 states (unnecessarily) that '[n]ational courts
shall have the power to apply Articles [101] and [102] of the Treaty'.[460] In
keeping with general rules, it is national remedies and procedures to which an
aggrieved undertaking turns.

13.113 The direct effect of articles 101(1) and 102 has two civil consequences.

- First, an agreement or a decision of an association of undertakings which
  is prohibited by article 101(1) and does not satisfy the conditions of article
  101(3) is, by virtue of article 101(2), 'automatically void' – or '*nul de plein
  droit*'; 'no prior decision to that effect [is] required'.[461] Article 102
  contains no provision equivalent to article 101(2), but its prohibition is
  absolute, again 'no prior decision to that effect being required',[462] and
  conduct infringing it cannot give rise to rights enforceable by the defaulting party – although the rights of other parties may be protected.[463]
- Second, breach of articles 101 and 102 is a civil wrong, and so third parties
  affected or injured by a prohibited agreement, decision, concerted practice
  or abusive conduct may be entitled to other civil remedies, such as
  declaratory relief, injunctive relief and/or damages.

In both cases, and as with administrative enforcement, it is for the party alleging
the infringment to make it out.[464]

---

458 For examples see, in Denmark, Konkurrenceloven, §§ 17 Stk 2, 18 Stk 8, 18a; in Germany, §§ 50–50c, 90a
     GWB; in France, Code de Commerce (version consolidée au 1 mai 2009), arts L462–8, L462–9; in Ireland,
     Competition Act, 2002, s. 46; in Luxembourg, loi du 17 mai 2004, arts 27–30.
459 Case 127/73 *Belgische Radio en Televisie* v *SABAM* [1974] ECR 313.
460 Regulation 1/2003, art. 6.
461 *Ibid.* art. 1(1).
462 *Ibid.* art. 1(3).
463 See Case 22/79 *Greenwich Film Production* v *SACEM* [1979] ECR 3275, *per* A-G Warner at 3296: '[I]n the
     case of an abuse of a dominant position, it would be unthinkable that Article [102] should be held
     indiscriminately to avoid contracts in a manner detrimental to the victims of the abuse or to third parties'.
464 Regulation 1/2003, art. 2.

There is otherwise little clarity or uniformity in this. Whilst an agreement **13.114** prohibited by article 101(1) is automatically void, there is little direction from the Court of Justice as to what exactly this ought to mean. It has said only that the nullity is 'absolute'[465] and

> [s]ince the nullity referred to in Article [101](2) is absolute, an agreement which is null and void by virtue of this provision has no effect as between the contracting parties and cannot be set up against [*n'est pas opposable aux*] third parties.[466]

Article 101(2) therefore requires at the least that the offending provisions of an agreement breaching article 101(1) cannot be enforced as between the parties and cannot be relied upon by them as against third parties, and that any relief sought by them which would have that purpose or effect – specific performance/implement, for example – must be declined. But it is otherwise for national courts to determine the legal consequences of its nullity in accordance with national law[467] (indeed, for the national court to determine the infringement in accordance with national standards of proof, which are left untouched by Regulation 1/2003);[468] other than the general requirements of equivalence and effectiveness of national remedies, the Court has resisted invitations to set a Union standard.

The entire agreement does not necessarily fall. The Court early on gave its **13.115** blessing to the doctrine of severance[469] and subsequently recognised that this too is a matter for national, not Union, law.[470] So, if national law permits the offending provisions of a contract to be severed by application of a 'blue pencil' test, the remaining provisions ('the residue') will be enforceable unless the contract is so changed in character as not to be of the sort that the parties on an objective basis intended to enter.[471] Third party rights may also remain unaffected: in English law, for example, the fact that a supplier party to a vertical agreement is also party to a horizontal price fixing agreement which is void does not make the vertical agreement itself void, and this is not inconsistent with article 101(2).[472] A judicial finding that an agreement (or part of an agreement)

---

465 Case 22/71 *Béguelin* v *GL Import Export* [1971] ECR 949, at para. 29; Case 319/82 *Société de Vente de Ciments et Bétons de l'Est* v *Kerpen & Kerpen* [1983] ECR 4173, at para. 11.

466 Case 22/71 *Béguelin, ibid.,* at para. 29.

467 Case 319/82 *Kerpen & Kerpen,* n. 465 above.

468 Regulation 1/2003, Preamble, 5th recital.

469 Cases 56 and 58/64 *Établissements Consten & Grundig-Verkaufs* v *EEC Commission* [1966] ECR 299; Case 56/65 *Société Technique Minière* v *Maschinenbau Ulm* [1966] ECR 235.

470 Case 319/82 *Kerpen & Kerpen,* n. 465 above.

471 E.g., *English, Welsh & Scottish Railway Ltd* v *E. ON UK and anor* [2007] EWHC 599 (Comm), [2007] All ER (D) 389.

472 See the discussion of Morgan J in *Bookmakers' Afternoon Greyhound Services and ors* v *Amalgamated Racing and ors* [2008] EWHC (Ch) 1978, [2009] LLR 25, at paras 409–10.

is void is the exclusive preserve of the national courts; the Court of Justice has no jurisdiction to annul an agreement concluded by a natural or legal person at the behest of one of the parties.[473]

13.116 Third parties injured by the operation of a prohibited agreement, decision or concerted practice or abusive conduct from a dominant undertaking have a remedy in declaratory and/or injunctive relief. In the United Kingdom, the courts have a marked preference for damages as an appropriate remedy generally,[474] but will grant an injunction (or similar) where a claimant can show that they are unlikely to prove adequate.[475] Urgency is a legitimate justification for immediate judicial intervention.[476] All examples hitherto have been orders for interlocutory/interim relief; owing to a marked propensity to settle, there has yet to be an injunction/interdict ordered in a final judgment in a UK court.[477]

13.117 As for damages, there was nothing in Community law which expressly required that they be available to parties injured by infringements of the competition rules, and the matter was therefore long left to national law[478] – which of course creates a risk of forum shopping. It was only in 2001, in *Courage* v *Crehan*, that the Court of Justice was moved to pronounce a view:

> The full effectiveness of Article [101] of the Treaty and, in particular, the practical effect of the prohibition laid down in Article [101](1) would be put at risk if it were not open

---

473 Case T-56/92R *Koelman* v *Commission* [1993] ECR II-1267. A national court may of course seek the intepretative assistance of the Court of Justice under art. 267, but the jurisdiction to determine an agreement to be void belongs to it alone.

474 See e.g., *Co-operative Insurance Society* v *Argyll Stores (Holdings)* [1998] AC 1 (HL).

475 See *Garden Cottage Foods* v *Milk Marketing Board* [1983] 2 All ER 292 (CA) (overturned by the House of Lords; see n. 478 below); *Cutsforth* v *Mansfield Inns* [1986] 1 All ER 577 (QBD); *Argyll Group* v *Distillers* 1987 SLT 514 (OH); *Millar and Bryce* v *Keeper of the Registers of Scotland* 1997 SLT 1000 (OH); *Greenalls Management Ltd* v *Canavan* [1998] EuLR 507 (CA); *Trent Taverns* v *Sykes* [1999] EuLR 492 (CA); *World Wildlife Fund for Nature and anor* v *World Wrestling Federation Entertainment* [2002] EWCA Civ 196, [2002] FSR 33, 530; *Leeds City Council* v *Watkins and Whiteley* [2003] EWHC 598 (Ch), [2003] LLR 477; *Lady Navigation* v *Lauritzenkool and anor* [2005] EWCA Civ 579, [2005] 2 Ll Rep 63; *Software Cellular Network* v *T-Mobile (UK) Ltd* (Truephone) [2007] EWHC 1790 (Ch), [2007] All ER (D) 14.

476 See e.g., *Truephone, ibid.*

477 For an Irish example see *HB Ice Cream* v *Masterfoods* [1993] ILRM 145 (HC).

478 The leading English case is *Garden Cottage Foods* v *Milk Marketing Board* [1984] AC 130, in which the House of Lords accepted that a breach of art. 102 could give rise to a cause of action for injured third parties. But the point was not authoritatively established, for the Lords merely discharged an interlocutory injunction granted by the Court of Appeal having determined that damages would be an available and preferable remedy; the parties settled before trial. The House of Lords identified the competent cause of action to be breach of statutory duty (but see the strong dissent of Lord Wilberforce, especially at 151–2). *Garden Cottage Foods* was subsequently cited by Parker LJ as 'clear authority that a private law action for breach of article [102] against an undertaking sounds in damages'; *Bourgoin* v *Minister for Agriculture, Fisheries and Food* [1985] 1 All ER 585 at 631 (CA); recognised (*obiter*) also in Scots law, *Argyll* v *Distillers* 1987 SLT 514 (OH). Breach of statutory duty appears equally to underlie an infringement of art. 101: *Norris* v *Government of the United States of America and ors* [2008] UKHL 16, [2008] 1 AC 920, at para. 32 (still *obiter*).

to any individual to claim damages for loss caused to him by a contract or by conduct liable to restrict or distort competition ...

[A]ctions for damages before the national courts can make a significant contribution to the maintenance of effective competition in the Community.

There should not therefore be any absolute bar to an action being brought .[479]

However, this was an uncommon case, the damages sought by a party to the agreement (a lease to a tied house) owing to loss caused by oppressive terms. It arose because in English law an agreement prohibited by article 101(1) is not only void but illegal,[480] so (in English law) barring recovery by a party to it either in reparation or in restitution,[481] and because by its construction through tort lenses the purpose of article 101 is to protect third parties:

[T]o whom is the duty implicit in Art. [101](1) owed? ... [It] seems to me ... that Art. [101](1) is designed to protect third-party competitors ... [T]he parties to [the agreement] offending Art. [101] are the cause, not the victims, of the distortion, restriction or prevention of competition.[482]

Upon being asked whether this was in any way incompatible with Community law, the Court of Justice presumed the availability of damages in English law generally, and the thrust of the judgment was that it would be unfair to deny them to a party to an anticompetitive agreement who was *non in pari delicto*. They were duly awarded by the Court of Appeal[483] but recalled by the House of Lords on appeal.[484] In any event *Crehan* is not direct authority for the availability of damages to injured third parties; that followed in *Manfredi* in 2006,[485] in which the Court confirmed:

---

479   Case C-453/99 *Courage* v *Crehan* [2001] ECR I-6297, at paras 26, 27, 29.

480   *Gibbs Mew* v *Gemmell* [1998] EuLR 588 (CA).

481   *Ibid.*, *per* Peter Gibson LJ at 606. As to later authority on bar to restitutionary claims in English law see *Devenish Nutrition and ors* v *Sanofi-Aventis and ors* [2008] EWCA Civ 1086, [2009] 3 All ER 27.

482   *Gibbs Mew*, n. 480 above, at 604.

483   *Crehan* v *Inntrepreneur Pub Company* [2004] EWCA Civ 637, [2004] All ER (D) 322.

484   The High Court had refused damages (*Crehan* v *Inntrepreneur Pub Company and anor* [2003] EWHC 1510 (Ch), [2003] All ER (D) 353) because it found the first *Delimitis* condition (market foreclosure) not to be met. The Court of Appeal reversed the High Court (*Crehan* v *Inntrepreneur Pub Company* [2004] EWCA Civ 637, [2004] All ER (D) 322), taking the view that the High Court was bound by a Commission decision in a related case which had found market foreclosure. The House of Lords reversed the Court of Appeal in turn (*Inntrepreneur Pub Company and ors* v *Crehan* [2006] UKHL 38, [2007] 1 AC 333), finding the Commission decision not to be binding upon the High Court so the High Court to have been competent to decide the *Delimitis 1* point itself, and reinstated its judgment. The issue of a duty to refer the point to the Court of Justice under art. 267 was put to their Lordships but batted aside peremptorily ('I see little point in [it]'; *per* Lord Hoffmann at para. 70 of his speech).

485   Cases C-295 etc./04 *Manfredi and ors* v *Lloyd Adriatico Assicurazioni and ors* [2006] ECR I-6619. Mr Manfredi fared better than Mr Crehan: his was a follow-on claim before a *Giudice di Pace*, who awarded him €889.10 in damages plus €500 costs; *Giudice di Pace di Bitoni*, sentenza del 21 maggio 2007, no. 172/2003.

(a)   there is a remedy in damages for injury suffered by a third party by a breach of article 101 where there is a 'causal relationship' between the two, causation to be determined by national law;

(b)   the principle of effectiveness requires that damages are available not only for actual loss (*damnum emergens*) but also for loss of profit (*lucrum cessans*); and

(c)   the principle of equivalence requires that exemplary damages be available if similar domestic remedies so provide, subject to prevention of unjustified enrichment.

It also follows that third party rights created by a contract (the *jus quaesitum tertio*) found to be void may be protected. Yet it remains that there is yet to be a successful final judgment awarding damages for breach of EU competition rules in a British court or tribunal.[486] The first case of a third party seeking damages to proceed to full trial and judgment was *Arkin* v *Borchard Lines*[487] in which no damages were awarded as the claimant failed to show a breach of either article 102 (the primary claim) or article 101; the case also stands as a good illustration of the risks of (English) litigation.[488] A subsequent judgment of the High Court finding a breach of article 102 was thought likely to be the first to yield damages[489] but it was overturned on its substance by the Court of Appeal.[490] A restitutionary award is probably unavailable in English law, but if it is, only exceptionally.[491] Damages have been awarded in other member states (most commonly in the Netherlands, in Germany and in France),[492] but on precious few occasions. Given the powers they have clearly had at their disposal since, at the latest, 1974,[493] the enforcement of articles 101 and 102 before national courts is still astonishingly underdeveloped – all the more surprising in that annual losses 'in the years to come' were estimated in 2007, in terms of unsought damages by 'victims' of infringements of articles 101 and 102, at between €5.7

---

486   Provision was made in 2002 for the availability of damages by a follow-on claim made before the Competition Appeal Tribunal for any loss or damage the result of an infringement of art. 101(1) or 102, an infringement of art. 101(1) or 102 or their UK equivalents (Competition Act 1998, s. 47A); the first damages (of £94,000, including, contentiously, £60,000 in exemplary damages) for an infraction of s. 18 (=art. 102) were awarded in 2012: *2 Travel Group v Cardiff City Transport* [2012] CAT 19.

487   [2003] EWHC 687, [2003] 2 Ll. Rep. 225. The Court referred throughout to the alleged 'breach of duty' and 'liability' of the defendants, but did not address the legal basis of such a claim, apparently presuming it to be competent.

488   Described subsequently by the Court of Appeal as a 'disastrous piece of litigation' (*Arkin v Borchard Lines and ors* [2005] EWCA 655, [2005] 3 All ER 613 at 615), the hearing lasted for 101 days and defendants' (unrecoverable) costs were around £6 million.

489   *Attheraces v British Horseracing Board* [2005] EWHC 3015 (Ch), [2006] FSR 336.

490   *Attheraces v British Horseracing Board* [2007] EWCA (Civ) 38, [2007] All ER (D) 26.

491   *Devenish Nutrition v Sanofi-Aventis (France) and ors* [2008] EWCA (Civ) 1086, [2009] 3 All ER 27.

492   See http://ec.europa.eu/comm/competition/elojade/antitrust/nationalcourts, part of the D-G Competition website at which (some) judgments of national courts applying arts 101 and 102 (in the language of the court only) are made available.

493   Case 127/73 *Belgische Radio en Televisie v SABAM* [1974] ECR 51.

thousand million and €23.3 thousand million.[494] At the end of 2005 the Commission adopted a Green Paper[495] discussing the issues, indicating enthusiasm for private enforcement and addressing possible steps to be taken; a (brief) White Paper was published in 2008.[496] A proposal for a Directive (the first to be proposed under article 103) was drawn up by the Commission in mid-2009 but subsequently disowned. A brave attempt was made in England by an undertaking to recover damages from its own directors and employees for the loss suffered in paying a penalty imposed under the Competition Act, but it came to naught.[497]

Most Union competition law is enforced in the civil or commercial courts. The **13.118** administrative courts are now involved insofar as they review the conduct of NCAs as and when the latter enforce articles 101 and 102; NCAs have a right to make representation before those courts even where national law does not allow it.[498] Generally the criminal courts have no part to play, although some member states have made various hardcore breaches of their own competition laws' criminal offences[499] and some have provided criminal sanctions for obstructing a Commission investigation.[500] In Ireland, uniquely, a breach of article 101 or of article 102 is in itself a criminal offence.[501]

---

494 Joint Impact Study, Centre for European Policy Studies, Erasmus University Rotterdam and Luiss Guido Carli, *Making Antitrust Damages Actions More Effective in the EU: Welfare Impact and Potential Scenarios* (21 December 2007), p. 11.
495 Damages actions for breach of the EC antitrust rules, COM(2005) 672 final.
496 Damages actions for breach of the EC antitrust rules, COM(2008) 165 final. See also the (more extensive) Commission Staff Working Paper accompanying the White Paper, SEC(2008) 404. As if to emphasise its resolve, in mid-2008 the Commission (on behalf of the Union) raised a claim for damages (of some €7 million) before the Brussels *Rechtbank van Koophandel* against the four parties to the lift/escalator cartel (Case COMP/38.823 [2008] OJ C75/19 (summary publication); resulting in a (then record) fine of €992 million; upheld almost entirely on review, in e.g. Case T-138/07 *Schindler Holding Ltd and ors v Commission*, judgment of 13 July 2011, not yet reported), they having supplied the lifts and escalators in various Union buildings. It raises interesting issues of (presumed) Commission reliance upon information it had itself gathered in the course of an investigation and a cartel the existence of which it had itself formally established. That question, amongst others, has now been referred to the Court of Justice: Case C-199/11 *European Union v Otis and ors*, pending.
497 *Safeway Stores and ors v Twigger and ors* [2010] EWCA Civ 1472, [2011] 2 All ER 841. The case involved a breach of s. 2 of the Competition Act (= art. 101) – and a prospective penalty of £10.7 million – but the principles would apply equally to a breach of EU law.
498 Case C-439/08 *Vlaamse federatie van verenigingen van Brood- en Banketbakkers, Ijsbereiders en Chocoladebewerkers v Raad voor de Mededinging and anor* [2010] ECR I-12471. The Commission too has a right to make representation, of its own initative if need be; Regulation 1/2003, art. 15(3); Case C-429/07 *Inspecteur van de Belastingdienst v X* [2009] ECR I-4833.
499 See e.g., (Czech) Zákon č. 40/2009 Sb., Zákon trestní zákoník, § 248.2; (Estonian) Karistusseadustik (as amended by RT I 2007, 13, 69), §§ 399–402; (French) Code de Commerce (version consolidée au 1er mai 2009), art. L. 420–6; (Irish) Competition Act, 2002, ss. 6 and 7; (Cypriot) Περί της Προστασίας του Ανταγωνισμού Νόμος 207/89, άρθ 32; (Hungarian) 1978. évi IV. törvény a Büntető Törvénykönyvről, 296/B.; (UK) Enterprise Act 2002, s. 188.
500 E.g., (UK) Competition Act 1998, ss. 42–4.
501 Competition Act, 2002, ss. 6 and 7. Note that penalties were increased significantly by the Competition (Amendment) Act, 2012 (No 18 of 2012).

5. Criminal enforcement?

13.119 Neither criminal law nor the rules of criminal procedure fell traditionally, 'as a general rule', within Community competences,[502] and fines imposed by the Commission by authority of Regulation 1/2003 are carefully circumscribed as being of a non-criminal character.[503] It was thus long understood that the Community had no constitutional authority to regulate competition matters by the means of criminal sanctions. A 2005 judgment of the Court of Justice[504] marked a sea change, recognising that the Community could compel the member states to adopt criminal sanctions in the prosecution of a Community policy where a number of conditions were satisfied.[505] Competition policy might satisfy the conditions, leaving this an option for the (indirect) criminal-isation of breaches of the competition rules. Alternatively, the Union is now competent:

(a) to approximate, by Directive, the criminal laws and regulations of the member states where it is essential to ensure the effective implementation of a Union policy in an area which has been subject to harmonisation measures.[506] This is an articulation/codification of the Community com-petence recognised by the Court in 2005. As such measures are to be adopted by the same procedure as the initial harmonising measure,[507] which is presumably by authority of article 103 in this case, they are a matter for the Council; or, the Council and Parliament are competent

(b) to establish, by Directive under the ordinary legislative procedure, mini-mum rules on the definition of criminal offences and sanctions in the areas of particularly serious crime with a cross-border dimension.[508] Although competition law does not now fall within the fields ('areas'; *domaines*) of crime recognised by the Treaties for these purposes,[509] the Council could, by unanimity and with the Parliament's consent, make it so provided it has come to light '[o]n the basis of developments in crime' and is a crime of sufficient ('particularly') seriousness.[510]

---

502 Case C-176/03 *Commission* v *Council* [2005] ECR I-7879, at para. 47; Case C-440/05 *Commission* v *Council* [2007] ECR I-9097, at para. 66; see 6.56 above.

503 Regulation 1/2003, art. 23(5); see n. 394 above.

504 Case C-176/03 *Commission* v *Council*, n. 502 above.

505 See Commission Communication to the European Parliament and the Council on the implications of the Court's judgment of 13 September 2005 (Case C 176/03 Commission v Council), COM(2005) 583 final; discussed at 6.57 above.

506 TFEU, art. 83(2).

507 *Ibid.*

508 *Ibid.* art. 83(1).

509 *Ibid.* art. 83(1), 2nd para.

510 *Ibid.* art. 83(1), 3rd para.

The Council could go further and, by unanimity and with Parliament's consent, **13.120** confer upon the European Public Prosecutor (should that office be created, also requiring a unanimous Council and the Parliament's consent)[511] authority to prosecute competition law crimes providing they are 'serious crime[s] having a cross-border dimension'.[512]

The Lisbon provisions add both new authority and complexity to the issues **13.121** opened in 2005. Should the institutions wish to resort to article 83(2) and/or article 83(1) as a means of addressing competition law it may be that they venture too far from the area of freedom, security and justice for which those provisions were designed and so act *ultra vires* – leaving Union competition law where Community competition law was prior to Lisbon. Alternatively the new provisions (particularly article 83(2)) displace the old rule and so form the correct base upon which now to proceed. It thus leaves delicately balanced questions both of correct legal base and of compatibility with the requirements of subsidiarity. There is also a wider debate as to the desirability, and workability, of drawing competition control into the field of criminal law; the criminal prohibitions in Irish (since 1996) and United Kingdom (2003) competition law have met with mixed fortunes.[513] There appears, for the present, to be little appetite in the Union to go down this route. But it may not always be so.

6. Union law and national law

Given that competition law has now, by choice or compulsion, been embraced **13.122** by all member states, there is a real likelihood of clash between Union and national competition law. In principle the Union rules are concerned with anticompetitive practices which affect trade between member states, whilst national rules are concerned with considerations peculiar to each member state and with practices in that context alone. But the two are not hermetically sealed, and can and do overlap. Problems are minimised where national law is overtly 'Union friendly',[514] but this is not always the case. Greatest friction has tended to arise in Germany owing to the existence there of a comprehensive body of

---

511 *Ibid.* art. 86(1).

512 *Ibid.* art. 86(4). Without such positive act the powers of the Public Prosecutor are restricted to offences against the Union's financial interests; TFEU, art. 86(2).

513 There have been a number of successful prosecutions brought in Ireland; discussed in *DDP* v *Duffy* [2009] IEHC 208. All sentences of imprisonment have been suspended. In the United Kingdom there has been one successful prosecution, in *R* v *Whittle, Allison and Brammar* [2008] EWCA 2560, [2008] All ER (D) 133, resulting in custodial sentences of 24, 20 and 30 months. But convictions were a result of guilty pleas, secured by agreement in order to avoid lengthier terms of imprisonment in the United States. A high profile criminal trial stemming from the fixing of fuel surcharges by British Airways and Virgin Atlantic on transatlantic routes (as a result of which BA was fined £121.5 million by the OFT, Virgin having secured immunity from fines) collapsed spectacularly in the face of the prosecution's incompetence; see (prior to its collapse) *IB* v *R* [2009] EWCA Crim 2575, [2010] All ER 728.

514 See e.g., the (UK) Competition Act 1998, s. 60 (the 'Europrinciples clause').

competition law (the GWB) which pre-dates the Community rules and in some measure diverges from them; but as more member states adopt and apply competition rules, and bearing in mind the obligation of an NCA to apply articles 101 and 102 (if joined) in any of their own investigations/decisions,[515] the problem is likely to become more widespread.

13.123 The application of the principle of the primacy of Union law in the field of competition was first considered in 1969 in *Wilhelm* v *Bundeskartellamt*.[516] The Court said that so long as legislation adopted by authority of article 103 of the Treaty did not seek to pre-empt or exclude national jurisdiction,

> national authorities may take action against an agreement in accordance with their national law, even when an examination of the agreement from the point of view of its compatibility with Community law is pending before the Commission, subject however to the condition that the application of national law may not prejudice the full and uniform application of Community law or the effects of measures taken to implement it.[517]

The test is therefore that national rules apply so long as they do not imperil the 'full and uniform application' of the Union rules. It is a principle the ambit of which is not yet clear. Where an agreement or practice is caught both by articles 101 and/or 102 and by national rules, the Union rules operate, but because national rules are not pre-empted the national prohibition may operate concurrently to the same set of circumstances and penalties provided by national law may apply.[518] This, of course, gives rise to problems of *non bis in idem*, recognised to be a general principle of Union law. The Court therefore said in *Wilhelm*:

> If, however, the possibility of two procedures being conducted separately were to lead to the imposition of consecutive sanctions, a general requirement of natural justice … demands that any previous punitive decision be taken into account in determining any sanction which is to be imposed.[519]

Alternatively,

> [t]he *ne bis in idem* principle must be complied with in proceedings for the imposition of fines under competition law. That principle precludes, in competition matters, an

---

515 Regulation 1/2003, art. 3(1).
516 Case 14/68 [1969] ECR 1.
517 *Ibid.*at para. 9. See further Cases 253/78 and 1–3/79 *Procureur de la République* v *Giry et Guerlain* (Perfume) [1980] ECR 2327.
518 Case 14/68 *Wilhelm*, n. 516 above.
519 *Ibid.* at para. 11.

undertaking from being found guilty or proceedings from being brought against it a second time on the grounds of anti-competitive conduct in respect of which it has been penalised or declared not liable by a previous unappealable decision. [520]

It is, perhaps surprisingly, not mentioned in Regulation 1/2003, but is codified in the law of some member states. [521] The problem becomes more acute with the compulsory co-application of Union rules and national rules by NCAs, [522] as it will become increasingly common for breaches of both to be found in the same proceedings and a single fine imposed. Further problems arise where a whistle-blower gains immunity from a Commission fine but there is no equivalent scheme in national law. To counter this leniency programmes have to date been adopted in all member states but Malta, although those which exist are not necessarily seamlessly compatible with the Union scheme.

Where an agreement or practice is caught by both article 101(1) and a national **13.124**
prohibition but satisfies the conditions of article 101(3), Regulation 1/2003 provides:

> The application of national competition law may not lead to the prohibition of agreements, decisions by associations of undertakings or concerted practices which may affect trade between Member States but which do not restrict competition within the meaning of Article [101](1) of the Treaty, or which fulfil the conditions of Article [101](3) of the Treaty or which are covered by a [block exemption]. [523]

This convoluted construction means, first, that the member states are now limited in their definition of anticompetitive conduct to that which mirrors an article 101(1) view, unless it falls below the Union's radar ('which may affect trade between Member States'); and second, an agreement or practice which avoids the prohibition of article 101(1) by virtue of article 101(3) must not suffer an equivalent prohibition in national law (in which article 101(3) criteria may be absent or a notification procedure in effect); this is application of what is called the 'double barrier theory' (*Zweischrankentheorie*) [524] and it produces a compulory system of 'parallel exemption', which was (previously voluntarily) codified in the law of some member states. [525] However, the Regulation goes on

---

520   Case C-17/10 *Toshiba Corporation and ors v Úřad pro ochranu hospodářské soutěže*, judgment of 14 February 2012, not yet reported, at para. 94.
521   E.g., (UK) Competition Act 1998, s. 38(9).
522   Regulation 1/2003, art. 3(1).
523   Regulation 1/2003, art. 3(2).
524   This was long supported by the Commission but never confirmed by the Court of Justice; see e.g., Case C-266/93 *Bundeskartellamt v Volkswagen* [1995] ECR I-3477.
525   E.g., Belgium (loi du 5 août 1991 sur la protection de la concurrence économique, art. 32); the Netherlands (Mededingingswet, arts 12, 14); the UK (Competition Act 1998, s. 10). Regulation 1/2003 occupies the field and renders this unnecessary. In England the High Court said *obiter* that the application of art. 101(3) to an

to provide that this rule does not 'preclude the application of provisions of national law that predominantly pursue an objective different from that pursued by Articles [101] and [102] of the Treaty'.[526] The Regulation provides oblique indication of what a 'predominantly different objective' might be,[527] but the whole could be taken as an open invitation to confusion and litigation.

E. OLIGOPOLIES

13.125 Liberal economists will identify control of oligopolistic markets as legitimate and necessary components of a competition law regime, but as a discrete concern it is relatively recent. An oligopolistic market is a market for goods or services marked by the presence of a small number of undertakings, no one of which is dominant, but which between or amongst them control the market or a large part of it. It may be created and maintained by statutory privileges, or it may exist or evolve naturally.

13.126 The difficulty for Union law is that articles 101 and 102 were not designed to address the problem of oligopolies: first, because their targets are cartels and monopolies respectively, and secondly, because both regulate market behaviour, whilst the anticompetitive weakness of oligopolies is the very structure of the market. The problem could be addressed by specific legislation, as exists in some member states,[528] but none has been adopted. It remains therefore to shoe-horn oligopolies into articles 101 and 102, and in many respects it is a poor fit.

1. Article 101 TFEU

13.127 An argument may be made that the price parallelism which marks an oligopolistic market falls within a concerted practice, even absent other evidence of collusion, and conduct which could be strengthened by an apparent disinclination to compete in other ways, and so be caught by the prohibition of article 101(1). But this ignores other criteria necessary to find a concerted practice. The Court of Justice has stressed that the prohibition of concerted practices 'does not deprive economic operators of the right to adapt themselves

---

agreement would pre-empt not only the Competition Act but also a common law tort (*in casu* restraint of trade); *Days Medical Aids v Pihsiang Machinery Manufacturing Co. and ors* [2004] EWHC 44 (Comm), [2004] 1 All ER (Comm) 991.

526 Regulation 1/2003, art. 3(3).
527 Preamble, recital 9.
528 E.g., § 19 III GWB; § 34 Ia (ö)KG.

intelligently to the existing and anticipated conduct of their competitors',[529] and this applies no less in an oligopolistic market.[530] In a transparent, oligopolistic market, this is precisely what occurs, even absent the contact, however desultory, amongst undertakings which is another prerequisite for a concerted practice,[531] owing to the simple fact that, because of the transparency of an oligopolistic market, much of the advantage normally gleaned from contact and, say, exchanges of information, is unnecessary. If a concerted practice lies in conduct which 'leads to conditions of competition which do not correspond to the normal conditions of the market', price parallelism is the normal condition of the market. This is the theory of 'oligopolistic interdependence', which marks the nature of many, but not all, oligopolistic markets.

Thus is the Commission shorn of one of its prime indicators for collusive conduct. It is sensitive to this lacuna, and is especially vigilant in oligopolistic markets to seek out corroboration. And, of course, should it find the existence of an agreement by which oligopolists have shared markets, fixed prices or set production quotas, then a breach of article 101(1) can fairly be found. But oligopolistic interdependence discourages recourse to agreements, for the same anticompetitive advantages which an agreement is designed to bring about are there on a plate. As a result, article 101 is impotent in significant measure for the control of oligopolies. **13.128**

2. Article 102 TFEU

It will be recalled that article 102 prohibits abuse 'by one or more undertakings' of a dominant position. The wording may owe its existence to nothing more than an attempt expressly to contemplate and accommodate the economic entity doctrine,[532] and early on the Court of Justice seemed to suggest that the problems presented by oligopolistic markets could not fall under article 102 owing to the construct (of its own making) that dominance is defined as a function of an ability to act independently of market forces:[533] But through a series of cases beginning in the early 1990s the Commission began to apply article 102 to oligopoly markets in which undertakings taken together enjoyed a 'joint' or 'collective' dominant position, and in this earned the support of the **13.129**

529 Cases 40 etc./73 *Coöperatieve Vereniging 'Suiker Unie' v Commission* [1975] ECR 1663, at para. 174; Case T-1/89 *Rhône-Poulenc v Commission* (Polypropylene) [1991] ECR II-867, at para. 103.
530 Cases 89 etc./85 *Åhlström v Commission* (Woodpulp) [1993] ECR I-1307, at para. 71.
531 Case T-1/89 *Polypropylene*, n. 529 above.
532 See 13.17 above.
533 See Case 85/76 *Hoffmann-La Roche v Commission* [1979] ECR 461.

Court.[534] The definition of the law of joint dominance is now best articulated in the *Compagnie Maritime Belge* appeal judgment of the Court of Justice:

> In terms of Article [102] of the Treaty, a dominant position may be held by several 'undertakings'. The Court of Justice has held, on may occasions, that the concept of 'undertaking' in the chapter of the Treaty devoted to the rules on competition presupposes the economic independence of the entity concerned.
>
> It follows that the expression 'one or more undertakings' in Article [102] of the Treaty implies that a dominant position may be held by two or more economic entities legally independent of each other, provided that from an economic point of view they present themselves or act together on a particular market as a collective entity. This is how the expression 'collective dominant position' ... should be understood ...
>
> In order to establish the existence of a collective entity as defined above, it is necessary to examine the economic links or factors which give rise to a connection between the undertakings concerned.
>
> In particular, it must be ascertained whether economic links exist between the undertakings which enable them to act together independently of their competitors, their customers and consumers ...
>
> Nevertheless, the existence of an agreement or other links in law is not indispensable to a finding of collective dominant position; such a finding may be based on other connecting factors and would depend on an economic assessment and, in particular, on an assessment of the structure of the market in question.[535]

Whether the necessary 'collective entity', which may be a function not only of links amongst the undertakings but 'other connecting factors' which depend 'in particular, on an assessment of the structure of the market in question', may exist in mere oligopolistic interdependence, which is a new element introduced in *Compagnie Maritime Belge*, will require further elaboration from the Court. It is equally unclear whether an undertaking which is collectively (but not individually) dominant can abuse that position unilaterally, or whether exploitative abuse can arise only in joint conduct; put another way, whether joint conduct is constitutive of dominance alone, or whether it is a necessary component also of abuse. The provisional answer favours the former proposition.[536]

---

534   See Cases T-68, 77 and 78/89 *Società Italiano Vetro* v *Commission* (Flat Glass) [1992] ECR II-1403; Case C-393/92 *Gemeente Almelo* v *Energiebedrijf IJsselmij* [1994] ECR I-1I-1477; Case C-323/93 *Société Civile Agricole du Centre d'Insémination de la Crespelle* v *Coopérative d'Elevage et d'Insérmination Artificielle du Département de la Mayenne* [1994] ECR I-5077; Case C-415/93 *Union Royale Belge des Sociétés de Football Association* v *Bosman* [1995] ECR I-4921, *per* A-G Lenz; Cases T-24 etc./93 *Compagnie Maritime Belge* v *Commission* [1996] ECR II-1201.

535   Cases C-395 and 396/96P *Compagnie Maritime Belge* v *Commission* [2000] ECR I-1365, at paras 35, 36, 41, 42 and 45.

536   Decision 97/624 (*Irish Sugar*) [1997] OJ L258/1; upheld on review in Case T-228/97 *Irish Sugar* v *Commission* [1999] ECR II-2969 and on appeal in Case C-497/99P *Irish Sugar* v *Commission* [2001] ECR I-5333.

Oligopolies may also fall for consideration as an aspect of Union control of **13.130** mergers, to which we now turn.

F. MERGERS AND TAKEOVERS

Although addressed in the European Coal and Steel Treaty,[537] the EEC Treaty **13.131** was, and the present Treaties are, silent on the matter of mergers and takeovers. It was therefore not at first clear which, if any, of the competition provisions of the Treaties applied to them. In 1973 the Court of Justice held that the acquisition of a competitor by a dominant undertaking, thereby diminishing competition still further, could constitute an abuse of its dominant position.[538] So, mergers are caught by article 102, but only insofar as an undertaking which is already dominant abuses that dominance by acquiring a competitor in the market in which it is dominant. This is fairly rudimentary merger control, but as dominance itself is not prohibited by article 102, merging of non-dominant undertakings into dominance is not proscribed, and article 102 can be stretched no further. As for article 101, it was long thought – not least by the Commission[539] – that it had no application to mergers. But in 1987 the Court of Justice found that certain aspects of concentration between undertakings which remain independent – here, a company acquiring an equity interest in, and so a degree of control of the operations of, a competitor – could in some circumstances fall within the prohibition of article 101(1).[540]

The parameters of the *Philip Morris* judgment were not fully explored.[541] But it, **13.132** combined with the pending completion of the internal market programme in 1992, led to pressure from industry for the adoption of comprehensive, clear and reliable rules on the regulation of mergers and acquisitions. This inspired the Commission to dust off a draft Regulation, first proposed in 1973,[542] and breathe new life into it. It was adopted by the Council in 1989[543] and entered into force in 1990. Unlike control of oligopolistic market structures and conduct, the Regulation marked a serious attempt at legislative consolidation of Treaty rules, intended to occupy much, but not all, of the field of merger control, at least at Union level. There was a significant overhaul of the

---

537 ECSC Treaty, arts 65–6.
538 Case 6/72 *Europemballage and Continental Can* v *Commission* [1973] ECR 215.
539 See e.g., *Memorandum on the Problems of Concentration in the Common Market*, Competition Series, Study No. 3 (Brussels, 1966) and *Fifteenth Report on Competition Policy* (1986), para. 26.
540 Cases 142 and 156/84 *BAT and Reynolds* v *Commission* (Philip Morris) [1987] ECR 4487.
541 But considered in Decision 93/252 (*Gillette/Wilkinson Sword*) [1993] OJ L116/21.
542 [1973] OJ C92/1.
543 Regulation 4064/89 [1989] OJ L395/1; revised text in [1990] OJ L257/14.

Regulation in 1998.[544] Then, following an *annus horribilis* in 2002 when the Court of First Instance annulled three key Commission decisions adopted under the Regulation,[545] it was replaced with a new Regulation which came into force, alongside Regulation 1/2003 and as the cornerstone of a 'comprehensive merger control reform package', in May 2004.[546]

1. Merger Regulation

13.133 The Regulation applies to 'concentrations', so embracing more than simply mergers/takeovers, but it is known universally as 'the Merger Regulation' (sometimes distinguishing between the 'old' and 'new' (or 'recast') Merger Regulation). A concentration arises where:

(a) two or more previously independent undertakings (or part of undertakings) merge, or

(b) one or more persons already controlling at least one undertaking, or one or more undertakings acquire, whether by purchase of securities or assets, by contract or by any other means, direct or indirect control of the whole or parts of one or more other undertakings.[547]

A concentration falling short of a merger requires that one undertaking acquire, at the least, 'decisive influence' (*influence déterminante*) over the commercial conduct of another.[548] A concentration may also exist in certain ('full function') joint ventures.[549] The Merger Regulation forms a 'composite whole' with articles 101 and 102 in pursuing the competition aims of the Treaties and so is to be interpreted in a manner consistently with them.[550]

---

544 Regulation 1310/97 [1997] OJ L180/1.

545 Case T-342/99 *Airtours* v *Commission* [2002] ECR II-2585 (annulling Decision 2000/276 (*Airtours/First Choice*) [2000] OJ L93/1); Case T-77/02 *Schneider Electric* v *Commission* [2002] ECR II-4201 (annulling Decision 2004/275 (*Schneider/Legrand*) [2004] OJ L101/1); Case T-5/02 *Tetra Laval* v *Commission* [2002] ECR II-4381 (annulling Case COMP/M.2416 *Tetra Laval/Sidel*, decision of 30 October 2001, not yet published). So flawed was the decision in *Airtours* ('vitiated by a series of errors of assessment as to factors fundamental to any [proper] assessment'; para. 294) that the undertaking precluded from the acquisition by it raised an action under art. 340 TFEU seeking damages from the Commission in the region of £500 million, but was rebuffed; Case T-212/03 *MyTravel Group* v *Commission* [2008] ECR II-1967. Schneider jumped on the bus subsequently but recovered only a fraction of damages sought; Case C-440/07P *Commission* v *Schneider Electric* [2009] ECR I-6413, as to which see 13.141 below.

546 Regulation 139/2004 [2004] OJ L24/1. The reforms consisted in important but not fundamental changes to the Regulation, otherwise in administrative reorganisation, primarily the break up of the 'Merger Task Force', its integration into sector specific directorates, and the appointment of a 'chief competition economist' and peer review panels.

547 Regulation 139/2004, art. 3(1).

548 *Ibid.* art. 3(2). For a detailed discussion of what constitutes a concentration see Case T-282/02 *Cementbouw Handel en Industrie* v *Commission* [2006] ECR II-319.

549 *Ibid.* art. 3(4).

550 Case T-22/97 *Kesko* v *Commission* [1999] ECR II-3775, at para. 106.

The Regulation further applies only to concentrations which have a 'Com- **13.134** munity dimension'. A concentration has a Community dimension if:

(a)   the combined aggregate worldwide turnover of all undertakings involved exceeds €5 thousand million;
(b)   the aggregate Union-wide turnover of each of at least two of the undertakings exceeds €250 million; and
(c)   the undertakings do not generate two-thirds of their turnover in a single member state.[551]

Alternatively,

(a)   the combined aggregate worldwide turnover of all undertakings involved exceeds €2,500 million;
(b)   the combined aggregate turnover of all undertakings concerned exceeds €100 million in at least three member states;
(c)   in each of the member states covered by (b), the aggregate turnover of each of at least two undertakings involved exceeds €25 million; and
(d)   the undertakings do not generate two-thirds of their turnover in a single member state.[552]

The means of calculating turnover are provided.[553]

It will be observed that 'Community dimension' is an attempt to limit the **13.135** application of the Regulation to large-scale concentrations, and those which involve at least two substantial undertakings (turnover of at least €250 million) within the Union, unless three or more member states are involved, in which case the figure drops to €25 million. And it excludes even large-scale concentrations which otherwise have a Community dimension but the preponderant impact of which is restricted to one member state (the 'two-thirds rule'), which then falls for consideration to the competition authorities of that state.[554] This is consistent with the principle of subsidiarity.[555]

---

551   Regulation 139/2004, art. 1(2).
552   *Ibid.* art. 1(3). This second set of criteria was introduced in the 1997 amendment.
553   *Ibid.* art. 5.
554   Except that the Merger Regulation provides for the possibility of referral by a national competition authority to the Commission of a concentration within its (the member state's) jurisdiction in order to be determined by the Commission in accordance with Community criteria; art. 22 (the 'Dutch clause'). Originally used only by member states (then) without merger control legislation, in 1997 Regulation 4064/89 was amended so as to allow for joint referrals (the 'Scandinavian clause'); in 2004 it became possible for the parties to request it prior to notification ('pre-notification referrals', art. 4(5)), and these are becoming more common.
555   The Merger Regulation also provides for the possibility of referral by the Commission to a national competition authority in a member state which requests it of a concentration (or part of a concentration) with

13.136 The scheme of the Merger Regulation is to occupy the field: a concentration with a Community dimension falls exclusively within Union competence, pre-empting the application of national law (except where the Regulation provides otherwise), and will be permitted only with Commission authorisation. Such a concentration is therefore required to be notified by the parties to it prior to its implementation;[556] failure to notify or supplying incomplete or misleading information may result in a fine.[557] As with Regulation 1/2003, the procedure for notification, the forms (Form CO or Form RS),[558] guidance as to their use and the rules regulating time limits and hearings are laid down by the Commission in an implementing Regulation,[559] and it has adopted a number of guidance notices on the manner in which it is likely to interpret various provisions of the Regulation;[560] it is bound by them unless they depart from the rules of the Treaty or of the Merger Regulation.[561] The Commission must examine a notification immediately it is received,[562] the purpose of which is to determine whether or not the concentration is 'compatible with the common market'.[563] It is required therefore to respond in the first instance in one of three ways:

(a)   conclude that the concentration does not fall within the scope of the Regulation, and adopt a decision to that effect (article 6(1)(a));

(b)   conclude that, although the concentration does fall within the scope of the Regulation, it does not raise serious doubts as to its compatibility with the common market, and adopt a decision to that effect (article 6(1)(b)); or

(c)   find that the concentration falls within the scope of the Regulation and does raise serious doubts as to its compatibility with the common market, and so decide to initiate proceedings – 'phase two' proceedings (article 6(1)(c)).

---

a Community dimension where the member state is a distinct market which will be affected significantly by the concentration, the referred concentration then to be determined in accordance with national law; art. 9 (the 'German clause'). Since 2004 this may be sought (and is frequently granted) by the parties prior to notification ('pre-notification referrals', art. 4(4)).

556   Regulation 139/2004, art. 4(1), subject to art. 4(4), *ibid.*; notification must be made jointly by the parties to a merger or by the undertaking acquiring joint control; art. 4(2).

557   *Ibid.* art. 14(1), (2); see e.g., Decision 1999/459 (*A.P. Møller*) [1999] OJ L183/29; Decision 1999/594 (*Samsung/AST Research*) [1999] OJ L225/12; Decision 2005/305 (*Tetra Laval/Sidel*) [2005] OJ L98/27.

558   Form RS ('reasoned submission') is used for pre-notification referrals, Form CO is the normal device. There is also a 'Short Form CO' for concentrations unlikely to be found objectionable.

559   Regulation 802/2004 [2004] OJ L133/1.

560   E.g., on the concept of a concentration ([1998] OJ C66/5); on assessment of horizontal mergers ([2004] OJ C31/5); on restrictions ancillary to a concentration ([2005] OJ C56/24); on the calculation of turnover ([1998] OJ C66/25).

561   Case T-114/02 *BaByliss* v *Commission* [2003] ECR II-1279, at para. 143; Case T-282/06 *Sun Chemical Group and ors* v *Commission* [2007] ECR II-2149, at para. 55.

562   Regulation 139/2004, art. 6(1).

563   *Ibid.* art. 2(1).

In order properly to consider the matter, the Commission is granted powers analogous to, but independent of, Regulation 1/2003 to request information, carry out investigations, liaise with the competent national authorities, hear the parties and third parties and impose fines.[564] Throughout the proceedings stage – during which the undertakings involved must do everything they can to facilitate the Commission's task and the Commission must act with 'the utmost diligence'[565] or 'with great care'[566] – an accommodation may be reached with the Commission, and in the light of any subsequent modification by, or structural and/or behavioural commitment from, the parties which dispel the serious doubts in the sense of article 6(1)(c), the Commission may by decision declare a concentration compatible with the common market as in article 6(1)(b).[567] It may attach conditions to a declaration of compatibility and/or to ensure compliance with any commitments agreed.[568] No concentration with a Community dimension may be put into effect before notification and until the Commission has acted;[569] should undertakings disobey and proceed, the Commission may order that the resulting concentration be dissolved and the *status quo ante*, and 'conditions of effective competition', restored.[570] But in the interests of expediency and legal certainty the Commission is subject to very short time limits: a phase one decision must be taken within 25 working days,[571] and, following initiation of phase two proceedings, a decision declaring a concentration incompatible with the common market must be adopted within 90 working days.[572] If the Commission fails to meet either of these deadlines the concentration is deemed to be unobjectionable[573] and so may proceed. Ultimately, if it concludes that the proposed concentration would be 'incompatible with the common market', the Commission may, by 'prohibition decision', veto it.[574]

To give an idea of the data: to September 2012 the Commission had received **13.137** 5,035 notifications under the Merger Regulation(s), almost one-half of which involved joint ventures, one-third acquisition of majority shareholding, and only about one-tenth outright mergers/takeovers. It adopted 4,685 final phase

---

564   *Ibid.* arts 11–15.
565   Case T-212/03 *MyTravel* v *Commission* [2008] ECR II-1967, at para. 119.
566   Case C-12/03 *Commission* v *Tetra Laval* [2005] ECR I-987, at para. 42; Case T-145/06 *Omya* v *Commission* [2009] ECR II-145, at para. 33.
567   Regulation 139/2004, arts 6(2), 8(2).
568   *Ibid.* For a comprehensive analysis of conditions and commitments see EC Commission, DG Competition, *Merger Remedies Study* (October 2005).
569   Regulation 139/2004, art. 7(1).
570   *Ibid.* art. 8(4), (5).
571   *Ibid.* art. 10(1); subject to extension in some circumstances.
572   *Ibid.* art. 10(3); also subject to extension in some circumstances.
573   *Ibid.* art. 10(6).
574   *Ibid.* art. 8(3).

one decisions, of which 52 were article 6(1)(a) decisions and 4,633 article 6(1)(b) decisions, 214 with commitments attached. Phase two proceedings under article 6(1)(c) were initiated in 211 cases, following which the concentration was found to be compatible with the common market in 148 cases, 97 with commitments attached. There were 44 partial and 114 full referrals to national competition authorities. Concentrations have been vetoed outright only 22 times,[575] and only thrice under the new Merger Regulation.[576]

13.138 A concentration is appraised 'with a view to establishing whether or not [it is] compatible with the common market'.[577] The test is whether:

> [it] would significantly impede effective competition in the common market or in a substantial part of it, in particular as a result of creation or strengthening of a dominant position.[578]

This is the so-called 'SIEC test', an amalgamation of the old (pre-2004) 'dominance test'[579] and the more flexible and comprehensive 'substantial lessening of competition' (SLC) test, as is used in a few member states,[580] but is largely faithful to the dominance test (which is used by most member states), merely reversing the word order so that the dominance test becomes a subset of a 'significant impediment to effective competition', but with a rider that this is intended to mean merely that the Regulation applies to a concentration in(to) an oligopolistic market.[581] It should be noted that, unlike article 102 from which much of it was borrowed, the Merger Regulation applies not only to the strengthening, but also to the creation, of a dominant position. And although it did not say so expressly, it was also held to apply to the creation of joint dominance;[582] the 2004 version so provides more expressly (if still

---

575 And on four of those the Commission was overturned by the Court of First Instance; see Case T-342/99 *Airtours* v *Commission* [2002] ECR II-2585; Case T-77/02 *Schneider Electric* v *Commission* [2002] ECR II-4201; Case T-5/02 *Tetra Laval* v *Commission* [2002] ECR II-4381; Case T-310/00 *MCI* v *Commission* [2004] ECR II-3253. See also the unsuccessful attempt to have annulled the last prohibition decision adopted under the old Merger Regulation, Case T-87/05 *Energias de Portugal* v *Commission* [2005] ECR II-3745. However, one of the last decisions taken under the old Regulation which approved a concentration was annulled by the Court for inadequate reasoning and manifest error of assessment; Case T-464/04 *Independent Music Publishers and Labels Assn (Impala)* v *Commission* [2006] ECR II-2289.
576 Case COMP/M.4439 *Ryanair/Aer Lingus* [2008] OJ C47/9 (summary publication), upheld in Case T-342/07 *Ryanair* v *Commission* [2010] ECR II-3457; Case COMP/M.5830 *Olympic/Aegean Airlines*, decision of 26 January 2011, not yet published; Case COMP/M.6166; Case COMP/M.6166 *Deutsche Börse/NYSE*, decision of 1 February 2012, not yet published.
577 Regulation 139/2004, art. 2(1).
578 *Ibid.* art. 2(2), (3).
579 Regulation 4064/89, art. 2(2), (3).
580 (Irish) Competition Act, 2002, ss. 21(2)(a), 22(3); (UK) Enterprise Act 2002, ss. 22(1)(b), 35(1)(b), 35(2).
581 Preamble, recital 25.
582 Cases C-68/94 and 30/95 *France and ors* v *Commission* (Kali + Salz) [1998] ECR I-1375; Case T-102/96 *Gencor* v *Commission* [1999] ECR II-753.

obliquely).[583] For purposes of the Merger Regulation, collective dominance comes into being if (on a necessarily prospective analysis) a concentration would produce a situation in which it is economically rational and preferable for undertakings to adopt a lasting common policy in the market without need of agreements or concerted practices to that end, and without effective competitive restraints from competitors, latent competition or powerful buyers.[584] In all events, in its 'discretionary margin implicit in the provisions of an economic nature which form part of the rules on concentrations',[585] the fact that the Commission finds only one in 24 concentrations to merit phase two proceedings, and only one in 229 a veto, suggests a fairly non-interventionist touch.

It should be self-evident, but bears mentioning, that if a concentration resulting **13.139** in a dominant position is declared to be compatible with the common market, it then becomes subject to the discipline of article 102.

2. Judicial control of the Commission

Measures adopted by the Commission under the Merger Regulation are subject **13.140** to review under article 263. The (relatively) generous title and interest of third parties to raise proceedings which is enjoyed in matters of competition law generally applies also here[586] but such is the breadth of discretion of complex economic assessment conferred upon the Commission by the Regulation that review is limited to ensuring compliance with the rules governing procedure and the statement of reasons, the substantive accuracy of the facts and the absence of manifest errors of assessment or misuse of powers.[587] Nevertheless

> that does not mean that the Community Courts must refrain from reviewing the Commission's interpretation of information of an economic nature. Not only must the Community Courts, *inter alia*, establish whether the evidence relied on is factually

---

583 Regulation 139/2004, art. 2(2), (3) with recital 25 of the Preamble. An earlier draft of art. 2(2) ([2003] OJ C20/4) was much clearer, providing that one or more undertakings are 'deemed to be in a dominant position if, without coordinating, they hold the economic power to influence appreciably and sustainably the parameters of competition ... or appreciably to foreclose competition', but it did not survive into the final text.

584 Case T-342/99 *Airtours* v *Commission* [2002] ECR II-2585, at para. 61; see also the the three conditions set out in para. 62.

585 Cases C-68/94 and 30/95 *Kali + Salz*, n. 582 above, at para. 224; Case T-102/96 *Gencor*, n. 582 above, at para. 165; Case T-22/97 *Kesko* v *Commission* [1999] ECR II-3775, at para. 142. In *Kesko* the words 'of appraisal' are inserted between 'margin' and 'implicit'.

586 E.g., Case T-102/96 *Gencor*, n. 582 above; Case T-310/00 *MCI* v *Commission* [2004] ECR II-3253; Case T-177/04 *easyJet* v *Commission* [2006] ECR II-1931.

587 Case T-342/00 *Petrolessence and anor* v *Commission* [2003] ECR II-1161, at para. 101; Case T-177/04 *easyJet*, *ibid.*, at para. 44; Case T-282/06 *Sun Chemical Group and ors* v *Commission* [2007] ECR II-2149, at para. 60.

accurate, reliable and consistent but also whether that evidence contains all the information which must be taken into account in order to assess a complex analysis and whether it is capable of substantiating the conclusions drawn from it,[588]

and

> [i]t is in the light of those considerations that the Court must examine whether the Commission's assessments ... are vitiated by a manifest error.[589]

Thus the Commission found itself struck down by the Court of First Instance on three key merger cases in the course of one year and a number since,[590] an account both remarkable and exprobrative. Nor is it impossible for a third party to attain the annulment of a decision approving a merger amongst its competitors,[591] but assuming the (approved) merger has proceeded, the victory is pyrrhic.

13.141 A party blocked from acquisition of another undertaking by a Commission decision which turned out to be badly flawed has recovered damages but only for loss incurred as a result of participation in the resumed procedure following annulment of the original Commission decision, the Court adopting a narrow view of causation.[592] Damages for serious flaws in the Commission's economic reasoning (sufficient to lead to the annulment of the decision) 'cannot be ruled out in principle'[593] but the breadth of Commission latitude and the article 340 requirement of a sufficiently serious breach appears to confer upon it (virtual) immunity.[594]

G. MISCELLANEOUS

1. Public and public service undertakings

13.142 The framers of the Treaties recognised that some undertakings would be in public ownership in various of the member states and that they, or other

---

588 Case C-12/03P *Commission* v *Tetra Laval* [2005] ECR I-987, at para. 39.
589 Case T-464/04 *Independent Music Publishers and Labels Association (Impala)* v *Commission* [2006] ECR II-2289, at para. 329.
590 See n. 575 above.
591 Case T-464/04 *Impala*, n. 589 above.
592 Case C-440/07P *Commission* v *Schneider Electric* [2009] ECR I-6413. The General Court had been more generous (Case T-351/03 *Schneider Electric* v *Commission* [2007] ECR II-2237), awarding damages for breach of Schneider's rights of defence and compensation for the cost of the additional clearance process before the Commission and for part of the price reduction that it was required to accept to delay the sales process.
593 Case T-212/03 *MyTravel Group* v *Commission* [2008] ECR II-1967, at para. 80.
594 Case T-212/03 *MyTravel, ibid.* On one view, if the Commission escaped liability in *MyTravel*, it will prove almost impossible to find it on a substantive matter in a merger case.

undertakings in private ownership, might be charged with special rights and duties in the public interest. The duties usually include the universal provision of goods or services throughout the whole or defined parts of the territory of the member state (the principle of universalilty) at identical or similar price (equality), the rights to various privileges, usually monopoly privileges and so a captive market and immunity from competition, in order to enable them properly or effectively to discharge their duties. In all events they are subject to significant state intervention, such as price controls and sometimes (massive) subsidies. Such undertakings are seen frequently to serve a desirable social function, for left to market forces undertakings would cream off profitable sectors (by service market or geographically) and leave others unsupplied or suppliable only at prohibitive cost. They are also seen to be more reliable in matters of public safety as they are less likely than the private sector to cut corners. Enthusiasm for them varies widely amongst the member states, and in some they are immunised from the rigours of (national) competition law.[595] They include first and foremost undertakings in the supply of utility, communications, transport and health services, but may extend into other areas as the state sees fit. The Treaties addresses them in two distinct ways: first, provision to ensure they do not escape the application of the competition rules (article 106(1)), and second, express authority to do precisely that in certain narrowly defined circumstances (article 106(2)).

(a) Article 106(1) TFEU

Article 106(1) admits of the state ownership of undertakings – it cannot do **13.143** otherwise, the Treaty reserving to the member states the rules governing the system of property ownership[596] – and of the close public regulation of undertakings charged with special duties. Its purpose is to ensure that publicly owned undertakings and undertakings enjoying statutory rights and duties (often, but not necessarily, one and the same) do not escape the strictures of the competition rules (and the rest of the Treaties). Article 106(1) therefore provides that, as regards these undertakings, member states 'shall neither enact nor maintain in force any measure contrary to the rules contained in the Treaties, in particular to those rules provided for in Article 18 and Articles 101 to 109'. By its clear terms it is of no independent effect, rather it is a *renvoi* device, defining the application of other Treaty provisions to a particular context. And it addresses not undertakings themselves but the member states, and is concerned not directly with the conduct of undertakings which distorts competition but with the legislation or regulation through which the member state permits, encourages or compels them to do so. In most circumstances, this

---

595   See e.g., §§ 103, 103a GWB (alte Fassung).
596   TFEU, art. 345 (ex art. 295 EC).

means legislation on public monopolies and the application of article 102. As under article 102 there is no reproach in the existence of a dominant position, there can be no reproach to the creation and existence of a statutory monopoly, and the Court is always quick to recognise this:

> [T]he simple fact of creating a dominant position … by granting an exclusive right within the meaning of Article [106](1) is not as such incompatible with Article [102] of the Treaty.[597]

But it is equally quick to add immediately that

> [a] Member State is in breach of the prohibition contained in those two provisions only if the undertaking in question, merely by exercising the exclusive right granted to it, cannot avoid abusing its dominant position.[598]

And so

> any measure adopted by a Member State which maintains in force a statutory provision that creates a situation in which a[n undertaking] cannot avoid infringing Article [102] is incompatible with the rules of the Treaty.[599]

The question is whether the law makes the infringement unavoidable; it is immaterial whether it in fact occurs.[600]

13.144   There is an uncommonly fine line between a lawful grant of monopoly rights and a breach of the Treaties under the combined provisions of articles 102 and 106(1), and the case law comes very close to finding the grant of exclusive rights to be *per se* an infringement.[601] It is not to be read that *all* exclusive rights enjoyed by monopolies will infringe article 106(1) (in concert with article 102), for it is only the more egregiously anticompetitive which have hitherto been challenged – frequently the reservation to the monopoly of ancillary activities remote from the legitimate services they may provide or blatant price/access

---

597   E.g., Case C-41/90 *Höfner and Elser* v *Macrotron* [1991] ECR I-1979, at para. 29; Case C-179/90 *Merci Convenzionali Porto di Genova* v *Siderurgica Gabrielli* [1991] ECR I-5889, at para. 16; Case C-55/96 *Job Centre Coop* [1997] ECR I-7119, at para. 31.

598   Cases cited above, at paras 29, 17 and 31, respectively; *Job Centre* substituting 'contravenes' for 'is in breach of'.

599   Cases cited n. 597 above, at paras 27 (*Höfner*) and 29 (*Job Centre*).

600   Case C-55/96 *Job Centre Coop*, n. 597 above, at para. 36; Case C-163/96 *Criminal proceedings against Raso and ors* [1998] ECR I-533, at para. 31.

601   See Case C-41/90 *Höfner*, n. 597 above; Case C-179/90 *Porto di Genova* v *Siderurgica Gabrielli*, n. 597 above; Case C-55/96 *Job Centre Coop*, n. 597 above; Case C-260/89 *Elliniki Radiophonia Tileorassi* v *Dimotiki Etairia Pliroforissis* [1991] ECR I-2925; Case 18/88 *Régie des Télégraphes et Téléphones* v *GB-Inno-BM* [1991] ECR I-5941; Case C-163/96 *Raso, ibid.*; Case C-49/07 *Motosykletistiki Omospondia Ellados* v *Elliniko Dimosio* [2008] ECR I-4863, *per* A-G Kokott at paras 82–106 of her opinion.

discrimination. But it can be taken to indicate that the Court interprets the requirements of article 106(1) very strictly. The prohibition is enforced by the Commission, by a national administrative authority[602] or, because it is directly effective,[603] by a national court.

(b) Article 106(2) TFEU

Article 106(2) provides undertakings with a degree of immunity from Treaty **13.145** rules, 'in particular … the rules on competition', where the application of those rules would obstruct the performance of their tasks. It is also a *renvoi* provision and applies to two categories of undertakings. The first is revenue-producing state monopolies, which used to be more prevalent on the continent and still exist to a limited extent; the most widely recognised is probably *Systembolaget* in Sweden.[604] They are specifically addressed by article 37, found in the Title on the free movement of goods, and it is normally in relation to immunity from article 37 (if a monopoly involving the provision of goods) that they arise for consideration under article 106(2). Secondly, article 106(2) applies to undertakings, public or private, which are 'entrusted with the operation of services of general economic interest' (SGEIs). Since such undertakings are frequently statutory monopolies it is usually in the context of immunity from article 102 that they fall to be considered – article 106(2) therefore constituting the one derogation from the burdens of article 102. This is a more complex construction than revenue producing monopolies, and three points in particular ought to be observed:

- services recognised to be in the general economic interest are not defined, but include, most commonly, the utilities (public water,[605] gas[606] and electricity[607] supply), the postal service,[608] a public telephone system (but not the provision of telephone equipment)[609] and other

---

602 Case C-198/01 *Consorzio Industrie Fiammiferi* v *Autorità Garante della Concorrenza del Marcato* [2003] ECR I-8055.

603 E.g., Case C-41/90 *Höfner*, n. 597 above; Case C-260/89 *Elliniki Radiophonia Tileorassi*, n. 601 above; Case C-179/90 *Porto di Genova* v *Siderurgica Gabrielli*, n. 597 above.

604 On the rules governing *Systembolaget* and their compatibility with the Treaty see Case C-189/95 *Criminal Proceedings against Franzén* [1997] ECR I-5909.

605 Cases 96 etc./82 *IAZ International Belgium* v *Commission* [1983] ECR 3369.

606 Case C-159/94 *Commission* v *France* [1997] ECR I-5815.

607 Case C-393/92 *Gemeente Almelo* v *Energiebedrijf IJsselmij* [1994] ECR I-1477; Case C-157/94; Case C-157/94 *Commission* v *Netherlands* [1997] ECR I-5699.

608 Cases C-48 and 66/90 *Netherlands and Koninklijke PTT* v *Commission* [1992] ECR I-565; Case C-230/91 *Criminal proceedings against Paul Corbeau* [1993] ECR I-2533; Cases C-147 and 148/97 *Deutsche Post* v *Gesellschaft für Zahlungssysteme* [2000] ECR I-825; Case C-340/99 *TNT Traco* v *Poste Italiane* [2001] ECR I-4109.

609 Case 18/88 *Régie des Télégraphes et Téléphones* v *GB-Inno-BM* [1991] ECR I-5941.

telecommunications services,[610] national public broadcasting (television) services,[611] ambulance services[612] and private medical insurance schemes.[613] Doubtless railways and other forms of universal public transport and health and related services meet the necessary test, and have not arisen for judgment simply because it is so obviously so;

- article 106(2) is directly effective. Despite apparent uncertainty early on, the Court has since confirmed the full direct effect of article 106(2) and so the competence of a national court to apply it in its entirety;[614]

- there is no procedure or necessity for notification and authorisation under article 106(2), and if its criteria are met any or all other Treaty provisions may be set aside. But because it represents an exception to the application of fundamental Treaty rules, it is strictly interpreted.[615]

13.146 Assuming these preconditions to be met, article 106(2) exempts undertakings providing an SGEI from the competition rules if those rules would 'obstruct the performance, in law or in fact, of the particular tasks assigned to them'.[616] The Court interpreted this test so strictly that there was for a long time no instance in which it found the conditions to be met. However, in the early 1990s it began to moderate its views,[617] and for the first time in 1998 expressly held article 106(2) to be satisfied.[618] It has done so again in subsequent cases,[619] and so says now

---

610 Decision 82/861 (*British Telecommunications*) [1982] OJ L360/36, upheld on review as Case 41/83 *Italy v Commission* [1985] ECR 873.

611 Case 155/73 *Sacchi* [1974] ECR 409; Case 260/89 *Elliniki Radiophonia Tileorassi v Dimotiki Etairia Pliroforissis* [1991] ECR I-2925; Case T-69/89 *Radio Telefis Éireann v Commission* [1991] ECR II-485; Cases T-258 etc./93 *Métropole Télévision v Commission* [1996] ECR II-649.

612 Case C-475/99 *Ambulanz Glöckner v Landkreis Südwestpfalz* [2001] ECR I-8089.

613 Case T-289/03 *BUPA v Commission* [2008] ECR II-81. A-G Ruiz-Jarabo Colomer set out a descriptive list in Case C-265/08 *Federutility Assogas and ors v Autorità per l'energia elettrica e il gas* [2010] ECR I-3377, at para. 53 of his opinion.

614 Case 260/89 *Elliniki Radiophonia Tileorassi v Dimotiki Etairia Pliroforissis* [1991] ECR I-2925; Case C-230/91 *Criminal proceedings against Corbeau* [1993] ECR I-2533; Case C-393/92 *Gemeente Almelo v Energiebedrijf IJsselmij* [1994] ECR I-1477.

615 Case 127/73 *Belgische Radio en Televisie v SABAM* [1974] ECR 313; Case 18/88 *Régie des Télégraphes et Téléphones v GB-Inno-BM* [1991] ECR I-5941; Case C-179/90 *Merci Convenzionali Porto di Genova v Siderurgica Gabrielli* [1991] ECR I-5889; Case C-242/95 *GT-Link v De Danske Statsbaner* [1997] ECR I-4449; Case C-157/94 *Commission v Netherlands* [1997] ECR I-5699. It is for the member state invoking the article to show its application is justified: Case C-160/08 *Commission v Germany* [2010] ECR I-3713, at para. 126 and case law cited.

616 Article 106(2) supplies a second test, that '[t]he development of trade [is] not … affected to such an extent as would be contrary to the interests of the Community', but this has been all but ignored by the Court of Justice.

617 See especially Case C-320/91 *Corbeau*, n. 614 above; Case C-157/94 *Commission v Netherlands*, n. 615 above; Case C-158/94 *Commission v Italy* [1997] ECR I-5789; Case C-159/94 *Commission v France* [1997] ECR I-5815; Case C-160/94 *Commission v Spain* [1997] ECR I-5851 (the *Electricity Supply* judgments).

618 Case C-266/96 *Corsica Ferries France v Gruppo Antichi Ormeggiatori del Porto di Genova* [1998] ECR I-3949.

619 Case C-67/96 *Albany International v Stichting Bedrijfspensioenfonds Textielindustrie* [1999] ECR I-5751; Cases C-147 and 148/97 *Deutsche Post v Gesellschaft für Zahlungssysteme* [2000] ECR I-825; Case C-209/98

it is not necessary ... that the financial balance or economic viability of the undertaking entrusted with the operation of a service of general economic interest should be threatened. It is sufficient that, in the absence of the exclusive rights at issue, it would not be possible for the undertaking to perform the particular tasks entrusted to it, defined by reference to the obligations and constraints to which it is subject, or that maintenance of those rights is necessary to enable the holder thereof to perform tasks of general economic interest which have been assigned to it under economically acceptable conditions.[620]

Thus the Court has lowered the bar significantly from earlier *dicta*, and come closer to adopting standard objective necessity and proportionality tests. It coincides with the introduction into the Treaties of article 14 TFEU by Amsterdam;[621] a general (and accelerating) Commission warming to services of general economic interest;[622] the Charter of Fundamental Rights, which notes that the Union 'recognises and respects access to services of general economic interest ... to promote social and territorial cohesion of the Union';[623] and, now, a new protocol introduced by Lisbon (at largely Dutch insistence, in order to safeguard the extensive social housing system there), which notes with approbation the 'essential role' played by services of general interest (*sic*; not general economic interest) as part of the 'shared values of the Union', and provides expressly (if unnecessarily) that the Treaties do not affect the competence of the member states to provide, commission and organise non-economic services of general interest.[624] All of these may be taken as indications that they can no longer (if ever they could) be dismissed as an irrelevance. Yet other than recognition by Advocates-General that these provisions are an 'expression of a fundamental value judgment of Community law'[625] and they indicate that such

---

Entreprenørforeningens Affalds/Miljøsektion v *Københavns Kommune* [2000] ECR I-3743 (probably); Case C-340/99 *TNT Traco* v *Poste Italiane* [2001] ECR I-4109 (probably); Case C-475/99 *Ambulanz Glöckner* v *Landkreis Südwestpfalz* [2001] ECR I-8089; Cases C-264 etc./01 *AOK Bundesverband and ors* v *Ichthyol-Gesellschaft Cordes and ors* [2004] ECR I-2493, *per* A-G Jacobs at paras 87–107 of his opinion; Case T-289/03 *BUPA* v *Commission* [2008] ECR II-81.

620   Case C-437/09 *AG2R Prévoyance* v *Beaudout Père et Fils*, judgment of 3 March 2011, not yet reported, at para. 76.

621   See 7.19 above.

622   See Communication on services of general economic interest in Europe, COM(96)443 final; Communication on services of general economic interest in Europe, COM(2000) 580 final; the (proactive) Green Paper on Services of General Economic Interest, COM(2003) 270 final; the 2004 White Paper on Services of General Interest, COM(2004) 374 final; part of the 'single market for the 21st century', Communication on services of general interest, including social services of general interest: a new European commitment, COM(2007) 725 final; Guide to the Application of the European Union Rules on State Aid, Public Procurement and the Internal Market to Services of General Economic Interest, and in particular to social services of general interest, SEC(2010) 1545 final.

623   EU Charter of Fundamental Rights, art. 36.

624   Protocol (No. 26) on Services of General Interest.

625   Case C-340/99 *TNT Traco*, n. 619 above, *per* A-G Albers at para. 94 of his opinion.

services 'have a special importance in the Community',[626] they have gone unremarked by the Court of Justice. But they may reasonably still be taken as a broader tolerance of public monopolies and the inroads they may make into competition law.

13.147 In late 2011 the Commission adopted a new 'package' on the application of the Union's state aid rules to SGEIs.[627]

2. Intellectual property rights

13.148 The exercise of an intellectual property right may fall foul of article 34, which is discussed above.[628] But it may also fall foul of the competition rules, and there has been a significant degree of cross-fertilisation between articles 34/36, on the one hand, and articles 101/102, on the other. In particular, the Court has come to rely upon the principles of specific subject matter, developed primarily in the context of the former, as an aid to the interpretation of the latter. Thus,

> Article [36], although it appears in the Chapter of the Treaty dealing with quantitative restrictions on trade between Member States, is based on a principle equally applicable to the question of competition.[629]

And

> [u]nder Article [36], as it has been interpreted by the Court of Justice in the light of the objectives pursued by Articles [101] and [102] …, only those restrictions on freedom of competition … which are inherent in the protection of the actual substance of the intellectual property right are permitted in Community law.[630]

In other words, the exercise of an intellectual property right in a manner which affects competition will not infringe articles 101 and 102 if it falls within the specific subject matter of the right. Beyond that, it may do so (yet may be exempted by application of article 101(3)). So, the exercise of an exhausted intellectual property right in a manner which is not saved by the specific subject matter test will fall foul of article 34, and may also fall foul of articles 101 and/or

---

626   Case C-575/99 *Ambulanz Glöckner*, n. 619 above, *per* A-G Jacobs at para. 175 of his opinion; see also Case C-126/01 *Ministre de l'économie, des finances et de l'industrie* v *GEMO* [2003] ECR I-13769, in which he refers (at para. 124) to 'the importance now attached to services of general interest, as recognised in Article [14 TFEU] and in Article 36 of the EU Charter of Fundamental Rights'.

627   See 13.168 below.

628   See 10.78–10.83 above.

629   Case 40/70 *Sirena* v *Eda* [1971] ECR 69, at para. 5.

630   Case T-69/89 *RTE* v *Commission* [1991] ECR II-485, at para. 69; Case T-70/89 *BBC* v *Commission* [1991] ECR II-535, at para. 56; Case T-76/89 *ITP* v *Commission* [1991] ECR II-575, at para. 54.

102. At the same time, there are circumstances in which the exercise of the right may skirt the prohibition of article 34 and fall to be considered in the context of articles 101 and 102 alone.

(a) Article 101 TFEU

The application of the competition rules to intellectual property rights was first **13.149** considered in *Consten and Grundig,*[631] in which the absolute territorial protection was secured for the French distributor not only by express contract terms but by the 'temporary assignment' of a French trade mark of which the German manufacturer was proprietor. The Court said:

> [T]he registration in France by Consten of the … trade mark … is intended to increase the protection inherent in the disputed agreement, against the risk of parallel imports into France of Grundig products, by adding the protection deriving from the law on industrial property rights…
>
> Consten's right under the contract to the exclusive user [sic] in France of the … trade mark … is intended to make it possible to keep under surveillance and to place an obstacle in the way of parallel imports. Thus, the agreement by which Grundig … authorized Consten to register it in France in its own name tends to restrict competition …
>
> That agreement therefore is one which may be caught by the prohibition in Article [101](1). The prohibition would be ineffective if Consten could continue to use the trade-mark to achieve the same object as that pursued by the agreement which has been held to be unlawful.[632]

So it was established from the start that a licensing agreement – which would come subsequently to attract the exhaustion of rights doctrine (first marketing by a proprietor or 'with his consent') and so the application of article 34 – could fall within the prohibition of article 101(1), vertical though it may be. But it may also apply to horizontal agreements or concerted practices the subjects of which are intellectual property rights, and some which may not be caught by article 34 – for example, an agreement to oppose the importation of protected goods from a member state in which the proprietor has not exhausted his right,[633] or an agreement between Union and non-Union undertakings which does not directly restirct the movement of goods between member states.[634] Of course, the mere exercise of an intellectual property is not enough to infringe

---

631 Cases 56 and 58/64 *Établissements Consten & Grundig-Verkaufs* v *EEC Commission* [1966] ECR 299; see 13.47 above.

632 *Ibid.* at 343, 345.

633 E.g., Case 40/70 *Sirena* v *Eda* [1971] ECR 69; Case 15/74 *Centrafarm* v *Sterling Drug* [1974] ECR 1147; Case 258/78 *Nungesser* v *Commission* (Maize Seeds) [1982] ECR 2015; Case 144/81 *Keurkoop* v *Nancy Kean Gifts* [1982] ECR 2853; Case C-9/93 *IHT Internationale Heiztechnik* v *Ideal Standard* [1994] ECR I-2789.

634 E.g., Case 51/75 *EMI* v *CBS* [1976] ECR 811; Case 28/77 *Tepea* v *Commission* [1978] ECR 1391.

article 101(1): it is further necessary to show an intention or effect, by agreement or concerted practice, to distort competition (usually, here, market partitioning). As the Court said early on,

> [T]he exercise of [intellectual property] rights cannot of itself fall … under Article [101](1), in the absence of any agreement, decision or concerted practice prohibited by that provision.[635]

And subsequently, in the context of voluntary assignment of a trade mark,

> [W]here undertakings independent of each other make trade-mark assignments following a market-sharing agreement, the prohibition of anti-competitive agreements under Article [101] applies and assignments which give effect to that agreement are consequently void. However, … that rule and the accompanying sanction cannot be applied mechanically to every assignment. Before a trade-mark assignment can be treated as giving effect to an agreement prohibited under Article [101], it is necessary to analyse the context, the commitments underlying the agreement, the intention of the parties and the consideration for the assignment.[636]

So, the standard analysis of the restrictive effects of agreements and concerted practices applies.

13.150 The most common type of agreement addressing the exercise of intellectual property rights is a licensing agreement. Generally they are pro-competitive, and many of their standard terms fall outwith the prohibition of article 101(1) because they do not distort competition within the meaning of article 101(1); others may do but are saved as falling within the specific subject matter of the right; and still others may go beyond that but satisfy the conditions of article 101(3).[637] There is therefore a block exemption covering technology transfer,[638] which governs most aspects of licensing. Some others may also fall within the ambit of the vertical agreements, the specialisation agreements and the research and development agreements block exemptions.[639]

(b) Article 102 TFEU

13.151 As title to an intellectual property right confers upon the proprietor a monopoly within the territory of a member state, and a member state may comprise a

---

635 Case 24/67 *Park, Davis* v *Probel* [1968] ECR 55, at 72.

636 Case C-9/93 *IHT Internationale Heiztechnik*, fn 633 above, at para. 59.

637 For consideration of these points see Case 258/78 *Nungesser* v *Commission* (Maize Seeds) [1982] ECR 2015; Case 193/83 *Windsurfing International* v *Commission* [1986] ECR 611; Case 27/87 *Erauw-Jacquery* v *La Hesbignonne* [1988] ECR 1919.

638 Regulation 772/2004 [2004] OJ L123/11 ('the new TTBER').

639 Regulations 2790/1999 [1999] OJ L336/21, 2658/2000 [2000] OJ L304/3 and 2659/2000 [2000] OJ L304/7, respectively.

substantial part of the internal market within the meaning of article 102, it may be that the proprietor is in a dominant position and so subject to the constraints of article 102. It is neither always nor necessarily so: the proprietor of a right 'does not enjoy a "dominant position" within the meaning of Article [102] merely because he is in a position to prevent third parties from putting into circulation, on the territory of a Member State, products [protected by the right]';[640] '[s]o far as dominant position is concerned … mere ownership of an intellectual property right cannot confer such a position'.[641] But upon a standard article 102 analysis the market privileges which ownership of an intellectual property right brings may be a material – and in some cases determinative – consideration in identification of a dominant position.

Some abuses of an intellectual property right are self-evident: excessive prices, restriction of output or sales artificially to inflate prices, oppressive or discriminatory contractual terms, for example. Tying (where the tied product is not protected) is a common abuse.[642] However, according to the Court of Justice the exercise by a dominant proprietor of an intellectual property right falls within the specific subject matter of the right, so that refusal to license a third party to manufacture or import a protected good, even where a reasonably royalty is offered, is not a breach of article 102.[643] However, the Court said that this does not hold in 'exceptional circumstances',[644] where   **13.152**

> the right is exercised in such ways as in fact to pursue an aim manifestly contrary to the objectives of Article [102]. In that event, the copyright is no longer exercised in a manner which corresponds to its essential function, within the meaning of Article 36 of the Treaty … In that case, the primacy of Community law, particularly as regards principles as fundamental as those of the free movement of goods and the freedom of competition, prevails over any use of a rule of national intellectual property law in a manner contrary to those principles.[645]

Such was the case, as in *Magill*, where the proprietor exercised the right to prevent the emergence on the market of new product for which there was clear demand, the absence of justification for it, and the resulting reservation to himself of the derivative market – so a variation of the essential facilities doctrine. For some time it was thought that the circumstances of *Magill* were so

---

640   Case 40/70 *Sirena* v *Eda* [1971] ECR 69, at para. 16.
641   Cases C-241–2/91P *RTE and ITP* v *Commission* (Magill) [1995] ECR I-743, at para. 46.
642   See e.g., Decision 2007/53 (*Microsoft*) [2007] OJ L32/23 (summary publication; full decision available at [2005] 4 CMLR 965).
643   Case 238/87 *Volvo* v *Veng* [1988] ECR 6211; Case 53/87 *CICRA* v *Renault* [1988] ECR 6039.
644   Cases C-241–2/91P *Magill*, n. 641 above, at para. 50.
645   Case T-69/89 *RTE* v *Commission* [1991] ECR II-485, at para. 71; Case T-70/89 *BBC* v *Commission* [1991] ECR II-535, at para. 58; Case T-76/89 *ITP* v *Commission* [1991] ECR II-575, at para. 56.

exceptional that it was a freak to be confined to its facts, but they have resurfaced, in the context of refusal to license a copyrighted database[646] and, in *Microsoft*, failure to provide competitors with 'interoperability information' to computer software and tying its software (the Windows Media Player) to its own operating system.[647] In the former case the Court of Justice said that

> the refusal by an undertaking which holds a dominant position and owns an intellectual property right … indispensable to [carrying out a downstream service] to grant a licence to use that [database] to another undertaking which also wishes to provide such [service] in the same Member State, constitutes an abuse of a dominant position within the meaning of Article [102] where the following conditions are fulfilled:
>
> – the undertaking which requested the licence intends to offer, on the market for the supply of the data in question, new products or services not offered by the owner of the intellectual property right and for which there is a potential consumer demand;
>
> – the refusal is not justified by objective considerations;
>
> – the refusal is such as to reserve to the owner of the intellectual property right the market for the supply of data on sales of pharmaceutical products in the Member State concerned by eliminating all competition on that market.[648]

The final test (elimination of all competition in the market) was watered down in *Microsoft*, the Court of First Instance finding an infringement made out where 'the refusal at issue entailed the risk of elimination of competition',[649] which lowers the bar significantly and may, or may not, be specific to *Microsoft*. A breach of article 102 was found subsequently by the English High Court on essential facilities reasoning.[650]

13.153 It ought finally to be noted that whilst as a general principle there is no obligation to license the exploitation of an intellectual property right to third parties, the Commission will sometimes impose such a duty as a condition for approval of a concentration under the Merger Regulation.[651]

---

646   Case C-418/01 *IMS Health* v *NDC Health* [2004] ECR I-5039; Decision 2003/741 (*NDC Health/IMS Health*) [2003] OJ L268/69.

647   Decision 2007/53 (*Microsoft*), n. 642 above; upheld in Case T-201/04 *Microsoft* v *Commission* [2007] ECR II-3601.

648   Case C-418/01 *IMS Health*, n. 646 above, at para. 52.

649   Case T-201/04 *Microsoft*, n. 647 above, at para. 620.

650   *Attheraces* v *British Horse Racing Board* [2005] EWHC 3015 (Ch), [2006] FSR 336; overturned on appeal (but not on that point), [2007] EWCA Civ 38, [2007] ECC 7.

651   E.g., Decision 98/526 (*Hoffmann–La Roche/Boehringer Mannheim*) [1998] OJ L234/14.

3. Extraterritorial application

There is a problem endemic in competition law a function of increasing **13.154** globalisation of economies, which is the extent to which the competition law of a state (or a Union) may apply to anticompetitive conduct outwith its territory. It is an issue primarily for public international law, in which general (and rudimentary) authority goes back to 1927.[652] In the sphere of competition law it is an authority seised most zealously in the United States with the development of the 'effects doctrine', a wide-ranging assertion of jurisdiction over the economic conduct of companies in third countries 'which has consequences within its borders which the State reprehends'.[653] Thus any anticompetitive conduct taking place outwith the United States may fall nonetheless within the strictures of the Sherman Act and the jurisdiction of the US civil and criminal courts so long as it produces effects there, even if they were incidental or secondary.[654] The effects doctrine has produced some enmity (and also some copying) abroad. Generally it is not an area given to harmony amongst states.

Articles 101 and 102 contain no express reference as to their (extra)territorial **13.155** application; they merely proscribe anticompetitive conduct 'within the internal market' which 'may affect trade between Member States'. In keeping with general principles its object or effect must be appreciable.[655] Thus an agreement between or amongst Union undertakings and their competitors in third countries which appreciably reduces the supply, within the Union, of goods or services originating in third countries is liable, at least potentially, to affect trade and distort competition between member states and so fall foul of article 101(1),[656] unless it can be shown that the effects are confined to one member state or to trade between one member state and one or more non-member states.[657] As for agreements and concerted practices the parties to which are all located outside the Union, the Court for a long time relied upon the economic entity doctrine, claiming jurisdiction over a foreign parent undertaking by virtue of the presence within the Union of a subsidiary indivisible from the

---

652 *France* v *Turkey* (The Lotus) [1927] PCIJ Ser A, No. 9.

653 *United States* v *Aluminum Company of America* (Alcoa) 148 F. 2d 416, 443 (2d Cir. 1945).

654 But owing to legislative intervention the effects must now be 'direct, substantial and reasonably foreseeable'; Foreign Trade Antitrust Improvements Act 1982; § 7 Sherman Act 15 USC § 6a.

655 See 13.35 above.

656 E.g., Case 22/71 *Béguelin* v *GL Import/Export* [1971] ECR 949; Case 71/74 *Frubo* v *Commission* [1975] ECR 563; Case 51/75 *EMI* v *CBS* [1976] ECR 811; Cases T-24 etc./93 *Compagnie Maritime Belge* v *Commission* [1996] ECR II-1201.

657 See 13.32 above.

parent.[658] When a case arose in which this device was not possible (an alleged concerted practice amongst undertakings all outwith, and many with no presence within, the Union), the Court laid down the Union view of its, the Union's, jurisdiction thus:

> It should be observed that an infringement of Article [101], such as the conclusion of an agreement which has had the effect of restricting competition within the common market, consists of conduct made up of two elements, the formation of the agreement, decision or concerted practice and the implementation thereof. If the applicability of prohibitions laid down under competition law were made to depend on the place where the agreement, decision or concerted practice was formed, the result would obviously be to give undertakings an easy means of evading those prohibitions. The decisive factor is therefore the place where it is implemented.

> The producers in this case implemented their pricing agreement within the common market. It is immaterial in that respect whether or not they had recourse to subsidiaries, agents, sub-agents, or branches within the Community in order to make their contacts with purchasers within the Community.

> Accordingly the Community's jurisdiction to apply its competition rules to such conduct is covered by the territoriality principle as universally recognized in public international law.[659]

13.156 So the Court steered shy of embracing the effects doctrine, cleaving instead to a less intrusive (objective) territorial principle 'as universally recognized in public international law'. An agreement formed or a practice existing abroad, so long as it is 'implemented' (*mis en oeuvre*, *durchgeführt*) within the Union – which it was in *Woodpulp* simply by sale of the product directly to Union buyers – and has appreciable effects there, falls within Union jurisdiction. By logical extension the abusive conduct of a dominant undertaking outwith the Union which is implemented within the Union in a manner which has an appreciable effect upon intra-Union trade is equally made subject to article 102.[660] There may be

---

658 E.g. Case 48/69 *ICI* v *Commission* (Dyestuffs) [1972] ECR 619; Cases 6–7/73 *Commercial Solvents* v *Commission* [1974] ECR 223; Case 27/76 *United Brands* v *Commission* [1978] ECR 207; Case T-30/89 *Hilti* v *Commission* [1991] ECR II-1439; and a host of cases involving Hoffmann-La Roche (based in Basel).

659 Cases 89 etc./85 *Åhlström and ors* v *Commission* (Woodpulp) [1988] ECR 5193, at paras 16–18. For a good discussion of the effects doctrine (which he recommended emulating) see the opinion of A-G Darmon.

660 The Commission has imposed fines upon a number of undertakings outwith the Union for breaches of art. 102, but the decisions were reasoned upon the economic entity doctrine (Decision 72/21 (*Continental Can*) [1972] JO L7/25; Decision 72/457 (*Commercial Solvents*) [1972] JO L299/51; Decision 76/353 (*Chiquita*) [1976] OJ L95/1; Decision 88/138 (*Hilti*) [1988] OJ L65/19), upon abusive conduct occasioned by unfair contract terms with undertakings within the Union (Decision 76/248 (*Hoffmann-La Roche*) [1976] OJ L51/7), or, following *Woodpulp*, normally with no express territorial justification (e.g., Decision 92/163 (*Tetra Pak II*) [1992] OJ L72/1; Decision 2007/53 (*Microsoft*) [2007] OJ L32/23).

little practical difference between the *Woodpulp* rule and the effects doctrine, but it remains that the Court has not, yet, recognised the latter.[661]

But whilst it is permissible in public international law for the Union to assume **13.157** this subject matter (or prescriptive) jurisdiction, it is another matter entirely whether that jurisdiction can be enforced (enforcement jurisdiction) abroad, which is not tolerated by public international law.[662] The Commission has no power to carry out an investigation of an undertaking in a third state unless the authorities there assist; unlike authorities within the Union (by virtue of Regulation 1/2003), they have no duty to assist, and are generally markedly unenthusiastic to do so. The Commission is therefore hampered in making out a breach of article 101 or 102. Whether it has authority to compel subsidiaries within the Union of a parent company outside it to disclose documents and information in the custody and control of the latter was before the Court but the action withdrawn.[663] Moreover, absent international treaty making it possible, no fine imposed by the Commission can be enforced in the territory of a third state. It is therefore shorn of its power of sanction/coercion. But it is consistent with the territorial principle that any property or assets within the Union of a third country undertaking upon which a fine has been imposed would, absent payment, be liable to seizure. This then is the only sanction, but one which has hitherto proved effective: undertakings in third states pay up – Hoffmann-La Roche (of Basel) stumped up, without murmur, €462 million for its part in the *Vitamins* cartel,[664] Microsoft (of Redmond, United States) paid its €497 million fine[665] and €1180 million in penalty payments[666] and Intel (Wilmington, United States) €1,060 million for fidelity rebates and loyalty payments[667] – because the Union market is too important to abandon.

The extraterritorial reach of Union competition law is now felt most particu- **13.158** larly in the field of merger control. A concentration anywhere in the world falls

---

661 It is claimed by some that the judgment of the Court of First Instance in Case T-102/96 *Gencor* v *Commission* [1999] ECR II-753 (a merger case) did so (at para. 82), but this is probably reading too much into a chance formulation.

662 See the *dictum* of the PCIJ in in the *The Lotus* [1927] PCIJ Ser A, No. 9, at p. 18: 'failing the existence of a permissive rule to the contrary [the state] may not exercise its power in any form in the territory of another State'.

663 Case T-140/07 *Chi Mei Optoelectronics Europe and anor* v *Commission*, removed from the register by order of 4 February 2011, unreported.

664 Decision 2003/2 (*Vitamins*) [2003] OJ L6/1. Perhaps it should have murmured: BASF was fined €296 million for its part in the cartel but managed to get €48 million shaved off by the Court of First Instance; Case T-15/02 *BASF* v *Commission* [2006] ECR II-497.

665 Decision 2007/53 (*Microsoft*) [2007] OJ L32/23 (summary publication).

666 Case COMP/37.792 *Microsoft*, decisions of 12 July 2006 and 27 February 2008, n. 390 above.

667 Case COMP/37.990 (*Intel*) [2009] OJ C227/13 (summary publication); under review as Case T-286/09 *Intel* v *Commission*, pending.

within the Merger Regulation so long as it involves at least two undertakings each with a turnover of €250 million in the Union or between them €100 million in at least three member states.[668] Multinational firms with this degree of penetration in the Union market are by no means rare. Many cases considered hitherto under the Merger Regulation have their centre of gravity elsewhere.[669] Yet the Commission has not been shy in using its powers: it imposed (not very burdensome) conditions upon the Boeing/McDonnell Douglas merger,[670] even though it had been approved by the Federal Trade Commission and occasioned strong-arm tactics from the Americans;[671] it vetoed the Gencor/Lonrho merger,[672] although it had been approved by the South African Competition Board; and it vetoed the takeover of Honeywell by General Electric, thought to be the world's largest industrial takeover agreement, worth $45 thousand million.[673]

Agreements with third countries

13.159 The Union has entered into an array of agreements with third countries, which are considered below.[674] Some of them contain competition provisions which address various of these problems. The most important are the following.

(i) European Economic Area

13.160 Article 53 of the EEA Agreement[675] is identical *mutatis mutandis* to article 101 TFEU, prohibiting restrictive practices 'between Contracting Parties' which distort competition 'within the territory covered by [the EEA] Agreement'; article 54 is identical to article 102 except that it applies to a dominant undertaking 'within the territory covered by this Agreement' insofar as it may affect trade 'between Contracting Parties'. Just as restrictive practices and potentially abusive conduct within a member state are, since 2004, to be

---

668 Regulation 139/2004, art. 1(2), (3).

669 E.g., Case M.1138 *Royal Bank/Bank of Montréal* [1998] OJ C74/32; Decision 97/816 (*Boeing/McDonnell Douglas*) [1997] OJ L336/16; Decision 97/26 (*Gencor/Lonrho*) [1997] OJ L11/30; Decision 2004/134 (*General Electric/Honeywell*) [2004] OJ L48/1; Case M.3349 *Toshiba/Samsung*, decision of 2 March 2004, not yet published.

670 Decision 97/816 (*Boeing/McDonnell Douglas*), *ibid*. The Commission also launched phase 2 proceedings over the subsequent acquisition by Boeing of the satellite interests of Hughes Electronics, but allowed it to proceed without conditions; Decision 2004/195 (*Boeing/Hughes*) [2004] OJ L63/53.

671 By a 416 to 2 vote, the US House of Representatives 'warned' the Community against 'an unwarranted and unprecedented interference in a United States business transaction' and called upon the President to make representation to the Commission; Congressional Record, July 22, 1997, p. H5517.

672 Decision 97/26 (*Gencor/Lonrho*), n. 669 above; upheld on review as Case T-102/96 *Gencor v Commission* [1999] ECR II-753 .

673 Decision 2004/134 (*General Electric/Honeywell*) [2004] OJ L48/1; upheld on review as Case T-209/01 *Honeywell Electric v Commission* [2005] ECR II-5527 and Case T-210/01 *General Electric Company v Commission* [2005] ECR II-5575.

674 See 14.82–14.102 below.

675 For the text see [1994] OJ L1/3.

assessed also in the light of articles 101 and 102 where the latter are joined, the Union rules are to be assessed in the light of articles 101 and 102 TFEU *and* of articles 53 and 54 of the EEA Agreement, so increasing the territorial scope in which (essentially the same) anticompetitive conduct is proscribed. The Agreement provides further rules governing public undertakings and state aids analogous to articles 106 and 107–9 TFEU.[676] According to the Agreement, the EEA competition rules are enforced by the Commission within the territory of the Union and by the EFTA Surveillance Authority within the (non-Swiss) territory of the EFTA states, where the latter enjoys 'equivalent powers and similar functions to those of the EC Commission, at the time of the signature of the Agreement, for the application of the competition rules of the EEC Treaty'.[677] Nevertheless, the Agreement establishes a 'one stop shop' in competition enforcement. The two institutions are required to cooperate closely,[678] and there are rules governing which of them ought to be competent to determine situations which fall within the territorial jurisdiction of both ('mixed' cases).[679] Each is required to carry out investigations within its territory at the request of the other and transmit to it the results,[680] and both may impose pecuniary sanctions enforceable by civil process throughout the territory of the EEA.[681] In the area of merger control the Commission enjoys legal as well as actual enforcement pre-eminence over the EFTA Surveillance Authority in the area of merger control, the Merger Regulation applying, the thresholds intact but 'adapted' for purposes of the EEA Agreement so that turnover criteria include that in the territories of the EFTA states, to concentrations with a 'Community or EFTA dimension'.[682] The Commission has 'sole competence' so long as the concentration is caught by the Merger Regulation;[683] it may therefore veto a concentration even if it creates or strengthens a dominant position within the territory of the EFTA and not within that of the Union. The EEA therefore marks a significant step towards international competition regulation and cooperation, noteworthy in particular for addressing and overcoming the bar in international law to the extraterritorial exercise of enforcement jurisdiction.

---

676   EEA Agreement, arts 59, 61–4.
677   *Ibid.* Protocol 21, art. 1; for the detail see the EFTA Surveillance Agreement of 2 May 1992, [1994] OJ L344/3, Protocol 4.
678   EEA Agreement, art. 58 and Protocols 23 and 24.
679   *Ibid.* art. 56.
680   *Ibid.* Protocol 23, art. 8(3), (5); Protocol 24, art. 8(4) for concentrations.
681   *Ibid.* art. 110.
682   *Ibid.* art. 57 and Annex XIV.
683   *Ibid.* art. 57(2)(a).

(ii)   Europe Agreements

13.161   Each of the Europe Agreements with the 2004 and 2007 accession countries contained identical competition provisions, declaring as incompatible with the agreement insofar as they affect trade between the contracting parties

(i)   all agreements between undertakings, decisions by associations of undertakings and concerted practices between undertakings which have as their object or effect the prevention, restriction or distortion of competition;

(ii)   abuse by one or more undertakings of a dominant position in the territories of the Community or of [the other contracting party] as a whole or in a substantial part thereof;

(iii)   any public aid which distorts or threatens to distort competition by favouring certain undertakings or the production of certain goods.[684]

They went on to provide that 'any practice contrary to this Article shall be assessed on the basis of criteria arising from the application of the rules of Articles [101, 102 and 107 TFEU]'.[685] Unlike articles 101 and 102 TFEU and articles 53 and 54 of the EEA Treaty, such practice or conduct was not 'prohibited', it was 'incompatible' with the agreement; further implementation of these provisions was left to the Association Council created by each agreement,[686] which normally provided for cooperation, consultation and exchange of information, but not mutual enforcement.

(iii)   Other agreements

13.162   The Union has entered into customs unions with a number of third states, some of which provide competition provisions. The custom union with Turkey has provisions identical to articles 53 and 54 of the EEA Agreement,[687] but they require further implementation (by 1998)[688] and none has yet been adopted. By comparison, the treaty establishing a customs union with San Marino contains no reference to competition. The free trade area agreement with Switzerland and partnership agreements with, for example, Russia and South Africa, have competition provisions[689] but nothing to suggest directly effective force, mutual enforcement jurisdiction or which could alter or limit the general application of articles 101 and 102. The exception is the free trade agreement with South

---

684   E.g., the Europe Agreement with Bulgaria [1994] OJ L358/3, art. 64.

685   *Ibid.* art. 64(2).

686   *Ibid.* art. 64(3). See e.g., Decision 2/97 of the Community/Bulgarian Association Council adopting implementing rules for competition provisions applicable to undertakings [1998] OJ L15/37.

687   Decision 1/95 of the EC/Turkey Association Council on implementing final provisions of the customs union [1996] OJ L35/1, arts 32–3.

688   *Ibid.* art. 37.

689   [1972] JO L350/13, art. 23 (Switzerland); [1997] OJ L327/3, arts 53–5 (Russia); [1999] OJ L331/3, art. 35 (South Africa).

Korea, in which the parties undertake to maintain and apply their respective competition rules to anticompetitive practices insofar as they may affect trade between them.[690] The Union has entered into agreements with the United States,[691] Canada,[692] Japan[693] and South Korea[694] (the 'first generation agreements'), another with Switzerland in the pipeline, and lesser agreements with Brazil[695] and Russia[696] designed to promote cooperation and coordination in the application of their respective competition laws, but they are essentially statements of intent, providing for exchange of information and not much more. The largest multilateral treaty to which the Union is party, the Cotonou Agreement, contains no provisions on competition.

H. STATE AID

Amongst the rules on competition in the Treaties, but forming a distinct section in the chapter and a *lex specialis*, are rules governing 'Aids granted by States', addressed in articles 107–109. That they are necessary, and logically to be addressed as part of the rules on competition, is self-evident: any subvention granted by a member state to an undertaking gives that undertaking a comparative advantage over its competitors. Subvention is legion notwithstanding various governments claiming to set their faces against it. The need increases with Union integration, the Treaties depriving member states of the tools with which they would traditionally combat foreign subvention (countervailing duties), and gathered even greater pace with economic and monetary union. That the rules are different is equally apparent: they address not the anti-competitive conduct of undertakings but the financial intervention of member states (which are not undertakings in this context) in the market.   **13.163**

Because the rules on state aids are different, a body of law has been developed by the Commission and the Court of Justice distinct to articles 107–109 both in substance and procedure. It is an important, highly sensitive and complex area of competition law, tightly bound up with industrial and regional policies (both   **13.164**

---

690 Free Trade Agreement of 6 October 2010 between the European Union, its Member States and the Republic of Korea [2011] OJ L127/6, arts 11.1–11.15; not yet in force but applied provisionally from 1 July 2011.
691 [1995] OJ L95/47.
692 [1999] OJ L175/50.
693 [2003] OJ L183/12.
694 [2009] OJ L202/36. The agreement will lapse with the entry into force of the free trade agreement, n. 690 above.
695 Memorandum of understanding between the Commission and the Direito da Concorrencia signed 8 October 2009.
696 Memorandum of understanding between the Commission and the Federal Antimonopoly Service (FAS) signed 10 March 2011.

national and Union), and raises fundamental economic questions of the viability and desirability of public services and public support for, for example, crisis industry, 'sunset' industries and remote industry – whether without permanent subvention undertakings in Sligo and Saaremaa can, and should, ever compete upon equal terms with those in the 'golden crescent'. It is also an issue very much to the fore in international deliberations in the World Trade Organization, especially trade in agricultural products.

1. The Treaty scheme

13.165 Article 107(1) provides:

> Save as otherwise provided in the Treaties, any aid granted by a Member State or through State resources in any form whatsoever which distorts or threatens to distort competition by favouring certain undertakings or the production of certain goods shall, insofar as it affects trade between Member States, be incompatible with the internal market.

Article 107(2) then goes on to list by way of exception state aids which are compatible with the internal market (those having a social character granted to individual consumers, those to make good damage caused by natural disasters or exception occurrences and those granted by Germany in order to compensate for economic disadvantages caused by the division of Germany)[697] and article 107(3) lists those which *may* be compatible with the internal market, that is:

- aids promoting the development of economically disadvantaged regions and of the Union's outermost regions;
- aids promoting the execution of important projects of common European interest or remedying a serious disturbance in the economy of a member state;
- aids facilitating the development of certain economic activities or regions;
- aids promoting culture and heritage conservation; and
- such other categories of aid as are determined by the Council.

Article 107(2) thus constitutes exceptions to the general prohibition (alongside state aids necessary to support services in the general economic interest which are excepted from the prohibition by article 106(2)), article 107(3) the possibility, across much broader categories of activity, of exemption from it. Article 108 vests the Commission with the duty of supervision of state aids to ensure

---

697 The continued provision of the special privileges enjoyed by Germany has been a bone of contention since reunification. The TFEU now provides (art. 107(2)(c)) that it may be repealed by the Council five years after the entry into force of Lisbon.

compliance with article 107 and confers upon it (almost)[698] sole power of exemption of article 107(3) aids. Article 109 provides the Council with authority to adopt Regulations to give effect to the application of articles 107 and 108. This is similar to the Treaty base in article 103, but unlike article 103, article 109 first saw action only in 1998, the Commission relying thitherto largely upon soft law devices.

2. The prohibition

Like article 101, the general approach of the Treaties is that state aids are *prima* **13.166** *facie* incompatible with the internal market. Although they are 'incompatible' with the internal market and not 'prohibited' as are breaches of articles 101 and 102, it has been construed by the Court to amount effectively to the same thing. In accordance with the terms of article 107(1), there are four elements necessary in order for article 107 to be joined:

- aid is granted by a member state or through public resources 'in any form whatsoever';
- it confers an (economic) advantage upon ('favours') the assisted under-taking(s);
- it distorts (or threatens to distort) competition; and
- it affects (or might affect) trade between member states.

They are cumulative, all four requiring to be fulfilled.[699] 'Aid' is not otherwise defined in the Treaties. The Court of Justice established early on (in a case under the ECSC Treaty, to which the same considerations apply) that it embraces not only subsidies but much wider state subvention, 'interventions which, in various forms, mitigate the charges which are normally included in the budget of an undertaking and which, without, therefore, being subsidies in the strict meaning of the word, are similar in character and have the same effect';[700] and so investment grants, free or reduced rental of premises, con-cessions on tax (exemption, reduced rate, rebates, deferment of payment) or national insurance/social security employer contributions, 'sweeteners' to attract a buyer, bonuses to attract new employees, preferential interest rates on loans, donations, lower energy prices, preferential conditions on the supply of goods or services or the award of contracts, various guarantees (cover for operating losses, export credits or exchange risks, dividend guarantees), debt write-offs and, in some circumstances, the acquisition of a holding in capital, granted directly or

---

698   See 13.176 below.
699   Case 142/87 *Belgium* v *Commission* (Tubemeuse) [1990] ECR I-959.
700   Case 30/59 *Gezamenlijke Steenkolenmijnen in Limburg* v *High Authority* [1961] ECR 1, at 19.

indirectly by or through any public authority. Generally the definition is very rigorous.[701] There is an (ill-defined) remoteness test for public works and general economic measures, otherwise, for example, a road building programme assists undertakings which will use those roads and a decrease in corporate taxation or a currency devaluation (an option no longer open to all member states) assists all exporters; this is usually considered under the rubric of the 'specificity' of the aid which is required in order that it confer an economic advantage. But, unlike article 101, there is no *de minimis* test built into article 107.[702]

13.167 There are particular problems with publicly owned undertakings and public support for public services. Investment in a publicly owned undertaking is not a state aid unless it exceeds that which would be secured privately under normal market conditions (the 'market investor principle', or market economy investor principle (MEIP) test).[703] Because aids are sometimes hidden (intentionally or otherwise) and difficult to detect, particularly so with publicly owned undertakings, the Transparency Directive which applies in the area of public procurement applies also here, requiring member states to make the books of those undertakings available to Commission inspection.[704] Where an undertaking, publicly or privately owned, benefits from subvention in order to discharge a public service obligation, it is a state aid only if it confers an 'economic advantage'; it does not do so, and is mere 'compensation' for that service, if the following cumulative criteria (the '*Altmark* criteria') are met:

- the recipient undertaking is actually required to discharge (clearly defined) public service obligations;
- the parameters for the calculation of compensation is established beforehand in an objective and transparent manner;
- it does not exceed what is necessary to cover all or part of the costs incurred in discharging the public service obligations; and
- where the undertaking is not chosen in a public procurement procedure, the level of compensation needed has been determined on the basis of an

---

701 Best guidance from the wealth of case law can probably be had from Case 78/76 *Steinike & Weinlig* v *Germany* [1977] ECR 595; Case 290/83 290/83 *Commission* v *France* [1985] ECR 439; Case C-379/98 *PreussenElektra* v *Schleswag* [2001] ECR I-2099); Case C-126/01 *Ministre de l'économie, des finances et de l'industrie* v *GEMO* [2003] ECR I-13769; Case C-345/02 *Pearle and ors* v *Hoofdbedrijfschap Ambachten* [2004] ECR I-7139; Cases C-266 etc./04 *Nazairdis and ors* v *Caisse Nationale de l'Organisation Autonome d'Assurance Vieillesse des Travailleurs non salariés des Professions Industrielles et Commerciales* [2005] ECR I-9481.
702 Discussed below.
703 For discussion of which see Cases T-228 and 233/99 *Westdeutsche Landebank Girozentrale* v *Commission* [2003] ECR II-435; Case T-20/03 *Kahla/Thüringen Porzellan* v *Commission* [2008] ECR II-2305, at paras 236–61; Case T-196/04 *Ryanair* v *Commission* [2008] ECR II-3643; Case T-156/04 *Électricité de France* v *Commission* [2009] ECR II-4503.
704 Directive 2006/111 [2006] OJ L318/17 (being a consolidation of Directive 80/723 [1980] OJ L195/35).

analysis of the costs which a typical undertaking, well run and adequately provided, would incur in discharging the assigned obligations, taking into account relevant receipts and a reasonable profit for doing so.[705]

It appears now, albeit equivocally, that the *Altmark* tests do not define and exhaust the immunity enjoyed by virtue of article 106(2) by undertakings providing services of general economic interest from the application of article 107.[706] At the same time the Commission seems to think this is not the case[707] and has muddied the water by adopting in 2005 a decision under article 106(3) on the application of article 106 to state aid in the form of public service compensation granted to undertakings providing SGEIs,[708] replacing it in 2011 as part of a new comprehensive 'package' on the application of state aid rules to SGEIs.[709] Exempted from any obligation to notify is subvention for the running of social services, more specifically health and long-term care, child care, access to and reintegration in the labour market, social housing and the care and social inclusion of vulnerable groups.[710] Other services (other than transport and transport infrastructure) receiving public compensation are exempted up to a cap of €15 million per year.[711] A communication sets out the manner in which the Commission will analyse cases falling outwith the decision and notified to it.[712]

Article 107 lays down no *de minimis* rule, and the Court of Justice declined to grant its imprimature to *de minimis* considerations as a means of avoiding the prohibition of article 107 as it has for that of article 101, although the Commission adopted *de minimis* principles as part of its reasoning on compatibility and grafted them to various notices.[713] In 1998 the Council adopted a **13.168**

---

705   Case C-280/00 *Altmark Trans and anor* v *Nahverkehrsgesellschaft Altmark* [2003] ECR I-7745; confirmed in Cases C-34 and 38/01 *Enrisorse* v *Ministero delle Finanze* [2003] ECR I-14243; Case C-345/02 *Pearle and ors* v *Hoofdbedrijfschap Ambachten* [2004] ECR I-7139; Case T-289/03 *BUPA* v *Commission* [2008] ECR II-81.

706   Case T-354/05 *Télévision Française 1* v *Commission* [2009] ECR II-471, at paras 124–47. For earlier discussion see Case C-53/00 *Ferring* v *Agence centrale des organismes de sécurité sociale* [2001] ECR I-9067; Case C-280/00 *Altmark, per* A-G Léger at para. 79 ff. of his opinion.

707   Case T-289/03 *BUPA*, n. 705 above, at para. 48; Regulation 2012/21, n. 709 below, Preamble, 5th indent.

708   Decision 2005/842 [2005] OJ L312/67. The decision was more of the nature of a block exemption (see immediately below) and so arguably improperly adopted under art. 106(3).

709   Decision 2012/21 [2012] OJ L7/3 on the application of Article 106(2) of the TFEU to state aid in the form of public service compensation granted to certain undertakings entrusted with the operation of SGEIs; also Communication on the application of European Union State aid rules to compensation granted for the provision of SGEIs [2012] OJ C8/4.

710   Decision 2012/21, *ibid.*, arts 2, 3.

711   *Ibid.* arts 2(1)(a), 3.

712   European Union framework for state aid in the form of public service compensation [2012] OJ C8/15.

713   E.g., Guidelines for State Aid for Small and Medium-sized Enterprises [1992] OJ C213/2; notice of the *de minimis* rule for state aids [1996] OJ C68/9.

Regulation (the Enabling Regulation, or ER)[714] authorising the Commission to adopt 'group exemption regulations' (GERs, or block exemptions), and using this power the Commission adopted GERs, declaring state aids to be compatible with the internal market without need of notification, for:

- *de minimis* aid (normally up to €200,000 to any single undertaking over a three-year period);[715]
- *de minimis* aid in the agricultural production sector;[716]
- *de minimis* aid in the fisheries production sector;[717]
- training aid;[718]
- aid for the creation of employment for disadvantaged and disabled workers;[719]
- aid to small and medium-sized enterprises;[720]
- aid to small and medium-sized enterprises for production of agricultural products;[721]
- aid to small and medium-sized enterprises for processing and marketing of agricultural products;[722]
- aid to small and medium-sized enterprises for production, processing and marketing of fisheries products;[723] and
- regional aid.[724]

Most (but not all) of these were realigned and consolidated into a single GER of general application (the General Block Exemption Regulation, GBER) in 2008,[725] covering regional aid (excluding the steel, shipbuilding and synthetic fibres sectors); SME investment and employment aid; aid for consultancy in favour of SMEs and SME participation in fairs; aid in the form of risk capital; aid for research, development and innovation; training aid; and aid for disadvantaged or disabled workers. It breaks new ground with provisions on aid for environmental protection and aid for the creation of enterprises by female entrepreneurs (*sic*), the latter which may, or may not, withstand scrutiny for

---

714 Regulation 994/98 [1998] OJ L142/1, authorising block exemption upon *de minimis* grounds and in the subject areas of small and medium-sized undertakings, research and development, environmental protection, employment and training, and aid to poorer regions.
715 Regulation 1998/2006 [2006] OJ L379/5. It is €100,000 in the road transport sector.
716 Regulation 1860/2004 [2004] OJ L325/4.
717 Regulation 875/2007 [2007] OJ L193/6.
718 Regulation 68/2001 [2001] OJ L10/20 (now lapsed).
719 Regulation 2204/2002 [2002] OJ L337/3 (now lapsed).
720 Regulation 70/2001 [2001] OJ L10/33 (now lapsed). SMEs are defined for Community purposes now in Regulation 800/2008 [2008] OJ L214/3, Annex I.
721 Regulation 1857/2006 [2006] OJ L358/3.
722 Regulation 1/2004 [2004] OJ L1/1.
723 Regulation 736/2008 [2008] OJ L201/16.
724 Regulation 1628/2006 [2006] OJ L302/29 (now repealed).
725 Regulation 800/2008 [2008] OJ L214/3.

compliance with Union rules on equal treatment.[726] The GBER is part of ongoing reform in the light of the Commission's State Aid Action Plan (or 'Monti package') adopted in 2005 with a view to 'less and better targeted' state aids and setting out its thinking on reform.[727] The final element of the 2011 package on SGEIs is a *de minimis* block exemption, exempting aid granted to undertakings providing SGEIs of up to €500,000 over a given three-year period.[728]

Article 34 TFEU

A state aid falls within article 107 but is not by that fact immunised from, and **13.169** may also fall within, the prohibition of article 34 TFEU; 'Article [107] may in no case be used to frustrate the rules of the Treaty on the free movement of goods'.[729] The evident problem here is that article 34 is an absolute (and directly effective) prohibition, whilst article 107 admits of significant discretionary derogation. The overlap is dealt with by a severability test: those aspects of a state aid which are so indissolubly linked to the object of the aid that it is impossible to evaluate them separately are to be assessed (for compatibility with the internal market) solely in accordance with the procedures of article 108. But if there exist conditions or factors which form part of the system but are nevertheless unnecessary for the attainment of the object of the state aid or for its proper functioning, they may be matter for article 34.[730]

3. Supervision of state aids

Article 108 TFEU imposes upon the Commission the task of supervision of **13.170** state aids to ensure compliance with the requirements of article 107. Its authority is, subject to review by the Court of Justice, (almost) exclusive;[731] thus a national court may not seek guidance from the Court of Justice under article 267 as to the compatibility with the Treaties of a given aid scheme.[732] Its exclusive competence also requires that where a complaint is made alleging the existence of an unlawful aid, the Commission is bound to conduct a diligent and

---

726 For the justification offered for this discrimination see recital 44 of the Preamble to the Regulation.

727 *State Aid Action Plan: Less and Better Targeted State Aids: A Roadmap for State Aid Reform 2005–2009*, COM(2005) 107 final.

728 Regulation 360/2012 [2012] OJ L114/8.

729 Case 103/84 *Commission* v *Italy* [1986] ECR 1759, at para. 19.

730 Case 74/76 *Ianelli & Volpi* v *Meroni* [1977] ECR 557, at para. 14. See also Case 249/81 *Commission* v *Ireland* [1982] ECR 4005; Case 18/84 *Commission* v *France* [1985] ECR 1339; Case 103/84 *Commission* v *Italy, ibid.*; Case 21/88 *Du Pont de Nemours Italiana* v *Unità Sanitaria Locale No. 2 di Carrara* [1990] ECR I-889; Case C-234/99 *Nygård* v *Svineafgiftsfonden* [2002] ECR I-3657.

731 Case C-39/94 *Syndicat Français de l'Express International* v *La Poste* [1996] ECR I-3547. As to the exception see 13.176 below.

732 Case C-297/01 *Sicilcassa and ors* v *IRA Costruzioni and ors* [2003] ECR I-7849.

impartial examination of it.[733] There is distinct treatment of 'new aids', in which the Commission exercises *a priori* control, and 'existing aids', those lawfully introduced prior to the entry into force of the Treaties or accession or in accordance with the procedures of article 108, where control is *ex post*.[734] Alteration of an existing aid is a new aid.[735] Rules applicable to the process of supervision developed over time through Commission procedure and case law of the Court of Justice; they were eventually codified and given greater precision in a 1999 Council Regulation (Regulation 659 or the Procedural Regulation).[736]

(a) Existing aids

13.171 Article 108(1) imposes upon the Commission a duty to

> keep under constant review all systems of aid existing in [the Member] States. It shall propose to the latter any appropriate measures required by the progressive development or by the functioning of the internal market.

It must therefore monitor all existing aids for continuing compatibility with article 107, including aids excepted under article 107(2). In order to assist, member states are required to submit annual reports on all existing aid schemes.[737] If the Commission determines that an existing aid no longer meets the criteria for exception or exemption it may recommend its termination[738] or order its termination within a reasonable period of time,[739] failing which it must initiate a formal investigation procedure.[740]

(b) New aids

13.172 Article 108(3) provides:

> The Commission shall be informed, in sufficient time to enable it to submit its comments, of any plans to grant or alter aid. If it considers that any such plan is not compatible with the internal market having regard to Article 107, it shall without delay initiate the procedure provided for in paragraph 2. The Member State concerned shall not put its proposed measures into effect until this procedure has resulted in a final decision.

---

733 Case T-395/04 *Air One* v *Commission* [2006] ECR II-1343.
734 On the difference between an existing and a new aid see Cases T-195 and 207/01 *Government of Gibraltar* v *Commission* [2002] ECR II-2309, at paras 105–31.
735 TFEU, art. 108(3), referring to 'plans to grant or alter aid'; Regulation 659, n. 736 below, art. 1(c).
736 Regulation 659/1999 [1999] OJ L83/1; see also Regulation 794/2004 [2004] OJ L140/1 (Implementing Regulation).
737 Regulation 659, art. 21(1); Regulation 794/2004, arts 5–7.
738 TFEU, art. 108(1); Regulation 659, art. 18.
739 TFEU, art. 108(2).
740 Regulation 659, art. 19(2).

There is therefore a 'standstill' clause, which is directly effective, prohibiting the introduction of a new aid (unless it falls within the terms of a block exemption) without the consent of the Commission.[741] Any proposal to grant a new aid is required to be notified to the Commission, which has adopted a standard form for that purpose, use of which is obligatory (and extensive).[742] It is required to respond to a proper notification with a preliminary examination 'with due expedition [*diligence*]' and within 'an appropriate period',[743] set by the Court at two months, after which absent a response Commission consent is deemed[744] and the Commission is barred from acting against it as a new aid.[745] This was codified in Regulation 659[746] which further provides, mimicking the procedures of the Merger Regulation, that the Commission must within two months of notification respond by a decision which (a) finds the notified measure not to constitute aid, (b) finds the measure to be compatible with the internal market in accordance with article 107(3), or (c) if it raises doubts as to its compatibility with the internal market, initiate a 'formal investigation procedure'.[747] The formal investigation procedure has developed through Commission practice and includes the publication of the notification in the *Official Journal* with an invitation to third parties to comment, the gathering of information, and as a general principle of Union law the hearing of interested parties, including all undertakings concerned by the aid.[748] Thoroughout the Commission must conduct a diligent and impartial examination of the case.[749] It is to assess the compatibility of the aid with the Treaties by applying any rules in force not at the time of notification but at the time it gives its decision.[750] The procedure is terminated by a decision (a) that the measure does not constitute aid; (b) that, with or without modification, the aid is compatible with the internal market ('positive decision'), which may have monitoring conditions imposed ('conditional decision'); or (c) that the aid is incompatible with the internal market ('negative decision').[751] The Commission should (must 'as far as possible endeavour') take the decision within a period of 18 months from the opening of

---

741 TFEU, art. 108(3), final sentence; Regulation 659, art. 2.
742 Regulation 794/2004, Annex.
743 Case 84/82 *Germany* v *Commission* [1984] ECR 1451, at para. 11.
744 Case 84/82 *Germany* v *Commission, ibid.*; also Case 120/73 *Lorenz* v *Germany* [1973] ECR 1471. The member state must inform the Commission of its intention to proceed.
745 Case C-312/90 *Spain* v *Commission* [1992] ECR I-4117.
746 Regulation 659, art. 4(5), (6).
747 *Ibid.* art. 4.
748 Cases 234/84 and 40/85 *Belgium* v *Commission* [1986] ECR 2263; Case 259/85 *France* v *Commission* [1987] ECR 4393; Case C-294/90 *British Aerospace* v *Commission* [1992] ECR I-493; codified in Regulation 659, arts 6, 20. The right to be heard is in the nature of an essential procedural requirement; Case C-334/07P *Commission* v *Freistaat Sachsen* [2008] ECR I-9465, at para. 55.
749 Case C-367/95P *Commission* v *Sytraval & Brink's France* [1998] ECR I-1719; Cases T-228 and 233/99 *Westdeutsche Landesbank and anor* v *Commission* [2003] ECR II-435.
750 Case C-334/07P *Freistaat Sachsen*, n. 748 above.
751 Regulation 659, art. 7(1)–(5).

the procedure,[752] and must, should the relevant member state so request, take a decision within two months thereafter, although should the information available to the Commission be insufficient to establish compatibility, there is a presumption of a negative decision.[753] As to determination of compatibility with the internal market, the Commission set out its stall and the criteria upon which it relies in 1983:[754]

(a) the aid ought to promote development which is in the interests of the Union as a whole; the promotion of national interest, which state aids generally subvent, is not enough to justify approval;

(b) the aid is necessary to achieve that development, and without it the measure in question would not be realised; for example, funds would be unlikely to be raised on the private capital markets (the 'market economy investor principle');

(c) the 'modalities' of the aid, its intensity, duration, displacement, the degree of distortion to competition, must be commensurate with the importance of the objective of the aid.

Because determination of compatibility with the internal market requires examination and appraisal of economic facts and circumstances which may be complex and liable to rapid change, the Commission necessarily enjoys a broad discretion.[755]

13.173 A failure to notify a new aid and proceeding with its introduction pending (timeous) preliminary examination or formal investigation by the Commission is a breach of article 108(3) irrespective of its merits[756] and renders the aid 'unlawful'.[757] The Commission may order the suspension of an unauthorised (and so unlawful) aid ('suspension injunction')[758] and may in cases of urgency order its recovery ('recovery injunction').[759] If the member state fails to comply the Commission may use a fast track procedure seeking a declaration from the Court of Justice that the failure constitutes an infringement of the Treaties.[760]

---

752 *Ibid.* art. 7(6).

753 *Ibid.* art. 7(7).

754 *XIIth Report on Competition Policy, 1982,* pp. 110–11.

755 E.g., Case 730/79 *Philip Morris* v *Commission* [1980] ECR 2671; Case C-301/87 *France* v *Commission* (Boussac) [1990] ECR I-307.

756 Case 120/73 *Lorenz* v *Germany* [1973] ECR 1471; Case C-39/94 *Syndicat Français de l'Express International* v *La Poste* [1996] ECR I-3547.

757 Regulation 659, art. 1(f).

758 *Ibid.* art. 11(1).

759 *Ibid.* art. 11(2).

760 TFEU, art. 108(2); Regulation 659, art. 12. Should the Court agree, and the member state still fail to comply, the Commission may pursue penalties against it in accordance with the procedures of art. 260; Regulation 659, art. 23(2). The disbursing member state may not defend a failure to comply with a decision by pleading its

The normal rule is that unlawful aid is required to be repaid by the recipient,[761] and the Commission is required to order repayment ('recovery decision') unless 'it would be contrary to a general principle of Community law'.[762] There is a legitimate expectation that an aid is lawful if it has been granted in a manner incompatible with requisite procedures in exceptional circumstances only.[763] The purpose is to ensure the recipient forfeits the competitive advantage conferred by the unlawful aid and to restore the *status quo ante*;[764] a recovery order is therefore a measure designed to restore a previously existing situation and is not penal in character.

If ordered, an aid must be repaid except in cases of 'absolute impossibility'.[765] Practical difficulties (for example, a requirement for France to recover aid in excess of €300 million disbursed to many thousands of individual producers of fruit and vegetables over the course of ten years and in the face of mass, organised resistance)[766] are irrelevant. Recovery gives rise to the peculiar legal situation in which the wrongdoer (the member state), which will in many (but not all) cases resist and obstruct efforts to force repayment, will end up being enriched. There is a limitation period of ten years.[767]

Because the standstill provisions of article 108(3) and Regulation 659 are **13.174** directly effective, actions of prohibition and recovery may also be taken to national courts.[768] But there may be difficulties in finding an appropriate national remedy. In order to provide guidance, in 2009 the Commission adopted a notice on enforcement of state aid law by national courts.[769]

---

illegality, that being a matter properly for art. 263; Case C-419/06 *Commission v Greece* (Olympic Airlines) [2008] ECR I-27*, at para. 52.

761　Case C-74/89 *Commission v Belgium* [1990] ECR I-492; Case C-39/94 *Syndicat Français de l'Express International* v *La Poste* [1996] ECR I-3547; Case C-232/05 *Commission v France* [2006] ECR I-10071.

762　Regulation 659, art. 14(1). But see Case T-318/00 *Freistaat Thüringen* v *Commission* [2005] ECR II-4179.

763　Case C-169/95 *Spain v Commission* [1997] ECR I-135; Case C-24/95 *Land Rheinland-Pfalz* v *Alcan Deutschland* [1997] ECR I-1591; Case C-408/04P *Commission v Salzgitter* [2008] ECR I-2797. For (rare) Commission recognition of such exceptional circumstances see Decision 2006/323 [2006] OJ L119/12 (*alumina mineral oils*) at paras 95–100.

764　Case 142/87 *Belgium* v *Commission* (Tubemeuse) [1990] ECR I-959.

765　Case 52/84 *Commission* v *Belgium* [1986] ECR 89; Case 301/87 *France* v *Commission* (Boussac) [1990] ECR I-307; Cases C-278–280/92 *Spain* v *Commission* [1994] ECR I-4103; Case T-67/94 *Ladbroke Racing* v *Commission* [1998] ECR II-1; Case C-75/97 *Belgium* v *Commission* [1999] ECR I-3671.

766　Decision 2009/402 (*'Contingency Plans' in the Fruit and Vegetable Sector*) [2009] OJ L127/11. The Commission allowed only (at para. 86) that should France encounter 'unforeseen difficulties' in recovery it may submit the problems for Commission 'consideration', and the two would then, owing to the mutual duty of sincere cooperation, require to work together in good faith 'with a view to overcoming the difficulties'.

767　Regulation 659, art. 15.

768　See below.

769　Notice on the enforcement of state aid law by national courts [2009] OJ C85/1 (the 'New Notice', replacing a previous Notice on cooperation between national courts and the Commission in the state aid field [1995] OJ C312/8).

13.175 Approval of an aid scheme by the Commission does not immunise it from other Treaty provisions of which it may fall foul.[770]

(c) Authority of the Council

13.176 As a nod to the importance and sensitivity of state aids, the Council may also declare a new or existing aid to be compatible with the internal market, upon a request from a member state, by unanimity, and if 'justified by exceptional circumstances'.[771] Because it requires Council unanimity it rarely happens, although the financial crisis of 2008 (and ongoing) has seen it brought into play.[772] If it happens as function of a dubious political expedient, for example where the Council approves a state aid after the Commission has declared it to be unlawful and ordered its repayment, it jeopardises legal certainty and is, in effect, an abuse of process.[773]

(d) Judicial control of the Commission

13.177 A decision taken under article 108 or under Regulation 659 is a decision (addressed always to the relevant member state) within the meaning of article 288 TFEU and so subject to review before the Court of Justice (more accurately the General Court) under article 263. Whilst the Commission enjoys a broad discretion in its powers, the administrative rules, in particular those on good administration, the right to be heard and sufficient (and sound) economic analysis and reasoning, which adhere to Regulation 1/2003, apply equally here. Unlike Regulation 1/2003, the initiation of an investigation *is* a reviewable act because it suspends aid disbursement.[774] A Commission decision may be challenged by any member state as of right or by the recipient of the aid, which by virtue of being the recipient is affected directly and individually by the decision,[775] and the Court is uncommonly generous in recognising individual concern enjoyed by third party competitors and trade associations,[776] although

---

770   Case 74/76 *Ianelli & Volpi* v *Meroni* [1977] ECR 557; Case 249/81 *Commission* v *Ireland* [1982] ECR 4005; Case 21/88 *Du Pont de Nemours Italiana* v *Unità Sanitaria Locale No. 2 di Carrara* [1990] ECR I-889; Case C-234/99 *Nygård* v *Svineafgiftsfonden* [2002] ECR I-3675.

771   TFEU, art. 108(2), 3rd para. Council intervention has the effect of suspending any Commission consideration of a case for three months.

772   E.g., Decision 2009/991 [2009] OJ L339/34.

773   Case C-110/02 *Commission* v *Council* (Portuguese Pigs) [2004] ECR I-6333; Case C-399/03 *Commission* v *Council* (Belgian Coordination Centres) [2006] ECR I-5629; Cases C-111/10, C-117/10, C-118/10 and C-121/10, each *Commission* v *Council*, involving the sale of agricultural land in Lithuania, Poland, Latvia and Hungary, respectively; all pending.

774   Case C-312/90 *Spain* v *Commission* [1992] ECR I-4117; Cases T-195 and 207/01 *Government of Gibraltar* v *Commission* [2002] ECR II-2309; Case T-332/06 *Alcoa Transformazioni* v *Commission* [2009] ECR II-29*.

775   Case C-188/92 *TWD Textilwerke Deggendorf* v *Germany* [1994] ECR I-833. However, the recipient is not a party to proceedings and there is no obligation for the Commission to notify it in the course of a procedure; Case C-276/03P *Scott* v *Commission* [2005] ECR I-8437.

776   E.g., Case 323/82 *Intermills* v *Commission* [1984] ECR 3809; Case C-198/91 *William Cook* v *Commission* [1993] ECR I-2487; Case C-225/91 *Matra* v *Commission* [1993] ECR I-3203; Case T-69/96 *Hamburger*

two Advocates-General have found the relevant case law to be 'plainly unsatisfactory'[777] and 'particulary complex and rather formalistic'.[778] Whilst the Commission alone enjoys the power to determine whether an article 107(3) aid is compatible with the internal market, the prohibition in article 108(3) of disbursement of an unauthorised, and *a fortiori* unnotified, aid is directly effective and so triggers the jurisdiction of the national courts which must make available such remedies as exist for the enforcement of equivalent rights in national law,[779] including damages.[780] The disbursing member state or an undertaking which enjoyed clear and unambiguous standing to raise an action of annulment against a Commission decision under article 263 (and so at least the actual and/or intended recipient of an aid) but failed to do so is barred from arguing the illegality of the decision in any national proceedings.[781]

The general rule that unlawful aids ought to be repaid applies equally in national courts, and the court ought in principle to make an appropriate order,[782] subject only to the proviso that in 'exceptional circumstances' it would be 'inappropriate' to do so.[783] However where an aid is unlawfully disbursed for want of a positive Commission decision, and that decision is subsequently forthcoming, a national court need not order recovery of the aid even in the absence of exceptional circumstances, but must order the recipient to pay interest in respect of the period of the unlawfulness.[784] If it is required to order recovery as a function of national law it may do so, but that is without prejudice to the member state's right to re-implement it subsequently.[785] A Commission decision wrongly prohibiting a state aid may give rise to a claim in damages for **13.178**

Hafen- und Lagerhaus and ors v *Commission* [2001] ECR II-1037; Case C-521/06P *Athinaïki Techniki* v *Commission* [2008] ECR I-5829; Case C-487/06P *British Aggegates Association* v *Commission* [2008] ECR I-10505 . If there are several parties to the same application it is appropriate to establish one applicant's right of action and, if established, there is no need to consider whether this is so for others; Cases T-273 and 297/06 *ISD Polska and anor* v *Commission* [2009] ECR II-2185, at para. 47 and case law there cited.

777 Case C-78/03P *Commission* v *Aktionsgemeinschaft Recht und Eigentum* [2005] ECR I-10737, *per* A-G Jacobs at para. 139 of his opinion.

778 Case C-487/06P *British Aggegates Association*, n. 776 above, *per* A-G Mengozzi at para. 71 of his opinion.

779 For English examples see *R* v *Attorney-General, ex parte ICI* [1987] 1 CMLR 72 (CA); *R* v *Commissioners of Customs and Excise, ex parte Lunn Poly* [1999] STC 350 (CA).

780 As to damages see Case C-199/06 *Centre d'exportation du livre français and anor* v *Société internationale de diffusion et d'édition* [2008] ECR I-469, at para. 55. It is not clear if the damages would lie against the subventing member state or the subvented undertaking, or if this may be a matter for national law.

781 Case C-188/92 *TWD Textilwerke Deggendorf* v *Germany* [1994] ECR I-833.

782 Case C-39/94 *Syndicat Français de l'Express International* v *La Poste* [1996] ECR I-3547.

783 *Ibid.* para. 71. See Case C-1/09 *Centre d'exportation du livre français and anor* v *Société internationale de diffusion et d'édition* [2010] ECR I-2099.

784 Case C-199/06 *Centre d'exportation du livre français and anor* v *Société internationale de diffusion et d'édition* [2008] ECR I-469. A recipient may even challenge for correctness the amount of aid disbursed in respect of the period predating the Commission decision; Case C-384/07 *Wienstrom* v *Bundesminister für Wirtschaft und Arbeit* [2008] ECR I-10393.

785 *Ibid.*

losses suffered but any relevant undertaking must act with reasonable diligence to avoid or minimise any loss.[786] General guidance may be had from the 2009 notice for national courts,[787] more specific guidance from a 2007 notice on effective implementation of Commission decisions ('the recovery notice').[788]

(e)   The 2008 financial crisis

13.179   That these rules are capable of some flexibility can be illustrated by the Commission response to the 2008 financial crisis. Not only did it approve a number of bank (and other financial institution) mergers which it might, in other circumstances, not have done,[789] it adopted a notice on state aids 'in the context of the current global financial crisis'[790] by which it noted that 'the level of seriousness that the current crisis in financial markets has reached' was such as to justify scrutiny of new aids not only under article 107(3)(c) (facilitating the development of certain economic activities or regions)[791] but article 107(3)(b) (remedying a serious disturbance in the economy of a member state),[792] a category normally available only sparingly, and set out (generous) parameters on its approach to guarantees covering the liabilities, recapitalisation, controlled winding up of, and other forms of liquidity assistance to, financial institutions, so long as 'undue distortions' to competition were avoided. The Commission adopted a number of 'temporary' communications as an aid to the (gentle) application of the state aids rules in the financial sector.[793] So generous has the

---

786   Case T-360/04 *FG Marine* v *Commission* [2007] ECR II-92*.

787   See n. 769 above.

788   Notice towards an effective implementation of Commission decisions ordering Member States to recover unlawful or incompatible aid [2007] OJ C272/4.

789   See Case COMP/M.5278 *Banque Fédérative du Crédit Mutuel/Citibank Private Banking Germany*, decision of 28 August 2008; Case COMP/M.5296 *Deutsche Bank/ABN Amro Assets*, decision of 1 October 2008; Case COMP/M.5360 *RBSK Group/DZ Bank Group/RZB Group/HVB Banca Pentru Locuinte*, decision of 3 December 2008; Case COMP/M.5384 *BNP Paribas/Fortis*, decision of 3 December 2008; Case COMP/M.5363 *Banco Santander/Bradford and Bingley Assets*, decision of 17 December 2008; Case COMP/M.5228 *Rabobank/Bank Gospodarki Żwnościowej*, decision of 11 February 2009. In a related manner the British government created an exemption in UK merger control legislation (the Enterprise Act 2002) in order to allow Lloyd's Bank to acquire Halifax/Bank of Scotland without competition scrutiny, which it would almost certainly not have passed; see the Enterprise Act 2002 (Specification of Additional Section 58 Consideration) Order 2008 (SI 2008/2645); *Merger Action Group* v *Secretary of State for Business, Enterprise and Regulatory Reform* [2008] CAT 36, 2009 SLT 10.

790   Communication from the Commission on the application of state aid rules to measures taken in relation to financial institutions in the context of the current global financial crisis [2008] OJ C270/8.

791   See e.g., Case N70/07 *Northern Rock Rescue Aid* [2008] OJ C43/1.

792   Commission Communication, n. 790 above, at para. 9. See e.g., Decision 2010/262 (*Northern Rock Restructuring Aid*) [2010] OJ L112/38 and the reasoning (at paras 102–3) for the switch from art. 107(3)(c), as in *Northern Rock Rescue Aid, ibid.*, to art. 107(3)(b).

793   The application of state aid rules to measures taken in relation to financial institutions in the context of the current global financial crisis (Banking Communication) [2008] OJ C270/8; Recapitalisation of financial institutions in the current financial crisis: limitation of the aid to the minimum necessary and safeguards against undue distortions of competition (Recapitalisation Communication) [2009] OJ C10/2; Treatment of impaired assets in the Community banking sector (Impaired Asset Communication) [2009] OJ C72/1;

Commission become it approved, under article 107(3)(b), impaired asset relief measures and the restructuring plan for the Royal Bank of Scotland of between €70–110 thousand million,[794] the largest amount of state aid disbursed in the Community/Union's history. It further undertook to respond swiftly to any complete notification of a state aid, 'if necessary within 24 hours and over a weekend'.[795] A Commission staff paper on its reaction to the crisis in the state aids sphere was published in 2011.[796]

(f) European Economic Area

It should be noted that because the free trade arrangements within the **13.180** European Economic Area echo (if less resoundingly) the concerns of the Union competition rules, provisions similar to articles 107 and 108 exist at EEA level. Article 61 of the EEA Agreement effectively replicates article 107 TFEU, article 62 is similar to article 108. The Commission enforces the EEA rules within the territory of the Union,[797] the EFTA Surveillance Authority within the (non-Swiss) territory of the EFTA,[798] their determinations then binding for the whole of the EEA (subject to judicial control of the Court of Justice and the EFTA Court of Justice). They are required to consult and cooperate closely in order to ensure a common approach.

(g) Reform

In Spring 2012 the Commission adopted a communication on state aid **13.181** modernisation (SAM),[799] intending to draw the state aid regime more effectively ('actively and positively') into the Europe 2020 programme. The three 'pillars' of the initiative are more focused and better quality aid, simplification, and shifting of the focus to a more structured policy approach. As a first step it has launched a review of the general block exemption regulation (GBER) with a view to proposing a revised version in 2013.

Temporary framework for state aid measures to support access to finance in the current financial and economic crisis [2009] OJ C83/1; Return to viability and the assessment of restructuring measures in the financial sector in the current crisis under the state aid rules (Restructuring Communication) [2009] OJ C195/9; Temporary Union framework for state aid measures to support access to finance in the current financial and economic crisis [2011] OJ C6/5; Application, from 1 January 2011, of state aid rules to support measures in favour of banks in the context of the financial crisis [2011] OJ C329/7.

794 Cases N422/2009 and N621/2009 *Royal Bank of Scotland* [2010] OJ C119/1.
795 Commission Communication, at para. 53.
796 *The Effects of Temporary State Aid Rules Adopted in the Context of the Financial and Economic Crisis*, SEC(2011) 1126 final.
797 EEA Agreement, art. 62(1)(a).
798 *Ibid.* art. 62(1)(b); Protocol 26; Agreement establishing a Surveillance Authority and an EFTA Court of Justice, art. 24.
799 COM(2012) 209 final.

14

OTHER POLICIES

Thus far we have considered Titles I–VII of Part Three of the Treaty, essentially **14.01** the four freedoms and competition law. The remainder of Part Three, comprising Titles VIII–XXIV, covers a number of areas in which the member states are bound to pursue common policies. Some existed from the beginning but many were added to the Treaty and/or refined by subsequent amending Treaties. Some are of great significance. It is impossible properly to understand the Union without taking them into account.

A. ECONOMIC AND MONETARY POLICY

1. General

From the beginning the EEC had as a means of achieving its 'task' the **14.02** approximation of the economic policies of the member states.[1] To this end the Treaty required the member states to regard their conjunctural policies as a matter of common concern,[2] authorising the Council to take, by unanimity, (unspecified) measures 'appropriate to the situation',[3] and to coordinate their economic policies to the extent necessary to ensure equilibrium in balance of payments and confidence in their currencies;[4] a provision introduced by the Single European Act spoke of further cooperation in convergence of economic and monetary policies.[5] These not very burdensome obligations were swept away by the Maastricht Treaty which incorporated into the EC Treaty the 'Delors proposals' for the achievement of economic and monetary union (EMU) and the necessary flanking measures. The general principles on economic and monetary policy are now laid down in article 119 TFEU and repeated in article 120 (for economic policy) and article 127 (for monetary policy); both, and for both the Union and the member states, are to be conducted

in accordance with the principle of an open market economy with free competition, favouring an efficient allocation of resources, and in compliance with the principles set out in Article 119.[6]

---

1 EEC Treaty, art. 2.
2 *Ibid.* art. 103(1).
3 *Ibid.* art. 103(2).
4 *Ibid.* arts 104, 105(1).
5 *Ibid.* art. 102a (subsequently art. 98 EC, art. 120 TFEU).
6 TFEU, arts 120 and 127(1) (ex arts 98 and 105(1) EC).

Articles 119 and 120 therefore 'establish the fundamental principles of economic policy of the Community system'.[7] Within these parameters, broad economic policy guidelines (BEPG) for both the Union and the member states are set annually by the Council, following discussion in the European Council, in the form of a recommendation.[8] Should a member state pursue economic policies inconsistent with these guidelines, or which 'risk jeopardising the proper functioning of economic and monetary union', the Council may, upon a Commission recommendation, make the 'necessary recommendations' to the member state.[9] It may make them public.[10] The sanction for disobedience is therefore to be 'named and shamed'.

14.03 The flagship of the Union's economic and monetary policy is of course EMU, which in 1993 was made both a 'task'[11] and an 'activity'[12] of the Community, and was to be achieved over a three stage transition period by 1999. In the present Treaties it merits inclusion at the outset: '[t]he Union shall establish an economic and monetary union whose currency is the euro'.[13] The Treaty provisions on EMU, and the institutional machinery intended to achieve it, are very complex, and will be considered here only briefly.

2. Background to EMU

14.04 The first concrete proposals for EMU came from an *ad hoc* committee of finance and central bank officials which was set up by the heads of state and government in 1969 and reported in 1970 (the Werner Report),[14] proposing a three-stage plan to create an economic and monetary union within a decade. The proposals were fairly uncontentious, formulated as they were within the environment of the monetary stability a product of the Bretton Woods system. However, the Bretton Woods system unravelled in 1971, and any progress upon implementation of the Werner proposals was forgotten.

14.05 In 1978 a Resolution of the European Council[15] established a European Monetary System (EMS), the purpose of which was to promote within the

---

7   Case C-451/03 *Servizi Ausiliari Dottori Commercialisti* v *Calafiori* [2006] ECR I-2941, at para. 20.
8   TFEU, art. 121(2) (ex art. 99(2) EC); for the present version (which is to 'remain stable' until 2014) see Recommendation 2010/410 on the broad economic policy guidelines of the Member States and of the Union [2010] OJ L191/28.
9   *Ibid.* art. 121(4).
10 *Ibid.*
11 EC Treaty, art. 2.
12 *Ibid.* art. 4.
13 TEU, art. 3(4).
14 *Report to the Council and the Commission on the Realisation by Stages of Economic and Monetary Union in the Community* (8 October 1970); summary in *Bulletin EC* 1970, Supplement 11.
15 *Bulletin EC* 12–1978, 10 ff.

Community the monetary stability which had been lost in 1971. EMS embraced a new mechanism for stabilising (but not fixing) exchange rates (the Exchange Rate Mechanism, or ERM) and a new unit of monetary value (the European currency unit, or ecu) based on a 'basket' of values of national currencies.[16] Within the EMS all participating currencies were permitted to fluctutate up to ± 2.25 per cent (for the *lira* ± 6 per cent) from the (nominal) value of the ecu ('the currency snake'); in the event of a risk of a currency exceeding these bounds, the appropriate national central bank(s) were obliged to intervene in order to (re)stabilise it.

The EMS was established within the context of the EEC but independently of **14.06** the Treaty, and was the first wholly voluntary Community initiative: member states could elect to join but were under no obligation to do so. Promulgated by the European Council, it was therefore doubly soft law, a 'non-act' adopted by a 'non-body'. Nevertheless all of the then nine member states save the United Kingdom joined from the outset (although the pound sterling was from the start part of the basket making up the ecu), Greece, Spain and Portugal upon accession in 1981 and 1986, and the United Kingdom in 1990 (the pound given a fluctuation limit, like the *lira*, of ± 6 per cent). In the meanwhile the political commitment to EMU was reconfirmed at the Hanover Summit in 1988, and the committee set up by it to study the matter (the Delors committee) reported in 1989,[17] identifying, in its turn, three stages necessary for the achievement of EMU and institutional machinery appropriate to it. The Delors proposals were considered by the economic and monetary intergovernmental conference (one of the two parallel IGCs) and incorporated into the Maastricht Treaty. However, seven months after its signature the ERM collapsed in the currency crisis of 1992 ('black Wednesday'); several currencies were sharply devalued, and Italy and the United Kingdom left it altogether. It was in this environment that the Maastricht Treaty, and its EMU provisions, entered into force.

3. Economic and monetary union

Economic and monetary union is not a common economic policy. Rather it **14.07** requires an unrestricted integrated market (such as is addressed elsewhere in the Treaties) together with close coordination of macroeconomic policies, including binding rules for budgetary policies (economic union) and irrevocable fixing of exchange rate parities or, preferably, a single currency area (monetary

---

16   The ecu was created and its value fixed by Regulation 3180/78 [1978] OJ L379/1, and a national currency varied in value to it with currency fluctuations. In the light of major shifts its currency composition (but not its external value) was realigned twice, in 1984 and 1989.

17   *Report of the Committee for the Study of Economic and Monetary Union* (1989) (Delors Report); summarised in *Bulletin EC* 4–1989, 8.

union).[18] According to the Court of Justice it was implicitly a Community goal even prior to the Maastricht texts.[19] In formal Treaty terms it is the 'close coordination of Member States' economic policies',[20] which are 'a matter of common concern',[21] within the framework of broad guidelines established by the Council upon the basis of a 'conclusion' established by the European Council,[22] and the irrevocable fixing of exchange rates leading to the introduction of a single currency and with it a single monetary and exchange rate policy.[23] In order to achieve it, both the Union and the member states were, and are, required to conduct their policies in a manner which complies with the 'guiding principles' of stable prices, sound public finances and monetary conditions and a sustainable balance of payments,[24] and the member states were, and are, further obliged to avoid excessive government deficits.[25]

4. The three stages

14.08 The first stage of the Delors Plan (1 July 1990–31 December 1993) required member states simply to comply with the Treaty provisions on the free movement of capital,[26] a precondition, or *sine qua non*, to EMU; to open up (if necessary) their financial institutions;[27] and to work towards lasting convergence in economic policy.[28] The second stage (1 January 1994–31 December 1998)[29] required all member states to adopt financial discipline[30] and ensure by the end of the stage (if necessary) that national legislation relating to central banks was made compatible with the Treaty and the ESCB/ECB Statute.[31] The currency composition of the ecu basket was fixed at the outset[32] and the European Monetary Institute (EMI) established in order to assist in and

---

18 *Ibid.* paras 22–30.

19 Opinion 1/91 *Re the EEA Agreement* [1991] ECR I-6079, at para. 17.

20 TFEU, art. 119(1).

21 *Ibid.* art. 121(1).

22 *Ibid.* arts 120 and 121(2); guidelines were first established by Recommendation 94/480 [1994] OJ L200/38.

23 *Ibid.* art. 119(2).

24 *Ibid.* art. 119(3).

25 See below.

26 1 July 1990 was identified as the start of the first stage (and recognised as such by the European Council at the 1989 Madrid Summit; see Conclusions of the Presidency, *Bulletin EC* 6–1989, para. B.3) even though it predates Maastricht texts, primarily because it is the day Directive 88/361 [1988] OJ L178/5 was required (for the most part) to be brought into force; see 12.04 above.

27 EC Treaty, arts 101 and 102 (now arts 123 and 124 TFEU); see also Regulation 3603/93 [1993] OJ L332/1 and Regulation 3604/93 [1993] OJ L332/4.

28 *Ibid.* art. 116(2); repealed by Lisbon.

29 *Ibid.* art. 116(1); repealed by Lisbon. The start of the second stage (1 January 1994) was the date on which the Treaty chapter on capital was replaced wholesale by Maastricht; see 12.05 above

30 *Ibid.* art. 104 (now art. 126 TFEU).

31 *Ibid.* art. 109 (now art. 131 TFEU).

32 *Ibid.* art. 118 (repealed by Lisbon); thus it is that the ecu never included as part of its composition the *schilling*, the *markka* or the Swedish *krona*.

monitor the development of and progress towards the third stage. The Council meeting as heads of state and government was required by the end of 1996 to decide whether a majority of member states fulfilled the necessary conditions for the adoption of a single currency, whether it was therefore appropriate to enter a third stage, and, if so, to set a date for the beginning of that stage,[33] which was in any event to start by 1 January 1999.[34]

5. The third stage

The requirements obtaining to the first and second stages applied and apply to all member states, irrespective of whether they proceed further. In order to proceed, a member state was, and is, required to meet the four 'convergence criteria' (or 'Maastricht criteria'), set out in the Treaties thus: **14.09**

- the achievement of a high degree of price stability; this will be apparent from a rate of inflation which is close to that of, at most, the three best performing Member States in terms of price stability;
- the sustainability of the government financial position; this will be apparent from having achieved a government budgetary position without a deficit that is excessive as determined in accordance with Article 126(6);
- the observance of the normal fluctuation margins provided for by the exchange-rate mechanism of the European Monetary System, for at least two years, without devaluing against the euro;
- the durability of convergence achieved by the Member State with a derogation and of its participation in the exchange-rate mechanism being reflected in the long-term interest-rate levels.[35]

In 1998 the Council determined that 11 of the 15 member states (Belgium, Germany,[36] Spain, France, Ireland, Italy, Luxembourg, the Netherlands, Austria, Portugal and Finland) met the criteria[37] and so entered the third stage on 1 January 1999. Greece and Sweden failed to meet the criteria, and did not. Denmark and the United Kingdom declined to proceed.[38]

The EC Treaty referred to monetary union based upon the ecu, it being the (nominal) common currency unit at the time of the Maastricht negotiations. It **14.10**

---

33   *Ibid.* art. 121(3); repealed by Lisbon.
34   *Ibid.* art. 121(4); repealed by Lisbon.
35   TFEU, art. 140(1) (ex art. 121(1) EC and Protocol on the Convergence Criteria referred to in Article 121 of the Treaty establishing the European Community).
36   Whilst it was not envisaged in (or permitted by) the Treaty, the Bundesverfassungsgericht said (BVerfG, 12. Oktober 1993 (*Maastricht*), BVerfGE 89, 155) that it would be unconstitutional for Germany to proceed to the third stage without further approval from the German parliament – which approval was duly obtained (Gesetz vom 9. Juni 1998 zur Einführung des Euro (Euro-Einführungsgesetz – EuroEG), BGBl. 1998 I S. 1242).
37   Decision 98/317 [1998] OJ L139/30.
38   See below.

continued to do so until Lisbon,[39] those responsible for subsequent amendments very wary of interfering even minimally the balance struck at Maastricht.[40] However, the political decision to christen the new currency the 'euro' was taken at the Madrid summit in 1995 and appropriate legislation was adopted in 1997,[41] thereafter '[e]very reference in a legal instrument to the ECU … replaced by a reference to the euro at a rate of one euro to one ECU'.[42] The euro is therefore a 'dual function currency', replacing both the ecu and the national currencies of participating member states. It replaced the latter with effect from the onset of the third stage[43] (the 'date of substitution'), immediately prior to which (on 31 December 1998) the Council adopted by unanimity of participating states the (irrevocable) conversion rates,[44] and thereafter became their currency in its own right. For three years the various national currencies alone remained in circulation, but were in law 'legacy' (sometimes 'yielded') currencies. Having satisfied the Council in 2000 that it met the convergence criteria,[45] Greece came on board with effect from 1 January 2001.[46] Euro notes and coins were introduced into circulation on 1 January 2002 ('€-day') and after a short period of dual currencies[47] the euro became the sole currency, *de facto* as well as *de jure*, of the 12 member states within the euro area, or 'eurozone' – those member states becoming, informally, the 'Eurogroup'.

14.11   In fact use of the euro extends further: Monaco, San Marino and the Vatican each had its own currency (the *franc monegasque*, the *lira sanmarinese*, the *lira vaticana*) but were historically in monetary union with France, Italy and Italy,

---

39   Treaty recognition of the euro came only with the Lisbon Treaty, art. 2(2)(h).

40   This is why various measures provided for under arts 98–130 EC continued to be adopted by the cooperation procedure, which was abandoned elsewhere in the Treaty by the Treaty of Amsterdam.

41   Regulation 1103/97 [1997] OJ L162/1.

42   *Ibid.* art. 2(1). The euro is 'euro' in all languages within the eurozone using the Latin alphabet, ευρω in Greek (see Regulation 1103/97, preamble, 2nd recital: 'whereas … the name of the single currency must be the same in all the official languages of the European Union, taking into account the existence of different alphabets'), both appearing on the banknotes. For phonetic reasons some of the 2004 accession member states pressed for additional spellings ('eiro' for the Latvians, 'euró' for the Hungarians, 'ewro' for the Maltese) but to no avail. The Bulgarians wanted евро (which approximates the Greek in pronunciation and reflects the common and natural Slavic predisposition to the word) but the Bank held out for еуро (which is used in the Bulgarian version of Regulation 1103/97), presumably because of its similarity with the written Greek; the Bulgarians seem to have prevailed, the Lisbon Treaty opting for евро (Договор от Лисабон, чл. 2.2.3). Others have had to make do with a unilateral declaration that the official (mis)spelling of the euro 'has no effect on the existing rules of the Latvian, Hungarian or Maltese languages'; Declaration (No. 58) by the Republic of Latvia, the Republic of Hungary and the Republic of Malta on the spelling of the name of the single currency in the Treaties.

43   Regulation 974/98 [1998] OJ L139/1.

44   Regulation 2866/98 [1998] OJ L359/1.

45   Decision 2000/427 [2000] OJ L167/19.

46   Regulation 2596/2000 [2000] OJ L300/2 (amending Regulation 974/98). The value at which the *drachma* was fixed was determined by Regulation 1478/2000 [2000] OJ L167/1 (amending Regulation 2866/98).

47   Each participating member state had the option of immediate use of the euro to the exclusion of all else (the 'big bang') or retaining concurrent use of a legacy currency for a time; most opted for, and all were completed within, a two-month period.

respectively; in 2000/2001 each abandoned its currency and entered into a monetary union with the Community[48] making the euro from €-day the official currency of each, and each issues its own euro coins (in small numbers). Andorra has no official currency, but with the withdrawal of the (semi-official) *peseta* and French *franc* the euro became its *de facto* currency in 2002. Negotiations on a monetary agreement with the Community began in 2004[49] and an agreement was signed in 2011,[50] which will enter into force on 1 January 2013 provided Andorra adopts into law before then an (extensive) list of Union measures on prevention of money laundering, fraud and counterfeiting and banking and finance.[51] The euro has also been adopted as the official currency, with Council agreement, in Mayotte and St Pierre-et-Miquelon[52] and, following its departure from the Union in 2012, in Saint-Barthélemy;[53] without Council agreement in the other French overseas collectivities other than New Caledonia, French Polynesia and Wallis-et-Futuna (which use the CFP franc, pegged to the euro); and, unilaterally, in Montenegro and Kosovo.

Immediately upon the setting of the date for the third stage the European **14.12** Central Bank (ECB) and the European System of Central Banks (ESCB) were established; they began to exercise their powers, in accordance with procedures established by the Council, from the first day of the third stage.[54] Thereafter these 'financial institutions' directed and controlled EMU through legislative and enforcement powers conferred upon them by the Treaty and their Statute,[55] and gained sole control of monetary policy within the eurozone. Like the German *Bundesbank*, the primary objective of the ESCB is price stability,[56] within which it is to contribute to the achievement of the objectives of EMU and define and implement monetary policy, foreign exchange and payment systems.[57] Within the participating member states the ECB enjoys the exclusive right to authorise the issue of banknotes;[58] the minting and issue of coinage is for the member states (on which each is permitted individual design on the

---

48 Monetary Agreement of 24 December 2001 between France, on behalf of the Community, and Monaco [2002] OJ L142/59; Monetary Agreement between Italy, on behalf of the Community, and San Marino [2001] OJ C209/1; Monetary Agreement of 29 December 2000 between Italy, on behalf of the Community, and the Vatican and the Holy See [2001] OJ C299/1. All three are, at the time of writing, under renegotiation.
49 See Council Decision 2004/548 [2004] OJ L244/47.
50 Monetary Agreement of 30 June 2011 between the European Union and the Principality of Andorra [2011] OJ C369/1.
51 *Ibid.* art. 2.
52 Decision 1999/95 [1999] OJ L30/29.
53 Decision 2011/433 [2011] OJ L189/1.
54 EC Treaty, art. 123(1); repealed by Lisbon.
55 See 4.04–4.11 above.
56 TFEU, art. 127(1) (ex art. 105(1) EC) and ESCB/ECB Statute, art. 2.
57 TFEU, art. 127(1), (2) and ESCB/ECB Statute, art. 3.
58 TFEU, art. 128(1) and ESCB/ECB Statute, art. 16.

'national side', the reverse of the 'common face') but subject to ECB approval of the volume.[59]

14.13 Ministers from Eurogroup member states have met informally since the launch of the third stage. With Lisbon meetings have been (partially) regularised, with a view to 'develop[ing] ever-closer coordination of economic policies within the euro area'.[60] Meetings are informal still but take place 'when necessary' to discuss questions related to the specific responsibilities they share with regard to the single currency;[61] at the end of 2011 it was agreed to meet at least twice annually.[62] The Commission takes part and the European Central Bank is invited to take part. The group has a president elected for a term of two and a half years.[63] The first president, from January 2010, is, as he was informally before, Mr Juncker.

14.14 There is no procedure for a Eurogroup member state to renounce the euro and re-establish its previous currency.

6. Derogation

14.15 The third stage applies automatically but only to those member states which meet the necessary convergence criteria. Other member states – 'member states with a derogation',[64] informally sometimes simply the 'outs' – do not take part. They continue to be bound by the obligations of the first two stages but they and their national central banks are excluded from rights and obligations within the ESCB and their voting rights within the Council on third stage matters suspended.[65] The Council 'abrogates' the derogation of a member state with a derogation which subsequently fulfils the criteria for sustainable economic convergence[66] and fixes the rate at which the euro is to be substituted for its currency,[67] after which that member state assumes full rights and obligations of EMU. In the meanwhile, stability of a sort was sought with the resuscitation in 1997 of the Exchange Rate Mechanism (now ERM-II or ERM Mark II) in

---

59 TFEU, art. 128(2).
60 TFEU, art. 137; Protocol (No. 14) on the Euro Group, preamble, 1st indent.
61 Protocol, art. 1.
62 European Council, Statement by the Euro Area heads of state or government, 9 December 2011, point 10.
63 *Ibid.* art. 2.
64 TFEU, art. 139(1) (ex art. 122(1) EC).
65 *Ibid.* art. 139(3)–(5). Equally, as with Denmark (and partly Ireland and the United Kingdom) under JLS matters, a member state with a derogation holding the presidency of the Council may yield it to another member state in the trio presidency.
66 *Ibid.* art. 140(2) (ex art. 122(2) EC).
67 *Ibid.* art. 140(3).

order to 'link currencies of Member States outside the euro area to the euro',[68] this time adopting the euro as the 'centre' of the new mechanism and fixing the permissible fluctuation margin of other currencies at ± 15 per cent. As with the original ERM, it was created by a European Council resolution only, and participation continued to be optional; all three then member states with a derogation could comfortably fit within the band prescribed (not surprisingly, with limits of ± 15 per cent), but only Denmark (the *krone* in fact within ± 2.25 per cent to the euro) opted in.

Alone amongst the member states, Denmark and the United Kingdom enjoy a **14.16** right of derogation as a price of their agreement to the scheme. In accordance with a Protocol attached to the Treaty,[69] even had it fulfilled the convergence criteria the United Kingdom was not bound to enter the third stage. It was entitled to do so, in which case it was obliged to notify the Council of that intention. Thus, it may 'opt in' to EMU, but bears no obligation; and in giving effect to the TEU (pre-Lisbon) within the United Kingdom, Parliament enacted a statutory bar restraining the government from submitting notification without the approval of an Act of Parliament.[70] Having (thus far) failed to do so, it enjoys in effect the status of member state with a permanent (or at least indefinite) derogation, and would now require to petition the Council for abrogation to alter it; the foreign secretary in the coalition government elected in 2010 has pledged that the United Kingdom will 'never' do so.[71] Denmark enjoys a similar right under the Treaty,[72] and although it was drafted in a manner which permitted Denmark to opt out of the third stage (as opposed to the drafting of the United Kingdom Protocol which presumed non-participation but permitted opting in), the Danish government straightaway submitted notification that Denmark would decline to participate in the third stage.[73] A subsequent referendum in 2000 indicated no change of heart, 53 per cent of Danes voting against joining. A second referendum was promised by the government in 2007, anticipated by 2011, but drifting now into 2012 and beyond.

---

68   Resolution of the European Council, 16 January 1997, Preamble [1997] OJ C236/5. See also the Agreement of 16 March 2006 between the ECB and the Central Banks of member states outside the euro area establishing ERM operating procedures [2006] OJ C73/21.

69   Protocol (No. 15) on Certain Provisions relating to the United Kingdom of Great Britain and Northern Ireland.

70   European Communities (Amendment) Act 1993, s. 2; now requiring prior approval by Act of Parliament and a referendum: European Union Act 2011, s. 6(1), (5)(e).

71   W. Hague, 'Draft letter from Foreign Secretary to Prime Minister', 9 May 2010. The coalition government's agreed position is that the United Kingdom 'will not join or prepare to join the Euro in this Parliament'; Conservative-Liberal Democrat Coalition Agreement, 11 May 2010, para. 9.

72   Protocol (No. 16) on Certain Provisions relating to Denmark.

73   European Council in Edinburgh, Conclusions of the Presidency, *Bulletin EC* 12–1992, 25.

14.17 Sweden secured no right of derogation under the Treaty when it acceded in 1995, and is bound in principle to sign up if it meets the convergence criteria. However, it is not a politically popular course of action: despite the support of all major political parties, in a 2003 referendum Swedes voted 56–42 per cent against joining. Since the third and fourth criteria require participation in the exchange rate mechanism for a period of at least two years, and participation in the ERM is wholly voluntary, Sweden can, and does, resist the siren call of EMU by the expedient (fortuitous or otherwise) simply of declining formally to join the ERM, and is likely to do so for the foreseeable future.

14.18 As for the 2004 and 2007 accession states, each participated immediately in EMU as a member state with a derogation,[74] and requires to meet the convergence criteria to the satisfaction of the Council to accede to EMU. Measures were adopted in 2005 in order to prepare the legal framework for it.[75] Slovenia met the criteria in 2006[76] (having joined ERM-II in 2004) and was admitted as from January 2007;[77] Cyprus and Malta (ERM-II in 2005) met the criteria in 2007[78] and were admitted as from January 2008;[79] Slovakia (ERM–II in 2005) met the criteria in 2008[80] and was admitted as from January 2009;[81] Estonia (ERM-II in 2004) met the criteria in 2010[82] and was admitted as from January 2011.[83] Lithuania (ERM-II in 2004), Bulgaria, the Czech Republic and Poland hope (or had hoped) to be admitted by 2012, Latvia (ERM-II in 2004), Hungary by 2013 and Romania by 2014;[84] all of these projections are subject to shifting and delay as a result of the ongoing financial and euro stability crisis. Immediately upon accession to the Union Croatia will be bound by the EMU rules as a member state with a derogation.[85]

---

74 2003 Act of Accession, art. 4; 2005 Act of Accession, art. 5.
75 Regulation 2169/2005 [2005] OJ L346/1 (amending Regulation 974/98); see also Guideline of the ECB on Frontloading and Sub-frontloading Preparatory to Changeover [2006] OJ L207/39 and Commission Recommendation 2008/78 [2008] OJ L23/30 on measures to facilitate future changeovers to the euro.
76 Decision 2006/495 [2006] OJ L195/25.
77 Regulation 1647/2006 [2006] OJ L309/2 (amending Regulation 974/98), the value of the *tolar* fixed by Regulation 1086/2006 [2006] OJ L195/1 (amending Regulation 2866/98).
78 Decision 2007/503 [2007] OJ L186/29 (Cyprus); Decision 2007/504 [2007] OJ L186/32 (Malta).
79 Regulation 835/2007 [2007] OJ L186/1 (Cyprus) and Regulation 836/2007 [2007] OJ L186/3 (Malta) (amending Regulation 974/98), the values of the *lira* fixed by Regulation 1134/2007 [2007] OJ L256/1 and the pound by Regulation 1135/2007 [2007] OJ L256/2 (amending Regulation 2866/98).
80 Decision 2008/608 [2008] OJ L195/24.
81 Regulation 693/2008 [2008] OJ L195/1 (amending Regulation 974/98), the value of the *koruna* fixed by Regulation 694/2008 [2008] OJ L195/3 (amending Regulation 2866/98).
82 Decision 2010/416 [2010] OJ L196/24.
83 Regulation 670/2010 [2010] OJ L196/1 (amending Regulation 974/98), the value of the *kroon* fixed by Regulation 671/2010 OJ L196/4 (amending Regulation 2866/98).
84 See Commission Communication, *Second Report on the Practical Preparations for the Future Enlargement of the Euro Area*, COM(2005) 545 final.
85 2011 Act of Accession, art. 5.

There remain two anomolies: with Cypriot accession in 2008 and the dis-   **14.19**
appearance of the pound the euro was also adopted in Akrotiri and Dhekelia[86]
even though part neither of Cyprus nor of the Union; they mark therefore the
only (first?) British territories in which the euro is the official currency.
Secondly, and on the other side of the coin, uniquely in the Union the official
currency of Bonaire, Sint Eustatius and Saba, reintegrated into the Netherlands
in 2010,[87] is, since 1 January 2011, the US dollar.[88]

7. Excessive government deficits: the stability and growth pact

The macroeconomic lever by which the member states could seriously jeopard-   **14.20**
ise EMU discipline still is public spending. The Treaties therefore oblige them
to avoid excessive government deficits[89] and provide (the bare bones of) a
mechanism for correcting them should they occur (the 'excessive deficit procedure').[90] From the start of the second stage member states have been required to
report regularly to the Commission on planned and actual government deficits,
public accounts budget deficits, estimate of the level of actual government debt,
government investment expenditure and interest expenditure, and forecast of
GDP and actual amount of GDP.[91] Then in 1997 at the Amsterdam Summit
the European Council adopted a resolution for the implementation of a
'stability and growth pact'.[92] The stability and growth pact consists of the
resolution creating it and two Regulations giving it effect, one on surveillance of
budgetary positions and surveillance and coordination of economic policies (the
'preventive' arm),[93] the other on speeding up and clarifying the implementation
of the excessive deficit procedure (the 'corrective' arm).[94]

Excessive government deficit is defined by two distinct (but economically   **14.21**
linked) criteria:

(a)   where the ratio of a planned or actual government deficit to GDP at
       market prices exceeds a 'reference value' of 3 per cent; and

---

86   Ordinance 18 of 2007 (Euro Ordinance), *Sovereign Base Areas Gazette* No. 1470 of 14 August 2007.
87   See 10.05 above, n. 39.
88   Wet van 30 september 2010, houdende regels met betrekking tot het geldstelsel van de openbare lichamen
     Bonaire, Sint Eustatius en Saba, alsmede enige voorzieningen van overgangsrechtelijke aard (Wet geldstelsel
     BES), stb 2010, 363.
89   TFEU, art. 126(1) (ex art. 104(1) EC).
90   Protocol (No. 12) on the Excessive Deficit Procedure.
91   Regulation 479/2009 [2009] OJ L145/1 (replacing ('codifying') Regulation 3605/93 [1993] OJ L332/7).
92   [1997] OJ C236/1.
93   Regulation 1466/97 [1997] OJ L209/1. The Council may, post-Lisbon, adopt measures to strengthen the
     coordination and surveillance of budgetary discipline (amongst eurozone member states only) and to set out
     economic policy guidelines for them; TFEU, art. 136.
94   Regulation 1467/97 [1997] OJ L209/6.

(b)   where the ratio of government debt to GDP at market prices exceeds a
       reference value of 60 per cent.[95]

However, should a member state fail in its obligation to avoid both of these it
cannot be made subject of normal enforcement proceedings, recourse to articles
258 and 259, uniquely in the Treaty, being ousted.[96] Rather the excessive deficit
procedure provides for an escalating scale of sanctions, as follows:[97]

- the Commission is required constantly to monitor the budgetary situation
  of each member state; where a member state breaches one or both of the
  discipline criteria, the Commission must prepare an economic report, and
  may prepare another report recording an opinion that there is a risk of an
  excessive government deficit in a member state (the 'early warning'; article
  126(3));
- the Economic and Financial Committee is consulted on the Commission
  report (article 126(4));
- if the Commission considers that an excessive deficit exists or may occur, it
  is required to address an opinion to the Council (article 126(5));
- the Council determines (by qualified majority vote) whether an excessive
  deficit exists (article 126(6));
- the Council makes recommendations to the defaulting member state(s)
  with a view to bringing the situation to an end within a prescribed period;
  the recommendations are not made public (article 126(7));
- failing an acceptable response within the period set, the Council may
  make its recommendations public (article 126(8)); this is the limit of the
  power of sanction over member states with a derogation;[98]
- if the failure persists, the Council may order ('decide to give notice to') the
  member state(s) to take measures for deficit reduction which it, the
  Council, thinks necessary to remedy the situation within a prescribed
  period; it may require the member state(s) to submit reports on their
  progress to this end (article 126(9));
- failing compliance, the Council may (article 126(11)):
    - require the member state(s) to publish additional information before
      issuing bonds and securities;
    - invite the EIB to reconsider its lending policy towards the member
      state(s);

---

95   TFEU, art. 126(2); Protocol on the Excessive Deficit Procedure, art. 1; ancillary rules and definitions set out in
     Regulation 479/2009, n. 91 above, and Regulation 1467/97, *ibid.*
96   *Ibid.* art. 126(10).
97   *Ibid.* art. 126.
98   *Ibid.* art. 122(3). See e.g., Decisions 2006/1014 [2006] OJ L414/81 and 2009/409 [2009] OJ L132/11
     declaring, respectively, the Polish and UK responses to art. 104(7) recommendations inadequate.

- require the member state(s) to make non-interest bearing deposit with the Union; and/or
- impose a fine.

Council action under article 126(6) to 126(9), 126(11) and 126(12) is adopted by a special qualified voting procedure excluding the votes of the member state(s) concerned[99] and member states with a derogation.[100] In all cases it acts upon a recommendation (*sic*) of the Commission.[101] If and when it is satisfied that a member state has corrected the situation the Council 'abrogates' any measure it has adopted and makes a public statement that the excessive deficit no longer exists.[102]

It will be seen that the whip hand is that of the Council – here the Ecofin Council. Even if a defaulting member state is excluded from voting in the later stages of the procedure, it is nevertheless sinners sitting in judgment of fellow sinners. And if the sinner is a large(r) member state, its authority is increased by its weighted share of the vote in the initial finding of an excessive deficit. A good example is the recommendation by the Commission in 2003 of Council action under article 126(8) and 126(9) against Germany and France, but none was taken simply because the Council declined to act. A judicial challenge of this failure taken by the Commission was largely unsuccessful.[103] **14.22**

By May 2004 the excessive deficit procedure had been initiated against five of the (then) 12 eurozone member states (Germany, Greece, France, the Netherlands and Portugal) and, within a fortnight of joining, six of the 2004 accession member states (the Czech Republic, Cyprus, Hungary, Malta, Poland and Slovakia).[104] The furthest the procedure has been taken is an article 126(9) direction, against Greece in 2005,[105] Germany in 2006[106] and Greece again in **14.23**

---

99 *Ibid.* art. 126(13).
100 *Ibid.* art. 139(4).
101 *Ibid.* art. 126(13).
102 *Ibid.* art. 126(12).
103 See Case C-27/04 *Commission* v *Council* [2004] ECR I-6649. The action (raised under art. 263) was inadmissible insofar as it libelled a failure formally to act, and successful only insofar as the Council decision held the procedure in abeyance, but this upon a narrow technical point; the Court was careful to express no view as to whether the Council was obliged to act where a member state fails to comply with an art. 126(8) recommendation (para. 90).
104 Proceedings against all but Hungary were terminated by the end of the year; Commission Communication of 22 December 2004, SEC(2004) 1630 final; further proceedings were subsequently initiated against Poland; see n. 98 above.
105 Decision 2005/441 [2005] OJ L153/29; abrogated by Decision 2007/465 [2007] OJ L176/21.
106 Decision 2006/344 [2006] OJ L126/20; abrogated by Decision 2007/490 [2007] OJ L183/23.

2010.[107] In 2005 changes were made to both implementing Regulations,[108] allowing the 3 per cent ceiling to be breached (which is permissible under the Treaties where 'exceptional and temporary'[109]) not only in the event of severe recession or natural disaster but also in the event of a negative annual growth rate or a very low GDP growth relative to potential,[110] and relaxing significantly the previously strict deadlines of the corrective Regulation for member state responses.

14.24 As they adapt to the 2008 financial crisis the growing deficits of an increasing number of member states are facing Union action: in the space of ten weeks in spring/summer 2009 the Council found excessive deficits (article 126(6)) to exist in nine member states (France, Greece, Ireland, Spain, Malta, Lithuania, Poland, Romania and Latvia)[111] and in early 2010 nine more (Austria, Belgium, the Czech Republic, Germany, Italy, the Netherlands, Portugal, Slovenia and Slovakia),[112] the Commission (article 126(5)) then adding yet five more (Bulgaria, Denmark, Cyprus, Luxembourg and Finland)[113] and the Council agreed (article 126(6)) in four cases (Bulgaria, Denmark, Cyprus and Finland).[114] In 2009 the Council issued recommendations (article 126(7)) to 13 member states to bring their excessive deficits to an end;[115] in 2009 and 2010 it made public the inadequacy of compliance with earlier recommendations by the United Kingdom[116] and by Greece[117] (article 126(8)); and it subsequently directed Greece (article 126(9)) to put an end to its deficit 'as rapidly as possible' and at the latest by 2014, and imposed stringent ('urgent', 'supporting' and 'other') fiscal surveillance measures and a timetable in order that it do so.[118] The only member states to have escaped Council/Commission discipline entirely are Estonia and Sweden.

---

107 Decision 2010/182 [2010] OJ L83/12.
108 Regulations 1055/2005 [2005] OJ L174/1 and 1056/2005 [2005] OJ L174/5, amending Regulations 1466/97 and 1467/97, respectively.
109 TFEU, art. 126(2)(a), 2nd indent.
110 Regulation 1467/97, art. 2(2) as amended.
111 See, respectively, Decisions 2009/414 [2009] OJ L135/19; 2009/415 [2009] OJ L135/21; 2009/416 [2009] OJ L135/23; 2009/417 [2009] OJ L135/23; 2009/587 [2009] OJ L202/42; 2009/588 [2009] OJ L202/44; 2009/589 [2009] OJ L202/46; 2009/590 [2009] OJ L202/48; 2009/591 [2009] OJ L202/50.
112 Decisions 2010/282, 2010/283, 2010/284, 2010/285, 2010/286, 2010/287, 2010/288, 2010/289, 2010/290 [2010] OJ L125/32, 34, 36, 38, 40, 42, 44, 46, 48.
113 Decisions of 12 May 2010, unpublished.
114 Decisions 2010/422 [2010] OJ L199/26; 2010/407 [2010] OJ L189/15; 2010/401 [2010] OJ L186/30 and 2010/408 [2010] OJ L189/17, respectively.
115 Decisions of 30 November 2009, Council Docs 15753–15765/09; the 13 were Austria, Belgium, Czech Republic, Germany, Italy, the Netherlands, Portugal, Slovenia, Slovakia, France, Ireland, Spain and the United Kingdom.
116 Decision 2009/409 [2009] OJ L132/11.
117 Decision 2010/291 [2010] OJ L125/50.
118 Decision 2010/320 [2010] OJ L145/6; amended several times and recast as Decision 2011/734 [2011] OJ L296/18.

The 2008 financial crisis and the ensuing eurozone debt crisis engendered a **14.25**
number of responses which come in a number of guises:

- a European Financial Stability Mechanism (EFSM) established by
  Council Regulation in 2010;[119] administered by the Commission with
  authority to raise up to €60 thousand million for loans or extension of
  credit to member states in difficulty;
- the European Financial Stability Facility (EFSF),[120] created in 2010 by
  the then 16 eurozone member states (Estonia not having yet joined); the
  EFSF is a company based in Luxembourg and owned by those 16 member
  states, with authority to borrow up to €440 thousand million in order to
  issue bonds to a eurozone member state in difficulty and guaranteed by
  them;
- Treaty amendment: there grew concurrently a (primarily German) impetus for a tightening of discipline and the creation of a permanent
  bail-out fund within the eurozone. In early 2011 the European Council
  adopted a decision for amendment of the TFEU, adding a new paragraph
  3 to article 136 so as to allow for the creation of a stability mechanism to
  be available 'if indispensable to safeguard the stability of the euro area as a
  whole'.[121] The amendment is hoped to secure the necessary ratifications
  by, and so be in force in, January 2013;[122]
- the European Stability Mechanism (ESM), created by extra-Union treaty
  amongst the eurozone member states,[123] to raise and mobilise funding
  and provide financial assistance to ESM members experiencing or threatened by severe financial problems. Ratification and entry into force is
  anticipated by the end of 2012. It will assume the tasks of the EFSM and
  the EFSF after June 2013; prior to that it may top up EFSF lending to a
  consolidated ceiling of €500 thousand million;
- a 'Euro Plus Pact', agreed in 2011 amongst the eurozone heads of state
  and government plus those of Bulgaria, Denmark, Latvia, Lithuania,
  Poland and Romania (so all but the Czech Republic, Hungary, Sweden
  and the United Kingdom) with a view to tighter economic coordination of
  national policies and so increasing competitiveness and convergence.[124] It
  addresses for the most part areas still within national competences and
  represents a political, not legal, undertaking;

---

119 Regulation 407/2010 [2010] OJ L118/1.
120 EFSF Framework Agreement, adopted 9 June 2010.
121 Decision 2011/199 [2011] OJ L91/1, art. 1.
122 *Ibid.* art. 2.
123 Treaties of 11 July 2011 and 2 February 2012 establishing the European Stability Mechanism. This because
   pending the entry into force of art. 136(3) TFEU the Treaties provide no authority for it.
124 Brussels European Council, 24/25 March 2011, Presidency Conclusions, Annex I.

- the 'economic governance package', six legislative measures adopted in autumn 2011 designed to reinforce the stability and growth pact, strengthen corrective action, set out minimum requirements for national budgetary frameworks and prevent and correct macroeconomic imbalances;[125]
- the 'Fiscal Compact'. At the close of 2011 the European Council met in order further to strengthen economic convergence in the euro area, improve budgetary discipline and deepen economic union. But discussion of appropriate Treaty amendment to this end was met with a British veto. The remaining member states[126] therefore resolved to enter into an extra-Union treaty establishing a new 'fiscal rule' involving balanced budgets entrenched in national law, automatic correction in the event of deviation subject to the control of the Commission and the Court of Justice, stricter and automatic controls of the excessive deficit procedure, deeper fiscal integration and adjustments to and acceleration of the ESM Treaty.[127] The Treaty was signed by 25 of them, the Czechs joining the British in staying out, in early 2012[128] and will enter into force on 1 January 2013 provided (an unlikely event) at least 12 eurozone member states have ratified it.[129] The Treaty is open to accession by the Czech Republic and the United Kingdom ('Member States of the European Union other than the Contracting Parties'),[130] the clear political intent is that this should happen 'as soon as possible',[131] and it anticipates such

---

125 The package contains six measures: Regulation 1173/2011 [2011] OJ L306/1 on effective enforcement of budgetary surveillance; Regulation 1174/2011 [2011] OJ L306/8 on enforcement measures to correct excessive macroeconomic imbalances; Regulation 1175/2011 [2011] OJ L306/12 on strengthening the surveillance of budgetary positions and surveillance and coordination of economic policies; Regulation 1176/2011 [2011] OJ L306/25 on prevention and correction of macroeconomic imbalances; Regulation 1177/2011 [2011] OJ L306/33 on speeding up and clarifying the implementation of the excessive deficit procedure; and Directive 2011/85 [2011] OJ L306/41 on requirements for budgetary frameworks of the member states.

126 Immediately agreement was reached there was a firm commitment from 23 member states (the 17 eurozone countries and six more) to proceed, with a provisional commitment but no promise from the Czech Republic, Hungary and Sweden.

127 European Council, 9 December 2011, Statement by the Euro Area heads of state or government.

128 Treaty of 2 March 2012 on Stability, Coordination and Governance in the Economic and Monetary Union ('Fiscal Compact').

129 *Ibid.* art. 14(2). The treaty was approved (by a majority of 60:40) in an Irish referendum in May 2012, by the *Conseil constitutionnel* in August (decision n° 2012–653 de 9 août 2012, p. 13283) and by the *Bundesverfassungsgericht* in September (BVerfG, 12. September 2012 (*Europäischer Stabilitätsmechanismus*)). But in the meanwhile the Supreme Court in Ireland (sitting as seven judges) has asked the Court of Justice whether Irish ratification of the treaty is compatible with its obligations under the Union Treaties: *Pringle* v *Government of Ireland* [2012] IESC 47, decision of 31 July 2012; lodged as Case C-370/12 *Pringle v Government of Ireland*, pending; which, even if the proceedings are accelerated (as the Supreme Court has requested), will delay ratification for months.

130 *Ibid.* art. 15.

131 Statement by the Euro Area heads of state or government, n. 127 above, p. 7.

agreement and incorporation of 'the substance of this Treaty' into the Union Treaties within five years of its entry into force 'at most'.[132]

B. SOCIAL POLICY

1. Introduction

The original EEC Treaty had, at best, modest social goals. In fact the European **14.26** Coal and Steel Treaty was, within its remit, more forthcoming.[133] Notwithstanding references to social interests in the Preamble,[134] no element of it figured in the Community's task, its activities included only the establishment of a European Social Fund 'to improve employment opportunities for workers and to contribute to the raising of their standard of living',[135] and although there was a separate Title on Social Policy[136] it was, other than the provisions establishing the Social Fund, anodyne: the Commission was charged with promoting cooperation amongst the member states in a number of social spheres, by (limited) means of producing studies, delivering opinions and arranging consultation.[137] There was no dedicated Treaty base for social legislation, and of possible interest only a lonely provision on, as between men and women, equal pay for equal work.[138] A reasonable silk purse was fashioned from this sow's ear: legislation setting out the detail of the free movement of workers included substantial social and social security elements, although generally seeking to ensure for the migrant worker simply the standards enjoyed by home workers;[139] and other legislation trenching heavily in the social sphere was adopted under articles 100 and/or 235 EEC (articles 115/352 TFEU), although not for that purpose, the social elements of this common market legislation (ostensibly) incidental only. Under the Treaty as it was, the Community could do no more.

---

132   Fiscal Compact Treaty, n. 128 above, art. 16.
133   See ECSC Treaty, art. 46 (re-employment of workers made redundant by market developments or technical change), art. 46(5) (improving working conditions and living standards) and arts 68–9 (wages and movement of workers).
134   EEC Treaty, preamble, 2nd indent ('Resolved to ensure the economic and social progress of their countries') and 3rd indent ('Affirming as the essential objective of their efforts the constant improvement of the living and working conditions of their peoples').
135   EEC Treaty, art. 2.
136   Title III, arts 117–28.
137   *Ibid.* art. 118.
138   *Ibid.* art. 119.
139   See especially Regulation 1612/68 [1968] JO L257/2 (now Regulation 492/2011 [2011] OJ L141/1), and especially art. 7(2): a migrant worker enjoys 'the same social ... advantages as national workers'. The irony is that, owing to the wholly internal rule, the rights enjoyed by migrant works in some circumstances eclipse those enjoyed by home workers.

14.27   By the time of Maastricht the ground had shifted significantly. Now the Community's task included the promotion of 'a high level of employment and of social protection, the raising of the standard of living and quality of life, and economic and social cohesion and solidarity among Member States'[140] and also included its activities being a policy in the social sphere[141] (on an equal Treaty footing with all Community activities) and the strengthening of economic and social cohesion.[142] The effect was liberating and substantial. As the Court of Justice was to say subsequently,

> according to Article 3(1)(c) and (j) EC, the activities of the Community are to include not only an 'internal market characterised by the abolition, as between Member States, of obstacles to the free movement of goods, persons, services and capital', but also 'a policy in the social sphere'. Article 2 EC states that the Community is to have as its task, *inter alia*, the promotion of 'a harmonious, balanced and sustainable development of economic activities' and 'a high level of employment and of social protection'.
>
> Since the Community has thus not only an economic but also a social purpose, the rights under the provisions of the Treaty on the free movement of goods, persons, services and capital must be balanced against the objectives pursued by social policy.[143]

Treaty authority for (minimal) harmonisation of legislation in relation to improvements in the working environment and the health and safety of workers had been provided by the Single European Act,[144] and a separate chapter on education, vocational training and youth added by Maastricht to the Title. Amsterdam was to add 'equality between men and women' as a Community task,[145] the 'eliminat[ion of] inequalities, and promot[ion of] equality, between men and women' as an integration clause covering all Community activities[146] and a new Title on employment.[147] It also extended Community legislative authority to social fields beyond health and safety.[148] In turn the TFEU marks another reorganisation, the result barely recognisable from the original EEC texts, providing now distinct Titles on

---

140   EC Treaty (pre-Amsterdam), art. 2.
141   *Ibid.* art. 3(i) (art. 3(1)(i) post-Amsterdam). The Social Fund was drawn into the social policy, the latter 'comprising' (*comprenant*) the Fund.
142   *Ibid.* art. 3(j) (art. 3(1)(j) post-Amsterdam).
143   Case C-438/05 *International Transport Workers' Union and anor* v *Viking Line* [2007] ECR I-10779, at paras 78–9.
144   EEC Treaty, art. 118a.
145   EC Treaty (post-Amsterdam), art. 2.
146   *Ibid.* art. 3(2).
147   *Ibid.* Title VIII, arts 125–30.
148   *Ibid.* art. 137(2).

- employment;[149]
- social policy;[150]
- the European Social Fund;[151]
- education, vocational training, youth and sport;[152] and
- economic, social and territorial cohesion,[153]

and adding integration clauses on promotion of high levels of employment, education, training and protection of human health; of adequate social protection; and combating social exclusion and discrimination based upon sex, racial or ethnic origin, religion or belief, disability, age or sexual orientation.[154]

Even as significant Community authority in the field of social policy emerged **14.28** and developed, there remained an implicit presumption of the pre-eminence of national policies. It is still the case, and is of course consistent with the principle of subsidiarity. Social policy ('for the aspects defined in this Treaty')[155] is an area of shared competence, a task borne by both ('[t]he Union and the Member States … shall have as their objectives … ').[156] Those objectives are

the promotion of employment, improved living and working conditions, so as to make possible their harmonisation while the improvement is being maintained, proper [*adéquate*, *angemessen*] social protection, dialogue between management and labour [the social dialogue], the development of human resources with a view to lasting high employment and the combating of exclusion,[157]

---

149 TFEU, Title IX, arts 145–50, first introduced into the Treaty by Amsterdam. But employment is, oddly, not numbered amongst the Union competences in arts 3, 4 and 6; it is therefore presumably a competence shared with the member states; TFEU, art. 4(1).
150 *Ibid.* Title X, arts 151–61.
151 *Ibid.* Title XI, arts 162–4.
152 *Ibid.* Title XII, arts 165–6.
153 *Ibid.* Title XVIII, arts 174–8.
154 *Ibid.* arts 9, 10.
155 *Ibid.* art. 4(2)(b).
156 *Ibid.* art. 151, 1st para.
157 *Ibid.* In all Union languages other than English, Latvian and Maltese (which reflect the English), dialogue between management and labour is rendered 'the social dialogue' or 'dialogue with social partners' (or, in Danish and Swedish, labour market partners). The social dialogue took formal shape in 1985 at Val Duchesse between the social partners, represented by the Union des Industries de la Communauté Européenne (UNICE) and the European Trade Union Confederation (ETUC), and was drawn into the Treaty (via the Social Agreement) in 1993. Recognised social partner representatives (and 'general cross-industry organisations') now include BUSINESSEUROPE (as UNICE became in 2007), ETUC, the Centre européen des entreprises à participation publique et des entreprises d'intérêt économique général (CEEP) and, sometimes, the Union Européenne de l'Artisanat et des Petites et Moyennes Entreprises (UEAPME).

whilst always taking adequate account of the diversity in national practices, in particular in the field of contractual relations, and the need to maintain the competitiveness of the Union's economy.[158]

14.29 The Union is to support and complement the activities of the Member States in the following fields:

(a) improvement in particular of the working environment to protect worker health and safety;

(b) working conditions;

(c) social security and social protection of workers;

(d) protection of workers where their employment contract is terminated;

(e) the information and consultation of workers;

(f) representation and collective defence of the interests of workers and employers, including co-determination;

(g) conditions of employment for third country nationals legally residing in Union territory;

(h) the integration of persons excluded from the labour market;

(i) equality between men and women with regard to labour market opportunities and treatment at work;

(j) the combating of social exclusion; and

(k) the modernisation of social protection systems.[159]

The Parliament and the Council may adopt measures to encourage cooperation between the member states (but excluding harmonisation of national laws) and, for fields (a)–(i), Directives on minimum requirements.[160] For the fields in (c), (d), (f) and (g) Council unanimity is required, although a mini-bridging clause provides for a unanimous Council to alter all of them but (c) to the ordinary legislative procedure.[161] At their joint request, implementation of a Directive may be entrusted to the social partners, subject to a right (and duty) of legislative override should it be necessary to guarantee the results imposed by the Directive.[162] The terms of a framework agreement adopted by them and given effect by a Directive may be directly effective (if they meet the standard tests) as 'an integral component' of the Directive.[163] As flanking measures the TFEU now requires (found oddly amongst the categories and areas of Union competences) the Union to take measures to ensure coordination of the

---

158   *Ibid.* Title XVIII, art. 151, 2nd para.
159   *Ibid.* art. 153(1).
160   *Ibid.* art. 153(2).
161   *Ibid.*
162   *Ibid.* art. 153(3).
163   Case C-268/06 *Impact* v *Minister for Agriculture and Food and ors* [2008] ECR I-2483, at para. 58.

member states' employment policies,[164] 'in particular' by defining guidelines[165] of which the member states must take account in their employment policies,[166] and may take 'initiatives' to ensure coordination of their social policies.[167] The Commission is to encourage and facilitate, through studies, opinions and consultation, cooperation between the member states and coordination of their action in all social policy fields addressed by the Treaties, particularly in matters relating to employment, labour law and working conditions, basic and advanced vocational training, social security, prevention of occupational accidents and diseases, occupational hygiene and rights of association and collective bargaining,[168] it being emphasised that these are essentially national competences and Union activity to be of 'a complementary nature'.[169]

2. Concurrent events

14.30 Whilst they were at the start modest in their social ambitions, events and forces were taking shape outside the Treaties, a mirror and product of the rapid introduction and expansion of social legislation in the 1970s and 1980s. The Treaties lagged behind but the Community was not unmindful of these developments, even though it did not set the pace.

(a) European Social Charter

14.31 In 1961 the Council of Europe adopted the European Social Charter in Turin.[170] Then, and still, external to the Community order, it is cited in the Treaties ('having in mind fundamental social rights such as those set out in the European Social Charter signed at Turin on 18 October 1961')[171] and the Court of Justice still refers to it from time to time.[172]

---

164 TFEU, art. 5(2).
165 *Ibid.*
166 *Ibid.* art. 148(2). The guidelines are drawn up annually by the Council; see most recently Decision 2011/308 [2011] OJ L138/56.
167 *Ibid.* art. 5(3).
168 *Ibid.* art. 156.
169 Declaration (No. 31) on Article 156 of the TFEU.
170 Convention of 18 October 1961, CETS No. 35, in force 26 February 1965; revised in 1996, CETS No. 163, in force 1 July 1999.
171 TFEU, art. 151, 1st para.
172 E.g., Case C-540/03 *Parliament v Council* (Family Reunification) [2006] ECR 5769, at para. 107; Case C-438/05 *International Transport Workers' Union v Viking Line* [2007] ECR I-10779, at para. 43; Case C-341/05 *Laval un partneri v Svenska Byggnadsarbetareförbundet and ors* (Vaxholm) [2007] ECR I-11767, at para. 90; Case C-268/06 *Impact v Minister for Agriculture and Food and ors* [2008] ECR I-2483, at para. 113; Cases C-395 and 396/08 *Istituto nazionale della previdenza sociale v Bruno and ors* [2010] ECR I-5119, at para. 31; Case C-282/10 *Dominguez v Centre informatique du Centre Ouest Atlantique and anor*, judgment of 24 January 2012, not yet reported, per A-G Trstenjak at para. 104 of her opinion.

(b)   Community Charter of the Fundamental Social Rights of Workers

14.32   Distinct from the European Social Charter, but confusingly commonly referred to as the Social Charter, is the Community Charter of the Fundamental Social Rights of Workers, adopted at the Strasbourg summit in 1989 in the form of a declaration approved by the heads of state and government of all (then) member states save the United Kingdom.[173] It too is cited in the Treaties as a source of social rights which the Union and the member states 'have in mind'.[174] The Charter is predicated on the belief that 'social consensus ... is an essential condition for ensuring sustained economic development' and that 'in the context of the establishment of the single European market, the same importance must be attached to the social aspects as to the economic aspects'.[175] It is not a legislative act, but a blueprint for the development of social legislation within the Community. At the same time the Commission adopted an Action Programme containing more specific guidelines and draft proposals for legislation.[176] The Social Charter and the Action Programme address areas such as freedom of movement, rights in employment, living and working conditions, social protection, freedom of association and collective bargaining, training, worker participation, health and safety and protection of children, adolescents, the elderly and the disabled. But both stress the pre-eminence of the member states rather than collective Community policy,[177] and here again subsidiarity plays an important role.

14.33   The legal and persuasive force of the Social Charter is best summed up by Advocate-General Kokott:

> The [Social Charter] was adopted at the European Council meeting in Strasbourg ... in the form of a declaration. It does not therefore have the legally binding status of primary legal acts as do the Treaty and ... the protocols annexed to it. Nor can the Charter be considered a binding instrument of secondary legislation because the European Council does not have legislative competence. It is simply a declaration of general socio-political aims the purpose of which is to provide the Union with impetus for its development in the field of social policy.
>
> Although, therefore, [it] is not a binding legal instrument as such, various provisions of Community law do nevertheless reveal a close connection with it that should reasonably be taken into account when interpreting and applying Community law. The Court of Justice has also already called on the Charter as an aid to interpretation with regard to provisions of this kind ...

---

173   Declaration of 9 December 1989; for the text see Social Europe 1/90.
174   TFEU, art. 151, 1st para.
175   Social Charter, Preamble, 5th and 2nd recitals.
176   COM(89) 568 final.
177   Social Charter, Preamble, recital 15 and point 27.

[Q]uite apart from such provisions that are closely linked to it by their specific socio-political content, the [Social Charter] does have to be taken into account when interpreting and applying Community law. The aims of social progress and a high level of social protection, as stated in Article 2 EC, in the second and third recitals in the preamble to the Treaty Establishing the European Community and in the eighth recital in the preamble to the Treaty on European Union, apply to all Community activities. The fourth recital in the preamble to the Treaty on European Union also makes such express reference to the Charter defining those aims.[178]

Various provisions of the Social Charter found their way eventually into the EU Charter of Fundamental Rights.

(c) Social Protocol and Agreement (1993–99)

At the intergovernmental conference which led to the adoption of the Treaty on European Union, 11 of the then 12 member states were, in the spirit of the Social Charter, keen to agree to more far-reaching provisions in the social sphere. To them social solidarity was an 'essential condition' of the single market,[179] the latter unthinkable absent due consideration given the former. But this was anathema to the Conservative government in the United Kingdom, leaving no possibility of incorporation of provisions of real substance into the general social provisions of the Treaty. The result was the adoption of a Protocol on Social Policy attached to the EC Treaty,[180] sometimes (wrongly) referred to as the 'Social Chapter'. The Protocol was an early example, *par excellence*, of primary variable geometry, or the enhanced cooperation which was to follow: it authorised the 11 member states other than the United Kingdom to pursue a social policy and to use Community institutions and procedures to that end, *but* the provisions adopted were not to apply to or in the United Kingdom. The areas addressed were set out in an Agreement annexed to the Protocol, hence occasional reference to 'the Social Protocol and Agreement'. The Agreement provided a framework for substantive rules following the objectives of the Social Charter but including also proper/adequate social protection, the social dialogue and the development of human resources.[181] The United Kingdom was (necessarily) a party to the Social Protocol but was *not* a party to the Agreement, it took no part in Council deliberations within the sphere of the Agreement for which there was a special system of weighted voting, and it bore none of the financial consequences other than administrative costs entailed for the institutions.[182] Misgivings at the risks in this early foray into primary

14.34

---

178   C-313/02 *Wippel* v *Peek and Kloppenburg* [2004] ECR I-9483, at paras 37–40 of her opinion.
179   Social Charter, Preamble, 5th recital.
180   Protocol No. 14 on Social Policy.
181   Agreement on Social Policy, art. 1.
182   Protocol on Social Policy, arts 2–3. On the financial consequences of the Social Protocol in the United Kingdom see *Monckton* v *Lord Advocate* 1995 SLT 1201 (OH).

variable geometry were overcome by recognition of UK intransigence making no other course possible. It also left the remaining 11 member states free to proceed more vigorously, liberated from the wrecking tactics frequently deployed by the United Kingdom in the social sphere.

14.35 Austria, Finland and Sweden acceded to the Social Agreement upon accession to the Union. Following election of the Labour government in 1997 the British antipathy dissolved, but the Social Protocol had been (intentionally) drafted in such a way as to make opting into the Agreement impossible. It was agreed at the intergovernmental conference which would lead to the Treaty of Amsterdam that the Social Protocol should be abandoned, and, not content to wait, at the Amsterdam summit in 1997 the European Council noted 'with great satisfaction' that the United Kingdom wished to accept the measures already adopted and so 'a means had to be found, in advance of the signature of the Amsterdam Treaty, to give legal effect to those wishes'.[183] Accordingly the existing Social Agreement measures – four Directives[184] – were extended (possibly unlawfully) to the United Kingdom ('the reunification of the fifteen') by Directives adopted (unanimously) by the Council under article 100 EC (article 115 TFEU).[185] The Protocol was then repealed by Amsterdam and the provisions of the Social Agreement grafted to various articles in the Treaty chapter on social policy.

(d)   EU Charter of Fundamental Rights

14.36 The EU Charter of Fundamental Rights, elevated by Lisbon to the same legal value as the Treaties,[186] has a Title IV on 'Solidarity'. The Union therefore 'recognises' as a right, a freedom or a principle:

- workers' rights to information and consultation within their employer undertaking;
- a right of collective bargaining and action;
- a right of access to free placement services;
- protection in the event of unjustified dismissal;
- fair and just working conditions;
- a prohibition of child labour and protection of young people at work;

---

183   European Council 16–17 June 1997, Conclusions of the Presidency, *Bulletin EU* 6–1997, para. 1.8.
184   Directive 94/45 [1994] OJ L254/64 on works councils for employee consultation; Directive 96/34 [1996] OJ L145/4 on a framework agreement on parental leave; Directive 97/80 [1998] OJ L14/6 on the burden of proof in cases of sex discrimination; Directive 97/81 [1998] OJ L14/9 on a framework agreement on part-time work.
185   Directive 97/74 [1998] OJ L10/22 (for Directive 94/45); Directive 97/75 [1998] OJ L10/24 (for Directive 96/34); Directive 98/23 [1998] OJ L34/10 (for Directive 97/81); Directive 98/52 [1998] OJ L205/66 (for Directive 97/80).
186   TEU, art. 6(1); see 6.116 above.

- social rights for the family, especially protection from dismissal for reasons of maternity and a right to paid maternity/parental leave;
- social security and social assistance;
- a right of access to preventive healthcare and to medical treatment.[187]

Title IV,

> relat[ing] to ... social fundamental rights and principles ... is regarded as one of the most controversial areas in the evolution of the Charter. There was dispute not only over the fundamental question whether social rights and principles should be incorporated into the Charter, but also how many social rights should be included, how they should be organised in detail, what binding force they should have, and whether they should be classified as fundamental rights or as principles.[188]

It remains to be seen if and how far this will influence both the Union legislator and the Court in the social sphere. It is Title IV from which Poland and the United Kingdom have in some measure opted (and the Czech Republic may opt) out, nothing in it creating justiciable rights there except insofar as such rights are provided in national law.[189]

3. Sex discrimination

Of all social matters addressed by Union law it is the area of sex discrimination **14.37** and pay which has deepest roots in the Treaties and keenest teeth. The original purpose of the rule was to ensure that undertakings in those member states (particularly France) which already provided for equal pay did not suffer through being required to compete with undertakings in other member states which did not proscribe pay differential based upon sex. The effect has gone well beyond that.

(a) Article 157 TFEU

Article 119 EEC required that member states ensure 'the principle that men **14.38** and women should receive equal pay for equal work'. As a reflection of intervening legislation and case law Amsterdam expanded this to equal pay for work of equal value. Article 157 TFEU now provides:

---

187 EU Charter, arts 27–35.
188 Cases C-411 and 493/10 *R (NS) & ME and ors* v *Secretary of State for the Home Department and ors*, judgment of 21 December 2011, not yet reported, per A-G Trstenjak at para. 172 of her opinion.
189 Protocol (No. 30) on the Application of the Charter of Fundamental Rights to Poland and to the United Kingdom, art. 1(2); see 6.118 above.

1. Each Member State shall ensure that the principle of equal pay for male and female workers for equal work or work of equal value is applied.
2. For the purpose of this Article, 'pay' means the ordinary basic or minimum wage or salary and any other consideration, whether in cash or in kind, which the worker receives directly or indirectly, in respect of his employment, from his employer.

Equal pay without discrimination based on sex means:

(a) that pay for the same work at piece rates shall be calculated on the basis of the same unit of measurement;
(b) that pay for work at time rates shall be the same for the same job.

There follows further Amsterdam additions, a Treaty base for legislation to ensure the application of the principle[190] and, drawn out of the Maastricht Social Agreement, tolerance of positive action in national (but not Union) measures for the specific advantage of an underrepresented sex making it easier to pursue a vocational activity or preventing or compensating for disadvantages in professional careers.[191] The Charter of Fundamental Rights now prohibits any discrimination on grounds of sex and enshrines the right to equal treatment between men and women 'in all areas, including employment, work and pay'.[192]

14.39 From the beginning this was visited by some confusion. The word 'pay' is too narrow a translation of terms used in the original language texts (*Entgelt, rémunérations, retribuzioni, beloning*) and has given rise to much misunderstanding. 'Pay' is defined by article 157 in very broad terms. Even 'consideration' in article 157(2) is shy of the mark, other texts using words (*avantages; Vergütungen; voordelen*) meaning advantage or recompense. Thus it is that favourable rates for railway travel for family employees,[193] pensions paid under a contracted-out private occupational scheme and any benefits paid by an employer to an employee in connection with his compulsory redundancy,[194] a severance grant[195] and compensation for unfair dismissal,[196] and maternity benefits,[197] have been held to be 'pay'.

---

190   TFEU, art. 157(3).
191   *Ibid.* art. 157(4). See n. 280 below and accompanying text.
192   EU Charter, arts 21 and 23.
193   Case 12/81 *Garland v British Rail Engineering Ltd* [1982] ECR 359; Case C-249/96 *Grant v South-West Trains* [1998] ECR I-621.
194   Case 171/88 *Rinner-Kühn v FWW Spezial-Gebäudereinigung* [1989] ECR 2743; Case 262/88 *Barber v Guardian Royal Exchange* [1990] ECR I-1889.
195   Case C-33/89 *Kowalska v Freie und Hansestadt Hamburg* [1990] ECR I-2591.
196   Case C-167/97 *R v Secretary of State for Employment, ex parte Seymour-Smith* [1999] ECR I-623.
197   Case C-342/93 *Gillespie v Northern Health and Social Services Boards* [1996] ECR I-475.

Long before social provisions were absorbed formally into the Treaties, article **14.40**
157 had the effect of an infectious agent drawing social concerns into Community law:

> Article [157] pursues a double aim.
>
> First ... the aim ... is to avoid a situation in which undertakings established in States which have actually implemented the principle of equal pay suffer a competitive disadvantage in intra-Community competition as compared with undertakings established in States which have not yet eliminated discrimination against women workers as regards pay.
>
> Secondly, this provision forms part of the social objectives of the Community, which is not merely an economic union, but is at the same time intended, by common action, to ensure social progress and seek the constant improvement of the living and working conditions of their peoples, as is emphasized by the Preamble to the Treaty. ...
>
> This double aim, which is at once economic and social, shows that the principle of equal pay forms part of the foundations of the Community.[198]

Thus social goals became part of Community policy with a parity with economic goals, and subsequently, in some measure, a priority:

> [T]he Court has repeatedly held that the right not to be discriminated against on grounds of sex is one of the fundamental human rights whose observance the Court has a duty to ensure. In view of that case-law, it must be concluded that the economic aim pursued by Article [157] of the Treaty, namely the elimination of distortions of competition between undertakings established in different Member States, is secondary to the social aim pursued by the same provision, which constitutes the expression of a fundamental human right.[199]

And its influence was not restricted simply to pay.

(b) Implementing legislation

The basic rule of the Treaties, which related originally only to the consideration **14.41**
received from an employer in respect of employment, was refined by subsequent legislation (to its critics, by dubious Treaty authority) and expanded out of all recognition from the intention of its framers. As will be apparent, the emphasis has been upon rights in employment law generally and combating sex discrimination in particular. A number of Directives provided for:

---

198 Case 43/75 *Defrenne* v *SABENA* (Defrenne II) [1976] ECR 455, at paras 8–12.
199 Case C-50/96 *Deutsche Telekom* v *Schröder* [2000] ECR I-743, at para. 57.

- equal pay for men and women for work of equal value;[200]
- equal treatment for men and women as regards access to employment, vocational training and promotion, and working conditions;[201]
- equal treatment in occupational social security schemes;[202] and
- burden of proof in cases of (alleged) discrimination based on sex.[203]

In 2006 they were consolidated into a single Directive, on the principle of equal opportunities and equal treatment of men and women in matters of employment and occupation (Gender Equality Directive).[204] The core of it is a prohibition of direct or indirect discrimination on grounds of sex (but including harassment, sexual or otherwise, irrespective of discrimination):

- in employment at all levels, public or private, including access, recruitment, selection and promotion;
- in access to all types and at all levels of vocational guidance and training, including work experience;
- in employment and working conditions, including dismissal, as well as pay; and
- in membership of, and involvement in, an organisation of workers or employers, or any organisation whose members carry on a particular profession.[205]

It also protects employment rights during and following maternity and paternity leave (but does not require the provision of paternity leave),[206] prohibits direct or indirect discrimination in occupational social security schemes for the working population (including self-employment) against sickness, invalidity, old age (including early retirement), industrial accidents and occupational diseases, unemployment, other social benefits in cash or in kind if consideration from an employer;[207] and lays down significant enforcement provisions.[208]

14.42 The Gender Equality Directive was adopted by authority of article 157(3) TFEU. There were other Directives left out of the consolidation exercise

---

200 Directive 75/117 [1975] OJ L45/19 (by authority of art. 100 EEC (art. 115 TFEU)).
201 Directive 76/207 [1976] OJ L39/40 (art. 235 EEC (art. 352 TFEU)).
202 Directive 86/378 [1986] OJ L225/40 (arts 100 and 235 EEC combined); also Directive 96/97 [1997] OJ L46/20 (art. 100 EC (pre-Amsterdam)).
203 Directive 97/80 [1998] OJ L14/6 (the Social Agreement).
204 Directive 2006/54 [2006] OJ L204/23 (art. 141(3) EC (art. 157(3) TFEU)).
205 *Ibid.* art. 14.
206 *Ibid.* arts 2(2)(c), 15, 16. But see Directive 2010/18 (n. 212 below), Annex, clause 2.2.
207 *Ibid.* arts 5–7.
208 *Ibid.* arts 17–19.

because they would (or might) require a different, and more onerous, Treaty base. They are Directives on:

- equal treatment for men and women in matters of social security;[209]
- equal treatment in self-employed occupations;[210]
- safety and health at work of pregnant workers and workers who have recently given birth or are breastfeeding;[211] and
- a framework agreement on parental leave.[212]

Of the three anti-discrimination Directives adopted to date under article 19 **14.43** TFEU, one addresses sex discrimination – a 2004 Directive on equal treatment between women and men in the access to and supply of goods and services (Goods and Services Directive).[213] It is the first legislation on gender equality to venture beyond the confines of the labour market (and employment and occupation expressly excluded from its ambit).[214] It is intended to ensure equal treatment between men and women in access to and supply of goods and services, free of direct discrimination based upon sex, including less favourable treatment of women for reasons of pregnancy and maternity; of indirect discrimination based on sex; and of harassment and sexual harassment.[215] The use of sex as a factor in the calculation of premiums and benefits for the purposes of insurance and related financial services may not result in differences in individuals' premiums and benefits.[216] Originally the Directive purported to permit exactly that 'where the use of sex is a determining factor in the assessment of risk based on relevant and accurate actuarial and statistical data'.[217] This was included at United Kingdom insistence and heralded as one of its periodic 'victories for common sense'. Advocate-General Kokott found it 'astonishing' (*erstaunlich*) that the provision could be argued to be compatible with the principle of equal treatment[218] (as it was argued by all six member states intervening and by the Council and the Commission),[219] and the Court duly set it aside with effect from December 2012.[220]

---

209 Directive 79/7 [1979] OJ L6/24 (arts 43 and 100 EEC combined).
210 Directive 86/613 [1986] OJ L359/56 (arts 100 and 235 combined); replaced by Directive 2010/41 [2010] OJ L180/1 (art. 157(3) TFEU) from August 2012.
211 Directive 92/85 [1992] OJ L348/1.
212 Directive 96/34 [1996] OJ L145/4; replaced by Directive 2010/18 [2010] OJ L68/13 (implementing the 2009 revised framework agreement on parental leave) from March 2012.
213 Directive 2004/113 [2004] OJ L373/37.
214 *Ibid.* art. 3(4).
215 *Ibid.* art. 4.
216 *Ibid.* art. 5(1).
217 *Ibid.* art. 5(2).
218 Case C-236/09 *Association Belge des Consommateurs Test-Achats and ors* v *Conseil des ministres*, judgment of 1 March 2011, not yet reported, at para. 22 of her opinion.
219 *Ibid.* at para. 25 of the opinion.
220 Case C-236/09 *Test-Achats*, n. 218 above.

4. Other social legislation

(a) General

14.44 The Council has adopted a number of other measures in the field of employment protection:

- a general Directive on health and safety at work;[221]
- the Working Time Directive, adopted in 1993 on health and safety grounds.[222] It provides for daily and weekly maximum working time and rest and break periods, with special rules on night work, and paid annual leave ('a particularly important principle of Community social law from which there can be no derogations'),[223] in all sectors of activity, both public and private, with a number of derogations for, for example, air, rail, road, sea, inland waterway and lake transport, sea fishing and seafarers (many of these being subject to other transport policy legislation), management, family workers, the clergy and the activities of doctors in training. It was challenged immediately and (essentially) unsuccessfully for incorrect Treaty base by the United Kingdom,[224] where it remains in some quarters contentious still. It was consolidated in 2003,[225] with the derogation for junior doctors (a particular sticking point with the United Kingdom) removed from August 2009;[226]
- a Directive on the protection of young people at work;[227]
- Directives on employee protection in part-time,[228] fixed-term[229] and agency[230] work. The first two implement social partner framework agreements in their respective fields, the third (the Agency Workers' Directive

---

221 Directive 89/391 [1989] OJ L183/1 (art. 118a EEC). The Directive called for more specific Directives to ensure health and safety as regards work equipment, personal protective equipment, work with visual display units, handling of heavy loads involving risk of back injury, temporary or mobile work sites and fisheries and agriculture but applies in their absence; art. 16 and Annex.

222 Directive 93/104 [1993] OJ L307/20 concerning certain aspects of the organisation of working time (art. 118a EEC).

223 Case C-173/99 *R* v *Secretary of State for Trade and Industry, ex parte Broadcasting, Entertainment, Cinematographic and Theatre Union* [2001] ECR I-4881, at para. 43; Cases C-350 and 520/06 *Schultz-Hoff* v *Deutsche Rentversicherung Bund* and *Stringer and ors* v *Her Majesty's Revenue and Customs* [2009] ECR I-179, at para. 22; Case C-282/10 *Dominguez* v *Centre informatique du Centre Ouest Atlantique and anor*, judgment of 24 January 2012, not yet reported, at para. 16 (substituting 'European Union' for 'Community').

224 Case C-84/94 *United Kingdom* v *Council* [1996] ECR I-5755. The Court annulled the Directive only insofar as it provided that the 'minimum uninterrupted rest period' of 24 hours should 'in principle' be on Sunday without justifying it on health and safety grounds.

225 Directive 2003/88 [2003] OJ L299/9 (art. 137(3) EC).

226 *Ibid.* art. 17(5).

227 Directive 94/33 [1993] OJ L216/12 (art. 118a EC (pre-Amsterdam)) – presumably compatible with rules on the prohibition of discrimination on the basis of age; see below.

228 Directive 97/81 [1998] OJ L14/9.

229 Directive 1999/70 [1999] OJ L175/43.

230 Directive 2008/104 [2008] OJ L327/9.

(AWD)) adopted following failure of the social partners to reach agreement follows the same pattern. They seek to ensure the application of a principle of non-discrimination, that, as much as possible, the part-time/fixed-term/agency worker is treated no less favourably than a comparable permanent worker unless different treatment is justified upon objective grounds[231] and to prevent abuse arising from, for example, the use of successive fixed-term employment contracts[232] or unnecessary prohibitions or restrictions on the use of temporary agency work;[233]

- a Directive on the protection of workers posted in another member state by an employer undertaking providing services there (Posted Workers Directive);[234]
- Directives harmonising the law on collective redundancy[235] and on safeguarding the rights of employees in the event of a transfer of ownership of their employer undertaking (TUPE Directive)[236] or insolvency of their employer;[237]
- the Directive on works councils,[238] requiring that all 'Community-scale undertakings' (any with at least 1,000 employees within the Union and at least 150 in each of at least two member states)[239] set up a European Works Council or an information and consultation procedure for informing and consulting employees, established by the central management and a special negotiating body acting 'in a spirit of cooperation with a view to reaching an agreement on the [necessary] detailed arrangements'.[240] For smaller undertakings (those with at least 50 or 20 employees in one member state, the choice left to the member states) there is a general framework setting out minimum requirements for the right to information and consultation of employees.[241] There are special rules on employee participation in the European Company (SE) and the European Cooperative Society (SCE), set out in Directives 'supplementing' the statutes providing for their creation, one for each.[242] A Directive on the

---

231 Directive 97/81, Annex (the framework agreement), clauses 1 and 4.1; Directive 1999/70, Annex (the framework agreement), clauses 1 and 4.1; Directive 2008/104, arts 2 and 5.

232 Directive 1999/70, Annex, clauses 1(a) and 5. See Case C-212/04 *Adeneler and ors* v *Ellinikos Organismos Galaktos* [2006] ECR I-6057; Case C-268/06 *Impact* v *Minister for Agriculture and Food and ors* [2008] ECR I-2483.

233 Directive 2008/104, art. 4.

234 Directive 96/71 [1997] OJ L18/1.

235 Directive 98/59 [1998] OJ L225/16.

236 Directive 2001/23 [2001] OJ L82/16 (updating Directive 77/187 [1977] OJ L61/26). See Case C-382/92 *Commission* v *United Kingdom* [1994] ECR I-2435.

237 Directive 2008/94 [2008] OJ L283/36 (updating Directive 80/987 [1980] OJ L283/23).

238 Directive 2009/38 [2009] OJ L122/28 (updating Directive 94/45 [1994] OJ L254/64).

239 *Ibid.* art. 2(1)(a).

240 *Ibid.* art. 6(1).

241 Directive 2002/14 [2002] OJ L80/29.

242 Directive 2001/86 [2001] OJ L294/22 (for SEs); Directive 2003/72 [2003] OJ L207/25 (for SCEs).

introduction of worker participation on the German model ('co-determination'/*Mitbestimmung*), the Fifth Company Law, or Vredeling, Directive, of which the Works Councils Directive is a watered down version, was proposed by the Commission in 1980[243] but has long gone cold.

(b) Anti-discrimination Directives

14.45 The EC Treaty was amended by Amsterdam to authorise the Council to adopt (by unanimity and, now, with the consent of the Parliament) legislation to combat discrimination based upon sex, racial or ethnic origin, religion or belief, disability, age or sexual orientation.[244] It is 'an expression of the commitment of the Community legal order to the principle of equal treatment and non-discrimination'.[245] Three Directives (the Anti-discrimination Directives) have been adopted to date. The first two are:

- Directive 2000/43 on equal treatment of persons irrespective of racial or ethnic origin (Race Directive);[246] and
- Directive 2000/78 on equal treatment in employment and occupation (Framework Employment Directive).[247]

The latter prohibits discrimination upon five grounds – religion, belief, disability, age and sexual orientation – so excluding nationality, sex, racial origin or ethnic origin, these subject to other measures. Both cover discrimination in employment and occupation, including conditions for access, selection criteria and recruitment, promotion, access to vocational guidance and (re)training, employment and working conditions, including dismissals and pay, and membership of workers' or employers' organisations.[248] But Directive 2000/78 does not cover social protection, including social security and healthcare, social advantages, education and access to and supply of publicly available goods and services, including housing, whilst Directive 2000/43 does.[249] Both were required to be implemented in 2003 but progress was patchy, causing the Commission to initiate enforcement proceedings against a number of member

---

243   [1980] OJ C297/33.
244   EC Treaty, art. 13; now TFEU, art. 19. Prior to Lisbon the Parliament was required only to be consulted.
245   Case C-303/06 *Coleman* v *Attridge Law and anor* [2008] ECR I-5603, per A-G Poiares Maduro at para. 8 of his opinion.
246   Directive 2000/43 [2000] OJ L180/22.
247   Directive 2000/78 [2000] OJ L303/16.
248   Directive 2000/43, art. 3(1)(a)–(d); Directive 2000/78, art. 3(1).
249   Directive 2000/43, art. 3(1)(e)–(h).

states.[250] In Slovakia the implementation of Directive 2000/43 led to a minor constitutional scuffle.[251] The rights contained in the Directives are to be interpreted broadly.[252]

The Third Directive adopted under article 19 is the 2004 Goods and Services **14.46** Directive, discussed above. A fourth (the Equal Treatment Directive), to close the gap between Directives 2000/43 and 2000/78 and extend the fields in which discrimination on grounds of religion and belief, disability, age and sexual orientation is prohibited beyond employment and occupation (Directive 2000/78) to education, social security, health care and housing, was proposed in 2008 and is, at the time of writing, still before the Council.[253]

5. Application of the rules

The social provisions have, not surprisingly, given rise to extensive litigation, **14.47** which has met with some complexity. The prohibition of discrimination set out in article 157 TFEU has, of itself, both vertical and horizontal direct effect.[254] Other than the competition rules which are addressed to private persons (undertakings) and so horizontally directly effective and only indirectly vertically directly effective,[255] this was unique in the Treaties until *Angonese* (2000).[256] *Why* this was made so is not immediately apparent: the language of the original article 119 EEC ('Each Member State shall ... ensure and ... maintain the application of the principle that men and women should receive equal pay for equal work') appears clearly to be addressed to the member states, barely passes the direct effect test, and provides no hint that it should enjoy the special (virtually unique) quality of horizontal direct effect. Yet it does. So rights arising from article 157 are enforceable in a competent national court or tribunal against any public or private person – *de facto* an employer. What is more, the Court has found Directive 75/117 on equal pay merely to restate the

---

250 E.g., Case C-320/04 *Commission* v *Luxembourg* and Case C-327/04 *Commission* v *Finland*, judgments of 24 February 2005, unreported; Case C-329/04 *Commission* v *Germany*, judgment of 28 April 2005, unreported; Case C-335/04 *Commission* v *Austria*, judgment of 4 May 2005, unreported.
251 See 6.19 above, n. 129.
252 See e.g., Case C-303/06 *Coleman* v *Attridge Law and anor* [2008] ECR I-5603.
253 Proposal for a Council Directive implementing the principle of equal treatment between persons irrespective of religion or belief, disability, age or sexual orientation, COM(2008) 426 final. The (necessary) parliamentary approval was obtained in 2009 (resolution of 2 April 2009, T6–0211/2009) but it is meeting staunch (particularly German) resistance in the Council.
254 Case 43/75 *Defrenne* v *SABENA* (No. 2) [1976] ECR 455.
255 See 11.140–11.144 above.
256 Case C-281/98 *Angonese* v *Cassa di Risparmio di Bolzano* [2000] ECR I-4139; see 11.141–11.144 above.

principles of article 119 and in no way to alter its content or scope,[257] the practical effect of which is that the provisions of that Directive (now absorbed into Directive 2006/54), including the principle of equal pay for work of equal value, also have vertical and horizontal direct effect.

14.48 Otherwise the Directives do not have horizontal direct effect. The uncomfortable result is that in the area of employment protection an employee of a public authority or an 'emanation of the state' may invoke a relevant Directive where its terms are unconditional and sufficiently precise (as for the most part they are), notwithstanding it has nothing to do with the employer authority's public functions, going instead to its private law relations as an employer;[258] but an employee of a private undertaking (which is 'often a matter of chance')[259] may not. As against a private employer the employee must rely upon the national legislation implementing the Directives (in the United Kingdom primarily the Equality Act 2010) although national courts and tribunals must, if at all possible, interpret and apply it in the light of the Directives.[260] If it is not possible, a remedy for injury may, by applying *Francovich* principles, lie in damages against the state.[261]

14.49 But one oddity has emerged by way of exception. In *Mangold* (2005)[262] an issue arose as to the horizontal application in Germany of the prohibition of discrimination on grounds of age (Directive 2000/78) prior to the deadline for implementation of the Directive and in the face of national legislation which in any event could not reasonably bear a Directive-friendly interpretation. The Court of Justice responded by finding that the prohibition, as set out in Directive 2000/78, 'must … be regarded as a general principle of Community law',[263] observance of this general principle (of equal treatment) cannot 'as such' be conditional upon the expiry of the period allowed for transformation of the Directive,[264] so that

---

257 Case 96/80 *Jenkins v Kingsgate (Clothing Productions) Ltd* [1981] ECR 911; Case C-243/95 *Hill and anor v Revenue Commissioners and anor* [1998] ECR I-3739; Case C-17/05 *Cadman v Health & Safety Executive* [2006] ECR I-9583.

258 Case 152/84 *Marshall v Southampton and Southwest Hampshire Area Health Authority* (No. 1) [1986] ECR 723, confirming that a public employee (here, of an emanation of the state, a local English health board) may rely upon the terms of a Directive (Directive 76/207) directly against her employer. See subsequently Case C-187/00 *Kutz-Bauer v Freie und Hansestadt Hamburg* [2003] ECR I-2741; Case C-268/06 *Impact v Minister for Agriculture and Food and ors* [2008] ECR I-2483; Case C-537/07 *Gómez-Limón Sánchez-Camacho v Instituto Nacional de la Seguridad Social and ors* [2009] ECR I-6525.

259 Case C-282/10 *Dominguez v Centre informatique du Centre Ouest Atlantique and anor*, judgment of 24 January 2012, not yet reported, per A-G Trstenjak at para. 118 of her opinion.

260 See 6.79 above. For an example of how far uniform interpretation may apply in this area, see Case 177/88 *Dekker v Stichting Vormingcentrum voor Jong Volwassenen Plus* [1990] ECR I-3941.

261 See 6.35–6.39 above.

262 Case C-144/04 *Mangold v Helm* [2005] ECR I-9981.

263 *Ibid.* at para. 75.

264 *Ibid.* at para. 76.

it is the responsibility of the national court to guarantee the full effectiveness of the general principle of non-discrimination in respect of age, setting aside any provision of national law which may conflict with Community law, even where the period prescribed for transposition of that directive has not yet expired.[265]

This was plucked from the ether and stands the case law on application of Directives on its head. It gave rise to an avalanche of litigation in which age discrimination in work was in issue, has been severely criticised, led to some rumbling from the German *Bundesverfassungsgericht*,[266] and is subject to re-evaluation.[267] With a defter touch the Court then in *Kücükdeveci*[268] recognised the *Mangold* rule that non-discrimination on grounds of age is itself a general principle of Union law, a specific application of the general principle of equal treatment,[269] but emphasises that it is one 'given expression in Directive 2000/78'[270] which thus marries the general principle to the substance of the Directive in a manner more clearly than *Mangold*. The Court then reiterated the standard formula of the duty of a national court to ensure the full effectiveness of a Directive by means of an *interprétation conforme*, yet went on nonetheless to confirm the direct effect of this general principle and its primacy over incompatible national legislation. The result seems to be a horizontally directly enforceable (and superior) right where there is a difference in treatment on grounds of age which is not objectively justified (in terms of Directive 2000/78) in a situation which falls within a field regulated by the Directive. How far age discrimination may (if at all) be reined in, or other rights (if any) set out in the anti-discrimination (or other) Directives extended in this manner, perhaps spliced to Charter rights now they constitute primary law, remains to be tested and seen. But it takes only a moment's reflection to appreciate the profound impact it would have upon the obligations of private persons should the principle come to gain wider currency. The issues were analysed at length by Advocate-General Trstenjak[271] but the answer is still unknown.

Common provisions

The Directives adopt a common approach in a number of respects: **14.50**

---

265 *Ibid.* at para. 78.
266 BVerfG, 6. Juli 2010 (*Honeywell*), BVerfGE 126, 286.
267 See in particular Case C-411/05 *Palacios de la Villa* v *Cortefiel Servicios* [2007] ECR I-8531, per A-G Mazák; Case C-427/06 *Bartsch* v *Bosch und Siemens Hausgeräte (BSH) Altersfürsorge* [2008] ECR I-7245, per A-G Sharpston.
268 Case C-555/07 *Kücükdeveci* v *Swedex* [2010] ECR I-365.
269 *Ibid.* at para. 50.
270 *Ibid.* at paras 51, 53, 55, 56 and in the *dispositif*.
271 Case C-282/10 *Dominguez*, n. 259 above – involving not an anti-discrimination Directive but entitlement to annual leave under the Working Time Directive (Directive 2003/88, n. 225 above); there was no consideration of the issues in the Court's judgment.

- They prohibit both direct and indirect discrimination.[272] Direct discrimination is justified only where expressly permitted, either by the terms of a Directive itself or by the application of overriding Treaty rules. Indirect discrimination is subject to broader exculpation of objective justification: it occurs, and is prohibited,

  > where an apparently neutral provision, criterion or practice would put persons of one sex [for example] at a particular disadvantage compared with persons of the other sex, unless that provision, criterion or practice is objectively justified by a legitimate aim, and the means of achieving that aim are appropriate and necessary.[273]

- They each contain a chapter providing for (horizontal) remedies and enforcement, and there is substantial case law on what is 'adequate' satisfaction in the event of breach of the rules, which must be real, effective and deterrent.[274] They also lay down strict rules on onus of proof: where a claimant can make a *prima facie* case, or show facts which justify a presumption that direct or indirect discrimination has occurred, the onus is on the respondent to show otherwise.[275]

- Most have an 'occupational requirement' exception. First appearing in the 1976 Directive on equal treatment in employment which provided that member states were free to exclude from it occupational activity in which the sex of the worker constituted a 'determining factor' (*eine unabdingbare Voraussetzung*),[276] by 2002 it had been narrowed considerably, the member states permitted (but not obliged) to exclude from its operation

---

272   Directive 2000/43, art. 2(1); Directive 2000/78, art. 2(1); Directive 2004/113, art. 4(1); Directive 2006/54, art. 4.

273   Directive 2004/113, art. 2(b); Directive 2006/54, art. 2(b); Directive 2010/41, art. 3(b). For 'of one sex' Directive 2000/43 substitutes 'persons of a racial or ethnic origin' (art. 2(b)), Directive 2000/78 substitutes 'having a particular religion or belief, a particular disability, a particular age, or a particular sexual orientation' (art. 2(b)); both then substitute 'of other persons' for 'of the other sex'.

274   E.g., Case 14/83 *Von Colson and Kamann* v *Land Nordrhein-Westfalen* [1984] ECR 1891; Case 177/88 *Dekker*, n. 260 above; Case 152/84 *Marshall 1*, n. 258 above; Case C-456/06 *Peek and Cloppenburg* v *Cassina* [2008] ECR I-2731; Case C-54/07 *Centrum voor gelijkheid van kansen en voor racismebestrijding* v *Firma Feryn* [2008] ECR I-5187.

275   Directive 2000/43, art. 8; Directive 2000/78, art. 10; Directive 2004/113, art. 9; Directive 2006/54, art. 19. This applies equally to art. 157 TFEU itself and to Directives 92/85 and 2010/18 insofar as discrimination based upon sex is concerned; Directive 2006/54, art. 19(4)(a). See Case 96/80 *Jenkins* v *Kingsgate (Clothing Productions) Ltd* [1981] ECR 911; Case 170/84 *Bilka-Kaufhaus* v *Weber von Hartz* [1986] ECR 1607; Case 171/88 *Rinner-Kühn* v *FWW Spezial-Gebäudereinigung* [1989] ECR 2743; Case C-127/92 *Enderby* v *Frenchay Health Authority* [1993] ECR I-5535.

276   Directive 76/207, art. 2(2). As to which see Case 165/82 *Commission* v *United Kingdom* (Male Midwives) [1982] ECR 3431; Case 170/84 *Bilka*; Case 222/84 *Johnston* v *Chief Constable of the RUC* [1986] ECR 1651; Case 171/88 *Rinner-Kühn*; Case C-273/97 *Sirdar* v *Army Board and anor* [1999] ECR I-7403; Case C-285/98 *Kreil* v *Bundesrepublik Deutschland* [2000] ECR I-69; Case C-186/01 *Dory* v *Bundesrepublik Deutschland* [2003] ECR I-2479. It might be noted that the Court became less illiberal (reactionary?) in its views as to what constituted a determining factor over time.

a difference of treatment which is based on characteristics relating to sex ... where, by reason of the particular occupational activities concerned or of the context in which they are carried out, such a characteristic constitutes a genuine and determining occupational requirement, provided that its objective is legitimate and the requirement is proportionate.[277]

The Gender Equality Directive (2006) re-adopted this text *verbatim*,[278] similar formulae are found in other Directives.[279]

- Many permit (but do not require) positive action to prevent or redress disadvantages linked to the grounds of their subject matter.[280] This first appeared in Directive 76/207 and the Social Agreement but applying only to the advantage of women ('[t]o make it easier for women to pursue a vocational activity or to prevent or compensate for disadvantages in their professional careers'[281] and 'by removing existing inequalities which affect women's opportunities'[282]), an odd thing to find in legislation promoting equality. The bias was never tested. Now permitted is positive action for the benefit of 'the under-represented sex'[283] or amending disadvantages linked 'to sex',[284] 'to racial or ethnic origin'[285] or 'any of the grounds referred to in [the Directive]',[286] although old habits die hard: in this context member states 'should, in the first instance, aim at improving the situation of women in working life'[287] and the promotion of entrepreneurship among women enjoys particular favour.[288]

Care should be taken that the employment Directives are normally for the **14.51** benefit of 'workers', but there is no single definition of worker for these

---

277   Directive 76/207 (as amended by Directive 2002/73 [2002] OJ L269/15), art. 2(6).

278   Directive 2006/54, art. 14(2).

279   E.g., Directive 2000/43, art. 4 ('a characteristic related to racial or ethnic origin'); Directive 2000/78, art. 4 ('a characteristic'); Directive 2004/113, art. 4(5).

280   Directive 2000/43, art. 5; Directive 2000/78, art. 7; Directive 2004/113, art. 6; Directive 2006/54, art. 3; Directive 2010/41, art. 5; made Treaty compatible by TFEU, art. 157(4). See further Case C-450/93 *Kalanke* v *Freie Hansestadt Bremen* [1995] ECR I-3051; Case C-409/95 *Marschall* v *Land Nordrhein-Westfalen* [1997] ECR I-6363; Case C-476/99 *Lommers* v *Minister van Landbouw, Natuurbeheer en Visserij* [2002] ECR I-2891; Case C-303/06 *Coleman* v *Attridge Law and anor* [2008] ECR I-5603 (confirming the prohibition of discrimination on grounds of disability in Directive 2000/78 to extend to a disabled child's primary carer); Case E-1/02 *EFTA Surveillance Authority* v *Norway* [2003] EFTA CR 1.

281   Social Agreement, art. 6.

282   Directive 76/207, art. 2(4).

283   Directive 2006/54, Preamble, 22nd indent.

284   Directive 2004/113, art. 6.

285   Directive 2000/43, art. 5.

286   Directive 2000/78, art. 7.

287   Directive 2006/54, Preamble, 22nd indent.

288   Directive 2010/41, art. 5. Similarly the 2008 general block exemption regulation for state aid exempts from the prohibition aid for the start-up of certain small undertakings created by female entrepreneurs (*sic*); Regulation 800/2008 [2008] OJ L214/3, art. 16.

purposes. In the field of equal treatment for male and female workers, for example, and under the Working Time Directive, it has an autonomous, Union meaning; but for the fixed-term work, part-time work and the TUPE Directives the meaning is to be derived solely from that laid down in national legislation.[289] A trap which must be avoided is a presumption that these are rights which adhere to workers within the meaning of article 45 TFEU, so that movement between member states is a prerequisite to their application. They do not, and it is not.

6. Pensions

14.52 An important (and costly) branch of social policy is the public provision and/or regulation of pensions. Under Union law a distinction is drawn between pensions paid under statutory social security schemes and those paid under occupational pension schemes. Social security pensions do not fall under article 157;[290] rather they are governed by Directive 79/7, which permits member states to maintain differential retirement ages for men and women, together with consequential discriminatory elements.[291] By contrast, pension payments under occupational schemes, whether contributory or non-contributory, and even if contracted out, are 'pay' and so fall under article 157.[292] The decisive test is, in terms of article 157 itself, whether the pension is paid directly or indirectly by the employer (i.e., funded wholly or partly by the employer) as part of the consideration in respect of the employment relationship.[293]

14.53 Men and women must have equal access to occupational pension schemes.[294] They must be treated equally in relation to retirement ages and pension benefits (but only in relation to periods of service after 17 May 1990).[295] It is the

---

289 See the discussion of A-G Kokott in Case C-393/10 *O'Brien* v *Ministry of Justice*, judgment of 1 March 2012, not yet reported, at paras 18–37 of her opinion.

290 Case 80/70 *Defrenne* v *Belgium* [1971] ECR 445.

291 Directive 79/7, art. 7(1)(a); see Case C-9/91 *R* v *Secretary of State for Social Security, ex parte Equal Opportunities Commission* [1992] ECR I-4297.

292 Case 170/84 *Bilka-Kaufhaus* v *Weber von Hartz* [1986] ECR 1607; Case 171/88 *Rinner-Kühn* v *FWW Spezial-Gebäudereinigung* [1989] ECR 2743; Case 262/88 *Barber* v *Guardian Royal Exchange* [1990] ECR I-1889.

293 Case C-7/93 *Bestuur van het Algemeen Burgerlijk Pensioenfonds* v *Beune* [1994] ECR I-4471.

294 Case 170/84 *Bilka*, n. 292 above, and, applying *Bilka*, Case C-57/93 *Vroege* v *NCIV Instituut voor Volkshuisvesting and Stichting Pensioenfonds NCIV* [1994] ECR I-4541 (exclusion of part-time workers) and Case C-128/93 *Fisscher* v *Voorhuis Hengelo and and Stichting Bedrijfspensioenfonds voor de Detailhandel* [1994] ECR I-4583 (exclusion of married women). See now Directive 2006/54, ch. 2.

295 That is, the date of the judgment in Case 262/88 *Barber*, n. 292 above. In *Barber* the Court limited the temporal effect of its judgment, accepting that the previous understanding of the member states of art. 157 was one to which they were reasonably entitled, and that legal certainty (and tacitly the huge cost to economies of retrospective adaptation) justified a limiting of its temporal effects: 'the direct effect of Article [157] may not be relied upon in order to claim entitlement to a pension with effect from a date prior to that of this judgment'

prospective periodic pension payments that constitute 'pay' for the purposes of article 157, not the employer's contributions (actuarially calculated according to the needs of the scheme) nor the employee's transfer benefits or lump-sum options (actuarially calculated upon the basis of accrued rights).[296] Article 157 applies to pensions paid to the spouses of deceased employees,[297] to 'top-up' schemes (supplementing the state pension)[298] and to 'contracted-out' schemes (in substitution for the state pension),[299] but not to single sex schemes.[300] Pension scheme trustees must, so far as is possible, administer their scheme in compliance with article 157 and, if necessary, have recourse to the employer and/or the courts in order to do so.[301] Employees and the surviving spouses and representatives of deceased employees can invoke the direct effect of article 157 against employers and trustees.[302]

C. ENVIRONMENTAL POLICY

Perusal of the original EEC Treaty reveals a studied ignorance of the environ- **14.54** ment and of its regulation. It seems astonishing today that instruments for the creation of an unrestricted Western European market in potential pollutants – steel, iron, coal and nuclear materials, plus agricultural and transport policies – should have nothing to say about the environment, but it is neither surprising nor uncommon for products of the 1950s. By the time, and partly as a result, of the Stockholm Conference on the Human Environment (1972) the issue had moved to the forefront of the national and international political agenda. The slow Community reaction to this was the adoption of the first (of many

---

(in the *dispositif*). Because pension entitlements accrue over the course of years and decades this was ambiguous, and was 'clarified' (with the adoption of the most limited of possible interpretations) by the 'Barber Protocol' (now Protocol (No. 33) concerning article 157 of the TFEU) added to the Treaties at Maastricht, by which '[f]or the purposes of Article 157 ..., benefits under occupational social security schemes shall not be considered as remuneration if and in so far as they are attributable to periods of employment prior to 17 May 1990'. See Case C-109/91 *Ten Oever* v *Stichting Bedrijfspensioenfonds voor het Glazenwassers- en Schoon-aakbedrijf* [1993] ECR I-4879 and Case C-7/93 *Beune*, n. 293 above, decided respectively before and after the entry into force of the protocol. This limitation in time relates to benefits only and does *not* apply to equality of access to pension schemes; Case C-57/93 *Vroege* and Case C-128/93 *Fisscher*, n. 294 above; Directive 2006/54, ch. 2.

296 Case C-152/91 *Neath* v *Hugh Steeper* [1993] ECR I-6935.
297 Case C-109/91 *Ten Oever* v *Stichting Bedrijfspensioenfonds voor het Glazenwassers- en Schoonaakbedrijf* [1993] ECR I-4879.
298 Case C-110/91 *Moroni* v *Firma Collo* [1993] ECR I-6591; Case C-147/08 *Römer* v *Frei und Hansestadt Hamburg*, judgment of 10 May 2011, not yet reported.
299 Case 262/88 *Barber* v *Guardian Royal Exchange* [1990] ECR I-1889.
300 Case C-200/91 *Coloroll Pension Trustees Ltd* v *Russell and ors* [1994] ECR I-4389.
301 *Ibid.*
302 *Ibid.*

sequential) environmental action programmes in 1973[303] and, notwithstanding the lack of direct Treaty authority, the adoption of legislation for harmonisation (or in some cases creation) of national environmental law under article 100 EEC (article 115 TFEU) and occasionally, where article 100 could not be stretched sufficiently, article 235 (article 352 TFEU).[304] By the mid-1980s the Court of Justice had come to recognise environmental protection, albeit still alien to the Treaty, to be 'one of the Community's essential objectives',[305] and it soon took its place amongst the mandatory requirements justifying derogation from article 34.[306] The Treaty breakthrough came in 1987 with the Single European Act and adoption of a new Title on 'Environment' amongst the policies of the Community.[307] It has been upgraded with each successive Treaty amendment, whilst all the while commanding increasing political attention and concern, from locally to globally.

14.55 The Union now 'work[s] for the sustainable development of Europe ... aiming at ... a high level of protection and improvement of the quality of the environment',[308] as an area of shared competence between the Union and the member states.[309] 'Environmental protection requirements' were the subject of the first, and until 1993 only, integration clause in the Treaty,[310] and now form the pre-eminent exemplar of the species in article 11 TFEU:

> Environmental protection requirements must be integrated into the definition and implementation of the Union policies and activities, in particular with a view to promoting sustainable development,

---

303 [1973] OJ C112/1. For the present (6th) Community Environmental Action Programme (EAP), to 2012, see Decision 1600/2002 [2002] OJ L242/1. A final assessment of the 6th EAP was produced in August 2011 (COM(2011) 531), the 7th in train and scheduled (optimistically) to be adopted in November 2012.

304 E.g., Directive 79/409 [1979] OJ L103/1 (on the conservation of wild birds), requiring recourse to art. 235 EEC. Treaty amendment in 1987 enabled the Council to adopt in 1992, by authority of (what is now) art. 192 TFEU, Directive 92/43 [1992] OJ L206/7 (on the conservation of natural habitats and of wild fauna and flora), and in 2009 update Directive 79/409 as Directive 2009/147 [2009] OJ L20/7. The two taken together (informally, the Wild Birds and the Habitats Directives, respectively) form the basis of Union nature conservation law still.

305 Case 240/83 *Procureur de la République* v *Association de défense des brûleurs d'huiles usages* [1985] ECR 531, at para. 13.

306 Case 302/86 *Commission* v *Denmark* (Returnable Bottles) [1988] ECR 4607. As to mandatory requirements see 10.40 above.

307 EEC Treaty, Title VII (arts 130r–130t). See also art. 100a(3).

308 TEU, art. 3(3).

309 TFEU, art. 4(2)(e).

310 EEC Treaty, art. 130r(2) ('Environmental protection requirements shall be a component of the Community's other policies').

which 'emphasises the fundamental nature of that objective and its extension across the range of those policies and activities'.[311] For good measure, additional emphasis is provided in the Charter of Fundamental Rights:

> A high level of environmental protection and the improvement of the quality of the environment must be integrated into the policies of the Union and ensured in accordance with the principle of sustainable development.[312]

This reflects a number of member state constitutions in which a right to a clean environment is, in varying terms, a fundamental and/or constitutionally guaranteed right.[313] It may mean the elevation of environmental protection to a general principle of Union law (insofar as that is distinct from the status it is accorded by article 11), but it has never (yet) been recognised as such.

There follows amongst the Union policies two primary Treaty bases for action in the sphere of the environment. **14.56**

1. Harmonisation of national laws

The Community's first foray into environmental matters was through the device of harmonisation of national law necessary for the proper functioning of the internal market. The legal base in the original Treaty was (what is now) article 115 TFEU, which required, and requires, unanimity in the Council. In tandem with its introduction of a title on the environment, the Single European Act also provided for harmonisation of laws by a qualified majority in the Council (through originally cooperation, subsequently co-decision, now the ordinary legislative procedure).[314] In proposing harmonisation measures under the new provision relating to, inter alia, environmental protection the Commission is required to take as a base a high level of protection,[315] and member states are permitted to maintain or introduce higher standards in the face of those measures, subject to strict limitations and significant scrutiny by the Commission.[316] All this is discussed above.[317] The Union still resorts to article 114 in the environmental sphere to regulate, for example, waste management, the classification, packaging and labelling of environmentally hazardous products and noise pollution. **14.57**

---

311 Case C-176/03 *Commission* v *Council* [2005] ECR I-7879, at para. 42; Case C-320/03 *Commission* v *Austria* [2005] ECR I-9871, at para. 73.
312 Charter of Fundamental Rights, art. 37.
313 E.g., the constitutions of Greece, art. 24; the Netherlands, art. 21; Finland, 20 §.
314 TFEU, art. 114 (ex art. 95 EC).
315 *Ibid.* art. 114(3).
316 *Ibid.* art. 114(4)–(7).
317 See 10.68–10.77 above.

2. Environmental policy

14.58 Since 1987 the Treaty contains a dedicated title (now Title XX) on, simply, 'Environment'. The purpose is 'to contribute to pursuit of the following objectives':

- preserving, protecting and improving the quality of the environment;
- protecting human health;
- prudent and rational utilisation of natural resources; and
- promoting measures at international level to deal with regional or world-wide environmental problems, and in particular combat climate change.[318]

Combined with the over-arching principle of sustainable development embraced by article 11, Union environmental policy is to incorporate a number of further co-mingling principles:

- a high level of protection (as with article 114), taking into account the diversity of situations in the various regions of the Union;
- the precautionary principle;
- the preventative principle;
- rectification at source; and
- polluter pays,[319]

which comprise 'fundamental principles of environmental protection'.[320] In its formulation account is to be taken of available scientific and technical data, environmental conditions in the various regions of the Union, the potential benefits and costs of action or lack of action and the economic and social development of the Union as a whole and the balanced development of its regions.[321] The Union's (new) competences in the field of energy are required to be carried out 'with regard for the need to preserve and improve the environment'.[322] The Council decides 'what action is to be taken by the Union in order to achieve [these] objectives', for the most part by the ordinary legislative procedure but with certain areas reserved to unanimity.[323] As with

---

318 TFEU, art. 191(1) (ex art. 174(1) EC).
319 TFEU, art. 191(2).
320 Case C-121/07 *Commission* v *France* [2008] ECR I-9159, at para. 74.
321 TFEU, art. 191(3).
322 *Ibid.* art. 194(1).
323 *Ibid.* art. 192(1), (2). Reserved are provisions primarily of a fiscal nature; measures affecting town and country planning, quantitative management of water resources or affecting, directly or indirectly, the availability of those resources, and land use, with the exception of waste management; and measures significantly affecting a member state's choice between different energy sources and the general structure of its energy supply

harmonisation legislation under article 114, member states are entitled to maintain or introduce 'more stringent protective measures' in the face of measures adopted under article 192;[324] they must be compatible with the Treaty and notified to the Commission.[325] There is sometimes a narrow line between legislation the pith and substance of which is internal market and the pith and substance of which is environmental protection, and much of the early case law on the correct legal base of Union legislation turned upon which was properly one or the other.[326] Some legislation – the Clean (or Renewable) Energy Directive,[327] for example – is adopted by authority of both.

A great many measures have been adopted under article 192, spanning a wide, **14.59** sometimes highly technical, field, from the Habitats Directive to water quality ('framework Directives' for Union action in the fields of water policy (Water Framework Directives, or WFD)[328] and marine environmental policy (Marine Strategy Framework Directive),[329] specific protection measures for bathing water,[330] groundwater,[331] drinking water,[332] shellfish water);[333] to waste control;[334] to carbon trading (the Union operating the world's largest emission trading scheme (ETS)[335] which is 'a cornerstone of European policy on climate change');[336] to a host of measures on the control and monitoring of discharge of effluent into air,[337] water and soil, and attempts to create an integrated programme of pollution prevention and control.[338] It should be noted that the

---

(art. 192(2)). One of the three bridging clauses in the EC Treaty allowed the Council to transfer (by unanimity) any of these matters to co-decision (art. 175(2), final para.); this disappeared with Lisbon but the matter is of course still open to bridging under the general bridging provision of TEU, art. 48(7).

324 TFEU, art. 193.

325 *Ibid.*

326 See e.g., Case C-300/89 *Commission* v *Council* (Titanium Dioxide) [1991] ECR I-2867; Case C-155/91 *Commission* v *Council* (Waste Disposal) [1993] ECR I-939.

327 Directive 2009/28 [2009] OJ L140/16.

328 Directive 2000/60 [2000] OJ L327/1; Directive 2008/105 [2008] OJ L348/84 (on environmental quality standards, consolidating and repealing a number of previous measures).

329 Directive 2008/56 [2008] OJ L164/19.

330 Directive 2006/7 [2006] OJ L64/37.

331 Directive 2006/118 [2006] OJ L372/19.

332 Directive 98/83 [1998] OJ L330/32.

333 Directive 2006/113 [2006] OJ L376/14.

334 Directive 2008/98 [2008] OJ L312/3 (Framework Directive on waste).

335 Directive 2003/87 [2003] OJ L275/32. It was linked to Kyoto mechanisms in 2005 (Directive 2004/101 [2004] OJ L338/18) and extends to aviation from 2012 (Directive 2008/101 [2009] OJ L8/3). For timing, administration and other aspects of auctioning of allowances see Regulation 1021/2010 [2010] OJ L302/1.

336 Case C-366/10 *R (Air Transport Association of America and ors)* v *Secretary of State for Energy and Climate Change*, judgment of 21 December 2011, not yet reported, per A-G Kokott at para. 1 of her opinion.

337 See in particular Directive 2001/81 [1981] OJ L309/22 (National Emission Ceilings for Certain Atmospheric Pollutants, or NEC, Directive); Directive 2008/50 [2008] OJ L152/1 on ambient air quality and cleaner air for Europe.

338 Primarily Directive 2008/1 [2008] OJ L24/8 (Integrated Pollution Prevention and Control, or IPPC, Directive).

Commission is thought sometimes to rely too heavily upon the business and industrial sectors in the formulation of legislation and the Council is too generous to them in its adoption. Environmental sustainability is an element of the Lisbon (and Europe 2020) agenda, but many would say insufficiently, and creeping ever lower down the pecking order.

14.60 Internationally, in which sphere competences are normally shared with the member states,[339] the Union is active, having entered into more than 30 multilateral (normally mixed) agreements, both universal and regional, for the environmental protection of, for example, the north east Atlantic,[340] the North Sea,[341] the Mediterranean,[342] the Baltic,[343] the Rhine,[344] the Danube,[345] the Elbe,[346] the Oder,[347] the Alps,[348] even the Antarctic.[349] Lisbon places new, especial emphasis upon the external dimension of Union environmental policy, introducing an express link between sustainable development and the Union's external relations in providing (or clarifying) amongst its basic objectives that '[i]n its relations with the wider world, the Union shall ... contribute to ... the sustainable development of the Earth'.[350] The Union has begun to develop and promote an Integrated Maritime Policy (IMP) with a view to maximising sustainable development, economic growth and social cohesion of the member states and sustainable use of the seas and oceans with regard to coastal, insular and outermost regions in the Union, as well as maritime sectors, through coherent maritime-related policies and relevant international cooperation.[351]

---

339   Case C-459/03 *Commission* v *Ireland* (MOX Plant) [2006] ECR I-4635, at para. 92.
340   Cooperation Agreement of 17 October 1990 for the Protection of the Coasts and Waters of the North-East Atlantic against Pollution (Lisbon Agreement) [1993] OJ L267/22; Convention of 22 September 1992 for the Protection of the Marine Environment of the North-East Atlantic (OSPAR, or Paris, Convention) [1998] OJ L104/3.
341   Agreement of 13 September 1983 for Cooperation in Dealing with Pollution of the North Sea by Oil and other Harmful Substances (Bonn Agreement) [1984] OJ L188/9.
342   Convention of 16 February 1976 on the Protection of the Mediterranean Sea Against Pollution (Barcelona Convention) [1977] OJ L240/3; Protocol of 21 January 2008 on Integrated Coastal Zone Management in the Mediterranean [2009] OJ L34/19; and many others.
343   Convention of 9 April 1992 on the Protection of the Marine Environment of the Baltic Sea Area, 1992 (revised Helsinki Convention) [1994] OJ L73/20.
344   Accord du 29 avril 1963 concernant la Commission internationale pour la protection du Rhin contre la pollution (Berne Convention), 993 UNTS 3.
345   Convention of 29 June 1994 on Cooperation for the Protection and Sustainable Use of the River Danube (Convention for the Protection of the Danube) [1997] OJ L342/19.
346   Convention of 8 October 1990 on the International Commission for the Protection of the Elbe [1991] OJ L321/25.
347   Convention of 11 April 1996 on the International Commission for the Protection of the Oder [1999] OJ L100/21.
348   Convention of 7 November 1991 on the Protection of the Alps (Alpine Convention) [1996] OJ L61/32.
349   Convention of 20 May 1980 on the Conservation of Antarctic Marine Living Resources [1981] OJ L252/27.
350   TEU, art. 3(5).
351   Regulation 1255/2011 [2011] OJ L321/1, art. 1.

Environmental protection is also, insofar as it is embraced by nuclear safety, writ **14.61** large in most of the activities of Euratom.

3. Enforcement

It will be apparent that most Union activity in the field is once removed. The **14.62** compulsory (article 115) and in all events preferred (articles 114 and 192) legislative measure which touches upon environmental matters is the Directive, with all the advantages (suppleness) and disadvantages (uniformity, timeous implementation, enforcement) it brings. For a variety of reasons the command and control structure does not always make for efficiency and uniformity of enforcement. National authorities, up to and including the courts, may be lukewarm in their enthusiasm for Union intervention, for successful implementation of environmental measures imposes costs upon industry. The struggle is against both intertia and sometimes powerful vested interests. Where national authorities fail to measure up to the mark, the corrective mechanism is enforcement proceedings under article 258, and as at the beginning of 2011 just over one-fifth of all enforcement cases under examination involved environmental matters,[352] making it the single most common subject matter of the procedure.

But it is not only time-consuming, it is shot through with the political **14.63** considerations which, fairly or otherwise, inform the Commission. It is, for example, not unmindful that sluggish implementation in Poland of an array of environmental Directives is a function at least in part of the fabulous amounts of money required, from a struggling economy, necessary to comply.[353] Nor was it, for some reason, minded vigorously to tackle Malta over the annual slaughter of birds unlucky enough to choose the mid-Mediterranean route for their spring migration, though failure to prohibit it is clearly contrary to the Wild Birds Directive.[354] As for private enforcement by individuals (or interested

---

352 *28th Annual Report on Monitoring the Application of Community Law (2010)*, COM(2011) 588 final, Accompanying Document, SEC(2011) 1094, Statistical Annexes I–III, p. 8 (209 of 739 own initiative cases, 120 of 883 cases arising from a complaint and 115 of 470 non-communication cases).

353 In 2000 a World Bank study calculated that Poland would require to spend US$22–43 thousand million in capital investment, with operating and maintenance costs US$5–11 thousand million annually, in order to implement the core environmental *acquis*; see *Poland: Complying with EU Environmental Legislation*, World Bank Technical Paper No. 454, p. ix.

354 The Directive permits derogation in the interests of public health and safety, for purposes of research and teaching, of repopulation, of re-introduction and for the breeding necessary for these purposes, and to permit, under strictly supervised conditions and on a selective basis, the capture, keeping or other judicious use of certain birds in small numbers 'where there is no other satisfactory solution' (Directive 2009/147, art. 9), and Malta continued, since accession, to permit the hunting of quail and turtle doves (but no other birds) by relying upon this derogation. It was four years before the Commission raised enforcement proceedings upon the basis that this reliance was an abuse; Case C-76/08 *Commission v Malta* [2009] ECR I-8213.

NGOs), the true target of most of these measures is of course the polluter, which, so long as he or she is a private person, goes untouched by the Directive itself[355] and so untouchable by other, affected persons. In many cases the latter will also lack both the information and the standing necessary to pursue action, although some inroads have been made here.[356] And whilst member states are sometimes persuaded to comply with Directives less out of duty to article 288 than out of fear of liability should they fail to do so, the *Francovich* rule[357] is in this context inadequate, for an environmental measure is normally one intended for the general good, so failing to meet the first of the *Francovich* (and *Brasserie du Pêcheur*)[358] tests of rights intended for the benefit of the individual. Yet the picture is not wholly bleak: in 2008 the High Court in England was persuaded to condemn (by declaration) the government for persistent failure to act in compliance with the requirements of the Directive on protection from pesticide spraying and order it to remedy its policy in the light of the judgment.[359] But it is gloomy: the judgment was set aside by the Court of Appeal.[360]

4. Environmental Liability Directive

14.64 The Council essayed a remedy to the problem in 2004 with adoption of the Environmental Liability Directive, or ELD.[361] The ELD seeks to establish a framework of environmental liability based upon the polluter pays principle in order to prevent and remedy environmental damage,[362] which is direct or indirect 'measurable adverse change of a natural resource or measurable impairment of a natural resource service'.[363] 'Measurable' is not defined. The Directive

---

355 However, some environmental Directives may give rise to a 'triangular situation' and so allow a measure of direct effect; see e.g., Case C-201/02 *R (Wells)* v *Secretary of State for Transport, Local Government and the Regions* [2004] ECR I-723.

356 For example, the Environmental Impact Assessment Directive (Directive 2011/92 [2012] OJ L26/1 (updating Directive 85/337 [1985] OJ L175/40)), which requires the holding of public inquiries into the likely effects any public or private project likely to produce significant environmental repercussions prior to any consent being given; Directive 2003/4 on public access to environmental information (Environmental Information Directive) [2003] OJ L41/26; Directive 2003/35 [2003] OJ L156/17 on public participation in environmental planning and access to justice (Public Participation Directive); Convention of 25 June 1998 on Access to Information, Public Participation in Decision-making and Access to Justice in Environmental Matters (Århus Convention), 2161 UNTS 450, implemented into Union law by Regulation 1367/2006 [2006] OJ L264/13.

357 Cases C-6 and 9/90 *Francovich and Bonifaci* v *Italy* [1991] ECR I-5357.

358 Cases C-46 and 48/93 *Brasserie du Pêcheur* v *Germany* and *R* v *Secretary of State for Transport, ex parte Factortame* (No. 3) [1996] ECR I-1029.

359 *R (Downs)* v *Secretary of State for Environment, Food and Rural Affairs* [2008] EWHC 2666 (Admin), [2008] 1 All ER (D) 145.

360 *Secretary of State for Environment, Food and Rural Affairs v Downs* [2009] EWCA Civ 664, [2009] All ER (D) 71.

361 Directive 2004/35 [2004] OJ L143/56.

362 *Ibid.* art. 1.

363 *Ibid.* art. 2(2).

requires an operator of an occupational activity[364] to take the measures necessary to prevent imminent damage,[365] to report situations in which an imminent threat is not dispelled (*ne disparaît pas*)[366] and to remedy damage which has occurred.[367] A competent authority must be nominated (or created) by the member states with powers to identify and assess environmental damage[368] and compel an operator to take preventative or remedial action,[369] absent which the necessary measures are to be adopted by the authority itself.[370] Preventative and remedial costs are to be borne by the operator;[371] costs incurred by the authority to that purpose are recoverable.[372] Affected individuals have a right to request a competent authority to take action in the event of damage or imminent threat thereof,[373] and the authority's action (or lack of it) must be reviewable,[374] but the Directive expressly excludes a civil right of action for injury caused by environmental damage, although does not harmonise away national legislation which provides for it.[375] It was hoped in some quarters that some form of enforcement authority might pass to the European Environment Agency, but they were to be disappointed.

14.65 The Directive was required to be implemented by May 2007. Few member states met the deadline.

5. Criminal sanctions

14.66 The Union is competent under article 192 to require member states to adopt effective, proportionate and dissuasive criminal penalties in order to combat serious environmental offences where they are an essential measure to that purpose and are necessary to make environmental protection fully effective[376] – and of course are justified by reference to subsidiarity. The practical difficulty is whether there is the necessary political will in the Council to do so,[377] being a function less of antipathy to effective environmental measures than to resistance

---

364 For definitions see art. 2(6), 3(1), Annex III.
365 *Ibid.* art. 5(1).
366 *Ibid.* art. 5(2).
367 *Ibid.* art. 6.
368 *Ibid.* art. 11.
369 *Ibid.* arts 5(3), 6, 7.
370 *Ibid.* arts 5(3)(d), (4) and 6(2)(e),(3).
371 *Ibid.* art. 8(1).
372 *Ibid.* art. 8(2).
373 *Ibid.* art. 12.
374 *Ibid.* art. 13.
375 *Ibid.* art. 3(3).
376 Case C-176/03 *Commission* v *Council* [2005] ECR I-7879; Case C-440/05 *Commission* v *Council* [2007] ECR I-9097.
377 See 6.57 above.

to Union incursion into the criminal sphere. However, in 2008 the Council adopted a Directive which requires member states to make criminal offences the intentional or seriously negligent commission, inciting, aiding or abetting of pollution which causes or is likely to cause death or serious injury to any person or substantial damage to environmental quality or to animals or plants,[378] and in 2009 the Council and Parliament amended an existing Directive on ship-source pollution to require breach of its provisions to be made criminal offences.[379] It is submitted that this power has not been extended by Lisbon, the cross-border dimension a test not excessively difficult to satisfy, but environmental degradation not (yet at any rate) an area of 'particularly serious crime' such as envisaged by article 82 TFEU.

D. THE UNION'S EXTERNAL ACTION

14.67 Part V of the TFEU addresses the Union's 'external action'. Part V is new with Lisbon, although its substance is not. Rather it is a significant reformulation and codification of rules developed over many years, rationalised as part of a coherent package and the handmaid of the Union's foreign policy, its operation thus made subject to the principles which inspire and guide its action on the international scene.[380] It consists of seven Titles: general provisions (which merely restate the obligation to comply with basic principles); common commercial policy; cooperation with third countries and humanitarian aid; restrictive measures; international agreements; relations with international organisations, third countries and Union delegations; and a solidarity clause.

1. Common Commercial Policy

14.68 The creation of a single market requires not only a common customs tariff[381] but a common approach to all aspects of trade with third states. A Common Commercial Policy (CCP) was therefore an 'activity' of the Community from the start,[382] second in sequence only to the prohibition of internal barriers to the free movement of goods, and is closely bound to, as the ancillary external manifestation of, the rules on the customs union. As the logic of the internal market dictates, the CCP is based upon 'uniform principles' in external Union trade, 'particularly' in regard to tariff rates, the conclusion of tariff and trade

---

378 Directive 2008/99 [2008] OJ L328/28.
379 Directive 2009/123 [2009] OJ L280/52. As this was primarily a transport measure it was adopted by authority of art. 80(2) EC (now art. 100(2) TFEU).
380 TEU, art. 21; TFEU, art. 205.
381 As to which see 10.11–10.14 above.
382 EEC Treaty, art. 3(b) (art. 3(1)(b) EC).

agreements in goods and services, commercial aspects of intellectual property, foreign direct investment, uniform liberalisation, export policy and protective measures in the event of dumping or subsidies.[383] The Treaties originally required member states to proceed 'only by common action' in respect of 'all matters of particular interest to the common market' within international organisations of an economic character.[384] This was deleted by Maastricht and replaced with a Union obligation to 'coordinate their action in international organisations and at international conferences' and 'uphold the common positions in such fora';[385] it was a more comprehensive stricture but was diminished by its transfer from the first to the second pillar. There is also an obligation to contribute towards international trade liberalisation.[386] Otherwise the Treaties provide little direction and confer wide latitude and discretion upon the Union institutions in shaping it. By comparison with the Common Customs Tariff which is an integral part of it, the CCP is a complex skein and a work in progress – indeed, in adaptation to global change and day-to-day events, a perpetual Union task. Nor are the issues immune from political considerations: it is worth noting that one of the Community's constitutional 'crises' arose in the context of the CCP and the pronounced German disinclination to adhere to the Community regime on banana imports.[387] With Lisbon the Common Commercial Policy is recognised to be a field of exclusive Union competence.[388]

Some of the measures which make up the CCP may be adopted unilaterally **14.69** ('autonomously') by the Union – for example, the adoption of the Common Customs Tariff[389] or the Community Customs Code,[390] the gathering of customs statistics,[391] the allocation and licensing of quotas,[392] export licences,[393] protective measures,[394] a vast complex of levies and measures regulating the import and export of agricultural products in particular, and so on – in effect, the internal implementation of the CCP. But the life of the CCP lies in active intercourse with third countries, and the Union's place in the wider

---

383 TFEU, art. 207(1) (ex art. 133(1) EC).
384 EEC Treaty, art. 116.
385 TEU (pre-Lisbon), art. 19(1).
386 TFEU, art. 206 (ex art. 131 EC).
387 See Case C-280/93 *Germany* v *Council* (Bananas) [1994] ECR I-4973; BVerfG, 7. Juni 2000 (*Bananenmarktordnung* or *Solange III*), BVerfGE 102, 147.
388 TFEU, art. 3(1)(e).
389 Regulation 2658/87 [1987] OJ L256/1.
390 Regulation 2913/92 [1992] OJ L302/1; Regulation 450/2008 [2008] OJ L145/1.
391 Regulation 451/2008 [2008] OJ L145/65; Regulation 471/2009 [2009] OJ L152/23; Regulation 113/2010 [2010] OJ L37/1.
392 Regulation 717/2008 [2008] OJ L198/1.
393 Regulation 116/2009 [2009] OJ L39/1 (export of cultural goods); Regulation 689/2008 [2008] OJ L204/1 (dangerous chemicals); Regulation 428/2009 [2009] OJ L134/1 ('dual use' goods).
394 See 14.103–14.112 below.

economic world; much of the internal implementation is in fact a product of that intercourse, contractual (or 'conventional') rather than autonomous.

2. Agreements between the Union and third countries

14.70 From the beginning the EEC was afforded the capacity to enter into:

- tariff, commercial and cooperation agreements with third countries;[395] and
- 'agreements establishing an association' with a third country, a group of countries or an international organisation.[396]

Whilst the former is a class not to be interpreted restrictively,[397] a matter fell within Community competence by virtue of article 113 EEC/133 EC only if it related specifically to international trade in that it is essentially intended to promote, facilitate or govern trade and has direct and immediate effects on trade in the products concerned.[398] In 1994 the Court of Justice found that it included cross-frontier services but only insofar as they do not involve the movement of natural or juristic persons, otherwise the matter was reserved to the member states;[399] to remedy this, a Treaty amendment made by Nice extended the operation of article 133 EC to agreements in the fields of trade in services and the commercial aspects of intellectual property.[400] An association agreement is more extensive, one which gives rise to specific (normally recipro- cal) rights and obligations, common action and special procedures; it usually provides for some form of institutional structure, sometimes extensive, com- petent to further the aims of the association and is normally comprehensive in regulating relations between the parties. An accession agreement with third European countries may address expressly, or imply, a gradual move towards eventual accession to the Union. In any event it is not restricted to commercial issues (the subject matter of article 207 agreements) but may address economic, political, technical, financial, cultural, environmental and other areas of cooperation. Some have provisions on free movement of persons. Since Lomé

---

395   EEC Treaty, art. 113; subsequently art. 133 EC; art. 207 TFEU.
396   EEC Treaty, art. 238; subsequently art. 310 EC; art. 217 TFEU.
397   Opinion 1/78 *Re the Agreement on Natural Rubber* [1979] ECR 2871, at para. 45.
398   Case C-347/03 *Regione autonoma Friuli-Venezia Giulia and anor* v *Ministero delle Politiche Agricole e Forestali* [2005] ECR I-3785, at para. 75; Cases C-402 and 415/05P *Kadi and Al Bakaraat* v *Council and Commission* (Kadi II) [2008] ECR I-6351, at para. 183; Case C-411/06 *Commission* v *Parliament and Council* (Shipment of Waste) [2009] ECR I-7585, at para. 71.
399   Opinion 1/94 *Re the World Trade Organization* [1994] ECR I-5267.
400   EC Treaty, art. 133(5). These matters were first addressed by the Treaty of Amsterdam but so as to confer upon the Council authority (upon which it never acted) to bring them into the field of art. 133 EC, not (as Nice did) do so with Treaty authority; the provisions are now subsumed in art. 207(1) TFEU.

III (1985–1990)[401] many have incorporated provisions in support of human rights, fundamental freedoms and good governance, now recognised as principles underlying the Union's external action.[402] Since the first such agreement in 1961 – an association with Greece[403] – the Union has entered into an extensive network of bilateral and multilateral association agreements with third countries. They are a very mixed bag, and considered below.

The treaty-making power is not restricted to those specific provisions and those **14.71** specific fields: in 1971 in *ERTA*,[404] a significant 'constitutional' judgment, the Court of Justice established that the Community enjoyed treaty-making power across the field of objectives identified in Part One of the EEC Treaty, at least insofar as the subject matter is regulated by common internal rules. External Union authority will therefore expand over time, and in areas in which Union rules occupy the field, Union treaty competence supplants that of the member states and is exclusive.[405] It also raises the issue of Union succession to treaty obligations into which a member state once entered, a course not necessarily acceptable to third country parties to it. *ERTA* was reflected in Maastricht, an express 'treaty-making power' being written into the Treaty in a number of new areas of Community competence.[406] Maastricht also provided authority to enter into formal agreements on an exchange rate system for the euro with non-Union currencies as a function of economic and monetary union[407] and Nice added a more general power, a new and distinct Title on economic, financial and technical cooperation with third countries authorising the Community to 'carry out [*mèner, durchführen*] within its spheres of competence, economic, financial and technical cooperation with third countries' in order to contribute to the development and consolidation of democracy, the rule of law and respect for human rights and fundamental freedoms.[408] These too underlie and inform the Union's external action. Finally, Lisbon added a general

---

401 See 14.97 below.

402 TEU, art. 21.

403 Treaty of 9 July 1961 (Athens Agreement) [1963] JO 26. The Turks followed suit two years later: Treaty of 12 September 1963 (Ankara Agreement) [1964] JO 217, which is therefore the oldest still operative association agreement with the Union.

404 Case 22/70 *Commission* v *Council* (European Road Transport Agreement) (ERTA) [1971] ECR 263.

405 Case 22/70 *ERTA, ibid.*, at paras 17–18; Opinion 1/75 *Re Export Credit Guarantee* [1975] 1355; Cases 3, 4 and 6/76 *Criminal proceedings against Kramer and ors* [1976] ECR 1279; Ruling 1/78 *Re the IAEA Draft Convention on the Physical Protection of Nuclear Materials, Facilities and Transports* [1978] ECR 2151; Opinion 1/94 *Re the World Trade Organization* [1994] ECR I-5267; Case C-45/07 *Commission* v *Greece* [2009] ECR I-701. The CCP itself is now such a field, and formally recognised as such by the Lisbon Treaty; TFEU, art. 3(1)(e).

406 EC Treaty (pre-Amsterdam), arts 126(3) (education); 127(3) (vocational training); 128(3) (culture); 129(3) (public health); 129c(3) (trans-European networks); 130r(4) (environment); 130y (development cooperation).

407 EC Treaty, art. 111(1) (art. 219(1) TFEU).

408 EC Treaty, art. 181a (art. 212 TFEU).

treaty-making power to conclude an agreement with one or more third countries or international organisations 'where the Treaties so provide or where the conclusion of an agreement is necessary in order to achieve, within the framework of the Union's policies, one of the objectives referred to in the Treaties, or is provided for in a legally binding Union act or is likely to affect common rules or alter their scope';[409] and recognises as an exclusive Union competence the conclusion of an international agreement where necessary to enable the Union to exercise its internal competences or insofar as its conclusion may affect common rules or alter their scope.[410] Presumably the *ERTA* rule remains alive within these strictures.

14.72 For all types of agreements the treaty-making authority is vested in the Council, although it is activated by a Commission recommendation (*sic*) (or a recommendation from the High Representative FASP where the agreement envisaged relates exclusively or principally to the CFSP) and the Commission conducts the negotiations in consultation with special committees appointed by the Council and within the framework of such Directives as the Council sees fit to issue.[411] The Council acts by qualified majority except for (a) commercial agreements concerning trade in services, commercial aspects of intellectual property and in the fields of cultural, audiovisual, social, education and health services; and (b) an association agreement which covers a field in which unanimity is required for the adoption of Union acts; for these unanimity is required.[412] The Parliament must consent to association agreements; agreement on Union accession to the European Convention; agreements establishing a specific institutional framework by organising cooperation procedures; agreements with important Union budgetary implications for the Union; and agreements covering fields to which either the ordinary legislative procedure applies, or the special legislative procedure where consent by the European Parliament is required.[413] Otherwise it is to be consulted.[414] There is a Treaty bar to agreements which include provisions which would exceed Union *vires* internally, particularly if leading to harmonisation of laws in areas which the Treaties exclude.[415] The view of the Court of Justice may be sought by the

---

409   TFEU, art. 216(1).

410   *Ibid.* art. 3(2).

411   *Ibid.* arts 207(3), 218 (ex arts 133(3), 300 EC). There are special procedures for agreements on exchange rate policy; art. 219 TFEU.

412   *Ibid.* arts 207(4), 218(8).

413   *Ibid.* art. 218(6)(a).

414   *Ibid.* art. 218(6)(b). For collaboration between Commission and Parliament on international agreements see Framework Agreement on relations between the European Parliament and the European Commission [2010] OJ L304/47, paras 23–5 and Annex III.

415   *Ibid.* art. 207(6).

Parliament, the Council, the Commission or a member state as to the compatibility with the Treaties of a proposed association agreement, and if found incompatible the Union may enter into it only if the agreement is altered to the extent necessary to accommodate the Court's objections or the Treaties themselves are amended to remove the incompatibility.[416]

Of course the assertion by a legal entity which is not a state of treaty-making **14.73** power does not of itself suffice to create it, it must also be recognised by other persons with international legal personality – for practical intents and purposes, third states. The EEC Treaty provided that '[t]he Community shall have legal personality'[417] which, combined with articles 113 and 238 EEC, seems intended and designed to meet the tests set out by the International Court of Justice in the *Reparations* case.[418] As for recognition, for many years the Soviet bloc states refused to recognise the Community or its institutions, but official relations were established with Comecon in 1988,[419] thereafter the Community was universally recognised as having the treaty-making power it asserts. It is a matter no longer contested.

(a) Mixed agreements

In order to enter into and give effect to a treaty with a third country or **14.74** international organisation the subject matter of which spans Union and national competences, there requires signature and ratification by both the Union in accordance with Treaty rules and by interested member states (some or all) in accordance with their constitutional rules. It is quite common, particularly for association agreements. It means, of course, that the Union institutions and the governments of the member states must collaborate, each within their respective spheres, in order to arrive at a mutually acceptable and compatible result. Even within their proper spheres of competence the member states are bound by article 4(3) TEU not to assume an international obligation which would frustrate or alter the scope of Treaty rules and objectives.[420] The

---

416   *Ibid.* art. 218(11) (ex art. 300(6) EC). An example of the former: in 1991 the Court barred the Community from ratifying the Agreement establishing the European Economic Area (Opinion 1/91 *Re the EEA Agreement* [1991] ECR I-6079), it doing so only after the Agreement was redrafted in order to overcome the Court's objections (see Opinion 1/92 *Re the EEA Agreement* (No. 2) [1993] ECR I-1061). As for the latter, the erstwhile Treaty bar to Community ratification of the European Convention (Opinion 2/94 *Re Accession to the ECHR* [1996] ECR I-1759) has now been removed by the Lisbon Treaty expressly providing for (and requiring) it; TEU, art. 6(2). As to accession to the ECHR see 6.113 above.

417   EEC Treaty, art. 210 (art. 47 TEU).

418   *Reparations for Injuries Suffered in the Service of the United Nations* [1949] ICJ Rep. 174.

419   Joint declaration of 25 June 1988 on the establishment of official relations between the European Economic Community and Council for Mutual Economic Assistance [1988] OJ L157/35.

420   Case 22/70 *Commission v Council* (ERTA) [1971] ECR 263, at paras 21–2. Advocate-General Poiares Maduro suggests that this extends to a duty of the member states, particularly those belonging to the Security Council, to prevent as far as possible the adoption of UN measures liable to enter into conflict with a core principle of

negotiation and adoption of these 'mixed agreements' is not always easy, even from the inside; a common position in the Council may be unachievable, or it may be at variance with the views of the participating member states. From the outside it is fraught, for it compels third countries to enter risky territory, perforce to interpret the constitutional (Treaty) competences of a foreign system, and in the event of success to agree an instrument which may be implemented, interpreted and applied on the Union side in 28 different ways. It is an issue which has long thwarted efficient treaty making by (and with) federal states, here made no less easy by the moving target of Union competences.[421]

14.75 It has just been made more difficult. The Court has identified a 'requirement' or 'principle' of 'unity in the international representation' of the Union and the Union and Member States[422] which derives from the duty of sincere cooperation of article 4(3) TEU: so much so that where a Union instrument provides a mechanism for a common approach to proposing additions to an Annex in a mixed agreement (an international convention on organic pollutants) but none had been adopted, a unilateral Swedish proposal (Sweden being a party to the Convention in its own right) 'resulted in splitting the international representation' of the Union,[423] dissociating Sweden from the 'concerted common strategy' of the Council,[424] so likely to compomise the principle of Union/member state unity in international representation (and so weaken the Union's negotiating power)[425] and so constitutes an infringment of article 4(3). Unspoken but implicit in the judgment is recognition and application of the closer collaboration in foreign policy required by the Treaty provisions on CFSP.

14.76 Where an international convention trenches (wholly or in part) upon Union jurisdiction but the Union cannot enter into it because accession is restricted to states, the Union may, exceptionally, authorise the member states to sign and

---

the Union legal order; see Cases C-402 and 415/05P *Kadi and Al Bakaraat v Council and Commission* (Kadi II) [2008] ECR I-6351, at para. 32 of his opinion.

421 An additional complexity, or a variation of mixed agreements, existed pre-Lisbon in circumstances in which the subject matter of an agreement spanned Community and Union competences, thus required to be signed by the Council acting by and in accordance with art. 24 TEU (pre-Lisbon) (for its CFSP elements) and/or art. 38 TEU (pre-Lisbon) (JHA elements), both for the Union, and by the Council by and in accordance with art. 300 EC for the Community. This at least had disappeared.

422 Opinion 1/91 *Re the EEA Agreement* [1993] ECR I-1061, at para. 36; Opinion 1/94 *Re the World Trade Organisation* [2004] ECR I-5267, at para. 108; Case C-246/07 *Commission v Sweden* [2010] ECR I-3317, at paras 55, 73, 104.

423 Case C-246/07 *Commission v Sweden, ibid.,* at para. 55.

424 *Ibid.* para. 91.

425 *Ibid.* para. 104.

ratify it.[426] But authorisation must be express, a presumption or a gentlemen's agreement will not suffice.[427] In 2009 the Community adopted regulations setting out compulsory procedures (Commission authorisation to negotiate and conclude the agreement, option to propose guidelines and participate as observer) by which member states may amend, renew or enter into treaty obligations with third countries in fields covered by the Rome I and Rome II Conventions (law applicable to contractual and non-contractual obligations)[428] and the Brussels II *bis* and maintenance Conventions (recognition, enforcement and cooperation in matrimonial and parental responsibility matters and in maintenance obligations).[429]

(b) Euratom

The Atomic Energy Community too has legal personality[430] and the power to **14.77** enter into association agreements with third states, groups of third states or international organisations within its spheres of activity.[431] It also has authority to enter into agreements with third states, international organisations or persons in third states 'within the limits of its powers and jurisdiction'.[432] This is essentially safety, security of materials and installations and supply of nuclear materials;[433] there is no authority to enter into commercial (external trade) agreements, which fall within Union competence even for materials, goods and products otherwise subject to Euratom.[434] Mixed agreements are envisaged and special rules are provided therefor.[435]

(c) Force of international agreements

Agreements concluded under article 216 are 'binding on the institutions of the **14.78** Union and on its Member States'.[436] This applies equally to agreements concluded not by the Union but by the member states, but to which the Union has succeeded.[437] Agreements concluded by the Union by authority of the

---

426 See e.g., Decision 2008/431 [2008] OJ L151/36, authorising (and compelling) member states to sign and ratify the Convention of 19 October 1996 on Jurisdiction, Applicable Law, Recognition, Enforcement, and Cooperation in respect of Parental Responsibility and Measures for the Protection of Children (1996 Hague Convention) [2008] OJ L151/39.

427 Case C-45/07 *Commission* v *Greece* [2009] ECR I-701.

428 Regulation 662/2009 [2009] OJ L200/25; as to the Rome Conventions see 11.169 above.

429 Regulation 664/2009 [2009] OJ L200/46; as to these Conventions see 11.169 above.

430 Euratom Treaty, art. 184.

431 *Ibid.* art. 206.

432 *Ibid.* art. 101, 1st para. Procedure is supplied in art. 101, 2nd and 3rd paras.

433 See Ruling 1/78 *Re the IAEA Draft Convention on the Physical Protection of Nuclear Materials, Facilities and Transports* [1978] ECR 2151.

434 Opinion 1/94 *Re the World Trade Organization* [1994] ECR I-5267.

435 Euratom Treaty, art. 102.

436 TFEU, art. 216(2) (ex art. 300(7) EC).

437 Cases 21 and 24/72 *International Fruit Company and ors* v *Produktschap voor Groenten en Fruit* [1972] ECR 1219; Case 38/75 *Douaneagent der Nederlandse Spoorwegen* v *Inspecteur der invoerrechten en accijnzen* [1975]

pre-Lisbon TEU[438] were also 'binding on the institutions of the Union'[439] but were governed not by Community law but by public international law, by their subject matter largely remote from the individual, and effective by such means as make international treaty law effective; the anomaly disappeared with Lisbon which provided express authority for agreements in CFSP fields with no dispensation from normal rules.[440]

14.79 From this it follows that a Union agreement forms an integral part of the Union legal order.[441] It is *not* to say its provisions are directly effective: that, as always, depends upon its terms. But the Union cleaves to a monist recognition of treaty law, attributed to article 216(2), and a great many association agreements into which the Union has entered (or succeeded) have been recognised as creating directly effective rights.[442] Advocate-General Sharpston observes that, as the effect of treaties in this context draws in part from the applicable rules of public international law, the test of direct effect as it applies to (internal) Union law differs slightly from that of an international treaty to which the Union is party or by which it is bound.[443] It is important to note that terms in a treaty provision may be identical to equivalent provisions in the TFEU yet it does *not* mean they mean the same thing, each to be interpreted in its context.[444] Nor, generally,

---

ECR 1439; Case C-308/06 *R (International Association of Independent Tanker Owners (Intertanko) and ors)* v *Secretary of State for Transport* [2008] ECR I-4057; Case C-366/10 *R (Air Transport Association of America and ors)* v *Secretary of State for Energy and Climate Change*, judgment of 21 December 2011, not yet reported, at para. 62. Where no such 'transfer' has occurred the agreement is not part of Union law; Case C-301/08 *Bogiatzi* v *Deutscher Luftpool and ors* [2009] ECR I-10185.

438 TEU (pre-Lisbon), arts 24 (for Title V) and 38 (for Title VI).
439 *Ibid.* art. 24(6); added by the Treaty of Nice.
440 TEU, art. 37.
441 Case C-459/03 *Commission* v *Ireland* (MOX) [2006] ECR I-4635, at para. 82; Case C-308/06 *Intertanko*, n. 437 above, at para. 53.
442 E.g., Case 181/73 *Haegemann* v *Belgian State* [1974] ECR 449 (association agreement with Greece); Case 104/81 *Hauptzollamt Mainz* v *Kupferberg* [1982] ECR 3641 (free trade agreement with Portugal); Case C-192/89 *Sevince* v *Staatssecretaris van Justitie* [1990] ECR I- 3461 (a measure adopted by institutions created under an association agreement with Turkey); Case C-432/92 *R* v *Secretary of State for Agriculture, Fisheries and Food, ex parte Anastasiou (Pissouri)* [1994] ECR I-3087 (association agreement with Cyprus); Case T-115/94 *Opel Austria* v *Council* [1997] ECR II-39 (EEA Agreement); Case C-63/99 *R* v *Secretary of State for the Home Department, ex parte Gloszczuk and anor* [2001] ECR I-6369 (Europe Agreement with Poland); Case C-438/00 *Deutscher Handballbund* v *Kolpak* [2003] ECR I-4135 (Europe Agreement with Slovakia); Case C-265/03 *Simutenkov* v *Ministerio de Educación y Cultura and anor* [2005] ECR I-2579 (partnership and cooperation agreement with Russia); Case C-366/10 *Air Transport Association of America*, n. 437 above (Open Skies air transport agreement with the United States).
443 Case C-240/09 *Lesoochranárske zoskupenie* v *Ministerstvo životného prostredia Slovenskej republiky*, judgment of 8 March 2011, not yet reported, at paras 39 and 85 of her opinion.
444 See e.g., Case 270/80 *Polydor* v *Harlequin Records* [1982] ECR 329: art. 14(2) of the 1972 free trade agreement with Portugal ('Quantitative restrictions ... and any measures having an effect equivalent to quantitative restrictions on imports shall be abolished') not to be construed in the same manner as art. 30 of the EEC Treaty (art. 34 TFEU). The agreement with the Swiss Confederation on the free movement of persons seems to merit a markedly different meaning in this context: see Case C-351/08 *Grimme* v *Deutsche Angesetellten-Krankenkasse* [2009] ECR I-10777; Case C-70/09 *Hengartner and Gasser* v *Landesregierung Vorarlberg* [2010]

does the Court appear to make reciprocity a condition for the direct effect, on the Union side, of a treaty provision.[445] A further function of monism, the provisions of an agreement with third countries enjoy primacy over incompatible Union legislation,[446] which can be set aside for that reason where the nature and broad logic of the agreement do not preclude it and its provisions are unconditional and sufficiently precise.[447] But they do not prevail over the law of the Treaties itself ('primary law'), and in particular the protection of fundamental rights.[448] This is because the Union reserves to itself (as it claims is its right in international law) the authority to determine the relationship between international law and the Union legal order and so subject the former to the latter.[449] This preserves the constitutional rules of the Union legal order from corruption by treaties, a courtesy the Union does not extend to those of the member states.

Where an international agreement affords no direct effect it nevertheless **14.80** continues to bind the Union, and there is (limited) authority for application of a principle of uniform interpretation by the courts.[450] In any event the Union is required by international law (and normally the express terms of the agreement itself) to take the measure necessary to comply with it. It might be observed that, unlike the rigour which it applies to member states in their compliance with Union law, the Union itself is sometimes very relaxed in its own compliance with wider rules set out by international treaty. Where the possibility exists it may be censured by other treaty partners, and fall within such enforcement mechanisms and sanctions as those treaties may provide.

ECR I-7229. The situation is different where there is express (or implied) direction in the agreement itself; see Case T-115/94 *Opel Austria*, n. 442 above: art. 10 of the EEA Agreement ('Customs duties on imports and exports, and any charges having equivalent effect, shall be prohibited between the Contracting Parties') to be interpreted as art. 12 EEC (art. 30 TFEU) *but* because the *acquis communautaire* was (by art. 6) expressly transposed into EEA law.

445 For example, the Swiss and Austrian courts generally did not accord direct effect to the free trade agreements with the EEC (e.g., Bundesgericht, 3. Mai 1978 (*Adams*), BGE 104 IV 175; 25. Januar 1979 (*Sunlight*), BGE 105 II 49; OGH, 10. Juli 1979 (*Austro-Mechana*), [1980] Öbl. 25) but it did not dissuade the Court of Justice from doing so. The Court takes a different approach in cases involving the World Trade Organization, putting greater store by reciprocity; see 14.102 below.

446 Case C-61/94 *Commission v Germany* [1996] ECR I-3989, at para. 52; Case C-311/04 *Algemene Scheeps Agentuur Dordrecht v Inspecteur der Belastingdienst – Douanedistrict Rotterdam* [2006] ECR I-609, at para. 25; Case C-344/04 *R (International Air Transport Association and anor) v Department for Transport* [2006] ECR I-403, at para. 35; Case C-308/06 *Intertanko*, n. 437 above, at para. 42; Case C-366/10 *Air Transport Association of America*, n. 437 above.

447 Case C-308/06 *Intertanko*, n. 437 above, at para. 45; Case C-366/10 *Air Transport Association of America*, n. 437 above, at paras 53–4.

448 Cases C-402 and 415/05P *Kadi and Al Bakaraat v Council and Commission* (Kadi II) [2008] ECR I-6351, at para. 308.

449 Per A-G Poiares Maduro at para. 24 of his opinion.

450 Case C-286/90 *Anklagemyndigheden v Poulsen and anor* [1992] ECR I-6019, at paras 9–10; Case C-308/06 *Intertanko*, n. 437 above, at para. 52. Such duty derives not from art. 4(3) TFEU (as it does in the intra-Union context) but from respect for international law.

14.81 Mixed agreements have the same status in the Union legal order as purely Union agreements as regards the provisions which fall within the scope of Union competence.[451]

3. The Agreements

14.82 Since 1961 the agreements into which the Community has entered are many, varied, sometimes comprehensive and frequently complex. Some are bilateral, some multilateral, and to some of the latter the Community/Union has acceded as a non-founding signatory or succeeded as it has assumed jurisdiction *ratione materiae* from the member states. A number are mixed agreements, with flanking ratification by the pre-Lisbon Union and/or the member states, and, depending upon the subject matter, the Atomic Energy Community may also be party to them. They may be grouped, in the manner of concentric circles looking outwards from the Union, as follows.

(a) Overseas countries and territories

14.83 The third countries with which the Union enjoys closest economic relations are not in fact third countries, but overseas territories of the member states (and in international law part of one or another member state) which although part of the Atomic Energy Community[452] are otherwise not part of the Union and, failing express reference (or perhaps necessary intendment), the general provisions of the Treaties and of Union law do not apply there.[453] From the beginning the EEC Treaty devoted a full Part (Part Four) to a special 'association' status envisaged for these overseas countries and territories (OCTs). The OCTs evolve and change over the years with acquisition by an OCT of independence from its metropolitan power, at which point it loses that status (gone, for example, are the French territories in Africa and there are no longer any Belgian or Italian territories to which Part Four applies),[454] and accession of

---

451 Case C-239/03 *Commission v France* [2004] ECR I-9325; see also the opinion of A-G Poiares Maduro in Case C-459/03 *Commission v Ireland* (MOX) [2006] ECR I-4635, at paras 20–42; Case C-240/09 *Lesoochranárske zoskupenie v Ministerstvo životného prostredia Slovenskej republiky*, judgment of 8 March 2011, not yet reported, and the extensive discussion of A-G Sharpston.

452 Euratom Treaty, art. 198; excluding Greenland and the British overseas territories; see 10.05 above, n. 42.

453 E.g., Case C-260/90 *Leplat v Territory of French Polynesia* [1992] ECR I-643; Case C-110/97 *Netherlands v Council* [2001] ECR I-8763.

454 OCT status lapses automatically with independence, the newly independent state free, by virtue of the 'clean slate' rule, unilaterally to alter any obligation it may have under Union law, but this does not remove it from the list of OCT states provided in the Treaty (Annex II), for that requires a positive act: prior to Lisbon formal Treaty amendment (which normally followed at the next round of Treaty amendment), now a decision of the (unanimous) European Council, TFEU (art. 355(6)), which was put to use first to sever Saint-Barthélemy from the Union and inscribe it in Annex II with effect from January 2012 (Decision 2010/718 [2010] OJ L325/4), subsequently to adapt the status of Mayotte in light of its becoming an overseas *department* (n. 457

new member states (principally the United Kingdom) which brought new territories into the fold. The present Treaty formulation confers OCT status upon 'non-European countries and territories which have special relations with Denmark, France, the Netherlands and the United Kingdom'.[455] They are:[456]

- Greenland;
- Mayotte, the French *collectivités d'outre-mer* (Saint-Pierre-et-Miquelon, Polynésie (Française), Wallis-et-Futuna, Saint-Barthélemy, but excluding Saint-Martin which is part of the Union), New Caledonia and the 'southern territories' (Terres Australes et Antarctiques Françaises);[457]
- Aruba, Curaçao and Sint Maarten and, for the present,[458] Bonaire, Saba and Sint Eustatius;
- Anguilla, the Cayman Islands, the Falkland Islands, South Georgia and the South Sandwich Islands, Montserrat, Pitcairn, Saint Helena and Dependencies, the British Antarctic Territory, the British Indian Ocean Territory, the Turks and Caicos Islands, the British Virgin Islands and Bermuda.

The object of Part Four association 'is to promote the economic and social **14.84** development of the [OCTs] and to establish close economic relations between them and the Union as a whole';[459] it 'serve[s]' primarily to further the interests and prosperity of the inhabitants of these countries and territories in order to lead them to the economic, social and cultural development to which they aspire'.[460] To this end the Treaties provide for admission of OCT goods into the Union as if they were Union goods ('the same treatment as [member states] accord each other pursuant to the Treaties'),[461] whilst the OCTs are required to

---

below). It is likely next to be redeployed to give effect to a political settlement of the evolving status of the erstwhile Netherlands Antilles.

455 TFEU, art. 198, 1st para. (ex art. 182, 1st para. EC).

456 Annex II.

457 Mayotte became an overseas *département* in 2011 (loi organique no. 2010–1486 du 7 décembre 2010 relative au Département de Mayotte, JO du 8 décembre 2010, p. 21458; in force 31 March 2011) and so an integral part of French territory but retains the OCT status it enjoyed previously as a *collectivité d'outre-mer* until upgraded to an outermost region within the Union by the European Council, upon a French recommendation (Declaration (No. 43) on Article 355(6) of the TFEU), with effect from 1 January 2014; Decision 2012/419 [2012] OJ L204/131. Although *collectivités d'outre-mer* upon withdrawal from the administrative jurisdiction of Guadeloupe in 2007, Lisbon expressly extended (or confirmed; see 2.75 above, n. 338 and accompanying text) the application of the Treaties to Saint-Martin and Saint-Barthélemy (TFEU, art. 355(1)), but the latter retroverted to OCT status (outside the Union) in 2012.

458 Aruba, Curaçao and Sint Maarten have been OCTs since 1964 as part of the Netherlands Antilles, retaining that status upon secession from (Aruba, 1986) and dissolution of (2010) the Antilles; upon dissolution Bonaire, Saba and Sint Eustatius were (re-)integrated into the European territory of the Netherlands but retain OCT status provisionally, until, it is anticipated, 2015; see n. 39 above.

459 TFEU, art. 198, 3rd para. (ex art. 182, 2nd para. EC).

460 *Ibid.* art. 198, 4th para.

461 *Ibid.* art. 199, 1st para. (ex art. 183, 1st para. EC).

treat Union goods (and goods from other OCTs) no less favourably than they accord goods from their metropole member state.[462] In particular, Union customs duties are expressly prohibited,[463] but an OCT may impose customs duties upon Union (or other OCT) goods insofar as they 'meet the needs of [its] development and industrialisation' or produce budget revenues and are no higher than those imposed upon goods imported from the metropole.[464] A right of establishment is extended to natural and juristic persons from an OCT in the manner of the Treaty chapter on establishment and upon a non-discriminatory basis[465] and the free movement of workers is addressed as a subject to be governed by future agreement.[466] However, since most of the peoples of the OCTs are also Union citizens,[467] any such agreement is, for them (and subject to the wholly internal rule as regards working in the mother country), otiose. Further detailed rules regulating association of OCTs with the Union are set out in a 2001 decision (Overseas Association Decision).[468] Closer 'partnership' arrangements with an individual OCT are possible.[469]

(b) European Economic Area

14.85 Commercial relations between the Union and the various member states of the European Free Trade Association (EFTA) were first governed by a series of free trade agreements entered into by the Community with each of the latter (the EFTA itself having no treaty-making power) in 1972/73. In order to advance the relationship, in 1992 the Community and its member states, on the one part, and the (then) EFTA member states (Iceland, Liechtenstein, Norway, Austria, Finland, Sweden and Switzerland) on the other, signed the treaty establishing the European Economic Area (EEA).[470] It entered into force, and, excluding Switzerland (which, following a (double) 'no' vote in a federal referendum,[471] declined to ratify it), the EEA came into being, on 1 January 1994. Whilst never an agreement between equals, with the accession of Austria, Finland and Sweden to the Union in 1995 the EFTA component of the EEA diminished further to a rump of Iceland, Liechtenstein and Norway. The balance was further distorted as the new (2004 and 2007) member states acceded to the EEA (as they must,[472] though requiring EFTA consent) upon

---

462 *Ibid.* art. 199, 2nd para.
463 *Ibid.* art. 200, 1st para. (ex 184, 1st para. EC).
464 *Ibid.* art. 200, 2nd and 3rd paras.
465 *Ibid.* art. 199, 5th para.
466 *Ibid.* art. 202 (ex art. 186 EC).
467 See 8.10 above.
468 Decision 2001/822 [2001] OJ L314/1.
469 See e.g., Decision 2006/526 [2006] OJ L208/28 on relations with Greenland.
470 Agreement of 2 May 1992 on the European Economic Area [1994] OJ L1/3 (EEA Agreement).
471 The Agreement required a double majority, approval by both electors and cantons (see now art. 142(2) (Sch)BV (of 18 April 1999)), and failed to achieve either.
472 EEA Agreement, art. 128.

(or shortly after) Union accession, as 'new contracting parties', subject to some transitional arrangements,[473] and will be distorted further still should Iceland be successful in its application for accession to the Union.

The purpose of the EEA is   **14.86**

> to promote a continuous and balanced strengthening of trade and economic relations between the Contracting Parties with equal conditions of competition, and the respect of the same rules, with a view to creating a homogenous European Economic Area.[474]

It is not otherwise defined and its nature is difficult to categorise. It is a sophisticated free trade area but includes also provisions on the free movement, of persons, services and capital, with a view to economic integration less profound than that of the Union but deeper than that of the EFTA. Two telling examples are the exhaustion of intellectual property rights within the EEA,[475] which did not apply in previous Community–EFTA trade;[476] and the EEA rules on the free movement of persons, a matter not or hardly addressed in other treaties, which are extensive, essentially (almost) the same as those which apply to free movement within the Union,[477] and Iceland, Liechtenstein and Norway are full parties to Schengen.[478] There has been extensive cooperation beyond the confines of the four freedoms. The EEA assumed the *acquis communautaire* as at the date of signature of the Agreement[479] insofar as the meaning of a Community provision identical in substance to an EEA provision had been established by the Court of Justice, which was then binding for the EEA; a determination by the Court of Justice after that date is to be accorded 'due consideration'.[480] The institutional machinery is the most sophisticated created by an association agreement: the EEA has its own institutions – a Council, a Joint Committee, a Parliamentary Committee, a Consultative Committee,[481] analogous to, respectively, the European Council, the Council, the Parliament and the Economic and Social Committee – one of which (the Joint Committee) may adopt binding acts, generally by agreement between the Union representatives and the EFTA representatives 'speaking with one voice'.[482] The

---

473   Agreement of 14 October 2003 [2004] OJ L130/11, in force 1 May 2004; agreement of 25 July 2007 [2007] OJ L221/15, in force 1 August 2007.
474   EEA Agreement, art. 1.
475   Protocol 28, art. 2; see 10.82 above.
476   Case 270/80 *Polydor v Harlequin Records* [1982] ECR 329.
477   See 11.149 above.
478   See 11.192–11.194 above.
479   EEA Agreement, art. 6.
480   EFTA Surveillance Agreement of 2 May 1992 establishing a Surveillance Authority and an EFTA Court of Justice, art. 3(2).
481   EEA Agreement, arts 90–6.
482   *Ibid.* art. 93(2).

Agreement also required the creation by the EFTA of a surveillance authority[483] and a court of justice (the EFTA Court)[484] to ensure fulfilment of EEA obligations on the EFTA side, which responsibilities are discharged by the Commission and the Court of Justice on the Union side. Thus it is that any (and extensive) Union legislation which may have a bearing upon a field of EEA activity now bears the notice 'text with EEA relevance'. The Agreement implies no cession of sovereignty. Once dubbed the 'European Waiting Room', from the German for EEA (*Europäischer Wirtschaftsraum*, EWR), it is thought to serve as a penultimate stage prior to Union accession (borne out within a year by Austrian, Finnish and Swedish accession). Iceland has now followed this trend, breaking ranks with a 2009 application for accession, but Liechtenstein and Norway at least show no inclination to rush to join, seeming rather to prefer a Europe *à la carte* which the EEA in some measure provides.

(c) Switzerland

14.87 With its failure to ratify the EEA Agreement, Community–Swiss relations continued to be governed by the 1972 free trade agreement between them.[485] With a view to building upon it, in 1999, following several years of negotiations, the two signed a series of agreements ('bilateral agreements I') in seven specific areas, or 'sectors': free movement of persons; technical trade barriers; public procurement; agriculture; overland transport; air transport; and research.[486] The most far-reaching is the agreement on the free movement of persons.[487] It was the degree of progress made here which prompted the overhaul of the constituent EFTA documents in the Vaduz Convention,[488] in order to bring EFTA law into line with what had been achieved between the Community and Switzerland. In 2004 nine further sectoral agreements ('bilateral agreements II') were signed, on taxation of savings income; cooperation in the fight against fraud; association of Switzerland to the Schengen *acquis*; Swiss participation in the Dublin and Eurodac regulations (asylum and electronic identification system); trade in processed agricultural products; Swiss participation in the European Environment Agency; statistical cooperation; Swiss participation in the Media Plus and Media programmes for training in the

---

483   *Ibid.* art. 108(1).
484   *Ibid.* art. 108(2).
485   Agreement of 22 July 1972 between the European Economic Community and the Swiss Confederation [1972] JO L300/191; in force 1 January 1973.
486   Agreements of 21 June 1999 between the European Community and its Member States, of the one part, and the Swiss Confederation, of the other part, [2002] OJ L114; in force 1 June 2002.
487   Agreement of 21 June 1999 between the European Community and its Member States, of the one part, and the Swiss Confederation, of the other part, on the Free Movement of Persons [2002] OJ L114/6. See 11.150 above.
488   Consolidated Version of the Convention Establishing the European Free Trade Area (Vaduz Convention of 21 June 2001), (Liechtensteinisches) LGBl. 2003 Nr. 189, in force 1 June 2002.

audiovisual sector; and on the avoidance of double taxation for retired Union *fonctionnaires* living in Switzerland. As of March 2009 Switzerland participates fully in Schengen.[489] The agreement on free movement of persons was subject to renewal in 2009,[490] and approved by (optional) referendum early that year;[491] had it been denounced by either party the remaining agreements would have died with it (the 'guillotine clause'),[492] as it is they now continue indefinitely.[493] In practice Switzerland closely shadows Union developments and, although it is not bound to do so, frequently conforms unilaterally to Union norms, through, for example, implementation of Directives – a process known there as *europäischer autonomer Nachvollzug*.

(d) Europe Agreements/Accession partnerships

Beginning with what were to become the 2004 accession countries and as part **14.88**
of the new 'accession strategy', in the 1990s the Community entered into 'Europe Agreements' with each, providing for the progressive development of economic integration preparatory to accession to the Community, considered, and formally expressed, to achieve 'gradual integration into the Community'.[494] They provide for rights of establishment and free movement of services, with limited rights for workers.[495] Each was accompanied later by an 'accession partnership', a 'new instrument ... constitut[ing] the key feature of the enhanced pre-accession strategy'[496] for making available financial resources within the framework of the relevant Europe Agreement. Both Europe Agreement and accession partnership lapse with accession, so that with the demise of the Europe Agreements with Romania[497] and Bulgaria,[498] none of the former now exists. In the cases of Turkey and of Croatia the latter leapfrogged the former, the Community adopting accession partnerships with each in 2006.[499] The past precedent of a Europe Agreement as a waystation on the road to accession was not followed with Croatia and may have died away. Special

---

489 See 11.193 above.
490 Agreement of 21 June 1999, n. 487 above, art. 25(2).
491 The Swiss Constitution provides for an 'optional' (*fakultativ*) referendum in areas such as this if demanded by 50,000 voters or 8 cantons; art. 141 (Sch)BV.
492 Agreement of 21 June 1999, n. 487 above, art. 25(4).
493 *Ibid.* art. 25(2).
494 E.g., Europe Agreement of 1 February 1994 with Romania [1994] OJ L357/2, art. 1.
495 See 11.155 above.
496 Regulation 622/98 [1998] OJ L85/1, preamble, 6th recital.
497 Europe Agreement of 1 February 1994, n. 494 above; accession partnership in Decision 2002/92 [2002] OJ L44/82.
498 Europe Agreement of 8 March 1993 [1994] OJ L358/3; accession partnership in Decision 2003/396 [2003] OJ L145/1.
499 Decision 2006/35 [2006] OJ L22/34 (Turkey); Decision 2006/145 [2006] OJ L55/30 (Croatia).

assistance ('pre-accession assistance') is made available to candidate countries in the run up to accession.[500]

(e)   Customs unions and free trade areas

14.89   The Union has entered into bilateral treaties creating customs unions with Andorra (partially),[501] San Marino,[502] Turkey[503] and the Færoe Islands.[504] There is no formal agreement with Monaco, but the 1963 Customs Convention with France means that the principality is, in effect, part of the territory of the EU's customs union.[505] Rather than any (difficult) renegotiation of uniform tariffs, they involve simply the adoption and extension of the Common Customs Tariff by and to these countries. But it should be noted that these arrangements do not bind third countries, so that, for example, Sanmarinese or Monegasque goods in free circulation in the Union have not acquired Union origin and so may be subjected to differential treatment upon re-export.

14.90   The Community/Union has entered into free trade agreements with a number of third countries and groups of third countries. In 2010 it broke new ground with conclusion of an extensive (1,421 pages in the *Official Journal*) free trade agreement with South Korea.[506] Even more ambitious negotiations are in train with Canada, Japan and India. But many of the other types of association agreements into which it has entered embrace elements of free trade in various fashions, as follows.

(f)   Union for the Mediterranean

14.91   A Euro-Mediterranean partnership (or 'Barcelona Process') started with the Barcelona Euro-Mediterranean Conference in 1995,[507] organised as a Union

---

500   Regulation 1085/2006 [2006] OJ L210/82 (IPA Regulation); Regulation 718/2007 [2007] OJ L170/1 implementing it.

501   Exchange of letters of 28 June 1990 [1990] OJ L374/14; in force 1 July 1991. The agreement applies reciprocally only to industrial goods (art. 2); agricultural goods of Andorran origin are admitted duty free into the Community (art. 11) but not vice versa.

502   Agreement of 16 December 1991 on Cooperation and Customs Union between the European Economic Community and the Republic of San Marino [2002] OJ L84/43; in force 1 April 2002.

503   Decision 1/95 of the EC-Turkey Association Council on implementing final provisions of the customs union [1996] OJ L35/1; in force 1 January 1996.

504   Agreement of 6 December 1996 between the European Community and the Government of Denmark and the Home Government of the Færoe Islands [1997] OJ L53/2; in force 1 January 1997.

505   Convention douanière de 18 mai 1963 entre le Gouvernement de la République française et le Gouvernement de la Principauté de Monaco, JORF du 23 août 1963, in force 1 September 1963; recognised as such in the Community Customs Code (Regulation 2913/92 [1992] OJ L302/1) and the Modernised Code (Regulation 450/2008 [2008] OJ L145/1), art. 3(2)(a). See discussion in Case C-291/09 *Francesco Guarnieri and Cie v Vandevelde Eddy VOF*, judgment of 7 April 2011, not yet reported.

506   Free Trade Agreement of 6 October 2010 between the European Union, its Member States and the Republic of Korea [2011] OJ L127/6; not yet in force but applied provisionally from 1 July 2011.

507   For the text of the 'Barcelona Declaration' see *Bulletin EU* 11–1995, 136.

initiative in order to strengthen relations with the non-Union countries of the Mediterranean littoral. The partnership came to comprise the Union and its member states plus Morocco, Algeria, Tunisia, Egypt, Palestine, Israel, Jordan, Lebanon, Syria and Turkey; Libya and Mauritania had observer status, leaving out only Monaco, the coastal states of (ex-)Yugoslavia and the Turkish Republic of Northern Cyprus. It had three principal objectives: the definition of a common area of peace and stability through the reinforcement of political and security dialogue (the political and security basket); the construction of a zone of shared prosperity through an economic and financial partnership and the gradual establishment of a free-trade area (the economic and financial basket); and a rapprochement between peoples through a social, cultural and human partnership aimed at encouraging understanding between cultures and exchanges between civil societies (the social, cultural and human basket). An essential feature has been the negotiation of Euro-Mediterranean association agreements to replace a (dated) series of 1970 cooperation agreements, with Tunisia (1998), Israel and Morocco (2000), Algeria (2001), Jordan and Lebanon (2002), Egypt and Syria (2004) and, upon an interim basis, with the Palestinian Authority (1997), to the extent of what are effectively free trade agreements with Israel[508] and with the Palestinian territories,[509] although the latter is a chimera so long as Gaza is under blockade and the West Bank borders subject *de facto* to Israeli control. In fact much of the partnership remains hostage to events in the Middle East. In order to impart a 'new impulse', in 2008 the Barcelona Process evolved into the 'Union for the Mediterranean' (UfM), approved in principle by the European Council in March of that year[510] and formally inaugurated at the 'Paris Summit for the Mediterranean' in July. It includes all existing members of the Barcelona Process plus Bosnia and Herzegovina, Croatia, Monaco and Montenegro – only Northern Cyprus still frozen out – and the active participation of the League of Arab States. The UfM is in the process of finding its feet.

(g) Partnership and cooperation agreements

Lisbon wrote into the Treaty a duty for the Union to   **14.92**

---

508   Euro-Mediterranean Agreement of 20 November 1995 establishing an Association between the European Communities and their Member States and Israel [2000] OJ L147/1. This developed out of a free trade area first established in 1975. 'Israel' is limited to the pre-1967 borders; Case C-386/08 *Brita v Hauptzollamt Hamburg-Hafen* [2010] ECR I-1289.

509   Euro-Mediterranean Interim Agreement of 24 February 1997 on Trade and Cooperation between the Community and the Palestine Liberation Organisation [1997] OJ L187/3. The agreement is restricted to the West Bank and Gaza, so excluding (for the present) East Jerusalem.

510   European Council, 13–14 March 2008, Conclusions of the Presidency, *Bulletin EU* 3–2008, Annex I.

develop a special relationship with neighbouring countries, aiming to establish an area of prosperity and good neighbourliness, founded on the values of the Union and characterised by close and peaceful relations based on cooperation.[511]

A species of this is partnership and cooperation agreements, a response to the dissolution of the Soviet Union. The first was signed with the Russian Federation in 1994 (in force 1997), subsequent PCAs with Moldova and the Ukraine (signed 1994; in force 1998), Kazakhstan and the Kyrgyz Republic (1995; 1999), Armenia, Azerbaijan, Georgia and Uzbekistan (1996; 1999) and Tajikistan (2004; 2010). Agreements have been signed with Belarus (1995) and Turkmenistan (1998) but are not yet in force. The PCAs constitute a framework for the promotion of political, commercial, economic, technical and cultural cooperation, and provide for some movement of persons and services.[512] A *leitmotif* is the transition of the PCA countries to a market economy, and the encouragement of trade and investment to that end. At the time of writing a new agreement with Russia is under negotiation.

(h)   Stabilisation and association partnerships

14.93 In response to the (violent) dismemberment of Yugoslavia, the European Council adopted the 'Thessaloniki Agenda' at the Thessaloniki summit in 2003 for a 'stabilisation and association process' (SAP) in the western Balkans, calling for the conclusion of a species of European partnerships (a stablisation and association agreement, SAA) with Albania, Bosnia and Herzegovina, Croatia, (the former Yugoslav Republic of) Macedonia and Serbia (including Kosovo) and Montenegro ('the partners').[513] Each is to provide a framework establishing the priorities, based upon a partner's individual circumstances and in light of criteria adopted by the European Council and the Council, for further integration with the Union, and the progress made in implementing the stabilisation and association process including stabilisation and association agreements, where appropriate, and monitoring.

14.94 Present terms are set in January 2006 on the principles, priorities and conditions contained in the SAAs with Albania, Bosnia and Herzegovina, Macedonia and Serbia and Montenegro. Following independence later in 2006, Montenegro entered into a separate SAA in 2007, entering into force in 2010; Kosovo has not yet done so. Croatia entered into an SAA in 2004, remaining part of the process but the relationship significantly overtaken by an accession partnership agreed in 2006[514] which will lapse with accession in 2013. The great attraction

---

511   TEU, art. 8.
512   See 11.156 above.
513   See Regulation 533/2004 [2004] OJ L86/1.
514   Decision 2006/145 [2006] OJ L55/30.

for the SAP partners is the carrot of accession, in the immediate (Croatia) or distant (Kosovo) future.

(i) European neighbourhood policy

Overlying the Union for the Mediterranean and the partnership and cooperation agreements is the European neighbourhood policy (ENP), developed in 2004.[515] The object is **14.95**

> to share the benefits of the EU's 2004 enlargement with neighbouring countries in strengthening stability, security and well-being for all concerned [in order] to prevent the emergence of new dividing lines between the enlarged EU and its neighbours and to offer them the chance to participate in various EU activities, through greater political, security, economic and cultural co-operation.[516]

It is therefore in part a mechanism for addressing the strategic objectives of the European Security Strategy agreed by the European Council in December 2003.[517] It offers each partner 'a privileged relationship', both political and economic, with the Union (and so 'a stake in the internal market'), the ambition and detail of which is a function of 'the existing status of relations with each country [and] its needs and capacities',[518] to be determined and agreed upon a bilateral basis (by 'action plans') and promoted, implemented and monitored through sub-committees. An ENP 'instrument' was adopted in 2006[519] to regulate Union assistance in promoting ENP goals, and since 2007 a partner may participate in Union agencies and programmes on their merits and where the legal base so allows. The ENP remains distinct from the process of enlargement although it does not prejudge how relations may develop in future, in accordance with Treaty provisions.

The ENP applies to the Union's 'immediate neighbours', all states party to the Union for the Mediterranean save Turkey plus Armenia, Azerbaijan, Belarus, Georgia, Libya, Moldova, Russia and the Ukraine. Since it builds upon existing agreements between the EU and the partner in question (Partnership and Cooperation Agreements, or Association Agreements in the framework of the EuroMediterranean Partnership), the ENP is not yet 'activated' for Belarus, Libya or Syria since no such Agreements are yet in force. In 2009 the ENP part evolved into a specialised 'Eastern Partnership Policy' (EPP) in order to build **14.96**

---

515 EC Commission, *Wider Europe – Neighbourhood: A New Framework for Relations with our Eastern and Southern Neighbours*, COM(2003) 104 final and *European Neighbourhood Policy: Strategy Paper*, COM(2004) 373 final.
516 *ENP Strategy Paper, ibid.*, p. 3.
517 *A Secure Europe in a Better World: European Security Strategy* (12 December 2003).
518 *ENP Strategy Paper*, n. 515 above, p. 3.
519 Regulation 1638/2006 [2006] OJ L310/1.

closer relations with a number of former Soviet countries of 'strategic importance': Armenia, Azerbaijan, Georgia, Moldova and the Ukraine, with Belarus
on the perimeter.

(j)   Cotonou Agreement

14.97   In 1963 an association agreement between the EEC and 18 African countries,
ex-colonies of the then member states which had recently gained their independence, was signed in Yaoundé (Cameroon). Dealing exclusively with trade
and economic relations, the Yaoundé Convention had a validity period of five
years; it was renewed (Yaoundé II) in 1969. British accession in 1973 altered
significantly the colonial heritage (and responsibilities) of the Community, and
arrangements grew to embrace a much larger number of African, Caribbean
and Pacific (ACP) countries, governed thereafter by a series of regularly
updated and renewed Lomé (Togo) Agreements, hence Lomé I (1975–80),
Lomé II (1980–85), Lomé III (1985–90) and Lomé IV (1990–2000). The
expiry of Lomé IV brought about another fundamental shift, and following 18
months of negotiations started in September 1998 a new partnership agreement, between the Community and the member states, on the one part and,
now, 79 ACP countries on the other (49 from sub-Saharan Africa, 15 from the
Caribbean and 15 from the Pacific) was concluded in February 2000 and signed
in June at Cotonou (Benin).[520] It is concluded for a 20-year period, to the end of
February 2020.[521] It is subject to 'revision' every five years,[522] as a result of which
some changes were agreed (the Luxembourg revision) in 2005, in force July
2008, and again (the second, or Oagodougou, revision) in 2010, not yet in force
but applied provisionally since signature.[523]

14.98   Cotonou is more ambitious than its predecessors. Generally it is a vehicle for
admission of identified (extensively) goods originating in ACP countries free of
customs duties, charges having equivalent effect and quantitative restrictions[524]
within the confines of the WTO; but its wider purpose is 'to promote and
expedite the economic, cultural and social development of the ACP States, with
a view to contributing to peace and security and to promoting a stable and

---

520   Partnership Agreement of 23 June 2000 between the members of the African, Caribbean and Pacific group of
states, of the one part, and the European Community and its Member States, of the other part [2000] OJ
L317/3; in force 1 April 2003. The agreement was signed by 77 ACP states, East Timor joined in 2003
following independence, South Africa in 2010. Cuba is recognised to be an ACP state but is not party to the
agreement; recent strong Spanish support for Cuban accession has met with resistance from a number of
Union member states.
521   *Ibid.* art. 95(1).
522   *Ibid.* art. 95(3).
523   Decision 2/2010 of the ACP-EU Council of Ministers [2010] OJ L287/68; applied as from 31 October 2010.
524   Cotonou Agreement, Annex V, arts 1 and 2.

democratic political environment',[525] to be achieved in accordance with four 'fundamental principles': equality of partners and ownership of development strategies; participation (of not only governments but civil society, the private sector, local government); dialogue and mutual obligations, in particular respect for human rights (concern for human rights in ACP states having developed in the Lomé days); and differentiation and regionalisation.[526] It is intended to be comprehensive and override any other bilateral or multilateral Union–ACP arrangement;[527] but special arrangements are permissible within Cotonou so long as they are not incompatible with it.[528]

(k) World Trade Organization

The World Trade Organization (WTO) came into being with the entry into **14.99** force of the Marrakech Agreement[529] on 1 January 1995. It grew out of, and absorbed, the General Agreement on Tariffs and Trade (GATT) (1947),[530] itself only a 'provisional' arrangement[531] until overtaken by the Havana Charter (1948)[532] which never came into force. The Community was never a signatory to the original GATT but purported to succeed to membership of the member states[533] and has since the 1960s discharged almost all GATT obligations in its own name without demur from other contracting parties. The 'original members' of the WTO were those contracting parties to GATT (as at January 1995) and the (European) Community which accepted its terms and conditions.[534] Subsequent accession, upon terms unique to and tailored to the needs of each

---

525   *Ibid.* art. 1.

526   *Ibid.* art. 2.

527   *Ibid.* art. 91.

528   E.g, the Economic Partnership Agreement of 15 October 2008 between [most of] the CARIFORUM States and the European Community and its Member States [2008] OJ L289/1/3. CARIFORUM is the 15 member states of the Caribbean Community plus the Domenican Republic; Haiti (a Caribbean Community member state) did not sign and remains outside the agreement; Interim Partnership Agreement of 30 July 2009 between the European Community and the Pacific States (Fiji and Papua New Guinea) [2009] OJ L272/2; Interim Partnership Agreement of 23 November and 12 December 2007 between the European Community and the Southern African Development Community states (Botswana, Lesotho, Mozambique, Namibia, Swaziland) [2009] OJ L319/3. Cotonou Agreement, art. 91.

529   Agreement of 15 April 1994 establishing the World Trade Organization, 1867 UNTS 154.

530   General Agreement on Tariffs and Trade of 30 October 1947, 55 UNTS 194; absorbed in to the WTO as Annex 1A of the WTO Agreement, the Multilateral Agreement on Trade in Goods or GATT 1994, being a revision of the original GATT.

531   Protocol on Provisional Application, 55 UNTS 308.

532   Charter of 24 March 1948 for an International Trade Organization, UN Doc. ICITO/1/4/1948.

533   Cases 21 and 24/72 *International Fruit Company and ors* v *Produktschap voor Groenten en Fruit* [1972] ECR 1219; Case 38/75 *Douaneagent der Nederlandse Spoorwegen* v *Inspecteur der invoerrechten en accijnzen* [1975] ECR 1439.

534   WTO Agreement, art. XI.1. Neither the ECSC nor Euratom were signatories to the WTO, for CCP measures fell within EC competence even for ECSC and Euratom products; Opinion 1/94 *Re the World Trade Organization* [1994] ECR I-5267. This gave rise to difficulties in that internal implementing measures may be a matter for one or another of the Communities as the case may be, but they have been largely neutered by the absorption of ECSC matters into the EC.

applicant country as agreed by the Ministerial Conference,[535] has led to a membership, as at January 2012, of 153. Russia applied for membership in 1993, abandoned bilateral accession negotiations in 2009 in favour of seeking first to form a customs union with Kazakhstan and Belarus, but in 2011 picked up a second wind, at the end of the year was admitted by a decision of the WTO ministerial conference and formally acceded in August 2012, bringing membership (with Vanuatu, also August 2012) to 157. There are also 30-odd 'observers', which (except for the Vatican) are required to enter into accession negotiations within five years of acquiring that status. Major countries still outside the WTO are Algeria, Iran, Iraq and Libya, all with observer status. Globally only 15 other (recognised) countries and territories have no formal link with the WTO.[536] The primary activity of the WTO is the administration of 60-odd agreements and commitments made by its members as part of the GATT 1994 (for trade in goods), the General Agreement on Trade in Services (GATS)[537] and the agreement on trade-related aspects of intellectual property rights (TRIPs).[538] It has legal personality.[539] Its seat is Geneva.

14.100 The Community and the member states were jointly original members of the WTO, which is just as well as accession is open to '[a]ny state or customs territory having full autonomy in the conduct of its trade policies'[540] which would bar both the Community (probably) and the member states (certainly). Prior to signature it proved necessary to consult the Court of Justice on the question of Community *vires*, which determined that it was solely for the Community to enter into the multilateral agreement on trade in goods, but that both the GATS and the TRIPs addressed areas of mixed competence.[541] This is no longer so.[542]

14.101 The WTO is an instrument for global trade liberalisation. It therefore speaks the same language as the Union, if in a far less sophisticated dialect, and the Court has recognised that there is a Treaty requirement of Union adherence to international trade liberalisation which mirrors that of the WTO.[543] The

---

535   *Ibid.* art. XII.
536   That is, East Timor, Eritrea, Kiribati, the Marshall Islands, Micronesia, Monaco, Nauru, North Korea, Palestine, Palau, San Marino, Somalia, Turkmenistan, Tuvalu, and the Western Sahara.
537   WTO Agreement, Annex 1B.
538   *Ibid.* Annex 1C.
539   *Ibid.* art. VIII.1.
540   *Ibid.* art. XII.
541   Opinion 1/94 *Re the World Trade Organization* [1994] ECR I-5267. The subject matters of the GATS and the TRIPs agreements remained within member state competence save for, respectively, cross-frontier services not involving the movement of natural or legal persons and the release of counterfeit goods into free circulation.
542   See n. 400 above and accompanying text.
543   TFEU, art. 206 (ex art. 131 EC); see Cases 21–24/72 *International Fruit Company and ors v Produktschap voor Groenten en Fruit* [1972] ECR 1219, at para. 13.

cornerstone is the most favoured nation (MFN) clause,[544] inherited from GATT 1947. A major innovation of the WTO was the dispute settlement procedure agreed at the Uruguay Round, addressed by the principal WTO Agreements[545] and the Dispute Settlement Understanding (DSU).[546] Essentially, parties to a dispute have recourse to DSU which provides for negotiation with a view to achieving a mutually acceptable settlement, failing which it is referred to a panel of the Dispute Settlement Body (DSB). Upon the panel's report the DSB may adopt a recommendation or ruling requiring the defaulting party to comply within a 'reasonable period of time',[547] may recommend compensation, compliance with which is 'voluntary',[548] and may authorise temporary suspension of WTO rights of the defaulting party,[549] so permitting retaliation.

An issue of significant contention, and not only for the Union, is the force of the **14.102** WTO Agreement, in particular whether its prohibitions can be, or should be, in Union terms, directly effective. The Court of Justice long set itself against the direct effect of the original GATT;[550] the question was then whether the WTO would suffer the same fate, in particular in light of the dispute settlement procedures, recognised by the Court itself as a significant 'strengthening of the system of safeguards and the mechanism for resolving disputes'.[551] It was the clear understanding of the Council that the Agreement confer no direct effect,[552] but no Union institution need be taught that the understanding, or even intention, of a contracting party to a treaty necessarily determines the meaning of its terms. The definitive answer of the Court was set out in 1999:

> [H]aving regard to their nature and structure, the WTO agreements are not in principle among the rules in the light of which the Court is to review the legality of measures adopted by the Community institutions.[553]

---

544 WTO Agreement, Annex 1A (GATT 1994), art. I; Annex 1B (GATS), art. II; Annex 1C (TRIPs), art. 4.

545 *Ibid.* Annex 1A, arts XXII and XXIII; Annex 1B, art. XXIII; Annex 1C, art. 64.

546 *Ibid.* Annex 2.

547 *Ibid.* art. 21.3.

548 *Ibid.* art. 22.1.

549 *Ibid.* art. 22.

550 Cases 21 and 24/72 *International Fruit Company and ors v Produktschap voor Groenten en Fruit* [1972] ECR 1219; Case 266/81 *Società Italiana per l'Oleodotto Transalpino v Ministero delle finanze and ors* [1983] ECR 731; Case C-469/93 *Amministrazione delle Finanze dello Stato v Chiquita Italia* [1995] ECR I-4533; Case C-280/93 *Germany v Council* (Bananas) [1994] ECR I-4973.

551 Case C-149/96 *Commission v Portugal* [1999] ECR I-8395, at para. 36.

552 See Decision 94/800 [1994] OJ L336/1 (by which the Council ratified the WTO Agreement), preamble, 12th indent: 'Whereas, by its nature, the Agreement establishing the World Trade Organization ... is not such as to be directly invoked in the Community or Member State courts'.

553 Case C-149/96 *Commission v Portugal*, n. 551 above, at para. 47.

The judgment was reasoned largely upon the basis of the DSU principle of settlement by negotiation rather than by law and, secondarily, reciprocity, the Court perceiving that the normal rule amongst other contracting parties to the Agreement was refusal to recognise direct effect. The result has been criticised – and was at variance with the opinion of Advocate-General Saggio[554] – but the Court has not wavered from it.[555] The exception is cases in which the Union intended to implement a particular obligation assumed in the context of the WTO or where a Union measure refers expressly to a particular provision of the WTO agreements.[556] Thus the Union anti-dumping Regulation, having the express purpose of giving effect in Union law to the WTO Anti-Dumping Agreement, must be implemented in accordance with it.[557] But a Union undertaking to comply with WTO rules following censure by a DSB decision is not intent to assume a particular obligation in the context of the WTO.[558] Advocate-General Alber argued that a Union court be bound to apply a decision of the DSB where the Union is censured for a breach of WTO rules and fails to comply with the recommendation or ruling within the prescribed period,[559] but the Court did not, and has not yet, followed him.

4. Protective measures

14.103 An aspect of the Common Commercial Policy which exerts a direct bearing upon individuals, but primarily those in third counties, is measures adopted in order to counteract injury to Union industries caused unfair trade practices. It is addressed by article 207 TFEU ('measures to protect trade such as those to be taken in the event of dumping or subsidies') which thus recognises it as part of the CCP and forms the legal base for such measures. It is an area informed by principles of trade law and competition law, in some measure falling uncomfortably between the two stools.

---

554 See paras 14–24 of his opinion.

555 Case C-377/98 *Netherlands* v *Parliament and Council* [2001 I-7079, at para. 52; Case C-93/02 *Biret International* v *Council* [2003] ECR I-10497, at para. 52; Case C-377/02 *Léon van Parys* v *Belgisch Interventie-en Restitutiebureau* [2005] ECR I-1465, at para. 39; Case C-351/04 *Ikea Wholesale* v *Commissioners of Customs and Excise* [2007] ECR I-7723, at para. 29; Cases C-120 and 121/06P *Fabbrica italiana accumulatori motocarri Montecchio (FIAMM) and anor* v *Council and Commission* [2008] ECR I-6513, at para. 111.

556 Case C-149/96 *Commission* v *Portugal* , n. 551 above, at para. 49; Case C-377/02 *Léon van Parys, ibid.*, at para. 40; Cases C-120 and 121/06P *FIAMM, ibid.*, at para. 112. These exceptions were developed in earlier case law involving the original GATT: Case 70/87 *Fediol* v *Commission* [1989] ECR 1781; Case C-69/89 *Nakajima* v *Council* [1991] ECR I-2069.

557 Case C-76/00P *Petrotub and Republica* v *Council* [2003] ECR I-79; as to anti-dumping see immediately below.

558 Case C-377/02 *Léon van Parys*, n. 555 above.

559 Case C-93/02 *Biret International*, n. 555 above.

(a) Antidumping and countervailing duties

14.104 The Union may adopt retaliatory measures against imports from third countries which benefit from unfair subsidies in their country of production or export (countervailing duties) or are dumped (anti-dumping duties), both permitted in international trade law.[560] Prior to 1996 the relevant Community rules were contained in a single instrument,[561] but in order to adapt to changes agreed within the Uruguay Round they were split into two, on 'protection against dumped imports'[562] and 'protection against subsidised imports'[563] – the 'basic Regulations'. They remain similar in construction and approach. They apply only partially to the importation of agricultural or processed agricultural goods.[564]

14.105 An imported product is dumped if its export price to the Union is less than a comparable price for the like product, in the ordinary course of trade, in the exporting country.[565] It is subsidised if it enjoys a financial contribution (a 'specific countervailable subsidy', defined broadly) by a government in the country of origin or export which confers upon it a benefit.[566] Where a product is dumped on the Union market the Union may impose an anti-dumping duty, the duty being the 'dumping margin', the difference by which the normal value exceeds the export price;[567] where it is subsidised the Union may impose a countervailing duty, calculated in terms of the benefit conferred upon the recipient.[568] In both cases the imposition of a duty must follow the initiation of an investigation (an 'administrative proceeding') by a complaint by a person acting on behalf of a Union industry[569] and it is a precondition of the imposition of a duty that the release into free circulation of the dumped/subsidised product causes 'material injury' to the Union industry.[570] Where a 'provisional affirmative affirmation' is made of the existence of dumping/

---

560 WTO, Annex 1A (GATT 1994), art. VI; Agreement on Subsidies and Countervailing Measures (SCM Agreement); Agreement on Implementation of Article VI of the General Agreement on Tariffs and Trade 1994 (AD Agreement; previously the Anti-Dumping Code).

561 Regulation 2423/88 [1988] OJ L209/1 (common rules for protection against dumped or subsidised imports).

562 Regulation 1225/2009 [2009] OJ L345/51 (replacing Regulation 384/96 [1996] OJ L56/1).

563 Regulation 597/2009 [2009] OJ L188/93 (replacing Regulation 2026/97 [1997] OJ L288/1).

564 Regulation 1225/2009, art. 22(b); Regulation 597/2009, art. 33(b).

565 Regulation 1225/2009, art. 1(2).

566 Regulation 597/2009, arts 1(1), 2(a), 3.

567 Regulation 1225/2009, art. 2. Criteria for computing all these data are set out in detail in the Regulation. Computation of a normal 'constructed' value, necessary (a) invariably for imports from (a dwindling number of) non-market economies and (b) usually where the product is not marketed in country of production, is particularly complex.

568 Regulation 597/2009, art. 5. This too is complex; for detail see arts 6, 7.

569 Regulation 1225/2009, art. 5; Regulation 597/2009, art. 10. The Commission may initiate an investigation absent a complaint but only in 'special circumstances … on the basis of sufficient evidence' which 'justify [it]'; arts 5(6) and 10(10), respectively. For the detail of the investigation see arts 6 and 11, respectively.

570 Regulation 1225/2009, arts 1(1), 3; Regulation 597/2009, arts 1(1), 8.

subsidy and consequent injury, the Commission may (unless overridden by the Council)[571] impose a provisional anti-dumping/countervailing duty where the Union interest justifies ('calls for') it.[572] A provisional anti-dumping duty may be imposed for up to six months, or nine months where it is requested by exporters representing a significant percentage of the relevant trade;[573] a provisional countervailing duty may be imposed for up to four months.[574] Voluntary undertakings may be accepted in lieu.[575]

14.106   Where the complaint is withdrawn in the course of an investigation or protective measures prove to be 'unnecessary', the proceedings are terminated.[576] Where the 'facts as finally established' by the investigation show the existence of dumping/subsidy, requisite injury, and 'the Community interest calls for intervention', the Council (upon a Commission proposal) imposes a definitive anti-dumping/countervailing duty.[577] An anti-dumping duty may not exceed the dumping margin and 'should be' less if the lesser duty would be adequate to relieve the injury.[578] Either duty is to remain in force only so long as, and to the extent that, it is necessary to counteract the dumping/subsidy which is causing injury.[579] They may be extended to imports from other third countries where producers seek to 'circumvent' them by setting up assembly operations elsewhere.[580] Duties lapse after five years unless it is determined in a review that such expiry would be likely to lead to a continuation or recurrence of the dumping/subsidy and injury.[581] The duties are collected upon importation by the competent customs authorities of the relevant member state.[582]

(b)   Safeguard measures

14.107   Also permitted by international trade law,[583] and preferred to anti-dumping or countervailing duties, are safeguard measures, a 'safety valve' permitting temporary restrictions on imports in the face of serious disruption to economies caused by surges in imports. For the Union they are regulated by a Regulation

---

571   Regulation 1225/2009, art. 7(6); Regulation 597/2009, art. 12(5).

572   Regulation 1225/2009, art. 7; Regulation 597/2009, art. 12.

573   Regulation 1225/2009, art. 7(7).

574   Regulation 597/2009, art. 12(6).

575   Regulation 1225/2009, art. 8; Regulation 597/2009, art. 13.

576   Regulation 1225/2009, art. 9(1)–(3); Regulation 597/2009, art. 14(1)–(3). Withdrawal of the complaint does not result in termination if it would 'not be in the Community interest'; arts 9(1) and 14(1), respectively. Protective measures are unnecessary if such injury as exists is negligible/*de minimis* (arts 9(3) and 14(3)).

577   Regulation 1225/2009, art. 9(4); Regulation 597/2009, art. 15(1). For the measure of sufficient Community interest see arts 21 and 31, respectively.

578   Regulation 1225/2009, art. 9(4).

579   Regulation 1225/2009, art. 11(1); Regulation 597/2009, art. 17.

580   Regulation 1225/2009, art. 13; Regulation 597/2009, art. 23.

581   Regulation 1225/2009, art. 11(2); Regulation 597/2009, art. 18(1).

582   Regulation 1225/2009, art. 14(1); Regulation 597/2009, art. 24(1).

583   WTO Agreement, Annex 1A (GATT 1994), art. XIX; Agreement on Safeguards (SG Agreement).

on 'common rules for imports',[584] which applies to all goods other than textiles[585] and those coming from certain non-WTO countries.[586] Safeguard measures are permitted where they are 'necessary' that is, '[w]here a product is imported into the Community in such greatly increased quantities and/or on such terms or conditions as to cause, or threaten to cause, serious injury to Community producers'.[587] 'Serious injury' means a significant overall impairment in the position of Union producers (taken as a whole) and 'threat of serious injury' means injury that is clearly imminent.[588] To discover it the Commission must, as a result of ongoing consultation with the member states as set out in the Regulation,[589] first launch a 'Community investigation procedure'.[590] If the investigation uncovers a threat of serious injury the Commission may initiate 'surveillance', either retrospective or prior;[591] products under surveillance may be put into free circulation only upon production of a 'surveillance document'.[592] Where necessary, appropriate safeguard measures, usually quotas or tariff increases, may be imposed by the Commission or, where the interests of the Union so require, by the Council, which may also confirm, amend or revoke a Commission measure.[593] Their duration is limited to a period of time necessary to prevent or remedy serious injury and to facilitate adjustment on the part of Union producers, and normally cannot exceed four years.[594] Provisional safeguard measures may be adopted by the Commission during an investigation or surveillance ('at any time') in 'critical circumstances' or where there is clear evidence of serious injury or threat thereof.[595] Surveillance and safeguard measures may be restricted to a part of the Union, but only exceptionally.[596]

14.108 The Union may also adopt measures to counteract 'illicit commercial practices' in third countries which are recognised by the WTO (or similar agreement) as 'obstacles to trade' and cause injury to a Union industry or enterprise, and are

---

584 Regulation 260/2009 [2009] OJ L84/1; replacing Regulation 3285/94 [1994] OJ L349/53.
585 Textiles are subject to Regulation 517/94 [1994] OJ L67/1.
586 That is, Armenia, Azerbaijan, Belarus, Kazakhstan, North Korea, Russia, Tajikistan, Turkmenistan, Uzbekistan, Vietnam (still, although Vietnam joined the WTO in 2007); subject to Regulation 519/94 [1994] OJ L67/89.
587 Regulation 260/2009, art. 16(1).
588 *Ibid.* art. 5(3).
589 *Ibid.* arts 2–4.
590 *Ibid.* arts 5–7.
591 *Ibid.* arts 11–15.
592 *Ibid.* art. 12(1).
593 *Ibid.* arts 16–22.
594 *Ibid.* art. 20(1).
595 *Ibid.* art. 8(1), 2nd para.
596 *Ibid.* arts 14, 16(5) and 18.

either prohibited by that agreement or it provides a right of action to seek their elimination.[597]

(c) Exports

14.109 The normal rule (the 'basic principle') is that export of goods from the Union is 'free', that is, subject to no quantitative restrictions.[598] Exceptions are the export of agricultural products, subject to significant financial intervention under the CAP;[599] and export of cultural goods,[600] dangerous chemicals[601] and 'dual use' goods.[602] Even generally, in the face of 'unusual developments on the market' the Commission may put in place a surveillance operation, and, where immediate intervention is called for, introduce a system of export authorisation in order to remedy a 'critical situation', or prevent it from arising, owing to a shortage of essential products;[603] to the same end and where the interests of the Union require it, the Council may adopt 'appropriate measures'.[604]

(d) Judicial protection

14.110 Whilst the adoption of safeguard measures is relatively rare and has not proved contentious, judicial review of anti-dumping or countervailing duties poses difficulties on several fronts. First, they are areas of highly complex economic analysis and political sensitivity: it is owing to the latter that much authority is reserved to the Council (which is rare in a largely administrative sphere), that challenges raised by natural or juristic persons under article 263 in the field were the last such transferred to the jurisdiction of the Court of First Instance,[605] and a definitive duty challenged by a member state fall within the (narrow) category of actions reserved still to the Court of Justice.[606] Then, the institutions must act always within the four corners of the basic Regulation(s) and are frequently challenged for failure to do so, although their complexity means that the tests in review are compliance with relevant procedural rules, accuracy of facts upon which the reasoning is based and whether there has been a manifest error in the appraisal of those facts or a misuse of powers.[607] Next, the most directly affected parties are, by definition, located in third countries, which effectively limits

---

597   Regulation 3286/94 [1994] OJ L349/71.
598   Regulation 1061/2009 [2009] OJ L291/1, art. 1.
599   See 10.105 above.
600   Regulation 116/2009 [2009] OJ L39/1.
601   Regulation 689/2008 [2008] OJ L204/1.
602   Regulation 428/2009 [2009] OJ L134/1. See the Commission Green Paper on Control of Export of Dual Use Goods, COM(2011) 393 final.
603   Regulation 428/2009, arts 5, 6.
604   *Ibid.* art. 7.
605   Decision 94/149 [1994] OJ L66/29.
606   Statute of the Court of Justice, art. 51; see 5.21 above.
607   Case 240/84 *NTN Toyo Bearing and ors* v *Council* [1987] ECR 1809; Case C-156/87 *Gestetner Holdings* v *Council and Commission* [1990] ECR I-781; Case C-150/94 *United Kingdom* v *Council* [1998] ECR I-7235.

their access to judicial protection to article 263; but as anti-dumping and countervailing duties are, and are required to be,[608] adopted in the form of Regulations, they have no addressee(s)[609] and this on its face ought to bar review proceedings under article 263 at the instance of a natural or juristic person altogether.[610] However, to counteract what might otherwise be a *déni de justice*, the Court of Justice has attributed to measures imposing anti-dumping or countervailing duties the character of a 'hybrid instrument', being a partly legislative and partly administrative act, and so easing the access of interested parties to article 263 and taking an unusually generous view of what constitutes individual concern thereunder.[611] An importer may have access to his national courts and so be able (with determination and luck) to engineer a declaration of invalidity under article 267, which leads to recovery of duties paid.[612] But in keeping with general principles an affected party which could have, but did not, raise annulment proceedings under article 263 is thereafter barred from pleading its illegality in national proceedings.[613]

Anti-dumping and countervailing duties and safeguard measures may be **14.111** challenged not only before the Court of Justice for compliance with the basic Regulations, but may be taken to the WTO dispute settlement body for compliance with the anti-dumping agreement or the subsidies and countervailing measures agreement.

5. Restrictive measures

Amsterdam inserted a new Treaty provision authorising the Community to **14.112** impose economic sanctions (interrupt or reduce, selectively, partly or completely, economic relations and/or the movement of capital and payments) against one or more third countries in implementation of a common position or joint action adopted by the Council under (then) Union CFSP provisions.[614] The power extended, at least in the context of combating terrorism, to imposing

---

608 Regulation 1225/2009, art. 14(1); Regulation 597/2009, art. 24(1).
609 Although a countervailing duty may, and must if practicable, specify a duty to be imposed for each supplier; Regulation 597/2009, art. 15(2).
610 See 5.77 above.
611 See e.g., Cases 239 and 275/82 *Allied Corporation and ors* v *Commission* [1984] ECR 1005; Case 264/82 *Timex* v *Council and Commission* [1985] ECR 849; Case C-358/89 *Extramet Industrie* v *Council* [1991] ECR I-2501. The partly administrative character of the measure means also that the effects of annulment will be restricted to the successful applicant and not to other concerned parties; see n. 529 above and accompanying text.
612 See e.g., Case C-351/04 *Ikea Wholesale* v *Commissioners of Customs and Excise* [2007] ECR I-7723.
613 Case C-239/99 *Nachi Europe* v *Hauptzollamt Krefeld* [2001] ECR I-1197.
614 EC Treaty, arts 60 and 301 (arts 75 and 215 TFEU). Article 60 EC was the legal base for the imposition of sanctions in the sphere of capital movements and payments, art. 301 for restrictive measures more generally. See e.g., Case T-184/95 *Dorsch Consult Ingenieurgesellschaft* v *Council and Commission* [1998] II-667; Cases T-246 and 332/08 *Melli Bank* v *Council* [2009] ECR II-2629.

sanctions against individuals.[615] Express provision is now made for the adoption of restrictive measures upon natural or juristic persons and groups or non-state entities.[616] The present rule is that, where a European Council or Council decision adopted under the CFSP provisions of the TEU (either pursuant to a UN Security Council resolution or autonomously) directs the restriction of economic and financial relations with one or more third countries, the Council is, upon a joint proposal from the Commission and the High Representative FASP, to adopt the necessary measures.[617] Prior to Lisbon the (EC) measure was subject to review by the Court of Justice, the CFSP (TEU) decision which directed that it be adopted was not; the loophole is now closed. Any measure adopted in the area must include provisions on legal safeguards.[618] Challenges hitherto have betrayed a degree of sloppiness, or at least indifference, to safeguards in the Council's administrative procedures.[619] Such actions are growing rapidly in number, from fewer than a dozen cases between 2000 and the end of 2009 to some seven dozen raised before the General Court in 2011, by both natural and juristic persons in, principally, Syria, Iran and (mostly) Côte-d'Ivoire.

6. Development cooperation and humanitarian aid

14.113 A Treaty chapter on development cooperation introduced by Maastricht[620] was absorbed by Lisbon into the Union's external action, addressed by a single Title on 'cooperation with third countries and humanitarian aid' and split into three chapters, on development cooperation, economic, financial and technical cooperation with third countries, and humanitarian aid.[621] Policies/operations in each are conducted within the framework of the principles and objectives of

---

615 Cases C-402 and 415/05P *Kadi and Al Bakaraat* v *Council and Commission* (Kadi II) [2008] ECR I-6351. Sanctions against 'rulers' of target third countries and 'individuals and entities associated with or controlled, directly or indirectly, by them' could be founded upon arts 60 and 301 EC (*Kadi II*, at para. 166) provided there was a 'sufficient link' with the regime (Case T-181/08 *Tay Za* v *Council* [2010] ECR II-1965, at para. 61); immediate family members cannot be presumed to meet the test: Case C-376/10P *Tay Za* v *Council*, judgment of 13 March 2012, not yet reported. For others additional recourse to art. 308 EC (art. 352 TFEU) was required.

616 TFEU, arts 75 and 215(2). The difference between the two as a legal base is discussed in Case C-130/10 *Parliament* v *Council*, judgment of 19 July 2012, not yet reported.

617 *Ibid.* art. 215(1).

618 *Ibid.* arts 75, 3rd para. and 215(3).

619 Case T-228/02 *Organisation des Modjahedines du peuple d'Iran* v *Council* [2006] ECR II-4665; Cases C-229/05P *Ocalan, on behalf of the Kurdistan Workers' Party (PKK) and anor* v *Council* [2007] ECR I-439; Cases C-402 and 415/05P *Kadi II*, n. 615 above; Case T-284/08 *People's Mojehadin Organization of Iran* v *Council* [2008] ECR II-3487 (upheld in Case C-27/09P *France* v *People's Mojahedin Organization of Iran*, judgment of 21 December 2011, not yet reported); Case T-341/07 *Sison* v *Council* [2009] ECR II-3625; Cases C-399 and 403/06P *Hassan and Ayadi* v *Council* [2009] ECR I-11393; Case T-348/07 *Stichting Al-Aqsa* v *Council* [2010] ECR II-4575.

620 EC Treaty, arts 177–81.

621 TFEU, arts 208–14.

the Union's external action.[622] Development cooperation has as its primary objective the reduction and, in the long term, eradication of poverty;[623] it, and humanitarian aid operations, are to comply with commitments and objectives approved in the context of the United Nations and other competent international organisations[624] and are to be coordinated (development cooperation) or may be coordinated (humanitarian aid operations) with national policies in the fields.[625] All three chapters impose a very light touch, and are there primarily to note a Union interest and, as the Treaties direct, provide competence to carry out activities, in particular to define and implement programmes, but never to trench upon member state authority in the fields.[626]

E. OTHER POLICIES

The remaining policies and internal actions addressed in Part Three of the **14.114** TFEU are, in the sum of Union endeavour, less pressing. Most were introduced into the Treaties by the Single European Act or the Maastricht Treaty. Their importance lay in establishing a legal basis for Community interest and (light touch) action but also in express provision of authority to treat with third countries in these areas.[627] Three fields (sport, space and administrative cooperation) are new with Lisbon. About half of them are areas of competences shared between the Union and the member states,[628] the rest ancillary Union competences only[629] save one (public health) which falls into both camps. Each is now addressed by a distinct Title in the TFEU, as follows.

1. Education, vocational training, youth and sport

The original EEC Treaty provided for the adoption of a common vocational **14.115** training policy.[630] This was read very broadly by the Court of Justice so as to cover most tertiary education[631] and Maastricht formally recognised a place for

---

622 *Ibid.* arts 208(1), 212(1) and 214(1).
623 *Ibid.* art. 208(1), 2nd para.
624 *Ibid.* arts 208(2), 214(7).
625 *Ibid.* arts 210, 214(6).
626 *Ibid.* art. 4(4).
627 EC Treaty, arts 149(3), 150(3), 151(3), 152(3), 155(3), 174(4), 181. These provisions codified for sake of certainty an international personality which existed in any event, as recognised in Case 22/70 *Commission v Council* (ERTA) [1971] ECR 263; see 14.71 above.
628 EC Treaty, art. 4.
629 *Ibid.* art. 6.
630 EEC Treaty, art. 128.
631 See in particular Case 293/83 *Gravier* v *Ville de Liège* [1985] ECR 593; Case 24/86 *Blaizot* v *University of Liège and ors* [1988] ECR 379; Case 263/86 86 *Belgium* v *Humbel and Edel* [1988] ECR 5365.

a Community contribution to 'quality' education[632] alongside the policy on vocational training.[633] The TFEU now provides education, vocational training, youth and sport with a distinct Title[634] and recognises them to be amongst the Union's ancillary competences,[635] authority therefore limited to supporting, coordinating and supplementing national action.[636] The Union is to contribute to the development of quality education still by developing a European dimension, encouraging mobility of students and teachers, promoting co-operation between institutions, developing information exchange and encouraging the development of distance education;[637] to encourage the development of youth exchanges and the participation of young people in democratic life in Europe;[638] and to develop a European dimension in sport, by promoting fairness and openness in competition and protecting the physical and moral integrity of sportsmen and sportswomen, especially the youngest.[639] To these ends the Parliament and the Council may adopt incentive measures[640] and the Council may adopt recommendations.[641] Harmonisation of national legislation is excluded.[642] Significant collaboration is pursued by competent national authorities outside the Union framework, for example through the Sorbonne declaration and the Bologna Process in higher education.[643]

14.116   Further issues of education and sport are discussed above.[644]

2. Culture

14.117   First Community tangency with culture was limited to numbering it amongst the mandatory requirements or imperative reasons in the general interest which could justify derogation from articles 34 and 56.[645] Maastricht introduced it as a

---

632   EC Treaty (pre-Amsterdam), arts 3(p) and 126.
633   *Ibid.* art. 127(1).
634   Title XII, arts 165–6.
635   *Ibid.* art. 6(e).
636   *Ibid.* arts 2(5), 6.
637   *Ibid.* art. 165(2).
638   *Ibid.*
639   *Ibid.*
640   *Ibid.* art. 165(4).
641   *Ibid.*
642   *Ibid.* arts 2(5), 165(4).
643   Sorbonne joint declaration of 25 May 1998 on harmonisation of the architecture of the European higher education system; Bologna Declaration of 19 June 1999 (towards a European higher education area).
644   See 11.65–11.68 and 11.81–11.85 above.
645   Cases 60–61/84 *Cinéthèque v Fédération National des Cinemas Français* [1985] ECR 2605; Case C-288/89 *Collectieve Antennevoorziening Gouda v Commissariaat voor de Media* [1991] ECR I-4007; Case C-148/91 *Vereniging Veronica Omroep Organisatie v Commissariaat voor de Media* [1993] ECR I-487; Case C-17/92 *Federación de Distribuidores Cinematográficos v Estado Español and anor* [1993] ECR I-2239. See also Case 379/87 *Groener v Minister for Education and anor* [1989] ECR 3967 on protection of language.

field of active Community interest, charging it with a contribution 'to the flowering [*épanouissement*] of the cultures of the Member States'.[646] Perhaps even more than education, culture is seen to be the legitimate preserve of the member states, or of regions within them, and Community intervention has been with the lightest of touches. Union authority in the field is now ancillary.[647] It is to contribute to the flowering of the cultures of the member states still, whilst respecting their national and regional diversity and at the same time bringing the common cultural heritage to the fore.[648] The Title contains an integration clause[649] and the Union is subject to a general obligation amongst its objectives to respect its rich cultural and linguistic diversity and ensure that Europe's cultural heritage is safeguarded and enhanced.[650] Harmonisation of legislation is excluded,[651] otherwise, as with education, the Parliament and Council may adopt incentive measures[652] and the Council recommendations.[653]

3. Public health

Public health too had its early running in the context of justification for **14.118** derogation from the free movement rules of the Treaty – being, uniquely, both an express Treaty exception under articles 36 and 52 and a mandatory requirement[654]/imperative reason in the general interest.[655] It broke into the Treaty first via the Single European Act which required that any harmonising legislation adopted under the new cooperation procedure 'concerning health' take as its base a high level of protection.[656] The Treaties now address public health as both an ancillary Union matter (as regards the 'protection and improvement of human health')[657] and a shared competence (as regards common safety concerns in public health matters).[658] Union action is to complement national policies and to be directed towards improving public health, preventing physical and mental illness and diseases, and obviating sources of danger to physical and mental health by promoting research, information and

---

646   EC Treaty (pre-Amsterdam), arts 3(p) and 128.
647   TFEU, art. 6(c).
648   *Ibid.* art. 167(1).
649   *Ibid.* art. 167(4).
650   TEU, art. 3(3).
651   TFEU, arts 2(5), 167(5).
652   *Ibid.* art. 167(5). This by the ordinary legislative procedure, previously it required Council unanimity; art. 151(5) EC.
653   *Ibid.* This too required Council unanimity, but no longer.
654   Case 120/78 *Rewe-Zentrale* v *Bundesmonopolverwaltung für Branntwein* (Cassis de Dijon) [1979] ECR 649.
655   See 11.118 and 11.128 above.
656   EEC Treaty, art. 100a(3) (art. 114(3) TFEU).
657   TFEU, art. 6(a).
658   *Ibid.* art. 4(2)(k).

education and monitoring cross-border threats to health.[659] It is to encourage cooperation, in particular so as to improve the complementarity of health services in cross-border areas (*régions frontalières*).[660] Several of the agencies established by the Council (the Medicines Agency, the Monitoring Centre for Drugs and Drug Addiction, the Food Safety Authority, the Centre for Disease Prevention and Control and the Executive Agency for Health and Consumers) are active in support of relevant programmes. In the (shared) field of safety in public health matters the Union may adopt measures setting high standards of quality and safety of organs and substances of human origin, blood and blood derivatives;[661] in the veterinary and phytosanitary fields which have as their direct objective the protection of public health; and setting high standards of quality and safety for medicinal products and devices for medical use.[662] Otherwise Union action is limited to incentive measures[663] and recommendations.[664]

14.119   In all events the Union must respect the responsibilities of the member states for the definition of their health policy and for the organisation and delivery of health services and medical care.[665] But these provisions do *not* immunise health care from Treaty freedoms, and there is a growing case law, and legislative intervention, on cross-frontier provision of health care.[666] Nor is public health protection ring-fenced from harmonisation legislation adopted under article 114,[667] otherwise article 114(3) ('proposals [for legislation] … concerning health … will take as a base a high level of protection') is meaningless. This is so even if public health protection is a decisive factor in the choices made in the Directive,[668] and it is sometimes difficult to resist the conclusion that harmonising legislation is, in some cases, in truth a public health measure; but the

---

659   *Ibid.* art. 168(1), 2nd para.

660   *Ibid.* art. 168(2), 1st para.

661   *Ibid.* art. 168(4)(a). But it cannot interfere with national rules on donation or medical use of organs and blood; art. 168(7). See e.g., measures on quality and safety for the collection, testing, processing, storage and distribution of human blood and blood components (Directive 2002/98 [2003] OJ L33/30), of human tissue and cells (Directive 2004/23 [2004] OJ L102/48) and of human organs intended for transplantation (Directive 2010/45 [2010] OJ L207/14).

662   *Ibid.* art. 168(4)(b), (c). Legislative authority in art. 168(4) matters was first introduced by the Treaty of Amsterdam; EC Treaty, art. 152(4).

663   *Ibid.* art. 168(5).

664   *Ibid.* art. 168(6).

665   *Ibid.* art. 168(7).

666   See 11.69–11.80 above.

667   Case C-376/98 *Germany v Parliament and Council* (Tobacco Advertising No. 1) [2000] ECR I-8419, at para. 78.

668   Case C-491/01 *R v Secretary of State for Health, ex parte British American Tobacco (Investments) and ors* [2002] ECR I-11453, at para. 62; Cases C-154 and 155/04 *R (Alliance for Natural Health and ors) v Secretary of State for Health and anor* [2005] ECR I-6451, at para. 30; Case C-380/03 *Germany v Parliament and Council* (Tobacco Advertising No. 2) [2006] ECR I-11573, at para. 39.

Court of Justice is prepared to give the legislature a wide leeway.[669] Protection of human health (at a 'high level') is an integration clause, repeated thrice over.[670] Honourable mention must go to a first instance judge in Namur, who used a case involving squaddies selling (duty free) tobacco rations off-base in order to orchestrate a reference to the Court of Justice to have the manufacture and sale of tobacco declared unlawful in Belgium as contrary to the Charter right to a high level of human health protection: it was a valiant and entertaining, but doomed, effort.[671]

14.120 The Euratom Treaty includes a chapter on 'health and safety' intended to provide for the protection of public health in the nuclear sector.[672]

4. Consumer protection

14.121 Like public health, consumer protection was recognised as a mandatory requirement in *Cassis de Dijon*.[673] First added to the Treaty by Maastricht, it is now an area of shared competence[674] although one in which the Union enjoys no dedicated legislative authority, rather it promotes consumer interests, ensures a high level of consumer protection, contributes to protecting the health, safety and economic interests of consumers, and promotes access to information, education and safeguarding consumer interests in the context of harmonisation legislation adopted under article 114.[675] The Parliament and Council may also adopt measures which support, supplement and monitor relevant national policies.[676] Consumer protection has its own integration clause.[677]

5. Economic, social and territorial cohesion

14.122 A Community commitment to economic and social cohesion, or put more simply a regional policy, was first made express by the Single European Act[678] and was made part of its task by Maastricht.[679] Economic, social and territorial

---

669   See the judgments *ibid.*

670   TFEU, arts 9, 168(1); EU Charter of Fundamental Rights, art. 35.

671   Cases C-267 and 268/10 *Rossius and Collard* v *État belge – Service public fédéral Finances*, order of 23 May 2011, not yet reported.

672   Euratom Treaty, Title II, Chapter 3, arts 30–9; Case 62/88 *Greece* v *Council* [1990] ECR I-1527, at para. 17.

673   Case 120/78 *Cassis de Dijon*, n. 654 above.

674   TFEU, art. 4(2)(f).

675   *Ibid.* art. 169(1), (2)(a). For examples see the Directives cited at n. 3 above.

676   *Ibid.* art. 169(2)(b).

677   *Ibid.* art. 12.

678   EEC Treaty, arts 130a–130e.

679   EC Treaty, art. 2.

cohesion ('territorial' new with Lisbon) is now an area of shared competence,[680] its promotion amongst the Union's objectives,[681] in pursuit of which it is charged with promoting overall harmonious development by strengthening (*renforcement*) its economic, social and territorial cohesion through its activities, in particular by reducing disparities between the levels of development of the various regions and the backwardness of the least favoured regions.[682] Rural areas, areas affected by industrial transition, and regions which suffer from severe and permanent natural or demographic handicaps such as the northern-most regions with very low population density and island, cross-border and mountain regions are singled out for particular attention.[683] The task acquired different dimensions with the 2004 and 2007 accessions.

14.123 The objectives set out are required to be taken into account in the formulation and implementation of Union policies generally and the implementation of the internal market specifically so that they contribute to their achievement.[684] Financial support is to come through the structural funds (the European Agricultural Guidance and Guarantee Fund, Guidance Section,[685] the European Social Fund and the European Regional Development Fund), the European Investment Bank and other existing financial instruments.[686] A Cohesion Fund was established to support projects in the fields of the environment and trans-European transport networks[687] but available only to member states with a *per capita* GNP of less than 90 per cent of the Union average,[688] that is the 2004 and 2007 accession member states plus Greece and Portugal. The task, priority objectives and organisation of the funds are set by Regulations adopted by the Parliament and Council;[689] structural spending now accounts for about one-third of the Union budget.[690] The member states are enjoined to the task, invited to conduct and coordinate their economic policies in such a way as to attain the objectives set out in article 174.[691] Union state aid

---

680 TFEU, art. 4(2)(c).
681 TEU, art. 3(3).
682 TFEU, art. 174.
683 *Ibid.* art. 174, 3rd para.
684 *Ibid.* art. 175, 1st para.
685 It is not clear why the Treaty refers to the FEOGA Guidance Section which disappeared in 2006 when replaced by the Agricultural Fund for Rural Development; see 10.112 above. Its inclusion dates back to the Single European Act, and it was presumably simply an oversight to reproduce it in the Lisbon texts.
686 TFEU, art. 175, 1st para.
687 *Ibid.* art. 177.
688 Protocol (No. 28) on Economic, Social and Territorial Cohesion.
689 *Ibid.*
690 €42,045 million appropriation for commitments in 2012; Definitive adoption of the general budget of the European Union for the financial year 2012, [2012] OJ L56, II/563.
691 TFEU art. 175, 1st para.

rules are applied in such a manner as to allow greater latitude to the less developed the member state/region.[692]

6. Trans-European networks

A function of economic, social and territorial cohesion specifically and of the cohesion of the internal market more generally, the Union is to contribute to the establishment and development of trans-European networks in the areas of transport, telecommunications and energy infrastructures, promoting the interconnection and interoperability of national networks and access to them.[693] Particular emphasis is placed upon linking island, landlocked and peripheral regions to the central regions of the Union.[694]

14.124

7. Industry

Industry is an ancillary Union competence,[695] the Union and the member states together ensuring that the conditions necessary for the competitiveness of their industries exist.[696] Combined action is aimed at speeding up the adjustment of industry to structural changes, encouraging an environment favourable to initiative and to the development of undertakings throughout the Union, particularly small and medium-sized undertakings, encouraging an environment favourable to cooperation between undertakings and fostering better exploitation of the industrial potential of policies of innovation, research and technological development.[697] It is to be achieved 'in accordance with a system of open and competitive markets',[698] and the third aim in particular does raise issues for the application of Union competition rules. The Commission may take any initiative to promote coordination of national action[699] and the Parliament and Council may adopt specific measures to support it, barring harmonisation of legislation.[700]

14.125

---

692 Regulation 800/2008 [2008] OJ L214/3 (Goup Block Exemption Regulation), ch. II, section 1; Guidelines on National Regional Aid for 2007–13 [2006] OJ C54/45.
693 TFEU, art. 170.
694 *Ibid.* art. 170(2).
695 *Ibid.* art. 6(b).
696 *Ibid.* art. 173(1).
697 *Ibid.*
698 *Ibid.*
699 *Ibid.* art. 173(2).
700 *Ibid.* art. 173(3).

8. Research and technological development and space

14.126 Research and technological development was first made an area of Community concern by the Single European Act.[701] Now a shared competence by default,[702] the Union is to strengthen its scientific and technological bases by developing a European research area in which researchers, scientific knowledge and technology circulate freely, and encourage it to become more competitive, including in its industry, while promoting the research activities deemed necessary by virtue of other provisions of the Treaties.[703] The Title therefore serves as a focus for R&D policy, and all Union research and technological development is to be pursued in accordance with it.[704] Union action 'complement[s] the activities carried out in the Member States',[705] must pay due respect to the fundamental orientations and choices of national research policies[706] and cannot result in the member states being prevented from exercising their own activities in the field[707] – a rare statement in the Treaties of the primacy of national rules. It consists in promoting cooperation with and between undertakings (again a possible clash with the competition rules), research centres and universities for the implementation of R&D and demonstration programmes; promotion of cooperation with third countries and international organisations; dissemination and optimisation of the results of Union R&D and demonstration; and stimulation (*Förderung*) of the training and mobility of researchers in the Union.[708] The Commission may, in close cooperation with the member states, 'take any useful initiative' to assist,[709] the Parliament and Council are to adopt a multiannual framework programme[710] and the Council may adopt specific programmes to implement it with the agreement of the relevant member state(s).[711]

14.127 Lisbon added 'space' to the Title. The Union is to draw up a European space policy, to which end it may promote joint initiatives, support research and technological development and coordinate the efforts needed for the exploration and exploitation of space.[712] The Parliament and Council are to establish

---

701   EEC Treaty, arts 130f–130p.
702   TFEU, art. 4(1).
703   *Ibid.* art. 179(1).
704   *Ibid.* art. 179(3).
705   *Ibid.* art. 179(3).
706   Declaration (No. 34) on Article 179 of the TFEU.
707   TFEU, *ibid.* art. 4(3).
708   *Ibid.* art. 180.
709   *Ibid.* art. 181(2).
710   *Ibid.* art. 182; see Decision 1982/2006 [2006] OJ L412/1, the Seventh Framework Programme (FP7) for research, technological development and demonstration activities (2007–13).
711   *Ibid.* arts 182(4), 188, 2nd para.
712   *Ibid.* art. 189(1).

(*erlassen*) the necessary measures, which may take the form of a European space programme, but excluding harmonisation of national laws.[713]

9. Energy, tourism and civil protection

Maastricht introduced as a Community activity measures in the spheres of **14.128** energy, civil protection and tourism[714] but added no subsequent operative Treaty provisions addressing them. A declaration attached to the Treaty stated that, in the view of the Commission, action in these spheres could be pursued under other provisions of the Treaty.[715] Lisbon redressed this with the introduction of a distinct Title for each.[716] Energy is a shared,[717] the other two ancillary[718] competences.

Energy not afforded greater prominence in the Treaties is perhaps surprising. It **14.129** was and is, after all, the prime concern of two of the three communities, its economics a major component of the internal market, and its vagaries a key element of Union policies on transport, the environment and climate change. Legislation has been adopted with a significant energy component, for example the greenhouse gas emission allowance trading scheme[719] (the Union operating the world's largest emission trading scheme which is 'a cornerstone of European policy on climate change')[720] and the Clean (or Renewable) Energy Directive,[721] both relying for a Treaty base upon the Title on the environment.[722] Yet achievement of the internal market in energy has long been thwarted by national intransigence,[723] this recognised by the European Council in 2011, which set out the objective of having a fully functioning internal energy market by 2014.[724]

---

713 *Ibid.* art. 189(2).
714 EC Treaty (pre-Amsterdam), art. 3(t).
715 Declaration (No. 1) on Civil Protection, Energy and Tourism.
716 TFEU, Title XXI, art. 194 (energy), Title XXII, art. 195 (tourism) and Title XXIII, art. 196 (civil protection).
717 *Ibid.* art. 4(2)(i).
718 *Ibid.* art. 6(d), (f).
719 Directive 2003/87 [2003] OJ L275/32.
720 Case C-366/10 *R (Air Transport Association of America and ors)* v *Secretary of State for Energy and Climate Change*, judgment of 21 December 2011, not yet reported, per A-G Kokott at para. 1 of her opinion.
721 Directive 2009/28 [2009] OJ L140/16.
722 Save that three articles of Directive 2009/87 on harmonising sustainability criteria biofuels and bioliquids required the additional Treaty base of art. 114.
723 The Commission, for example, was moved to send on a single occasion in 2010 a total of 35 reasoned opinions to 20 member states (all but Denmark, Estonia, Cyprus, Latvia, Lithuania, Malta and Finland) for failure to comply with Regulations on conditions for access to electricity and gas transmission networks; see IP/10/836.
724 European Council, 4 February 2011, Presidency Conclusions, paras 2–15.

14.130   Even before Lisbon, Community activity gathered pace. In 2007 the Commission adopted an important, wide-ranging and ambitious energy package comprising an energy policy,[725] an internal market review and third liberalisation package,[726] further network interconnection,[727] a 'renewable energy roadmap',[728] strategic energy research,[729] and, under Euratom authority, a rudimentary policy on nuclear power.[730] Post-Lisbon the 'Union policy on energy' has the aim, 'in a spirit of solidarity between Member States', of ensuring the functioning of the energy market; ensuring the security of energy supply in the Union; promoting energy efficiency and energy saving and the development of new and renewable forms of energy; and promoting the interconnection of energy networks.[731] The Parliament and Council may establish (*erlassen*) the measures necessary to achieve these ends[732] but no measure may affect a member state's right to determine the conditions for exploiting its energy resources, its choice between different energy sources and the general structure of its energy supply[733] or the right to ensure its energy supplies,[734] which is a matter of public security under article 36 which may justify derogation from the rules on free movement.[735] Perhaps the primary importance of the new Title is to enhance the Union's international personality (and, in accordance with *ERTA*,[736] treaty-making powers) in the sphere.

14.131   More hands off is Union activity in the fields of tourism and civil protection, being limited, for tourism, to complementing national action, in particular by promoting the competitiveness of Union undertakings in the sector;[737] and, for civil protection, to encouraging cooperation between member states in order to improve the effectiveness of systems for preventing and protecting against natural or man-made disasters through supporting and complementing national/local action and promoting operational cooperation and consistency in the field.[738]

---

725   An Energy Policy for Europe, SEC(2007) 12.
726   Proposals for the Internal Gas and Electricity Markets, COM(2006) 841 final.
727   Priority Interconnection Plan, COM(2006) 846 final.
728   *Renewable Energies in the 21st Century: Building a More Sustainable Future*, COM(2006) 848 final; also *Sustainable Power Generation from Fossil Fuels*, COM(2006) 843 final.
729   *Towards a European Strategic Energy Technology Plan*, COM(2006) 847 final.
730   Nuclear Illustrative Programme, COM(2006) 844 final.
731   TFEU, art. 194(1).
732   *Ibid.* art. 194(2).
733   *Ibid.* art. 194(2), 2nd para.
734   Declaration (No. 35) on Article 194 of the TFEU.
735   Case 72/82 Campus *Oil and ors v Minister for Industry and Energy and ors* [1984] ECR 2727.
736   Case 22/70 *Commission v Council* (ERTA) [1971] ECR 263; see 14.71 above.
737   TFEU, art. 195(1).
738   *Ibid.* art. 196(1).

10. Administrative cooperation

A new Title on administrative cooperation notes that effective implementation **14.132** of Union law by the member states is essential for the proper functioning of the Union, and so is to be regarded as a matter of common interest.[739] As an ancillary competence[740] the Union may support national efforts in improving their administrative capacity to implement Union law, including facilitating the exchange of information and of civil servants and supporting training schemes,[741] but there is no obligation of a member state to avail itself of such support.[742] The Parliament and Council are to establish (*erlassen*) the necessary measures, barring, as always, harmonisation of national laws and regulations.[743]

---

739   *Ibid.* art. 197(1).
740   *Ibid.* art. 6(g).
741   *Ibid.* art. 197(2).
742   *Ibid.*
743   *Ibid.*

ANNEX I

THE SCHUMAN DECLARATION

of 9 May 1950

The peace of the world cannot be safeguarded without creative efforts commensurate with the dangers which threaten it. The contribution an organised and living Europe can bring to civilisation is indispensable to the maintenance of peaceful relations. In assuming for more than 20 years the role of champion of a united Europe, France has always had as her essential aim the service of peace. Europe was not achieved – and we had war.

Europe will be made neither at a stroke, nor according to a uniform model: it will be built through concrete achievements which first create a *de facto* solidarity. The coming together of the European nations requires that the age-old enmity of France and Germany be eliminated. Any action taken must first and foremost embrace France and Germany. In pursuit of this goal, the French government proposes that action be taken immediately on one limited but decisive point.

The French government proposes that the entirety of Franco-German production of coal and steel be placed under a common High Authority, within an organisation open to the participation of the other countries of Europe. The pooling of coal and steel production will provide immediately for the establishment of common foundations for economic development, a first step in the federation of Europe, and will change the destiny of those regions long devoted to the manufacture of munitions of war, of which they have been the most constant victims.

The solidarity in production thus established will make it plain that any war between France and Germany becomes not merely unthinkable, but materially impossible. The establishment of this powerful productive unit, open to all countries wishing to take part and bound ultimately to provide all the member countries with the basic elements of industrial production on the same terms, will lay a true foundation for their economic unification.

This production will be offered to the world as a whole with neither distinction nor exception, as a contribution to raising living standards and to promoting peaceful achievements. With her resources thus increased, Europe will be able to pursue one of her essential tasks: the development of the African continent.

In this way there will be brought about simply and speedily that fusion of interests which is indispensable to the establishment of a common economic system; it may be the leaven from which may grow a wider and deeper community between countries long riven by bloody division.

By pooling basic production and by instituting a new High Authority, whose decisions will bind France, Germany and other member countries, this proposal will lead to the realisation of the first concrete foundations of a European federation indispensable to the preservation of peace.

To pursue the achievement of the objectives thus defined, the French Government is ready to open negotiations on the following bases.

The task entrusted to this common High Authority will be that of securing in the shortest possible time: the modernisation of production and the improvement of its quality; the supply of coal and steel on identical terms to the French and German markets, as well as to those of other member countries; the development in common of exports to other countries; equalisation in improvement of the living conditions of workers in these industries.

To achieve these objectives, starting out from the very different conditions in which the production of member countries currently finds itself, it is proposed that certain transitional measures should be put in place, including the application of a production and investment plan, the establishment of compensating machinery for equating prices, and the creation of a restructuring fund to facilitate the rationalisation of production. The movement of coal and steel between member countries will be freed immediately from all customs duties, and will not be affected by differential transport tariffs. Conditions will gradually be created which will provide spontaneously for the more rational distribution of production at the highest level of productivity.

In contrast with international cartels, which tend to impose restrictive practices on distribution and the exploitation of national markets, and to maintain high profits, the proposed organisation will ensure the fusion of markets and the expansion of production.

The essential principles and undertakings defined above will be the subject of a treaty signed between the States and submitted for the ratification of their parliaments. The negotiations required to settle implementing details will be carried out with the help of an arbitrator appointed by common agreement; he will be entrusted with the task of ensuring that the agreements reached conform with principles, and, in the event of a deadlock, will decide upon the solution to be adopted.

The common High Authority entrusted with the management of the scheme will be composed of independent persons appointed upon a balanced basis by the governments; a president will be chosen by common agreement of the governments; its decisions will be enforceable in France, in Germany and in other member countries. Appropriate measures will be provided for means of review of the decisions of the High Authority. A representative of the United Nations accredited to the Authority will be charged with making a public report to the United Nations twice yearly, giving an account of the working of the new organisation, particularly as concerns the safeguarding of its peaceful objectives.

The creation of the High Authority will in no way prejudice the system of company ownership. In discharging its task, the common High Authority will take into account the powers conferred upon the International Ruhr Authority and the obligations of all kinds imposed upon Germany, so long as these remain in force.

ANNEX II

ADMINISTRATIVE STRUCTURE OF THE COMMISSION

The Directorates-General

Policies

Agriculture and Rural Development (AGRI)

Budget (BUDG)

Climate Action (CLIMA)

Communication (COMM)

Communications Networks, Content and Technology (CNECT)

Competition (COMP)

Economic and Financial Affairs (ECFIN)

Education and Culture (EAC)

Employment, Social Affairs and Inclusion (EMPL)

Energy (ENER)

Enlargement (ELARG)

Enterprise and Industry (ENTR)

Environment (ENV)

EuropAid Development & Cooperation (DEVCO)

Eurostat (ESTAT)

Health and Consumers (SANCO)

Home Affairs (HOME)

Humanitarian Aid (ECHO)

Human Resources and Security (HR)

Informatics (DIGIT)

Internal Market and Services (MARKT)

Interpretation (SCIC)

Joint Research Centre (JRC)

Justice (JUST)

Maritime Affairs and Fisheries (MARE)

Mobility and Transport (MOVE)

Regional Policy (REGIO)

Research and Innovation (RTD)

Secretariat General (SG)

Service for Foreign Policy Instruments (FPI)

Taxation and Customs Union (TAXUD)

Trade (TRADE)

Translation (DGT)

Services

Bureau of European Policy Advisers (BEPA)

Central Library

European Anti-Fraud Office (OLAF)

European Commission Data Protection Officer

Historical archives

Infrastructures and Logistics – Brussels (OIB)

Infrastructures and Logistics – Luxembourg (OIL)

Internal Audit Service (IAS)

Legal Service (SJ)

Office for Administration and payment of individual entitlements (PMO)

Publications Office (OP)

ANNEX III

WEIGHTING OF MEMBER STATES FOR PURPOSES OF QUALIFIED MAJORITY VOTING IN THE COUNCIL*

Belgium	12
Bulgaria	10
Czech Republic	12
Denmark	7
Germany	29
Estonia	4
Greece	12
Spain	27
France	29
[Croatia	7]
Ireland	7
Italy	29
Cyprus	4
Latvia	4
Lithuania	7
Luxembourg	4
Hungary	12
Malta	3
Netherlands	13
Austria	10
Poland	27
Portugal	12
Romania	14
Slovenia	4
Slovakia	7
Finland	7
Sweden	10
United Kingdom	29
	—
Total	345 [352]

* From EC Treaty, art. 205(2) as amended; made applicable 2009–14, and exceptionally 2014–17, by TEU and TFEU, Protocol (No. 36) on Transitional Provisions, art. 3(3).

ANNEX IV

FINDING JUDGMENTS OF THE COURT OF JUSTICE

Judgments of the Court of Justice (together with the opinions of the Advocates-General) and of the General Court are reported officially in the European Court Reports (ECR), which exist in 22 official languages.[1] Since the creation of the Court of First Instance (now the General Court) in 1989, ECR has been divided into two parts, Part I (judgments of the Court of Justice) and Part II (General Court).

Judgments of the Court of Justice and the General Court are normally cited (in English) by reference to case number (which is assigned sequentially by the Registrar), the names of the parties and the page reference in ECR. So: Case C-224/01 *Köbler* v *Austria* [2003] ECR I-10239; Case T-228/02 *Organisation des Modjehedines du peuple d'Iran* v *Council* [2006] ECR II-4665. 'C-' (for *Cour de Justice*) identifies a judgment of the Court of Justice, 'T-' (for *Tribunal*) a judgment of the General Court; the 'I' and 'II' indicate Parts I and II of the ECR, in which the respective judgments are reported. Citation in other languages varies with their traditions, but usually includes the date of judgment. Since judgments are published in ECR in strict chronological order, it is not difficult to trace the report of a case from its date.

Since 2004 reporting of judgments has been selective, the Court of Justice deciding not to report in the ECR judgments in direct actions of chambers of (a) three judges and (b) five judges if the latter are cases decided without an Advocate-General's opinion; in both cases unless the formation giving judgment, in exceptional circumstances, directs otherwise;[2] but it seems since to have followed no recognisable pattern. Most (but not all) orders of the Court disposing of a case are reported, most (but not all) interlocutory orders are not. Since 2005 judgments of the full court, the Grand Chamber and chambers of five judges of the General Court are reported, others are not, unless the formation of the Court directs otherwise on a case by case basis.

---

1 The ECR is published in most languages from the date of accession of the relevant member state(s); however following the 1973 accessions it was produced in an English version which goes back to 1952. The Commission organised the translation of 136 'historic case law' judgments into the nine 2004 accession languages and, to date, 57 into the two 2007 accession languages, available from the Court's website. There has never been an Irish version.

2 See (the annual) *Report on Proceedings of the Court of Justice, 2004*, p. 11.

Since 2005 (General Court) and 2006 (Court of Justice) some (not many, and normally only those arising from uncontentious enforcement proceedings raised under article 258 TFEU) chambers judgments are reported in the ECR in summary form (identified by an asterisk at the page cited; so, for example, Case C-457/08 *Commission v United Kingdom* [2009] ECR I-137*). The *dispositif* of each judgment and order is published in the *Official Journal*, normally within a month or two of judgment.

Judgments in staff cases are, since 1994, reported in a specialist series of the ECR (ECR-SC). Since its creation in 2005 a judgment of the Civil Service Tribunal can be identified by case number 'F-' (for *Fonction publique*). ECR-SC includes appeal judgments of the General Court and the Court of Justice in staff cases. Except in summary form, they are normally reported only in the language of the case.

All judgments, opinions and orders since 1997 are available in full from the date of judgment (but not immediately in all languages) in electronic form on the Court's website, http://curia.europa.eu/jcms/jcms/Jo1_6308/ecran-d-accueil.

Orders are published, if published, only after they have been notified to the parties.

The opinion of the Advocate-General (if there is one) is reported with the judgment of the Court. Until 1994 the 'Report for the Hearing' (*Rapport d'Audience*), sometimes in earlier reports called 'Issues of Fact and of Law', was also normally published with the judgment; but it is no longer, and is now available only in the language of proceedings and directly from the Court.

ANNEX V

TABLE OF EQUIVALENCE OF RENUMBERED TREATY ARTICLES

(from: article 12 of the Treaty of Amsterdam; new numbering effective 1 May 1999 and article 5 of the Treaty of Lisbon; new numbering effective 1 December 2009) (adapted from [1997] OJ C340/85 and [2010] OJ C83/361)

A. TREATY ON EUROPEAN UNION

Treaty on European Union (1993–99)	Treaty on European Union (1999–2009)	Treaty on European Union (2009–)
TITLE I	TITLE I	TITLE I
Article A	Article 1	Article 1
	Article 2	
Article B	Article 2	Article 3
Article C	Article 3 (repealed)	
Article D	Article 4 (repealed)	
Article E	Article 5 (repealed)	
Article 5 EC	*Article 10 EC (replaced)*	Article 4
Article 3b EC	*Article 5 EC (replaced)*	Article 5
Article F	Article 6	Article 6
	Article 7	Article 7
	Article 8	
TITLE II	TITLE II	TITLE II
Article G	Article 8 (repealed)	
	Article 9	
	Article 10	
	Article 11	
	Article 12	
TITLE III	TITLE III	TITLE III
Article H	Article 9 (repealed)	
	Article 7 EC (replaced)	Article 13
	Article 8 EC (replaced)	Article 14

940

Treaty on European Union (1993–99)	Treaty on European Union (1999–2009)	Treaty on European Union (2009–)
	Article 15	
	Article 16	
	Article 17	
	Article 18	
	Article 19	
TITLE IV	TITLE IV	TITLE IV
Article I	Article 10 (repealed)	
	Article 20	
TITLE V	TITLE V	TITLE V
	Article 21	
	Article 22	
	Article 23	
Article J.1	Article 11	Article 24
Article J.2	Article 12	Article 25
Article J.3	Article 13	Article 26
	Article 27	
Article J.4	Article 14	Article 28
Article J.5	Article 15	Article 29
Article J.12	*Article 22*	Article 30
Article J.13	*Article 23*	Article 31
Article J.6	Article 16	Article 32
Article J.7	Article 17	*Article 42*
Article J.8	Article 18	Article 33
Article J.9	Article 19	Article 34
Article J.10	Article 20	Article 35
Article J.11	Article 21	Article 36
	Article 22	*Article 30*
	Article 23	*Article 31*
	Article 24	Article 37
	Article 25	Article 38
	Article 39	
Article M	*Article 47*	Article 40
	Article 26 (repealed)	
	Article 27 (repealed)	
	Articles 27a–27e	*Article 20*
	Article 28	Article 41

Treaty on European Union (1993–99)	Treaty on European Union (1999–2009)	Treaty on European Union (2009–)
	Article 17 (replaced)	Article 42
	Article 43	
	Article 44	
	Article 45	
	Article 46	
TITLE VI	TITLE VI	TITLE VI
Article K.1	Article 29 (replaced)	*Article 67 TFEU*
Article K.2	Article 30 (replaced)	*Articles 87, 88 TFEU*
Article K.3	Article 31 (replaced)	*Articles 82, 83, 85 TFEU*
Article K.4	Article 32 (replaced)	*Article 89 TFEU*
Article K.5	Article 33 (replaced)	*Article 72 TFEU*
Article K.6	Article 34 (repealed)	
Article K.7	Article 35 (repealed)	
Article K.8	Article 36 (replaced)	*Article 71 TFEU*
Article K.9	Article 37 (repealed)	
	Article 38 (repealed)	
	Article 39 (repealed)	
	Article 40 (replaced)	*Article 20*
	Article 40a (replaced)	*Article 20*
	Article 40b (replaced)	*Article 20*
	Article 41 (repealed)	
	Article 42 (repealed)	
TITLE VII	TITLE VII	
	Article 43 (replaced)	*Article 20*
	Article 43a (replaced)	*Article 20*
	Article 43b (replaced)	*Article 20*
	Article 44 (replaced)	*Article 20*
	Article 44a (replaced)	*Article 20*
	Article 45 (replaced)	*Article 20*
	TITLE VIII	
Article L	Article 46 (repealed)	
	Article 47	
Article M	Article 47 (replaced)	*Article 40*
Article N	Article 48	Article 48

Treaty on European Union (1993–99)	Treaty on European Union (1999–2009)	Treaty on European Union (2009–)
Article O	Article 49	Article 49
	Article 50	
	Article 311 EC (replaced)	Article 51
	Article 299(1) EC (replaced)	Article 52
Article P	Article 50 (repealed)	
Article Q	Article 51	Article 53
Article R	Article 52	Article 54
Article S	Article 53	Article 55

B. TREATY ESTABLISHING THE EUROPEAN (ECONOMIC) COMMUNITY/ TREATY ON THE FUNCTIONING OF THE EUROPEAN UNION

Treaty establishing the European Economic Community/ European Community (1958–99)	Treaty establishing the European Community (1999–2009)	Treaty on the Functioning of the European Union (2009–)
PART ONE	PART ONE	PART ONE
Article 1	Article 1 (repealed)	
	Article 1	
Article 2	Article 2 (repealed)	
	Article 2	
	Article 3	
	Article 4	
	Article 5	
	Article 6	
	Article 7	
Article 3	Article 3(1) (repealed)	
	Article 3(2)	Article 8
Article 3a	Article 4	*Article 119*
Article 3b	Article 5 (replaced)	*Article 5 TEU*
	Article 9	
	Article 10	
	Article 6	Article 11
	Article 153(2)	Article 12

943

Treaty establishing the European Economic Community/ European Community (1958–99)	Treaty establishing the European Community (1999–2009)	Treaty on the Functioning of the European Union (2009–)
	Article 13	
Article 4	Article 7 (replaced)	*Article 13 TEU*
Article 4a	Article 8 (replaced)	*Article 13 TEU, Article 282*
Article 4b	Article 9 (repealed)	
Article 5	Article 10 (replaced)	*Article 4(3) TEU*
	Article 11 (replaced)	*Articles 326 to 334*
	Article 11a (replaced)	*Articles 326 to 334*
Article 6	Article 12	*Article 18*
	Article 13	*Article 19*
Article 7 (repealed)		
Article 7a	Article 14	*Article 26*
Article 7b (repealed)		
Article 7c	Article 15	*Article 27*
	Article 16	Article 14
	Article 255	Article 15
	Article 286 (replaced)	Article 16
	Article 17	
PART TWO	**PART TWO**	**PART TWO**
Article 6	*Article 12*	Article 18
	Article 13	Article 19
Article 8	Article 17	Article 20
Article 8a	Article 18	Article 21
Article 8b	Article 19	Article 22
Article 8c	Article 20	Article 23
Article 8d	Article 21	Article 24
Article 8e	Article 22	Article 25
PART THREE	**PART THREE**	**PART THREE**
Article 7a	*Article 14*	Article 26
Article 7c	*Article 15*	Article 27
Article 9	Article 23	Article 28
Article 10	Article 24	Article 29
Article 11 (repealed)		
Articles 12, *17*	Article 25	Article 30

Treaty establishing the European Economic Community/ European Community (1958–99)	Treaty establishing the European Community (1999–2009)	Treaty on the Functioning of the European Union (2009–)
Articles 13–27 (repealed)		
Article 28	Article 26	Article 31
Article 29	Article 27	Article 32
Article 116	*Article 135*	Article 33
Article 30	Article 28	Article 34
Articles 31–33 (repealed)		
Article 34	Article 29	Article 35
Article 35 (repealed)		
Article 36	Article 30	Article 36
Article 37	Article 31	Article 37
Article 38	Article 32	Article 38
Article 39	Article 33	Article 39
Article 40	Article 34	Article 40
Article 41	Article 35	Article 41
Article 42	Article 36	Article 42
Article 43	Article 37	Article 43
Articles 44–45 (repealed)		
Article 46	Article 38	Article 44
Article 47 (repealed)		
Article 48	Article 39	Article 45
Article 49	Article 40	Article 46
Article 50	Article 41	Article 47
Article 51	Article 42	Article 48
Article 52	Article 43	Article 49
Article 53 (repealed)		
Article 54	Article 44	Article 50
Article 55	Article 45	Article 51
Article 56	Article 46	Article 52
Article 57	Article 47	Article 53
Article 58	Article 48	Article 54
	Article 294	Article 55
Article 59	Article 49	Article 56
Article 60	Article 50	Article 57
Article 61	Article 51	Article 58
Article 62 (repealed)		

Treaty establishing the European Economic Community/ European Community (1958–99)	Treaty establishing the European Community (1999–2009)	Treaty on the Functioning of the European Union (2009–)
Article 63	Article 52	Article 59
Article 64	Article 53	Article 60
Article 65	Article 54	Article 61
Article 66	Article 55	Article 62
Articles 67–73a (repealed)		
Article 73b	Article 56	Article 63
Article 73c	Article 57	Article 64
Article 73d	Article 58	Article 65
Article 73e (repealed)		
Article 73f	Article 59	Article 66
Article 73g	Article 60	*Article 75*
Article 73h (repealed)		
	Article 61, *Article 29 TEU*	Article 67
	Article 68	
	Article 69	
	Article 70	
	Article 71	
	Article 64(1), Article 33 TEU	Article 72
	Article 73	
	Article 66	Article 74
Article 73g	*Article 60*	Article 75
	Article 76	
	Article 62	Article 77
	Article 63, points 1 and 2	Article 78
	Article 63, points 3 and 4	Article 79
	Article 80	
	Article 64(1) (replaced)	*Article 72*
	Article 64(2)	*Article 78*
	Article 65	Article 81
	Article 66 (replaced)	*Article 74*
	Article 67 (repealed)	
	Article 68 (repealed)	
	Article 69 (repealed)	

Treaty establishing the European Economic Community/ European Community (1958–99)	Treaty establishing the European Community (1999–2009)	Treaty on the Functioning of the European Union (2009–)
	Article 31 TEU (replaced)	Article 82
	Article 31 TEU (replaced)	Article 83
	Article 84	
	Article 31 TEU (replaced)	Article 85
	Article 86	
	Article 30 TEU (replaced)	Article 87
	Article 30 TEU (replaced)	Article 88
	Article 32 TEU (replaced)	Article 89
Article 74	Article 70	Article 90
Article 75	Article 71	Article 91
Article 76	Article 72	Article 92
Article 77	Article 73	Article 93
Article 78	Article 74	Article 94
Article 79	Article 75	Article 95
Article 80	Article 76	Article 96
Article 81	Article 77	Article 97
Article 82	Article 78	Article 98
Article 83	Article 79	Article 99
Article 84	Article 80	Article 100
Article 85	Article 81	Article 101
Article 86	Article 82	Article 102
Article 87	Article 83	Article 103
Article 88	Article 84	Article 104
Article 89	Article 85	Article 105
Article 90	Article 86	Article 106
Article 91 (repealed)		
Article 92	Article 87	Article 107
Article 93	Article 88	Article 108
Article 94	Article 89	Article 109
Article 95	Article 90	Article 110
Article 96	Article 91	Article 111
Article 97 (repealed)		
Article 98	Article 92	Article 112
Article 99	Article 93	Article 113
Article 100	Article 94	*Article 115*

Treaty establishing the European Economic Community/ European Community (1958–99)	Treaty establishing the European Community (1999–2009)	Treaty on the Functioning of the European Union (2009–)
Article 100a	Article 95	*Article 114*
Articles 100b–100d (repealed)		
Article 101	Article 96	Article 116
Article 102	Article 97	Article 117
	Article 118	
Article 3a	*Article 4*	Article 119
Article 102a	Article 98	Article 120
Article 103	Article 99	Article 121
Article 103a	Article 100	Article 122
Article 104	Article 101	Article 123
Article 104a	Article 102	Article 124
Article 104b	Article 103	Article 125
Article 104c	Article 104	Article 126
Article 105	Article 105	Article 127
Article 105a	Article 106	Article 128
Article 106	Article 107	Article 129
Article 107	Article 108	Article 130
Article 108	Article 109	Article 131
Article 108a	Article 110	Article 132
Article 109	Article 111(1)–(3), (5)	*Article 219*
	Article 111(4)	*Article 138*
	Article 133	
Article 109a	Article 112	*Article 283*
Article 109b	Article 113	*Article 284*
Article 109c	Article 114	Article 134
Article 109d	Article 115	Article 135
	Article 136	
	Article 137	
	Article 111(4)	Article 138
Article 109e	Article 116 (repealed)	
	Article 139	
Article 109f	Article 117(1), (2)(6th), (3)–(9) (repealed)	
	Article 117(2)(1st–5th indents)	*Article 141(2)*

Treaty establishing the European Economic Community/ European Community (1958–99)	Treaty establishing the European Community (1999–2009)	Treaty on the Functioning of the European Union (2009–)
	Article 121(1)	Article 140(1)
	Article 122(2), 2nd sentence	Article 140(2), 1st para
	Article 123(5)	Article 140(3)
Artice 109g	Article 118 (repealed)	
	Article 123(3)	Article 141
	Article 124(1)	Article 142
Article 109h	Article 119	Article 143
Article 109i	Article 120	Article 144
	Article 121(1)	*Article 140(1)*
Article 109j	Article 121(2)–(4) (repealed)	
Article 109k	Article 122(1), (2, 1st), (3)–(6) (repealed)	
	Article 122(2), 2nd sentence	*Article 140(2), 1st para*
Article 109l	Article 123(1), (2), (4) (repealed)	
	Article 123(3)	*Article 141(1)*
	Article 123(5)	*Article 140(3)*
Article 109m	Article 124(1)	*Article 142*
	Article 124(2) (repealed)	
	Article 125	Article 145
	Article 126	Article 146
	Article 127	Article 147
	Article 128	Article 148
	Article 129	Article 149
	Article 130	Article 150
Article 110	Article 131	*Article 206*
Article 111 (repealed)		
Article 112	Article 132 (repealed)	
Article 113	Article 133	*Article 207*
Article 114 (repealed)		
Article 115	Article 134 (repealed)	
Article 116 (repealed)		
	Article 135	*Article 33*

Treaty establishing the European Economic Community/ European Community (1958–99)	Treaty establishing the European Community (1999–2009)	Treaty on the Functioning of the European Union (2009–)
Article 117	Article 136	Article 151
	Article 152	
Articles 118, 118a (replaced)	Article 137	Article 153
Article 118b	Article 138	Article 154
Article 118b	Article 139	Article 155
	Article 140	Article 156
Article 119	Article 141	Article 157
	Article 142	Article 158
Article 120	Article 143	Article 159
Article 121	Article 144	Article 160
Article 122	Article 145	Article 161
Article 123	Article 146	Article 162
Article 124	Article 147	Article 163
Article 125	Article 148	Article 164
Article 126	Article 149	Article 165
Article 127	Article 150	Article 166
Article 128	Article 151	Article 167
Article 129	Article 152	Article 168
Article 129a	Article 153(1), (3)–(5)	Article 169
	Article 153(2)	*Article 12*
Article 129b	Article 154	Article 170
Article 129c	Article 155	Article 171
Article 129d	Article 156	Article 172
Article 130	Article 157	Article 173
Article 130a	Article 158	Article 174
Article 130b	Article 159	Article 175
Article 130c	Article 160	Article 176
Article 130d	Article 161	Article 177
Article 130e	Article 162	Article 178
Article 130f	Article 163	Article 179
Article 130g	Article 164	Article 180
Article 130h	Article 165	Article 181
Article 130i	Article 166	Article 182
Article 130j	Article 167	Article 183
Article 130k	Article 168	Article 184

Treaty establishing the European Economic Community/ European Community (1958–99)	Treaty establishing the European Community (1999–2009)	Treaty on the Functioning of the European Union (2009–)
Article 130l	Article 169	Article 185
Article 130m	Article 170	Article 186
Article 130n	Article 171	Article 187
Article 130o	Article 172	Article 188
	Article 189	
Article 130p	Article 173	Article 190
Article 130q (repealed)		
Article 130r	Article 174	Article 191
Article 130s	Article 175	Article 192
Article 130t	Article 176	Article 193
	Article 194	
	Article 195	
	Article 196	
	Article 197	
Article 130u	Article 177	*Article 208*
Article 130v	Article 178 (repealed)	
Article 130w	Article 179	*Article 209*
Article 130x	Article 180	*Article 210*
Article 130y	Article 181	*Article 211*
	Article 181a	*Article 212*
PART FOUR	PART FOUR	PART FOUR
Article 131	Article 182	Article 198
Article 132	Article 183	Article 199
Article 133	Article 184	Article 200
Article 134	Article 185	Article 201
Article 135	Article 186	Article 202
Article 136	Article 187	Article 203
Article 136a	Article 188	Article 204
		PART FIVE
	Article 205	
	Article 131	Article 206
	Article 133	Article 207
	Article 177	Article 208

Treaty establishing the European Economic Community/ European Community (1958–99)	Treaty establishing the European Community (1999–2009)	Treaty on the Functioning of the European Union (2009–)
	Article 179	Article 209
	Article 180	Article 210
	Article 181	Article 211
	Article 181a	Article 212
	Article 213	
	Article 214	
	Article 301	Article 215
	Article 216	
	Article 310	Article 217
	Article 300	Article 218
	Article 111(1)–(3), (5)	Article 219
	Articles 302 to 304	Article 220
	Article 221	
	Article 222	
PART FIVE	PART FIVE	PART SIX
Article 137	Article 189 (repealed)	
Article 138	Article 190(1)–(3) (repealed)	
	Article 190(4)–(5)	Article 223
Article 138a	Article 191, 1st para. (repealed)	
	Article 191, 2nd para	Article 224
Article 138b	Article 192, 1st para. (repealed)	
	Article 192, 2nd para	Article 225
Article 138c	Article 193	Article 226
Article 138d	Article 194	Article 227
Article 138e	Article 195	Article 228
Article 139	Article 196	Article 229
Article 140	Article 197, 1st para. (repealed)	
	Article 197, 2nd, 3rd, 4th paras	Article 230
Article 141	Article 198	Article 231

Treaty establishing the European Economic Community/ European Community (1958–99)	Treaty establishing the European Community (1999–2009)	Treaty on the Functioning of the European Union (2009–)
Article 142	Article 199	Article 232
Article 143	Article 200	Article 233
Article 144	Article 201	Article 234
Article 145	Article 202 (repealed)	
Article 146	Article 203 (repealed)	
	Article 235	
	Article 236	
Article 147	Article 204	Article 237
Article 148	Article 205(1), (3)	Article 238
	Article 205(2), (4) (repealed)	
Article 149 (repealed)		
Article 150	Article 206	Article 239
Article 151	Article 207	Article 240
Article 152	Article 208	Article 241
Article 153	Article 209	Article 242
Article 154	Article 210	Article 243
Article 155	Article 211 (repealed)	
Article 156	Article 212	*Article 249(2)*
	Article 244	
Article 157	Article 213	Article 245
Article 158	Article 214 (repealed)	
Article 159	Article 215	Article 246
Article 160	Article 216	Article 247
Article 161	Article 217 (replaced)	*Article 17 TEU*, Article 248
Article 162	Article 218(1) (repealed)	
	Article 218(2)	Article 249
Article 163	Article 219	Article 250
Article 164	Article 220 (repealed)	
Article 165	Article 221(1) (repealed)	
	Article 221(2), (3)	Article 251
Article 166	Article 222	Article 252
Article 167	Article 223	Article 253
Article 168	Article 224	Article 254
	Article 255	

Treaty establishing the European Economic Community/ European Community (1958–99)	Treaty establishing the European Community (1999–2009)	Treaty on the Functioning of the European Union (2009–)
Article 168a	Article 225	Article 256
	Article 225a	Article 257
Article 169	Article 226	Article 258
Article 170	Article 227	Article 259
Article 171	Article 228	Article 260
Article 172	Article 229	Article 261
	Article 229a	Article 262
Article 173	Article 230	Article 263
Article 174	Article 231	Article 264
Article 175	Article 232	Article 265
Article 176	Article 233	Article 266
Article 177	Article 234	Article 267
Article 178	Article 235	Article 268
	Article 269	
Article 179	Article 236	Article 270
Article 180	Article 237	Article 271
Article 181	Article 238	Article 272
Article 182	Article 239	Article 273
Article 183	Article 240	Article 274
	Article 275	
	Article 276	
Article 184	Article 241	Article 277
Article 185	Article 242	Article 278
Article 186	Article 243	Article 279
Article 187	Article 244	Article 280
Article 188	Article 245	Article 281
	Article 282	
	Article 112	Article 283
	Article 113	Article 284
Article 188a	Article 246	Article 285
Article 188b	Article 247	Article 286
Article 188c	Article 248	Article 287
Article 189	Article 249	Article 288
	Article 289	
	Article 290	

Treaty establishing the European Economic Community/ European Community (1958–99)	Treaty establishing the European Community (1999–2009)	Treaty on the Functioning of the European Union (2009–)
	Article 291	
	Article 292	
Article 189a	Article 250	Article 293
Article 189b	Article 251	Article 294
Article 189c	Article 252 (repealed)	
	Article 295	
Article 190	Article 253	Article 296
Article 191	Article 254	Article 297
	Article 298	
	Article 255	*Article 15*
Article 192	Article 256	Article 299
	Article 300	
Article 193	Article 257 (replaced)	Article 300(2)
Article 194	Article 258 (replaced)	Article 300(4), Article 301
Article 195	Article 259	Article 302
Article 196	Article 260	Article 303
Article 197	Article 261 (repealed)	
Article 198	Article 262	Article 304
Article 198a	Article 263(1), (5) (replaced)	*Article 300(3), (4)*
	Article 263(2)–(4)	Article 305
Article 198b	Article 264	Article 306
Article 198c	Article 265	Article 307
Article 198d	Article 266	Article 308
Article 198e	Article 267	Article 309
Article 199	Article 268	Article 310
Article 200 (repealed)		
Article 201	Article 269	Article 311
Article 201a	Article 270 (repealed)	
	Article 312	
Article 202	Article 271	*Article 316*
Article 203	Article 272(1)	Article 313
	Article 272(2)–(10)	Article 314
Artile 204	Article 273	Article 315
	Article 271	Article 316

Treaty establishing the European Economic Community/ European Community (1958–99)	Treaty establishing the European Community (1999–2009)	Treaty on the Functioning of the European Union (2009–)
Artile 205	Article 274	Article 317
Article 205a	Article 275	Article 318
Article 206	Article 276	Article 319
Article 206a (repealed)		
Article 207	Article 277	Article 320
Article 208	Article 278	Article 321
Article 209	Article 279	Article 322
	Article 323	
	Article 324	
Article 209a	Article 280	Article 325
	Articles 11 and 11a	Article 326
	Articles 11 and 11a	Article 327
	Articles 11 and 11a	Article 328
	Articles 11 and 11a	Article 329
	Articles 11 and 11a	Article 330
	Articles 11 and 11a	Article 331
	Articles 11 and 11a	Article 332
	Articles 11 and 11a	Article 333
	Articles 11 and 11a	Article 334
PART SIX	PART SIX	PART SEVEN
Article 210	Article 281 (replaced)	*Article 52 TEU*
Article 211	Article 282	Article 335
Article 212 (repealed)		
	Article 283	Article 336
Article 213	Article 284	Article 337
	Article 285	Article 338
	Article 286 (replaced)	*Article 16*
Article 214	Article 287	Article 339
Article 215	Article 288	Article 340
Article 216	Article 289	Article 341
Article 217	Article 290	Article 342
Article 218 (repealed)		
	Article 291	Article 343
Article 219	Article 292	Article 344

Treaty establishing the European Economic Community/ European Community (1958–99)	Treaty establishing the European Community (1999–2009)	Treaty on the Functioning of the European Union (2009–)
Article 220	Article 293 (repealed)	
Article 221	Article 294	*Article 55*
Article 222	Article 295	Article 345
Article 223	Article 296	Article 346
Article 224	Article 297	Article 347
Article 225	Article 298	Article 348
Article 226 (repealed)		
Article 227	Article 299(1) (replaced)	*Article 52 TEU*
	Article 299(2) 2nd–4th paras	Article 349
	Article 299(2) 1st para, (3)–(6)	*Article 355*
Article 228	Article 300 (replaced)	*Article 218*
Article 228a	Article 301 (replaced)	*Article 215*
Article 229	Article 302 (replaced)	*Article 220*
Article 230	Article 303 (replaced)	*Article 220*
Article 231	Article 304 (replaced)	*Article 220*
Article 232	Article 305 (repealed)	
Article 233	Article 306	Article 350
Article 234	Article 307	Article 351
Article 235	Article 308	Article 352
Article 236 (replaced)	*Article 48 TEU*	*Article 48 TEU*
Article 237 (replaced)	*Article 49 TEU*	*Article 49 TEU*
	Article 353	
	Article 309	Article 354
Article 238	Article 310	*Article 217*
Article 239	Article 311 (replaced)	*Article 51 TEU*
Article 353		
	Article 299(2) 1st para, (3)–(6)	Article 355
Article 240	Article 312	Article 356
Articles 241–246 (repealed)		

Treaty establishing the European Economic Community/ European Community (1958–99)	Treaty establishing the European Community (1999–2009)	Treaty on the Functioning of the European Union (2009–)
Article 247	Article 313	Article 357
Artile 248	Article 314 (replaced)	*Article 55 TEU*
	Article 358	

INDEX

Scotland 3.36, 5.127, 5.130, 5.132, 5.136,
  5.152, 6.16, 6.18, 6.29, 6.39, 6.72, 8.12,
  10.89, 11.42, 11.66, 11.91, 11.101,
  13.117
seals 5.82, 10.31, 10.60, 10.71
secession 1.20, 2.60, 2.75–2.77, 2.78, 3.42,
  3.65
self-employment 6.125, 11.03, 11.06, 11.07,
  11.17, 11.19, 11.24, 11.26, 11.28, 11.30,
  11.31, 11.36, 11.93, 11.113, 11.120,
  11.167, 14.41, 14.42
'selling arrangements' 10.46–10.49, 10.51,
  13.44
semi-privileged applicant 5.73, 5.74, 5.75
Serbia 2.73, 8.06, 11.90, 14.93, 14.94
services *see* free movement
Services Directive 10.31, 11.45–11.48, 11.75,
  11.114, 11.130
services of general (economic) interest 7.19,
  11.46, 11.89, 11.217, 13.145–13.147,
  13.165, 13.167, 13.168
severance 5.85, 5.101, 6.69, 10.97, 13.106,
  13.115, 13.169
sex discrimination *see* discrimination
shared competence *see* competence
Sharpston, Eleanor 5.26, 5.49, 5.53, 5.83,
  5.122, 5.131, 6.13, 6.45, 6.73, 6.102,
  6.105, 6.125, 6.135, 6.138, 10.13, 10.30,
  10.70, 10.102, 10.112, 11.31, 11.43,
  11.75, 11.82, 11.95, 11.98, 11.102,
  11.104, 11.106, 11.108, 11.112, 11.127,
  11.128, 11.131, 13.99, 14.49, 14.79,
  14.81
sickness insurance 11.12, 11.17, 11.66, 11.103,
  11.104, 11.134, 13.15, 13.145
simplified revision procedure *see* amendment
sincere cooperation 2.22, 5.30, 6.01, 6.31,
  13.92, 13.173, 14.75
Single CMO Regulation *see* Common
  Agricultural Policy
Single European Act 1.24–1.27, 1.32, 2.03,
  2.08, 2.34, 2.45, 2.47, 2.63, 2.64, 3.01,
  3.45, 3.65, 4.61, 5.03, 6.128, 7.11, 7.16,
  8.04, 9.04, 9.05, 10.21, 10.68, 10.69,
  14.02, 14.27, 14.54, 14.57, 14.114,
  14.118, 14.122, 14.126

Single European sky *see* Common Transport
  Policy, Air
single market 7.03, 9.03, 9.05, 9.07, 10.80,
  11.35, 13.05, 13.10, 14.34
Sint Eustatius 2.73, 10.05, 14.19, 14.83
Sint Maarten 10.05, 11.183, 14.83
Slovakia 1.47, 1.50, 1.51, 2.12, 2.66, 2.73, 2.76,
  4.04, 5.05, 5.48, 6.19, 6.20, 8.06, 8.12,
  11.125, 11.196, 13.09, 14.18, 14.23,
  14.24, 14.45, 14.79
Slovenia 1.47, 1.50, 1.52, 2.12, 2.46, 2.73,
  2.76, 3.40, 3.74, 5.05, 5.38, 5.148,
  11.125, 11.173, 11.196, 13.09, 14.18,
  14.24
Slynn, Gordon 5.104, 11.66
small and medium sized undertakings (SMEs)
  4.09, 11.45, 11.217, 13.35, 13.45, 13.51,
  13.168, 14.125
Snus 2.02, 10.60, 10.72
social advantages 11.12, 11.21, 11.90, 14.45
Social Charter *see* Community Charter of the
  Fundamental Social Rights of Workers;
  European Social Charter
social dumping *see* dumping, social
social policy 1.33, 3.43, 6.127, 6.128, 7.08,
  7.13, 9.05, 10.33, 11.04, 11.28, 11.130,
  11.200, 14.26–14.53
Social Protection Committee 4.17
Social Protocol (and Agreement) 2.67, 6.118,
  14.34–14.35
social security 10.40, 11.04, 11.24–11.29,
  11.66, 11.70–11.75, 11.97, 11.99,
  11.101, 11.108, 11.130, 11.164, 13.14,
  13.164, 14.26, 14.29, 14.36, 14.41,
  14.42, 14.45, 14.46, 14.52, 14.53
Societas Cooperativa Europæa see European
  Cooperative Society
Societas Europæa see European Company
Societas Privata Europæa see European Private
  Company
soft law 6.02, 6.135, 11.132, 13.111, 13.165,
  14.06
Solange 6.18, 6.19, 6.54, 6.130, 10.104, 14.68
solidarity 2.08, 2.09, 2.19, 2.20, 2.45, 2.50,
  2.59, 5.96, 6.96, 6.105, 6.114, 6.118,
  6.164, 13.15, 14.27, 14.34, 14.36, 14.67,
  14.130